IVAN GOGIN
Graphics by Alexander Dashyan

FIGHTING SHIPS
OF
WORLD WAR TWO
1937 - 1945

Volume II

United States of America

Gatchina
2023

Contents

Foreword

The second volume of the 'Fighting ships of World War Two' series focuses on the United States Navy - the largest and most powerful navy of its day, and the largest navy ever to have existed. The first volume contains information about the Royal Navy and Commonwealth navies: Canadian, Australian, New Zealand, Indian, South African and Burmese Government ships.

The reference contains the maximum possible number of side views, reduced from the point of view of common sense and space limitation, in uniform 1:1250 scale. The format of the publication, is forced to limit us to information on merchant and fishing vessels with less with a capacity of less than 500 grt, performing patrol, minesweeping and other combat duties, and purpose-built craft with the displacement of less than 10 t.

Ship data blocks contain the name of the ship (Builder, laid down, launched, completed or commissioned -reason and date of deletion from the fleet list). If only two dates are present in the group "laid down - launched - commissioned", then they mean the dates of launching and commissioning. If there is only one date, then it indicates the date of commissioning.

Tables containing data on civilian ships converted into combat ones contain the following columns: Name (previous names); date of launching / commissioning by the Navy; capacity in grt (if the number is indicated in *Italic*, then the displacement is in t); length x width x draft, m; maximum speed, knots; armament; fate.

Technical data blocks include the standard / full load displacement in tons (usually long tons) or surface / submerged displacement for submarines, length overall (oa) (if the length between the perpendiculars is indicated, it is written pp, if the length by the waterline is wl) x breadth x mean draught in meters (or maximal draught (max)), composition of the machinery (if necessary, number of shafts in brackets), maximum power of the main engines in horsepower, maximum speed in knots, maximum fuel capacity in tons, maximum cruising range in nautical miles at cruising speed in knots (in brackets), complement, maximum operating depth for submarines in meters. Armor protection is described briefly, the reader can find a detailed description of the protection arrangement in the text below. Armament is described according to the following system: Artillery - number of mounts x number of guns in the mount - caliber of guns in millimeters/barrel length in calibers and the mark or common name of the gun. If the ship had gun mounts with a different gun number, then these mounts are marked with «+» sign. For example, (2 x 4 + 1 x 2) — 356/45 BL Mk I means that the ship was armed with two quadruple and one twin mount with 356/45 Mk I breech-loading guns. Machine guns with a caliber of less than

Preamble. Why 1937?

20 mm are marked without barrel length and gun mark. Torpedoes: number of torpedo banks x number of tubes in the bank - torpedo caliber for rotating turntable mounts or number of tubes - torpedo caliber for fixed tubes (for example, on submarines, MTBs or old ships). The numbers in brackets after the number of DCTs and DCRs are the total number of depth charges carried.

The aircraft data should be read as follows:

Hellcat Mk II: 13.08 x 10.17 x 4.11 m, 31.0 m², 4155 / 6400 kg, 1 Pratt & Whitney R-2800-10W, 2200 hp, 611 km/h, 2600 (270) km, 15.1 m/s, 11500 m, 1 seat; 6 x 12.7 MG or (2 x 20 guns + 4 x 12.7 MG), 6 x 127-mm rockets or 908-kg bombs (2 x 454-kg).
Means: Hellcat Mk II model data: wingspan 13.08m, length 10.17m, height 4.11m, wing area 31.0m², empty weight 4155 kg / maximum takeoff weight 6400 kg, 1 Pratt & Whitney R-2800-10W engine with 2200-hp power, maximal speed 611 km/h, flying range 2600 km at a speed of 270 km/h, maximum rate of climb 15.1 m/s, service ceiling 11500 m, 1 seat; armament consisted of 6 12.7-mm MGs or 2 20-mm guns and 4 12.7-mm MGs, 6 127-mm rockets or 908 kg of bombs.

Hellcat Mk II (fighter-bomber, 854 transferred spring 1944- 1945 (including FR Mk II and PR Mk II), serv. spring 1944-8.1946, USN F6F-5, Pratt & Whitney R-2800-10W (2200hp), strengthened armor, 6 x 12.7 MG or 2 x 20 guns and 4 x 12.7 MG, 6 x 127mm rockets or 908 kg bombs (2 x 454-kg));
Means: Hellcat Mk II modification, fighter-bomber assignment, 865 served in the RN, entered the Navy in the spring 1944-1945 and served in the spring 1944 - August 1946. Further, the differences from the previous modification are briefly described.

The first echoes of the thunderstorm, which subsequently swept the whole world and remained in the memory of mankind as the most destructive and deadly war, were heard on October 25, 1936, when Germany and Japan signed the Agreement against the Communists International, which provided for the destruction of communism in general and the Soviet Union in particular. 11/6/1937 Italy joins the pact. An Axis was formed, with the goal of creating a new order. The order in which German Nazis, Japanese militarists and Italian fascists were to be given the right to decide which of the peoples inhabiting the planet would live.

The Axis initially faced little resistance to aggression. In 1935-1936, Italy invaded Ethiopia. In 1936, German troops occupied the Rhine demilitarized zone. Germany annexed Austria in March 1938, the Sudetenland in October, and Czechoslovakia in March 1939. But the war broke out at the other end of Eurasia.

Back in 1931-1932, Japanese troops captured Chinese Manchuria, creating a puppet state on its territory. The League of Nations did not react in any way to the aggression. Creeping aggression associated with constant armed clashes and the seizure of new territories continued for another five years, but in 1937 Japan switched to full-scale military operations. Armies of millions clashed in a vast theater of operations that engulfed the entire eastern China. On July 7, 1937, World War II began.

Based on the fact that in July 1937 the first large-scale conflict began, which was undoubtedly part of the Second World War and lasted until September 1945, we propose to consider the incident on the Marco Polo bridge on July 7, 1937 as its actual beginning. And so, our series is an overview of all warships in the world from July 1937 to September 1945.

Abbreviations

AA - anti-aircraft
AEW - airborne early warning
AP - armor-piercing
ASW - anti-submarine warfare
ASWRL - anti-submarine warfare rocket launcher
aw - above water
BDE - British destroyer escort
bhp - brake horsepower
BL - breech-loading
brt - British registered tons
BU - broken up
CIC - combat information center
CMB - coastal motor boat
Compl. - complement
CT - conning tower
CTL - constructive total loss
cwt - hundredweight
cyl - cylinder
DC - depth charge
DC - reciprocating engine, diagonal, compound
DCR - depth charge rack
DCT - depth charge thrower
DE - destroyer escort
DP - dual-purpose
DSE - reciprocating engine, diagonal, single expansion
DTE - reciprocating engine, diagonal, triple expansion
DYd - dockyard
ECM - electronic countermeasures
FY - Fiscal Year
GM - metacentric height
grt - gross registered tons
HA - high angle
HDML - harbour defence motor launch
HMS - His/Her Majesty's Ship
hp - horse power(s)
HP - high pressure
HQ – headquarters
HC - reciprocating engine, horizontal, compound
HSE - reciprocating engine, horizontal, single expansion
HTE - reciprocating engine, horizontal, triple expansion
ihp - indicated horsepower

kt(s) - knot(s)
LA - low angle
lb - pound(s)
LCA - Landing Craft, Assault
LCF - Landing Craft, Flak
LCG - Landing Craft, Gun
LCG(L) - Landing Craft, Gun (Large)
LCG(M) - Landing Craft, Gun (Medium)
LCI(G) - Landing Craft, Infantry (Gun)
LCI(L) - Landing Craft, Infantry (Large)
LCI(S) - Landing Craft, Infantry (Small)
LCM - Landing Craft, Mechanical
LCP - Landing Craft, Personnel
LCP(R) - Landing Craft, Personnel (Rocket)
LCS - Landing Craft, Support
LCS(L) - Landing Craft, Support (Large)
LCS(M) - Landing Craft, Support (Medium)
LCS(S) - Landing Craft, Support (Small)
LCT - Landing Craft, Tank
LCT(R) - Landing Craft, Tank (Rocket)
LCV - Landing Craft, Vehicle
LCV(P) - Landing Craft, Vehicle (Personnel)
LP - low pressure
LSC - Landing Ship, Carrier
LSD - Landing Ship, Dock
LSF - Landing Ship, Fighter Direction
LSG - Landing Ship, Gantry
LSH(L) - Landing Ship, Headquarters (Large)
LSI - Landing Ship, Infantry
LSI(H) - Landing Ship, Infantry (Hand)
LSI(L) - Landing Ship, Infantry (Large)
LSI(M) - Landing Ship, Infantry (Medium)
LSI(S) - Landing Ship, Infantry (Small)
LSS - Landing Ship, Stern Chute
LST - Landing Ship, Tank
MA/SB - Motor anti-submarine boat
max - maximum
MG - machine gun
MGB - motor gunboat
Mk - Mark
ML - motor launch
MMS - motor minesweeper

Mod - model
MTB - motor torpedo boat
nm - nautical mile(s)
No(s) - number(s)
N Yd - Navy Yard
oa - overall
pdr - pounder(s)
pp - between perpendiculars
QF - quick-firing
RAN - Royal Australian Navy
RCMP - Royal Canadian Mounted Police
RCN - Royal Canadian Navy
RIM - Royal Indian Marine
RIN - Royal Indian Navy
RN - Royal Navy
RNVR - Royal Naval Volunteer Reserve
RNZN - Royal New Zealand Navy
RSAN - Royal South African Navy
SAN - South African Navy
SAP - semi-armor piercing
SB - Shipbuilding
SE - single-ended
shp - shaft horsepower
std - standard
sub - submerged
t — ton(s)
TC - torpedo cradle
TNT - trinitrotoluene
TS - training ship
TT - torpedo tube(s)
US - United States
USCG - United States Coast Guard
USN - United States Navy
VC – reciprocating engine, vertical, compound.
VQE - reciprocating engine, vertical, quadruple expansion
VQuE - reciprocating engine, vertical, quintuple expansion
VTE - reciprocating engine, vertical, triple expansion
Wks - Works

Dear reader!

I created the Navypedia project in 2003, and since then all my free time and effort has been devoted to the development of the site, which has since become, according to many users, the largest database of warships in the world. However, only in 2019 I was offered to start writing and publishing books, in 2020 the first attempts appeared, including in collaboration with other authors, in the same year I learned about the incredible opportunities that the Amazon KDP program gives to independent authors. In 2021, a theme and format were found that resonated with readers: illustrated reference books in an encyclopedic format. I understand that they are far from perfect. But I really want to do something that will please the majority of readers! And I think you, my dear reader, can help me. I am very attentive to the feedback posted by readers on Amazon after reading my books, and I try to meet the requirements of readers to the greatest extent possible by rewriting, redesigning and correcting my books in accordance with them. I invite you to dialogue, my dear reader. You will write to me in a review about what you liked and what you didn't. And I will respond by adjusting the formats of books and entire series. And, I hope, such a democracy will allow you and me, dear reader, to create the format that you and I will like.

Organization of the United States Navy during the World War Two

At the time of the Japanese attack on Pearl Harbor, the war in the Pacific region had been going on for 10 years, since September 18, 1931, when Japan began to invade Chinese Manchuria from Korea. In 1937, hostilities resumed, now in central China. The years 1940-1941 were marked by the occupation of French Indochina and Japan's acquisition of Thailand as an ally. The US Navy began to redeploy its forces for the war with Japan in early 1941, when the main forces of the Pacific Fleet moved from San Diego to Pearl Harbor. The United States put an end to the question of the beginning of the war on November 26, 1941, when the so-called Hull Note was presented to the Ambassador of Japan. This note contained ultimatum demands that Japan could not afford - the withdrawal of all troops from China (except Manchukuo) and Indochina, the withdrawal from the Tripartite Pact. By that time, the United States had already imposed trade sanctions against Japan, frozen Japanese financial assets on its territory, and imposed an embargo on oil supplies to Japan. On November 26, 1941, the United States made war with Japan inevitable.

On December 1, Emperor Hirohito gave final permission to attack Pearl Harbor. At 9:30 p.m. on December 6, US President Roosevelt read a Japanese note he had recently received and said, "This is war." However, the Pacific Fleet learned about its beginning only by the sound of Japanese aircraft engines over Pearl Harbor. Even the detection of the coastal radar of the first wave of aircraft 50 minutes before the attack did not make the command raise an alarm ...

The US began to prepare for war with Japan in 1932, so most of the naval forces were concentrated in the Pacific. Two fleets were based there - the Pacific Fleet at the beginning of 1941 moved to a forward base in Pearl Harbor, Hawaii, and the Asian Fleet, based in the Philippines, which at that time was an autonomous territory within the United States. The functions of the escort service within the framework of the so-called "armed neutrality" in the Atlantic were performed by the Atlantic Fleet. Coastal protection was subordinated to the naval districts.

The combat ships of the Pacific Fleet were

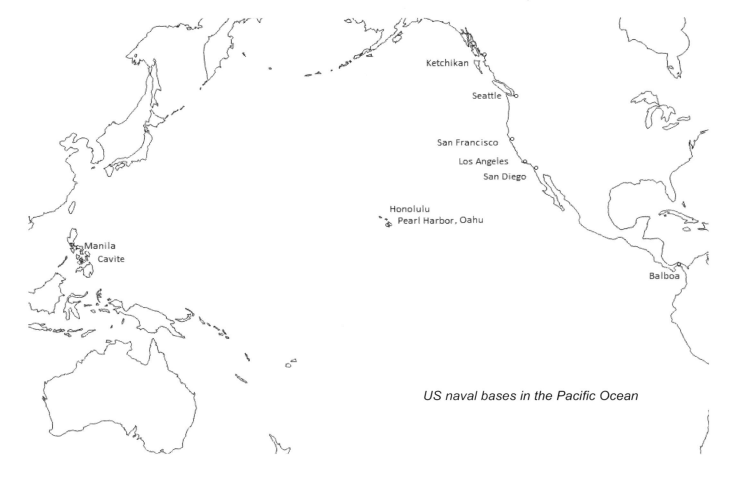

US naval bases in the Pacific Ocean

US naval bases in the Atlantic Ocean

concentrated in two large formations with HQs in Pearl Harbor – Battle Force and Scouting Force.

Battle Force included Battleship Division 1 (BatDiv 1, Pearl Harbor, BB36 *Nevada*, BB38 *Pennsylvania* and BB39 *Arizona* (F)), BatDiv 2 , Pearl Harbor(BB37 *Oklahoma*, BB43 *Tennessee* (F), BB44 *California*) and BatDiv 4 (Pearl Harbor, BB45 *Colorado,* BB46 *Maryland*, BB48 *West Virginia* (F)), Carrier Division 1 (CarDiv 1, Pearl Harbor, CV2 *Lexington* (F), CV3 *Saratoga*), CarDiv 2 (Pearl Harbor, CV6 *Enterprise* (F)), Cruiser Division 3 (CruDiv 3, Pearl Harbor, CL9 *Richmond*, CL10 *Concord* (F), CL11 *Trenton*), CruDiv 9 (Pearl Harbor, CL46 *Phoenix*, CL47 *Boise*, CL48 *Honolulu* (F)(FC), CL49 *St. Louis*, CL50 *Helena*). Light forces included Destroyer Flotilla 1 (DesFlot 1, Pearl Harbor, CL7 *Raleigh* (FF)), consisted of Destroyer Squadron 1 (DesRon 1, Pearl Harbor, destroyer *Phelps* and 8 destroyers of *Farragut* class), DesRon 3 (Pearl Harbor, destroyer *Clark* and 8

destroyers of *Mahan* class) and DesRon 5 (destroyers *Porter* and 8 destroyers of *Mahan* class), DesFlot 2 (Pearl Harbor, CL8 *Detroit* (FF)(DBFF)) with DesRon 4 (Pearl Harbor, destroyers *Selfridge* and 8 destroyers of *Bagley* class) and DesRon 6 (Pearl Harbor, destroyer *Balch*, 4 destroyers of *Gridley* class, 2 of *Mahan* class and 2 of *Benham* class), separate DesDiv 50 (4 flushdeckers), Mine Squadron 1 (MinRon 1, Pearl Harbor, minelayer *Oglala* (F) and 8 flushdeckers-minelayers) and MinRon 2 (Pearl Harbor, 13 flushdeckers-minesweepers).

Scouting Force had CruDiv 4 (Pearl Harbor, CA24 *Pensacola*, CA25 *Salt Lake City*, CA29 *Chicago* (F), CA35 *Indianapolis* (CF)), CruDiv 5 (Pearl Harbor, CA26 *Northampton* (F), CA27 *Chester*, CA28 *Louisville*, CA33 *Portland*), CruDiv 6 (Pearl Harbor, CA32 *New Orleans*, CA34 *Astoria* (F), CA36 *Minneapolis*, CA38 *San Francisco*), Patrol Wing 1 (Pearl Harbor, tender AV1 *Wright* (F), 1 *Auk*-class and 2 flushdeckers), Patrol Wing

2 (Pearl Harbor, tenders AV4 *Curtiss* (F), AV8 *Tangier*, 2 *Auk*-class and 2 flushdeckers), Patrol Wing 4 (Pearl Harbor, 2 *Auck*-class and 2 flushdeckers), Submarine Squadron 4 (SubRon 4, San Diego/Pearl Harbor, 1 flushdecker, 6 *S*-class, *Argonaut*, 2 *Narwhal*-class, *Dolphin*, 2 *Cashalot*-class, 3 *Perch*-class submarines), SubRon 6 (Pearl Harbor, 9 *Tambor*-class submarines), SubRon 8 (Pearl Harbor, no submarines)

Combat ships of Pacific Fleet Base Force included MinDiv 10 (Pearl Harbor, 4 *Auks*) and MinDiv 11 (Pearl Harbor, 4 *Auks*) from Service Squadron 6 (SerRon 6).

Asiatic Fleet (Manila) had cruisers CA30 *Houston* and CL13 *Marblehead*. Light forces included DesRon 29 (Manila Bay, 13 flushdeckers), Patrol Wing 10 (Manila Bay, tender AV3 *Langley*, 1 *Auk*-class and 2 flushdeckers), SubRon 20 (Manila Bay, 6 *S*-class, 2 *Porpoise*-class, 2 *Shark*-class, 3 *Perch*-class, 6 *Salmon*-class, 10 *Sargo*-class submarines) and MinRon 3 (Manila Bay, 6 *Auk*-class minesweepers).

Atlantic Fleet (Norfolk, CA31 *Augusta*) included BatDiv 3 (Norfolk, BB40 *New Mexico*, BB41 *Mississippi*, BB42 *Idaho* (F)), BatDiv 5 (Norfolk, BB33 *Arkansas*, BB34 *New York* (F), BB35 *Texas*), BatDiv 6 (Norfolk, BB55 *North Carolina*, BB56 *Washington* (F)), CarDiv 3 (Norfolk, CV4 *Ranger* and CV7 *Wasp*), carriers CV5 *Yorktown* and CV8 *Hornet*, escort carrier AVG1 *Long Island*, CruDiv 2 (Norfolk, CL4 *Omaha*, CL5 *Milwaukee*, CL6 *Cincinnati*, CL13 *Memphis* (F)), CruDiv 7 (Norfolk, CA37 *Tuscaloosa*, CA39 *Quincy*, CA44 *Vincennes*, CA45 *Wichita* (F)), CruDiv 8 (Norfolk, CL40 *Brooklyn*, CL41 *Philadelphia* (F)(CF), CL42 *Savannah*, CL43 *Nashville*), Patrol Wing 3 (Coco Solo, 2 *Auks* and 2 flushdeckers), Patrol Wing 5 (Norfolk, 2 *Auks* and 2 flushdeckers), Patrol Wing 7 (Norfolk, tenders AV5 *Albermarle*, AV9 *Pocomoke* and 1 *Auk*-class), Patrol Wing 8 (Norfolk, 1 *Auk*-class and 2 flushdeckers), Patrol Wing 9 (1 *Auk*-class), destroyer *Noa* as flagship of destroyers, DesFlot 3 (Norfolk/Argentia/Halifax//Hvalfjordur, 3 *Porter*-class, 5 *Somers*-class, 2 *Sims*-class, 24 *Benson*-class, 1 *Bristol*-class), DesFlot 4 (Norfolk/Boston/Bermuda, 10 *Sims*-class, 8 *Benham*-class, 18 *Bristol*-class), DesFlot 8 (Argentia/Boston, 26 flushdeckers), SubRon 1 (New London, 7 *O*-class, 11 *R*-class, 3 *S*-class, *Mackerel*, *Marlin* submarines), SubRon 3 (Coco Solo, 8 *S*-class and 3 *Barracuda*-class submarines), SubRon 5 (New London, 12 *S*-class submarines), SubRon 7 (New London, 7 *R*-class, 2 *S*-class, 3 *Tambor*-class), TranDiv 11 of SerRon 3 (Norfolk, 6 APD-flushdeckers), SerRon 9 (Norfolk, 5 flushdeckers-minesweepers, 7 old *Auk*-class, 2 *Raven*-class and new *Auk* minesweepers, 23 auxiliary minesweepers)

Coastal defense was entrusted to the Naval Districts.

1st Naval District (Boston) had 2 gunboats, 3 patrol escorts, 4 patrol yachts and 5 USCG cutters.

3rd Naval District (New York) had 4 minesweepers, 2 patrol escorts, 1 patrol yacht and 5 cutters.

4th Naval District (Philadelphia): 4 minesweepers, 1 patrol escort, 1 cutter.

5th Naval District (Norfolk): 9 minesweepers, 2 gunboats, 1 patrol yacht, 2 cutters, 1 minelayer.

6th Naval District (Charleston): 2 patrol yachts, 1 cutter.

7th Naval District (Jacksonville): 2 minesweepers, 2 patrol yachts, 6 cutters.

8th Naval District (New Orleans): 3 minesweepers, 1 patrol yacht, 3 cutters.

9th Naval District (Great Lakes): 1 patrol yacht, 2 gunboats.

10th Naval District (San Juan): 5 minesweepers, 2 patrol yachts, 9 cutters).

11th Naval District (San Diego): DesDiv 70 (4 flushdeckers), 8 minesweepers, 2 patrol yachts, 3 cutters

12th Naval District (San Francisco): DesDiv 83 (4 flushdeckers), 8 minesweepers, 1 patrol escort, 5 cutters.

13th Naval District (Seattle): DesDiv 82 (5 flushdeckers), 7 minesweepers, 1 patrol escort, 1 patrol yacht, 2 cutters, 1 seaplane tender of *Auk* class.

14th Naval District (Honolulu): MinDiv (4 minesweepers), DesDiv 80 (4 flushdeckers), MTBRon 1 (12 MTBs), 2 gunboats

15th Naval District (Balboa): DesRon 33 (10 flushdeckers), 5 minesweepers, 1 gunboat, 4 patrol yachts.

16th Naval District (Cavite): 7 gunboats, 6 MTBs.

One patrol yacht served on Potomac (at Bellevue).

Ships of the US Coast Guard were allocated to Boston, New York, Philadelphia, Norfolk, Charleston, Jacksonville, New Orleans, St. Louis, Cleveland, Chicago, San Juan, Los Angeles, San Francisco, Seattle, Ketchikan and Honolulu districts.

This organization, of course, changed during the war. The Asian Fleet all but disappeared with the fall of the Philippines in May 1942, and the survived ships retreated to Australia and later became part of the Southwest Pacific Command. On March 15, 1943, the US Navy underwent a massive reorganization. Instead of two Fleets, the Pacific and the Atlantic, 9 Fleets appeared. Each Fleet could include up to 10 Task Forces. A Task Force could be created for a temporary specific task or a permanent task (for example, in 1943 the 1st Fleet included TF12 (main forces), TF13 (amphibious training command), TF15 (destroyers), TF16 (service force), TF17 (submarines) and TF19 (air force) but in 1945 it consisted of TF11 (South Pacific Force), TF13 (Amphibious Force), TF14 (Fleet Operation Training Command), TF15 (Cruisers and Destroyers, Pacific Fleet), TF16 (Service Force, Pacific Fleet), TF17 (Submarines, Pacific Fleet), TF18 (Minecraft, Pacific

Fleet) and TF19 (Air Force)). In the second half of the war, the 3rd and 5th Fleets really were indeed the same Fleet, commanded by Admiral Halsey as the 3rd Fleet or by Admiral Spruance as the 5th Fleet and included almost all USN major surface combatants in Pacific.

There is a list of numbered Fleets of US Navy that existed during World War Two:

1st Fleet – the main force of the Pacific Fleet (TF10-19), created 15.3.1943.

2nd Fleet – the main force of the Atlantic Fleet (TF20-29), created 15.3.1943.

3rd Fleet - South Pacific (TF30-39), created 15.3.1943, included British Pacific Fleet as TF37 from November 1944.

4th Fleet - South Atlantic (TF40-49), created 15.3.1943.

5th Fleet - Central and North Pacific (TF50-59), created 15.3.1943, included British Pacific Fleet as TF57 from November 1944.

6th Fleet - Central and North Atlantic (TF60-69), created 15.3.1943.

7th Fleet - Southwest Pacific (TF70-79), created 15.3.1943.

8th Fleet - Northwest Africa (TF80-89), created 15.3.1943 on the basis of Northwest African Force.

9th Fleet - Southeast Pacific (TF93), Naval Transportation Service (TF94), Western Sea Frontier (TF96), Northwest Sea Frontier (TF97), Naval Forces in Europe (TF99, later TF92), created 15.3.1943, redesignated 11th Fleet 15.8.1943.

9th Fleet - North Pacific (TF90-92), Strategic Air Force (TF93), Forward Area, Central Pacific (TF94), Marshall-Gilbert Islands (TF96), Hawaii (TF97, 98), created 1944.

10th Fleet - Anti-submarine forces in the Atlantic, created 20.5.1943.

11th Fleet - Southeast Pacific (TF113), Naval Transportation Service (TF114), Western Sea Frontier (TF116), Northwest Sea Frontier (TF117), former 9th Fleet, renumbered 15.8.1943.

12th Fleet - US naval forces in Europe, created 1.10.1943.

Some TFs were created 15.3.1943 under the control of the Commander-in-Chief of the US Fleet:

TF00 and 01 - Cominch (CiC, US Fleet),

TF02 - Eastern Sea Frontier,

TF03 - Gulf Sea Frontier,

TF04 - Caribbean Sea Frontier,

TF05 - Panama Sea Frontier.

United States Navy and United States Coast Guard order of battle, December 7, 1941

Pacific Fleet
(1 OS2U-1)

Battle Force

Battleships (Pearl Harbor)

BatDiv 1 (Pearl Harbor) – BB36 *Nevada*, BB38 *Pennsylvania*, BB39 *Arizona* (F), VO-1 (8 OS2U-3)

BatDiv 2 (Pearl Harbor) – BB37 *Oklahoma*, BB43 *Tennessee* (F), BB4 *California*, VO-2 (9 OS2U-3)

BatDiv 4 (Pearl Harbor) – BB45 *Colorado*, BB46 *Maryland*, BB48 *West Virginia* (F), VO-4 (9 OS2U-3)

Aircraft (Pearl Harbor, 1 OS2U-2, 2 SBD-2, 1 SNJ-2)

CarDiv 1 (Pearl Harbor, 1 SBD-2, 1 SNJ-2) – CV2 *Lexington* (F), VF-2 (16 F2A-3), VB-2 (15 SBD-2), VS-2 (1 SBD-2, 14 SBD-3), VT-2 (12 TBD-1), 2 F2A-3, 2 J2F-1, 1 SBD-2, 1 SBD-3, 1 SOC-3, 2 TBD-1, VMSB-231 (18 SB2U-3), CV3 *Saratoga*, VF-3 (7 F4F-3, 2 F4F-3A, 1 XF4F-4), VB-3 (22 SBD-3), VS-3 (21 SBD-3), VT-3 (12 TBD-1), 6 J2F-5, 1 N2Y-1, 5 OS2U-1/3, 3 SBD-1/3, 5 SOC-1/2, 3 SON-1

CarDiv 2 (Pearl Harbor, 1 SBD-3, 1 SNJ-2) – CV6 *Enterprise* (F), VF-6 (16 F4F-3A), VB-6 (17 SBD-2), VS-6 (10 SBD-2, 8 SBD-3), VT-6 (18 TBD-1, 2 SNJ-3), 3 F4F-3, 2 J2F-2, 6 SBD-2/3, 2 SOC-3, 4 TBD-1

Battle Force Pool (Pearl Harbor, San Diego, Alameda, 15 F2A-2/3, 10 F3F-2, 7 F4F-3, 4 J2F-5, 40 OS2U-1/3, 2 SF-2, 13 SBC-3/4, 34 SBD-1/3, 8 TBD-1, 24 SOC-1/3, 1 SON-1, 1 R3D-2)

Fleet Air Photo Unit (San Diego, 1 F2A-3, 1 SNJ-3)

Advanced Carrier Training Group (San Diego, 2 F2A-2/3, 1 N3N-1, 1 OS2U-2, 21 SBD-2/3, 10 SNJ-2/3)

Cruisers (Pearl Harbor)

CruDiv 3 (Pearl Harbor) – CL9 *Richmond*, CL10 *Concord* (F), CL11 *Trenton*, VCS-3 (3 SOC-3, 3 SON-1)

CruDiv 9 (Pearl Harbor) – CL46 *Phoenix*, CL47 *Boise*, CL48 *Honolulu* (F)(FC), CL49 *St. Louis*, CL50 *Helena*, VCS-9 (16 SOC-3, 4 SON-1)

Destroyers (Pearl Harbor)

DesFlot 1 (Pearl Harbor) - CL7 *Raleigh*, AD3 *Dobbins*, AD4 *Whitney*, 2 SOC-3

DesRon 1 (Pearl Harbor) –

DD360 *Phelps* (SF)

DesDiv 1 – DD349 *Dewey* (F), DD350 *Hull*, DD351 *MacDonough*, DD352 *Worden*

DesDiv 2 – DD348 *Farragut* (F), DD353 *Dale*, DD354 *Monaghan*, DD355 *Aylwin*

DesRon 3 (Pearl Harbor) – DD361 *Clark* (SF)

DesDiv 5 – DD369 *Reid*, DD371 *Conyngham*, DD372 *Cassin* (F), DD375 *Downes*

DesDiv 6 – DD365 *Cummings*, DD370 *Case* (F), DD373 *Shaw*, DD374 *Tucker*

DesRon 5 (Pearl Harbor) – DD356 *Porter* (SF)

DesDiv 9 – DD364 *Mahan*, DD366 *Drayton* (F), DD367 *Lamson*, DD368 *Flusser*

DesDiv 10 – DD376 *Cushing* (F), DD377 *Perkins*, DD378 *Smith*, DD379 *Preston*

DesFlot 2 (Pearl Harbor) – CL8 *Detroit* (DBFF)(FF), AD14 *Dixie*, 1 SOC-3, 1 SON-1

DesRon 4 (Pearl Harbor) – DD357 *Selfridge* (SF)

DesDiv 7 – DD386 *Bagley*, DD387 *Blue* (F), DD388 *Helm*, DD391 *Henley*

DesDiv 8 – DD389 *Mugford* (F), DD390 *Ralph Talbot*, DD392 *Patterson*, DD393 *Jarvis*

DesRon 6 (Pearl Harbor) – DD363 *Balch* (SF)

DesDiv 11 – DD380 *Gridley*, DD382 *Craven*, DD400 *McCalla*, DD401 *Maury* (F)

DesDiv 12 – DD384 *Dunlap* (F), DD385 *Fanning*, DD397 *Benham*, DD398 *Ellet*

DesDiv 50 (San Diego) – DD113 *Rathburne* (F), DD114 *Talbot*, DD115 *Waters*, DD116 *Dent*

Minecraft (Pearl Harbor)

MinRon 1 (Pearl Harbor) – CM4 *Oglala* (SF)

MinDiv 1 – DM19 *Tracy*, DM20 *Preble*, DM21 *Sicard*, DM22 *Pruitt* (F)

MinDiv 2 – DM15 *Gamble*, DM16 *Ramsay*, DM17 *Montgomery* (F), DM18 *Breese*

MinRon 2 (Pearl Harbor) – DMS13 *Hopkins* (SF)

MinDiv 4 – DMS14 *Zane*, DMS15 *Wasmuth*, DMS16 *Trever*, DMS17 *Perry* (F)

MinDiv 5 – DMS9 *Chandler*, DMS10 *Southard* (F), DMS11 *Hovey*, DMS12 *Long*

MinDiv 6 – DMS1 *Dorsey* (F), DMS2 *Lamberton*, DMS3 *Boggs*, DMS4 *Elliott*

Scouting Force

Cruisers (Pearl Harbor) – 4 SOC-1/3

CruDiv 4 (Pearl Harbor) – CA24 *Pensacola*, CA25 *Salt Lake City*, CA29 *Chicago* (F), CA35 *Indianapolis* (CF), VCS-4 (16 SOC-1/2)

CruDiv 5 (Pearl Harbor) – CA26 *Northampton* (F), CA27 *Chester*, CA28 *Louisville*, CA33 *Portland*, VCS-5 (16 SOC-1/2)

CruDiv 6 (Pearl Harbor) – CA32 *New Orleans*, CA34 *Astoria* (F), CA36 *Minneapolis*, CA38 *San Francisco*, VCS-6 (15 SOC-1/2)

Aircraft (Pearl Harbor) – 2 OS2U-2, 1 JRB-2, 1 SNJ-2

PatWing 1 (Pearl Harbor, 1 OS2U-2) – AV1 *Wright* (SF), AVP4 *Avocet*, AVD6 *Hulbert* (F), AVD10 *Ballard*, VP-11 (12 PBY-5), VP-12 (12 PBY-5), VP-14 (12 PBY-5)

PatWing 2 (Pearl Harbor, 1 SU-3, 1 SOC-1) – AV4 *Curtiss* (F), AV8 *Tangier*, AVP7 *Swan*, AVP12 *Casco*, AVD11 *Thornton*, AVD14 *McFarland*, VP-22 (14 PBY-3), VP-23 (12 PBY-5), VP-24 (7 PBY-5)

PatWing 4 (Seattle, 1 OS2U-2) – AVP5 *Teal*, AVP6 *Pelican*, AVD2 *Williamson* (F), AVD12 *Gillis*, VP-41 (6 PBY-4/5), VP-42 (6 PBY-5), VP-43 (6 PBY-5), VP-44 (6 PBY-5)

Scouting Force Pool – 2 PBY-3, 1 PBY-5

Transition Training Group – 1 J2F-1, 27 PBY-4/5, VP-13 (4 PBY-5)

Submarines (Submarine Base, Oahu) – AM30 *Seagull*

SubRon 4 (Submarine Base, Oahu) – DD336 *Litchfield*, ASR1 *Widgeon*

SubDiv 41 (San Diego) – SS123 *S18* (SF), SS128 *S23*, SS132 *S27*, SS133 *S28*, SS139 *S34*, SS140 *S35*

SubDiv 42 (Submarine Base, Oahu) – SM1 *Argonaut* (F), SS167 *Narwhal* (F), SS168 *Nautilus*, SS169 *Dolphin*, SS170 *Cachalot*, SS171 *Cuttlefish*

SubDiv 43 (Submarine Base, Oahu) – SS179 *Plunger* (F), SS180 *Pollack*, SS181 *Pompano*

SubRon 6 (Submarine Base, Oahu) – AS14 *Pelias*, ASR5 *Ortolan*

SubDiv 61 (Submarine Base, Oahu) – SS198 *Tambor* (F), SS199 *Tautog*, SS200 *Thresher*, SS201 *Triton*, SS202 *Trout*, SS203 *Tuna*

SubDiv 62 (Submarine Base, Oahu) – SS206 *Gar*, SS209 *Grayling*, SS211 *Gudgeon*

SubRon 8 (Submarine Base, Oahu) – AS11 *Fulton*

Base Force (Pearl Harbor)

SerRon 2 (Pearl Harbor) – AH5 *Solace*,

AP37 *President Jackson*, AP38 *President Adams*, AP39 *President Hayes*, AP40 *Crescent City*, AR1 *Medusa*, AR4 *Vestal*, AR11 *Rigel*, AT12 *Sonoma*, AT30 *Sciota*, AT33 *Pinola*, AT38 *Keosanqua*, AT64 *Navajo*, AT65 *Seminole*

SerRon 4 (Pearl Harbor) – AK23 *Alchiba*, AP1 *Henderson*, AP5 *Chaumont*, AP6 *William W. Burrowa*, AP8 *Harris* (F), AP9 *Zeilin*, AP29 *Ulysses S. Grant*, AP32 *St. Mihiel*, AP33 *Republic*

SerRon 6 (Pearl Harbor)

MinDiv 10 – AM20 *Bobolink*, AM43 *Grebe*, AM25 *Kingfisher*, AM52 *Vireo*

MinDiv 11 – AM3 *Robin*, AM13 *Turkey*, AM26 *Rail*, AM31 *Tern*

UtWing 4 (1 OS2U-2) – VU-1 (9 J2F, 9 JRS), VU-2 (10 J2F, 4 PBY-1), VU-3 (4 JRB-1, 2 BT-1, 2 JRF-1, 1 J2F-4, 11 TDN-1)

Service Force Pool (3 J2F-1, 7 J2F-5, 1 O3U-6, 11 BG-1, 1 PBY-1)

AA Artillery School – AG16 *Utah*

SerRon 8 (Pearl Harbor) – AE1 *Pyro*, AE3 *Lassen*, AF1 *Bridge*, AF7 *Arctic*, AF9 *Boreas*, AF10 *Aldebaran*, AKS1 *Castor*, AKS3 *Antares* (F), AO1 *Kanawha*, AO3 *Cuyama*, AO4 *Brazos*, AO5 *Naches*, AO21 *Tippecanoe*, AO23 *Neosho*, AO24 *Platte*, AO25 *Sabine*, AO27 *Kaskaskia*

AG31 *Argonne* (SF), AG32 *Sumner*, AK42 *Mercury*, AK44 *Aroostook*, AO12 *Ramapo*, AO20 *Sepulga*, ARD1, AP30 Henry T. Allen

2nd Marine Aircraft Wing (San Diego/Ewa Field, 1 JRF-4, 1 SBC-4, 1 SBD-1) – MVF-211 (20 F4F-3, 1 SNJ-3), MVF-221 (14 F2A-3, 1 SNJ-3), VMSB-231 (24 SB2U-3), VMSB-232 (19 SBD-1, 3 SBD-2), VMO-251 (1 J2F-4, 2 OS2U-3, 2 SNJ-3), VMJ-252 (1 J2F-4, 1 JRS-1, 1 R3D-2, 1 JO-2, 1 SBD-1, 1 SB2U-3)

NAS San Diego – HSS-2 (4 JF-2, 1 JRB-2, 1 R2D-1, 4 SBC-4, 2 SB2U-3)

Asiatic Fleet

(Manila, 1 OS2U-1, 5 SOC-1/3, 1 SON-1) – CA30 *Houston* (FF), CL13 *Marblehead*

Destroyers (Manila Bay)

DesRon 29 (Manila Bay) – DD230 *Paul Jones* (SF), AD9 *Blackhawk*

DesDiv 57 – DD211 *Alden*, DD216 *John D. Edwards* (F), DD217 *Whipple*, DD219 *Edsall*

DesDiv 58 – DD213 *Barker*, DD218 *Parrott*, DDD222 *Bulmer*, DD224 *Stewart* (F)

DesDiv 59 – DD225 *Pope*, DD226 *Peary*, DD227 *Pillsbury*, DD228 *John D. Ford* (F)

Aircraft (Manila Bay)

PatWing 10 (Manila Bay) – AV3 *Langley*, 2 SOC-1/2, AVP2 *Heron*, AVD1 *Childs*, AVD7 *William B.*

Preston, VP-101 (18 PBY-4), VP-102 (18 PBY-4), VU-110 (4 J3F-2/4, 5 OS2U-2, 1 SOC)

Submarines (Manila Bay)

SubRon 20 (Manila Bay) – AS3 *Holland*, AS9 *Canopus*, AS20 *Otus*, ASR6 *Pigeon*

SubDiv 21 – SS182 *Salmon* (F), SS183 *Seal*, SS184 *Skipjack*, SS188 *Sargo* (SF), SS189 *Saury*, SS190 *Spearfish*

SubDiv 22 – SS185 *Snapper* (F), SS186 *Stingray*, SS187 *Sturgeon*, SS191 *Sculpin*, SS192 *Sailfish*, SS193 *Swordfish*

SubDiv 201 – SS141 *S36*, SS142 *S37*, SS143 *S38*, SS144 *S39*, SS145 *S40*, SS146 *S41*

SubDiv 202 – SS194 *Seadragon*, SS195 *Sealion*, SS196 *Searaven*, SS197 *Seawolf*

SubDiv 203 – SS172 *Porpoise*, SS173 *Pike*, SS174 *Shark*, SS175 *Tarpon*, SS176 *Perch*, SS177 *Pickerel*, SS178 *Permit*

Service Train (Cavite N Yd)

MinRon 3 (Cavite N Yd)

MinDiv 8 - AM9 *Finch*, AM36 *Bittern*

MinDiv 9 – AM5 *Tanager*, AM15 *Quail*, AM21 *Lark*, AM35 *Whippoorwill*

AO6 *Pecos*, AO13 *Trinity*, PY10 *Isabel*, s/s *President Madison*, s/s *President Harrison*

Atlantic Fleet

(Newport, 1 JRF-4, 4 SOC-1/2)

Battleships (Norfolk)

BatDiv 3 (Norfolk) – BB40 *New Mexico*, BB41 *Mississippi*, BB42 *Idaho* (F), VO-3 (11 OS2U-1/3)

BatDiv 5 (Norfolk) – BB33 *Arkansas*, BB34 *New York* (F), BB35 *Texas*, VO-5 (9 OS2U-3)

BatDiv 6 (Norfolk) – BB55 *North Carolina*, BB56 *Washington* (F), VO-6 (6 OS2U-3)

Aircraft (Norfolk, 1 JRF-5, 2 SOC-2/3, 2 SNJ-2/3)

CarDiv 3 (Norfolk) – CV4 *Ranger*, VF-41 (17 F4F-3, 2 SNJ-3), VF-42 (18 F4F-3), VS-41 (10 SB2U-1/2, 3 TBD-1), VS-42 (15 SB2U-1/2), utility unit (2 J2F-5, 2 SOC-1), CV7 *Wasp*, VF-71 (18 F4F-3), VF-72 (17 F4F-3, 2 SB2U-2, 1 SNJ-3), SC-71 (17 SB2U-1/2, 2 TBD-1), VS-72 (18 SB2U-2), utility unit (2 J2F-2/3, 1 OS2U-1, 1 SB2U-2, 1 SON-1)

CV5 *Yorktown* (Norfolk), VF-5 (18 F4F-3), VB-5 (19 SBD-3), VS-5 (19 SBD-3, 2 SNJ-3), VT-5 (14 TBD-1), utility unit (2 J2F-5, 1 SBD-3, 1 SOC-1)

CV8 *Hornet* (Norfolk), VF-8 (21 F4F-3, 2 SNJ-3), VB-8 (19 SBC-4), VS-8 (20 SBC-4), VT-8 (8 TBD-1, 7 SBN-1), utility unit (2 J2F-5, 2 OS2U-2)

AVG1 *Long Island* (Norfolk), VS-201 (7 F2A-2/3, 12 SOC-3A, 1 SOC-1A)

Fleet Air Photo Unit (2 J2F-5, 1 SBD-3)
Advanced Carrier Training Group (12 F4F-3, 1 J2F-5, 5 SBC-4, 2 SBD-3, 3 SBN-1, 5 SB2U-1/2, 6 SNJ-2/3, 1 SOC-3, 2 TBD-1)
Fleet Tactical Unit (1 SBD-3, 1 SNJ-3)
Cruisers (Norfolk)
CruDiv 2 (Norfolk) – CL4 *Omaha*, CL5 *Milwaukee*, CL6 *Cincinnati*, CL13 *Memphis* (F), VCS-2 (4 SOC-1/3, 2 SON-1)
CruDiv 7 (Norfolk) – CA37 *Tuscaloosa*, CA39 *Quincy*, CA44 *Vincennes*, CA45 *Wichita* (F), VCS-7 (12 SOC-1/3, 4 SON-1)
CruDiv 8 (Norfolk) – CL40 *Brooklyn*, CL41 *Philadelphia* (F), CL42 *Savannah*, CL43 *Nashville*, VCS-8 (6 SOC-1/3, 10 SON-1)
Patrol Wings (Norfolk, 1 XPBS-1, 1 XPBY-5)
PatWing 3 (Coco Solo, Canal Zone) – AVP1 *Lapwing*, AVP9 *Sandpiper*, AVD4 *Clemson*, AVD9 *Osmond Ingram*, VP-31 (11 PBY-5), VP-32 (13 PBY-5)
PatWing 5 (Norfolk, 4 OS2U-2) – AVP3 *Thrush*, AVP8 *Gannet*, AVD5 *Goldsborough*, AVD13 *Greene*, VP-51 (12 PBY-1/5), VP-52 (12 PBY-5)
PatWing 7 (Argentia, Newfoundland, 1 JRF-5, 1 PBY-5) – AV5 *Albermarle*, 2 OS2U-2, AV9 *Pocomoke*, 2 OS2U-2, AVP11 *Biscayne*, 1 OS2U-1, VP-71 (11 PBY-5), VP-72 (12 PBY-5), VP-73 (13 PBY-5), VP-74 (13 PBM-1)
PatWing 8 (Norfolk) – AVP10 *Barnegat*, AVD3 *George E. Badger*, AVD8 *Belknap*, VP-81 (8 PBY-5), VP-82 (14 PBO-1), VP-83 (10 PBY-5)
PatWing 9 (Quonset Point) – AVP21 *Humboldt*, VP-91 (6 PBY-5)
Transition Training Squadron – 1 OS2U-3, 6 PBM-1, 2 PBO-1
Destroyers (Norfolk, 1 DB-2, 1 JRF-5) – DD343 *Noa*, AD2 *Melville*, AD11 *Altair*, AD12 *Denebola* (F), AD15 *Prairie*, AD20 *Hamul*, AD21 *Markab*, 1 SOC-1
DesFlot 3
DesRon 7 (Norfolk) – DD431 *Plunkett* (SF)
DesDiv 13 – DD421 *Benson*, DD422 *Mayo*, DD423 *Gleaves*, DD424 *Niblack* (F)
DesDiv 14 – DD425 *Madison* (F), DD426 *Lansdale*, DD427 *Hilary P. Jones*, DD428 *Charles F. Hughes*
DesRon 8 (Trinidad) – DD395 *Davis* (SF)
DesDiv 17 – DD381 *Somers*, DD383 *Warrington*, DD396 *Jouett*
DesDiv 18 – DD358 *McDougal* (F), DD359 *Winslow*, DD362 *Moffett*, DD394 *Sampson*
DesRon 11 (Hvalfjordur, Iceland) – DD418 *Roe* (SF)
DesDiv 21 – DD423

Livermore (F), DD430 *Eberle*, DD432 *Kearny*, DD440 *Ericsson*
DesDiv 22 – DD433 *Gwin* (F), DD434 *Meredith*, DD435 *Grayson*, DD436 *Monssen*
DesRon 13 (Norfolk) – DD420 *Buck* (SF)
DesDiv 25 – DD437 *Woolsey* (F), DD438 *Ludlow*, DD439 *Edison*, DD453 *Bristol*
DesDiv 26 – DD441 *Wilkes* (F), DD442 *Nicholson*, DD443 *Swanson*, DD444 *Ingraham*
DesFlot 4
DesRon 2 (Boston) – DD417 *Morris* (SF)
DesDiv 3 – DD409 *Sims*, DD410 *Hughes*, DD411 *Anderson* (F), DD412 *Hammann*
DesDiv 4 – DD413 *Mustin* (F), DD414 *Russell*, DD415 *O'Brien*, DD416 *Walke*
DesRon 8 (Bermuda) – DD419 *Wainwright* (SF)
DesDiv 15 – DD399 *Lang* (F), DD406 *Stack*, DD407 *Sterett*, DD408 *Wilson*
DesDiv 16 – DD402 *Mayrant* (F), DD403 *Trippe*, DD404 *Rhind*, DD405 *Rowan*
DesRon 10 (Norfolk) – DD454 *Ellyson* (SF)
DesDiv 19 – DD455 *Hambleton* (F), DD456 *Rodman*, DD457 *Emmons*, DD458 *Macomb*
DesDiv 20 – DD461 *Forrest* (F), DD462 *Fitch*, DD463 *Corry*, DD464 *Hobson*
DesRon 12 (Norfolk) – DD491 *Farenholt* (SF)
DesDiv 23 – DD459 *Laffey* (F), DD460 *Woodworth*, DD483 *Aaron Ward*, DD484 *Buchanan*
DesDiv 24 – DD485 *Duncan* (F), DD486 *Lansdowne*, DD487 *Lardner*, DD488 *McCalla*
DesFlot 8
DesRon 27 (Argentia) – DD341 *Decatur* (SF)
DesDiv 53 – DD126 *Badger* (F), DD128 *Babbitt*, DD158 *Leary*, DD159 *Schenck*
DesDiv 54 – DD130 *Jacob Jones*, DD147 *Roper* (F), DD157 *Dickerson*, DD160 *Herbert*
DesRon 30 (Argentia) – DD199 *Dallas* (SF)
DesDiv 60 – DD152

Dupont, DD153 Bernadou, DD154 Ellis (F), DD155 Cole

DesDiv 61 – DD118 Lea, DD142 Tarbell, DD144 Upshur, DD145 Greer (F)

DesRon 31 (Argentia) – DD220 MacLeish (SF)

DesDiv 62 – DD239 Overton, DD240 Sturtevant, DD246 Bainbridge (F)

DesDiv 63 – DD210 Broome, DD221 Simpson, DD223 McCormick (F), DD229 Truxtun

WPG31 Bibb, WPG32 Campbell, WPG33 Duane, WPG34 Alexander Hamilton, WPG35 Ingham, WPG36 Spencer

Submarines (New London) – AD2 Melville (F)

SubRon 1 (New London) – AG24 Semmes, ASR2 Falcon

SubDiv 11 - SS63 O2, SS64 O3, SS65 O4, SS67 O6, SS68 O7, SS69 O8, SS71 O10, SS157 S46, SS158 S47, SS159 S48

SubDiv 12 - SS79 R2, SS81 R4, SS82 R5, SS83 R6, SS84 R7, SS86 R9, SS87 R10, SS88 R11, SS90 R13, SS91 R14, SS97 R20, SS204 Mackerel, SS205 Marlin

SubRon 3 (Coco Solo, Canal Zone) – AS21 Antaeus, ASR4 Mallard

SubDiv 31 – SS105 S1, SS116 S11, SS117 S12, SS118 S13, SS119 S14, SS120 S15, SS121 S16, SS122 S17

SubDiv 32 – SS163 Barracuda, SS164 Bass, SS165 Bonita

SubRon 5 (New London/Argentia) – AS13 Griffin

SubDiv 51 – SS125 S20, SS126 S21, SS127 S22, SS129 S24, SS134 S29

SubDiv 52 – SS135 S30, SS136 S31, SS138 S33

SubDiv 53 – SS153 S42, SS154 S43, SS155 S44, SS156 S45

SubRon 7 (New London) – AS5 Beaver, ASR3 Chewink

SubDiv 71 – SS89 R12, SS92 R15, SS93 R16, SS94 R17, SS95 R18, SS96 R19, SS207 Grampus, SS208 Grayback, SS210 Grenadier

SubDiv 72 – SS78 R1, SS131 S26, SS137 S32

Train (Norfolk)

SerRon 1 (Norfolk) – AG17 Wyoming, AH1 Relief, AR5 Vulcan, ARS4 Redwing, ARS11 Warbler, ARS12 Willet, AT23 Kalmia, AT34 Algorma, AT37 Iuka, AT66 Cherokee

SerRon 3 (Norfolk)

TraDiv 1 – AK31 Markab, AP11 Barnett, AP13 George F. Elliott, AP16 Neville (F)

TraDiv 3 – AK30 Hamul, AP10 McCawley (F), AP12 Heywood, AP14 Fuller

TraDiv 5 – AK26 Alhena, AP15 William P. Biddle (F), AP17 Harry Lee

TraDiv 7 – AK29 Delta, AP25 Leonard Wood (F), AP26 Joseph T. Dickman, AP27 Hunter Liggett

TraDiv 9 – AK27 Almaack, AP21 Wakefield, AP22 Mount Vernon, AP23 West Point, AP24 Orizaba

TraDiv 11 – APD1 Manley, APD2 Colhoun, APD3 Gregory, APD4 Little, APD5 McKean, APD6 Stringham (F)

SerRon 5 (Norfolk)

MinRon 7 (Norfolk) – DMS18 Hamilton (F)

MinDiv 19 – DMS5 Palmer, DMS6 Hogan (F), DMS7 Howard, DMS8 Stansbury

MinDiv 20 – AM16 Partridge, AM24 Brant, AM70 Flicker, AM71 Albatros, AM72 Bluebird, AM76 Linnet

MinDiv 21 – AM2 Owl, AM55 Raven, AM56 Osprey, AM57 Auk

MinRon 9 (Argentia/Newport/New York/Boston)

MinDiv 25 – AM73 Grackle, AM74 Gull, AM75 Kite, AM77 Goldfinch (F)

MinDiv 26 – detached to the 1st Naval District

MinDiv 27 – detached to the 1st Naval Dsitrict

AM40 Cormorant, AM66 Bullfinch, AM67 Cardinal, AM80 Goldcrest, AMc78 Energy, AMc84 Heroic

SerRon 7 (Norrfolk) – AE2 Nitro, AE4 Kilauea, AF9 Yukon, AF11 Polaris, AF12 Mizar, AF13 Tarazed, AK18 Arcturus, AK23 Alchiba, AK25 Algorab, AK28 Betelgeuse, AKS2 Pollux, AO9 Patoka, AO11 Sarpelo, AO15 Kaweah, AO16 Laramie, AO17 Mattole, AO18 Rapidan, AO19 Salinas, AO22 Cimarron, AO26 Salamonee, AO30 Chemung, AO32 Guadalupe

SerRon 9 (Norfolk)

UtWing 1 (Norfolk) (1 OS2U-2) – VU-4 (16 J2F-1/3/4/5, 3 PBY-1), VU-5 (7 BG-1, 2 BT-1, 3 F2A-3, 3 F4B-4, 5 J2F-2/4/5, 5 JRB-1)

SubChasDiv 31 – SC449 – 452 (SC451 as flagship)

AG30 Bowditch, AGS4 Alcor (F), AK13 Capella, AK46 Pleiades, AP28 Kent, AP31 Chateau Thierry, AP41 Stratford, AO2 Maumee

1st Marine Aircraft Wing (Quantico, 1 JRB-2, 1 SBC-4, 2 SBD-1) – MVF-111 (15 F4F-3A, 2 SNJ-3), MVF-121 (20 F4F-3A, 2 SNJ-3), VMSB-131 (23 SB2U-3), VMSB-132 (19 SBD-1), VMO-151 (12 SBC-4, 2 J2F-4), VMJ-152 (1 J2F-1, 3 J2F-4, 2 R3D-2, 1 JD-2, 1 SB2U-3)

NAS Quantico – HSS-1 (1 FF-2, 2 F4F-3, 1

JF-2, 1 J2F-1, 2 SU-2, 1 XSBC-4, 3 SBC-4, 4 SBD-1, 2 SB2U-3, 5 SNJ-2/3)

1st Naval District (Boston)

Local Defense Force – YN15 *Elder*, YN18 *Mahogany*, YN19 *Mango*, YN20 *Hackberry*, YN23 *Palm*, YN24 *Hazel*, YN33 *Nutmeg*

Naval Coastal Force – PG5 *Williamsburg*, PG54 *St. Augustine*, PE19, PE27, PE38, PY13 *Syren*, PY16 *Zircon*, PYc2 *Sapphire*, PYc12 *Sardonyx*, WPG47 *Mojave*

MinDiv 26 – AMc36 *Accentor*, AMc37 *Bateleur*, AMc42 *Chimango*, AMc43 *Cotinga*, AMc46 *Fulmar*, AMc50 *Marabout*

MinDiv 27 – AMc29 *Puffin*, AMc38 *Barbet*, AMc39 *Brambling*, AMc47 *Jacamar*, AMc56 *Kingbird*, AMc72 *Courier*, AMc75 *Detector*

Naval Air Station (Quonset Point, 1 JF-1, 2 JRF-5, 6 OS2U-2, 1 SNJ-3, 1 SOC-1)

Naval Training Center (Newport, 1 J2F-1)

Naval Torpedo Station (Newport, 1 JF-1, 3 N3N-1, 2 OS3U-3, 1 PBY-3, 1 TBD-1)

Naval Reserve Air Base (Squanton, 1 GB-1, 1 JF-1, 4 JF-2/3/4, 23 N3N-1/3)

ATO26 *Wandank*, IX20 *Constellation*, IX21 *Constitution*

Boston Coast Guard District

CG Base South Portland – WAGL218 *Hibiscus*, WAGL222 *Ilex*, CG456, 468

CG Base Boston – WAGL229 *Lotus*, CG409, 410, 415, 450, 453 – 455, 472, 474

CG Air Station (Salem, 1 JRF-2, 1 J4F-1, 1 RD-4)

CG Patrol (Boston) – WPC100 *Argo*, WSC132 *Cartigan*, WSC136 *Dix*, WSC140 *General Greene*, WSC141 *Harriet Lane*

District vessels – WAGL56 *Kickapoo*, WAL502, 510, 528, WARC58 *Pequot*, CG158

Lightship Stations – WAL501, 503, 507, 511, 514, 520, 521, 525, 532, 534

CG Station South West Harbor - CG155, 211

CG Station Woods Hole – WAGL202 *Anemone*, WAGL203 *Arbutus*

CG Station Newport – CG461

CG Station Bristol – WAGL244 *Shrub*

3rd Naval District (New York)

Local Defense Force – AM81 *Chaffinch*, AMc48 *Limpkin*, AMc49 *Lorikeet*, AMc74 *Demand*, YN16 *Larch*, YN17 *Locust*

Naval Coastal Force – PE48, PE55, PY42 *Sylph*, WPC128 *Bedloe*

Part of MinDiv 27 – AMc61 *Acme*, AMc76 *Dominant*

New York N Yd – IX39 *Seattle*

Underwater Sound Lab (New London) – IX54 *Galaxy*

Naval Air Station (New York, 37 F2A-3, 2 GB-1/2, 1 JE-1, 22 J2F-2/5, 78 OS2U-2, 1 R3D-1, 1 SNJ-2)

District vessels – AT20 *Sagamore*, IX28 *Wheeling*, IX42 *Camden*, IX46 *Transfer*

Naval Reserve Air Base (New York, 22 N3N-1/3, 1 GB-1), VS-103 (12 OS2U-3)

Naval Reserve Midshipmen School – IX15 *Prairie State*

New York Coast Guard District

CG Base New London – WAGL215 *Hawthorn*, CG147, 157, 416

CG Air Station (Brooklyn, 2 PH-2, 2 JRF-3, 1 J4F-1, 1 N3N-1, 1 XR30-1, 1 R50-1)

CG Patrol (New York) – WPG112 *Nourmahal*, WPC110 *Icarus*, WPC128 *Antietam*, WSC125 *Active*, WSC143 *Kimball*

District vessels – WAGL205 *Beech*, WAGL219 *Hickory*, WAGL239 *Oak*, WAGL249 *Tulip*, WAL505, WYT87 *Hudson*, WYT88 *Navesink*, WYT91 *Mahoning*, WYT95 *Manhattan*, CG139, 156, 171, 172, 176, 178, 190, 213, 406 – 408, 439, 451, 452, 457, 469, 476

Lightship Stations – WAL512, 533, 536, 539

4th Naval District (Philadelphia)

Local Defense Force – AMc23 *Blue Jay*, AMc52 *Roller*, AMc53 *Skimmer*, WPG78 *Mohawk*

Naval Coastal Force – PE56

Naval Aircraft Factory (Philadelphia, 4 BG-1, 1 XBT-2, 23 F4B-4, 1 FF-2, 2 F2A-2/3, 2 F4F-3, 1 XF4F-5, 1 GB-1, 1 GH-1, 4 JRB-1/2, 1 XN3N-1, 2 N3N-3, 1 XN5N-1, 1 N2S-2, 2 OS2U-2/3, 9 O3U-1/3/6, 1 PBM-1, 1 XPBM-2, 1 XPBY-1, 1 PBY-5, 10 SU-4, 3 SF-1, 1 XBC-3, 1 SBC-3, 1 SBD-1, 2 SBN-1, 1 XSB2U-3, 1 SNJ-2, 1 SNC-1, 1 XOS2U-1, 1 TBD-1, 3 TG-1/2, 1 T4M-1)

Naval Air Station (Lakehurst, 1 Sf3F-1, 1 SNJ-3)

Lighter Than Air School (airships Nos G3, L1-3, K2-5, TC13, 14)

Naval Air Station (Cape May, 1 SU-4) – VS-104 (2 OS2U-2)

District vessels – AN5 *Keokuk*, AT19 *Allegheny*, IX40 *Olympia*

Naval Reserve Air Base (Philadelphia, 14 N3N-1/3)

Philadelphia Coast Guard District

CG Base Edgemour – WAGL227 *Lilac*, WAGL255 *Zinnia*
CG Patrol (Philadelphia) – WSC133 *Colfax*
Lightship Stations – WAL506, 524, 530
District vessels – WAL519, WYT92 *Naugatuck*
CG Station Atlantic City – WAGL260 *Elm*
CG Station Cape May – CG159, 214, 226, 464, 471

5th Naval District (Norfolk)

Local Defense Force – AMc5 *Kestrel*, AMc6 *Heath Hen*, AMc22 *Flamingo*, AMc24 *Egret*, AMc25 *Canary*, AMc62 *Adamant*, AMc63 *Advance*, AMc64 *Aggressor*, YN26 *Rosewood*, YN27 *Sandalwood*
Naval Coastal Force – PG17 *Dubuque*, PG18 *Paducah*, PY20 *Tourmaline*, WPG107 *Dione*
Naval Air Station Bermuda (Bermuda, 1 OS2U-2, 1 SOC-1)
Naval Air Station Norfolk (Norfolk, 3 F2A-1/2/3, 1 SF2A-2, 3 FF-2, 1 XF3F-1, 19 F3F-1/2/3, 20 F4F-3/4, 1 GB-1, 13 J2F-1/3/4/5, 3 JRB-2, 1 JRF-4, 12 OS2U-1/2/3, 1 O3U-3, 1 XJO-3, 2 PBO-1, 2 PBY-1, 3 PBY-5, 1 XPB2Y-1, 1 PB2Y-2, 1 SF-1, 1 SU-4, 2 SB2U-2, 4 SBC-3, 6 SNJ-2/3, 18 SOC-1/2/3, 4 SON-1, 8 TBD-1)
Naval Aircraft Depot (Norfolk, 1 JF-1, 1 TG-2)
Mine Warfare School (Yorktown) – CMc3 *Wassuc*, AMc26 *Humming Bird*, AMc28 *Mockingbird*
District vessels – AG1 *Hannibal*, AT24 *Kewaydin*, AT63 *Acushnet*, IX13 *Hartford*, IX25 *Reina Mercedes*

Norfolk Coast Guard District

CG Base Baltimore – WAGL250 *Violet*, WAGL254 *Wistaria*, WYT74 *Tioga*, CG140, 470
CG Base Norfolk – WSC142 *Jackson*, WSC144 *Legare*, WPG183 *Mayflower*, WAT55 *Carrabasset*, WYT84 *Winnisimmett*, WYT86 *Calumet*, CG462, 463, 475
CG Patrol (Norfolk) – WPC107 *Dione*, WSC157 *Cuyahoga*
Lightship Stations – WAL527, WAL529, WAL538
District vessels – CG128, 143, 218, 288, 440, 441, WAL515
CG Air Station (Elizabeth City, 2 PH-2, 2 JRF-3, 1 J4F-1, 1 N3N-3, 1 J2K-1, 1 J2K-2, 1 N4Y-1, 1 R3Q-1)
CG Station Virginia Beach – CG473
CG Depot, Portsnouth – WAGL237 *Mistletoe*,

WAGL238 *Narcissus*, WAGL240 *Orchid*, WAGL245 *Speedwell*

6th Naval District (Charleston)

Local Defense Force – YN21 *Mimosa*
Naval Coastal Force – PY21 *Ruby*, PYc1 *Emerald*
District vessels – AT25 *Umpqua*
Marine Corps Air Station (Parris Island, 1 SBC-4, 1 JF-1)
Naval Reserve Air Base (Atlanta, 1 GB-1, 22 N3N-3)

Charleston Coast Guard District

CG Base Charleston – WAGL211 *Cypress*, WAGL232 *Mangrove*, WAGL265 *Palmetta*, WSC126 *Agassiz*
CG Patrol (Charleston) – WPG52 *Tallapoosa*
Lightship Stations – WAL518, WAL537
District vessels – WAGL228 *Linden*, WAL518, WPR57 *Pamlico*, CG228

7th Naval District (Jacksonville)

Local Defense Force – AMc54 *Tapacola*, AMc55 *Turaco*, YN14 *Holly*
Naval Coastal Force – PY15 *Coral*, PY19 *Carnelian*, WPC113 *Pandora*
Naval Air Station (Jacksonville, 1 J2F-3, 1 JRF-5, 33 N3N-3, 99 NR-1, 108 N2S-1/3, 97 OS2U-2/3, 31 PBY-1/2, 19 SNC-1, 90 SNJ-2/3, 1 JRB-2)
Naval Air Station (Miami, 33 BT-1, 15 F2A-2/3, 16 F2F-1, 50 F3F-1/2/4, 1 JF-1, 1 JRF-4, 1 JRB-2, 10 N3N-3, 55 SBC-3, 96 SNJ-2/3)
Naval Air Station (Banana River, 1 JF-1)
Naval Air Station (Key West, 1 JF-1)
Naval Reserve Air Base (Opalocka) – VS7R07 (13 N3N-1/3)

Jacksonville Coast Guard District

CG Base Fort Lauderdale – WAGL266 *Poinciana*, CG212, 244
CG Base Key West – WAGL224 *Juniper*, WAGL266 *Pandora*, CG185
CG Patrol (Jacksonville) – WPC108 *Galatea*, WPA111 *Nemesis*, WPC115 *Thetis*, WSC154 *Vigilant*
District vessels – WAL522, WAGL223 *Althea*, CG131, CG186
Lightship Stations – WAL509
CG Station, Miami – WAGL160 *Forward*
CG Air Station, Miami (2 PH-2, 1 RD-4, 3 SOC-4)

CG Station, St. Petersburg – WAGL256 *Birch*
CG Air Station, St. Petersburg (1 J4F-1, 1 RD-4, 2 N3N-3)

8th Naval District (New Orleans)

Local Defense Force – AMc44 *Courlain*, AMc45 *Develin*, AMc51 *Ostrich*
Naval Coastal Force – PYc5 *Onyx*, WPC130 *Boutwell*, WPC154 *Vigilant*
Naval Air Station (Pensacola, 7 F2F-1, 1 GB-1, 2 GK-1, 1 JF-1, 1 JRF-4, 39 NJ-1, 409 N3N-1/3, 1 XN3N-3, 42 NS-1, 87 N2S-1/3, 87 OS2U-1/2/3, 56 O3U-1/3, 12 PBY-2, 3 P3M-2, 41 P2Y-2/3, 2 R2D-1, 1 R4D-2, 1 R5D-2, 49 SU-1/2/3, 1 XSBU-1, 73 SBU-1/2, 63 SNJ-1/2/3, 9 SOC-1/2, 1 XTBD-1, 1 JRB-2)
Naval Air Station (Corpus Christi, 30 F3F-2/3, 1 XF3F-3, 1 GB-1, 185 N3N-1/3, 279 N2S-1/2/3, 1 JRF-4, 89 OS2U-3, 141 PBY-1/2/3, 34 SBC-4, 10 SBU-1, 128 SNC-1, 39 SNJ-3, 35 SNV-1)
Naval Aircraft Depot (Pensacola, 1 GB-2, 1 J2F-4)
Naval Reserve Air Base (New Orleans, 1 GB-1, 21 N3N-3)
Naval Reserve Air Base (Dallas, 22 N3N-1, 18 NP-1)
Naval Reserve Air Base (Kansas City, 1 GB-1, 11 N3N-1/3, 13 NP-1)

New Orleans Coast Guard District

CG Base Mobile – WAGL226 *Larkspur*, WAGL231 *Magnolia*, WAGL269 *Aster*, CG240
CG Base Galveston – WSC155 *Woodbury*, WAGL247 *Sunflower*, WAGL257 *Bluebonnet*, WAGL263 *Myrtle*
CG Air Station (Biloxi, 2 PH-2, 1 JRF-2, 1 J4F-1, 2 JF-2)
CG Patrol (New Orleans) – WPC112 *Nike*, WPC116 *Triton*, WSC130 *Boutwell*
District vessels – WARC58 *Pequot*, CG130, 170
CG Depot (New Orleans) – WAGL206 *Camellia*, WAGL261 *Jasmine*, WYT81 *Davey*, WYT89 *Tuckahoe*

9th Naval District (Chicago)

District vessels – PYc14 *Truant*, IX30 *Dover*
Naval Reserve Air Base (St. Louis, 14 N3N-1/3, 9 NP-1)
Naval Reserve Air Base (Glenview, 1 GB-1, 5 GH-1, 23 N3N-1/3, 14 NP-1, 1 SU-2)
Naval Reserve Air Base (Grosse Isle, 1 GB-1, 26 N3N-1/3, 10 NP-1)

Naval Reserve Air Base (Minneapolis, 1 J2F-3, 14 N3N-1/3)

Saint Louis Coast Guard District

District vessels – WAGL213 *Goldenrod*, WAGL214 *Greenbriar*, WAGL251 *Wakerobin*, WAGL259 *Dogwood*, WAGL268 *Sycamore*
CG Depot (Chattanooga) – WAGL209 *Cottonwood*
CG Depot (Memphis) – WAGL253 *Willow*
CG Depot (St. Louis) – USCGC *Minneapolis*, WAGL241 *Poplar*

Cleveland Coast Guard District

CG Base Buffalo – WAGL258 *Cherry*
CG Base Detroit – WAGL235 *Marigold*, WAGL288 *Dahlia*, CG153, 172, 192
CG Base Sault Ste. Marie – WAGL204 *Aspen*
CG Air Patrol Detachment (Traverse City, 1 JRF-3, 1 J4F-1)
CG Patrol (Cleveland) – WPR50 *Ossipee*, WPG80 *Tahoma*
District vessels – WAGL234 *Maple*, WAGL248 *Tamarisk*, CG219
Lightship Stations – WAL526
CG Station (Alpena) – WAGL161 *Phlox*
CG Station (Duluth) – WAGL201 *Amaranth*
CG Station (Toledo) – WAGL210 *Crocus*

Chicago Coast Guard District

CG Base Milwaukee – WAGL220 *Hollyhock*, WAGL221 *Hyacinth*
District vessels – WAGL264 *Oleander*, CG119

10th Naval District (San Juan)

Local Defense Force – AM14 *Woodcock*, AM16 *Partridge*, AMc41 *Chachalaca*, AMc73 *Defiance*, AMc77 *Endurance*, YN22 *Mulberry*, YN25 *Redwood*
Naval Coastal Force – PY18 *Turquoise*, PYc8 *Opal*, WSC128 *Agassiz*, WSC133 *Colfax*, WSC136 *Dix*, WSC144 *Legare*, WSC151 *Rush*, WSC157 *Cuyahoga*
Naval Air Station (Guantanamo, 1 JRF-5, 1 N3N-2)
Naval Operation Base Trinidad – YP63, 64
Naval Air Station (Trinidad, 1 JRF-5)
Naval Air Station (san Juan, 1 JRF-4, 1 SOC-3)
District vessels – AT26 *Wandank*, AT39 *Montcalm*

San Juan Coast Guard District

CG Patrol (San Juan) – WPG53 *Unalga*, WSC134 *Crawford*, WSC145 *Marion*
District vessels – WAGL406 *Acacia*, WAGL246 *Spruce*, CG458, 460
CG Station Charlotte Amalie – CG459

11ᵗʰ Naval District (San Diego)

DesDiv 70 – DD109 *Crane* (F), DD137 *Kilty*, DD138 *Kennison*, DD164 *Crosby*
Local Defence Force – AMc3 *Plover*, AMc11 *Sanderling*, AMc12 *Grouse*, AMc32 *Courser*, AMc33 *Firecrest*, AMc35 *Road Runner*, AMc37 *Bateleur*, AMc59 *Ruff*, YN5 *Chestnut*, YN9 *Buckthorn*
Naval Coastal Force – PYc3 *Amethyst*, PYc13 *Jasper*
AT21 *Bagaduce*, YW56
Naval Air Station (North Island, 1 BT-1, 1 GB-1, 1 JK-1, 4 JRF-1/5, 1 XPB2Y-3, 1 R3D-1, 1 SF-1, 7 SBC-3/4, 1 SNJ-2, 2 SOC-1/3, 1 TBD-1, 1 TG-2)
Naval Destroyer Base – ARD1, IX44
Naval Ammunition Depot (1 JF-1)
Naval Reserve Air Base (Long Beach) – VS16RD11 (1 GB-1, 2 JF-3, 24 N3N-1/3)

Los Angeles Coast Guard District

CG Patrol (Los Angeles) – WPC109 *Hermes*, WSC131 *Cahoone*, WSC135 *Diligence*, WSC137 *Ewing*
District vessels – CG442
CG Base Los Angeles – CG254, 411
CG Air Station (San Diego, 1 JF-2, 2 PH-2/3, 1 RD-4)

12ᵗʰ Naval District (San Francisco)

DesDiv 83 – DD236 *Humphreys*, DD242 *King*, DD243 *Sands*, DD250 *Lawrence*
Local Defence Force – AMc7 *Bunting*, AMc13 *Hornbill*, AMc15 *Waxbill*, AMc16 *Chatterer*, AMc19 *Grosbeak*, AMc21 *Killdeer*, AMc34 *Parrakeet*, AMc58 *Rhea*, YN1 *Aloe*, YN5 *Catalpa*, YN10 *Ebony*, YN12 *Chinquapin*
Naval Coastal Force – PE32
Receiving Station (Yerba Buena Is) – IX2 *Dispatch*
Naval Net Depot (Tiburon) – YNG20 *Elder*, YNG21 *Dreadnought*
Naval Air Station (Alameda, 2 J2F-1/4, 1 JRF-4, 9 PBY-1/2/3, 1 SF-1, 1 SNJ-3, 7 SOC-1/2, 2 SON-1)
Naval Reserve Air Base (Oakland, 1 GB-1, 1 JF-3, 15 N3N-1/3)

San Francisco Coast Guard District

CG Patrol (San Francisco) – WPC101 *Ariadne*, WPC106 *Daphne*, WSC127 *Alert*, WSC147 *Morris*, WSC149 *Pulaski*
District vessels – WAT54 *Shawnee*, WAL504, CG412, 443
CG Base Alameda – CG255, 262, 401, 405
CG Station San Francisco – WYT94 *Golden Gate*, WAGL208 *Columbine*, WAGL230 *Lupine*, WAGL243 *Sequoia*
Lightship Stations – WAL508, WAL523
CG Air Station (San Francisco, 1 JF-2, 1 J4F-1, 1 PBY-5, 1 PH-3, 2 RD-4)

13ᵗʰ Naval District (Seattle)

DesDiv 82 – DD231 *Hatfield*, DD232 *Brooks*, DD233 *Gilmer* (F), DD234 *Fox*, DD235 *Kane*
Local Defence Force – AM7 *Oriole*, AM79 *Goshawk*, AMc17 *Pintail*, AMc20 *Crow*, AMc27 *Frigate Bird*, AMc57 *Phoebe*, AMc111 *Agile*, YP166 *Nightingale*, YN3 *Boxwood*, YN4 *Butternut*, YN8 *Buckeye*, YN11 *Eucalyptus*
Naval Coastal Force – PYc6 *Amber*, PE57, WPC109 *Hermes*, WPC114 *Perseus*
District vessels – AK16 *Spica*, AT27 *Tatnuck*, AT29 *Mahopac*, IX22 *Oregon*
Navy Yard (Puget Sound) – AVP12 *Casco*
Alaskan Sector (Dutch Harbor) – PG51 *Charleston* (F) (1 SOC-1)
Alaska Patrol (Dutch Harbor) – YP72 (F), YP73, YP74
Naval Air Station (Dutch Harbor, 1 OS2U-1)
Naval Air Station (Sitka, 1 J2F-1, 1 OS2U-2)
Naval Air Station (Kodiak, 1 F2F-1, 1 JRF-5)
Naval Air Station (Seattle, 1 F3F-3, 1 J2F-4, 1 JRF-1, 2 OS2U-1, 3 PBY-1/2, 1 SNJ-2, 2 SU-4)
Naval Air Station (Tongue Point, 1 JF-1)
Naval Reserve Air Base (Seattle) – VN15RD13 (1 GB-1, 1 JF-3, 14 N3N-1/3)

Seattle Coast Guard District

CG Patrol (Seattle) – WPG79 *Onondaga*, WPC102 *Atalanta*
District vessels – WAGL267 *Rhododendron*, WAL516, CG270, 271, 402, 404, 413, 414, *Invincible*
CG Base Astoria – WAGL233 *Manzanita*, WAGL242 *Rose*
CG Base Seattle – WAGL212 *Fir*, WYT *Guard*

Lightship Stations – WAL513, 517, 535

CG Air Station (Port Angeles, 1 JF-2, 1 J4F-1, 1 PBY-5, 2 PH-3, 2 RD-4)

Ketchikan Coast Guard District

CG Patrol – WPG45 *Haida*, WPC103 *Aurora*, WPC105 *Cyane*, WPC114 *Perseus*, WSC129 *Bonham*, WSC146 *McLane*, WSC148 *Nemaha*

CG Base Ketchikan – WAGL207 *Cedar*, WAGL216 *Alder*, WAGL217 *Hemlock*

14th Naval District (Honolulu)

DesDiv 80 (Pearl Harbor) – DD66 *Allen*, DD103 *Schley*, DD106 *Chew*, DD139 *Ward*

MinDiv (Pearl Harbor) – AMc8 *Cockatoo*, AMc9 *Crossbill*, AMc14 *Condor*, AMc30 *Reedbird*

MTBRon 1 (Pearl Harbor) – PT20 – 30, 42

Local Defence Force (Pearl Harbor) – YN2 *Ash*, YN7 *Cinchona*

Naval Coastal Force (Pearl Harbor) – PG19 *Sacramento*, PG52 *Niagara*

District vessels – AG33 *Kaula*, AK14 *Regulus*, ARS1 *Viking*, ARS3 *Discoverer*, AT28 *Sunnadin*, IX52 *Chenango*

Navy Yard Pearl Harbor – YP108, 109 etc

Naval Air Station (Pearl Harbor, 3 F2A-3, 1 F3F-2, 1 F4F-3, 4 J2F-2/4, 1 JRF-1, 5 OS2U-2, 1 RD-3, 1 R3D-2, 3 SBD-2)

Naval Air Station (Kaneohe, 1 J2F-1)

Johnston Island Command

Naval Air Station (1 J2F-2, 2 PBY-3)

Midway Island Command

Naval Air Station (1 J2F-2)

21 USN (PatWing 2) (10 PBY-3)

Palmyra Island Command

Naval Air Station (1 J2F-2)

Wake Island Command

Naval Submarine Base – YCK1

VMF-211 (12 F4F-3)

Honolulu Coast Guard District (1 JF-2)

CG Patrol – WPG37 *Taney* (1 JF-2), WSC150 *Reliance*, WSC152 *Tiger*

CG Depot – WAGL225 *Kukui*, WAGL252 *Walnut*, CG8, 27, 400, 403, 517, 4818

15th Naval District (Balboa, Canal Zone)

DesRon 33 – DD215 *Borie* (SF)

DesDiv 66 – DD148 *Brackinridge* (F), DD149 *Barney*, DD150 *Blakeley*, DD151 *Biddle*

DesDiv 67 – DD125 *Tattnall*, DD156 *J. Fred Talbott*, DD187 *Dahlgren*, DD247 *Goff* (F), DD248 *Barry*

Local Defence Force – AM68 *Catbird*, AM69 *Curlew*, AMc1 *Pipit*, AMc2 *Magpie*, AMc10 *Longspur*

Naval Coastal Force – PG50 *Erie* (1 SOC-1), PY17 *Jade*, PYc4 *Agate*, PYc9 *Moonstone*, PYc10 *Topaz*

District vessels – ARS2 *Crusader*, YP26

Naval Air Station (Colo Colo, 1 JF-1, 2 J2F-1, 1 JRF-1, 5 PBY-1/2/3, 1 RD-3)

16th Naval District (Cavite, Philippines)

MTBRon 3 – PT31 – 35, 41

Naval Inshore Patrol – PG21 *Asheville*, PG22 *Tulsa*, PR3 *Wake*, PR4 *Tutuila*, PR6 *Oahu*, PR7 *Luzon*, PR8 *Mindanao*, PY *Lankai*

District vessels – AT32 *Napa*, AT55 *Genesee*

Naval Yard Cavite – YP16, 17, 97 *etc*

Aircraft Detachment (2 J2F-5, 7 SOC-1/2/3)

Potomac River Naval Command (Washington)

Naval Air Station (Anacostia, 1 F2A-2, 2 F4F-2, 1 GK-1, 1 XJW-1, 2 GB-2, 3 JRF-4/5, 1 N3N-1, 1 XN3N-2, 1 OS2U-2, 1 R4D-2, 1 XR2D-1, 4 R5D-1/3, 4 SBD-2/3, 1 SBN-1, 20 SNJ-2/3, 1 SNV-1, 4 SOC-1/2, 1 XSO3C-1, 2 SON-1, 1 XTBF-1)

Fleet Test Unit (Anacostia, 1 F2A-3, 1 F4F-4, 1 XF4F-6, 3 J2F-5)

Naval Research Laboratory (Bellevue) – PYc7 *Aquamarine*, (2 JRB)

Naval Proving Ground (Dahlgren, 1 BD-1, 1 J2F-1, 2 N3N-3, 2 TBD-1, 1 TG-2)

Naval Reserve Air Base (Washington, 1 GB-1, 12 N3N-1/3)

Severn River Naval Command (Annapolis)

US Naval Academy – IX8 *Cumberland*, IX43 *Freedom*, IX48 *Highland Light* (2 J2F-1/3, 2 N3N-3, 3 O3U-3, 1 XOSN-1, 1 XOS2U-1)

BATTLESHIPS

WYOMING class battleship

Arkansas	BB33	New York SB, Camden	25.1.1910	14.1.1911	17.9.1912	nuclear tests 26.7.1946

Arkansas 1942

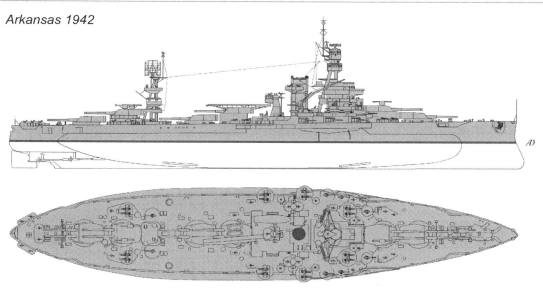

26066 / 30610 t, 171.3 x 32.3 x 9.1 m, 4 Parsons steam turbines, 12 Babcock & Wilcox boilers, 28000 hp, 21 kts, 3786 t oil, 14000 nm (10 kts), complement 1242; belt 280-229, deck 119-67, bulkheads 280-229, barbettes 280-114, turrets up to 305, CT 292; 6 x 2 – 305/50 Mk 7, 16 x 1 – 127/51 Mk 7.8, 8 x 1 – 76/52 Mk 10, 1 catapult, 3 seaplanes (SOC/SON, 1941- OS2U, late 1944- OS2U/SC)

Built according to the 1909 Program, paired with the sister BB32 *Wyoming*. The 305-mm main battery was chosen in 1909, in large part because the largest ship with these guns could be docked in existing shipyards on both coasts, whereas the 356-mm-gunned ship could be docked only on the Pacific coast. As compensation, a new, more powerful 305-mm/50 gun was designed. In 1926-1927, both ships underwent modernization: they received new bulges and new boilers, the horizontal armor protection was strengthened, and part of the secondary guns was moved to the upper deck. In 1931 *Wyoming* became a gun training ship AG17, armed with only 6 305-mm/50, 16 127-mm/51 and 2 76-mm/50 guns, no armor belt and only part of the boilers.

The main belt, 122-m long, had a depth of 2.44 m (1.3 m above and 1.14 m below the waterline) abreast citadel and was ha a thickness at the top of 280 mm, tapering to 229 mm at the lower edge. The belt was connected to the end barbettes with 280-mm fore and 229-mm aft bulkheads. There was a narrow 127-mm belt between the No 6 barbette and the stern. The upper belt had a depth of 2.21 m, being 280 mm at the lower and 229 mm at the upper edge, it was closed with 229-mm bulkheads.

The casemate had 165-mm armor and was connected to the No 2 and No 3 barbettes with diagonal 165-mm bulkheads. The funnel uptakes had 165-mm protection. The old flat armored deck (the splinter deck after the modernization) was connected to the upper edge of the main belt and had 57-mm thickness over the boilers and 76-mm over the magazines. The main deck over the turbines (between No 4 and No 5 barbettes) was not protected. This deck had 38-mm thickness between the citadel and the stem. It was 51-mm aft of the citadel and was reinforced over the steering gear up to 76 mm with 76-mm slopes. The new main deck (the old battery deck) was connected to the upper edge of the upper belt and was 114-mm over the magazines, 120-mm over the boilers and 132-mm over the turbines. Main gun turrets had 305-mm faces, 203-mm sides and rears and 120-mm crowns. The barbettes were 254-mm at the upper and 102-mm at the lower edge. CT had 292-mm sides

Arkansas 1945

and 120-mm roof. Underwater protection was 9.0-m deep. There was 38-mm longitudinal bulkhead.

7.1942: maximal 305-mm guns elevation angle was increased to 30°. - 10 x 1 – 127/51; + 2 x 1 – 76/50 Mk 20, 4 x 4 – 28/75 Mk 1, 20 x 1 – 20/70 Oerlikon, SC, SG, SK, FC (Mk 3) radars. 9.1942, *Arkansas*: + 2 x 4 – 28/75

Mk 1. 12.1942, *Arkansas*: + 2 x 4 – 28/75 Mk 1, 6 x 1 – 20/70 Oerlikon.

5.1943: - 8 x 4 – 28/75; + 8 x 4 – 40/56 Bofors.

5.1944: - 4 x 1 – 20/70; + 2 x 4 – 20/70 Oerlikon. 11.1944, *Arkansas*: + 2 x 1 – 76/50 Mk 20, 1 x 4 – 40/56 Bofors, 6 x 1 – 20/70 Oerlikon, SG (2nd), 2 Mk 19 radars.

NEW YORK class battleships

New York	BB34	New York N Yd, Brooklyn	11.9.1911	30.10.1912	15.4.1914	sunk as target 8.7.1948
Texas	BB35	Newport News	17.4.1911	18.5.1912	12.3.1914	stricken 4.1948

New York 1942

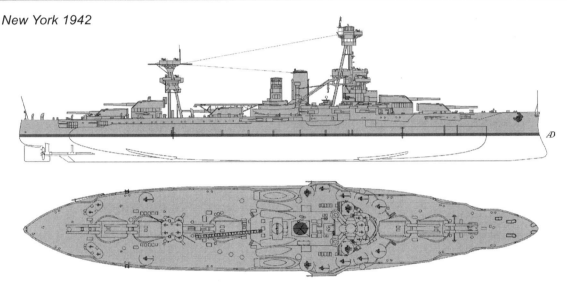

27000 / 31924 t, 174.7 x 32.3 x 9.2 m, 2 VTE, 6 Bureau Express boilers, 28100 hp, 21 kts, 2810 t oil, 15400 nm (10 kts), complement 1290; belt 305-254, deck 114-88, barbettes 305-127, turrets up to 356, CT 305; 5 x 2 – 356/45 Mk 8, 16 x 1 – 127/51 Mk 7.8, 8 x 1 – 76/52 Mk 10.18, 8 x 1 – 12.7 MG, 1 catapult, 3 seaplanes (SOC/ SON, 1941- OS2U, late 1944- OS2U/SC).

The ships of the 1911 Program were originally planned to be armed with 5 triple 305-mm turrets, but later, when 343-mm guns appeared in the Royal Navy, they were redesigned for 356-mm guns. It was a design that was originally developed in 1908-1909 as an alternative to the *Wyoming*. Turbine machinery plans were drawn up, but trials of the *North Dakota* showed that the turbines were generally unsatisfactory: it was estimated that

New York 1938

the new ship would only be able to reach about 5605 nm at 12 kts with turbines, compared to 7060 nm with reciprocating engines. In 1925-1927 both ships underwent modernization: they received new bulges, new boilers, horizontal armor protection was reinforced, secondary guns were partly moved one deck up.

The main belt, 122-m-long, had 2.44-m depth (1.3 m above and 1.14 m below the waterline) abreast citadel and was 305-mm thick in the upper part tapering to 254 mm at the lower edge. The belt was connected to the end barbettes with 254-mm fore and 280-mm aft bulkheads. There was a narrow 229-mm belt between No 5 barbette and the stern. The upper belt, 280-mm at the lower and 229-mm at the upper edges, was closed with 280 / 229-mm bulkheads. The casemate had 165-mm armor and was connected to the No 2 and No 3 barbettes with diagonal 165-mm bulkheads. The funnel uptakes had 165-mm protection. The old flat armored deck (splinter deck after the modernization) was connected to the upper edge of the main belt and was 51-mm over the boilers and 76-mm over the magazines. The main deck over the turbines (between No 3 and No 4 barbettes) was not protected. This deck had 38-mm thickness between the citadel and the stem. It was 51-mm aft of the citadel and was reinforced over the steering gear up to 120 mm with 76-mm slopes. The new main deck (old battery deck) was connected to the upper edge of the upper belt and was 114-mm over the magazines and turbines and 132-mm over the boilers. The main gun turrets had 305-mm faces, 203-mm sides and rears and 146-mm crowns. The barbettes were 305-mm at the upper and 127-mm at the lower edges. CT had 305-mm sides and 146-mm roof. The depth of underwater protection was 9.2 m. There was a 38-mm longitudinal bulkhead.

12.1938, *Texas*: + XAF radar

1.1939, *New York*: + CXZ radar

Early 1941, both: maximal angle of main guns elevation was increased up to 30°. Mid-1941, both: - 6 x 1 – 127/51; + 2 x 1 – 76/50 Mk 20, 4 x 4 – 28/75 Mk 1.

Early 1942, *Texas*: - XAF radar; + SG, SK, FC (Mk 3) radars. Early 1942, *New York*: - CXZ radar; + SG, SK, FC (Mk 3) radars. 8.1942, both: - 10 x 1 – 127/51; + 4 x 4 – 28/75 Mk 1, 42 x 1 – 20/70 Oerlikon.

1943, both: - 4 x 4 – 28/75; + 4 x 4 – 40/56 Bofors.

Texas

1944, both: - 4 x 4 – 28/75; + 4 x 4 – 40/56 Bofors. Autumn 1944, both: + 2 x 4 – 40/56 Bofors, (1 x 2 + 2 x 1) – 20/70 Oerlikon, 2 Mk 19 radars.

Supporting the Normandy landing, *Texas* 26.6.1944 received several hits of 280- and 240-mm shells from German coast batteries and spent a month under repair.

NEVADA class battleships

Nevada	BB36	Fore River, Quincy	4.11.1912	11.7.1914	11.3.1916	nuclear tests 2.1946
Oklahoma	BB37	New York SB, Camden	26.10.1912	23.3.1914	2.5.1916	sunk 7.12.1941

Oklahoma 1941

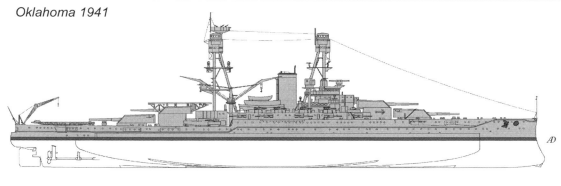

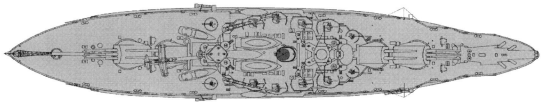

29067 / 31706t, 177.7 x 32.9 x 9.0 m, 2 sets Parsons geared steam turbines, 6 Bureau Express boilers (BB36) or 2 VTE, 6 Bureau Express boilers (BB37), 25000 hp, 20.5 kts, 3148 t oil, 15700 nm (10 kts), complement 1374; belt 343-203, bulkheads 330-203, deck 127, splinter deck 51-25, barbettes 330, turrets up to 457 (triple) or 406 (twin), CT 406; (2 x 3 + 2 x 2) – 356/45 Mk 9, 12 x 1 – 127/51 Mk 8, 8 x 1 – 127/25 Mk 10/11/13, 2 catapults, 3 seaplanes (SOC/SON, 1941- OS2U, late 1944- OS2U/SC)

The ships of the 1912 Program were the first USN battleships designed with 'all-or-nothing' protection, intended for long range artillery duels. The concept provided for the maximum possible protection of critical parts of the ship. The citadel, turrets, conning tower, and steering gear were covered with the thickest possible armor, the rest of the ship was not armored at all. Like the previous class, they carried 10 356-mm guns,

Oklahoma 1920

Nevada 1944

but their location changed: the ships lost the middle turret, instead of it, the end one became triple. Mass savings went to enhance protection. The ships had different machineries to compare the advantages and disadvantages of turbines of *Nevada* and reciprocating engines of *Oklahoma*. In 1927-1930, both ships were modernized: new main engines and boilers were fitted, horizontal protection was strengthened, secondary guns were partly moved to the upper deck, the maximum elevation angle of the main guns was increased to 30°.

The main belt, 122-m long, had 5.3-m depth and was 343-mm thick in the upper part tapering to 203 mm at the lower edge. The belt was connected to the end barbettes with 320-mm bulkheads. 2.6-m-deep 203-mm belt at 18.3-m length aft of the aft bulkhead protected the steering gear; it was closed aft with 229-mm

bulkhead. The flat main armor deck was connected to the upper edge of the belt and was 127-mm over the citadel. There was 38-mm splinter deck with 76-mm slopes one level down, the slopes were connected to the lower edge of the belt. This deck was 63-mm thick aft of the citadel, protecting the steering gear. The main gun turrets had 457-mm (triple) or 406-mm (twin) faces, 254-229-mm sides, 229-mm rears and 127-mm crowns. The barbettes were 330-mm above and 114-mm below the main deck. CT had 406-mm sides and 203-mm roof. The depth of the underwater protection was 5.8 m. There was 38-mm longitudinal bulkhead.

1941, *Oklahoma*: + 4 x 1 – 76/50 Mk 20.

(12.1941-10.1942), *Nevada*: - 12 x 1 – 127/51, 8 x 1 – 127/25, 1 catapult; + 8 x 2 – 127/38 Mk 12, 8 x 4 – 40/56 Bofors, 16 x 1 – 20/70 Oerlikon, SC, SG, Mk 3, 4 Mk 4 radars; full displacement was 35400 t.

Summer 1944, *Nevada*: + 1 x 4 – 40/56 Bofors, 22 x 1 – 20/70 Oerlikon. 11.1944, *Nevada*: - 33 x 1 – 20/70; + 1 x 4 – 40/56 Bofors, 20 x 2 – 20/70 Oerlikon.

Oklahoma was sunk in Pearl Harbor by B5N2 bombers from Japanese carrier *Akagi*: she received 4 torpedoes, capsized and sank. Later, 6.11.1943, the wreck was salvaged and used until 1947 as a hulk. *Nevada* 7.12.1941 was badly damaged during Japanese aircraft raid on Pearl Harbor; she received hits of one air torpedo and 2-3 bombs and ran aground. *Nevada* was salvaged 12.2.1942 and was under repair until March 1943.

Nevada 1944

PENNSYLVANIA class battleships

Pennsylvania	BB38	Newport News	27.10.1913	16.3.1915	12.6.1916	nuclear tests 2.1946
Arizona	BB39	New York N Yd, Brooklyn	16.3.1914	19.6.1915	17.10.1916	sunk 7.12.1941

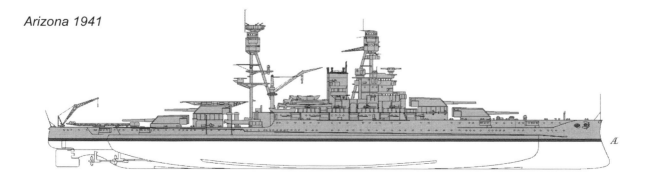

Arizona 1941

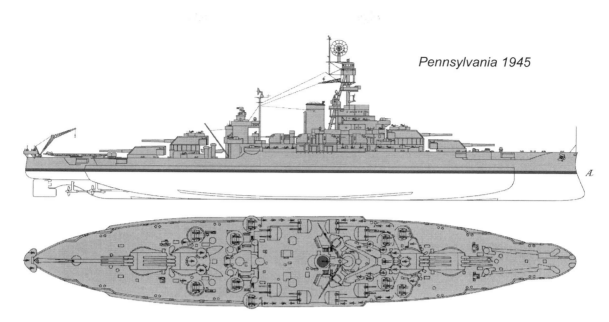

Pennsylvania 1945

33384 / 35929 t, 185.3 x 32.4 x 9.2 m, 4 sets Westinghouse geared steam turbines, 5 White-Foster & 1 Bureau Express boilers (*BB38*) or 2 Parsons steam turbines + 2 sets Westinghouse geared steam turbines, 6 Bureau Express boilers (*BB39*), 33375 hp, 21 kts, 3778 t oil, 19900 nm (10 kts), complement 1052; belt 343-203, bulkheads 330, deck 121, splinter deck 51-25, barbettes 330-114, turrets 457-229, CT 406; 4 x 3 – 356/45 Mk 10, 12 x 1 – 127/51 Mk 8/15, 8 x 1 – 127/25 Mk 10/11/13, 2 catapults, 3 seaplanes (SOC/SON, 1941- OS2U, late 1944- OS2U/SC).

The ships of the 1913 (BB38) and 1914 (BB39) Programs became essentially enlarged *Nevadas* with four triple turrets instead of the previous two twin and two triple mounts and 22 127-mm guns. 4000 t of additional protection was used for strengthened artillery and special underwater protection, consisting of a 76-mm torpedo bulkhead at a distance of 2.9 m from the plating, and a retaining bulkhead 0.8 m inboard of it. It was planned that this system would be able to withstand the explosion of 136 kg of TNT. *Pennsylvania* was ordered as a flagship, with a special two-level CT. In 1929-1931, both ships were modernized: they received new main engines and boilers and reinforced horizontal protection, secondary guns were partly moved to the upper deck, the maximum elevation angle of the main guns was increased to 30°.

The main belt, 125-m-long, had 5.3-m depth and was 343-mm thick in the upper part tapering to 203 mm at the lower edge. The belt was connected to the end barbettes with 320-mm bulkheads. There was 2.6-m-deep 203-mm belt at 18.3-m length aft of the aft bulkhead, protecting the steering gear; it was closed aft with 343-mm bulkhead. The flat main armor deck was connected to the upper edge of the belt and was 121-mm over the citadel. There was 38-mm splinter deck with 76-mm slopes one level down; the slopes were connected to the lower edge of the belt. This deck was 63-mm thick aft of the citadel, protecting the steering gear. The main gun turrets had 457-mm faces, 254-229-mm sides, 229-mm rears and 127-mm crowns. The barbettes were 330-mm above and 114-mm below the main deck. CT had 406-mm sides and 203-mm roof. The underwater protection was 5.8-m deep. There was 76-mm longitudinal bulkhead.

Mid-1941, both: + (8 - 9) x 1 - 12.7 MG. Mid-1941, *Pennsylvania*: + 4 x 1 - 76/50 Mk 20.

Early 1942, *Pennsylvania*: - 4 x 1 - 76/50; + 4 x 4 - 28/75 Mk 1, 16 x 1 - 20/70 Oerlikon, CXAM, Mk 3 radars.

1.1943, *Pennsylvania*: CT was removed; - 12 x 1 - 127/51, 8 x 1 - 127/25, 4 x 4 - 28/75, 1 catapult, CXAM

Arizona 1920

Pennsylvania 1945

radar; + 8 x 2 - 127/38 Mk 12, 10 x 4 - 40/56 Bofors, 34 x 1 - 20/70 Oerlikon, SG, SK, SR, Mk 3 (2nd), 2 Mk 4 radars.
7.1945, *Pennsylvania*: - 23 x 1 - 20/70, Mk 3 radar; + 1 x 2 - 40/56 Bofors, 22 x 2 - 20/70 Oerlikon, SC-2, SP, Mk 8 radars.
Arizona was hit in Pearl Harbor by 1 torpedo and

5-8 bombs from B5N2 bombers from Japanese carrier *Kaga*, was hit by a bomb in the magazine, blown up and sank. *Pennsylvania* was lightly damaged 7.12.1941 during Japanese air raid on Pearl Harbor and was under repair until the end of March 1942; 12.8.1945 damaged by a Japanese air torpedo; partial repairs were completed in October 1945.

NEW MEXICO class battleships

New Mexico	BB40	New York N Yd, Brooklyn	14.10.1915	23.4.1917	20.5.1918	stricken 2.1947
Mississippi	BB41	Newport News	5.4.1915	25.1.1917	18.12.1917	gunnery test ship 2.1946
Idaho	BB42	New York SB, Camden	20.1.1915	30.6.1917	24.3.1919	stricken 11.1947

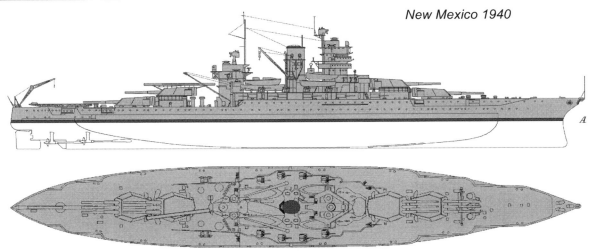

New Mexico 1940

33420 / 36157 t, 190.2 x 32.4 x 9.4 m, 4 sets Westinghouse geared steam turbines, 4 White Forster (BB40) or 6 Bureau Express (BBB41, 42) boilers, 40000 hp, 22 kts, 5402 t oil, 22000-26000 nm (10 kts), complement 1443; belt 343-203, bulkheads 343-203, deck 140, splinter deck 70, barbettes 320, turrets 457-127, CT 406; 4 x 3 – 356/50 Mk 7/11, 12 x 1 – 127/51 Mk 8, 8 x 1 – 127/25 Mk 10/11/13, 2 catapults, 3 seaplanes (SOC/SON, 1941-OS2U, late 1944- OS2U/SC).
Under the 1915 Program, three battleships of this class were built. Design began in the spring of 1913. Initially,

New Mexico 1943

it was planned to equip them with the latest 406-mm/45 guns in twin turrets and 152-mm secondary artillery, but in the middle of the year it was decided to return to 356-mm guns, which at existing combat distances were practically not inferior in armor penetration to 406 mm, but at the same time were noticeably faster. The choice of the design was finally decided in January 1914, when Secretary of the Navy Josephus Daniels ordered the building of new ships repeating the *Pennsylvania* class. After the approval of the design in July 1914, the armament was strengthened by replacing the 356-mm/45 guns with more powerful 356-mm/50. At the same time, the bow was redesigned from straight to clipper, which significantly improved seaworthiness, the thickness of the transverse bulkheads was raised from 320 to 343 mm and the deck from 76 to 89 mm. *New Mexico* received experimental turboelectric machinery, replaced with geared turbines during modernization. In 1931-1934 all three ships underwent modernization: they received new main engines and boilers and enhanced horizontal protection; the maximum elevation angle of the main guns was increased to 30°.
The belt was 125-m long and 5.2-m deep and was 343-mm thick in the upper part tapering to 203 mm at the lower edge. The belt was connected to the end

barbettes with 343-mm bulkheads. There was a 203-mm belt 2.6-m high at 18.3-m length aft of the aft bulkhead, protecting the steering gear, it was closed aft with 343-mm bulkhead. The flat main armored deck was connected to the upper edge of the belt and was 140-mm over the citadel. 70-mm splinter deck with 51-mm slopes was one level down, the slopes were connected to the lower edge of the belt. This deck was 63-mm thick aft of the citadel, protecting the steering gear. The main gun turrets had 457-mm faces, 254-229-mm sides, 229-mm rears and 127-mm crowns. The barbettes were 320-mm above and 114-mm below the main deck. CT had 406-mm sides and 127-mm roof. The depth of underwater protection was 6.7 m. There was a 76-mm longitudinal bulkhead.

Mid-1941, all: - 2 x 1 - 127/51; + 4 x 1 - 76/50 Mk 20, (8 - 10) x 1 - 12.7 MG.

12.1941 – 1.1942, all: - 4 x 1 - 76/50, (4 - 6) x 1 - 12.7 MG; + 4 x 4 - 28/75 Mk 1, 8 x 1 - 20/70 Oerlikon, SC, Mk 3 radars. 11.1942, *New Mexico, Mississippi*: - 4 x 1 - 127/51, 4 x 1 - 12.7 MG, 1 catapult; + 2 x 4 - 40/56 Bofors, 6 x 1 - 20/70 Oerlikon, SG radar. 12.1942, *Idaho*: - 10 x 1 - 127/51, 4 x 4 - 28/75, 4 x 1 - 12.7 MG, 1 catapult; + 10 x 4 - 40/56 Bofors, 16 x 1 - 20/70 Oerlikon. 2.1943, *Idaho*: + 19 x 1 - 20/70 Oerlikon. 10.1943, *New Mexico*: - 4 x 4 - 28/75, SC radar; + (2 x 4 + 2 x 2) - 40/56 Bofors, 10 x 1 - 20/70 Oerlikon, Mk 3 (2nd), SG (2nd), SK radars. 10.1943, *Mississippi*: - 4 x 4 - 28/75, SC radar; + (2 x 4 + 2 x 2) - 40/56 Bofors, 15 x 1 - 20/70 Oerlikon, Mk

Mississippi 1945

3 (2nd), SG (2nd), SK radars.

1.1944, *New Mexico*: + 19 x 1 - 20/70 Oerlikon. 1.1944, *Mississippi*: + 21 x 1 - 20/70 Oerlikon. Late 1944, *New Mexico, Mississippi*: - Mk 3 radar; + 6 x 4 - 40/56 Bofors, Mk 8, Mk 27, 2 Mk 28 radars.

1.1945, *Idaho*: - 8 x 1 - 127/25, Mk 3 radar; + 10 x 1 - 127/38 Mk 12, Mk 8, Mk 27, 2 Mk 28 radars. 4.1945, *Mississippi*: CT was replaced by lighter one with 38mm armor; - 6 x 1 - 127/51, 10 x 1 - 20/70; + 8 x 1 - 127/25 Mk 10/11/13, 2 x 4 - 40/56 Bofors. Mid-1945, *Mississippi*: - 6 x 1 - 20/70; + 1 x 4 - 40/56 Bofors.

New Mexico was 6.1.1945 damaged by kamikaze and was under repair until March 1945; 12.5.1945 she was again badly damaged by kamikaze and was under repair until August 1945. *Mississippi* was 9.1.1945 damaged by kamikaze and was repaired in March-April 1945; 5.6.1945 she was again damaged by kamikaze and was under repair for a month.

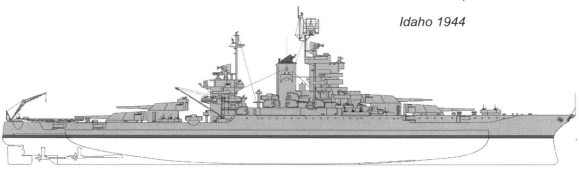

Idaho 1944

TENNESSEE class battleships

Tennessee	BB43	New York N Yd, Brooklyn	14.5.1917	30.4.1919	3.6.1920	stricken 3.1959
California	BB44	Mare Island N Yd, Vallejo	25.10.1916	20.11.1919	10.8.1921	stricken 3.1959

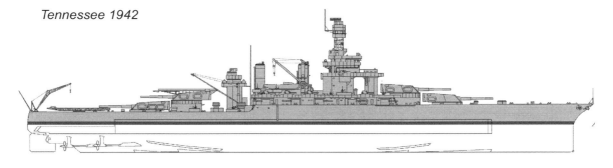

Tennessee 1942

Tennessee 1921

32300 / 33190 t, 190.2 x 29.7 x 9.2 m, 4 electric motors, 2 Westinghouse (BB43) or General Electric (BB44) turbo-generators, 8 Babcock & Wilcox (BB43) or Bureau Express (BB44) boilers, 26800 hp, 21 kts, 1900 t oil, 20500 nm (10 kts), complement 1083; belt 343-203, deck 89, splinter deck 38, barbettes 320, turrets 457-229, CT 406; 4 x 3 – 356/50 Mk 4, 12 x 1 – 127/51 Mk 8, 8 x 1 – 127/25 Mk 10/11, 8 x 1 – 12.7 MG, 2 – 533 TT (beam), 2 catapults, 3 seaplanes (SOC/SON, 1941- OS2U, late 1944- OS2U/SC).

Two battleships of the 1916 Program were planned to be built as a repetition of the previous class. After the order was issued in October 1915, a number of changes were made to their design. In December 1915, it was decided to equip them with a turboelectric machinery, and in February 1916, a new four-layer underwater protection system with 5.3-m depth was approved, capable, according to calculations, of withstanding an explosion of 181 kg of TNT. At the same time, the plates of the main belt were not installed on the shelf, but were attached to the plating, which freed up more space for underwater protection. The number of 127-mm guns was reduced to 14. Due to the refusal to install them at the ship ends, the lines of the forecastle and poop became even, without breaks in the casemates. The final design was ready in March 1916.

The belt, 125-m long, had 5.2-m depth and was 343-mm thick in the upper 3.2-m part, tapering to 203 mm at the lower edge. The belt was connected to the end barbettes with 343-mm bulkheads. 203-mm belt with 2.6-m depth was placed at 18.3-m length aft of the aft bulkhead, protecting the steering gear, it was closed aft with 343-mm bulkhead. The flat main armored deck was

California 1944

connected to the upper edge of the belt and was 89-mm over the citadel. The flat 38-mm splinter deck was placed one level down. This deck was 159-mm at flat with 159-mm slopes aft of the citadel, protecting the steering gear and was closed with 203-mm bulkhead. The TTs were protected by 127-mm deck at the level of the main belt lower edge. The main gun turrets had 457-mm faces, 254-mm sides, 229-mm rears and 127-mm crowns. The barbettes were 320-mm above and 102-114-mm below the main deck. CT had 406-mm sides and 152-mm roof. The funnel uptakes were protected by 229-mm armor. The depth of underwater protection was 5.3 m.

Late 1941, both: - 2 x 1 - 127/51; + 4 x 1 - 76/50 Mk 20. 3.1942, *Tennessee*: - 4 x 1 - 76/50; + 4 x 4 - 28/75 Mk 1, 16 x 1 - 20/70 Oerlikon, SC, FC (Mk 3) radars. 6.1942, *Tennessee*; + 2 x 4 - 28/75 Mk 1.

(9.1942-5.1943) *Tennessee*, (6.1942-1.1944) *California*: were modernized as follows: 34858 / 40345 t, 190.2 x 34.8 x 10.1 m, 4 electric motors, 2 Westinghouse (BB43) or General Electric (BB44) turbo-generators, 8 Babcock & Wilcox (BB43) or Bureau Express (BB44) boilers, 29500 hp, 20.5 kts, 4700 t oil, 9700 nm (18 kts), complement 2375; belt 343-203, deck 165-140, splinter deck 38, barbettes 320, turrets 457-229, CT 127; 4 x 3 – 356/50 Mk 7/11, 8 x 2 – 127/38 Mk 12, 10 (BB43) or 14 (BB44) x 4 – 40/56 Bofors, 43 (BB43) or 52 (BB44) x 1 – 20/70 Oerlikon, 1 catapult, 3 (BB43) or 4 (BB44) seaplanes (SO3C or OS2U), SC-2, SG, 2 Mk 8, 4 Mk 4 radars.

After the modernization: The belt, 125-m long, had 5.2-m depth and was 343-mm thick in the upper 3.2-m part, tapering to 203 mm at the lower edge. The belt was connected to the end barbettes with 343-mm bulkheads. 203-mm belt with 2.6-m depth was placed at 18.3-m length aft of the aft bulkhead, protecting the steering gear, it was closed aft with 343-mm bulkhead. The flat main armored deck was connected to the upper edge of the belt and was 140-mm over the citadel, increasing up to 165 mm over the magazines. The flat 38-mm splinter deck was placed one level down. This deck was 159-mm at flat with 159-mm slopes aft of the citadel, protecting the steering gear and was closed with 203-mm bulkhead. The main gun turrets had 457-mm faces, 254-mm sides, 229-mm rears and 178-mm crowns. The barbettes were 320-mm above and 102-114-mm below the main deck. CT had 127-mm sides. The funnel uptakes were protected by 229-mm armor. The depth of underwater protection was 8.0 m.

1945, *Tennessee*: - Mk 8 radar; + Mk 13 radar. 1945, *California*: - 52 x 1 - 20/70, Mk 8 radar; + 40 x 2 - 20/70 Oerlikon, Mk 13 radar.

During a raid of Japanese carrier aircraft on Pearl Harbor 7.12.1941, *Tennessee* was damaged by two bombs and ensuring fire, repairs lasted until March 1942; 12.4.1945 she was badly damaged by kamikaze and spent a month under repair. *California* during a

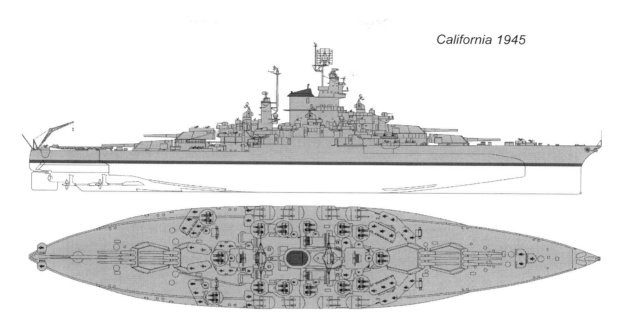

California 1945

raid of Japanese aircraft on Pearl Harbor 7.12.1941, received hits of two torpedoes and several bombs and ran aground. She was salvaged 26.3.1942 and was under repair and modernization until January 1944; 6.1.1945 she was damaged by kamikaze and was under repair until May 1945.

COLORADO class battleships

Colorado	BB45	New York N Yd, Brooklyn	29.5.1919	22.3.1921	30.8.1923	stricken 3.1959
Maryland	BB46	Newport News	24.4.1917	20.3.1920	21.7.1921	stricken 3.1959
West Virginia	BB48	Newport News	12.4.1920	19.11.1921	1.12.1923	stricken 3.1959

Maryland 1941

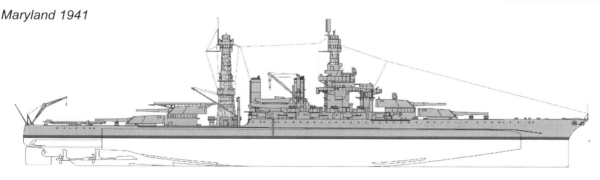

32600 / 33590 t, 190.2 x 29.7 x 9.2 m, 4 electric motors, 2 Westinghouse (BB45, 46) or General Electric (BB48) turbo-generators, 8 Babcock & Wilcox boilers, 28900 hp, 21 kts, 1900 t oil, 21100 nm (10 kts), complement 1080; belt 343-203, deck 89, splinter deck 38, barbettes 320, turrets 457-229, CT 406; 4 x 2 – 406/45 Mk 1, 12 x 1 – 127/51 Mk 8, 8 x 1 – 127/25 Mk 10/11, 8 x 1 – 12.7 MG, 2 – 533 TT (beam), 2 catapults, 3 seaplanes (SOC/SON, 1941- OS2U, late 1944- OS2U/SC).

According to the plans of the General Board, the battleships of the 1917 Program were to switch from 356-mm to 406-mm main guns. It was even possible to prepare a design of such a ship with 10 406-mm guns, but in June 1916, Secretary of the Navy ordered the building of the *BB45-48* as copies of the *Tennessee* class, but the designers were given the opportunity to choose the caliber of the main guns. This was decided in August 1916, when the replacement of 356-mm guns with 406-mm guns was approved. Building of *BB47 Washington* was cancelled due to the decisions of the Washington Naval Conference.

The belt, 125-m long, had 5.2-m depth and was 343-mm thick in the upper 3.2-m part tapering to 203 mm at the lower edge. The belt was connected to the end barbettes with 343-mm bulkheads. 2.6-m deep 203-mm belt at 18.3-m length was placed aft of the aft bulkhead, protecting the steering gear, it was closed aft with 343-mm bulkhead. The flat main armored deck was connected to the upper edge of the belt and was 89-mm over the citadel. The flat 38-mm splinter deck was placed one level down. This deck was 159-mm thick at flat with 159-mm slopes aft of the citadel, protecting the

Maryland 1945

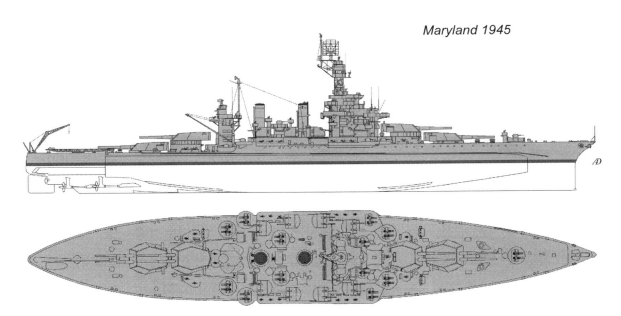

steering gear and was closed with 203-mm bulkhead. The TTs were protected by 127-mm deck at the level of the main belt lower edge. The main gun turrets had 457-mm faces, 254-mm sides, 229-mm rears and 127-mm crowns. The barbettes were 320-mm above and 102-114-mm below the main deck. CT had 406-mm sides and 203-mm roof. The funnel uptakes were protected by 229-mm armor. Underwater protection was 5.3-m deep. 7.1941, *West Virginia*: - 2 x 1 - 127/51; + 4 x 1 - 76/50 Mk 20.

(1941-12.1941), *Maryland*; (6.1941-1.1942), *Colorado*; (6.1942-9.1944), *West Virginia*: were modernized as follows: 34000 / 39100 (BB45, 46) or 37000 / 40396 (BB48) t, 190.2 x 32.9 (BB45, 46) or 34.8 (BB48) x 10.7-10.8 m, 4 electric motors, 2 Westinghouse (BB45, 46) or General Electric (BB48) turbo-generators, 8 Babcock & Wilcox boilers, 28900 hp, 20.5 kts, 4700 t oil, 9700 nm (18 kts), complement 2375; belt 343-203, upper deck 37 (BB45, 46), deck 89 (BB45, 46) or 165-140 (BB48), splinter deck 38, barbettes 320, turrets 457-229, CT 406 (BB45, 46) or 127 (BB48); 4 x 2 – 406/45 Mk 5/8, 10 x 1 – 127/51 Mk 8/15 (BB45, 46), 8 x 1 – 127/25 Mk 10/11/13 (BB45, 46) or 8 x 2 – 127/38 Mk 12 (BB48), 10 x 4 – 40/56 Bofors (BB48), 4 x 4 – 28/75 Mk 1 (BB45, 46), 14 (BB45) or 50 (BB48) x 1 – 20/70 Oerlikon, 8 (BB45) or 10 (BB46) x 1 – 12.7 MG, 2 (BB45, 46) or 1 (BB48) catapults, 3 seaplanes (OS2U on BB45, 46 and OS2U or SO3C on BB48); SC (BB45), SC-2 (BB48), SG (BB48), 1 (BB46) or 2 (BB48) FC (Mk 3), 2 Mk 8 (BB48),

4 Mk 4 (BB48) radars

After the modernization: The belt, 125-m long, had 5.2-m depth and was 343-mm thick in the upper 3.2-m part tapering to 203 mm at the lower edge. The belt was connected to the end barbettes with 343-mm bulkheads. 2.6-m deep 203-mm belt at 18.3-m length was placed aft of the aft bulkhead, protecting the steering gear, it was closed aft with 343-mm bulkhead. The flat main armored deck was connected to the upper edge of the belt and was 89 (BB45 and 46) or 140 (BB48)-mm over the citadel. On BB48 its thickness over the magazines was increased up to 165 mm. The flat 38-mm splinter deck was placed one level down. This deck was 159-mm thick at flat with 159-mm slopes aft of the citadel, protecting the steering gear and was closed with 203-mm bulkhead. Ex-TT rooms were protected by 127-mm deck at the level of the main belt lower edge. An additional 38-mm deck laid over the turbines, one level above the main deck. The main gun turrets had 457-mm faces, 254-mm sides, 229-mm rears and 127 (BB45, 46) or 184 (BB48)-mm crowns. The barbettes were 320-mm above and 102-114-mm below the main deck. CT on BB45 and 46 had 406-mm sides and 203-mm roof, BB48 had light CT with only 127-mm sides. The funnel uptakes were protected by 229-mm armor. Underwater protection was 8.0-m deep on BB45 and 46 and 9.0-m on BB48.

2.1942, *Maryland*: + 16 x 1 - 20/70 Oerlikon, SC radar. Early 1942, *Colorado, Maryland*: - 1 catapult. 11.1942, *Colorado*: + 8 x 1 - 20/70 Oerlikon. 2.1943, *Maryland*: + 2 x 4 - 28/75 Mk 1, 32 x 1 - 20/70 Oerlikon. 11.1943, *Colorado*: - 2 x 1 - 127/51, 4 x 4 - 28/75, 8 x 1 - 12.7 MG; + (6 x 4 + 4 x 2) - 40/56 Bofors, 20 x 1 - 20/70 Oerlikon. 11.1943, *Maryland*: - 2 x 1 - 127/51, 6 x 4 - 28/75, 8 x 1 - 20/70, 10 x 1 - 12.7 MG; + (6 x 4 + 4 x 2) - 40/56 Bofors. Spring 1944, *Colorado*: - 2 x 2 - 40/56, 7 x 1 - 20/70, Mk

Colorado pre-war

3 radar; + 2 x 4 - 40/56 Bofors, 1 x 4 - 20/70 Oerlikon, Mk 8 radar. Spring 1944, *Maryland*: - 2 x 2 - 40/56, 4 x 1 - 20/70, Mk 3 radar; + 2 x 4 - 40/56 Bofors, 1 x 4 - 20/70 Oerlikon, Mk 8 radar. 10.1944, *Colorado*: - Mk 8 radar; + (8 x 2 + 4 x 1) - 20/70 Oerlikon, Mk 13 radar.

Summer 1945, *Maryland*: - 8 x 1 - 127/51, 8 x 1 - 127/25, 34 x 1 - 20/70, Mk 8 radar; + 8 x 2 - 127/38 Mk 12, 4 x 4 - 40/56 Bofors, 19 x 2 - 20/70 Oerlikon, Mk 13 radar. 1945, *West Virginia*: - Mk 8 radar; + (1 x 4 + 1 x 2 + 8 x 1) - 20/70 Oerlikon, Mk 13 radar.

7.12.1941, during a raid of Japanese carrier aircraft on Pearl Harbor, *Maryland* was damaged by hits of two bombs and was under repair until February 1942; 22.6.1944 she was damaged by Japanese air torpedo and was repaired until August 1944; 29.11.1944 she was again damaged by kamikaze and was under repair until March 1945; she was again badly damaged by kamikaze 7.4.1945 and returned to service in August

Colorado 1944

1945. 7.12.1941, during a raid of Japanese carrier aircraft on Pearl Harbor, *West Virginia* received hits of 6-7 torpedoes and 2 bombs and sank. She was salvaged in May 1942 and recommissioned after repair and modernization in July 1944. *Colorado* was damaged 24.7.1944 by Japanese coastal battery (22 hits) and was under repair until October 1944.

West Virginia 1945

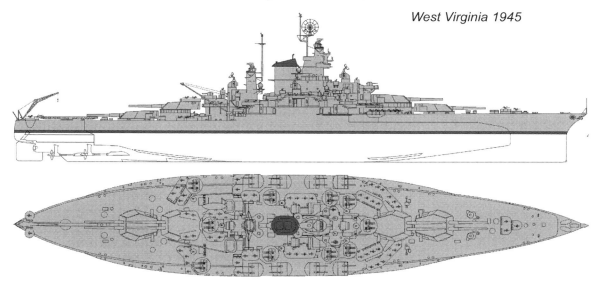

NORTH CAROLINA class battleships

North Carolina	BB55	New York N Yd, Brooklyn	27.10.1937	13.6.1940	9.4.1941	stricken 6.1960
Washington	BB56	Philadelphia N Yd	14.6.1938	1.6.1940	15.5.1941	stricken 6.1960

37484 / 44377 t, 222.1 x 33.0 x 10.0 m, 4 sets General Electric geared steam turbines, 8 Babcock & Wilcox boilers, 121000 hp, 28 kts, 6260 t oil, 17450 nm (15 kts), complement 1880; belt 305-168, main deck 140-127, upper deck 37, splinter deck 19-16, bulkheads 279, barbettes 406-292, turrets 406-249, secondary gunmounts 51, CT 406-373; 3 x 3 – 406/45 Mk 6, 10 x 2 – 127/38 Mk 12, 4 x 4 – 28/75 Mk 1, 12 x 1 – 12.7 MG, 2 catapults, 3 seaplanes (OS2U, late 1944- OS2U/SC). The first USN battleships built after the "battleship holiday". For the first time, it was envisaged to build ships with characteristics close to those of 'standard' battleships. The design was focused on providing protection and powerful armament at a fairly moderate

Washington 1944

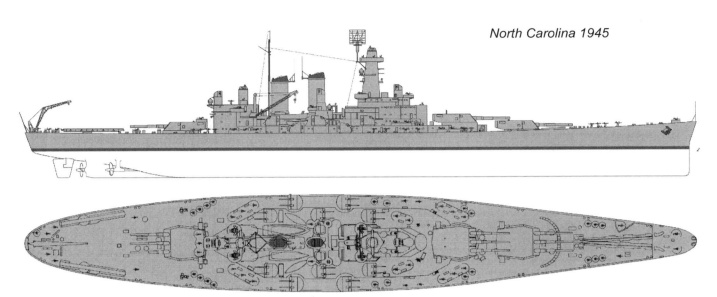

North Carolina 1945

speed. In 1935, the General Board revised the requirements for future battleships: now, additionally to the protection and armament, considerable attention was paid to the speed. Several versions of the design with a contractual 35000-t displacement and a 27-30-kt speed were prepared. General Board was leaning towards a variant with 30-kt speed and nine 356-mm guns in three turrets, however, for further study the design of slower (27 kts) ship with 11 356-mm guns in triple and quadruple turrets (soon the gun number was increased to 12, with replacing of a triple turret by a quadruple) was chosen.

The armor provided protection against 356-mm shells: the maximum caliber stipulated by the restrictions of the 1936 London Naval Conference (35000-t standard displacement, 356-mm guns). Since only United Kingdom, the USA and France signed the final protocol, it was provided that if Japan did not sign the treaty within a year, these restrictions would lose their force and new ones would come into force: 45000 t and 406-mm guns.

When it became clear, that Japan would not comply with the decisions of the Conference, the design of the new USN battleships was changed to reflect the changed situation. The caliber of the main guns was increased to 406 mm (quadruple turrets were replaced by triple with smaller barbette diameter), but it was not possible to increase the protection: this was possible only with a complete redesign of the hull (it was decided to do it on the next class). Under 356-mm shells, *North Carolina* and *Washington* had immune zone between 100 and 154 cables, under 406-mm shells it narrowed to 116-130 cables (105-135 cables for magazines). The armor arrangement was made according to the "all-or-nothing" scheme, traditional for the US Navy, with an increase in the number of armored decks to three: in addition to the main and splinter decks, there was also an upper deck for triggering a

bomb fuse. External armor belt was declined outward by 15°, which increased its strength at long distances.

Heavy AA armament of the new ships was designed to be very powerful: 10 twin 127-mm/38 mounts amidships, placed on two levels in the shape of the letter "W", became the standard for subsequent classes of US Navy battleships. Light AA armament was worse and consisted of 28-mm MGs nicknamed "Chicago pianos", which were distinguished by whimsical and unreliable. Almost immediately after the commissioning, they were replaced by quadruple 40-mm Bofors and 12.7-mm MGs were replaced by 20-mm Oerlikons.

The belt, 136-m long, inclined at angle of 15° to the vertical, had 5.5-m depth and a thickness of 305 mm (on 19-mm STS-steel plating) in the upper part tapering to 168 mm at the lower edge. The belt was connected to the end barbettes with 282-mm bulkheads. The steering gear compartment had its own 378-mm belt with 282-mm bulkheads. The flat main armored deck was connected to the upper edge of the belt and was 140-127-mm over the citadel. 38-mm upper deck was placed one level up. Its thickness decreased to 25-19 mm fwd of the No1 barbette. Flat 19-16-mm splinter deck was placed one level below. This deck extended aft of No 3 barbette and was 152-mm over the steering gear. The main gun turrets had 406-mm faces, 249-mm sides, 300-mm rears and 178-mm crowns. The barbettes above the main deck were 373-mm at the end parts, 406-mm at the sides and 292-mm at the inner parts. They consisted of two rings (73-mm outer and 37-mm inner) below the main deck. CT had 406-mm sides, 373-mm fore and aft parts, 178-mm roof and 102-mm deck. Underwater protection consisted of 5 compartments and could withstand an explosion of 317 kg of TNT. The longitudinal bulkhead had 95-51-mm thickness abreast magazines only.

Late 1941, *North Carolina*: + 1 x 4 - 28/75 Mk 1.

3.1942, *North Carolina*: + 33 x 1 - 20/70 Oerlikon, CXAM, 2 Mk 3, 3 Mk 4 radars. 4.1942, *North Carolina*:

+ 7 x 1 - 20/70 Oerlikon. 4.1942, *Washington*: + 20 x 1 - 20/70 Oerlikon, CXAM, 2 Mk 3, 3 Mk 4 radars. 7.1942, both: + 16 x 1 - 12.7 MG; 9.1942, *Washington*: + 20 x 1 - 20/70 Oerlikon. 11.1942, *North Carolina*: - 5 x 4 - 28/75, 28 x 1 - 12.7 MG, CXAM radar; + 10 x 4 - 40/56 Bofors, 6 x 1 - 20/70 Oerlikon, SG, Mk 4 (4th) radars. 11.1942, *Washington*: - 5 x 1 - 20/70, 28 x 1 - 12.7 MG, CXAM radar; + 2 x 4 - 28/75 Mk 1, SG, Mk 4 (4th) radars. 4.1943, *Washington*: + 29 x 1 - 20/70 Oerlikon. 6.1943, *North Carolina*: + 4 x 4 - 40/56 Bofors. 7.1943, *Washington*: - 6 x 4 - 28/75; + 10 x 4 - 40/56 Bofors. 8.1943, *Washington*: + 5 x 4 - 40/56 Bofors. 11.1943, *North Carolina*: + 1 x 4 - 40/56 Bofors. 3.1944, *North Carolina*: - Mk 3 radar; + 7 x 1 - 20/70 Oerlikon, SG (2nd), SK, 2 Mk 8, Mk 27 radars. 4.1944, *Washington*: - 1 x 1 - 20/70, Mk 3 radar; + 1 x 4 - 20/70 Oerlikon, SG (2nd), SK, 2 Mk 8, Mk 27 radars. 9.1944, *North Carolina*: - SK, 4 Mk 4 radars; + SK-2, 4 Mk 12/22 radars, TDY ECM suite. 9.1944, *Washington*: - 4 Mk 4 radars; + 4 Mk 12/22 radars, TDY ECM suite.

North Carolina 1946

Summer 1945, *North Carolina*: - 33 x 1 - 20/70; + 9 x 4 - 40/56 Bofors, 8 x 2 - 20/70 Oerlikon, SR, SCR-720 radars; 46700-t displacement (full). Autumn 1945, *Washington*: + 8 x 2 - 20/70 Oerlikon, SR, SCR-720 radars; 46796-t displacement (full).
North Carolina 15.9.1942 was damaged by a torpedo from Japanese submarine; repair lasted until the end of a year.

SOUTH DAKOTA class battleships

South Dakota	BB57	New York SB, Camden	5.7.1939	7.6.1941	20.3.1942	stricken 6.1962
Indiana	BB58	Newport News	20.11.1939	21.11.1941	30.4.1942	stricken 6.1962
Massachusetts	BB59	Bethlehem, Quincy	20.7.1939	23.9.1941	12.5.1942	stricken 6.1962
Alabama	BB60	Norfolk N Yd, Portsmouth	1.2.1940	16.2.1942	16.8.1942	stricken 6.1962

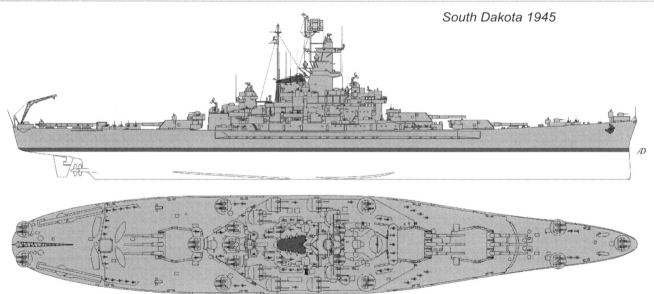

South Dakota 1945

37970 / 44519 t, 207.3 x 33.0 x 10.7 m, 4 sets General Electric geared steam turbines, 8 Babcock & Wilcox boilers, 130000 hp, 27.5 kts, 6959 t oil, 15000 nm (15 kts), complement 1793; belt 310, lower belt 310, deck 152-146, upper deck 38, splinter deck 19, bulkheads 287, barbettes 439-287, turrets 457-241, CT 406; 3 x 3 – 406/45 Mk 6, 8 (BB57) or 10 (BB58-60) x 2 – 127/38 Mk 12, 6 x 4 – 40/56 Bofors (BB58-60), 7 x 4 – 28/75 Mk 1 (BB57), 16 (BB57, 58) or 35 (BB59) or 22 (BB60) x 1 – 20/70 Oerlikon, 8 x 1 – 12.7 MG (BB57), 2 catapults, 3 seaplanes (OS2U, late 1944- OS2U/SC); SC, SG, 2 Mk 3 (BB57) or 2 Mk 8 (BB58-60), 4 Mk 4 radars.

When designing the battleships of the FY39 Program (future *South Dakota* class), the designers were tasked with providing protection against 406-mm shells, correcting the main drawback of the previous *North Carolina* class. In addition, it was required to fit the new ship into 35000-t standard displacement, avoiding

South Dakota 1943

noticeable drop in speed. To solve such a complex problem, it was necessary to start designing almost from scratch, borrowing only structure and arrangement of the armament from the previous design. Design began in 1937. The new hull shape became significantly shorter with the same breadth. Due to more cramped machinery, the total machinery spaces length was reduced by 17 m, which, in turn, made it possible to reduce the length of the protected spaces. Although the thickness of the armor was increased slightly compared to the predecessors, the new armor distribution scheme provided much better protection. The main belt (310-mm armor on 19-mm STS steel plating) was located at an 19° angle outward deep in the hull and extended to the bottom, gradually narrowing to 25 mm and connecting to the anti-torpedo bulkhead (It was assumed that the new underwater protection would withstand explosion of a torpedo with a charge of 317 kg of TNT). Thus, the external side plating (19-mm) served as an APC destroyer. The thickness and arrangement of armored decks differed from the *North Carolina* class. In general, the new scheme turned out to be more reliable than on the predecessors, and provided an immune zone under 406-mm shells in the 90-150 cables interval (4 times wider than on the *North Carolina* class). A short hull with a lower L/B ratio required the installation of more powerful, than on the *North Carolina* class, machinery,

Indiana 1944

but the speed still fell by half a knot.

Initially, it was originally supposed to order two ships (BB57 and BB58), switching from BB59 to a new design (the future *Iowa* class), but in June 1938 a decision was made to build two more 35000-t battleships, since the design of a new high-speed battleship was carried out more slowly than originally expected.

The lead-ship (BB57) was supposed to become the flagship and differed from the other three in a larger conning tower. Due to the increased upper weight, the number of 127-mm mounts on her was reduced to eight (it was partly offset by an increase in the number of 28-mm MGs).

The 28-mm MGs envisaged by the design, during fitting out were replaced with quadruple 40-mm Bofors, and 12.7-mm MGs by 20-mm Oerlikons.

The inner belt, 113.4-m long, inclined at 19° to the vertical, had 3.2-m depth and had a thickness of 310 mm (on 51-mm cement layer and 22-mm plating). 19°-inclined lower belt was connected to the main belt and tapered from 310 mm at the upper edge to 152 mm 2.1 m below and then to 25 mm at the lower edge. The belt was connected to the end barbettes with bulkheads. The thickness of the fore bulkhead was 287 mm, but at lower part of the bulkhead it was decreased to 25 mm (as a lower belt). The aft bulkhead had 287-mm thickness only on one level below the main deck, its lower part was only 16-mm thick, but it was connected to the steering gear belt. The steering gear compartment had 343-mm 19°-inclined belt and 287-mm bulkhead expanded up to the lower (splinter) deck. The flat main armored deck was connected to the upper edge of the belt and was 154 (near the sides)-146-mm (near the center line) over the citadel. 38-mm upper deck was placed one level up. Its thickness was decreased to 25-19 mm fwd of the No1 barbette. Flat 19-mm splinter deck was placed one level down. This deck extended aft of the No3 barbette and was 157-121-mm over the steering gear belt. The main gun turrets had 457-mm faces, 305-mm sides, 300-mm rears and 184-mm crowns. The barbettes above the main deck were 294-mm at the center line and 440-mm at the sides. They consisted of two rings (73-mm outer and 37-mm inner) below the main deck. CT had 406-mm sides, 373-mm fore and aft parts, 178-mm roof and 102-mm deck. 5.45-m deep underwater protection consisted of 4 compartments and could withstand an explosion of 317 kg of TNT. As the 3rd longitudinal bulkhead, the inner main and lower belts were used.

10.1942, *South Dakota*: - 2 x 4 - 28/75, 8 x 1 - 12.7 MG; + 4 x 4 - 40/56 Bofors, 20 x 1 - 20/70 Oerlikon. 11.1942, *Indiana*: + 4 x 4 - 40/56 Bofors. 12.1942, *Massachusetts*: + 4 x 4 - 40/56 Bofors, 13 x 1 - 20/70 Oerlikon.

1943, all: - SC, 4 Mk 4 radars; + SG (2nd), SK, 4 Mk 12/22 radars. 1.1943, *Indiana*: + 37 x 1 - 20/70 Oerlikon. 2.1943, *South Dakota*: - 5 x 4 - 28/75, 1 x 1 - 20/70;

+ 13 x 4 - 40/56 Bofors. 2.1943, *Indiana*: + 2 x 4 - 40/56 Bofors. 2.1943, *Massachusetts*: + 2 x 4 - 40/56 Bofors, 13 x 1 - 20/70 Oerlikon. 2.1943, *Alabama*: + 4 x 4 - 40/56 Bofors. 5.1943, *Alabama*: + 38 x 1 - 20/70 Oerlikon. 9.1943, *Massachusetts*: - 18 x 1 - 20/70. 11.1943, *Alabama*: + 2 x 4 - 40/56 Bofors. 12.1943, *Indiana*: + 7 x 1 - 20/70 Oerlikon. 1943, *South Dakota*: - 2 Mk 3 radars; + 2 Mk 8 radars.
1944, all: + Mk 27 radar, TDY ECM suite. 4.1944, *Indiana*: + 3 x 1 - 20/70 Oerlikon. 7.1944, *Indiana*: - 16 x 1 - 20/70; + 4 x 2 - 20/70 Oerlikon. 10.1944, *Massachusetts*: - 17 x 1 - 20/70; + (1 x 4 + 1 x 2) - 20/70 Oerlikon. 12.1944, *South Dakota*: + 37 x 1 - 20/70 Oerlikon. 12.1944, *Indiana*: - 3 x 1 - 20/70; 12.1944, *Massachusetts*: + 6 x 4 - 40/56 Bofors, 6 x 1 - 20/70 Oerlikon. 12.1944, *Alabama*: - 8 x 1 - 20/70.
3.1945, *South Dakota*: + 5 x 1 - 20/70 Oerlikon. 1945, *South Dakota, Massachusetts*: - SK, 2 Mk 8

Massachusetts 1944

radars; + SK-2, SR, 2 Mk 13 radars. 1945, *Indiana*: - 2 Mk 8 radars; + SP, 2 Mk 13 radars. 1945, *Alabama*: - SG, SK, 2 Mk 8 radars; + SK-2, SR, SU, 2 Mk 13 radars. Summer 1945, *Massachusetts*: - 1 x 1 - 20/70. Summer 1945, *Alabama*: + 4 x 1 - 20/70 Oerlikon.
South Dakota 15.11.1942 was damaged by Japanese ships in the battle of Guadalcanal and was under repair until February 1943; 19.6.1944 she was again damaged by Japanese aircraft (1 bomb hit) and was recommissioned in August 1944.

IOWA class battleships

Iowa	BB61	New York N Yd, Brooklyn	27.6.1940	27.8.1942	22.2.1943	stricken 3.2006
New Jersey	BB62	Philadelphia N Yd	16.9.1940	7.12.1942	23.5.1943	stricken 1.1999
Missouri	BB63	New York N Yd, Brooklyn	6.1.1941	29.1.1944	11.6.1944	stricken 1.1995
Wisconsin	BB64	Philadelphia N Yd	25.1.1941	7.12.1943	16.4.1944	stricken 3.2006
Illinois	BB65	Philadelphia N Yd	6.12.1942	-	-	cancelled 8.1945
Kentucky	BB66	Norfolk N Yd, Portsmouth	6.12.1942	20.1.1950	-	suspended 2.1947

48110 / 57540 t, 270.4 x 33.0 x 11.0 m, 4 sets General Electric geared steam turbines, 8 Babcock & Wilcox boilers, 212000 hp, 32.5 kts, 7621 t oil, 15000 nm (15 kts), complement 1921; belt 307, lower belt 307, main deck 178, upper deck 38, splinter deck 25-16, bulkheads 287-216 (BB61,62) or 368-297 (BB63, 64), barbettes 439-295, turrets 495-260, CT 440; 3 x 3 – 406/50 Mk 7, 10 x 2 – 127/38 Mk 12, 15 (BB61) or 20 (BB62-64) x 4 – 40/56 Bofors, 60 x 1 (BB61) or 49 x 1 (BB62, 63) or (2 x 2 + 49 x 1) (BB64) – 20/70 Oerlikon, 2 catapults, 3 seaplanes (OS2U, late 1944- OS2U/SC); SK (BB61, 62, 64) or SK-2 (BB63), 2 SG, Mk 3 (BB61, 62) or Mk 27 (BB63, 64), 2 Mk 8, 4 Mk 4 (BB61, 62) or 4 Mk 12/22 (BB63, 64) radars.
The design of the *Iowa* class began in 1938. In defining their data elements, the General Board reverted to the idea of a battleship to support and defend a fast carrier force against Japanese heavy and battle-cruisers (the *North Carolina* class battleships were originally designed for this task and should have 30-kt speed). By the time the design work began, the limitations of the 1936 London Naval Conference, due to Japan's refusal to sign the document, were increased from 35000 to 45000 t of standard displacement, and 406-mm caliber of the artillery instead of 356-mm. This made it possible to create a ship with protection and armament that were not inferior to accepted on the *South Dakota* class, taking advantage of the increase in

displacement to fit more powerful machinery. In the *Iowa* design, the hull was lengthened by almost 70 m with the same breadth (the limited width of the Panama Canal). The increased L/B ratio, together with 60% more powerful machinery, should provide 33-kt speed. The increase in the length of the protected citadel led to a growth of an armor weight, although the thickness of its elements, in comparison with the *South Dakota* class, remained practically unchanged. The only difference was the thickness of the transverse bulkheads increased to 368 mm, starting with the third ship of the class.
Iowa class ships received new 406-mm/50 guns. The appearance of this artillery system was rather curious: with protection and armament similar to the *South Dakota*, an increase in displacement by 10000 t went only to increase speed by 6 knots, which could serve as a subject of criticism of the new design. At the same

Iowa 1947

time, a large number of ready-made 406-mm/50 guns (manufactured in the early twenties for battleships and battlecruisers that became victims of the Washington Conference) were ready or almost ready in the naval arsenals. The use of these guns in the new design made it possible both to save finances and to justify the increase in displacement due to the transition to a new artillery system. But it turned out that the fitting of 406mm-/50 guns would lead to an additional increase in displacement (by about another 2000 t). The way out was found in the manufacture of new guns, since there was a backlog for the design. As on the predecessors, heavy AA armament was represented by 20 127-mm guns in twin mountings, supplemented by 4 x 4 28-mm Mk 1 guns and 12 12.7-mm MGs.

The design was approved in June 1938, the following year an order was issued for BB61 and BB62 under the FY40 Program. In July 1939, the decision to build BB63 and BB64 (FY40) followed, and in September 1939 building of BB65 and BB66 was approved.

The building of battleships was carried out very quickly, and in 1943 the first pair was ready. BB61 was supposed to be the flagship and had larger CT. During the building, light AA armament was changed: instead of 28-mm and 12.7-mm MGs, the ships received 40-mm Bofors and 20-mm Oerlikons.

The second pair was commissioned in 1944, then the building of BB65 and BB66 was first suspended and then cancelled.

The inner belt, 141.4-m long, inclined at an angle of 19° to the vertical, had 3.2-m depth and a thickness of 307 mm (on 51-mm cement layer and 22-mm plating). This belt was covered by a vertical 38-mm outer belt. An 8.5-m high lower belt was inclined at an angle of 19°, was connected to the main belt and was tapered from 307 mm at the upper edge to 41 mm at the lower edge. The belt was connected to the end barbettes with bulkheads. The thickness of the fore bulkhead was 287

mm on BB61 and 62 and 368 mm on BB63 and 64, but in the lower part of the bulkhead it was decreased to 216 mm on BB61 and 62 and 297 mm on BB63 and 64. The aft bulkhead had 287-mm (on BB61 and 62) or 368-mm (on BB63 and 64) thickness only up to one level below the main deck, its lower part was only 16-mm thick, but adjacent to the steering gear belt. The steering gear compartment had 343-mm 19°-inclined belt and 287-mm bulkhead extended to the lower (splinter) deck. The flat main armored deck was connected to the upper edge of the belt and was 178 (near the sides)-152-mm (near the center line) over the citadel. 38-mm upper deck was placed one level up. Flat 16-mm (25-mm over the magazines) splinter deck was placed one level down. This deck extended aft of the No 3 barbette and was 157-142-mm over the steering gear belt. The main gun turrets had 432-mm (on 63-mm plating) faces, 241-mm (on 19-mm plating) sides, 300-mm rears and 184-mm crowns. The barbettes above the main deck were 294-mm at the center line and 440-mm at the sides, but its thickness decreased to 76-38 mm below the main deck. CT had 440-mm sides and 184-mm roof. 5.45-m deep underwater protection consisted of 4 compartments and could withstand an explosion of 317 kg of TNT. As the 3rd longitudinal bulkhead, the inner main and lower belts were used.

7.1943, *Iowa*: - 8 x 1 - 20/70; + 4 x 4 - 40/56 Bofors.
3.1945, *Iowa*: - SG, SK, Mk 3, 2 Mk 8, 4 Mk 4 radars; + 8 x 2 - 20/70 Oerlikon, Mk 4, SC-2, SK-2, SP, SU, 2 Mk 13, 4 Mk 12/22, Mk 27 radars, TDY ECM suite.
5.1945, *Missouri*: + 8 x 2 - 20/70 Oerlikon, SP radar, TDY ECM suite. 5.1945, *Wisconsin*: - 2 Mk 8 radars; + 6 x 2 - 20/70 Oerlikon, SR, 2 Mk 13 radars, TDY ECM suite. 6.1945, *New Jersey*: - SG, SK, Mk 3, 2 Mk 8, 4 Mk 4 radars; + 8 x 2 - 20/70 Oerlikon, SK-2, SP, 2 Mk 13, 4 Mk 12/22, Mk 27 radars, TDY ECM suite.
Iowa was damaged during a storm 17.12.1944 and was under repair until March 1945.

MONTANA class battleships

60500 / 70500 hp, 281.9 x 36.9 x 11.2 m, 4 sets geared steam turbines, 8 boilers, 172000 hp, 28 kts, 7300 t oil, 15000 nm (16 kts), complement 2149; belt 409-259, lower belt 183-25, main deck 187-152, splinter deck 19-16, bulkheads 457-387, barbettes 541-457, turrets 572-254, CT 457; 4 x 3 – 405/50 Mk 7, 10 x 2 – 127/54 Mk 16, 8 x 4 – 40/56 Bofors, 20 x 1 – 20/70 Oerlikon, 2 catapults, 3 seaplanes (OS2U-3).
Relatively slow ships protected from new 406-mm shells. At first, 457-mm guns were considered, later they were replaced by 12 406-mm/50 (but in quadruple turrets to save length). Finally, the ships were to have a *North Carolina*-style hull, four main triple turrets, and new 127-mm/54 secondary guns. As a result, new very heavily protected and heavily armed ships could not

pass existing locks of the Panama Canal, and at the same time funds were allocated for the third set of locks. 5 ships were authorized in accordance with the Act of 19.7.1940, but suspended by Presidential decree in April 1942 due to lack of steel; the new Panama Canal locks were also cancelled. Finally, all five ships, *Montana* and *Ohio* (Philadelphia N Yd), *Maine* and *New Hampshire* (New York N Yd) and *Louisiana* (Norfolk N Yd) were cancelled 21.7.1943.

The main belt, inclined at an angle of 19° to the vertical, was to be 409-mm thick (on 25-mm STS plating) in the upper part tapering to 259 mm at the lower edge. The belt was connected to the end barbettes with 457-mm fore and 387-mm aft bulkheads. The lower belt, inclined at an angle of 10°, had 183-mm (abreast the machinery)-

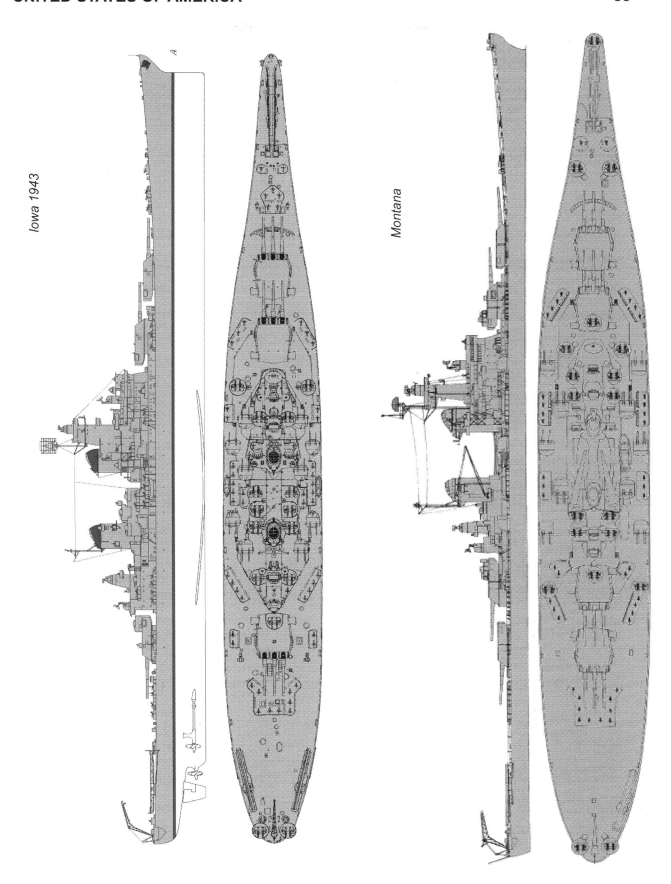

Iowa 1943

Montana

216-mm (abreast the magazines) thickness at the upper edge tapering to 25 mm at the lower edge. The flat main armored deck was connected to the upper edge of the belt and was 147-mm (on 57-mm plating) over the citadel. 38-mm upper deck was placed one level up.

Flat 19-16-mm splinter deck was placed one level down. The steering gear had the own belt and roof. The main gun turrets had 572-mm faces. Fore barbettes above the main deck were 572-mm at the sides, the aft barbettes had protection up to 457-mm.

AIRCRAFT CARRIERS

LEXINGTON class aircraft carriers

Lexington	CV2	Bethlehem, Quincy	8.1.1921	3.10.1925	14.12.1927	sunk 8.5.1942
Saratoga	CV3	New York SB, Camden	25.9.1920	7.4.1925	16.11.1927	nuclear tests 25.7.1946

37681 / 43055 t, 270.7 x 32.1 x 10.2 m, 4 electric motors, 4 General Electric turbo-generators, 16 Yarrow boilers, 180000 hp, 33.2 kts, 3600 t oil, 10500 nm (15 kts), complement 2327; belt 178-127, lower deck 32, CT 51; 4 x 2 – 203/55 Mk 9, 12 x 1 – 127/25 Mk 10/11/13, 28 x

1 – 12.7 MG, 63 aircraft (F4B, F11C, F2F, F3F fighters, BG, BM, SBU dive bombers, TG, TBD torpedo bombers, O2C, O3U/SU, SOC/SON reconnaissance planes, JF, J2F amphibians)

Year	fighters	dive bombers	torpedo bombers	reconnaissance	amphibians
1937 Lexington	18 F2F-1, 18 F4B-4	18 BG-1, 20 SBU-1	-	3 O2U-3	2 JF-1
12.1941 Lexington	18 F2A-3	17 SBD-2, 15 SBD-3, 18 SB2U-3	14 TBD-1	1 SOC-3	2 J2F-1
12.1941 Saratoga	7 F4F-3, 2 F4F-3A, 1 XF4F-4	46 SBD-3	12 TBD-1	5 SOC-1/2, 3 SON-1, 5 OS-2U-1/3, 1 N2Y-1	6 J2F-5
5.1942 Lexington	22 F4F-3/3A	36 SBD-2/3	13 TBD-1	-	-
8.1942 Saratoga	27 F4F-4, 1 F4F-7	33 SBD-3	13 TBF-1	-	-
11.1943 Saratoga	33 F6F	22 SBD	16 TBF	-	-
4.1944 Saratoga	27 F6F	24 SBD	18 TBF	-	-

Flight deck: 268.2 x 27.4 m. Hangar: 129.2 x 22.6 x 6.4 m. Elevators: fore (9.0 x 18.1 m, 7.3 t) and aft (8.9 x 10.6 m, 2.7 t). Aircraft fuel stowage in 1942: 520 500 l.
The largest and fastest aircraft carriers of their time.

Lexington 1931

They were laid down as battlecruisers, but after the Washington Naval Conference they were reordered as aircraft carriers (CV2 and 3 22.11.1922 and 30.10.1922 respectively). In terms of applied design and architectural solutions, *Lexington* and *Saratoga* markedly influenced the further development of aircraft carriers. Their flight deck and hangar sides were designed as part of the hull construction involved in providing longitudinal strength (unlike subsequent ships, in which the flight deck and hangar were a superstructure). Such a constructive solution provided a certain gain in the mass of the hull and made it possible to make a single-level hangar completely closed. Repair shops placed aft of the hangar, holds were arranged below for dismantled spare planes. Two elevators were arranged quite close to each other. The aft one was intended only for fighters,

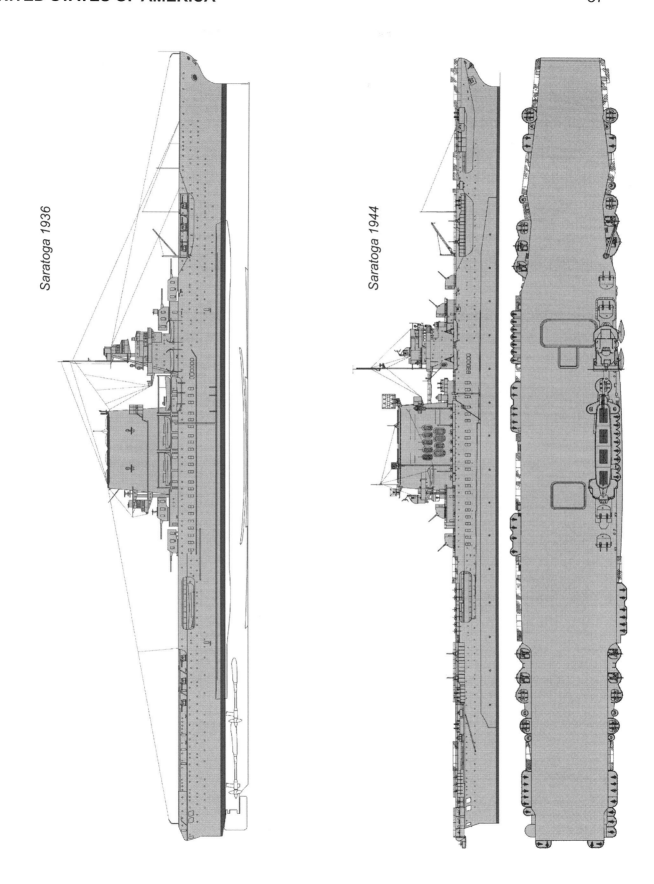

Saratoga 1936

Saratoga 1944

Saratoga 1945

and the fore one for heavy planes. A curious feature of the fore elevator was that it could lift aircraft whose fuselage length exceeded the length of the elevator, due to an additional folding 6 x 8-m hatch. At the same time, the presence of only two elevators on such huge ships was a serious miscalculation of the designers and later negatively affected on the effectiveness of the combat usage of the air group.

Lexington and Saratoga had unusual turbo-electric machinery with huge 180000-hp power. Turbine generators were installed in the central compartments, and boiler rooms alongside. According to the tactical doctrines of the 1920s, the carriers were armed with 8 203-mm guns in four turrets.
The main 178-mm belt had 161.5-m length and 2.9-m depth. It was connected to the flat 51-mm main deck at its upper edge. Underwater protection had 4.8-m depth and included 4 compartments.
Spring 1940, both: + 4 x 1 - 12.7 MG, CXAM-1 radar. 1940, both: - 4 x 1 - 12.7 MG; + 5 x 1 - 76/50 Mk 20.

1941, both: - 5 x 1 - 76/50; + 5 x 4 - 28/75 Mk 1.
Early 1942, Saratoga: - 28 x 1 - 12.7 MG; + 4 x 4 - 28/75 Mk 1, 32 x 1 - 20/70 Oerlikon. 4.1942, Lexington: - 4 x 2 - 203/55; + 7 x 4 - 28/75 Mk 1, 32 x 1 - 20/70 Oerlikon, 2 Mk 4 radars. 5.1942, Saratoga: - 4 x 2 - 203/55, 12 x 1 - 127/25, 4 x 4 - 28/75, 2 x 1 - 20/70; + (4 x 2 + 8 x 1) - 127/38 Mk 12, 4 x 4 - 40/56 Bofors, 2 H II catapults, SC, 2 Mk 4 radars. Breadth was increased by starboard bulge to 34.1 m, and displacement rose to 40000 / 48552 t. Flight deck was lengthened, length oa became 277.2 m. Maximal fuel stowage rose to 9748 t. Complement became 3373. 10.1942, Saratoga: - 5 x 4 - 28/75; + 5 x 4 - 40/56 Bofors, 22 x 1 - 20/70 Oerlikon.
1.1944, Saratoga: - 36 x 1 - 20/70; + (14 x 4 + 2 x 2) - 40/56 Bofors, SK radar. Summer 1944, Saratoga: + SM radar.
5.1945, Saratoga: aft elevator was deleted, new fore elevator was fitted.
Lexington 7.5.1942 during the battle of the Coral Sea was badly damaged by Japanese carrier aircraft from the carriers Shokaku and Zuikaku, received two torpedo and two 60-kg bomb hits, abandoned by the crew and torpedoed by destroyer Phelps. Foundered 8.5.1942. Saratoga 11.1.1942 was damaged by a torpedo from Japanese submarine I16 and was under repair until the end of May 1942; 31.8.1942 she was again torpedoed by Japanese submarine I26 and returned to the service at the end of November 1942; during Iwo Jima landing 21.2.1945 she was badly damaged by Japanese aircraft (hit by four bombs and two kamikazes), returned to service in May 1945; later she was used in nuclear tests at Bikini, damaged 1.7.1946 and sank after explosion 25.7.1946.

RANGER aircraft carrier

Ranger	CV4	Newport News	26.9.1931	25.2.1933	4.7.1934	stricken 10.1946

14575 / 17577 t, 234.4 x 33.4 x 6.8 m, 2 sets Curtis (HP) / Parsons (LP) geared steam turbines, 6 Babcock & Wilcox boilers, 53500 hp, 29.2 kts, 2350 t oil, 7000 nm (15 kts), complement 1788; belt abreast aircraft ammunition holds 51, bulkheads 51, deck 25; 8 x 1 – 127/25 Mk 10/11/13, 40 x 1 – 12.7 MG, 76 aircraft (F4B, F11C, F2F, F3F fighters, BG, BM, SBU dive bombers, TG, TBD torpedo bombers, O2C, O3U/SU, SOC/SON reconnaissance planes, JF, J2F amphibians).

Year	fighters	dive bombers	torpedo bombers	reconnaissance	amphibians
12.1941	17 F4F-3	25 SB2U-1/2	3 TBD-1	2 SNJ-3, 2 SOC-1	2 J2F-5
11.1942	54 F4F-4	18 SBD-3	1 TBF-1	-	-
10.1943	27 F4F	27 SBD	18 TBF	-	-

Flight deck: 216.1 x 26.2 m. Hangar: 168.2 x 19.8 x 5.77 m. Three elevators (fore and mid: 15.8 x 12.5 m, 6.8 t and aft: 12.1 x 10.6 m, 4.1 t). Aircraft fuel stowage: 514 400 l.
First USN ship originally laid down as an aircraft carrier. The design was developed practically without using the experience of operating carrier aircraft, relatively small, compared to the Lexington class, dimensions were determined by the desire to have the

largest number of aircraft carriers within the limits of total displacement, allowed by the Washington Treaty of 1922. The decision to build a CV4 with 13800-t displacement was taken in 1930. Initially, she was supposed to be a flush-deck ship without an island superstructure, but during the building the design was modified. Six folding funnels (three on each side) were a distinctive feature of the ship. Originally planned turbine-electric machinery was abandoned in favor of more

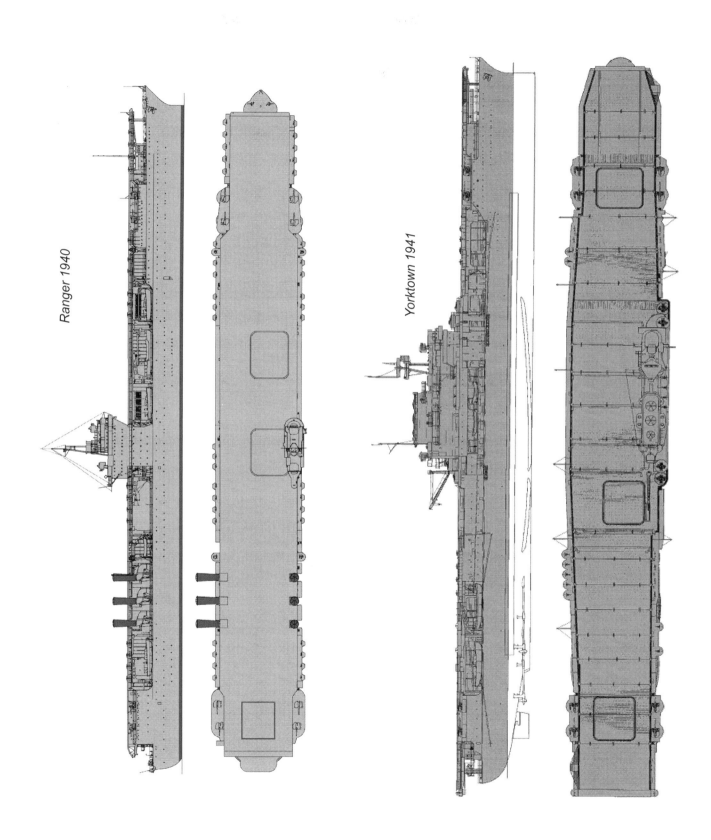

Ranger 1940

Yorktown 1941

Ranger 1938

compact geared turbines.

In general, *Ranger* turned out to be unsuccessful: the

small dimensions and the irrational arrangement of the elevators greatly hampered the air group operation. She suffered from insufficient seaworthiness, low stability, and lack of underwater protection.

Aircraft armament holds had box-shaped vertical protection with 51-mm belt and 51-mm bulkheads. The flight deck over the hangar was 25-mm thick.

9.1941: - 16 x 1 - 12.7 MG; + 6 x 4 - 28/75 Mk 1.

8.1942: + 30 x 1 - 20/70 Oerlikon.

1.1943: the flight deck was lengthened to 228.6 m; - 6 x 4 - 28/75, 24 x 1 - 12.7 MG; + 6 x 4 - 40/56 Bofors, 16 x 1 - 20/70 Oerlikon, SC-2, SP, 2 Mk 4 radars. Autumn 1943: - 6 x 1 - 20/70.

7.1944: - 8 x 1 - 127/25, 2 Mk 4 radars; + 1 catapult H-II-1, SM radar.

Ranger was used as a training carrier from 4.1944.

YORKTOWN class aircraft carriers

Yorktown	CV5	Newport News	21.5.1934	4.4.1936	30.9.1937	sunk 7.6.1942
Enterprise	CV6	Newport News	16.7.1934	3.10.1936	12.5.1938	stricken 10.1956
Hornet	CV8	Newport News	25.9.1939	14.12.1940	20.10.1941	sunk 24.10.1942

19875 / 25484 t, 246.6 (251.4 max) x 33.4 x 7.9 m, 4 sets Westinghouse geared steam turbines, 9 Babcock & Wilcox boilers, 120000 hp, 32.5 kts, 4360 t oil, 12000 nm (15 kts), complement 2175; belt 102-64, deck 38, bulkheads 102, CT 102; 8 x 1 – 127/38 Mk 12, 4 x 4 – 28/75 Mk 1, 24 x 1 – 12.7 MG, 96 aircraft (F11C (CV5, 6), F4B (CV5), F2F (CV5, 6), F3F (CV5, 6), F2A (CV8), F4F (CV8) fighters, BFC (CV5, 6), BF2C (CV5, 6), BG (CV5, 6), SBU (CV5, 6), SBC, SB2U (CV6), BM (CV5, 6), BT (CV6), SBD (CV8) dive bombers, T4M (CV5), TG (CV5), TBD torpedo bombers, O3U (CV5, 6), SU (CV5, 6), SOC/SON reconnaissance planes, JF, J2F amphibians); SC radar (CV8).

Flight deck: 244.6 (CV5, 6) or 248.3 (CV8) x 29.9 m. Hangar: 166.4 x 19.2 x 5.25 m. Three elevators (14.6 x 13.7 m, 7.7 t) and 3 H II catapults (2 on the flight deck and 1 doubled athwartship catapult in the hangar). Aircraft fuel stowage: 673 900 l.

After the *Ranger* order, the remaining US Navy aircraft carriers, according to the Washington Treaty, could have a total displacement of 55000 t. In this limit, it was possible to build three 18500-t or two 27000-t ships. Naval staff would have preferred to have three carriers, but, as world experience had shown, the limited dimensions of carrier drastically reduced her combat capabilities. As a result, they came to a compromise: it was decided to build two 20700-t ships and a smaller one (future CV7 *Wasp*). CV5 and 6 were laid down

in 1934; four years later, after the cancellation of the Washington Treaty, Congress decided to build the third ship of class, CV8.

The design of *Yorktown* turned out to be much more successful than the predecessor (*Ranger*), harmoniously combining offensive and defensive qualities. The hangar was designed for a large air group (96 planes at the time of designing, subsequently, due to increase in the size of the planes, their number was reduced). In addition to two catapults on the flight deck, there was also a third one deck below: with its help, it was possible to launch planes directly from the hangar through special ports. Alas, the original idea did not justify itself, and hangar catapult was removed in 1942. The carriers had good armor protection, comparable to protection of 'Washington' cruisers. Unlike *Ranger*, *Yorktown* received underwater protection. However, this protection could withstand the explosion of 180 kg of TNT, while battleships were able to withstand an explosion of 320 kg of TNT.

There was 102-64-mm armor belt, connected to the 38-mm armored main deck and closed by 102-mm transverse bulkheads. CT had 102-mm sides and 51-mm roof.

1940, *Yorktown*: + CXAM radar. 1940, *Enterprise*: +

Yorktown 1940

Year	fighters	dive bombers	torpedo bombers	reconnaissance	amphibians
6.1938 Enterprise	20 F3F	21 SBC, 13 BT	20 TBD	2 O3U	-
12.1941 Yorktown	-	39 SBD-3	14 TBD-1	2 SNJ-3, 1 SOC-1	2 J2F-5
12.1941 Enterprise	3 F4F-3, 16 F4F-3A	31 SBD-2, 10 SBD-3	22 TBD-1	2 SNJ-3, 2 SOC-3	2 J2F-2
12.1941 Hornet	21 F4F-3	39 SBC-4, 7 SBN-1	8 TBD-1	2 SNJ-3, 2 OS2U-2	2 J2F-5
5.1942 Yorktown	18 F4F-3	35 SBD-3	13 TBD-1	-	-
6.1942 Yorktown	27 F4F-4	37 SBD-3	13 TBD-1	-	-
6.1942 Enterprise	27 F4F-4	37 SBD-2/3	14 TBD-1	-	-
6.1942 Hornet	27 F4F-4	35 SBD-3	15 TBD-1	-	-
8.1942 Enterprise	28 F4F-4, 1 F4F-7	35 SBD-3	16 TBF-1	-	-
10.1942 Enterprise	36 F4F-4	44 SBD-3	15 TBF-1	-	-
10.1942 Hornet	37 F4F-4	30 SBD-3	15 TBF-1	-	-
2.1944 Enterprise	32 F6F, 4 F4U	30 SBD	16 TBF	-	-
6.1944 Enterprise	31 F6F, 3 F4U	21 SBD	14 TBF	-	-
10.1944 Enterprise	35 F6F-5, 4 F6F-3N	34 SB2C-3	19 TBM-1C	-	-

CXAM-1 radar.
Mid-1942, *Yorktown, Hornet*: - 24 x 1 - 12.7 MG; + 24 x 1 - 20/70 Oerlikon, 2 Mk 4 radars. Mid-1942, *Enterprise*: - 24 x 1 - 12.7 MG; + 32 x 1 - 20/70 Oerlikon, 2 Mk 4 radars. 8,1942, *Enterprise*: + 1 x 4 - 28/75 Mk 1, 6 x 1 - 20/70 Oerlikon, SC-2 radar. 8.1942, *Hornet*: + 1 x 4 - 28/75 Mk 1, 8 x 1 - 20/70 Oerlikon. 11.1942, *Enterprise*: - 4 x 1 - 28/75; + 4 x 4 - 40/56 Bofors, 8 x 1 - 20/70 Oerlikon.
10.1943, *Enterprise*: bulges were fitted, breadth by the waterline increased from 25.3 to 29.1 m, displacement to 24128 / 29882 t and fuel stowage to 6511 t. - 1 x 4 - 28/75, CXAM-1, 2 Mk 4 radars; + (2 x 4 + 8 x 2) - 40/56 Bofors, (1 x 3 + 1 x 2 + 2 x 1) - 20/70 Oerlikon, SK, SM, 2 Mk 12/22 radars; 2 H II catapults were replaced by 2 H 2-1. Late 1943, *Enterprise*: - (1 x 3 + 1 x 2) - 20/70; + 2 x 1 - 20/70 Oerlikon.
9.1945, *Enterprise*: - 3 x 2 - 40/56, 50 x 1 - 20/70; + 5 x 4 - 40/56 Bofors, 16 x 2 - 20/70 Oerlikon, SU, 8 Mk 19 radars.
Yorktown during battle of the Coral Sea 7.5.1942 was damaged by a hit of Japanese 250-kg air bomb. She was urgently repaired in Pearl Harbor and took part in the battle of Midway 4.6.1942. She was badly damaged by the air group of Japanese carrier *Hiryu*, receiving 3 bomb and 2 torpedo hits. 6.6.1942 she was hit by two more torpedoes

from Japanese submarine *I168* and foundered the next day morning. *Enterprise* during the battle of the Eastern Solomons 24.8.1942 received serious damage as result of hits of three 250-kg air bombs and three close misses, returned to service in mid-October 1942; in battle of Santa Cruz 26.10.1942 she received hits of three 250-kg air bombs and was under repair until mid-November 1942; during Okinawa landing 14.5.1945 she was damaged by kamikaze and never entered service until the end of the war. *Hornet* in battle of Santa Cruz 26.10.1942 was badly damaged by air groups of Japanese aircraft carriers *Shokaku* and *Zuikaku*, receiving hits of two torpedoes, four bombs and two downed planes, after a hit of one more torpedo and several air bombs she was abandoned by the crew and torpedoed by destroyers of her escort, however remained afloat. At the night 27.10.1942 the wreck of *Hornet* was discovered and sunk by Japanese destroyers.

Enterprise 1942

WASP aircraft carrier

Wasp	CV7	Bethlehem, Quincy	1.4.1936	4.4.1939	25.4.1940	sunk 15.9.1942

15752 / 19116 t, 219.5 x 30.5 x 7.1 m, 2 sets Parsons geared steam turbines, 6 Yarrow boilers, 70000 hp, 29.5 kts, 1602 t oil, 7500 nm (15 kts), complement 2167; belt 16 (plating), deck 32; 8 x 1 – 127/38 Mk 12, 4 x 4 – 28/75 Mk 1, 24 x 1 – 12.7 MG, 76 aircraft (F2F, F3F, F2A fighters, BG, SBU, SBC, SB2U, BT dive bombers, TBD torpedo bombers, SOC/SON reconnaissance planes, JF, J2F amphibians).

Year	fighters	dive bombers	torpedo bombers	reconnaissance	amphibians
12.1941	47 F4F-3	38 SB2U-1/2	2 TBD-1	1 SNJ-3, 1 OS2U-1, 1 SON-1	2 J2F-2/3
8.1942	25 F4F-4	27 SBD-3	10 TBF-1	-	1 J2F-3

Flight deck: 226.0 x 30.5 m. Hangar: 159.1 x 19.2 x 5.23 m. Two elevators (14.6 x 13.4 m, 7.7 t) and 4 H 2 catapults (2 on the flight deck and 1 doubled athwartships catapult in the hangar). Aircraft fuel stowage: 613 500 l.

The decision to build CV7 Wasp was made 27.3.1934, at the same time as the decision to convert CV1 Langley to airplane transport. In order to avoid exceeding the total displacement of aircraft carriers allowed by Washington Treaty, the US Navy had to limit the displacement of the new ship to 14700 t. However, US politicians cheated a little: speaking of the freed-up tonnage, they indicated the full displacement of Langley, and standard displacement of Wasp. The ship was ordered 19.9.1935. The design had

Wasp 1940

some original features. The asymmetric hull became a unique feature of the ship: in this way, the designers compensated for the weight of the island superstructure without placing ballast on the port side. In addition, she was distinguished by the unusual arrangement of engine and boiler rooms en echelone; this was repeated later in the Essex design. As an experiment, an additional T-shaped deck-edge elevator was fitted in the fore part on the port side. There were 4 catapults: two on the flight deck and two more, arranged transverse, in the hangar for launching the planes through the side ports. Due to the limited displacement, the armor protection was very weak.

Only the lower (main) deck over the machinery had 32-mm protection. The steering gear compartment was protected by 87-mm belt and 32-mm deck.

1.1942: + CXAM-1 radar; Spring 1942: - 18 x 1 - 12.7 MG; + 1 x 1 - 40/56 Bofors, 32 x 1 - 20/70 Oerlikon.

15.9.1942 Wasp was hit S of Guadalcanal by 3 torpedoes from Japanese submarine I19 and sunk by destroyer Lansdowne 6 hours later.

ESSEX class aircraft carriers

Essex	CV9	Newport News	28.4.1941	31.7.1942	31.12.1942	stricken 6.1975
Yorktown (ex-Bon Homme Richard)	CV10	Newport News	1.12.1941	21.1.1943	15.4.1943	stricken 6.1973
Intrepid	CV11	Newport News	1.12.1941	26.4.1943	16.8.1943	stricken 2.1982
Hornet (ex-Kearsarge)	CV12	Newport News	3.8.1942	30.8.1943	29.11.1943	stricken 7.1989
Franklin	CV13	Newport News	7.12.1942	14.10.1943	31.1.1944	stricken 10.1964
Ticonderoga (ex-Hancock)	CV14	Newport News	1.2.1943	7.2.1944	8.5.1944	stricken 11.1973
Randolph	CV15	Newport News	10.5.1943	29.6.1944	9.10.1944	stricken 6.1973
Lexington (ex-Cabot)	CV16	Bethlehem, Quincy	15.9.1941	26.9.1942	17.2.1943	stricken 11.1991
Bunker Hill	CV17	Bethlehem, Quincy	15.9.1941	7.12.1942	20.5.1943	stricken 11.1966
Wasp (ex-Oriskany)	CV18	Bethlehem, Quincy	18.3.1942	17.8.1943	24.11.1943	stricken 7.1972
Hancock (ex-Ticonderoga)	CV19	Bethlehem, Quincy	26.1.1943	17.8.1943	15.4.1944	stricken 1.1976
Bennington	CV20	Newport News	15.12.1942	26.2.1944	6.8.1944	stricken 9.1989
Boxer	CV21	Newport News	13.9.1943	14.12.1944	16.4.1945	stricken 12.1969

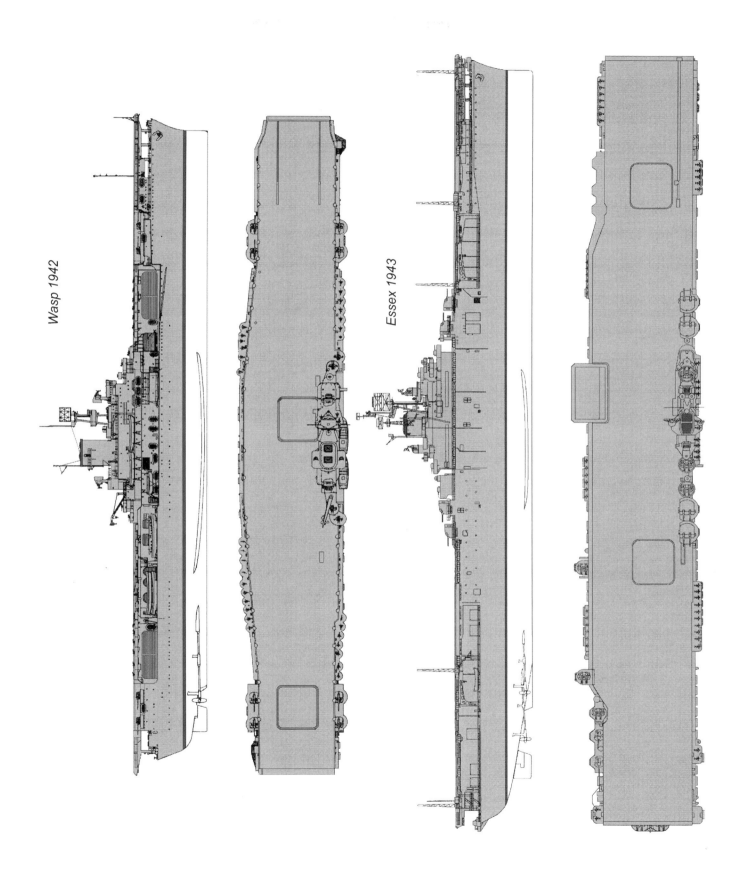

Wasp 1942

Essex 1943

Bon Homme Richard	CV31	New York N Yd, Brooklyn	1.2.1943	29.4.1944	26.11.1944	stricken 9.1989
Leyte (ex-Crown Point)	CV32	Newport News	21.2.1944	23.8.1945	11.4.1946	stricken 6.1969
Kearsarge	CV33	New York N Yd, Brooklyn	1.3.1944	5.5.1945	2.3.1946	stricken 5.1973
Oriskany	CV34	New York N Yd, Brooklyn	1.5.1944	13.10.1945	25.9.1950	stricken 7.1989
Reprisal	CV35	New York N Yd, Brooklyn	1.7.1944	1946	-	cancelled 8.1945
Antietam	CV36	Philadelphia N Yd	15.3.1943	20.8.1944	28.1.1945	stricken 5.1973
Princeton (ex-Valley Forge)	CV37	Philadelphia N Yd	14.9.1943	8.7.1945	18.11.1945	stricken 1.1970
Shangri La	CV38	Norfolk N Yd, Portsmouth	15.1.1943	24.2.1944	15.9.1944	stricken 7.1982
Lake Champlain	CV39	Norfolk N Yd, Portsmouth	15.3.1943	2.11.1944	3.6.1945	stricken 12.1969
Tarawa	CV40	Norfolk N Yd, Portsmouth	1.3.1944	12.5.1945	8.12.1945	stricken 6.1967
Valley Forge	CV45	Philadelphia N Yd	7.9.1944	18.11.1945	3.11.1946	stricken 1.1970
Iwo Jima	CV46	Newport News	29.1.1945	-	-	cancelled 8.1945
Philippine Sea (ex-Wright)	CV47	Bethlehem, Quincy	19.8.1944	5.9.1945	11.5.1946	stricken 12.1969

27208 / 34881 t, 265.8 (CV9-13, 16-18, 20, 31) - 270.7 (CV14, 15, 17-19, 21, 32-40, 45-47) x 45.0 x 8.4 m, 4 sets Westinghouse geared steam turbines, 8 Babcock & Wilcox boilers, 150000 hp, 32.7 kts, 6330 t oil, 15440 nm (15 kts), complement 2682; belt 102-64, hangar deck 64, main deck 38; (4 x 2 + 4 x 1) – 127/38 Mk 12, 8 (CV9-14, 16-19) or 10 (CV15, 20, 31, 38) or 18 (CV21, 32, 33, 36, 37, 39, 40, 45, 47) x 4 – 40/56 Bofors, 46 x 1 (CV9-14, 16-19) or 57 x 1 (CV15, 20, 31, 38) or 35 x 2 (CV21, 32, 33) or (16 x 2 + 23 x 1) (CV36, 37, 39, 40, 45, 47) – 20/70 Oerlikon, 91 aircraft (F4F (CV9-21, 31, 36-39), F4U, F6F (CV10-21, 31-33, 36-40, 45, 47), F7F (CV13-15, 19-21, 31-33, 36-40, 45, 47), FR (CV21, 32, 33, 37, 39, 40, 45, 47), F8F (CV32, 33, 37, 39, 40, 45, 47) fighters, SB2U (CV9), SB2C, SBD (CV9-20, 31, 38) dive bombers, TBF/TBM torpedo bombers, SOC/ SON (CV9-21, 31, 36, 38, 39) reconnaissance planes, J2F amphibians); SK (CV9-12, 16-18), SK-2 (CV13-15, 19-21, 31-33, 36-40, 45, 47), SC-2 (CV9-20, 31, 38), SR (CV21, 32, 33, 36, 37, 39, 40, 45, 47), 1 or 2 SG, SG-6 (CV21, 32, 33, 36, 37, 39, 40, 45, 47), SP (partly CV21, 32, 33, 36, 37, 39, 40, 45, 47), SX (CV21, 32, 33, 36, 37, 39, 40, 45, 47), SM (CV10-20, 31, 38), 2 Mk 4 (CV9), 2 Mk 12/22 (CV10-21, 31-33, 36-40, 45, 47), 2 Mk 29 (CV21, 32, 33, 36, 37, 39, 40, 45, 47), 6 Mk 39 (CV21, 32, 33, 36, 37, 39, 40, 45, 47), 9 Mk 28 (CV21, 32, 33, 36, 37, 39, 40, 45, 47) radars, TDY ECM suite (CV21, 32, 33, 36, 37, 39, 40, 45, 47).

Flight deck: 262.8 (CV9-13, 16-18, 20, 31) or 257.4 (CV14, 15, 19, 21, 32-40, 45-47) x 32.9 m. Hangar: 199.4 x 21.3 x 5.35 m. Two elevators on the center line (12.7 t, 14.7 x 13.5 m) and one deck-edge (12.7 t, 18.3 x 10.4 m). No catapults (CV9) or one on the flight deck H4B and one doubled athwartships H4A catapults (CV10-13, 17, 18) or two on the flight deck H4B catapults (CV14, 15, 19-21, 31-40, 45-47) or one H4B catapult on the flight deck (CV16). Aircraft fuel stowage: 908 900 l.

CV34 as completed: 28404 / 40600 t, 273.8 x 46.3 x 9.1 m, 4 sets Westinghouse geared steam turbines, 8 Babcock & Wilcox boilers, 150000 hp, 30 kts, 15000 nm (15 kts), complement 2905; belt 37, hangar deck 64, main deck 38; 8 x 1 - 127/38 Mk 12, 14 x 2 - 76/50 Mk 22, 16 x 2 - 20/70 Oerlikon, ~80 aircraft (F4U/FG, F6F, F7F, F8F, F2H, F9F, F6U fighters, AD, AM attackers, TBF/TBM torpedo bombers, F4U-P, F6F-P, F8F-P, F2H-P, F9F-P reconnaissance planes, TBM-3S ASW planes, AD-Q, AM-Q ECM planes, TBM-3W, AD-W AEW planes, TBM-3R cargo planes, HUK, HUP, HO4S/HRS helicopters); SPS-6, SR, SX, SPN-6, SPN-8, 4 Mk 25, 4 Mk 35 radars, SLR-2 ECM suite.

Year	fighters	dive bombers	torpedo bombers
11.1943 Essex	36 F6F-3	36 SBD-5	19 TBF-1
11.1943 Bunker Hill	24 F6F, 24 F4U	33 SB2C	18 TBF
2.1944 Essex	36 F6F	34 SBD	19 TBF
2.1944 Yorktown	37 F6F, 4 F6F-N	36 SBD	18 TBF

2.1944 Intrepid	37 F6F, 4 F4U-N	36 SBD	19 TBF
2.1944 Bunker Hill	38 F6F, 4 F4U-N	31 SB2C	20 TBF
6.1944 Essex	42 F6F	36 SB2C	20 TBF
6.1944 Yorktown	46 F6F	40 SB2C, 4 SBD	17 TBF
6.1944 Hornet	41 F6F	33 SB2C	18 TBF
6.1944 Lexington	41 F6F	34 SBD	18 TBF
6.1944 Bunker Hill	42 F6F	33 SB2C	18 TBF
6.1944 Wasp	34 F6F-3, 5 F6F-3N	32 SB2C	18 TBF-1
10.1944 Essex	22 F6F-3, 3 F6F-3N, 2 F6F-3P, 23 F6F-5, 1 F6F-5N	25 SB2C-3	15 TBF-1C, 5 TBM-1C
10.1944 Intrepid	36 F6F-5, 5 F6F-5N, 3 F6F-5P	28 SB2C-3	18 TBM-1C
10.1944 Hornet	11 F6F-3, 2 F6F-3N, 1 F6F-3P, 21 F6F-5, 2 F6F-5N, 3 F6F-5P	25 SB2C-3	1 TBF-1C, 17 TBM-1C
10.1944 Franklin	1 F6F-3, 1 F6F-3N, 30 F6F-5, 1 F6F-5N, 4 F6F-5P	31 SB2C-3	18 TBM-1C
10.1944 Lexington	14 F6F-3, 2 F6F-3N, 2 F6F-3P, 23 F6F-5, 1 F6F-5N	30 SB2C-3	18 TBM-1C
10.1944 Bunker Hill	27 F6F-3, 4 F6F-3N, 14 F6F-5, 4 F6F-5N	17 SB2C-1C, 3 SBF-1, 1 SBW-1	17 TBM-1C, 2 TBM-1D
10.1944 Wasp	33 F6F-3, 3 F6F-3N, 2 F6F-3P, 14 F6F-5, 1 F6F-5N	25 SB2C-3	5 TBF-1C, 1 TBF-1D, 11 TBM-1C, 1 TBM-1D
10.1944 Hancock	37 F6F-5, 4 F6F-5N	30 SB2C-3, 12 SB2C-3E	18 TBM-1C
1.1945 Essex	27 F6F-3, 17 F6F-5, 36 F4U-1D	-	18 TBM-1C
3.1945 Randolph	49 F6F-5, 4 F6F-5N, 2 F6F-5E, 2 F6F-5P	15 SB2C-4E	15 TBM-3
7.1945 Essex	36 F6F, 36 F4U	15 SB2C	15 TBF
7.1945 Yorktown	73 F6F	16 SB2C	7 TBF
7.1945 Randolph	57 F6F	16 SB2C	15 TBF
7.1945 Hancock	72 F6F	12 SB2C	10 TBF
7.1945 Bennington	37 F6F, 37 F4U	15 SB2C	15 TBF
7.1945 Bon Homme Richard	37 F6F-5N	-	18 TBM-3

Flight deck: 257.4 x 32.9 m. Hangar: 199.4 x 21.3 x 5.35 m. Two elevators on the center line (fore and aft, 20.9 t, 17.7 x 13.4 m) and one deck-edge (20.9 t, 18.3 x 10.4 m). Two H 8 catapults. Aircraft fuel stowage: 1 143 900 l (petrol)

The most famous aircraft carriers of the US Navy, which made an invaluable contribution to the victory over Japan in the Second World War. The fact that 24 heavy aircraft carriers were built in a very short period of time is truly unique in the history of world naval shipbuilding. The design of *Essex* was developed in 1939-1940 on the basis of the *Yorktown* class and was distinguished by increased dimensions, strengthened AA armament, improved horizontal protection, more powerful catapults, improved machinery and a number of other innovations. The number of carried airplanes also increased, which led to an increase in the capacity of aircraft magazines and petrol tanks.

The dimensions of the flight deck of *Essex* and 8 more ships were 262.8 x 32.9 m, aircraft carriers of the second group (CV14, 15, 19, 21, 32-40, 45-47) had hulls lengthened by 4.9 m, and the flight decks shortened to 257.4 m; this was done to increase the elevation angles of the 40-mm guns on the bow and stern. According to the design, each ship was supposed to carry three catapults: two on the flight deck and one transverse in the hangar. In fact, *Essex* was commissioned without the catapults, following ships with one deck and

Essex 1945

Yorktown 1944

one hangar catapults (the latter was mounted on six ships only: CV10, 12-14, 17 and 18). By the end of 1943, all ships, both commissioned and built, had two deck catapults, all hangar catapults were removed.

An important innovation was the fitting of the deck-edge elevator, placed outside the deck contour. This increased the useful area of the hangar, increased the strength of the flight deck by eliminating additional cutouts in it, and made it possible to lift planes that exceed the dimensions of the elevator. The other two elevators were ordinary, located along the center line. Horizontal protection of the *Essex*, compared to the *Yorktown*, was significantly strengthened by thickening the hangar deck to 64 mm. However, unlike British fleet carriers, the flight deck was left unprotected. The depth of underwater protection was 5.1 m. The propulsive plant of the new carriers was arranged *en echelon* and was unified with the machinery of the *Atlanta* class cruisers, representing, as it were, a double version of the latter. In general, the machinery of all ships turned out to be quite successful: they were highly reliable and could work smoothly at full speed for a long time. So, in November 1945, *Lake Champlain* crossed the Atlantic in four days and 9 hours at an average speed of 32.048 kts. As a result, the *Essex* class carriers were highly successful ships, often referred to as the best carriers in history. At the same time, they had a number of drawbacks: a weak flight deck, poor seaworthiness, poor ventilation of the internal compartments, and congestion in the habitable spaces. Due to the lack of an armored flight deck, these carriers suffered from kamikaze attacks with heavy crew losses.

At the end of the war, the *Essexes* were found to be unable to support the new jets. Incomplete *Oriskany* was suspended pending completion of the new design and completed in 1950 to the revised SCB-27A design.

The main 38-mm deck was connected to the upper edge of 102-64-mm armor belt, the hangar deck had 64-mm thickness. There was 5.1-m deep underwater protection. By summer 1945, *Essex*: - SK, SC-2, 2 Mk 4 radars; + 3 x 4 - 40/56 Bofors, 15 x 1 - 20/70 Oerlikon, SG-6, SK-

Lexington 1943

2, SX, 2 Mk 12/22, 2 Mk 29, 6 Mk 39, 9 Mk 28 radars, TDY ECM suite, 2 flight deck catapults. By the summer 1945, *Yorktown, Intrepid*: - SK, SC-2, SM radars, double athwartships catapult; + 9 x 4 - 40/56 Bofors, 15 x 1 - 20/70 Oerlikon, SG-6, SK-2, SR, SP, SX, 2 Mk 29, 6 Mk 39, 9 Mk 28 radars, TDY ECM suite, 1 flight deck catapult. By summer 1945, *Hornet*: - 11 x 1 - 20/70, SK, SC-2, SM radars, double athwartships catapult; + 2 x 4 - 40/56 Bofors, SG-6, SK-2, SR, SP, SX, 2 Mk 29, 6 Mk 39, 9 Mk 28 radars, TDY ECM suite, 1 flight deck catapult. By summer 1945, *Ticonderoga*: - 46 x 1 - 20/70, SC-2, SM radars; + 10 x 4 - 40/56 Bofors, 35 x 2 - 20/70 Oerlikon, SG-6, SR, SP, SX, 2 Mk 29, 6 Mk 39, 9 Mk 28 radars, TDY ECM suite. By summer 1945, *Randolph*: - 1 x 1 - 20/70, SC-2, SM radars; + 8 x 4 - 40/56 Bofors, SG-6, SR, SP, SX, 2 Mk 29, 6 Mk 39, 9 Mk 28 radars, TDY ECM suite. By summer 1945, *Lexington*: - 46 x 1 - 20/70, SK, SC-2, SM radars; + 9 x 4 - 40/56 Bofors, 30 x 2 - 20/70 Oerlikon, 6 x 4 - 12.7 MG, SG-6, SK-2, SR, SP, SX, 2 Mk 29, 6 Mk 39, 9 Mk 28 radars, TDY ECM suite, 1 flight deck catapult. By summer 1945, *Bunker Hill*: - 46 x 1 - 20/70, SK, SC-2, SM radars; + 9 x 4 - 40/56 Bofors, 35 x 2 - 20/70 Oerlikon, SG-6, SK-2, SR, SP, SX, 2 Mk 29, 6 Mk 39, 9 Mk 28 radars, TDY ECM suite, 1 flight deck catapult. By summer 1945, *Wasp*: - 46 x 1 - 20/70, SK, SC-2, SM radars, double athwartships catapult; + 9 x 4 - 40/56 Bofors, 29 x 2 - 20/70 Oerlikon, 6 x 4 - 12.7 MG, SG-6, SK-2, SR, SP, SX, 2 Mk 29, 6 Mk 39, 9 Mk 28 radars, TDY ECM suite, 1 flight deck catapult. By summer 1945, *Hancock*: - SC-2, SM radars; + 10 x 4 - 40/56 Bofors, 13 x 1 - 20/70 Oerlikon, SG-6, SR, SP, SX, 2 Mk 29, 6 Mk 39, 9 Mk 28 radars, TDY ECM suite. By summer 1945, *Bennington*: - SC-2, SM radars; + 8 x 4 - 40/56 Bofors, 3 x 1 - 20/70 Oerlikon, SG-6, SR, SP, SX, 2 Mk 29, 6 Mk 39, 9 Mk 28 radars, TDY ECM suite. By summer 1945, *Bon Homme Richard*: - 1 x 1 - 20/70, SC-2, SM radars; + 7 x 4 - 40/56 Bofors, SG-6, SR, SP, SX, 2 Mk 29, 6 Mk 39, 9 Mk 28 radars, TDY ECM suite. By summer 1945, *Shangri La*: - 50 x 1 - 20/70, SC-2, SM radars; + 1 x 4 - 40/56 Bofors, 53 x 2 - 20/70 Oerlikon, SG-6, SR, SP, SX, 2 Mk 29, 6 Mk 39, 9 Mk 28 radars, TDY ECM suite. 1945, many (temporarily): + SO-11 or APS-6A or SCR-720 radar.

11.4.1945 *Essex* was damaged by kamikaze hit near on the port side and was under repair until June 1945. *Intrepid* 17.2.1944 was damaged by Japanese air torpedo and returned to service in July 1944; she was 25.11.1944 badly damaged again as a result of attack of two kamikazes and was under repair until February 1945; next time she was 16.4.1945 badly damaged by direct hit of kamikaze and one near miss of blown kamikaze and was under repair until August 1945. *Hornet* was badly damaged 5.6.1945 during a storm and was under repair until the end of the war. *Franklin* was damaged by kamikaze 30.10.1944, returned to service

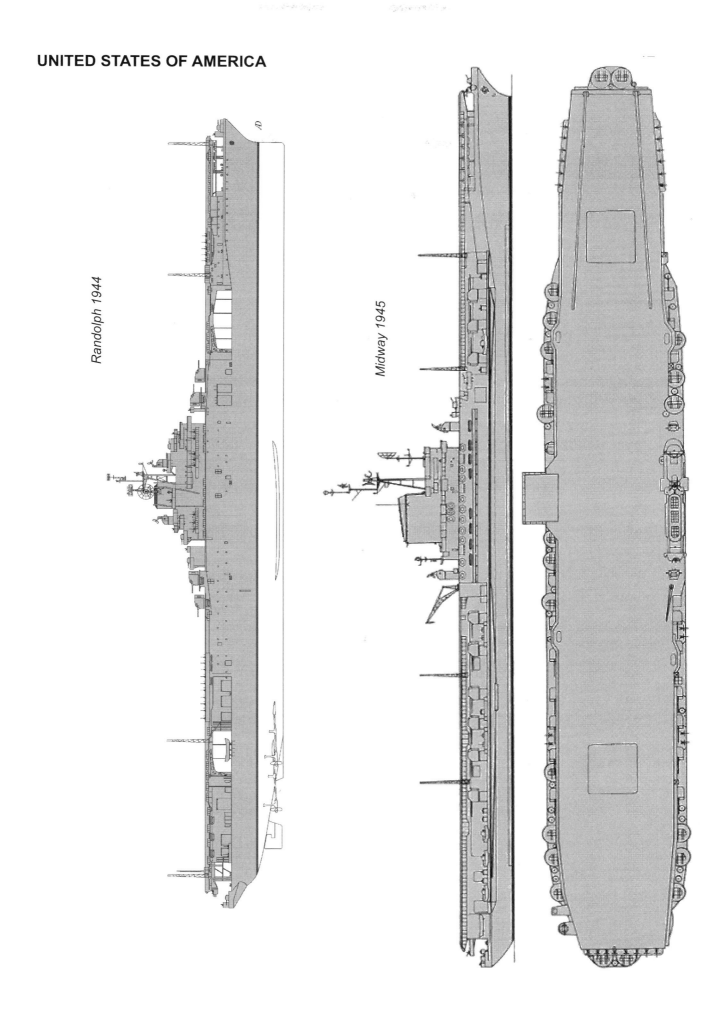

Randolph 1944

Midway 1945

in January 1945, very badly damaged 19.3.1945 by two Japanese air bombs and was under repair until the end of the war. *Ticonderoga* 21.1.1945 was damaged by hits of two kamikazes and was repaired until May 1945. *Randolph* 11.3.1945 was damaged by a hit of kamikaze, her repair lasted until the beginning of April 1945. *Lexington* 4.12.1943 was damaged by Japanese air torpedo and returned to service in March 1944. *Bunker Hill* 11.5.1945 was badly damaged by two kamikazes and was under repair until the end of the war. *Wasp* 19.3.1945 was damaged by a hit of Japanese air bomb, re-commissioned after repairs in June 1945.

MIDWAY class aircraft carriers

Midway	CVB41	Newport News	27.10.1943	20.3.1945	10.9.1945	stricken 3.1997
Franklin D.	CVB42	New York N Yd,	1.12.1943	29.4.1945	27.10.1945	stricken 10.1977
Roosevelt (ex-*Coral Sea*)		Brooklyn				
Coral Sea	CVB43	Newport News	10.7.1944	2.4.1946	1.10.1947	stricken 4.1990

47387 / 59901 t, 295.0 x 41.5 x 10.5 m, 4 sets Westinghouse geared steam turbines, 12 Babcock & Wilcox boilers, 212000 hp, 33 kts, 10032 t oil, 15000 nm (15 kts), complement 4104; belt 193/178, upper belt 51, flight deck 89, hangar deck 51, main deck 51, bulkheads 160; 18 CVB41, 42) or 14 (CVB43) x 1 – 127/54 Mk 16, 21 (CVB41, 42) or 19 (CVB43) x 4 – 40/56 Bofors, 28 x 1 – 20/70 Oerlikon (CVB41, 42), 137 aircraft (F4F (CVB41, 42), F4U, F6F, F7F, FR, F8F, FH (CVB43) fighters, SB2C dive bombers, TBF/TBM torpedo bombers, AD (CVB43) attackers, F-4F-P (CVB41, 42), F4U-P, F6F-P, F8F-P reconnaissance planes, TBM-S (CVB43) ASW planes, AD-Q (CVB43) ECM planes, TBM-W (CVB43) AEW planes, TBM-R (CVB43) cargo planes, HNS helicopters); SK-2 (CVB41, 42), SR-2, SR-3 (CVB43), SX, 2 SG, 4 Mk 25 radars, TDY ECM suite

Year	fighters	dive bombers
9.1945 Midway	64 F4U-4, 4 F6F-5N, 4 F6F-5P	64 SB2C-5

Midway 1945

Flight deck: 281.6 x 34.4 m. Hangar: 210.9 x 28.9 x 5.33 m. Two center-line elevators (12 t, 16.5 x 14 m) and one deck-edge elevator (8.2 t, 17.1 x 10.4 m). Two H 4-1 catapults. Aircraft fuel stowage: 1 255 000 l.

Very large aircraft carriers with an armored flight deck (a first in the US Navy). The large size of these ships was the result of an attempt to provide an armored flight deck in addition to the armored hangar and main decks. It was necessary to provide protection against 203-mm shells from Japanese heavy cruisers: in 1942, when designing these ships, it was still believed that an aircraft carrier could become a victim of cruisers attacking her at night or in bad weather. Thus, the characteristics of the designed ships required an immune zone under the fire of 203-mm/55 guns with heavy shells between 74 and 108 cables. In addition, they received battleship-scale underwater protection and the machinery, arranged like on the *Montana* class battleships. The carriers received new 127-mm/54 guns.

At first, 4 carriers were planned, but the President considered that they would not be ready by the end of the war, and decided to order additional escort carriers instead. At first, only CVB41 and 42 were approved and CVB44 was cancelled 11.1.1943. Two more carriers, CVB56 and 57 from the aborted 1945 Program, were cancelled 28.3.1945. In 1945 there was a general agreement that such huge ships were too expensive and very large air groups were too large for efficient operation. However, for some time after the war, they were the only carriers large enough to operate jets and new AJ strategic bombers.

The main 51-mm deck was connected to the upper edge of 156-m long 193-178-mm armor belt. The main belt had 193-mm thickness on the port side and 178 mm on the starboard side, which compensated for the mass of the island superstructure. The thickness of the main belt was decreased to 76 mm at the lower edge. There was 5.2-m deep underwater protection, consisted of 4 compartments. The thickness of the main longitudinal bulkhead was 32 mm. The belt was closed with 160-mm transverse bulkheads. The thickness of the bulkheads was decreased to 25 mm above the main deck. The steering gear compartment had 193-mm belt, 160-mm bulkheads, 127-mm roof and 63-mm deck. CT had 165-mm sides and 87-mm roof. Communication tubes of the CT were protected by 102-mm armor.

INDEPENDENCE class light aircraft carriers

Independence (ex-CL59 Amsterdam)	CV22, 7.1943-CVL22	New York SB, Camden	1.5.1941	22.8.1942	1.1.1943	stricken 8.1946
Princeton (ex-CL61 Tallahassee)	CV23, 7.1943-CVL23	New York SB, Camden	2.6.1941	18.10.1942	25.2.1943	sunk 24.10.1944
Belleau Wood (ex-CL76 New Haven)	CV24, 7.1943-CVL24	New York SB, Camden	11.8.1941	6.12.1942	31.3.1943	to France 9.1953 (Bois Belleau)
Cowpens (ex-CL77 Huntington)	CV25, 7.1943-CVL25	New York SB, Camden	17.12.1941	17.1.1973	28.5.1943	stricken 11.1959
Monterey (ex-CL78 Dayton)	CV26, 7.1943-CVL26	New York SB, Camden	29.12.1941	28.2.1943	17.6.1943	stricken 6.1970
Langley (ex-Crown Point, ex-CL85 Fargo)	CVL27	New York SB, Camden	11.4.1942	22.5.1943	31.8.1943	to France 1.1951 (La Fayette)
Cabot (ex-CL79 Wilmington)	CVL28	New York SB, Camden	13.3.1942	4.4.1943	24.7.1943	to Spain 8.1967 (Dédalo)
Bataan (ex-CL99 Buffalo)	CVL29	New York SB, Camden	31.8.1942	1.8.1943	17.11.1943	stricken 9.1959
San Jacinto (ex-Reprisal, ex-CL100 Newark)	CVL30	New York SB, Camden	26.10.1942	26.9.1943	15.12.1943	stricken 6.1970

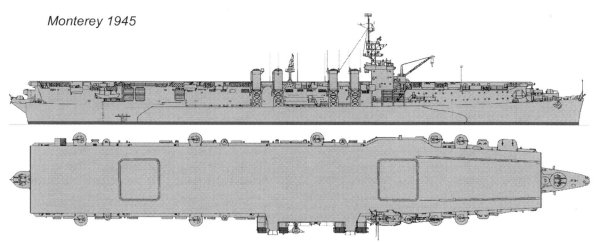

Monterey 1945

10622 / 14751 t, 189.7 x 33.3 x 7.4 m, 4 sets General Electric geared steam turbines, 4 Babcock & Wilcox boilers, 100000 hp, 31.6 kts, 2633 t oil, 13000 nm (15 kts), complement 1569; belt 127 (CVL24-30), bulkheads 127, main deck 51; (2 x 4 + 8 x 2) – 40/56 Bofors, 22 x 1 – 20/70 Oerlikon, 30 aircraft (F4F, F4U, F6F fighters, SB2U (CVL22, 23), SBD, SB2C dive bombers, TBF/TBM torpedo bombers, SOC/SON reconnaissance planes, JF, J2F amphibians); SK, SC-2, SG radars.

Independence 1943

Year	fighters	torpedo bombers
11.1943 Independence	36 F6F-3	9 TBF-1
11.1943 Princeton	19 F6F	7 TBF
2.1944 Belleau Wood	24 F6F	8 TBF
2.1944 Cowpens	24 F6F	9 TBF
2.1944 Monterey	25 F6F	9 TBF
2.1944 Cabot	26 F6F	9 TBF
6.1944 Princeton	24 F6F	9 TBF
6.1944 Belleau Wood	26 F6F	9 TBF
6.1944 Cowpens	23 F6F	9 TBF
6.1944 Monterey	21 F6F-3	8 TBM-1
6.1944 Langley	23 F6F	9 TBF
6.1944 Cabot	26 F6F	9 TBF
6.1944 Bataan	24 F6F	9 TBF
6.1944 San Jacinto	24 F6F	8 TBF
10.1944 Independence	3 F6F-3, 2 F6F-5, 14 F6F-5N	18 TBM-1D
10.1944 Princeton	18 F6F-3, 7 F6F-5	9 TBM-1C
10.1944 Belleau Wood	24 F6F-5, 1 F6F-5P	9 TBM-1C
10.1944 Cowpens	25 F6F-5, 1 F6F-5P	9 TBF-1C
10.1944 Monterey	21 F6F-5, 2 F6F-5P	9 TBM-1C
10.1944 Langley	19 F6F-3, 6 F6F-5	9 TBM-1C
10.1944 Cabot	3 F6F-3, 18 F6F-5	1 TBF-1C, 8 TBM-1C
10.1944 San Jacinto	14 F6F-3, 5 F6F-5	7 TBM-1C
7.1945 Independence	25 F6F	8 TBF/TBM
7.1945 Belleau Wood	25 F6F-5	9 TBM-3
7.1945 Cowpens	25 F6F	9 TBF/TBM
7.1945 Monterey	25 F6F	9 TBF/TBM
7.1945 Bataan	24 F6F	12 TBF/TBM
7.1945 San Jacinto	25 F6F	9 TBF/TBM

Flight deck: 169.2 x 22.3 m. Hangar: 78.6 x 16.7 x 5.3 m. Two center line elevators (12.7 t, 12.8 x 13.4 m). One H 2-1 catapult. Aircraft fuel stowage: 462 700 l.

In 1942, it became clear that the US Navy would not be able to receive fleet aircraft carriers until 1944 (planned date of the completion of *Essex*). The President ordered the Navy to convert the *Cleveland* class cruisers to carriers. This made it possible to receive new aircraft carriers already at the beginning of 1943.

Cleveland class light cruisers were used as a design base. The hulls were blistered, which improved stability and increased the breadth by about 1.5 m. Only seven ships had armor belt, the first two had no side armor. The internal arrangement was slightly altered; the machinery remained unaltered. Despite the increase in displacement, breadth and draught, the speed decreased slightly. The flight deck received one catapult (all ships received one more in 1944-1945). The dimensions of the hangar were smaller than on the *Bogue* and *Casablanca* classes escort carriers, which predetermined the main design flaw, the small size of the air group. According to the design, the artillery included two 127-mm/38 DP guns, 8 twin 40-mm and 16 single 20-mm guns. However, after trials of the *Independence*, 127-mm guns were replaced by two quadruple 40-mm Bofors, and all subsequent ships were commissioned with this armament. In general, *Independence* class carriers turned out to be quite successful, but too cramped ships. Their air groups were three times smaller, than of the *Essex*, and the endurance twice. In addition, *Essex* class carriers (for which the *Independence* class was built as a temporary replacement) were being built much faster than originally planned, and the *Essex* was commissioned earlier, than the *Independence*.

127-mm belt (on CV24-30, CV22 and 23 had only 16-mm side plating) on 16-mm plating was closed near ship ends with 127-mm bulkheads and was connected to the 51-mm main deck.

1944-1945, all survived: + 1 H-II-1 catapult (2nd).

By 1945, *Independence, Belleau Wood, Bataan*: - 18 x 1 - 20/70, SC-2 radar; + 2 x 2 - 40/56 Bofors, SP radar. By 1945, *Cowpens, Langley, Cabot*: - 2 x 4 - 40/56, 22 x 1 - 20/70, SC-2 radar; + 1 x 2 - 40/56 Bofors, 5 x 2 - 20/70 Oerlikon, SP radar. By 1945, *Monterey*: - 2 x 4 - 40/56, 22 x 1 - 20/70, SC-2 radar; + 1 x 2 - 40/56 Bofors, 8 x 2 - 20/70 Oerlikon, SP radar. By 1945, *San Jacinto*: - 2 x 4 - 40/56, SC-2 radar; + 1 x 2 - 40/56 Bofors, SP radar.

Princeton 24.10.1944 was badly damaged by a 250-kg air bomb hit from Japanese D4Y bomber and ensuing fire. She was finally torpedoed by light cruiser *Reno*. *Independence* 20.11.1943 was damaged by a hit of Japanese air torpedo and was under repair until August 1944. *Belleau Wood* 30.10.1944 was badly damaged by a kamikaze and returned to service in January 1945.

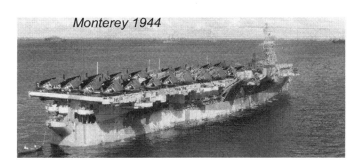
Monterey 1944

SAIPAN class light aircraft carriers

Saipan	CVL48	New York SB, Camden	10.7.1944	8.7.1945	14.7.1946	stricken 8.1975
Wright	CVL49	New York SB, Camden	21.8.1944	1.9.1945	9.2.1947	stricken 12.1977

Saipan 1946

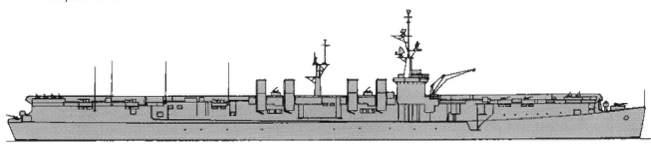

15118 / 18750 t, 208.4 x 32.9 x 8.2 m, 4 sets General Electric geared steam turbines, 4 Babcock & Wilcox boilers, 120000 hp, 33 kts, 2400 t oil, 13000 nm (15 kts), complement 1821; belt 102 on 16-mm plating, bulkheads 102, main deck 64; (5 x 4 + 10 x 2) – 40/56 Bofors, 16 x 2 – 20/70 Oerlikon, 48 aircraft (F4U, F6F, F7F, FR, F8F fighters, SB2C dive bombers, AD (CVL49) attackers, TBF/TBM torpedo bombers, F4U-P, F6F-P, F8F-P reconnaissance planes, TBM-S ASW planes, TBM-W AEW planes, TBM-R cargo planes, HNS helicopters); SP, SK-2 (CVL48), SG (CVL48), SR (CVL49), SR-2 (CVL49), SG radars, TDY ECM suite.

Flight deck: 186.2 x 24.4 m. Hangar: 86.6 x 20.7 x 5.4 m. Two center line elevators (13.6 t, 14.6 x 13.4 m). Two H 2-1 catapults. Aircraft fuel stowage: 543 100 l.

In 1943, Admiral King ordered to the building of two light aircraft carriers a year to make up for the expected losses, two new ships were to be completed in December 1945. The new ships were to be based on the hull of the *Baltimore* heavy cruiser. There were no plans to convert existing cruisers, but using of already produced hull would simplify design and building. Indeed, an entirely new hull was designed, without bulges. The protection was generally at the level of the *Essex* carrier and was stronger than of *Baltimore*; the flight deck was reinforced to receive 9-t aircraft, a new island was provided, like on *Commencement Bay*. Only two ships were built, by the time another pair could be ordered, the war was over. Both ships were cramped for jet aircraft and were soon laid up.

102-mm belt was closed by 102-mm bulkheads and a 64-mm main deck. The steering gear compartment was protected by a 102-mm belt and bulkheads, a 64-mm roof and a 19-mm deck. The thickness of the main bulkheads above the main deck was reduced to 37 mm. There was light underwater protection.

Saipan 1955

LONG ISLAND escort aircraft carrier

| **Long Island** (ex-Mormacmail) | AVG1, 8.1942- ACV1, 7.1943- CVE1 | Sun SB, Chester / Newport News | 7.7.1939 | 11.1.1940 | 2.6.1941 | aircraft ferry 2.1944, stricken 4.1946 |

Long Island 1944

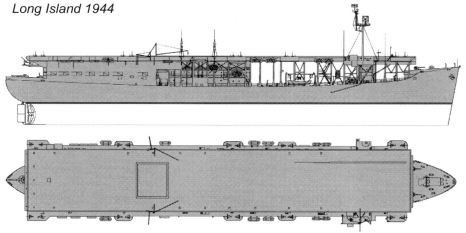

11300 / 14050 t, 150.0 x 31.1 x 7.7 m, 4 Bush-Sulzer diesels (1 shaft), 8500 hp, 16.5 kts, 1365 t diesel oil, complement 408; 1 x 1 – 102/50 Mk 9, 2 x 1 – 76/50 Mk 20, 4 x 1 – 12.7 MG, 16 aircraft (F3F, F2A fighters, SOC/SON reconnaissance planes, JF, J2F amphibians).

Year	fighters	dive bombers	reconnaissance
1941	-	6 SBC	10 SOC
12.1941	7 F2A-2/3	-	1 SOC-1A, 12 SOC-3A

Flight deck: 109.7 x 21.3 m. Hangar: 29.9 x 16.5 x 5.3 m. One center line elevator (3.4 t, 11.6 x 10.4 m). One H 2 catapult. Aircraft fuel stowage: 379 000 l.

The first USN escort aircraft carrier, converted from a C-3 type cargo m/s *Mormacmail* before the USA entered the Second world war. Conversion was started 6.3.1941 and completed in 88 days. The design was reminiscent of the British *Audacity* (commissioned around the same time) but was more austere carrier. *Long Island* had a small hangar, an elevator and a catapult. To increase stability, 1650 t of lead ballast were laid in the hold. The hull had primitive underwater protection, which included a 25-mm longitudinal bulkhead.

The flight deck was 19-mm thick.

9.1941: - 4 x 1 - 12.7 MG; + 4 x 1 - 20/70 Oerlikon.

1942: flight deck was lengthened to 127.4 m, - 1 x 1 - 102/50; + 1 x 1 - 127/38 Mk 12, 16 x 1 - 20/70 Oerlikon, SC radar.

2.1944 as aviation ferry: the catapult was replaced by more powerful one; the flight deck was lightened. - SC radar; + SC-2 radar.

1945: - 20 x 1 -20/70; + 20 x 2 - 20/70 Oerlikon.

In February 1944 the ship was converted to aircraft ferry: the flight deck was lightened; catapult and arresting gear were removed.

Long Island 1943

CHARGER escort aircraft carrier

| **Charger** (ex-BAVG4, ex-Rio de la Plata) | AVG30, 8.1942- ACV30, 7.1943- CVE30 | Sun SB, Chester / Newport News | 19.1.1940 | 1.3.1941 | 3.3.1942 | stricken 3.1946 |

11800 / 16000 t, 150.0 x 33.9 x 7.7 m, 2 Sun-Doxford diesels (1 shaft), 8500 hp, 16.5 kts, 3061 t diesel oil, 26340 nm (15 kts), complement 856; 1 x 1 – 127/38 Mk 12, 2 x 1 – 76/50 Mk 20, 10 x 1 – 20/70 Oerlikon, 36 aircraft (F2A fighters, SOC/SON reconnaissance planes, JF, J2F amphibians); SC radar.

Charger 1942

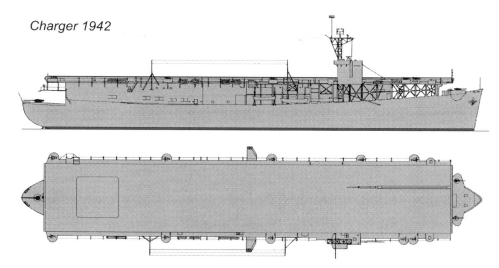

Flight deck: 134.0 x 23.8 m. Hangar: 29.9 x 16.5 x 5.3 m. One center line elevator (3.4 t, 11.6 x 10.4 m). One H 2 catapult. Aircraft fuel stowage: 341 000 l.

One of five *Archer* class ships, built in the US for the UK. 4.10.1940, already after launching, it was decided to leave one ship in the USA and use her for training British naval pilots. The ship was commissioned by the RN 2.10.1941 and 4.10.1941 returned under the USN flag with the British name. *Charger* was converted from cargo m/s *Rio de la Plata* (C-3 type). Structurally, she was very much close to *Long Island*, but had an enlarged flight deck, a small island superstructure and a smaller supply of aviation petrol. At the same time, the fuel stowage was more than doubled, due to the disappearance of the

Charger 1942

need to load the lead ballast, as had to be done on *Long Island*.

BOGUE class escort aircraft carriers

Altamaha (ex-Mormacmail)	ACV6	Ingalls, Pascagoula	15.4.1941	4.4.1942	(15.11.1942)	to the UK 10.1942 (Battler)
Barnes (ex-Steel Artisan)	ACV7	Western Pipe & Steel, San Francisco	17.4.1941	27.9.1942	(10.10.1942)	to the UK 9.1942 (Attacker)
Block Island (ex-Mormacpenn)	ACV8	Ingalls, Pascagoula	15.5.1941	22.5.1942	(11.1.1943)	to the UK 1.1943 (Hunter)
Bogue *(ex-Steel Advocate)*	ACV9, 7.1943- CVE9	Seattle-Tacoma, Seattle	1.101941	15.1.1942	26.9.1942	stricken 3.1959
Breton (ex-Mormacgulf)	ACV10	Ingalls, Pascagoula	28.6.1941	15.2.1942	(9.4.1943)	to the UK 4.1943 (Chaser)
Card	ACV11, 7.1943-CVE11	Seattle-Tacoma, Seattle	27.10.1941	21.2.1942	8.11.1942	stricken 9.1970
Copahee (ex-Steel Architect)	AVG12, 8.1942-ACV12, 7.1943-CVE12	Seattle-Tacoma, Seattle	18.6.1941	21.10.1941	15.6.1942	stricken 3.1959

Core	ACV13, 7.1943-CVE13	Seattle-Tacoma, Seattle	2.1.1942	15.5.1942	10.12.1942	stricken 9.1970
Croatan	ACV14	Western Pipe & Steel, San Francisco	5.9.1941	4.4.1942	20.2.1943	to the UK 2.1943 (Fencer)
Hamlin	ACV15	Western Pipe & Steel, San Francisco	6.10.1941	5.3.1942	(30.12.1942)	to the UK 12.1942 (Stalker)
Nassau	ACV16, 7.1943-CVE16	Seattle-Tacoma, Seattle	27.11.1941	4.4.1942	20.8.1942	stricken 3.1959
St. George (ex-Mormacland)	ACV17	Ingalls, Pascagoula	31.7.1941	18.7.1942	(14.6.1943)	to the UK 6.1943 (Pursuer)
Altamaha	ACV18, 7.1943-CVE18	Seattle-Tacoma, Seattle	19.12.1941	22.5.1942	15.9.1942	stricken 3.1959
Prince William	ACV19	Western Pipe & Steel, San Francisco	15.12.1941	7.5.1942	(29.4.1943)	to the UK 4.1943 (Striker)
Barnes	ACV20, 7.1943-CVE20	Seattle-Tacoma, Seattle	19.1.1942	22.5.1942	20.2.1943	stricken 3.1959
Block Island	ACV21, 7.1943-CVE21	Seattle-Tacoma, Seattle	19.1.1942	6.6.1942	8.3.1943	sunk 29.5.1944
	ACV22	Seattle-Tacoma, Seattle	20.2.1942	20.6.1942	(8.4.1943)	to the UK 4.1943 (Searcher)
Breton	ACV23, 7.1943-CVE23	Seattle-Tacoma, Seattle	25.2.1942	27.6.1942	12.4.1943	stricken 8.1971
	ACV24	Seattle-Tacoma, Seattle	11.4.1942	16.7.1942	(26.4.1943)	to the UK 4.1943 (Ravager)
Croatan	ACV25, 7.1943-CVE25	Seattle-Tacoma, Seattle	15.4.1942	3.8.1942	28.4.1943	stricken 9.1970
Prince William	ACV31, 7.1943-CVE31	Seattle-Tacoma, Seattle	19.5.1942	23.8.1942	9.4.1943	stricken 3.1959
Chatham	CVE32	Seattle-Tacoma, Seattle	25.5.1942	19.9.1942	(11.8.1943)	to the UK 8.1943 (Slinger)
Glacier	ACV33, 7.1943-CVE33	Seattle-Tacoma, Seattle	9.6.1942	7.9.1942	3.7.1943	to the UK 8.1943 (Atheling)
Phybus	ACV34, 7.1943-CVE34	Seattle-Tacoma, Seattle	23.6.1942	7.10.1942	31.5.1943	to the UK 8.1943 (Emperor)
Baffins	ACV35, 7.1943-CVE35	Seattle-Tacoma, Seattle	18.7.1942	18.10.1942	28.6.1943	to the UK 7.1943 (Ameer)
Bolinas	CVE36	Seattle-Tacoma, Seattle	3.8.1942	11.11.1942	22.7.1943	to the UK 8.1943 (Begum)
Bastian	CVE37	Seattle-Tacoma, Seattle	25.8.1942	15.12.1942	(4.8.1943)	to the UK 8.1943 (Trumpeter)

Carnegie	CVE38	Seattle-Tacoma, Seattle	9.9.1942	30.12.1942	(13.8.1943)	to the UK 8.1943 (Empress)
Cordova	CVE39	Seattle-Tacoma, Seattle	30.12.1942	30.1.1943	23.8.1943	to the UK 8.1943 (Khedive)
Delgada	CVE40	Seattle-Tacoma, Seattle	9.10.1942	20.2.1943	(20.11.1943)	to the UK 11.1943 (Speaker)
Edisto	CVE41	Seattle-Tacoma, Seattle	20.10.1942	22.3.1943	(7.9.1943)	to the UK 9.1943 (Nabob)
Estero	CVE42	Seattle-Tacoma, Seattle	31.10.1942	22.3.1943	(3.11.1943)	to the UK 11.1943 (Premier)
Jamaica	CVE43	Seattle-Tacoma, Seattle	13.11.1942	21.4.1943	(27.9.1943)	to the UK 9.1943 (Shah)
Keweenaw	CVE44	Seattle-Tacoma, Seattle	27.11.1942	6.5.1943	(25.10.1943)	to the UK 10.1943 (Patroller)
McClure	CVE45	Seattle-Tacoma, Seattle	17.12.1942	18.5.1943	(17.1.1944)	to the UK 1.1944 (Rajah)
Niantic	CVE46	Seattle-Tacoma, Seattle	5.1.1943	2.6.1943	(8.11.1943)	to the UK 11.1943 (Ranee)
Perdido	CVE47	Seattle-Tacoma, Seattle	1.1.1943	17.6.1943	(31.1.1944)	to the UK 1.1944 (Trouncer)
Sunset	CVE48	Seattle-Tacoma, Seattle	22.2.1943	15.7.1943	(19.11.1943)	to the UK 11.1943 (Thane)
St. Andrews	CVE49	Seattle-Tacoma, Seattle	12.3.1943	2.8.1943	(7.12.1943)	to the UK 12.1943 (Queen)
St. Joseph	CVE50	Seattle-Tacoma, Seattle	25.3.1943	21.8.1943	(22.12.1943)	to the UK 12.1943 (Ruler)
St. Simon	CVE51	Seattle-Tacoma, Seattle	26.4.1943	9.9.1943	(31.12.1943)	to the UK 12.1943 (Arbiter)
Vermillion	CVE52	Seattle-Tacoma, Seattle	10.5.1943	27.9.1943	(20.1.1944)	to the UK 1.1944 (Smiter)
Willapa	CVE53	Seattle-Tacoma, Seattle	21.5.1943	5.2.1944	(5.2.1944)	to the UK 2.1944 (Puncher)
Winjah	CVE54	Seattle-Tacoma, Seattle	5.6.1943	22.11.1943	(21.2.1944)	to the UK 2.1944 (Reaper)

9393 / 13891 t, 151.1 x 34.0 x 7.1 m, 1 set Allis-Chalmers geared steam turbines, 2 Foster-Wheeler boilers, 8500 hp, 16.5 kts, 3420 t oil, 26300 nm (15 kts), complement 890; 2 x 1 – 127/51 Mk 15 or 2 x 1 – 127/38 Mk 12 (ACV31), 2 x 2 – 40/56 Bofors (ACV31), 10 x 1 or 10 x 2 (ACV31) – 20/70 Oerlikon, 28 aircraft (F4F, F4U (ACV11, 13, 20, 21, 23, 25, 31) fighters, SBD dive bombers, TBD (ACV12, 16), TBF/TBM torpedo bombers, SOC/SON, F4F-P, F4U-P (ACV11, 13, 20, 21, 23, 25, 31) reconnaissance planes, JF, J2F amphibians); SC, SG radars.

Year	fighters	torpedo bombers	reconnaissance planes
5.1943 Nassau	26 F4F-4	-	3 F4F-3P, 1 SOC-3A
1943 - 1945 ASW carriers	9 F4F-8/FM-2	10 - 12 TBF-1/TBM-3	-

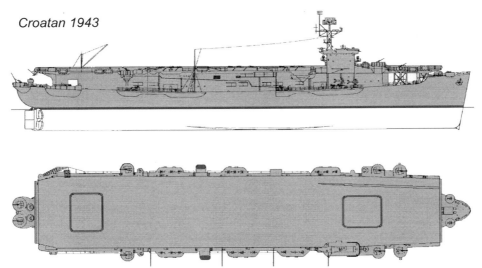

Croatan 1943

Flight deck: 133.1 x 24.4 m or 141.7 x 23.9 m (ACV31). Hangar: 79.6 x 18.9 x 5.3 m. Two center line elevators (6.3 t, 12.6 x 10.1 m). One H 2 catapult. Aircraft fuel stowage: 341 000 l or 225 000 l (ACV31)

The decision to mass convert merchant vessel hulls to escort aircraft carriers was made immediately after the Japanese attack on Pearl Harbor. A C-3-S type turbine-engined cargo vessel was chosen as the basis for the new design. The *Long Island* and *Charger* conversion experience was used, but with some modifications. So, the flight deck and a hangar increased in size, there were two elevators instead of one.

The *Bogue* class carriers were built in two series. The first included 21 ships: 10 for the USN and 11 for the RN (*Attacker* class). The second (24 ships of *Ameer* class) was built specifically for the Royal Navy, but one ship, *Prince William*, remained with the USN. The main difference of 2nd series ships was the lengthening of the flight deck to 141.7 m and a smaller supply of aviation fuel.

1943, *Bogue, Card, Core, Nassau, Altamaha, Barnes, Block Island, Breton*: - 2 x 1 - 127/51; + 2 x 1 - 127/38 Mk 12, 4 x 2 - 40/56 Bofors, 17 x 1 - 20/70 Oerlikon. 1943, *Card*: - 2 x 1 - 127/51; + 2 x 1 - 127/38 Mk 12, 4 x 2 - 40/56 Bofors, 15 x 1 - 20/70 Oerlikon. 1943, *Copahee, Croatan*: - 2 x 1 - 127/51; + 2 x 1 - 127/38 Mk 12, 8 x 2 - 40/56 Bofors, 17 x 1 - 20/70 Oerlikon.

By 1945, *Bogue, Card, Core, Nassau, Altamaha, Barnes, Breton*: + 6 x 2 - 40/56 Bofors. By 1945, *Copahee, Croatan*: + 2 x 2 - 40/56 Bofors. By 1945, *Prince William*: + 8 x 2 - 40/56 Bofors, 7 x 1 - 20/70 Oerlikon.

Block Island 29.5.1944 420 nm S of the Azores, was torpedoed by German submarine *U549*, broke in half and sank one hour after three torpedo hits.

Bogue 1942

Core 1944

SANGAMON class escort aircraft carriers

Sangamon (ex-AO28, ex-Esso Trenton)	ACV26, 7.1943-CVE26	Federal, Kearny / Newport News	13.3.1939	4.11.1939	(1940) / 25.8.1942	damaged 4.5.1945, never repaired
Suwanee (ex-AO33, ex-Markay)	ACV27, 7.1943-CVE27	Federal, Kearny / Newport News	3.6.1939	4.4.1940	(1940) / 24.9.1942	stricken 3.1959
Chenango (ex-AO31, ex-Esso New Orleans)	ACV28, 7.1943-CVE28	Sun SB, Chester / Bethlehem, Staten Is	10.7.1938	1.4.1939	(1939) / 19.9.1942	stricken 3.1959

Santee *(ex-AO29, ex-*	ACV29,	Sun SB,	31.5.1938	4.3.1939	(1939) /	stricken 3.1959
Seakay)	7.1943-	Chester / Norfolk			24.8.1942	
	CVE29	N Yd				

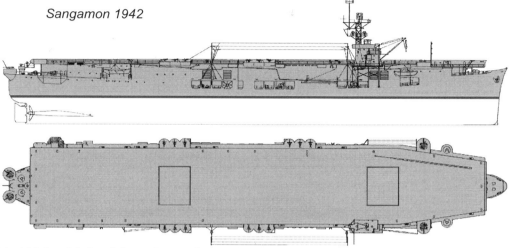

Sangamon 1942

10494 / 23875 t, 168.6 x 32.1 x 9.3 m, 2 sets General Electric geared steam turbines, 4 Babcock & Wilcox boilers, 13500 hp, 18 kts, 4780 t oil, 23900 nm (15 kts), complement 1080; 2 x 1 – 127/51 Mk 15, 4 x 2 – 40/56 Bofors, 12 x 1 – 20/70 Oerlikon, 31 aircraft (F4F fighters, SBD dive bombers, TBD (ACV26, 29), TBF/TBM torpedo bombers, SOC/SON, F4F-P reconnaissance planes, JF, J2F amphibians), SC, SG radars.

Year	fighters	dive bombers	torpedo bombers
11.1942 Sangamon	12 F4F-4	9 SBD-3	9 TBF-1
11.1942 Suwanee	29 F4F-4	-	9 TBF-1
11.1942 Santee	14 F4F-4	9 SBD-3	8 TBF-1
7.1943 Santee	12 F4F-4	9 SBD-5	13 TBF-1
11.1943 Sangamon	12 F6F-3	9 SBD-5	9 TBF-1
10.1944 Sangamon	12 F6F-3, 5 F6F-5	-	9 TBM-1C
10.1944 Suwanee	22 F6F-3	-	9 TBM-1C
10.1944 Chenango	24 F6F-3	-	9 TBM-1C
10.1944 Santee	24 FM-2	-	6 TBF-1C, 3 TBM-1C
4.1945 Santee	18 F6F-5	-	12 TBM-1C

Flight deck: 153.0 x 25.9 m. Hangar: 60.4 x 21.0 x 5.33 m. Two center line elevators (6.3 t, 10.4 x 12.8 m). One H 2 catapult. Aircraft fuel stowage: 674 100 l.

These carriers were laid down as T-3 type oilers. They were later acquired by the Navy and commissioned as AO28, 29, 31 and 33. *Esso Trenton* (*Sangamon*) and *Seakay* (*Santee*) were purchased by the USN 22.10.1940, *Esso New Orleans* (*Chenango*) 31.5.1941 and *Markay* (*Suwanee*) 26.6.1941. They all were commissioned as fleet oilers in the summer of 1941.

In early 1942, it was decided to convert them to escort aircraft carriers, and on February 14 they were reclassified as AVG (subsequently the index was changed to CVE). The work was carried out from February to August 1942. The *Sangamons* were much larger than the ships converted from C-3 type hulls. Cargo tanks were preserved: each ship could carry 12876 t of fuel oil, but in practice this opportunity was not used. By the end of the war, part of the cargo tanks began be used for

storing ship fuel oil, which increased the total fuel supply to 4780 t; the cruising range accordingly increased to 23900 nm (15 kts). Compared to escort carriers rebuilt from dry cargo ships, the *Sangamons* had better resistance to damage (due to the better compartments arrangement), long endurance and, thanks to the large size of the flight deck, could carry heavier aircraft. However, planned in 1942 conversion of the same class tankers to aircraft carriers was abandoned due to the crisis in oiler tonnage, preference was given to cheaper ships of the *Casablanca* class in dry cargo vessel hulls.

Sangamon 1942

1943, all: - 2 x 1 - 127/51; + 2 x 1 - 127/38 Mk 12.
1944, all: - SC radar; + 1 H 2 catapult (2ⁿᵈ), SC-2 radar. By 1945, *Sangamon, Suwanee, Chenango*: + (2 x 4 + 6 x 2) - 40/56 Bofors, 9 x 1 - 20/70 Oerlikon. By 1945, *Santee*: + (2 x 4 + 6 x 2) - 40/56 Bofors, 7 x 1 - 20/70 Oerlikon.

    Sangamon 4.5.1945 was badly damaged by a kamikaze hit and was not repaired. *Suwannee* 25.10.1944 was damaged by a kamikaze hit, the next day she was hit by an air bomb hit and returned to service in February 1945; 24.5.1945 she was damaged by an internal explosion and was under repair for about a month. *Santee* 25.10.1944 was damaged by kamikaze and a hit of torpedo from Japanese submarine *I56*, she was badly damaged and returned to service in March 1945.

CASABLANCA class escort aircraft carriers

Casablanca *(ex-Alazon Bay, ex-Ameer)*	ACV55, 7.1943- CVE55	Kaiser, Vancouver	3.11.1942	5.4.1943	8.7.1943	stricken 7.1946
Liscombe Bay	CVE56	Kaiser, Vancouver	9.12.1942	19.4.1943	7.8.1943	sunk 24.11.1943
Coral Sea *(ex-Alikula Bay)*, 9.1944- **Anzio**	CVE57	Kaiser, Vancouver	12.12.1942	1.5.1943	27.8.1943	stricken 3.1959
Corregidor *(ex-Anguilla Bay, ex-Atheling)*	CVE58	Kaiser, Vancouver	17.12.1942	12.5.1943	31.8.1943	stricken 10.1958
Mission Bay *(ex-Atheling)*	CVE59	Kaiser, Vancouver	28.12.1942	26.5.1943	13.9.1943	stricken 9.1958
Guadalcanal *(ex-Astrolabe Bay)*	CVE60	Kaiser, Vancouver	5.1.1943	5.6.1943	25.9.1943	stricken 5.1958
Manila Bay *(ex-Bucareli Bay)*	CVE61	Kaiser, Vancouver	15.1.1943	10.7.1943	5.10.1943	stricken 5.1958
Natoma Bay *(ex-Begum)*	CVE62	Kaiser, Vancouver	17.1.1943	20.7.1943	14.10.1943	stricken 9.1958
Midway *(ex-Chapin Bay)*, 9.1944 - **St. Lo**	CVE63	Kaiser, Vancouver	23.1.1943	17.8.1943	23.10.1943	sunk 25.10.1944
Didrickson Bay, 11.1943- **Tripoli**	CVE64	Kaiser, Vancouver	1.2.1943	2.9.1943	31.10.1943	stricken 2.1959
Wake Island *(ex-Dolomi Bay)*	CVE65	Kaiser, Vancouver	6.2.1943	15.9.1943	7.11.1943	stricken 4.1946
White Plains *(ex-Elbour Bay)*	CVE66	Kaiser, Vancouver	11.2.1943	27.9.1943	15.11.1943	stricken 7.1958
Solomons *(ex-Nassuk Bay, ex-Emperor)*	CVE67	Kaiser, Vancouver	19.3.1943	6.10.1943	21.11.1943	stricken 6.1946
Kalinin Bay	CVE68	Kaiser, Vancouver	26.4.1943	15.10.1943	27.11.1943	damaged 25.10.1944, repaired as aircraft tender
Kassan Bay	CVE69	Kaiser, Vancouver	11.5.1943	24.10.1943	4.12.1943	stricken 3.1959
Fanshaw Bay	CVE70	Kaiser, Vancouver	18.5.1943	1.11.1943	9.12.1943	stricken 3.1959
Kitkun Bay	CVE71	Kaiser, Vancouver	31.5.1943	8.11.1943	15.12.1943	stricken 5.1946
Tulagi *(ex-Fortaleza Bay)*	CVE72	Kaiser, Vancouver	7.6.1943	15.11.1943	21.12.1943	stricken 5.1946
Gambier Bay	CVE73	Kaiser, Vancouver	10.7.1943	22.11.1943	28.12.1943	sunk 25.10.1944
Nehenta Bay *(ex-Khedive)*	CVE74	Kaiser, Vancouver	20.7.1943	28.11.1943	3.1.1944	stricken 8.1959

Hoggatt Bay	CVE75	Kaiser, Vancouver	17.8.1943	4.12.1943	11.1.1944	stricken 9.1959
Kadashan Bay	CVE76	Kaiser, Vancouver	2.9.1943	11.12.1943	18.1.1944	stricken 8.1959
Marcus Island (ex-Kanalku Bay)	CVE77	Kaiser, Vancouver	15.9.1943	16.12.1943	26.1.1944	stricken 9.1959
Savo Island (ex-Kaita Bay)	CVE78	Kaiser, Vancouver	27.9.1943	22.12.1943	3.2.1944	stricken 9.1959
Ommaney Bay	CVE79	Kaiser, Vancouver	6.10.1943	29.12.1943	11.2.1944	sunk 4.1.1945
Petrof Bay	CVE80	Kaiser, Vancouver	15.10.1943	5.1.1944	18.2.1944	stricken 6.1958
Rudyard Bay	CVE81	Kaiser, Vancouver	24.10.1943	12.1.1944	25.2.1944	stricken 8.1959
Saginaw Bay	CVE82	Kaiser, Vancouver	1.11.1943	19.1.1944	2.3.1944	stricken 8.1959
Sargent Bay	CVE83	Kaiser, Vancouver	8.11.1943	31.1.1944	9.3.1944	stricken 6.1958
Shamrock Bay	CVE84	Kaiser, Vancouver	15.11.1943	4.2.1944	15.3.1944	stricken 6.1958
Shipley Bay	CVE85	Kaiser, Vancouver	22.11.1943	12.2.1944	21.3.1944	stricken 3.1959
Sitkoh Bay	CVE86	Kaiser, Vancouver	23.11.1943	19.2.1944	28.3.1944	stricken 4.1960
Steamer Bay	CVE87	Kaiser, Vancouver	4.12.1943	26.2.1944	4.4.1944	stricken 3.1959
Cape Esperance (ex-Tananek Bay)	CVE88	Kaiser, Vancouver	11.12.1943	3.3.1944	9.4.1944	stricken 3.1959
Takanis Bay	CVE89	Kaiser, Vancouver	16.12.1943	10.3.1944	15.4.1944	stricken 8.1959
Thetis Bay	CVE90	Kaiser, Vancouver	22.12.1943	16.3.1944	21.4.1944	stricken 3.1964
Makassar Strait (ex-Ulitaka Bay)	CVE91	Kaiser, Vancouver	29.12.1943	22.3.1944	29.4.1944	stricken 9.1958
Wyndham Bay	CVE92	Kaiser, Vancouver	5.1.1944	29.3.1944	3.5.1944	stricken 2.1959
Makin Island (ex-Woodcliff Bay)	CVE93	Kaiser, Vancouver	12.1.1944	5.4.1944	9.5.1944	stricken 7.1947
Lunga Point (ex-Alazon Bay)	CVE94	Kaiser, Vancouver	19.1.1944	11.4.1944	14.5.1944	stricken 4.1960
Bismarck Sea (ex-Alikula Bay)	CVE95	Kaiser, Vancouver	31.1.1944	17.4.1944	20.5.1944	sunk 21.2.1945
Salamaua (ex-Anguilla Bay)	CVE96	Kaiser, Vancouver	4.2.1944	22.4.1944	26.5.1944	stricken 9.1946
Hollandia (ex-Astrolabe Bay)	CVE97	Kaiser, Vancouver	12.2.1944	28.4.1944	1.6.1944	stricken 4.1960
Kwajalein (ex-Bucareli Bay)	CVE98	Kaiser, Vancouver	19.2.1944	4.5.1944	7.6.1944	stricken 4.1960
Admiralty Islands (ex-Chapin Bay)	CVE99	Kaiser, Vancouver	26.2.1944	10.5.1944	13.6.1944	stricken 5.1946
Bougainville (ex-Didrickson Bay)	CVE100	Kaiser, Vancouver	3.3.1944	16.5.1944	18.6.1944	stricken 4.1960
Matanikau (ex-Dolomi Bay)	CVE101	Kaiser, Vancouver	10.3.1944	22.5.1944	24.6.1944	stricken 4.1960

Attu (ex-Elbour Bay)	CVE102	Kaiser, Vancouver	16.3.1944	27.5.1944	30.6.1944	stricken 7.1946
Roi (ex-Alava Bay)	CVE103	Kaiser, Vancouver	22.3.1944	2.6.1944	6.7.1944	stricken 5.1946
Munda (ex-Tonowek Bay)	CVE104	Kaiser, Vancouver	29.3.1944	8.6.1944	8.7.1944	stricken 9.1958

Nehenta Bay 1944

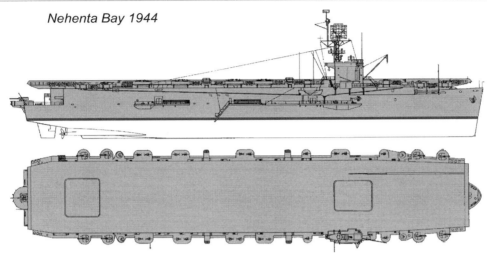

8188 / 10902 t, 156.1 x 32.9 x 6.3 m, 2 Skinner Uniflow VQuiE, 4 Babcock & Wilcox boilers, 9000 hp, 19 kts, 2228 t oil, 10200 nm (15 kts), complement 860; 1 x 1 – 127/38 Mk 12, 4 x 2 – 40/56 Bofors, 12 x 1 – 20/70 Oerlikon, 27 aircraft (F4F, F4U, F6F fighters, SBD dive bombers, TBF/TBM torpedo bombers, SOC/SON, F4F-P, F4U-P, F6F-P reconnaissance planes, JF, J2F amphibians); SG, SK radars.

Year	fighters	torpedo bombers
1943 - 1945 ASW carriers	9 F4F-8/FM-2	10 - 12 TBF-1/TBM-3
8.1944 Kasaan Bay	24 F6F-5, 7 F6F-3N	-
10.1944 Manila Bay	16 FM-2	12 TBM-1C
10.1944 St. Lo	17 FM-2	12 TBM-1C
10.1944 Natoma Bay	16 FM-2	12 TBM-1C
10.1944 White Plains	16 FM-2	12 TBM-1C
10.1944 Kalinin Bay	16 FM-2	1 TBF-1C, 11 TBM-1C
10.1944 Fanshaw Bay	16 FM-2	12 TBM-1C
10.1944 Kitkun Bay	14 FM-2	12 TBM-1C
10.1944 Gambier Bay	18 FM-2	12 TBM-1C
10.1944 Kadashan Bay	15 FM-2	11 TBM-1C
10.1944 Marcus Island	15 FM-2	11 TBM-1C
10.1944 Savo Island	16 FM-2	12 TBM-1C
10.1944 Ommaney Bay	16 FM-2	11 TBM-1C
10.1944 Petrof Bay	16 FM-2	10 TBM-1C
10.1944 Saginaw Bay	15 FM-2	12 TBM-1C
4.1945 Fanshaw Bay	24 FM-2	6 TBM-3
4.1945 Savo Island	20 FM-2	11 TBM-1C, 4 TBM-3

Flight deck: 144.5 x 24.4 m. Hangar: 78.0 x 17.1 x 5.3 m. Two center line elevators (fore, 6.3 t, 12.6 x 10.1 m and aft, 6.3 t, 12.7 x 11.5 m). One H 2 catapult. Aircraft fuel stowage: 378 500 l.

In the early summer 1942, the owner of a shipyard in Vancouver (WA), Henry John Kaiser, proposed to the US government to organize the mass building of escort carriers, undertaking to build 100 ships a year. By that time, Kaiser had already mastered the mass building of merchant vessels, and now it was planned to extend the technology of continuous assembly to warships. President Roosevelt became interested in the project, and Kaiser received an order for 50 aircraft carriers at once. The *Casablanca* was in many ways similar to the *Bogue*, but had a smaller displacement, two shafts, and was faster. The design was based on a fast dry cargo carrier of the S4-S2BB-3 type, but, unlike their predecessors, the new carriers were built completely new, instead of earlier ships converted from merchant hulls. The construction period for the first 10 ships was 241-287 days, the last ships of the class were built in 101-112 days. The machinery included two original 'Uniflow' five-cylinder steam engines, often referred to as turbines.

By 1945, all survived: + 4 x 2 - 40/56 Bofors, 8 x 1 - 20/70 Oerlikon.

Liscombe Bay off Makin Atoll 24.11.1943 was torpedoed by Japanese submarine *I175*. As a result of explosion of gasoline steam and ammunition, she sank 23 minutes after the attack. *St. Lo* 25.10.1944 during the Battle of Samar received a hit of A6M kamikaze plane, followed by many internal explosions. *Gambier Bay* 25.10.1944 during the Battle of Samar was sunk by gunfire from Japanese cruisers *Chikuma*, *Chokai*, *Haguro* and *Tone*. *Ommaney Bay* 4.1.1945 S of Mindoro was damaged by a kamikaze hit, abandoned by her crew, and sunk by destroyer *Barnes*. *Bismarck Sea* 21.2.1945 off Iwo Jima was hit by two kamikazes, causing numerous fires and explosions. She sank 2 hours after the attack. *Corregidor* 20.4.1945 was damaged by a storm and was under repair for about two months, later she was used for training of naval pilots. *Manila Bay* 5.1.1945 was damaged by kamikaze and was under repair until March 1945. *Wake Island* 3.4.1945 was damaged by kamikaze hit and returned to service only at the end of the war. *White Plains* 25.10.1944 during the Battle of Samar was damaged by kamikaze blown up near the stern and close underwater explosion of a shell fired by Japanese battleship, repair lasted until March 1945. *Kalinin Bay* 25.10.1944 during the Battle of Samar received 15 hits of 203-mm shells from Japanese cruisers and two kamikaze hits, was

Mission Bay 1944

damaged and never repaired. *Fanshaw Bay* 25.10.1944 in the Battle of Samar was heavily damaged by gunfire from Japanese cruisers (6 203-mms shell hits) and was under repair until March 1945. *Kitkun Bay* 8.1.1945 was damaged by a kamikaze hit and was under repair until March 1945. *Hoggatt Bay* 15.1.1945 was damaged by an internal explosion, returned to service in June 1945. *Kadashan Bay* 8.1.1945 was damaged by a kamikaze hit, after repairs she was used as TS. *Wyndham Bay* was badly damaged during a storm 5.6.1945 and was under repair until the end of the war. *Salamaua* 13.1.1945 was damaged by a kamikaze hit, repair lasted until March 1945; 5.6.1945 she was badly damaged during a storm and was under repair until the end of the war. *Kwajalein* received weather damage 18.12.1944 and spent several months under repair.

Guadalcanal 1944

COMMENCEMENT BAY class escort aircraft carriers

Commencement Bay (ex-*St. Joseph Bay*)	CVE105	Todd-Pacific, Tacoma	23.9.1943	9.5.1944	27.11.1944	stricken 4.1971
Block Island (ex-*Sunset Bay*)	CVE106	Todd-Pacific, Tacoma	25.10.1943	10.6.1944	30.12.1944	stricken 7.1959
Gilbert Islands (ex-*St. Andrews Bay*)	CVE107	Todd-Pacific, Tacoma	29.11.1943	20.7.1944	5.2.1945	stricken 10.1976
Kula Gulf (ex-*Vermillion Bay*)	CVE108	Todd-Pacific, Tacoma	16.12.1943	15.8.1944	12.5.1945	stricken 9.1970
Cape Gloucester (ex-*Willapa Bay*)	CVE109	Todd-Pacific, Tacoma	10.1.1944	12.9.1944	5.3.1945	stricken 4.1971
Salerno Bay (ex-*Winjah Bay*)	CVE110	Todd-Pacific, Tacoma	7.2.1944	26.9.1944	19.5.1945	stricken 6.1961
Vella Gulf (ex-*Totem Bay*)	CVE111	Todd-Pacific, Tacoma	7.3.1944	19.10.1944	9.4.1945	stricken 12.1970

Siboney *(ex-Frosty Bay)*	CVE112	Todd-Pacific, Tacoma	1.4.1944	9.11.1944	14.5.1945	stricken 6.1970
Puget Sound *(ex-Hobart Bay)*	CVE113	Todd-Pacific, Tacoma	12.5.1944	30.11.1944	18.6.1945	stricken 6.1960
Rendova *(ex-Mosser Bay)*	CVE114	Todd-Pacific, Tacoma	15.6.1944	28.12.1944	22.10.1945	stricken 4.1971
Bairoko *(ex-Portage Bay)*	CVE115	Todd-Pacific, Tacoma	25.7.1944	25.1.1945	16.7.1945	stricken 4.1960
Badoeng Strait *(ex-San Alberto Bay)*	CVE116	Todd-Pacific, Tacoma	18.8.1944	15.2.1945	14.11.1945	stricken 12.1970
Saidor *(ex-Saltery Bay)*	CVE117	Todd-Pacific, Tacoma	29.9.1944	17.3.1945	4.9.1945	stricken 12.1970
Sicily *(ex-Sandy Bay)*	CVE118	Todd-Pacific, Tacoma	23.10.1944	14.4.1945	27.2.1946	stricken 7.1960
Point Cruz *(ex-Trocadero Bay)*	CVE119	Todd-Pacific, Tacoma	4.12.1944	18.5.1945	16.10.1945	stricken 9.1970
Mindoro	CVE120	Todd-Pacific, Tacoma	2.1.1945	27.6.1945	4.12.1945	stricken 12.1959
Rabaul	CVE121	Todd-Pacific, Tacoma	29.1.1945	14.7.1945	30.8.1946	stricken 9.1971
Palau	CVE122	Todd-Pacific, Tacoma	19.2.1945	6.8.1945	15.1.1946	stricken 4.1960
Tinian	CVE123	Todd-Pacific, Tacoma	20.3.1945	5.9.1945	30.7.1946	stricken 6.1970
Bastogne	CVE124	Todd-Pacific, Tacoma	2.4.1945	-	-	cancelled 8.1945
Eniwetok	CVE125	Todd-Pacific, Tacoma	20.4.1945	-	-	cancelled 8.1945
Lingayen	CVE126	Todd-Pacific, Tacoma	1.5.1945	-	-	cancelled 8.1945
Okinawa	CVE127	Todd-Pacific, Tacoma	22.5.1945	-	-	cancelled 8.1945

Commencement Bay 1945

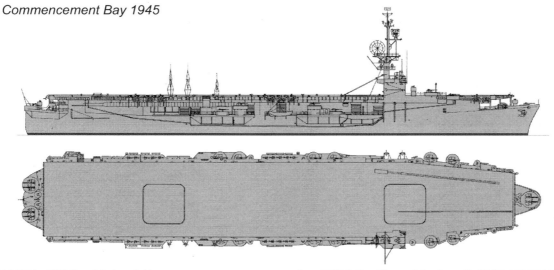

18908 / 21397 t, 169.9 x 32.1 x 8.5 m, 2 sets Allison-Chalmers geared steam turbines, 4 Combustion Engineering boilers, 16000 hp, 19 kts, 1789 t oil, 10000 nm (15 kts), complement 1066; 2 x 1 – 127/38 Mk 12, (3 x 4 + 12 x 2) – 40/56 Bofors, 20 x 1 – 20/70 Oerlikon, 33 aircraft (F4F (CVE105-117, 119), F4U, F6F, FR (CVE108-123), F8F (CVE108, 110, 112-123) fighters, SB2C dive bombers, TBF/TBM torpedo bombers, TBM-S ASW planes, TBM-W AEW planes, SOC/SON, F4F-P (CVE105-117, 119), F4U-P, F6F-P,

F8F-P (CVE108, 110, 112-123) reconnaissance planes,   J2F (CVE105-119) amphibians)

Year	fighters	torpedo bombers
6.1945 Block Island	20 F4U-1D and F6F-5N	9 TBM-3

Flight deck: 152.7 x 24.4 m. Hangar: 65.8 x 21.0 x 5.33 m. Two center line elevators (7.7 t, 13.4 x 12.8 m). One H 2 and one H 4C catapults. Aircraft fuel stowage: 700 000 l.

The largest and most successful US-built escort aircraft carriers. The design was an improved *Sangamon*. The hull repeated the hull of the T-3 oiler, but was thoroughly modified and rearranged; the number of watertight bulkheads was increased. The aft arrangement of the engine and boiler rooms was preserved, but the machinery became to be arranged *en echelon*, its power was also increased. The area of the flight deck was somewhat decreased compared to the *Sangamon*, but the hangar became larger.

Commencement Bay 1945

SEAPLANE TENDERS AND AIRCRAFT TRANSPORTS

WRIGHT seaplane tender

Wright	AV1	American SB, Hog Island / Tietjen & Lang, Hoboken	1919	28.4.1920	12.1921	auxiliary 10.1944

11500 t, 136.6 x 17.7 x 7.0 m, 1 steam turbine, 6 boilers, 6000 hp, 15 kts, 1630 t oil, complement 228; 2 x 1 – 127/51 Mk 7/8, 2 x 1 – 76/50 Mk 10, 12 seaplanes (OL (till 1938), O3U (till 1942), SOC/SON, JF, J2F, 1940- also OS2U, 1942- also SO3C)

Year	reconnaissance
12.1941	2 OS2U-2

Former *Hog Island* class transport, commissioned in mid-1922 as a balloon tender. Converted to a "pure" seaplane tender at Norfolk N Yd, Portsmouth in 7-12.1926. In 1944 *Wright* was reclassified to an auxiliary AG79 and was used as a command ship in the Pacific, renamed *San Clemente* 3.2.1945.

Wright 1931

LANGLEY seaplane tender

Langley (ex-*Jupiter*)	AV3	Mare Island N Yd, Vallejo / Norfolk N Yd	18.10.1911	24.8.1912	(7.4.1913) / 20.3.1922	sunk 27.2.1942

13990 / 15150 t, 165.3 x 19.9 x 6.3 m, 2 electric motors, 2 General Electric turbo-generators, 3 Yarrow boilers, 6500 hp, 15.5 kts, 2300 t coal, complement 468; 4 x 1 – 127/51 Mk 7/8, 34 aircraft (F4B, F11C, F2F, F3F fighters, BG, BM, SBU dive bombers, TG, TBD torpedo bombers, O2C, O3U/SU, SOC/SON reconnaissance planes, JF, J2F amphibians)

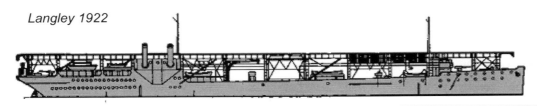

Langley 1922

Year	reconnaissance
12.1941	2 SOC-1/2

Flight deck: ~109 x 19.5 m. Open hangar and one elevator (13.9 x 11.0 m, 4.5 t). Aircraft fuel stowage: 929 000 l.

Langley 1937

USN's first aircraft carrier. She was laid down as the collier *Jupiter* for the US Navy and commissioned in 1913. An unusual feature of the vessel was a twin-shaft turbo-electric machinery. In July 1919, a design was completed to convert her to an aircraft carrier. The conversion was carried out at Norfolk N Yd in March 1920-March 1922.

Langley had a rectangular flight deck. The space between the flight deck and the upper deck could be called a hangar with big caveat: it was open on both sides to its full length. There was one aircraft elevator, in addition, seaplanes were handled by special cranes. Tanks for aviation gasoline and aviation ammunition magazines were placed in the former cargo holds. Too slow to serve with the battlefleet, *Langley* was used as an experimental ship, which tested various technical innovations. So, initially the carrier was equipped with one funnel on the port side, but due to the heavy smoke on the flight deck, it had to be replaced with two funnels folded down. In October 1936 – February 1937 *Langley* was converted to a seaplane tender. The fwd third of the flight deck was removed. One seaplane squadron could be based. Ship could carry up to 55 planes as an aircraft transport

Langley was badly damaged by Japanese G4M land-based bombers 27.2.1942 75 nm S of Java (receiving five direct bomb hits) and sunk by destroyer *Whipple*.

CURTISS class seaplane tenders

Curtiss	AV4	New York SB, Camden	3.1938	20.4.1940	11.1940	stricken 7.1963
Albemarle	AV5	New York SB, Camden	6.1939	13.7.1940	12.1940	auxiliary 3.1965

12053 / 14900 t, 160.7 x 21.1 x 6.5 m, 2 sets Parsons geared steam turbines, 4 Babcock & Wilcox boilers, 12000 hp, 18 kts, 2164 t oil, complement 1195; 4 x 1 –

127/38 Mk 12, 10 x 1 – 12.7 MG, 30 seaplanes (O3U (till 1942), SOC/SON, OS2U, JF, J2F, 1942-1944- also SO3C, 1944- also SC)

Year	reconnaissance
12.1941, both	2 OS2U-2

The first USN modern purpose-built seaplane tenders. According to the design, each of them should maintain two seaplane squadrons and provide minor aircraft repairs. To do this, the deck aft was freed up to accommodate aircraft in need of repair, and a hangar with the necessary

Curtiss 1940

equipment appeared in the superstructure. Seaplanes were handled by three heavy cranes (one aft of the aviation deck and two on the superstructure). The hull had a 4-compartment underwater protection; aviation fuel tanks were placed below the waterline. The total supply of aviation fuel significantly exceeded the allowable for aircraft carriers (1 020 500 l).

1941, *Curtiss*: + CXAM-1 radar.
1942-1943, both: - 10 x 1 - 12.7 MG; + 2 x 4 - 40/56 Bofors, 12 x 1 - 20/70 Oerlikon, Mk 26 radar.
1944-1945, both: + 2 x 4 - 40/56 Bofors, SG, SK radars
1945, *Curtiss*: - CXAM-1 radar.
Curtiss was badly damaged 21.6.1945 by kamikaze off Okinawa.

PATOKA seaplane tender

Patoka	AV6	Newport News	12.1918	26.7.1919	(10.1919) / 11.1939	oiler 6.1940

5400 / 16800 t, 136.6 x 18.4 x 8.4 m, 1 VQE, 2 boilers, 2800 hp, 11.2 kts, complement 301; 2 x 1 − 127/38, 2 seaplanes (SOC)

Former oiler, used in 1924 − 1933 as a tender for the airships ZR1 *Shenandoah*, ZR3 *Los Angeles* and ZRS4 *Akron*. A huge mooring mast was installed in the stern. She was decommissioned in 1933 but recommissioned in 1939 as a temporary seaplane tender intended to supply large patrol flying boats. The mooring mast was removed in 1940.

Patoka 1940

CURRITUCK class seaplane tenders

Currituck	AV7	Philadelphia N Yd	14.12.1942	11.9.1943	26.6.1944	stricken 4.1971
Norton Sound	AV11	Todd, San Pedro	7.9.1942	28.11.1943	8.1.1945	test ship 8.1951
Pine Island	AV12	Todd, San Pedro	16.11.1942	26.2.1944	26.4.1945	stricken 2.1971
Salisbury Sound (ex-*Puget Sound*)	AV13	Todd, San Pedro	10.4.1943	18.6.1944	26.11.1945	stricken 1971

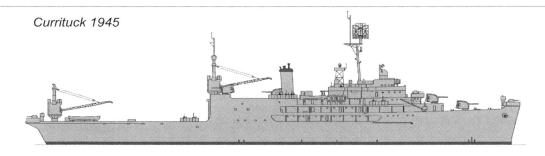
Currituck 1945

12100 / 15092 t, 164.7 x 21.1 x 6.8 m, 2 sets Parsons geared steam turbines, 4 Babcock & Wilcox boilers, 12000 hp, 19.2 kts, 2324 t oil, complement 1247; 4 x 1 − 127/38 Mk 12, 4 x 4 − 40/56 Bofors, 30 seaplanes (SOC/SON, OS2U, SC (AV11-13) (AV7 also since 1944), J2F); SG, SK, Mk 26 radars.

Development of the *Curtiss* class. The main difference was the increased size of the aviation deck aft. The hangar was moved fwd, which, in turn, required the redesign of the funnels, trunking them into one. This became the most visible visual difference with two-funneled *Curtiss* class. The next changes made to the design were a transverse catapult on the aviation deck and increased supply of aviation fuel. When designing in 1941, it was supposed to protect the ships with a 51-mm armored deck (the hull beam was to be increased by 0.7 m), but these plans were not implemented. AA armament, in comparison with the predecessors, was significantly strengthened: 2 quadruple 28-mm MG mounts and 4 12.7-mm MGs were provided. Already before completion, unsuccessful 28-mm MGs were

replaced by 40-mm Bofors. Aircraft fuel stowage was 1 052 200 l. There were 3 heavy cranes for handling seaplanes and a transverse catapult H-5. Marine Corps dive bombers could be launched from a catapult and land on coastal airfields. There was a 4-compartment underwater protection.

Currituck 1944

TANGIER class seaplane tenders

Tangier (ex-Sea Arrow)	AV8	Moore, Oakland	13.3.1939	15.9.1939	25.8.1940	stricken 6.1961
Pocomoke (ex-Exchequer)	AV9	Ingalls, Pascagoula	14.8.1938	8.6.1940	18.7.1941	stricken 6.1961

Tangier 1942

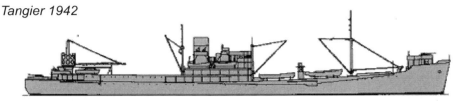

11760 / 13500 t, 150.0 x 21.2 x 7.2 m, 1 set geared steam turbines, 2 boilers, 8500 hp, 16.5 kts, 1310 t oil, complement 1075; 4 x 1 – 127/51 Mk 7/8/15, 8 x 1 – 12.7 MG, 24 seaplanes (O3U (till 1942), SOC/SON, OS2U, JF, J2F, 1942-1944- also SO3C, 1944- also SC).

Year	reconnaissance
12.1941 Tangier	3 OS2U-2
12.1941 Pocomoke	2 OS2U-2

Tangier 1941

Seaplane tenders in standard C3-S type cargo hulls. They were purchased by the Navy already after launching and converted during outfitting. The aviation deck for seaplane maintenance was arranged aft of the superstructure and rose one level over the cargo deck. The crane for aircraft handling was placed at the stern. Cargo holds were arranged to store various aviation equipment and aviation fuel. Aircraft fuel stowage was 1 101 500 l

1942-1943, both: - 4 x 1 - 127/51, 8 x 1 - 12.7 MG; + 1 x 1 - 127/38 Mk 12, 4 x 1 - 76/50 Mk 20, 4 x 2 - 40/56 Bofors, 15 x 1 - 20/70 Oerlikon, SG, SK, Mk 26 radars.

CHANDELEUR seaplane tender

Chandeleur	AV10	Western Pipe & Steel, San Francisco	29.5.1941	29.11.1941	11.1942 stricken 4.1971

Chandeleur 1945

11500 / 13700 t, 150.0 x 21.2 x 7.2 m, 1 set geared steam turbines, 2 boilers, 9350 hp, 17 kts, 1309 t oil, complement 1077; 1 x 1 – 127/38 Mk 12, 4 x 1 – 76/50 Mk 18/20, 4 x 2 – 40/56 Bofors, 15 x 1 – 20/70 Oerlikon, 24 seaplanes (SOC/SON, OS2U, SO3C (till 1944), JF, J2F, 1944- also SC)

Another seaplane tender built in a standard merchant hull, this time C3-S-A2. The crane for handling seaplanes at the stern, 1 180 900 l of aviation petrol.

1943-1945: + SG, SK, Mk 26 radars.

KENNETH WHITING class seaplane tenders

Kenneth Whiting	AV14	Todd, Tacoma	19.6.1943	15.12.1943	8.5.1944	stricken 7.1961
Hamlin	AV15	Todd, Tacoma	19.7.1943	11.1.1944	26.6.1944	stricken 7.1963
St. George	AV16	Todd, Tacoma	4.8.1943	14.2.1944	24.7.1944	stricken 7.1963
Cumberland Sound	AV17	Todd, Tacoma	25.8.1943	11.1.1944	21.8.1944	stricken 7.1961
Kenneth Whiting	AV18	Todd, Tacoma	1944	-	-	cancelled 8.1945
Hamlin	AV19	Puget Sound N Yd	1944	-	-	cancelled 10.1944
St. George	AV20	Charleston N Yd	1944	-	-	cancelled 10.1944

10500 / 12610 t, 150.0 x 21.2 x 7.2 m, 1 set geared steam turbines, 2 boilers, 8500 hp, 16.5 kts, 1556 (AV14-17) or 1309 (AV19) t oil, complement 1077; 2 x 1 – 127/38 Mk 12, (2 x 4 + 2 x 2) – 40/56 Bofors, 16 x 1 – 20/70 Oerlikon, 24 seaplanes (SOC/SON, OS2U, 1944- also SC, J2F); SG, SK, Mk 26 radars.

The latest and most numerous class of seaplane tenders built in standard merchant hulls, now the C3-S-A1 type. The crane for handling seaplanes at the stern, 1 180 900 l of aviation petrol.

Cumberland Sound 1944

'BIRD' class small seaplane tenders

Lapwing	AVP1	Todd SB, Brooklyn	10.1917	14.3.1918	6.1918	stricken 1946
Heron	AVP2	Standard SB, Shooters Is	8.1917	18.3.1918	10.1918	stricken 12.1946
Thrush	AVP3	Pusey & Jones, Wilmington	5.1918	15.9.1918	4.1919	stricken 1.1946
Avocet	AVP4	Baltimore SB	9.1917	9.3.1918	9.1919	stricken 1946
Teal	AVP5	Sun SB, Chester	10.1917	25.5.1918	8.1918	stricken 12.1946
Pelican	AVP6	Gas Engine & Power Co, Morris Heights	11.1917	12.6.1918	10.1918	stricken 12.1945
Swan	AVP7	Alabama SB & DD Co, Mobile	12.1917	4.7.1918	1.1919	stricken 1.1946
Gannet	AVP8	Todd SB, Brooklyn	10.1918	19.3.1919	7.1919	sunk 7.6.1942
Sandpiper	AVP9	Philadelphia N Yd	11.1918	28.4.1919	10.1919	stricken 4.1946

950 / 1400 t, 57.6 x 10.8 x 3.8 m, 1 VTE, 2 Babcock & Wilcox boilers, 1400 hp, 13.5 kts, coal, 6850 nm (8 kts), complement 85; 2 x 1 – 76/50 Mk 3/5/6, 2 x 1 – 7.6 MG, 1 seaplane 12 seaplanes (OL (till 1938), O3U (till 1942), SOC/SON, JF, J2F, 1940- also OS2U, 1942- also SO3C)
9 minesweepers of the 'Bird' class were converted to seaplane tenders in 1936: minesweeping equipment was removed, the mast with heavy derrick was installed, ships received ability to support one squadron of large flying boats such as PBY.
1942-1943, all survived: + 4 x 1 - 20/70 Mk 4, 2 DCR, SO or SU radar.
Gannet 7.6.1942 was sunk by German submarine *U653* off Bermuda.

Thrush 1943

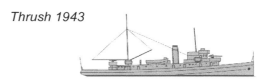

Teal 1942

BARNEGAT class small seaplane tenders

Barnegat	AVP10	Puget Sound N Yd, Bremerton	10.1939	23.5.1941	7.1941	stricken 5.1958
Biscayne	AVP11, 10.1944- AGC18	Puget Sound N Yd, Bremerton	1939	23.5.1941	7.1941	amphibious command ship 4.1943, stricken 7.1968
Casco	AVP12	Puget Sound N Yd, Bremerton	5.1940	12.11.1941	12.1941	stricken 3.1969
Mackinac	AVP13	Puget Sound N Yd, Bremerton	5.1940	15.11.1941	1.1942	stricken 7.1968
Humboldt	AVP21, 7.1945- AG121, 9.1945- AVP21	Boston N Yd, Charlestown	9.1940	17.3.1941	7.1941	stricken 9.1969

Matagorda	AVP22, 7.1945-AG122, 9.1945-AVP22	Boston N Yd, Charlestown	9.1940	18.3.1941	12.1941	stricken 7.1968
Absecon	AVP23	Lake Washington, Houghton	7.1941	8.3.1942	1.1943	to South Vietnam 6.1972 (Phạm Ngũ Lão)
Chincoteague	AVP24	Lake Washington, Houghton	7.1941	15.4.1942	4.1943	to South Vietnam 6.1972 (Lý Thường Kiệt)
Coos Bay	AVP25	Lake Washington, Houghton	8.1941	15.5.1942	5.1943	stricken 9.1967
Half Moon	AVP26	Lake Washington, Houghton	3.1942	12.7.1942	6.1943	stricken 7.1969
Mobjack	AVP27	Lake Washington, Houghton	2.1942	2.8.1942	(10.1943)	completed as motor torpedo boat depot ship
Oyster Bay	AVP28	Lake Washington, Houghton	4.1942	7.9.1942	(11.1943)	completed as motor torpedo boat depot ship
Rockaway	AVP29	Associated, Seattle	6.1941	14.2.1942	1.1943	stricken 1.1972
San Pablo	AVP30	Associated, Seattle	7.1941	31.3.1942	3.1943	survey vessel 8.1949
Unimak	AVP31	Associated, Seattle	2.1942	27.5.1942	12.1943	stricken 4.1988
Yakutat	AVP32	Associated, Seattle	4.1942	2.7.1942	3.1944	to South Vietnam 1.1971 (Trần Nhật Duật)
Barataria	AVP33	Lake Washington, Houghton	4.1943	2.10.1943	8.1944	sold 10.1970
Bering Strait	AVP34	Lake Washington, Houghton	6.1943	15.1.1944	7.1944	to South Vietnam 1.1971 (Trần Quang Khải)
Castle Rock	AVP35	Lake Washington, Houghton	7.1943	11.3.1944	10.1944	to South Vietnam 12.1971 (Trần Bình Trọng)
Cook Inlet	AVP36	Lake Washington, Houghton	8.1943	13.5.1944	11.1944	to South Vietnam 12.1971 (Trần Quốc Toản)
Corson	AVP37	Lake Washington, Houghton	10.1943	15.7.1944	12.1944	stricken 4.1966
Duxbury Bay	AVP38	Lake Washington, Houghton	1.1944	2.10.1944	12.1944	stricken 5.1966
Gardiners Bay	AVP39	Lake Washington, Houghton	3.1944	2.12.1944	2.1945	to Norway 5.1958 (Haakon VII)

Floyds Bay	AVP40	Lake Washington, Houghton	5.1944	28.1.1945	3.1945	stricken 3.1960
Greenwich Bay	AVP41	Lake Washington, Houghton	7.1944	18.3.1945	5.1945	stricken 7.1966
Onslow	AVP48	Lake Washington, Houghton	5.1942	20.9.1942	12.1943	stricken 6.1960
Orca	AVP49	Lake Washington, Houghton	7.1942	4.10.1942	1.1944	to Ethiopia 1.1962 (ኢትዮጵያ [Ethiopia])
Rehoboth	AVP50	Lake Washington, Houghton	8.1942	8.11.1942	2.1944	survey vessel 11.1949
San Carlos	AVP51	Lake Washington, Houghton	9.1942	20.12.1942	3.1944	oceanographic research ship 12.1958
Shelikof	AVP52	Lake Washington, Houghton	9.1942	31.3.1943	4.1944	stricken 5.1960
Suisun	AVP53	Lake Washington, Houghton	10.1942	14.3.1943	9.1944	stricken 4.1966
Timbalier	AVP54	Lake Washington, Houghton	11.1942	18.4.1943	5.1946	stricken 5.1960
Valcour	AVP55	Lake Washington, Houghton	12.1942	5.7.1943	7.1946	stricken 1.1973
Wachapreague	AVP56	Lake Washington, Houghton	2.1943	10.7.1943	(5.1944)	completed as motor torpedo boat depot ship
Willoughby	AVP57	Lake Washington, Houghton	3.1943	21.8.1943	(6.1944)	completed as motor torpedo boat depot ship

2040 / 2410-2620 t, 94.7 x 12.5 x 3.8 m, 4 Fairbank-Morse 38D8⅛ x10 diesel-generators, 2 electric motors, 6080 hp, 20 kts, 260 t diesel oil, 6000 nm (12 kts), complement 367; 2 (AVP10-13, 21, 22, 52-55) or 4 (AVP23-26, 29-33, 48-51) or 1 (AVP34-41) x 1 – 127/38 Mk 12, (1 x 4 + 2 x 2) – 40/56 Bofors (AVP34-41), 4 x 2 (AVP23-26, 29-33, 48-55) or 6 x 1 (AVP34-41) – 20/70 Oerlikon, 4 x 1 – 12.7 MG (AVP10-13, 21, 22), 2 DCT (AVP23-26, 29-41, 48-55), 2 DCR (AVP23-26, 29-41, 48-55), 12 seaplanes (O3U (AVP10-13, 21, 22), SOC/SON, OS2U/OS2N, SO3C (AVP23-26, 29-32, 48-51), other 1942-1944), SC (AVP35-41, 52-55, other since 1944), J2F); SA, SF or SL or SU, Mk 26 radars, QCJ sonar.

The only USN purpose-built small seaplane tenders. Designed for seaplane maintenance on distant Pacific islands and atolls with shallow harbor, which predetermined the inclusion of severe draught

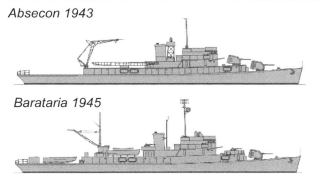

Absecon 1943

Barataria 1945

restrictions in the design assignment. Since in wartime these ships were supposed to be involved in escorting large tenders, the design provided for the fitting of anti-submarine armament and sonar.

Small seaplane tenders could tend a single seaplane squadron. The designed armament was limited to two DP 127-mm/38 guns and 4 12.7-mm MGs, but in

Yakutat 1944

1942, when the first ships of the class were already commissioned, a new armament was approved: 4 127-mm/38, 8 20-mm Oerlikons and 2 DCTs. Ships were actually commissioned with one to four 127-mm guns and 6-8 20-mm MGs. Aircraft fuel stowage was 303 000 l. There was one crane for handling seaplanes.

A total of 39 ships of this class were ordered, four were completed as PT depot ships (AGP6-9). Ordered from Lake Washington AVP42 *Hatteras*, AVP43 *Hempstead*, AVP44 *Kamishak*, AVP45 *Magothy*, AVP46 *Matanzas*, and AVP47 *Metomkin* were never laid down and cancelled in April 1943.

1943, *Absecon*: was converted to the training ship for cruiser air groups. One catapult was fitted. - 2 x 1 -127/38, 2 DCT, 2 DCR. 1943-1944, *Barnegat, Biscayne, Casco, Mackinac, Humboldt, Matagorda*: - 4 x 1 - 12.7 MG; + 4 x 2 - 20/70 Oerlikon, 2 DCT, 2 DCR. 1943-1944, *Chincoteague, Half Moon, Rockaway, San Pablo, Unimak, Yakutat, Onslow, Orca, Rehoboth, San Carlos, Barataria*: - 2 x 1 - 127/38. 1943-1944, *Coos Bay*: - 2 x 1 - 127/38; + 2 x 4 - 178 Mousetrap ASWRL.

1944-1945, many ships: - 1 x 1 -127/38, QCJ sonar; + 1 x 4 - 40/56 Bofors. QGA sonar.

Chincoteague 17.7.1943 was damaged by Japanese aircraft. *Orca* 5.1.1945 was damaged by kamikaze.

KITTY HAWK class aircraft transports

Kitty Hawk (*ex-Seatrain New York*)	APV1, 9.1943- AKV1	Sun SB, Chester	21.2.1932	14.9.1932	(1932) / 26.11.1941	stricken 2.1946
Hammondsport (*ex-Seatrain Havana*)	APV2, 9.1943- AKV2	Sun SB, Chester	20.1.1932	26.9.1932	(1932) / 11.12.1941	stricken 4.1946

Kitty Hawk 1942

10900 / 16480 t, 145.8 x 19.4 x 8.0 m, 1 set De Laval geared steam turbines, 3 Babcock & Wilcox boilers, 8000 hp, 16 kts, complement 255; 1 x 1 – 127/38 Mk 12, 4 x 1 – 76/50 Mk 20/21, 2 x 2 – 40/56 Bofors, (8 x 2 + 16 x 1) – 20/70 Oerlikon (as in 1945)

Former train ferries converted to aircraft transports. They were used for carrying of land-based aircraft to island bases. Fully assembled airplanes could be carried in large open holds.

LAKEHURST aircraft transport

Lakehurst (*ex-Seatrain New Jersey*)	APV3, 12.1942- APM9	Sun SB, Chester	1940	26.3.1940	(7.1940) / 13.10.1942	mechanized artillery transport 12.1942, stricken 1946

Lakehurst 1942

10900 /16480 t, 147.3 x 19.4 x 8.0 m, 1 set De Laval geared steam turbines, 3 Babcock & Wilcox boilers, 8000 hp, 16 kts, complement 255; 1 x 1 – 127/38 Mk 12, 4 x 1 – 76/50 Mk 20/21, 2 x 2 – 40/56 Bofors, 8 x 1 – 20/70 Oerlikon (as in 1945)

Semi-sister-ship of the previous pair.

LAFAYETTE aircraft transport

Lafayette	APV4	C A de Penhöet, St-Nazaire, France	26.1.1931	29.10.1932	(1935)	stricken incomplete 10.1945

66400 / 68350 t, 313.6 x 35.9 x 11.2 m, 4 electric motors, 4 steam turbine generators, 29 boilers, 160000 hp, 29 kts.

The largest ship in the world at the time of completion. She was laid up at New York in 1939, acquired 24.12.1941 as a transport AP53 but burned down and capsized at the berth 9.2.1942. 15.9.1943 she received hull symbol APV4, but conversion to aircraft transport was cancelled, and the ship was stricken in October 1945.

CRUISERS

ROCHESTER armored cruiser

Rochester (ex-Saratoga, ex-New York)	CA2	Cramp, Philadelphia	30.9.1890	2.12.1891	1.8.1893	stricken 10.1938

New York 1900

8200 / 9021 t, 117.0 x 19.8 x 7.3 m, 4 VTE, 8 Babcock & Wilcox boilers (2 shafts), 5300 hp, 13.5 kts, 1290 t coal, 4000 nm (10 kts), complement 566; Nickel steel, belt 102, deck 152-64, barbettes 152-102, turrets 165 (Krupp steel), casemates 102, CT 190; 2 x 2 – 203/45 Mk 6, 8 x 1 – 127/50 Mk 6, 2 x 1 – 76/50 Mk 10.

The first US armored cruiser, decommissioned only 29.4.1933 after an active and varied career. In 1905-1909, the ship was completely rearmed. In 1927 8 boilers from 12 were removed and the maximum speed was reduced from 20 to 13.5 kts.

The main 102-mm belt protected only machinery. The armored deck over the citadel was 76-mm in the flat part and was connected to the lower edge of the main belt by 152-mm slopes. The thickness of the main deck was 64 mm at ship ends. The main gun turrets had 165-mm

Krupp cemented steel sides and shallow 152-102-mm barbettes. Ammunition tubes were protected by 127-mm steel.

Rochester was stricken 28.10.1938 in the Philippines and was scuttled to avoid capture by the Japanese.

Rochester late 1920s

PENSACOLA class heavy cruisers

Pensacola	CA24	New York N Yd, Brooklyn	10.1926	25.4.1929	6.2.1930	target 7.1946
Salt Lake City	CA25	New York SB, Camden	6.1927	23.1.1929	11.12.1929	target 7.1946

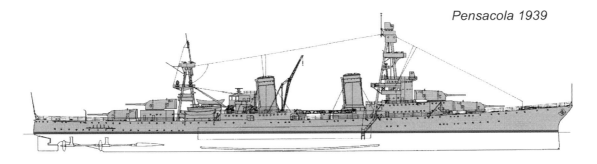

Pensacola 1939

Pensacola 1943

9097 / 11512 t, 178.5 x 19.9 x 5.9 m, 4 sets Parsons geared steam turbines, 8 White-Forster boilers, 107000 hp, 32.5 kts, 2116 t oil, 10000 nm (15 kts), complement 631; belt 102-64, deck 45-25, bulkheads 64-25, barbettes 19, turrets 64-19, CT 32; (2 x 3 + 2 x 2) – 203/55 Mk 9/10/11/13/14, 4 x 1 – 127/25 Mk 10/11/13, 8 x 1 – 12.7 MG, 2 catapults, 4 seaplanes (SOC, 1942- also OS2U, 1942-1944- also SO3C, 1944- also SC)

The first USN 'Washington' cruisers. Design work began in the USA in 1919, but the final version was ready only by 1925. Powerful armament consisted of 10 203-mm guns in twin and triple turrets was provided, armor protected machinery and magazines from fire from 130-mm guns on medium distances. This ensured invulnerability from destroyer guns, and the central fire control system made it possible to deal with light cruisers armed with 152-mm guns at long distances, at which their backfire would be ineffective. At the same time, the ships were vulnerable at any distances under fire from 203-mm guns. The flush-decked hull with a noticeable deck sheer was very narrowed at the ship ends. This decision made it possible to reduce the weight of the hull by several percent and increase the speed, but it also had negative consequences: the wide barbettes of the triple turrets did not fit into the narrow hull lines. As a result, cruisers received a rather unusual arrangement of main gun turrets: end twin turrets and superfiring triple ones. The armament also included 4 127-mm/25 AA guns and 2 x 3 533-mm TTs, removed in 1930s. Two catapults for

seaplanes were placed amidships.

Soon after commissioning, their very strong roll appeared. During fixing of this problem, bilge keels were increased.

The main belt extended up to 1.5 m below the waterline and to the 2nd deck abreast the machinery and to the 3rd deck abreast the magazines. The middle part of the belt abreast the machinery had 64-mm thickness, end parts abreast the magazines were 102-mm. The belt was closed with 64-mm bulkheads; midship and end parts were separated by 25-mm bulkheads. The armored deck over the main belt was 45-mm over the magazines and 25-mm over the machinery. The barbettes were 19-mm thick. The turrets had 64-mm faces, 25-mm sides, 19-mm rears and 51-mm crowns. CT had 32-mm sides. 1940, *Pensacola*: + CXAM radar.

Early 1941, both: - 8 x 1 - 12.7 MG; + 4 x 1 - 127/25 Mk 10/11/13. 11.1941, both: + 2 x 4 - 28/75 Mk 1.

1942, both: + 2 x 4 - 28/75 Mk 1, 8 x 1 - 20/70 Oerlikon. Late 1942, both: - 4 x 4 - 28/75; + 4 x 4 - 40/56 Bofors, 4 x 1 - 20/70 Oerlikon.

1943, *Pensacola*: - CXAM radar; + SG, SK, Mk 3, Mk 4 radars. 1943, *Salt Lake City*: + SC, SG, Mk 3, Mk 4 radars.

1944, both: - 1 catapult; + 2 x 4 - 40/56 Bofors, (8 - 9) x 1 - 20/70 Oerlikon.

By 1945, *Pensacola*: - 20 x 1 - 20/70; + 1 x 4 - 40/56 Bofors, 9 x 2 - 20/70 Oerlikon. By 1945, *Salt Lake City*: - 2 x 1 - 20/70 (19 at all). Late 1945, *Pensacola*: - 4 x 1 - 127/25, 1 x 4 - 40/56, 4 x 2 - 20/70, 1 catapult.

Pensacola 30.11.1942 in the Battle of Tassafaronga was badly damaged by a torpedo from Japanese ship and was under repair until November 1943. *Salt Lake City* 11.10.1942 in the Battle of Cape Esperance was damaged by three shells from Japanese ships, repair lasted until February 1943; in the Battle of Commander Islands 26.3.1943 she received heavy damage from the gunfire of Japanese cruisers (4 shells) and returned to service in October 1943.

NORTHAMPTON class heavy cruisers

Northampton	CA26	Bethlehem, Quincy	12.4.1928	5.9.1929	5.1930	sunk 1.12.1942
Chester	CA27	New York SB, Camden	6.3.1928	3.7.1929	6.1930	stricken 3.1959
Louisville	CA28	Puget Sound N Yd, Bremerton	4.7.1928	1.9.1930	3.1931	stricken 3.1959
Chicago	CA29	Mare Island N Yd, Vallejo	10.9.1928	10.4.1930	3.1931	sunk 30.1.1943
Houston	CA30	Newport News	1.5.1928	7.9.1929	6.1930	sunk 1.3.1942
Augusta	CA31	Newport News	2.7.1928	1.2.1930	1.1931	stricken 3.1959

9006 / 11420 t, 183.0 x 20.1 x 5.9 m, 4 sets Parsons geared steam turbines, 8 White-Forster boilers, 107000 hp, 32.5 kts, 2108 t oil, 10000 nm (15 kts), complement 617 (CA26-28) or 734-748 (CA29-31, inc. flag); belt 95-76, deck 51-25, barbettes 38, turrets 64-19, CT 32; 3 x 3 – 203/55 Mk 9/10/11/13/14, 4 x 1 – 127/25 Mk 10/11/13,

8 x 1 – 12.7 MG, 2 catapults, 4 seaplanes (SOC, 1942- also OS2U, 1942-1944- also SO3C, 1944- also SC).

When discussion at the General Board (February 1926) the specification of the cruisers planned for building, it was proposed to redesign the *Pensacola* class, improving protection by machinery re-

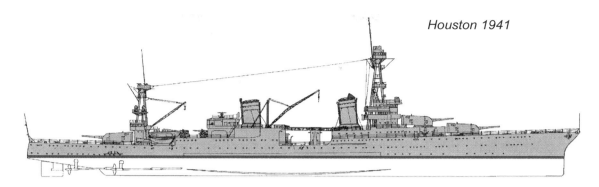

Houston 1941

arrangement into larger number of compartments, and increasing seaworthiness using a forecastle. In addition, it was recommended to improve the conditions for maintenance and storage of seaplanes by fitting a hangar. To keep the displacement at the same level, it was considered possible to reduce the number of the main guns to eight or nine, like most of the 'Washington' cruisers of other navies. In April, two basic designs were presented to the Board for consideration: the first with four twin turrets, and the second with three triple ones. The latter was chosen, since the armament weight in triple turrets turned out to be less, than in twin ones. In addition, four-turret arrangement, compared to the three-turret one, was too cramped. In the final version, the armament consisted of 3 x 3 203-mm/55 main guns, 4 x 1 127-mm/25 AA guns and 2 x 3 533-mm TTs.

The protection of the new design differed little from the *Pensacola* class. When designing, an immune zone was not determined, however, the calculations of 1933 showed that protection against 130-mm shells at a distance of more than 40 cables was provided, the immune zone against 152-mm shells laid in the 50-105 cables interval, but only for magazines, since the belt abreast the machinery was not penetrated at distance above 65 cables, when the deck already became penetrable for 152-mm shell. Under 203-mm shells, the immune zone was absent. When designing, it was proposed to strengthen the armor, providing at least protection for the magazines from 203-mm shells, but the work was limited only to splinter-proof protection of the ammunition elevators.

All 6 ships were built according to FY29 program. CA29, CA30 and CA31 were designed as flag ships and visually differed from the rest by a forecastle, lengthened to the catapults, including additional accommodations.

The main belt was extended to 1.5 m below and 3 m above the waterline. The midship part of the belt abreast the machinery was 76-mm, and end parts abreast the magazines were 95-mm. The belt was closed with 64-mm bulkheads; midship and end parts were separated by 25-mm bulkheads. The armored deck over the main belt was 51-mm thick over the magazines and 25-mm over the machinery. The barbettes were 38-mm thick.

The turrets had 64-mm faces, 25-mm sides, 19-mm rears and 51-mm crowns. CT had 32-mm sides.
1938-1939, all: + 4 x 1 – 127/25 Mk 10/11/13.
1940, *Northampton, Chester, Chicago*: + CXAM radar.
Mid-1941, *Northampton*: + 4 x 1 - 76/50 Mk 20. Mid-1941, *Chester, Louisville, Chicago, Augusta*: + 4 x 4 - 28/75 Mk 1. Mid-1941, *Houston*: + 3 x 1 - 76/50 Mk 20, 1 x 4 - 28/75 Mk 1. Late 1941, *Northampton*: - 4 x 1 - 76/50; + 4 x 4 - 28/75 Mk 1. Late 1941, *Houston*: - 3 x 1 - 76/50; + 3 x 4 - 28/75 Mk 1.
Early 1942, *Augusta*: + CXAM-1 radar. 1942, *Northampton, Louisville, Chicago, Augusta*: - 8 x 1 - 12.7 MG; + 14 x 1 - 20/70 Oerlikon, Mk 3, Mk 4 radars. 1942, *Chester*: - 2 x 4 - 28/75, 8 x 1 - 12.7 MG; + 13 x 1 - 20/70 Oerlikon, Mk 3, Mk 4 radars. Late 1942, *Augusta*: - CXAM-1 radar; + SG, SK radars.
Early 1943, *Chester*: - 2 x 4 - 28/75, 1 x 1 - 20/70, CXAM radar; + 4 x 4 - 40/56 Bofors, SG, SK, SP radars. Early 1943, *Louisville*: - 4 x 4 - 28/75, 2 x 1 - 20/70; + 4 x 4 - 40/56 Bofors, SG, SK, SP radars. Early 1943, *Augusta*: - 4 x 4 - 28/75, 2 x 1 - 20/70; + 4 x 4 - 40/56 Bofors, SP radar.
1944-1945, *Chester*: - 12 x 1 - 20/70, 1 catapult; + (1 x 4 + 2 x 2) - 40/56 Bofors, 13 x 2 - 20/70 Oerlikon. 1944-1945, *Louisville, Augusta*: - 1 catapult; + 4 x 2 - 40/56 Bofors, 8 x 1 - 20/70 Oerlikon; full displacement was 14000 t.
Houston 4.2.1942 was damaged by Japanese aircraft (a bomb hit No3 turret); 27.2.1942 in the Battle of the Java Sea she was damaged by gunfire from Japanese cruisers and 1.3.1942 was sunk by gunfire and torpedoes from Japanese cruisers *Mogami* and *Mikuma* in the Sunda Strait. *Northampton* in the Battle of Tassafaronga 30.11.1942, shortly before midnight, received 2 torpedo

Augusta 1942

hits from Japanese destroyer *Oyashio*. After 3 hours, she was abandoned by the crew and sank. *Chicago* 9.8.1942 in the Battle of Savo Island was damaged by a Japanese torpedo and was under repair until the end of the year; 29.1.1943 she was damaged by two Japanese air torpedoes near Rennell Island and lost speed; she was taken in tow, but the next day received 4 more air torpedo hits from G4M bombers and quickly sank.

Chester 1.2.1942 was damaged by Japanese aircraft (1 bomb hit) and was under repair until May 1942; 20.10.1942 she was damaged by a torpedo from Japanese submarine *I176* and was repaired until June 1943; 19.2.1945 she was again damaged in a collision with auxiliary vessel *Estes* and returned to service in May 1945. *Louisville* 5.1.1945 and 8.1.1945 was damaged by hits of two kamikazes; repair lasted until April 1945; 5.6.1945 she was again damaged by kamikaze and returned to service in August.

PORTLAND class heavy cruisers

Portland	CA33	Bethlehem, Quincy	17.2.1930	21.5.1932	23.2.1933	stricken 3.1959
Indianapolis	CA35	New York SB, Camden	31.3.1930	7.11.1931	15.11.1932	sunk 29.7.1945

Indianapolis 1945

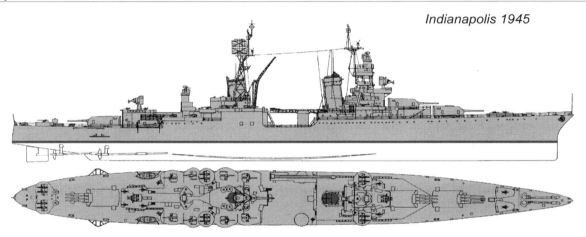

10258 / 12755 t, 185.9 x 20.1 x 6.4 m, 4 sets Parsons geared steam turbines, 8 Yarrow boilers, 107000 hp, 32.5 kts, 2125 t oil, 10000 nm (15 kts), complement 807 (CA33) or 917 (CA35, inc. flag); belt 146-83, bulkheads 32-25, deck 64-54, barbettes 38, turrets 64-19, CT 32; 3 x 3 – 203/55 Mk 9/10/11/13/14, 8 x 1 – 127/25 Mk 10/11/13, 8 x 1 – 12.7 MG, 2 catapults, 4 seaplanes (SOC, 1942- also OS2U, 1942-1944- also SO3C, 1944- also SC).

The original design of the *Portland* class cruisers, approved in 1929, was almost an exact copy of

Indianapolis 1939

the *Northampton*, only 3 m longer. It was planned to build five ships (CL32-36, subsequently the index was replaced by CA). Already with the approval of the design of new cruisers, it turned out, that their prototype, the *Northampton*, was underloaded and a displacement reserve could be used to strengthen the protection. In this regard, it was decided to limit the class to only two ships according to the modified design and build other ships according to the new one (the future *New Orleans* class). Redesigning of the *Portland* class resulted in an increase in the thickness of the deck over the machinery and better protection of the magazines. These innovations made it possible to provide more reliable protection of the machinery from 152-mm shells, and for the first time USN ships received an immune zone under 203-mm shells, however only for magazines (for fore magazines between 60 and 115 cables, and for aft ones between 60 and 102 cables). In addition to more reliable protection, the *Portland* class differed from the predecessors by the absence of TTs and doubled number of 127-mm AA guns.

The main belt reached 1.5 m below and 3 m over the waterline. Midship part of the belt abreast the machinery was 127-mm thick (83 mm at the lower edge) on 19-mm STS plating, and the end parts abreast the magazines were 146-mm. The belt was closed with 64-mm bulkheads; midship and end parts were separated by 25-mm bulkheads. The armored deck over the main belt was 54-mm over the magazines and 64-mm over the machinery. The barbettes were 38-mm thick. The turrets had 64-mm faces, 25-mm sides, 19-mm rears and 51-mm crowns. CT had 32-mm sides.

Early 1942, both: - 8 x 1 - 12.7 MG; + 4 x 4 - 28/75 Mk 1, 12 x 1 - 20/70 Oerlikon, SC, Mk 3, Mk 4 radars.

5.1943, both: - 4 x 4 - 28/75, 1 catapult, SC radar; + 4 x 4 - 40/56 Bofors, SG, SK radars. *Portland* could carry 2 seaplanes and *Indianapolis* 3.

Autumn 1944, both: - Mk 3, Mk 4 radars; + Mk 8, Mk 18 radars. 1944-1945, *Portland*: + 4 x 2 - 40/56 Bofors, 5 x 1 - 20/70 Oerlikon. 1944-1945, *Indianapolis*: - 12 x 1 - 20/70; + 2 x 4 - 40/56 Bofors, 8 x 2 - 20/70 Oerlikon, full displacement exceeded 15000 t.

Indianapolis was damaged 30.3.1945 by a kamikaze and was under repair until July 1945; 30.7.1945 she was sunk by three torpedoes from Japanese submarine *I58* in the Philippine Sea. *Portland* 13.11.1942 in the Battle of Guadalcanal received one torpedo hit from Japanese ship, was damaged and was under repair until May 1943.

NEW ORLEANS class heavy cruisers

New Orleans	CA32	New York N Yd, Brooklyn	14.3.1931	12.4.1933	18.4.1934	stricken 3.1959
Astoria	CA34	Puget Sound N Yd, Bremerton	1.9.1930	16.12.1933	1.6.1934	sunk 9.8.1942
Minneapolis	CA36	Philadelphia N Yd	27.6.1931	6.9.1933	20.6.1934	stricken 3.1959
Tuscaloosa	CA37	New York SB, Camden	3.9.1931	15.11.1933	17.8.1934	stricken 3.1959
San Francisco	CA38	Mare Island N Yd, Vallejo	9.9.1931	9.3.1933	23.4.1934	stricken 3.1959
Quincy	CA39	Bethlehem, Quincy	15.11.1933	19.6.1935	9.6.1936	sunk 9.8.1942
Vincennes	CA44	Bethlehem, Quincy	2.1.1934	21.5.1936	24.2.1937	sunk 9.8.1942

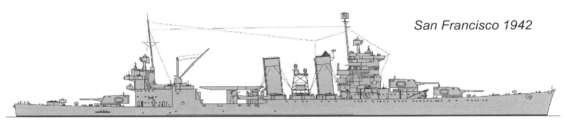

San Francisco 1942

10136 / 12463 t, 179.2 x 18.8 x 6.9 m, 4 sets Westinghouse geared steam turbines, 8 Babcock & Wilcox boilers, 107000 hp, 32.7 kts, 1861 t oil, 10000 nm (15 kts), complement 868; belt 127-76, bulkheads 76-38, deck 57, barbettes 127 (CA32, 34, 36) or 152 (CA37, 38) or 133 (CA39, 44), turrets 203-38, CT 127; 3 x 3 – 203/55 Mk 9/11/13/14 (CA32, 34, 36) or Mk 12/15 (CA37-39, 44), 8 x 1 – 127/25 Mk 10/11/13, 8 x 1 – 12.7 MG, 2 catapults, 4 seaplanes (SOC, 1942- also OS2U, 1942-1944- also SO3C, 1944- also SC)

Starting to design a successor to the *Portland* class under the 1929 Program (CA37-41), the USN staff decided that the protection of the early heavy cruisers was insufficient. After much deliberation, the General Board abandoned plans of a modified *Northampton* class in favor of a better protected ship. Her creation became possible due to the fact that the *Northampton* class cruisers had a standard displacement of about 1000 t less than the limit set by the Washington Conference, and this reserve could be spent on strengthening protection. The structure (but not an arrangement) of the machinery of the new cruisers remained unchanged, but the hull was quite new and became noticeable shorter and narrower compared to the predecessors. The reduction in length was achieved by abandoning the machinery arrangements *en echelon* in favor of a linear one. In addition, the length of

the machinery rooms was reduced. This made it possible to shorten a waterline belt and increase its thickness to 127 mm. Unlike the predecessors, the turrets received protection from 203-mm shells. The protection weight was 15% of the standard displacement. As result, the immune zone under the fire of 203-mm guns at a relative 60° bearing laid in a band between 60 and 120 cables.

Initially, it was planned to build 5 ships (CA37-41) according to this design, but they exceeded the *Northampton* class (CA32-36) so much that it was decided to build CA32, 34 and 36, the order for which was received by the Naval Yards, according to the new design (at the same time, building of CA39-41 was suspended). The first three cruisers of the *New Orleans* class (CA32, 34 and 36) were built under the

Minneapolis 1943

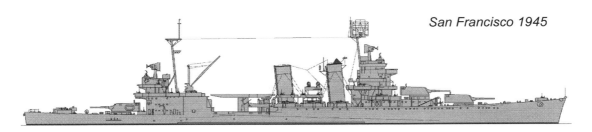

San Francisco 1945

FY29 Program. They were followed by three ships of the FY30 Program (CA37-39), not much different from the previous three. CA37 and CA38 had more protected barbettes and new, lighter 203-mm guns in more compact turrets. On CA39 it provided for the possibility of fitting of the 28-mm AA MGs in the future, which required a margin of displacement. To do this, it was necessary to reduce the thickness of the barbettes. The last ship of the class, CA44, was built under the FY31 Program and completely repeated the CA39 design.

By the middle of the war, stability approached a dangerous limit, and further modernizations were accompanied by additional lead ballast. In addition, the ships lost their CTs, and the bridges were rebuilt. The main belt abreast the machinery reached 1.5 m below and 2.86 m over the waterline. It was 127-mm thick (76-mm at lower edge) on 19-mm STS plating. There were narrow belts abreast the magazines. The thickness of these belts was 102 mm decreasing to 76 mm at the lower edge. The magazines were protected by 37-mm bulkheads fore and aft, the machinery and magazines were separated by 76-51-mm bulkheads. The armored deck over the main belt was 57-mm over the machinery (on 2nd deck level) and the magazines (on the 1st platform level). Its thickness decreased to 32 mm fwd of the fore magazine. The barbettes were 127-mm (CA32, 34, 36) or 152-mm (CA37, 38) or 133-mm (CA39, 44) thick. The turrets had 203-mm faces, 95-38-mm sides, 38-mm

rears and 70-mm crowns.
6.1941, *Astoria*; 11.1941, *New Orleans, Minneapolis*; 12.1941-4.1942, *Tuscaloosa, San Francisco, Quincy, Vincennes*: + 4 x 4 - 28/75 Mk 1.
Mid-1942, all: - 8 x 1 - 12.7 MG; + 6 x 1 - 20/70 Oerlikon, SC, Mk 3 radars. Late 1942, all survived: + (6 - 10) x 1 - 20/70 Oerlikon.
Late 1943, all survived: - 4 x 4 - 28/75, 1 catapult, SC radar; + 6 x 4 - 40/56 Bofors, 2 SG, SK, Mk 4 radars. CT was removed.
1944, *Minneapolis*: - 3 x 3 - 203/55; + 3 x 3 - 203/55 Mk 12/15, SP radar. 1944-1945, *New Orleans*: - (12 - 16) x 1 - 20/70; + 14 x 2 - 20/70 Oerlikon. 1944-1945, *Minneapolis*: - (12 - 16) x 1 - 20/70; + 8 x 2 - 20/70 Oerlikon. 1944-1945, *Tuscaloosa*: - (12 - 16) x 1 - 20/70; + 28 x 1 - 20/70 Oerlikon. 1944-1945, *San Francisco*: - (12 - 16) x 1 - 20/70; + 26 x 1 - 20/70 Oerlikon.
Vincennes, Quincy and *Astoria* were sunk by gunfire and torpedoes from Japanese heavy cruisers 9.8.1942 in the Battle of Savo Island (Guadalcanal). *New Orleans* 30.11.1942 was damaged by Japanese torpedo (fore end was cut off to the No2 turret) and returned to service in July 1943. *Minneapolis* was damaged 30.11.1942 by two torpedoes from Japanese destroyers. The fore end to the No1 turret was cut off, repair lasted until September 1943. *San Francisco* 13.11.1942 was badly damaged by gunfire from Japanese ships (up to 45 shell hits) and was under repair until February 1943.

WICHITA heavy cruiser

Wichita	CA45	Philadelphia N Yd / New York SB, Camden	28.10.1935	16.11.1937	16.2.1939	stricken 3.1959

Wichita 1942

10589 / 13015 t, 185.4 x 18.8 x 7.2 m, 4 sets Parsons geared steam turbines, 8 Babcock & Wilcox boilers, 100000 hp, 33 kts, 1984 t oil, 10000 nm (15 kts), complement 929; belt 152-102, bulkheads 152, deck 57, barbettes 178, turrets 203-38, CT 152; 3 x 3 – 203/55 Mk 12/15, 8 x 1 – 127/38 Mk 12, 8 x 1 – 12.7 MG, 2 catapults, 4 seaplanes (SOC, 1942- also OS2U, 1942-1944- also SO3C, 1944- also SC).
According to the decisions of the London Naval Conference of 1930, the USA could lay down one heavy cruiser in 1934 (CA44 *Vincennes* of the *New Orleans* class) and one more in 1935. In March 1934,

Wichita 1945

a decision was made to build the latter according to the new design, based on the *Brooklyn*, with the replacement of 152-mm guns with 203-mm ones. The thickness of the main belt was increased to 152 mm, and barbettes to 178 mm. The main disadvantage of the previous 203-mm turrets was too much projectile dispersion due to insufficient distance between the barrels. In the new turrets, this distance was increased without increasing of barbette diameter (the barbettes were made conical, not cylindrical). The structure and arrangement of the machinery were the same as on the last two ships of the *Brooklyn* class: the boiler room with six of the eight boilers was placed before the fore engine room, and two remained boilers were installed in the boiler room arranged between two engine rooms. The armor protection provided the ship with an immune zone under the fire of 203-mm guns in a band between 50 and 110 cables. In addition to 203-mm guns, the cruiser carried new 127-mm/38 DP guns, placed not along the sides, but in a diamond pattern, which significantly improved the firing sectors. Since the design called for much lighter 127-mm/25 AA guns, stability after

the installation of 127-mm/38 guns became a serious concern. The way out was found in 200 t of lead ballast. The main belt abreast the machinery reached 1.5 m below and 2.86 m over the waterline. It was 152-mm thick (76-mm at the lower edge) on 16-mm STS plating. There were narrow belts abreast the magazines. The thickness of these belts was 102 mm, decreasing to 76 mm at the lower edge. The magazines were protected by 152-mm bulkheads fore and aft, the machinery and magazines were separated by 152-mm bulkheads. The armored deck over the main belt was 57-mm. The barbettes were 178-mm thick. The turrets had 203-mm faces, 95-mm sides, 38-mm rears and 70-mm crowns. The CT had 152-mm sides and 57-mm roof.

7.1941: + 2 x 4 - 28/75 Mk 1, CXAS Mk 1 radar.

4.1942: - 8 x 1 - 12.7 MG, CXAS Mk 1 radar; + 12 x 1 - 20/70 Oerlikon, SC, 2 Mk 4, Mk 8 radars.

11.1943: - 2 x 4 - 28/75, SC, Mk 8 radars; + (4 x 4 + 2 x 2) - 40/56 Bofors, 6 x 1 - 20/70 Oerlikon, SG, SK-1, Mk 13 radars.

1945: - 2 Mk 4 radars; + 2 x 2 - 40/56 Bofors, 2 Mk 25 radars, full displacement was 14611 t.

BALTIMORE class heavy cruisers

Baltimore subclass						
Baltimore	CA68	Bethlehem, Quincy	26.5.1941	28.7.1942	15.4.1943	stricken 2.1971
Boston	CA69	Bethlehem, Quincy	30.6.1941	26.8.1942	30.6.1943	stricken 4.1974
Canberra (ex-*Pittsburgh*)	CA70	Bethlehem, Quincy	3.9.1941	19.4.1943	14.10.1943	stricken 7.1978
Quincy (ex-*St. Paul*)	CA71	Bethlehem, Quincy	9.10.1941	23.6.1943	15.12.1943	stricken 10.1973
Pittsburgh (ex-*Albany*)	CA72	Bethlehem, Quincy	3.2.1943	22.2.1944	10.10.1944	stricken 7.1973
St. Paul (ex-*Rochester*)	CA73	Bethlehem, Quincy	3.2.1943	16.9.1944	17.2.1945	stricken 7.1978
Columbus	CA74	Bethlehem, Quincy	28.6.1943	30.11.1944	8.6.1945	stricken 8.1976

Helena (*ex-Des Moines*)	CA75	Bethlehem, Quincy	9.9.1943	28.4.1945	4.9.1945	stricken 1.1974
Bremerton	CA130	New York SB, Camden	1.2.1943	2.7.1944	29.4.1945	stricken 10.1973
Fall River	CA131	New York SB, Camden	12.4.1943	13.8.1944	1.7.1945	stricken 2.1971
Macon	CA132	New York SB, Camden	14.6.1943	15.10.1944	26.8.1945	stricken 11.1969
Toledo	CA133	New York SB, Camden	13.9.1943	6.5.1945	27.10.1946	stricken 1.1974
Los Angeles	CA135	Philadelphia N Yd	28.7.1943	20.8.1944	22.7.1945	stricken 1.1974
Chicago	CA136	Philadelphia N Yd	28.7.1943	20.8.1944	10.1.1945	stricken 1.1984

Oregon City (Baltimore 1942) subclass

Oregon City	CA122	Bethlehem, Quincy	8.4.1944	9.6.1945	16.2.1946	stricken 11.1970
Albany	CA123	Bethlehem, Quincy	6.3.1944	30.6.1945	15.6.1946	stricken 6.1985
Rochester	CA124	Bethlehem, Quincy	29.5.1944	28.8.1945	20.12.1946	stricken 10.1973
Northampton	CLC1 (*ex-CA125*)	Bethlehem, Quincy	31.8.1944	27.1.1951	7.3.1953	commissioned as command ship, stricken 12.1977
Kansas City	CA128	Bethlehem, Quincy	9.7.1945	-	-	cancelled 8.1945
Norfolk	CA137	Philadelphia N Yd	27.12.1944	-	-	cancelled 8.1945
Scranton	CA138	Philadelphia N Yd	27.12.1944	-	-	cancelled 8.1945

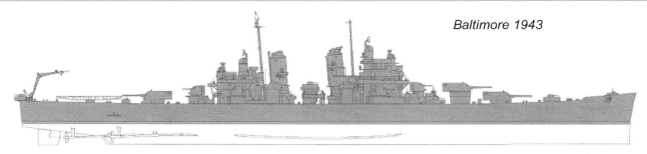

Baltimore 1943

14472 / 17031 t, 205.3 x 21.6 x 7.3 m, 4 sets General Electric geared steam turbines, 4 Babcock & Wilcox boilers, 120000 hp, 33 kts, 2250 t oil, 10000 nm (15 kts), complement 2039; belt 152-102, deck 65, barbettes 160, turrets 203-38, CT 152 (CA74, 75, 122-133, 135-138); 3 x 3 – 203/55 Mk 12/15, 6 x 2 – 127/38 Mk 12, 12 x 4 (CA68-71) or (11 x 4 + 2 x 2) (CA72-75, 122-124, 130-133, 135, 136) – 40/56 Bofors, 24 x 1 (CA68-71) or 22 x 1 (CA72-75) or 10 x 2 (CA122-124) or 14 x 2 (CA130-133, 135, 136) – 20/70 Oerlikon, 2 catapults, 4 (CA68-71) or 2 seaplanes (SOC, 1942- also OS2U, 1942-1944- also SO3C, 1944- also SC); SG-1 (CA68-73, 130, 136), SG-3 (CA74, 75, 122-124, 131, 132, 135), SK (CA68-71), SK-2 (CA72-75, 122-124, 130-132, 135, 136), SP (CA72-75, 122-124, 130-132, 135, 136), Mk 8 (CA68-73, 130, 136), Mk 13 (CA74, 75, 122-124, 131, 132, 135), 2 Mk 12/22 radars.

Work on the *Baltimore* design began in September 1939. The war in Europe lifted all restrictions that made it possible to return to the building of cruisers with 203-mm guns. The newly built *Wichita* was taken as the basis, her only drawback was unsatisfactory stability. Initially, it was supposed to be limited to increasing the hull beam by 0.6 m, but it was soon decided to go for a more significant design change, strengthening AA armament by placing 127-mm/38 guns in twin mounts on accepted on the *Cleveland* class light cruisers diamond-shaped scheme, and installing multi-barreled automatic

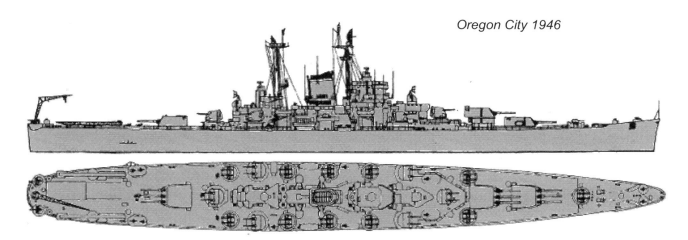

Oregon City 1946

guns (originally 4 x 4 28-mm "Chicago pianos", later replaced by 40-mm/56 Bofors). It was also envisaged to lengthen a waterline belt. As a result, the new ship grew noticeably; the standard displacement reached 13600 t, and almost the entire increase in displacement was aimed at strengthening AA armament and ensuring better seaworthiness and stability. Protection, in comparison with *Wichita*, was not changed much: only the deck thickness was increased to 65 mm, and the waterline belt became longer. The immune zone under the fire from 203-mm guns stretched from 77.5 to 120 cables. The engine power was increased by 20%, as the displacement increased dramatically compared to the prototype.

The order for the first four ships (CA68-71) was placed in July 1940; in September, an order for the next four (CA72-75) followed. The last series of 16 ships (CA122-138) was ordered in August 1943. The first ship was commissioned only in the spring of 1943, and war experience was taken in the account during her construction, therefore, after commissioning, the ships were practically not modernized throughout the war. In 1942, an improved design was created, characterized by a reduction in the number of funnels to one and improved sectors of antiaircraft artillery fire. It was decided to modify on the "1942 design" incomplete CA122-129, CA137 and CA138. In the end of the war, CA134 was re-ordered as the cruiser of the new class with automatic 203-mm guns (the future *De Moines* class), 12.8.1945 the orders for CA126 *Cambridge*, CA127 *Bridgeport* and CA129 *Tulsa* (all – Bethlehem, Quincy) were cancelled (as were orders for laid down CA128, 137 and 138), CA125 was completed after the war as a command ship. The main belt abreast the machinery reached 1.5 m below and 2.86 m over the waterline. It was 152-mm thick (76-mm at the lower edge) on 16-mm STS plating. There were narrow belts abreast the magazines. The thickness of these belts was 76 mm decreasing to 51 mm at the lower edge. The magazines were protected by 140-mm fore and 127-mm aft bulkheads, the

Baltimore 1944

machinery and magazines were separated by 152-mm bulkheads. The armored deck over the main belt was 65-mm. The barbettes were 178-mm thick. The turrets had 203-mm faces, 83-38-mm sides, 38-mm rears and 76-mm crowns. The CT on all ships instead of CA68-73 had 152-mm sides and 76-mm roof.

Canberra 13.10.1944 was damaged by a Japanese air torpedo and returned to service in October 1945. *Pittsburgh* 5.6.1945 was badly damaged during a typhoon (she lost fore end to the No1 turret) and was under repair until September 1945.

Oregon City 1946

ALASKA class large cruisers

Alaska	CB1	New York SB, Camden	17.12.1941	15.8.1943	17.6.1944	stricken 1.6.1960
Guam	CB2	New York SB, Camden	2.2.1942	12.11.1943	17.9.1944	stricken 1.6.1960
Hawaii	CB3	New York SB, Camden	20.12.1943	11.3.1945	-	suspended 9.1947

29779 / 34253 t, 246.4 x 27.8 x 9.7 m, 4 sets General Electric geared steam turbines, 4 Babcock & Wilcox boilers, 150000 hp, 33 kts, 3619 t oil, 12000 nm (15 kts), complement 1517; belt 229-127, main deck 102-97, upper deck 36, splinter deck 16, barbettes 330-378, turrets 325-127, CT 269; 3 x 3 – 305/50 Mk 8, 6 x 2 – 127/38 Mk 12, 14 x 4 – 40/56 Bofors, 34 x 1 – 20/70 Oerlikon, 2 catapults, 4 seaplanes (OS2U, 1944- SC); SK, 2 SG-1, 2 Mk 8, 2 Mk 12/22 radars.

The large cruisers *Alaska* and *Guam*, due to their size and armament, often referred to the class of battleships, however, they were descended from the 'Washington' cruisers, being their direct successors. The origin of these ships was due to several factors. Firstly, with the outbreak of war in Europe, all treaties restrictions became invalid, secondly, the financing of new shipbuilding programs did not meet with a response from Congress, and thirdly, at that time the concept of a "super-cruiser" that could replace the existing 'Washington' cruisers with 203-mm main guns, was popular. Design (a new CB subclass was even created for her) was started in 1940. As result of the

disappearance of restrictions, the ship became huge. The requirement for high speed predetermined a large L/B ratio, which did not allow for any effective underwater protection, in addition, the presence of only one rudder instead of two (which was practiced on battleships) predetermined poor maneuverability. In the early design stages, it was supposed to be protected only from 203-mm shells (except for magazines, traditionally better protected), but then the armor was strengthened, and as a result, the ships received an immune zone under the fire from 305-mm guns in the range of 90-120 cables at a relative 60° bearing. Initially, it was planned to arm ships with 8 305-mm/50 guns in twin and triple turrets, but in the end, it was decided to place all the guns in triple turrets so as not to waste time designing turrets of two types.

The FY40 Program provided for building of six ships of the class (CB1-6), but by 1943 opinion about this design began to change for the worse, and three ships (CB4 *Philippines*, CB5 *Puerto Rico* and CB6 *Samoa*, all were planned to be built by New York SB) were cancelled. Building of CB3 *Hawaii* was suspended in 1947.

The main 134-m armor belt was 4.6-m deep. It was 229-mm thick (127-mm at the lower edge) and was inclined at 10° to the vertical. The belt was closed with 260-mm bulkheads. The steering gear compartment had 270-mm sides and bulkheads. The depth of underwater protection was 3.0-2.4 m. The main deck was 102-96-mm thick over the machinery and 108-mm over the magazines. The 19-16-mm splinter deck was placed one level lower and the 36-mm upper deck was one level higher. The steering gear compartment had 38-mm roof. The thickness of the second deck over the steering gear compartment was 102 mm. The barbettes were 330-278-mm thick. The turrets had 325-mm faces, 152-133-mm sides, 133-mm rears and 127-mm crowns. The CT had 269-mm sides and 127-mm roof.

Guam 1944

DES MOINES class heavy cruisers

Des Moines	CA134	Bethlehem, Quincy	28.5.1945	27.9.1946	17.11.1948	stricken 7.1991
Salem	CA139	Bethlehem, Quincy	4.6.1945	25.3.1947	9.5.1949	stricken 7.1991
Dallas	CA140	Bethlehem, Quincy	15.10.1945	-	-	cancelled 6.1946
Newport News	CA148	Newport News	1.10.1945	6.3.1947	29.1.1949	stricken 7.1978

17255 / 20934 t, 218.4 x 23.0 x 7.9 m, 4 sets General Electric geared steam turbines, 4 Babcock & Wilcox boilers, 120000 hp, 33 kts, 3006 t oil, 10500 nm (15 kts), complement 1799; belt 152-102, deck 95, upper deck 25, bulkheads 127-102, barbettes 160, turrets 203-38,

bridge 165-140; 3 x 3 – 203/55 Mk 16, 6 x 2 – 127/38 Mk 12, 12 x 2 – 76/50 Mk 22, 12 x 2 – 20/70 Oerlikon; SG-6, SK-3, SPS-6, 2 Mk 13, 4 Mk 25, 4 Mk 35 radars.

The final design for the US gun cruiser. These ships were designed around the new Mk 16 203-mm/55 rapid-

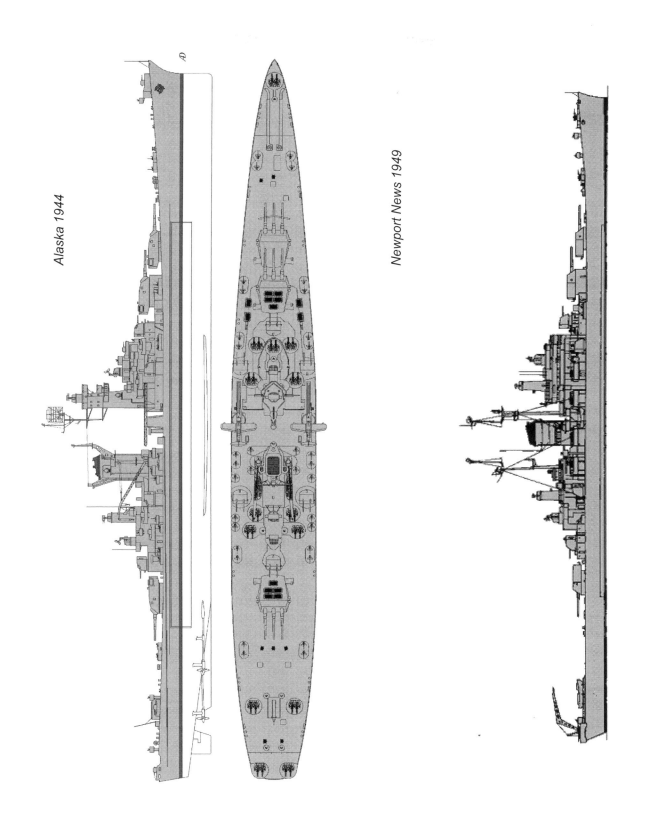

Alaska 1944

Newport News 1949

Des Moines 1951

firing guns, which were theoretically three times faster than the previous Mk 12 and Mk 15. It was calculated that this increase in rate of fire made it possible to more successfully conduct night operations against fast Japanese ships. In July 1943, the detailed weights of the twin and triple turrets with these guns were calculated, and design of the new class began immediately. An initial proposal for a "modified *Baltimore*" with twin turrets (their barbettes were similar in diameter to those of the triple turrets on previous class) was rejected due to lack of armament as a result, and a decision was made to

create a completely new ship with a greater beam and stronger armor. The immune zone from 203-mm shells tanged from 77 to 138 cables.

In total, it was planned to build 12 ships of this class. Already in July 1943, CA139-142 were ordered. In October 1943, it was decided to build CA134 under this design, and later the former light cruisers CL143, 148 and 149 were reordered as the *Des Moines* class. Another 4 ships, CA150-153, were envisaged by the 1945 Program, which was not approved by the President. The main belt between the end barbettes had 3.1-m depth. It was 152-mm thick (102-mm at the lower edge). There were 6 127-mm transverse bulkheads (2 external and 4 internal), dividing the ship into 5 zones. The armored deck over the main belt was 95 mm. The upper 25-mm deck was placed one level higher. The barbettes were 178-mm thick. The turrets had 203-mm faces, 90-51-mm sides, 38-mm rears and 102-mm crowns. The armored bridge had 165-140-mm sides.

OMAHA class light cruisers

Omaha	CL4	Todd, Tacoma	6.12.1918	14.12.1920	24.2.1923	stricken 11.1945
Milwaukee	CL5	Todd, Tacoma	13.12.1918	24.3.1921	20.6.1923	to the USSR 4.1944 (Murmansk)
Cincinnati	CL6	Todd, Tacoma	15.5.1920	23.5.1921	1.1.1924	stricken 11.1945
Raleigh	CL7	Bethlehem, Quincy	16.8.1920	25.10.1922	6.2.1924	stricken 11.1945
Detroit	CL8	Bethlehem, Quincy	10.11.1920	29.6.1922	31.7.1923	stricken 1.1946
Richmond	CL9	Cramp, Philadelphia	16.2.1920	29.9.1921	2.7.1923	stricken 1.1946
Concord	CL10	Cramp, Philadelphia	29.3.1920	15.12.1921	3.11.1923	stricken 12.1945
Trenton	CL11	Cramp, Philadelphia	18.8.1920	16.4.1923	19.4.1924	stricken 1.1946
Marblehead	CL12	Cramp, Philadelphia	4.8.1920	9.10.1923	8.9.1924	stricken 11.1945
Memphis	CL13	Cramp, Philadelphia	14.10.1920	17.4.1924	4.2.1925	stricken 1.1946

Detroit 1945

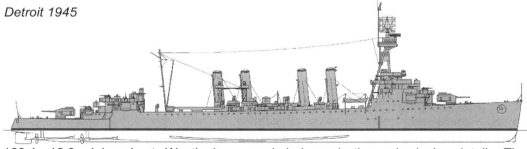

7050 / 9508 t, 169.4 x 16.9 x 4.1 m, 4 sets Westinghouse geared steam turbines, 12 Yarrow boilers, 90000 hp, 34 kts, 1852 t oil, 8460 nm (10 kts), complement 458; belt 76, deck 38, CT 32; (2 x 2 + 8 x 1) (CL4, 5, 10, 11, 13) or (2 x 2 + 6 x 1) (CL6-9) or (2 x 2 + 7 x 1) (CL12) – 152/53 Mk 12/14/18, 4 x 1 – 76/50 Mk 10/18, 2 x 3 – 533 TT, 2 catapults, 2 seaplanes (SOC, 1942- also OS2U, 1942-1944- also SO3C, 1944- also SC).

The *Omaha* class cruisers were built as part of an ambitious shipbuilding program of 1916. One of the main requirements for a 7000-t cruiser-scout was 35-kt speed. This circumstance predetermined a noticeable

imbalance in the main design details. The hull was as narrow as possible, with slender "destroyer" lines. To save weight, ship's framing was maximally lightened, which, combined with powerful and, as a result, heavy-weight machinery, led to vibration at full speed. The excessive thrust to achieve high speed led to the fact that the displacement spent on armament and protection turned out to be noticeably less than on foreign contemporaries: for example, only 8% of the displacement was allocated for protection. In addition, the desire to ensure maximum fire forward and aft led to the introduction of a dubious arrangement of the

Richmond 1945

main artillery in two-level casemates fore and aft: they noticeably weighed the ends but had only splinter-proof protection. According to the design, the new cruiser was supposed to have a displacement of 7050 t, a speed of 35 knots, armament consisted of 10 152-mm/53 guns (4 in the fore casemates, 4 aft and 2 more guns on open mounts amidships), 2 76-mm/50 AA guns and 2 twin 533-mm TTs.

The building contract was signed 8.7.1916, but the first ships were laid down only two years later, after the design was substantially revised, mainly due to criticism about insufficient armament. The 152-mm open mounts were abandoned, but twin turrets appeared at the ship ends, further increasing a local overload. The torpedo armament was strengthened, adding to the two twin TTs on the main deck (removed immediately after commission) two more triple ones on the upper deck, fwd of the aft casemate. The originally planned quarterdeck catapult was abandoned, replaced by two rotating on the upper deck. Structural changes led to an increase in displacement by about 400 t, which reduced the speed by 1 knot. For the first time in USN practice, the machinery was arranged *en echelon*: the engine rooms were placed between fore and stern boiler rooms groups. Turbines and boilers were produced by different companies, which led to a noticeable spread in performance, and the ships were divided into "high endurance" group (CL9-13) and "low endurance" group (CL4-8). However, the planned cruising range (10000 nm at 10 kts) was never achieved.

In 1940, it was planned to convert the *Omahas* to air defense cruisers armed with 2 twin 152-mm/53 guns, 7 single 127-mm/38 DP guns and 6 quadruple 28-mm MGs, but their stability in this configuration caused concern, and modernization was cancelled.

The main 5.8-m deep belt protected only the machinery and was closed by 38-mm fore and 76-mm aft bulkheads. The main deck consisted of 22-mm STS steel and 15-mm plating. The guns had only 6-mm protection.

1941, *Omaha, Milwaukee, Detroit, Richmond, Trenton, Marblehead, Memphis*: + 4 x 1 - 76/50 Mk 20, 8 x 1 - 12.7 MG. 1941, *Cincinnati, Raleigh, Concord*: + 2 x 4 - 28/75 Mk 1

1942, *Omaha, Milwaukee, Trenton, Memphis*: - 2 x 1 - 152/53, 1 x 1 - 76/50, 8 x 1 - 12.7 MG; + 2 x 4 - 28/75 Mk 1, 8 x 1 - 20/70 Oerlikon, SC, Mk 3 radars. 1942, *Cincinnati, Raleigh*: - 8 x 1 - 12.7 MG; + 3 x 1 - 76/50 Mk 20, 8 x 1 - 20/70 Oerlikon, SC, Mk 3 radars.

1942, *Detroit, Richmond, Marblehead*: - 1 x 1 - 76/50, 8 x 1 - 12.7 MG; + 2 x 4 - 28/75 Mk 1, 8 x 1 - 20/70 Oerlikon, SC, Mk 3 radars. 1942, *Concord*: - 2 x 1 - 152/53, 8 x 1 - 12.7 MG; + 3 x 1 - 76/50 Mk 20, 8 x 1 - 20/70 Oerlikon, SC, Mk 3 radars. Late 1942, *Cincinnati, Memphis*: - SC radar; + SK radar.

1943 - 1944, *Omaha, Milwaukee, Detroit, Concord, Trenton, Marblehead*: - 1 x 1 - 76/50, 2 x 4 - 28/75, SC radar; + 3 x 2 - 40/56 Bofors, 4 x 1 - 20/70 Oerlikon, SK, 2 SG, Mk 3 (2nd) radars. 1943 - 1944, *Cincinnati*: - 2 x 4 - 28/75, 2 x 3 - 533 TT; + 1 x 1 - 76/50 Mk 20, (3 x 2 + 2 x 1) - 40/56 Bofors, 2 SG, Mk 3 (2nd) radars. 1943 - 1944, *Raleigh*: - 2 x 4 - 28/75, SC radar; + 1 x 1 - 76/50 Mk 20, 2 SG, SK, Mk 3 (2nd) radars. 1943 - 1944, *Richmond*: - 1 x 1 - 76/50, 2 x 4 - 28/75; + 3 x 2 - 40/56 Bofors, 4 x 1 - 20/70 Oerlikon, 2 SG, Mk 3 (2nd) radars. 1943 - 1944, *Memphis*: - 2 x 4 - 28/75; + 2 x 2 - 40/56 Bofors, 4 x 1 - 20/70 Oerlikon, 2 SG, Mk 3 (2nd) radars.

1945, *Detroit*: - 2 x 1 - 152/53, 2 x 3 - 533 TT; + 2 x 2 - 40/56 Bofors.

Raleigh was badly damaged in Pearl Harbor 7.12.1941 by a Japanese air torpedo and was under repair until July 1942. *Marblehead* 5.1.1942 received 2 direct bomb hits and several near-misses and was under repair until the end of 1942.

Richmond 1944

Omaha 1943

BROOKLYN class light cruisers

Brooklyn	CL40	New York N Yd, Brooklyn	12.3.1935	30.11.1936	18.7.1938	to Chile 1.1951 (O'Higgins)
Philadelphia	CL41	Philadelphia N Yd	28.5.1935	17.11.1936	28.7.1938	to Brazil 1.1951 (Barroso)
Savannah	CL42	New York SB, Camden	31.5.1934	8.5.1937	30.8.1938	stricken 3.1959
Nashville	CL43	New York SB, Camden	24.1.1935	2.10.1937	25.11.1938	to Chile 1.1951 (Capitán Prat)
Phoenix	CL46	New York SB, Camden	15.4.1935	12.3.1938	18.3.1939	to Argentina 1.1951 (Diecisiete de Octubre)
Boise	CL47	Newport News	1.4.1935	3.12.1936	1.2.1939	to Argentina 1.1951 (Nueve de Julio)
Honolulu	CL48	New York N Yd, Brooklyn	10.9.1935	26.8.1937	7.9.1938	stricken 3.1959
St. Louis	CL49	Newport News	10.12.1936	15.4.1938	12.1939	to Brazil 1.1951 (Tamandaré)
Helena	CL50	New York N Yd, Brooklyn	9.12.1936	28.8.1938	14.12.1939	sunk 6.7.1943

Brooklyn 1941

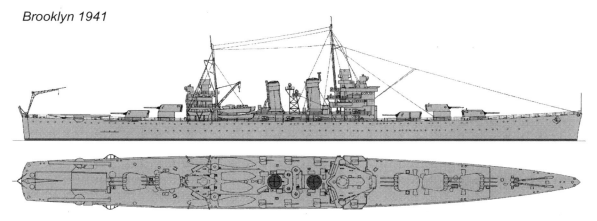

9800 (CL40-43, 46-48) or 10560 (CL49,50) / 12243-12700 (CL40-43, 46-48) or 13327 (CL49,50) t, 185.4 x 18.8 x 6.5-6.9 (CL40-43, 46-48) or 7.0-7.4 (CL49,50) m, 4 sets Westinghouse geared steam turbines, 8 Babcock & Wilcox boilers, 100000 hp, 32.5 kts, 10000 nm (15 kts), complement 868; belt 127-83, magazines belts 51 (fore) – 120 (aft), bulkheads 127-51, deck 51, barbettes 152, turrets 165-32, secondary gun mounts 32-25 (CL49, 50), CT 127; 5 x 3 – 152/47 Mk 16, 8 x 1 – 127/25 Mk 10/11/13 (CL40-43, 46-48) or 4 x 2 – 127/38 Mk 12 (CL49, 50), 8 x 1 – 12.7 MG, 2 catapults, 4 seaplanes (SOC, 1942- also OS2U, 1942-1944- also SO3C, 1944- also SC).

The London Naval Conference of 1930 limited the number of cruisers with 203-mm guns, and the attention of shipbuilders was forced to switch to ships with 152-mm guns. Initially, there was an opinion in the USA that, within the limits of 10000-t displacements, it was realistic to create a ship with a dozen of 152-mm guns and better protection, than on existing 203-mm cruisers. Such a ship could theoretically win a duel with a more armed enemy due to the higher rate of fire of 152-mm guns. However, this calculation was based on a duel with the

first generation 'Washington' cruiser. The appearance of well-protected *New Orleans* class ships led to the that in the cruisers of the new design an emphasis was placed on increasing the number of 152-mm guns to the detriment of protection. Design work began in the fall of 1930. Of the six proposed options with a displacement of 6000 to 10000 t and 6 to 15 152-mm guns, in 1931 a design of a 9600-t ship with 12 guns in four triple turrets was selected. The armor scheme basically repeated that adopted on the *New Orleans* class. It was supposed to include building of such a ship into the FY33 Program, but for a number of reasons this did not happen. It was proposed to provide for the installation of 28-mm MGs. The search for a place for them led to the moving of the catapults and the hangar to the stern.

In March 1932, new designs for a cruiser with 152-mm guns (10000-t displacement, from 12 to 16 152-mm guns, 127-mm belt) were presented for discussion by the General Board. In the end, they decided to build a variant with 15 152-mm guns in five triple turrets. The choice was influenced by Japanese-built cruisers of *Mogami* class with 8500-t displacement and 15 155-mm guns (the maximum caliber allowed by the London

Conference). The design, approved in 1933, had many innovations. The hull lines resembled the *New Orleans*, but the lengthening of the forecastle aft to the stern frame converted it into a flush-decked one. The ship received a longitudinal framing, which allowed to save weight. The rise of the upper deck in the stern made it possible to place the hangar and catapults on the quarterdeck, freeing up space around the superstructure. Some design flaws were caused primarily by the need to comply with treaty limitations. So, machinery arrangement remained linear, as well as on the *New Orleans*. The hull was too weak and required to be strengthened. The armor scheme basically repeated that adopted on the *New Orleans*, but in some elements it was thinner. The immune zone of the new cruisers under the fire from 152-mm guns at a relative 60° bearing was in the band between 40 and 115 cables. In addition to the new 152-mm/47 Mk 16 guns, the cruisers were armed with 8 127-mm/25 AA guns. The 28-mm MGs envisaged by the design were not ready, and close AA armament consisted only of 12.7-mm MGs.

Under the emergency FY33 Program 4 ships (CL40-44) were ordered, 3 more in FY34 (CL46-48). Later, two more ships were added (CL49 and 50) to replace the first cruisers of *Omaha* class; they were built to an improved design. The use of new compact high-pressure boilers allowed to reduce the size of boiler rooms. This, in turn, made it possible to rearrange machinery, returning to *en echelon* scheme. Besides, the single 127-mm/25 AA guns were replaced by new 127-mm/38 DP guns in twin mounts.

The main belt abreast the machinery was 4.2-m deep. It was 127-mm thick (83-mm at the lower edge) on 16-mm STS plating. There were narrow belts abreast the magazines. The thickness of the fore belt was 51 mm, and aft inner belt had a thickness of 120 mm. The magazines were protected by 93-mm bulkheads fore and aft; the machinery and magazines were separated by 127-51-mm bulkheads. The armored deck over the main belt was 51-mm. The barbettes were 152-mm thick. The turrets had 165-mm faces, 32-mm sides, 32-mm rears and 51-mm crowns. The CT had 127-mm sides and 57-mm roof.

Mid-1941, all: + 2 x 1 - 76/50 Mk 20; 2 x 4 - 28/75 Mk 1. Late 1941, *Philadelphia, Helena*; 12.1941, *Honolulu*: - 2 x 1 - 76/50; + 2 x 4 - 28/75 Mk 1, Mk 3 radar. 12.1941, *Phoenix*: + 2 x 4 - 28/75 Mk 1, Mk 3 radar. 12.1941, *Helena*: - 4 x 4 - 28/75.

1.1942, *Honolulu*: + 8 x 1 - 20/70 Oerlikon, Mk 3 radar. 1.1942, *Brooklyn, St. Louis*; 4.1942, *Nashville*; 6.1942, *Boise*: - 2 x 1 - 76/50; + 2 x 4 - 28/75 Mk 1, 8 x 1 - 20/70 Oerlikon, Mk 3 radar. Late 1942, all: - 8 x 1 - 12.7 MG; + SC, SG, 2 Mk 4 radars. 8.1942, *Savannah*; 2.1943, *Phoenix*: - 2 x 1 - 76/50, 4 x 4 - 28/75; + (4 x 4 + 4 x 2) - 40/56 Bofors, 12 x 1 - 20/70 Oerlikon, Mk 3 radar. Late 1942, *St. Louis*: - 4 x 4 - 28/75; + (4 x 4 + 4 x 2) -

Nashville 1939

40/56 Bofors, 4 x 1 - 20/70 Oerlikon. Late 1942, *Helena*: + (4 x 4 + 4 x 2) - 40/56 Bofors, 12 x 1 - 20/70 Oerlikon. Early 1943, *Brooklyn, Nashville, Boise*: - 4 x 4 - 28/75; + (4 x 4 + 4 x 2) - 40/56 Bofors, 4 x 1 - 20/70 Oerlikon. Early 1943, *Philadelphia*: - 4 x 4 - 28/75; + (4 x 4 + 4 x 2) - 40/56 Bofors, 12 x 1 - 20/70 Oerlikon. 11.1943, *Honolulu*: - 4 x 4 - 28/75; + (4 x 4 + 4 x 2) - 40/56 Bofors, 4 x 1 - 20/70 Oerlikon. 1943-1945, *Brooklyn, Phoenix*: - SC radar; + SK radar. 1943-1945, *Philadelphia*: - SC, Mk 3 radars; + SK, Mk 13 radars. 1943-1945, *Savannah, Honolulu*: - SC, Mk 3 radars; + SK, Mk 8 radars. 1943-1945, *Nashville, Boise*: - SC, Mk 3, 2 Mk 4 radars; + SK, Mk 13, 2 Mk 28 radars. 1943-1945, *St. Louis*: - SC, Mk 3, 2 Mk 4 radars; + SK-2, Mk 8, 2 Mk 28 radars.

1944-1945, *Brooklyn, Philadelphia, Savannah, Honolulu*: - 12 x 1 - 20/70; + 2 x 2 - 40/56 Bofors, 10 x 2 - 20/70 Oerlikon, CT was removed. 1944-1945, *Nashville*: - 12 x 1 - 20/70; + 2 x 2 – 40/56 Bofors, 9 x 2 - 20/70 Oerlikon, CT was removed. 1944-1945, *Phoenix*: + 7 x 1 - 20/70 Oerlikon, CT was removed. 1944-1945, *Boise*: + 6 x 1 - 20/70 Oerlikon, CT was removed. 1944-1945, *St. Louis*: - 4 x 1 - 20/70; + 2 x 2 - 40/56 Bofors, CT was removed. 9.1944, *Savannah*: new bulges were fitted, breadth increased to 21.2 m; - 8 x 1 - 127/25, 2 Mk 4 radars; + 4 x 2 - 127/38 Mk 12, 2 Mk 12/22 radars.

1945, *Brooklyn, Philadelphia, Honolulu*: new bulges were fitted, breadth increased to 21.2 m.

Helena 7.12.1941 in Pearl Harbor received an air torpedo hit, was repaired until May 1942; 6.7.1943 in the Battle of Kula Bay she received three torpedo hits from Japanese destroyers *Tanikaze* and *Suzukaze*, broken in half and sank. *Brooklyn* off the coast of Sicily was damaged by a mine 14.7.1943 and was under repair until December 1943. *Savannah* 11.9.1943 was badly damaged off Salerno by German glide air bomb, was under repair until September 1944. *Nashville* 12.5.1943

Helena 1940

was damaged by internal explosion of gun turret No1 and returned to service in August 1943; 13.12.1944 she was damaged by kamikaze and was under repair until April 1945. *Boise* ran ashore 21.1.1942 and was under repair until June 1942; 11.10.1942 in the Battle of Cape Esperance she was badly damaged by gunfire from Japanese ships and returned to service in March 1943. *Honolulu* 13.7.1943 was damaged by a torpedo from Japanese ship, fore end by a capstan was broken

off; repair lasted until November 1943; 20.10.1944 she was damaged by Japanese air torpedo and was under repair until October 1945. *St. Louis* 13.7.1943 was damaged by a torpedo from Japanese destroyer, fore end was broken off, repairs lasted until November 1943; 14.2.1944 she was damaged by Japanese air bomb and was under repair until May 1944; 27.11.1944 she was damaged by kamikaze and returned to service in March 1945.

ATLANTA class light cruisers

Atlanta	CL51	Federal, Kearny	22.4.1940	6.9.1941	24.12.1941	sunk 13.11.1942
Juneau	CL52	Federal, Kearny	27.5.1940	25.10.1941	14.2.1942	sunk 13.11.1942
San Diego	CL53	Bethlehem, Quincy	27.3.1940	26.7.1941	10.1.1942	stricken 3.1959
San Juan	CL54	Bethlehem, Quincy	15.5.1940	6.9.1941	28.2.1942	stricken 3.1959
Oakland	CL95	Bethlehem, San Francisco	13.7.1941	23.10.1942	17.7.1943	stricken 3.1959
Reno	CL96	Bethlehem, San Francisco	12.8.1941	23.12.1942	28.12.1943	stricken 3.1959
Flint *(ex-Spokane)*	CL97	Bethlehem, San Francisco	23.10.1942	25.1.1944	31.8.1944	stricken 9.1965
Tucson	CL98	Bethlehem, San Francisco	23.11.1942	3.9.1944	3.2.1945	stricken 6.1966
Juneau	CL119	Federal, Kearny	15.9.1944	15.7.1945	15.2.1946	stricken 11.1959
Spokane	CL120	Federal, Kearny	15.11.1944	22.9.1945	17.5.1946	test ship 4.1966
Fresno	CL121	Federal, Kearny	12.2.1945	5.3.1946	27.11.1946	stricken 4.1965

San Diego 1942

6590 (CL51-54, 95-98) or -6700 (CL119-121) / 8100 (CL51-54, 95-98) or 8450 (CL119-121) t, 165.1 x 16.2 x 6.3 m, 2 sets Westinghouse geared steam turbines, 4

San Diego 1944

Babcock & Wilcox boilers, 75000 hp, 32.5 kts, 1360 t oil, 8500 nm (15 kts), complement 623; belt 95, bulkheads 95, magazines 95-28, deck 32, turrets 32-35, CT 63 (CL51-54); 8 (CL51-54) or 6 (CL95-98, 119-121) x 2 – 127/38 Mk 12, 8 x 2 (CL95-98) or (6 x 4 + 4 x 2) (CL119-121) – 40/56 Bofors, 3 (CL51, 52) or 4 (CL53, 54) x 4 – 28/75 Mk 1, 8 x 1 (CL53, 54) or 14 x 1 (CL95) or 16 x 1 (CL96-98) or 8 x 2 (CL119-121) – 20/70 Oerlikon, 2 x 4 – 533 TT (CL51-54, 95-98), 2 DCR (CL51-54); SC (CL95-98, 119-121), SG (CL95-98, 119-121), 2 Mk 12/22 (CL95-98, 119-121) radars, QCJ sonar (CL51-54). The second London Naval Conference limited the displacement of cruisers to 8000 t. Initially, it was planned to create a ship within these limits (8000 t and 152-

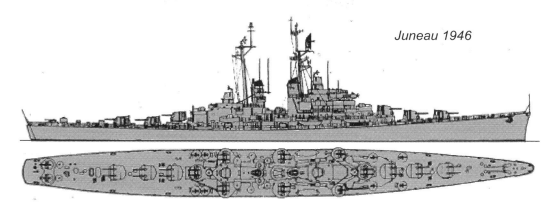

Juneau 1946

mm guns), but for various reasons, at the end of 1937, priority was returned to the creation of a smaller cruiser with 127-mm artillery, intended to operate together with destroyers. The draft design of 6000-t ship armed with 127-mm guns in twin mounts was ready by July 1938. The armor protection provided an immune zone from the fire of 130-mm guns between 30 and 80 cables at a 60° relative bearing. The armor belt was part of the hull construction and partially had no plating underneath.

The ships were significantly overloaded: on the lead CL51 it exceeded 700 t, and the design speed of 35 kts was never reached. 4 ships were built according to the original design (CL51-54), the next 4 were completed according to the modified design: two 127-mms mounts (and 28-mm MGs) were replaced by 40-mm Bofors. The last three ships had no TTs and redesigned superstructures.

The main belt abreast the machinery was 4.2-m deep. It was 95-mm thick on 16-mm STS plating. There were narrow belts abreast the magazines. The fore belt was 28-mm thick, but the aft belt had 95-46-mm thickness. The belt was closed with 95-mm bulkheads. The armored deck over the main belt was 32-mm. Gun mounts had 32-25-mm protection, CT on first 4 ships had 63-mm sides.

Early 1942, *Atlanta, Juneau*: + 1 x 4 - 28/75 Mk 1. Mid-1942, *Atlanta, Juneau*: - 2 DCR, QCJ sonar; + SC, SG, 2 Mk 4 radars. Mid-1942, *San Diego, San Juan*: - 2 DCR, QCJ sonar; + SC, SG, 2 Mk 12/22 radars.

12.1943, *San Diego, San Juan*: - 4 x 4 - 28/75; + (1 x 4 + 3 x 2) - 40/56 Bofors, 7 x 1 - 20/70 Oerlikon.

1945, *San Juan*: + 2 x 2 - 40/56 Bofors. 4.1945, *Oakland*:

- 6 x 2 - 40/56, 14 x 1 - 20/70, 2 x 4 - 533 TT; + 4 x 4 - 40/56 Bofors, 8 x 2 - 20/70 Oerlikon. 1945, *Tucson*: - 2 x 4 - 533 TT.

Atlanta 12.11.1942 was badly damaged in the Battle of Guadalcanal by a torpedo from Japanese destroyer *Akatsuki*, gunfire from Japanese destroyers *Akatsuki, Inazuma, Ikazuchi* and friendly fire from cruiser *San Francisco*; she sank next morning. *Juneau* 12.11.1942 was badly damaged in the Battle of Guadalcanal by a torpedo and gunfire from Japanese ships and 13.11.1942 S of Guadalcanal sunk by torpedo from Japanese submarine *I26*. *Reno* 4.11.1944 was damaged by a torpedo from Japanese submarine *I41* and was under repair until the end of the war.

Juneau 1951

CLEVELAND class light cruisers

Cleveland subclass

Cleveland	CL55	New York SB, Camden	1.7.1940	1.11.1941	15.6.1942	stricken 3.1959
Columbia	CL56	New York SB, Camden	19.8.1940	17.12.1941	29.6.1942	stricken 11.1959
Montpelier	CL57	New York SB, Camden	2.12.1940	12.2.1942	9.9.1942	stricken 3.1959

Denver	CL58	New York SB, Camden	26.12.1940	4.4.1942	15.10.1942	sold 2.1960
Amsterdam	CL59	New York SB, Camden	1.5.1941	22.8.1942	-	completed as CVL22
Santa Fe	CL60	New York SB, Camden	7.6.1941	10.6.1942	24.11.1942	stricken 3.1959
Tallahassee	CL61	New York SB, Camden	2.6.1941	18.10.1942	-	completed as CVL23
Birmingham	CL62	Newport News	17.2.1941	20.3.1942	29.1.1943	stricken 3.1959
Mobile	CL63	Newport News	14.4.1941	15.5.1942	24.3.1943	stricken 3.1959
Vincennes *(ex-Flint)*	CL64	Bethlehem, Quincy	7.3.1942	17.7.1943	21.1.1944	stricken 4.1966
Pasadena	CL65	Bethlehem, Quincy	6.2.1943	28.12.1943	8.6.1944	stricken 12.1970
Springfield	CL66	Bethlehem, Quincy	13.2.1943	9.3.1944	9.9.1944	stricken 9.1978
Topeka	CL67	Bethlehem, Quincy	21.4.1943	19.8.1944	23.12.1944	stricken 9.1973
New Haven	CL76	New York SB, Camden	11.8.1942	6.11.1942	-	completed as CVL24
Huntington	CL77	New York SB, Camden	17.12.1941	17.1.1943	-	completed as CVL25
Dayton	CL78	New York SB, Camden	29.12.1941	28.2.1943	-	completed as CVL26
Wilmington	CL79	New York SB, Camden	13.3.1942	4.4.1943	-	completed as CVL28
Biloxi	CL80	Newport News	9.7.1941	23.2.1943	21.8.1943	stricken 9.1961
Houston *(ex-Vicksburg)*	CL81	Newport News	4.8.1941	19.6.1943	20.12.1943	stricken 3.1959
Providence	CL82	Bethlehem, Quincy	27.7.1943	28.12.1944	15.5.1945	stricken 7.1978
Manchester	CL83	Bethlehem, Quincy	25.9.1944	5.3.1946	29.10.1946	stricken 4.1960
Fargo	CL85	New York SB, Camden	11.4.1942	22.5.1943	-	completed as CVL27
Vicksburg *(ex-Cheyenne)*	CL86	Newport News	26.10.1942	14.12.1943	12.6.1944	stricken 10.1962
Duluth	CL87	Newport News	9.11.1942	13.1.1944	18.9.1944	stricken 11.1960
Miami	CL89	Cramp, Philadelphia	2.8.1941	12.8.1942	28.12.1943	stricken 9.1961
Astoria *(ex-Wilkes-Barre)*	CL90	Cramp, Philadelphia	6.9.1941	6.3.1943	17.5.1944	stricken 11.1969
Oklahoma City	CL91	Cramp, Philadelphia	8.3.1942	20.2.1944	22.12.1944	stricken 12.1979
Little Rock	CL92	Cramp, Philadelphia	6.3.1943	27.8.1944	17.6.1945	stricken 11.1976
Galveston	CLG3 (ex-CL93)	Cramp, Philadelphia	20.2.1944	22.4.1945	28.5.1958	stricken 12.1973
Youngstown	CL94	Cramp, Philadelphia	4.9.1944	-	-	cancelled 8.1945
Buffalo	CL99	New York SB, Camden	31.8.1942	1.8.1943	-	completed as CVL29

Newark	CL100	New York SB, Camden	26.10.1942	26.9.1943	-	completed as CVL30
Amsterdam	CL101	Newport News	3.3.1943	25.4.1944	8.1.1945	stricken 1.1971
Portsmouth	CL102	Newport News	28.6.1943	20.9.1944	25.6.1945	stricken 12.1970
Wilkes-Barre	CL103	New York SB, Camden	14.12.1942	24.12.1943	1.7.1944	stricken 1.1971
Atlanta	CL104	New York SB, Camden	25.1.1943	6.2.1944	3.12.1944	stricken 10.1962
Dayton	CL105	New York SB, Camden	8.3.1943	19.3.1944	7.1.1945	stricken 9.1961

Fargo (Cleveland 1942) subclass

Fargo	CL106	New York SB, Camden	23.8.1943	25.3.1945	9.12.1945	stricken 3.1970
Huntington	CL107	New York SB, Camden	4.10.1943	8.4.1945	23.2.1946	stricken 9.1961
Newark	CL108	New York SB, Camden	17.1.1944	14.12.1945	-	cancelled 8.1945
New Haven	CL109	New York SB, Camden	28.2.1944	-	-	cancelled 8.1945
Buffalo	CL110	New York SB, Camden	3.4.1944	-	-	cancelled 8.1945
Wilmington	CL111	Cramp, Philadelphia	5.3.1945	-	-	cancelled 8.1945
Tallahassee	CL116	Newport News	31.1.1944	-	-	cancelled 8.1945
Cheyenne	CL117	Newport News	29.5.1944	-	-	cancelled 8.1945
Chattanooga	CL118	Newport News	9.10.1944	-	-	cancelled 8.1945

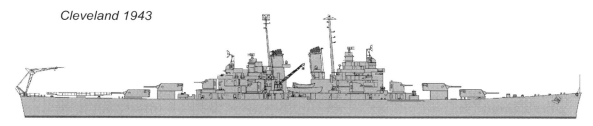

Cleveland 1943

11130-11734 or 11890 (CL106-118) / 13897-14144 or 14464 (CL106-118) t, 186.0 x 20.2 x 7.5 m, 4 sets General Electric geared steam turbines, 4 Babcock & Wilcox boilers, 100000 hp, 32.5 kts, 2100 t oil, 11000 nm (15 kts), complement 1285; belt 127-89, bulkheads 127-51, deck 51, barbettes 152, turrets 165-32, secondary gun mounts 32-35, CT (CL55-63) 127; 4 x 3 – 152/47 Mk 16, 6 x 2 – 127/38 Mk 12, 4 x 2 (CL55, 56) or (4 x 4 + 4 x 2) (CL57, 58, 60, 64-66, 80, 81) or (4 x 4 + 6 x 2) (CL62, 63, 67, 82, 83, 86, 87, 89-92, 101-105) or (6 x 4 + 2 x 2) (CL106, 107) – 40/56 Bofors, 13 x 1 (CL55, 56) or 17 x 1 (CL57, 58) or 21 x 1 (CL60, 62-66, 80, 81) or 10 x 1 (CL67, 82, 83, 86, 87, 89-92, 101-105) or 14 x 2 (CL106, 107) – 20/70 Oerlikon, 2 (CL55-58, 60, 62-67, 80-82, 86, 87, 89-92, 101-105) or 1 (CL83, 106, 107) catapults, 4 seaplanes (SOC, OS2U, SO3C till 1944, 1944- also SC); SC (CL55-58, 60) or SK (CL62-64, 80, 81, 89) or SK-2, SG, Mk 8 (CL55-58) or Mk 13, 2 Mk 12/22 (CL55-58, 60, 62-64, 80, 81, 89) or 2 Mk 25 radars.

CLG3 *Galveston as completed*: 11066 / 15152 t, 186.0 x 20.2 x 7.8 m, 4 sets General Electric geared steam turbines, 4 Babcock & Wilcox boilers, 100000 hp, 32 kts, 2661 t oil, 8000 nm (15 kts), complement 1382; belt 127-89, bulkheads 127-51, deck 51, barbettes 152, turrets 165-32, secondary guns 32-35; 1 x 2 Talos SAM (46 RIM-8), 2 x 3 – 152/47 Mk 16, 3 x 2 – 127/38 Mk 12, SPS-8B, SPS-29, SPS-39, 2 SPG-49/SPW-2, Mk 13, Mk 25 radars, WLR-1, ULQ-6 ECM suites.

The most numerous class of cruisers in history: 29 ships out of 52 ordered entered service as cruisers, another 9

Cleveland 1942

Fargo 1945

were completed as light aircraft carriers.

The history of these ships began in 1938, when a decision was made to build two 8000-t light cruisers under the FY40 Program in accordance with the limit set by 1936 London Conference. In May 1939, a design of a new ship was ready (8000 t, 173 m, 5 x 2 152-mm/47 guns, 5 x 4 28-mm MGs, 1 catapult and 2 x 3 TT), outwardly resembling the moderated *Brooklyn*. The disadvantage of this option that arose during the discussion in the General Board was a very cramped arrangement that did not involve any alterations. It was proposed to create a new design, but in September the war began in Europe, treaty limitations disappeared and, in order not to waste time, it was decided to use the design of cruiser *Helena*, strengthening her heavy antiaircraft armament. The hull of the new cruiser had a greater breadth than the prototype to compensate for the increased top weight and keep acceptable stability. For the same purpose, the construction of superstructures provided for the use of aluminum alloys. Paradoxically, the latter circumstance ultimately had an unfavorable effect: in wartime conditions, the shortage of aluminum forced it to be replaced with steel from CL66, which only worsened the situation with stability. The main caliber of the new cruisers consisted of 12 152-mm Mk 16 guns in four triple turrets. The antiaircraft armament was strong: 12 127-mm/38 DP guns in six twin mounts. A successful arrangement according to a diamond-shaped scheme provided wide arcs of fire, allowing massive fire from at least six guns in any direction. Light AA armament initially was limited to 12.7-mm MGs, the question arose of installing of 28-mm MGs. Low stability required to accompany this operation with ballast laying. Even before the commissioning of the first cruiser, the unreliable 28-mm MGs were replaced by

Fargo 1946

twin 40-mm Bofors. The protection was the same as *Helena*, with better protected aft magazines. The immune zone under the fire of 152-mm guns at a relative 90° bearing laid between 47 and 108 cables. The structure and arrangement scheme of the machinery did not differ from those adopted on *Helena*, but the length of the engine rooms was increased to get rid of crowding.

The first 2 ships, CL55 and 56, were ordered 23.3.1940. Prior to the US entry into the Second World War, orders were placed for 28 ships, CL59-CL67 and CL76-CL94. After 7.12.1941 new orders followed, and before 1942 orders were placed for additional 20 ships, CL99-CL118.

Since the CL64 cruisers were commissioned with a new open bridge and without armored CT. Since 1942, work was carried out to improve the design, in which, due to the lower arrangement of 127-mm guns and 40-mm MGs, stability was increased. At the same time, it was supposed to reduce the number of the funnels to one, which would provide AA MGs with better firing angles. In August 1942, a decision was made to build CL106-118 according to a modified design, but due to the reduction in shipbuilding at the end of the war, only two ships were completed according to the new design.

At the beginning of 1942, in order to speed up the building of aircraft carriers, it was decided to convert 9 ships, ordered to New York SB, to light aircraft carriers of the *Independence* class. The orders for CL84 *Buffalo* and CL88 *Newark* were cancelled 16.12.1940 to allow Federal, Kearny to concentrate on destroyers. In 1944-1945 orders for ships at an early stage of building or not yet laid down were cancelled: CL112 *Vallejo*, CL113 *Helena*, CL114 *Roanoke* and CL115 (all - New York SB, Camden) 5.10.1944; CL94, 109-111 and 116-118 12.8.1945. CLG3 *(ex-CL93) Galveston* was completed in 1958 as a missile cruiser.

The main belt abreast the machinery was 4.1-m deep. It was 127-mm thick (83-mm at the lower edge) on 16-mm STS plating. There were narrow belts abreast the magazines. The fore belt was 51-mm thick, but aft internal belt had 120-mm thickness. The magazines were protected by 93-mm bulkheads fore and aft; the machinery and magazines were separated by 127-51-mm bulkheads. The armored deck over the main belt was 51-mm. The barbettes were 152-mm thick. The turrets had 152-mm faces, 76-mm sides, 32-mm rears and 76-mm crowns. The CT on CL55-63 had 127-mm sides and 57-mm roof.

11.1942, *Cleveland, Columbia*: + 2 x 2 - 40/56 Bofors.
1945, all completed: - 1 catapult.

Columbia on January 6 and 9, 1945 was badly damaged by kamikazes, repairs lasted until May 1945. *Denver* 13.11.1943 was damaged by a Japanese air torpedo and was under repair until June 1944. *Birmingham* 8.11.1943 was badly damaged by a Japanese aircraft (bombs and torpedo) and was under repair until February 1944; 24.10.1944 she was damaged by an explosion on the aircraft carrier *Princeton,* was under repair until January 1945; 3.5.1945 she was damaged by kamikaze and returned to service in August 1945. *Biloxi* 26.3.1945 was damaged by kamikaze and was under repair until July 1945. *Houston* 14.10.1944 was badly damaged by Japanese air torpedo, damaged again by an air torpedo while under tow 16.10.1944 and returned to service in October 1945. *Duluth* was badly damaged in a typhoon 5.6.1945 and returned to service in August 1945.

WORCESTER class light cruisers

Worcester	CL144	New York SB, Camden	29.1.1945	4.2.1947	25.6.1948	stricken 1.12.1970
Roanoke	CL145	New York SB, Camden	15.5.1945	16.6.1947	4.4.1949	stricken 1.12.1970
Vallejo	CL146	New York SB, Camden	16.7.1945	-	-	cancelled 12.8.1945

Worcester 1948

14700 / 17997 t, 207.1 x 21.5 x 7.5 m, 4 sets General Electric geared steam turbines, 4 Babcock & Wilcox boilers, 120000 hp, 33 kts, 2400 t oil, 8000 nm (15 kts), complement 1401; belt 127-76, magazines 127-51, deck 89 + 25-22, bulkheads 127-51, barbettes 127, turrets 165-51, CT 127; 6 x 2 – 152/47 Mk 16, (11 x 2 + 2 x 1) – 76/50 Mk 22, 6 x 2 – 20/70 Oerlikon, SR-2, SR-6, SG-6, SP-2, 4 Mk 25, 6 Mk 27, 4 Mk 35 radars.

The largest light cruisers in history were designed to carry the new 152-mm/47 automatic DP guns, originally intended to be the main battery of the *Cleveland* class cruisers according to the original 1939 design. In 1941, the design was revised. It turned out to be a kind of "air defense barrage" cruiser with 12 heavy long-range 152-mm anti-aircraft guns, strong horizontal protection, and high speed. Later, the armor belt returned to the design. The immune zone against 152-mm shells ranged from 46 to 138 cables, the ship was invulnerable to 454-kg SAP bombs and 454-kg AP bombs dropped from an altitude of less than 2300 m. The final design was approved in 1944, at that time the armament included 12 quadruple 40-mm Bofors and 20 20-mm Oerlikons, however, the ships entered service with a modified composition of anti-aircraft artillery. CL147 *Gary* (New York SB) was cancelled 12.8.1945 before she was laid down.

The main belt abreast the machinery was 4.4-m deep. It was 127-mm thick (76-mm at the lower edge) on 16-mm STS plating. There were narrow 51-mm underwater belts abreast fore and No 4 magazines. The underwater belt protecting aft magazines was 127-mm thick. The magazines were protected by 93-mm bulkheads fore and aft; the machinery and magazines were separated by 127-51-mm bulkheads. The main deck over the main belt was 89-mm. There was 22-25-mm upper deck one deck level higher. The barbettes were 127-mm thick. The turrets had 165-mm faces, 76-51-mm sides, 76-51-mm rears and 102-mm crowns. The CT had 127-mm sides and 57-mm roof.

Worcester 1949

DESTROYERS

SAMPSON class destroyer

Allen	DD66	Bath Iron Wks	5.1915	5.12.1916	1.1917	stricken 11.1945

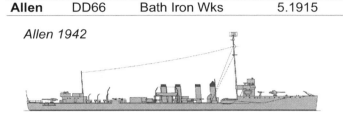

Allen 1942

1100 / 1225 t, 96.1 x 9.1 x 2.9 m, 2 Curtis steam turbines / 1 steam turbine for cruising, 4 Yarrow boilers (2 shafts), 17500 hp, 29.5 kts, 310 t oil, 4300 nm (14 kts), complement 99; 4 x 1 – 102/50 Mk 9, 2 x 1 – 12.7 MG, 4 x 3 – 533 TT, 1 DCT, 2 DCR.

The last of the 'thousand tonners', authorized in June 1914, had a new triple 533-mm TTs.

1942-1943: - 2 x 1 - 12.7 MG, 2 x 3 - 533 TT, 1 DCT; + 6 x 1 - 20/70 Oerlikon, 6 DCT, presumably SA, SE radars, sonar; the displacement was 1152 / 1433 t.

CALDWELL class destroyers

Craven, 11.1939- **Conway**	DD70	Norfolk N Yd, Portsmouth	11.1917	29.6.1918	10.1918	to the UK 10.1940 (Lewes)
Conner	DD72	Cramp, Philadelphia	10.1916	21.8.1917	1.1918	to the UK 10.1940 (Leeds)
Stockton	DD73	Cramp, Philadelphia	10.1916	17.7.1917	11.1917	to the UK 10.1940 (Ludlow)
Manley	DD74, 11.1938- AG28, 8.1940- APD1, 6.1945- DD74	Bath Iron Wks	8.1916	23.8.1917	10.1917	auxiliary 11.1938, fast amphibious transport 8.1940, destroyer 6.1945, stricken 12.1945

Stockton 1917

Craven 1918

Manley 1940

1120 / 1187 t, 96.2 x 9.3 x 2.7 m, 2 sets Parsons geared steam turbines, 4 Thornycroft boilers (DD70) or 3 Curtis steam turbines / 1 geared steam turbine for cruising, 4 Yarrow boilers (3 shafts) (DD72, 73) or 2 sets Parsons geared steam turbines, 4 Normand boilers, 18500 hp, 30 kts, 310 t oil, 2500 nm (20 kts), complement 100; 4 x 1 – 102/50 Mk 9, 2 x 1 – 12.7 MG, 4 x 3 – 533 TT, 1 DCT, 2 DCR.

The history of the 'flush-deckers' dates back to 1915, when the main elements of the ships of the FY16 Program (DD69-74) were identified. The composition and arrangement of the armament were borrowed from the *Sampson* class, but the hull was designed in a new way. At the initiative of the C & R Bureau, it was made on a flush-deck scheme with a significant lowering from bow to stern. The breadth of the hull in the midship area was slightly increased, while the draught of the ship, on the contrary, decreased. Due to the new flush-deck architecture, the Americans tried to reduce the susceptibility of the new destroyers to pitching and rolling (due to some lightening of the ship's ends) and to increase the longitudinal strength. Since, due to the reduced draught, the propeller blades protruded below the keel line, the latter received a characteristic drag in the stern. Unlike the twin-shaft machinery of the *Sampsons,* the design of the new destroyer provided for the transition to a triple-shaft one, where a high-pressure turbine with a cruising stage worked on the central shaft. A similar solution allowed to increase the efficiency of power plant, receiving additionally 1000 hp of its power. The draft design provided for three funnels (a wide middle one was supposed to unite two boiler smoke ducts).

Of the six FY16 destroyers, only two were built according to the original design (DD72 and 73), some improvements were made to the working drawings of the rest, in particular the triple-shaft scheme with direct transmission was replaced with a twin-shaft geared turbines and returned to the previously accepted practice

of individual funnels for all boilers, then, there were four funnels again. The exception was the three-funneled DD71.

(11.1938-2.1939, New York N Yd), *Manley* was converted to fast transport with data as follows: 1315 / 1793 t, 96.2 x 9.3 x 3.8 m, 2 sets Parsons geared steam turbines, 4 Normand boilers, 18500 hp, 30 kts, 310 t oil, 101p; 4 x 1 – 102/50 Mk 9; 6 LCP(L) or LCP(R), 2 DCR.

Early 1940, *Manley*: 2 boilers were removed, boiler rooms were converted to accommodations, 9250 hp, 22-24 kts, ~400 t oil; - 2 LCP(L)/CLP(R); + 120 troops.

1941, *Manley*: - 1 x 1 – 102/50; + 2 x 1 – 20/70 Oerlikon, 6 DCT, QCJ sonar.

7.1943, *Manley*: - 3 x 1 - 102/50; + 4 x 1 - 76/50 Mk 20, presumably SA, SE radars.

WICKES class destroyers

Name	Hull no.	Builder	Laid down	Launched	Commissioned	Fate
Wickes	DD75	Bath Iron Wks	6.1917	25.6.1918	7.1918	to the UK 10.1940 (Montgomery)
Philip	DD76	Bath Iron Wks	9.1917	25.7.1918	8.1918	to the UK 10.1940 (Lancaster)
Evans	DD78	Bath Iron Wks	12.1917	30.10.1918	11.1918	to the UK 10.1940 (Mansfield)
Little	DD79, 8.1940- APD4	Fore River, Quincy	6.1917	11.11.1917	4.1918	fast transport 8.1940, sunk 5.9.1942
Sigourney	DD81	Fore River, Quincy	8.1917	16.12.1917	5.1918	to the UK 11.1940 (Newport)
Gregory	DD82, 8.1940- APD3	Fore River, Quincy	8.1917	27.1.1918	6.1918	fast transport 11.1940, sunk 5.9.1942
Stringham	DD83, 8.1940- APD6, 6.1945- DD83	Fore River, Quincy	9.1917	30.3.1918	7.1918	fast transport 12.1940, destroyer 6.1945, stricken 12.1945
Colhoun	DD85, 8.1940- APD2	Fore River, Quincy	9.1917	21.2.1918	7.1918	fast transport 12.1940, sunk 30.8.1942
Robinson	DD88	Union Iron Wks, San Francisco	10.1917	28.3.1918	10.1918	to the UK 11.1940 (Newmarket)
Ringgold	DD89	Union Iron Wks, San Francisco	10.1917	14.4.1918	11.1918	to the UK 11.1940 (Newark)
McKean	DD90, 8.1940- APD5	Union Iron Wks, San Francisco	2.1918	4.7.1918	2.1919	fast transport 12.1940, sunk 17.11.1943
Fairfax	DD93	Mare Island N Yd, Vallejo	7.1917	15.12.1917	4.1918	to the UK 10.1940 (Richmond)
Taylor	DD94	Mare Island N Yd, Vallejo	10.1917	27.12.1917	7.1918	stricken 12.1938
Schley	DD103, 2.1943- APD14, 7.1945- DD103	Union Iron Wks, San Francisco	10.1917	28.3.1918	9.1918	fast transport 2.1943, destroyer 7.1945, stricken 12.1945
Chew	DD106	Union Iron Wks, San Francisco	1.1918	26.5.1918	12.1918	stricken 11.1945

Williams	DD108	Union Iron Wks, San Francisco	3.1918	4.7.1918	3.1919	to Canada 9.1940 (St. Clair)
Crane	DD109	Union Iron Wks, San Francisco	1.1918	4.7.1918	4.1919	stricken 12.1945
Rathburne	DD113, 5.1944- APD25, 7.1945- DD113	Cramp, Philadelphia	7.1917	27.12.1917	6.1918	fast transport 5.1944, destroyer 7.1945, stricken 11.1945
Talbot	DD114, 3.1943- APD7, 7.1945- DD114	Cramp, Philadelphia	7.1917	20.2.1918	7.1918	fast transport 10.1942, destroyer 7.1945, stricken 10.1945
Waters	DD115, 2.1943- APD8, 8.1945- DD115	Cramp, Philadelphia	7.1917	9.3.1918	8.1918	fast transport 10.1942, destroyer 8.1945, stricken 10.1945
Dent	DD116, 3.1943- APD9	Cramp, Philadelphia	8.1917	23.3.1918	9.1918	fast transport 10.1942, stricken 1.1946
Dorsey	DD117, 11.1940- DMS1	Cramp, Philadelphia	9.1917	9.4.1918	9.1918	fast minesweeper 11.1940, wrecked 9.10.1945
Lea	DD118	Cramp, Philadelphia	9.1917	29.4.1918	10.1918	stricken 8.1945
Lamberton	AG21, 11.1940- DMS2	Newport News	10.1917	30.3.1918	8.1918	target vessel, fast minesweeper 11.1940, stricken 1.1947
Montgomery	DM17	Newport News	10.1917	23.3.1918	7.1918	fast minelayer, damaged 17.10.1944, never repaired
Breese	DM18	Newport News	11.1917	11.5.1918	10.1918	fast minelayer, stricken 2.1946
Gamble	DM15	Newport News	11.1917	11.5.1918	11.1918	fast minelayer, damaged 18.2.1945, never repaired
Ramsay	DM16	Newport News	12.1917	8.6.1918	2.1919	fast minelayer, auxiliary 6.1945
Tattnall	DD125, 7.1943- APD19	New York SB, Camden	12.1917	5.9.1918	6.1919	fast transport 7.1943, stricken 1.1946
Badger	DD126	New York SB, Camden	1.1918	14.8.1918	5.1919	stricken 8.1945
Twiggs	DD127	New York SB, Camden	1.1918	28.9.1918	7.1919	to the UK 10.1940 (Leamington)
Babbitt	DD128	New York SB, Camden	2.1918	30.9.1918	10.1919	auxiliary 6.1945
Jacob Jones	DD130	New York SB, Camden	2.1918	20.11.1918	10.1919	sunk 28.2.1942
Buchanan	DD131	Bath Iron Wks	6.1918	2.1.1919	1.1919	to the UK 9.1940 (Campbelltown)
Aaron Ward	DD132	Bath Iron Wks	8.1918	10.4.1919	4.1919	to the UK 9.1940 (Castleton)
Hale	DD133	Bath Iron Wks	10.1918	29.5.1919	6.1919	to the UK 9.1940 (Caldwell)
Crowninshield	DD134	Bath Iron Wks	11.1918	24.7.1919	8.1919	to the UK 9.1940 (Chelsea)
Tillman	DD135	Charleston N Yd	7.1918	7.7.1919	4.1920	to the UK 11.1940 (Wells)

Boggs	IX36, 11.1940- DMS3	Mare Island N Yd, Vallejo	11.1917	25.4.1918	9.1918	target vessel, fast minesweeper 11.1940, auxiliary 6.1945
Kilty	DD137, 3.1943 - APD15, 7.1945 - DD137	Mare Island N Yd, Vallejo	12.1917	25.4.1918	12.1918	fast transport 1.1943, destroyer 7.1945, stricken 11.1945
Kennison	DD138	Mare Island N Yd, Vallejo	2.1918	8.6.1918	4.1919	auxiliary 10.1944
Ward *(ex-Cowell)*	DD139, 2.1943- APD16	Mare Island N Yd, Vallejo	5.1918	1.6.1918	7.1919	fast transport 1.1943, sunk 7.12.1944
Claxton	DD140	Mare Island N Yd, Vallejo	4.1918	14.1.1919	9.1919	to the UK 11.1940 (Salisbury)
Hamilton	DD141, 10.1941- DMS18	Mare Island N Yd, Vallejo	6.1918	15.1.1919	11.1919	fast minesweeper 10.1941, auxiliary 6.1945
Tarbell	DD142	Cramp, Philadelphia	12.1917	28.5.1918	11.1918	stricken 8.1945
Yarnall	DD143	Cramp, Philadelphia	2.1918	19.1.1918	11.1918	to the UK 10.1940 (Lincoln)
Upshur	DD144	Cramp, Philadelphia	2.1918	4.7.1918	12.1918	auxiliary 6.1945
Greer	DD145	Cramp, Philadelphia	2.1918	1.8.1918	12.1918	stricken 8.1945
Elliot	DD146, 11.1940- DMS4	Cramp, Philadelphia	2.1918	4.7.1918	1.1919	fast minesweeper 11.1940, auxiliary 6.1945
Roper	DD147, 10.1943- APD20	Cramp, Philadelphia	3.1918	17.8.1918	2.1919	fast transport 10.1943, stricken 10.1945
Breckinridge	DD148	Cramp, Philadelphia	3.1918	17.8.1918	2.1919	auxiliary 6.1945
Barney	DD149	Cramp, Philadelphia	3.1918	5.9.1918	3.1919	auxiliary 6.1945
Blakeley	DD150	Cramp, Philadelphia	3.1918	19.9.1918	5.1919	stricken 8.1945
Biddle	DD151	Cramp, Philadelphia	4.1918	3.10.1918	4.1919	auxiliary 6.1945
Du Pont	DD152	Cramp, Philadelphia	5.1918	22.10.1918	4.1919	auxiliary 9.1944
Bernadou	DD153	Cramp, Philadelphia	6.1918	7.11.1918	5.1919	stricken 8.1945
Ellis	DD154	Cramp, Philadelphia	7.1918	30.11.1918	6.1919	auxiliary 6.1945
Cole	DD155	Cramp, Philadelphia	6.1918	11.1.1919	6.1919	auxiliary 6.1945
J. Fred Talbott	DD156	Cramp, Philadelphia	7.1918	14.12.1918	6.1919	auxiliary 9.1944
Dickerson	DD157, 8.1943- APD21	New York SB, Camden	5.1918	12.3.1919	9.1919	fast transport 8.1943, sunk 4.4.1945
Leary	DD158	New York SB, Camden	3.1918	18.12.1918	12.1919	sunk 24.12.1943
Schenck	DD159	New York SB, Camden	3.1918	23.4.1919	10.1919	auxiliary 9.1944
Herbert	DD160, 12.1943- APD22	New York SB, Camden	4.1918	8.5.1919	11.1919	fast transport 12.1943, stricken 10.1945
Palmer	DD161, 11.1940- DMS5	Fore River, Quincy	5.1918	18.8.1918	11.1918	fast minesweeper 11.1940, sunk 7.1.1945

Thatcher	DD162	Fore River, Quincy	6.1918	31.8.1918	1.1919	to Canada 9.1940 (Niagara)
Walker	DD163	Fore River, Quincy	6.1918	14.9.1918	1.1919	water barge 3.1938
Crosby	DD164, 2.1943- APD17	Fore River, Quincy	6.1918	28.9.1918	1.1919	fast transport 1.1943, stricken 10.1945
Cowell	DD167	Fore River, Quincy	7.1918	23.11.1918	3.1919	to the UK 9.1940 (Brighton)
Maddox	DD168	Fore River, Quincy	7.1918	27.10.1918	3.1919	to the UK 9.1940 (Georgetown)
Foote	DD169	Fore River, Quincy	8.1918	14.12.1918	3.1919	to the UK 9.1940 (Roxburgh)
Kalk *(ex-Rodgers)*	DD170	Fore River, Quincy	8.1918	21.12.1918	3.1919	to Canada 9.1940 (Hamilton)
Mackenzie	DD175	Union Iron Wks	7.1918	29.9.1918	7.1919	to Canada 9.1940 (Annapolis)
Hogan	DD178, 11.1940- DMS6	Union Iron Wks	11.1918	12.4.1919	10.1919	fast minesweeper 11.1940, auxiliary 6.1945
Howard	DD179, 11.1940- DMS7	Union Iron Wks	12.1918	26.4.1919	1.1920	fast minesweeper 11.1940, auxiliary 6.1945
Stansbury	DD180, 11.1940- DMS8	Union Iron Wks	12.1918	16.5.1919	1.1920	fast minesweeper 11.1940, auxiliary 6.1945
Hopewell	DD181	Newport News	1.1918	8.6.1918	3.1919	to the UK 9.1940 (Bath)
Thomas	DD182	Newport News	3.1918	4.7.1918	4.1919	to the UK 9.1940 (St. Albans)
Haraden	DD183	Newport News	3.1918	4.7.1918	6.1919	to Canada 9.1940 (Columbia)
Abbot	DD184	Newport News	4.1918	4.7.1918	6.1919	to the UK 9.1940 (Charlestown)
Bagley, 12.1939- **Doran**	DD185	Newport News	5.1918	19.10.1918	8.1919	to the UK 9.1940 (St. Mary's)

Ward 1943

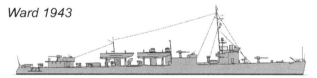

1090 / 1247 t, 95.8 x 9.4 x 2.8 m, 2 sets Parsons geared steam turbines, 4 Normand boilers (DD75, 76, 78, 131-134) or 2 Curtis steam turbines / 1 geared steam turbine for cruising, 4 Yarrow boilers (2 shafts) (DD79, 81-83, 85, 161-164, 167-170) or 2 sets General Electric

Stringham 1942

Curtis geared steam turbines, 4 Yarrow boilers (DD88-90, 103, 106-109, 175, 178-180) or 2 sets Parsons geared steam turbines, 4 Normand boilers (DD93, 94, 135, IX36, DD137-141) or 2 sets Parsons geared steam turbines, 4 White-Forster boilers (DD113-118, 125-128, 130, 142-160) or 2 sets General Electric Curtis geared steam turbines, 4 Thornycroft boilers (AG21, DM15-18, DD181-185), 27000 (DD75, 76, 78, 79, 81-83, 85, 88-90, 93, 103, 106, 108, 109, 113-118, AG21, DM15-18, DD131-135, IX36, DD137-156, 161, 162, 164, 167-170, 175, 178-185) or 24900 (DD125-128, 130) or 26000 (DD157-160) hp, 35 kts, 225 t oil, 3800 nm (15 kts)nm, complement 114;
Destroyers: 4 x 1 – 102/50 Mk 9, 1 x 1 – 76/23 Mk 14, 2 x 1 – 12.7 MG, 4 x 3 – 533 TT, 1 DCT, 2 DCR (15).
Fast minelayers: 4 x 1 – 102/50 Mk 9, 2 x 1 – 12.7 MG, 2 DCR (15), 80 mines.
The "prototypes", as the first six flush-deckers were called, were followed by an order for "improved" type destroyers. From the lead ship, the entire series became known as the *Wickes* class. Their main difference from

their predecessors was the machinery power increased by one and a half times, which made it possible to increase the speed from 30 to 35 knots. The greater weight of the machinery led to an increase in displacement by 90 - 100 tons. The rest of the design repeated the four-funneled "prototypes". The only changes in the architecture of the hull were the rejection of the cruising stern and a keel without the drag, characteristic for the predecessors.

It was originally planned to build 50 "improved" destroyers: an order for the first 20 units was issued in November 1916 (DD75-94), a second order for the remaining 30 (DD95-124) followed a month later. The ships were built as part of a FY16 three-year Program. The US entry into the First World War led to an increase in the order for another 61 ships (DD125-185). Destroyers of the *Wickes* class were built according to two detailed designs: one was developed by Bethlehem and was used by its shipyards (DD79-92, 95-112, 161-185), the other by the Bath Iron Works and was used by all shipyards, except Bethlehem, and became known as "Liberty" (DD75-78, 93-94, 113-160, 181-185). Between themselves, these designs differed both in the type of boilers and turbines, and in many technological features. The use of different machineries led to the fact that the ships built by different shipyards differed significantly in cruising range. The Bath Iron Works 'Liberty' covered 3178 miles at 20 knots, Bethlehems' building by the Fore River - 3400 miles at 15 knots, the ships from the other Bethlehem yards made only 2300-2400 nm at the same speed.

1940-1942, almost all survived: + QCJ or QCL sonar.
1940, fast minesweepers *Dorsey, Lamberton, Boggs, Elliot, Palmer, Hogan, Howard, Stansbury*; 1941, *Hamilton*: - 4 x 1 - 102/50, 1 x 1 - 76/23, 4 x 3 - 533 TT, 1 DCT; + 4 x 1 - 76/50 Mk 20, 2 x 1 - 12.7 MG, (2 - 4) DCT, minesweeping gear, one boiler was removed (25 kts max).
1940, *Little, Gregory, Stringham, Colhoun, McKean*; 1942, *Talbot, Waters, Dent*; 1943, *Schley, Tattnall, Kilty, Ward, Roper, Dickerson, Herbert, Crosby*; 1944, *Rathburne* were converted to fast attack transports with data as follows: 1315 / 1793 t, 95.7 x 11.3 x 3.8 m, 2 Curtis steam turbines / 1 geared steam turbine for cruising, 2 Yarrow boilers (APD2-4, 6, 17) or 2 sets General Electric Curtis geared steam turbines, 2 Yarrow boilers (APD5, 14) or 2 sets Parsons geared steam turbines, 2 White-Forster boilers (APD7-9, 19, 20-22, 25) or 2 sets Parsons geared steam turbines, 2 Normand boilers (APD15, 16), 13000 hp, 22-24 kts, 429 t oil, complement 101; 3 x 1 – 102/50 Mk 9 (APD2-6) or 3 x 1 – 76/50 Mk 20, 1 x 2 – 40/56 Bofors (APD14-17, 19-22, 25), 6 (APD7-9) or 5 (APD14-17, 19-22, 25) x 1 – 20/70 Oerlikon, 6 x 1 – 12.7 MG (APD2-6), 4 DCT, 2 DCR; 4 LCP(L) or LCP(R), 144 troops; SA, SE radars (since 1942-1943), QCJ or QCL sonar.
1941-1942, *Lea, Badger, Babbitt, Jacob Jones, Tarbell,*

Howard 1944

Greer, Roper, Dupont, Bernadou, Ellis, Cole, Dickerson, Leary, Schenck, Herbert: - 4 x 1 - 102/50, 1 x 1 - 76/23, 2 x 3 - 533 TT; + 6 x 1 - 76/50 Mk 20, 2 x 1 - 12.7 MG.
1942, *McKean, Stringham*: - 3 x 1 - 102/50, 6 x 1 - 12.7 MG; + 3 x 1 - 76/50 Mk 20, 6 x 1 - 20/70 Oerlikon.
1942, *Lea, Badger, Babbitt, Tarbell, Greer, Roper, Dupont, Bernadou, Ellis, Cole, Dickerson, Leary, Schenck, Herbert*: - 4 x 1 - 12.7 MG, 1 DCT; + 5 x 1 - 20/70 Oerlikon, 6 DCT.
1942 - 1943, *Gamble, Montgomery, Breese, Ramsay*: - 4 x 1 - 102/50, 1 x 1 - 76/23, 2 x 1 - 12.7 MG; + 4 x 1 - 76/50 Mk 20, 4 x 1 - 20/70 Oerlikon. 1942-1943, almost all survived: + SA, SE radars. 1942-1944, *Dorsey, Lamberton, Boggs, Elliot, Palmer, Hogan, Howard, Stansbury, Hamilton*: - (1 - 2) x 1 - 76/50, 2 x 1 - 12.7 MG; + 1 x 2 - 40/56 Bofors (on ships with 2 76mm guns), (3 - 5) x 1 - 20/70 Oerlikon.
1943, *McKean, Stringham, Talbot, Waters, Dent*: - 1 x 1 - 20/70, + 1 x 2 - 40/56 Bofors. 1943, almost all survived: no more than 3 boilers (25 kt max), fuel stowage was increased. 1943, *Crane, Lea, Badger, Babbitt, Tarbell, Upshur, Greer*: - (1 - 2) x 1 - 20/70 (4 x 1 Oerlikons on board), 2 DCT; + 1 x 24 - 178 Hedgehog Mk 10 ASWRL.
1945, *Schley, Rathburne, Talbot, Waters, Kilty*: - landing craft and landing capacity.

Jacob Jones 28.2.1942 was sunk at coast of Delaware by German submarine *U578*. *Colhoun* 30.8.1942 off Guadalcanal was sunk by Japanese bombers. *Little* and *Gregory* 5.9.1942 were sunk off Guadalcanal by Japanese destroyers *Yudachi, Hatsuyuki* and *Murakumo*. *McKean* 17.11.1942 was sunk in Empress Augusta Bay by a Japanese air torpedo. *Leary* 24.12.1943 was sunk in the North Atlantic by German submarines *U275* and *U382*. *Ward* 7.12.1944 was sunk by kamikaze in Ormoc Bay. *Palmer* 7.1.1945 was sunk by Japanese aircraft off Luzon. *Dickerson* 2.4.1945 was badly damaged by kamikaze off Okinawa and scuttled by own crew two days later.

Chew 1945

Blakeley 25.5.1942 was damaged by a torpedo from German submarine off Martinique and was under repair until September 1942. *Stansbury* 8.11.1942 was damaged by a mine during operation "Torch". *Montgomery* 17.10.1944 was badly damaged by a mine E of Palau. *Talbot* 10.11.1944 was damaged by an explosion of ammunition aboard the cargo vessel *Mount Hood*. *Gamble* 18.2.1945 was badly damaged by

Japanese aircraft off Iwo Jima, for various reasons her repairs were not started and 16.7.1945 she was scuttled off Guam.

As a result of attacks by Japanese aircraft and kamikazes off Okinawa following ships received damages of various severity: *Dorsey* (26.3.1945, heavy), *Rathburne* (27.4.1945, heavy), *Tattnall* (20.5.1945), *Roper* (25.5.1945, heavy).

CLEMSON class destroyers

Clemson	DD186, 11.1939- AVP17, 8.1940- AVD4, 12.1943- DD186, 3.1944- APD31, 7.1945 - DD186	Newport News	5.1918	5.9.1918	12.1919	seaplane tender 11.1939, destroyer 12.1943, fast transport 5.1944, destroyer 7.1945, stricken 10.1945
Dahlgren	DD187	Newport News	6.1918	20.11.1918	1.1920	auxiliary 3.1945
Goldsborough	DD188, 11.1939- AVP18, 8.1940- AVD5, 12.1943- DD188, 3.1944- APD32, 7.1945- DD188	Newport News	6.1918	20.11.1918	1.1920	seaplane tender 11.1939, destroyer 12.1943, fast transport 3.1944, destroyer 7.1945, stricken 10.1945
Satterlee	DD190	Newport News	7.1918	21.12.1918	12,1919	to the UK 10.1940 (Belmont)
Mason	DD191	Newport News	7.1918	8.3.1919	2.1920	to the UK 10.1940 (Broadwater)
Abel P. Upshur	DD193	Newport News	8.1918	14.2.1920	11.1920	to the UK 9.1940 (Clare)
Hunt	DD194	Newport News	8.1918	14.2.1920	11.1920	to the UK 10.1940 (Broadway)
Welborn C. Wood	DD195	Newport News	9.1918	6.3.1920	1.1921	to the UK 9.1940 (Chesterfield)
George E. Badger	DD196, 10.1939- AVP16, 8.1940- AVD3, 12.1943- DD196, 4.1944 - APD33, 7.1945- DD196	Newport News	9.1918	6.3.1920	7.1920	seaplane tender 10.1939, destroyer 11.1943, fast transport 5.1944, destroyer 7.1945, stricken 10.1945
Branch	DD197	Newport News	10.1918	19.4.1919	7.1920	to the UK 10.1940 (Beverley)
Herndon	DD198	Newport News	11.1918	31.5.1919	9.1920	to the UK 9.1940 (Churchill)
Dallas, 3.1945- Alexander Dallas	DD199	Newport News	11.1918	31.5.1919	10.1920	stricken 8.1945
Chandler	DD206, 11.1940- DMS9	Cramp, Philadelphia	8.1918	19.3.1919	9.1919	fast minesweeper 11.1940, auxiliary 6.1945
Southard	DD207, 11.1940- DMS10	Cramp, Philadelphia	8.1918	31.3.1919	9.1919	fast minesweeper 11.1940, wrecked 9.10.1945

Hovey	DD208, 11.1940- DMS11	Cramp, Philadelphia	9.1918	26.4.1919	10.1919	fast minesweeper 11.1940, sunk 7.1.1945
Long	DD209, 11.1940- DMS12	Cramp, Philadelphia	9.1918	26.4.1919	10.1919	fast minesweeper 11.1940, sunk 6.1.1945
Broome	DD210	Cramp, Philadelphia	10.1918	14.5.1919	10.1919	auxiliary 5.1945
Alden	DD211	Cramp, Philadelphia	10.1918	7.6.1919	11.1919	stricken 8.1945
Barker	DD213	Cramp, Philadelphia	4.1919	11.9.1919	12.1919	stricken 8.1945
Tracy	DM19	Cramp, Philadelphia	4.1919	12.8.1919	3.1920	fast minelayer, stricken 2.1946
Borie	DD215	Cramp, Philadelphia	4.1919	4.10.1919	3.1920	sunk 2.11.1943
John D. Edwards (ex-Stewart)	DD216	Cramp, Philadelphia	5.1919	18.10.1919	4.1920	stricken 8.1945
Whipple	DD217	Cramp, Philadelphia	6.1919	6.11.1919	4.1920	auxiliary 6.1945
Parrott	DD218	Cramp, Philadelphia	7.1919	25.11.1919	5.1920	collision 2.5.1944
Edsall	DD219	Cramp, Philadelphia	9.1919	29.7.1920	11.1920	sunk 1.3.1942
MacLeish	DD220	Cramp, Philadelphia	8.1919	18.12.1919	8.1920	auxiliary 1.1945
Simpson	DD221	Cramp, Philadelphia	10.1919	28.4.1920	11.1920	auxiliary 5.1945
Bulmer	DD222	Cramp, Philadelphia	8.1919	22.1.1920	8.1920	auxiliary 11.1944
McCormick	DD223	Cramp, Philadelphia	8.1919	14.2.1920	8.1920	auxiliary AG118 6.1945
Stewart	DD224	Cramp, Philadelphia	9.1919	4.3.1920	9.1920	scuttled 2.3.1942, commissioned by Japan (Dai 102-go)
Pope	DD225	Cramp, Philadelphia	9.1919	23.3.1920	10.1920	sunk 1.3.1942
Peary	DD226	Cramp, Philadelphia	9.1919	6.4.1920	10.1920	sunk 19.2.1942
Pillsbury	DD227	Cramp, Philadelphia	10.1919	3.8.1920	12.1920	sunk 1.3.1942
John D. Ford (ex-Ford)	DD228	Cramp, Philadelphia	11.1919	2.9.1920	12.1920	auxiliary 6.1945
Truxtun	DD229	Cramp, Philadelphia	12.1919	28.9.1920	2.1921	wrecked 18.2.1942
Paul Jones	DD230	Cramp, Philadelphia	12.1919	30.9.1920	4.1921	auxiliary 6.1945
Hatfield	DD231	New York SB, Camden	6.1918	17.3.1919	4.1920	auxiliary 10.1944
Brooks	DD232, 12.1942- APD10	New York SB, Camden	6.1918	24.4.1919	6.1920	fast transport 10.1942, damaged 6.1.1945, never repaired

Gilmer	DD233, 1.1943- APD11	New York SB, Camden	6.1918	24.5.1919	4.1920	fast transport 10.1942, stricken 2.1946
Fox	DD234	New York SB, Camden	6.1918	12.6.1919	5.1920	auxiliary 10.1944
Kane	DD235, 3.1943- APD18	New York SB, Camden	7.1918	12.8.1919	6.1920	fast transport 1.1943, stricken 2.1946
Humphreys	DD236, 12.1942- APD12, 7.1945- DD236	New York SB, Camden	7.1918	28.7.1919	7.1920	fast transport 10.1942, destroyer 7.1945, stricken 11.1945
McFarland	DD237, 8.1940- AVD14, 12.1943- DD237	New York SB, Camden	7.1918	30.3.1920	9.1920	seaplane tender 8.1940, destroyer 12.1943, stricken 12.1945
Overton	DD239, 8.1943- APD23	New York SB, Camden	10.1918	10.7.1919	6.1920	fast transport 8.1943, stricken 8.1945
Sturtevant	DD240	New York SB, Camden	11.1918	29.7.1920	9.1920	sunk 26.4.1942
Childs	DD241, 7.1938- AVP14, 8.1940- AVD1	New York SB, Camden	3.1919	15.9.1920	10.1920	seaplane tender 7.1938, stricken 1.1946
King	DD242	New York SB, Camden	4.1919	14.10.1920	12.1920	stricken 11.1945
Sands	DD243, 12.1942- APD13	New York SB, Camden	3.1919	28.10.1919	11.1920	fast transport 12.1942, stricken 11.1945
Williamson	DD244, 7.1938- AVP15, 8.1940- AVD2, 12.1943- DD244	New York SB, Camden	3.1919	16.10.1919	10.1920	seaplane tender 7.1938, destroyer 12.1943, stricken 12.1945
Reuben James	DD245	New York SB, Camden	4.1919	4.10.1919	9.1920	sunk 30.10.1941
Bainbridge	DD246	New York SB, Camden	5.1919	12.6.1920	2.1921	stricken 8.1945
Goff	DD247	New York SB, Camden	7.1919	2.6.1920	1.1921	stricken 8.1945
Barry	DD248, 1.1944- APD29	New York SB, Camden	7.1919	28.10.1920	12.1920	fast transport 1.1944, sunk 25.5.1945
Hopkins	DD249, 11.1940- DMS13	New York SB, Camden	7.1919	26.6.1920	3.1921	fast minesweeper 11.1940, stricken 1.1946
Lawrence	DD250	New York SB, Camden	8.1919	10.7.1920	4.1921	stricken 8.1945
Belknap	DD251, 8.1940- AVD8, 12.1943- DD251, 6.1944- APD34	Fore River, Quincy	7.1918	14.1.1919	4.1919	seaplane tender 8.1940, destroyer 12.1943, fast transport 6.1944, damaged 11.1.1945, never repaired
McCook	DD252	Fore River, Quincy	9.1918	31.1.1919	4.1919	to Canada 9.1940 (St. Croix)
McCalla	DD253	Fore River, Quincy	9.1918	28.3.1919	5.1919	to the UK 10.1940 (Stanley)
Rodgers *(ex-Kalk)*	DD254	Fore River, Quincy	9.1918	26.4.1919	7.1919	to the UK 10.1940 (Sherwood)

Name	Number	Builder	Laid down	Launched	Completed	Fate
Osmond Ingram (ex-Ingram)	DD255, 8.1940- AVD9, 12.1943- DD255, 6.1944- APD35	Fore River, Quincy	10.1918	28.2.1919	6.1919	seaplane tender 8.1940, destroyer 12.1943, fast transport 6.1944, stricken 1.1946
Bancroft	DD256	Fore River, Quincy	11.1918	21.3.1919	6.1919	to Canada 9.1940 (St. Francis)
Welles	DD257	Fore River, Quincy	11.1918	8.5.1919	9.1919	to the UK 9.1940 (Cameron)
Aulick	DD258	Fore River, Quincy	12.1918	11.4.1919	7.1919	to the UK 10.1940 (Burnham)
Gillis	DD260, 8.1940- AVD12	Fore River, Quincy	12.1918	29.4.1919	9.1919	seaplane tender 8.1940, stricken 11.1945
Laub	DD263	Bethlehem, Squantum	4.1918	25.8.1918	3.1919	to the UK 10.1940 (Burwell)
McLanahan	DD264	Bethlehem, Squantum	4.1918	22.9.1918	4.1919	to the UK 10.1940 (Bradford)
Edwards	DD265	Bethlehem, Squantum	4.1918	10.10.1918	4.1919	to the UK 10.1940 (Buxton)
Greene (ex-Anthony)	DD266, 8.1940- AVD13, 12.1943- DD266, 2.1944- APD36	Bethlehem, Squantum	6.1918	2.11.1918	5.1919	seaplane tender 8.1940, destroyer 12.1943, fast transport 2.1944, wrecked 9.10.1945, never repaired
Ballard	DD267, 8.1940- AVD10	Bethlehem, Squantum	6.1918	7.12.1918	6.1919	seaplane tender 8.1940, stricken 1.1946
Shubrick	DD268	Bethlehem, Squantum	6.1918	31.12.1918	7.1919	to the UK 11.1940 (Ripley)
Bailey	DD269	Bethlehem, Squantum	6.1918	5.2.1919	6.1919	to the UK 11.1940 (Reading)
Thornton	DD270, 8.1940- AVD11	Bethlehem, Squantum	6.1918	22.3.1919	7.1919	seaplane tender 8.1940, damaged 5.4.1945, never repaired
Swasey	DD273	Bethlehem, Squantum	8.1918	7.5.1919	8.1919	to the UK 11.1940 (Rockingham)
Meade	DD274	Bethlehem, Squantum	9.1918	24.5.1919	9.1919	to the UK 11.1940 (Ramsey)
Litchfield	DD336	Mare Island N Yd, Vallejo	1.1919	12.8.1919	5.1920	auxiliary 3.1945
Zane	DD337, 11.1940- DMS14	Mare Island N Yd, Vallejo	1.1919	12.8.1919	2.1921	fast minesweeper 11.1940, auxiliary 6.1945
Wasmuth	DD338, 11.1940- DMS15	Mare Island N Yd, Vallejo	8.1919	15.9.1919	12.1921	fast minesweeper 11.1940, sunk 29.12.1942
Trever	DD339, 11.1940- DMS16	Mare Island N Yd, Vallejo	8.1919	15.9.1920	8.1922	fast minesweeper 11.1940, auxiliary 6.1945
Perry	DD340, 11.1940- DMS17	Mare Island N Yd, Vallejo	9.1920	29.10.1921	8.1922	fast minesweeper 11.1940, sunk 13.9.1944
Decatur	DD341	Mare Island N Yd, Vallejo	9.1920	29.10.1921	8.1922	stricken 8.1945

Hulbert	DD342, 8.1940- AVP19, 8.1940- AVD6, 12.1943- DD342	Norfolk N Yd, Portsmouth	11.1918	28.6.1919	10.1920	seaplane tender 8.1940, destroyer 12.1943, stricken 11.1945
Noa	DD343, 8.1943- APD24	Norfolk N Yd, Portsmouth	11.1918	28.6.1919	2.1921	fast transport 8.1943, collision 12.9.1944
William B. Preston	DD344, 8.1940- AVP20, 8.1940- AVD7	Norfolk N Yd, Portsmouth	11.1918	9.9.1919	8.1920	seaplane tender 8.1940, stricken 1.1946
Preble	DM20	Bath Iron Wks	4.1919	8.3.1920	3.1920	fast minelayer, auxiliary 6.1945
Sicard	DM21	Bath Iron Wks	6.1919	20.4.1920	6.1920	fast minelayer, auxiliary 6.1945
Pruitt	DM22	Bath Iron Wks	7.1919	28.3.1920	9.1920	fast minelayer, auxiliary 6.1945

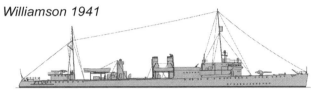

Williamson 1941

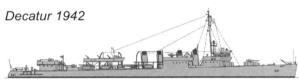

Decatur 1942

Clemson 1942

Overton 1943

1190 / 1308 t, 95.8 x 9.4 x 3.0 m, DD186 - 199, 231 - 250: 2 sets Westinghouse geared steam turbines, 4 White-Forster boilers (DD186-188, 190, 191, 193-199, 231-237, 239-250) or 2 sets Parsons geared steam turbines, 4 White-Forster boilers (DD206-211, 213-230) or 2 Curtis steam turbines / 1 geared steam turbine for cruising, 4 Yarrow boilers (2 shafts) (DD251-258, 260, 263-270, 273, 274) or 2 sets Parsons geared steam turbines, 4 Normand boilers (DD336-344, DM20-22), 27000 hp, 35 kts, 225 t oil, 2500 nm (20 kts), complement 114;

Destroyers: 4 x 1 – 102/50 Mk 9 or 4 x 2 – 102/50 Mk 9 (DD208, 209) or 4 x 1 – 127/51 Mk 8 (DD231-235), 1 x 1 – 76/23 Mk 14, 2 x 1 – 12.7 MG, 4 x 3 – 533 TT, 1 DCT, 2 DCR (15).

Fast minelayers: 4 x 1 – 102/50 Mk 9, 1 x 1 – 76/23 Mk 14, 2 x 1 – 12.7 MG, 2 DCR (15), 80 mines.

Almost simultaneously with an order for 111 *Wickes*-class destroyers, an order for 162 *Clemson*-class ships followed in 1918. Their main difference was the increased fuel supply by about 100 tons and, accordingly, the increased full displacement. Wartime left its mark on the conditions for the delivery of ships to the navy: high-speed trials were excluded from the contract; they were replaced by the requirement to reach design power. These destroyers were built according to three slightly different designs: Bethlehem (DD251-335), Bath (DD206-250, 336-347) and Newport News (DD186-205, the order for the last six was cancelled).

Several ships of the *Clemson* class, received strengthened armament, which was explained by the appearance at the end of the World War I of German submarines armed with heavy 150-mm guns. Five ships (DD231-235) received four 127-mm/51 instead of 102-mm guns, and on two more (DD208 and 209) 102-mm guns were mounted in paired mounts with a single cradle.

1938, *Childs, Williamson*; 1939, *Clemson, Goldsborough, George E. Badger, Hulbert, William B. Preston*; 1940, *McFarland, Belknap, Osmond Ingram, Gillis, Greene, Ballard, Thornton*: were converted to seaplane tenders: 2 boilers and their funnels were removed (with following data: 1202 / 1699 t, 12500-13500 hp, 25 kt, 429 t oil, complement 101, 2 x 1 - 102/50 Mk 9, 4 x 1 - 12.7 MG, equipment for support an air squadron (12 patrol bombers such as PBY), 113 550 l of aviation petrol).

1940-1942, almost all survived: + QCJ or QCL sonar. 1940, *Noa*: - 2 x 3 - 533 TT; + 1 seaplane. 1940, *Chandler, Southard, Hovey, Long, Hopkins, Zane, Wasmuth, Trever, Perry*: - 4 x 1 - 102/50, 1 x 1 - 76/23, 4 x 3 - 533 TT, 1 DCT (Y-gun); + 4 x 1 - 76/50 Mk 20, 2 x 1 - 12.7 MG, (2 - 4) DCT, minesweeping gear, one boiler was removed (25 kt max).

1941 - 1942, *Dallas, Broome, McLeish, Simpson, McCormick, Truxtun, Overton, Sturtevant, Reuben James, Bainbridge, Decatur*: - 4 x 1 - 102/50, 1 x 1 - 76/23, 2 x 3 - 533 TT; + 6 x 1 - 76/50 Mk 20, 2 x 1 - 12.7 MG.

1942, *Brooks, Gilmer, Humphreys, Sands*; 1943, *Kane, Overton, Noa*; 1944, *Clemson, Goldsborough, George E. Badger, Barry, Belknap, Osmond Ingram, Greene* were converted to fast attack transports with data as follows: 1315 / 1793 t, 95.7 x 11.3 x 3.8 m, 2 sets Westinghouse geared steam turbines, 2 White-Forster boilers (APD10-13, 18, 23, 29, 31 – 33) or 2 sets Parsons geared steam turbines, 2 Normand boilers (APD24) or 2 Curtis steam turbines / 1 geared steam turbine for cruising, 2 Yarrow boilers (2 shafts) (APD34 – 36), 13000 hp, 22-24 kts, 429 t oil, complement 101; 3 x 1 – 76/50 Mk 20, 1 x 2 – 40/56 Bofors (APD18, 23, 24, 29, 31-36), 6 (APD10-13) or 5 (APD18, 23, 24, 29, 31-36) x 1 – 20/70 Oerlikon, 4 DCT, 2 DCR, 4 LCP(L) o LCP(R), 144 troops; SA, SE radars, QCJ or QCL sonar.

1942 - 1943, *Clemson, Goldsborough, George E. Badger, McFarland, Childs, Williamson, Belknap, Osmond Ingram, Gillis, Greene, Ballard, Thornton, Hulbert, William B. Preston*: - 2 x 1 - 102/50, 4 x 1 - 12.7 MG; + 2 x 1 - 76/50 Mk 20, (4 - 6) x 1 - 20/70 Oerlikon, (2 - 4) DCT, 2 DCR. 1942, *Dallas, Broome, McLeish, Simpson, McCormick, Overton, Bainbridge, Decatur*: - 4 x 1 - 12.7 MG, 1 DCT (Y-gun); + 5 x 1 - 20/70 Oerlikon, 6 DCT. 1942-1943, almost all survived: + SA, SE radars.

1942 - 1943, *Tracy, Preble, Sicard, Pruitt*: - 4 x 1 - 102/50, 1 x 1 - 76/23, 2 x 1 - 12.7 MG; + 4 x 1 - 76/50 Mk 20, 4 x 1 - 20/70 Oerlikon. 1942 - 1944, *Chandler, Southard, Hovey, Long, Hopkins, Zane, Wasmuth, Trever, Perry*: - (1 - 2) x 1 - 76/50, 2 x 1 - 12.7 MG; + 1 x 2 - 40/56 Bofors (on ships with 2 76-mm guns), (3 - 5) x 1 - 20/70 Oerlikon. 1942-1943, *Dahlgren, Alden, Barker, Borie, John D. Edwards, Whipple, Parrott, Bulmer, John D. Ford, Paul Jones, Hatfield, Brooks, Gilmer, Fox, Kane, Humphreys, King, Sands, Goff, Barry, Lawrence*: - 4 x 1 - 12.7 MG, 2 x 3 - 533 TT, 1 DCT ("Y"-gun); + 6 x 1 - 20/70 Oerlikon, 6 DCT.

1943, *Brooks, Gilmer, Humphreys, Sands*: - 1 x 1 - 20/70; + 1 x 2 - 40/56 Bofors. 1943, almost all survived: no more than 3 boilers (25 kts max), fuel stowage was

Hovey 1942

increased. 1943, *McLeish, McCormick, Bainbridge, Decatur*. - (1 - 2) x 1 - 20/70 (4 x 1 - 20/70 Oerlikon on board), 2 DCT; + 1 x 24 - 178 Hedgehog ASWRL. 1943, *Clemson, Goldsborough, George E. Badger, McFarland, Williamson, Belknap, Osmond Ingram, Greene, Hulbert*: - 2 x 1 - 102/50, 4 x 1 - 12.7 MG, equipment for seaplanes; + 2 x 1 - 76/50 Mk 20, (4 - 6) x 1 - 20/70 Oerlikon, (2 - 4) DCT, (1 - 2) DCR.

1944, *McLeish, McCormick*: - 2 x 3 - 533 TT; + 1 x 1 - 40/56 Bofors.

1945, *Clemson, Goldsborough, George E. Badger, Humphreys*: - landing craft and landing capacity.

Reuben James 31.10.1941 was sunk in the North Atlantic by German submarine *U552* a month before the US official entered the Second World War. *Truxtun* 18.2.1942 was wrecked during a storm off the coast of Newfoundland. *Peary* 19.2.1942 was sunk at Darwin (Australia) by Japanese D3A bombers from aircraft carriers *Akagi, Kaga, Soryu* and *Hiryu. Pillsbury* 1.3.1942 was sunk S of Java by Japanese cruisers *Atago* and *Maya* and destroyers. *Edsall* 1.3.1942 was sunk S of Java by Japanese battlecruisers *Hiei* and *Kirishima. Pope* 1.3.1942 was sunk in the Java Sea by Japanese cruisers *Myoko* and *Ashigara. Stewart* 20.2.1942 was damaged in the Badoeng Strait by Japanese ships and docked in Surabaya for repairs, where 20.2.1942 she capsized and received further damage 1.3.1942 during a Japanese air raid. 2.3.1942, when Surabaya surrendered, she was scuttled. In February 1943, she was salvaged by Japanese, repaired and under the number *102* in September 1943 was commissioned by the IJN. After the Japanese capitulation, she returned to the USA and in October 1945 formally commissioned with the same hull number DD224. She was stricken in April 1946 and was sunk as a target 24.5.1946. *Sturtevant* 26.4.1942 was lost off the coast of Florida, blown up by an US mine. *Wasmuth* 29.12.1942 off the Aleutian Islands sank after an explosion of own DCs during a storm. *Borie* 2.11.1943 was lost N of the Azores being rammed by German submarine *U405. Noa* 12.9.1944 was lost off Palau after a collision with destroyer *Fullman. Perry* was lost 13.9.1944 on mines near Palau. *Hovey* and *Long* were sunk by Japanese aircraft 6.1.1945 off Leyte.

McFarland 16.10.1942 was damaged off Guadalcanal by Japanese aircraft. *Parrott* 2.5.1944 was badly damaged near Norfolk in a collision with s/s *John Morton*, never repaired and laid up in June 1944. *Brooks* 6.1.1945 was damaged by kamikaze off Luzon. *Clemson* 10.1.1945 was damaged in collision with battleship *Pennsylvania*. *Belknap* was damaged by kamikaze at coast of the Philippines 11.1.1945 and was never repaired. *Thornton* 5.4.1945 was badly damaged in a collision with oilers *Ashtabula* and *Escalante*, ran ashore and was never repaired.

As a result of Japanese air and kamikaze attacks off Okinawa following ships received damages of various severity level: *Gilmer* (25.3.1945), *Southard* (27.3.1945 and 27.5.1945), *Hopkins* (4.5.1945), *Barry* (25.5.1945, heavy). It was decided not to repair the last ship, but use her as decoy for Japanese aircraft, she was sunk in this role 21.6.1945.

AG24 *Semmes* was used as an escort during the war and was armed with 1 x 1 – 76/50 Mk 10/19/21, 4 DCT, 2 DCR.

FARRAGUT class destroyers

Farragut (ex-Smith, ex-Farragut)	DD348	Bethlehem, Quincy	9.1932	15.3.1934	6.1934	stricken 1.1947
Dewey (ex-Phelps, ex-Dewey)	DD349	Bath Iron Wks	12.1932	28.7.1934	10.1934	stricken 11.1945
Hull	DD350	New York N Yd, Brooklyn	3.1933	31.1.1934	1.1935	foundered 18.12.1944
MacDonough	DD351	Boston N Yd, Charlestown	5.1933	22.8.1934	3.1935	stricken 11.1945
Worden	DD352	Puget Sound N Yd, Bremerton	12.1932	27.10.1934	1.1935	wrecked 12.1.1943
Dale	DD353	New York N Yd, Brooklyn	2.1934	23.1.1935	6.1935	stricken 11.1945
Monaghan	DD354	Boston N Yd, Charlestown	11.1933	9.1.1935	4.1935	foundered 18.12.1944
Aylwin	DD355	Philadelphia N Yd	9.1933	10.7.1934	3.1935	stricken 11.1945

Aylwin 1940

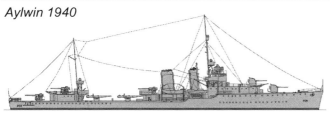

1358 / 2064 t, 104.0 x 10.4 x 3.5 m, 2 sets Curtis geared steam turbines, 4 Yarrow boilers, 42800 hp, 36.5 kts, 600 t oil, 6500 nm (12 kts), complement 160; 5 x 1 – 127/38 Mk 12, 4 x 1 – 12.7 MG, 2 x 4 – 533 TT, QCA sonar.

With the mass building of the *Clemson* and *Wickes* classes destroyers at the end of the First World War and shortly thereafter, the USN destroyer development line was interrupted for many years. All funds went to the building of aircraft carriers, 'Washington' cruisers and the modernization of battleships. The usual practice, explained by the reluctance of Congress to spend money on "unpresentable" ships, and the vague views of seamen on what kind of destroyers they need, led to the fact that in the early 1930th 'flush-deckers', which formed a basis of light naval forces, became outdated.

Work on design of a new generation destroyer began in the first half of 1928 after by the General Board determined the main specifications: 4 127-mm/51 main guns, one 76-mm AA gun, 12 TTs, larger, than the previous classes, dimensions (to improve seaworthiness and endurance). The use of machinery with increased steam parameters was envisaged. However, it soon became clear that it was not worth rushing with design works, since it became known that Congress did not plan to allocate funds for the building of destroyers either in FY28 or in FY29. Supporters of the installing DP guns on the destroyers took advantage of this, insisting on replacing the single purpose 127-mm/51 with AA 127-mm/25 guns with an appropriate fire control system. Such a replacement was confirmed by the fact that firing of a destroyer at long distances is unlikely to be effective due to her instability as a gun platform, and at close ranges, short-barreled antiaircraft 127-mm/25 guns were not inferior to long-barreled 127-mm/51 ones.

The designers returned to design work in the

Farragut 1935

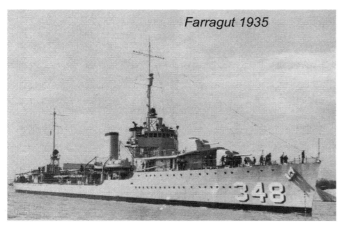

early 1930. By the end of the year, several options were ready with a standard displacement of 1350 to 1850 t. 127-mm/25 AA guns were used as the main caliber, but they were soon abandoned: by this time, the new DP 127-mm/38 gun was ready which so exceeded short-barreled 127-mm/25 gun that because of this, an immediate decision was made to rearm the designed ships. At the same time, three triple TTs gave way to two quadruples.

The final version of a new destroyer design was ready in March 1931. There was a complete rejection of the ideas embodied in the 'flush-deckers': all armament was placed on the centerline; the flush deck hull was abandoned in favor of a more traditional one with a forecastle. In order to save displacement as much as possible, a longitudinal framing and widespread use of welding instead of a riveting were provided. For the same reasons, only two fwd guns had enclosed mounts, while the aft guns had open mounts. Light AA armament was limited to 4 12.7-mm MGs, and anti-submarine equipment to a sonar and two DC racks (in a wartime installation of additional DCTs was planned, for which the deck had necessary reinforcement).

The working design was developed by Bethlehem (usual practice in the US naval shipbuilding of that time: Bureau of Construction prepared a sketch design, and detailed design was completed by one of the private contractors).

Mid-1941, all: + 2 DCR (14).

1942-1944, almost all survived: + SC, SG, Mk 12/22 radars. 5-9.1942, all: - 1 x 1 - 127/38 (No 3), 4 x 1 - 12.7 MG; + 8 x 1 - 20/70 Oerlikon, 4 DCT (48 DC at all). Late 1942, all: - 3 x 1 - 20/70; + 2 x 2 - 40/56 Bofors. Full displacement was 2307-2335 t.

Worden during landing on the Aleutian Islands 12.1.1943 was wrecked on the coastal rocks at Amchitka Island. *Hull* and *Monaghan* 18.12.1944 were lost during a typhoon off Luzon.

MacDonough 10.5.1943 was damaged in collision with destroyer-minelayer *Sicard* (engine rooms and aft boiler room were foundered) and was under repair until the end of the year.

PORTER class destroyers

Porter	DD356	New York SB, Camden	12.1933	12.12.1935	8.1936	sunk 26.10.1942
Selfridge	DD357	New York SB, Camden	12.1933	18.4.1936	11.1936	stricken 11.1945
McDougal	DD358	New York SB, Camden	12.1933	17.7.1936	12.1936	auxiliary 9.1945
Winslow	DD359	New York SB, Camden	12.1933	21.9.1936	2.1937	auxiliary 9.1945
Phelps	DD360	Bethlehem, Quincy	1.1934	18.7.1935	2.1936	stricken 1.1947
Clark	DD361	Bethlehem, Quincy	1.1934	15.10.1935	5.1936	stricken 11.1945
Moffett	DD362	Bethlehem, Quincy	1.1934	11.12.1935	8.1936	stricken 1.1947
Balch	DD363	Bethlehem, Quincy	5.1934	24.3.1936	10.1936	stricken 11.1945

1834 / 2597 t, 116.2 x 11.3 x 4.0 m, 2 sets geared steam turbines, 4 Babcock & Wilcox boilers, 50000 hp, 37 kts, 635 t oil, 6500 nm (12 kts), complement 194; 4 x 2 – 127/38 Mk 12, 2 x 4 – 28/75 Mk 1, 2 x 1 – 12.7 MG, 2 x 4 – 533 TT (16), 2 DCR (14); QCA sonar.

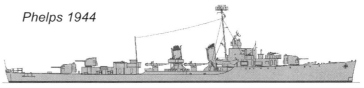
Phelps 1944

The ships of the *Porter* class became the first USN destroyer leaders. The need for such ships became clear to the General Board in 1917, when, along with the building of a large number of 'flush deckers', the design of a ship intended to fulfil a role of flotilla leader was started: larger than a destroyer, and carrying stronger artillery. FY21 program provided for the building of five such ships (2200 t, 35 kts, 5 127-mm guns, 4 triple TTs), but Congress did not allocate the necessary funds, citing the fact that at the end of the war there were many destroyers in the US Navy. The design of leaders with a displacement of 1600 to 2900 t was started again only in the late twenties.

In 1930, the London Naval Conference established a maximum 1850-t standard displacement for leaders, and the General Board, previously inclined in favor of a ship with moderate dimensions, decided to raise the displacement of future leaders to the permitted limit. The increase in dimensions was supposed to be directed to improving seaworthiness, additional equipment necessary for a command ship, and improvement habitation conditions. By November 1930, the Bureau of Construction had prepared a draft design for the new ship. With 1850-t standard displacement, the armament consisted of 4 single 127-mm/25 DP guns and 2 quadruple TTs, the speed reached 35.5 kts. An important innovation was the use of light 12.7-mm armor

Selfridge 1936

for the machinery and the bridge.

Although the design satisfied the General Board, work on the leader for was delayed for a number of reasons: in particular, the emergence of a new 127-mm/38 DP gun which required a significant revision of the design, played a significant role. It was resubmitted for consideration in January 1932, and the number of 127-mm/38 DP guns was increased to five; two months later, during design correction, a sixth was added. In the middle of the same year, when, it would seem, all possible comments were taken into account, the Bureau of Construction was able to insist on replacing the DP main guns with SP twin mounts, which made it possible to increase the number of guns to eight. As compensation, 2 quadruple 28-mm AA MGs were provided.

The abandonment of the DP main guns in the early 1930th was presented not too big a sacrifice for the sake of two additional main guns, and in this version the armament was approved by the General Board. The replacement of the artillery allowed for another alteration in the armament structure: to place around the aft funnel a storehouse for eight spare torpedoes, which made the *Porter* class stand out among the remaining USN destroyers. The machinery arrangement of the new leaders did not fundamentally differ from the *Farragut* class, only the turbines were placed in separate rooms.

All eight ships of this class were built under the FY33 Program. The detailed design was carried out by New York Shipbuilding Co.

Mid-1941-early 1942, all: - 2 x 1 - 12.7 MG, spare torpedoes; + 3 x 1 - 20/70 Oerlikon.

1942-1943, almost all survived: + SC, SG, Mk 3 radars.

10-12.1943, all survived: - 2 x 4 - 28/75; + 3 x 2 - 40/56 Bofors, 3 x 1 - 20/70 Oerlikon. 3.1943-3.1944, *McDougal, Winslow, Phelps, Clark, Moffett, Balch*: - 1 x 2 - 127/38 (No 3); + 1 x 4 - 40/56 Bofors, 4 DCT (in total 48 DC).

Late 1944-early 1945, *Selfridge*: - 4 x 2 - 127/38, 1 x 2 - 40/56, Mk 3 radar; + (2 x 2 + 1 x 1) - 127/38 Mk 12 (DP), 1 x 4 - 40/56 Bofors, 4 DCT (in total 48 DC), Mk 12/22 radar. Late 1944-early 1945, *McDougal, Winslow, Phelps*: - 3 x 2 - 127/38, Mk 3 radar, 1 x 2 - 40/56; + (2 x 2 + 1 x 1) - 127/38 Mk 12 (DP), Mk 12/22 radar.

8.1945, *Selfridge, Winslow, Phelps*: - 6 x 1 - 20/70, 2 x 4 - 533 TT, 2 DCT, 1 DCR (22 DC in total); + 2 x 4 - 40/56 Bofors, 2 x 2 - 20/70 Oerlikon, displacement increased to 2154 / 2857 t.

Porter was sunk 26.10.1942 by Japanese submarine *I21* during the Battle of Santa Cruz.

Selfridge on the night 6-7.10.1943 in the Battle of Vella Lavella received a torpedo hit from Japanese destroyer, was badly damaged (the fore end was broken off); repairs lasted until the beginning of 1944.

McDougal and *Winslow* were converted to radar picket destroyers in September 1945, receiving SP and SG-6 radars.

MAHAN class destroyers

Mahan subclass

Mahan	DD364	Bethlehem, Staten I, Port Richmond	6.1934	15.10.1935	9.1936	sunk 7.12.1944
Cummings	DD365	Bethlehem, Staten I, Port Richmond	6.1934	11.12.1935	11.1936	stricken 1.1947
Drayton	DD366	Bath Iron Wks	3.1934	26.3.1936	9.1936	stricken 10.1945
Lamson	DD367	Bath Iron Wks	3.1934	17.6.1936	10.1936	nuclear tests 25.7.1946
Flusser	DD368	Federal, Kearny	6.1934	28.9.1935	10.1936	stricken 4.1947
Reid	DD369	Federal, Kearny	6.1934	11.1.1936	11.1936	sunk 11.12.1944
Case	DD370	Boston N Yd, Charlestown	9.1934	14.9.1935	9.1936	stricken 1.1947
Conyngham	DD371	Boston N Yd, Charlestown	9.1934	14.9.1935	11.1936	stricken 6.1948
Cassin	DD372	Philadelphia N Yd	10.1934	28.10.1935	8.1936	destroyed 7.12.1941
Cassin *(ii)*	DD372	Mare Island N Yd, Vallejo	6.1942	25.6.1943	2.1944	stricken 1.1947
Shaw	DD373	Philadelphia N Yd	10.1934	28.10.1935	9.1936	stricken 10.1945
Tucker	DD374	Norfolk N Yd, Portsmouth	8.1934	26.2.1936	7.1936	sunk 4.8.1942
Downes	DD375	Norfolk N Yd, Portsmouth	8.1934	22.4.1936	1.1937	destroyed 7.12.1941
Downes *(ii)*	DD375	Mare Island N Yd, Vallejo	6.1942	22.5.1943	11.1943	stricken 1.1947
Cushing	DD376	Puget Sound N Yd, Bremerton	8.1934	31.12.1935	8.1936	sunk 13.11.1942
Perkins	DD377	Puget Sound N Yd, Bremerton	8.1934	31.12.1935	9.1936	collision 29.11.1943
Smith	DD378	Mare Island N Yd, Vallejo	10.1934	20.2.1936	9.1936	stricken 2.1947
Preston	DD379	Mare Island N Yd, Vallejo	10.1934	22.4.1936	10.1936	sunk 14.11.1942

Dunlap subclass

Dunlap	DD384	Bethlehem, Staten I, Port Richmond	4.1935	18.4.1936	6.1937	stricken 1.1947
Fanning	DD385	Bethlehem, Staten I, Port Richmond	4.1935	18.9.1936	10.1937	stricken 1.1947

1488 / 2103 t, 104.0 x 10.7 x 3.8 m, 2 sets General Electric geared steam turbines, 4 Babcock & Wilcox boilers, 49000 hp, 36.5 kts, 522 t oil, 6500 nm (12 kts), complement 158; 5 x 1 – 127/38 Mk 12, 4 x 1 – 12.7 MG, 3 x 4 – 533 TT, 2 DCR (14), QCA sonar.
DD372(ii) and 375 (ii): 4 x 1 – 127/38 Mk 12, 2 x 2 – 40/56 Bofors, 6 x 1 – 20/70 Oerlikon, 2 x 4 – 533 TT, 4 DCT, 2 DCR (44), SC-3, SG-1, Mk 12/22 radars, QCA sonar.

Even at the design stage, destroyers of the *Farragut* class were criticized by the USN chief staff for insufficient, from their point of view, torpedo armament. When discussing at the General Board the requirements for new destroyers to be built under the FY33 Program, the opinion of supporters of strengthening of torpedo armament prevailed, and it was proposed to prepare a design with 12 TTs. Soon a draft design was prepared with 4 triple TT banks, arranged on each beam, and 5 single 127-mm/38 SP guns. The latter circumstance caused sharp criticism from the chief of the Department of Naval Operations (analogue of HQ chief) and this design was rejected.

In March 1933, a new compromise was ready. Due to a slight increase in a hull breadth and replanning of an armament arrangement (No 3 main gun was transferred to the aft superstructure, and two of three TTs were placed on either beam aft of the aft funnel), the desired result was achieved, but a wider hull led to a decrease in speed, which was considered unacceptable. A way out was found by Gibbs and Cox Co., which developed the compact machinery with sufficient high-pressure boilers and the first-ever (on destroyers) double-reduction geared turbines. Alhough the new machinery turned out to be almost 30 t heavier than on the *Farragut* class, it was several thousand hp more powerful and much more sufficient: with 50 t less fuel stowage *Mahan* had the same cruising range as *Farragut*.

Under the FY33 Program 16 ships were built, two more (DD384 and 385) under the FY34 Program. The latter ships differed from other ships of the class having both fwd guns installed in ring-based mounts for the first time in USN; this made it possible to simplify the ammunition feeding and make a mount completely enclosed. Often these ships were singled out as a separate *Dunlap* class.

During the Japanese air raid on Pearl Harbor 7.12.1941 *Downes* and *Cassin*, laying in dry dock, were badly damaged by fire. When the dock was flooded, they received additional damage. The hulls of both destroyers

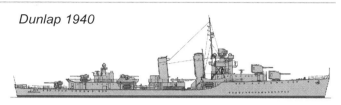

Dunlap 1940

were so deformed, that they could not be repaired. Only the machinery and part of armament were relatively undamaged. Formally, both destroyers were repaired: although hulls were built anew, they had the same numbers, so from a bureaucratic point of view, the ships remained the same. Both new-built ships differed from other destroyers of the class with a low open "Admiralty" bridge, two TTs on the centerline and a new fire control system.

Early 1942, *Mahan, Cummings, Drayton, Lamson, Flusser, Reid, Case, Tucker, Cushing, Perkins, Smith, Preston, Dunlap, Fanning*: - 1 x 1 - 127/38, 4 x 1 - 12.7 MG; + 7 x 1 - 20/70 Oerlikon, 4 DCT (44 DC at all). Early 1942, *Conyngham*: - 1 x 1 - 127/38, 2 x 1 - 12.7 MG; + 2 x 1 - 20/70 Oerlikon, 4 x 2 - 12.7 MG, 4 DCT (44 DC at all). Late 1942, *Shaw*: - 1 x 1 - 127/38, 2 x 1 - 12.7 MG; + 1 x 4 - 28/75 Mk 1, 4 x 1 - 20/70 Oerlikon, 4 DCT (44 DC at all). 1942-1944, almost all survived (except *Cassin (ii), Downes (ii)*): + SC, SG, Mk 12/22 radars.

1.1943-mid-1944, *Mahan, Cummings, Drayton, Lamson, Flusser, Reid, Case, Perkins, Smith, Dunlap, Fanning*: - 2 x 1 - 20/70; + 2 x 2 - 40/56 Bofors. Spring 1943, *Conyngham*: - (4 x 2 + 2 x 1) - 12.7 MG; + 2 x 2 - 40/56 Bofors, 3 x 1 - 20/70 Oerlikon. Late 1943-mid-1944, *Shaw*: - 1 x 4 - 28/75; + 2 x 2 - 40/56 Bofors, 1 x 1 - 20/70 Oerlikon.

1944, *Dunlap*: - 1 x 4 - 533 TT.
1.1945, *Lamson*: - 2 x 2 - 40/56, 2 x 4 - 533 TT; + 2 x 4 - 40/56 Bofors. 6.1945, *Shaw*: - 1 x 1 - 127/38, 5 x 1 - 20/70, 3 x 4 - 533 TT; + 2 x 4 - 40/56 Bofors, 2 x 2 - 20/70 Oerlion. 8.1945, *Lamson*: - 1 x 4 - 533 TT.

Drayton 1944

During the Japanese air raid on Pearl Harbor 7.12.1941 *Downes* and *Cassin*, laying in a drydock, were badly damaged by fire. When the dock was flooded, they received additional damage. *Tucker* 4.8.1942 was lost on US minefield in the New Hebrides area. *Cushing* 13.11.1942 off Guadalcanal was sunk by Japanese battleship *Hiei*, cruiser *Nagara* and destroyer *Teruzuki*. *Preston* off Guadalcanal 14.11.1942 was sunk by Japanese cruiser *Nagara* and destroyers. *Perkins* 29.11.1943 was lost in a collision with Australian cargo vessel *Duntroon* off New Guinea. *Mahan* was damaged 27.10.1942 in collision with battleship *South Dakota*, 7.12.1944 off the coast of the Philippines she received hits of three kamikazes and then had to be scuttled. Almost

in the same place and at the same time, during kamikaze attacks, following ships received damages of various severity: *Drayton* (December 4 and 5), *Lamson* (7.12.1944). *Reid* 11.12.1944 was sunk by kamikaze off Mindanao.

Fanning 22.1.1942 was damaged in collision with destroyer *Gridley*. *Shaw* 7.12.1941 during Japanese air raid on Pearl Harbor received an air bomb hit, a fire caused an explosion of fore magazines, the fore end was destroyed; repairs lasted until the end of 1942; 2.4.1945 she was damaged when she ran ashore, and so heavy that her repair was deemed inexpedient. *Smith* 26.10.1942 was damaged by Japanese aircraft and was under repair until the spring of 1943.

GRIDLEY class destroyers

Gridley	DD380	Bethlehem, Quincy	6.1935	1.12.1936	6.1937	stricken 2.1947
Craven	DD382	Bethlehem, Quincy	6.1935	25.2.1937	9.1937	stricken 2.1947
McCall	DD400	Bethlehem, San Francisco	3.1936	20.11.1937	6.1938	stricken 1.1947
Maury	DD401	Bethlehem, San Francisco	3.1936	14.2.1938	8.1938	stricken 11.1945

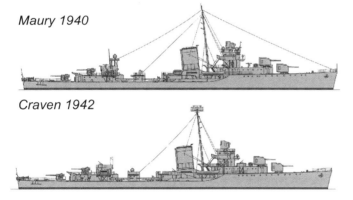

Maury 1940

Craven 1942

1590 / 2219 t, 103.9 x 10.7 x 3.9 m, 2 sets Bethlehem geared steam turbines, 4 Yarrow boilers, 50000 hp, 38.5 kts, 525 t oil, complement 158; 4 x 1 – 127/38 Mk 12, 4 x 1 – 12.7 MG, 4 x 4 – 533 TT, 2 DCR (14), QCA sonar. The FY34 program included the building of two leaders and 12 destroyers. The latter were originally supposed to be built according to the *Dunlap* design (an improved *Mahan* with part of the guns in enclosed mounts), but a number of experts refused the centerline TT bank with threats that during torpedo launch from it

at small relative bearings, the torpedo could hit the tail on the upper deck. The remark was taken into account, and the General Board decided to build two destroyers, ordered to Bethlehem, according to its design based on the *Mahan* class, considering the wishes of supporters of strengthening torpedo armament, with four TTs, placed on either beam. The number of guns was reduced from five to four.

A distinctive feature of the *Gridley* class destroyers was a huge funnel conducting smoke from all four boilers. The boilers produced a steam with higher parameters, tan the boilers of the *Mahan* class. The Use of more compact machinery made it possible to increase its power without increasing its dimensions, so destroyers of this class became the fastest destroyers in the US Navy: DD380 on trials with 1774-t displacement reached 38.99-kt speed.

Two ships, DD30 and 382, were built under the FY34 Program, two more (DD400 and 401) were built under the FY35 Program.

The strength of the hulls of this class turned out to be insufficient, as well as the stability, which did not allow for a serious armament modernization.

Early 1942, all: - 4 x 1 - 12.7 MG; + 6 x 1 - 20/70 Oerlikon. 1942, all: + 4 DCT (44 DC at all). 1942 - 1944, almost all: + SC, SG, Mk 12/22 radars.

Mid-1943, all: + 1 x 1 - 20/70 Oerlikon. Late 1943, *Gridley, Craven, McCall*: + 1 x 1 - 20/70 Oerlikon.

Spring 1945, all: - 2 x 4 - 533 TT, full displacement was 2400 t

Gridley 22.1.1942 was damaged in collision with destroyer *Fanning*.

Craven 1945

BAGLEY class destroyers

Bagley	DD386	Norfolk N Yd, Portsmouth	7.1935	3.9.1936	6.1937	stricken 2.1947
Blue	DD387	Norfolk N Yd, Portsmouth	9.1935	27.5.1937	8.1937	sunk 22.8.1942
Helm	DD388	Norfolk N Yd, Portsmouth	9.1935	27.5.1937	10.1937	stricken 2.1947
Mugford	DD389	Boston N Yd, Charlestown	10.1935	31.10.1936	8.1937	nuclear tests 7.1946
Ralph Talbot	DD390	Boston N Yd, Charlestown	10.1935	31.10.1936	10.1937	nuclear tests 7.1946
Henley	DD391	Mare Island N Yd, Vallejo	10.1935	11.1.1937	8.1937	sunk 3.10.1943
Patterson	DD392	Puget Sound N Yd, Bremerton	7.1935	6.5.1937	9.1937	stricken 2.1947
Jarvis	DD393	Puget Sound N Yd, Bremerton	8.1935	6.5.1937	10.1937	sunk 9.8.1942

1646 / 2245 t, 104.0 x 10.8 x 3.9 m, 2 sets General Electric geared steam turbines, 4 Babcock & Wilcox boilers, 49000 hp, 38.5 kts, 504 t oil, 6500 nm (12 kts), complement 158; 4 x 1 – 127/38 Mk 12, 4 x 1 – 12.7 MG, 4 x 4 – 533 TT, 2 DCR (14); QCA sonar.

These ships were built under the FY34 Program and were similar to the Bethlehem-designed *Gridley,* but redesigned to suit the capabilities of the navy yards. They were distinguished by a more durable hull and machinery, repeating those fitted on the *Mahan* class. Although the *Bagley* class destroyers proved to be slower than the *Gridley* class, they were considered by naval experts as much more successful.

Early 1942, all: - 4 x 1 - 12.7 MG; + 6 x 1 - 20/70 Oerlikon. Late 1942, all survived: + 1 x 1 - 20/70 Oerlikon, 4 DCT (44 DC at all). 1942 - 1944, almost all survived: + SC, SG, Mk 12/22 radars.

1944, all survived: + 1 x 2 - 40/56 Bofors.

Jarvis 8.8.1942 during landing on Guadalcanal was damaged by a Japanese air torpedo from G4M bomber and sunk next day by Japanese aircraft S of Guadalcanal. *Blue* 22.8.1942 was badly damaged by a torpedo from Japanese destroyer *Kawakaze* and was scuttled next day off Guadalcanal. *Henley* 3.10.1943 was sunk off coast of New Guinea by Japanese submarine *RO108.*

Mugford 7.8.1942 was damaged by Japanese

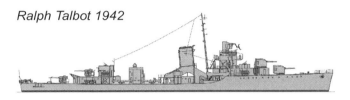

Ralph Talbot 1942

Mugford 1937

aircraft during landing on Guadalcanal and was under repair until the end of the year; 16.9.1944 she was damaged by mine, repairs lasted until November 1944; she was again damaged by kamikaze 5.12.1944 and 5.1.1945. *Helm* was damaged by kamikaze 5.1.1945. *Patterson* and *Ralph Talbot* in the Battle of Savo Island 9.8.1942 were damaged by Japanese ships and were under repair until the end of the year. *Ralph Talbot* was badly damaged by kamikaze 27.4.1945.

SOMERS class destroyers

Somers	DD381	Federal, Kearny	6.1935	13.3.1937	12.1937	stricken 1.1947
Warrington	DD383	Federal, Kearny	10.1935	15.5.1937	2.1938	foundered 13.9.1944
Sampson	DD394	Bath Iron Wks	4.1936	16.4.1937	8.1938	stricken 11.1945
Davis	DD395	Bath Iron Wks	7.1936	30.7.1938	11.1938	stricken 11.1945
Jouett	DD396	Bath Iron Wks	3.1936	24.9.1938	1.1939	stricken 11.1945

2047 / 2767 t, 116.1 x 11.3 x 3.8 m, 2 sets General Electric geared steam turbines, 4 Babcock & Wilcox boilers, 52000 hp, 37 kts, 627 t oil, 7500 nm (15 kts), complement 294; 4 x 2 – 127/38 Mk 12, 2 x 4 – 28/75 Mk 1, 2 x 1 – 12.7 MG, 3 x 4 – 533 TT, 2 DCR (14), QCE sonar.

It was originally planned that under the FY34 Program the next two leaders of the *Porter* class (DD381 and 383) would be built. However, the emergence of

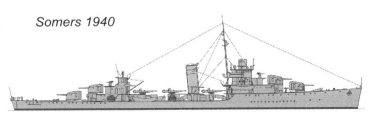

Somers 1940

Somers 1938

the *Mahan* class with new efficient machinery with compact high-pressure boilers and double-reduction gears, has led to a redesign of the leaders with similar machinery. The new machinery made it possible to raise the full speed by half a knot and significantly increase cruising range t the same fuel supply. The rejection of a massive aft superstructure with a director allowed to change the structure of the torpedo armament: a third TT was placed on the centerline (which was also facilitated by the reduction of all smoke ducts into one funnel). This put the new leaders in the first place in the US Navy (and for a time in the world, before the advent of Japanese "torpedo" cruisers) in torpedo salvo. However, spare torpedoes, unlike the leaders of the *Porter* class, were not carried.

A delay in design modification resulted in DD381 and 383 being moved from the FY34 Program to the following year. Three more leaders were built under the FY36 Program.

1942, all: - 2 x 4 - 28/75, 2 x 1 - 12.7 MG, 1 x 4 - 533 TT; + 2 x 2 - 40/56 Bofors, 5 x 1 - 20/70 Oerlikon, 6 DCT (62 DC at all). 1942-1943, almost all survived: + SC, SG, Mk 3 radars.

1943, *Warrington, Sampson, Davis*; autumn 1944, *Somers*: - 1 x 2 - 127/38; + 1 x 2 - 40/56 Bofors, 1 x 1 - 20/70 Oerlikon.

Spring 1944, *Jouett*: - 1 x 2 - 127/38, 1 x 1 - 20/70; + 2 x 2 - 40/56 Bofors. Late 1944, *Davis*: - 3 x 2 - 127/38, 6 x 1 - 20/70, 2 DCT (50 DC at all), Mk 3 radar; + (2 x 2 + 1 x 1) - 127/38 Mk 12 (DP), 2 x 4 - 40/56 Bofors, 2 x 2 - 20/70 Oerlikon, Mk 12/22 radar.

Summer 1945, *Jouett*: - 3 x 2 - 127/38, 1 x 2 - 40/56, 4 x 1 - 20/70, 2 DCT (50 DC at all), Mk 3 radar; + (2 x 2 + 1 x 1) - 127/38 Mk 12 (DP), 2 x 4 - 40/56 Bofors, 2 x 2 - 20/70 Oerlikon, Mk 12/22 radar.

Warrington 13.9.1944 foundered during a storm 175 nm SE of the Bahamas. *Davis* 21.6.1944 was damaged by mine off the coast of Normandy.

BENHAM class destroyers

Benham	DD397	Federal, Kearny	6.1936	16.4.1938	2.1939	sunk 15.11.1942
Ellet	DD398	Federal, Kearny	12.1936	11.6.1938	2.1939	stricken 11.1945
Lang	DD399	Federal, Kearny	4.1937	27.8.1938	3.1939	stricken 11.1945
Mayrant	DD402	Boston N Yd, Charlestown	4.1937	14.5.1938	9.1939	nuclear tests 7.1946
Trippe	DD403	Boston N Yd, Charlestown	4.1937	14.5.1938	11.1939	nuclear tests 7.1946
Rhind	DD404	Philadelphia N Yd	9.1937	28.7.1938	11.1939	nuclear tests 7.1946
Rowan	DD405	Norfolk N Yd, Portsmouth	6.1937	5.5.1938	9.1939	sunk 10.9.1943
Stack	DD406	Norfolk N Yd, Portsmouth	6.1937	5.5.1938	11.1939	nuclear tests 7.1946
Sterett	DD407	Charleston N Yd	12.1936	27.10.1938	8.1939	stricken 2.1947
Wilson	DD408	Puget Sound N Yd, Bremerton	3.1937	12.4.1939	7.1939	nuclear tests 7.1946

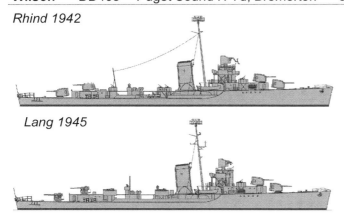

Rhind 1942

Lang 1945

1657 / 2250 t, 103.9 x 10.8 x 3.9 m, 2 sets Westinghouse geared steam turbines, 3 Babcock & Wilcox boilers, 50000 hp, 38.5 kts, 484 t oil, 6500 nm (12 kts), complement 184; 4 x 1 – 127/38 Mk 12, 4 x 1 – 12.7 MG, 4 x 4 – 533 TT, 2 DCR (10), QCE sonar.

The *Benham* class destroyers were built under the FY35 Program and were similar to the *Bagley* class, but with improved machinery with changed structure, and with three larger boilers. The machinery power was increased to 50000 hp to achieve a speed of 38.5 kts, as on the *Gridley* class. Thanks to the presence of only three smoke ducts trunked to the funnel, its size was smaller compared to the previous class. The placement of all main guns in ring-based mounts was the only difference in armament in comparison with predecessors, however, only forward mounts were completely enclosed. Although the *Benham* class ships nominally belonged to a series of so-called 1500-t destroyers (the *Mahan, Bagley,* and *Gridley* classes), their actual standard displacement greatly exceeded the official 1500 t.

1941, *Lang, Mayrant, Trippe, Rhind, Rowan, Stack, Sterett, Wilson*: - 2 x 4 - 533 TT; + 3 x 1 - 12.7 MG, 4

DCT (46 DC at all).

Early 1942, *Benham, Ellet*: - 4 x 1 - 12.7 MG, 2 x 4 - 533 TT; + 6 x 1 - 20/70 Oerlikon, 4 DCT (44 DC at all). Early 1942, *Lang, Mayrant, Trippe, Rhind, Rowan, Stack, Sterett, Wilson*: - 7 x 1 - 12.7 MG; + 6 x 1 - 20/70 Oerlikon. 1942 - 1944, almost all survived: + SC, SG, Mk 12/22 radars. 8.1942-early 1943, all survived: - 2 x 1 - 20/70; + 2 x 2 - 40/56 Bofors.

Summer 1945, *Lang, Sterett, Wilson*: - 4 x 1 - 20/70, 2 x 4 - 533 TT; + 2 x 2 - 40/56 Bofors, 4 x 2 - 20/70 Oerlikon. *Benham* 14.11.1942 in the Battle of Guadalcanal was torpedoed by a Japanese destroyer and sank next day. *Rowan* 11.9.1943 was sunk off Salerno by German MTBs of 7th Flotilla. *Mayrant* 26.7.1943 was damaged by German aircraft. *Sterett* 13.11.1942 was damaged by Japanese ships in the Battle of Guadalcanal and

Ellet 1939

was under repair until February 1943; 9.4.1945 again damaged by kamikaze off Okinawa. *Wilson* 15.4.1945 was damaged off Okinawa by kamikaze.

SIMS class destroyers

Sims	DD409	Bath Iron Wks	7.1937	8.4.1938	8.1939	sunk 7.5.1942
Hughes	DD410	Bath Iron Wks	9.1937	17.6.1939	9.1939	nuclear tests 7.1946
Anderson	DD411	Federal, Kearny	11.1937	4.2.1939	5.1939	nuclear tests 7.1946
Hammann	DD412	Federal, Kearny	1.1938	4.2.1939	8.1939	sunk 6.6.1942
Mustin	DD413	Newport News	12.1937	8.12.1938	9.1939	nuclear tests 7.1946
Russell	DD414	Newport News	12.1937	8.12.1938	11.1939	stricken 11.1945
O`Brien	DD415	Boston N Yd, Charlestown	5.1938	20.10.1939	3.1940	sunk 19.10.1942
Walke	DD416	Boston N Yd, Charlestown	5.1938	20.10.1939	4.1940	sunk 14.11.1942
Morris	DD417	Norfolk N Yd, Portsmouth	6.1938	1.6.1939	3.1940	damaged 6.4.1945, never repaired
Roe	DD418	Charleston N Yd	4.1938	21.6.1939	1.1940	stricken 11.1945
Wainwright	DD419	Norfolk N Yd, Portsmouth	6.1938	1.6.1939	4.1940	nuclear tests 7.1946
Buck	DD420	Philadelphia N Yd	4.1938	22.5.1939	5.1940	sunk 9.10.1943

1764 / 2313 t, 106.2 x 11.0 x 3.9 m, 2 sets Westinghouse geared steam turbines, 3 Babcock & Wilcox boilers, 50000 hp, 35 kts, 459 t oil, 6500 nm (12 kts), complement 192; 5 x 1 – 127/38 Mk 12, 4 x 1 – 12.7 MG, 3 (DD409-413) or 2 (DD414-420) x 4 – 533 TT (16 on DD409-413 or 8 on DD414-420), 2 DCR (10), QCE sonar.

O'Brien 1942

The 12 destroyers of the FY37 Program were originally planned to be built according to a slightly modified design of the *Benham* class, but after lengthy discussions at the General Board, supporters of strong artillery managed to return the fifth 127-mm gun by reducing the number of quadruple TTs to 3. The design of the new destroyer began in the spring of 1936. Initially, her standard displacement was determined by the "treaty" 1500 t, but in May 1936 the Senate ratified the final document of the London Naval Conference, according to which the upper limit of the destroyer's displacement was raised to 3000 t. By this time, the design work was in a phase where significant changes were not possible, so the standard displacement of the new destroyer was increased by 70 t: simply, the real overload included in the design, was officially announced. The armament

arrangement of the new destroyer repeated that adopted on the *Mahan* class. The main difference was that all main guns were installed in base-ring mounts (and No1, 2 and 5 guns in fully enclosed mounts). An important innovation was the emergence of a new Mk 37 fire control system. Besides, in addition to three TT banks, four spare torpedoes were available.

When the first ships went to the trials, it turned out that the building overload reached 120 t and the stability was low. In addition, the experience of service in the North Atlantic showed that side-mounted TTs on the destroyers were prone to severe corrosions and risk of damage by wave impacts. 25.9.1939, shortly after the commissioning of the first ships of the *Sims* class, the Secretary of Navy approved the dismantling of the side TT banks and the transfer of one of them to

Mustin 1942

the centerline and, in addition, the placement of 60 t of ballast. Freed TTs were installed on *Atlanta* class cruisers. Many destroyers were already completed with the modified TT arrangement, and already completed ships changed the TT arrangement in the summer of 1940.

Summer 1940, *Sims, Hughes, Anderson, Hammann, Mustin*: - 1 x 4 - 533 TT.

Summer 1941, all: - 1 x 1 - 127/38; + 4 x 1 - 12.7 MG, 1 DCT ("Y"-gun) (38 DC at all). Late 1941, all: - 8 x 1 - 12.7 MG; + 6 x 1 - 20/70 Oerlikon.

Early 1942, all: - 1 DCT ("Y"-gun); + 4 DCT ("K"-gun) (58 DC at all). 1942 - 1944, almost all survived: + SC, SG, Mk 4 or Mk 12/22 radars.

1-10.1943, all survived: - 2 x 1 - 20/70; + 2 x 2 - 40/56 Bofors.

3.1944, *Wainwright*: - 1 x 4 - 533 TT; + 3 x 1 - 40/56 Bofors.

Spring 1945, *Wainwright*: - 3 x 1 - 40/56; + 1 x 4 - 533 TT. Summer 1945, *Mustin, Morris*: - 2 x 4 - 533 TT; + 2 x 2 - 40/56 Bofors. Summer 1945, *Russell*: - 2 x 1 - 20/70, 2 x 4 - 533 TT; + 2 x 2 - 40/56 Bofors, 2 x 2 - 20/70 Oerlikon. *Sims* 7.5.1942 was sunk in the Coral Sea by Japanese D3A bombers from aircraft carriers *Shokaku* and *Zuikaku* (three direct bomb hits). *Hammann* 6.6.1942 was sunk by Japanese submarine *I168* off Midway. *O'Brien* 15.9.1942 was damaged by a torpedo from Japanese submarine *I15* off Espiritu Santo, was temporarily repaired, but on passage to the USA for final repairs broke in half and foundered off Samoa 19.10.1942. *Buck* was badly damaged 22.8.1942 in the North Atlantic as a result of a collision with s/s *Awatea* and was under repair until 1943, 9.10.1943 she was sunk off Salerno by German submarine *U616*. *Walke* was sunk in the Battle of Guadalcanal 14.11.1942 by gunfire and torpedo from Japanese cruiser *Nagara* and destroyers *Ayanami* and *Uranami*. *Anderson* 1.11.1944 was hit by kamikaze in Leyte Gulf. 10.12.1944 *Hughes* was badly damaged by kamikaze in Leyte Gulf. *Morris* 6.4.1945 off Okinawa was badly damaged by kamikaze, repairs were deemed inexpedient.

BENSON and GLEAVES classes destroyers

Benson subclass						
Benson	DD421	Bethlehem, Quincy	5.1938	15.11.1939	7.1940	to Taiwan 2.1954 (Lo Yang)
Mayo	DD422	Bethlehem, Quincy	5.1938	26.3.1940	9.1940	stricken 12.1970
Madison	DD425	Boston N Yd, Charlestown	9.1938	20.10.1939	8.1940	stricken 6.1968
Lansdale	DD426	Boston N Yd, Charlestown	12.1938	20.10.1939	9.1940	sunk 20.4.1944
Hilary P. Jones	DD427	Charleston N Yd	11.1938	14.12.1939	9.1940	to Taiwan 2.1954 (Han Yang)
Charles F. Hughes	DD428	Puget Sound N Yd, Bremerton	1.1939	16.5.1940	10.1940	stricken 6.1968
Gleaves subclass						
Gleaves	DD423	Bath Iron Wks	5.1938	9.12.1939	6.1940	stricken 11.1969
Niblack	DD424	Bath Iron Wks	8.1938	18.5.1940	8.1940	stricken 7.1968
Livermore (ex-*Grayson*)	DD429	Bath Iron Wks	3.1939	3.8.1940	10.1940	stricken 7.1956
Eberle	DD430	Bath Iron Wks	4.1939	14.9.1940	12.1940	to Greece 1.1951 (Niki)
Plunkett	DD431	Federal, Kearny	3.1939	9.3.1940	7.1940	to Taiwan 2.1959 (Nan Yang)
Kearny	DD432	Federal, Kearny	3.1939	9.3.1940	9.1940	stricken 6.1971

Gwin	DD433	Boston N Yd, Charlestown	6.1939	25.5.1940	1.1941	sunk 13.7.1943
Meredith	DD434	Boston N Yd, Charlestown	6.1939	24.4.1940	3.1941	sunk 15.10.1942
Grayson (ex-Livermore)	DD435	Charleston N Yd	7.1939	7.8.1940	4.1941	stricken 6.1971
Monssen	DD436	Puget Sound N Yd, Bremerton	7.1939	16.5.1940	3.1941	sunk 13.11.1942
Woolsey	DD437	Bath Iron Wks	10.1939	12.2.1941	5.1941	stricken 7.1971
Ludlow	DD438	Bath Iron Wks	12.1939	11.11.1940	3.1941	to Greece 1.1951 (Δόξα [Doxa])
Edison	DD439	Federal, Kearny	3.1940	23.11.1940	1.1941	stricken 4.1966
Ericsson	DD440	Federal, Kearny	3.1940	23.11.1940	3.1941	stricken 6.1970
Wilkes	DD441	Boston N Yd, Charlestown	11.1939	31.5.1940	6.1941	stricken 3.1971
Nicholson	DD442	Boston N Yd, Charlestown	11.1939	31.5.1940	6.1941	to Italy 1.1951 (Aviere)
Swanson	DD443	Charleston N Yd	11.1939	2.11.1940	5.1941	stricken 3.1971
Ingraham	DD444	Charleston N Yd	11.1939	15.2.1941	7.1941	collision 22.8.1942

1911 / 2591 (*Benson* subclass) or 1838 / 2572 (*Gleaves* subclass) t, 106.2 x 11.0 x 4.0 m, 2 sets Westinghouse geared steam turbines, 4 Babcock & Wilcox boilers, 50000 hp, 35 kts, 453 t oil, 3630-3880 nm (20 kts), complement 208; 5 x 1 – 127/38 Mk 12, 6 x 1 – 12.7 MG, 2 x 5 – 533 TT (14), 2 DCR (10), SC, Mk 4 radars (since spring 1941), QCE sonar.

The FY38 program called for the building of eight destroyers, DD421-428. Their design was developed on the basis of the *Sims* class with the replacement of the linear machinery arrangement with *en echelon*. Thus, the number of boilers increased from three to four and there were two funnels. Re-planning of the machinery led to an increase in the standard displacement by 50 t, up to 1620 t. The armament structure was initially the same as on the *Sims* class: 5 127-mm/38 guns, 4 12.7-mm MGs and 3 quadruple 533-mm TTs, 2 of which would be installed on each beam on the upper deck. The detailed study of the design was carried out by two builders, Bethlehem (DD421, 422 and 425-428) and Gibbs & Cox (DD423 and 424), so the ships differed from each other, mainly in the machinery structure. The shape of the funnels was the only noticeable external difference between Bethlehem and Gibbs & Cox designs. The first had funnels with flat sides, the second – round ones. Besides, the latter ships were officially 10 t heavier.

While the design work was going on, negative feedback began to come from existing ships about the arrangement of TTs on either beam: they were exposed to waves, which led to breakdowns and severe corrosion. In this regard, it was decided, starting with the ships of the FY39 Program, which were to be built according to the FY38 design, to rearrange all TTs to the center line,

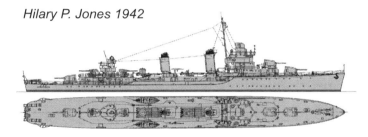

Hilary P. Jones 1942

reducing their number to two, thus providing a place for spare torpedoes. By this time, new quintuple TTs had already appeared, which even made it possible to increase a side torpedo salvo. It is curious that, due to bureaucratic delays, the number of spare torpedoes according to the specification was limited to four. Another important innovation introduced was a machinery with the increased steam parameters. The number of 12.7-mm MGs was increased to six.

Almost all changes in the design were made on the first 8 ships, thanks to a revision of the FY38 Program. They were commissioned with ten TTs and six MGs, and DD423 and 424 received also a new machinery. 8 ships of the *Benson* class were built under the FY40 Program on Gibbs & Cox design. At the time of commission all destroyers of the *Benson* class were heavily overloaded: standard 1620-t displacement was exceeded by 250-300 t.

1941, all: + 1 DCT ("Y"-gun) (22 DC in total).
Early 1942, all: - 6 x 1 - 12.7 MG, 1 x 5 - 533 TT, 1 DCT ("Y"-gun); + 6 x 1 - 20/70 Oerlikon, (4 - 6) DCT (44 - 50 DC at all). 1942, some survived: - 1 x 1 - 127/38; + 1 x 4 - 28/75 Mk 1, 1 x 1 - 20/70 Oerlikon. 1942 - 1944, almost all survived earlier ships: + SC, SG, Mk 4 or Mk 12/22 radar. 1942-1944, almost all survived later ships:

Gleaves 1941

+ SG radar.
1943, some survived: -1 x 4 - 28/75 Mk 1, 1 x 1 - 20/70; + 1 x 1 - 127/38.
Early 1944, all survived: were armed with 4 x 1 - 127/38 Mk 12, 2 x 2 - 40/56 Bofors, 4 x 1 - 20/70 Oerlikon, 2 x 5 - 533 TT, (4 - 6) DCT, 2 DCR (44 - 50). 3.1944, *Benson, Mayo, Gleaves, Niblack, Madison, Lansdale, Hilary P. Jones, Charles F. Hughes, Livermore, Eberle, Plunkett, Kearny, Woolsey, Ludlow, Edison, Ericsson*: - 1 x 5 - 533 TT; + 2 x 1 - 40/56 Bofors, 4 x 1 - 20/70 Oerlikon.
11.1944, *Benson, Mayo, Gleaves, Niblack, Madison, Hilary P. Jones, Charles F. Hughes, Livermore, Eberle, Plunkett, Kearny, Woolsey, Ludlow, Edison, Ericsson*: - 2 x 1 - 40/56, 4 x 1 - 20/70; + 1 x 5 - 533 TT.

Summer 1945, *Gleaves, Niblack, Livermore, Eberle, Plunkett, Kearny, Grayson, Woolsey, Ludlow, Edison, Ericsson, Swanson*: - 4 x 1 - 20/70, 2 x 5 - 533 TT; + 2 x 4 - 40/56 Bofors, 2 x 2 - 20/70 Oerlikon.
Before the US entered the Second World War, 17.10.1941 *Kearny* was torpedoed by German submarine *U568* and was under repair until early 1942.
Ingraham 22.8.1942, escorting AT20 convoy, was lost off Halifax as result of collision with oiler *Chemung* and the explosion of own DCs. *Meredith* 15.10.1942 was sunk by Japanese B5N bombers from *Zuikaku* aircraft carrier off San Cristobal, while escorting a convoy to Guadalcanal. *Monssen* 12.11.1942 was sunk between Savo and Guadalcanal by gunfire from Japanese battleships and destroyers *Asagumo*, *Murasame* and *Samidare*. *Gwin* on the night 14-15.11.1942 was damaged by gunfire from Japanese ships and was under repair until the spring 1943, 13.7.1943 in the Battle of Kolombangara she was sunk by a torpedo from Japanese destroyer *Mikazuki* or *Yukikaze*. *Lansdale* 20.4.1944 was sunk by German air torpedo from Ju 88 bomber off the coast of Algeria.

BRISTOL and LAFFEY classes destroyers

Bristol subclass

Bristol	DD453	Federal, Kearny	12.1940	25.7.1941	10.1941	sunk 12.10.1943
Ellyson	DD454, 11.1944- DMS19	Federal, Kearny	12.1940	25.7.1941	11.1941	fast minesweeper 11.1944, to Japan 19.10.1954 (Asakaze)
Hambleton	DD455, 11.1944- DMS20	Federal, Kearny	12.1940	26.9.1941	12.1941	fast minesweeper 11.1944, stricken 6.1971
Rodman	DD456, 12.1944- DMS21	Federal, Kearny	12.1940	26.9.1941	1.1942	fast minesweeper 12.1944, to Taiwan 7.1955 (Hsien Yang)
Emmons	DD457, 11.1944- DMS22	Bath Iron Wks	11.1940	23.8.1941	12.1941	fast minesweeper 11.1944, sunk 6.4.1945
Macomb	DD458, 11.1944- DMS23	Bath Iron Wks	9.1940	23.9.1941	1.1942	fast minesweeper 11.1944, to Japan 10.1954 (Hatakaze)
Forrest	DD461, 11.1944- DMS24	Boston N Yd, Charlestown	1.1941	14.6.1941	1.1942	fast minesweeper 11.1944, stricken 12.1945
Fitch	DD462, 11.1944- DMS25	Boston N Yd, Charlestown	1.1941	14.6.1941	2.1942	fast minesweeper 11.1944, stricken 7.1971
Corry	DD463	Charleston N Yd	9.1940	28.7.1941	12.1941	sunk 6.6.1944
Hobson	DD464, 11.1944- DMS26	Charleston N Yd	11.1940	8.9.1941	1.1942	fast minesweeper 11.1944, collision 26.4.1952

Aaron Ward	DD483	Federal, Kearny	2.1941	22.11.1941	3.1942	sunk 7.4.1943
Buchanan	DD484	Federal, Kearny	2.1941	22.11.1941	3.1942	to Turkey 4.1949 (Gelibolu)
Duncan	DD485	Federal, Kearny	7.1941	20.2.1942	4.1942	sunk 12.10.1942
Lansdowne	DD486	Federal, Kearny	7.1941	20.2.1942	4.1942	to Turkey 4.1949 (Gaziantep)
Lardner	DD487	Federal, Kearny	9.1941	20.3.1942	5.1942	to Turkey 4.1949 (Gemlik)
McCalla	DD488	Federal, Kearny	9.1941	20.3.1942	5.1942	to Turkey 4.1949 (Giresun)
Mervine	DD489, 5.1945-DMS31	Federal, Kearny	11.1941	3.5.1942	6.1942	fast minesweeper 5.1945, stricken 7.1968
Quick	DD490, 6.1945-DMS32	Federal, Kearny	11.1941	3.5.1942	7.1942	fast minesweeper 6.1945, stricken 1.1972
Carmick	DD493, 6.1945-DMS33	Seattle-Tacoma, Seattle	5.1941	8.3.1942	12.1942	fast minesweeper 6.1945, stricken 7.1971
Doyle	DD494, 6.1945-DMS34	Seattle-Tacoma, Seattle	5.1941	17.3.1942	1.1943	fast minesweeper 6.1945, stricken 12.1970
Endicott	DD495, 5.1945-DMS35	Seattle-Tacoma, Seattle	5.1941	5.4.1942	2.1943	fast minesweeper 5.1945, stricken 11.1969
McCook	DD496, 5.1945-DMS36	Seattle-Tacoma, Seattle	5.1941	30.4.1942	3.1943	fast minesweeper 5.1945, stricken 1.1972
Frankford	DD497	Seattle-Tacoma, Seattle	6.1941	17.5.1942	3.1943	stricken 6.1971
Davison	DD618, 6.1945-DMS37	Federal, Kearny	2.1942	19.7.1942	9.1942	fast minesweeper 6.1945, stricken 1.1972
Edwards	DD619	Federal, Kearny	2.1942	19.7.1942	9.1942	stricken 7.1971
Glennon	DD620	Federal, Kearny	3.1942	26.8.1942	10.1942	sunk 10.6.1944
Jeffers	DD621, 11.1944-DMS27	Federal, Kearny	3.1942	26.8.1942	11.1942	fast minesweeper 11.1944, stricken 7.1971
Maddox	DD622	Federal, Kearny	5.1942	15.9.1942	10.1942	sunk 10.7.1943
Nelson	DD623	Federal, Kearny	5.1942	15.9.1942	11.1942	stricken 3.1968
Baldwin	DD624	Seattle-Tacoma, Seattle	7.1941	14.6.1942	4.1943	wrecked 19.4.1961
Harding	DD625, 11.1944-DMS28	Seattle-Tacoma, Seattle	7.1941	28.6.1942	5.1943	fast minesweeper 11.1944, damaged 6.4.1945, never repaired
Satterlee	DD626	Seattle-Tacoma, Seattle	9.1941	17.7.1942	7.1943	stricken 12.1970
Thompson	DD627, 5.1945-DMS38	Seattle-Tacoma, Seattle	9.1941	10.8.1942	7.1943	fast minesweeper 5.1945, stricken 7.1971
Welles	DD628	Seattle-Tacoma, Seattle	9.1941	7.9.1942	8.1943	stricken 3.1968

Cowie	DD632, 5.1945- DMS39	Boston N Yd, Charlestown	3.1941	27.9.1941	7.1942	fast minesweeper 5.1945, stricken 12.1970
Knight	DD633, 6.1945- DMS40	Boston N Yd, Charlestown	3.1941	27.9.1941	6.1942	fast minesweeper 6.1945, stricken 6.1967
Doran	DD634, 5.1945- DMS41	Boston N Yd, Charlestown	6.1941	10.12.1941	8.1942	fast minesweeper 5.1945, stricken 1.1972
Earle	DD635, 6.1945- DMS42	Boston N Yd, Charlestown	6.1941	10.12.1941	9.1942	fast minesweeper 6.1945, stricken 12.1969
Butler	DD636, 11.1944- DMS29	Philadelphia N Yd	9.1941	12.2.1942	8.1942	fast minesweeper 11.1944, damaged 25.5.1945, never repaired
Gherardi	DD637, 11.1944- DMS30	Philadelphia N Yd	9.1941	12.2.1942	9.1942	fast minesweeper 11.1944, stricken 6.1971
Herndon	DD638	Norfolk N Yd, Portsmouth	8.1941	5.2.1942	12.1942	stricken 7.1971
Shubrick	DD639	Norfolk N Yd, Portsmouth	2.1942	18.4.1942	2.1943	damaged 28.5.1945, never repaired
Beatty	DD640	Charleston N Yd	9.1941	20.12.1941	5.1942	sunk 6.11.1943
Tillman	DD641	Charleston N Yd	9.1941	20.12.1941	6.1942	stricken 6.1970
Stevenson	DD645	Federal, Kearny	7.1942	11.11.1942	12.1942	stricken 6.1968
Stockton	DD646	Federal, Kearny	7.1942	11.11.1941	1.1943	stricken 7.1971
Thorn	DD647	Federal, Kearny	11.1942	28.2.1943	3.1943	stricken 7.1971
Turner	DD648	Federal, Kearny	11.1942	28.2.1943	4.1943	internal explosion 3.1.1944
Laffey subclass						
Laffey	DD459	Bethlehem, San Francisco	1.1941	29.11.1941	3.1942	sunk 13.11.1942
Woodworth	DD460	Bethlehem, San Francisco	4.1941	29.11.1941	4.1942	to Italy 5.1951 (Artigliere)
Farenholt	DD491	Bethlehem, Staten I, Port Richmond	12.1940	19.11.1941	4.1942	stricken 6.1971
Bailey	DD492	Bethlehem, Staten I, Port Richmond	1.1941	19.12.1941	5.1942	stricken 6.1968
Bancroft	DD598	Bethlehem, Quincy	5.1941	31.12.1941	4.1942	stricken 6.1971
Barton	DD599	Bethlehem, Quincy	5.1941	31.1.1942	5.1942	sunk 13.11.1942
Boyle	DD600	Bethlehem, Quincy	12.1941	15.6.1942	8.1942	stricken 6.1971
Champlin	DD601	Bethlehem, Quincy	1.1942	25.6.1942	9.1942	stricken 1.1971
Meade	DD602	Bethlehem, Staten I, Port Richmond	3.1941	15.2.1942	6.1942	stricken 6.1971
Murphy	DD603	Bethlehem, Staten I, Port Richmond	5.1941	29.4.1942	7.1942	stricken 11.1970
Parker	DD604	Bethlehem, Staten I, Port Richmond	6.1941	12.5.1942	8.1942	stricken 7.1971
Caldwell	DD605	Bethlehem, San Francisco	3.1941	15.1.1942	6.1942	stricken 5.1965
Coghlan	DD606	Bethlehem, San Francisco	3.1941	12.2.1942	7.1942	stricken 7.1971

Frazier	DD607	Bethlehem, San Francisco	7.1941	17.3.1942	7.1942	stricken 7.1971
Gansevoort	DD608	Bethlehem, San Francisco	6.1941	11.4.1942	8.1942	stricken 7.1971
Gillespie	DD609	Bethlehem, San Francisco	6.1941	8.5.1942	9.1942	stricken 7.1971
Hobby	DD610	Bethlehem, San Francisco	6.1941	4.6.1942	11.1942	stricken 7.1971
Kalk	DD611	Bethlehem, San Francisco	6.1941	18.7.1942	10.1942	stricken 6.1968
Kendrick	DD612	Bethlehem, San Pedro	5.1941	2.4.1942	9.1942	stricken 5.1966
Laub	DD613	Bethlehem, San Pedro	5.1941	28.4.1942	10.1942	stricken 7.1971
Mackenzie	DD614	Bethlehem, San Pedro	5.1941	27.6.1942	11.1942	stricken 7.1971
McLanahan	DD615	Bethlehem, San Pedro	5.1941	7.9.1942	12.1942	stricken 7.1971
Nields	DD616	Bethlehem, Quincy	6.1942	1.10.1942	1.1943	stricken 9.1970
Ordronaux	DD617	Bethlehem, Quincy	7.1942	9.11.1942	2.1943	stricken 7.1971

1900 / 2600 t, 106.2 x 11.0 or 11.3 (DD634, 635) x 4.9 m, 2 sets Westinghouse geared steam turbines, 4 Babcock & Wilcox boilers, 500000 hp, 35 kts, 453 t oil, 3630-3880 nm (20 kts), complement 208; 4 x 1 – 127/38 Mk 12, (1 x 4 – 28/75 Mk 1, 5 x 1 – 20/70 Oerlikon) (many completed early 1942) or 6 x 1 – 20/70 Oerlikon (completed from early 1942) or (2 x 2 – 40/56 Bofors, 4 x 1 – 20/70 Oerlikon) (completed from autumn 1942) or (2 x 2 – 40/56 Bofors, 7 x 1 – 20/70 Oerlikon) (completed from 11.1942), 1 x 5 – 533 TT, 6 DCT, 2 DCR (62), SC, SG (from spring 1942), Mk 4 or Mk 12/22 (from mid-1943) radars, QCJ sonar.

Despite the appearance of the *Fletcher* design, in order to strengthen the Navy as soon as possible, it was decided in parallel with these large destroyers to continue building the *Benson* class ships, which, due to their smaller dimensions, turned out to be easier to manufacture and could be built faster. The first 12 ships (DD453-464) were ordered in May 1940; 15 more (DD483-497) in September of that year. Almost immediately after the US entered the war, an order was placed for another 41 ships (DD598-628 and 632-641); in February 1942 the last 4 (DD645-648) were ordered. The last two series should be built according to a modified design with 28-mm quadruple MG instead of 127-mm gun No 3.

At the beginning of 1941, it was decided that destroyers, starting with DD453, would be armed not with five, but four 127-mm/38 guns in enclosed mounts. The specification included also two twin 40-mm Bofors and 4 single 20-mm Oerlikons. Since the production of 40-mm guns was started only, as a temporary measure, the installation of quadruple 28-mm MG was envisaged. At the same time, the ASW armament was significantly strengthened: all these destroyers were intended for

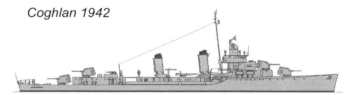

Coghlan 1942

service in the Atlantic and the *Fletchers* for the Pacific). Two DCRs aft (32 DCs) were reinforced by a single DCT (Y-gun) on the quarterdeck (10 DCs). The increased weight of AA and ASW armament led to the fact that the TT had to be abandoned from the stern; this decision was made in August 1941. Nevertheless, the overload caused concern, and in the latest series it was supposed to increase a hull breadth, but in reality, this was only done on the DD634 and 635.

Like their predecessors, the ships of *Bristol* class were built to two detailed designs by Bethlehem (DD459, 460, 491, 492 and 598-617) and Gibbs & Cox (DD453-458, 461-464, 483-497, 618-641 and 645-648). While keeping external differences (funnels with flat sides on the former and round in the section on the latter), the machinery was arranged according to the Gibbs & Cox design. To simplify building and reduce building time, ships of the later series (DD493-497, 618-628 and 645-648) received a superstructure with more technologically advanced rectangular fore part instead of a cylindrical one and a director placed directly on the

Hambleton 1944

Lardner 1945

chart room roof, instead of on a special curbstone.

The first destroyers were commissioned without 40-mm guns, instead of which they received additional Oerlikons (6 guns in total), or temporarily carried 28-mm quadruple mount. Standard Bofors first appeared on DD606. In November 1942, the final armament composition of these destroyers was determined: in addition to 4 Bofors, they had 7 Oerlikons. All earlier destroyers were also rearmed in such a way, and by early 1944 the process was complete.

1942 - 1944, almost all survived earlier ships: + SG radar.

1943, *Carmick, Gillespie, Glennon, Maddox, Nelson, Earle, Gherardi, Herndon, Shubrick, Stockton, Thorn, Turner*: + 3 x 8 - 178 Mousetrap ASWRL.

Early 1944, all survived: were armed by 4 x 1 - 127/38 Mk 12, 2 x 2 - 40/56 Bofors, 7 x 1 - 20/70 Oerlikon, 1 x 5 - 533 TT, 6 DCT, 2 DCR (62). Spring 1944, *Carmick, Glennon, Nelson, Earle, Gherardi, Herndon, Shubrick, Stockton, Thorn*; summer 1945, *Gillespie*: - 3 x 8 - 178 Mousetrap ASWRL. 11-12.1944, DMS *Ellyson, Hambleton, Rodman, Emmons, Macomb, Forrest, Fitch, Hobson, Jeffers, Harding, Butler, Gherardi*: - 1 x 1 - 127/38 (No 4), 1 x 5 - 533 TT, 4 DCT (34 DC at all); + minesweeping gear.

5-6.1945, DMS *Mervine, Quick, Carmick, Doyle, Endicott, McCook, Davison, Thompson, Cowie, Knight, Doran, Earle*: - 1 x 1 - 127/38 (No 4), 5 x 1 - 20/70, 1 x 5 - 533 TT, 6 DCT (32 DC at all); + 2 x 4 - 40/56 Bofors, 2 x 2 - 20/70 Oerlikon, minesweeping gear. Summer 1945, *Frankford, Boyle, Champlin, Murphy, Parker, Gansevoort, Hobby, Kendrick, Laub, Mackenzie, Nields, Ordronaux, Nelson, Baldwin, Welles*: - 5 x 1 - 20/70, 1 x 5 - 533 TT; + 2 x 4 - 40/56 Bofors, 2 x 2 - 20/70 Oerlikon. Summer 1945, *McLanahan*: - 5 x 1 - 20/70, 1 x 5 - 533 TT; + 2 x 2 - 40/56 Bofors, 2 x 2 - 20/70 Oerlikon.

Duncan 11.10.1942 in the Battle of Cape Esperance was badly damaged by Japanese cruiser *Furutaka* and destroyer *Hatsuyuki* and sank next day. *Laffey* 13.11.1942 in the battle of Guadalcanal received hit of Japanese 356-mm shell from battlecruiser *Hiei* and one torpedo from destroyer *Teruzuki*, exploded and sank. *Barton* 13.11.1942 in the Battle of Guadalcanal received two torpedo hits from Japanese destroyer *Yudachi* and sank. *Aaron Ward* 13.11.1942 was badly damaged by gunfire from Japanese ships and was under repair until the beginning of spring 1943; 7.4.1943 she was sunk by Japanese D3A carrier bombers off Guadalcanal while escorting a convoy. *Bailey* 26.3.1943 was badly damaged by 203-mm shell from Japanese heavy cruiser and was under repair until Summer 1943. *Maddox* 10.7.1943 during the landing in Sicily was sunk by German bombers. *Bristol* 12.10.1943 was sunk off the coast of Algeria by German submarine *U371*. *Beatty* 6.11.1943 was sunk in the central Mediterranean by a German air torpedo from Ju 88 bomber. *Turner* 3.1.1944 was lost in New York harbor after a magazine explosion. *Corry* 6.6.1944 during landing in Normandy was blown up by a German mine, broken in half and sank. *Glennon* 8.6.1944 was mined off the coast of Normandy and sunk by German coastal artillery two days later. *Emmons* 6.4.1945 was sunk off Okinawa after hits of 5 kamikazes.

Farenholt 11.10.1942 was badly damaged by Japanese ships and was under repair until March of the following year. *Buchanan* 12.11.1942 was accidentally badly damaged by gunfire from USN ships and was under repair until the following spring. *Hambleton* 11.11.1942 was damaged by a torpedo from German submarine and was repaired until mid-1943. *Murphy* 21.10.1943 was badly damaged SE of New York in a collision with oiler *Bulkoil*, broken in half, the bow sank, the ship was under repair until mid-1944. *Nelson* 11.6.1944 was damaged by German torpedo and was repaired until the end of the year. *Caldwell* 27.6.1945 hit a mine and was under repair until the end of the war. The following ships were attacked and damaged by kamikaze off Okinawa: *Hambleton* (3.4.1945), *Rodman* (6.4.1945, heavy), *Harding* (6.4.1945, heavy), *Jeffers* (12.4.1945, heavy), *Hobson* (16.4.1945, heavy), *Macomb* (3.5.1945, heavy), *Butler* (28.4.1945 and heavy damages 25.5.1945), *Forrest* (27.5.1945, heavy) and *Shubrick* (28.5.1945, heavy). The damage to *Forrest, Harding, Butler* and *Shubrick* proved to be so severe that it was deemed impractical to repair them.

FLETCHER class destroyers

Fletcher	DD445	Federal, Kearny	10.1941	3.5.1942	6.1942	stricken 8.1967
Radford	DD446	Federal, Kearny	10.1941	3.5.1942	7.1942	stricken 15.7.1969
Jenkins	DD447	Federal, Kearny	11.1941	21.6.1942	7.1942	stricken 7.1969
La Vallette	DD448	Federal, Kearny	11.1941	21.6.1942	8.1942	stricken 2.1974

Nicholas	DD449	Bath Iron Wks	3.1941	19.2.1942	6.1942	stricken 1.1970
O'Bannon	DD450	Bath Iron Wks	3.1941	14.3.1942	6.1942	stricken 1.1970
Chevalier	DD451	Bath Iron Wks	4.1941	11.4.1942	7.1942	sunk 7.10.1943
Saufley	DD465	Federal, Kearny	1.1942	19.7.1942	8.1942	stricken 9.1966
Waller	DD466	Federal, Kearny	2.1942	15.8.1942	10.1942	stricken 7.1969
Strong	DD467	Bath Iron Wks	4.1941	17.5.1942	8.1942	sunk 5.7.1943
Taylor	DD468	Bath Iron Wks	8.1941	7.6.1942	8.1942	to Italy 7.1969 (Lanciere)
De Haven	DD469	Bath Iron Wks	9.1941	28.6.1942	9.1942	sunk 1.2.1943
Bache	DD470	Bethlehem, Staten I, Port Richmond	11.1941	27.7.1942	11.1942	stricken 3.1968
Beale	DD471	Bethlehem, Staten I, Port Richmond	12.1941	24.8.1942	12.1942	stricken 10.1968
Guest	DD472	Boston N Yd, Charlestown	9.1941	20.2.1942	12.1942	to Brazil 6.1959 (Pará)
Bennett	DD473	Boston N Yd, Charlestown	12.1941	16.4.1942	2.1943	to Brazil 12.1959 (Paraiba)
Fullam	DD474	Boston N Yd, Charlestown	12.1941	16.4.1942	3.1943	stricken 6.1962
Hudson	DD475	Boston N Yd, Charlestown	2.1942	3.6.1942	3.1943	stricken 12.1972
Hutchins	DD476	Boston N Yd, Charlestown	9.1941	20.2.1942	11.1942	damaged 26.4.1945, repair incomplete
Pringle	DD477	Charleston N Yd	7.1941	2.5.1942	9.1942	sunk 3.5.1945
Stanly	DD478	Charleston N Yd	12.1941	2.5.1942	10.1942	stricken 12.1970
Stevens	DD479	Charleston N Yd	12.1941	24.6.1942	2.1943	stricken 12.1972
Halford	DD480	Puget Sound N Yd, Bremerton	6.1941	29.10.1942	4.1943	stricken 5.1968
Leutze	DD481	Puget Sound N Yd, Bremerton	6.1941	29.10.1942	3.1943	damaged 6.4.1945, never repaired
Philip	DD498	Federal, Kearny	5.1942	13.10.1942	11.1942	stricken 10.1968
Renshaw	DD499	Federal, Kearny	5.1942	13.10.1942	12.1942	stricken 1.1970
Ringgold	DD500	Federal, Kearny	6.1942	11.11.1942	12.1942	to West Germany 7.1959 (Z2)
Schroeder	DD501	Federal, Kearny	6.1942	11.11.1942	1.1943	stricken 10.1972
Sigsbee	DD502	Federal, Kearny	7.1942	7.12.1942	1.1943	stricken 12.1974
Conway	DD507	Bath Iron Wks	11.1941	16.8.1942	10.1942	stricken 11.1969
Cony	DD508	Bath Iron Wks	12.1941	16.8.1942	10.1942	stricken 7.1969
Converse	DD509	Bath Iron Wks	2.1942	30.8.1942	11.1942	to Spain 7.1959 (Almirante Valdéz)
Eaton	DD510	Bath Iron Wks	3.1942	20.9.1942	12.1942	stricken 7.1969
Foote	DD511	Bath Iron Wks	4.1942	11.10.1942	12.1942	stricken 10.1972
Spence	DD512	Bath Iron Wks	5.1942	27.10.1942	1.1943	foundered 18.12.1944
Terry	DD513	Bath Iron Wks	6.1942	22.11.1942	1.1943	stricken 4.1974
Thatcher	DD514	Bath Iron Wks	6.1942	6.12.1942	2.1943	damaged 15.7.1945, repair incomplete
Anthony	DD515	Bath Iron Wks	8.1942	20.12.1942	2.1943	to West Germany 1.1958 (Z1)
Wadsworth	DD516	Bath Iron Wks	8.1942	10.1.1943	3.1943	to West Germany 10.1959 (Z3)
Walker	DD517	Bath Iron Wks	8.1942	31.1.1943	4.1943	to Italy 7.1969 (Fante)

Brownson	DD518	Bethlehem, Staten I, Port Richmond	2.1942	24.9.1942	2.1943	sunk 26.12.1943
Daly	DD519	Bethlehem, Staten I, Port Richmond	4.1942	24.10.1942	3.1943	stricken 12.1974
Isherwood	DD520	Bethlehem, Staten I, Port Richmond	5.1942	24.10.1942	4.1943	to Peru 12.1960 (Almirante Guise)
Kimberly	DD521	Bethlehem, Staten I, Port Richmond	7.1942	4.2.1942	5.1943	to Taiwan 6.1967 (An Yang)
Luce	DD522	Bethlehem, Staten I, Port Richmond	8.1942	6.3.1943	6.1943	sunk 3.5.1945
Abner Read	DD526	Bethlehem, San Francisco	10.1941	18.8.1942	2.1943	sunk 1.11.1944
Ammen	DD527	Bethlehem, San Francisco	11.1941	17.9.1942	3.1943	stricken 10.1960
Mullany (ex-Beatty)	DD528	Bethlehem, San Francisco	1.1942	10.10.1942	4.1943	to Taiwan 10.1971 (Chiang Yang)
Bush	DD529	Bethlehem, San Francisco	2.1942	27.10.1942	5.1943	sunk 6.4.1945
Trathen	DD530	Bethlehem, San Francisco	3.1942	22.10.1942	5.1943	stricken 11.1972
Hazelwood	DD531	Bethlehem, San Francisco	4.1942	20.11.1942	6.1943	stricken 12.1974
Heermann	DD532	Bethlehem, San Francisco	5.1942	5.12.1942	7.1943	to Argentina 8.1961 (Almirante Brown)
Hoel	DD533	Bethlehem, San Francisco	6.1942	19.12.1942	7.1943	sunk 25.10.1944
McCord	DD534	Bethlehem, San Francisco	7.1942	10.1.1943	8.1943	stricken 10.1972
Miller	DD535	Bethlehem, San Francisco	8.1942	7.3.1943	8.1943	stricken 12.1974
Owen	DD536	Bethlehem, San Francisco	9.1942	21.3.1943	9.1943	stricken 4.1973
The Sullivans (ex-Putnam)	DD537	Bethlehem, San Francisco	10.1942	4.4.1943	9.1943	stricken 12.1974
Stephen Potter	DD538	Bethlehem, San Francisco	10.1942	28.4.1943	10.1943	stricken 12.1972
Tingey	DD539	Bethlehem, San Francisco	10.1942	28.5.1943	11.1943	stricken 11.1965
Twining	DD540	Bethlehem, San Francisco	11.1942	11.7.1943	12.1943	to Taiwan 10.1971 (Kwei Yang)
Yarnall	DD541	Bethlehem, San Francisco	12.1942	25.7.1943	12.1943	to Taiwan 6.1968 (Kuen Yang)
Boyd	DD544	Bethlehem, San Pedro	4.1942	29.10.1942	5.1943	to Turkey 10.1969 (İskenderun)
Bradford	DD545	Bethlehem, San Pedro	4.1942	12.12.1942	6.1943	to Greece 9.1962 (Thyella)
Brown	DD546	Bethlehem, San Pedro	6.1942	21.2.1943	7.1943	to Greece 9.1962 (Navarino)
Cowell	DD547	Bethlehem, San Pedro	9.1942	18.3.1943	8.1943	to Argentina 8.1971 (Almirante Storni)
Capps	DD550	Gulf SB, Chickasaw	7.1941	31.5.1942	6.1943	to Spain 5.1957 (Lepanto)
David W. Taylor	DD551	Gulf SB, Chickasaw	7.1941	4.7.1942	6.1943	to Spain 5.1957 (Almirante Ferrándiz)

Evans	DD552	Gulf SB, Chickasaw	7.1941	4.10.1942	12.1943	damaged 11.5.1945, repair incomplete
John D. Henley	DD553	Gulf SB, Chickasaw	7.1941	15.11.1942	12.1943	stricken 5.1968
Franks	DD554	Seattle-Tacoma, Seattle	3.1942	7.12.1942	6.1943	stricken 12.1974
Haggard	DD555	Seattle-Tacoma, Seattle	3.1942	9.2.1943	8.1943	damaged 29.4.1945, never repaired
Hailey	DD556	Seattle-Tacoma, Seattle	4.1942	9.3.1943	9.1943	to Brazil 7.1961 (Pernambuco)
Johnston	DD557	Seattle-Tacoma, Seattle	5.1942	25.3.1943	10.1943	sunk 24.10.1944
Laws	DD558	Seattle-Tacoma, Seattle	5.1942	22.4.1943	11.1943	stricken 4.1973
Longshaw	DD559	Seattle-Tacoma, Seattle	6.1942	4.6.1943	12.1943	sunk 18.5.1945
Morrison	DD560	Seattle-Tacoma, Seattle	6.1942	4.7.1943	12.1943	sunk 3.5.1945
Prichett	DD561	Seattle-Tacoma, Seattle	7.1942	31.7.1943	1.1944	to Italy 1.1970 (Geniere)
Robinson	DD562	Seattle-Tacoma, Seattle	8.1942	28.8.1943	1.1944	stricken 12.1974
Ross	DD563	Seattle-Tacoma, Seattle	9.1942	10.9.1943	2.1944	stricken 12.1974
Rowe	DD564	Seattle-Tacoma, Seattle	12.1942	30.9.1943	3.1944	stricken 12.1974
Smalley	DD565	Seattle-Tacoma, Seattle	2.1943	17.10.1943	3.1944	stricken 4.1965
Stoddard	DD566	Seattle-Tacoma, Seattle	3.1943	19.11.1943	4.1944	stricken 6.1975
Watts	DD567	Seattle-Tacoma, Seattle	3.1943	31.12.1943	4.1944	stricken 2.1974
Wren	DD568	Seattle-Tacoma, Seattle	4.1943	29.1.1944	5.1944	stricken 12.1974
Aulick	DD569	Consolidated, Orange	5.1941	2.3.1942	10.1942	to Greece 8.1959 (Sfendoni)
Charles Ausburne	DD570	Consolidated, Orange	5.1941	6.3.1942	11.1942	to West Germany 4.1960 (Z6)
Claxton	DD571	Consolidated, Orange	7.1941	1.4.1942	12.1942	to West Germany 12.1959 (Z4)
Dyson	DD572	Consolidated, Orange	7.1941	15.4.1942	12.1942	to West Germany 12.1960 (Z5)
Harrison	DD573	Consolidated, Orange	7.1941	7.5.1942	1.1943	to Mexico 5.1968 (Cuauhtémoc)
John Rodgers	DD574	Consolidated, Orange	7.1941	7.5.1942	2.1943	to Mexico 5.1968 (Cuitláhuac)
McKee	DD575	Consolidated, Orange	3.1942	2.8.1942	3.1943	stricken 10.1972
Murray	DD576	Consolidated, Orange	3.1942	16.8.1942	4.1943	stricken 6.1965
Sproston	DD577	Consolidated, Orange	4.1942	31.8.1942	5.1943	stricken 10.1968
Wickes	DD578	Consolidated, Orange	4.1942	13.9.1942	6.1943	stricken 11.1972
William D. Porter	DD579	Consolidated, Orange	5.1942	27.9.1942	7.1943	sunk 10.6.1945
Young	DD580	Consolidated, Orange	5.1942	11.10.1942	7.1943	stricken 5.1968
Charrette	DD581	Boston N Yd, Charlestown	2.1942	3.6.1942	5.1943	to Greece 6.1959 (Velos)
Conner	DD582	Boston N Yd, Charlestown	4.1942	18.7.1942	6.1943	to Greece 9.1959 (Aspis)
Hall	DD583	Boston N Yd, Charlestown	4.1942	18.7.1942	7.1943	to Greece 2.1960 (Lonchi)
Halligan	DD584	Boston N Yd, Charlestown	11.1942	19.3.1943	8.1943	sunk 26.3.1945
Haraden	DD585	Boston N Yd, Charlestown	11.1942	19.3.1943	9.1943	stricken 11.1972
Newcomb	DD586	Boston N Yd, Charlestown	3.1943	4.7.1943	11.1943	damaged 6.4.1945, never repaired
Bell	DD587	Charleston N Yd	2.1942	24.6.1942	3.1943	stricken 11.1972
Burns	DD588	Charleston N Yd	5.1942	8.8.1942	4.1943	stricken 11.1972

Izard	DD589	Charleston N Yd	5.1942	8.8.1942	5.1943	stricken 5.1968
Paul Hamilton	DD590	Charleston N Yd	1.1943	7.4.1943	10.1943	stricken 5.1968
Twiggs	DD591	Charleston N Yd	1.1943	7.4.1943	11.1943	sunk 16.6.1945
Howorth	DD592	Puget Sound N Yd, Bremerton	11.1941	10.1.1943	4.1944	stricken 3.1962
Killen	DD593	Puget Sound N Yd, Bremerton	11.1941	10.1.1943	5.1944	stricken 1.1963
Hart (ex-Mansfield)	DD594	Puget Sound N Yd, Bremerton	8.1943	25.9.1944	11.1944	stricken 4.1973
Metcalfe	DD595	Puget Sound N Yd, Bremerton	8.1943	25.9.1944	11.1944	stricken 1.1971
Shields	DD596	Puget Sound N Yd, Bremerton	8.1943	25.9.1944	2.1945	to Brazil 7.1972 (Maranhão)
Wiley	DD597	Puget Sound N Yd, Bremerton	8.1943	25.9.1944	2.1945	stricken 5.1968
Abbot	DD629	Bath Iron Wks	9.1942	17.2.1943	4.1943	stricken 12.1974
Braine	DD630	Bath Iron Wks	10.1942	7.3.1943	5.1943	to Argentina 8.1961 (Domecq García)
Erben	DD631	Bath Iron Wks	10.1942	21.3.1943	5.1943	to South Korea 5.1963 (Chungmu)
Hale	DD642	Bath Iron Wks	11.1942	4.4.1943	6.1943	to Columbia 12.1960 (Antioquia)
Sigourney	DD643	Bath Iron Wks	12.1942	24.4.1943	6.1943	stricken 12.1974
Stembel	DD644	Bath Iron Wks	12.1942	8.5.1943	7.1943	to Argentina 8.1961 (Rosales)
Albert W. Grant	DD649	Charleston N Yd	12.1942	29.5.1943	11.1943	stricken 4.1971
Caperton	DD650	Bath Iron Wks	1.1943	22.5.1943	7.1943	stricken 12.1974
Cogswell	DD651	Bath Iron Wks	2.1943	5.6.1943	8.1943	to Turkey 10.1969 (İzmit)
Ingersoll	DD652	Bath Iron Wks	2.1943	28.6.1943	8.1943	stricken 1.1970
Knapp	DD653	Bath Iron Wks	3.1943	10.7.1943	9.1943	stricken 3.1972
Bearss	DD654	Gulf SB, Chickasaw	7.1942	25.7.1943	4.1944	stricken 12.1974
John Hood	DD655	Gulf SB, Chickasaw	10.1942	25.10.1943	7.1944	stricken 12.1974
Van Valkenburgh	DD656	Gulf SB, Chickasaw	11.1942	19.12.1943	8.1944	to Turkey 2.1967 (İzmir)
Charles J. Badger	DD657	Bethlehem, Staten I, Port Richmond	9.1942	3.4.1943	7.1943	stricken 1.1974
Colahan	DD658	Bethlehem, Staten I, Port Richmond	10.1942	3.5.1943	8.1943	stricken 8.1966
Dashiell	DD659	Federal, Kearny	10.1942	6.2.1943	3.1943	stricken 12.1974
Bullard	DD660	Federal, Kearny	10.1942	28.2.1943	4.1943	stricken 12.1972
Kidd	DD661	Federal, Kearny	10.1942	28.2.1943	4.1943	stricken 12.1974
Bennion	DD662	Boston N Yd, Charlestown	3.1943	4.7.1943	12.1943	stricken 4.1971
Heywood L. Edwards	DD663	Boston N Yd, Charlestown	7.1943	6.10.1943	1.1944	to Japan 3.1959 (Ariake)
Richard P. Leary	DD664	Boston N Yd, Charlestown	7.1943	6.10.1943	2.1944	to Japan 3.1959 (Yugure)
Bryant	DD665	Charleston N Yd	12.1942	29.5.1943	12.1943	stricken 6.1968
Black	DD666	Federal, Kearny	11.1942	28.3.1943	5.1943	stricken 9.1969
Chauncey	DD667	Federal, Kearny	11.1942	28.3.1943	5.1943	stricken 10.1972
Clarence K. Bronson	DD668	Federal, Kearny	12.1942	18.4.1943	6.1943	to Turkey 1.1967 (İstanbul)

Cotten	DD669	Federal, Kearny	2.1943	12.6.1942	7.1943	stricken 12.1974
Dortch	DD670	Federal, Kearny	3.1943	20.6.1943	8.1943	to Argentina 8.1961 (Espora)
Gatling	DD671	Federal, Kearny	3.1943	20.6.1943	8.1943	stricken 12.1974
Healy	DD672	Federal, Kearny	3.1943	4.7.1943	9.1943	stricken 12.1974
Hickox	DD673	Federal, Kearny	3.1943	4.7.1943	9.1943	to South Korea 11.1968 (Pusan)
Hunt	DD674	Federal, Kearny	3.1943	1.8.1943	9.1943	stricken 12.1974
Lewis Hancock	DD675	Federal, Kearny	3.1943	1.8.1943	9.1943	to Brazil 8.1967 (Piauí)
Marshall	DD676	Federal, Kearny	4.1943	29.8.1943	10.1943	stricken 7.1969
McDermut	DD677	Federal, Kearny	6.1943	17.10.1943	11.1943	stricken 4.1965
McGowan	DD678	Federal, Kearny	6.1943	14.11.1943	12.1943	to Spain 11.1960 (Jorge Juan)
McNair	DD679	Federal, Kearny	6.1943	14.11.1943	1.1944	stricken 12.1974
Melvin	DD680	Federal, Kearny	7.1943	17.10.1943	11.1943	stricken 12.1974
Hopewell	DD681	Bethlehem, San Pedro	10.1942	2.5.1943	9.1943	stricken 1.1970
Porterfield	DD682	Bethlehem, San Pedro	10.1942	13.6.1943	10.1943	stricken 3.1975
Stockham	DD683	Bethlehem, San Francisco	12.1942	25.6.1943	2.1944	stricken 12.1974
Wedderburn	DD684	Bethlehem, San Francisco	1.1943	1.8.1943	3.1944	stricken 10.1969
Picking	DD685	Bethlehem, Staten I, Port Richmond	11.1942	1.6.1943	9.1943	stricken 3.1975
Halsey Powell	DD686	Bethlehem, Staten I, Port Richmond	2.1943	30.6.1943	10.1943	to South Korea 4.1968 (Seoul)
Uhlmann	DD687	Bethlehem, Staten I, Port Richmond	3.1943	30.7.1943	11.1943	stricken 7.1972
Remey	DD688	Bath Iron Wks	3.1943	25.7.1943	9.1943	stricken 12.1974
Wadleigh	DD689	Bath Iron Wks	4.1943	7.8.1943	10.1943	to Chile 7.1962 (Blanco Encalada)
Norman Scott	DD690	Bath Iron Wks	4.1943	28.8.1943	11.1943	stricken 4.1973
Mertz	DD691	Bath Iron Wks	5.1943	11.9.1943	11.1943	stricken 10.1970
Callaghan	DD792	Bethlehem, San Pedro	2.1943	1.8.1943	11.1943	sunk 28.7.1945
Cassin	DD793	Bethlehem, San Pedro	3.1943	12.9.1943	12.1943	stricken 12.1974
Irwin	DD794	Bethlehem, San Pedro	5.1943	31.10.1943	2.1944	to Brazil 5.1968 (Santa Catharina)
Preston	DD795	Bethlehem, San Pedro	6.1943	12.12.1943	3.1944	to Turkey 11.1969 (İçel)
Benham	DD796	Bethlehem, Staten I, Port Richmond	4.1943	30.8.1943	12.1943	to Peru 10.1961 (Villar)
Cushing	DD797	Bethlehem, Staten I, Port Richmond	5.1943	30.9.1943	1.1944	to Brazil 7.1961 (Parana)
Monssen	DD798	Bethlehem, Staten I, Port Richmond	6.1943	30.10.1943	2.1944	stricken 2.1963
Jarvis	DD799	Seattle-Tacoma, Seattle	6.1943	14.2.1944	6.1944	to Spain 11.1960 (Alcalá Galiano)
Porter	DD800	Seattle-Tacoma, Seattle	7.1943	13.3.1944	6.1944	stricken 10.1972
Colhoun	DD801	Seattle-Tacoma, Seattle	8.1943	10.4.1944	7.1944	sunk 6.4.1945
Gregory	DD802	Seattle-Tacoma, Seattle	8.1943	8.5.1944	7.1944	stricken 5.1966
Little	DD803	Seattle-Tacoma, Seattle	9.1943	22.5.1944	8.1944	sunk 3.5.1945
Rooks	DD804	Seattle-Tacoma, Seattle	10.1943	6.6.1944	9.1944	to Chile 7.1962 (Cochrane)

La Vallette 1942

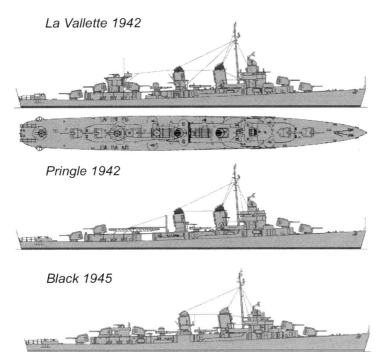

Pringle 1942

Black 1945

2276-2325 / 2924-3005 t, 114.7 x 12.1 x 4.2 m, 2 sets General Electric geared steam turbines, 4 Babcock & Wilcox boilers, 60000 hp, 38 kts, 492 t oil, 6500 nm (15 kts), complement 273; 5 x 1 – 127/38 Mk 12, 1 (DD466, 469, 477-480, 507, 508, 569) or 2 (DD470-472, 476, 498-502, 509-513, 570-573) or 3 (DD473-475, 481, 514-521, 526-530, 544, 574-577, 581, 587-589, 629-631, 659-661, 666, 667) or 5 (DD522, 531-541, 545-547, 550-568, 578-580, 582-586, 590, 591-597, 642-644, 649-658, 662-665, 668-691, 792-804) x 2 – 40/56 Bofors, 1 x 4 – 28/75 Mk 1 (DD445-451, 465, 467, 468), 4 (DD445-451, 465-469, 478, 507, 508, 569) or 6 (DD470-472, 476, 498-502, 509-513, 550-553, 570-573, 578-580, 592, 593) or 7 (DD522, 531-541, 545-547, 554-568, 582-586, 590, 591, 594-597, 642-644, 649-658, 662-665, 668-691, 792-804) or 8 (DD477, 479, 480) or 10 (DD518-521, 526-530, 544, 581, 587-589, 629-631, 659-661, 666, 667) or 11 (DD473-475, 481, 514-517, 574-577) x 1 – 20/70 Oerlikon, 2 or 1 (DD477, 479, 480) x 5 – 533 TT, 6 DCT, 2 DCR (56), 1 catapult,

Fletcher 1942

1 seaplane (SOC, SO3C) (DD477, 479, 480); SC or SR (from 11.1944), SG, Mk 4 or Mk 12/22 (from 5.1943) radars, QCJ sonar.

The most famous destroyers of the US Navy. The history of their creation dates back to October 1939, when the war, that began in Europe led to the abolition of any restrictions on the construction of new ships, and the question arose before the General Board: which destroyers to build next. Initially, the decision was in favor of medium-sized destroyers, which were cheaper and faster to built. According to the initial requirements (displacement not more than 1600 t, at least four 127-mm guns and 10 TTs, 36-ks maximum speed) 6 variants were prepared, not much different from the previous *Benson* and *Sims* classes. However, at the end of the year, the restriction of 1600 t was removed, as it became clear that it was impossible to implement additional requirements within this displacement. This meant that a place had to be found for a 28-mm quadruple MG mount and strengthened anti-submarine armament. Under the changed requirements of the Bureau of Construction, a new design was prepared, with the displacement increased to 2100 t. The Secretary of the Navy approved it already 27.1.1940. In the design, for the first time in 20 years, the designers returned to a flush-deck hull shape with a noticeable deck sheer. This decision provided some savings in the estimated hull weight, but reduced the internal volume, "squeezing out" a part of the spaces into superstructures; by the way, the large size of the fore superstructure became almost the only reason for design criticism. The power of the machinery was increased to 60000 hp to achieve 38-kt speed. At that time there was an opinion that the speed of the destroyer should exceed the speed of the ships escorted by her by at least 5 kts. Unfortunately, the overload did not allow to approach the coveted value: with a displacement close to full, it was rarely possible to exceed 34 kts. At first glance, the armament structure compared to the previous *Benson* class changed slightly: 28-mm MGs and 4 DCTs were added, but it is important, that at the design stage the *Fletcher* had a displacement reserve for new weapons systems. Splinter-proof armor was another important innovation: the sides and the deck over the machinery were protected by 13-mm armor plates, the directors had 19-mm protection.

An order for the first 24 ships (DD445-451 and 465-481) was placed in June-July 1940. An order for 100 ships (DD498-597) followed in September. 16.12.1940, the order for seven ships was cancelled (DD523-525, 542, 543, 548 and 549), but 6 new ships of the class were ordered (DD629-631 and 642-644). In February 1941, the order for DD503 *Stevenson*, DD504 *Stockton*, DD505 *Thorn* and DD506 *Turner* (Federal, Kearny) was cancelled, instead of which 4 *Benson* class destroyers were to be built (DD645-648). When the US entered the war, 56 more destroyers were ordered (DD649-691 and 792-804). In 1941, summarizing the experience of the war in Europe, it was concluded that an open bridge was preferred over a traditional closed one, from which it was inconvenient to monitor the air. Open bridges were received by DD518-522, 526-541, 544-547, 554-568, 581-591, 594-597, 629-644, 649-691 and 792-804.

With the designed composition of light AA armament (1 quadruple 28-mm and 4 single 20-mm guns), only the very first ships were commissioned: from September 1942, all destroyers received twin 40-mm Bofors instead of "Chicago pianos". Soon the number of Oerlikons was increased to 6, and many destroyers received the second Bofors on the quarterdeck; the last position was subsequently recognized as unsuccessful and by the beginning of 1943 that Bofors was replaced by three Oerlikons. In February 1943, a new standard for *Fletchers* AA armament was set: three twin Bofors (two abeam the aft funnel and one between No 2 and 3 guns) and 10 (on destroyers with an open bridge) or 11 (with a closed bridge) Oerlikons. The variant adopted in June 1943, with five twin Bofors, (the additional pair was installed fwd of the fore superstructure) and 7 Oerlikons became the definitive standard for this class. Many destroyers were commissioned with this arrangement of small-caliber guns. Many earlier ships were converted to this standard: by the end of 1944, 157 destroyers out of 166 operable *Fletchers* were armed in this way.

Six ships (DD476-481) were planned to be equipped with catapult for seaplanes. It was mounted on the superstructure aft of the aft funnel in the place of the removed No 2 TT and No 3 127-mm gun. Three ships were commissioned with a catapult. Operating experience showed that a seaplane aboard a destroyer was not really needed, and the remained three destroyers were completed in standard configuration. By the second half of 1944, the former "aircraft-carriers" also lost their catapults and received standard armament.

DD482 *Watson* and DD452 *Persival* (both Federal, Kearny) were to be built as test ships with experimental machinery: diesel on the first and turbines with high-parameter steam on the second. In connection with the outbreak of the war, work on them was suspended, and in January 1946 their building was ultimately cancelled. Autumn 1942, all completed and survived except *Pringle, Stevens, Halford*: were armed with 5 x 1 - 127/38 Mk 12, 1 x 2 - 40/56 Bofors, 4 x 1 - 20/70 Oerlikon, 2 x 5 - 533 TT, 6 DCT, 2 DCR (56). Late 1942, all completed and survived except *Pringle, Stevens, Halford*: were armed with 5 x 1 - 127/38 Mk 12, 2 x 2 - 40/56 Bofors, 6 x 1 - 20/70 Oerlikon, 2 x 5 - 533 TT, 6 DCT, 2 DCR (56). Early 1943, all completed and survived except *Pringle, Stevens, Halford*: were armed with 5 x 1 - 127/38 Mk 12, 1 x 2 - 40/56 Bofors, 9 x 1 - 20/70 Oerlikon, 2 x 5 - 533 TT, 6 DCT, 2 DCR (56). 1943-1944, all completed and survived: were armed with 5 x 1 - 127/38 Mk 12, 3 x 2 -

Ringgold 1944

40/56 Bofors, (10 - 11) x 1 - 20/70 Oerlikon, 2 x 5 - 533 TT, 6 DCT, 2 DCR (56). 1943-1944, *Fletcher, Radford, Jenkins, La Valette, Nicholas, O`Bannon, Chevalier, Saufley, Waller, Strong, Taylor, Bache, Beale, Guest, Hutchins, Pringle, Stanly, Stevens, Halford, Philip, Renshaw, Ringgold, Scroeder, Sigsbee, Cottway, Cony, Converse, Eaton, Foote, Spence, Terry, Aulick, Charles Ausburne, Claxton, Dyson, Harrison*: were armed with 5 x 1 - 127/38 Mk 12, 3 x 2 - 40/56 Bofors, 11 x 1 - 20/70 Oerlikon, 2 x 5 - 533 TT, 6 DCT, 2 DCR (56). Late 1943, all completed and survived: were armed with 5 x 1 - 127/38 Mk 12, 5 x 2 - 40/56 Bofors, 7 x 1 - 20/70 Oerlikon, 2 x 5 - 533 TT, 6 DCT, 2 DCR (56).

Summer 1945, *Fletcher, Radford, Jenkins, La Valette, Bennet, Stanly, Renshaw, Sigsbee, Isherwood, Kimberly, Mullany, Trathen, Hazelwood, McCord, Miller, Owen, The Sullivans, Stephen Potter, Tingey, Twining, Capps, Franks, Hailey, Ross, Sproston, Wickes, Young, Izard, Howorth, Sigourney, Charles J. Badger, Kidd, Bryant, Clarence K. Bronson, Cotten, Gatling, Healy, Hickox, Hunt, Lewis Hancock, Marshall, Hopewell, Porterfield, Picking, Halsey Powell, Porter, Gregory, Rooks*: were armed with 5 x 1 - 127/38 Mk 12, (2 x 4 + 3 x 2) - 40/56 Bofors, (4 x 2 + 3 x 1) - 20/70 Oerlikon, 1 x 5 - 533 TT, 6 DCT, 2 DCR (56).

De Haven 1.2.1943 was sunk by Japanese D3A bombers (3 bombs) off Cape Esperance. *Strong* 5.7.1943 in the Battle of New Georgia was sunk by a torpedo from Japanese destroyer *Minazuki, Mocjizuki* or *Kawakaze. Chevalier* 6.10.1943 received a torpedo hit from Japanese destroyer *Yugumo*, badly damaged and 7.10.1943 sunk by a torpedo from destroyer *La Vallette. Brownson* 26.12.1943 was sunk off Cape Gloucester by Japanese D3A bombers. *Hoel* and *Johnston* 25.10.1944 were sunk in the Battle of Samar by gunfire from Japanese battlecruiser *Kongo* and

Wadsworth 1944

Cushing 1944

cruiser *Haguro. Abner Read* 1.11.1944 was sunk by kamikaze off Samar. *Spence* 18.12.1944 off Luzon capsized and foundered during a typhoon. *Halligan* 26.3.1945 was mined off Okinawa, her magazines detonated, wreck was washed ashore at Takashiki Island and destroyed by gunfire. *Longshaw* 18.5.1945 during landing on Okinawa ran aground at Ose Reef, could not be salvaged, badly damaged by Japanese coastal guns and abandoned by the own crew after the detonation of fore magazines. *Twiggs* 16.6.1945 was sunk by a Japanese air torpedo from G4M bomber off Okinawa.

Bush, Mullany and *Colhoun* (6.4.1945) were sunk by kamikaze off Okinawa. *Little, Pringle* (3.5.1945), *Luce* and *Morrison* (4.5.1945), *William D. Porter* (10.6.1945) and *Callaghan* (28.7.1945) followed them later. *La Vallette* 30.1.1943 was damaged by a Japanese air torpedo and was under repair until August 1943.

O'Bannon 6.10.1943 was damaged in collision with destroyer *Chevalier* (the bow was destroyed) and was repaired until December 1943. *Abner Read* 18.8.1943 was damaged by Japanese mine (the stern was broken off), repair lasted until the beginning of 1944. *Cony* 27.10.1943 was damaged by Japanese aircraft (2 bombs), later she was repaired. *Foote* 2.11.1943 was damaged by a torpedo from Japanese destroyer, repairs lasted about half a year. *Wadleigh* 16.9.1944 was damaged by a Japanese mine and was repaired until the end of the

year. *Fullam* 12.9.1944 was damaged in collision with APD (ex-DD) *Noa* and was under repair for over two months. *Ross* 19.10.1944 was damaged by a Japanese mine. *Morrison* 24.10.1944 was damaged in collision with aircraft carrier *Princeton* during salvage operations, she lost both funnels and a mast, was under repair for more than a month. *Albert W. Grant* 24.10.1944 during the Battle of the Surigao Strait was mistakenly badly damaged by gunfire from USN ships. *David W. Taylor* 5.1.1945 was damaged by a Japanese mine. *Philips* 10.1.1945 was damaged by Japanese explosive boat.

La Vallette and *Radford* 14.2.1945 were damaged by Japanese mines. *Renshaw* 21.2.1945 was damaged by a torpedo from Japanese submarine *RO43*, repaired until October 1945. *Charles J. Badger* 8.4.1945 was badly damaged by explosive boat. *Jenkins* 30.4.1945 was damaged by a mine.

During the landing in the Philippines, kamikaze damaged *Claxton* and *Ammen* (1.11.1944), *Saufley* and *Aulick* (29.11.1944), *Haraden* (13.12.1944), *Paul Hamilton* and *Howorth* (15.12.1944), *Foote* (21.12.1944) and *Bryant* (22.12.1944), *Pringle* (29.12.1944), *Newcomb* and *Richard P. Leary* (6.1.1945).

During landing on Okinawa, kamikaze damaged *Halsey Powell* (20.3.1945), *Kimberly* (25.3.1945), *Porterfield* (26.3.1945), *Pritchett* (2.4.1945, another time 28.7.1945), *Franks* (2.4.1945), *Sproston* (3.4.1945), *Leutze, Harrison, Howorth, Newcomb* and *Bennett* (6.4.1945), *Longshaw* (7.4.1945), *Hutchins* (6.4.1945 and 26.4.1945), *Gregory* (8.4.1945), *Bullard* and *Kidd* (11.4.1945), *Stanly* (12.4.1945), *Cassin Young* (12.4.1945 and repeatedly 29.7.1945), *Sigsbee, Hunt* and *Dashiell* (14.4.1945), *Bryant* (16.4.1945), *Benham* (17.4.1945), *Isherwood* (22.4.1945), *Hudson* (22.4.1945, repeatedly 4.5.1945), *Wadsworth* (22.4.1945 and 28.4.1945), *Daly* and *Twiggs* (28.4.1945), *Bennion* (28.4.1945, second time 30.4.1945), *Hazelwood* and *Haggard* (29.4.1945), *Bache* (3.5.1945 and 13.5.1945), *Cowell* (4.5.1945 and 25.5.1945), *Brown* (10.5.1945), *Evans* (11.5.1945), *Thatcher* (20.5.1945, repeatedly 19.7.1945), *Guest* (24.5.1945), *Anthony* (26.5.1945 and 7.6.1945) and *Braine* (26.5.1945). The damage to *Leutze, Newcomb* and *Haggard* were so severe that repairs were deemed impractical.

Cogswell 1945

ALLEN M. SUMNER class destroyers

Allen M. Sumner	DD692	Federal, Kearny	7.1943	15.12.1943	1.1944	stricken 8.1973
Moale	DD693	Federal, Kearny	8.1943	16.1.1944	2.1944	stricken 7.1973
Ingraham	DD694	Federal, Kearny	8.1943	16.1.1944	3.1944	to Greece 7.1971 (Miaoulis)
Cooper	DD695	Federal, Kearny	8.1943	9.2.1944	3.1944	sunk 3.12.1944
English	DD696	Federal, Kearny	10.1943	27.2.1944	5.1944	to Taiwan 8.1970 (Huei Yang)

Charles S. Sperry	DD697	Federal, Kearny	10.1943	13.3.1944	5.1944	to Chile 1.1974 (Ministro Zenteno)
Ault	DD698	Federal, Kearny	11.1943	26.3.1944	5.1944	stricken 7.1973
Waldron	DD699	Federal, Kearny	11.1943	26.3.1944	6.1944	to Colombia 10.1973 (Santander)
Haynsworth	DD700	Federal, Kearny	12.1943	15.4.1944	6.1944	to Taiwan 5.1970 (Yuen Yang)
John W. Weeks	DD701	Federal, Kearny	1.1944	21.5.1944	7.1944	stricken 8.1970
Hank	DD702	Federal, Kearny	1.1944	21.5.1944	8.1944	to Argentina 7.1972 (Seguí)
Wallace L. Lind	DD703	Federal, Kearny	2.1944	14.6.1944	9.1944	to South Korea 12.1973 (Daegu)
Borie	DD704	Federal, Kearny	2.1944	4.7.1944	9.1944	to Argentina 7.1972 (Bouchard)
Compton	DD705	Federal, Kearny	3.1944	17.9.1944	11.1944	to Brazil 9.1972 (Matto Grosso)
Gainard	DD706	Federal, Kearny	3.1944	17.9.1944	11.1944	stricken 2.1971
Soley	DD707	Federal, Kearny	4.1944	8.9.1944	12.1944	stricken 2.1970
Harlan R. Dickson	DD708	Federal, Kearny	5.1944	17.12.1944	2.1945	stricken 7.1972
Hugh Purvis	DD709	Federal, Kearny	5.1944	17.12.1944	3.1945	to Turkey 2.1972 (Zafer)
Barton	DD722	Bath Iron Wks	5.1943	10.10.1943	12.1943	stricken 10.1968
Walke	DD723	Bath Iron Wks	6.1943	27.10.1943	1.1944	stricken 2.1974
Laffey	DD724	Bath Iron Wks	6.1943	21.11.1943	2.1944	stricken 3.1975
O'Brien	DD725	Bath Iron Wks	12.1943	8.12.1943	2.1944	stricken 2.1972
Meredith	DD726	Bath Iron Wks	7.1943	21.12.1943	3.1944	sunk 9.6.1944
De Haven	DD727	Bath Iron Wks	8.1943	9.1.1944	3.1944	to South Korea 12.1973 (Incheon)
Mansfield	DD728	Bath Iron Wks	8.1943	29.1.1944	4.1944	to Argentina 6.1974 (spares)
Lyman K. Swenson	DD729	Bath Iron Wks	9.1943	12.2.1944	5.1944	to Taiwan 5.1974 (spares)
Collett	DD730	Bath Iron Wks	10.1943	5.3.1944	5.1944	to Argentina 6.1974 (Piedra Buena)
Maddox	DD731	Bath Iron Wks	10.1943	19.3.1944	6.1944	to Taiwan 7.1972 (Po Yang)
Hyman	DD732	Bath Iron Wks	11.1943	8.4.1944	6.1944	stricken 11.1969
Mannert L. Abele	DD733	Bath Iron Wks	12.1943	23.4.1944	7.1944	sunk 12.4.1945
Purdy	DD734	Bath Iron Wks	12.1943	7.5.1944	7.1944	stricken 7.1973
Robert H. Smith	DM23	Bath Iron Wks	1.1944	25.5.1944	8.1944	minelayer, stricken 2.1971
Thomas E. Fraser	DM24	Bath Iron Wks	1.1944	10.6.1944	8.1944	minelayer, stricken 11.1970
Shannon	DM25	Bath Iron Wks	2.1944	24.6.1944	9.1944	minelayer, stricken 11.1970
Harry F. Bauer	DM26	Bath Iron Wks	3.1944	9.7.1944	9.1944	minelayer, stricken 8.1971
Adams	DM27	Bath Iron Wks	3.1944	23.7.1944	10.1944	minelayer, stricken 12.1970

Tolman	DM28	Bath Iron Wks	4.1944	13.8.1944	10.1944	minelayer, stricken 12.1970
Drexler	DD741	Bath Iron Wks	4.1944	3.9.1944	11.1944	sunk 28.5.1945
Blue	DD744	Bethlehem, Staten I, Port Richmond	1.1943	28.11.1943	3.1944	stricken 2.1974
Brush	DD745	Bethlehem, Staten I, Port Richmond	6.1943	28.12.1943	4.1944	to Taiwan 12.1969 (Hsiang Yang)
Taussig	DD746	Bethlehem, Staten I, Port Richmond	8.1943	25.1.1943	5.1944	to Taiwan 5.1974 (Lo Yang)
Samuel N. Moore	DD747	Bethlehem, Staten I, Port Richmond	9.1943	23.2.1944	6.1944	to Taiwan 12.1969 (Heng Yang)
Harry E. Hubbard	DD748	Bethlehem, Staten I, Port Richmond	10.1943	24.3.1944	7.1944	stricken 10.1969
Henry A. Wiley	DM29	Bethlehem, Staten I, Port Richmond	11.1943	21.4.1944	8.1944	minelayer, stricken 10.1970
Shea	DM30	Bethlehem, Staten I, Port Richmond	12.1943	20.5.1944	9.1944	minelayer, stricken 9.1973
J. William Ditter	DM31	Bethlehem, Staten I, Port Richmond	1.1944	4.7.1944	10.1944	minelayer, damaged 6.6.1945, never repaired
Alfred A. Cunningham	DD752	Bethlehem, Staten I, Port Richmond	2.1944	3.8.1944	11.1944	stricken 2.1974
John R. Pierce	DD753	Bethlehem, Staten I, Port Richmond	3.1944	1.9.1944	12.1944	stricken 2.7.1973
Frank E. Evans	DD754	Bethlehem, Staten I, Port Richmond	4.1944	3.10.1944	2.1945	collision 2.6.1969
John A. Bole	DD755	Bethlehem, Staten I, Port Richmond	5.1944	1.11.1944	3.1945	to Taiwan 5.1974 (spares)
Beatty	DD756	Bethlehem, Staten I, Port Richmond	7.1944	30.11.1944	3.1945	to Venezuela 8.1972 (Carabobo)
Putnam	DD757	Bethlehem, San Francisco	7.1943	26.3.1944	10.1944	stricken 8.1973
Strong	DD758	Bethlehem, San Francisco	7.1943	23.4.1944	3.1945	to Brazil 10.1973 (Rio Grande de Norte)
Lofberg	DD759	Bethlehem, San Francisco	11.1943	12.8.1944	4.1945	to Taiwan 5.1974 (spares)
John W. Thomason	DD760	Bethlehem, San Francisco	11.1943	30.9.1944	10.1945	to Taiwan 5.1974 (Nan Yang)
Buck	DD761	Bethlehem, San Francisco	2.1944	11.3.1945	6.1946	to Brazil 7.1973 (Alagoas)
Henley	DD762	Bethlehem, San Francisco	2.1944	8.4.1945	10.1946	stricken 7.1973
Lowry	DD770	Bethlehem, San Pedro	8.1943	6.2.1944	7.1944	to Brazil 10.1973 (Espírito Santo)
Lindsey	DM32	Bethlehem, San Pedro	9.1943	5.3.1944	8.1944	minelayer, stricken 10.1970
Gwin	DM33	Bethlehem, San Pedro	10.1943	9.4.1944	9.1944	minelayer, to Turkey 8.1971 (Muavenet)
Aaron Ward	DM34	Bethlehem, San Pedro	12.1943	5.5.1944	10.1944	minelayer, damaged 3.5.1945, never repaired
Hugh W. Hadley	DD774	Bethlehem, San Pedro	2.1944	16.7.1944	11.1944	damaged 11.5.1945, never repaired

Willard Keith	DD775	Bethlehem, San Pedro	3.1944	29.8.1944	12.1944	to Colombia 7.1972 (Caldas)
James C. Owens	DD776	Bethlehem, San Pedro	4.1944	1.10.1944	2.1945	to Brazil 7.1973 (Sergipe)
Zellars	DD777	Todd-Pacific, Seattle	12.1943	19.7.1944	10.1944	to Iran 3.1971 (Babr)
Massey	DD778	Todd-Pacific, Seattle	1.1944	19.8.1944	11.1944	stricken 9.1973
Douglas H. Fox	DD779	Todd-Pacific, Seattle	1.1944	30.9.1944	12.1944	to Chile 1.1974 (Ministro Portales)
Stormes	DD780	Todd-Pacific, Seattle	2.1944	4.11.1944	1.1945	to Iran 2.1972 (Palang)
Robert K. Huntington	DD781	Todd-Pacific, Seattle	2.1944	5.12.1944	3.1945	to Venezuela 10.1973 (Falcon)
Bristol	DD857	Bethlehem, San Pedro	5.1944	29.10.1944	3.1945	to Taiwan 9.1969 (Hua Yang)

2610 / 3218 t, 114.8 x 12.5 x 4.3 m, 2 sets General Electric geared steam turbines, 4 Babcock & Wilcox boilers, 60000 hp, 36.5 kts, 504 t oil, 3300 nm (20 kts), complement 336; 3 x 2 – 127/38 Mk 12, (2 x 4 + 2 x 2) or (3 x 4 + 2 x 2) (DD760-762) – 40/56 Bofors, 11 x 1 or 10 x 2 (DD760-762) – 20/70 Oerlikon, 2 or 1 (DD760-762) x 5 – 533 TT, 6 DCT, 2 DCR (56); SC or SR (from 6.1944), SG, Mk 12/22 radars, QGA sonar.

Minelayers: 3 x 2 – 127/38 Mk 12, (2 x 4 + 2 x 2) – 40/56 Bofors, 8 x 1 – 20/70 Oerlikon, 4 DCT, 2 DCR (56), 120 mines; SG, SR, Mk 12/22 radars, QGA sonar.

With all the advantages, *Fletchers* did not fully meet the requirements of the US Navy. Firstly, the noticeable side profile, which at that time was considered unacceptable for destroyers, was criticized (this claim was also made to their predecessors, the *Benson* class). The creation of a new design of a "barely visible" destroyer, which was supposed to be armed with automatic 127-mm/54 DP guns (still in the design stage), was seriously considered. Since the design from scratch required too much time, they resorted to a much more rational way: they reworked the existing design of the *Fletcher* class, replacing the bow 127-mm guns with one twin, which allowed to reduce the size of the fore superstructure. Alas, it turned out that there was no place for most systems and equipment. The impossibility of reducing the outline profile without a radical alteration was recognized, but the work done was not in vain. By this time, it became necessary to redesign the *Fletcher* to accommodate additional AA armament. On existing ships, this proved inconvenient both because of the threat of reduced stability and the lack of space on the upper deck and superstructures. The way out was supposed to be the replacement of single 127-mm mounts with twin ones in the "barely visible" destroyer design. After the installation of three twin gun mounts instead of five single ones, it became possible to place TTs separately from each other, reducing the risk of their simultaneous destruction, and allocate space for additional AA MGs. To keep the stability, the hull was increased by 0.4 m

De Haven 1944

in breadth. Approved by the Secretary of Navy in April 1942, the design provided for armament consisted of 3 twin 127-mm/38 DP mounts, 2 twin 40-mm/56 and 4 20-mm/70 AA guns and 2 quintuple 533-mm TTs. In August, the order for 69 ships followed; one more, DD857, was laid down as the *Gearing* class but completed as *Allen M. Sumner* class.

In the summer of 1943, changes were made to the design regarding AA armament: in addition to the twin 40-mm/56 Bofors two quadruple were added, and a number of 20-mm Oerlikons was increased to 11. During the trials, overloaded ships could not approach the design speed of 36.5 kts; with a displacement close to full, they barely reached 31 kts, and with normal displacement they were hardly faster, making 33 kts.

In the summer of 1944, it was decided to complete 12 destroyers of the *Allen M Sumner* class (DD735-740, 749-751 and 771-773, hull indexes were changed to DM23-34 respectively) as fast minelayers. Mine rails for 120 mines were fitted on the quarter deck. To compensate for the top weight increased by more than 100 t, it was planned to remove both TTs, three Oerlikons aft and two to six DCT. Despite the measures taken, the

Allen M. Sumner 1944

Henry A. Wiley 1944

177 bombers. *Cooper* 3.12.1944 was sunk by a torpedo from Japanese destroyer *Kuwa* in Ormoc Bay. *Mannert L. Abele* 12.4.1945 at Okinawa received hits of two kamikazes (include one Ohka jet) and sank. *Drexler* 28.5.1945 was sunk by the kamikaze off Okinawa.

The following destroyers were badly damaged off Okinawa as a result of kamikaze actions: *O'Brien* (26.3.1945), *Haynsworth* (6.4.1945), *Purdy*, *Zellars* (12.4.1945), *Laffey* (15.4.1945), *Hugh W. Hadley* (11.5.1945), *Douglas H. Fox* (17.5.1945), *Stormes* (25.5.1945), *Robert H. Smith* (25.3.1945), *Adams* (27.3.1945 and 31.3.1945), *Lindsey* (12.4.1945), *Shannon* (29.4.1945), *Shea* (22.4.1945 and 3.5.1945), *Aaron Ward* (3.5.1945), *Gwin* (4.5.1945), *J. William Ditter* (6.6.1945); all were repaired, except *Hugh W. Hadley*, *J. William Ditter* and *Aaron Ward*, who were deemed not worth repairing.

stability of ships with a full mine load caused concern and were practically not used for their intended purpose.

In 1945, the AA armament of the class was significantly strengthened: the aft TT was replaced by the third quadruple Bofors, and single Oerlikons by 10 twins.

Summer 1945, all completed and survived destroyers: - 11 x 1 - 20/70, 1 x 5 - 533 TT; + 1 x 4 - 40/56 Bofors, 10 x 2 - 20/70 Oerlikon.

Meredith 8.6.1944 hit a mine off the coast of Normandy and sank next day by German He

Borie 2.4.1945 was damaged in a collision, 9.8.1945 damaged by kamikaze, repaired after the war. *Harry F. Bauer* 5.4.1945 was damaged by a Japanese air torpedo off Okinawa. She was urgently repaired, but from 29.4.1945 to 6.6.1945 she was three times damaged by kamikazes and repaired after the war.

GEARING class destroyers

Gearing	DD710	Federal, Kearny	8.1944	18.2.1945	5.1945	stricken 7.1973
Eugene A. Greene	DD711	Federal, Kearny	8.1944	18.3.1945	6.1945	to Spain 8.1972 (Churucca)
Gyatt	DD712	Federal, Kearny	9.1944	15.4.1945	7.1945	stricken 10.1969
Kenneth D. Bailey	DD713	Federal, Kearny	9.1944	17.6.1945	7.1945	to Iran 1.1975 (spares)
William R. Rush	DD714	Federal, Kearny	10.1944	8.7.1945	9.1945	to South Korea 7.1978 (Gangwon)
William M. Wood	DD715	Federal, Kearny	11.1944	29.7.1945	11.1945	stricken 12.1976
Wiltsie	DD716	Federal, Kearny	3.1945	31.8.1945	1.1946	to Pakistan 4.1977 (Tariq)
Theodore E. Chandler	DD717	Federal, Kearny	4.1945	20.10.1945	3.1946	stricken 4.1975
Hamner	DD718	Federal, Kearny	4.1945	24.11.1945	7.1946	to Taiwan 2.1981 (Yun Yang)
Epperson	DDE719	Federal, Kearny	5.1945	22.12.1945	3.1949	to Pakistan 4.1977 (Taimur)
Castle	DD720	Federal, Kearny	7.1945	1946	-	cancelled 2.1946
Woodrow R. Thompson	DD721	Federal, Kearny	8.1945	1946	-	cancelled 2.1946
Frank Knox	DD742	Bath Iron Wks	5.1944	17.9.1944	12.1944	to Greece 1.1971 (Themistoklis)
Southerland	DD743	Bath Iron Wks	5.1945	5.10.1944	12.1944	stricken 2.1981
William C. Lawe	DD763	Bethlehem, San Francisco	3.1944	21.5.1945	12.1946	stricken 1.1983
Lloyd Thomas	DD764	Bethlehem, San Francisco	3.1944	5.10.1945	3.1947	to Taiwan 10.1972 (Dang Yang)

Keppler	DD765	Bethlehem, San Francisco	4.1944	24.6.1946	5.1947	to Turkey 6.1972 (Tınaztepe)
Lansdale	DD766	Bethlehem, San Francisco	4.1944	20.12.1946	-	cancelled 1.1946
Seymour D. Owens	DD767	Bethlehem, San Francisco	4.1944	24.2.1947	-	cancelled 1.1946
Hoel	DD768	Bethlehem, San Francisco	4.1944	-	-	cancelled 9.1946
Abner Read	DD769	Bethlehem, San Francisco	5.1944	-	-	cancelled 9.1946
Rowan	DD782	Todd-Pacific, Seattle	3.1944	29.12.1944	3.1945	to Taiwan 12.1975 (Chao Yang)
Gurke	DD783	Todd-Pacific, Seattle	7.1944	15.2.1945	5.1945	to Greece 3.1977 (Tompazis)
McKean	DD784	Todd-Pacific, Seattle	9.1944	31.3.1945	6.1945	to Turkey 11.1982 (spares)
Henderson	DD785	Todd-Pacific, Seattle	10.1944	28.5.1945	8.1945	to Pakistan 9.1980 (Tughril)
Richard B. Anderson	DD786	Todd-Pacific, Seattle	12.1944	7.7.1945	10.1945	to Taiwan 6.1977 (Kai Yang)
James E. Kyes	DD787	Todd-Pacific, Seattle	12.1944	4.8.1945	2.1946	to Taiwan 4.1973 (Chien Yang)
Hollister	DD788	Todd-Pacific, Seattle	1.1945	9.10.1945	3.1946	stricken 10.1979
Eversole	DD789	Todd-Pacific, Seattle	2.1945	8.1.1946	5.1946	to Turkey 7.1973 (Gayret)
Shelton	DD790	Todd-Pacific, Seattle	3.1945	8.3.1946	6.1946	to Taiwan 4.1973 (Lao Yang)
Seaman	DD791	Todd-Pacific, Seattle	7.1945	20.5.1946	-	cancelled 3.1961
Chevalier	DD805	Bath Iron Wks	6.1944	29.10.1944	1.1945	to South Korea 7.1972 (Chungbuk)
Higbee	DD806	Bath Iron Wks	6.1944	12.11.1944	1.1945	stricken 7.1979
Benner	DD807	Bath Iron Wks	7.1944	30.11.1944	2.1945	stricken 2.1974
Dennis J. Buckley	DD808	Bath Iron Wks	7.1944	20.12.1944	3.1945	stricken 7.1973
Corry	DD817	Consolidated, Orange	4.1945	28.7.1945	2.1946	to Greece 7.1981 (Kriezis)
New	DD818	Consolidated, Orange	4.1945	18.8.1945	4.1946	to South Korea 2.1977 (Daejeon)
Holder	DD819	Consolidated, Orange	4.1945	25.8.1945	5.1946	to Ecuador 9.1978 (Presidente Eloy Alfaro)
Rich	DD820	Consolidated, Orange	5.1945	5.10.1945	7.1946	stricken 12.1977
Johnston	DD821	Consolidated, Orange	6.1945	19.10.1945	8.1946	to Taiwan 2.1981 (Zheng Yang)
Robert H. McCard	DD822	Consolidated, Orange	6.1945	9.11.1945	10.1946	to Turkey 6.1980 (Kılıç Ali Paşa)
Samuel B. Roberts	DD823	Consolidated, Orange	6.1945	30.11.1945	12.1946	stricken 11.1970
Basilone	DDE824	Consolidated, Orange	7.1945	22.12.1945	7.1949	stricken 11.1977
Carpenter	DDK825	Consolidated, Orange	7.1945	28.12.1945	12.1949	to Turkey 2.1981 (Anıttepe)
Agerholm	DD826	Bath Iron Wks	9.1945	30.3.1946	6.1946	stricken 12.1978
Robert A. Owens	DDK827	Bath Iron Wks	10.1945	15.7.1946	9.1949	to Turkey 2.1982 (Alçıtepe)

Timmerman	EDD828	Bath Iron Wks	10.1945	19.5.1951	9.1952	auxiliary 1.1954
Myles C. Fox	DD829	Bath Iron Wks	8.1944	13.1.1945	3.1945	to Greece 8.1980 (Apostolis)
Everett F. Larson	DD830	Bath Iron Wks	9.1944	28.1.1945	4.1945	to South Korea 10.1972 (Jeonbuk)
Goodrich	DD831	Bath Iron Wks	9.1944	25.2.1945	4.1945	stricken 2.1974
Hanson	DD832	Bath Iron Wks	10.1944	11.3.1945	5.1945	to Taiwan 4.1973 (Liao Yang)
Herbert J. Thomas	DD833	Bath Iron Wks	10.1944	25.3.1945	5.1945	to Taiwan 5.1974 (Han Yang)
Turner	DD834	Bath Iron Wks	11.1944	8.4.1945	6.1945	stricken 9.1969
Charles P. Cecil	DD835	Bath Iron Wks	12.1944	22.4.1945	6.1945	to Greece 8.1980
George K. Mackenzie	DD836	Bath Iron Wks	12.1944	13.5.1945	7.1945	stricken 10.1976
Sarsfield	DD837	Bath Iron Wks	1.1945	27.5.1945	7.1945	to Taiwan 10.1977 (Te Yang)
Ernest G. Small	DD838	Bath Iron Wks	1.1945	14.6.1945	8.1945	to Taiwan 4.1971 (Fu Yang)
Power	DD839	Bath Iron Wks	2.1945	30.6.1945	9.1945	to Taiwan 10.1977 (Shen Yang)
Glennon	DD840	Bath Iron Wks	3.1945	14.7.1945	10.1945	stricken 10.1976
Noa	DD841	Bath Iron Wks	3.1945	30.7.1945	11.1945	to Spain 10.1973 (Blas de Lezo)
Fiske	DD842	Bath Iron Wks	4.1945	8.9.1945	11.1945	to Turkey 6.1980 (Piyale Paşa)
Warrington	DD843	Bath Iron Wks	4.1945	27.9.1945	12.1945	to Taiwan 4.1973 (spares)
Perry	DD844	Bath Iron Wks	5.1945	25.10.1945	1.1946	stricken 7.1973
Baussell	DD845	Bath Iron Wks	5.1945	19.11.1945	2.1946	stricken 5.1978
Ozbourn	DD846	Bath Iron Wks	6.1945	22.12.1945	3.1946	stricken 6.1975
Robert L. Wilson	DD847	Bath Iron Wks	7.1945	5.1.1946	3.1946	stricken 9.1974
Witek	DD848	Bath Iron Wks	7.1945	2.2.1946	4.1946	stricken 9.1968
Richard E. Kraus	DD849	Bath Iron Wks	7.1945	2.3.1946	5.1946	to South Korea 10.1972 (Gwangju)
Joseph P. Kennedy, Jr.	DD850	Bethlehem, Quincy	4.1945	26.7.1945	12.1945	stricken 7.1973, preserved
Rupertus	DD851	Bethlehem, Quincy	5.1945	21.9.1945	3.1946	to Greece 7.1973 (Kountouriotis)
Leonard F. Mason	DD852	Bethlehem, Quincy	8.1945	4.1.1946	6.1946	to Taiwan 3.1978 (Sui Yang)
Charles H. Roan	DD853	Bethlehem, Quincy	9.1945	15.3.1946	9.1946	to Turkey 9.1973 (Mareşal Fevzi Çakmak)
Robert A. Owens	DD854	Bethlehem, Staten I, Port Richmond	7.1945	-	-	cancelled 1945
	DD855	Bethlehem, Staten I, Port Richmond	8.1945	-	-	cancelled 1945
Fred T. Berry	DD858	Bethlehem, San Pedro	7.1944	28.1.1945	5.1945	stricken 9.1970
Norris	DD859	Bethlehem, San Pedro	8.1944	25.2.1945	6.1945	to Turkey 7.1974 (Kocatepe)
McCaffery	DD860	Bethlehem, San Pedro	10.1944	12.4.1945	7.1945	stricken 9.1973
Harwood	DD861	Bethlehem, San Pedro	10.1944	22.5.1945	9.1945	to Turkey 12.1971 (Kocatepe)

Vogelgesang	DD862	Bethlehem, Staten I, Port Richmond	8.1944	15.1.1945	4.1945	to Mexico 2.1982 (Quetzalcóatl)
Steinaker	DD863	Bethlehem, Staten I, Port Richmond	9.1944	13.2.1945	5.1945	to Mexico 2.1982 (Netzahualcóyotl)
Harold J. Ellison	DD864	Bethlehem, Staten I, Port Richmond	10.1944	14.3.1945	6.1945	to Pakistan 10.1983 (Shah Jahan)
Charles R. Ware	DD865	Bethlehem, Staten I, Port Richmond	11.1944	12.4.1945	7.1945	stricken 12.1974
Cone	DD866	Bethlehem, Staten I, Port Richmond	11.1944	10.5.1945	8.1945	to Pakistan 10.1982 (Alamgir)
Stribling	DD867	Bethlehem, Staten I, Port Richmond	1.1945	8.6.1945	9.1945	stricken 7.1976
Brownson	DD868	Bethlehem, Staten I, Port Richmond	2.1945	7.7.1945	11.1945	stricken 9.1976
Arnold J. Isbell	DD869	Bethlehem, Staten I, Port Richmond	3.1945	6.8.1945	1.1946	to Greece 12.1973 (Sachtouris)
Fechteler	DD870	Bethlehem, Staten I, Port Richmond	4.1945	19.9.1945	3.1946	stricken 9.1970
Damato	DD871	Bethlehem, Staten I, Port Richmond	5.1945	21.11.1945	4.1946	to Pakistan 9.1980 (Tippu Sultan)
Forrest Royal	DD872	Bethlehem, Staten I, Port Richmond	6.1945	17.1.1946	6.1946	to Turkey 3.1971 (Adatepe)
Hawkins *(ex-Beatty)*	DD873	Consolidated, Orange	5.1944	7.10.1944	2.1945	stricken 10.1979
Duncan	DD874	Consolidated, Orange	5.1944	27.10.1944	2.1945	stricken 9.1973
Henry W. Tucker	DD875	Consolidated, Orange	5.1944	8.11.1944	3.1945	to Brazil 12.1973 (Marcílio Dias)
Rogers	DD876	Consolidated, Orange	6.1944	20.11.1944	3.1945	to South Korea 8.1981 (Jeonju)
Perkins	DD877	Consolidated, Orange	6.1944	7.12.1944	4.1945	to Argentina 1.1973 (Py)
Vesole	DD878	Consolidated, Orange	7.1944	29.12.1944	4.1945	stricken 12.1976
Leary	DD879	Consolidated, Orange	8.1944	20.1.1945	5.1945	to Spain 10.1973 (Lángara)
Dyess	DD880	Consolidated, Orange	8.1944	26.1.1945	5.1945	to Greece 7.1981 (Themistoklis)
Bordelon	DD881	Consolidated, Orange	9.1944	3.3.1945	6.1945	stricken 2.1977
Furse	DD882	Consolidated, Orange	9.1944	9.3.1945	7.1945	to Spain 8.1972 (Gravina)
Newman K. Perry	DD883	Consolidated, Orange	10.1944	17.1.1945	7.1945	to South Korea 7.1981 (Gueonggi)
Floyd B. Parks	DD884	Consolidated, Orange	10.1944	31.3.1945	7.1945	stricken 7.1973
John R. Craig	DD885	Consolidated, Orange	11.1944	14.4.1945	8.1945	stricken 7.1979
Orleck	DD886	Consolidated, Orange	11.1944	12.5.1945	9.1945	to Turkey 10.1982 (Yücetepe)
Brinkley Bass	DD887	Consolidated, Orange	12.1944	26.5.1945	10.1945	to Brazil 12.1973 (Mariz e Barros)
Stickell	DD888	Consolidated, Orange	1.1945	16.6.1945	10.1945	to Greece 7.1972 (Kanaris)
O`Hare	DD889	Consolidated, Orange	1.1945	22.6.1945	11.1945	to Spain 10.1973 (Méndez Núñez)
Meredith	DD890	Consolidated, Orange	1.1945	28.6.1945	10.1945	to Turkey 6.1979 (Savaştepe)

Gearing 1945

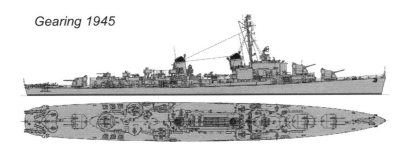

Eugene A. Green 1945

2616 / 3460 t, 119.0 x 12.5 x 4.4 m, 2 sets General Electric geared steam turbines, 4 Babcock & Wilcox boilers, 60000 or 100000 (DD828) hp, 36.8 kts, 740 t oil, 4500 nm (20 kts), complement 336; 3 x 2 – 127/38 Mk 12, (2 x 4 + 2 x 2) (DD742, 743, 782, 805-808, 829-831, 862, 873-878) or (3 x 4 + 2 x 2) (DD710-718, 763-765, 783-790, 817-823, 826, 828, 832-853, 858-861, 863-872, 879-890) – 40/56 Bofors, 11 x 1 – 20/70 Oerlikon, 2 (DD742, 743, 782, 808, 862) or 1 (DD710-718, 763-765, 783-790, 805-807, 817-823, 826, 828-831, 836-853, 858-861, 863-878, 884-890) x 5 – 533 TT, 6 DCT, 2 DCR

McKean 1945

(56); SG (except DD764, 765), SG-6 (DD764, 765), SP (DD742, 743, 805-808, 829-835, 873-883), SR, Mk 12/22 (except DD764, 765), Mk 25 (DD764, 765) radars, QGA sonar.

DDE and *DDK*: 3182 t, 119.2 x 12.5 x 4.3 m, 2 sets General Electric geared steam turbines, 4 Babcock & Wilcox boilers, 60000 hp, 32 kts, 740 t oil; 2 x 2 – 127/38 Mk 12 (DDE), 2 x 2 – 76/50 Mk 22, 4 x 2 – 20/70 Oerlikon, 4 – 533 TT (10) (DDE) or 4 x 1 – 533 TT (DDK), 1 (DDE) or 2 (DDK) x 1 Weapon Alfa ASWRL, 2 (DDE) or 1 (DDK) x 24 Hedgehog ASWRL, 4 DCT (DDK), 2 DCR, SPS-6, SPS-10, Mk 25 (DDE), Mk 35 radars, QHb sonar, 4 Mk 31 torpedo decoy launchers, FXE torpedo decoy.

In the design of the *Gearing* class, the fundamental flaw of the *Allen M. Sumner* class ships, their overload caused by the installation of additional antiaircraft armament was corrected. Due to the inserted midship 4.3-m section the fuel supply was increased by almost one and a half times. Besides, the higher L/B ratio allowed even a slight increase in speed, although the *Gearing* never exceed 32 kts at full displacement.

A total of 153 ships (of which 98 were completed) were ordered. DD857 was completed on the *Allen M. Sumner* design. An order for 47 unlaid ships (DD809-816, 854-856, 891-926), was cancelled in 1945, 2 more ships (DD768 and 769) were broken up on the stocks, and 5 incomplete destroyers (DD720, 721, 766, 767 and 791) were suspended and sold for scrap later. *Epperson, Basilone, Carpenter,* and *Robert A. Owens* were completed as escort destroyers (DDE) and ASW destroyers (DDK).

Summer 1945, all completed and survived: - 1 x 5 - 533 TT; + 1 x 4 - 40/56 Bofors.

DESTROYER ESCORTS

'GMT' (EVARTS) class destroyer escorts

Bayntun	DE1	Boston N Yd, Charlestown	4.1942	27.6.1942	(1.1943) / 8.1945	to the UK 1.1943-8.1945 (Bayntun), stricken 11.1945
Bazely	DE2	Boston N Yd, Charlestown	4.1942	27.6.1942	(2.1943) / 8.1945	to the UK 2.1943-8.1945 (Bazely), stricken 11.1945
	DE3	Boston N Yd, Charlestown	9.1942	23.11.1942	(3.1943)	to the UK 3.1943 (Berry)
	DE4	Boston N Yd, Charlestown	9.1942	23.11.1942	(3.1943)	to the UK 3.1943 (Blackwood)
Evarts	DE5	Boston N Yd, Charlestown	10.1942	7.12.1942	4.1943	stricken 10.1945
Wyffels	DE6	Boston N Yd, Charlestown	10.1942	7.12.1942	4.1943	to China 8.1945 (Tai Kang)
Griswold	DE7	Boston N Yd, Charlestown	11.1942	9.1.1943	4.1943	stricken 12.1945
Steele	DE8	Boston N Yd, Charlestown	11.1942	9.1.1943	4.1943	stricken 12.1945
Carlson	DE9	Boston N Yd, Charlestown	11.1942	9.1.1943	5.1943	stricken 1.1946
Bebas	DE10	Boston N Yd, Charlestown	11.1942	9.1.1943	5.1943	stricken 11.1945
Crouter	DE11	Boston N Yd, Charlestown	12.1942	26.1.1943	5.1943	stricken 12.1945
	DE12	Boston N Yd, Charlestown	12.1942	26.1.1943	(6.1943)	to the UK 6.1943 (Burges)
Brennan *(ex-Bentinck)*	DE13	Mare Island N Yd, Vallejo	2.1942	22.8.1942	1.1943	stricken 10.1945
Doherty *(ex-Berry)*	DE14	Mare Island N Yd, Vallejo	2.1942	29.8.1942	2.1943	stricken 1.1946
Austin *(ex-Duckworth)*	DE15	Mare Island N Yd, Vallejo	3.1942	25.9.1942	5.1943	stricken 1.1946
Edgar G. Chase *(ex-Burges)*	DE16	Mare Island N Yd, Vallejo	3.1942	26.9.1942	3.1943	stricken 11.1945
Edward C. Daly *(ex-Byard)*	DE17	Mare Island N Yd, Vallejo	4.1942	21.10.1942	4.1943	stricken 1.1946
Gilmore *(ex-Halder)*	DE18	Mare Island N Yd, Vallejo	4.1942	22.10.1942	4.1943	stricken 1.1946
Burden R. Hastings *(ex-Duckworth)*	DE19	Mare Island N Yd, Vallejo	4.1942	20.11.1942	5.1943	stricken 11.1945
Le Hardy *(ex-Duff)*	DE20	Mare Island N Yd, Vallejo	4.1942	21.11.1942	5.1943	stricken 11.1945
Harold C. Thomas *(ex-Essington)*	DE21	Mare Island N Yd, Vallejo	4.1942	18.12.1942	5.1943	stricken 11.1945
Wileman	DE22	Mare Island N Yd, Vallejo	4.1942	19.12.1942	6.1943	stricken 11.1945

Charles R. Greer	DE23	Mare Island N Yd, Vallejo	9.1942	18.1.1943	6.1943	stricken 11.1945
Whitman	DE24	Mare Island N Yd, Vallejo	9.1942	19.1.1943	7.1943	stricken 11.1945
Wintle	DE25	Mare Island N Yd, Vallejo	10.1942	18.2.1943	7.1943	stricken 11.1945
Dempsey	DE26	Mare Island N Yd, Vallejo	10.1942	19.2.1943	7.1943	stricken 11.1945
Duffy	DE27	Mare Island N Yd, Vallejo	10.1942	16.4.1943	8.1943	stricken 11.1945
Emery *(ex-Eisner)*	DE28	Mare Island N Yd, Vallejo	10.1942	17.4.1943	8.1943	stricken 11.1945
Stadtfeld	DE29	Mare Island N Yd, Vallejo	11.1942	17.5.1943	8.1943	stricken 11.1945
Martin	DE30	Mare Island N Yd, Vallejo	11.1942	18.5.1943	9.1943	stricken 12.1945
Sederstrom *(ex-Gillette)*	DE31	Mare Island N Yd, Vallejo	12.1942	15.6.1943	9.1943	stricken 11.1945
Fleming	DE32	Mare Island N Yd, Vallejo	12.1942	16.6.1943	9.1943	stricken 11.1945
Tisdale	DE33	Mare Island N Yd, Vallejo	1.1943	28.6.1943	10.1943	stricken 11.1945
Eisele	DE34	Mare Island N Yd, Vallejo	1.1943	29.6.1943	10.1943	stricken 11.1945
Fair	DE35	Mare Island N Yd, Vallejo	2.1943	27.7.1943	10.1943	stricken 11.1945
Manlove	DE36	Mare Island N Yd, Vallejo	2.1943	28.7.1943	11.1943	stricken 11.1945
Greiner	DE37	Puget Sound N Yd, Bremerton	9.1942	20.5.1943	8.1943	stricken 12.1945
Wyman	DE38	Puget Sound N Yd, Bremerton	9.1942	3.6.1943	9.1943	stricken 1.1946
Lovering	DE39	Puget Sound N Yd, Bremerton	9.1942	18.6.1943	9.1943	stricken 11.1945
Sanders	DE40	Puget Sound N Yd, Bremerton	9.1942	18.6.1943	10.1943	stricken 1.1946
Brackett	DE41	Puget Sound N Yd, Bremerton	1.1943	1.8.1943	10.1943	stricken 12.1945
Reynolds	DE42	Puget Sound N Yd, Bremerton	1.1943	1.8.1943	11.1943	stricken 12.1945
Mitchell	DE43	Puget Sound N Yd, Bremerton	1.1943	1.8.1943	11.1943	stricken 12.1945
Donaldson	DE44	Puget Sound N Yd, Bremerton	1.1943	1.8.1943	12.1943	stricken 12.1945
Andres	DE45	Philadelphia N Yd	2.1942	24.7.1942	3.1943	stricken 11.1945
Drury *(ex-Cockburn)*	DE46	Philadelphia N Yd	2.1942	24.7.1942	(4.1943) / 8.1945	to the UK 4.1943-8.1945 (Cockburn), stricken 11.1945
Decker	DE47	Philadelphia N Yd	4.1942	24.7.1942	5.1943	to China 8.1945 (Tai Ping)
Dobler	DE48	Philadelphia N Yd	4.1942	24.7.1942	5.1943	stricken 10.1945
Doneff	DE49	Philadelphia N Yd	4.1942	24.7.1942	6.1943	stricken 1.1946
Engstrom *(ex-Drury)*	DE50	Philadelphia N Yd	4.1942	24.7.1942	6.1943	stricken 1.1946

Seid	DE256	Boston N Yd, Charlestown	1.1943	22.2.1943	6.1943	stricken 1.1946
Smartt	DE257	Boston N Yd, Charlestown	1.1943	22.2.1943	6.1943	stricken 10.1945
Walter S. Brown	DE258	Boston N Yd, Charlestown	1.1943	22.2.1943	6.1943	stricken 10.1945
William C. Miller	DE259	Boston N Yd, Charlestown	1.1943	22.2.1943	7.1943	stricken 1.1946
Cabana	DE260	Boston N Yd, Charlestown	1.1943	10.3.1943	7.1943	stricken 1.1946
Dionne	DE261	Boston N Yd, Charlestown	1.1943	10.3.1943	7.1943	stricken 2.1946
Canfield	DE262	Boston N Yd, Charlestown	2.1943	6.4.1943	7.1943	stricken 1.1946
Deede	DE263	Boston N Yd, Charlestown	2.1943	6.4.1943	7.1943	stricken 1.1946
Eldon	DE264	Boston N Yd, Charlestown	2.1943	6.4.1943	8.1943	stricken 2.1946
Cloues	DE265	Boston N Yd, Charlestown	2.1943	6.4.1943	8.1943	stricken 12.1945
Wintle	DE266	Boston N Yd, Charlestown	3.1943	22.4.1943	(8.1943)	to the UK 8.1943 (Capel)
Dempsey	DE267	Boston N Yd, Charlestown	3.1943	22.4.1943	(8.1943)	to the UK 8.1943 (Cooke)
Duffey	DE268	Boston N Yd, Charlestown	4.1943	19.5.1943	(8.1943)	to the UK 8.1943 (Dacres)
Eisner	DE269	Boston N Yd, Charlestown	4.1943	19.5.1943	(9.1943)	to the UK 9.1943 (Domett)
Foley *(ex-Gillette)*	DE270	Boston N Yd, Charlestown	4.1943	19.5.1943	(9.1943) / 8.1945	to the UK 9.1943-8.1945 (Foley), stricken 11.1945
Garlies *(ex-Fleming)*	DE271	Boston N Yd, Charlestown	4.1943	19.5.1943	(9.1943) / 8.1945	to the UK 9.1943-8.1945 (Garlies), stricken 11.1945
Lovering	DE272	Boston N Yd, Charlestown	4.1943	4.6.1943	(9.1943)	to the UK 9.1943 (Gould)
Grindall *(ex-Sanders)*	DE273	Boston N Yd, Charlestown	4.1943	4.6.1943	(9.1943) / 8.1945	to the UK 9.1943-8.1945 (Grindall), stricken 11.1945
O`Toole	DE274	Boston N Yd, Charlestown	5.1943	8.7.1943	(9.1943)	to the UK 9.1943 (Gardiner)
Reybold	DE275	Boston N Yd, Charlestown	5.1943	8.7.1943	(10.1943)	to the UK 10.1943 (Goodall)
George	DE276	Boston N Yd, Charlestown	5.1943	8.7.1943	(10.1943)	to the UK 10.1943 (Goodson)
Herzog	DE277	Boston N Yd, Charlestown	5.1943	8.7.1943	(10.1943)	to the UK 10.1943 (Gore)
Tisdale	DE278	Boston N Yd, Charlestown	6.1943	17.7.1943	(10.1943)	to the UK 10.1943 (Keats)
Trumpeter	DE279	Boston N Yd, Charlestown	6.1943	17.7.1943	(10.1943)	to the UK 10.1943 (Kempthorne)

Kingsmill	DE280	Boston N Yd, Charlestown	7.1943	13.8.1943	(10.1943) / 8.1945	to the UK 10.1943-8.1945 (Kingsmill), stricken 11.1945
Lake	DE301	Mare Island N Yd, Vallejo	4.1943	18.8.1943	2.1944	stricken 12.1945
Lyman	DE302	Mare Island N Yd, Vallejo	4.1943	19.8.1943	2.1944	stricken 12.1945
Crowley	DE303	Mare Island N Yd, Vallejo	5.1943	22.9.1943	3.1944	stricken 12.1945
Rall	DE304	Mare Island N Yd, Vallejo	5.1943	23.9.1943	4.1944	stricken 1.1946
Halloran	DE305	Mare Island N Yd, Vallejo	6.1943	14.1.1944	5.1944	stricken 11.1945
Connolly	DE306	Mare Island N Yd, Vallejo	6.1943	15.1.1944	7.1944	stricken 12.1945
Finnegan	DE307	Mare Island N Yd, Vallejo	7.1943	22.2.1944	8.1944	stricken 12.1945
Creamer	DE308	Mare Island N Yd, Vallejo	7.1943	23.2.1944	-	cancelled 9.1944
Ely	DE309	Mare Island N Yd, Vallejo	8.1943	10.4.1944	-	cancelled 9.1944
Delbert W. Halsey	DE310	Mare Island N Yd, Vallejo	8.1943	11.4.1944	-	cancelled 9.1944
Keppler	DE311	Mare Island N Yd, Vallejo	8.1943	-	-	cancelled 3.1944
Lloyd Thomas	DE312	Mare Island N Yd, Vallejo	8.1943	-	-	cancelled 3.1944
William C. Lawe	DE313	Mare Island N Yd, Vallejo	1.1944	-	-	cancelled 3.1944
Willard Keith	DE314	Mare Island N Yd, Vallejo	1.1944	-	-	cancelled 3.1944
	DE315	Mare Island N Yd, Vallejo	3.1944	-	-	cancelled 3.1944
	DE516	Boston N Yd, Charlestown	7.1943	13.8.1943	(11.1943)	to the UK 11.1943 (Lawford)
	DE517	Boston N Yd, Charlestown	7.1943	13.8.1943	(11.1943)	to the UK 11.1943 (Louis)
	DE518	Boston N Yd, Charlestown	7.1943	13.8.1943	(11.1943)	to the UK 11.1943 (Lawson)
Pasley *(ex-Lindsay)*	DE519	Boston N Yd, Charlestown	7.1943	30.8.1943	(11.1943) / 8.1945	to the UK 11.1943-8.1945 (Pasley), stricken 11.1945
	DE520	Boston N Yd, Charlestown	7.1943	30.8.1943	(11.1943)	to the UK 11.1943 (Loring)
Hoste	DE521	Boston N Yd, Charlestown	8.1943	24.9.1943	(12.1943) / 8.1945	to the UK 12.1943-8.1945 (Mitchell), stricken 11.1945
	DE522	Boston N Yd, Charlestown	8.1943	24.9.1943	(12.1943)	to the UK 12.1943 (Moorsom)
	DE523	Boston N Yd, Charlestown	8.1943	24.9.1943	(12.1943)	to the UK 12.1943 (Manners)

	DE524	Boston N Yd, Charlestown	8.1943	24.9.1943	(12.1943)	to the UK 12.1943 (Mounsey)
	DE525	Boston N Yd, Charlestown	9.1943	2.11.1943	(12.1943)	to the UK 12.1943 (Inglis)
	DE526	Boston N Yd, Charlestown	9.1943	2.11.1943	(1.1944)	to the UK 1.1944 (Inman)
O`Toole	DE527	Boston N Yd, Charlestown	9.1943	2.11.1943	1.1944	stricken 11.1945
John J. Powers	DE528	Boston N Yd, Charlestown	9.1943	2.11.1943	2.1944	stricken 11.1945
Mason	DE529	Boston N Yd, Charlestown	10.1943	17.11.1943	3.1944	stricken 11.1945
John M. Bermingham	DE530	Boston N Yd, Charlestown	10.1943	17.11.1943	4.1944	stricken 11.1945

1192 / 1416 t, 88.7 x 10.7 x 3.1 m, 4 General Motors diesel-generators, 2 electric motors, 6000 hp, 19.5 kts, 131-197 t diesel oil, 6000 nm (12 kts), complement 156; 3 x 1 – 76/50 Mk 20, 1 x 4 – 28/75 Mk 1 (DE13-18, 45) or 1 x 2 – 40/56 Bofors, 9 x 1 – 20/70 Oerlikon, 1 x 24 Hedgehog ASWRL, 8 DCT, 2 DCR (120); SC, SF or SL radars, QGa sonar.

The need to build smaller and cheaper ships along with destroyers, was put forward by a number of officers and admirals of the US Navy in 1939. Such "2nd rank" destroyers could successfully escort convoys and solve many auxiliary tasks when using of destroyers was inappropriate. Initially, the General Board did not approve the building of such ships, but the following year the situation changed dramatically, and as a result, some designs were prepared. US designers tried to take the path of reducing the displacement of a conventional destroyer to 1000-1200 t, while retaining the main armament. A very cramped arrangement with unsatisfactory combination of leading particulars became a result.

Despite the fact, that the design was not yet completed, in January 1941 it was decided to build 50 of these destroyers. In order to somehow speed up the design process, the General board in February changed the requirements for speed (initially, at least 25 kts) and armament (the installation of 127-mm DP guns was previously envisaged). Soon a new design was ready: 1140-t displacement, 85.3-m length, 24-kt speed, 2 single 102-mm/50 or 127-mm/38 SP guns, 1 quadruple 40-mm Bofors, 2 single 20-mm Oerlikons and 1 triple TT. The General Board approved the design, but in this form, it was never implemented; in May 1941, this program was cancelled. Probably the destroyer escort would not have appeared at all, but unexpectedly help came from Britain. The British commission expressed interest in the project and 23.6.1941 sent a request for the possibility of building 100 such ships, with the replacement of the 102- or 127-mm SP guns by 3 single 76-mm/50 AA guns, twin rudders to improve maneuverability and reconfiguring the bridge to the British standard. These corrections were

Bebas 1944

made to the design, and already 15.8.1941, Roosevelt approved a plan to build 50 ships for the UK. At the same time, the US Navy HQ convinced the President to start building similar ships for the own navy, but this proposal was rejected. Only in November 1941 did an order for the first DEs for the US Navy follow.

After the US entered the war, the overload of industry with various defense orders led to the need to make significant changes to the design regarding machinery. The originally envisaged 12000-hp twin-shaft geared steam turbine plant was replaced by diesel, diesel-electric or turbo-electric machinery and only a small part of the ships were equipped with geared turbines. Besides, new machinery required a more spacious engine room and, as a result, lengthening of the hull.

The design included a displacement reserve to strengthen the armament (replacement of three 76-mm open-standing guns with two 127-mm in enclosed mounts) , as was implemented in later series.

There were six series of destroyer escorts in total:

Evarts class (GMT): 6000-hp diesel-electric machinery (4 1500-hp diesel-generators, 2 electric motors), 76-mm guns, "short" hull.

Wyffels 1943

Halloran 1944

Cannon class (DET): 6000-hp diesel-electric machinery (4 1500-hp diesel-generators, 2 electric motors), 76-mm guns, "long" hull.

Edsall class (FRM): 6000-hp diesel machinery (4 1500-hp diesels working through gears on 2 shafts), 76-mm guns, "long" hull.

Buckley class (TE): 12000-hp turbo-electric machinery, 76-mm guns, "long" hull.

Rudderow class (TEV): 12000-hp turbo-electric machinery, 127-mm guns, "long" hull.

John C. Butler class (WGT): 12000-hp geared steam turbine machinery, 127-mm guns, "long" hull.

In 1944, when the number of escorts in the Atlantic was deemed sufficient, a large number of DEs of *Buckley* and *Rudderow* classes were converted to fast landing transports for service in the Pacific. So, they received a superstructure expanded to the sides, all anti-submarine armament, (except two DC racks, part of the artillery and torpedoes were removed. After conversion, such a transport could carry up to 162 rangers, there were 4 LCVP for the landing.

A total of 105 ships of GMT class were ordered. The building of eight of them was cancelled in 1944 (DE308-315). It was originally planned to transfer the first 50 ships, DE1-50, to the Royal Navy, however, the shortage of escorts in the USN has led to the fact that some of them remained under the US flag, and the Royal Navy received escorts from later orders.

1944-1945, *Brennan, Doherty, Edgar G. Chase, Edward C. Daly, Gilmore, Andres*: - 1 x 4 - 28/75; + 1 x 2 - 40/56 Bofors.

During attacks by Japanese aircraft and kamikazes off Okinawa, the following ships received damage of varying severity: *Manlove* (11.4.1945), *Rail* (12.4.1945, heavy), *Connolly* (13.4.1945) and *Halloran* (21.6.1945).

'TE' (BUCKLEY) class destroyer escorts

Buckley	DE51	Bethlehem, Hingham	6.1942	9.1.1943	4.1943	stricken 6.1968
Bull	DE52	Bethlehem, Hingham	6.1942	3.2.1943	(5.1943)	to the UK 5.1943 (Bentinck)
Charles Lawrence	DE53, 10.1944-APD37	Bethlehem, Hingham	8.1942	16.2.1943	5.1943	fast transport 10.1944, stricken 9.1964
Daniel T. Griffin	DE54, 10.1944-APD38	Bethlehem, Hingham	9.1942	23.2.1943	6.1943	fast transport 10.1944, to Chile 11.1966 (Uribe)
Donaldson	DE55	Bethlehem, Hingham	10.1942	6.3.1943	(6.1943)	to the UK 6.1943 (Byard)
Donnell	DE56	Bethlehem, Hingham	11.1942	13.3.1943	6.1943	damaged 3.5.1944, repaired as auxiliary
Fogg	DE57	Bethlehem, Hingham	12.1942	20.3.1943	7.1943	stricken 1.1965
Formoe	DE58	Bethlehem, Hingham	12.1942	27.3.1943	(7.1943)	to the UK 7.1943 (Calder)
Foss	DE59	Bethlehem, Hingham	12.1942	10.4.1943	7.1943	stricken 1.1965
Gantner	DE60, 2.1945-APD42	Bethlehem, Hingham	12.1942	17.4.1943	7.1943	fast transport 2.1945, stricken 1.1966
Thomas J. Gary	DE61	Bethlehem, Hingham	1.1943	1.5.1943	(8.1943)	to the UK 8.1943 (Duckworth)
George W. Ingram	DE62, 2.1945-APD43	Bethlehem, Hingham	2.1943	8.5.1943	8.1943	fast transport 2.1945, stricken 1.1967

Ira Jeffery	DE63, 2.1945-APD44	Bethlehem, Hingham	2.1943	15.5.1943	8.1943	fast transport 2.1945, stricken 6.1960
Lamons	DE64	Bethlehem, Hingham	2.1943	22.5.1943	(8.1943)	to the UK 8.1943 (Duff)
Lee Fox	DE65, 2.1945-APD45	Bethlehem, Hingham	3.1943	29.5.1943	8.1943	fast transport 2.1945, stricken 9.1964
Amesbury	DE66, 2.1945-APD46	Bethlehem, Hingham	3.1943	5.6.1943	8.1943	fast transport 2.1945, stricken 6.1960
Essington	DE67	Bethlehem, Hingham	3.1943	19.6.1943	(9.1943)	to the UK 9.1943 (Essington)
Bates	DE68, 7.1944-APD47	Bethlehem, Hingham	3.1943	6.6.1943	9.1943	fast transport 7.1944, sunk 25.5.1945
Blessman	DE69, 7.1944-APD48	Bethlehem, Hingham	3.1943	19.6.1943	9.1943	fast transport 7.1944, stricken 6.1967
Joseph E. Campbell	DE70, 7.1944-APD49	Bethlehem, Hingham	3.1943	26.6.1943	9.1943	fast transport 7.1944, to Chile 11.1966 (Riquelme)
Oswald	DE71	Bethlehem, Hingham	4.1943	30.6.1943	(9.1943)	to the UK 9.1943 (Affleck)
Harmon	DE72	Bethlehem, Hingham	4.1943	10.7.1943	(9.1943)	to the UK 9.1943 (Aylmer)
McAnn	DE73	Bethlehem, Hingham	4.1943	10.7.1943	(10.1943)	to the UK 10.1943 (Balfour)
Elbert	DE74	Bethlehem, Hingham	4.1943	17.7.1943	(10.1943)	to the UK 10.1943 (Bentley)
Eisele	DE75	Bethlehem, Hingham	5.1943	26.7.1943	(10.1943)	to the UK 10.1943 (Bickerton)
Liddle	DE76	Bethlehem, Hingham	5.1943	31.7.1943	(10.1943)	to the UK 10.1943 (Blight)
Straub	DE77	Bethlehem, Hingham	5.1943	31.7.1943	(11.1943)	to the UK 11.1943 (Braithwaite)
	DE78	Bethlehem, Hingham	5.1943	7.8.1943	(10.1943)	to the UK 10.1943 (Bullen)
	DE79	Bethlehem, Hingham	5.1943	14.8.1943	(10.1943)	to the UK 10.1943 (Byron)
	DE80	Bethlehem, Hingham	6.1943	21.8.1943	(10.1943)	to the UK 10.1943 (Conn)
	DE81	Bethlehem, Hingham	6.1943	21.8.1943	(11.1943)	to the UK 11.1943 (Cotton)
	DE82	Bethlehem, Hingham	6.1943	28.8.1943	(11.1943)	to the UK 11.1943 (Cranstoun)
	DE83	Bethlehem, Hingham	6.1943	11.9.1943	(11.1943)	to the UK 11.1943 (Cubitt)
	DE84	Bethlehem, Hingham	6.1943	18.9.1943	(11.1943)	to the UK 11.1943 (Curzon)
	DE85	Bethlehem, Hingham	6.1943	18.9.1943	(11.1943)	to the UK 11.1943 (Dakins)
	DE86	Bethlehem, Hingham	6.1943	25.9.1943	(11.1943)	to the UK 11.1943 (Deane)

	DE87	Bethlehem, Hingham	7.1943	2.10.1943	(11.1943)	to the UK 11.1943 (Ekins)
	DE88	Bethlehem, Hingham	8.1943	1.9.1943	(10.1943)	to the UK 10.1943 (Fitzroy)
	DE89	Bethlehem, Hingham	7.1943	2.10.1943	(11.1943)	to the UK 11.1943 (Redmill)
	DE90	Bethlehem, Hingham	7.1943	9.10.1943	(12.1943)	to the UK 12.1943 (Retalick)
	DE91	Bethlehem, Hingham	7.1943	14.10.1943	(11.1943)	to the UK 11.1943 (Halsted)
	DE92	Bethlehem, Hingham	8.1943	23.10.1943	(12.1943)	to the UK 12.1943 (Riou)
	DE93	Bethlehem, Hingham	8.1943	23.10.1943	(12.1943)	to the UK 12.1943 (Rutherford)
	DE94	Bethlehem, Hingham	8.1943	20.10.1943	(12.1943)	to the UK 12.1943 (Cosby)
	DE95	Bethlehem, Hingham	8.1943	30.10.1943	(12.1943)	to the UK 12.1943 (Rowley)
	DE96	Bethlehem, Hingham	8.1943	31.10.1943	(12.1943)	to the UK 12.1943 (Rupert)
	DE97	Bethlehem, Hingham	8.1943	31.10.1943	(12.1943)	to the UK 12.1943 (Stockham)
	DE98	Bethlehem, Hingham	9.1943	1.11.1943	(12.1943)	to the UK 12.1943 (Seymour)
Reuben James	DE153	Norfolk N Yd, Portsmouth	9.1942	6.2.1943	4.1943	stricken 6.1968
Sims	DE154, 9.1944-APD50	Norfolk N Yd, Portsmouth	9.1942	6.2.1943	4.1943	fast transport 9.1944, stricken 6.1960
Hopping	DE155, 9.1944-APD51	Norfolk N Yd, Portsmouth	12.1942	10.3.1943	5.1943	fast transport 9.1944, stricken 9.1964
Reeves	DE156, 9.1944-APD52	Norfolk N Yd, Portsmouth	2.1943	22.4.1943	6.1943	fast transport 9.1944, stricken 6.1960
Fechteler	DE157	Norfolk N Yd, Portsmouth	2.1943	22.4.1943	7.1943	sunk 4.5.1944
Chase	DE158, 11.1944-APD54	Norfolk N Yd, Portsmouth	3.1943	24.4.1943	7.1943	fast transport 11.1944, damaged 20.5.1945, repair incomplete
Laning	DE159, 11.1944-APD55	Norfolk N Yd, Portsmouth	4.1943	4.7.1943	8.1943	fast transport 11.1944, stricken 3.1975
Loy	DE160, 10.1944-APD56	Norfolk N Yd, Portsmouth	4.1943	4.7.1943	9.1943	fast transport 10.1944, stricken 9.1964
Barber	DE161, 10.1944-APD57	Norfolk N Yd, Portsmouth	4.1943	20.5.1943	10.1943	fast transport 10.1944, stricken 11.1968
Lovelace	DE198	Norfolk N Yd, Portsmouth	5.1943	4.7.1943	11.1943	stricken 7.1967
Manning	DE199	Charleston N Yd	2.1943	1.6.1943	10.1943	stricken 7.1968
Neuendorf	DE200	Charleston N Yd	2.1943	1.6.1943	10.1943	stricken 7.1967
James E. Craig	DE201	Charleston N Yd	4.1943	22.7.1943	11.1943	stricken 6.1968

Eichenberger	DE202	Charleston N Yd	4.1943	22.7.1943	11.1943	stricken 12.1972
Thomason	DE203	Charleston N Yd	6.1943	23.8.1943	12.1943	stricken 6.1968
Jordan	DE204	Charleston N Yd	6.1943	23.8.1943	12.1943	collision 18.9.1945, repair incomplete
Newman	DE205, 7.1944-APD59	Charleston N Yd	6.1943	9.8.1943	11.1943	fast transport 7.1944, stricken 9.1964
Liddle	DE206, 7.1944-APD60	Charleston N Yd	6.1943	9.8.1943	12.1943	fast transport 7.1944, stricken 4.1967
Kephart	DE207, 7.1944-APD61	Charleston N Yd	5.1943	6.9.1943	1.1944	fast transport 7.1944, stricken 5.1967
Cofer	DE208, 7.1944-APD62	Charleston N Yd	5.1943	6.9.1943	1.1944	fast transport 7.1944, stricken 4.1966
Lloyd	DE209, 7.1944-APD63	Charleston N Yd	7.1943	23.10.1943	2.1944	fast transport 7.1944, stricken 6.1966
Otter	DE210	Charleston N Yd	7.1943	23.10.1943	2.1944	stricken 11.1969
Joseph C. Hubbard	DE211, 6.1945-APD53	Charleston N Yd	8.1943	11.11.1943	3.1944	fast transport 6.1945, stricken 5.1969
Hayter	DE212, 6.1945-APD80	Charleston N Yd	8.1943	11.11.1943	3.1944	fast transport 6.1945, stricken 12.1966
William T. Powell	DE213	Charleston N Yd	8.1943	27.11.1943	3.1944	stricken 11.1965
Scott	DE214	Philadelphia N Yd	1.1943	3.4.1943	7.1943	stricken 7.1965
Burke	DE215, 1.1945-APD65	Philadelphia N Yd	1.1943	3.4.1943	7.1943	fast transport 1.1945, stricken 6.1968
Enright	DE216, 1.1945-APD66	Philadelphia N Yd	2.1943	29.5.1943	9.1943	fast transport 1.1945, to Ecuador 7.1967 (Veinteicinco de Julio)
Coolbaugh	DE217	Philadelphia N Yd	2.1943	29.5.1943	10.1943	stricken 7.1972
Darby	DE218	Philadelphia N Yd	2.1943	29.5.1943	11.1943	stricken 9.1968
J. Douglas Blackwood	DE219	Philadelphia N Yd	2.1943	29.5.1943	12.1943	stricken 1.1970
Francis M. Robinson	DE220	Philadelphia N Yd	2.1943	29.5.1943	1.1944	stricken 7.1972
Solar	DE221	Philadelphia N Yd	2.1943	29.5.1943	2.1944	internal explosion 30.4.1946
Fowler	DE222	Philadelphia N Yd	4.1943	3.7.1943	3.1944	stricken 7.1965
Spangenberg	DE223	Philadelphia N Yd	4.1943	3.7.1943	3.1944	stricken 11.1965
	DE563	Bethlehem, Hingham	9.1943	16.10.1943	(1.1944)	to the UK 1.1944 (Spragge)
	DE564	Bethlehem, Hingham	9.1943	6.11.1943	(12.1943)	to the UK 12.1943 (Stayner)
	DE565	Bethlehem, Hingham	9.1943	13.11.1943	(12.1943)	to the UK 12.1943 (Thornborough)
	DE566	Bethlehem, Hingham	9.1943	20.11.1943	(1.1944)	to the UK 1.1944 (Trollope)
	DE567	Bethlehem, Hingham	10.1943	20.11.1943	(1.1944)	to the UK 1.1944 (Tyler)

	DE568	Bethlehem, Hingham	9.1943	27.11.1943	(1.1944)	to the UK 1.1944 (Torrington)
	DE569	Bethlehem, Hingham	10.1943	27.11.1943	(1.1944)	to the UK 1.1944 (Narbrough)
	DE570	Bethlehem, Hingham	10.1943	4.12.1943	(1.1944)	to the UK 1.1944 (Waldegrave)
	DE571	Bethlehem, Hingham	10.1943	12.12.1943	(1.1944)	to the UK 1.1944 (Whitaker)
	DE572	Bethlehem, Hingham	10.1943	18.12.1943	(1.1944)	to the UK 1.1944 (Holmes)
	DE573	Bethlehem, Hingham	10.1943	18.12.1943	(2.1944)	to the UK 2.1944 (Hargood)
	DE574	Bethlehem, Hingham	11.1943	21.12.1943	(2.1944)	to the UK 2.1944 (Hotham)
Ahrens	DE575	Bethlehem, Hingham	11.1943	21.12.1943	2.1944	stricken 4.1965
Barr	DE576, 10.1944-APD39	Bethlehem, Hingham	11.1943	28.12.1943	2.1944	fast transport 10.1944, stricken 6.1960
Alexander J. Luke	DE577	Bethlehem, Hingham	11.1943	28.12.1943	2.1944	stricken 5.1970
Robert I. Paine	DE578	Bethlehem, Hingham	11.1943	30.12.1943	2.1944	stricken 6.1968
Foreman	DE633	Bethlehem, San Francisco	3.1943	1.8.1943	10.1943	stricken 11.1965
Whitehurst	DE634	Bethlehem, San Francisco	3.1943	5.9.1943	11.1943	stricken 7.1969
England	DE635	Bethlehem, San Francisco	4.1943	26.9.1943	12.1943	damaged 9.5.1945, never repaired
Witter	DE636	Bethlehem, San Francisco	4.1943	17.10.1943	12.1943	damaged 6.4.1945, repair incomplete
Bowers	DE637, 6.1945-APD40	Bethlehem, San Francisco	5.1943	31.10.1943	1.1944	fast transport 6.1945, to the Philippines 4.1961 (Rajah Soliman)
Willmarth	DE638	Bethlehem, San Francisco	6.1943	21.11.1943	3.1944	stricken 12.1966
Gendreau	DE639	Bethlehem, San Francisco	8.1943	12.12.1943	3.1944	stricken 12.1972
Fieberling	DE640	Bethlehem, San Francisco	8.1943	2.4.1944	4.1944	stricken 3.1972
William C. Cole	DE641	Bethlehem, San Francisco	9.1943	29.12.1943	5.1944	stricken 3.1972
Paul G. Baker	DE642	Bethlehem, San Francisco	9.1943	12.3.1944	5.1944	stricken 12.1969
Damon M. Cummings	DE643	Bethlehem, San Francisco	10.1943	18.4.1944	6.1944	stricken 3.1972
Vammen	DE644	Bethlehem, San Francisco	8.1943	21.5.1944	7.1944	stricken 7.1969
Jenks	DE665	Dravo, Pittsburgh	5.1943	11.9.1943	6.1944	stricken 2.1966
Durik	DE666	Dravo, Pittsburgh	6.1943	9.10.1943	3.1944	stricken 6.1965
Wiseman	DE667	Dravo, Pittsburgh	7.1943	6.11.1943	4.1944	stricken 4.1973

Weber	DE675, 12.1944- APD75	Bethlehem, Quincy	2.1943	1.5.1943	6.1943	fast transport 12.1944, stricken 6.1960
Schmitt	DE676, 1.1945- APD76	Bethlehem, Quincy	2.1943	29.5.1943	7.1943	fast transport 1.1945, stricken 5.1967
Frament	DE677, 12.1944- APD77	Bethlehem, Quincy	5.1943	28.6.1943	8.1943	fast transport 12.1944, stricken 1.1960
Harmon	DE678	Bethlehem, Quincy	5.1943	25.7.1943	8.1943	stricken 8.1965
Greenwood	DE679	Bethlehem, Quincy	6.1943	21.8.1943	9.1943	stricken 2.1967
Loeser	DE680	Bethlehem, Quincy	7.1943	11.9.1943	10.1943	stricken 8.1968
Gillette	DE681	Bethlehem, Quincy	8.1943	25.9.1943	10.1943	stricken 12.1972
Underhill	DE682	Bethlehem, Quincy	9.1943	15.10.1943	11.1943	sunk 24.7.1945
Henry R. Kenyon	DE683	Bethlehem, Quincy	9.1943	30.10.1943	11.1943	stricken 12.1969
Bull	DE693, 7.1944- APD78	Defoe, Bay City	12.1942	25.3.1943	8.1943	fast transport 7.1944, stricken 6.1966
Bunch	DE694, 7.1944- APD79	Defoe, Bay City	2.1943	29.5.1943	8.1943	fast transport 7.1944, stricken 4.1964
Rich	DE695	Defoe, Bay City	3.1943	22.6.1943	10.1943	sunk 8.6.1944
Spangler	DE696	Defoe, Bay City	4.1943	15.7.1943	10.1943	stricken 3.1972
George	DE697	Defoe, Bay City	5.1943	14.8.1943	11.1943	stricken 11.1969
Raby	DE698	Defoe, Bay City	6.1943	4.9.1943	12.1943	stricken 6.1968
Marsh	DE699	Defoe, Bay City	6.1943	25.9.1943	1.1944	stricken 4.1973
Currier	DE700	Defoe, Bay City	7.1943	14.10.1943	2.1944	stricken 12.1966
Osmus	DE701	Defoe, Bay City	8.1943	4.11.1943	2.1944	stricken 12.1972
Earl V. Johnson	DE702	Defoe, Bay City	9.1943	24.11.1943	3.1944	stricken 5.1967
Holton	DE703	Defoe, Bay City	9.1943	15.12.1943	5.1944	stricken 11.1972
Cronin	DE704	Defoe, Bay City	10.1943	5.1.1944	5.1944	stricken 6.1970
Frybarger	DE705	Defoe, Bay City	11.1943	25.1.1944	5.1944	stricken 12.1972
Tatum	DE789, 12.1944- APD81	Consolidated, Orange	4.1943	7.8.1943	11.1943	fast transport 12.1944, stricken 6.1960
Borum	DE790	Consolidated, Orange	4.1943	14.8.1943	11.1943	stricken 8.1965
Maloy	DE791	Consolidated, Orange	5.1943	18.8.1943	12.1943	stricken 6.1965
Haines	DE792, 12.1944- APD84	Consolidated, Orange	5.1943	26.8.1943	12.1943	fast transport 12.1944, stricken 6.1960
Runels	DE793, 1.1945- APD85	Consolidated, Orange	6.1943	4.9.1943	1.1944	fast transport 1.1945, stricken 6.1960
Hollis	DE794, 1.1945- APD86	Consolidated, Orange	7.1943	11.9.1943	1.1944	fast transport 1.1945, stricken 9.1974

Gunason	DE795	Consolidated, Orange	8.1943	16.10.1943	2.1944	stricken 9.1973
Major	DE796	Consolidated, Orange	8.1943	23.10.1943	2.1944	stricken 12.1972
Weeden	DE797	Consolidated, Orange	8.1943	27.10.1943	2.1944	stricken 6.1968
Varian	DE798	Consolidated, Orange	8.1943	6.11.1943	2.1944	stricken 12.1972
Scroggins	DE799	Consolidated, Orange	9.1943	6.11.1943	3.1944	stricken 7.1965
Jack W. Wilke	DE800	Consolidated, Orange	10.1943	18.12.1943	3.1944	stricken 8.1972

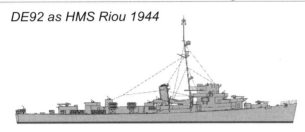

DE92 as HMS Riou 1944

1432 /1823 t, 93.3 x 11.3 x 3.4 m, DE51 - 98, 563 - 578, 665 - 673: 2 General Electric steam turbine-generators, 2 electric motors, 2 Foster Wheeler (DE51-98, 563- 578, 665-673) or Babcock & Wilcox (DE153, 154, 156-161, 198, 214-223, 789-800) or Combustion Engineering (DE155, 199-213, 633-644, 675-683, 693-705) boilers, 12000 hp, 23 kts, 359 t oil, 5000-5500 nm (15 kts), complement 186; 3 x 1 – 76/40 Mk 20, 1 x 4 – 28/75 Mk 1 (DE51, 153, 154) or 1 x 2 – 40/56 Bofors or (1 x 2 + 4 x 1) – 40/56 Bofors (DE575-578), 6 (DE51, 153, 154) or 8 x 1 – 20/70 Oerlikon, 1 x 3 – 533 TT (except DE575-578), 1 x 24 Hedgehog ASWRL, 8 DCT, 2 DCR (120); SC, SF or SL or SU radars, QGa sonar.

A total of 154 destroyer escorts of TE class were ordered.

43 ships were converted to fast personnel landing transports: 6 ships (APD69-74, ex-DE668-673) were commissioned as landing ships, other (DE53, 54, 576, 637, 60, 62, 63, 65, 66, 68-70, 154-156, 211, 158-161, 205-209, 215, 216, 675-677, 693, 694, 212, 789, 792-794 were re-classified as APD37-40, 42-57, 59-63, 65, 66, 75-81 and 84-86 respectively) were converted after the service as destroyer escorts.

For some reasons, work on the conversion of seven more ships (DE635, 636, 214, 665, 666, 790 and 791, for which the numbers APD41, 58, 64, 67, 68, 82 and 83 were reserved) was not started.

Mid-1943, *Buckley, Reuben James, Sims*: - 1 x 4 - 28/75; + 1 x 2 - 40/56 Bofors, 2 x 1 - 20/70 Oerlikon.

1944 - 1945, APD *Charles Lawrence, Daniel T. Griffin, Gantner, George W. Ingram, Ira Jeffery, Lee Fox, Amesbury, Bates, Blessman, Joseph E. Campbell, Sims, Hopping, Reeves, Chase, Laning, Loy, Barber, Newman, Liddle, Kephart, Cofer, Lloyd, Joseph C. Hubbard, Hayter, Burke, Enright, Barr, Bowers, Weber, Schmitt, Frament, Bull, Bunch, Tatum, Haines, Runels, Hollis*: - 3 x 1 - 76/50, 1 x 3 - 533 TT, 1 x 24 Hedgehog, 8 DCT; + 1 x 1 - 127/38 Mk 12, 2 x 2 - 40/56 Bofors, 4 LCVP, 162 troops.

1945, *Ahrens, Alexander J. Luke, Robert I. Paine*: - 4 x 1 - 40/56; + 2 x 2 - 40/56 Bofors. Autumn 1945, *Coolbaugh, Darby, J. Douglas Blackwood, Harmon, Greenwood, Loeser, Spangler, George, Raby, Currier, Osmus*: - 3 x 1 - 76/50, 2 x 1 - 20/70, 1 x 3 - 533 TT; + 2 x 1 - 127/38 Mk 12, (1 x 4 + 2 x 2) - 40/56 Bofors, Mk 25 radar. 1945, *Buckley, Fogg, Reuben James, William T. Powell, Spangenberg*: - 3 x 1 - 76/50, 2 x 1 - 20/70, 1 x 3 - 533 TT; + 2 x 1 - 127/38 Mk 12, (1 x 4 + 2 x 2) - 40/56 Bofors, SPS-6, Mk 25 radars. 1945, *Alexander J. Luke, Robert I. Paine*: - 3 x 1 - 76/50, 2 x 1 - 20/70; + 2 x 1 - 127/38 Mk 12, 1 x 4 - 40/56 Bofors, SPS-6, Mk 25 radars.

DE668 - 673 were completed as fast landing transports APD69 - 74. *Fechteler* 5.5.1944 was sunk NW of Oran by German submarine *U967. Rich* 8.6.1944 was lost off the coast of Normandy on a mine. *Bates* 25.5.1945 was sunk by three kamikazes off Okinawa. *Underhill* 24.7.1945 was sunk off the Philippines by Japanese *Kaiten* human torpedo, launched from submarine *I53*.

Fogg 20.12.1944 was damaged by a torpedo from German submarine. *Donnell* 3.5.1944 was badly damaged N of Ireland by a torpedo from German submarine *U765*, was never fully repaired and was used as a floating power station at Cherbourg from July 1944. *Barr* 29.5.1944 was damaged by German submarine *U549* and was for two months under repair. *Frament* 15.11.1944 was damaged off Bermuda

Buckley 1944

in a collision with Italian submarine *Luigi Settembrini* and was for a month under repair. *Vammen* 1.4.1945 was damaged off Okinawa on a mine. *Blessman* 18.2.1945 was damaged by Japanese 225-kg air bomb.

During attacks by Japanese aircraft and kamikaze off Okinawa following ships received damage of varying severity: *Foreman* (26.3.1945 and 2.4.1945), *Witter* (6.4.1945), *Fieberling* (6.4.1945), *Whitehurst*

(12.4.1945), *Bowers* (16.4.1945), *England* (27.4.1945 and 9.5.1945, never repaired), *Chase* (20.5.1945), *Sims* (24.5.1945), *William C. Cole* (24.5.1945), *Loy* (27.5.1945). *Gendreau* 9.6.1945 was damaged at Okinawa by Japanese coastal guns.

Jordan collided with s/s *John Sherman* off Miami 18.9.1945, was never completely repaired and stricken in January 1946.

'DET' (CANNON) class destroyer escorts

Cannon	DE99	Dravo, Wilmington	11.1942	25.5.1943	9.1943	to Brazil 12.1944 (Baependi)
Christopher	DE100	Dravo, Wilmington	12.1942	19.6.1943	10.1943	to Brazil 12.1944 (Benavente)
Alger	DE101	Dravo, Wilmington	1.1943	8.7.1943	11.1943	to Brazil 3.1945 (Babitonga)
Thomas	DE102	Dravo, Wilmington	1.1943	31.7.1943	11.1943	to China 12.1948 (Tai Ho)
Bostwick	DE103	Dravo, Wilmington	2.1943	30.8.1943	12.1943	to China 12.1948 (Tai Tsang)
Breeman	DE104	Dravo, Wilmington	3.1943	4.9.1943	12.1943	to China 10.1948 (Tai Hu)
Burrows	DE105	Dravo, Wilmington	3.1943	2.10.1943	12.1943	to the Netherlands 6.1950 (Van Amstel)
Corbesier	DE106	Dravo, Wilmington	4.1943	11.11.1943	(1.1944)	to France 1.1944 (Sénégalais)
Cronin	DE107	Dravo, Wilmington	5.1943	27.11.1943	(1.1944)	to France 1.1944 (Algérien)
Crosley	DE108	Dravo, Wilmington	6.1943	17.12.1943	(2.1944)	to France 2.1944 (Tunisien)
	DE109	Dravo, Wilmington	9.1943	1.1.1944	(2.1944)	to France 2.1944 (Marocain)
	DE110	Dravo, Wilmington	9.1943	22.1.1944	(3.1944)	to France 3.1944 (Hova)
	DE111	Dravo, Wilmington	10.1943	12.2.1944	(4.1944)	to France 4.1944 (Somali)
Carter	DE112	Dravo, Wilmington	11.1943	29.2.1944	5.1944	to China 12.1948 (Tai Chao)
Clarence L. Evans	DE113	Dravo, Wilmington	12.1943	22.3.1944	6.1944	to France 3.1952 (Berbère)
Levy	DE162	Federal, Newark	10.1942	28.3.1943	5.1943	stricken 8.1973
McConnell	DE163	Federal, Newark	10.1942	28.3.1943	5.1943	stricken 10.1972
Osterhaus	DE164	Federal, Newark	11.1942	18.4.1943	6.1943	stricken 11.1972
Parks	DE165	Federal, Newark	11.1942	18.4.1943	6.1943	stricken 7.1972
Baron	DE166	Federal, Newark	11.1942	9.5.1943	7.1943	to Uruguay 5.1952 (Uruguay)
Acree	DE167	Federal, Newark	11.1942	9.5.1943	7.1943	stricken 7.1972
Amick	DE168	Federal, Newark	1.1943	27.5.1943	7.1943	to Japan 6.1955 (Asahi)
Atherton	DE169	Federal, Newark	1.1943	27.5.1943	8.1943	to Japan 6.1955 (Hatsuhi)

Booth	DE170	Federal, Newark	1.1943	21.6.1943	9.1943	to the Philippines 12.1967 (Datu Kalantiaw)
Carroll	DE171	Federal, Newark	1.1943	21.6.1943	10.1943	stricken 8.1965
Cooner	DE172	Federal, Newark	2.1943	25.7.1943	8.1943	stricken 7.1972
Eldridge	DE173	Federal, Newark	2.1943	25.7.1943	8.1943	to Greece 1.1951 (Leon)
Marts	DE174	Federal, Newark	4.1943	8.8.1943	9.1943	to Brazil 3.1945 (Bocaina)
Pennewill	DE175	Federal, Newark	4.1943	8.8.1943	9.1943	to Brazil 8.1944 (Bertioga)
Micka	DE176	Federal, Newark	5.1943	22.8.1943	9.1943	stricken 8.1965
Reybold	DE177	Federal, Newark	5.1943	22.8.1943	9.1943	to Brazil 8.1944 (Bracuí)
Herzog	DE178	Federal, Newark	5.1943	5.9.1943	10.1943	to Brazil 8.1944 (Beberibe)
McAnn	DE179	Federal, Newark	5.1943	5.9.1943	10.1943	to Brazil 8.1944 (Bauru)
Trumpeter	DE180	Federal, Newark	6.1943	19.9.1943	10.1943	stricken 8.1973
Straub	DE181	Federal, Newark	6.1943	19.9.1943	10.1943	stricken 8.1973
Gustafson	DE182	Federal, Newark	7.1943	3.10.1943	11.1943	to the Netherlands 10.1950 (Van Ewijck)
Samuel S. Miles	DE183	Federal, Newark	7.1943	3.10.1943	11.1943	to France 8.1950 (Arabe)
Wesson	DE184	Federal, Newark	7.1943	17.10.1943	11.1943	to Italy 1.1951 (Andromeda)
Riddle	DE185	Federal, Newark	7.1943	17.10.1943	11.1943	to France 8.1950 (Kabyle)
Swearer	DE186	Federal, Newark	8.1943	31.10.1943	11.1943	to France 9.1950 (Bambara)
Stern	DE187	Federal, Newark	8.1943	31.10.1943	12.1943	to the Netherlands 3.1951 (Van Zijll)
O`Neill	DE188	Federal, Newark	8.1943	14.11.1943	12.1943	to the Netherlands 10.1950 (Dubois)
Bronstein	DE189	Federal, Newark	8.1943	14.11.1943	12.1943	to Uruguay 5.1952 (Artigas)
Baker (ex-Raby)	DE190	Federal, Newark	9.1943	28.11.1943	12.1943	to France 3.1952 (Malgache)
Coffman	DE191	Federal, Newark	9.1943	28.11.1943	12.1943	stricken 7.1972
Eisner	DE192	Federal, Newark	9.1943	12.12.1943	1.1944	to the Netherlands 3.1951 (De Zeeuw)
Garfield Thomas (ex-William G. Thomas)	DE193	Federal, Newark	9.1943	12.12.1943	1.1944	to Greece 1.1951 (Panthir)
Wingfield	DE194	Federal, Newark	10.1943	30.12.1943	1.1944	to France 9.1950 (Sakalave)
Thornhill	DE195	Federal, Newark	10.1943	30.12.1943	2.1944	to Italy 1.1951 (Aldebaran)
Rinehart	DE196	Federal, Newark	10.1943	9.1.1944	2.1944	to the Netherlands 6.1950 (De Bitter)

Roche	DE197	Federal, Newark	10.1943	9.1.1944	2.1944	damaged 22.9.1945, never repaired
Bangust	DE739	Western Pipe & Steel, San Pedro	2.1943	6.6.1943	10.1943	to Peru 2.1952 (Castilla)
Waterman	DE740	Western Pipe & Steel, San Pedro	2.1943	20.6.1943	11.1943	to Peru 2.1952 (Aguirre)
Weaver	DE741	Western Pipe & Steel, San Pedro	3.1943	4.7.1943	12.1943	to Peru 2.1952 (Rodríguez)
Hilbert	DE742	Western Pipe & Steel, San Pedro	3.1943	18.7.1943	2.1944	stricken 8.1972
Lamons	DE743	Western Pipe & Steel, San Pedro	4.1943	1.8.1943	2.1944	stricken 8.1972
Kyne	DE744	Western Pipe & Steel, San Pedro	4.1943	15.8.1943	4.1944	stricken 8.1972
Snyder	DE745	Western Pipe & Steel, San Pedro	4.1943	29.8.1943	5.1944	stricken 8.1972
Hemminger	DE746	Western Pipe & Steel, San Pedro	5.1943	12.9.1943	5.1944	to Thailand 7.1959 (Pin Clao)
Bright	DE747	Western Pipe & Steel, San Pedro	6.1943	26.9.1943	6.1944	to France 11.1950 (Touareg)
Tills	DE748	Western Pipe & Steel, San Pedro	6.1943	3.10.1943	8.1944	stricken 9.1968
Roberts	DE749	Western Pipe & Steel, San Pedro	7.1943	14.11.1943	9.1944	stricken 9.1968
McClelland	DE750	Western Pipe & Steel, San Pedro	7.1943	28.11.1943	9.1944	stricken 8.1972
Gaynier	DE751	Western Pipe & Steel, San Pedro	8.1943	30.1.1944	-	cancelled 9.1944
Curtis W. W. Howard	DE752	Western Pipe & Steel, San Pedro	8.1943	26.3.1944	-	cancelled 9.1944
John J. van Buren	DE753	Western Pipe & Steel, San Pedro	8.1943	16.1.1944	-	cancelled 9.1944
Willard Keith	DE754	Western Pipe & Steel, San Pedro	9.1943	-	-	cancelled 1943
Paul G. Baker	DE755	Western Pipe & Steel, San Pedro	9.1943	-	-	cancelled 1943
Cates	DE763	Tampa SB	3.1943	10.10.1943	12.1943	to France 11.1950 (Soudanais)
Gandy	DE764	Tampa SB	3.1943	12.12.1943	2.1944	to Italy 1.1951 (Altair)
Earl K. Olsen	DE765	Tampa SB	3.1943	13.2.1944	4.1944	stricken 8.1972
Slater	DE766	Tampa SB	3.1943	13.2.1944	5.1944	to Greece 3.1951 (Aetos)
Oswald	DE767	Tampa SB	4.1943	25.4.1944	6.1944	stricken 8.1972
Ebert	DE768	Tampa SB	4.1943	11.5.1944	6.1944	to Greece 3.1951 (Ierax)
Neal A. Scott	DE769	Tampa SB	6.1943	4.6.1944	7.1944	stricken 6.1968
Muir	DE770	Tampa SB	6.1943	4.6.1944	8.1944	to South Korea 2.1956 (Gyeonggi)
Sutton	DE771	Tampa SB	8.1943	6.8.1944	12.1944	to South Korea 2.1956 (Gangwon)
Milton Lewis	DE772	Tampa SB	8.1943	6.8.1944	-	cancelled 9.1944
George M. Campbell	DE773	Tampa SB	10.1943	15.10.1944	-	cancelled 9.1944

Russell M. Cox	DE774	Tampa SB	10.1943	-	-	cancelled 9.1944

Cannon 1943

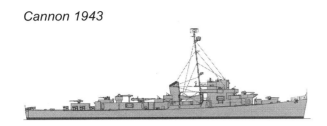

Breeman 1944

1253 / 1602 t, 93.3 x 11.2 x 3.2m, 4 General Motors diesel-generators, 2 electric motors, 6000 hp, 21 kts, 320 t diesel oil, 11500 nm (11 kts), complement 186; 3 x 1 – 76/50 Mk 20, 1 x 2 – 40/56 Bofors, 8 or 10 (DE740-756, 765-774) x 1 – 20/70 Oerlikon, 1 x 3 – 533 TT, 1 x 24 Hedgehog ASWRL, 8 DCT, 2 DCR (120); SC, SF or SL or SU radars, QGa sonar.

A total of 116 ships of DET class were ordered. Building of 44 units was cancelled in 1943 (DE114-128, 754-762, 775-788, ordered to Western Pipe & Steel DE756 was named _Damon Cummings_) and in 1944 (DE751-753 and 772-774). The level of readiness of some of them at the moment of cancelling was quite high, five were even launched.

1945, some ships: - 1 x 3 - 533 TT; + 4 x 1 - 40/56 Bofors. During the kamikaze attacks off Okinawa following ships received damage of varying severity: _Samuel S. Miles_ (11.4.1945), _Wesson_ (7.4.1945, heavy), _Riddle_ (12.4.1945, heavy), _O'Neill_ (24.5.1945, heavy) and _Bright_ (13.5.1945, heavy). _Roche_ hit a mine off Tokyo Bay 22.9.1945, was never repaired and scuttled off Yokosuka 11.3.1946.

'FMR' (EDSALL) class destroyer escorts

Edsall	DE129	Consolidated, Orange	7.1942	1.11.1942	4.1943	stricken 6.1968
Jacob Jones	DE130	Consolidated, Orange	6.1942	29.11.1942	4.1943	stricken 1.1971
Hammann (ex-_Langley_)	DE131	Consolidated, Orange	7.1942	13.12.1942	5.1943	stricken 10.1972
Robert E. Peary	DE132	Consolidated, Orange	6.1942	3.1.1943	5.1943	stricken 7.1966
Pillsbury	DE133	Consolidated, Orange	7.1942	10.1.1943	6.1943	stricken 7.1965
Pope	DE134	Consolidated, Orange	7.1942	12.1.1943	6.1943	stricken 1.1971
Flaherty	DE135	Consolidated, Orange	11.1942	17.1.1943	6.1943	stricken 4.1965
Frederick C. Davis	DE136	Consolidated, Orange	11.1942	24.1.1943	7.1943	sunk 24.4.1945
Herbert C. Jones	DE137	Consolidated, Orange	11.1942	19.1.1943	7.1943	stricken 7.1972
Douglas L. Howard	DE138	Consolidated, Orange	12.1942	24.1.1943	7.1943	stricken 10.1972
Farquhar	DE139	Consolidated, Orange	12.1942	13.2.1943	8.1943	stricken 10.1972
J. R. Y. Blakely	DE140	Consolidated, Orange	12.1942	7.3.1943	8.1943	stricken 1.1971
Hill	DE141	Consolidated, Orange	12.1942	28.2.1943	8.1943	stricken 10.1972
Fessenden	DE142	Consolidated, Orange	1.1943	9.3.1943	8.1943	stricken 9.1966

Fiske	DE143	Consolidated, Orange	1.1943	14.3.1943	8.1943	sunk 2.8.1944
Frost	DE144	Consolidated, Orange	1.1943	21.3.1943	8.1943	stricken 4.1965
Huse	DE145	Consolidated, Orange	1.1943	23.3.1943	8.1943	stricken 8.1973
Inch	DE146	Consolidated, Orange	1.1943	4.4.1943	9.1943	stricken 10.1972
Blair	DE147	Consolidated, Orange	1.1943	6.4.1943	9.1943	stricken 12.1972
Brough	DE148	Consolidated, Orange	1.1943	10.4.1943	9.1943	stricken 11.1965
Chatelaine	DE149	Consolidated, Orange	1.1943	21.4.1943	9.1943	stricken 8.1973
Neunzer	DE150	Consolidated, Orange	1.1943	27.4.1943	9.1943	stricken 7.1972
Poole	DE151	Consolidated, Orange	2.1943	8.5.1943	9.1943	stricken 1.1971
Peterson	DE152	Consolidated, Orange	2.1943	15.5.1943	9.1943	stricken 8.1973
Stewart	DE238	Brown SB, Houston	7.1942	22.11.1942	5.1943	stricken 10.1972
Sturtevant	DE239	Brown SB, Houston	7.1942	3.12.1942	6.1943	stricken 12.1972
Moore	DE240	Brown SB, Houston	7.1942	21.12.1942	7.1943	stricken 8.1973
Keith (*ex-Scott*)	DE241	Brown SB, Houston	8.1942	21.12.1942	7.1943	stricken 11.1972
Tomich	DE242	Brown SB, Houston	9.1942	28.12.1942	7.1943	stricken 11.1972
J. Richard Ward (*ex-James R. Ward*)	DE243	Brown SB, Houston	9.1942	6.1.1943	7.1943	stricken 1.1971
Otterstetter	DE244	Brown SB, Houston	11.1942	19.1.1943	8.1943	stricken 8.1974
Sloat	DE245	Brown SB, Houston	11.1942	21.1.1943	8.1943	stricken 1.1971
Snowden	DE246	Brown SB, Houston	12.1942	19.2.1943	8.1943	stricken 9.1968
Stanton	DE247	Brown SB, Houston	12.1942	21.2.1943	8.1943	stricken 12.1970
Swasey	DE248	Brown SB, Houston	12.1942	18.3.1943	8.1943	stricken 11.1972
Marchand	DE249	Brown SB, Houston	12.1942	20.3.1943	9.1943	stricken 1.1971
Hurst	DE250	Brown SB, Houston	1.1943	14.4.1943	8.1943	stricken 12.1972
Camp	DE251	Brown SB, Houston	1.1943	16.4.1943	9.1943	to South Vietnam 2.1971 (Trần Hưng Đạo)
Howard D. Crow	DE252	Brown SB, Houston	2.1943	26.4.1943	9.1943	stricken 9.1968
Pettit	DE253	Brown SB, Houston	2.1943	28.4.1943	9.1943	stricken 8.1973
Picketts	DE254	Brown SB, Houston	3.1943	10.5.1943	10.1943	stricken 11.1972
Sellstrom	DE255	Brown SB, Houston	3.1943	12.5.1943	10.1943	stricken 11.1965
Harveston	DE316	Consolidated, Orange	3.1943	22.5.1943	10.1943	stricken 12.1966
Joyce	DE317	Consolidated, Orange	3.1943	26.5.1943	9.1943	stricken 12.1972
Kirkpatrick	DE318	Consolidated, Orange	3.1943	5.6.1943	10.1943	stricken 8.1974
Leopold	DE319	Consolidated, Orange	3.1943	12.6.1943	10.1943	sunk 10.3.1944
Menges	DE320	Consolidated, Orange	3.1943	15.6.1943	10.1943	stricken 1.1971
Mosley	DE321	Consolidated, Orange	4.1943	26.6.1943	10.1943	stricken 1.1971

Newell	DE322	Consolidated, Orange	4.1943	29.6.1943	10.1943	stricken 9.1968
Pride	DE323	Consolidated, Orange	4.1943	3.7.1943	11.1943	stricken 1.1971
Falgout	DE324	Consolidated, Orange	5.1943	24.7.1943	11.1943	stricken 6.1975
Lowe	DE325	Consolidated, Orange	5.1943	28.7.1943	11.1943	stricken 9.1968
Thomas J. Gary (ex-Gary)	DE326	Consolidated, Orange	6.1943	21.8.1943	11.1943	to Tunisia 10.1973 (President Bourguiba)
Brister	DE327	Consolidated, Orange	6.1943	24.8.1943	11.1943	stricken 9.1968
Finch	DE328	Consolidated, Orange	6.1943	28.8.1943	12.1943	stricken 2.1974
Kretchmer	DE329	Consolidated, Orange	6.1943	31.8.1943	12.1943	stricken 10.1973
O`Reilly	DE330	Consolidated, Orange	7.1943	2.10.1943	12.1943	stricken 1.1971
Koiner	DE331	Consolidated, Orange	7.1943	5.10.1943	12.1943	stricken 9.1968
Price	DE332	Consolidated, Orange	8.1943	30.10.1943	1.1944	stricken 8.1974
Strickland	DE333	Consolidated, Orange	8.1943	2.11.1943	1.1944	stricken 12.1972
Forster	DE334	Consolidated, Orange	8.1943	13.11.1943	1.1944	to South Vietnam 9.1971 (Trần Khánh Dư)
Daniel	DE335	Consolidated, Orange	8.1943	16.11.1943	1.1944	stricken 1.1971
Roy O. Hale	DE336	Consolidated, Orange	9.1943	20.11.1943	2.1944	stricken 8.1974
Dale W. Peterson	DE337	Consolidated, Orange	10.1943	22.12.1943	2.1944	stricken 1.1971
Martin H. Ray	DE338	Consolidated, Orange	10.1943	29.12.1943	2.1944	stricken 5.1966
Ramsden	DE382	Consolidated, Orange	3.1943	24.5.1943	10.1943	stricken 8.1974
Mills	DE383	Consolidated, Orange	3.1943	26.5.1943	10.1943	stricken 8.1974
Rhodes	DE384	Consolidated, Orange	4.1943	29.6.1943	10.1943	stricken 8.1974
Richey	DE385	Consolidated, Orange	4.1943	30.6.1943	10.1943	stricken 6.1968
Savage	DE386	Consolidated, Orange	4.1943	15.7.1943	10.1943	stricken 6.1975
Vance	DE387	Consolidated, Orange	4.1943	16.7.1943	11.1943	stricken 6.1975
Lansing	DE388	Consolidated, Orange	5.1943	2.8.1943	11.1943	stricken 2.1974
Durant	DE389	Consolidated, Orange	5.1943	3.8.1943	11.1943	stricken 4.1974
Calcaterra	DE390	Consolidated, Orange	5.1943	16.8.1943	11.1943	stricken 7.1973

Chambers	DE391	Consolidated, Orange	5.1943	17.8.1943	11.1943	stricken 3.1975
Merrill	DE392	Consolidated, Orange	7.1943	29.8.1943	11.1943	stricken 4.1971
Haverfield	DE393	Consolidated, Orange	7.1943	30.8.1943	11.1943	stricken 6.1969
Swenning	DE394	Consolidated, Orange	7.1943	13.9.1943	12.1943	stricken 7.1972
Willis	DE395	Consolidated, Orange	7.1943	14.9.1943	12.1943	stricken 7.1972
Janssen	DE396	Consolidated, Orange	8.1943	4.10.1943	12.1943	stricken 7.1972
Wilhoite	DE397	Consolidated, Orange	8.1943	5.10.1943	12.1943	stricken 7.1969
Cockrill	DE398	Consolidated, Orange	8.1943	29.10.1943	12.1943	stricken 8.1973
Stockdale	DE399	Consolidated, Orange	8.1943	30.10.1943	12.1943	stricken 7.1972
Hissem	DE400	Consolidated, Orange	10.1943	26.12.1943	1.1944	stricken 6.1975
Holder	DE401	Consolidated, Orange	10.1943	27.12.1943	1.1944	sunk 11.4.1944

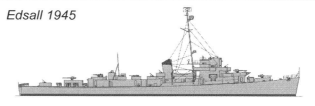

Edsall 1945

1253 / 1602 t, 93.3 x 11.2 x 3.2m, 4 Fairbanks Morse diesels (2 shafts), 6000 hp, 21 kts, 320 t diesel oil, 9000 nm (12 kts), complement 186; 3 x 1 – 76/50 Mk 20, 1 x 2 – 40/56 Bofors, 8 x 1 – 20/70 Oerlikon, 1 x 3 – 533 TT, 1 x 24 Hedgehog ASWRL, 8 DCT, 2 DCR (120); SC, SF or SL or SU radars, QGa sonar.

A total of 85 ships of FMR class were ordered. 4.1945, *Camp*: - 3 x 1 - 76/50, 2 x 1 - 20/70, 1 x 3 - 533 TT; + 2 x 1 - 127/38 Mk 12, (1 x 4 + 2 x 2 + 2 x 1) - 40/56 Bofors, Mk 25 radar. 1945, some ships: - 1 x 3 - 533 TT; + 4 x 1 - 40/56 Bofors.

Leopold 9.3.1944 was torpedoed S of Iceland by German submarine *U255* and sank the next day. *Fiske* 2.8.1944 was sunk N of the Azores by German submarine *U804*. *Frederick C. Davis* 24.4.1945 was sunk in the North Atlantic by German submarine *U546*.

Holder 11.4.1944 was damaged off the Algerian coast by German Ju 88 bomber and was not repaired. *Herbert C. Jones* 15.2.1944 was damaged off Anzio by German guided glide bomb. *Menges* 3.5.1944 was damaged in the Mediterranean by German submarine *U371*. *Haverson* 25.11.1943 was damaged

in a collision with Canadian s/s *O.K. Service*, 15.12.1943 she was again damaged in collision with British s/s *William T. Barry*.

Edsall 1943

'TEV' (RUDDEROW) class destroyer escorts

Rudderow	DE224	Philadelphia N Yd	7.1943	14.10.1943	5.1944	stricken 11.1969
Day	DE225	Philadelphia N Yd	7.1943	14.10.1943	6.1944	stricken 6.1968
Chaffee	DE230	Charleston N Yd	8.1943	27.11.1943	5.1944	stricken 8.1946
Hodges	DE231	Charleston N Yd	9.1943	9.12.1943	5.1944	stricken 12.1972
Riley	DE579	Bethlehem, Hingham	10.1943	29.12.1943	3.1944	to Taiwan 7.1968 (Tai Yuan)

Leslie L. B. Knox	DE580	Bethlehem, Hingham	11.1943	8.1.1944	3.1944	stricken 1.1972
McNulty	DE581	Bethlehem, Hingham	11.1943	8.1.1944	3.1944	stricken 3.1972
Metivier	DE582	Bethlehem, Hingham	11.1943	12.1.1944	4.1944	stricken 6.1968
George A. Johnson	DE583	Bethlehem, Hingham	11.1943	12.1.1944	4.1944	stricken 11.1965
Charles J. Kimmel	DE584	Bethlehem, Hingham	12.1943	15.1.1944	4.1944	stricken 6.1968
Daniel A. Joy	DE585	Bethlehem, Hingham	12.1943	15.1.1944	4.1944	stricken 5.1965
Lough	DE586	Bethlehem, Hingham	12.1943	22.1.1944	5.1944	stricken 11.1969
Thomas F. Nickel	DE587	Bethlehem, Hingham	12.1943	22.1.1944	6.1944	stricken 12.1972
Peiffer	DE588	Bethlehem, Hingham	12.1943	26.1.1944	6.1944	stricken 12.1966
Tinsman	DE589	Bethlehem, Hingham	12.1943	29.1.1944	6.1944	stricken 11.1969
DeLong	DE684	Bethlehem, Quincy	10.1943	23.11.1943	12.1943	stricken 8.1969
Coates	DE685	Bethlehem, Quincy	11.1943	9.12.1943	1.1944	stricken 1.1970
Eugene E. Elmore	DE686	Bethlehem, Quincy	11.1943	23.12.1943	2.1944	stricken 6.1968
Holt	DE706	Defoe, Bay City	11.1943	15.2.1944	6.1944	to South Korea 6.1963 (Chungnam)
Jobb	DE707	Defoe, Bay City	12.1943	4.3.1944	7.1944	stricken 11.1969
Parle	DE708	Defoe, Bay City	1.1944	25.3.1944	7.1944	stricken 7.1970
Bray	DE709, 7.1945-APD139	Defoe, Bay City	1.1944	15.4.1944	9.1944	fast transport 7.1945, stricken 6.1960

1430 / 1811 t, 93.3 x 11.3 x 3.4 m, 2 General Electric turbine-generators, 2 electric motors, 2 Babcock & Wilcox (DE224, 225) or Combustion Engineering (DE230, 231, 684-686, 706-709) or Foster Wheeler (DE579-589) boilers, 12000 hp, 23 kts, 348 t oil, 5500 nm (15 kts), complement 156; 2 x 1 – 127/38 Mk 12, 2 x 2 – 40/56 Bofors, 8 (DE684-686) or 10 x 1 – 20/70 Oerlikon, 1 x 3 – 533 TT, 1 x 24 Hedgehog ASWRL, 8 DCT, 2 DCR (100);

SC, SF or SL or SU, Mk 25 radars, QGa sonar.

A total of 252 destroyer escorts of TEV class were ordered. Building of 180 ships was cancelled in 1943 (DE647-664, 725-738, 905-1005) and in 1944 (DE284-300, 607-632, 645, 646, 723, 724). Some ships were named: planned to be built on Charleston NYd DE284 *Vogelgesang*, DE285 *Weekes,* DE286 *Sutton*, DE287 *William M. Wood*, DE288 *William R. Rush*, DE290 *Williams* and ordered from Dravo, Pittsburgh, DE723 *Walter X. Young.*

51 destroyer escorts were converted to fast personnel landing transports. 50 (DE226-229, 232-237, 281-283, 590-606, 674, 721, 722, 687-692 and 710-720, reclassified 17.7.1944 as APD87-136 respectively) were commissioned already in this capacity, one more (DE709, reclassified as APD139 16.7.1945) was converted after service in a destroyer escort role. For some reason, work on the conversion of two more ships (DE684 and 685 were to become APD137 and 138) was not started.

7.1945, *Bray*: - 1 x 1 - 127/38, 2 x 1 - 20/70, 1 x 3 - 533 TT, 1 x 24 Hedgehog ASWRL, 8 DCT; + 1 x 2 - 40/56

Rudderow 1944

Bofors, 4 LCVP, 162 troops
Hodges 9.1.1945 was damaged by kamikaze off the

Philippines. *Knudson* 25.3.1945 was damaged by Japanese aircraft off Okinawa.

'WGT' (JOHN C. BUTLER) class destroyer escorts

John C. Butler	DE339	Consolidated, Orange	10.1943	11.12.1943	3.1944	stricken 6.1970
O`Flaherty	DE340	Consolidated, Orange	10.1943	14.12.1943	4.1944	stricken 12.1972
Raymond	DE341	Consolidated, Orange	11.1943	8.1.1944	4.1944	stricken 7.1972
Richard W. Suesens	DE342	Consolidated, Orange	11.1943	11.1.1944	4.1944	stricken 3.1972
Abercrombie	DE343	Consolidated, Orange	11.1943	14.1.1944	5.1944	stricken 5.1967
Oberrender	DE344	Consolidated, Orange	11.1943	18.1.1944	5.1944	sunk 9.5.1945
Robert Brazier	DE345	Consolidated, Orange	11.1943	22.1.1944	5.1944	stricken 1.1968
Edwin A. Howard	DE346	Consolidated, Orange	11.1943	25.1.1944	5.1944	stricken 12.1972
Jesse Rutherford	DE347	Consolidated, Orange	11.1943	29.1.1944	5.1944	stricken 1.1968
Key	DE348	Consolidated, Orange	12.1943	12.2.1944	6.1944	stricken 3.1972
Gentry	DE349	Consolidated, Orange	12.1943	15.2.1944	6.1944	stricken 1.1972
Traw	DE350	Consolidated, Orange	12.1943	12.2.1944	6.1944	stricken 8.1967
Maurice J. Manuel	DE351	Consolidated, Orange	12.1943	19.2.1944	6.1944	stricken 5.1966
Naifeh	DE352	Consolidated, Orange	12.1943	29.2.1944	7.1944	stricken 1.1966
Doyle C. Barnes	DE353	Consolidated, Orange	1.1944	4.3.1944	7.1944	stricken 12.1972
Kenneth M. Willett	DE354	Consolidated, Orange	1.1944	7.3.1944	7.1944	stricken 7.1972
Jaccard	DE355	Consolidated, Orange	1.1944	18.3.1944	7.1944	stricken 11.1967
Lloyd E. Acree	DE356	Consolidated, Orange	1.1944	21.3.1944	8.1944	stricken 1.1972
George E. Davis	DE357	Consolidated, Orange	2.1944	8.4.1944	8.1944	stricken 12.1972
Mack	DE358	Consolidated, Orange	2.1944	11.4.1944	8.1944	stricken 3.1972
Woodson	DE359	Consolidated, Orange	3.1944	29.4.1944	8.1944	stricken 7.1965
Johnnie Hutchins	DE360	Consolidated, Orange	3.1944	2.5.1944	8.1944	stricken 7.1972
Walton	DE361	Consolidated, Orange	3.1944	20.5.1944	9.1944	stricken 9.1968
Rolf	DE362	Consolidated, Orange	3.1944	23.5.1944	9.1944	stricken 12.1972
Pratt	DE363	Consolidated, Orange	4.1944	1.6.1944	10.1944	stricken 3.1972
Rombach	DE364	Consolidated, Orange	4.1944	6.6.1944	9.1944	stricken 3.1972
McGinty	DE365	Consolidated, Orange	5.1944	5.8.1944	9.1944	stricken 9.1968
Alvin C. Cockrell	DE366	Consolidated, Orange	5.1944	8.8.1944	10.1944	stricken 9.1968
French	DE367	Consolidated, Orange	5.1944	17.6.1944	10.1944	stricken 5.1972
Cecil J. Doyle	DE368	Consolidated, Orange	5.1944	1.7.1944	10.1944	stricken 7.1967
Thaddeus Parker	DE369	Consolidated, Orange	5.1944	26.8.1944	10.1944	stricken 9.1967
John L. Williamson	DE370	Consolidated, Orange	5.1944	29.8.1944	10.1944	stricken 9.1970
Presley	DE371	Consolidated, Orange	6.1944	19.8.1944	11.1944	stricken 6.1968
Williams	DE372	Consolidated, Orange	6.1944	22.8.1944	11.1944	stricken 7.1967
William C. Lawe	DE373	Consolidated, Orange	6.1944	-	-	cancelled 6.1944
Lloyd Thomas	DE374	Consolidated, Orange	6.1944	-	-	cancelled 6.1944
Keppler	DE375	Consolidated, Orange	6.1944	-	-	cancelled 6.1944
Kleinsmith	DE376	Consolidated, Orange	6.1944	-	-	cancelled 6.1944
Henry W. Tucker	DE377	Consolidated, Orange	6.1944	-	-	cancelled 6.1944
Weiss	DE378	Consolidated, Orange	6.1944	-	-	cancelled 6.1944
Francovich	DE379	Consolidated, Orange	6.1944	-	-	cancelled 6.1944
Richard S. Bull	DE402	Brown SB, Houston	8.1943	16.11.1943	2.1944	stricken 6.1968
Richard M. Rowell	DE403	Brown SB, Houston	8.1943	17.11.1943	3.1944	stricken 6.1968
Eversole	DE404	Brown SB, Houston	9.1943	3.12.1943	3.1944	sunk 28.10.1944
Dennis	DE405	Brown SB, Houston	9.1943	4.12.1943	3.1944	stricken 12.1972
Edmonds	DE406	Brown SB, Houston	11.1943	17.12.1943	4.1944	stricken 5.1972

Shelton	DE407	Brown SB, Houston	11.1943	18.12.1943	4.1944	sunk 3.10.1944
Straus	DE408	Brown SB, Houston	11.1943	30.12.1943	4.1944	stricken 5.1966
La Prade	DE409	Brown SB, Houston	11.1943	31.12.1943	4.1944	stricken 1.1972
Jack Miller	DE410	Brown SB, Houston	11.1943	10.1.1944	4.1944	stricken 6.1968
Stafford	DE411	Brown SB, Houston	11.1943	11.1.1944	4.1944	stricken 3.1972
Walter C. Wann	DE412	Brown SB, Houston	12.1943	19.1.1944	5.1944	stricken 6.1968
Samuel B. Roberts	DE413	Brown SB, Houston	12.1943	20.1.1944	4.1944	sunk 25.10.1944
Le Ray Wilson	DE414	Brown SB, Houston	12.1943	28.1.1944	5.1944	stricken 5.1972
Lawrence C. Taylor	DE415	Brown SB, Houston	12.1943	29.1.1944	5.1944	stricken 12.1972
Melvin R. Nawman	DE416	Brown SB, Houston	1.1944	7.2.1944	5.1944	stricken 7.1972
Oliver Mitchell	DE417	Brown SB, Houston	1.1944	8.2.1944	6.1944	stricken 3.1972
Tabberer	DE418	Brown SB, Houston	1.1944	18.2.1944	5.1944	stricken 7.1972
Robert F. Keller	DE419	Brown SB, Houston	1.1944	19.2.1944	6.1944	stricken 7.1972
Leland E. Thomas	DE420	Brown SB, Houston	1.1944	28.2.1944	6.1944	stricken 12.1972
Chester T. O`Brien	DE421	Brown SB, Houston	1.1944	29.2.1944	7.1944	stricken 7.1972
Douglas A. Munro	DE422	Brown SB, Houston	1.1944	8.3.1944	7.1944	stricken 12.1965
Dufilho	DE423	Brown SB, Houston	1.1944	9.3.1944	7.1944	stricken 12.1972
Haas	DE424	Brown SB, Houston	2.1944	20.3.1944	8.1944	stricken 7.1966
Corbesier	DE438	Federal, Newark	11.1943	13.2.1944	3.1944	stricken 12.1972
Conklin	DE439	Federal, Newark	11.1943	13.2.1944	4.1944	stricken 10.1970
McCoy Reynolds	DE440	Federal, Newark	11.1943	22.2.1944	5.1944	to Portugal 2.1957 (Corte Real)
William Seiverling	DE441	Federal, Newark	12.1943	7.3.1944	6.1944	stricken 12.1972
Ulvert M. Moore	DE442	Federal, Newark	12.1943	7.3.1944	7.1944	stricken 12.1965
Kendall C. Campbell	DE443	Federal, Newark	12.1943	19.3.1944	7.1944	stricken 1.1972
Goss	DE444	Federal, Newark	12.1943	19.3.1944	8.1944	stricken 3.1972
Grady	DE445	Federal, Newark	1.1944	2.4.1944	9.1944	stricken 6.1968
Charles E. Brannon	DE446	Federal, Newark	1.1944	23.4.1944	11.1944	stricken 9.1968
Albert T. Harris	DE447	Federal, Newark	1.1944	16.4.1944	11.1944	stricken 9.1968
Cross	DE448	Federal, Newark	3.1944	4.7.1944	1.1945	stricken 7.1966
Hanna	DE449	Federal, Newark	3.1944	4.7.1944	1.1945	stricken 12.1972
Joseph E. Connolly	DE450	Federal, Newark	4.1944	6.8.1944	2.1945	stricken 6.1970
Woodrow R. Thompson	DE451	Federal, Newark	5.1944	-	-	cancelled 6.1944
Steinaker	DE452	Federal, Newark	6.1944	-	-	cancelled 6.1944
Gilligan *(ex-Donaldson)*	DE508	Federal, Newark	11.1943	22.2.1944	5.1944	stricken 3.1972
Formoe	DE509	Federal, Newark	1.1944	2.4.1944	10.1944	to Portugal 2.1957 (Diogo Cão)
Heyliger	DE510	Federal, Newark	4.1944	6.8.1944	3.1945	stricken 5.1966
Edward H. Allen	DE531	Boston N Yd, Charlestown	8.1943	7.10.1943	12.1943	stricken 7.1972
Tweedy	DE532	Boston N Yd, Charlestown	8.1943	7.10.1943	2.1944	stricken 6.1969
Howard F. Clark	DE533	Boston N Yd, Charlestown	10.1943	8.11.1943	5.1944	stricken 5.1972
Silverstein	DE534	Boston N Yd, Charlestown	10.1943	8.11.1943	7.1944	stricken 12.1972
Lewis	DE535	Boston N Yd, Charlestown	11.1943	7.12.1943	9.1944	stricken 1.1966
Bivin	DE536	Boston N Yd, Charlestown	11.1943	7.12.1943	10.1944	stricken 6.1968

Rizzi	DE537	Boston N Yd, Charlestown	11.1943	7.12.1943	6.1945	stricken 8.1972
Osberg	DE538	Boston N Yd, Charlestown	11.1943	7.12.1943	12.1945	stricken 8.1972
Wagner	DER539	Boston N Yd, Charlestown	11.1943	27.12.1943	11.1955	stricken 11.1974
Vandivier	DER540	Boston N Yd, Charlestown	11.1943	27.12.1943	10.1955	stricken 11.1974
Sheehen	DE541	Boston N Yd, Charlestown	11.1943	27.12.1943	-	cancelled 1.1946
Oswald A. Powers	DE542	Boston N Yd, Charlestown	11.1943	27.12.1943	-	cancelled 1.1946
Groves	DE543	Boston N Yd, Charlestown	12.1943	27.1.1944	-	cancelled 9.1944
Alfred Wolf	DE544	Boston N Yd, Charlestown	12.1943	27.1.1944	-	cancelled 9.1944
Harold J. Ellison	DE545	Boston N Yd, Charlestown	1944	-	-	cancelled 6.1944
Myles C. Fox	DE546	Boston N Yd, Charlestown	1944	-	-	cancelled 6.1944
Charles R. Ware	DE547	Boston N Yd, Charlestown	1944	-	-	cancelled 6.1944
Carpellotti	DE548	Boston N Yd, Charlestown	1944	-	-	cancelled 6.1944
Eugene A. Greene	DE549	Boston N Yd, Charlestown	1944	-	-	cancelled 6.1944
Gyatt	DE550	Boston N Yd, Charlestown	1944	-	-	cancelled 6.1944
Benner	DE551	Boston N Yd, Charlestown	1944	-	-	cancelled 6.1944
Kenneth D. Bailey	DE552	Boston N Yd, Charlestown	1944	-	-	cancelled 6.1944
Dennis J. Buckley	DE553	Boston N Yd, Charlestown	1944	-	-	cancelled 6.1944
Everett F. Larson	DE554	Boston N Yd, Charlestown	1944	-	-	cancelled 6.1944

1430 / 1811 t, 93.3 x 11.3 x 3.4 m,2 sets Westinghouse geared steam turbines, 2 Combustion Engineering (DE339-372, 402-424) or Babcock & Wilcox boilers, 12000 hp, 23 kts, 348 t oil, 4650 nm (12 kts), complement 156; 2 x 1 – 127/38 Mk 12, 2 x 2 or (1 x 4 + 3 x 2) (DE537, 538, DER539, 540) – 40/56 Bofors, 10 x 1 or (3 x 2 + 10 x 1) (DE448-450, 510) or 6 x 1 (DER539, 540) – 20/70 Oerlikon, 1 x 3 – 533 TT (except DE448-450, 510, 537, 538, DER539, 540), 1 x 24 Hedgehog ASWRL, 8 DCT, 2 DCR (100); SC (except DER539, 540), SF or SL or SU (except DER539, 540), SPS-10 (DER539, 540), SPS-29 (DER539, 540), Mk 25 radars, QGa sonar.

A total of 293 destroyer escorts of WGT class were ordered. The building of 208 ships was cancelled in 1943 (DE478-507, 801-904), in 1944 (DE373-381, 425-437, 451-477, 512-515, 543-562) and in 1946 (DE541 and 542). Three planned for building on Boston N Yd ships were named: DE555 Rogers Blood, DE556 William R.

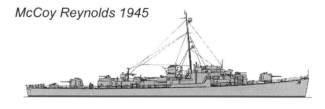

McCoy Reynolds 1945

Rush and DE557 *William M. Wood*.

The building of two ships (DE539 *Wagner* and DE540 *Vandivier*) was suspended

O'Flaherty 1944

in 1946 and resumed only in 1954: ships were completed as radar pickets.

Shelton 3.10.1944 was sunk off Morotai by Japanese submarine *RO41*. *Samuel B. Roberts* 25.10.1944 was sunk in the Battle of Samar (Leyte Gulf) by Japanese cruisers *Tone* and *Haguro*. *Richard M. Rowell* 25.10.1944 was damaged in Leyte Gulf by Japanese aircraft. *Eversole* 25.10.1944 was damaged in Leyte Gulf by Japanese ships and 28.10.1944 sunk E of Leyte Gulf by Japanese submarine *I45*.

Dennis 25.10.1944 was damaged in the Battle of Samar (Leyte Gulf) by Japanese ships. During kamikaze attacks off the Philippines following ships received damages of varying severity: *Stafford* (5.1.1945), *Leray Wilson* (10.1.1945), *Richard W. Suesens* (12.1.1945) and *Gilligan* (12.1.1945).

During attacks by Japanese aircraft and kamikazes off Okinawa following ships were damaged: *Walter C. Wann* (12.4.1945), *Oberrender* (9.5.1945, heavy damages, not repaired and sank as a target 6.11.1945), *John C. Butler* (20.5.1945, heavy), *Gilligan* (27.5.1945).

SUBMARINES

'O' class submarines

O1	SS62	Portsmouth N Yd	3.1917	9.7.1918	11.1918	stricken 3.1938
O2	SS63	Puget Sound N Yd, Bremerton	7.1917	24.5.1918	10.1918	stricken 8.1945
O3	SS64	Fore River, Quincy	12.1916	29.9.1917	6.1918	stricken 10.1945
O4	SS65	Fore River, Quincy	12.1916	20.10.1917	5.1918	stricken 10.1945
O6	SS67	Fore River, Quincy	12.1916	25.11.1917	6.1918	stricken 9.1945
O7	SS68	Fore River, Quincy	2.1917	16.12.1917	7.1918	stricken 7.1945
O8	SS69	Fore River, Quincy	2.1917	21.12.1917	7.1918	stricken 10.1945
O9	SS70	Fore River, Quincy	2.1917	27.1.1918	7.1918	foundered 20.6.1941
O10	SS71	Fore River, Quincy	2.1917	21.2.1918	8.1918	stricken 10.1945

O8 1943

O10 1922

521 / 629 t, 52.5 x 5.5 x 4.4 m, 2 NLSE diesels / 2 electric motors, 600 / 550 hp, 13 / 11 kts, 88 t diesel oil, 5500 nm (11.5 kts) /, complement 25, 60 m; 1 x 1 – 76/23 Mk 9, 4 – 450 TT (bow, 8), SC sonar.

The effective design of the submarine, completed after much experimentation with many classes. Development of the 'N' class. There were two subgroups: 10 submarines of the first were built according to the Holland design (*O1-10*), 6 submarines of the second (*O11-16*) according to the Lake design. The latter submarines were unsuccessful. Saddle-tank hull.

1939-1940, most survived: - 1 x 1 - 76/23; + 1 x 1 - 12.7 MG, JK sonar.

1940s, most survived: + SD or SJ radar

O9 foundered after a technical accident 20.6.1941 15 nm of Portsmouth.

'R' class submarines

R1	SS78	Fore River, Quincy	10.1917	24.8.1918	12.1918	stricken 11.1945
R2	SS79	Fore River, Quincy	10.1917	23.9.1918	1.1919	stricken 11.1945
R3	SS80	Fore River, Quincy	12.1917	18.1.1919	4.1919	to the UK 1.1941 (P511)
R4	SS81	Fore River, Quincy	10.1917	26.10.1918	3.1919	stricken 7.1945
R5	SS82	Fore River, Quincy	10.1917	24.11.1918	4.1919	stricken 10.1945
R6	SS83	Fore River, Quincy	12.1917	1.3.1919	5.1919	stricken 10.1945

R7	SS84	Fore River, Quincy	12.1917	5.4.1919	6.1919	stricken 10.1945
R9	SS86	Fore River, Quincy	3.1918	24.5.1919	7.1919	stricken 10.1945
R10	SS87	Fore River, Quincy	3.1918	28.6.1919	8.1919	stricken 7.1945
R11	SS88	Fore River, Quincy	3.1918	12.7.1919	9.1919	stricken 10.1945
R12	SS89	Fore River, Quincy	3.1918	15.8.1919	9.1919	foundered 12.6.1943
R13	SS90	Fore River, Quincy	3.1918	27.8.1919	10.1919	stricken 10.1945
R14	SS91	Fore River, Quincy	11.1918	10.10.1919	12.1919	stricken 5.1945
R15	SS92	Union Iron Wks, San Francisco	4.1917	10.12.1917	7.1918	stricken 10.1945
R16	SS93	Union Iron Wks, San Francisco	4.1917	15.12.1917	8.1918	stricken 7.1945
R17	SS94	Union Iron Wks, San Francisco	5.1917	24.12.1917	8.1918	to the UK 3.1942-9.1944 (P512), stricken 6.1945
R18	SS95	Union Iron Wks, San Francisco	6.1917	8.1.1918	9.1918	stricken 11.1945
R19	SS96	Union Iron Wks, San Francisco	6.1917	28.1.1918	10.1918	to the UK 3.1942 (P514)
R20	SS97	Union Iron Wks, San Francisco	6.1917	21.8.1918	10.1918	stricken 10.1945

569 / 680 t, 56.8 x 5.5 x 4.4 m, 2 NLSE diesels / 2 electric motors, 1200 / 940 hp, 13.5 / 11 kts, 75 t diesel oil, 4700 nm (6 kts) /, complement 29, 60 m; 1 x 1 – 76/50 Mk 6, 4 – 533 TT (bow, 8), SC sonar.

Quite successful boats, the development of the previous 'O' class, but faster and with a long-barrel gun. 20 submarines entered service: the first group (R1-20), wase built according to the Holland design, the second seven submarines (R21-27) were built according to the Lake design. The last group was unsuccessful. Saddle-tank hull.

1939-1940, most survived: - 1 x 1 - 76/50; + 1 x 1 - 12.7 MG, JK sonar.

1940s, most survived: - SC sonar; + SD or SJ radar, QB or QC, JP sonars

R12 was lost 12.6.1943 off Key West (Florida) during a training dive.

R13 1940

R4 1920s

'S' class submarines, 1st group

S1	SS105	Fore River, Quincy	12.1917	26.10.1918	6.1920	to the UK 4.1942 (P552)
S18	SS123	Bethlehem, Quincy	8.1918	29.4.1920	4.1924	stricken 11.1945
S19	SS124	Bethlehem, Quincy	8.1918	21.6.1920	8.1921	stricken 12.1938
S20	SS125	Bethlehem, Quincy	8.1918	9.6.1920	11.1922	stricken 7.1945
S21	SS126	Bethlehem, Quincy	12.1918	18.8.1920	8.1921	to the UK 9.1942-7.1944 (P553), sunk as target 23.3.1945
S22	SS127	Bethlehem, Quincy	1.1919	15.7.1920	6.1924	to the UK 6.1942-7.1944 (P554), stricken 8.1945
S23	SS128	Bethlehem, Quincy	1.1919	27.10.1920	10.1923	stricken 11.1945
S24	SS129	Bethlehem, Quincy	11.1918	27.6.1922	8.1923	to the UK 8.1942-1944 (P555), sunk as target 25.8.1947
S25	SS130	Bethlehem, Quincy	10.1918	29.5.1922	7.1923	to the UK 11.1941 (P551)
S26	SS131	Bethlehem, Quincy	11.1919	22.8.1922	10.1923	collision 24.1.1942
S27	SS132	Bethlehem, Quincy	4.1919	18.10.1922	1.1924	wrecked 19.6.1942
S28	SS133	Bethlehem, Quincy	4.1919	20.9.1922	12.1923	foundered 4.7.1944
S29	SS134	Bethlehem, Quincy	4.1919	9.11.1922	5.1924	to the UK 6.1942 (P556)

S30	SS135	Union Iron Wks, San Francisco	4.1918	21.11.1918	10.1920	stricken 10.1945
S31	SS136	Union Iron Wks, San Francisco	4.1918	28.12.1918	5.1922	stricken 11.1945
S32	SS137	Union Iron Wks, San Francisco	4.1918	11.1.1919	6.1922	stricken 11.1945
S33	SS138	Union Iron Wks, San Francisco	6.1918	5.12.1918	4.1922	stricken 11.1945
S34	SS139	Union Iron Wks, San Francisco	5.1918	13.2.1919	7.1922	stricken 11.1945
S35	SS140	Union Iron Wks, San Francisco	6.1918	27.2.1919	8.1922	sunk as target 4.4.1946
S36	SS141	Union Iron Wks, San Francisco	12.1918	3.6.1919	4.1923	scuttled 21.1.1942
S37	SS142	Union Iron Wks, San Francisco	12.1918	20.6.1919	7.1923	sunk as target 20.2.1945
S38	SS143	Union Iron Wks, San Francisco	1.1919	17.6.1919	5.1923	stricken 1.1945
S39	SS144	Union Iron Wks, San Francisco	1.1919	2.7.1919	9.1923	wrecked 14.8.1942
S40	SS145	Bethlehem, San Francisco	3.1919	5.1.1921	11.1923	stricken 11.1945
S41	SS146	Bethlehem, San Francisco	4.1919	21.2.1921	1.1924	stricken 2.1946

S25 1941

854 / 1062 t, 66.9 x 6.3 x 4.8 m, 2 NLSE diesels / 2 electric motors, 1200 / 1500 hp, 14 / 11 kts, 168 t diesel oil, 3420 nm (6.5 kts) /, complement 38, 60 m; 1 x 1 – 102/50 Mk 9, 4 – 533 TT (bow, 12), SC sonar.

Further development of the 'R' class submarines. They were built to three distinctly differed designs by Holland, Lake and the Bureau of Construction & Repair. After the acquisition of these designs by the General board in 1917, one submarine was built on each of them as a "prototype" (*S1, 2* and *3* respectively). Lake's variant (*S2*) was unsuccessful, and later Lake built submarines according to the Bureau's design.

Serial building was developed on two designs: 24 submarines (*S18-41*) under the Holland design and 14 (*S4-17*) under the Bureau design. They were followed by 10 almost identical boats of the second series (*S42-47* Holland and *S48-51* Bureau).

The main difference between the Holland and Bureau designs was in the construction of the hull: in the first case, it was made single-hulled, in the second double-hulled. The diving depth was the same. Submarines built by Lake had additional stern TT. When these submarines were designed, an opinion was dominated that it was necessary to ensure the highest submerged speed, and the CT was made as much as possible streamlined. On trials, the "prototypes" showed outstanding results, reaching speeds from 12.5 to 13 kts in a submerged position. The experience of the First World War, however, showed that the extra 2-3 knots were not so necessary compared to the safety of the crew, therefore, already during the completion the serial-built submarines received less streamlined, but much more comfortable CTs.

Although the *'S'* class submarines were noticeably superior to their predecessors in most characteristics, the naval authorities in 1925 recognized them as unsuccessful due to insufficient endurance for the service in the Pacific.

1939, all: + 1 x 1 – 12.7 MG, JK sonar.
1940s, most survived: - SC sonar; + 1 x 1 - 20/70 Oerlikon, SJ radar, QB sonar. 1940s, *S27, S28*: - SC sonar; + 1 x 1 – 20/70 Oerlikon, SJ radar, QC sonar.

S36 20.1.1942 was damaged in a beaching at Celebes and was scuttled by the own crew the next day. *S26* 24.1.1942 was lost off the Gulf of Panama in a collision with *PC460*. *S27* 19.6.1942 ran aground at Cape St. Macarius (Amchitka Island) and was abandoned by the crew. *S39* 14.8.1942 ran aground at Russell Island and was abandoned 16.8.1942. *S28* 4.7.1944 foundered off Pearl Harbor during a training dive.

S18 26.8.1944 was damaged off San Diego in a collision with *LSM135*.

S1

'S' class submarines, 2nd group

S42	SS153	Bethlehem, Quincy	12.1920	30.4.1923	11.1924	stricken 11.1945
S43	SS154	Bethlehem, Quincy	12.1920	31.3.1923	12.1924	stricken 11.1945
S44	SS155	Bethlehem, Quincy	2.1921	27.10.1923	2.1925	sunk 7.10.1943
S45	SS156	Bethlehem, Quincy	12.1920	26.6.1923	3.1925	stricken 11.1945
S46	SS157	Bethlehem, Quincy	2.1921	11.9.1923	6.1925	stricken 11.1945
S47	SS158	Bethlehem, Quincy	2.1921	5.1.1924	9.1925	stricken 11.1945

906 / 1126 t, 68.7 x 6.3 x 4.9 m, 2 NLSE diesels / 2 electric motors, 1200 / 1200 hp, 14.5 / 11 kts, 168 t diesel oil, 2510 nm (6.5 kts) /, complement 38, 60 m; 1 x 1 – 102/50 Mk 9, 4 – 533 TT (bow, 12), SC sonar.
1939, all: + 1 x 1 – 12.7 MG, JK sonar.
1940s, most survived: - SC, JK sonars; + 1 x 1 - 20/70 Oerlikon, SD, SJ radars, QB, QC, JP sonars.

S42 1924

S44 7.10.1943 was sunk off Paramushir Island by Japanese escort *Ishigaki*.

'S' class submarines, 4th group

S11	SS116	Portsmouth N Yd	12.1919	7.2.1921	1.1923	stricken 10.1945
S12	SS117	Portsmouth N Yd	1.1920	4.8.1921	4.1923	stricken 5.1945
S13	SS118	Portsmouth N Yd	2.1920	20.10.1921	7.1923	stricken 10.1945
S14	SS119	Lake, Bridgeport	12.1917	22.10.1919	2.1921	stricken 5.1945
S15	SS120	Lake, Bridgeport	12.1917	8.3.1920	1.1921	stricken 6.1946
S16	SS121	Lake, Bridgeport	3.1918	23.12.1919	12.1920	stricken 10.1944
S17	SS122	Lake, Bridgeport	3.1918	22.5.1920	3.1921	stricken 11.1944

876 / 1092 t, 70.4 x 6.7 x 4.0 m, 2 MAN diesels / 2 electric motors, 2000 / 1200 hp, 15 / 11 kts, 148 t diesel oil, 5000 nm (10 kts) / , complement 38, 60 m; 1 x 1 – 102/50 Mk 9, 5 – 533 TT (4 bow, 1 stern, 14) (SS116-118) or 4 – 533 TT (bow, 12) (SS119-122), SC sonar.
1939-1940, all survived: + 1 x 1 - 12.7 MG, JK sonar.
1940s, most survived: - SC sonar; + SD radar, QB or QC sonars.
S16 13.7.1942 was mistakenly damaged off the coast of Panama by US aircraft. She was laid up to reserve 4.10.1944 and sunk as target 3.4.1945 off Key West (Florida).

lead S3 1919

S15 1921

'S' class submarine, 5th group

S48	SS159	Lake, Bridgeport	10.1920	26.2.1921	10.1922	stricken 9.1945

903 / 1230 t, 73.2 x 6.6 x 4.1 m, 2 Bush-Sulzer diesels / 2 electric motors, 1800 / 1500 hp, 14.5 / 11 kts, 177 t diesel oil, 8000 nm (10 kts) /, complement 38, 60 m; 1 x 1 – 102/50 Mk 9, 5 – 533 TT (4 bow, 1 stern, 14), SC sonar.
1939: + 1 x 1 - 12.7 MG, JK sonar.

S48 1921

1940s: - SC sonar; + SD radar, QB or QC sonars.

BARRACUDA (ex-V1) class submarines

Barracuda *(ex-V1)*	SS163	Portsmouth N Yd	10.1921	17.7.1924	10.1924	sold 11.1945
Bass *(ex-V2)*	SS164	Portsmouth N Yd	10.1921	27.12.1924	9.1925	stricken 3.1945
Bonita *(ex-V3)*	SS165	Portsmouth N Yd	11.1921	9.6.1925	5.1926	stricken 3.1945

Bonita 1940

2119 / 2506 t, 102.0 x 8.4 x 4.6 m, 2 Sulzer diesels + 2

Bonita 1930s

Sulzer diesel-generators / 2 electric motors, 6200 / 2400 hp, 18.7 / 9 kts, 364 t diesel oil, 12000 nm (11 kts) / 10 nm (8 kts), complement 85, 60 m; 1 x 1 – 76/50 Mk 17/18, 6 – 533 TT (4 bow, 2 stern, 12); SC sonar.

The design of ocean-going submarines was developed on the basis of the latest series of the *S* class. Built according to the 1916 Program. Double-hulled. The machinery was of a combined type: in addition to main propulsion diesels with direct drive, there were two diesels-generators used both for battery recharging and for cruising using an electric drive.

Despite the noticeable greater autonomy, cruising range and higher speed, compared to the *S* class submarines, these ships were considered rather mediocre due to poor maneuverability. At the beginning of the war, they were supposed to be converted to transports, but this idea was abandoned.

1940, all: Sulzer diesel-generators were replaced by more powerful MAN; - SC sonar; + WBA sonar.

1943, all: - 1 x 1 - 76/50; + 2 x 1 - 20/70 Oerlikon, SD, SJ radars.

Bass in August 1942 was badly damaged by a fire in the engine room.

ARGONAUT (ex-V4) submarine

Argonaut *(ex-V4)*	SS166, 9.1942-APS1	Portsmouth N Yd	5.1925	10.11.1927	4.1928	transport submarine 9.1942, sunk 10.1.1943

Argonaut 1942

2878 / 4045 t, 116.1 x 10.3 x 4.9 m, 2 MAN diesels + 2 MAN diesel-generators / 2 electric motors, 3175 / 2200 hp, 13.6 / 7.4 kts, 696 t diesel oil, 18000 nm (10 kts) / 50 nm (5 kts), complement 86, 95 m; 2 x 1 – 152/53 Mk 12/14, 2 x 1 – 7.6 MG, 4 – 533 TT (bow, 8), 60 mines; SC, JK sonars.

A unique purpose-built minelaying submarine of the US Navy. The naval commanders proposed to increase the displacement in order to ensure the cruising range necessary in the conditions of the Pacific theater, and in some cases, this was quite absurd: for example, in one of the draft designs there was a "monster" with a displacement of 20500 t. Finally, the Bureau of Construction & Repair prepared in 1922 a draft design of a submarine with a surface displacement of just over 2500 t, armed with two 152-mm/53 guns of cruiser caliber, four bow TTs and two mine tubes in the stern for 60 mines, which was supposed to operate at sea for 90 days, and with 18000-nm surface cruising range. The hull of the future *Argonaut* was designed for a diving depth of 95 m instead of 60 m for the previous classes. When designing, in addition to using some technical solutions used on *S* and *Barracuda* classes submarines, US designers probably took full account of the German experience in building submarine cruisers during the First World War. In the early stages of design, the fore end was planned to be made with a characteristic bulbous stem as on *Barracuda*, but in the final version featured the characteristic sharp "German" bow.

Double-hulled, the machinery was of combined type (the main diesels directly connected to the shafts, and auxiliary diesel-generators for recharging batteries). The advantages of this submarine include, perhaps, only endurance and good habitability conditions (which, however, was important for three-month voyage). In remaining, submarine was quite mediocre: she had poor maneuverability and slow surface speed.

1940: diesels were replaced by more powerful Fairbank-Morse (6000 hp, 15 kts surfaced); - SC sonar: + QCD sonar.

9.1942, *Argonaut* was converted to a cargo submarine, the mine deck and spare torpedo compartment were rebuilt as cargo holds; + SD, SJ radars.

10.1.1943 *Argonaut* was sunk by Japanese destroyers *Isokaze* and *Maikaze* between Bougainville and New Britannia.

NARWHAL (ex-V5) class submarines

Narwhal *(ex-V5)*	SS167	Portsmouth N Yd	5.1927	17.12.1927	3.1930	stricken 5.1945
Nautilus *(ex-V6)*	SS168	Mare Island N Yd, Vallejo	5.1927	15.3.1930	7.1930	stricken 7.1945

2987 / 3960 t, 113.1 x 10.1 x 5.2 m, 2 MAN diesels + 2 MAN diesel-generators / 2 electric motors, 5633 / 1600 hp, 17.4 / 8 kts, 732 t diesel oil, 18000 nm (10 kts) / 50 nm (5 kts), complement 90, 100 m; 2 x 1 – 152/53 Mk 12/14, 2 x 1 – 12.7 MG, 6 – 533 TT (4 bow, 2 stern, 12); JK sonar.

The largest USN submarines before the nuclear-powered *Nautilus*. They were built according to a slightly modified *Argonaut* design, in which the stern mine tubes were replaced by two TTs. Double-hulled.

These submarines had most of the shortcomings of the *Argonaut*: insufficient maneuverability and too long dive time. At the same time, a large internal volume allowed to use these submarines for sabotage landings. 1940-1941, *Narwhal*: main diesels were replaced by more powerful Fairbank-Morse diesel-generators (6000 hp); + QCH sonar. 1940-1941, *Nautilus*: main diesels were replaced by more powerful Fairbank-Morse diesel-

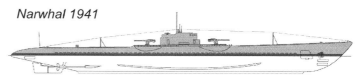
Narwhal 1941

generators (6000 hp); + QCD sonar.
1942, *Nautilus*; 1943, *Narwhal*: + 2 x 1 - 20/70 Oerlikon, 4 - 533 TT (2 ext bow, 2 ext stern, 16 torpedoes totally), SD, SJ radars.

Narwhal 1931

DOLPHIN submarine

Dolphin *(ex-V7)*	SS169	Portsmouth N Yd	6.1930	8.3.1932	7.1932	stricken 10.1945

1688 / 2215 t, 97.3 x 8.5 x 4.0 m, 2 MAN diesels + 2 MAN diesel-generators / 2 electric motors, 3500 / 1750 hp, 17 / 8 kts, 412 t diesel oil, 6000 nm (10 kts) / 50 nm (5 kts), complement 63, 75 m; 1 x 1 – 76/50 Mk 17/18, 2 x 1 – 12.7 MG, 6 – 533 TT (4 bow, 2 stern, 18); QB, JK sonars.

By the end of 1920th in the USA, there was a withdrawal from the previously usual trend towards an increase in the displacement of submarines. A surface displacement of up to 3000 t, of course, allowed to ensure high endurance, but at the same time all other characteristics unnecessarily deteriorated. In 1927, the basic requirements for a submarine for operations in the Eastern Pacific were prepared, according to which the cruising range was reduced to 12000 nm, and endurance to 60 days. Speed was considered less important than maneuverability and torpedo armament. At the same time, artillery armament was considered possible to reduce to one 102-mm gun. Surface displacement was limited to 1600 t.

In accordance with these requirements, the design of *Dolphin* was prepared. The first attempt to

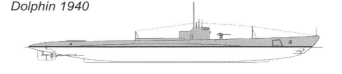
Dolphin 1940

create an ocean patrol submarine was not entirely successful: *Dolphin* was notable for her insufficient hull strength and cruising range less than designed.

Double-hulled. The machinery consisted of two main diesels with direct drive and two diesel-generators for battery recharging. The 102-mm/50 gun shortly after completion was replaced with a lighter 76-mm gun.
Late 1930s: - QB sonar; + QC, JG sonars.
1940s: + SD, SJ radars.

Dolphin 1932

CACHALOT class submarines

Cachalot	SS170	Portsmouth N Yd	10.1931	19.10.1933	12.1933	stricken 11.1945
Cuttlefish	SS171	Electric Boat, Groton	10.1931	21.11.1933	6.1934	stricken 7.1946

Cachalot 1940

1120 / 1650 t, 82.9 x 7.5 x 4.3 m, 2 MAN diesels / 2 electric motors, 2770 / 1600 hp, 17 / 8 kts, 333 t diesel oil, 9000 nm (12 kts) / 50 nm (5 kts), complement 51, 75 m; 1 x 1 – 76/50 Mk 17/18, 3 x 1 – 12.7 MG, 6 – 533 TT (4 bow, 2 stern, 16); QC, JK sonars.

The appearance of these boats with a small, compared to previous US designs, displacements can be explained by several reasons. First, the limitation of the total

Cuttlefish 1934

displacement of submarines adopted by the London Naval Conference of 1930 left only one way to increase the number of these ships: reducing their dimensions. Secondly, the comparison of the *Dolphin* with one of the best German submarines of the First World War, the *U135*, was not in favor of the USN submarine, which, with a significantly larger displacement, surpassed the German counterpart only in cruising range, inferior in most other characteristics.

Taking into account these factors, the design of a new submarine with German "roots" was ready, but made at a new technological level, with extensive use of welding instead of traditional riveting. Double-hulled, diesels drove the shafts directly.

Although some experts spoke of *Cachalot* as a not entirely successful ship, she became the ancestor of most of the later fleet submarines of the US Navy.
1938, both: diesels were replaced by more powerful ones (3100 hp).
1940s, both: + SD, SJ radars.

PORPOISE class submarines

| Porpoise | SS172 | Portsmouth N Yd | 10.1933 | 20.6.1935 | 8.1935 | stricken 8.1956 |
| Pike | SS173 | Portsmouth N Yd | 12.1933 | 12.9.1935 | 12.1935 | stricken 2.1956 |

Pike 1943

Porpoise 1936

1316 / 1934 t, 91.8 x 7.6 x 4.3 m, 4 Winton diesel-generators / 2 electric motors, 4300 / 2085 hp, 19 / 10 kts, 347 t diesel oil, 10000 nm (10 kts) / 42 nm (5 kts), complement 54, 75 m; 1 x 1 – 76/50 Mk 17/18, 2 x 1 – 12.7 MG, 6 – 533 TT (4 bow, 2 stern, 16); QC, JK sonars. Based on the *Cachalot* class submarines. The dimensions and displacement were noticeably increased, which made it possible to install more powerful diesels and make the engine room more spacious compared to the *Cachalot* engine room, which was very cramped

and inconvenient for servicing the diesels. An important innovation of this class was the rejection of the rigid connection of diesel with the propeller shaft and the transition to an electrical drive. The introduction of generators on diesel shafts was partially offset by the abandonment of the use of an auxiliary diesel-generator, serving only to recharge the battery. The new scheme provided much more flexible use of the machinery, allowing to significantly speed up the process of recharging or recharge battery at almost full speed. The advantage of diesel-electric gear was manifested in a noticeable reduction in vibration. On the boats of this class, special attention was paid to improving habitability conditions, in particular, they received air conditioning for the first time. Double-hulled.

Funding for the building of this class came from the National Industrial Recovery Act passed in 1933. There were two detailed designs developed by the Bureau of Construction & Repair (SS172 and 173) and Electric Boat (SS174 and 175).
1942-1943, both: CT was rebuilt; - 2 x 1 - 12.7 MG; + 2 x 1 - 20/70 Oerlikon, 2 - 533 TT (ext stern, 18 torpedoes totally), SD, SJ radars.

SHARK class submarines

| Shark | SS174 | Electric Boat, Groton | 10.1933 | 21.5.1935 | 1.1936 | sunk 11.2.1942 |
| Tarpon | SS175 | Electric Boat, Groton | 12.1933 | 4.9.1935 | 3.1936 | stricken 9.1956 |

1315 / 1968 t, 90.8 x 7.6 x 4.6 m, 4 Winton diesel-generators / 2 electric motors, 4300 / 2085 hp, 19.5 / 8 kts, 347 t diesel oil, 10000 nm (10 kts) / 42 nm (5 kts), complement 54, 75 m; 1 x 1 – 76/50 Mk 17/18, 2 x 1 – 12.7 MG, 6 – 533 TT (4 bow, 2 stern, 16); QC, JK sonars.
1942-1943, *Tarpon*: CT was rebuilt; - 2 x 1 - 12.7 MG; + 2 x 1 - 20/70 Oerlikon, 2 - 533 TT (ext stern, 18 torpedoes totally), SD, SJ radars.
Shark was sunk 11.2.1942 120 nm E of Celebes by Japanese destroyer *Yamakaze*.

Tarpon 1944

Tarpon 1937

PERCH class submarines

Perch	SS176	Electric Boat, Groton	2.1935	9.5.1936	11.1936	sunk 3.3.1942
Pickerel	SS177	Electric Boat, Groton	3.1935	7.7.1936	1.1937	sunk 3.4.1943
Permit (ex-Pinna)	SS178	Electric Boat, Groton	6.1935	5.10.1936	3.1937	stricken 7.1956
Plunger	SS179	Portsmouth N Yd	7.1935	8.7.1936	11.1936	stricken 7.1956
Pollack	SS180	Portsmouth N Yd	10.1935	15.9.1936	1.1937	stricken 10.1946
Pompano	SS181	Mare Island N Yd, Vallejo	1.1936	11.3.1937	6.1937	sunk 8-9.1943

1330 / 1997 t, 91.6 x 7.7 x 4.6 m, 4 Winton or Fairbank-Morse (SS180) or Hoover, Owens, Rentschler (SS181) diesel-generators / 2 electric motors, 4300 / 2366 hp, 19.2 / 8 kts, 373 t diesel oil, 10000 nm (10 kts) / 42 nm (5 kts), complement 54, 75 m; 1 x 1 – 76/50 Mk 17/18, 2 x 1 – 12.7 MG, 6 – 533 TT (4 bow, 2 stern, 16); QC, JK sonars.
These submarines were built under the FY35 Program. They differed little from *Porpoise*, except for the use of more powerful diesels.
1942, *Pickerel, Permit*: + 2 - 533 TT (ext stern, 18 torpedoes totally). 1942-1943, all survived: CT was rebuilt; - 2 x 1 - 12.7 MG; + 2 x 1 - 20/70 Oerlikon, SD, SJ radars.
Perch 1.3.1942 was damaged by the DCs from Japanese destroyers *Amatsukaze* and *Hatsukaze* and 3.3.1942 was scuttled E of Surabaya having received additionally damage from Japanese destroyer *Yukikaze*. *Pickerel* in

Pompano 1937

April 1943 was lost off the N coast of Japan (most likely, 3.4.1943 N of Honshu Island she was sunk by Japanese aircraft, destroyer *Shirakami* and auxiliary patrol *Bunzan Maru*). *Pompano* was lost to an unknown cause in August-September 1943, probably off the coast of Honshu or Hokkaido, probably hit by a mine.

Pompano 1938

SALMON class submarines

Salmon	SS182	Electric Boat, Groton	4.1936	12.6.1937	3.1938	stricken 10.1945
Seal	SS183	Electric Boat, Groton	5.1936	25.8.1937	4.1938	stricken 5.1956
Skipjack	SS184	Electric Boat, Groton	7.1936	23.10.1937	6.1938	nuclear tests 7.1946
Snapper	SS185	Portsmouth N Yd	7.1936	24.8.1937	12.1937	stricken 4.1948
Stingray	SS186	Portsmouth N Yd	10.1936	6.10.1937	3.1938	stricken 7.1946
Sturgeon	SS187	Mare Island N Yd, Vallejo	10.1936	15.3.1938	6.1938	stricken 3.1948

1449 / 2210 t, 93.9 x 8.0 x 4.8 m, 4 Hoover, Owens, Rentschler diesels / 4 electric motors (2 shafts), 5500 / 2660 hp, 21 / 9 kts, 384 t diesel oil, 11000 nm (10 kts) / 96 nm (2 kts), complement 59, 75 m; 1 x 1 – 76/50 Mk 17/18, 2 x 1 – 12.7 MG, 8 – 533 TT (4 bow, 4 stern, 24 torpedoes or 32 mines); QCC, JK sonars.
The *Salmon* class submarines were an enlarged version of the *Porpoise* class with more powerful machinery,

Salmon 1938

two additional stern TTs (8 in total) and increased to 24 torpedo stowage. In their construction, the designers returned to diesels with mechanical shaft drive (through a special hydraulic clutches). This decision was a tribute

Skipjack 1938

to the concerns expressed by some experts about the lack of reliability of electrical transmission, which could easily fail if any damage to the power cable. Double-hulled, built according to the FY36 Program.
1942-1943, all survived: CT was rebuilt; - 1 x 1 - 76/50, 2 x 1 - 12.7 MG; + 1 x 1 - 102/50 Mk 9 or 1 x 1 - 127/25 Mk 17, 2 x 1 - 20/70 Oerlikon, SD, SJ radars.

SARGO and SEADRAGON classes submarines

Sargo subclass

Sargo	SS188	Electric Boat, Groton	5.1937	6.6.1938	2.1939	stricken 7.1946
Saury	SS189	Electric Boat, Groton	6.1937	20.8.1938	4.1939	stricken 7.1946
Spearfish	SS190	Electric Boat, Groton	9.1937	29.10.1938	7.1939	stricken 7.1946
Sculpin	SS191	Portsmouth N Yd	9.1937	27.7.1938	1.1939	sunk 18.11.1943
Squalus, 5.1940- **Sailfish**	SS192	Portsmouth N Yd	10.1937	14.9.1939	3.1939	stricken 4.1948

Seadragon subclass

Swordfish	SS193	Mare Island N Yd, Vallejo	10.1937	1.4.1939	7.1939	lost 1.1945
Seadragon	SS194	Electric Boat, Groton	4.1938	21.4.1939	10.1939	stricken 4.1948
Sealion	SS195	Electric Boat, Groton	6.1938	25.5.1939	11.1939	sunk 25.12.1941
Searaven	SS196	Portsmouth N Yd	8.1938	21.6.1939	10.1939	sunk as target 11.9.1948
Seawolf	SS197	Portsmouth N Yd	9.1938	15.8.1939	12.1939	sunk 3.10.1944

Sargo 1940

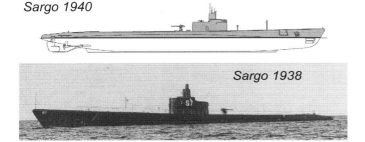
Sargo 1938

1450 / 2198 t, 94.6 x 8.2 x 5.1 m, 4 Hoover, Owens, Rentschler (SS188-191) or General Electric (SS192) diesels / 4 electric motors or 4 General Electric (SS193-195, 197) or Hoover, Owens, Rentschler (SS196) diesel-generators / 4 electric motors (2 shafts), 5500 / 2740 (SS188-192) or 5200 / 2740 (SS193-197) hp, 20 / 8.7 kts, 428 t diesel oil, 11000 nm (10 kts) / 96 nm (2 kts), complement 59, 75 m; 1 x 1 – 76/50 Mk 17/18, 2 x 1 – 12.7 MG, 8 – 533 TT (4 bow, 4 stern, 24 torpedoes or 32 mines); QCD, JK sonars.
As part of the FY37 and FY38 Programs, the *Salmon*

class was continued by 10 more boats of the similar *Sargo* class. Due to a slight increase in the fuel stowage, they had an increased cruising range. The four boats of the FY38 Program (SS194-197) were often identified as a separate *Seadragon* subclass. They again had diesel-electrical machinery, besides, almost 30% more battery capacity allowed them to go 48 hrs at 2-kt speed in a submerged position.
1942-1943, all survived: CT was rebuilt; - 1 x 1 - 76/50, 2 x 1 - 12.7 MG; + 1 x 1 - 102/50 Mk 9 or 1 x 1 - 127/25 Mk 17, 2 x 1 - 20/70 Oerlikon, SD, SJ radars.
Squalus foundered 23.5.1939 during trials, salvaged and commissioned in May 1940 under a new name.
Sealion 10.12.1941 was damaged by Japanese aircraft and 25.12.1941 scuttled at Cavite (Philippines). *Sculpin* 18.11.1943 was scuttled N of Truk being damaged by Japanese destroyer *Yamagumo*. *Seawolf* 3.10.1944 was sunk by mistake by destroyer escort *Richard M. Rowel*. *Swordfish* was lost of unknown cause in the Pacific in January 1945.

TAMBOR class submarines

Tambor	SS198	Electric Boat, Groton	1.1939	20.12.1939	6.1940	stricken 9.1959
Tautog	SS199	Electric Boat, Groton	3.1939	27.1.1940	7.1940	stricken 9.1959
Thresher	SS200	Electric Boat, Groton	4.1939	27.3.1940	8.1940	stricken 12.1947
Triton	SS201	Portsmouth N Yd	7.1939	25.3.1940	8.1940	sunk 15.3.1943

Trout	SS202	Portsmouth N Yd	8.1939	21.5.1940	11.1940	sunk 29.2.1944
Tuna	SS203	Mare Island N Yd, Vallejo	7.1939	2.10.1940	1.1941	sunk as target 24.9.1948
Gar	SS206	Electric Boat, Groton	12.1939	7.11.1940	4.1941	stricken 5.1959
Grampus	SS207	Electric Boat, Groton	2.1940	23.12.1940	5.1941	sunk 5.3.1943
Grayback	SS208	Electric Boat, Groton	4.1940	31.1.1941	6.1941	sunk 26.2.1944
Grayling	SS209	Portsmouth N Yd	12.1939	4.9.1940	3.1941	sunk 9.9.1943
Grenadier	SS210	Portsmouth N Yd	4.1940	29.11.1940	5.1941	sunk 22.4.1943
Gudgeon	SS211	Mare Island N Yd, Vallejo	11.1939	25.1.1941	4.1941	sunk 18.4.1944

1475 / 2370 t, 93.6 x 8.3 x 4.6 m, 4 General Electric diesels / 4 electric motors (2 shafts), 5400 / 2740 hp, 20 / 8.7 kts, 374-385 t diesel oil, 10000 nm (10 kts) / 60 nm (5 kts), complement 60, 75 m; 1 x 1 – 127/51 Mk 9 (SS198-200, 203, 206, 209) or 1 x 1 – 76/50 Mk 21 (SS201, 202, 207, 208, 210), 2 x 1 – 12.7 MG, 10 – 533 TT (6 bow, 4 stern, 24 or 4 torpedoes + 40 mines); QCG, JK sonars.
The *T* class design was developed on the basis of the *Salmon* and *Sargo* classes with an increased to 10 number of TTs and strengthened pressure hull. Otherwise, they were close to the prototype. Double-hulled, actual operational diving depth was 90 m; designed operational diving depth was 75 m, and designed destruction depth was 150 m. The diesels were directly connected to the propeller shafts.

They were built under the FY39 (SS198-203) and FY40 Programs (SS206-211).
1942-1943, all survived: CT was rebuilt; - 1 x 1 - 76/50 or 1 x 1 - 127/51, 2 x 1 - 12.7 MG; + 1 x 1 - 102/50 Mk 9 or 1 x 1 - 127/25 Mk 17, (1 x 1 - 40/56 Bofors, 1 x 1 - 20/70 Oerlikon) or 2 x 1 - 20/70 Oerlikon, SD, SJ radars.
Grampus was lost of unknown cause in February-March 1943, probably sunk 5.3.1943 off Kolombangara by Japanese destroyers *Minegumo* and *Murasame*. *Triton* 15.3.1943 was sunk N of the Admiralty Islands by

Tuna 1943

Japanese destroyers. *Grenadier* 21.4.1943 was damaged by Japanese aircraft in the Strait of Malacca by Japanese aircraft and 22.4.1943 was scuttled by her own crew at Penang. *Grayling* was lost of unknown cause in August-September 1943, possibly sunk by Japanese passenger vessel *Hokusu Maru* 9.9.1943 off the coast of Luzon. *Trout* 29.2.1944 was sunk SE of Okinawa by Japanese destroyers *Asashimo*, *Kisninami* and *Okinami*. *Grayback* was lost in February-March 1944, possibly sunk 26.2.1944 in the East China Sea by Japanese B5N torpedo bomber. *Gudgeon* in April-May 1944 was lost for an unknown cause off the Mariana Islands, probably sunk by Japanese aircraft.

Thresher 1940

MACKEREL and MARLIN submarines

Mackerel	SS204	Electric Boat, Groton	10.1939	28.9.1940	3.1941	stricken 11.1945
Marlin	SS205	Portsmouth N Yd	5.1940	29.1.1941	8.1941	stricken 11.1945

Mackerel: 940 / 1190 t, 74.1 x 6.7 x 4.3 m, 4 Electric Boat diesels / 4 electric motors (2 shafts), 3360 / 1500 hp, 16.2 / 11 kts, 116 t diesel oil, 6500 nm (10 kts) /, complement 42, 75 m; 1 x 1 – 76/50 Mk 21, 2 x 1 – 12.7 MG, 6 – 533 TT (4 bow, 2 stern, 12); WBA, JK sonars.
Marlin: 910 / 1165 t, 72.8 x 6.6 x 4.0 m, 4 Electric Boat diesel-generators / 4 electric motors (2 shafts), 3400 / 1500 hp, 16.5 / 11 kts, 116 t diesel oil, 7400 nm (10 kts) /, complement 42, 75 m; 1 x 1 – 76/50 Mk 21, 2 x 1 – 12.7 MG, 6 – 533 TT (4 bow, 2 stern, 12); WBA, JK sonars.
The *Mackerel*, or 'M' class submarines were designed as a cheaper alternative for large *P, S* and *T* classes, whose dimensions were criticized by some members of the

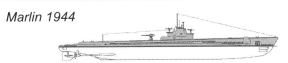
Marlin 1944

General Board. It was believed that it was submarines with a smaller displacement compared to the "fleet" submarines of *P* and *T* classes, that would replace the outdated *S* class.

The FY40 Program provided for the building of two "prototypes" of the *M* class. The detailed design of the first (SS204) was completed by Electric Boat, the second (SS205) by the Bureau of Construction & Repair. Being similar, the designs had many fundamental differences,

Mackerel 1941

in particular, SS204 had machinery with a direct drive, and SS205 was diesel-electrical driven. Double-hulled.

Submarines were unsuccessful: with armament strong enough for their displacement, their endurance turned out to be insufficient for operations in the Pacific, besides, the limited dimensions predetermined insufficient, according to the USN, habitability. The planned building of a large series was abandoned and, the "prototypes" commissioned in 1941 were used mainly for training. 1942-1943, both: CT was rebuilt; - 1 x 1 - 76/50, 2 x 1 - 12.7 MG; + 1 x 1 - 127/25 Mk 17, 2 x 1 - 20/70 Oerlikon, SD, SJ radars.

GATO and BALAO classes submarines

Gato subclass

Gato	SS212	Electric Boat, Groton	10.1940	21.8.1941	12.1941	stricken 3.1960
Greenling	SS213	Electric Boat, Groton	11.1940	20.9.1941	1.1942	stricken 3.1960
Grouper	SS214	Electric Boat, Groton	12.940	27.10.1941	2.1942	auxiliary 5.1958
Growler	SS215	Electric Boat, Groton	2.1941	22.11.1941	3.1942	sunk 8.11.1944
Grunion	SS216	Electric Boat, Groton	3.1941	22.12.1941	4.1942	sunk 30.7.1942
Guardfish	SS217	Electric Boat, Groton	4.1941	20.1.1942	5.1942	stricken 10.1960
Albacore	SS218	Electric Boat, Groton	4.1941	17.2.1942	6.1942	sunk 7.11.1944
Amberjack	SS219	Electric Boat, Groton	5.1941	6.3.1942	6.1942	sunk 16.2.1943
Barb	SS220	Electric Boat, Groton	6.1941	2.4.1942	7.1942	to Italy 12.1954 (Enrico Tazzoli)
Blackfish	SS221	Electric Boat, Groton	7.1941	18.4.1942	7.1942	stricken 9.1958
Bluefish	SS222	Electric Boat, Groton	6.1942	21.2.1943	5.1943	stricken 6.1959
Bonefish	SS223	Electric Boat, Groton	6.1942	7.3.1943	5.1943	sunk 18.6.1945
Cod	SS224	Electric Boat, Groton	7.1942	21.3.1943	6.1943	auxiliary 12.1962
Cero	SS225	Electric Boat, Groton	8.1942	4.4.1943	7.1943	stricken 6.1967
Corvina	SS226	Electric Boat, Groton	9.1942	9.5.1943	8.1943	sunk 16.11.1943
Darter	SS227	Electric Boat, Groton	10.1942	6.6.1943	9.1943	wrecked 24.10.1944
Drum	SS228	Portsmouth N Yd	9.1940	12.5.1941	11.1941	auxiliary 12.1962
Flying Fish	SS229	Portsmouth N Yd	12.1940	9.7.1941	12.1941	auxiliary 11.1950
Finback	SS230	Portsmouth N Yd	2.1941	25.8.1941	1.1942	stricken 9.1958
Haddock	SS231	Portsmouth N Yd	3.1941	20.10.1941	3.1942	stricken 6.1960
Halibut	SS232	Portsmouth N Yd	5.1941	3.12.1941	4.1942	damaged 14.11.1944, never repaired
Herring	SS233	Portsmouth N Yd	7.1941	15.1.1942	5.1942	sunk 1.6.1944
Kingfish	SS234	Portsmouth N Yd	8.1941	2.3.1942	5.1942	stricken 3.1960
Shad	SS235	Portsmouth N Yd	10.1941	15.4.1942	6.1942	stricken 4.1960
Silversides	SS236	Mare Island N Yd, Vallejo	11.1940	26.8.1941	12.1941	auxiliary 11.1962
Trigger	SS237	Mare Island N Yd, Vallejo	2.1941	22.10.1941	1.1942	sunk 28.3.1945
Wahoo	SS238	Mare Island N Yd, Vallejo	6.1941	14.2.1942	5.1942	sunk 11.10.1943
Whale	SS239	Mare Island N Yd, Vallejo	6.1941	14.3.1942	6.1942	stricken 3.1960
Angler	SS240	Electric Boat, Groton	11.1942	4.7.1943	10.1943	auxiliary 7.1963
Bashaw	SS241	Electric Boat, Groton	12.1942	25.7.1943	10.1943	auxiliary 9.1962
Bluegill	SS242	Electric Boat, Groton	12.1942	8.8.1943	11.1943	auxiliary 4.1966

Bream	SS243	Electric Boat, Groton	2.1943	17.10.1943	1.1944	auxiliary 4.1965
Cavalla	SS244	Electric Boat, Groton	3.1943	14.11.1943	2.1944	auxiliary 7.1963
Cobia	SS245	Electric Boat, Groton	3.1943	28.11.1943	3.1944	auxiliary 12.1962
Croaker	SS246	Electric Boat, Groton	4.1943	19.12.1943	4.1944	auxiliary 5.1967
Dace	SS247	Electric Boat, Groton	7.1942	25.4.1943	7.1943	to Italy 1.1955 (Leonardo da Vinci)
Dorado	SS248	Electric Boat, Groton	8.1942	23.5.1943	8.1943	sunk 12.10.1943
Flasher	SS249	Electric Boat, Groton	9.1942	20.6.1943	9.1943	stricken 6.1959
Flier	SS250	Electric Boat, Groton	10.1942	11.7.1943	10.1943	sunk 13.8.1944
Flounder	SS251	Electric Boat, Groton	12.1942	22.8.1943	11.1943	stricken 6.1959
Gabilan	SS252	Electric Boat, Groton	1.1943	19.9.1943	12.1943	stricken 6.1959
Gunnel	SS253	Electric Boat, Groton	7.1941	17.5.1942	8.1942	stricken 9.1958
Gurnard	SS254	Electric Boat, Groton	9.1941	1.6.1942	9.1942	stricken 5.1961
Haddo	SS255	Electric Boat, Groton	10.1941	21.6.1942	10.1942	stricken 8.1958
Hake	SS256	Electric Boat, Groton	11.1941	17.7.1942	10.1942	auxiliary 12.1962
Harder	SS257	Electric Boat, Groton	12.1941	19.8.1942	12.1942	sunk 24.8.1944
Hoe	SS258	Electric Boat, Groton	1.1942	17.9.1942	12.1942	stricken 5.1960
Jack	SS259	Electric Boat, Groton	2.1942	16.10.1942	1.1943	to Greece 4.1958 (Amfitriti)
Lapon	SS260	Electric Boat, Groton	2.1942	27.10.1942	1.1943	to Greece 8.1957 (Poseidon)
Mingo	SS261	Electric Boat, Groton	3.1942	30.11.1942	2.1943	to Japan 8.1955 (Kuroshio)
Muskallunge	SS262	Electric Boat, Groton	4.1942	13.12.1942	3.1943	to Brazil 1.1957 (Humaitá)
Paddle	SS263	Electric Boat, Groton	5.1942	30.12.1942	3.1943	to Brazil 1.1957 (Riachuelo)
Pargo	SS264	Electric Boat, Groton	5.1942	24.1.1943	4.1943	stricken 12.1960
Peto	SS265	Manitowoc SB	6.1941	30.4.1942	11.1942	stricken 8.1960
Pogy	SS266	Manitowoc SB	9.1941	23.6.1942	1.1943	stricken 9.1958
Pompon	SS267	Manitowoc SB	11.1941	15.8.1942	3.1943	stricken 4.1960
Puffer	SS268	Manitowoc SB	2.1942	22.11.1942	4.1943	stricken 7.1960
Rasher	SS269	Manitowoc SB	5.1942	20.12.1942	6.1943	auxiliary 7.1960
Raton	SS270	Manitowoc SB	5.1942	24.1.1943	7.1943	auxiliary 7.1960
Ray	SS271	Manitowoc SB	7.1942	28.2.1943	7.1943	stricken 4.1960
Redfin	SS272	Manitowoc SB	9.1942	4.4.1943	8.1943	auxiliary 6.1963
Robalo	SS273	Manitowoc SB	10.1942	9.5.1943	9.1943	sunk 26.7.1944
Rock	SS274	Manitowoc SB	12.1942	20.6.1943	1.1943	auxiliary 8.1959
Runner	SS275	Portsmouth N Yd	12.1941	30.5.1942	7.1942	lost 1.7.1943
Sawfish	SS276	Portsmouth N Yd	1.1942	23.6.1942	8.1942	stricken 4.1960
Scamp	SS277	Portsmouth N Yd	3.1942	20.7.1942	9.1942	sunk 16.11.1944
Scorpion	SS278	Portsmouth N Yd	3.1942	20.7.1942	10.1942	sunk 1.2.1944
Snook	SS279	Portsmouth N Yd	4.1942	15.8.1942	10.1942	lost 8.4.1945
Steelhead	SS280	Portsmouth N Yd	6.1942	11.9.1942	12.1942	stricken 4.1960
Sunfish	SS281	Mare Island N Yd, Vallejo	9.1941	2.5.1942	7.1942	stricken 5.1960
Tunny	SS282	Mare Island N Yd, Vallejo	11.1941	30.6.1942	9.1942	stricken 6.1969
Tinosa	SS283	Mare Island N Yd, Vallejo	2.1942	7.10.1942	1.1943	stricken 9.1958
Tullibee	SS284	Mare Island N Yd, Vallejo	4.1942	11.11.1942	2.1943	sunk 26.3.1944

Golet	SS361	Manitowoc SB	1.1943	1.8.1943	11.1943	sunk 14.6.1944
Guavina	SS362	Manitowoc SB	3.1943	29.8.1943	12.1943	oiler 2.1950
Guitarro	SS363	Manitowoc SB	4.1943	26.9.1943	1.1944	to Turkey 8.1954 (Preveze)
Hammerhead	SS364	Manitowoc SB	5.1943	24.10.1943	3.1944	to Turkey 10.1954 (Cerbe)

Balao subclass

Balao	SS285	Portsmouth N Yd	6.1942	27.10.1942	2.1943	auxiliary 4.1960
Billfish	SS286	Portsmouth N Yd	7.1942	12.11.1942	4.1943	auxiliary 12.1962
Bowfin	SS287	Portsmouth N Yd	7.1942	7.12.1942	5.1943	auxiliary 12.1962
Cabrilla	SS288	Portsmouth N Yd	8.1942	24.12.1942	5.1943	auxiliary 12.1962
Capelin	SS289	Portsmouth N Yd	9.1942	20.1.1943	6.1943	lost 12.1943
Cisco	SS290	Portsmouth N Yd	10.1942	24.12.1942	5.1943	sunk 28.9.1943
Crevalle	SS291	Portsmouth N Yd	11.1942	22.2.1943	6.1943	auxiliary 4.1960
Devilfish	SS292	Cramp, Philadelphia	3.1942	30.5.1943	9.1944	auxiliary 12.1962
Dragonet	SS293	Cramp, Philadelphia	4.1942	18.4.1943	3.1944	stricken 6.1961
Escolar	SS294	Cramp, Philadelphia	6.1942	18.4.1943	6.1944	lost 10.1944
Hackleback	SS295	Cramp, Philadelphia	8.1942	30.5.1943	11.1944	auxiliary 12.1962
Lancetfish	SS296	Cramp, Philadelphia	12.1942	15.8.1943	2.1945	foundered 15.3.1945, never repaired
Ling	SS297	Cramp, Philadelphia	11.1942	15.8.1943	6.1945	auxiliary 12.1962
Lionfish	SS298	Cramp, Philadelphia	12.1942	7.11.1943	11.1944	auxiliary 12.1962
Manta	SS299	Cramp, Philadelphia	1.1943	7.11.1943	12.1944	target 8.1949
Moray	SS300	Cramp, Philadelphia	4.1943	14.5.1944	1.1945	auxiliary 12.1962
Roncador	SS301	Cramp, Philadelphia	4.1943	14.5.1944	3.1945	auxiliary 12.1962
Sabalo	SS302	Cramp, Philadelphia	6.1943	4.6.1944	6.1945	stricken 7.1971
Sablefish	SS303	Cramp, Philadelphia	6.1943	4.6.1944	12.1945	auxiliary 6.1969
Seahorse	SS304	Mare Island N Yd, Vallejo	8.1942	9.1.1943	3.1943	auxiliary 12.1962
Skate	SS305	Mare Island N Yd, Vallejo	8.1942	4.3.1943	4.1943	nuclear tests 7.1946
Tang	SS306	Mare Island N Yd, Vallejo	1.1943	17.8.1943	10.1943	sunk 24.10.1944
Tilefish	SS307	Mare Island N Yd, Vallejo	3.1943	25.10.1943	12.1943	to Venezuela 12.1960 (Carite)
Apogon (ex-Abadejo)	SS308	Portsmouth N Yd	12.1942	10.3.1943	7.1943	nuclear tests 7.1946
Aspro (ex-Acedia)	SS309	Portsmouth N Yd	12.1942	7.4.1943	7.1943	auxiliary 7.1960
Batfish (ex-Acoupa)	SS310	Portsmouth N Yd	12.1942	5.5.1943	8.1943	auxiliary 12.1962
Archerfish	SS311	Portsmouth N Yd	1.1943	28.5.1943	9.1943	auxiliary 2.1960
Burrfish (ex-Arnillo)	SS312	Portsmouth N Yd	2.1943	18.6.1943	9.1943	to Canada 5.1961 (Grilse)
Perch	SS313	Electric Boat, Groton	1.1943	12.9.1943	1.1944	auxiliary 6.1971
Shark	SS314	Electric Boat, Groton	1.1943	17.10.1943	2.1944	sunk 24.10.1944
Sealion	SS315	Electric Boat, Groton	2.1943	31.10.1943	4.1944	stricken 3.1977
Barbel	SS316	Electric Boat, Groton	3.1943	14.11.1943	4.1944	sunk 4.2.1945
Barbero	SS317	Electric Boat, Groton	3.1943	12.12.1943	4.1944	stricken 7.1964
Baya	SS318	Electric Boat, Groton	4.1943	2.1.1944	5.1944	auxiliary 8.1949
Becuna	SS319	Electric Boat, Groton	4.1943	30.1.1944	5.1944	auxiliary 10.1969
Bergall	SS320	Electric Boat, Groton	5.1943	12.2.1944	6.1944	to Turkey 10.1958 (Turgut Reis)

Besugo	SS321	Electric Boat, Groton	5.1943	27.2.1944	6.1944	auxiliary 12.1962
Blackfin	SS322	Electric Boat, Groton	6.1943	12.3.1944	7.1944	stricken 9.1972
Caiman (ex-Blanquillo)	SS323	Electric Boat, Groton	6.1943	30.3.1944	7.1944	to Turkey 7.1972 (Dumlupınar)
Blenny	SS324	Electric Boat, Groton	7.1943	9.4.1944	7.1944	auxiliary 1964
Blower	SS325	Electric Boat, Groton	7.1943	23.4.1944	8.1944	to Turkey 11.1950 (Dumlupınar)
Blueback	SS326	Electric Boat, Groton	7.1943	7.5.1944	8.1944	to Turkey 5.1948 (İkinçi İnönü)
Boarfish	SS327	Electric Boat, Groton	8.1943	21.5.1944	9.1944	to Turkey 5.1948 (Sakarya)
Charr (ex-Bocaccio)	SS328	Electric Boat, Groton	8.1943	18.6.1944	9.1944	auxiliary 1966
Chub (ex-Bonaci)	SS329	Electric Boat, Groton	9.1943	18.6.1944	10.1944	to Turkey 5.1948 (Gür)
Brill	SS330	Electric Boat, Groton	9.1943	25.6.1944	10.1944	to Turkey 5.1948 (Birinçi İnönü)
Bugara	SS331	Electric Boat, Groton	10.1943	2.7.1944	11.1944	auxiliary 1969
Bullhead	SS332	Electric Boat, Groton	10.1943	16.7.1944	12.1944	sunk 6.8.1945
Bumper	SS333	Electric Boat, Groton	11.1943	6.8.1944	12.1944	to Turkey 11.1950 (Çanakkale)
Cabezon	SS334	Electric Boat, Groton	11.1943	27.8.1944	12.1944	auxiliary 1962
Dentuda (ex-Capidoli)	SS335	Electric Boat, Groton	11.1943	10.9.1944	12.1944	auxiliary 1962
Capitaine	SS336	Electric Boat, Groton	12.1943	1.10.1944	1.1945	auxiliary 7.1960
Carbonero	SS337	Electric Boat, Groton	12.1943	15.10.1944	2.1945	stricken 12.1970
Carp	SS338	Electric Boat, Groton	12.1943	12.11.1944	2.1945	auxiliary 3.1968
Catfish	SS339	Electric Boat, Groton	1.1944	19.11.1944	3.1945	to Argentina 7.1971 (Santa Fé)
Entemedor (ex-Chickwick)	SS340	Electric Boat, Groton	2.1944	17.12.1944	4.1945	to Turkey 7.1972 (Preveze)
Chivo	SS341	Electric Boat, Groton	2.1944	14.1.1945	4.1945	to Argentina 7.1971 (Santiago del Estero)
Chopper	SS342	Electric Boat, Groton	3.1944	4.2.1945	5.1945	auxiliary 1969
Clamagore	SS343	Electric Boat, Groton	3.1944	25.2.1945	6.1945	stricken 6.1975
Cobbler	SS344	Electric Boat, Groton	4.1944	1.4.1945	8.1945	to Turkey 11.1973 (Çanakkale)
Cochino	SS345	Electric Boat, Groton	4.1944	20.4.1945	8.1945	foundered 25.8.1949
Corporal	SS346	Electric Boat, Groton	4.1944	10.6.1945	11.1945	to Turkey 11.1973 (İkinçi İnönü)
Cubera	SS347	Electric Boat, Groton	5.1944	17.6.1945	12.1945	to Venezuela 1.1972 (Tiburón)
Cusk	SS348	Electric Boat, Groton	5.1944	28.7.1945	2.1946	auxiliary 9.1969
Diodon	SS349	Electric Boat, Groton	6.1944	10.9.1945	3.1946	stricken 1.1971
Dogfish	SS350	Electric Boat, Groton	6.1944	27.10.1945	4.1946	to Brazil 7.1972 (Guanabara)
Greenfish (ex-Doncella)	SS351	Electric Boat, Groton	6.1944	21.12.1945	6.1946	to Brazil 12.1973 (Amazonas)
Halfbeak (ex-Dory)	SS352	Electric Boat, Groton	7.1944	19.2.1946	7.1946	stricken 7.1971
Hardhead	SS365	Manitowoc SB	7.1943	12.12.1943	4.1944	to Greece 7.1972 (Papanikolis)

Hawkbill	SS366	Manitowoc SB	8.1943	9.1.1944	5.1944	to the Netherlands 4.1953 (Zeeleuw)
Icefish	SS367	Manitowoc SB	9.1943	20.2.1944	6.1944	to the Netherlands 2.1953 (Walrus)
Jallao	SS368	Manitowoc SB	9.1943	12.3.1944	7.1944	to Spain 6.1974 (S35)
Kete	SS369	Manitowoc SB	10.1943	9.4.1944	7.1944	lost 3.1945
Kraken	SS370	Manitowoc SB	12.1943	30.4.1944	9.1944	to Spain 10.1959 (Almirante García de los Reyes)
Lagarto	SS371	Manitowoc SB	1.1944	28.5.1944	10.1944	sunk 3.5.1945
Lambrey	SS372	Manitowoc SB	2.1944	18.6.1944	11.1944	to Argentina 8.1960 (Santa Fé)
Lizardfish	SS373	Manitowoc SB	3.1944	16.7.1944	12.1944	to Italy 1.1960 (Evangelista Torricelli)
Loggerhead	SS374	Manitowoc SB	4.1944	13.8.1944	2.1945	auxiliary 12.1962
Macabi	SS375	Manitowoc SB	5.1944	19.9.1944	3.1945	to Argentina 11.1960 (Santiago del Estero)
Mapiro	SS376	Manitowoc SB	5.1944	9.11.1944	4.1945	to Turkey 3.1960 (Piri Reis)
Menhaden	SS377	Manitowoc SB	6.1944	20.12.1944	6.1945	stricken 8.1973
Mero	SS378	Manitowoc SB	7.1944	17.1.1945	8.1945	to Turkey 4.1960 (Hızır Reis)
Sand Lance (ex-Ojanco, ex-Orca)	SS381	Portsmouth N Yd	3.1943	25.6.1943	10.1943	to Brazil 9.1963 (Rio Grande do Sul)
Picuda (ex-Obispo)	SS382	Portsmouth N Yd	3.1943	12.7.1943	10.1943	to Spain 10.1972 (Narciso Monturiol)
Pampanito	SS383	Portsmouth N Yd	3.1943	12.7.1943	11.1943	auxiliary 12.1962
Parche	SS384	Portsmouth N Yd	4.1943	24.7.1943	11.1943	auxiliary 12.1962
Bang	SS385	Portsmouth N Yd	4.1943	30.8.1943	12.1943	to Spain 10.1972 (Cosme García)
Pilotfish	SS386	Portsmouth N Yd	5.1943	30.8.1943	12.1943	nuclear tests 25.7.1946
Pintado	SS387	Portsmouth N Yd	5.1943	15.9.1943	1.1944	auxiliary 12.1962
Pipefish	SS388	Portsmouth N Yd	5.1943	12.10.1943	1.1944	auxiliary 12.1962
Piranha	SS389	Portsmouth N Yd	6.1943	27.10.1943	2.1944	auxiliary 12.1962
Plaice	SS390	Portsmouth N Yd	6.1943	15.11.1943	2.1944	to Brazil 9.1963 (Bahia)
Pomfret	SS391	Portsmouth N Yd	7.1943	27.10.1943	2.1944	to Turkey 7.1971 (Oruç Reis)
Sterlet (ex-Pudiano)	SS392	Portsmouth N Yd	7.1943	27.10.1943	3.1944	stricken 10.1968
Queenfish	SS393	Portsmouth N Yd	7.1943	30.11.1943	3.1944	auxiliary 7.1960
Razorback	SS394	Portsmouth N Yd	9.1943	27.1.1944	4.1944	to Turkey 11.1970 (Murat Reis)
Redfish	SS395	Portsmouth N Yd	9.1943	27.1.1944	4.1944	auxiliary 7.1960
Ronquil	SS396	Portsmouth N Yd	9.1943	27.1.1944	4.1944	to Spain 7.1971 (Isaac Peral)
Scabbardfish	SS397	Portsmouth N Yd	9.1943	27.1.1944	4.1944	to Greece 2.1965 (Triaina)
Segundo	SS398	Portsmouth N Yd	10.1943	5.2.1944	5.1944	stricken 8.1970
Sea Cat	SS399	Portsmouth N Yd	10.1943	30.2.1944	5.1944	auxiliary 6.1968
Sea Devil	SS400	Portsmouth N Yd	11.1943	28.2.1944	5.1944	auxiliary 7.1960

Sea Dog	SS401	Portsmouth N Yd	11.1943	28.3.1944	6.1944	auxiliary 12.1962
Sea Fox	SS402	Portsmouth N Yd	11.1943	28.3.1944	6.1944	to Turkey 12.1970 (Burak Reis)
Atule	SS403	Portsmouth N Yd	11.1943	6.3.1944	6.1944	stricken 8.1973
Spikefish (ex-Shiner)	SS404	Portsmouth N Yd	1.1944	26.4.1944	6.1944	auxiliary 7.1962
Sea Owl	SS405	Portsmouth N Yd	2.1944	7.5.1944	7.1944	auxiliary 6.1969
Sea Poacher	SS406	Portsmouth N Yd	2.1944	20.5.1944	7.1944	stricken 8.1973
Sea Robin	SS407	Portsmouth N Yd	3.1944	25.5.1944	7.1944	stricken 10.1970
Sennet	SS408	Portsmouth N Yd	3.1944	6.6.1944	8.1944	stricken 12.1968
Piper (ex-Awa)	SS409	Portsmouth N Yd	3.1944	26.6.1944	8.1944	auxiliary 6.1967
Threadfin (ex-Sole)	SS410	Portsmouth N Yd	3.1944	26.6.1944	8.1944	to Turkey 8.1972 (Birinçi İnönü)
Spadefish	SS411	Mare Island N Yd, Vallejo	5.1943	8.1.1944	3.1944	auxiliary 12.1962
Trepang (ex-Senoria)	SS412	Mare Island N Yd, Vallejo	6.1943	8.1.1944	5.1944	auxiliary 12.1962
Spot	SS413	Mare Island N Yd, Vallejo	8.1943	19.5.1944	8.1944	to Chile 1.1962 (Simpson)
Springer	SS414	Mare Island N Yd, Vallejo	10.1943	3.8.1944	10.1944	to Chile 1.1961 (Thomson)
Stickleback	SS415	Mare Island N Yd, Vallejo	3.1944	1.1.1945	3.1945	collision 29.5.1958
Tiru	SS416	Mare Island N Yd, Vallejo	4.1944	16.6.1947	9.1948	stricken 7.1975

1810 / 2410 (SS212-284, 361-364) or 1845 / 2415 (SS285-360, 365-415) t, 95.0 x 8.3 x 4.7 m, 4 General Electric (SS212-227, 327, 328, 331, 333, 337,338) or Fairbank-Morse (SS228-237, 275-284, 292-312, 381-416, 425, 426) or General Motors (SS238-252, 265-274, 285-291, 313-326, 329, 330, 332, 334-336, 339-352, 361-380) or Hoover, Owens, Rentschler (SS253-264) diesel-generators / 4 electric motors (2 shafts), 5400 / 2740 hp, 20.2 / 8.7 kts, 378-472 t diesel oil, 11000 nm (10 kts) / 96 nm (2 kts), complement 60, 90 (SS212-284, 361-364) or 120 (SS285-360, 365-415) m; 1 x 1 – 127/51 Mk 9 (SS256), 1 x 1 – 127/25 Mk 17 (SS224, 292-352, 361-378, 381-415), 1 x 1 – 102/50 Mk 9 (SS225-227, 240-252, 257-274, 280, 283-291), 1 x 1 – 76/50 Mk 17/18 (SS212-223, 228-239, 253-255, 275-279, 281, 282), 1 x 1 – 40/56 Bofors (SS313-352, 361-378, 381-415), 2 (SS225-227, 240-252, 257-274, 280, 283-312) or 1 (SS313-352, 361-378, 381-415) x 1 – 20/70 Oerlikon, 2 x 1 – 12.7 MG (SS212-224, 228-239, 253-256, 275-279, 281, 282), 10 – 533 TT (6 bow, 4 stern, 24 torpedoes or 40 mines); SD (SS212-295, 298, 299, 304-335, 361-373, 381-414), SJ (SS220-227, 240-296, 298-301, 304-342, 361-376, 381-415), SS (SS297, 302, 303, 343-352, 377, 378), ST (SS292, 295, 296-303, 322-352, 368-378, 405-410, 413-415), SV (SS296, 297, 300-303, 336-352, 374-378, 415) radars, (WCA or WDA) (SS212-219, 228-239), WDA (SS220-227, 240-296, 298-301, 304-342, 361-376, 381-415), WFA (SS297, 302, 303, 343-352,

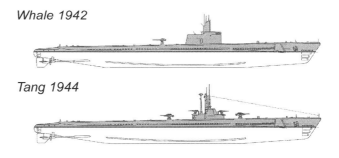

Whale 1942

Tang 1944

377, 378), JK (SS212-219, 228-239), JP (SS220-227, 240-296, 298-301, 304-342, 361-376, 381-415), JT (SS297, 302, 303, 343-352, 377, 378) sonars, APR-1 ECM suite (SS292, 295-303, 322-352, 368-378, 405-410, 413-415)

Electronic equipment data is given presumably.
SS416: 1870 / 2440 t, 93.6 x 8.2 x 5.2 m, 4 Fairbanks-Morse diesel-generators / 4 electric motors (2 shafts), 4610 / 5400 hp, 18 / 16 kts, 472 t diesel oil, 11000 nm (10 kts) / 96 nm (2 kts), complement 82, 120 m; 10 – 533

Gato 1945

Cero late war

TT (6 bow, 4 stern, 24 torpedoes or 40 mines); SS, ST, SV radars, BQR-2, BQS-2, JT or SQR-3 sonars, APR-1 ECM suite.

The FY41 Program called for the building of eight *Gato* class submarines (SS212-219). Basically, they repeated the predecessors of the *Gar* class, the main difference was the return to a diesel-electric drive and slight increase in length to improve the hull subdivision into compartments and the division of the engine room by a watertight bulkhead.

A decision to build 28 more (SS220-247) *Gato* class submarines followed in May 1940, and 37 more boats (SS248-284) were ordered two months later. The "Emergency" 1942 Program provided for the building of another 132 submarines of the somewhat improved *Balao* class (SS285-416), but in 1944 an order for 10 boats (SS353 *Dugong*, SS354 *Eel*, SS355 *Espada*, SS356 *Jawfish (ex-Fanegal)*, SS357 *Ono (ex-Friar)*, SS358 *Garlopa*, SS359 *Garrupa*, SS360 *Goldring*, ordered for Electric Boat and SS379 *Needlefish* and SS380 *Nerka* from Manitowoc's order) was cancelled 23.10.1944 (the first three) and 29.7.1944 (the rest).

Double-hulled. Starting with SS285 *Balao*, the design received many improvements in hull construction (mostly technological), which made it possible to simplify building and at the same time led to some weight savings. This weight reserve was used to strengthen the pressure hull, after which the diving depth was increased to 120 m. The diving depth was a reason for the selection of *Balao* the class submarines as the separate group. Since the submarines of both classes were built in parallel throughout the second half of the war, the differences between submarines of the same group were often greater than between the *Balao* and *Gato* classes (with the exception of diving depth).

The first *Gato* class submarines were commissioned with traditional large and streamlined CT, but by the end of 1942 the CT was replaced by new smaller one, with the special platform for AA guns. Subsequently, earlier submarines also received CTs rebuilt according to this principle.

The designed artillery consisted of 76-mm/50 gun and two 12.7-mm MGs, and the first *Gatos* were completed in this way. From the end of 1942, submarines

Flasher late war

received stronger artillery consisting of 102-mm/50 gun and two 20-mm Oerlikons. In 1943, submarines were commissioned with one-two 127-mm/25 guns and two 20-mm Oerlikons. On part of the boats, one or both 20-mm MGs replaced by 40-mm Bofors. SS416 *Tiru*, commissioned in 1948, was completed modernized according to the GUPPY II design.

1943, *Greenling, Grouper, Flying Fish, Kingfish*: CT was rebuilt; - 1 x 1 - 76/50, 2 x 1 - 12.7 MG; + 1 x 1 - 127/25 Mk 17, 2 x 1 - 20/70 Oerlikon. 1943-1944, many earlier submarines: CT was rebuilt; - 1 x 1 - 76/50, 2 x 1 - 12.7 MG; + (1 - 2) x 1 - 127/25 Mk 17, (1 x 1 - 40/56 Bofors, 1 x 1 - 20/70 Oerlikon) or 2 x 1 - 20/70 Oerlikon.

1944-1945, many submarines: - 1 x 1 - 102/50; + (1 - 2) x 1 - 127/25 Mk 17.

1945, many submarines: - 1 x 1 - 20/70; + 1 x 1 - 40/56 Bofors. 1945, *Flying Fish, Entemedor, Sea Cat, Sea Dog, Sea Poacher, Sea Robin, Sennet*: were armed with 2 x 1 - 127/25 Mk 17, 2 x 1 - 40/56 Bofors, 10 - 533 TT (24 torpedoes or 40 mines, 6 bow, 4 stern), SJ, ST, SV radars, WFA, JT sonars. 1945, *Barb, Chivo, Chopper*: + 6 x 12 - 127 Mk 51 RL.

Grunion in June-July 1942 was lost for an unknown cause in the North Pacific (presumably sunk by Japanese submarine *I25*). *Amberjack* 16.2.1943 was sunk off Rabaul by Japanese torpedo boat *Hiyodori* and submarine chaser *Ch18*. *Wahoo* 11.10.1943 was sunk in the La Perouse Strait by Japanese aircraft and submarine chasers *Ch15* and *Ch43*. *Dorado* in October 1943 was lost for an unknown cause off the E Coast of North America (presumably by mistake by US Navy patrol aircraft). *Corvina* 16.11.1943 was sunk off Truk by Japanese submarine *I176*. *Runner* in May-June 1943 was lost for an unknown cause off the coast of Japan (possibly mined off Hokkaido). *Cisco* 28.9.1943 was sunk in the Sula Sea by Japanese aircraft and river gunboat *Karatsu*. *Capelin* in December 1943 was lost for an unknown cause in the Pacific (probably mined). *Scorpion* in January-February 1944 was lost for an unknown cause in the Yellow Sea (probably mined). *Tullibee* 26.3.1944 was sunk N of Palau by her own torpedo. *Herring* 1.6.1944 was sunk off Matua Island by Japanese coastal battery. *Golet* 14.6.1944 was sunk NE of Honshu by Japanese ships. *Robalo* 26.7.1944 was lost in a minefield off Palawan. *Flier* 13.8.1944 was mined in the Balabac Strait. *Harder* 24.8.1944 was sunk in the South China Sea by Japanese escort *CD22*. *Tang* 24.10.1944 was lost in the Taiwan Strait as result of her own torpedo hit. *Shark* 24.10.1944 was sunk off Luzon by Japanese destroyer *Harukaze*. *Darter* 24.10.1944 ran aground at Palawan, was abandoned by her crew and sunk by submarine *Dace*. *Escolar* in October-November 1944 was lost for an unknown cause in the area of the Tsushima Strait, probably mined. *Albacore* 7.11.1944 was lost in a minefield off Hokkaido. *Growler* 8.11.1944 was sunk off Luzon by Japanese destroyer *Shigure* and escorts *Chiburi* and *CD19*. *Scamp* 11.11.1944 was sunk N of the Bonin Islands by Japanese aircraft and escort *CD4*. *Barbel* 4.2.1945 was sunk SW of Palawan by Japanese aircraft. *Kete* in March 1945 was lost by unknown cause between Okinawa and Midway, probably mined or sunk by Japanese submarine *RO41*. *Trigger* 28.3.1945 was sunk in the East China Sea by Japanese aircraft and escort *Micura*. *Snook* in April 1945 was lost by unknown cause E of Taiwan, probably mined. *Lagarto* 3.5.1945 was sunk in the Gulf of Siam by Japanese minelayer *Hatsutaka*. *Lancetfish* 15.3.1945 foundered at the pier in Boston, salvaged 23.3.1945, never completely repaired and formally stricken in June 1958. *Bonefish* was sunk 18.6.1945 off the coast of Japan by Japanese escorts *Okinawa*, *CD63, 75, 158* and *207*. *Bullhead* 6.8.1945

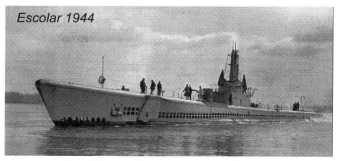

Escolar 1944

was sunk N of Bali by Japanese aircraft.
Barbero 27.12.1944 was damaged by Japanese aircraft and was under repair until the end of the war. *Halibut* 14.11.1944 was damaged by Japanese aircraft and never repaired. *Bergall* 13.6.1945 was damaged in the Gulf of Siam by a Japanese mine.

TENCH class submarines

Tench	SS417	Portsmouth N Yd	4.1944	7.7.1944	10.1944	stricken 8.1973
Thornback	SS418	Portsmouth N Yd	4.1944	7.7.1944	10.1944	to Turkey 7.1971 (Uluç Ali Reis)
Tigrone	SS419	Portsmouth N Yd	5.1944	20.7.1944	10.1944	auxiliary 12.1963
Tirante	SS420	Portsmouth N Yd	4.1944	9.8.1944	11.1944	stricken 10.1973
Trutta (ex-*Tomatate*)	SS421	Portsmouth N Yd	5.1944	18.8.1944	11.1944	to Turkey 7.1972 (Cerbe)
Toro	SS422	Portsmouth N Yd	5.1944	23.8.1944	12.1944	auxiliary 7.1962
Torsk	SS423	Portsmouth N Yd	6.1944	6.9.1944	12.1944	auxiliary 5.1968
Quillback (ex-*Trembler*)	SS424	Portsmouth N Yd	6.1944	1.10.1944	12.1944	stricken 3.1973
Trumpetfish	SS425	Cramp, Philadelphia	8.1943	13.5.1945	1.1946	to Brazil 10.1973 (Goiás)
Tusk	SS426	Cramp, Philadelphia	8.1943	8.7.1945	4.1946	to Taiwan 10.1973 (Hai Pao)
Turbot	SS427	Cramp, Philadelphia	11.1943	12.4.1946	-	cancelled 8.1945
Ulua	SS428	Cramp, Philadelphia	11.1943	23.4.1946	-	cancelled 8.1945
Corsair	SS435	Electric Boat, Groton	3.1945	3.5.1946	11.1946	auxiliary 4.1960
Unicorn	SS436	Electric Boat, Groton	4.1945	1.8.1946	9.1946	stricken 6.1958
Walrus	SS437	Electric Boat, Groton	6.1945	20.9.1946	10.1946	stricken 6.1958
Argonaut	SS475	Portsmouth N Yd	6.1944	1.10.1944	1.1945	to Canada 12.1968 (Rainbow)
Runner	SS476	Portsmouth N Yd	7.1944	17.10.1944	2.1945	auxiliary 2.1969
Conger	SS477	Portsmouth N Yd	7.1944	17.10.1944	2.1945	auxiliary 3.1962
Cutlass	SS478	Portsmouth N Yd	7.1944	5.11.1944	3.1945	to Taiwan 4.1973 (Hai Shih)
Diablo	SS479	Portsmouth N Yd	8.1944	1.12.1944	3.1945	auxiliary 7.1962
Medregal	SS480	Portsmouth N Yd	8.1944	15.12.1944	4.1945	stricken 8.1970
Requin	SS481	Portsmouth N Yd	8.1944	1.1.1945	4.1945	auxiliary 6.1968
Irex	SS482	Portsmouth N Yd	10.1944	26.1.1945	5.1945	auxiliary 6.1969
Sea Leopard	SS483	Portsmouth N Yd	11.1944	2.3.1945	6.1945	to Brazil 3.1973 (Bahia)
Odax	SS484	Portsmouth N Yd	12.1944	10.4.1945	7.1945	to Brazil 7.1972 (Rio de Janeiro)
Sirago	SS485	Portsmouth N Yd	1.1945	11.5.1945	8.1945	stricken 6.1972

Pomodon	SS486	Portsmouth N Yd	1.1945	12.6.1945	9.1945	stricken 8.1970
Remora	SS487	Portsmouth N Yd	3.1945	12.7.1945	1.1946	to Greece 10.1973 (Katsonis)
Sarda	SS488	Portsmouth N Yd	4.1945	24.8.1945	4.1946	auxiliary 7.1962
Spinax	SS489	Portsmouth N Yd	5.1945	20.11.1945	9.1946	auxiliary 6.1969
Volador	SS490	Portsmouth N Yd	6.1945	17.1.1946	10.1948	to Italy 8.1972 (Gianfranco Gazzana Priaroggia)
Pompano	SS491	Portsmouth N Yd	7.1945	-	-	cancelled 8.1945
Wahoo	SS516	Portsmouth N Yd	5.1944	-	-	cancelled 7.1.1946
	SS517	Portsmouth N Yd	5.1944	-	-	cancelled 29.7.1944
Amberjack	SS522	Boston N Yd, Charlestown	2.1944	15.12.1944	3.1946	to Brazil 10.1972 (Ceará)
Grampus	SS523	Boston N Yd, Charlestown	2.1944	15.12.1944	10.1947	to Brazil 7.1972 (Rio Grande do Sul)
Pickerel	SS524	Boston N Yd, Charlestown	2.1944	15.12.1944	4.1949	to Italy 8.1972 (Primo Longobardo)
Grenadier	SS525	Boston N Yd, Charlestown	2.1944	15.12.1944	2.1951	to Venezuela 5.1973 (Picua)
Dorado	SS526	Boston N Yd, Charlestown	1944	-	-	cancelled 29.7.1944

Trutta 1945

1845 / 2415 t, 95.0 x 8.3 x 4.7 m, 4 Fairbanks-Morse (SS417-424, 475-491, 522-525) or General Motors (SS435-437) diesel-generators / 4 electric motors (2 shafts), 5400 / 2740 hp, 20.2 / 8.7 kts, 472 t diesel oil, 11000-12000 nm (10 kts) / 96 nm (2 kts), complement 60, 120 (SS417-437) or 135 (SS475-529) m; 1 (SS417-426, 435-437) or 2 (SS475-488, 522) x 1 – 127/25 Mk 17, 1 x 1 – 40/56 Bofors, 1 x 1 – 20/70 Oerlikon, 10 – 533 TT (6 bow, 4 stern, 24 torpedoes or 40 mines for SS417-437 or 28 torpedoes or 40 mines for SS475-526); SD (SS417-424), SJ (SS417-424, 475-482), SS (SS425, 426, 435, 483-488, 522), ST, SV (SS425, 426, 435, 475-488, 522) radars, WDA (SS417-424, 475-482), WFA (SS425, 426, 435, 483-488, 522), JP (SS417-424, 475-482), JT (SS425, 426, 435, 483-488, 522) sonars, APR-1 ECM suite.
Electronic equipment data is given presumably.

SS489: 1525 / 2410 t, 95.1x8.3x4.7m, 4 Fairbanks-Morse diesel-generators / 4 electric motors (2 shafts), 4610 / 1750 hp, 17 / 8 kts, 472 t diesel oil, 12000 nm (10 kts) /, complement 90, 135 m; 1 x 1 – 40/56 Bofors, 4 – 533 TT (bow, 12); SS, SV-1, SV-2 radars, WFA, JT sonars, APR-1 ECM suite.

SS490, 523-525: 1870 / 2440 t, 93.6 x 8.2 x 5.2 m,

4 Fairbanks-Morse diesel-generators / 4 electric motors (2 shafts), 4610 / 5400 hp, 18 / 16 kts, 378-472 t diesel oil, 11000 nm (10 kts) / 96 nm (2 kts), complement 82, 135 m; 10 – 533 TT (6 bow, 4 stern, 28 torpedoes or 40 mines); SS, ST, SV radars, BQR-2, BQS-2, JT or SQR-3 sonars, APR-1 ECM suite.

Further development of the *Gato* and *Balao* classes. The design of a new submarine received an enhanced internal subdivision into compartments, a strengthened hull, which led to an increase in displacement by about 35-40 t. Otherwise, they differed little from predecessors. The latest series, starting with SS475, was designed for a greater operating diving depth (135 m, maximum allowable 225 m), in addition, they had increased to 28 torpedo stowage.

In total, 146 new submarines were ordered (SS417-562) in 1942-1943, but in 1944-1945 the building of 112 boats (SS427-434, 438-474, 491-515, 517-521 and 526-562) was cancelled. Some cancelled submarines were named (SS429 *Unicorn*, SS430 *Vandace*, SS431 *Walrus*, SS432 *Whitefish*, SS433 *Whiting*, SS434 *Wolffish* – all Cramp, cancelled 29.7.1944, SS492 *Grayling*, SS493 *Needlefish*, SS494 *Sculpin* – all Portsmouth N Yd, cancelled 12.8.1945, SS527 *Comber*, SS528 *Sea Panther*, SS529 *Tiburon* - all Boston N Yd, cancelled 29.7.1944). 1946 also saw the cancellation of SS516, and building of SS436 and 437 was suspended and they were eventually sold for scrap without commission. As a result, 31 submarines were completed. SS489 *Spinax* was commissioned as a radar picket submarine under the Migraine project, SS490 and 523-525 were commissioned under the GUPPY II design of modernization.
1945, *Requin*: + 6 x 12 - 127 Mk 51 RL.

Torsk 1945

ESCORT AND PATROL SHIPS

WILMINGTON patrol gunboat

Wilmington	PG8	Newport News	10.1894	19.10.1895	5.1897	auxiliary 1.1941

1397 / 1689 t, 76.4 x 12.5 x 2.7 m, 2 VTE, 4 Babcock & Wilcox boilers, 1900 hp, 15 kts, 277 t coal, 5500 nm (10 kts), complement 199; belt 25, deck 38; 1 x 1 – 102/50 Mk 9, 5 x 1 – 76/50 Mk 10.
Shallow-draught ship, one of the two built in the class. Served as TS.
There was a strip of 25-mm armor amidships on the waterline.

Wilmington 1897

DUBUQUE class patrol gunboats

Dubuque	AG6, 11.1940-PG17	Gas Engine & Power, Morris Heights	9.1903	15.8.1904	6.1905	TS, gunboat 1.1940, stricken 9.1945
Paducah	AG7, 11.1940-PG18	Gas Engine & Power, Morris Heights	9.1903	11.10.1904	9.1905	auxiliary, gunboat 11.1940, stricken 9.1945

1084 / 1237 t, 61.1 x 10.7 x 4.1 m, 2 VTE, 2 Babcock & Wilcox boilers, 1250 hp, 13 kts, 200 t coal, complement 184-198; 1 x 1 – 127/38 Mk 12, 2 x 1 – 102/50 Mk 7, 1 x 1 – 76/50 Mk 10.
Composite-hulled colonial gunboats, similar to the RN sloops. Both ships since 1919 served on the Great Lakes with reduced armament, training naval reservists. In November 1940, they were again reclassified as gunboats and rearmed. During the Second World War, they were used to train the armed guards of merchant

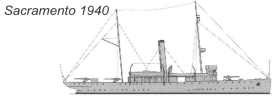
Dubuque 1914

vessels.
1943-1944, *Dubuque*: + 3 x 1 – 20/70 Oerlikon. 1943-1944, *Paducah*: + 5 x 1 – 20/70 Oerlikon.

SACRAMENTO patrol gunboat

Sacramento	PG19	Cramp, Philadelphia	4.1913	21.2.1914	4.1914	for disposal 2.1946

1425 / 1592 t, 69.0 x 12.5 x 3.5 m, 1 VTE, 2 Babcock & Wilcox boilers, 950 hp, 12.5 kts, 428 t coal, 4000 nm (10 kts), complement 163; 2 x 1 – 102/50 Mk 9, 1 x 1 – 76/50 Mk 10.
Cheap alternative to a small cruiser: the oceangoing colonial gunboat.

Sacramento 1940

ASHEVILLE class patrol gunboats

Asheville	PG21	Charleston N Yd	6.1917	4.7.1918	7.1920	sunk 3.3.1942
Tulsa, 12.1944- **Tacloban**	PG22	Charleston N Yd	12.1919	25.8.1922	12.1923	stricken 4.1946

1575 / 1760 t, 73.5 x 12.6 x 3.4 m, 1 set Parsons geared steam turbines, 3 Thornycroft boilers, 850 hp, 12 kts, 420 t coal, 2000 nm (10 kts), complement 159; 3 x 1 – 102/50 Mk 9, 60 passengers.
The last conventional gunboats built for the US Navy, the later *Erie* and *Charleston* were partly conceived as small

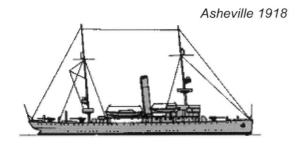

Asheville 1918

cruisers. A modified *Sacramentos*, the main changes being the accommodations for approximately 60 more troops and 3 rather than two boilers. The lines repeated those of the previous ship, but 4.6-m ong section was added amidships.
1942, both: - 3 x 1 – 102/50; + 5 x 1 - 76/50 Mk 20
1943-1944, *Tulsa*: + 6 x 1 – 20/70 Oerlikon.
Asheville 3.3.1942 was sunk S of Java by Japanese destroyers *Arashi* and *Nowaki*.

ERIE class patrol gunboats

Erie	PG50	New York N Yd, Brooklyn	12.1934	29.1.1936	7.1936	beached 12.11.1942
Charleston	PG51	Charleston N Yd	10.1934	25.2.1936	7.1936	for disposal 5.1946

Erie 1940

2000 / 2800 t, 100.1 x 12.6 x 3.5 m, 2 sets Parsons geared steam turbines, 2 Babcock & Wilcox boilers, 6200 hp, 20 kts, 489 t oil, 8000 nm (12 kts), complement 236; belt 89, deck 32-25, upper belt 76-51, CT: sides 102, roof 32; 4 x 1 – 152/47 Mk 17, 4 x 4 – 28/75 Mk 1, 1 seaplane (SOC).
The appearance of two gunboats of the *Erie* class was the result of the London Conference of 1930. The final document, approved by all the great world naval powers, allowed to build ships in any quantity with a standard displacement of less than 2000 t, speed no more than 20 kts, armed with up to 155-mm guns. With these characteristics as a guide, US designers set about designing a multipurpose 'sloop', called to solve a wide range of tasks: from fire support for marines during amphibious operations (in 1930th, US interests in the Caribbean were often accompanied by armed

interventions) to protection convoys from surface raiders and submarines in wartime. The minelaying ability was also envisaged.
The hull of the new gunboats (this is how the new ships were classified) had rather unusual shape with an oblong clipper bow to reduce splashing and a stern with a significant overhang for the convenience of minelaying and placing of anti-submarine armament.
The main artillery consisted of four 152-mm/47 guns in deck mounts, placed two each in the bow and stern. Since it was impossible to place 127-mm DP guns in addition to 152-mm guns, the *Erie* and *Charleston* became one of the first USN ships armed with 28-mm MGs. It was possible to place even one seaplane, which could be used both for reconnaissance and for gunfire correction. A seaplane could take off only from the water: there was no place for a catapult. Despite their modest dimensions, the new gunboats were well protected.
Although the new gunboats were positively evaluated by naval commanders, this class did not receive further development: they were too expensive for peacetime.
The main belt protecting the machinery was 89-mm thick. The fore magazines were protected by the 73-mm local upper belt, and aft magazines were protected by 76-51-mm one. The main deck was connected to the upper edge of the belt and was 32-mm thick over the machinery and 25-mm over the magazines.
1942, both: - 4 x 4 - 28/75; + 6 x 1 - 20/70 Oerlikon, 2 DCR.
Erie was torpedoed 12.11.1942 in the Caribbean Sea by German submarine *U163*, towed to the harbor of Willemstad, where she sank 5.12.1942.

Erie 1938

auxiliary patrol gunboats

Niagara (*ex-Hi-Esmaro*)	PG52	7.6.1929 / 1.1941	*1922*	81.4 x 10.8 x 5.2	16	2 - 76/50	auxiliary 1.1943

Name	No.	Date	Displ.	Dimensions	Speed	Armament	Fate
Vixen *(ex-Orion)*	PG53	1929 / 2.1941	*3774*	101.6 x 14.2 x 4.9	15	4 - 76/50, 2 DCR	stricken 7.1946
St. Augustine *(ex-Noparo)*	PG54	1929 / 1.1941	*1720*	83.0 x 11.0 x 4.4	14	2 - 76/50	collision 5.1.1944
Jamestown *(ex-Alder)*	PG55	1928 / 5.1941	*2250*	89.6 x 11.6 x 4.9	15	2 - 76/50, 6 - 20	auxiliary 1.1943
Williamsburg *(ex-Aras)*	PG56	8.12.1930 / 101941	*1820*	74.3 x 11.0 x 4.3	16	2 - 76/50, 3 DCT	yacht 11.1945
Plymouth *(ex-Alva)*	PG57	1931 / 4.1942	*1500*	80.6 x 14.1 x 5.8	15	1 - 102/50, 2 - 76/50	sunk 5.8.1943
Hilo *(ex-Moana)*	PG58	18.7.1931 / 61942	*2350*	75.4 (pp) x 11.6	14.5	1 - 76/50	auxiliary 1.1943
San Bernardino *(ex-Vanda)*	PG59	3.10.1928 / 6.1942	*1768*	73.2 x 11.1 x 4.9	17	2 - 76/50, 2 – 40	stricken 5.1946
Beaumont *(ex-Carola)*	PG60	1930 / 6.1942	*1434*	68.9 x 10.6 x 3.9	15.5	2 - 76/50, 2 - 40	for disposal 2.1947
Dauntless *(ex-Delphine)*	PG61	2.4.1921 / 5.1942	*1950*	78.5 x 10.7 x 5.0	16	2 - 76/50	for disposal 6.1946
Nourmahal	WPG72, 4.1943-PG72, 12.1943-WPG122	1928 / 8.1940	*2250*	65.7 x 12.7 x 6.7	15	2 - 102/50, 2 DCR	Coast Guard cutter, to the Navy 6.1942, to the Coast Guard 12.1943, for disposal 7.1948
Corsair	PG85	1899 / 4.1942	*1136*	92.7 x 10.2	19	2 - 76/50	auxiliary 8.1942

Numbers written in *Italic* indicate displacement
Yachts purchased by the US Navy and classified as gunboats.
Plymouth was torpedoed 15.8.1943 by German submarine *U566* off Cape Henry. *St. Augustine* was sunk 5.1.1944 off Cape May after collision with oiler *Camas Meadows*.

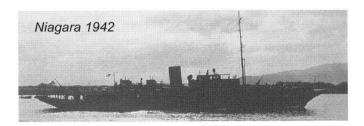
Niagara 1942

ASHEVILLE class patrol frigates

Name	No.	Builder	Laid down	Launched	Commissioned	Fate
Asheville *(ex-Adur)*	PG101, 4.1943 - PF1	Canadian Vickers, Montreal, Canada	10.1941	22.8.1942	12.1942	stricken 2.1946
Natchez *(ex-Annan)*	PG102, 4.1943 - PF2	Canadian Vickers, Montreal, Canada	3.1942	12.9.1942	12.1942	to the Maritime Commission 11.1945

1412 / 2150 t, 91.9 x 11.1 x 4.0 m, 2 VTE, 2 Admiralty 3-drum boilers, 5500 hp, 20 kts, 674 t oil, complement 190; 3 x 1 – 76/50 Mk 20, 2 x 2 – 40/56 Bofors, 4 x 1 – 20/70 Oerlikon, 1 x 24 Hedgehog ASWRL, 8 DCT, 2 DCR (100), SA, SL radars, Type 144 sonar.
In the early years of the war, the USA experienced a

Asheville 1942

Natchez 1943

shortage of ships to escort Atlantic convoys. In early 1942, the United States and the United Kingdom reached

an agreement on the delivery of 10 newest frigates of *River* class. British shipyards were overwhelmed with military orders, and the order was transferred to Canada. By the time the frigates were commissioned, the need for Allied assistance had disappeared, and the US Navy commissioned only two ships.

Asheville, 1944: - 1 x 24 Hedgehog ASWRL; + 1 x 3 Squid Mk 3 ASWRL, Type 147B sonar (temporarily for tests, replaced again by Hedgehog in 1944).

TACOMA class patrol frigates

Tacoma	PF3	Kaiser, Richmond	3.1943	7.7.1943	11.1943	to the USSR 8.1945 (EK-11)
Sausalito	PF4	Kaiser, Richmond	4.1943	20.7.1943	3.1944	to the USSR 8.1945 (EK-16)
Hoquiam	PF5	Kaiser, Richmond	4.1943	31.7.1943	5.1944	to the USSR 8.1945 (EK-13)
Pasco	PF6	Kaiser, Richmond	7.1943	17.8.1943	4.1944	to the USSR 8.1945 (EK-12)
Albuquerque	PF7	Kaiser, Richmond	1943	14.9.1943	12.1943	to the USSR 8.1945 (EK-14)
Everett	PF8	Kaiser, Richmond	1943	29.9.1943	1.1944	to the USSR 8.1945 (EK-15)
Pocatello	PF9	Kaiser, Richmond	8.1943	17.10.1943	2.1944	BU 9.1947
Brownsville	PF10	Kaiser, Richmond	9.1943	14.11.1943	5.1944	BU 9.1947
Grand Forks	PF11	Kaiser, Richmond	9.1943	27.11.1943	3.1944	stricken 6.1946
Casper	PF12	Kaiser, Richmond	10.1943	27.12.1943	3.1944	BU 5.1947
Pueblo	PF13	Kaiser, Richmond	11.1943	20.1.1944	5.1944	sold 9.1947
Grand Island	PF14	Kaiser, Richmond	11.1943	19.2.1944	5.1944	to Cuba 6.1947 (Máximo Gómez)
Annapolis	PF15	American SB, Lorain	5.1943	16.10.1943	12.1944	stricken 6.1946
Bangor	PF16	American SB, Lorain	5.1943	6.11.1943	11.1944	to Mexico 11.1947 (General José María Morelos)
Key West	PF17	American SB, Lorain	6.1943	29.12.1943	11.1944	BU 4.1947
Alexandria	PF18	American SB, Lorain	6.1943	15.1.1944	3.1945	stricken 5.1946
Huron	PF19	American SB, Cleveland	5.1943	3.7.1943	9.1944	sold 5.1947
Gulfport	PF20	American SB, Cleveland	1943	21.8.1943	9.1944	stricken 6.1946
Bayonne	PF21	American SB, Cleveland	1943	11.9.1943	2.1945	to the USSR 9.1945 (EK-25)
Gloucester	PF22	Walter Butler, Superior	1943	12.7.1943	12.1943	to the USSR 9.1945 (EK-26)
Shreveport	PF23	Walter Butler, Superior	3.1943	15.7.1943	12.1943	stricken 6.1946
Muskegon	PF24	Walter Butler, Superior	5.1943	25.7.1943	2.1944	to France 3.1947 (Mermoz)
Charlottesville	PF25	Walter Butler, Superior	5.1943	30.7.1943	4.1944	to the USSR 7.1945 (EK-1)
Poughkeepsie	PF26	Walter Butler, Superior	6.1943	12.8.1943	9.1944	to the USSR 9.1945 (EK-27)
Newport	PF27	Walter Butler, Superior	6.1943	15.8.1943	9.1944	to the USSR 9.1945 (EK-28)

Emporia	PF28	Walter Butler, Superior	7.1943	30.8.1943	10.1944	to France 3.1947 (Le Verrier)
Groton	PF29	Walter Butler, Superior	7.1943	14.9.1943	9.1944	to Columbia 3.1947 (Almirante Padilla)
Hingham	PF30	Walter Butler, Superior	7.1943	27.8.1943	11.1944	BU 8.1947
Grand Rapids	PF31	Walter Butler, Superior	7.1943	10.9.1943	10.1944	BU 4.1947
Woonsocket	PF32	Walter Butler, Superior	8.1943	27.9.1943	9.1944	stricken 5.1947
Dearborn (ex-*Toledo*)	PF33	Walter Butler, Superior	8.1943	27.9.1943	9.1944	BU 7.1947
Long Beach	PF34	Consolidated Steel, Wilmington	3.1943	5.5.1943	9.1943	to the USSR 7.1945 (EK-2)
Belfast	PF35	Consolidated Steel, Wilmington	3.1943	20.5.1943	11.1943	to the USSR 7.1945 (EK-3)
Glendale	PF36	Consolidated Steel, Wilmington	4.1943	28.5.1943	10.1943	to the USSR 6.1945 (EK-6)
San Pedro	PF37	Consolidated Steel, Wilmington	4.1943	11.6.1943	10.1943	to the USSR 7.1945 (EK-5)
Coronado	PF38	Consolidated Steel, Wilmington	5.1943	17.6.1943	11.1943	to the USSR 7.1945 (EK-8)
Ogden	PF39	Consolidated Steel, Wilmington	5.1943	23.6.1943	12.1943	to the USSR 7.1945 (EK-10)
Eugene	PF40	Consolidated Steel, Wilmington	6.1943	6.7.1943	1.1944	stricken 7.1946
El Paso	PF41	Consolidated Steel, Wilmington	6.1943	16.7.1943	12.1943	BU 10.1947
Van Buren	PF42	Consolidated Steel, Wilmington	6.1943	27.7.1943	12.1943	stricken 6.1946
Orange	PF43	Consolidated Steel, Wilmington	7.1943	6.8.1943	1.1944	stricken 4.1947
Corpus Christi	PF44	Consolidated Steel, Wilmington	7.1943	17.8.1943	1.1944	BU 10.1947
Hutchinson	PF45	Consolidated Steel, Wilmington	1943	27.8.1943	2.1944	stricken 10.1946
Bisbee	PF46	Consolidated Steel, Wilmington	1943	7.9.1943	2.1944	to the USSR 8.1945 (EK-17)
Gallup	PF47	Consolidated Steel, Wilmington	8.1943	17.9.1943	2.1944	to the USSR 8.1945 (EK-22)
Rockford	PF48	Consolidated Steel, Wilmington	8.1943	27.9.1943	3.1944	to the USSR 8.1945 (EK-18)
Muskogee	PF49	Consolidated Steel, Wilmington	9.1943	18.10.1943	3.1944	to the USSR 8.1945 (EK-19)
Carson City	PF50	Consolidated Steel, Wilmington	9.1943	13.11.1943	3.1944	to the USSR 8.1945 (EK-20)
Burlington	PF51	Consolidated Steel, Wilmington	1943	7.12.1943	4.1944	to the USSR 8.1945 (EK-21)
Allentown	PF52	Froemming, Milwaukee	1943	3.7.1943	3.1944	to the USSR 7.1945 (EK-9)
Machias	PF53	Froemming, Milwaukee	5.1943	22.8.1943	3.1944	to the USSR 7.1945 (EK-4)
Sandusky	PF54	Froemming, Milwaukee	7.1943	5.10.1943	4.1944	to the USSR 7.1945 (EK-7)
Bath	PF55	Froemming, Milwaukee	8.1943	14.11.1943	9.1944	to the USSR 7.1945 (EK-29)

Covington	PF56	Globe, Superior	3.1943	15.7.1943	10.1944	stricken 4.1947
Sheboygan	PF57	Globe, Superior	4.1943	31.7.1943	5.1944	to Belgium 3.1947 (Lieutenant ter Zee Victor Billet)
Abilene (ex-Bridgeport)	PF58	Globe, Superior	5.1943	21.8.1943	10.1944	to the Netherlands 5.1947 (Cirrus)
Beaufort	PF59	Globe, Superior	7.1943	9.10.1943	8.1944	BU 4.1947
Charlotte	PF60	Globe, Superior	8.1943	10.10.1943	10.1944	sold 5.1947
Manitowoc	PF61	Globe, Duluth	8.1943	30.11.1943	12.1944	to France 3.1947 (Le Brix)
Gladwyne (ex-Worcester)	PF62	Globe, Duluth	10.1943	7.1.1944	11.1944	stricken 10.1946
Moberly (ex-Scranton)	PF63	Globe, Duluth	11.1943	26.1.1944	12.1944	stricken 4.1947
Knoxville	PF64	Leatham D. Smith SB, Superior	4.1943	10.7.1943	4.1944	to Dominican Republic 9.1947 (Presidente Troncoso)
Uniontown (ex-Chattanooga)	PF65	Leatham D. Smith SB, Superior	4.1943	7.8.1943	10.1944	stricken 1.1946
Reading	PF66	Leatham D. Smith SB, Superior	5.1943	28.8.1943	8.1944	stricken 1.1946
Peoria	PF67	Leatham D. Smith SB, Superior	5.1943	2.10.1943	1.1945	stricken 6.1946
Brunswick	PF68	Leatham D. Smith SB, Superior	7.1943	6.11.1943	10.1944	stricken 6.1946
Davenport	PF69	Leatham D. Smith SB, Superior	8.1943	8.12.1943	2.1945	BU 6.1946
Evansville	PF70	Leatham D. Smith SB, Superior	8.1943	27.11.1943	12.1944	to the USSR 9.1945 (EK-30)
New Bedford	PF71	Leatham D. Smith SB, Superior	10.1943	29.12.1943	11.1944	BU 11.1947
Hallowell (ex-Machias)	PF72	Walsh-Kaiser, Providence	4.1943	14.7.1943	(10.1943)	to the UK 10.1943 (Anguilla)
Hammond	PF73	Walsh-Kaiser, Providence	1943	26.7.1943	(11.1943)	to the UK 11.1943 (Antigua)
Hargood	PF74	Walsh-Kaiser, Providence	1943	6.8.1943	(11.1943)	to the UK 11.1943 (Ascension)
Hotham	PF75	Walsh-Kaiser, Providence	1943	17.8.1943	(12.1943)	to the UK 12.1943 (Bahamas)
Halstead	PF76	Walsh-Kaiser, Providence	1943	27.8.1943	(12.1943)	to the UK 12.1943 (Barbados)
Hannam	PF77	Walsh-Kaiser, Providence	1943	6.9.1943	(12.1943)	to the UK 12.1943 (Caicos)
Harland	PF78	Walsh-Kaiser, Providence	1943	6.9.1943	(1.1944)	to the UK 1.1944 (Cayman)
Harman	PF79	Walsh-Kaiser, Providence	1943	14.9.1943	(1.1944)	to the UK 1.1944 (Dominica)
Harvey	PF80	Walsh-Kaiser, Providence	1943	21.9.1943	(2.1944)	to the UK 2.1944 (Labuan)
Holmes	PF81	Walsh-Kaiser, Providence	1943	27.9.1943	(8.1944)	to the UK 8.1944 (Tobago)
Hornby	PF82	Walsh-Kaiser, Providence	1943	27.9.1943	(8.1944)	to the UK 8.1944 (Montserrat)

Hoste	PF83	Walsh-Kaiser, Providence	1943	6.10.1943	(7.1944)	to the UK 7.1944 (Nyasaland)
Howett	PF84	Walsh-Kaiser, Providence	1943	10.10.1943	(7.1944)	to the UK 1.1944 (Papua)
Pilford	PF85	Walsh-Kaiser, Providence	1943	15.10.1943	7.1944	to the UK 7.1944 (Pitcairn)
Pasley	PF86	Walsh-Kaiser, Providence	9.1943	20.10.1943	(2.1944)	to the UK 2.1944 (St. Helena)
Patton	PF87	Walsh-Kaiser, Providence	10.1943	25.10.1943	(2.1944)	to the UK 2.1944 (Sarawak)
Peard	PF88	Walsh-Kaiser, Providence	10.1943	30.10.1943	(2.1944)	to the UK 2.1944 (Seychelles)
Phillimore	PF89	Walsh-Kaiser, Providence	1943	5.11.1943	(2.1944)	to the UK 2.1944 (Perim)
Popham	PF90	Walsh-Kaiser, Providence	1943	11.11.1943	(2.1944)	to the UK 2.1944 (Somaliland)
Peyton	PF91	Walsh-Kaiser, Providence	10.1943	16.11.1943	(5.1944)	to the UK 5.1944 (Tortola)
Prowse	PF92	Walsh-Kaiser, Providence	10.1943	21.11.1943	(6.1944)	to the UK 6.1944 (Zanzibar)
Lorain (ex-Roanoke)	PF93	American SB, Lorain	10.1943	18.3.1944	1.1945	to France 3.1947 (La Place)
Milledgeville (ex-Sitka)	PF94	American SB, Lorain	11.1943	5.4.1944	1.1945	stricken 4.1947
Orlando	PF99	American SB, Cleveland	8.1943	1.12.1943	11.1944	stricken 7.1946
Racine	PF100	American SB, Cleveland	9.1943	15.3.1944	1.1945	stricken 7.1946
Greensboro	PF101	American SB, Cleveland	1943	9.3.1944	1.1945	stricken 4.1947
Forsyth	PF102	American SB, Cleveland	12.1943	20.5.1944	2.1945	to the Netherlands 7.1947 (Cumulus)

1509 / 2238 t, 92.6 x 11.4 x 3.9 m, 2 VTE, 3 boilers, 5500 hp, 20 kts, 768 t oil, 9500 nm (12 kts), complement 190 (frigates) or 176 (weather ships);

Frigates PF3-16, 19, 21, 22, 25-27, 34-39, 42-65, 70: 3 x 1 – 76/50 Mk 20/21, 2 x 2 – 40/56 Bofors, 9 x 1 – 20/70 Oerlikon, 1 x 24 Hedgehog ASWRL, 8 DCT, 2 DCR (100); SA, SL radars, QGA sonar.

Weather ships PF17, 18, 20, 23, 24, 28-33, 40, 41, 66-69, 71, 93, 94, 99-102: 2 x 1 – 76/50 Mk 20/21, 2 x 2 – 40/56 Bofors, 4 x 1 – 20/70 Oerlikon, 1 x 24 Hedgehog ASWRL, 8 DCT, 2 DCR (100), balloons; SA, SL radars, QGA sonar.

The shortage of escort forces to serve in the Atlantic at the start of the war prompted the USA to follow the path tried by the UK: the building of warships in non-specialized shipyards with no experience in naval shipbuilding. In order not to waste time on developing a new design, at the suggestion of the Maritime Commission, the 'River' class frigate, designed in 1941 according to the merchant standard, taking in the account the capabilities of small shipbuilders, was chosen as a sample; in addition, the

Tacoma 1944

US Navy was supposed to receive 10 of these Canadian-built ships under the "reverse" Lend-Lease. Initially, the new ships were to be classified as gunboats (PG), but then a new type was invented for them: 'patrol frigate' (PF).

Unfortunately, when revising the design for the capabilities of the US industry, the desire to simplify construction for the sake of manufacturability led to the

Tacoma 1943

Greensboro 1945

fact that, in comparison with the British sample, the US ship turned out to be noticeably worse. The replacement of a riveted hull with all-welded was not accompanied by a corresponding strength recalculation, and, as a result, the hulls of new ships "cracked" in a wake. Already after the commissioning of all frigates, it was necessary to strengthen the longitudinal braces, but even after that, the strength of the hull left much to be desired.

In addition to problems with a hull strength, these ships had many other disadvantages, such as poor maneuverability and uncomfortable by the standards of the US Navy habitability conditions. The disadvantages of the *Tacoma* class were especially noticeable against the background of escort destroyers designed to solve the same tasks and carried the same armament.

A total of 100 ships of this class were ordered in 1942. PF95 *Stamford*, PF96 *Macon* and PF98 *Vallejo (ex-Milledgeville)* were cancelled in December 1943, PF97 *Lorain (ex-Sitka)* in January 1944 (all were to be built by American SB, Lorain).

EAGLE class patrol vessels

Eagle No10	PE10	Ford Motors, Detroit	7.1918	9.11.1918	10.1919	sunk as target 19.8.1937
Eagle No19	PE19	Ford Motors, Detroit	8.1918	30.1.1919	6.1919	stricken 3.1945
Eagle No26	PE26	Ford Motors, Detroit	9.1918	1.3.1919	9.1919	sold 8.1938
Eagle No27	PE27	Ford Motors, Detroit	10.1918	1.3.1919	7.1919	sold 6.1946
Eagle No32	PE32	Ford Motors, Detroit	11.1918	15.3.1919	8.1919	sold 3.1947
Eagle No35	PE35	Ford Motors, Detroit	1.1919	22.3.1919	8.1919	sold 6.1938
Eagle No38	PE38	Ford Motors, Detroit	1.1919	29.3.1919	7.1919	sold 3.1947
Eagle No39	PE39	Ford Motors, Detroit	2.1919	29.3.1919	9.1919	sold 6.1938
Eagle No44	PE44	Ford Motors, Detroit	2.1919	24.5.1919	9.1919	stricken 5.1938
Eagle No48	PE48	Ford Motors, Detroit	3.1919	24.5.1919	9.1919	sold 10.1946
Eagle No51	PE51	Ford Motors, Detroit	3.1919	14.6.1919	9.1919	sold 8.1938
Eagle No52	PE52	Ford Motors, Detroit	3.1919	9.7.1919	9.1919	sold 8.1938
Eagle No55	PE55	Ford Motors, Detroit	3.1919	22.7.1919	9.1919	sold 3.1947
Eagle No56	PE56	Ford Motors, Detroit	3.1919	15.8.1919	10.1919	sunk 23.4.1945
Eagle No57	PE57	Ford Motors, Detroit	3.1919	29.7.1919	9.1919	sold 3.1947
Eagle No58	PE58	Ford Motors, Detroit	3.1919	2.8.1919	10.1919	stricken 6.1940
Eagle No59	PE59	Ford Motors, Detroit	3.1919	12.4.1919	9.1919	sold 8.1938
Eagle No60	PE60	Ford Motors, Detroit	3.1919	13.8.1919	10.1919	sold 8.1938

PE19 1941

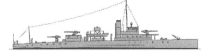

500 / 615 t, 61.2 x 10.1 x 2.6 m, 1 set Poole geared steam turbines, 2 Bureau Express boilers, 2500 hp, 18.3 kts, 105 t coal + 45 t oil, 3500 nm (10 kts), complement 61; 2 x 1 – 102/50 Mk 9, 1 x 1 – 76/50 Mk 10, 1 DCT.

Purpose-built ASW ships built shortly after the US entered the First World War as an alternative to more expensive destroyers. New ships were supposed to carry armament sufficient to fight a surfaced submarine, have a speed of at least 18 kts and acceptable for operations in the conditions of the North Atlantic seaworthiness. A total of 100 ships were to be built for the USN and another 12 for Italy. The contract for building of the entire series was received by Henry Ford Auto company. To reduce production costs and in consideration of the contractor's lack of sufficient experience in shipbuilding, the design was simplified as much as possible, the number of curved surfaces was minimized, replacing them, if possible, with the flat ones. The hull was flush-decked. In the early design stages, it was planned to arm new ships with two 76-mm/50 guns and twin 533-mm TT, however, against the 150-mm guns of German submarine cruisers, such armament looked too weak, so the TT soon disappeared from the design, and the artillery was strengthened. Originally designed diesels were abandoned at Ford's request in favor of lighter steam turbines: the changes made to the design led to an increase in displacement, which cast doubt on the possibility of achieving a 18-kt speed.

Under the terms of the contract, all 100 ships of *Eagle* class for the US Navy were to be commissioned before the end of 1918, however, due to the corrections of the design, the lead *PE1* was commissioned by the Navy only in October 1918. A month later, the war ended, the need for *Eagles* has disappeared, and the building of 72 ships, including all Italians, was cancelled. 1942-1943, most survived: - 2 x 1 - 102/50, 1 DCT; + 1 x 24 Hedgehog ASWRL, 2 DCR, SE or SF radar.

PE17 was wrecked off Long Island 19.5.1922 in heavy gale. *PE56* was sunk by German submarine *U853* 23.4.1945 off Portland (US Atlantic coast).

'FLOWER' class patrol gunboats

1st group

Temptress (ex-*Veronica*)	PG62	Smith's Dock, South Bank, UK	7.1940	17.10.1940	(2.1941) / 3.1942	to the UK 8.1945
Surprise (ex-*Heliotrope*)	PG63	Crown, Sunderland, UK	10.1939	5.6.1940	(9.1940) / 3.1942	to the UK 8.1945
Spry (ex-*Hibiscus*)	PG64	Harland & Wolff, Belfast, UK	11.1939	6.4.1940	(5.1940) / 5.1942	to the UK 8.1945
Saucy (ex-*Arabis*)	PG65	Harland & Wolff, Belfast, UK	10.1939	14.2.1940	(4.1940) / 4.1942	to the UK 8.1945 (Snapdragon)
Restless (ex-*Periwinkle*)	PG66	Harland & Wolff, Belfast, UK	10.1939	24.2.1940	(4.1940) / 3.1942	to the UK 8.1945
Ready (ex-*Calendula*)	PG67	Harland & Wolff, Belfast, UK	10.1939	21.3.1940	(5.1940) / 3.1942	to the UK 8.1945
Impulse (ex-*Begonia*)	PG68	Cook, Welton & Gemmel, Beverley, UK	3.1940	18.9.1940	(3.1941) / 3.1942	to the UK 8.1945
Fury (ex-*Larkspur*)	PG69	Fleming & Ferguson, Paisley, UK	3.1940	5.9.1940	(1.1941) / 3.1942	to the UK 8.1945
Courage (ex-*Heartsease*)	PG70	Harland & Wolff, Belfast, UK	11.1939	20.4.1940	(6.1940) / 4.1942	to the UK 8.1945
Tenacity (ex-*Candytuft*)	PG71	Grangemouth, UK	10.1939	8.7.1940	(10.1940) / 6.1942	to the UK 8.1945

2nd group

Action (ex-*Comfrey*)	PG86	Collingwood, Canada	1.1942	28.7.1942	11.1942	sold 2.1946
Alacrity (ex-*Cornel*)	PG87	Collingwood, Canada	1.1942	4.9.1942	12.1942	stricken 10.1945
Beacon (ex-*Dittany*)	PG88	Collingwood, Canada	1942	31.10.1942	(5.1943)	to the UK 3.1943 (Dittany)
Brisk (ex-*Flax*)	PG89	Kingston, Canada	1942	15.6.1942	12.1942	sold 10.1946
Caprice (ex-*Honesty*)	PG90	Kingston, Canada	1942	28.9.1942	(5.1943)	to the UK 5.1943 (Honesty)
Clash (ex-*Linaria*)	PG91	Midland, Canada	1942	18.11.1942	(6.1943)	to the UK 6.1943 (Linaria)
Haste (ex-*Mandrake*)	PG92	Morton, Quebec City, Canada	11.1941	22.8.1942	4.1943	disposed 10.1945
Intensity (ex-*Milfoil*)	PG93	Morton, Quebec City, Canada	11.1941	5.8.1942	3.1943	disposed 10.1945
Might (ex-*Musk*)	PG94	Morton, Quebec City, Canada	11.1941	15.7.1942	12.1942	stricken 10.1945
Pert (ex-*Nepeta*)	PG95	Morton, Quebec City, Canada	7.1942	27.11.1942	7.1943	stricken 10.1945
Prudent (ex-*Privet*)	PG96	Morton, Quebec City, Canada	8.1942	4.12.1942	6.1943	stricken 11.1945
Splendor (ex-*Rosebay*)	PG97	Collingwood, Canada	1942	11.2.1943	(7.1943)	to the UK 7.1943 (Rosebay)
Tact (ex-*Smilax*)	PG98	Collingwood, Canada	1942	24.12.1942	(6.1943)	to the UK 6.1943 (Smilax)

Vim (ex-Statice)	PG99	Collingwood, Canada	1942	10.4.1943	(9.1943)	to the UK 9.1943 (Statice)
Vitality (ex-Willowherb)	PG100	Midland, Canada	1942	24.3.1943	(8.1943)	to the UK 8.1943 (Willowherb)

Intensity 1943

1st group: 940 / 1180 t, 62.5 x 10.1 x 4.5 m, 1 VTE, 2 cylindrical boilers, 2750 hp, 16 kts, 230 t oil, 3500 nm (12 kts), complement 87; 1 x 1 – 102/50 Mk 9, 1 x 1 – 76/50 Mk 20, 4 x 1 – 20/70 Oerlikon, 4 DCT, 2 DCR (72); Type 271 radar, Type 128 sonar.

Alacrity 1943

2nd group: 1015 / 1375 t, 63.5 x 10.1 x 4.5 m, 1 VTE, 2 Admiralty 3-drum boilers, 2800 hp, 16 kts, 337 t oil, 7400 nm (10 kts), complement 90; 2 x 1 – 76/50 Mk 20, 4 x 1 – 20/70 Oerlikon, 1 x 24 Hedgehog ASWRL, 4 DCT, 2 DCR (72); SG or SL radar, Type 144 sonar.

In early 1942, the United Kingdom transferred to the USA 10 corvettes of the '*Flower*' class, reclassified by the USN as gunboats (PG62-71). At the same time, another 15 ships were ordered in Canada according to the advanced design. Only eight ships of the 2nd group were commissioned by the USN, since by the time they were completed, the need for foreign-built ships, which still had to be re-equipped according to the standards adopted by the US Navy, had disappeared. The remaining seven (PG88, 90, 91 and 97-100) were transferred to the Royal Navy under Lend-Lease.

1942-1943, 1st group ships: - Type 271 radar; + SG or SL radar.

1943-1944, *Temptress, Surprise, Spry, Saucy, Restless, Ready, Impulse, Fury, Courage, Tenacity*: + 1 x 24 Hedgehog ASWRL.

PCE class patrol ships

PCE827	Pullman Standard Car, Chicago	10.1942	2.5.1943	(7.1943)	to the UK 7.1943 (Kilbirnie)
PCE828	Pullman Standard Car, Chicago	11.1942	15.5.1943	(7.1943)	to the UK 7.1943 (Kilbride)
PCE829	Pullman Standard Car, Chicago	12.1942	27.5.1943	(8.1943)	to the UK 8.1943 (Kilchattan)
PCE830	Pullman Standard Car, Chicago	12.1942	13.6.1943	(8.1943)	to the UK 8.1943 (Kilchrenan)
PCE831	Pullman Standard Car, Chicago	1.1943	26.6.1943	(9.1943)	to the UK 9.1943 (Kildary)
PCE832	Pullman Standard Car, Chicago	2.1943	10.7.1943	(9.1943)	to the UK 9.1943 (Kildwick)
PCE833	Pullman Standard Car, Chicago	2.1943	2.8.1943	(10.1943)	to the UK 10.1943 (Kilham)
PCE834	Pullman Standard Car, Chicago	3.1943	19.8.1943	(10.1943)	to the UK 10.1943 (Kilkenzie)
PCE835	Pullman Standard Car, Chicago	3.1943	3.9.1943	(10.1943)	to the UK 10.1943 (Kilkhampton)
PCE836	Pullman Standard Car, Chicago	4.1943	17.9.1943	(11.1943)	to the UK 11.1943 (Kilmalcolm)
PCE837	Pullman Standard Car, Chicago	4.1943	1.10.1943	(11.1943)	to the UK 11.1943 (Kilmarnock)
PCE838	Pullman Standard Car, Chicago	5.1943	13.10.1943	(11.1943)	to the UK 11.1943 (Kilmartin)
PCE839	Pullman Standard Car, Chicago	5.1943	23.10.1943	(12.1943)	to the UK 12.1943 (Kilmelford)

PCE840	Pullman Standard Car, Chicago	5.1943	2.11.1943	(12.1943)	to the UK 12.1943 (Kilmington)
PCE841	Pullman Standard Car, Chicago	6.1943	9.11.1943	(12.1943)	to the UK 12.1943 (Kilmore)
PCE842	Pullman Standard Car, Chicago	6.1943	14.11.1943	1.1944	stricken 6.1961
PCE843	Pullman Standard Car, Chicago	6.1943	24.11.1943	1.1944	stricken 7.1960
PCE844	Pullman Standard Car, Chicago	7.1943	1.12.1943	2.1944	to Mexico 1947 (Pedro Sainz de Baranda)
PCE845	Pullman Standard Car, Chicago	7.1943	1.12.1943	3.1944	stricken 6.1964
PCE846	Pullman Standard Car, Chicago	8.1943	20.12.1943	3.1944	to Ecuador 11.1960 (Esmeraldas)
PCE847	Pullman Standard Car, Chicago	8.1943	27.12.1943	3.1944	to Mexico 1947 (David Porter)
PCE(R)848	Pullman Standard Car, Chicago	9.1943	21.1.1944	3.1944	stricken 3.1946
PCE(R)849	Pullman Standard Car, Chicago	9.1943	31.1.1944	4.1944	stricken 4.1966
PCE(R)850	Pullman Standard Car, Chicago	10.1943	8.2.1944	4.1944	stricken 5.1968
PCE(R)851	Pullman Standard Car, Chicago	10.1943	22.2.1944	5.1944	stricken 12.1968
PCE(R)852	Pullman Standard Car, Chicago	10.1943	1.3.1944	5.1944	to South Vietnam 7.1966 (Ngọc Hồi)
PCE(R)853	Pullman Standard Car, Chicago	11.1943	18.3.1944	6.1944	to South Vietnam 6.1970 (Van Kiếp II)
PCE(R)854	Pullman Standard Car, Chicago	1943	1944	7.1944	sold 1946
PCE(R)855	Pullman Standard Car, Chicago	12.1943	10.4.1944	11.1944	stricken 3.1970
PCE(R)856	Pullman Standard Car, Chicago	12.1943	21.4.1944	11.1944	stricken 7.1970
PCE(R)857	Pullman Standard Car, Chicago	12.1943	4.5.1944	4.1945	stricken 1970?
PCE(R)858	Pullman Standard Car, Chicago	1.1944	13.5.1944	5.1945	sold 12.1947
PCE(R)859	Pullman Standard Car, Chicago	1.1944	28.11.1944	3.1945	sold ~1946
PCE(R)860	Pullman Standard Car, Chicago	1.1944	30.5.1944	3.1945	sold 12.1947
PCE867	Albina, Portland	7.1942	3.12.1942	6.1943	to China 2.1948 (Yung Tai)
PCE868	Albina, Portland	8.1942	29.1.1943	8.1943	to Mexico 12.1947 (Virgilio Uribe)
PCE869	Albina, Portland	9.1942	6.2.1943	9.1943	to China 2.1946 (Yong Xing)
PCE870	Albina, Portland	11.1942	27.2.1943	10.1943	to South Korea 12.1961 (Byeokpa)

	PCE871	Albina, Portland	12.1942	10.3.1943	10.1943	to Mexico 1947 (Blas Godínez)
	PCE872	Albina, Portland	1.1943	24.3.1943	11.1943	to Cuba 11.1947 (Caribe)
	PCE873, 8.1945- PCE(C)873	Albina, Portland	2.1943	5.5.1943	12.1943	to South Korea 9.1955 (Hansan)
	PCE874	Albina, Portland	3.1943	11.3.1943	12.1943	stricken 5.1959
	PCE875	Albina, Portland	3.1943	27.5.1943	1.1944	to Mexico 1947 (Tomás Marín)
	PCE876	Albina, Portland	5.1943	30.9.1943	(6.1944)	completed as degaussing vessel
	PCE877, 8.1945- PCE(C)877	Albina, Portland	5.1943	11.8.1943	2.1944	stricken 7.1970
6.1944- **Buttress**	PCE878, 6.1944- ACM4	Albina, Portland	5.1943	26.8.1943	3.1944	minelayer 6.1944, stricken 3.1947
	PCE879	Albina, Portland	5.1943	30.9.1943	(7.1944)	completed as degaussing vessel
	PCE880	Albina, Portland	8.1943	27.10.1943	4.1944	stricken 7.1970
	PCE881	Albina, Portland	8.1943	10.11.1943	7.1944	to the Philippines 7.1948 (Cebu)
	PCE882, 8.1945- PCE(C)882	Albina, Portland	8.1943	3.12.1943	2.1945	to South Korea 2.1955 (Noryang)
	PCE883	Albina, Portland	1943	1944	(11.1944)	completed as degaussing vessel
	PCE884	Albina, Portland	10.1943	24.2.1944	3.1945	to the Philippines 7.1948 (Negros Occidental)
	PCE885	Albina, Portland	2.1944	20.6.1944	4.1945	to the Philippines 7.1948 (Leyte)
	PCE886, 8.1945- PCE(C)886	Albina, Portland	3.1944	10.7.1944	5.1945	stricken ~1970
	PCE891	Willamette Iron & Steel, Portland	10.1943	24.4.1944	6.1944	to the Philippines 7.1948 (Pangasinan)
	PCE892	Willamette Iron & Steel, Portland	10.1943	1.5.1944	7.1944	to South Korea 12.1961 (Yulpo)
	PCE893	Willamette Iron & Steel, Portland	10.1943	8.5.1944	7.1944	to Cuba 11.1947 (Siboney)
	PCE894	Willamette Iron & Steel, Portland	12.1943	15.5.1944	8.1944	to Burma 6.1965 (Yan Taing Aung)
	PCE895	Willamette Iron & Steel, Portland	12.1943	18.5.1944	10.1944	to South Vietnam 11.1961 (Đống Đa II)
	PCE896, 8.1945- PCE(C)896	Willamette Iron & Steel, Portland	12.1943	22.5.1944	11.1944	to South Korea 2.1955 (Myengnyang)

PCE897	Willamette Iron & Steel, Portland	12.1943	30.8.1944	1.1945	to the Philippines 7.1948 (Iloilo)
PCE898, 8.1945-PCE(C)898	Willamette Iron & Steel, Portland	12.1943	30.8.1944	1.1945	to South Korea 9.1955 (Okpo)
PCE899	Willamette Iron & Steel, Portland	1.1944	11.8.1944	3.1945	auxiliary 7.1964
PCE900	Willamette Iron & Steel, Portland	1.1944	11.8.1944	4.1945	stricken 2.1960
PCE901	Willamette Iron & Steel, Portland	5.1943	8.7.1943	(10.1944)	completed as transport
PCE902	Willamette Iron & Steel, Portland	1.1944	28.8.1944	4.1945	stricken 6.1970
PCE903	Willamette Iron & Steel, Portland	2.1944	6.9.1944	5.1945	stricken 6.1961
PCE904	Willamette Iron & Steel, Portland	2.1944	9.9.1944	5.1945	BU 6.1960

795 / 903 t, 56.2 x 10.1 x 2.9 m, 2 diesels, 2000 hp, 15.1 kts, 140 t diesel oil, 8500 nm (12 kts), complement 96; 1 x 1 – 76/50 Mk 20/21, (2 - 3) (PCE) or 1 (PCE(C), PCE(R)) x 2 – 40/56 Bofors, (2 – 5) (PCE) or 4 (PCE(C), PCE(R)) x 1 – 20/70 Oerlikon, 1 x 24 Hedgehog ASWRL, 4 DCT, 2 DCR, SG or SL radar, QHA sonar.

Admirable class ocean minesweepers, redesigned as escorts, were required by both the Royal, and the US Navy. The removal of the minesweeping equipment allowed to install the sonar, the Hedgehog and DCTs. Although the escorts in the minesweeper hulls were too slow, their merits included good seaworthiness and strong armament. In any case, they were superior to the British anti-submarine trawlers, successfully used throughout the war.

In November 1941, 20 PCEs were ordered, another 15 PCEs were intended for the RN. A total of 108 PCE (PCE827-934) were ordered. PCE861-866 (Pullman Standard Car), PCE887-890 (Albina), PCE905-910 (Puget Sound Bridge), PCE911-934 (Willamette Iron & Steel) were cancelled in June 1944. PCE935-976 were planned to be built by Willamette Iron & Steel, but never ordered.

1944, *PCE882, 884 - 886, 897 - 900, 902 - 904*; mid-

PCE867 1943

1945, *PCE842, 844 - 847, 870, 871, 874, 880, 881, 893 - 896*: were converted to aircraft rescue ships PCE(R) and weather reconnaissance ships PCE(C) with armament consisted of 1 x 1 - 76/50 Mk 20/21, 1 x 2 - 40/60 Bofors, 4 x 1 - 20/70 Oerlikon, 1 x 24 - 178 Hedgehog ASWRL, 4 DCT, 2 DCR, SF or SO or SU radar, QHA sonar; 6.1944, *Buttress*: - 1 x 24 Hedgehog ASWRL, 4 DCT, 2 DCR; + mines.

PCE877 1946

PC451 patrol craft

PC451	Defoe, Bay City	9.1939	23.5.1940	8.1940	disposed 1.1947

270 (std) t, 52.9 x 6.3 x 2.0 m, 2 diesels, 2880 hp, 18.5 kts, 49 t diesel oil, 4800 nm (12 kts), complement 65; 1 x 1 – 76/50 Mk 20; QC sonar.

The first, diesel-engined, prototype of a huge series of PC class submarine chasers, built for comparative trials.

PC451 1940

PC452 patrol craft

| PC452 | Defoe, Bay City | 3.1940 | 23.8.1940 | 5.1944 | auxiliary 3.1945 |

280 (std) t, 52.9 x 6.9 x 2.4 m, 2 sets geared steam turbines, 2 boilers, 22.5 kts, 50 t oil, 4800 nm (12 kts), complement 65; 1 x 1 – 76/50 Mk 20; QC sonar.

The second, turbine-engined, prototype of a huge series of PC class submarine chasers, built for comparative trials. Ultimately commissioned by the Navy much later than the start of the building of a large series.

PC461 class patrol craft

PC461	Geo Lawley, Neponset	7.1941	23.12.1941	3.1942	stricken 9.1957
PC462, 8.1945- PC(C)462	Geo Lawley, Neponset	7.1941	24.1.1942	4.1942	disposed 2.1947
PC463, 8.1945- PC(C)463	Geo Lawley, Neponset	8.1941	27.2.1942	4.1942	sunk as target 20.7.1953
PC464	Geo Lawley, Neponset	8.1941	27.2.1942	5.1942	sold 1.1947
PC465	Geo Lawley, Neponset	8.1941	27.3.1942	5.1942	stricken 7.1960
PC466	Geo Lawley, Neponset	9.1941	29.4.1942	6.1942	BU 1960
PC467	Geo Lawley, Neponset	10.1941	29.4.1942	6.1942	to Norway 9.1942 (Kong Haakon VII)
PC468	Geo Lawley, Neponset	1.1942	30.4.1942	6.1942	to the Netherlands 8.1942 (Queen Wilhelmina)
PC469, 8.1945- PC(C)469	Geo Lawley, Neponset	1.1942	10.6.1942	7.1942	disposed 6.1949
PC470	Geo Lawley, Neponset	2.1942	27.6.1942	7.1942	stricken 7.1960
PC471	Defoe, Bay City	4.1941	15.9.1941	11.1941	to France 6.1944 (L'Eveillé)
PC472	Defoe, Bay City	7.1941	14.11.1941	12.1941	to France 6.1944 (Le Rusé)
PC473	Defoe, Bay City	8.1941	19.11.1941	12.1941	to France 7.1944 (L'Ardent)
PC474	Defoe, Bay City	8.1941	15.9.1941	2.1942	to France 6.1944 (L'Indiscret)
PC475	Defoe, Bay City	9.1941	16.12.1941	12.1941	to France 6.1944 (Le Résolu)
PC476	Defoe, Bay City	10.1941	1.1.1942	3.1942	stricken 12.1947
PC477	Defoe, Bay City	11.1941	28.1.1942	3.1942	sold 12.1946
PC478	Defoe, Bay City	12.1941	20.2.1942	4.1942	stricken 10.1946
PC479	Defoe, Bay City	1.1942	10.3.1942	4.1942	stricken 11.1946
PC480	Defoe, Bay City	1941	25.10.1941	4.1942	to France 7.1944 (L'Emorté)
PC481	Defoe, Bay City	2.1942	31.3.1942	4.1942	to France 6.1944 (L'Effronté)
PC482	Defoe, Bay City	2.1942	9.4.1942	4.1942	to France 7.1944 (L'Ehjoué)
PC483	Consolidated SB, New York	12.1940	25.10.1941	3.1942	stricken 7.1960
PC484	Consolidated SB, New York	4.1941	6.12.1941	4.1942	stricken 7.1960
PC485	Consolidated SB, New York	5.1941	20.12.1941	4.1942	to South Korea 1.1952 (Hanlasan)
PC486	Consolidated SB, New York	10.1941	25.1.1942	5.1942	stricken 5.1959
PC487	Consolidated SB, New York	12.1941	28.2.1942	6.1942	stricken 7.1960
PC488	Sullivan, Brooklyn	3.1941	20.12.1941	8.1942	auxiliary 4.1943

PC489	Sullivan, Brooklyn	3.1941	20.12.1941	7.1942	disposed 11.1948
PC490	Dravo, Pittsburgh	5.1941	18.10.1941	3.1942	to Taiwan 8.1948 (Wu Song)
PC491	Dravo, Pittsburgh	5.1941	6.12.1941	4.1942	sold 2.1948
PC492	Dravo, Pittsburgh	6.1941	29.12.1941	5.1942	to Taiwan 6.1948 (Huang Pu)
PC493	Dravo, Pittsburgh	8.1941	24.1.1942	5.1942	to Thailand 5.1947
PC494	Dravo, Pittsburgh	8.1941	24.1.1942	5.1942	sold 2.1948
PC495	Dravo, Wilmington	6.1941	30.12.1941	4.1942	to Thailand 1951 (Sarasin)
PC496	Leatham D. Smith SB, Sturgeon Bay	4.1941	22.11.1941	2.1942	sunk 4.6.1943
PC542	Defoe, Bay City	2.1942	20.4.1942	5.1942	to France 9.1944 (Le Tirailleur)
PC543	Defoe, Bay City	3.1942	5.5.1942	5.1942	to France 6.1944 (Le Volontaire)
PC544	Defoe, Bay City	3.1942	30.5.1942	6.1942	to Brazil 9.1942 (Guaporé)
PC545	Defoe, Bay City	3.1942	8.5.1942	6.1942	to France 10.1944 (Goumier)
PC546	Defoe, Bay City	4.1942	15.5.1942	7.1942	to France 10.1944 (Franc-Tireur)
PC547	Defoe, Bay City	4.1942	22.5.1942	7.1942	to Brazil 9.1942 (Gurupi)
PC548	Defoe, Bay City	4.1942	29.5.1942	8.1942	nuclear tests 7.1946
PC549, 8.1945- PC(C)549	Defoe, Bay City	5.1942	6.6.1942	8.1942	disposed 4.1948
PC550	Leatham D. Smith SB, Sturgeon Bay	6.1941	8.3.1942	4.1942	to France 6.1944 (Le Vigilant)
PC551	Leatham D. Smith SB, Sturgeon Bay	7.1941	12.4.1942	5.1942	to France 10.1944 (Mameluck)
PC552	Sullivan, Brooklyn	5.1941	13.2.1942	7.1942	disposed 12.1946
PC553	Sullivan, Brooklyn	12.1941	30.5.1942	10.1942	stricken 9.1957
PC554	Sullivan, Brooklyn	12.1941	1.5.1942	9.1942	to Brazil 10.1943 (Goiana)
PC555, 1944- PC(C)555	Sullivan, Brooklyn	2.1942	30.5.1942	2.1943	disposed 1946
PC556	Luders Marine, Stamford	10.1941	23.6.1942	9.1942	to France 10.1944 (Carabinier)
PC557	Luders Marine, Stamford	10.1941	2.8.1942	10.1942	to France 10.1944 (Dragon)
PC558	Luders Marine, Stamford	10.1941	13.9.1942	11.1942	sunk 9.5.1944
PC559	Jeffersonville	10.1941	2.1.1942	5.1942	to France 10.1944 (Voltigeur)
PC560	Jeffersonville	11.1941	17.3.1942	6.1942	stricken 9.1957
PC561	Jeffersonville	1.1942	1.5.1942	7.1942	to Brazil 11.1943 (Graúna)
PC562	Jeffersonville	2.1942	4.6.1942	8.1942	to France 6.1944 (L'Attentif)
PC563, 8.1945- PC(C)563	Consolidated SB, New York	12.1941	17.3.1942	6.1942	sold 11.1946
PC564	Consolidated SB, New York	1.1942	12.4.1942	7.1942	to South Korea 1.1964 (Seolaksan)

PC565	Brown, Houston	8.1941	27.2.1942	4.1942	to Venezuela 7.1960 (Alcatraz)
PC566	Brown, Houston	8.1941	21.3.1942	6.1942	stricken 7.1960
PC567	Brown, Houston	9.1941	11.4.1942	6.1942	to USAF 4.1960
PC568	Brown, Houston	9.1941	25.4.1942	7.1942	to USAF 4.1960
PC569	Albina, Portland	9.1941	22.1.1942	5.1942	stricken 7.1960
PC570	Albina, Portland	9.1941	5.1.1942	4.1942	to Thailand 6.1953 (Longlom)
PC571	Albina, Portland	9.1941	12.2.1942	5.1942	stricken 11.1957
PC572	Albina, Portland	9.1941	23.2.1942	6.1942	stricken 7.1960
PC573	Dravo, Pittsburgh	10.1941	5.3.1942	6.1942	disposed 6.1948
PC574	Dravo, Wilmington	12.1941	30.3.1942	7.1942	sold 12.1946
PC575	Dravo, Wilmington	2.1942	5.5.1942	8.1942	to Thailand 3.1947 (Thayanchon)
PC576	Dravo, Wilmington	4.1942	13.6.1942	9.1942	sold 2.1947
PC577	Dravo, Wilmington	5.1942	25.7.1942	10.1942	sunk at tests 12.11.1948
PC578, 8.1945- PC(C)578	Albina, Portland	12.1941	29.4.1942	7.1942	sold 4.1948
PC579	Albina, Portland	1.1942	29.4.1942	8.1942	stricken 7.1960
PC580	Albina, Portland	1.1942	29.4.1942	9.1942	to Indonesia 3.1960 (Hiu)
PC581	Albina, Portland	2.1942	8.7.1942	10.1942	to Indonesia 3.1960 (Torani)
PC582, 8.1945- PC(C)582	Albina, Portland	2.1942	15.7.1942	10.1942	to Venezuela 7.1960 (Albatros)
PC583	Defoe, Bay City	5.1942	12.6.1942	9.1942	disposed 7.1948
PC584	Defoe, Bay City	5.1942	18.6.1942	8.1942	wrecked 9.10.1945
PC585	Defoe, Bay City	5.1942	8.7.1942	9.1942	disposed 7.1948
PC586	Defoe, Bay City	5.1942	15.7.1942	10.1942	stricken 4.1959
PC587	Defoe, Bay City	6.1942	1.8.1942	9.1942	disposed 4.1948
PC588, 6.1945- PC(C)588	Leatham D. Smith SB, Sturgeon Bay	11.1941	3.5.1942	6.1942	stricken 4.1959
PC589, 6.1945- PC(C)589	Leatham D. Smith SB, Sturgeon Bay	3.1942	7.6.1942	7.1942	stricken 4.1959
PC590	Leatham D. Smith SB, Sturgeon Bay	4.1942	4.7.1942	10.1942	wrecked 9.10.1945
PC591	Leatham D. Smith SB, Sturgeon Bay	5.1942	2.8.1942	10.1942	to France 10.1944 (Spahi)
PC592	Dravo, Pittsburgh	3.1942	27.6.1942	11.1942	stricken 4.1959
PC593	Dravo, Pittsburgh	4.1942	22.8.1942	12.1942	to China 8.1948
PC594	Dravo, Pittsburgh	5.1942	7.9.1942	3.1943	disposed 12.1947
PC595	Dravo, Pittsburgh	5.1942	9.10.1942	4.1943	to China 6.1948
PC596	Commercial Iron Wks, Portland	4.1942	8.8.1942	1.1943	BU 11.1946
PC597	Commercial Iron Wks, Portland	5.1942	7.9.1942	2.1943	stricken 9.1957
PC598, 8.1945- PC(C)598	Commercial Iron Wks, Portland	5.1942	7.9.1942	3.1943	sold 11.1946
PC599	Commercial Iron Wks, Portland	8.1942	26.9.1942	5.1943	disposed 4.1948
PC600	Consolidated SB, New York	2.1942	9.5.1942	8.1942	to South Korea 1.1952 (Myohyangsan)
PC601	Consolidated SB, New York	3.1942	23.5.1942	9.1942	stricken 7.1960

PC602	Consolidated SB, New York	4.1942	13.6.1942	9.1942	stricken 7.1960
PC603	Consolidated SB, New York	5.1942	30.6.1942	10.1942	stricken 7.1960
PC604	Luders Marine, Stamford	2.1942	24.10.1942	3.1943	to Brazil 6.1943 (Guaíba)
PC605	Luders Marine, Stamford	3.1942	19.11.1942	5.1943	to Brazil 6.1943 (Gurupá)
PC606	Luders Marine, Stamford	4.1942	8.1.1943	8.1943	stricken 9.1957
PC607	Luders Marine, Stamford	7.1942	11.2.1943	8.1943	to Brazil 10.1943 (Guajará)
PC608	Brown, Houston	1.1942	16.5.1942	8.1942	disposed 7.1948
PC609	Brown, Houston	1.1942	30.5.1942	9.1942	to Thailand 5.1947 (Khamronsin)
PC610	Brown, Houston	2.1942	19.6.1942	9.1942	wrecked 7.6.1950
PC611	Brown, Houston	2.1942	19.6.1942	10.1942	disposed 7.1948
PC612	Gibbs Gas Engine, Jacksonville	6.1942	7.9.1942	5.1943	disposed 3.1948
PC613	Gibbs Gas Engine, Jacksonville	7.1942	27.10.1942	6.1943	stricken 5.1946
PC614	Gibbs Gas Engine, Jacksonville	7.1942	23.12.1942	7.1943	to Mexico 1947 (GC32)
PC615	Gibbs Gas Engine, Jacksonville	7.1942	17.2.1943	7.1943	stricken 7.1947
PC616	Geo Lawley, Neponset	2.1942	4.7.1942	8.1942	to Thailand 1952 (Tongpliu)
PC617	Geo Lawley, Neponset	3.1942	18.7.1942	8.1942	stricken 9.1957
PC618	Geo Lawley, Neponset	4.1942	1.8.1942	9.1942	stricken 11.1965
PC619	Geo Lawley, Neponset	4.1942	15.8.1942	9.1942	to Venezuela 1960 (Gaviota)
PC620	Nashville Bridge	2.1942	12.8.1942	1.1943	stricken 9.1957
PC621	Nashville Bridge	3.1942	22.5.1942	12.1942	to France 10.1944 (Fantassin)
PC622	Nashville Bridge	5.1942	7.7.1942	3.1943	to Greece 6.1944 (Vasilefs Georgios II)
PC623	Nashville Bridge	6.1942	24.9.1942	4.1943	sold 11.1946
PC624	Jeffersonville	3.1942	4.7.1942	8.1942	damaged 12.3.1944, repaired as water barge
PC625	Jeffersonville	5.1942	22.7.1942	9.1942	to France 10.1944 (Grenadier)
PC626	Jeffersonville	6.1942	18.8.1942	10.1942	to France 11.1944 (Lansquenet)
PC627	Jeffersonville	6.1942	7.9.1942	11.1942	to France 10.1944 (Cavalier)
PC776	Commercial Iron Wks, Portland	8.1942	27.10.1942	3.1943	BU 9.1960
PC777	Commercial Iron Wks, Portland	9.1942	12.11.1942	4.1943	stricken 4.1959
PC778	Commercial Iron Wks, Portland	9.1942	26.11.1942	4.1943	stricken 4.1959
PC779	Commercial Iron Wks, Portland	9.1942	7.12.1942	5.1943	stricken 4.1959
PC780	Commercial Iron Wks, Portland	10.1942	10.12.1942	6.1943	BU 9.1959

PC781	Commercial Iron Wks, Portland	11.1942	24.12.1942	7.1943	stricken 11.1959
PC782	Commercial Iron Wks, Portland	11.1942	31.12.1942	7.1943	stricken 4.1959
PC783	Commercial Iron Wks, Portland	12.1942	13.1.1943	8.1943	disposed 1948?
PC784	Commercial Iron Wks, Portland	12.1942	18.1.1943	8.1943	disposed 3.1948
PC785	Commercial Iron Wks, Portland	12.1942	23.1.1943	10.1943	stricken 1959?
PC786	Commercial Iron Wks, Portland	12.1942	6.2.1943	10.1943	to Taiwan 5.1954 (Xian Jiang)
PC787	Commercial Iron Wks, Portland	1.1943	12.2.1943	11.1943	to Indonesia 3.1960 (Alu Alu)
PC788	Commercial Iron Wks, Portland	1.1943	5.3.1943	2.1944	disposed ~1948
PC789	Commercial Iron Wks, Portland	1.1943	13.3.1943	3.1944	disposed ~1948
PC790	Commercial Iron Wks, Portland	2.1943	22.3.1943	3.1944	to Cuba 1956 (Baire)
PC791	Commercial Iron Wks, Portland	3.1943	17.4.1943	3.1944	disposed ~1948
PC792	Commercial Iron Wks, Portland	3.1943	24.4.1943	4.1944	disposed ~1948
PC793	Commercial Iron Wks, Portland	4.1943	22.5.1943	5.1944	disposed ~1948
PC794	Commercial Iron Wks, Portland	4.1943	29.5.1943	5.1944	to Mexico 1947 (GC34)
PC795	Commercial Iron Wks, Portland	5.1943	24.7.1943	6.1944	disposed ~1948
PC796	Commercial Iron Wks, Portland	5.1943	3.7.1943	6.1944	to France 1949 (Pnom-Penh)
PC797	Commercial Iron Wks, Portland	7.1943	21.8.1943	7.1944	to France 1950 (Hué)
PC798	Commercial Iron Wks, Portland	7.1943	14.8.1943	7.1944	to France 1949 (Luang-Prabang)
PC799	Commercial Iron Wks, Portland	7.1943	14.8.1943	8.1944	to South Korea 6.1950 (Geumgangsan)
PC800	Commercial Iron Wks, Portland	7.1943	28.8.1943	9.1944	disposed ~1948
PC801	Commercial Iron Wks, Portland	8.1943	18.9.1943	12.1944	disposed ~1948
PCC802, 8.1945- PC(C)802	Commercial Iron Wks, Portland	8.1943	25.9.1943	1.1945	to South Korea 1950 (Samgaksan)
PCC803, 8.1945- PC(C)803	Commercial Iron Wks, Portland	8.1943	2.10.1943	1.1945	disposed ~1948
PC804, 4.1945- PC(C)804	Commercial Iron Wks, Portland	8.1943	16.10.1943	2.1945	disposed 7.1948
PC807	Commercial Iron Wks, Portland	10.1943	6.11.1943	2.1945	disposed ~1948
PC808	Commercial Iron Wks, Portland	10.1943	29.11.1943	3.1945	stricken 4.1959
PC809	Commercial Iron Wks, Portland	10.1943	4.12.1943	3.1945	to Portugal 1948 (Sal)

PC810	Commercial Iron Wks, Portland	10.1943	11.12.1943	4.1945	stricken 5.1946
PC811	Commercial Iron Wks, Portland	11.1943	18.12.1943	4.1945	to Portugal 1948 (Madeira)
PC812	Commercial Iron Wks, Portland	11.1943	11.2.1944	5.1945	to Portugal 1948 (Flores)
PC813	Commercial Iron Wks, Portland	12.1943	27.3.1944	5.1945	to Mexico 1947 (GC33)
PC814	Commercial Iron Wks, Portland	2.1944	13.5.1944	6.1945	wrecked 10.10.1945
PC815	Albina, Portland	10.1942	5.12.1942	4.1943	collision 11.9.1945
PC816	Albina, Portland	12.1942	8.1.1943	6.1943	disposed ~1948
PC817	Albina, Portland	1.1943	4.3.1943	7.1943	stricken 4.1959
PC818	Albina, Portland	3.1943	30.3.1943	8.1943	disposed ~1948
PC819	Albina, Portland	3.1943	19.5.1943	8.1943	to Mexico 1952 (GC37)
PC820	Albina, Portland	5.1943	2.8.1943	9.1943	to Mexico 1952 (GC30)
PC821	Leatham D. Smith SB, Sturgeon Bay	9.1943	23.10.1943	6.1944	sold 6.1948
PC822	Leatham D. Smith SB, Sturgeon Bay	10.1943	27.12.1943	6.1944	stricken 4.1959
PC823	Leatham D. Smith SB, Sturgeon Bay	11.1943	15.1.1944	7.1944	merchant TS 5.1948
PC824	Leatham D. Smith SB, Sturgeon Bay	3.1944	10.5.1944	8.1944	to Mexico 1948 (GC35)
PC825	Leatham D. Smith SB, Sturgeon Bay	3.1944	28.5.1944	9.1944	disposed ~1948
PC1077	Albina, Portland	2.1942	29.7.1942	12.1942	stricken ~1959
PC1078	Albina, Portland	4.1942	8.8.1942	2.1943	to Taiwan 5.1954 (Zi Jiang)
PC1079	Albina, Portland	4.1942	25.8.1942	3.1943	stricken 7.1960
PC1080	Albina, Portland	4.1942	27.8.1942	3.1943	disposed ~1948
PC1081	Albina, Portland	7.1942	29.8.1942	4.1943	stricken ~1959
PC1082	Albina, Portland	8.1942	10.10.1942	5.1943	sold 11.1946
PC1083	Geo Lawley, Neponset	8.1942	7.9.1942	8.1943	sold ~1946
PC1084	Geo Lawley, Neponset	9.1942	31.10.1942	8.1943	sold ~1946
PC1085	Geo Lawley, Neponset	1.1943	27.3.1943	10.1943	sold ~1946
PC1086	Geo Lawley, Neponset	2.1943	24.4.1943	1.1944	to France 3.1951 (Flamberge)
PC1087	Geo Lawley, Neponset	4.1943	21.8.1943	5.1944	to Taiwan 7.1957 (Dong Jiang)
PC1119	Defoe, Bay City	6.1942	11.8.1942	12.1942	BU 7.1958
PC1120	Defoe, Bay City	6.1942	24.8.1942	1.1943	stricken 4.1959
PC1121	Defoe, Bay City	6.1942	27.8.1942	12.1942	to the Philippines 1947 (Camarines Sur)
PC1122	Defoe, Bay City	7.1942	7.9.1942	1.1943	disposed ~1948
PC1123	Defoe, Bay City	7.1942	7.9.1942	2.1943	disposed ~1948
PC1124	Defoe, Bay City	1942	1942	5.1943	damaged 24.11.1944, repaired as auxiliary
PC1125	Defoe, Bay City	8.1942	15.10.1942	5.1943	stricken ~1959

PC1126, 8.1945- PC(C)1126	Defoe, Bay City	8.1942	31.10.1942	5.1943	wrecked 9.10.1945, repair incomplete
PC1127	Defoe, Bay City	9.1942	2.11.1942	5.1943	disposed ~1948
PC1128	Defoe, Bay City	9.1942	19.11.1942	5.1943	wrecked 9.10.1945
PC1129	Defoe, Bay City	9.1942	11.1942	6.1943	sunk 31.1.1945
PC1130	Defoe, Bay City	10.1942	10.12.1942	6.1943	to France 1951 (L'Intrépide)
PC1131	Defoe, Bay City	10.1942	17.12.1942	7.1943	to the Philippines 1947 (Bohol)
PC1132	Defoe, Bay City	11.1942	29.12.1942	8.1943	disposed ~1948
PC1133	Defoe, Bay City	11.1942	9.1.1943	8.1943	to the Philippines 1948 (Zamboanga del Sur)
PC1134	Defoe, Bay City	12.1942	18.1.1943	9.1943	to the Philippines 7.1948 (Batangas)
PC1135	Defoe, Bay City	12.1942	3.2.1943	10.1943	stricken ~1959
PC1136	Defoe, Bay City	12.1942	5.3.1943	11.1943	sold 3.1960
PC1137, 8.1945- PC(C)1137	Defoe, Bay City	12.1942	29.3.1943	10.1943	stricken 3.1959
PC1138	Defoe, Bay City	1.1943	19.4.1943	9.1943	stricken 4.1959
PC1139	Defoe, Bay City	1.1943	10.5.1943	11.1943	disposed ~1948
PC1140	Defoe, Bay City	2.1943	14.6.1943	1.1944	stricken 7.1960
PC1141	Defoe, Bay City	3.1943	22.6.1943	12.1943	to Indonesia 10.1958 (Tjakalang)
PC1142	Defoe, Bay City	3.1943	20.8.1943	6.1944	to Taiwan 7.1957 (Bei Jiang)
PC1143	Defoe, Bay City	4.1943	22.9.1943	5.1944	to France 3.1951 (Trident)
PC1144	Defoe, Bay City	5.1943	4.10.1943	5.1944	to France 1951 (Mousquet)
PC1145	Defoe, Bay City	6.1943	27.10.1943	6.1944	stricken 6.1960
PC1146	Defoe, Bay City	9.1943	15.11.1943	7.1944	to France 1951 (Glaive)
PC1147	Defoe, Bay City	10.1943	2.12.1943	8.1944	disposed ~1948
PC1149	Defoe, Bay City	11.1943	11.1.1944	6.1944	to Taiwan 7.1957 (Xi Jiang)
PC1167	Sullivan, Brooklyn	4.1943	3.7.1943	12.1943	to France 1951 (L'Ardent)
PC1168	Sullivan, Brooklyn	4.1943	3.7.1943	12.1943	to Taiwan 5.1954 (Qing Jiang)
PC1169, 1944- PC(C)1169	Sullivan, Brooklyn	7.1943	16.10.1943	1.1944	stricken 7.1960
PC1170	Sullivan, Brooklyn	7.1943	16.10.1943	2.1944	stricken 7.1960
PC1171	Leatham D. Smith SB, Sturgeon Bay	3.1943	15.5.1943	9.1943	to France 1951 (L'Inconstant)
PC1172	Leatham D. Smith SB, Sturgeon Bay	3.1943	5.6.1943	10.1943	stricken 7.1960
PC1173	Leatham D. Smith SB, Sturgeon Bay	4.1943	27.6.1943	11.1943	stricken 7.1960
PC1174	Leatham D. Smith SB, Sturgeon Bay	5.1943	22.7.1943	11.1943	stricken 1957

PC1175	Leatham D. Smith SB, Sturgeon Bay	6.1943	7.8.1943	12.1943	to Taiwan 7.1957 (Gan Jiang)
PC1176	Leatham D. Smith SB, Sturgeon Bay	6.1943	28.8.1943	11.1943	stricken 7.1960
PC1177, 8.1945- PC(C)1177	Leatham D. Smith SB, Sturgeon Bay	7.1943	18.9.1943	12.1943	stricken 7.1960
PC1178, 8.1945- PC(C)1178	Leatham D. Smith SB, Sturgeon Bay	8.1943	2.10.1943	1.1944	stricken 11.1959
PC1179	Leatham D. Smith SB, Sturgeon Bay	9.1943	6.11.1943	1.1944	to Taiwan 1957 (Liu Jiang)
PC1180	Leatham D. Smith SB, Sturgeon Bay	10.1943	27.11.1943	2.1944	stricken 7.1960
PC1181	Gibbs Gas Engine, Jacksonville	10.1942	15.4.1943	9.1943	stricken 4.1959
PC1182	Gibbs Gas Engine, Jacksonville	10.1942	14.6.1943	10.1943	to Taiwan 7.1954 (Yuan Jiang)
PC1183	Gibbs Gas Engine, Jacksonville	10.1942	7.7.1943	12.1943	disposed ~1948
PC1184	Gibbs Gas Engine, Jacksonville	1.1943	4.8.1943	1.1944	disposed ~1948
PC1185	Gibbs Gas Engine, Jacksonville	3.1943	27.8.1943	4.1944	to Thailand 1952 (Phali)
PC1186	Gibbs Gas Engine, Jacksonville	4.1943	27.9.1943	6.1944	stricken 4.1959
PC1187	Gibbs Gas Engine, Jacksonville	6.1943	26.11.1943	7/1944	disposed ~1948
PC1188	Gibbs Gas Engine, Jacksonville	7.1943	31.1.1944	9.1944	to Israel 1948 (Nogah 2)
PC1190	Gibbs Gas Engine, Jacksonville	9.1943	29.6.1944	2.1945	disposed ~1948
PC1191	Consolidated SB, New York	5.1942	25.7.1942	11.1942	stricken 3.1959
PC1192	Consolidated SB, New York	6.1942	8.8.1942	11.1942	disposed ~1948
PC1193	Consolidated SB, New York	6.1942	29.8.1942	1.1943	BU 9.1959
PC1194	Consolidated SB, New York	7.1942	19.9.1942	2.1943	sold ~1946
PC1195	Consolidated SB, New York	8.1942	3.10.1942	3.1943	sold ~1946
PC1196	Consolidated SB, New York	8.1942	24.10.1942	4.1943	stricken 4.1959
PC1197	Consolidated SB, New York	9.1942	14.11.1942	4.1943	sold ~1946
PC1198	Consolidated SB, New York	10.1942	12.12.1942	5.1943	stricken 4.1959
PC1199	Consolidated SB, New York	10.1942	2.1.1943	5.1943	sold ~1946
PC1200	Consolidated SB, New York	11.1942	23.1.1943	5.1943	disposed ~1946
PC1201	Consolidated SB, New York	12.1942	14.2.1943	6.1943	BU 10.1959
PC1202	Consolidated SB, New York	1.1943	27.2.1943	6.1943	to Dominican Republic 1947 (Capitán Wenceslao Arvelo)
PC1203	Consolidated SB, New York	1.1943	14.3.1943	7.1943	sold ~1946
PC1204	Consolidated SB, New York	2.1943	14.4.1943	8.1943	sold ~1946
PC1205	Consolidated SB, New York	3.1943	29.4.1943	8.1943	disposed ~1948
PC1206	Consolidated SB, New York	6.1943	21.7.1943	10.1943	disposed ~1948
PC1207	Consolidated SB, New York	6.1943	18.8.1943	11.1943	sold 12.1945

PC1208	Consolidated SB, New York	7.1943	15.9.1943	11.1943	to Taiwan 7.1954 (Li Jiang)
PC1209	Consolidated SB, New York	8.1943	7.10.1943	5.1944	BU 10.1959
PC1210	Consolidated SB, New York	9.1943	30.10.1943	5.1944	to Mexico 1952 (GC38)
PC1211	Luders Marine, Stamford	8.1942	12.3.1943	8.1943	to Spain 10.1956 (Javier Quiroga)
PC1212	Luders Marine, Stamford	9.1942	23.4.1943	9.1943	stricken 4.1959
PC1213	Luders Marine, Stamford	11.1942	22.5.1943	10.1943	stricken 4.1959
PC1214	Luders Marine, Stamford	2.1943	28.6.1943	10.1943	disposed ~1948
PC1215	Luders Marine, Stamford	3.1943	29.7.1943	11.1943	disposed 6.1948
PC1216	Luders Marine, Stamford	4.1943	29.8.1943	12.1943	stricken ~1959
PC1217	Luders Marine, Stamford	5.1943	26.9.1943	4.1944	disposed 3.1948
PC1218	Luders Marine, Stamford	7.1943	24.10.1943	5.1944	to Thailand 6.1948 (Sukrip)
PC1219	Luders Marine, Stamford	8.1943	21.11.1943	7.1944	sold ~1946
PC1220	Luders Marine, Stamford	9.1943	22.12.1943	7.1944	disposed ~1948
PC1221	Penn-Jersey, Camden	5.1942	29.8.1943	4.1944	disposed 7.1948
PC1222	Penn-Jersey, Camden	10.1942	25.9.1943	7.1944	sold 6.1947
PC1223	Penn-Jersey, Camden	9.1943	9.1.1944	11.1944	sold 11.1946
PC1224	Penn-Jersey, Camden	8.1943	9.7.1944	1.1945	to Mexico 1948 (GC36)
PC1225	Leatham D. Smith SB, Sturgeon Bay	6.1942	7.9.1942	1.1943	stricken 9.1957
PC1226	Leatham D. Smith SB, Sturgeon Bay	7.1942	7.9.1942	1.1943	to France 11.1944 (Légionnaire)
PC1227	Leatham D. Smith SB, Sturgeon Bay	1942	17.10.1942	1943	to France 11.1944 (Lancier)
PC1228	Leatham D. Smith SB, Sturgeon Bay	9.1942	18.11.1942	5.1943	stricken 9.1957
PC1229	Leatham D. Smith SB, Sturgeon Bay	9.1942	19.12.1942	6.1943	stricken 9.1957
PC1230	Leatham D. Smith SB, Sturgeon Bay	12.1942	10.3.1943	7.1943	sold 1960s
PC1231	Sullivan, Brooklyn	9.1942	12.12.1942	7.1943	stricken ~1959
PC1232	Sullivan, Brooklyn	9.1942	12.12.1942	8.1943	to Taiwan 6.1954 (Zhang Jiang)
PC1233	Sullivan, Brooklyn	9.1942	11.1.1943	9.1943	to Taiwan 7.1954 (Gong Jiang)
PC1234	Sullivan, Brooklyn	1942	1943	6.1943	to Uruguay 5.1944 (Maldonado)
PC1235	Sullivan, Brooklyn	1942	1943	7.1943	to France 10.1945 (Hussard)
PC1236	Sullivan, Brooklyn	1.1943	24.4.1943	8.1943	to Brazil 11.1943 (Grajaú)
PC1237	Consolidated SB, New York	2.1943	3.4.1943	7.1943	stricken 4.1959
PC1238	Consolidated SB, New York	4.1943	15.5.1943	9.1943	wrecked 9.10.1945, never repaired
PC1239	Consolidated SB, New York	4.1943	9.6.1943	9.1943	sold ~1946
PC1240	Consolidated SB, New York	5.1943	26.6.1943	10.1943	stricken 4.1959
PC1241	Nashville Bridge	9.1942	24.12.1942	5.1943	to the Philippines 10.1948 (Nueva Esija)
PC1242	Nashville Bridge	9.1942	25.1.1943	7.1943	stricken 12.1959

PC1243	Nashville Bridge	12.1942	15.3.1943	9.1943	stricken 4.1946
PC1244, 8.1945- PC(C)1244	Nashville Bridge	1.1943	8.5.1943	10.1943	stricken 7.1960
PC1245	Nashville Bridge	3.1943	29.5.1943	10.1943	disposed ~1948
PC1246	Nashville Bridge	5.1943	3.7.1943	11.1943	stricken 2.1957
PC1247	Nashville Bridge	5.1943	7.8.1943	12.1943	to China 6.1948 (Chia Ling)
PC1248	Nashville Bridge	6.1943	18.8.1943	(1.1944)	to France 1.1944 (Sabre)
PC1249	Nashville Bridge	8.1943	6.11.1943	(2.1944)	to France 2.1944 (Pique)
PC1250	Nashville Bridge	8.1943	18.12.1943	(3.1944)	to France 3.1944 (Cimeterre)
PC1251, 8.1945- PC(C)1251	Brown, Houston	6.1942	12.9.1942	2.1943	stricken 7.1960
PC1252	Brown, Houston	6.1942	30.9.1942	3.1943	stricken 7.1960
PC1253	Brown, Houston	6.1942	14.10.1942	4.1943	to Thailand 1952 (Liulom)
PC1254	Brown, Houston	6.1942	31.10.1942	4.1943	to Taiwan 5.1954 (Bo Jiang)
PC1255, 12.1944- PGM18	Luders Marine, Stamford	9.1943	23.1.1944	9.1944	gunboat 12.1944, sunk 7.4.1945
PC1256	Luders Marine, Stamford	10.1943	21.5.1944	10.1944	to Portugal 1948 (São Tomé)
PC1257	Luders Marine, Stamford	11.1943	23.7.1944	12.1944	to Portugal 1948 (Santiago)
PC1258	Luders Marine, Stamford	12.1943	23.9.1944	1.1945	disposed 6.1948
PC1259	Luders Marine, Stamford	1.1944	7.10.1944	3.1945	to Portugal 1948 (São Vicente)
PC1260	Leatham D. Smith SB, Sturgeon Bay	10.1942	16.1.1943	4.1943	stricken ~1959
PC1261	Leatham D. Smith SB, Sturgeon Bay	1943	1943	4.1943	sunk 6.6.1944
PC1262	Leatham D. Smith SB, Sturgeon Bay	1.1943	27.3.1943	6.1943	to Taiwan 6.1954 (Chang Jiang)
PC1263	Leatham D. Smith SB, Sturgeon Bay	3.1943	19.4.1943	7.1943	to Taiwan 7.1959 (Tuo Jiang)
PC1264	Consolidated SB, New York	10.1943	28.11.1943	4.1944	disposed 3.1948
PC1265	Consolidated SB, New York	10.1943	19.12.1943	5.1944	disposed 12.1946
PC1546	Consolidated SB, New York	11.1943	30.1.1944	6.1944	to South Korea 11.1960 (Geumjeongsan)
PC1547	Consolidated SB, New York	12.1943	8.2.1944	7.1944	stricken ~1959
PC1548, 7.1944- PGM9	Consolidated SB, New York	12.1943	13.2.1944	7.1944	gunboat 7.1944, wrecked 9.10.1945
PC1549	Consolidated SB, New York	1.1944	12.3.1944	7.1944	to China 5.1946 (Qian Tang)
PC1560	Leatham D. Smith SB, Sturgeon Bay	11.1943	3.2.1944	(4.1944)	to France 4.1944 (Coutelas)
PC1561	Leatham D. Smith SB, Sturgeon Bay	1943	1944	(6.1944)	to France 6.1944 (Dague)

PC1562	Leatham D. Smith SB, Sturgeon Bay	1.1944	4.3.1944	(6.1944)	to France 6.1944 (Javelot)
PC1563	Leatham D. Smith SB, Sturgeon Bay	2.1944	24.3.1944	6.1944	to the Philippines 5.1945 (Negros Oriental)
PC1564	Leatham D. Smith SB, Sturgeon Bay	2.1944	19.4.1944	8.1944	to the Philippines 7.1947 (Capiz)
PC1569	Leatham D. Smith SB, Sturgeon Bay	9.1944	9.12.1944	3.1945	stricken 6.1960

PC466 1945

PC472 1942

PC815 1943

PC552 1944

280-414 / 330-463 t, 52.9 x 7.1 x 2.4-3.3 m, 2 diesels, 2880 hp, 19-21 kts, 49 t diesel oil, 3000-4800 nm (12 kts), complement 59-65; 2 (to 1943) or 1 (from 1943) x 1 – 76/50 Mk 20/21, 1 x 1 – 40/56 Bofors (from 1943), 3 – 4 x 1 – 20/70 Oerlikon (from 1943), 3 x 1 – 12.7 MG (to 1943), 2 x 4 Mousetrap ASWRL (from 1943), 2 DCT, 2 DCR; SF (from late 1942) or SO (from late 1942) or SCR-517A (late 1942 – early 1944) or SU (from early 1944) radar, QHA sonar.

In 1938, requirements were prepared for a small patrol ship (PC, patrol craft), which was supposed to replace the morally and physically obsolete 'Eagle' class ships. The main purpose of this ship was to escort coastal convoys and anti-submarine service in the coastal zone. The task provided a speed of at least 22 kts and 3000-nm cruising range at 12-kt speed. Under the FY38 Program, two prototypes were built: a 173-ft flush-decked turbine-engined PC452 and a 165-ft diesel-engined PC451 with a forecastle. On trials in 1940, the PC452 showed the better seaworthiness and higher speed, but the low reliability of her experimental machinery did not allow mass-building of this, in remaining the successful, ship. At the same time, the diesel-powered version, PC451, also did not suit a series: unsatisfactory seaworthiness made her very difficult to use armament. It was not possible to correct this drawback by increasing the dimensions due to the inevitable decrease in speed. At that time, there were no diesels in the USA suitable for installation on small ships with more than 1500-hp power. In addition to the difficulties with the choice of the machinery, President Roosevelt made his contribution to the list of design problems, demanding the installation of a second 76-mm gun.

The way out was found after working out a variant with diesels in the hull of a 173-ft prototype. Thus, 22 knots had to be abandoned. The contract speed was reduced by 2 knots, and on trials the lead PC461 reached 21.16 kts, however, with a displacement close to the standard one. The increase in hull breadth by 0.2 m compared to the prototype made it possible to place heavier armament. The design was ready at the beginning of 1941, and in March 1942 the Navy received the first serial ships.

The ships of the early series were commissioned with design armament, later the aft 76-mm gun was replaced by 40-mm Bofors, and 12.7-mm MGs by 20-mm Oerlikons. Plans to fit the Hedgehog had to be abandoned, as this could only be done by dismantling the fore gun. As a temporary alternative, a variant with two Mousetraps was accepted: this could be done without removing the 76-mm gun. Subsequently, this scheme was approved as ultimate. In August 1945, 35 PCs were converted to PC(C) – Submarine Chaser (Patrol Craft) (Control) – they were intended to command and control landing craft during a planned landing in Japan.

PC1092-1118 (Geo Lawley) were cancelled in

November (PC1092-1105) and September (PC1106-1118) 1943. PC1150-1166 (Defoe) were cancelled in September 1943. PC1570-1585 (Leatham D. Smith) were cancelled in September (PC1570-1575, 1582-1585) and November (PC1576-1581) 1943.

1943-1944, almost all survived early PC: - 1 x 1 - 76/50, 3 x 1 - 12.7 MG; + 1 x 1 - 40/56 Bofors, (3 - 4) x 1 - 20/70 Oerlikon, 2 x 4 - 178 Mousetrap ASWRL.

August 1945, 35 PC were converted to PC(C): - 1 x 1 - 40/56, (3 - 4) x 1 - 20/70; additional communication and HQ accommodations were mounted.

PC496 was mined 4.6.1943, *PC558* was sunk by German submarine *U230* 9.5.1944, *PC1129* by Japanese ships 31.1.1945.

PC1594 1944

PCS class patrol craft

PCS1376	Wheeler, Brooklyn	10.1942	3.4.1943	9.1943	stricken 9.1957
PCS1377	Wheeler, Brooklyn	2.1943	14.10.1943	1.1944	stricken ~1947
PCS1378	Wheeler, Brooklyn	2.1943	18.12.1943	2.1944	stricken 9.1957
PCS1379, 8.1945- PCS(C)1379	Wheeler, Brooklyn	2.1943	4.2.1944	3.1944	stricken ~1946
PCS1380	Wheeler, Brooklyn	2.1943	25.2.1944	3.1944	stricken 9.1957
PCS1381	Wheeler, Brooklyn	1943	1944	4.1944	stricken ~1947
PCS1382	Wheeler, Brooklyn	3.1943	16.3.1944	5.1944	stricken ~1947
PCS1383	Wheeler, Brooklyn	3.1943	23.6.1944	8.1944	stricken 7.1956
PCS1384	Wheeler, Brooklyn	4.1943	7.8.1944	9.1944	stricken ~1957
PCS1385	Wheeler, Brooklyn	5.1943	26.8.1944	10.1944	stricken 7.1970
PCS1386	Wheeler, Brooklyn	5.1943	28.9.1944	11.1944	stricken 7.1959
PCS1387	Wheeler, Brooklyn	5.1943	10.10.1944	11.1944	stricken 7.1967
PCS1388	Robert Jacob, New York	12.1942	17.7.1943	12.1943	survey vessel 2.1945
PCS1389, 8.1945- PCS(C)1389	Robert Jacob, New York	2.1943	18.9.1943	1.1944	stricken ~1946
PCS1390, 8.1945- PCS(C)1390	Robert Jacob, New York	3.1943	13.9.1943	2.1944	damaged 6.4.1945, never repaired
PCS1391, 8.1945- PCS(C)1391	Robert Jacob, New York	3.1943	8.10.1943	2.1944	disposed 4.1948
PCS1392	Robert Jacob, New York	4.1943	13.10.1943	3.1944	stricken ~1957
PCS1393	Robert Jacob, New York	5.1943	26.2.1944	(6.1944)	commissioned as minesweeper
PCS1394	Robert Jacob, New York	6.1943	18.3.1944	(6.1944)	commissioned as minesweeper
PCS1395	Robert Jacob, New York	6.1943	27.3.1944	(7.1944)	commissioned as minesweeper
PCS1396	South Coast, Newport Beach	1943	7.8.1943	3.1944	survey vessel 3.1945

PCS1397	South Coast, Newport Beach	5.1943	25.9.1943	5.1944	stricken ~1947
PCS1398	South Coast, Newport Beach	6.1943	29.2.1944	(7.1944)	commissioned as minesweeper
PCS1399	South Coast, Newport Beach	8.1943	15.4.1944	11.1944	to the Philippines 1.1948 (Tarlac)
PCS1400	South Coast, Newport Beach	9.1943	20.5.1944	1.1945	stricken 7.1956
PCS1401	South Coast, Newport Beach	1943	22.7.1944	2.1945	stricken 8.1962
PCS1402, 8.1945- PCS(C)1402	Colberg, Stockton	3.1943	11.8.1943	1.1944	stricken ~1946
PCS1403, 8.1945- PCS(C)1403	Colberg, Stockton	4.1943	28.9.1943	2.1944	to the Philippines 1.1948 (Laguna)
PCS1404	Colberg, Stockton	1943	12.11.1943	3.1944	survey vessel 3.1945
PCS1405	Greenport Basin	5.1943	21.8.1943	2.1944	survey vessel 8.1946
PCS1406	Greenport Basin	7.1943	2.10.1943	(6.1944)	commissioned as minesweeper
PCS1407	Greenport Basin	8.1943	23.10.1943	(6.1944)	commissioned as minesweeper
PCS1408	Greenport Basin	8.1943	13.11.1943	(7.1944)	commissioned as minesweeper
PCS1409	Greenport Basin	10.1943	11.12.1943	(8.1944)	commissioned as minesweeper
PCS1410	Greenport Basin	11.1943	8.1.1944	(9.1944)	commissioned as minesweeper
PCS1411	Greenport Basin	12.1943	12.2.1944	(10.1944)	commissioned as minesweeper
PCS1412	Greenport Basin	1.1944	8.4.1944	(10.1944)	commissioned as minesweeper
PCS1413	Stadium, Cleveland	1.1943	21.8.1943	11.1943	stricken ~1957
PCS1414	Stadium, Cleveland	2.1943	14.9.1943	11.1943	stricken ~1957
PCS1415	Stadium, Cleveland	6.1943	4.12.1943	(5.1944)	completed as minesweeper
PCS1416	Stadium, Cleveland	6.1943	8.1.1944	(6.1944)	completed as minesweeper
PCS1417	Dachel-Carter, Benton Harbor	3.1943	7.8.1943	1.1944	stricken ~1947
PCS1418, 8.1945- PCS(C)1418	Dachel-Carter, Benton Harbor	4.1943	4.9.1943	2.1944	wrecked 9.10.1945
PCS1419	Dachel-Carter, Benton Harbor	6.1943	31.10.1943	3.1944	stricken ~1947
PCS1420	Dachel-Carter, Benton Harbor	6.1943	20.11.1943	4.1944	stricken ~1947
PCS1421, 8.1945- PCS(C)1421	William F. Stone, Oakland	5.1943	1.11.1943	2.1944	stricken ~1946
PCS1422	William F. Stone, Oakland	6.1943	24.1.1944	4.1944	stricken ~1947
PCS1423	Burger, Manitowoc	12.1942	22.5.1943	11.1943	stricken 3.1962

PCS1424	Burger, Manitowoc	2.1943	19.6.1943	12.1943	stricken 5.1946
PCS1425	Hiltebrant, Kingston	1.1943	20.7.1943	2.1944	stricken ~1947
PCS1426	Hiltebrant, Kingston	3.1943	31.8.1943	4.1944	to South Korea 1952 (Suseong)
PCS1427	Hiltebrant, Kingston	4.1943	11.10.1943	(6.1944)	commissioned as minesweeper
PCS1428	Hiltebrant, Kingston	5.1943	21.3.1944	(7.1944)	commissioned as minesweeper
PCS1429, 8.1945- PCS(C)1429	Gibbs Gas Engine, Jacksonville	2.1943	16.7.1943	2.1944	stricken ~1946
PCS1430	Gibbs Gas Engine, Jacksonville	2.1943	6.8.1943	3.1944	stricken ~1947
PCS1431	Gibbs Gas Engine, Jacksonville	5.1943	2.11.1943	3.1944	stricken 7.1965
PCS1432	Gibbs Gas Engine, Jacksonville	5.1943	9.12.1943	(6.1944)	commissioned as minesweeper
PCS1433	Gibbs Gas Engine, Jacksonville	6.1943	4.1.1944	(6.1944)	commissioned as minesweeper
PCS1434	Gibbs Gas Engine, Jacksonville	6.1943	22.1.1944	(7.1944)	commissioned as minesweeper
PCS1435	Gibbs Gas Engine, Jacksonville	6.1943	22.2.1944	(8.1944)	commissioned as minesweeper
PCS1436	Gibbs Gas Engine, Jacksonville	6.1943	23.3.1944	(8.1944)	commissioned as minesweeper
PCS1437	Gibbs Gas Engine, Jacksonville	7.1943	17.3.1944	(9.1944)	commissioned as minesweeper
PCS1438	Gibbs Gas Engine, Jacksonville	8.1943	5.4.1944	(10.1944)	commissioned as minesweeper
PCS1439	Gibbs Gas Engine, Jacksonville	9.1943	23.5.1944	(10.1944)	commissioned as minesweeper
PCS1440	Gibbs Gas Engine, Jacksonville	9.1943	21.6.1944	(11.1944)	commissioned as minesweeper
PCS1441	Harbor Boat, Terminal I	2.1943	15.9.1943	4.1944	stricken ~1947
PCS1442	Harbor Boat, Terminal I	3.1943	11.11.1943	5.1944	stricken ~1947
PCS1443	Harbor Boat, Terminal I	5.1943	22.4.1944	(8.1944)	commissioned as minesweeper
PCS1444	Harbor Boat, Terminal I	5.1943	23.5.1944	12.1944	stricken 9.1957
PCS1445	San Diego Marine	1.1943	19.6.1943	3.1944	to South Korea 5.1952 (Geumseong)
PCS1446	San Diego Marine	1.1943	21.7.1943	4.1944	to South Korea 1952 (Mokseong)
PCS1447	San Diego Marine	4.1943	23.5.1944	(8.1944)	commissioned as minesweeper
PCS1448	San Diego Marine	4.1943	14.6.1944	11.1944	to South Korea 6.1952 (Hwaseong)
PCS1449	Burger, Manitowoc	2.1943	17.7.1943	12.1943	stricken ~1946
PCS1450	Burger, Manitowoc	2.1943	14.8.1943	2.1944	survey vessel 8.1946
PCS1451	Tacoma Boat	3.1943	3.7.1943	1.1944	stricken ~1947

	PCS1452, 8.1945- PCS(C)1452	Tacoma Boat	4.1943	28.8.1943	2.1944	stricken ~1946
	PCS1453	Tacoma Boat	7.1943	6.11.1943	(7.1944)	commissioned as minesweeper
	PCS1454	Tacoma Boat	9.1943	8.1.1944	(8.1944)	commissioned as minesweeper
	PCS1455, 8.1945- PCS(C)1455	Mojean & Ericson, Tacoma	3.1943	4.9.1943	2.1944	stricken ~1947
	PCS1456	Mojean & Ericson, Tacoma	4.1943	30.9.1943	(7.1944)	commissioned as minesweeper
	PCS1457	Ballard, Seattle	5.1943	6.9.1943	2.1944	survey vessel 3.1945
	PCS1458	Ballard, Seattle	4.1943	6.11.1943	(5.1944)	commissioned as survey vessel
	PCS1459	Western, Tacoma	3.1943	2.7.1943	12.1943	stricken ~1947
	PCS1460, 8.1945- PCS(C)1460	Western, Tacoma	4.1943	28.8.1943	2.1944	stricken ~1946
	PCS1461, 8.1945- PCS(C)1461	Bellingham Iron Wks	3.1943	15.9.1943	2.1944	wrecked 9.10.1945
	PCS1462	Bellingham Iron Wks	5.1943	20.11.1943	(3.1944)	commissioned as degaussing vessel
	PCS1463	Bellingham Iron Wks	5.1943	20.11.1943	(3.1944)	commissioned as minesweeper
1.1945- **Medrick**	PCS1464, 1.1945- AMc203	Astoria Marine	5.1943	11.10.1943	1.1944	minesweeper 1.1945, stricken 8.1946
1.1945- **Minah**	PCS1465, 1.1945- AMc204	Astoria Marine	6.1943	27.12.1943	2.1944	minesweeper 1.1945, stricken 11.1959

PCS1376 1943

251 / 278 t, 41.5 x 7.5 x 2.4 m, 2 diesels, 800 hp, 14 kts, 3000 nm (12 kts), complement 57; 1 x 1 – 76/50 Mk 20/21, 1 x 1 – 40/56 Bofors, 2 x 1 – 20/70 Oerlikon, 2 x 4 Mousetrap ASWRL, 4 DCT, 2 DCR; SF or SO or SU radar, QHA sonar.

The shortage of submarine chasers in the early stages of the war forced the US naval commanders to take emergency action to deal with this crisis. One of them was the program to create submarine chasers in the hulls of the YMS class minesweepers. In June 1942, an order for 100 of these ships followed. It was supposed to increase the fuel supply and the cruising range by removing the diesel-generator, to install a second 76-mm gun, the Hedgehog and increase to 52 DC stowage. However, calculations showed that in this case the ship would be overloaded, and the work was limited to the adding of single 40mm Bofors and Mousetrap launchers. The new chasers were unsuccessful: having 14-kt speed and the weakest armament among other ASW ships, they were not very suitable for an anti-submarine role, and the building program began to be curtailed already at the end of 1942. Only 90 ships were really ordered, subsequently building of 31 of them was cancelled. Many submarine chasers were converted to minesweepers during building: PCS1393-1395 (Robert Jacobs, later YMS446-448), PCS1398 (South Coast, later YMS449), PCS1406-1412 (Greenport Basin, later YMS453-459), PCS1415 and 1416 (Stadium, later YMS460 and 461), PCS1427 and 1428 (Hiltebrant, later YMS462 and 463), PCS1432-1440 (Gibbs Gas Engine, later YMS464-

PCS1387 post-war

472), PCS1443 (Harbor Boat, later YMS473), PCS1447 (San Diego Marine, later YMS475), PCS1453 and 1454 (Tacoma Boat, later YMS477 and 478), PCS1456 (Mojean & Ericson, later YMS479) and PCS1463 (Bellingham Iron Wks, later YMS481).

1944, *PCS1377, 1378, 1380 - 1387, 1392, 1417, 1423, 1424, 1426, 1431, 1441, 1442, 1445, 1446, 1448, 1449*: were converted to ASW TS: - 1 x 1 - 76/50; + 1 x 24 Hedgehog ASWRL

1945, *PCS(C)1379, 1389 - 1391, 1402, 1403, 1418, 1421, 1429, 1452, 1455, 1460, 1461*; were converted to amphibious command ships: - 1 x 1 - 40/56; additional communication equipment and HQ accommodations were fitted.

1.1945, AMc203 *Medrick*, AMc204 *Minah*: were converted to minehunters: - 1 x 1 - 40/56, 1 x 1 - 20/70, 2 x 4 Mousetrap ASWWRL, 4 DCT, 2 DCR; + FM sonar, equipment for divers.

Patrol yachts

More than 1000 t displacement

Name	PY no.	Built / comm.	Displ.	Dim.	Speed	Armament	Fate
Mayflower (*ex-Ogden Goelet*)	PY1, 10.1943-WPG183	1896 / 3.1898	*2690*	83.2 x 11.0	17	6 - 57	Coast Guard 10.1943, for disposal 1.1947
Nokomis (*ex-Nokomis II*)	PY6	1914 / 12.1917	*1265*	74.1 x 9.7	16	4 - 76	stricken 5.1938
Niagara	PY9	1898 / 4.1918	*2690*	86.0 x 13.1	12	4 - 102, 1 DCT	stricken 12.1931
Zircon (*ex-Nakhoda*)	PY16	1929 / 1941	*1220*	71.7 x 10.4	14	2 - 76/50, 2 - 20, 2 DCR	stricken 6.1946
Azurlite (*ex-Vogabondia*)	PY22	1928 / 3.1942	*1080*	64.3 x 10.4	12	2 - 76/50	for disposal 1.1947
Beryl (*ex-Rene*)	PY23	1929 / 3.1942	*1400*	68.6 x 10.4	14	2 - 76/50	to Maritime Commission 10.1946
Crystal (*ex-Vida*)	PY25	1929 / 2.1942	*1400*	68.6 x 10.4	18	2 - 76/50	to Maritime Commission 4.1947
Cythera (*ex-Agawa*)	PY26	20.9.1906 / 3.1942	*1000*	65.5 x 8.4	12	3 - 76	sunk 2.5.1942
Marcasite (*ex-Ramsis*)	PY28	1925 / 5.1942	*1130*	68.6 x 9.9	12	2 - 76/50, 1 DCT	stricken 10.1944
Hydrographer	PY30	1928	*1135*	51.1 x 9.6	10	1 - 76/50	commissioned as survey vessel 5.1942
Southern Seas	PY32	1920 / 12.1942	*1116*	69.5 x 9.5	11	small guns	foundered 9.10.1945

500 – 1000 t displacement

PY2 **Hawk** (1891 / 4.1898, 545 t – stricken 1940)

PY10 **Isabel** (1917 / 12.1917, 710 t - stricken 2.1946)

PY12 **Sylph** (*ex-Intrepid*) (1929 / 10.1940, 810 t, 2 – 76/50 - stricken 1.1946)

PY13 **Siren** (*ex-Lotosland*) (1929 / 11.1940, 720 t, 2 – 76/50 - stricken 11.1945)

PY14 **Argus** (*ex-Haida*) (1929 / 2.1941, 890 t, 1 – 76/50 - stricken 5.1946)

PY15 **Coral** (*ex-Yankee Clipper, ex-Sialia*) (1914 / 2.1941, 790 t, 2 – 76/50 - stricken 7.1947)

PY17 **Jade** (*ex-Dr. Brinkley*) (1926 / 3.1941, 562 t, 1 – 76/50 - to Ecuador 3.1943 - 1.1944, stricken 1.1945)

PY18 **Turquoise** (*ex-Entropy*) (1922 / 2.1941, 565 t, 1 – 76/50 – to Ecuador 1.1944 (9 de Octobre))

PY19 **Carnelian** (*ex-Seventeen*) (1930 / 6.1941, 500 t – stricken 10.1946)

PY20 **Tourmaline** (*ex-Sylvia*) (1930 / 9.1941, 750 t, 2 – 76/50 - stricken 8.1945)

PY21 **Ruby** (*ex-Placida*) (1929 / 9.1941, 500 t, 2 – 76/50 - stricken 8.1945)

PY24 **Almandite** (*ex-Happy Days*) (1927 / 4.1942, 705 t, 1 – 76/50 - stricken 12.1946)

PY27 **Girasol** (*ex-Firenza*) (1926 / 5.1942, 700 t, 1 – 76/50 - stricken 2.1946)

PY29 **Mizpah** (*ex-Allegro*) (1927 / 10.1942, 607 t, 2 – 76/50 - stricken 9.1946)

PY31 **Cythera** (*ex-Abryl*) (1931 / 10.1942, 800 t, 1 – 76/50 – stricken 11.1946)

Isabel 1942

Cythera 1942

Numbers written in *Italic* indicate displacement
Yachts purchased by the USN during the war and used as patrols.
1943, *Mayflower* was armed with 1 - 127/51, 2 - 76/50, 6 - 20/70 guns, 1 x 24 Hedgehog ASWRL, 4 DCT, 2 DCR.
Cythera was sunk by German submarine *U402* off the coast of North Carolina 2.5.1942.

Coastal patrol yachts

More than 1000 t displacement

Chalcedony *(ex-Velero III)*	PYc16	1931 / 2.1942	*1000*	59.5 x 9.1	11.5	1 - 76/23　for disposal 10.1946

500-1000 t displacement
PYc2 **Sapphire** (*ex-Buccaneer*) (1922 / 6.1941, 500 t, 2 – 76/50 – stricken 9.1946)
PYc3 **Amethyst** (*ex-Samona II*) (1931 / 2.1941, 525 t – USCG 3.1944)
PYc8 **Opal** (*ex-Coronet*) (1928 / 6.1941, 590 t, 1 – 76/23 – to Ecuador 9.1943 (Manabi))
PYc9 **Moonstone** (*ex-Lone Star*) (1929 / 4.1941, 645 t, 1 – 76/50 – collision 16.10.1943)

PYc12 **Sardonyx** (*ex-Queen Anne*) (1928 / 8.1941, 640 t, 1 – 76/50 - stricken 10.1946)
PYc19 **Rhodolite** (*ex-Seapine*) (1931 / 3.1942, 588 t, 1 – 76/50 – stricken 1.1946)
PYc26 **Cymophane** (*ex-Seaforth*) (1926 / 8.1942, 523 t, 1 – 76/50 – stricken 6.1948)
PYc40 **Captor** (*ex-Wave*) (1938 / 4.1942, 520 t, 1 – 102/50 - stricken 10.1944).

100-500t displacement
Requisitioned: 1 (1940), 7 (1941), 22 (1942), 9 (1943)
Discarded: 2 (1942), 1 (1943), 17 (1944), 9 (1945), 10

(post-war)
Moonstone collided with destroyer *Greer* 16.10.1943.

Patrol craft, converted from merchant vessels

More than 500 t displacement
PC459 (*ex-Entropy*) (1922 / 12.1940, 565 t, 1 – 76/50 –

patrol yacht PY18 2.1941)

100-500 t displacement
Requisitioned: 3 (1940), 3 (1941), 1 (1942)

Discarded: 6 (1943)
Lost: 1 (1941)

COASTAL FORCES

PALOS class river gunboat

Monocacy	PR2	Mare Island N Yd, Vallejo / Kiangnan Dock, Shanghai, China	4.1913	27.4.1914	6.1914	stricken 1.1939

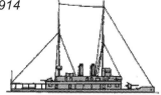

Monocacy 1914

190 / 204 t, 48.8 x 7.5 x 0.7 m, 2 VTE, 2 Babcock & Wilcox boilers, 800 hp, 13.3 kts, 34 t coal, complement 47; 2 x 1 – 57/50 Mk 8/11, 6 x 1 – 7.6 MG.
The first class of USN gunboats for the service on the Chinese rivers.

GUAM class river gunboats

Guam, 1.1941- **Wake**	PR3	Kiangnan Dock, Shanghai, China	1926	28.5.1927	12.1927	captured by Japan 8.12.1941 (Tatara), returned 8.1945, to China 1946 (Tai Yuan)
Tutuila	PR4	Kiangnan Dock, Shanghai, China	10.1926	14.6.1927	3.1928	to China 2.1942 ([Mei Yuan)

370 / 395 t, 48.6 x 8.3 x 1.6 m, 2 VTE, 2 Thornycroft boilers, 1950 hp, 14.5 kts, complement 70; 2 x 1 – 76/50 Mk 6, 8 x 1 – 7.6 MG.
Built under the FY25 Program for service on the Yangtze River in China to protect US interests.
1941, both: + 8 x 1 - 7.6 MG.

Wake 1941

Wake 7.12.1941 was captured in Shanghai by Japanese and commissioned by the IJN as *Tatara*.

PANAY class river gunboats

Panay	PR5	Kiangnan Dock, Shanghai, China	1927	10.11.1927	9.1928	sunk 12.12.1937
Oahu	PR6	Kiangnan Dock, Shanghai, China	12.1926	26.11.1927	10.1928	scuttled 6.5.1942

450 / 474 t, 58.2 x 8.6 x 1.6 m, 2 VTE, 2 Thornycroft boilers, 2250 hp, 15 kts, complement 70; 2 x 1 – 76/50 Mk 6.
Built under the FY25 Program for service on the Yangtze River in China to protect US interests.
1941: + 8 x 1 - 7.6 MG.
Panay was mistakenly sunk 12.12.1937 by Japanese

Panay 1937

aircraft. *Oahu* 6.5.1942 was scuttled at Corregidor to avoid capture by Japanese.

LUZON class river gunboats

Luzon	PR7	Kiangnan Dock, Shanghai, China	11.1926	12.9.1927	6.1928	scuttled 6.5.1942, to Japan (Karatsu)
Mindanao	PR8	Kiangnan Dock, Shanghai, China	11.1926	28.9.1927	7.1928	sunk 5.5.1942

Built under the FY25 Program for service on the Yangtze River in China to protect US interests.
1941, both: + 10 x 1 - 7.6 MG.
Luzon 6.5.1942 was scuttled at Corregidor, salvaged by Japanese, commissioned them as *Karatsu*. 3.3.1944 she was sunk by an US submarine. *Mindanao* 5.5.1942

Luzon 1942

was sunk at Corregidor by Japanese aircraft.

PT1 class motor torpedo boats

Fogal Boat, Miami: PT1, 2 (1941)
Discarded: PT1, 2 (1941)
25 / 30 t, 17.7 x 4.9 x 1.3 m, 2 petrol engines, 2000 hp,

30 kts, complement 17; 2 x 1 – 28/75 Mk 1 (fitted for), 2 – 533 TT.
Experimental boats; served as MTBs for only one month.

PT3 class motor torpedo boats

Fisher Boat Works, Detroit: PT3, 4 (1940)
Transferred: United Kingdom – PT3, 4 (1941)
25 / 30 t, 17.7 x 4.9 x 1.3 m, 2 petrol engines, 2400 hp, 32 kts, complement 17; 2 x 1 – 28/75 Mk 1 (fitted for),

2 – 533 TT.
Experimental MTBs that did not have armament in the US Navy. Both were transferred to the RN under Lend-Lease and were used as MTBs.

PT5 class motor torpedo boats

PT6 1941

Higgins, New Orleans: PT6 (i) (1940), PT5, 6 (ii) (1941)
Transferred: United Kingdom – PT5, 6 (i), 6 (ii) (1941)

30 / 34 t, 24.7 m, 3 petrol engines, 3000 (PT5, 6 (i)) – 3600 (PT6 (ii)) hp, 31 (PT5, 6 (i)) – 36 (PT6 (ii)) kts, complement 17; 2 x 2 – 12.7 MG, 2 – 533 TT.
Experimental MTBs built according to the Higgins design may be the truly armed USN MTBs. All of them were transferred to the RN under Lend-Lease and were commissioned by the RN as MTBs (2 boats) and MGB (1 boat).

PT7 class motor torpedo boats

PT8

Philadelphia N Yd: PT7, PT8 (1941- YP110) (1941)

Transferred: United Kingdom – PT7 (1941)
Discarded: YP110 (~1945)
32 (std) t, 24.7 m, 4 (2 shafts) (PT7) or 2 (PT8) petrol engines, 3600 hp, 30 kts, complement 17; 2 x 2 – 12.7 MG, 2 – 533 TT.
Experimental MTBs designed and built by the Navy.
10.1941, *YP110*: - 2 - 533 TT.
PT8 was reclassified as the patrol boat *YP110* in October 1941. Discarding date is unknown.

PT9 motor torpedo boat

PT9 1940

British Power Boat, Hythe, UK: PT9 (1940)
Transferred: United Kingdom – PT9 (1941)
30 / 40 t, 21.3 x 6.1 m, 3 petrol engines, 3000 hp, 45 kts, complement 17; 2 x 2 – 12.7 MG, 4 – 450 TT.
Scott-Payne design.

PT10 class motor torpedo boats

PT12

ELCO, Bayonne: PT10-19 (1940)
Transferred: United Kingdom – PT10-19 (1941)
32 / 40 t, 21.3 x 6.1 x 1.4 m, 3 petrol engines, 3600 hp, 45 kts, complement 17; 2 x 2 – 12.7 MG, 4 - 450 TT.
First serial-built US MTBs, 70-ft ELCO design. Wooden hull.

PT20 class motor torpedo boats

ELCO, Bayonne: PT20-48 (1941), PT49-68 (1942)
Lost: PT33 (1941), PT31, 32, 34, 35, 41, 44 (1942), PT22, 28, 37, 43, 67, 68 (1943), PT63 (1944)
Transferred: United Kingdom – PT49-58 (1942)
Discarded: PT21, 23, 25, 26 (1943), PT20, 24, 27, 29,

30, 36, 38-40, 42, 45-48, 59-61 (1944), PT62, 64-66 (1945)
35 / 46 t, 23.5 x 6.1 x 1.4 m, 3 petrol engines, 4050 hp, 41 kts, 1400 nm (30 kts), complement 17; 1 x 1 – 20/70 Oerlikon (PT45-48, 59-68), 1 (PT49-58) or 2 (PT20-48, 59-68) x 2 – 12.7 MG, 2 x 2 – 7.7 MG (PT49-58), 1 x 1 – 7.6 MG (PT46-48), (4 – 533 TT or (2 – 533 TT, 2 DCR (8))) (PT20-48, 59-68) or 2 – 533 TT (PT49-58).
ELCO 77-ft type. Development of the 70-ft type. Due to the increase in dimensions, the number of TTs was increased from two to four.
1941, *PT20-27, 29, 36-40, 42-45*: + 1 x 1 - 7.6 MG.
1941, *PT31-35, 41*: + 2 x 1 - 7.6 MG.

PT20 1941

1942, *PT22, 24, 26, 27*: + 1 x 1 - 20/70 Oerlikon.
1942, *PT65-68*: + 1 x 1 - 7.6 MG.

1943, *PT59-61*: - 4 - 533 TT; + 2 x 1 - 40/56 Bofors, 6 x 2 - 12.7 MG

PT69 motor torpedo boat

Huckins Yacht, Jacksonville: PT69 (1941- YP106) (1941)
Discarded: YP106 (~1945)
32 / 40 t, 21.9 x 6.1 m, 3 petrol engines, 3600 hp, 42 kts, complement 17; 2- 533 TT.
Prototype MTB, 72-ft Huckins type.
1941: - 2 - 533 TT; + 2 x 1 - 12.7 MG, DC.
The MTB was reclassified as a patrol boat in 1941, discarding date is unknown.

PT69 1941

PT70 motor torpedo boat

Higgins, New Orleans: PT70 (1941- YP107) (1941)
Discarded: YP107 (~1945)
32 / 40 t, 21.9 x 6.1 m, 3 petrol engines, 3600 hp, 42 kts, complement 17; 2 x 2 – 12.7 MG, 4 – 533 TT.

Prototype MTB of the 76-ft Higgins type.
1941: - 4 - 533 TT; + DC.
The MTB was reclassified as patrol boat in September 1941, discarding date is unknown.

PT71 class motor torpedo boats

Higgins, New Orleans: PT71-80, 82-94 (1942), PT81, 197-254, 265-307 (1943), PT308-313, 450-485, 625, 626 (1944), PT627-660, 791-796 (1945), PT797-808 (incomplete)
Lost: PT219, 239 (1943), PT200, 202, 218, 247, 251, 279, 283, 300, 301, 311 (1944), PT73, 77, 79 (1945)
Transferred: Soviet Union – PT85-87, 89, 197, 198, 265-276, 289-294 (1943), PT625-656 (1945); United Kingdom – PT88, 90-94, 201, 203-217 (1943)
Discarded: PT71, 72, 74 - 76, 78, 80 - 84, 197 - 199, 220 - 238, 240 - 246, 248 - 250, 252 - 254, 277 - 278, 280 - 282, 284 - 288, 295 - 299, 302 - 310, 312, 313, 450 - 485, 657 - 660, 791 – 796 (1945-1946)
35 / 43-48 t, 23.9-24.0 x 6.1 x 1.6 m, 3 petrol engines, 4050-4500 hp, 41 kts, 500 nm (20 kts), complement 17; 1 x 1 – 40/56 Bofors (PT450-485, 625-660, 791-796), 1 (PT71-94, 197-254, 265-313) or 2 (PT450-485, 635-660, 791-796) – 20/70 Oerlikon, 2 x 2 - 12.7 MG (PT71-94,

PT265 1944
1:625 scale

one of PT791-796 1945

197-254, 265-313), 4 – 533 TT; SO or SCR-517A radar.
78-ft Higgins type, the development of British Power Boats design.
1944-1945, survived early boats: - 2 x 2 – 12.7 MG; + 1 x 1 – 40/56 Bofors, 1 x 1 – 20/70 Oerlikon.

PT95 class motor torpedo boats

Huckins Yacht, Jacksonville: PT95-102 (1942), PT255-264 (1943)
Discarded: PT95-102, 255-264 (1945-1946)
35 / 46 t, 23.8 x 5.9 x 1.5 m, 3 petrol engines, 4050 hp, 42 kts, 500 nm (20 kts), complement 17; 1 x 1 – 20/70 Oerlikon, 2 x 2 - 12.7 MG, 4 – 533 TT; SO or SCR-517A radar.
A Huckins 78-ft type, used primarily for training.

PT96 1942

PT103 class motor torpedo boats

PT103 1942
1:625 scale

ELCO, Bayonne: PT103-171 (1942), PT172-196, 314-361, 372-383, 486, 488-502, 546-563, 565-570 (1943), PT487, 503-545, 571-575, 731-752 (1944), PT576-622, 753-760 (1945), PT623, 624, 761-790 (incomplete)
Harbor Boat, Long Beach: PT362-367 (1943)
Lost: PT109, 111-113, 117-119, 121, 123, 136, 147, 153, 158, 164-166, 172, 173, 322 (1943), PT107, 110, 133, 135, 145, 193, 320, 321, 323, 337-339, 346, 347, 353, 363, 493, 509, 555 (1944)
Transferred: Soviet Union – PT499, 500, 503, 504, 510-513 (1944), PT498, 501, 502, 506-508, 510-521, 552-554, 556, 560-563, 731-760 (1945)
Discarded: PT103-106, 108, 114-116, 120, 122, 124-132, 134, 137, 138, 142-144, 146, 148-152, 154-157, 159-163, 167-171, 174-192, 194-196, 318, 319, 324-336, 340-345, 348-352, 354-362, 364-367, 372-383, 488-492, 494-497, 522-551, 565-600 (1945), PT139 - 141, 314 - 317, 486, 487, 505, 557 - 559, 601 - 612, 614, 615, 617, 618, 621, 622 (1946)
38 / 54-61 t, 24.4 x 6.3 x 1.6 m, 3 petrol engines, 4050-4500 hp, 41-43 kts, 500 nm (20 kts), complement 17; 1 (PT174, 196, 515) or 2 (PT560-563) x 1 – 40/56 Bofors, 1 x 1 – 37/71 M9 (PT565-624), 1 (PT103-196, 314-367, 372-383, 515, 565-624) or 2 (PT486-514, 516-555, 731-760) x 1 – 20/70 Oerlikon or (1 x 4 + 1 x 1) – 20/70 Oerlikon (PT556-559), 2 x 2 – 12.7 MG, 2 x 1 – 127 RL (PT565-624), 2 (PT515, 556-559) or 4 (PT486-514, 516-555, 565-624) – 572 TR, 2 (PT196, 731-760) or 4 (PT103-195, 314-367, 372-383, 560-563) – 533 TT, 2 DC (PT515); SO or SCR-517A radar.
80-ft ELCO type. Further development of 77-ft ELCO.

PT117 1942

1942, PT138: + 1 x (4 - 20/70 Oerlikon + 2 - 12.7 MG). 1942, PT160: + 1 x 4 - 20/70 Oerlikon.
1943, PT109: + 1 x 1 - 37/61 M3. 1943, PT149: + 2 x 1 - 12.7 MG. 1943, PT157: - 1 x 2 - 12.7 MG; + 1 x 1 - 20/70 Oerlikon. 1943, PT187-192: - 1 x 2 - 12.7 MG; + 2 x 1 - 20/70 Oerlikon. 1943, PT193-195: - 1 x 2 - 12.7 MG; + 1 x 1 - 40/56 Bofors, 1 x 1 - 20/70 Oerlikon. 1943, PT331: + 1 x 1 - 37/61 M4, 1 x 1 - 20/70 Oerlikon. 1943, PT353, 354, 374-377: - 1 x 1 - 20/70; + 1 x 1 - 40/56 Bofors.
1944, PT115: - 1 x 2 - 12.7 MG, 4 - 533 TT; + 1 x 1 - 20/70 Oerlikon, 4 - 572 TR. 1944, PT129: - 4 - 533 TT; + 1 x 1 - 40/56 Bofors, 1 x 1 - 37/61 M4, 2 x 12 - 127 RL, 4 - 572 TR. 1944, PT143: - 4 - 533 TT; + 1 x 1 - 40/56 Bofors, 1 x 1 - 37/71 M9, 2 x 1 - 20/70 Oerlikon, 1 x 1 - 60/12 M19 mortar, 4 - 572 TR, 4 DC. 1944, PT154: - 1 x 2 - 12.7 MG, 4 - 533 TT; + 1 x 1 - 40/56 Bofors, 1 x 1 - 37/71 M9, 1 x 1 - 20/70 Oerlikon, 2 - 572 TR, 2 DC. 1944, PT161: - 4 - 533 TT; + 1 x 1 - 40/56 Bofors, 1 x 1 - 37/61 M4, 4 - 572 TR. 1944, PT167: + 1 x 1 - 37/61 M4. 1944, PT168: - 4 - 533 TT; + 1 x 1 - 57/70 recoilless, 1 x 1 - 37/61 M4, 4 - 572 TR. 1944, PT169: - 4 - 533 TT; + 1 x 1 - 37/61 M4, 4 - 572 TR. 1944, PT174: - 4 - 533 TT; + 4 - 572 TR. 1944, PT178: - 4 - 533 TT; + 1 x 1 - 40/56 Bofors, 1 x 1 - 37/61 M4, 1 x 1 - 20/70 Oerlikon, 4 - 572 TR. 1944, PT330: - 4 - 533 TT; + 1 x 1 - 40/56 Bofors, 1 x 1 - 37/61 M4, 2 x 1 - 12.7 MG, 4 - 572 TR, 2 DC. 1944, PT334: + 1 x 1 - 75/31 M4. 1944, PT343: - 4 - 533 TT; + 1 x 1 - 40/56 Bofors, 1 x 1 - 37/71 M9, 1 x 1 - 20/70 Oerlikon, 4 - 572 TR, 2 DC. 1944, PT349: - 4 - 533 TT; + 1 x 1 - 37/71 M9, 2 x 1 - 7.6 MG, 2 x 12 - 127 RL, 2 - 572 TR, 2 DC. 1944, PT352: - 4 - 533 TT; + 1 x 1 - 40/56 Bofors, 1 x 1 - 20/70 Oerlikon, 2 x 12 - 114 RL, 2 - 572 TR, 2 DC. 1944, PT491: + 1 x 1 - 40/56 Bofors, 1 x 1 - 37/61 M4, 1 x 1 - 20/70 Oerlikon. 1944, PT506, 512: - 1 x 1 - 20/70, 2 - 572 TR; + 1 x 1 - 40/56 Bofors, 2 DC. 1944, PT515, 520: + 1 x 1 - 37/71 M9. 1944, PT517: - 2 x 1 - 20/70, 2 - 572 TR; + 1 x 1 - 40/56 Bofors, 1 x 1 - 37/71 M9, 2 DC. 1944, PT519: - 1 x 1 - 20/70, 2 - 572 TR; + 1 x 1 - 40/56 Bofors, 1 x 1 - 37/71 M9, 2 DC. 1944, PT523: - 2 - 572 TR; + 1 x 1 - 40/56 Bofors, 1 x 1 - 37/71 M9, 1 x 1 - 20/70 Oerlikon, 2 x 1 - 7.6 MG, 2 x 1 - 60/12 M9 mortars. 1944, PT525: + 2 x 1 - 7.6 MG. 1944, PT533 - 544: - 2 - 572 TR; + 1 x 1 - 20/70 Oerlikon. 1944, PT552 - 555: - 1 x 1 - 20/70; + 1 x 1 - 40/56 Bofors.

PT368 class motor torpedo boats

Canadian Power Boat, Montreal, Canada: PT368-371 (1943)
Lost: PT368, 371 (1944)
Discarded: PT369, 370 (1945)
33 / 45 t, 21.4 x 5.8 x 1.5 m, 3 petrol engines, 4500 hp, 41 kts, 570 nm (20 kts), complement 12; 1 x 1 – 20/70 Oerlikon, 2 x 2 – 12.7 MG, 4 – 533 TT; SO or SCR-517A radar.
70-ft Canadian Power Boat type, built under the license of Scott-Paine.

PT384 class motor torpedo boats

Robert Jacob, New York: PT384-399 (1944)
Annapolis Yacht: PT400-429, 661-682 (1944), PT683-730 (1945)
Herreshoff, Bristol: PT430-449 (1944)
Transferred: United Kingdom – PT384-399 (1944), Soviet Union – PT400-449, 661-677 (1944), PT678-692 (1945), Cuba – PT715, 716 (1946)
Discarded: PT729, 730 (1945), PT693-714 (1946),

PT717-728 (1947)
33 / 45 t, 22.1 x 5.9 x 1.7 m, 3 petrol engines, 3375 hp, 39 kts, 570 nm (20 kts), complement 10-12; 1 x 1 – 20/70 Oerlikon (PT661-692), 1 (PT384-449) or 2 (PT661-692) x 2 – 12.7 MG, 2 – 533 TT, 2 DC; SO or SCR-517A radar. 72-ft Vosper type, the boats were built under the license of Vosper. PT693-730 were never commissioned and never were armed.

PT564 motor torpedo boat

Higgins, New Orleans: PT564 (1943)
Discarded: PT564 (1948)
40 t, 21.3 x 6.1 x 1.4 m, 3 Packard petrol engines, 13500 hp, 46 kts, complement 11; 1 x 1 – 20/70 Oerlikon, 2 x 2 – 12.7 MG, 4 – 572 TR, SO radar.
70-ft prototype "Higgins Hellcat" MTB with high speed and low silhouette.

PT564

PGM9 class motor gunboats

PGM10 (ex-PC805)	Commercial Iron Wks, Portland	9.1943	27.10.1943	11.1944	to the Philippines 1950
PGM11 (ex-PC806)	Commercial Iron Wks, Portland	9.1943	30.10.1943	12.1944	disposed ~1948
PGM12 (ex-PC1088)	Geo Lawley, Neponset	8.1943	18.1.1945	4.1945	to China 8.1948 (Tung Ping)
PGM13 (ex-PC1089)	Geo Lawley, Neponset	1.1945	12.4.1945	6.1945	to China 6.1948 (Tung Ting)
PGM14 (ex-PC1090)	Geo Lawley, Neponset	4.1945	15.6.1945	8.1945	to China 6.1948
PGM15 (ex-PC1091)	Geo Lawley, Neponset	6.1945	31.7.1945	10.1945	to China 6.1948 (Kan Tang)
PGM16 (ex-PC1148)	Defoe, Bay City	10.1943	19.12.1943	10.1944	to Greece 8.1947 (Antipliarchos Laskos)
PGM17 (ex-PC1189)	Gibbs Gas Engine, Jacksonville	8.1943	14.4.1944	11.1944	wrecked 4.5.1945, never repaired
PGM19 (ex-PC1550)	Consolidated SB, New York	2.1944	11.4.1944	12.1944	disposed 6.1949
PGM20 (ex-PC1551)	Consolidated SB, New York	3.1944	7.5.1944	12.1944	to China 6.1948 (Pao Ying)
PGM21 (ex-PC1552)	Consolidated SB, New York	4.1944	25.5.1944	11.1944	to Greece 8.1947 (Antipliarchos Pezopoulos)
PGM22 (ex-PC1553)	Consolidated SB, New York	5.1944	25.6.1944	12.1944	to Greece 8.1947 (Plotarchis Meletopoulos)
PGM23 (ex-PC1554)	Consolidated SB, New York	5.1944	16.7.1944	12.1944	disposed ~1948
PGM24 (ex-PC1555)	Consolidated SB, New York	7.1944	13.8.1944	1.1945	disposed ~1948
PGM25 (ex-PC1556)	Consolidated SB, New York	7.1944	16.9.1944	2.1945	to Greece 8.1947 (Plotarchis Arsanoglou)

PGM26 (ex-PC1557)	Consolidated SB, New York	8.1944	25.9.1944	2.1945	to China 6.1948 (Hung Tse)
PGM27 (ex-PC1558)	Consolidated SB, New York	6.1944	28.10.1944	3.1945	wrecked 9.10.1945
PGM28 (ex-PC1559)	Consolidated SB, New York	6.1944	19.11.1944	4.1945	to Greece 8.1947 (Plotarchis Blessas)
PGM29 (ex-PC1565)	Leatham D. Smith SB, Sturgeon Bay	5.1944	16.7.1944	11.1944	to Greece 8.1947 (Plotarchis Chadzikonstandis)
PGM30 (ex-PC1566)	Leatham D. Smith SB, Sturgeon Bay	5.1944	12.8.1944	12.1944	disposed 4.1947
PGM31 (ex-PC1567)	Leatham D. Smith SB, Sturgeon Bay	7.1944	23.9.1944	1.1945	to Taiwan 3.1954 (Zhu Jiang)
PGM32 (ex-PC1568)	Leatham D. Smith SB, Sturgeon Bay	8.1944	14.10.1944	2.1945	sold 10.1947

PGM10 1944

PGM25

414 / 463 t, 52.9 x 7.1 x 3.3 m, 2 diesels, 2880 hp, 19 kts, 49 t diesel oil, 3000 nm (12 kts), complement 59-65;

(1 x 1 – 76/50 Mk 20/21, 1 x 1 – 40/56 Bofors) or 2 x 2 – 40/56 Bofors, 6 x 1 – 20/70 Oerlikon, 1 x 2 – 60/19 M19 mortar, 2 x 1 – 12.7 MG; SF or SO or SU radar.

In 1944, 24 173-ft submarine chasers, due to the dismantling of ASW equipment, received strengthened gun armament and were reoriented from the ASW role to combat Japanese small craft. Although the armament was the only difference between these ships and standard PC, they were outlined into a separate subclass of motor gunboats with new hull indexes.

PGM17 struck a reef off Kouri Island, Okinawa, 4.5.1945. PGM18 was mined 7.4.1945.

SC1 class submarine chasers

SC64 1941

SC2

New York N Yd, Brooklyn: SC64 (1918)
ELCO, Bayonne: SC102 (1918)
International SB, Upper Nyack: SC185 (1918)
New York Yacht, Launch & Engine, Morris Heights: SC229 (8.1942- USCG WPC335 Boone), SC231 (8.1942- USCG WPC336 Blaze), SC238 (7.1943- USCG

WPC365 Bowstring) (1918)
Geo Lawley, Neponset: WPC372 Belleville (ex-SC258) (USCG) (1917/1942)
Burger Boat, Sturgeon Bay: SC330 (1918)
Clayton SB: SC412 (1919)
Matthews Boat, Port Clinton: SC432, SC433 (ex-Kingelhoefer) (1918), SC431 (ex-Knudsen, ex-SC431) (1919)
Rocky River: SC437 (ex-Boyce, ex-SC437) (1919)
Wheeler, Brooklyn: SC440 (1919)
Lost: SC433 (1938), SC185 (1940)
Discarded: SC64, 440 (1942) WPC365, WPC372, SC432 (1945), WPC335, 336, SC330, 412, 431 (1946), SC102, 437 (1947)

75 / 85 t, 33.5 x 4.5 x 1.7 m, 3 Standard petrol engines, 660 hp, 18 kts, 1000 nm (12 kts), complement 27; 1 x 1 – 76/24 Mk 15 (SC64) or 1 x 1 – 76/23 Mk 14 (other), 2 x 1 – 7.6 MG, 1 DCT.

110-ft submarine chasers built in a huge series for their time. Wooden-hulled.

PC449 submarine chaser

PC449, 9.1942- SC449	Luders Marine, Stamford	7.1939	14.5.1940	9.1940	stricken 7.1949

85 / 132 t, 33.5 x 4.5 x 1.7 m, 2 Cooper Besssemer diesels, 800 hp, 18 kts, complement 27; 1 x 1 – 76/23 Mk 14, 2 x 1 – 7.6 MG, 1 DCT; QC sonar.
Experimental submarine chaser, built according to the FY38 Program.

PC449 1941

PC450 submarine chaser

PC450, 9.1942- SC450	American Car & Foundry, Wilmington	8.1939	14.3.1940	5.1940	to the Maritime Comm. 5.1947

85 / 120 t, 33.5 x 4.5 x 1.7 m, 2 General Motors diesels, 800 hp, 15.6 kts, complement 27; 1 x 1 – 76/23 Mk 14, 2 x 1 – 7.6 MG, 1 DCT; QC sonar.
Experimental submarine chaser, built under the FY38 Program.

PC450 1940

PC453 submarine chaser

PC453, 4.1943- SC453	Fisher Boat Wks, Detroit	9.1940	3.5.1941	8.1941	Coast Guard SAR cutter 11.1945

100 (std) t, 33.5 x 5.5 x 1.8 m, 2 diesels, 1540 hp, 17 kts, complement 27; 1 x 1 – 76/23 Mk 14, 2 x 1 – 7.6 MG, 1 DCT; QC sonar.
An experimental submarine chaser, built under the FY38 Program. Designed by the Navy, became the basis for the design of a huge class. She differed from her WWI-era predecessor by increased breadth and stronger hull structure with steel framing.

PC497 class submarine chasers

PC497, 9.1942- SC497	Westergard, Rockport	3.1941	4.7.1941	4.1942	to France 3.1944 (Ch96)
PC498, 9.1942- SC498	Westergard, Rockport	3.1941	21.7.1941	4.1942	to France 10.1944 (Ch142)
PC499, 9.1942- SC499	Fisher, Detroit	2.1941	24.10.1941	3.1942	USCG 8.1945
PC500, 9.1942- SC500	Fisher, Detroit	2.1941	11.10.1941	3.1942	to the USSR 6.1945 (BO-319)
PC501, 9.1942- SC501	Seabrook Yacht, Houston	4.1941	24.1.1942	4.1942	auxiliary 4.1943
PC502, 9.1942- SC502	Seabrook Yacht, Houston	5.1941	31.1.1942	6.1942	to the MarCom 3.1948
PC503, 9.1942- SC503	Rice Bros, E. Boothbay	1.1941	14.3.1942	4.1942	to France 11.1944 (Ch112)
PC504, 9.1942- SC504	Rice Bros, E. Boothbay	1.1941	14.3.1942	5.1942	to the MarCom 9.1946
PC505, 9.1942- SC505	Luders Marine, Stamford	2.1941	23.2.1942	4.1942	to the MarCom 5.1947
PC506, 9.1942- SC506	Luders Marine, Stamford	3.1941	30.1.1942	4.1942	to France 9.1944 (Ch113)
PC507, 9.1942- SC507	Mathis Yacht, Camden	2.1941	30.6.1941	1.1942	to France 11.1944 (Ch85)
PC508, 9.1942- SC508	Mathis Yacht, Camden	2.1941	25.7.1941	3.1942	to France 3.1944 (Ch95)
PC511, 9.1942- SC511	American Cruiser, Detroit	8.1941	1.4.1942	6.1942	USCG 8.1945

PC512, 9.1942- SC512	American Cruiser, Detroit	8.1941	26.3.1942	7.1942	USCG 10.1945
PC513, 9.1942- SC513	Quincy Adams, Quincy	5.1941	20.1.1942	3.1942	to the MarCom 10.1945
PC514, 9.1942- SC514	Quincy Adams, Quincy	6.1941	7.3.1942	4.1942	to the MarCom 3.1948
PC515, 9.1942- SC515	Elizabeth City	4.1941	20.9.1941	4.1942	to France 10.1944 (Ch121)
PC516, 9.1942- SC516	Elizabeth City	5.1941	11.10.1941	5.1942	to France 3.1944 (Ch81)
PC517, 9.1942- SC517	Elizabeth City	5.1941	11.10.1941	5.1942	to France 3.1944 (Ch82)
PC518, 9.1942- SC518	Elizabeth City	6.1941	12.11.1941	5.1942	destroyed 13.7.1948
PC519, 9.1942- SC519	Vineyard, Milford	6.1941	14.3.1942	4.1942	to France 3.1944 (Ch83)
PC520, 9.1942- SC520	Vineyard, Milford	7.1941	18.4.1942	5.1942	to the MarCom 9.1947
PC521, 9.1942- SC521	Annapolis Yacht	5.1941	1.2.1942	4.1942	foundered 10.7.1945
PC522, 9.1942- SC522	Annapolis Yacht	5.1941	18.2.1942	4.1942	to France 9.1944 (Ch111)
PC524, 9.1942- SC524	Mathis Yacht, Camden	5.1941	19.9.1941	4.1942	to France 10.1944 (Ch101)
PC525, 9.1942- SC525	Mathis Yacht, Camden	7.1941	21.11.1941	5.1942	to France 10.1944 (Ch102)
PC526, 9.1942- SC526	Mathis Yacht, Camden	7.1941	30.12.1941	5.1942	to France 9.1944 (Ch114)
PC527, 9.1942- SC527	Mathis Yacht, Camden	9.1941	21.1.1942	5.1942	stricken 2.1946
PC528, 9.1942- SC528	Mathis Yacht, Camden	10.1941	17.2.1942	6.1942	for disposal 2.1947
PC529, 9.1942- SC529	Mathis Yacht, Camden	11.1941	16.3.1942	6.1942	to France 3.1944 (Ch84)
PC530, 9.1942- SC530	Westergard, Rockport	3.1941	16.8.1941	5.1942	to France 11.1944 (Ch115)
PC531, 9.1942- SC531	Westergard, Rockport	3.1941	4.9.1941	5.1942	to the MarCom 2.1948
PC532, 9.1942- SC532	Luders Marine, Stamford	4.1941	7.4.1942	5.1942	to France 11.1944 (Ch103)
PC533, 9.1942- SC533	Luders Marine, Stamford	5.1941	13.4.1942	6.1942	to France 10.1944 (Ch104)
PC534, 9.1942- SC534	Luders Marine, Stamford	5.1941	27.4.1942	7.1942	to France 10.1944 (Ch122)
PC535, 9.1942- SC535	Luders Marine, Stamford	6.1941	9.7.1942	7.1942	to France 11.1944 (Ch143)
PC536, 9.1942- SC536	Peterson Boat, Sturgeon	4.1941	5.3.1942	4.1942	USCG 2.1946
PC537, 9.1942- SC537	Peterson Boat, Sturgeon	4.1941	21.3.1942	5.1942	to the USSR 6.1945 (BO-304)
PC538, 9.1942- SC538	Peterson Boat, Sturgeon	5.1941	1.4.1942	5.1942	to the USSR 8.1945 (BO-321)
PC539, 9.1942- SC539	Peterson Boat, Sturgeon	5.1941	7.4.1942	5.1942	USCG 12.1945

PC540, 9.1942- SC540	Robinson Marine, Benton Harbor	7.1941	7.4.1942	4.1942	USCG 4.1945
PC541, 9.1942- SC541	Robinson Marine, Benton Harbor	8.1941	11.4.1942	5.1942	USCG 10.1945
PC628, 9.1942- SC628, 8.1945- SCC628	Quincy Adams, Quincy	8.1941	15.4.1942	4.1942	to the MarCom 5.1947
PC629, 9.1942- SC629, 8.1945- SCC629	Quincy Adams, Quincy	9.1941	27.4.1942	5.1942	to the MarCom 3.1949
PC630, 9.1942- SC630, 8.1945- SCC630	Mathis Yacht, Camden	12.1941	18.4.1942	6.1942	to the MarCom 3.1948
PC631, 9.1942- SC631	Mathis Yacht, Camden	1.1942	19.6.1942	8.1942	to the MarCom 3.1948
SC632	Mathis Yacht, Camden	2.1942	25.6.1942	9.1942	wrecked 16.9.1945
SC633	Mathis Yacht, Camden	3.1942	3.7.1942	9.1942	destroyed 4.4.1946
SC634	Mathis Yacht, Camden	4.1942	10.7.1942	9.1942	to the USSR 6.1945 (BO-309)
SC635	Mathis Yacht, Camden	6.1942	12.10.1942	10.1942	USCG 10.1945
PC636, 9.1942- SC636	Vineyard, Milford	1.1942	14.5.1942	7.1942	wrecked 9.10.1945
PC637, 9.1942- SC637	Vineyard, Milford	12.1941	10.6.1942	7.1942	for disposal 10.1948
PC638, 9.1942- SC638	Elizabeth City	8.1941	20.12.1941	6.1942	to France 9.1944 (Ch116)
PC639, 9.1942- SC639	Elizabeth City	8.1941	31.12.1941	6.1942	to France 5.1944 (Ch93)
PC640, 9.1942- SC640	Elizabeth City	8.1941	17.1.1942	7.1942	to the MarCom 12.1946
PC641, 9.1942- SC641	Elizabeth City	10.1941	12.2.1942	7.1942	to the MarCom 3.1948
PC642, 9.1942- SC642	Peterson Boat, Sturgeon	10.1941	30.5.1942	8.1942	USCG 1.1946
PC643, 9.1942- SC643	Peterson Boat, Sturgeon	11.1941	10.6.1942	8.1942	to the USSR 8.1945 (BO-322)
SC644, 12.1943- PGM1	Peterson Boat, Sturgeon	11.1941	27.6.1942	10.1942	gunboat 12.1943, for disposal 5.1947
SC645	Peterson Boat, Sturgeon	1.1942	26.7.1942	9.1942	to the MarCom 3.1948
PC646, 9.1942- SC646	Robinson Marine, Benton Harbor	9.1941	21.5.1942	7.1942	to the USSR 5.1945 (BO-310)
PC647, 9.1942- SC647	Robinson Marine, Benton Harbor	9.1941	27.6.1942	8.1942	to the USSR 5.1945 (BO-308)
PC648, 9.1942- SC648	Delaware Bay, Leesburg	10.1941	18.4.1942	7.1942	to China 6.1948
PC649, 9.1942- SC649	Delaware Bay, Leesburg	10.1941	18.4.1942	7.1942	to France 6.1944 (Ch91)
PC650, 9.1942- SC650	Westergard, Rockport	10.1941	30.4.1942	7.1942	for disposal 1.1947
PC651, 9.1942- SC651	Westergard, Rockport	11.1941	14.5.1942	8.1942	to France 11.1944 (Ch135)
PC652, 9.1942- SC652	Julius Peterson, Nyack	12.1941	18.4.1942	6.1942	for disposal 5.1947

PC653, 9.1942- SC653	Julius Peterson, Nyack	12.1941	18.4.1942	7.1942	USCG 10.1945
PC654, 9.1942- SC654	Westergard, Rockport	9.1941	4.5.1942	7.1942	sunk as target 18.12.1945
PC655, 9.1942- SC655	Westergard, Rockport	10.1941	12.5.1942	8.1942	to France 10.1944 (Ch144)
PC656, 9.1942- SC656	Snow, Rockland	12.1941	2.5.1942	8.1942	USCG 1.1946
SC657	Snow, Rockland	12.1941	22.6.1942	9.1942	to the USSR 6.1945 (BO-307)
PC658, 9.1942- SC658	American Cruiser, Detroit	12.1941	6.6.1942	8.1942	to the MarCom 1.1948
SC659	American Cruiser, Detroit	12.1941	29.6.1942	10.1942	USCG 10.1945
SC660	Burger, Manitowoc	12.1941	20.6.1942	9.1942	to the USSR 6.1945 (BO-311)
SC661	Burger, Manitowoc	12.1941	26.6.1942	10.1942	to the USSR 5.1945 (BO-303)
PC662, 9.1942- SC662	Fisher, Detroit	11.1941	11.4.1942	6.1942	USCG 10.1945
PC663, 9.1942- SC663	Fisher, Detroit	11.1941	22.4.1942	7.1942	to the USSR 6.1945 (BO-318)
PC664, 9.1942- SC664	Dachel-Carter, Benton Harbor	11.1941	21.5.1942	8.1942	for disposal 12.1946
PC665, 9.1942- SC665	Dachel-Carter, Benton Harbor	11.1941	12.5.1942	8.1942	sold 6.1950
SC666	Weaver, Orange	10.1941	17.3.1942	9.1942	to France 9.1944 (Ch134)
SC667, 8.1945- SCC667	Weaver, Orange	10.1941	4.4.1942	9.1942	to the MarCom 3.1948
PC668, 9.1942- SC668	Daytona Beach	11.1941	12.3.1942	7.1942	sold 11.1946
PC669, 9.1942- SC669	Daytona Beach	11.1941	21.3.1942	7.1942	to the MarCom 3.1947
SC670	Inland Waterways, Duluth	11.1941	6.7.1942	9.1942	USCG 3.1946
SC671	Inland Waterways, Duluth	11.1941	8.8.1942	10.1942	sold 12.1946
PC672, 9.1942- SC672	Walter E. Abrams, Halesite	10.1941	2.5.1942	6.1942	USCG 10.1945
PC673, 9.1942- SC673	Walter E. Abrams, Halesite	11.1941	16.5.1942	7.1942	to the USSR 6.1945 (BO-316)
PC674, 9.1942- SC674	Hiltebrant, Kingston	10.1941	13.3.1942	8.1942	to the USSR 5.1945 (BO-306)
SC675	Hiltebrant, Kingston	11.1941	19.3.1942	9.1942	to the USSR 6.1945 (BO-314)
PC676, 9.1942- SC676	W. A. Robinson, Ipswich	1.1942	23.6.1942	7.1942	to France 10.1944 (Ch105)
PC677, 9.1942- SC677	W. A. Robinson, Ipswich	2.1942	27.7.1942	8.1942	disposed 3.1946
SC678	Walter E. Abrams, Halesite	3.1942	17.8.1942	11.1942	disposed 4.1948
SC679	Walter E. Abrams, Halesite	3.1942	29.8.1942	12.1942	to France 3.1951 (Ch736)
SC680	Walter E. Abrams, Halesite	3.1942	7.9.1942	1.1943	to the MarCom 11.1946
SC681	Walter E. Abrams, Halesite	3.1942	30.9.1942	3.1943	to the MarCom 11.1946
SC682	American Cruiser, Detroit	4.1942	18.9.1942	11.1942	USCG 10.1945
SC683	American Cruiser, Detroit	4.1942	14.10.1942	11.1942	to Norway 10.1943 (Hessa)

SC684	American Cruiser, Detroit	7.1942	21.11.1942	1.1943	USCG 1.1946
SC685	American Cruiser, Detroit	7.1942	25.3.1943	5.1943	to the USSR 7.1945 (BO-302)
SC686, 8.1945- SCC686	American Cruiser, Detroit	11.1942	15.4.1943	7.1943	wrecked 9.10.1945
SC687	American Cruiser, Detroit	1.1943	5.6.1943	8.1943	to the USSR 5.1945 (BO-301)
SC688	Annapolis Yacht	4.1942	22.8.1942	11.1942	to the MarCom 10.1946
SC689	Annapolis Yacht	4.1942	15.8.1942	11.1942	to the MarCom 9.1946
SC690	Annapolis Yacht	5.1942	7.9.1942	12.1942	to France 10.1944 (Ch106)
SC691	Annapolis Yacht	5.1942	19.9.1942	12.1942	to France 9.1944 (Ch132)
SC692	Calderwood, Manchester	3.1942	25.9.1942	11.1942	to France 11.1944 (Ch131)
SC693	Calderwood, Manchester	5.1942	24.10.1942	1.1943	to France 9.1944 (Ch107)
SC694	Daytona Beach	3.1942	25.5.1942	9.1942	sunk 23.8.1943
SC695	Daytona Beach	3.1942	4.7.1942	10.1942	to France 11.1944 (Ch133)
SC696	Daytona Beach	3.1942	6.8.1942	11.1942	sunk 23.8.1943
SC697	Daytona Beach	3.1942	15.8.1942	12.1942	to France 5.1944 (Ch92)
SC698	Delaware Bay, Leesburg	3.1942	7.8.1942	9.1942	to China 6.1949 (Chu Chien 103)
SC699	Delaware Bay, Leesburg	3.1942	7.9.1942	10.1942	to the Philippines 7.1948
SC700	Delaware Bay, Leesburg	3.1942	7.9.1942	11.1942	fire 10.3.1944
SC701	Delaware Bay, Leesburg	4.1942	17.9.1942	12.1942	to the MarCom 3.1948
SC702	Delaware Bay, Leesburg	5.1942	10.10.1942	12.1942	to the MarCom 12.1946
SC703	Delaware Bay, Leesburg	5.1942	28.11.1942	1.1943	to China 9.1947
SC704	Elizabeth City	3.1942	6.4.1942	9.1942	for disposal 10.1948
SC705	Elizabeth City	3.1942	24.4.1942	10.1942	to the MarCom 9.1946
SC706	Elizabeth City	3.1942	26.6.1942	10.1942	to the MarCom 9.1946
SC707	Elizabeth City	4.1942	10.6.1942	10.1942	to the MarCom 8.1946
SC708	Elizabeth City	5.1942	26.6.1942	11.1942	to China 9.1947 (Chu Chien 102)
SC709	Elizabeth City	6.1942	15.7.1942	11.1942	grounded 21.1.1943
SC710	Dooleys Basin, Fort Lauderdale	3.1942	7.9.1942	11.1942	USCG 8.1945
SC711	Dooleys Basin, Fort Lauderdale	4.1942	17.10.1942	1.1943	USCG 10.1945
SC712, 8.1945- SCC712	Fisher, Detroit	3.1942	25.7.1942	9.1942	to the MarCom 2.1948
SC713	Fisher, Detroit	4.1942	25.7.1942	10.1942	to the USSR 5.1945 (BO-313)
SC714	Fisher, Detroit	4.1942	17.9.1942	11.1942	USCG 12.1945
SC715	Fisher, Detroit	5.1942	23.10.1942	12.1942	USCG 1.1946
SC716	Fisher, Detroit	5.1942	20.11.1942	1.1943	stricken 5.1950
SC717	Fisher, Detroit	7.1942	14.12.1942	5.1943	USCG 10.1945
SC718	Fisher, Detroit	9.1942	31.3.1943	5.1943	to Norway 10.1943 (Hitra)
SC719	Fisher, Detroit	9.1942	3.4.1943	7.1943	to the USSR 8.1943 (BO-210)
SC720	Fisher, Detroit	11.1942	10.4.1943	8.1943	to the USSR 9.1943 (BO-211)
SC721	Fisher, Detroit	11.1942	17.4.1943	8.1943	to the USSR 9.1943 (BO-212)

SC722	Harbor Boat, Terminal Island	3.1942	15.5.1942	11.1942	to China 6.1948
SC723	Harbor Boat, Terminal Island	3.1942	10.6.1942	12.1942	to China 6.1948
SC724	Harbor Boat, Terminal Island	4.1942	2.7.1942	12.1942	to the MarCom 12.1946
SC725	Harbor Boat, Terminal Island	4.1942	23.7.1942	1.1943	to the MarCom 12.1946
SC726	Harbor Boat, Terminal Island	4.1942	12.8.1942	1.1943	to the MarCom 11.1946
SC727, 8.1945- SCC727	Harbor Boat, Terminal Island	5.1942	7.9.1942	2.1943	for disposal 5.1947
SC728	Harbor Boat, Terminal Island	5.1942	30.11.1942	3.1943	to the MarCom 12.1946
SC729	Harbor Boat, Terminal Island	5.1942	25.1.1943	4.1943	to the MarCom 3.1948
SC730	Hiltebrant, Kingston	3.1942	5.6.1942	11.1942	to the MarCom 12.1946
SC731	Hiltebrant, Kingston	4.1942	27.6.1942	12.1942	to the Philippines 6.1948 (Cagayan)
SC732	Hiltebrant, Kingston	4.1942	27.6.1942	12.1942	to the Philippines 7.1948
SC733	Hiltebrant, Kingston	6.1942	10.8.1942	1.1943	to the MarCom 4.1948
SC734	Al Larson, Terminal Island	4.1942	18.7.1942	12.1942	for disposal 4.1947
SC735	Al Larson, Terminal Island	4.1942	29.8.1942	3.1943	to China 6.1948
SC736	Liberty, Brooklyn	4.1942	29.10.1942	2.1943	to the Philippines 7.1948 (Mountain Province)
SC737	Liberty, Brooklyn	4.1942	15.12.1942	5.1943	for disposal 8.1947
SC738	Julius Peterson, Nyack	3.1942	27.6.1942	10.1942	for disposal 12.1947
SC739	Julius Peterson, Nyack	3.1942	4.7.1942	10.1942	to the Philippines 7.1948 (Ilocos Sur)
SC740	Julius Peterson, Nyack	3.1942	14.7.1942	11.1942	grounded 17.6.1943
SC741	Julius Peterson, Nyack	4.1942	3.8.1942	12.1942	for disposal 8.1946
SC742	Julius Peterson, Nyack	4.1942	17.8.1942	1.1943	to the Philippines 7.1948
SC743	Julius Peterson, Nyack	4.1942	26.8.1942	2.1943	to the Philippines 7.1948
PC744, 9.1942- SC744	Quincy Adams, Quincy	2.1942	23.5.1942	7.1942	sunk 27.11.1944
PC745, 9.1942- SC745	Quincy Adams, Quincy	3.1942	15.6.1942	8.1942	for disposal 2.1948
PC746, 9.1942- SC746	Quincy Adams, Quincy	4.1942	8.7.1942	8.1942	for disposal 4.1948
SC747	Quincy Adams, Quincy	4.1942	28.7.1942	9.1942	to the Philippines 7.1948 (Surigao)
SC748	Quincy Adams, Quincy	4.1942	21.8.1942	9.1942	for disposal 1.1948
SC749	Quincy Adams, Quincy	5.1942	7.9.1942	10.1942	for disposal 4.1948
SC750	Quincy Adams, Quincy	6.1942	26.9.1942	11.1942	to the Philippines 7.1948 (Isabella)
SC751	Quincy Adams, Quincy	8.1942	15.10.1942	11.1942	grounded 22.6.1943
SC752	Robinson Marine, Benton Harbor	5.1942	7.12.1942	2.1943	to the USSR 8.1945 (BO-325)
SC753	Robinson Marine, Benton Harbor	5.1942	4.1.1943	4.1943	USCG 12.1945
SC754	Robinson Marine, Benton Harbor	6.1942	23.2.1943	5.1943	to the USSR 8.1945 (BO-324)
SC755	Robinson Marine, Benton Harbor	6.1942	3.4.1943	5.1943	to the MarCom 1.1948
SC756	Robinson Marine, Benton Harbor	7.1942	15.5.1943	7.1943	to the USSR 9.1945 (BO-335)
SC757, 12.1943- PGM2	Robinson Marine, Benton Harbor	7.1942	17.6.1943	8.1943	gunboat 12.1943, stricken 6.1946
SC758	Robinson Marine, Benton Harbor	8.1942	28.7.1943	9.1943	USCG 1.1946

SC759	Robinson Marine, Benton Harbor	8.1942	26.8.1943	10.1943	to the MarCom 1.1948
SC760, 8.1945- SCC760	W. A. Robinson, Ipswich	3.1942	11.8.1942	9.1942	to the MarCom 2.1948
SC761	W. A. Robinson, Ipswich	3.1942	24.8.1942	9.1942	to the MarCom 3.1948
SC762	W. A. Robinson, Ipswich	3.1942	14.9.1942	10.1942	to Brazil 12.1942 (Jutaí)
SC763	W. A. Robinson, Ipswich	3.1942	25.9.1942	10.1942	to Brazil 12.1942 (Javari)
SC764	W. A. Robinson, Ipswich	4.1942	12.10.1942	10.1942	to Brazil 12.1942 (Juruá)
SC765	W. A. Robinson, Ipswich	4.1942	12.11.1942	12.1942	to Brazil 2.1943 (Jaguarão)
SC766	W. A. Robinson, Ipswich	4.1942	27.10.1942	11.1942	to Brazil 12.1942 (Juruena)
SC767	W. A. Robinson, Ipswich	4.1942	7.12.1942	1.1943	to Brazil 2.1943 (Jaguaribe)
SC768	Seabrook Yacht	4.1942	8.8.1942	11.1942	for disposal 4.1948
SC769	Seabrook Yacht	4.1942	23.8.1942	12.1942	to the Philippines 7.1948
SC770	Seabrook Yacht	7.1942	18.10.1942	12.1942	to France 10.1944 (Ch141)
SC771	Seabrook Yacht	8.1942	5.11.1942	1.1943	to France 11.1944 (Ch124)
SC772	Peyton, Newport Beach	5.1942	7.9.1942	4.1943	USCG 12.1945
SC773	Peyton, Newport Beach	5.1942	17.10.1942	5.1943	to the MarCom 2.1948
SC774	Peyton, Newport Beach	6.1942	27.10.1942	6.1943	to the USSR 8.1945 (BO-323)
SC775	Peyton, Newport Beach	6.1946	28.11.1942	7.1943	USCG 3.1946
SC977	Simms Bros, Dorchester	4.1942	10.10.1942	11.1942	to France 5.1944 (Ch94)
SC978	Simms Bros, Dorchester	5.1942	10.10.1942	12.1942	to France 10.1944 (Ch145)
SC979	Simms Bros, Dorchester	5.1942	9.12.1942	1.1943	to France 10.1944 (Ch146)
SC980	Simms Bros, Dorchester	6.1942	9.12.1942	2.1943	to the MarCom 9.1946
SC981	Vineyard, Milford	3.1942	14.8.1942	10.1942	disposed 1.1946
SC982	Vineyard, Milford	4.1942	7.9.1942	11.1942	to the Philippines 7.1948 (Cavite)
SC983	Vineyard, Milford	5.1942	5.11.1942	1.1943	to the MarCom 4.1947
SC984	Vineyard, Milford	6.1942	19.12.1942	2.1943	grounded 9.4.1944
SC985	John E. Matton, Waterford	4.1942	18.9.1942	12.1942	USCG 10.1945
SC986	John E. Matton, Waterford	4.1942	13.11.1942	4.1943	to the USSR 6.1945 (BO-305)
SC987	John E. Matton, Waterford	6.1942	10.4.1943	6.1943	USCG 10.1945
SC988	John E. Matton, Waterford	11.1942	1.6.1943	7.1943	USCG 10.1945
SC989	John E. Matton, Waterford	12.1942	25.6.1943	8.1943	USCG 10.1945
SC990	Geo W. Kneass, San Francisco	8.1942	9.12.1942	3.1943	to the MarCom 3.1948
SC991	Geo W. Kneass, San Francisco	8.1942	20.1.1943	4.1943	to the MarCom 3.1948
SC992	Geo W. Kneass, San Francisco	8.1942	31.3.1943	6.1943	to the MarCom 10.1946
SC993	Geo W. Kneass, San Francisco	11.1942	1.5.1943	6.1943	to the MarCom 3.1948
SC994	Geo W. Kneass, San Francisco	11.1942	24.5.1943	7.1943	to the MarCom 10.1946

SC995	Geo W. Kneass, San Francisco	11.1942	5.6.1943	8.1943	to the MarCom 11.1946
SC996	Island Docks, Kingston	3.1942	7.9.1942	11.1942	USCG 10.1945
SC997	Island Docks, Kingston	4.1942	21.10.1942	12.1942	to the USSR 8.1945 (BO-326)
SC998	Island Docks, Kingston	4.1942	13.11.1942	1.1943	to the MarCom 2.1948
SC999, 8.1945- SCC999	Island Docks, Kingston	4.1942	9.12.1942	5.1943	wrecked 9.10.1945, never repaired
SC1000	Dingle Boat, St. Paul	4.1942	22.10.1942	5.1943	for disposal 7.1947
SC1001	Dingle Boat, St. Paul	5.1942	5.11.1942	3.1943	for disposal 7.1947
SC1002	Dingle Boat, St. Paul	7.1942	3.4.1943	5.1943	to the MarCom 9.1946
SC1003	Fellows & Stewart, Wilmington	4.1942	25.7.1942	12.1942	USCG 11.1945
SC1004	Fellows & Stewart, Wilmington	4.1942	1.8.1942	1.1943	USCG 12.1945
SC1005	Fellows & Stewart, Wilmington	4.1942	15.8.1942	2.1943	to the MarCom 9.1946
SC1006	Fellows & Stewart, Wilmington	4.1942	7.9.1942	5.1943	to the MarCom 3.1946
SC1007	Fellows & Stewart, Wilmington	5.1942	14.11.1942	5.1943	to the USSR 8.1945 (BO-332)
SC1008	Fellows & Stewart, Wilmington	5.1942	19.11.1942	6.1943	to the MarCom 1.1948
SC1009	Fellows & Stewart, Wilmington	7.1942	25.11.1942	6.1943	USCG 4.1946
SC1010	Fellows & Stewart, Wilmington	7.1942	12.12.1942	7.1943	USCG 12.1945
SC1011	Fellows & Stewart, Wilmington	8.1942	16.12.1942	7.1943	to the USSR 8.1945 (BO-327)
SC1012, 8.1945- SCC1012	Fellows & Stewart, Wilmington	9.1942	28.12.1942	8.1943	wrecked 9.10.1945, never repaired
SC1013	Luders Marine, Stamford	3.1942	22.7.1942	9.1942	USCG 10.1945
SC1014	Luders Marine, Stamford	4.1942	26.7.1942	9.1942	for disposal 5.1947
SC1015	Luders Marine, Stamford	5.1942	30.8.1942	10.1942	USCG 10.1945
SC1016	Luders Marine, Stamford	6.1942	4.9.1942	12.1942	USCG 10.1945
SC1017	Luders Marine, Stamford	6.1942	28.10.1942	12.1942	USCG 10.1945
SC1018, 8.1945- SCC1018	Luders Marine, Stamford	7.1942	21.11.1942	1.1943	for disposal 1.1947
SC1019	Luders Marine, Stamford	7.1942	1.12.1942	2.1943	wrecked 22.4.1945
SC1020	Luders Marine, Stamford	8.1942	23.12.1942	5.1943	to the MarCom 1.1948
SC1021	Luders Marine, Stamford	8.1942	1.2.1943	4.1943	to the USSR 6.1945 (BO-312)
SC1022	Luders Marine, Stamford	8.1942	23.3.1943	6.1943	USCG 10.1945
SC1023	Mathis Yacht, Camden	6.1942	28.11.1942	12.1942	USCG 10.1945
SC1024	Mathis Yacht, Camden	6.1942	28.11.1942	12.1942	collision 2.3.1943
SC1025	Mathis Yacht, Camden	8.1942	17.12.1942	1.1943	to the MarCom 3.1948
SC1026	Mathis Yacht, Camden	9.1942	8.1.1943	1.1943	to the MarCom 2.1948
SC1027	Mathis Yacht, Camden	9.1942	26.1.1943	2.1943	USCG 12.1945
SC1028	Mathis Yacht, Camden	10.1942	21.2.1943	3.1943	USCG 1.1946
SC1029	Donovan, Burlington	4.1942	31.8.1942	11.1942	to France 10.1944 (Ch123)
SC1030	Donovan, Burlington	5.1942	31.8.1942	11.1942	to France 10.1944 (Ch136)

SC1031	Peterson Boat, Sturgeon	4.1942	3.10.1942	2.1943	to the USSR 8.1945 (BO-328)
SC1032	Peterson Boat, Sturgeon	5.1942	17.10.1942	2.1943	USCG 11.1945
SC1033	Peterson Boat, Sturgeon	6.1942	12.11.1942	4.1943	USCG 12.1945
SC1034	Peterson Boat, Sturgeon	8.1942	2.1.1943	4.1943	to the MarCom 3.1948
SC1035, 12.1943- PGM3	Peterson Boat, Sturgeon	9.1942	12.4.1943	5.1943	gunboat 12.1943, for disposal 5.1947
SC1036	Peterson Boat, Sturgeon	9.1942	10.5.1943	6.1943	to the MarCom 2.1948
SC1037	Peterson Boat, Sturgeon	10.1942	29.5.1942	7.1943	USCG 1.1946
SC1038	Peterson Boat, Sturgeon	11.1942	12.6.1943	7.1943	USCG 1.1946
SC1039	Rice Bros, E. Boothbay	4.1942	28.7.1942	10.1942	to the MarCom 2.1948
SC1040	Rice Bros, E. Boothbay	4.1942	1.8.1942	10.1942	to the MarCom 2.1948
SC1041	Rice Bros, E. Boothbay	5.1942	13.8.1942	11.1942	to the MarCom 3.1948
SC1042	Rice Bros, E. Boothbay	5.1942	15.8.1942	11.1942	to the MarCom 3.1948
SC1043	Rice Bros, E. Boothbay	8.1942	15.10.1942	12.1942	to France 10.1944 (Ch125)
SC1044	Rice Bros, E. Boothbay	8.1942	17.10.1942	1.1943	to France 11.1944 (Ch126)
SC1045	Rice Bros, E. Boothbay	8.1942	19.11.1942	2.1943	to the MarCom 3.1948
SC1046	Rice Bros, E. Boothbay	8.1942	21.11.1942	3.1943	to the MarCom 3.1948
SC1047	Ventnor, Atlantic City	4.1942	15.1.1943	1.1943	to the MarCom 4.1947
SC1048	Ventnor, Atlantic City	4.1942	12.12.1942	4.1943	to the MarCom 11.1946
SC1049, 8.1945- SCC1049	Ventnor, Atlantic City	5.1942	2.5.1943	6.1943	destroyed 4.12.1945
SC1050	Ventnor, Atlantic City	5.1942	9.5.1943	8.1943	to the MarCom 11.1946
SC1051	Ventnor, Atlantic City	5.1942	19.6.1943	7.1943	to the MarCom 3.1947
SC1052	Ventnor, Atlantic City	5.1942	26.6.1943	9.1943	to the MarCom 10.1946
SC1053, 12.1943- PGM4	Wilmington Boat	4.1942	7.9.1942	3.1943	gunboat 12.1943, for disposal 6.1947
SC1054	Wilmington Boat	4.1942	10.9.1942	4.1943	USCG 2.1946
SC1055	Wilmington Boat	5.1942	10.10.1942	5.1943	USCG 11.1945
SC1056, 12.1943- PGM5	Wilmington Boat	5.1942	11.11.1942	5.1943	gunboat 12.1943, for disposal 5.1947
SC1057	Gulf Marine Ways, Galveston	5.1942	11.11.1942	5.1943	sold 7.1948
SC1058	Gulf Marine Ways, Galveston	5.1942	1.12.1942	6.1943	to the MarCom 9.1946
SC1059	Burger, Manitowoc	5.1942	28.11.1942	3.1943	wrecked 12.12.1944
SC1060	Burger, Manitowoc	7.1942	1.12.1942	4.1943	to the USSR 6.1945 (BO-317)
SC1061	Harris & Parsons, Greenwich	5.1942	26.9.1942	1.1943	to Norway 10.1943 (Vigra)
SC1062	Harris & Parsons, Greenwich	6.1942	23.12.1942	2.1943	USCG 10.1945
SC1063	Victory, Holland	6.1942	28.11.1942	2.1943	USCG 10.1945
SC1064	Victory, Holland	7.1942	16.1.1943	5.1943	USCG 10.1945
SC1065	Perkins & Vaughan, Wickford	5.1942	17.10.1942	12.1942	to the MarCom 2.1948
SC1066, 8.1945- SCC1066	Perkins & Vaughan, Wickford	6.1942	14.11.1942	2.1943	for disposal 5.1947
SC1067	Mathis Yacht, Camden	11.1942	9.3.1943	4.1943	foundered 19.11.1943
SC1068	Mathis Yacht, Camden	12.1942	26.3.1943	4.1943	USCG 2.1946
SC1069	Mathis Yacht, Camden	12.1942	17.4.1943	4.1943	USCG 12.1945

SC1070	Mathis Yacht, Camden	1.1943	3.5.1943	5.1943	USCG 12.1945
SC1071, 12.1943- PGM6	Mathis Yacht, Camden	2.1943	20.5.1943	6.1943	gunboat 12.1943, stricken 2.1946
SC1072, 12.1943- PGM7	Mathis Yacht, Camden	3.1943	17.6.1943	6.1943	gunboat 12.1943, stricken 2.1946
SC1073	Mathis Yacht, Camden	3.1943	30.6.1943	7.1943	to the USSR 8.1943 (BO-206)
SC1074	Mathis Yacht, Camden	4.1943	12.7.1943	7.1943	to the USSR 9.1943 (BO-207)
SC1075	Mathis Yacht, Camden	5.1943	27.7.1943	8.1943	to the USSR 9.1943 (BO-208)
SC1076	Mathis Yacht, Camden	5.1943	12.8.1943	8.1943	to the USSR 9.1943 (BO-209)
SC1266	Quincy Adams, Quincy	7.1942	9.11.1942	2.1943	to the MarCom 4.1948
SC1267	Quincy Adams, Quincy	8.1942	12.12.1942	2.1943	to the Philippines 7.1948 (Alert)
SC1268	Quincy Adams, Quincy	9.1942	24.2.1943	4.1943	to the MarCom 9.1946
SC1269	Quincy Adams, Quincy	9.1942	24.2.1943	4.1943	to the Philippines 7.1948
SC1270	Quincy Adams, Quincy	10.1942	24.2.1943	4.1943	to the MarCom 11.1946
SC1271	Quincy Adams, Quincy	11.1942	31.3.1943	5.1943	to the MarCom 11.1946
SC1272, 8.1945- SCC1272	Quincy Adams, Quincy	12.1942	19.4.1943	6.1943	to the MarCom 10.1947
SC1273, 8.1945- SCC1273	Quincy Adams, Quincy	12.1942	8.5.1943	6.1943	to the MarCom 3.1947
SC1274	Quincy Adams, Quincy	1.1943	22.5.1943	7.1943	to the Philippines 7.1948 (Ilocos Norte)
SC1275	Quincy Adams, Quincy	1.1943	5.6.1943	8.1943	to the Philippines 7.1948
SC1276	Elizabeth City	9.1942	27.10.1942	3.1943	to the MarCom 11.1946
SC1277	Elizabeth City	9.1942	27.10.1942	3.1943	to the MarCom 11.1946
SC1278, 8.1945- SCC1278	Elizabeth City	9.1942	7.12.1942	3.1943	to the Philippines 7.1948
SC1279	Elizabeth City	9.1942	7.12.1942	4.1943	to the MarCom 9.1946
SC1280	Elizabeth City	10.1942	30.12.1942	4.1943	disposed 5.1948
SC1281, 8.1945- SCC1281	Elizabeth City	10.1942	6.2.1943	5.1943	to the MarCom 12.1946
SC1282	Elizabeth City	12.1942	6.2.1943	5.1943	to the MarCom 9.1946
SC1283	Elizabeth City	12.1942	20.2.1943	6.1943	to the USSR 7.1943 (BO-201)
SC1284	Elizabeth City	2.1943	26.3.1943	6.1943	to the USSR 7.1943 (BO-202)
SC1285	Elizabeth City	2.1943	17.4.1943	7.1943	to the USSR 8.1943 (BO-203)
SC1286	Elizabeth City	2.1943	15.5.1943	7.1943	to the USSR 8.1943 (BO-204)
SC1287	Elizabeth City	4.1943	5.6.1943	7.1943	to the USSR 9.1943 (BO-205)
SC1288	W. A. Robinson, Ipswich	7.1942	24.12.1942	2.1943	to Brazil 5.1943 (Jacuí)
SC1289	W. A. Robinson, Ipswich	8.1942	8.2.1943	3.1943	to Brazil 4.1943 (Jundiaí)
SC1290	W. A. Robinson, Ipswich	8.1942	16.3.1943	4.1943	for disposal 6.1947
SC1291	W. A. Robinson, Ipswich	9/1942	30.3.1943	5.1943	to Cuba 6.1947 (Habana)
SC1292	W. A. Robinson, Ipswich	10.1942	17.4.1943	5.1943	to the MarCom 3.1946
SC1293	W. A. Robinson, Ipswich	10.1942	24.4.1943	6.1943	to the MarCom 8.1946
SC1294	W. A. Robinson, Ipswich	12.1942	4.6.1943	7.1943	to the MarCom 9.1947

SC1295	W. A. Robinson, Ipswich	1.1943	23.7.1943	8.1943	to the USSR 6.1945 (BO-320)
SC1296	W. A. Robinson, Ipswich	2.1943	20.8.1943	9.1943	USCG 8.1945
SC1297	W. A. Robinson, Ipswich	3.1943	2.9.1943	10.1943	USCG 10.1945
SC1298, 8.1945- SCC1298	Perkins & Vaughan, Wickford	9.1942	19.3.1943	4.1943	destroyed 6.3.1946
SC1299	Perkins & Vaughan, Wickford	9.1942	10.4.1943	6.1943	to the MarCom 8.1946
SC1300	Perkins & Vaughan, Wickford	9.1942	8.5.1943	7.1943	to the MarCom 3.1948
SC1301	Perkins & Vaughan, Wickford	9.1942	15.5.1943	8.1943	for disposal 8.1947
SC1302	Daytona Beach	8.1942	31.10.1942	3.1943	to the MarCom 10.1946
SC1303	Daytona Beach	9.1942	28.11.1942	5.1943	to the MarCom 9.1946
SC1304	Daytona Beach	9.1942	16.1.1943	6.1943	to the MarCom 10.1946
SC1305	Daytona Beach	9.1942	15.2.1943	8.1943	to the MarCom 1.1946
SC1306, 8.1945- SCC1306	Daytona Beach	10.1942	25.3.1943	9.1943	wrecked 9.10.1945, never repaired
SC1307	Daytona Beach	10.1942	15.4.1943	10.1943	USCG 2.1946
SC1308	Daytona Beach	11.1942	15.5.1943	11.1943	to the MarCom 4.1948
SC1309, 8.1945- SCC1309	Annapolis Yacht	9.1942	26.2.1943	5.1943	Sea Scouts TS 9.1946
SC1310	Annapolis Yacht	9.1942	28.2.1943	5.1943	to the MarCom 9.1946
SC1311, 8.1945- SCC1311	Annapolis Yacht	9.1942	10.4.1943	6.1943	to the MarCom 12.1946
SC1312, 8.1945- SCC1312	Annapolis Yacht	10.1942	10.4.1943	7.1943	to the MarCom 3.1947
SC1313	Annapolis Yacht	10.1942	3.5.1943	7.1943	to the MarCom 9.1945
SC1314, 8.1945- SCC1314	Annapolis Yacht	3.1943	12.6.1943	8.1943	to the MarCom 9.1946
SC1315, 8.1945- SCC1315	Julius Peterson, Nyack	8.1942	3.3.1943	6.1943	to the MarCom 3.1948
SC1316, 8.1945- SCC1316	Julius Peterson, Nyack	8.1942	11.3.1943	6.1943	to the US Army 12.1946
SC1317	Julius Peterson, Nyack	9.1942	20.3.1943	7.1943	to the MarCom 11.1946
SC1318	Julius Peterson, Nyack	9.1942	2.4.1943	8.1943	to the MarCom 11.1946
SC1319	Julius Peterson, Nyack	9.1942	12.4.1943	8.1943	to the MarCom 3.1948
SC1320	Julius Peterson, Nyack	10.1942	17.5.1943	9.1943	to the MarCom 12.1946
SC1321	Harris & Parsons, Greenwich	9.1942	6.2.1943	5.1943	to the MarCom 3.1946
SC1322	Harris & Parsons, Greenwich	9.1942	8.4.1943	6.1943	to the MarCom 1.1948
SC1323, 8.1945- SCC1323	Harris & Parsons, Greenwich	12.1942	15.5.1943	8.1943	to the MarCom 3.1948
SC1324	Harris & Parsons, Greenwich	2.1943	22.7.1943	9.1943	to the USSR 6.1945 (BO-315)
SC1325	Delaware Bay, Leesburg	9.1942	11.2.1943	4.1943	to the MarCom 4.1948
SC1326, 8.1945- SCC1326	Delaware Bay, Leesburg	9.1942	24.2.1943	5.1943	to the MarCom 12.1946
SC1327	Delaware Bay, Leesburg	10.1942	24.3.1943	6.1943	to the MarCom 1.1947
SC1328	Delaware Bay, Leesburg	10.1942	21.4.1943	6.1943	to the MarCom 9.1946
SC1329	Simms Bros, Dorchester	10.1942	19.4.1943	5.1943	USCG 2.1946
SC1330	Simms Bros, Dorchester	10.1942	19.4.1943	5.1943	to the MarCom 9.1947

SC1331	Simms Bros, Dorchester	12.1942	2.6.1943	7.1943	to France 4.1944 (Ch6)
SC1332	Simms Bros, Dorchester	12.1942	17.7.1943	8.1943	to the MarCom 7.1948
SC1333	Thomas Knutson, Halesite	8.1942	24.4.1943	6.1943	to the MarCom 6.1946
SC1334	Thomas Knutson, Halesite	8.1942	8.5.1943	7.1943	to the MarCom 8.1948
SC1335	Thomas Knutson, Halesite	9.1942	5.6.1943	8.1943	to France 11.1943 (Ch52)
SC1336	Thomas Knutson, Halesite	9.1942	22.5.1943	8.1943	to France 11.1943 (Ch51)
SC1337	Thomas Knutson, Halesite	9.1942	19.7.1943	9.1943	to France 12.1943 (Ch71)
SC1338, 8.1945- SCC1338	Thomas Knutson, Halesite	10.1942	7.8.1943	10.1943	to the MarCom 1.1948
SC1339	Thomas Knutson, Halesite	10.1942	21.8.1943	11.1943	USCG 11.1945
SC1340	Thomas Knutson, Halesite	11.1942	18.9.1943	12.1943	USCG 10.1945
SC1341, 8.1945- SCC1341	Rice Bros, E. Boothbay	10.1942	14.1.1943	5.1943	disposed 2.1947
SC1342	Rice Bros, E. Boothbay	10.1942	16.1.1943	8.1943	disposed 7.1946
SC1343	Rice Bros, E. Boothbay	11.1942	20.2.1943	8.1943	disposed 8.1946
SC1344	Rice Bros, E. Boothbay	11.1942	27.3.1943	8.1943	to France 11.1943 (Ch62)
SC1345	Rice Bros, E. Boothbay	1.1943	10.4.1943	9.1943	to France 12.1943 (Ch61)
SC1346	Rice Bros, E. Boothbay	1.1943	29.4.1943	10.1943	to France 1.1944 (Ch72)
SC1347	Fisher, Detroit	2.1943	15.7.1943	9.1943	USCG 11.1945
SC1348	Fisher, Detroit	2.1943	12.8.1943	10.1943	USCG 10.1945
SC1349, 8.1945- SCC1349	Fisher, Detroit	4.1943	11.9.1943	10.1943	destroyed 21.8.1946
SC1350, 8.1945- SCC1350	Fisher, Detroit	4.1943	6.10.1943	11.1943	for disposal 1.1947
SC1351	Vineyard, Milford	9.1942	11.3.1943	4.1943	to Honduras 9.1946 (Sanchez)
SC1352	Vineyard, Milford	9.1942	21.4.1943	6.1943	disposed 10.1946
SC1353	Vineyard, Milford	11.1942	3.6.1943	8.1943	to Honduras 10.1946 (Mella)
SC1354	Vineyard, Milford	12.1942	10.8.1943	9.1943	disposed 11.1946
SC1355	Luders Marine, Stamford	11.1942	12.4.1943	7.1943	USCG 10.1945
SC1356	Luders Marine, Stamford	1.1943	7.6.1943	8.1943	USCG 10.1945
SC1357	Luders Marine, Stamford	2.1943	21.6.1943	8.1943	USCG 10.1945
SC1358	Calderwood, Manchester	10.1942	22.2.1943	4.1943	survey boat 9.1946
SC1359	Calderwood, Manchester	11.1942	3.4.1943	6.1943	to France 8.1944 (Ch5)
SC1360, 8.1945- SCC1360	Calderwood, Manchester	2.1943	22.6.1943	8.1943	disposed 10.1947
SC1361	Calderwood, Manchester	4.1943	24.7.1943	10.1943	USCG 10.1945
SC1362	Peyton, Newport Beach	11.1942	24.4.1943	9.1943	USCG 2.1946
SC1363	Peyton, Newport Beach	11.1942	29.5.1943	9.1943	disposed 1.1946
SC1364	Peyton, Newport Beach	11.1942	10.7.1943	11.1943	to the USSR 8.1945 (BO-331)
SC1365	Peyton, Newport Beach	4.1943	29.9.1943	1.1944	to the USSR 8.1945 (BO-329)
SC1366, 12.1943- PGM8	Wilmington Boat Works	11.1942	1.5.1943	8.1943	gunboat 12.1943, for disposal 5.1947
SC1367	Wilmington Boat Works	11.1942	27.5.1943	9.1943	USCG 1.1946
SC1368	Wilmington Boat Works	11.1942	21.6.1943	10.1943	disposed 1.1948
SC1369	Wilmington Boat Works	12.1942	19.7.1943	11.1943	USCG 7.1948
SC1370	Fellows & Stewart, Wilmington	12.1942	20.5.1943	9.1943	disposed 1.1948
SC1371	Fellows & Stewart, Wilmington	12.1942	22.5.1943	9.1943	disposed 1.1948

SC1372	Fellows & Stewart, Wilmington	12.1942	18.6.1943	11.1943	disposed 2.1948
SC1373	Fellows & Stewart, Wilmington	12.1942	19.6.1943	11.1943	USCG 1.1946
SC1374	Fellows & Stewart, Wilmington	12.1942	5.7.1943	11.1943	disposed 3.1948
SC1375	Fellows & Stewart, Wilmington	12.1942	31.7.1943	11.1943	disposed 1.1948
SC1474, 8.1945- SCC1474	Quincy Adams, Quincy	6.1943	11.1.1944	4.1944	sold 2.1947
SC1475	Quincy Adams, Quincy	6.1943	8.2.1944	4.1944	to the USSR 6.1944 (BO-219)
SC1476	Quincy Adams, Quincy	6.1943	8.3.1944	5.1944	to the USSR 7.1944 (BO-223)
SC1477	Quincy Adams, Quincy	7.1943	22.3.1944	6.1944	to the USSR 7.1944 (BO-230)
SC1478	Quincy Adams, Quincy	7.1943	25.4.1944	7.1944	to the USSR 9.1944 (BO-238)
SC1479	Quincy Adams, Quincy	8.1943	5.6.1944	8.1944	to the USSR 10.1944 (BO-244)
SC1480	Rice Bros, E. Boothbay	4.1943	1.10.1943	4.1944	to the USSR 5.1944 (BO-214)
SC1481	Rice Bros, E. Boothbay	4.1943	16.10.1943	5.1944	to the USSR 6.1944 (BO-221)
SC1482	Rice Bros, E. Boothbay	5.1943	14.12.1943	6.1944	to the USSR 8.1944 (BO-232)
SC1483	Rice Bros, E. Boothbay	5.1943	16.12.1943	7.1944	to the USSR 9.1944 (BO-239)
SC1484	Daytona Beach	7.1943	27.10.1943	4.1944	to the USSR 5.1944 (BO-213)
SC1485	Daytona Beach	7.1943	30.11.1943	5.1944	to the USSR 7.1944 (BO-229)
SC1486	Daytona Beach	8.1943	15.1.1944	7.1944	to the USSR 8.1944 (BO-235)
SC1487	Daytona Beach	9.1943	11.3.1944	9.1944	to the USSR 10.1944 (BO-245)
SC1488	Elizabeth City	7.1943	24.8.1943	4.1944	to the USSR 5.1944 (BO-216)
SC1489	Elizabeth City	8.1943	25.9.1943	4.1944	to the USSR 5.1944 (BO-217)
SC1490	Elizabeth City	8.1943	16.10.1943	5.1944	to the USSR 6.1944 (BO-220)
SC1491	Elizabeth City	8.1943	30.10.1943	7.1944	to the USSR 8.1944 (BO-237)
SC1492	Simms Bros, Dorchester	6.1943	8.12.1943	4.1944	to the USSR 6.1944 (BO-218)
SC1493	Simms Bros, Dorchester	6.1943	22.2.1943	6.1944	to the USSR 7.1944 (BO-231)
SC1494	Simms Bros, Dorchester	6.1943	-	-	cancelled 9.1943
SC1495	Simms Bros, Dorchester	6.1943	-	-	cancelled 9.1943
SC1496	Vineyard, Milford	6.1943	1.12.1943	4.1944	to the USSR 5.1944 (BO-215)
SC1497	Vineyard, Milford	8.1943	4.5.1944	7.1944	to the USSR 8.1944 (BO-236)

SC1498	Thomas Knutson, Halesite	8.1943	21.3.1944	5.1944	to the USSR 6.1944 (BO-222)
SC1499	Thomas Knutson, Halesite	9.1943	27.4.1944	8.1944	to the USSR 9.1944 (BO-242)
SC1502	Calderwood, Manchester	7.1943	27.11.1943	6.1944	to the USSR 7.1944 (BO-227)
SC1503	Calderwood, Manchester	8.1943	22.5.1944	8.1944	to the USSR 9.1944 (BO-243)
SC1504	Donovan, Burlington	7.1943	16.4.1944	5.1944	to the USSR 7.1944 (BO-228)
SC1505	Donovan, Burlington	7.1943	30.4.1944	6.1944	to the USSR 8.1944 (BO-234)
SC1506	Donovan, Burlington	8.1943	14.5.1944	7.1944	to the USSR 9.1944 (BO-241)
SC1507	Harris & Parsons, Greenwich	7.1943	26.1.1944	5.1944	to the USSR 7.1944 (BO-224)
SC1508	Harris & Parsons, Greenwich	8.1943	8.5.1944	7.1944	to the USSR 9.1944 (BO-240)
SC1510	Perkins & Vaughan, Wickford	7.1943	9.12.1943	5.1944	to the USSR 7.1944 (BO-226)
SC1511	Perkins & Vaughan, Wickford	7.1943	3.4.1944	7.1944	to the USSR 8.1944 (BO-233)
SC1512	Perkins & Vaughan, Wickford	7.1943	15.6.1944	9.1944	to the USSR 10.1944 (BO-246)
SC1517	Peterson Boat, Sturgeon	8.1943	12.4.1944	6.1944	to the USSR 7.1944 (BO-225)

SC677 1943

98-121 / 117-136 t, 33.8 x 5.2-5.5 x 1.9-2.0 m, 2 General Motors diesels, 1000 or 2400 hp, 16 or 21 kts, 18 t diesel oil, 1500 nm (12 kts), complement 27; 1 x 1 – 76/23 Mk 14 (to 1942-1943) or 1 x 1 – 76/50 Mk 10/18 (built 1942-1943) or 1 x 1 – 40/56 Bofors (from 1943-1944), 2 (built 1942-1943) or 3 (from 1942-1943) x 1 – 20/70 Oerlikon, 2 x 1 -12.7 MG (to 1942), 2 x 4 Mousetrap ASWRL (from 1942), 2 DCT (14) (to 1942-1943) or (2 DCT, 1 DCR (34) (built 1942-1943) or (2 DCT, 2 DCR (34)) (from 1943-1944); SF or SO or SU or SCR-517A or SW-1C radar

(not on all), QC sonar.
SC497, 498, 501-505, 513-515, 518, 520-522, 527, 528, 530-535, 628, 629, 636, 637, 639-641, 648, 650, 654, 667-669, 676-681, 688, 691-693, 696-708, 712, 713, 722-750, 760, 761, 768, 769, 978, 980-984, 990-995, 1000-1002, 1039-1052, 1057, 1058, 1266-1282, 1290-1293, 1298-1323, 1325, 1326, 1328-1330, 1332-1334, 1337, 1341-1344, 1351-1354, 1358-1361, 1480-1560 (totally 231 boats): 1000 hp, 16 kts.
SC499, 500, 507, 508, 511, 512, 536-541, 630-635, 642-647, 652, 653, 656-665, 670-675, 682-687, 710, 711, 714-718, 720, 721, 752-759, 772-775, 985-989, 996-999, 1003-1023, 1025-1038, 1053-1056, 1059-1073, 1075, 1076, 1283-1287, 1294-1297, 1324, 1335, 1338-1340, 1347-1350, 1355-1357, 1362-1375, 1474-1479, 1507-1517 (totally 204 boats): 2400 hp, 21 kts.
SC506, 516, 517, 519, 524-526, 529, 638, 649, 651, 655, 666, 689, 690, 694, 695, 709, 719, 751, 762-767, 770, 771, 977, 979, 1024, 1074, 1288, 1289, 1327, 1331, 1336, 1345, 1346: 1000 or 2400 hp.

During the First World War, a large number of 110-ft submarine chasers were built in the USA. Secretary of the Navy Roosevelt (the future President) participated in the development of the building of this huge series on small shipyards. When in 1937 the main characteristics of an ASW ship intended for patrolling coastal areas and on fleet anchorages were determined, Roosevelt insisted

SC1302 1943

on returning to a twenty-year-old design, which during building was criticized for the small displacement and insufficient endurance. Perhaps the only concessions to technical progress were the choice of diesels as the main engines and the installation of sonar.

Three experimental chasers of various designs (SC449, SC450 and SC453) were built under the FY38 Program. The third, designed by the Navy, formed the basis of serial-built chasers. She differed from the WWI-era predecessor by increased breadth and stronger hull with steel framing.

Chasers differed in the armament structure. Only a few lead boats received design armament, since 1942, the Mousetrap was fitted, and 12.7-mm MGs were replaced by 20-mm Oerlikons; since 1943, newly built ships received 76-mm/50 guns instead of the obsolete 76-mm/23 guns, and ASW armament was strengthened by two DCTs. In 1944, the replacement of 76-mm/23 guns with 40-mm Bofors began, and by the next year only 4 chasers had old short-barreled guns. The shortage of diesels of suitable power led to the fact that 231 chasers received 500-hp diesels instead of 1200-hp ones. The maximum speed of such boats was limited to 16 kts. SC1500 and 1501 (Thomas Knutson, Halesite), SC1509 (Harris & Parsons, Greenwich), SC1513-1516 (Perkins & Vaughan, Wickford) and SC1518-1520 (Peterson Boat, Sturgeon Bay) were cancelled in September 1943.

In 1944 eight chasers were converted to motor gunboats PGM1-8 for operations against Japanese boats. After rearming their armament consisted of single 76-mm/23 gun and single 40-mm/56 Bofors or 2 single 40-mm/56 Bofors; 4 twin 12.7-mm MGs, 1 single 60-mm mortar and multi-barreled 83-mm Bazooka.

SC1297 1944

In 1944 35 SCs were converted to command-and-control ships of amphibious forces SC(C).
1942, earlier boats were re-armed as newly built ones.
1942-1943, earlier boats were re-armed as newly built ones.
12.1943, *SC644, 757, 1035, 1053, 1056, 1071, 1072* and *1366* were converted to motor gunboats *PGM1-8*, armed with: (1 x 1 - 76/23 Mk 14, 1 x 1 - 40/56 Bofors) or 2 x 1 - 40/56 Bofors, 4 x 2 - 12.7 MG, 1 x 1 - 60/12 M19 mortar, 1 x 4 – 57/27 M9A1 Bazooka grenade launcher.
1943-1944, earlier boats were re-armed as newly built ones.
1944, 35 units were converted to SC(C) amphibious command ships: - 2 x 1 - 20/70, 2 DCT, 2 DCR.
SC694 and *SC696* were sunk by German aircraft 23.8.1943. *SC744* was sunk by kamikaze 27.11.1944.
SC521 (10.7.1945), *SC632* (16.9.1945), *SC709* (21.1.1943), *SC740* (17.6.1943), *SC751* (22.6.1943), *SC984* (9.4.1944), *SC1019* (22.4.1945), *SC1024* (2.3.1943), *SC1059* (12.12.1944), *SC1067* (19.11.1943) were lost due to navigational incidents. *SC700* (10.3.1944) was destroyed by fire.

PC1466 class submarine chasers

Leblanc SB, Weymouth, Canada: PC1466-1473 (1943-SC1466-1473) (1942/1942)
Lost: SC1470 (1943)
Transferred: Mexico – SC1466, 1469, 1471 (1943)
Discarded: SC1467 (1946), SC1468, 1472, 1473 (1948)
76 / 86 t, 34.8 x 5.6 x 1.5 m, 2 Hall-Scott petrol engines, 1120 hp, 18 kts, complement 28; 1 x 1 – 76/23 Mk 14, 2 x 1 – 20/70 Oerlikon, 2 x 4 Mousetrap ASWRL, 2 DCT, 2

SC1467 1943

DCR (18); Type 134 sonar.
'Fairmile B' class motor launches, built under reverse Lend-Lease.
1943, all: - 1 x 1 – 76/23; + 1 x 1 – 76/50 Mk 18/20.

PTC1 class motorboat submarine chasers

ELCO, Bayonne: PTC1-12 (1941)
Transferred: United Kingdom – PTC1-12 (1941)
32 / 40 t, 21.3 x 6.1 x 1.4 m, 3 petrol engines, 3600 hp, 45 kts, complement 17; 2 x 2 – 12.7 MG, 2 DCT, 2 DCR (24).

PTC boats were built in MTB hulls for ASW service. Wooden hulls, 70-ft ELCO design. Additional identical PTC13-36 (built by ELCO), PTC37-66 (built by Trumpy, Gloucester City), and RPC1-50 (built by Miami SB) were built for the Soviet Union.

Former USCG 75-ft cutters

Lake Union, Seattle: YP7 (ex-CG272), YP16 (ex-CG267), YP17 (ex-CG275), YP37 (ex-CG273), YP38 (ex-CG269), YP39 (ex-CG276) (1925)
Portsmouth N Yd: YP8 (ex-CG191) (1925)
Mathis Yacht, Camden: YP9 (ex-CG105), YP23 (ex-CG286), YP24 (ex-CG106), YP36 (ex-CG280), YP48 (ex-CG103), YP50 (ex-CG278), YP57 (ex-CG112), YP67 (ex-CG100) (1925)
Chance Marine, Annapolis: YP10 (ex-CG194), YP11 (ex-CG196), YP21 (ex-CG199) (1925)
Kingston Dry Dock: YP12 (ex-CG204), YP32 (ex-CG208), YP59 (ex-CG203), YP60 (ex-CG207) (1925)
Defoe, Bay City: YP13 (ex-CG123) (1925)
Southern SY, Newport News: YP14 (ex-CG181), YP49 (ex-CG182), YP58 (ex-CG183) (1925)

Dachel-Carter, Benton Harbor: YP15 (ex-CG149), YP25 (ex-CG142), YP46 (ex-CG146) (1925)
Rice Bros, East Boothbay: YP19 (ex-CG177), YP29 (ex-CG116), YP40 (ex-CG175) (1925)
New York Yacht, Launch & Engine, Morris Heights: YP20 (ex-CG163), YP31 (ex-CG167), YP52 (ex-CG160), YP54 (ex-CG168), YP55 (ex-CG169) (1925)
Vinyard, Milford: YP22 (ex-CG221), YP35 (ex-CG222) (1925)
Gibbs Gas Engine, Jacksonville: YP26 (ex-CG252), YP27 (ex-CG301) (1925)
Colonna's SY, Norfolk: YP28 (ex-CG225) (1925)
A. W. De Young, Alameda: YP33 (ex-CG253), YP34 (ex-CG258)1925)
Crowninshield SB, Fall River: YP45 (ex-CG133) (1925)
Soule Steel, Freeport: YP47 (ex-CG152)
Losses: YP16, 26 (1942), YP47 (1943)
Discarding: YP50 (1940), YP7, 10, 13 (1941), YP49 (1943), YP11 (1944), YP33, 37, 39, 55 (1945)
37 (trials) t, 22.9 x 4.2 x 1.2 m, 1 petrol engine, 400 hp, 13.5 kts; 1 x 1 – 37/50 Mk 4.
Former coastal USCG patrol boats, transferred to the USN in 1933-1934.
1940s, all survived: - 1 x 1 - 37/50; + 1 x 1 - 20/70 Oerlikon, 2 DCR

Former USCG CORWIN class cutters

(ex-Mahoning)	YP41	Defoe, Bay City	1926	1926	1926	sold 1946
(ex-Gallatin)	YP42	Defoe, Bay City	1926	1926	1926	sold 12.1946
(ex-Naugatuck)	YP56	Defoe, Bay City	1926	1926	1926	sold 1947
(ex-Dallas)	YP61	Defoe, Bay City	1925	1925	10.1925	sold 5.1946
(ex-Corwin)	YP62	Defoe, Bay City	1925	1925	1925	sold 5.1946
(ex-Dexter)	YP63	Defoe, Bay City	1925	1925	1925	sold 7.1946
(ex-Eagle)	YP64	Defoe, Bay City	1925	1925	11.1925	sold 1946

210 (std) t, 30.4 x 7.0 x 1.4 m, 2 Grey diesels, 300 hp, 12 kts, complement 15; 1 x 1 – 76/23 Mk 9/13.
Former 100-ft USCG patrol cutters, transferred to the USN in 1935-1936. One more craft, Patriot, was transferred to the USN in March 1938 as YP69 (see Coast Guard).

75-ft patrol boats

Hutchinson Boat Wks, Alexandria Bay: YP78, 79 (1941), YP242-246 (1942), YP583-591 (1943)
Elscot Boat: YP80-82 (1941), YP99 (1942)
Discarded: YP78-82, 246, 583 (1946), YP588 (1972), YP584, 585 (1974), YP586 (1975), YP589, 590 (1976),
YP587 (1977), YP591 (1978)
Transferred: Peru – YP99, 242-245 (1958)
51 (std) t, 22.9 x 4.9 m, 2 diesels, 400 hp.
Small patrol boats, used for training.

YP600 class patrol boats

Bristol Yachts, South Bristol: YP600, 601 (1943)
Discarded: YP600, 601 (1946)
92 (std) t, 23.8 m.
Small patrol craft.

128-ft patrol craft

YP617	Harbor BB, Terminal Island	1945	stricken 1948
YP618	Harbor BB, Terminal Island	1945	stricken 1949
YP619	Fulton, Antioch	1945	stricken 1949
YP620	Fulton, Antioch	1945	stricken 1949
YP621	Hodgson-Greene, Long Beach	1945	stricken 1949
YP622	Hodgson-Greene, Long Beach	1945	stricken 1948
YP623	Astoria Marine	1945	stricken 1940s
YP624	Astoria Marine	1945	destroyed 1946
YP625	Tacoma Boat	1945	stricken 1949
YP626	Tacoma Boat	1945	stricken 1949
YP627	Western BB, Tacoma	1945	stricken 1949
YP628	Western BB, Tacoma	1945	stricken 1949
YP629	Seattle SB & DD	1945	auxiliary ~1949
YP630	Seattle SB & DD	1945	stricken 1949
YP631	Sagstad, Seattle	1945	stricken 1949
YP632	Sagstad, Seattle	1945	stricken 1948
YP633	Chilman, Hoquiam	1945	stricken 1948
YP634	Chilman, Hoquiam	1945	stricken 1949
YP635	Ballard, Seattle	1945	stricken 1948
YP636	Ballard, Seattle	1945	lost 1946
YP637	Martinac, Seattle	1945	stricken 1949
YP638	Martinac, Seattle	1945	stricken 1948
YP639	South Coast SB, Newport Beach	1945	stricken 1949
YP640	South Coast SB, Newport Beach	1945	stricken 1948
YP641	Bellingham Iron Wks	1945	stricken 1949
YP642	Bellingham Iron Wks	1945	stricken 1949
YP643	Everett Marine Wks	1945	stricken 1949
YP644	Everett Marine Wks	1945	stricken 1949
YP645	Colberg, Stockton	1945	stricken 1949
YP646	Colberg, Stockton	1945	stricken 1948

403 t, 39.0 x 9.3 x 4.3 m, 1 diesel, 560 hp, complement 25.

Patrol craft, used for training.

Patrol boats, converted from civilan vessels

100-500t displacement
Requisitioned: 1 (1940), 26 (1941), 80 (1942), 1 (1943)

Lost: 3 (1942), 7 (1943), 2 (1944), 2 (1945)
Discarded: 2 (1942), 14 (1944), 7 (1945), 71 (post-war)

MINE WARFARE SHIPS

BALTIMORE minelayer

Baltimore	CM1	Cramp, Philadelphia	5.5.1887	6.10.1888	7.1.1890	stricken 10.1937

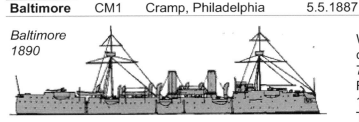

Baltimore 1890

4413 / 5436 t, 102.1 x 14.8 x 5.9 m, 2 THE, 8 Babcock &

Wilcox, 10750 hp, 19 kts, 1144 t coal, 5000 nm (10 kts), complement 386; Steel, deck 64 with 102mm slopes, CT 76; 4 x 1 – 127/51 Mk 8, 2 x 1 – 76/50 Mk 10, 180 mines. Former protected cruiser converted to the minelayer in 1914.
The protective deck was 64-mm in the flat with 102-mm slopes amidships. The CT had 76-mm sides.

TERROR minelayer

Terror	CM5	Philadelphia N Yd	9.1940	6.6.1941	7.1942	stricken 11.1970

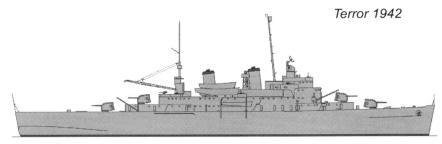

Terror 1942

Terror

5875 / 8640 t, 138.6 x 18.3 x 6.0 m, 2 sets General Electric geared steam turbines, 4 boilers, 11000 hp, 20 kts, 1834 t oil, 10000 nm (15 kts), complement 481; 4 x 1 – 127/38 Mk 12, 4 x 4 – 28/75 Mk 1, 900 mines; SC, SG, Mk 4 radars.

A unique USN purpose-built minelaying ship. In the early design stages, a 25-kt version was considered, but a slower but much more capacious version was preferred.

The mine deck was completely covered, six mine rails were designed to carry 648 mines, another 548 mines were stored on the lower decks. Two elevators were used to handle them. Designed mine capacity was almost 1200 pieces, but with new mines, their number ranged from 800 to 875.

Although the ship did not have armor, damage resistance was ensured by cruiser standards: the double bottom turned into a double side, and on two following minelayers of modified design (future LSV *Catskill* and *Ozark*), the armor deck was provided.

1942-1943: + 14 x 1 – 20/70 Oerlikon.
1943-1944: - 4 x 4 - 28/75; + 4 x 4 - 40/56 Bofors.
30.4.1945 *Terror* was badly damaged by kamikaze off Okinawa.

CHIMO class coastal minelayers

Chimo (ex-Col. Charles W. Bundy)	ACM1	Marietta, Point Pleasant	1943	1943	(1943) / 4.1944	to War Shipping Adm. 9.1948
Planter (ex-Col. George Ricker)	ACM2	Marietta, Point Pleasant	4.1941	1942	(1942) / 4.1944	stricken 12.1947
Barricade (ex-Col. John Storey)	ACM3	Marietta, Point Pleasant	10.1941	11.1942	(1942) / 4.1944	USCG auxiliary 6.1946

Barbican (ex-Col. George Armistead)	ACM5	Marietta, Point Pleasant	1941	1942	(1942) / 3.1945	USCG auxiliary 6.1946
Bastion (ex-Col. Henry J. Hunt)	ACM6	Marietta, Point Pleasant	1941	1942	(1942) / 4.1945	USCG auxiliary 6.1946
Obstructor (ex-1st Lt. William G. Sylvester)	ACM7	Marietta, Point Pleasant	1941	1942	(1942) / 4.1945	USCG auxiliary 6.1946
Picket (ex-Gen. Henry Knox)	ACM8	Marietta, Point Pleasant	1941	1942	(1942) / 3.1945	USCG auxiliary 6.1946
Trapper (ex-MG Arthur Murray)	ACM9	Marietta, Point Pleasant	1943	1943	(1944) / 3.1945	USCG auxiliary 6.1946

880 / 1320 t, 57.4 x 11.3 x 3.8 m, 2 Skinner Uniflow QEV, 2 Combustion Engineering boilers, 1200 hp, 12.5 kts, complement 69; 1 x 1 – 40/56 Bofors, 4 x 1 – 20/70 Oerlikon, mines; SC or SO radar.

Small coastal minelayers transferred to the USN by the US Army. 6 more ships were transferred by the Army to the Navy in 1950-1951, two more spent all service time

Chimo 1945

under the Army flag.

minelayers converted from merchant vessels

Aroostok (ex-Bunker Hill)	CM3	1907 / 12.1917	4200	120.4 x 15.9 x 4.9	20	5 x 1 – 76/50, 300 mines	cargo ship 5.1941
Oglala (ex-Shawmut, ex-Massachusetts)	CM4	1907 / 7.12.1917	4200	120.4 x 15.9 x 4.9	20	5 x 1 – 76/50, 300 mines	sunk 7.12.1941
Keokuk (ex-Columbia Heights)	CM8	1914 / 5.1942	6150	107.6 x 17.4 x 5.2	12	3 x 1 - 76/50, 2 x 2 - 40, mines	net cargo ship 11.1943
Salem (ex-Joseph R. Parrott), 8.1945- **Shawmut**	CM11	1916 / 8.1942	5300	106.7 x 17.4 x 4.6	12	3 x 1 - 76/50, 19 - 20, mines	stricken 1.1946
Weehawken (ex-Estrada Palma)	CM12	1920 / 9.1942	6525	106.7 x 17.4 x 5.2	12	3 x 1 - 76/50, 4 - 20, mines	wrecked 9.10.1945, never repaired
Wassuc (ex-Yale)	CMc3	1924 / 5.1941	1830	70.3 x 12.8 x 3.1	13	2 x 1 - 76/50, mines	stricken 11.1945
Monadnock (ex-Cavalier)	CMc4, 5.1942- CM9, 7.1945- ACM10	1938 / 12.1941	3110	89.0 x 14.9 x 5.0	17.5	2 x 1 - 76/50, 2 x 2 - 40, 10 x 1 - 20, 2 DCR, mines	stricken 7.1946
Miantonomah (ex-Quaker)	CMc5, 5.1942- CM10	1938 / 11.1941	3110	89.0 x 14.8 x 5.0	17.5	2 x 1 - 76/50, 2 x 2 - 40, 10 x 1 - 20, 2 DCR, mines	sunk 25.7.1944

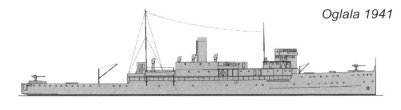

Oglala 1941

Weehawken 1943

Numbers written in *Italic* indicate displacement
Former merchant vessels, converted to minelayers (CM), coastal minelayers (CMc) and auxiliary minelayers (ACM).
7.12.1941 *Oglala* was sunk in Pearl Harbor by Japanese aircraft, in 1942 she was salvaged and commissioned again in May 1943 as internal combustion engine repair ship. *Miantonomah* was mined off Le Havre 25.7.1944.

'BIRD' class minesweepers

Owl	AM2	Todd SB, Brooklyn	10.1917	4.3.1918	7.1918	tug 6.1942
Robin	AM3	Todd SB, Brooklyn	3.1918	17.6.1918	8.1918	tug 6.1942
Swallow	AM4	Todd SB, Brooklyn	3.1917	4.7.1918	10.1918	wrecked 19.2.1938
Tanager	AM5	Staten Is SB, Port Richmond	9.1917	2.3.1918	6.1918	sunk 4.5.1942
Oriole	AM7	Staten Is SB, Port Richmond	3.1918	3.7.1918	11.1918	tug 6.1942
Finch	AM9	Standard SB, Shooters Is	8.1917	30.3.1918	9.1918	sunk 6.5.1942, captured by Japanese (Dai 103-go)
Turkey	AM13	Chester SB	8.1917	30.4.1918	12.1918	tug 6.1942
Woodcock	AM14	Chester SB	10.1917	12.5.1918	2.1919	tug 6.1942
Quail	AM15	Chester SB	5.1918	6.10.1918	4.1919	sunk 6.5.1942
Partridge	AM16	Chester SB	5.1918	15.10.1918	6.1919	tug 6.1942
Eider	AM17	Pusey & Jones, Wilmington	9.1917	26.5.1918	1.1919	gate vessel 10.1940
Bobolink	AM20	Baltimore SB	10.1917	15.6.1918	1.1919	tug 6.1942
Lark	AM21	Baltimore SB	3.1918	6.8.1918	4.1919	tug 3.1944
Brant	AM24	Sun SB, Chester	12.1917	30.5.1918	9.1918	tug 6.1942
Kingfisher	AM25	Puget Sound N Yd, Bremerton	12.1917	30.3.1918	5.1918	tug 6.1942
Rail	AM26	Puget Sound N Yd, Bremerton	12.1917	25.4.1918	6.1918	tug 6.1942
Seagull	AM30	Gas Engine & Power Co, Morris Heights	6.1918	24.12.1918	3.1919	tug 6.1942
Tern	AM31	Gas Engine & Power Co, Morris Heights	9.1918	22.3.1919	5.1919	tug 6.1942
Penguin	AM33	New Jersey DD & T Co, Gloucester City	11.1918	12.6.1919	11.1919	sunk 8.12.1941
Whippoorwill	AM35	Alabama SB & DD Co, Mobile	12.1917	4.7.1919	4.1919	tug 3.1944
Bittern	AM36	Alabama SB & DD Co, Mobile	12.1917	15.2.1919	5.1919	sunk 10.12.1941
Cormorant	AM40	Todd SB, Brooklyn	9.1918	5.2.1919	5.1919	tug 6.1942
Grebe	AM43	Staten Is SB, Port Richmond	5.1918	17.12.1918	5.1919	tug 6.1942
Peacock	AM46	Staten Is SB, Port Richmond	8.1918	8.4.1919	12.1919	collision 24.8.1940
Vireo	AM52	Philadelphia N Yd	11.1918	26.5.1919	10.1919	tug 6.1942
Warbler	AM53	Philadelphia N Yd	4.1919	30.7.1919	12.1919	rescue vessel 9.1941
Willet	AM54	Philadelphia N Yd	5.1919	11.9.1919	1.1920	rescue vessel 9.1941

Owl 1918

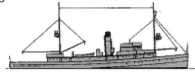

950 / 1400 t, 57.6 x 10.8 x 3.8 m, 1 VTE, 2 Babcock & Wilcox boilers, 1400 hp, 13.5 kts, coal, 6850 nm (8 kts), complement 85; 2 x 1 – 76/50 Mk 3/5/6, 2 x 1 – 7.6 MG, sweeps, mines.

Multipurpose seagoing ships that could be used for minesweeping, patrolling, towing and SAR duties. 1916 design.
1942-1943, all survived: + 4 x 1 - 20/70 Oerlikon, SO or SU radar
Swallow ran aground at Kanaga Island (Aleutian) 19.2.1938. *Peacock* collided with Norwegian s/s *Hindonger* 24.8.1940. *Penguin* 8.12.1941 foundered in Guam harbor after being damaged by Japanese aircraft. *Bittern* 10.12.1941 was

damaged by Japanese aircraft and 8.4.1942 scuttled off Corregidor. *Tanager* 4.5.1942 was scuttled at Manila. *Finch* 6.5.1942 was sunk at Corregidor (according to other sources, 10.4.1942 she was lost off coast of the Philippines), salvaged by Japanese, repaired and commissioned by the IJN in April 1943 as patrol ship *No.103*; she was sunk 12.1.1945 by US aircraft. *Quail* 6.5.1942 was scuttled at Corregidor. *Gannet* 7.6.1942 off Bermuda was sunk by German submarine *U653*.

RAVEN and AUK classes minesweepers

Raven subclass						
Raven	AM55	Norfolk N Yd, Portsmouth	6.1939	24.8.1940	11.1940	stricken 5.1967
Osprey	AM56	Norfolk N Yd, Portsmouth	6.1939	24.8.1940	11.1940	sunk 5.6.1944
Auk subclass						
Auk	AM57	Norfolk N Yd, Portsmouth	4.1941	26.8.1941	1.1942	stricken 8.1956
Broadbill	AM58	Defoe, Bay City	7.1941	21.5.1942	10.1942	stricken 7.1972
Chickadee	AM59	Defoe, Bay City	8.1941	20.7.1942	11.1942	to Uruguay 8.1966 (Comandante Pedro Campbell)
Nuthatch	AM60	Defoe, Bay City	5.1942	16.9.1942	11.1942	stricken 12.1966
Pheasant	AM61	Defoe, Bay City	7.1942	24.10.1942	12.1942	stricken 12.1966
Sheldrake	AM62	General Engineering, Alameda	6.1941	12.2.1942	10.1942	survey ship 4.1952
Skylark	AM63	General Engineering, Alameda	7.1941	12.3.1942	11.1942	sunk 28.3.1945
Starling	AM64	General Engineering, Alameda	7.1941	11.4.1942	12.1942	stricken 7.1972
Swallow	AM65	General Engineering, Alameda	7.1941	6.5.1942	1.1943	sunk 22.4.1945
Heed	AM100	General Engineering, Alameda	2.1942	19.6.1942	2.1943	stricken 3.1967
Herald	AM101	General Engineering, Alameda	3.1942	4.7.1942	3.1943	stricken 7.1972
Motive	AM102	General Engineering, Alameda	4.1942	17.8.1942	4.1943	stricken 12.1966
Oracle	AM103	General Engineering, Alameda	5.1942	30.9.1942	5.1943	stricken 12.1966
Pilot	AM104	Pennsylvania SY, Beaumont	10.1941	5.7.1942	2.1943	stricken 7.1972
Pioneer	AM105	Pennsylvania SY, Beaumont	10.1941	26.7.1942	2.1943	stricken 7.1972
Portent	AM106	Pennsylvania SY, Beaumont	11.1941	16.8.1942	4.1943	sunk 22.1.1944
Prevail	AM107	Pennsylvania SY, Beaumont	11.1941	13.9.1942	4.1943	survey ship 4.1952
Pursuit	AM108	Winslow Marine	11.1941	12.6.1942	4.1943	survey ship 8.1951
Requisite	AM109	Winslow Marine	11.1941	25.7.1942	6.1943	survey ship 8.1951
Revenge *(ex-Right)*	AM110	Winslow Marine	6.1942	7.11.1942	7.1943	stricken 11.1966
Sage	AM111	Winslow Marine	7.1942	21.11.1942	8.1943	stricken 7.1972
Seer	AM112	American SB, Lorain	11.1941	23.5.1942	10.1942	to Norway 12.1962 (Uller)
Sentinel	AM113	American SB, Lorain	11.1941	23.5.1942	11.1942	sunk 12.7.1943

Staff	AM114	American SB, Lorain	11.1941	17.6.1942	11.1942	stricken 3.1967
Skill	AM115	American SB, Lorain	11.1941	22.6.1942	11.1942	sunk 25.9.1943
Speed	AM116	American SB, Cleveland	11.1941	18.4.1942	10.1942	to South Korea 11.1967 (Suncheon)
Strive	AM117	American SB, Cleveland	11.1941	16.5.1942	10.1942	to Norway 10.1959 (Gor)
Steady	AM118	American SB, Cleveland	11.1941	6.6.1942	11.1942	stricken 2.1968
Sustain	AM119	American SB, Cleveland	11.1941	23.6.1942	11.1942	to Norway 10.1959 (Tyr)
Sway	AM120	John H. Mathis, Camden	11.1941	29.9.1942	7.1943	stricken 7.1972
Swerve	AM121	John H. Mathis, Camden	5.1942	25.2.1943	1.1944	sunk 9.7.1944
Swift	AM122	John H. Mathis, Camden	6.1942	5.12.1942	12.1943	stricken 7.1972
Symbol	AM123	Savannah Machine & Foundry Co.	11.1941	2.7.1942	12.1942	stricken 7.1972
Threat	AM124	Savannah Machine & Foundry Co.	12.1941	15.8.1942	3.1943	stricken 7.1972
Tide	AM125	Savannah Machine & Foundry Co.	3.1942	7.9.1942	5.1943	sunk 7.6.1944
Token	AM126	Gulf SB, Madisonville	7.1941	28.3.1942	12.1942	stricken 12.1966
Tumult	AM127	Gulf SB, Madisonville	7.1941	19.4.1942	2.1943	stricken 5.1967
Velocity	AM128	Gulf SB, Madisonville	7.1941	15.4.1942	4.1943	stricken 7.1972
Vital	AM129	Gulf SB, Madisonville	1.1942	7.9.1942	(5.1943)	to the UK 5.1943 (Strenuous)
Usage	AM130	Gulf SB, Madisonville	1.1942	4.10.1942	(6.1943)	to the UK 6.1943 (Tourmaline)
Zeal	AM131	Gulf SB, Madisonville	1.1942	15.9.1942	7.1943	stricken 12.1966
Champion (ex-Akbar)	AM314	General Engineering, Alameda	7.1942	12.12.1942	9.1943	stricken 7.1972
Chief (ex-Alice)	AM315	General Engineering, Alameda	7.1942	5.1.1943	10.1943	stricken 7.1972
Competent (ex-Amelie)	AM316	General Engineering, Alameda	8.1942	30.1.1943	11.1943	stricken 7.1972
Defense (ex-Amity)	AM317	General Engineering, Alameda	10.1942	18.2.1943	1.1944	stricken 7.1972
Devastator (ex-Augusta)	AM318	General Engineering, Alameda	12.1942	19.4.1943	1.1944	stricken 7.1972
Gladiator (ex-Blaze)	AM319	General Engineering, Alameda	1.1943	1.5.1943	2.1944	stricken 7.1972
Impeccable (ex-Brutus)	AM320	General Engineering, Alameda	2.1943	21.5.1943	4.1944	stricken 7.1972
Overseer (ex-Elfreda)	AM321	Associated, Seattle	9.1942	25.1.1943	(12.1943)	to the UK 12.1943 (Elfreda)
Spear (ex-Errant)	AM322	Associated, Seattle	10.1942	25.2.1943	12.1943	stricken 7.1972
Triumph (ex-Espoir)	AM323	Associated, Seattle	10.1942	25.2.1943	2.1944	to Norway 1.1961 (Brage)
Vigilance (ex-Exploit)	AM324	Associated, Seattle	11.1942	5.4.1943	2.1944	stricken 12.1966

Ardent *(ex-Buffalo)*	AM340	General Engineering, Alameda	2.1943	22.6.1943	5.1944	stricken 7.1972
Dextrous *(ex-Sepoy)*	AM341	Gulf SB, Madisonville	1943	17.6.1943	9.1943	to South Korea 12.1967 (Geoje)
Minivet	AM371	Savannah Machine & Foundry Co.	7.1944	8.11.1944	5.1945	sunk 29.12.1945
Murrelet	AM372	Savannah Machine & Foundry Co.	8.1944	29.12.1944	8.1945	stricken 12.1964
Peregrine	AM373	Savannah Machine & Foundry Co.	10.1944	17.2.1945	9.1945	auxiliary 2.1964
Pigeon	AM374	Savannah Machine & Foundry Co.	11.1944	28.3.1945	10.1945	stricken 12.1966
Pochard	AM375	Savannah Machine & Foundry Co.	2.1944	11.6.1944	11.1944	stricken 12.1966
Ptarmigan	AM376	Savannah Machine & Foundry Co.	3.1944	15.7.1944	1.1945	to South Korea 7.1963 (Sinseong)
Quail	AM377	Savannah Machine & Foundry Co.	4.1944	20.8.1944	3.1945	stricken 12.1966
Redstart	AM378	Savannah Machine & Foundry Co.	6.1944	18.10.1944	4.1945	to Taiwan 7.1963 (Wu Sheng)
Roselle	AM379	Gulf SB, Madisonville	2.1944	29.8.1944	2.1945	stricken 7.1972
Ruddy	AM380	Gulf SB, Madisonville	2.1944	29.10.1944	4.1945	to Peru 11.1960 (Gálvez)
Scoter	AM381	Gulf SB, Madisonville	4.1944	26.9.1944	3.1945	stricken 7.1972
Shoveller	AM382	Gulf SB, Madisonville	4.1944	10.12.1944	5.1945	to Peru 11.1960 (Diez Canseco)
Surfbird	AM383	American SB, Lorain	2.1944	31.8.1944	11.1944	degaussing vessel 6.1957
Sprig	AM384	American SB, Lorain	2.1944	15.9.1944	4.1945	stricken 7.1972
Tanager	AM385	American SB, Lorain	3.1944	9.12.1944	7.1945	sold 11.1972
Tercel	AM386	American SB, Lorain	5.1944	16.12.1944	8.1945	stricken 7.1972
Toucan	AM387	American SB, Cleveland	2.1944	15.9.1944	11.1944	to Taiwan 12.1964 (Jian Men)
Towhee	AM388	American SB, Cleveland	3.1944	6.1.1945	3.1945	survey vessel 4.1964
Waxwing	AM389	American SB, Cleveland	5.1944	10.3.1945	8.1945	to Taiwan 10.1965 (Ju Yong)
Wheatear	AM390	American SB, Cleveland	5.1944	21.4.1945	10.1945	stricken 7.1972

Raven class: 810 / 1040 t, 67.1 x 9.8 x 2.8 m, 2 diesels, 2880 hp, 18 kts, 200 t diesel oil, 6370 nm (16.5 kts), complement 105; 2 x 1 - 76/50 Mk 20, 4 x 1 – 12.7 MG, 2 DCR, 80 mines (overloaded), sweeps; QCU sonar.

Auk class: 890 / 1250 t, 67.4 x 9.8 x 3.3 m, 2 electric motors, 2 diesel-generators, 2880 hp, 18 kts, 200 t diesel oil, 6370 nm (15 kts), complement 105; 2 or 1 (AM371-390) x 1 – 76/50 Mk 20, 2 x 1 – 40/56 Bofors (AM371-390), 4 (AM58-65, 100-131, 314-324, 340, 341) or 8 (AM371-390) x 1 – 20/70 Oerlikon, 4 x 1 – 12.7 MG (AM57), 1 x 24 Hedgehog ASWRL (except AM57), 4 DCT (except AM57), 2 DCR, 80 mines (overloaded), sweeps (inc. magnetic and acoustic); SF or SO or SU

Prevail 1943

radar, QCU sonar.

By the end of 1930th, the *Bird* class minesweepers, which formed the basis of the US Navy's minesweeping forces, were completely obsolete. To replace them, in 1938, the design of new ships began, which, according to the Naval Staff, in addition to their main purpose, solve a number of tasks from ASW service to minelaying.

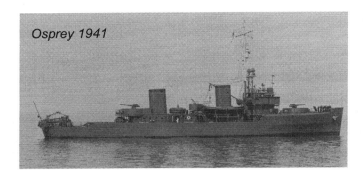

Osprey 1941

Such versatility was bought by the increase in displacement. In addition to minesweeping equipment, the new minesweeper could carry 80 mines, a sonar and two stern DC racks. The artillery consisted of two 76-mm/50 DP guns and four 12.7-mm MGs.

The experience of the early stage of the war in Europe unexpectedly revealed serious design flaw: the new minesweepers were not able to deal with magnetic mines. The tight layout prevented the installation of a diesel-generator required for the magnetic minesweeping gear. The problem was solved by replacing diesel machinery with diesel-electric one. Despite the different machineries, outwardly diesel and diesel-electric-powered ships practically did not differ

Pioneer 1943

from each other.

Only two ships (*Raven* class) were built according to the original design, and all subsequent ships were already improved versions (*Auk* class).

During the building of the first minesweepers, the armament structure underwent some changes: 12.7-mm MGs were replaced by 20-mm/70 Oerlikons, and ASW armament was strengthened with the Hedgehog and 4 DCTs. Many ships in 1944-45 had 2 single 40-mm/56 Bofors instead of the aft 76-mm/50 gun and up to 8 Oerlikons.

A total of 101 *Ravens* and *Auks* were ordered, but six were cancelled in 1943. 22 ships were transferred to the RN under Lend-Lease.

1942-1943, AM55-57: - 4 x 1 - 12.7 MG; + 4 x 1 - 20/70 Oerlikon.

1944-1945, most of survived early (AM55 - 65, 100 - 131, 314 - 324, 340, 341) ships: - 1 x 1 - 76/50; + 2 x 1 - 40/56 Bofors.

1945, most of survived early (AM55 - 65, 100 - 131, 314 - 324, 340, 341) ships: + 4 x 1 - 20/70 Oerlikon.

Sentinel 10.7.1943 was sunk off Sicily by German aircraft. *Skill* 25.9.1943 was sunk off Salerno by German submarine *U593*. *Portent* was mined 22.1.1944 off Anzio. *Osprey* and *Tide* were mined off the coast of Normandy 5.6.1944 and 7.6.1944, respectively. *Swerve* was mined 9.7.1944 off Anzio. *Skylark* 28.3.1945 was mined off Okinawa. *Swallow* was sunk 22.4.1945 off Okinawa by kamikaze.

Following ships were damaged by kamikazes off Okinawa: *Champion* (17.2.1945 and 16.4.1945), *Defense* (6.4.1945), *Devastator* (6.4.1945), *Gladiator* (12.4.1945 and 22.4.1945).

ADROIT class minesweepers

Adroit, 6.1944- *unnamed*	AM82, 6.1944- PC1586	Commercial Iron Wks, Portland	7.1941	21.2.1942	7.1942	patrol craft 6.1944, stricken 1.1946
Advent, 6.1944- *unnamed*	AM83, 6.1944- PC1587	Commercial Iron Wks, Portland	8.1941	12.3.1942	7.1942	patrol craft 6.1944, stricken 2.1946
Annoy, 6.1944- *unnamed*	AM84, 6.1944- PC1588	Commercial Iron Wks, Portland	12.1941	6.4.1942	9.1942	patrol craft 6.1944, stricken 3.1946
Conflict, 6.1944- *unnamed*	AM85, 6.1944- PC1589	Commercial Iron Wks, Portland	1.1942	18.4.1942	9.1942	patrol craft 6.1944, stricken 1946
Constant, 6.1944- *unnamed*	AM86, 6.1944- PC1590	Commercial Iron Wks, Portland	2.1942	9.5.1942	9.1942	patrol craft 6.1944, stricken 1954
Daring, 6.1944- *unnamed*	AM87, 6.1944- PC1591	Commercial Iron Wks, Portland	3.1942	23.5.1942	10.1942	patrol craft 6.1944, stricken 1946

Dash, 6.1944- *unnamed*	AM88, 6.1944- PC1592	Commercial Iron Wks, Portland	4.1942	20.6.1942	10.1942	patrol craft 6.1944, stricken 1946
Despite, 6.1944- *unnamed*	AM89, 6.1944- PC1593	Dravo, Pittsburgh	11.1941	28.3.1942	8.1942	patrol craft 6.1944, stricken 1946
Direct, 6.1944- *unnamed*	AM90, 6.1944- PC1594	Dravo, Pittsburgh	12.1941	25.4.1942	8.1942	patrol craft 6.1944, stricken 1946
Dynamic, 6.1944- *unnamed*	AM91, 6.1944- PC1595	Dravo, Pittsburgh	1.1942	26.5.1942	9.1942	patrol craft 6.1944, stricken 1946
Effective, 6.1944- *unnamed*	AM92, 6.1944- PC1596	Dravo, Pittsburgh	1.1942	12.6.1942	10.1942	patrol craft 6.1944, stricken 1946
Engage, 6.1944- *unnamed*	AM93, 6.1944- PC1597	Dravo, Pittsburgh	2.1942	11.7.1942	10.1942	patrol craft 6.1944, to Dominican Republic 1946 (Cibas)
Excel, 6.1944- *unnamed*	AM94, 6.1944- PC1598	Jakobson, Oyster Bay	12.1941	10.5.1942	12.1942	patrol craft 6.1944, to the MarCom 6.1947
Exploit, 6.1944- *unnamed*	AM95, 6.1944- PC1599, 8.1945- PCC1599	Jakobson, Oyster Bay	5.1942	7.9.1942	2.1943	patrol craft 6.1944, to the MarCom 3.1949
Fidelity, 6.1944- *unnamed*	AM96, 6.1944- PC1600	Nashville Bridge	10.1941	28.2.1942	9.1942	patrol craft 6.1944, to the MarCom 6.1948
Fierce, 6.1944- *unnamed*	AM97, 6.1944- PC1601, 8.1945- PCC1601	Nashville Bridge	10.1941	5.3.1942	10.1942	patrol craft 6.1944, stricken 1946
Firm, 6.1944- *unnamed*	AM98, 6.1944- PC1602, 8.1945- PCC1602	Penn-Jersey, Camden	10.1941	29.5.1942	4.1943	patrol craft 6.1944, to the MarCom 6.1948
Force, 6.1944- *unnamed*	AM99, 6.1944- PC1603	Penn-Jersey, Camden	11.1941	7.9.1942	6.1943	patrol craft 6.1944, sunk 21.5.1945

295 / 370 t, 52.9 x 7.1 x 2.5 m, 2 diesels, 1800 hp, 16 kts, 49 t diesel oil, 4800 nm (12 kts), complement 59-65; 1 x 1 – 76/50 Mk 20, 1 x 1 – 40/56 Bofors, sweeps (inc. magnetic and acoustic); SF or SO or SCR-517A radar.

In November 1940, even before the completion of work on the 173-ft PC design, it was decided to build minesweepers in 173-ft hulls. A total of 18 minesweepers of the *Adroit* class were completed. By installing less powerful diesels and reducing the speed to 16 kts, it was possible to get a place for the diesel-generator for magnetic sweep. As minesweepers, these ships were unsuccessful and in June 1944, they were re-classified

Similar PC466 1945

as patrols.

6.1944, all: were converted to PC, - sweeps; + (3 - 4) x 1 - 20/70 Oerlikon, 2 x 4 Mousetrap ASWRL, 2 DCT, 2 DCR

Mid-1944, PC(C)1599, 1601, 1602: - 1 x 1 - 40/56, (3 - 4) x 1 - 20/70; additional communication and HQ accommodations were mounted.

PC1603 was sunk by kamikaze off Okinawa 21.5.1945.

ADMIRABLE class minesweepers

Admirable	AM136	Tampa SB	4.1942	18.10.1942	4.1943	to the USSR 7.1945 (T-331)
Adopt	AM137	Tampa SB	4.1942	18.10.1942	5.1943	to the USSR 7.1945 (T-332)
Advocate	AM138	Tampa SB	4.1942	1.11.1942	(6.1943)	to the USSR 6.1943 (T-111 Starshiy Leytenant Liekarev)
Agent	AM139	Tampa SB	4.1942	1.11.1942	(7.1943)	to the USSR 7.1943 (T-112 Starshiy Leytenant Vladyimirov)
Alarm	AM140	Tampa SB	6.1942	7.12.1942	(8.1943)	to the USSR 8.1943 (T-113)
Alchemy	AM141	Tampa SB	6.1942	7.12.1942	(8.1943)	to the USSR 8.1943 (T-114)
Apex	AM142	Tampa SB	6.1942	7.12.1942	(8.1943)	to the USSR 8.1943 (T-115)
Arcade	AM143	Tampa SB	6.1942	7.12.1942	(8.1943)	to the USSR 8.1943 (T-116)
Arch	AM144	Tampa SB	10.1942	7.12.1942	(9.1943)	to the USSR 9.1943 (T-117)
Armada	AM145	Tampa SB	10.1942	7.12.1942	(9.1943)	to the USSR 9.1943 (T-118)
Aspire	AM146	Tampa SB	11.1942	27.12.1942	(9.1943)	to the USSR 9.1943 (T-119)
Assail	AM147	Tampa SB	11.1942	27.12.1942	(10.1943)	to the USSR 10.1943 (T-120)
Astute	AM148	Tampa SB	12.1942	23.2.1943	1.1944	to the USSR 7.1945 (T-333)
Augury	AM149	Tampa SB	12.1942	23.2.1943	3.1944	to the USSR 7.1945 (T-334)
Barrier	AM150	Tampa SB	12.1942	23.2.1943	5.1944	to the USSR 7.1945 (T-335)
Bombard	AM151	Tampa SB	12.1942	23.2.1943	5.1944	to the USSR 7.1945 (T-336)
Bond	AM152	Willamette Iron & Steel, Portland	4.1942	21.10.1942	8.1943	to the USSR 8.1945 (T-285)
Buoyant	AM153	Willamette Iron & Steel, Portland	4.1942	24.11.1942	9.1943	to China 5.1946
Candid	AM154	Willamette Iron & Steel, Portland	4.1942	14.10.1942	10.1943	to the USSR 8.1945 (T-283)
Capable	AM155	Willamette Iron & Steel, Portland	5.1942	16.11.1942	12.1943	to the USSR 8.1945 (T-339)
Captivate	AM156	Willamette Iron & Steel, Portland	5.1942	1.12.1942	12.1943	to the USSR 8.1945 (T-338)
Caravan	AM157	Willamette Iron & Steel, Portland	5.1942	27.10.1942	1.1944	to the USSR 8.1945 (T-337)
Caution	AM158	Willamette Iron & Steel, Portland	5.1942	7.12.1942	2.1944	to the USSR 8.1945 (T-284)
Change	AM159	Willamette Iron & Steel, Portland	5.1942	15.12.1942	2.1944	stricken 1960
Clamour	AM160	Willamette Iron & Steel, Portland	5.1942	15.12.1942	3.1944	stricken 1959
Climax	AM161	Willamette Iron & Steel, Portland	5.1942	9.1.1943	3.1944	stricken 1959
Compel	AM162	Willamette Iron & Steel, Portland	5.1942	16.1.1943	4.1944	stricken 1959
Concise	AM163	Willamette Iron & Steel, Portland	6.1942	6.2.1943	4.1944	stricken 1959
Control	AM164	Willamette Iron & Steel, Portland	6.1942	28.1.1943	5.1944	stricken 1958
Counsel	AM165	Willamette Iron & Steel, Portland	6.1942	17.2.1943	5.1944	stricken 7.1972
Crag *(ex-Craig)*	AM214	Tampa SB	12.1942	21.3.1943	8.1944	to Mexico 1962 (DM15)
Cruise	AM215	Tampa SB	12.1942	21.3.1943	9.1944	stricken 7.1972

Deft	AM216	Tampa SB	12.1942	28.3.1943	4.1944	to China 8.1948
Delegate	AM217	Tampa SB	12.1942	28.3.1943	4.1944	to China 5.1946 (Yung Ho)
Density	AM218	Tampa SB	3.1943	6.2.1944	6.1944	sold 2.1955
Design	AM219	Tampa SB	3.1943	6.2.1944	6.1944	stricken 1955
Device	AM220	Tampa SB	7.1943	21.5.1944	7.1944	to Mexico 1962 (DM11)
Diploma	AM221	Tampa SB	7.1943	21.5.1944	7.1944	to Mexico 1962 (DM17)
Disdain	AM222	American SB, Lorain	10.1943	25.3.1944	12.1944	to the USSR 5.1945 (T-271)
Dour	AM223	American SB, Lorain	10.1943	25.3.1944	11.1944	stricken 5.1962
Eager	AM224	American SB, Lorain	12.1943	10.6.1944	11.1944	stricken 5.1962
Elusive	AM225	American SB, Lorain	12.1943	10.6.1944	2.1945	to China 5.1946 (Yung Kang)
Embattle	AM226	American SB, Lorain	4.1944	17.9.1944	4.1945	to China 5.1946 (Yung Hsing)
Execute	AM232	Puget Sound Bridge	3.1944	22.6.1944	11.1944	stricken 5.1962
Facility	AM233	Puget Sound Bridge	3.1944	22.6.1944	11.1944	stricken 5.1962
Fancy	AM234	Puget Sound Bridge	5.1944	4.9.1944	12.1944	to the USSR 5.1945 (T-272)
Fixity	AM235	Puget Sound Bridge	5.1944	4.9.1944	12.1944	to the MarCom 1.1948
Garland	AM238	Commercial Ship Repair, Winslow	10.1943	20.2.1944	8.1944	stricken 4.1960
Gayety	AM239	Commercial Ship Repair, Winslow	11.1943	19.3.1944	9.1944	to South Vietnam 4.1962 (Chi Lăng II)
Hazard	AM240	Commercial Ship Repair, Winslow	2.1944	21.5.1944	10.1944	BU 10.1968
Hilarity	AM241	Commercial Ship Repair, Winslow	3.1944	30.7.1944	11.1944	to Mexico 8.1962 (DM02)
Inaugural	AM242	Commercial Ship Repair, Winslow	5.1944	1.10.1944	12.1944	stricken 3.1967
Implicit	AM246	Savannah Machine & Foundry Co.	3.1943	6.9.1943	1.1944	to China 6.1948 (Yung Chia)
Improve	AM247	Savannah Machine & Foundry Co.	6.1943	26.9.1943	2.1944	sold 2.1949
Incessant	AM248	Savannah Machine & Foundry Co.	7.1943	22.10.1943	3.1944	to the MarCom 11.1948
Incredible	AM249	Savannah Machine & Foundry Co.	9.1943	21.11.1943	4.1944	stricken 12.1959
Indicative	AM250	Savannah Machine & Foundry Co.	9.1943	12.12.1943	6.1944	to the USSR 5.1945 (T-273)
Inflict	AM251	Savannah Machine & Foundry Co.	10.1943	16.1.1944	8.1944	to the MarCom 10.1948
Instill	AM252	Savannah Machine & Foundry Co.	11.1943	5.3.1944	5.1944	stricken 5.1962
Intrigue	AM253	Savannah Machine & Foundry Co.	12.1943	8.4.1944	7.1944	stricken 5.1962
Invade	AM254	Savannah Machine & Foundry Co.	1.1944	6.2.1944	9.1944	stricken 5.1962
Jubilant	AM255	American SB, Lorain	10.1942	20.2.1943	8.1943	stricken 5.1962
Knave	AM256	American SB, Lorain	10.1942	13.3.1943	10.1943	to Mexico 10.1962 (DM13)
Lance	AM257	American SB, Lorain	10.1942	10.4.1943	11.1943	to China 8.1945 (Yung Sheng)
Logic	AM258	American SB, Lorain	10.1942	10.4.1943	11.1943	to China 8.1945 (Yung Shun)
Lucid	AM259	American SB, Lorain	2.1943	5.6.1943	12.1943	to China 8.1945 (Yung Ting)
Magnet	AM260	American SB, Lorain	3.1943	5.6.1943	3.1944	to China 8.1945 (Yung Ning)

Mainstay	AM261	American SB, Lorain	4.1943	31.7.1943	4.1944	stricken 12.1959
Marvel	AM262	American SB, Lorain	4.1943	31.7.1943	6.1944	to the USSR 5.1945 (T-274)
Measure	AM263	American SB, Lorain	6.1943	23.10.1943	5.1944	to the USSR 5.1945 (T-275)
Method	AM264	American SB, Lorain	6.1943	23.10.1943	7.1944	to the USSR 5.1945 (T-276)
Mirth	AM265	American SB, Lorain	7.1943	24.12.1943	8.1944	to the USSR 5.1945 (T-277)
Nimble	AM266	American SB, Lorain	8.1943	24.12.1943	9.1944	to China 6.1948
Notable	AM267	Gulf SB, Madisonville	9.1942	12.6.1943	12.1943	to China 5.1946
Nucleus	AM268	Gulf SB, Madisonville	9.1942	12.6.1943	12.1943	to the USSR 5.1945 (T-278)
Opponent	AM269	Gulf SB, Madisonville	9.1942	26.6.1943	2.1944	stricken 4.1960
Palisade	AM270	Gulf SB, Madisonville	9.1942	26.6.1943	3.1944	to the USSR 5.1945 (T-279)
Penetrate	AM271	Gulf SB, Madisonville	1.1943	11.9.1943	3.1944	to the USSR 5.1945 (T-280)
Peril	AM272	Gulf SB, Madisonville	2.1943	25.7.1943	4.1944	to the USSR 5.1945 (T-281)
Phantom	AM273	Gulf SB, Madisonville	2.1943	25.7.1943	5.1944	to China 6.1948 (Yung Ming)
Pinnacle	AM274	Gulf SB, Madisonville	2.1943	11.9.1943	5.1944	to China 6.1948 (Yung Hsiu)
Pirate	AM275	Gulf SB, Madisonville	7.1043	16.12.1943	6.1944	sunk 12.10.1950
Pivot	AM276	Gulf SB, Madisonville	7.1943	11.11.1943	7.1944	to China 8.1948 (Yung Shou)
Pledge	AM277	Gulf SB, Madisonville	7.1943	23.12.1943	7.1944	sunk 12.10.1950
Project	AM278	Gulf SB, Madisonville	7.1943	20.11.1943	8.1944	stricken 9.1947
Prime	AM279	Gulf SB, Madisonville	9.1943	22.1.1944	9.1944	to China 5.1946 (Yung Feng)
Prowess	AM280	Gulf SB, Madisonville	9.1943	17.2.1944	9.1944	auxiliary 3.1966
Quest	AM281	Gulf SB, Madisonville	11.1943	16.3.1944	10.1944	stricken 9.1947
Rampart	AM282	Gulf SB, Madisonville	11.1943	30.3.1944	11.1944	to the USSR 5.1945 (T-282)
Ransom	AM283	General Engineering, Alameda	4.1943	18.9.1943	8.1944	stricken 5.1962
Rebel	AM284	General Engineering, Alameda	5.1943	28.10.1943	9.1944	stricken 5.1962
Recruit	AM285	General Engineering, Alameda	5.1943	11.12.1943	11.1944	stricken 5.1962
Reform	AM286	General Engineering, Alameda	6.1943	29.1.1944	2.1945	to China 6.1948
Refresh	AM287	General Engineering, Alameda	9.1943	12.4.1944	4.1945	to China 6.1948 (Yung Chang)
Reign	AM288	General Engineering, Alameda	10.1943	29.5.1944	10.1946	stricken 11.1959
Report	AM289	General Engineering, Alameda	12.1943	8.7.1944	7.1946	auxiliary 4.1963
Reproof	AM290	General Engineering, Alameda	12.1943	8.8.1944	(1947)	completed mercantile
Risk	AM291	General Engineering, Alameda	4.1944	7.11.1944	(1947)	completed mercantile
Salute	AM294	Commercial Ship Repair, Winslow	11.1942	6.2.1943	12.1943	sunk 8.6.1945
Saunter	AM295	Commercial Ship Repair, Winslow	11.1942	20.2.1943	1.1944	stricken 11.1945
Scout	AM296	Commercial Ship Repair, Winslow	2.1943	2.5.1943	3.1944	stricken 5.1962
Scrimmage	AM297	Commercial Ship Repair, Winslow	2.1943	16.5.1943	4.1944	stricken 4.1960
Scuffle	AM298	Commercial Ship Repair, Winslow	5.1943	8.8.1943	5.1944	stricken 5.1962

Sentry	AM299	Commercial Ship Repair, Winslow	5.1943	15.8.1943	5.1944	stricken 2.1962
Serene	AM300	Commercial Ship Repair, Winslow	8.1943	31.10.1943	6.1944	to South Vietnam 1.1964 (Nhut Tảo)
Shelter	AM301	Commercial Ship Repair, Winslow	8.1943	14.11.1943	7.1944	to South Vietnam 1.1964 (Chí Linh)
Signet	AM302	Associated, Seattle	4.1943	16.8.1943	6.1944	to Dominican Republic 1.1965 (Tortuguero)
Skirmish	AM303	Associated, Seattle	4.1943	16.8.1943	6.1944	to Dominican Republic 1.1965 (Separación)
Scurry (ex-Skurry)	AM304	Associated, Seattle	5.1943	1.10.1943	7.1944	stricken 5.1967
Spectacle	AM305	Associated, Seattle	5.1943	1.10.1943	6.1944	damaged 24.5.1945, never repaired
Specter	AM306	Associated, Seattle	5.1943	15.2.1944	8.1944	stricken 7.1972
Staunch	AM307	Associated, Seattle	9.1943	15.2.1944	9.1944	stricken 4.1967
Strategy	AM308	Associated, Seattle	10.1943	28.3.1944	9.1944	stricken 10.1967
Strength	AM309	Associated, Seattle	10.1943	28.3.1944	9.1944	stricken 4.1967
Success	AM310	Associated, Seattle	2.1944	11.5.1944	10.1944	stricken 5.1962
Superior	AM311	Associated, Seattle	2.1944	11.5.1944	11.1944	stricken 7.1972
Adjutant	AM351	Willamette Iron & Steel, Portland	8.1943	17.6.1944	-	cancelled 11.1945
Bittern	AM352	Willamette Iron & Steel, Portland	9.1943	21.6.1944	-	cancelled 11.1945
Breakhorn	AM353	Willamette Iron & Steel, Portland	9.1943	4.7.1944	-	cancelled 11.1945
Cariama	AM354	Willamette Iron & Steel, Portland	10.1943	1.7.1944	-	cancelled 11.1945
Chukor	AM355	Willamette Iron & Steel, Portland	12.1943	15.7.1944	-	cancelled 11.1945
Creddock	AM356	Willamette Iron & Steel, Portland	11.1943	22.7.1944	12.1945	to Burma 1967 (Yan Gyi Aung)
Dipper	AM357	Willamette Iron & Steel, Portland	11.1943	26.7.1944	12.1945	sold 1.1961
Dotterel	AM358	Willamette Iron & Steel, Portland	11.1943	5.8.1944	-	cancelled 11.1945
Drake	AM359	Willamette Iron & Steel, Portland	11.1943	12.8.1944	(8.1945)	commissioned as degaussing vessel
Driver	AM360	Willamette Iron & Steel, Portland	11.1943	5.8.1944	-	cancelled 11.1945
Dunlin	AM361	Puget Sound Bridge	1.1943	26.8.1943	2.1945	to China 5.1946
Gadwall	AM362	Puget Sound Bridge	5.1943	15.7.1943	6.1945	stricken 4.1967
Gavia	AM363	Puget Sound Bridge	7.1943	18.9.1943	7.1945	to China 5.1946 (Yung Chun)
Graylag	AM364	Puget Sound Bridge	7.1943	4.12.1943	8.1945	stricken 10.1967
Harlequin	AM365	Puget Sound Bridge	8.1943	3.6.1944	8.1945	stricken 5.1962
Harrier	AM366	Puget Sound Bridge	8.1943	7.6.1944	10.1945	stricken 12.1959
Albatross	AM391	Defoe, Bay City	1945	-	-	cancelled 11.1945
Bullfinch	AM392	Defoe, Bay City	8.1945	-	-	cancelled 11.1945
Cardinal	AM393	Defoe, Bay City	10.1945	-	-	cancelled 11.1945

Admirable 1943

825 / 945 t, 56.2 x 10.1 x 3.0 m, 2 diesels, 2000 hp, 15.1 kts, 140 t diesel oil, 8500 nm (12 kts), complement 96; 1 x 1 – 76/50 Mk 20/21 (except AM214, 215), (2 x 1 – 40/56 Bofors + 4 x 1 – 20/70 Oerlikon) or 2 x 2 – 40/56 Bofors or 2 x 1 Bofors (AM214, 215), sweeps (inc. magnetic and acoustic) or magnetic sweeps only (AM214, 215); SF or SO or SU radar, QCU sonar.

Raven/Auk class minesweepers, due to the desire of the US Navy to get multi-purpose ships, turned out to be too large, difficult to build and, as a result, expensive. In the spring of 1940, work began on the creation of a simpler and cheaper purpose-built minesweeper, which had to meet two main requirements: seaworthiness and the ability to work with a minesweeping gear in bad weather conditions and a simple design, allowing minesweepers to be built in large quantities at minimal cost.

As a starting point for the creation of a new ship, a design of a radically "simplified" *Raven/Auk* was set. The double bottom was abandoned, and in order to keep resistance to damage, the hull was increased in height and breadth. A separate diesel-generator was fitted for

the magnetic sweep, abandoning the diesel-electric machinery adopted on the *Auk* class.

Calculations showed that the new ships could be built faster than the *Raven/Auk* class and would cost a third less. Initially, there was no order for their building for the USN; according to some members of the General Bureau, they did not fully meet the requirements for minesweepers. The design was proposed to the Royal Navy for delivery under Lend-Lease. According to the requirements of the Admiralty, they received new bridges, other improvements were made, but the British were still not enthusiastic about the project: they liked the larger ships of the *Auk* class more

In November 1941, an order for the first 30 ships of the *Admirable* class followed. A total of 174 ships were ordered (AM136-165, 214-311, 351-366 and 391-420). In June 1944, building of most incomplete ships was cancelled. Some ships received names: AM227 *Embroil*, AM228 *Enhance*, AM229 *Equity*, AM230 *Esteem* and AM231 *Event* (American SB, Lorain), AM236 *Flame* and AM237 *Fortify* (Puget Sound Bridge), AM243 *Illusive*, AM244 *Imbue* and AM245 *Impervious* (Commercial Ship Repair), AM292 *Rival* and AM293 *Sagacity* (General Engineering), AM367 *Hummer*, AM368 *Jackdaw*, AM369 *Medrick* and AM370 *Minah* (Puget Sound Bridge). In November 1945, some ships built by Willamette Iron & Steel, and AM394 *Firecrest* and AM395 *Goldfinch*, planned to be laid down by Defoe, were also cancelled. *Salute* 8.6.1945 was mined N of Borneo. Following ships were damaged by Japanese aircraft and kamikazes off Okinawa: *Facility* (6.4.1945), *Gayety* (4.5.1945 and 27.5.1945), *Ransom* (6.4.1945 and 22.4.1945), *Skirmish* (26.3.1945 and 1.4.1945) and *Spectacle* (24.5.1945 heavy damages, the ship was never repaired).

Prime 1945

Minesweepers converted from civilian vessels

More than 500 t displacement.
AM66 **Bullfinch** (*ex-Villanova*) (1937 / 10.1940, 516 t, 1 - 76/50 - stricken 9.1944)
AM67 **Cardinal** (*ex-Jeanne d`Arc*) (1937 / 11.1940, 516 t, 1 - 76/50 – stricken 9.1944)
AM68 **Catbird** (*ex-Bittern*) (1938 / 11.1940, 570 t, 1 - 76/50 – stricken 8.1944)
AM69 **Curlew** (*ex-Kittiwake*) (1938 / 11.1940, 570 t, 1 - 76/50 – stricken 6.1944)
AM70 **Flicker** (*ex-Delaware*) (1937 / 10.1940, 510 t, 1 - 76/23 – stricken 4.1944)
AM71 **Albatross** (*ex-Illinois*) (1931 / 11.1940, 510 t, 1 - 76/50 – stricken 6.1944)
AM72 **Bluebird** (*ex-Maine*) (1931 / 11.1940, 520 t, 1 - 76/50 - stricken 6.1944)
AM73 **Grackle** (*ex-Notre Dame*) (1919 / 2.1941, 525 t,

1 - 76/23 - stricken 9.1944)
AM79 **Goshawk** (*ex-Penobscot*) (1919 / 3.1941, 585 t, 1 - 76/50 – stricken 10.1944)
AM132 **Eagle** (*ex-Wave*) (1938 / 3.1942, 520 t, 1 - 102/50 – patrol yacht 4.1942)
AM133 **Hawk** (*ex-Gale*) (1937 / 5.1942, 530 t - stricken 9.1944)
AM134 **Ibis** (*ex-Tide*) (1937 / 5.1942, 590 t - stricken 9.1944)
AM135 **Merganser** (*ex-Ocean*) (1937 / 5.1942, 590 t – stricken 9.1944)

100-500t displacement
Requisitioned: 1 (1940); 5 (1941)
Discarded: 4 (1944), 2 (post-war)

FLAMINGO class coastal minesweepers

Flamingo *(ex-Harriet N. Eldridge)*	AMc22	Morse, Thomaston	1940	6.1941	auxiliary 7.1944
Canary *(ex-John G. Murley)*	AMc25	Morse, Thomaston	1939	6.1941	diving tender 1.1944

199 t, 28.4 x 5.9 x 3.7 m, 1 Cooper diesel, 180 hp, 9 kts; 1 x 1 – 76/50 Mk 20/21, 1 x 1 – 20/70 Oerlikon, sweeps.

Wooden-hulled trawlers purchased by the USN before the completion.

ACCENTOR class coastal minesweepers

Accentor	AMc36	W. A. Robinson, Ipswich	1.1941	10.5.1941	7.1941	stricken 7.1946
Bateleur	AMc37	W. A. Robinson, Ipswich	1.1941	12.5.1941	8.1941	sold 1946
Barbet	AMc38	W. A. Robinson, Ipswich	1.1941	24.7.1941	9.1941	sold 8.1947
Brambling	AMc39	W. A. Robinson, Ipswich	2.1941	17.8.1941	10.1941	sold 1946
Caracara	AMc40	Bristol YB	12.1940	23.8.1941	12.1941	stricken 1.1946
Charcalaca	AMc41	Bristol YB	12.1940	11.6.1941	9.1941	stricken 5.1946
Chimango	AMc42	Gibbs Gas Engine, Jacksonville	1.1941	8.3.1941	6.1941	sold 1946
Cotinga	AMc43	Gibbs Gas Engine, Jacksonville	1.1941	25.3.1941	6.1941	sold 1946
Courlan	AMc44	Gibbs Gas Engine, Jacksonville	1.1941	4.4.1941	7.1941	sold 1947
Develin	AMc45	Gibbs Gas Engine, Jacksonville	1.1941	10.4.1941	9.1941	stricken 7.1946
Fulmar	AMc46	Greenport Basin	12.1940	25.2.1941	6.1941	sold 1946
Jacamar	AMc47	Greenport Basin	2.1941	10.3.1941	6.1941	sold 1946
Limpkin	AMc48	Greenport Basin	2.1941	5.4.1941	8.1941	stricken 5.1946
Morikeet	AMc49	Greenport Basin	2.1941	19.4.1941	8.1941	stricken 1.1946
Marabout	AMc50	Herreshoff, Bristol	12.1940	17.2.1941	7.1941	sold 7.1946
Ostrich	AMc51	Herreshoff, Bristol	2.1941	29.3.1941	7.1941	stricken 1.1946
Roller	AMc52	Snow Shipyards, Rockland	12.1940	14.5.1941	8.1941	stricken 5.1946
Skimmer	AMc53	Snow Shipyards, Rockland	1.1941	7.6.1941	8.1941	stricken 8.1946
Tapacola	AMc54	Snow Shipyards, Rockland	1.1941	3.6.1941	9.1941	stricken 10.1946
Turaco	AMc55	Snow Shipyards, Rockland	1.1941	28.7.1941	10.1941	stricken 12.1945
Acme	AMc61	Greenport Basin	3.1941	31.5.1941	9.1941	stricken 1.1946
Adamant	AMc62	Greenport Basin	3.1941	7.6.1941	9.1941	stricken 1.1946
Advance	AMc63	Greenport Basin	4.1941	28.6.1941	10.1941	stricken 1.1946
Aggressor	AMc64	Greenport Basin	4.1941	19.7.1941	10.1941	stricken 1.1946
Assentive	AMc65	Bristol YB	4.1941	19.11.1941	3.1942	stricken 12.1945
Avenge	AMc66	Bristol YB	5.1941	17.2.1942	4.1942	stricken 1.1946
Bold	AMc67	Bristol YB	8.1941	2.4.1942	5.1942	sold 1946
Bulwark	AMc68	Hogdon Bros., Goudy & Stevens, East Boothbay	4.1941	12.9.1941	2.1942	sold 9.1946
Combat	AMc69	Hogdon Bros., Goudy & Stevens, East Boothbay	4.1941	6.10.1941	2.1942	sold 1946
Conqueror	AMc70	Warren Fish Co., Pensacola	5.1941	1941	3.1942	sold 1946

Conquest	AMc71	Warren Fish Co., Pensacola	5.1941	25.8.1941	3.1942	sold 1946
Courier	AMc72	Warren Fish Co., Pensacola	3.1941	17.5.1941	10.1941	sold 1946
Defiance	AMc73	Warren Fish Co., Pensacola	4.1941	21.6.1941	11.1941	sold 1946
Demand	AMc74	Gibbs Gas Engine, Jacksonville	3.1941	22.5.1941	9.1941	stricken 12.1945
Detector	AMc75	Gibbs Gas Engine, Jacksonville	3.1941	29.5.1941	9.1941	sold 1946
Dominant	AMc76	Gibbs Gas Engine, Jacksonville	4.1941	6.6.1941	9.1941	sold 1946
Endurance	AMc77	Gibbs Gas Engine, Jacksonville	4.1941	19.6.1941	10.1941	sold 1946
Energy	AMc78	W. A. Robinson, Ipswich	1941	20.9.1941	1.1942	degaussing vessel 2.1943
Exultant	AMc79	W. A. Robinson, Ipswich	4.1941	27.9.1941	1.1942	degaussing vessel 2.1943
Fearless	AMc80	W. A. Robinson, Ipswich	4.1941	1941	1942	degaussing vessel 2.1943
Fortitude	AMc81	W. A. Robinson, Ipswich	5.1941	1941	(1942)	commissioned as degaussing vessel
Governor	AMc82	Camden SB	5.1941	26.7.1941	1.1942	sold 4.1947
Guide	AMc83	Camden SB	5.1941	20.9.1941	3.1942	sold 4.1947
Heroic	AMc84	Warren Boat Yard, Pensacola	1941	5.5.1941	3.1942	sold 1946
Ideal	AMc85	Warren Boat Yard, Pensacola	6.1941	20.9.1941	4.1942	sold 1946
Industry	AMc86	Fulton Shipyard, Antioch	5.1941	6.9.1941	12.1941	wrecked 9.10.1945
Liberator	AMc87	Fulton Shipyard, Antioch	5.1941	6.9.1941	2.1942	auxiliary 12.1944
Loyalty	AMc88	Fulton Shipyard, Antioch	5.1941	23.8.1941	1.1942	wrecked 16.9.1945, never repaired
Memorable	AMc89	Fulton Shipyard, Antioch	7.1941	24.12.1941	3.1942	stricken 1.1946
Merit	AMc90	Fulton Shipyard, Antioch	8.1941	4.1.1942	3.1942	stricken 5.1946
Observer	AMc91	Fulton Shipyard, Antioch	9.1941	15.1.1942	4.1942	stricken 5.1946
Paramount	AMc92	Delaware Bay SB, Leesburg	4.1941	9.8.1941	12.1941	stricken 2.1946
Peerless	AMc93	Delaware Bay SB, Leesburg	4.1941	9.8.1941	2.1942	stricken 3.1946
Pluck	AMc94	Noank SB	6.1941	4.4.1942	10.1942	stricken 5.1946
Positive	AMc95	Noank SB	6.1941	7.3.1942	8.1942	stricken 5.1946
Reaper *(ex-Power)*	AMc96	Noank SB	6.1941	15.4.1942	11.1942	stricken 11.1945
Prestige	AMc97	Anderson & Cristofani, San Francisco	5.1941	16.8.1941	12.1941	stricken 7.1946
Progress	AMc98	Anderson & Cristofani, San Francisco	5.1941	6.9.1941	1.1942	stricken 7.1946
Radiant	AMc99	Anderson & Cristofani, San Francisco	6.1941	27.9.1941	2.1942	stricken 3.1946
Reliable	AMc100	Anderson & Cristofani, San Francisco	8.1941	14.2.1942	3.1942	stricken 9.1946
Rocket	AMc101	Anderson & Cristofani, San Francisco	9.1941	23.2.1942	3.1942	stricken 1.1946

Royal	AMc102	Anderson & Cristofani, San Francisco	11.1941	19.3.1942	4.1942	stricken 1.1946
Security	AMc103	H. G. Marr, Damariscotta	4.1941	27.9.1941	3.1942	stricken 11.1945
Skipper	AMc104	H. G. Marr, Damariscotta	5.1941	16.1.1941	5.1942	stricken 2.1946
Stalwart	AMc105	Snow Shipyards, Rockland	3.1941	28.8.1941	1.1942	auxiliary 8.1945
Summit	AMc106	Snow Shipyards, Rockland	3.1941	20.9.1941	1.1942	auxiliary 8.1945
Trident	AMc107	Snow Shipyards, Rockland	4.1941	8.10.1941	2.1942	stricken 11.1945
Valor	AMc108	Snow Shipyards, Rockland	5.1941	8.11.1941	3.1942	collision 29.6.1944
Victor	AMc109	Snow Shipyards, Rockland	7.1941	6.12.1941	4.1942	stricken 11.1945
Vigor	AMc110	Snow Shipyards, Rockland	8.1941	19.1.1942	5.1942	stricken 11.1945

Barbet

205 / 221 t, 29.6 x 6.7 x 2.8 m, 1 Superior or Cooper Bessemere diesel, 400 hp, 10 kts, complement 17; 1 or 2 x 1 – 12.7 MG, sweeps.
Small coastal minesweepers. Wooden-hulled.
~1942 - 1943, *Industry, Loyalty, Prestige, Progress*: were converted to minehunters: FM sonar and diving equipment were fitted.
Valor was rammed by destroyer escort *Richard W. Suessens* 29.6.1944 in Buzzards Bay, Massachusetts. *Loyalty* struck a reef and grounded 16.9.1945 off Okinawa.

RHEA class coastal minesweepers

Rhea	AMc58	Martinolich SB, Tacoma	1940	9.8.1941	10.1941	stricken 2.1946
Ruff *(ex-Speaker)*	AMc59	Martinolich SB, Tacoma	1940	24.4.1941	10.1941	stricken 2.1946

307 t, 30.0 x 7.3 x 3.4 m, 1 Superior diesel, 465 hp, 10 kts, complement 17; 2 x 1 – 12.7 MG, sweeps.

Wooden-hulled trawlers purchased by the USN during building.

AGILE class coastal minesweepers

Agile	AMc111	Petersen SB, Tacoma	1940	1941	12.1941	auxiliary 12.1944
Affray	AMc112	Tacoma Boat	1940	1941	12.1941	stricken 1.1946

215 t, 29.3 x 7.3 x 2.1 m, 1 Atlas diesel, 275 hp, 10 kts, complement 17; 2 x 1 – 12.7 MG, 2 x 1 – 7.6 MG, sweeps.

Wooden-hulled trawlers purchased by the USN during building.

Coastal minesweepers, converted from civilian vessels

100-500 t displacement
Requisitioned: 7 (1940), 27 (1941), 1 (1942)
Lost: 2 (1942), 1 (1943)

Stricken: 2 (1941), 16 (1944), 1 (1945), 13 (post-war)
Wooden-hulled trawlers requisitioned by the US Navy and served as minesweepers.

YMS class motor minesweepers

YMS1	Henry B. Nevins, New York	3.1941	10.1.1942	3.1942	stricken 4.1946
YMS2	Henry B. Nevins, New York	3.1941	28.1.1942	4.1942	stricken 2.1947
YMS3	Henry B. Nevins, New York	3.1941	13.4.1942	4.1942	to France 10.1944 (D334)
YMS4	Henry B. Nevins, New York	8.1941	14.3.1942	5.1942	stricken 6.1946
YMS5	Henry B. Nevins, New York	8.1941	13.4.1942	4.1942	stricken 4.1946
YMS6	Henry B. Nevins, New York	8.1941	19.5.1942	6.1942	stricken 6.1946
YMS7	Henry B. Nevins, New York	10.1941	11.5.1942	6.1942	stricken 6.1947
YMS8	Henry B. Nevins, New York	1.1942	2.6.1942	6.1942	stricken 6.1946
YMS9	Henry B. Nevins, New York	2.1942	15.6.1942	7.1942	stricken 6.1946
YMS10	Henry B. Nevins, New York	3.1942	30.6.1942	7.1942	stricken 6.1946
YMS11	Henry B. Nevins, New York	4.1942	20.7.1942	8.1942	stricken 6.1946
YMS12	Rice Bros, E. Boothbay	4.1941	14.3.1942	7.1942	stricken 4.1946
YMS13	Rice Bros, E. Boothbay	4.1941	2.5.1942	8.1942	to France 10.1944 (D317)
YMS14	Rice Bros, E. Boothbay	7.1941	13.6.1942	10.1942	collision 11.1.1945
YMS15	Rice Bros, E. Boothbay	7.1941	16.7.1942	12.1942	to France 10.1944 (D338)
YMS16	Rice Bros, E. Boothbay	3.1942	7.9.1942	2.1943	to France 10.1944 (D322)
YMS17	Rice Bros, E. Boothbay	5.1942	24.10.1942	4.1943	stricken 6.1946
YMS18	Herreshoff, Bristol	6.1941	8.12.1941	5.1942	to France 10.1944 (D332)
YMS19	Herreshoff, Bristol	6.1941	27.12.1941	6.1942	sunk 24.9.1944
YMS20	Greenport Basin	6.1941	1.11.1941	4.1942	to France 10.1944 (D327)
YMS21	Greenport Basin	6.1941	25.11.1941	4.1942	sunk 1.9.1944
YMS22	Greenport Basin	7.1941	31.12.1941	5.1942	stricken 7.1946
YMS23	Greenport Basin	7.1941	13.12.1941	5.1942	to France 3.1944 (D201)
YMS24	Greenport Basin	11.1941	10.1.1942	5.1942	sunk 16.8.1944
YMS25	Greenport Basin	11.1941	28.1.1942	6.1942	stricken 7.1947
YMS26	Greenport Basin	12.1941	28.2.1942	6.1942	to France 3.1944 (D211)
YMS27	Greenport Basin	12.1941	7.3.1942	6.1942	to France 10.1944 (D333)
YMS28	Greenport Basin	1.1942	31.3.1942	7.1942	to France 10.1944 (D315)
YMS29	Greenport Basin	1.1942	11.4.1942	7.1942	to France 10.1944 (D335)
YMS30	Greenport Basin	1942	1942	8.1942	sunk 25.1.1944
YMS31	Greenport Basin	3.1942	23.5.1942	8.1942	to France 3.1944 (D212)
YMS32	Hiltebrant, Kingston	5.1941	1.10.1941	5.1942	stricken 6.1946
YMS33	Hiltebrant, Kingston	5.1941	8.10.1941	6.1942	to the USSR 8.1945 (T-603)
YMS34	Hiltebrant, Kingston	5.1941	21.10.1941	6.1942	to France 10.1944 (D311)
YMS35	Hiltebrant, Kingston	5.1941	7.11.1941	7.1942	stricken 7.1947
YMS36	Hiltebrant, Kingston	10.1941	21.1.1942	7.1942	to France 10.1944 (D321)
YMS37	Hiltebrant, Kingston	10.1941	28.1.1942	8.1942	to France 10.1944 (D316)
YMS38	Hiltebrant, Kingston	5.1941	24.1.1942	4.1942	to the USSR 7.1945 (T-593)
YMS39	Robert Jacob, New York	5.1941	23.12.1941	3.1942	sunk 26.6.1945
YMS40	Robert Jacob, New York	6.1941	14.3.1942	4.1942	stricken 5.1946
YMS41	Robert Jacob, New York	6.1941	14.4.1942	5.1942	stricken 6.1946
YMS42	Wheeler, Brooklyn	6.1941	17.3.1942	4.1942	to the USSR 7.1945 (T-592)
YMS43	Wheeler, Brooklyn	6.1941	30.3.1942	5.1942	to France 10.1944 (D324)
YMS44	Wheeler, Brooklyn	6.1941	10.4.1942	5.1942	stricken 6.1946
YMS45	Wheeler, Brooklyn	6.1941	20.4.1942	6.1942	stricken ~1957
YMS46	Wheeler, Brooklyn	6.1941	30.4.1942	6.1942	stricken 6.1947
YMS47	Wheeler, Brooklyn	6.1941	7.5.1942	7.1942	stricken 10.1945
YMS48	Wheeler, Brooklyn	6.1941	15.5.1942	7.1942	sunk 14.2.1945
YMS49	Wheeler, Brooklyn	6.1941	22.5.1942	7.1942	stricken 7.1946
YMS50	Wheeler, Brooklyn	7.1941	6.6.1942	8.1942	sunk 18.6.1945

YMS51	Wheeler, Brooklyn	7.1941	22.6.1942	8.1942	stricken 6.1947
YMS52	Wheeler, Brooklyn	8.1941	15.6.1942	8.1942	stricken 6.1946
YMS53	Wheeler, Brooklyn	8.1941	24.7.1942	8.1942	stricken 7.1946
YMS54	Gibbs Gas Engine, Jacksonville	5.1941	1.11.1941	2.1942	stricken 6.1946
YMS55	Gibbs Gas Engine, Jacksonville	5.1941	22.11.1941	3.1942	to France 9.1944 (D331)
YMS56	Gibbs Gas Engine, Jacksonville	5.1941	6.12.1941	3.1942	stricken 1946
YMS57	Gibbs Gas Engine, Jacksonville	6.1941	15.12.1941	3.1942	stricken 6.1946
YMS58	Gibbs Gas Engine, Jacksonville	6.1941	22.12.1941	4.1942	to France 10.1944 (D313)
YMS59	Gibbs Gas Engine, Jacksonville	7.1941	30.12.1941	4.1942	to the USSR 6.1945 (T-521)
YMS60	Gibbs Gas Engine, Jacksonville	9.1941	19.1.1942	5.1942	stricken 6.1947
YMS61	Gibbs Gas Engine, Jacksonville	9.1941	3.2.1942	6.1942	stricken 6.1946
YMS62	Gibbs Gas Engine, Jacksonville	11.1941	25.2.1942	5.1942	to France 10.1944 (D323)
YMS63	Gibbs Gas Engine, Jacksonville	11.1941	6.3.1942	6.1942	to France 10.1944 (D312)
YMS64	Gibbs Gas Engine, Jacksonville	1.1942	25.3.1942	6.1942	to France 10.1944 (D336)
YMS65	Gibbs Gas Engine, Jacksonville	1.1942	30.3.1942	7.1942	stricken 6.1947
YMS66	Weaver, Orange	7.1941	30.9.1941	6.1942	stricken 5.1946
YMS67	Weaver, Orange	7.1941	17.2.1942	7.1942	stricken 7.1946
YMS68	Weaver, Orange	7.1941	24.2.1942	8.1942	stricken 7.1946
YMS69	Weaver, Orange	7.1941	5.3.1942	8.1942	to France 9.1944 (D337)
YMS70	Weaver, Orange	7.1941	12.3.1942	9.1942	wrecked 17.10.1944
YMS71	Weaver, Orange	7.1941	26.3.1942	9.1942	sunk 3.4.1945
YMS72	Weaver, Orange	7.1941	9.4.1942	1.1943	stricken 3.1946
YMS73	Weaver, Orange	7.1941	23.4.1942	1.1943	stricken 6.1947
YMS74	Weaver, Orange	7.1941	30.4.1942	2.1943	stricken 6.1946
YMS75	Weaver, Orange	7.1941	26.5.1942	2.1943	to the USSR 7.1945 (T-590)
YMS76	Stadium, Cleveland	4.1941	8.11.1941	6.1942	stricken 5.1946
YMS77	Stadium, Cleveland	5.1941	11.10.1941	5.1942	to France 3.1944 (D202)
YMS78	Stadium, Cleveland	5.1941	11.12.1941	6.1942	to France 10.1944 (D318)
YMS79	Stadium, Cleveland	6.1941	27.12.1941	6.1942	stricken 2.1948
YMS80	Stadium, Cleveland	6.1941	5.5.1942	7.1942	stricken 3.1958
YMS81	Stadium, Cleveland	7.1941	30.5.1942	7.1942	stricken 6.1947
YMS82	Stadium, Cleveland	10.1941	13.6.1942	8.1942	to France 10.1944 (D325)
YMS83	Stadium, Cleveland	10.1941	27.6.1942	8.1942	to France 10.1944 (D326)
YMS84	Henry C. Grebe, Chicago	6.1941	3.3.1942	5.1942	sunk 9.7.1945
YMS85	Henry C. Grebe, Chicago	6.1941	19.3.1942	6.1942	to the USSR 8.1945 (T-604)
YMS86	Al Larson, Terminal I	6.1941	31.1.1942	5.1942	stricken 4.1946
YMS87	Al Larson, Terminal I	7.1941	31.3.1942	8.1942	stricken 4.1946
YMS88	South Coast, Newport Beach	6.1941	18.10.1941	5.1942	to the USSR 8.1945 (T-608)
YMS89	South Coast, Newport Beach	7.1941	22.11.1941	6.1942	stricken 5.1946
YMS90	South Coast, Newport Beach	7.1941	19.12.1941	7.1942	wrecked 9.10.1945, never repaired

YMS91	South Coast, Newport Beach	10.1941	7.3.1942	8.1942	sold 1948
YMS92	South Coast, Newport Beach	11.1941	14.5.1942	9.1942	stricken 10.1945
YMS93	South Coast, Newport Beach	12.1941	16.5.1942	10.1942	sold 2.1947
YMS94	Colberg, Stockton	6.1941	15.12.1941	3.1942	stricken 6.1947
YMS95	Colberg, Stockton	6.1941	16.12.1941	3.1942	stricken 6.1946
YMS96	Colberg, Stockton	6.1941	20.2.1942	4.1942	stricken 1.1946
YMS97	Colberg, Stockton	6.1941	16.2.1942	4.1942	stricken 2.1947
YMS98	Colberg, Stockton	6.1941	31.12.1941	4.1942	wrecked 16.9.1945
YMS99	Colberg, Stockton	6.1941	11.3.1942	4.1942	stricken 1.1946
YMS100	Astoria Marine	7.1941	12.4.1942	6.1942	to the USSR 8.1945 (T-602)
YMS101	Astoria Marine	7.1941	20.6.1942	7.1942	stricken 6.1946
YMS102	Astoria Marine	6.1941	1.8.1942	8.1942	stricken 6.1947
YMS103	Astoria Marine	7.1941	29.8.1942	9.1942	sunk 8.4.1945
YMS104	Frank L. Sample, Boothbay Harbor	5.1941	17.2.1942	5.1942	stricken 7.1946
YMS105	Frank L. Sample, Boothbay Harbor	5.1941	10.3.1942	7.1942	stricken 5.1946
YMS106	Frank L. Sample, Boothbay Harbor	5.1941	19.4.1942	8.1942	stricken 6.1947
YMS107	Burger, Manitowoc	5.1941	28.3.1942	8.1942	stricken 4.1946
YMS108	Burger, Manitowoc	5.1941	18.4.1942	8.1942	stricken 7.1946
YMS109	Burger, Manitowoc	5.1941	16.5.1942	9.1942	stricken 11.1959
YMS110	Burger, Manitowoc	8.1941	16.7.1942	10.1942	stricken 4.1946
YMS111	Burger, Manitowoc	8.1941	25.7.1942	10.1942	stricken 4.1946
YMS112	Burger, Manitowoc	8.1941	5.8.1942	11.1942	stricken 7.1946
YMS113	San Diego Marine	6.1941	13.2.1942	8.1942	stricken 11.1959
YMS114	San Diego Marine	6.1941	13.3.1942	8.1942	stricken 11.1959
YMS115	San Diego Marine	6.1941	3.4.1942	9.1942	stricken 7.1946
YMS116	San Diego Marine	6.1941	20.4.1942	10.1942	stricken 8.1946
YMS117	Harbor Boat, Terminal I	5.1941	23.8.1942	4.1942	stricken 6.1947
YMS118	Harbor Boat, Terminal I	5.1941	27.10.1941	5.1942	stricken 4.1946
YMS119	Harbor Boat, Terminal I	7.1941	2.3.1942	6.1942	stricken 6.1947
YMS120	Harbor Boat, Terminal I	8.1941	4.4.1942	8.1942	stricken 11.1959
YMS121	Kruse & Banks, North Bend	5.1941	14.3.1942	7.1942	stricken 7.1946
YMS122	Kruse & Banks, North Bend	5.1941	2.6.1942	9.1942	stricken 4.1946
YMS123	Kruse & Banks, North Bend	7.1941	14.3.1942	8.1942	stricken 4.1946
YMS124	Kruse & Banks, North Bend	12.1941	6.6.1942	10.1942	stricken 4.1946
YMS125	J. M. Martinac, Tacoma	1941	18.12.1941	7.1942	stricken 1946
YMS126	J. M. Martinac, Tacoma	7.1941	3.3.1942	9.1942	stricken 4.1946
YMS127	J. M. Martinac, Tacoma	10.1941	2.5.1942	10.1942	wrecked, CTL 10.1.1944
YMS128	J. M. Martinac, Tacoma	12.1941	27.6.1942	12.1942	stricken 4.1946
YMS129	Tacoma Boat	5.1941	18.12.1941	7.1942	stricken 5.1946
YMS130	Tacoma Boat	6.1941	18.12.1941	8.1942	stricken 4.1946
YMS131	Tacoma Boat	7.1941	4.3.1942	10.1942	stricken 4.1946
YMS132	Tacoma Boat	7.1941	2.5.1942	11.1942	stricken 4.1946
YMS133	Western, Tacoma	7.1941	18.12.1941	7.1942	wrecked 21.2.1943
YMS134	Western, Tacoma	8.1941	16.3.1942	9.1942	stricken 4.1946
YMS135	Astoria Marine	5.1942	26.12.1942	2.1943	to the USSR 9.1945 (T-606)
YMS136	Astoria Marine	7.1942	8.2.1943	3.1943	stricken 11.1959
YMS137	Astoria Marine	8.1942	19.3.1943	(4.1943)	to the UK 4.1943 (BYMS137)
YMS138	Astoria Marine	8.1942	17.4.1943	6.1943	stricken 6.1946
YMS139	Astoria Marine	1.1943	19.5.1943	6.1943	to the USSR 7.1945 (T-594)

YMS140	Astoria Marine	2.1943	19.6.1943	8.1943	stricken 6.1947
YMS141	Astoria Marine	3.1943	19.7.1943	(8.1943)	to the UK 8.1943 (BYMS141)
YMS142	Astoria Marine	4.1943	16.8.1943	(9.1943)	to the UK 9.1943 (BYMS142)
YMS143	San Diego Marine	4.1942	30.6.1942	2.1943	to the USSR 5.1945 (T-522)
YMS144	San Diego Marine	4.1942	30.7.1942	3.1943	to the USSR 5.1945 (T-523)
YMS145	San Diego Marine	5.1942	7.9.1942	4.1943	to the USSR 5.1945 (T-524)
YMS146	San Diego Marine	6.1942	30.9.1942	6.1943	wrecked 9.10.1945
YMS147	Western, Tacoma	5.1942	24.10.1942	2.1943	stricken 2.1947
YMS148	Western, Tacoma	6.1942	29.11.1942	(5.1943)	to the UK 5.1943 (BYMS148)
YMS149	Western, Tacoma	10.1942	4.4.1943	(8.1943)	to the UK 8.1943 (BYMS149)
YMS150	Western, Tacoma	12.1942	5.4.1943	(8.1943)	to the UK 8.1943 (BYMS150)
YMS151	Campbell, San Diego	6.1942	31.3.1943	10.1943	wrecked 9.10.1945
YMS152	Campbell, San Diego	8.1942	17.4.1943	(11.1943)	to the UK 11.1943 (BYMS152)
YMS153	Campbell, San Diego	8.1942	31.7.1943	(11.1943)	to the UK 11.1943 (BYMS153)
YMS154	Campbell, San Diego	8.1942	4.9.1943	(1.1944)	to the UK 1.1944 (BYMS154)
YMS155	Burger, Manitowoc	6.1942	27.10.1942	(2.1943)	to the UK 2.1943 (BYMS155)
YMS156	Burger, Manitowoc	6.1942	12.11.1942	(3.1943)	to the UK 3.1943 (BYMS156)
YMS157	Burger, Manitowoc	7.1942	1.12.1942	(4.1943)	to the UK 4.1943 (BYMS157)
YMS158	Burger, Manitowoc	8.1942	26.12.1942	5.1943	stricken 6.1946
YMS159	Burger, Manitowoc	8.1942	16.1.1943	6.1943	stricken 8.1946
YMS160	Burger, Manitowoc	8.1942	30.1.1943	7.1943	to the Philippines 5.1945
YMS161	Burger, Manitowoc	12.1942	3.4.1943	(7.1943)	to the UK 7.1943 (BYMS161)
YMS162	Burger, Manitowoc	12.1942	24.4.1943	(8.1943)	to the UK 8.1943 (BYMS162)
YMS163	Dachel-Carter, Benton Harbor	4.1942	27.10.1942	3.1943	stricken 2.1947
YMS164	Dachel-Carter, Benton Harbor	4.1942	28.11.1942	3.1943	stricken 1.1960
YMS165	Dachel-Carter, Benton Harbor	5.1942	16.1.1943	4.1943	stricken 2.1947
YMS166	Dachel-Carter, Benton Harbor	5.1942	30.1.1943	5.1943	stricken 7.1946
YMS167	Dachel-Carter, Benton Harbor	8.1942	12.6.1943	(7.1943)	to the UK 7.1943 (BYMS167)
YMS168	Dachel-Carter, Benton Harbor	9.1942	4.7.1943	(8.1943)	to the UK 8.1943 (BYMS168)
YMS169	Dachel-Carter, Benton Harbor	9.1942	24.4.1943	6.1943	to France 8.1944 (D301)
YMS170	Dachel-Carter, Benton Harbor	9.1942	29.5.1943	7.1943	stricken 6.1960
YMS171	Henry C. Grebe, Chicago	5.1942	21.11.1942	(3.1943)	to the UK 3.1943 (BYMS171)
YMS172	Henry C. Grebe, Chicago	5.1942	26.11.1942	(4.1943)	to the UK 4.1943 (BYMS172)
YMS173	Henry C. Grebe, Chicago	5.1942	7.12.1942	(5.1943)	to the UK 5.1943 (BYMS173)
YMS174	Henry C. Grebe, Chicago	6.1942	19.12.1942	(5.1943)	to the UK 5.1943 (BYMS174)
YMS175	Henry C. Grebe, Chicago	6.1942	9.1.1943	(6.1943)	to the UK 6.1943 (BYMS175)
YMS176	Henry C. Grebe, Chicago	7.1942	23.1.1943	7.1943	stricken 9.1946
YMS177	Henry C. Grebe, Chicago	9.1942	20.3.1943	7.1943	stricken 9.1946
YMS178	Henry C. Grebe, Chicago	9.1942	24.4.1943	7.1943	to the USSR 7.1945 (T-588)
YMS179	Henry C. Grebe, Chicago	10.1942	8.5.1943	7.1943	stricken 11.1959
YMS180	Henry C. Grebe, Chicago	10.1942	5.6.1943	8.1943	to the USSR 8.1945 (T-609)
YMS181	Henry C. Grebe, Chicago	1.1943	24.6.1943	(9.1943)	to the UK 9.1943 (BYMS181)
YMS182	Henry C. Grebe, Chicago	1.1943	15.7.1943	(9.1943)	to the UK 9.1943 (BYMS182)
YMS183	Greenport Basin	3.1942	25.6.1942	1.1943	stricken 6.1947
YMS184	Greenport Basin	5.1942	18.7.1942	1.1943	to the USSR 7.1945 (T-595)
YMS185	Greenport Basin	5.1942	8.8.1942	(2.1943)	to the UK 2.1943 (BYMS185)
YMS186	Greenport Basin	5.1942	22.8.1942	(2.1943)	to the UK 2.1943 (BYMS186)
YMS187	Greenport Basin	6.1942	7.9.1942	(3.1943)	to the UK 3.1943 (BYMS187)
YMS188	Greenport Basin	7.1942	26.9.1942	(3.1943)	to the UK 3.1943 (BYMS188)
YMS189	Greenport Basin	8.1942	14.10.1942	(5.1943)	to the UK 5.1943 (BYMS189)
YMS190	Greenport Basin	8.1942	31.10.1942	(5.1943)	to the UK 5.1943 (BYMS190)
YMS191	Greenport Basin	9.1942	14.11.1942	(6.1943)	to the UK 6.1943 (BYMS191)

YMS192	Greenport Basin	9.1942	5.12.1942	6.1943	to Japan 3.1955 (Ujishima)
YMS193	Greenport Basin	10.1942	2.1.1943	6.1943	stricken 10.1968
YMS194	Greenport Basin	11.1942	30.1.1943	(7.1943)	to the UK 7.1943 (BYMS2194)
YMS195	Hiltebrant, Kingston	4.1942	10.8.1942	3.1943	survey vessel 3.1945
YMS196	Hiltebrant, Kingston	4.1942	14.8.1942	4.1943	to the Philippines 5.1946
YMS197	Hiltebrant, Kingston	4.1942	24.8.1942	5.1943	to the UK 6.1943 (BYMS197)
YMS198	Hiltebrant, Kingston	5.1942	7.9.1942	5.1943	stricken 8.1946
YMS199	Hiltebrant, Kingston	8.1942	10.10.1942	6.1943	stricken 2.1947
YMS200	Hiltebrant, Kingston	8.1942	26.10.1942	7.1943	stricken 6.1946
YMS201	Hiltebrant, Kingston	8.1942	19.11.1942	7.1943	stricken 11.1959
YMS202	Hiltebrant, Kingston	9.1942	9.12.1942	(8.1943)	to the UK 8.1943 (BYMS202)
YMS203	Hiltebrant, Kingston	10.1942	15.1.1943	(8.1943)	to the UK 8.1943 (BYMS203)
YMS204	Hiltebrant, Kingston	11.1942	2.3.1943	(9.1943)	to the UK 9.1943 (BYMS204)
YMS205	Hiltebrant, Kingston	11.1942	31.3.1943	(9.1943)	to the UK 9.1943 (BYMS205)
YMS206	Hiltebrant, Kingston	12.1942	29.4.1943	(10.1943)	to the UK 10.1943 (BYMS206)
YMS207	Robert Jacob, New York	4.1942	1.8.1942	1.1943	to the UK 3.1943 (BYMS207)
YMS208	Robert Jacob, New York	4.1942	8.8.1942	2.1943	to the UK 3.1943 (BYMS208)
YMS209	Robert Jacob, New York	4.1942	15.8.1942	(3.1943)	to the UK 3.1943 (BYMS209)
YMS210	Robert Jacob, New York	5.1942	7.9.1942	(4.1943)	to the UK 4.1943 (BYMS210)
YMS211	Robert Jacob, New York	5.1942	10.10.1942	(5.1943)	to the UK 5.1943 (BYMS211)
YMS212	Robert Jacob, New York	5.1942	16.10.1942	(5.1943)	to the UK 5.1943 (BYMS212)
YMS213	Robert Jacob, New York	6.1942	13.11.1942	(6.1943)	to the UK 6.1943 (BYMS213)
YMS214	Robert Jacob, New York	8.1942	26.2.1943	(7.1943)	to the UK 7.1943 (BYMS214)
YMS215	Robert Jacob, New York	8.1942	22.2.1943	7.1943	stricken 11.1959
YMS216	J. M. Martinac, Tacoma	6.1942	17.10.1942	2.1943	to the USSR 7.1945 (T-596)
YMS217	J. M. Martinac, Tacoma	6.1942	21.11.1942	(4.1943)	to the UK 4.1943 (BYMS217)
YMS218	J. M. Martinac, Tacoma	7.1942	23.12.1942	6.1943	to South Korea 1.1956 (Geumhwa)
YMS219	J. M. Martinac, Tacoma	10.1942	23.1.1943	7.1943	stricken 1.1960
YMS220	J. M. Martinac, Tacoma	11.1942	6.3.1943	8.1943	stricken 6.1946
YMS221	J. M. Martinac, Tacoma	12.1942	22.4.1943	(9.1943)	to the UK 9.1943 (BYMS221)
YMS222	Mojean & Ericson, Tacoma	5.1942	11.11.1942	4.1943	stricken 5.1946
YMS223	Mojean & Ericson, Tacoma	6.1942	27.12.1942	(4.1943)	to the UK 4.1943 (BYMS223)
YMS224	Mojean & Ericson, Tacoma	11.1942	28.2.1943	8.1943	stricken 6.1946
YMS225	Mojean & Ericson, Tacoma	1.1943	25.4.1943	(10.1943)	to the UK 10.1943 (BYMS225)
YMS226	Frank L. Sample, Boothbay Harbor	3.1942	31.8.1942	1.1943	to the UK 3.1943 (BYMS226)
YMS227	Frank L. Sample, Boothbay Harbor	4.1942	7.9.1942	3.1943	to France 3.1944 (D273)
YMS228	Frank L. Sample, Boothbay Harbor	4.1942	2.10.1942	5.1943	to Turkey 2.1948 (Kemer)
YMS229	Frank L. Sample, Boothbay Harbor	9.1942	11.1.1943	(6.1943)	to the UK 6.1943 (BYMS229)
YMS230	Frank L. Sample, Boothbay Harbor	9.1942	20.2.1943	(7.1943)	to the UK 7.1943 (BYMS230)
YMS231	Frank L. Sample, Boothbay Harbor	10.1942	3.4.1943	8.1943	to Japan 3.1955 (Etajima)
YMS232	Frank L. Sample, Boothbay Harbor	1.1943	26.4.1943	(9.1943)	to the UK 9.1943 (BYMS232)
YMS233	Frank L. Sample, Boothbay Harbor	2.1943	22.7.1943	(10.1943)	to the UK 10.1943 (BYMS233)

YMS234	Frank L. Sample, Boothbay Harbor	4.1943	4.9.1943	(11.1943)	to the UK 11.1943 (BYMS234)
YMS235	Stadium, Cleveland	7.1942	15.2.1943	7.1943	stricken 8.1946
YMS236	Stadium, Cleveland	7.1942	16.1.1943	(6.1943)	to the UK 6.1943 (BYMS236)
YMS237	Stadium, Cleveland	6.1942	7.9.1942	11.1942	to the USSR 7.1945 (T-589)
YMS238	Stadium, Cleveland	5.1942	12.9.1942	11.1942	stricken 11.1959
YMS239	Stadium, Cleveland	5.1942	27.10.1942	4.1943	to Turkey 2.1948 (Kerempe)
YMS240	Stadium, Cleveland	4.1942	31.10.1942	(5.1943)	to the UK 5.1943 (BYMS240)
YMS241	Tacoma Boat	5.1942	7.9.1942	2.1943	to the USSR 7.1945 (T-591)
YMS242	Tacoma Boat	6.1942	10.10.1942	3.1943	survey vessel 3.1945
YMS243	Tacoma Boat	6.1942	10.11.1942	5.1943	stricken 1.1946
YMS244	Tacoma Boat	10.192	18.12.1942	(7.1943)	to the UK 7.1943 (BYMS244)
YMS245	Tacoma Boat	10.1942	6.2.1943	7.1943	stricken 6.1946
YMS246	Tacoma Boat	11.1942	11.3.1943	(8.1943)	to the UK 8.1943 (BYMS246)
YMS247	Weaver, Orange	5.1942	14.10.1942	5.1943	to Norway 5.1945 (NYMS247)
YMS248	Weaver, Orange	5.1942	14.10.1942	6.1943	stricken 6.1946
YMS249	Weaver, Orange	5.1942	24.10.1942	6.1943	stricken 7.1946
YMS250	Weaver, Orange	5.1942	9.12.1942	7.1943	stricken 6.1947
YMS251	Weaver, Orange	5.1942	24.12.1942	8.1943	stricken 7.1946
YMS252	Weaver, Orange	5.1942	24.6.1943	(9.1943)	to the UK 9.1943 (BYMS252)
YMS253	Weaver, Orange	5.1942	3.7.1943	(10.1943)	to the UK 10.1943 (BYMS253)
YMS254	Weaver, Orange	5.1942	31.1.1943	(11.1943)	to the UK 11.1943 (BYMS254)
YMS255	Weaver, Orange	5.1942	22.5.1943	(11.1943)	to the UK 11.1943 (BYMS255)
YMS256	Weaver, Orange	6.1942	2.8.1943	(12.1943)	to the UK 12.1943 (BYMS256)
YMS257	Weaver, Orange	10.1942	30.9.1943	(1.1944)	to the UK 1.1944 (BYMS2257)
YMS258	Weaver, Orange	10.1942	28.10.1943	(2.1944)	to the UK 2.1944 (BYMS2258)
YMS259	South Coast, Newport Beach	5.1942	21.8.1942	3.1943	stricken 9.1947
YMS260	South Coast, Newport Beach	5.1942	6.9.1942	4.1943	to the USSR 8.1945 (T-527)
YMS261	South Coast, Newport Beach	6.1942	25.9.1942	(7.1943)	to the UK 7.1943 (BYMS261)
YMS262	South Coast, Newport Beach	9.1942	24.12.1942	8.1943	survey vessel 3.1945
YMS263	South Coast, Newport Beach	8.1942	2.11.1942	8.1943	survey vessel 3.1945
YMS264	South Coast, Newport Beach	9.1942	16.1.1943	(10.1943)	to the UK 10.1943 (BYMS264)
YMS265	Kruse & Banks, North Bend	5.1942	25.11.1942	3.1943	stricken 6.1947
YMS266	Kruse & Banks, North Bend	5.1942	24.12.1942	4.1943	to the USSR 8.1945 (T-601)
YMS267	Kruse & Banks, North Bend	7.1942	6.3.1943	6.1943	stricken 6.1947
YMS268	Kruse & Banks, North Bend	12.1942	15.4.1943	6.1943	stricken 11.1959
YMS269	Bellingham Iron Wks	4.1942	7.9.1942	2.1943	stricken 6.1947
YMS270	Bellingham Iron Wks	5.1942	7.9.1942	3.1943	stricken 6.1947
YMS271	Bellingham Iron Wks	7.1942	17.10.1942	4.1943	stricken 10.1968
YMS272	Bellingham Iron Wks	7.1942	14.11.1942	5.1943	to the USSR 7.1945 (T-597)
YMS273	Bellingham Iron Wks	7.1942	26.12.1942	7.1943	to the USSR 7.1945 (T-598)
YMS274	Bellingham Iron Wks	9.1942	9.1.1943	7.1943	stricken 6.1947
YMS275	Bellingham Iron Wks	11.1942	4.2.1943	8.1943	wrecked 9.10.1945
YMS276	Bellingham Iron Wks	11.1942	5.3.1943	9.1943	stricken 2.1947
YMS277	J. M. Martinac, Tacoma	2.1943	19.6.1943	(10.1943)	to the UK 10.1943 (BYMS277)
YMS278	J. M. Martinac, Tacoma	3.1943	17.7.1943	(11.1943)	to the UK 11.1943 (BYMS278)
YMS279	Henry C. Grebe, Chicago	1.1943	29.7.1943	(10.1943)	to the UK 10.1943 (BYMS279)
YMS280	Henry C. Grebe, Chicago	1.1943	12.8.1943	(10.1943)	to the UK 10.1943 (BYMS280)
YMS281	San Diego Marine	7.1942	30.10.1942	7.1943	stricken 10.1946
YMS282	San Diego Marine	8.1942	30.11.1942	(8.1943)	to the UK 8.1943 (BYMS282)
YMS283	San Diego Marine	9.1942	30.12.1942	9.1943	stricken 2.1947
YMS284	San Diego Marine	10.1942	17.2.1943	(10.1943)	to the UK 10.1943 (BYMS284)

YMS285	Northwestern, Bellingham	6.1942	20.3.1943	6.1943	to the USSR 9.1945 (T-610)
YMS286	Northwestern, Bellingham	6.1942	20.3.1943	6.1943	stricken 9.1946
YMS287	Associated, Seattle	7.1942	27.10.1942	3.1943	to the USSR 9.1945 (T-611)
YMS288	Associated, Seattle	8.1942	28.11.1942	3.1943	to the USSR 8.1945 (T-600)
YMS289	Associated, Seattle	10.1942	26.1.1943	6.1943	to Turkey 1947 (Kilimli)
YMS290	Associated, Seattle	11.1942	27.2.1943	7.1943	stricken 11.1959
YMS291	Associated, Seattle	1.1943	20.4.1943	8.1943	stricken 10.1968
YMS292	Associated, Seattle	3.1943	8.6.1943	10.1943	stricken 2.1947
YMS293	Associated, Seattle	4.1943	7.7.1943	10.1943	stricken 9.1946
YMS294	Associated, Seattle	6.1943	11.8.1943	9.1943	stricken 7.1959
YMS295	Associated, Seattle	7.1943	11.8.1943	11.1943	to the USSR 7.1945 (T-599)
YMS296	Associated, Seattle	8.1943	3.11.1943	12.1943	stricken 6.1947
YMS297	Tacoma Boat	1.1943	24.4.1943	9.1943	stricken 10.1946
YMS298	Tacoma Boat	2.1943	16.6.1943	10.1943	stricken 7.1946
YMS299	William F. Stone, Oakland	6.1942	14.11.1942	4.1943	stricken 11.1959
YMS300	William F. Stone, Oakland	6.1942	7.12.192	7.1943	stricken 2.1947
YMS301	William F. Stone, Oakland	11.1942	1.5.1943	9.1943	to the USSR 8.1945 (T-605)
YMS302	William F. Stone, Oakland	12.1942	12.6.1943	11.1943	stricken 1.1948
YMS303	Rice Bros, E. Boothbay	5.1942	21.7.1943	8.1943	stricken 7.1946
YMS304	Rice Bros, E. Boothbay	6.1942	10.8.1943	10.1943	sunk 30.7.1944
YMS305	Rice Bros, E. Boothbay	7.1942	30.9.1943	11.1943	to Norway 5.1945 (NYMS305)
YMS306	Rice Bros, E. Boothbay	9.1942	27.11.1943	1.1944	stricken 11.1957
YMS307	Rice Bros, E. Boothbay	10.1942	31.12.1943	2.1944	to Turkey 2.1948 (Kirte)
YMS308	Henry B. Nevins, New York	2.1943	21.7.1943	8.1943	stricken 1.1946
YMS309	Henry B. Nevins, New York	4.1943	17.8.1943	9.1943	stricken 6.1946
YMS310	Henry B. Nevins, New York	4.1943	11.9.1943	10.1943	stricken 6.1946
YMS311	Henry B. Nevins, New York	5.1943	6.10.1943	11.1943	stricken 8.1961
YMS312	Henry B. Nevins, New York	6.1943	9.11.1943	12.1943	stricken 3.1963
YMS313	Harbor Boat, Terminal I	5.1942	23.2.1943	6.1943	stricken 6.1947
YMS314	Harbor Boat, Terminal I	6.1942	17.3.1943	7.1943	stricken 6.1947
YMS315	Harbor Boat, Terminal I	6.1942	14.4.1943	8.1943	stricken 6.1946
YMS316	Harbor Boat, Terminal I	6.1942	1.5.1943	8.1943	stricken 6.1947
YMS317	South Coast, Newport Beach	10.1942	27.2.1943	11.1943	stricken 11.1959
YMS318	South Coast, Newport Beach	12.1942	1.5.1943	12.1943	stricken 1946
YMS319	South Coast, Newport Beach	1.1943	5.6.1943	2.1944	stricken 3.1948
YMS320	Al Larson, Terminal I	7.1942	9.1.1943	8.1943	stricken 6.1946
YMS321	Al Larson, Terminal I	8.1942	20.2.1943	10.1943	wrecked 21.9.1963
YMS322	Al Larson, Terminal I	1.1943	31.5.1943	11.1943	stricken 4.1946
YMS323	Al Larson, Terminal I	2.1943	15.7.1943	12.1943	stricken 6.1946
YMS324	Al Larson, Terminal I	6.1943	14.10.1943	2.1944	stricken 3.1959
YMS325	Al Larson, Terminal I	7.1943	11.1.1944	4.1944	stricken 3.1947
YMS326	Ballard, Seattle	6.1942	17.11.1942	3.1943	stricken 6.1947
YMS327	Ballard, Seattle	6.1942	5.12.1942	4.1943	stricken 11.1969
YMS328	Ballard, Seattle	7.1942	19.12.1942	5.1943	stricken 10.1946
YMS329	Ballard, Seattle	11.1942	23.2.1943	7.1943	stricken 6.1946
YMS330	Ballard, Seattle	12.1942	27.3.1943	8.1943	stricken 6.1946
YMS331	Ballard, Seattle	12.1942	24.4.1943	9.1943	stricken 10.1946
YMS332	Ballard, Seattle	3.1943	5.6.1943	10.1943	to the USSR 9.1945 (T-607)
YMS333	Ballard, Seattle	6.1943	4.8.1943	12.1943	stricken 10.1946
YMS334	Seattle SB	6.1942	24.10.1942	3.1943	stricken 6.1946
YMS335	Seattle SB	7.1942	21.11.1942	4.1943	stricken 9.1947
YMS336	Seattle SB	10.1942	19.12.1942	5.1943	stricken 6.1946

YMS337	Seattle SB	11.1942	20.2.1943	7.1943	stricken 8.1946
YMS338	Seattle SB	1.1943	20.3.1943	8.1943	stricken 6.1946
YMS339	Seattle SB	3.1943	8.5.1943	9.1943	to China 6.1948
YMS340	Seattle SB	3.1943	26.6.1943	10.1943	stricken 6.1947
YMS341	Seattle SB	5.1943	21.8.1943	12.1943	wrecked 16.9.1945
YMS342	Bellingham Iron Wks	1.1943	5.4.1943	10.1943	stricken 8.1946
YMS343	Bellingham Iron Wks	2.1943	1.5.1943	11.1943	stricken 3.1947
YMS344	Bellingham Iron Wks	3.1943	4.6.1943	(1944)	completed as degaussing vessel
YMS345	Bellingham Iron Wks	4.1943	14.8.1943	12.1943	stricken 7.1946
YMS346	Gibbs Gas Engine, Jacksonville	8.1942	5.1.1943	8.1943	stricken 6.1946
YMS347	Gibbs Gas Engine, Jacksonville	9.1942	7.1.1943	8.1943	stricken 6.1946
YMS348	Gibbs Gas Engine, Jacksonville	9.1942	9.2.1943	9.1943	stricken 2.1948
YMS349	Gibbs Gas Engine, Jacksonville	9.1942	5.3.1943	9.1943	stricken 2.1947
YMS350	Gibbs Gas Engine, Jacksonville	10.1942	29.1.1943	9.1943	sunk 2.7.1944
YMS351	Gibbs Gas Engine, Jacksonville	10.1942	21.2.1943	10.1943	stricken 6.1946
YMS352	Gibbs Gas Engine, Jacksonville	1.1943	14.5.1943	10.1943	stricken 7.1946
YMS353	Gibbs Gas Engine, Jacksonville	1.1943	20.5.1943	11.1943	stricken 7.1946
YMS354	Gibbs Gas Engine, Jacksonville	1.1943	29.5.1943	11.1943	stricken 1.1947
YMS355	Gibbs Gas Engine, Jacksonville	1.1943	8.6.1943	11.1943	stricken 5.1946
YMS356	Gibbs Gas Engine, Jacksonville	2.1943	6.9.1943	12.1943	stricken 6.1946
YMS357	Gibbs Gas Engine, Jacksonville	3.1943	16.9.1943	12.1943	stricken 8.1946
YMS358	Robert Jacob, New York	9.1942	22.3.1943	8.1943	stricken 1.1947
YMS359	Robert Jacob, New York	9.1942	9.4.1943	8.1943	stricken 4.1946
YMS360	Robert Jacob, New York	10.1942	16.6.1943	9.1943	stricken 4.1946
YMS361	Robert Jacob, New York	10.1942	11.6.1943	9.1943	stricken 5.1946
YMS362	Robert Jacob, New York	11.1942	22.5.1943	10.1943	stricken 10.1957
YMS363	Wheeler, Brooklyn	11.1942	8.6.1943	8.1943	stricken 6.1946
YMS364	Wheeler, Brooklyn	11.1942	25.6.1943	8.1943	stricken 3.1948
YMS365	Wheeler, Brooklyn	12.1942	26.6.1943	8.1943	sunk 26.6.1945
YMS366	Wheeler, Brooklyn	12.1942	5.7.1943	9.1943	stricken 6.1946
YMS367	Wheeler, Brooklyn	12.1942	15.7.1943	9.1943	to China 10.1948
YMS368	Wheeler, Brooklyn	12.1942	17.7.1943	9.1943	stricken 6.1947
YMS369	Wheeler, Brooklyn	1.1943	24.7.1943	10.1943	to Japan 3.1955 (Nuwajima)
YMS370	Wheeler, Brooklyn	1.1943	7.8.1943	10.1943	stricken 6.1946
YMS371	Weaver, Orange	11.1942	27.11.1943	2.1944	stricken 11.1959
YMS372	Weaver, Orange	12.1942	23.12.1943	3.1944	stricken 2.1959
YMS373	Weaver, Orange	12.1942	23.1.1944	4.1944	to Brazil 1.1960 (Juruá)
YMS374	Weaver, Orange	1.1943	17.2.1944	5.1944	to South Korea 1.1956 (Gimpo)
YMS375	Greenport Basin	12.1942	27.2.1943	7.1943	stricken 2.1948
YMS376	Greenport Basin	1.1943	13.3.1943	8.1943	to Japan 2.1955 (Ninoshima)
YMS377	Greenport Basin	2.1943	3.4.1943	8.1943	to Norway 3.1945 (NYMS377)

YMS378	Greenport Basin	3.1943	27.4.1943	9.1943	sunk 30.7.1944
YMS379	Greenport Basin	3.1943	29.5.1943	9.1943	to Norway 3.1945 (NYMS379)
YMS380	Greenport Basin	4.1943	29.5.1943	9.1943	to Norway 3.1945 (NYMS380)
YMS381	Greenport Basin	5.1943	17.7.1943	10.1943	to Norway 3.1945 (NYMS381)
YMS382	Greenport Basin	6.1943	21.8.1943	11.1943	to Norway 3.1945 (NYMS382)
YMS383	Seattle SB	4.1942	29.9.1942	2.1943	wrecked 9.10.1945
YMS384	Seattle SB	4.1942	17.10.1942	4.1943	wrecked 9.10.1945, never repaired
YMS385	Seattle SB	6.1942	27.10.1942	4.1943	sunk 1.10.1944
YMS386	Seattle SB	10.1942	23.3.1943	7.1943	stricken 7.1946
YMS387	Seattle SB	10.1942	16.4.1943	8.1943	stricken 7.1946
YMS388	Seattle SB	11.1942	10.5.1943	9.1943	stricken 6.1946
YMS389	Stadium, Cleveland	11.1942	6.3.1943	8.1943	stricken 7.1947
YMS390	Stadium, Cleveland	11.1942	3.4.1943	8.1943	stricken 6.1947
YMS391	Stadium, Cleveland	11.1942	8.5.1943	9.1943	stricken 6.1947
YMS392	Stadium, Cleveland	11.1942	10.6.1943	10.1943	stricken 6.1946
YMS393	Harbor Boat, Terminal I	6.1942	29.5.1943	9.1943	stricken 6.1947
YMS394	Harbor Boat, Terminal I	7.1942	24.6.1943	10.1943	stricken 9.1946
YMS395	Harbor Boat, Terminal I	7.1942	15.7.1943	11.1943	stricken 10.1968
YMS396	Harbor Boat, Terminal I	7.1942	9.8.1943	1.1944	stricken 6.1947
YMS397	Henry B. Nevins, New York	6.1942	5.12.1942	1.1943	stricken 3.1947
YMS398	Henry B. Nevins, New York	6.1942	4.1.1943	3.1943	stricken 3.1947
YMS399	Henry B. Nevins, New York	6.1942	8.2.1943	4.1943	stricken 6.1947
YMS400	Henry B. Nevins, New York	7.1942	24.3.193	5.1943	sunk 1.10.1950
YMS401	Henry B. Nevins, New York	7.1942	1.4.1943	6.1943	stricken 2.1947
YMS402	Henry B. Nevins, New York	7.1942	17.4.1943	6.1943	stricken 11.1959
YMS403	Henry B. Nevins, New York	8.1942	22.5.1943	7.1943	stricken 6.1947
YMS404	Henry B. Nevins, New York	8.1942	26.5.1943	8.1943	stricken 2.1947
YMS405	Henry C. Grebe, Chicago	1.1943	24.8.1943	11.1943	stricken 2.1947
YMS406	Henry C. Grebe, Chicago	1.1943	6.9.1943	11.1943	to Norway 5.1945 (NYMS406)
YMS407	Henry C. Grebe, Chicago	4.1943	16.9.1943	12.1943	stricken 7.1946
YMS408	Henry C. Grebe, Chicago	4.1943	9.10.1943	12.1943	stricken 7.1947
YMS409	Henry C. Grebe, Chicago	5.1943	27.10.1943	1.1944	wrecked 14.9.1944
YMS410	Bellingham Iron Wks	9.1943	22.2.1944	9.1944	stricken 11.1946
YMS411	Bellingham Iron Wks	10.1943	22.4.1944	8.1944	stricken 8.1946
YMS412	Bellingham Iron Wks	11.1943	3.6.1944	9.1944	stricken 5.1947
YMS413	Bellingham Iron Wks	1.1944	4.7.1944	10.1944	stricken 1.1947
YMS414	Stadium, Cleveland	9.1943	11.3.1944	9.1944	stricken 5.1947
YMS415	Stadium, Cleveland	10.1943	15.4.1944	10.1944	to Japan 4.1955 (Yurishima)
YMS416	Stadium, Cleveland	1.1944	28.5.1944	10.1944	stricken 2.1947
YMS417	Stadium, Cleveland	1.1944	29.6.1944	11.1944	stricken 5.1959
YMS418	Henry C. Grebe, Chicago	9.1943	22.2.1944	9.1944	stricken 2.1947
YMS419	Henry C. Grebe, Chicago	9.1943	23.3.1944	11.1944	to South Korea 1.1956 (Gochang)
YMS420	Henry C. Grebe, Chicago	9.1943	8.4.1944	2.1945	stricken 1.1950
YMS421	Henry C. Grebe, Chicago	9.1943	15.4.1944	3.1945	wrecked 15.9.1945
YMS422	Astoria Marine	10.1943	1.6.1944	9.1944	to Japan 3.1955 (Yakushima)
YMS423	Astoria Marine	12.1943	5.8.1944	10.1944	stricken 2.1947
YMS424	Astoria Marine	1.1944	12.8.1944	11.1944	wrecked 9.10.1945, never repaired
YMS425	Astoria Marine	6.1944	6.9.1944	12.1944	stricken 10.1968
YMS426	Mojean & Ericson, Tacoma	9.1943	9.2.1944	9.1944	stricken 6.1947
YMS427	Mojean & Ericson, Tacoma	11.1943	25.3.1944	11.1944	stricken 2.1947

YMS428	Mojean & Ericson, Tacoma	2.1944	5.6.1944	1.1945	to the USSR 5.1945 (T-525)
YMS429	Mojean & Ericson, Tacoma	3.1944	30.11.1944	3.1945	stricken 2.1947
YMS430	Tacoma Boat	11.1943	23.3.1944	10.1944	stricken 11.1959
YMS431	Tacoma Boat	1.1944	20.5.1944	11.1944	stricken 8.1946
YMS432	Tacoma Boat	3.1944	8.7.1944	12.1944	stricken 2.1947
YMS433	Tacoma Boat	6.1944	30.9.1944	2.1945	stricken 8.1946
YMS434	J. M. Martinac, Tacoma	10.1943	10.5.1944	11.1944	stricken 6.1947
YMS435	J. M. Martinac, Tacoma	5.1944	30.9.1944	3.1945	to the USSR 5.1945 (T-526)
YMS436	J. M. Martinac, Tacoma	6.1944	15.3.1945	5.1945	stricken 3.1947
YMS437	J. M. Martinac, Tacoma	10.1944	22.4.1945	7.1945	sunk 2.2.1951
YMS438	Robert Jacob, New York	11.1943	7.7.1944	10.1944	stricken 3.1947
YMS439	Robert Jacob, New York	10.1943	14.7.1944	11.1944	stricken 7.1946
YMS440	Robert Jacob, New York	11.1943	28.10.1944	12.1944	stricken 8.1946
YMS441	Robert Jacob, New York	11.1943	13.11.1944	2.1945	to Japan 4.1955 (Ogishima)
YMS442	Hiltebrant, Kingston	10.1943	20.4.1944	10.1944	stricken 10.1968
YMS443	Hiltebrant, Kingston	10.1943	5.5.1944	11.1944	stricken 11.1959
YMS444	Hiltebrant, Kingston	11.1943	20.7.1944	12.1944	stricken 10.1968
YMS445	Hiltebrant, Kingston	3.1944	28.9.1944	3.1945	stricken 3.1947
YMS446	Robert Jacob, New York	5.1943	26.2.1944	6.1944	stricken 11.1959
YMS447	Robert Jacob, New York	6.1943	18.3.1944	6.1944	to the USSR 3.1945 (T-181)
YMS448	Robert Jacob, New York	6.1943	27.3.1944	7.1944	to the USSR 4.1945 (T-185)
YMS449	South Coast, Newport Beach	6.1943	29.2.1944	7.1944	stricken 7.1946
YMS450	South Coast, Newport Beach	8.1943	15.4.1944	(11.1944)	commissioned as submarine chaser
YMS451	South Coast, Newport Beach	9.1943	20.5.1944	(12.1944)	commissioned as submarine chaser
YMS452	South Coast, Newport Beach	1943	23.6.1944	(2.1945)	commissioned as submarine chaser
YMS453	Greenport Basin	7.1943	2.10.1943	6.1944	to the USSR 5.1945 (T-189)
YMS454	Greenport Basin	8.1943	23.10.1943	6.1944	wrecked 9.10.1945, never repaired
YMS455	Greenport Basin	8.1943	13.11.1943	7.1944	to the USSR 5.1945 (T-190)
YMS456	Greenport Basin	9.1943	11.12.1943	8.1944	to the USSR 5.1945 (T-191)
YMS457	Greenport Basin	11.1943	8.1.1944	9.1944	to the USSR 5.1945 (T-182)
YMS458	Greenport Basin	12.1943	12.2.1944	10.1944	stricken 2.1947
YMS459	Greenport Basin	1.1944	8.4.1944	10.1944	stricken 1.1946
YMS460	Stadium, Cleveland	6.1943	4.12.1943	5.1944	to the USSR 3.1945 (T-183)
YMS461	Stadium, Cleveland	6.1943	8.1.1944	6.1944	to Japan 4.1955 (Yugeshima])
YMS462	Hiltebrant, Kingston	4.1943	11.10.1943	6.1944	to the USSR 4.1945 (T-184)
YMS463	Hiltebrant, Kingston	5.1943	21.3.1944	7.1944	to South Korea 5.1947 (Gangneung])
YMS464	Gibbs Gas Engine, Jacksonville	5.1943	9.12.1943	6.1944	to the USSR 5.1945 (T-188)
YMS465	Gibbs Gas Engine, Jacksonville	6.1943	4.1.1944	6.1944	to the USSR 5.1945 (T-187)
YMS466	Gibbs Gas Engine, Jacksonville	6.1943	22.1.1944	7.1944	to the USSR 5.1945 (T-192)
YMS467	Gibbs Gas Engine, Jacksonville	6.1943	22.2.1944	8.1944	stricken 2.1947
YMS468	Gibbs Gas Engine, Jacksonville	6.1943	23.3.1944	8.1944	stricken 2.1948

YMS469	Gibbs Gas Engine, Jacksonville	7.1943	17.3.1944	9.1944	to the USSR 4.1945 (T-186)
YMS470	Gibbs Gas Engine, Jacksonville	8.1943	5.4.1944	10.1944	stricken 11.1959
YMS471	Gibbs Gas Engine, Jacksonville	9.1943	23.5.1944	10.1944	stricken 11.1959
YMS472	Gibbs Gas Engine, Jacksonville	9.1943	21.6.1944	11.1944	wrecked 16.9.1945
YMS473	Harbor Boat, Terminal I	5.1943	22.4.1944	8.1944	stricken 6.1946
YMS474	Harbor Boat, Terminal I	5.1943	23.5.1944	(12.1944)	commissioned as submarine chaser
YMS475	San Diego Marine	4.1943	23.5.1944	8.1944	stricken 10.1946
YMS476	San Diego Marine	4.1943	14.6.1944	(11.1944)	commissioned as submarine chaser
YMS477	Tacoma Boat	7.1943	6.11.1943	7.1944	stricken 8.1946
YMS478	Tacoma Boat	9.1943	8.1.1944	8.1944	wrecked 8.10.1945, never repaired
YMS479	Mojean & Ericson, Tacoma	4.1943	30.9.1943	7.1944	stricken 11.1959
YMS480	Bellingham Iron Wks	5.1943	20.11.1943	(3.1944)	commissioned as degaussing vessel
YMS481	Bellingham Iron Wks	5.1943	20.11.1943	3.1944	sunk 2.5.1945

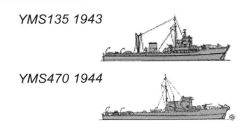

YMS135 1943

YMS470 1944

270 / 320 t, 41.5 x 7.5 x 2.4 m, 2 diesels, 800 hp, 14 kts, 2000 nm (12 kts), complement 60; 1 x 1 – 76/50 Mk 20/21, 2 x 1 – 20/70 Oerlikon, 2 DCT, 2 DCR, sweeps (inc. magnetic and acoustic); SF or SO or SU radar.

Designing a minesweeper to protect the bases from mine danger began after the appearance in the UK of 105-ft minesweeper. This ship made good impression on the US Navy authorities with her simplicity of design and low cost. It was decided to create a similar ship for the US Navy, which could be built in large numbers by almost any small shipbuilder. At first, they wanted to build minesweeper in the hull of 110-ft submarine chaser, but this idea was abandoned due to the inability to place a diesel-generator necessary for magnetic sweep. The hull had to be redesigned. To improve seaworthiness, a short forecastle was provided. As in the case of submarine chasers, wood was chosen as the construction material

to reduce the cost of the ship.

YMS class minesweepers were sectioned into three practically identical sub-classes, the main difference between which was the number of funnels: there were two on YMS1-134, one on YMS135-445 and 481, and there was no funnel on remaining ships. The UK additionally received 80 minesweepers (BYMS1-80), built specially for the Royal Navy.

YMS133 foundered 20.2.1943 off Coos Bay, Oregon. YMS127 ran aground 10.1.1944 at Aleutian Islands. YMS30 was mined off Anzio 25.1.1944. YMS350 was mined 2.7.1944 off the coast of Normandy. YMS304 and YMS378 were mined 30.7.1944 off the coast of Normandy. YMS24 was mined off St. Tropez 16.8.1944. YMS21 was mined off Toulon 1.9.1944. YMS409 foundered in a hurricane off Cape Hatteras 12.9.1944. YMS19 was mined in the Palau Islands area 24.9.1944. YMS385 was mined off Ulithi, Caroline Islands, 1.10.1944. YMS70 foundered in a storm off Leyte 17.10.1944. YMS14 sank in a collision in Boston Harbor 11.1.1945. YMS48 was damaged by Japanese coastal guns at Corregidor 14.2.1945 and sunk by destroyer *Fletcher*. YMS71 was mined off Borneo 3.4.1945. YMS103 was mined at Okinawa 8.4.1945, beached and abandoned by her crew. YMS481 was sunk by Japanese coastal guns off Tarakan, Borneo, 2.5.1945. YMS50 was mined off Balikpapan 18.6.1945. YMS39 was mined off Balikpapan 26.6.1945. YMS365 struck a mine at Balikpapan 26.6.1945 and sunk by US aircraft. YMS84 was mined off Balikpapan 9.7.1945. YMS98, YMS341, YMS421 and YMS472 foundered during a typhoon off Okinawa 16.9.1945.

YMS143 1943

MSB1 class minesweeping boats

Norfolk N Yd, Portsmouth: MSB1, 2 (1946)
Mare Is N Yd, Vallejo: MSB3, 4 (1946)
Transferred: South Korea – MSB2 (1961), Taiwan – MSB4 (1961)
Discarded: MSB1, 3 (early 1960s)

42 t, 17.5 x 4.8 x 1.3 m, 2 diesels, 300 hp, 12 kts, 16 t diesel oil, complement 6, sweeps.
Small minesweeping boats built for the US Army and transferred to the USN in 1949.

AMPHIBIOUS SHIPS

APPALACHIAN class amphibious forces command ships

Appalachian	AGC1	Federal, Kearny / Todd, Brooklyn	11.1942	29.1.1943	10.1943	stricken 3.1959
Blue Ridge	AGC2	Federal, Kearny / Bethlehem, Brooklyn	12.1942	7.3.1943	9.1943	stricken 1.1960
Rocky Mount	AGC3	Federal, Kearny / Bethlehem, Hoboken	12.1942	7.3.1943	10.1943	stricken 7.1960
Catoctin (ex-Mary Whitridge)	AGC5	Moore, Oakland / Philadelphia N Yd	1942	23.1.1943	1.1944	stricken 12.1959

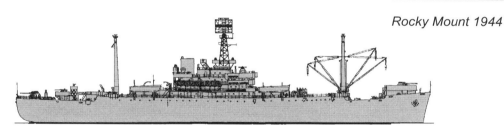

Rocky Mount 1944

8700 / 13910 t, 140.0 x 19.2 x 7.3 m, 1 set General Electric r De Laval (AGC3) geared steam turbines, 2 Combustion Engineering or Foster Wheeler (AGC5) boilers, 6600 hp, 17 kts, 3305 t oil, 48460 nm (15 kts), complement 875; 2 x 1 – 127/38 Mk 12, 4 x 2 – 40/56 Bofors, 14 x 1 – 20/70 Oerlikon, 165 persons of HQ, 2 LCV(P), 4 LCP(L), 2 LCP(R), 2 LCC, SA or SC or SR, SG or SU, SK, SM or SP radars.

Amphibious command ships (sometimes also called as command ships) were equipped with a wide range of communication equipment, the commander of landing controlled all the forces from these ships: from fire support ships to fighter aircraft. The *Appalachian* class

Blue Ridge 1943

ships were converted from standard C2-S-B1 cargo hulls.

ANCON amphibious forces command ship

Ancon	AGC4	Bethlehem, Quincy	24.9.1938	(6.1939) / 4.1943	stricken 4.1946

Ancon 1945

9946 / 13144 t, 150.3 x 19.5 x 8.0 m, 2 sets Bethlehem geared steam turbines, 2 Yarrow boilers, 10000 hp, 18 kts, 1186 t oil, 10852 nm (15 kts), complement 707; 2 x 1 – 127/38 Mk 12, 4 x 2 – 40/56 Bofors, 14 x 1 – 20/70 Oerlikon, 195 persons of HQ, 6 LCV(P), 4 LCP(L), 2 LCP(R), 2 LCC, SA or SC, SG, SK, SM radars.

Former s/s of Panama Rail Road Co., acquired by the Army in January 1942 and used as a transport (with the Navy from August 1942 as AP66). Ship was converted to AGC in February-April 1943.

MOUNT MCKINLEY class amphibious forces command ships

Mount McKinley (ex-Cyclone)	AGC7	North Carolina SB, Wilmington / Philadelphia N Yd	7.1943	27.9.1943	5.1944	stricken 3.1970
Mount Olympus (ex-Eclipse)	AGC8	North Carolina SB, Wilmington / Boston N Yd, Charlestown	8.1943	3.10.1943	5.1944	stricken 6.1961
Wasatch (ex-Fleetwing)	AGC9	North Carolina SB, Wilmington / Norfolk N Yd, Portsmouth	8.1943	8.10.1943	5.1944	stricken 1.1960
Auburn (ex-Kathay)	AGC10	North Carolina SB, Wilmington / Bethlehem, Hoboken	8.1943	19.10.1943	7.1944	stricken 7.1960
Eldorado (ex-Monsoon)	AGC11	North Carolina SB, Wilmington / Bethlehem, Brooklyn	1943	26.10.1943	8.1944	stricken 11.1972
Estes (ex-Morning Star)	AGC12	North Carolina SB, Wilmington / Norfolk N Yd, Portsmouth	1943	1.11.1943	10.1944	stricken 7.1976
Panamint (ex-Northern Light)	AGC13	North Carolina SB, Wilmington / Todd, Hoboken	9.1943	9.11.1943	10.1944	stricken 7.1960
Teton (ex-Witch of the Wave)	AGC14	North Carolina SB, Wilmington / Bethlehem, Brooklyn	11.1943	5.2.1944	10.1944	stricken 6.1961
Adirondack	AGC15	North Carolina SB, Wilmington / Philadelphia N Yd	11.1944	13.1.1945	9.1945	stricken 6.1961
Pocono	AGC16	North Carolina SB, Wilmington / Boston N Yd, Charlestown	11.1944	25.1.1945	12.1945	stricken 12.1976
Taconic	AGC17	North Carolina SB, Wilmington / Atlantic Basin IW, Portsmouth	12.1944	10.2.1945	1.1946	stricken 12.1976

Eldorado 1944

8700 / 12560 t, 139.9 x 19.2 x 7.6 m, 1 set General Electric geared steam turbines, 2 Babcock & Wilcox (AGC7-10, 14) or Combustion Engineering boilers, 6600 hp, 17 kts, 3273 t oil, 43948 nm (12 kts), complement 1063; 2 x 1 – 127/38 Mk 12, 4 x 2 – 40/56 Bofors, 14 (AGC7-14) or 12 (AGC15-17) x 1 – 20/70 Oerlikon, 336 (AGC7-14) or 317 (AGC15-17) persons of HQ, 2 LCV(P)

(AGC7-14), 4 LCP(L), 2 (AGC7-14) or 1 (AGC15-17) LCP(R), 2 LCC (AGC7-14), SA or SC or SR, SG or SU, SK, SM or SP radars.

The *Mount McKinley* class ships were converted from standard C2-S-AJ1 cargo hulls.

Some ships were also classified as AGCs during the WWII. There were former *Treausury* class USCG cutter AGC6 (WAGC33, ex-WPG33) *Duane* (since 10.1944), former *Barnegat* class seaplane tender AGC18 (ex-AVP11) *Dexter* (since 10.1944) and former auxiliary gunboat AGC369 (ex-PG56) *Williamsburg* (since 11.1945). The latter really served as the Presidential yacht and was officially classified as general communication vessel since November 1945.

Mount Olympus 1944

ASHLAND class dock landing ships

Ashland subclass

Ashland	LSD1	Moore, Oakland	6.1942	21.12.1942	6.1943	stricken 11.1969
Belle Grove	LSD2	Moore, Oakland	10.1942	17.2.1943	8.1943	stricken 11.1969
Carter Hall	LSD3	Moore, Oakland	10.1942	4.3.1943	9.1943	stricken 10.1969
Epping Forest	LSD4	Moore, Oakland	11.1942	2.4.1943	10.1943	stricken 11.1968
Gunston Hall	LSD5	Moore, Oakland	1942	1.5.1943	11.1943	to Argentina 5.1970 (Candido de Lasala)
Lindenwald	LSD6	Moore, Oakland	2.1943	11.6.1943	12.1943	stricken 12.1967
Oak Hill	LSD7	Moore, Oakland	3.1943	25.6.1943	1.1944	stricken 10.1969
White Marsh	LSD8	Moore, Oakland	4.1943	19.7.1943	1.1944	to Taiwan 11.1960 (Dong Hai)

Casa Grande subclass

Casa Grande *(ex-Portway, ex-Spear)*	LSD13	Newport News	11.1943	11.4.1944	6.1944	stricken 10.1976
Rushmore *(ex-Swashway, ex-Sword)*	LSD14	Newport News	12.1943	14.5.1944	7.1944	stricken 11.1976
Shadwell *(ex-Waterway, ex-Tomahawk)*	LSD15	Newport News	1.1944	24.5.1944	7.1944	stricken 11.1976
Cabildo	LSD16	Newport News	7.1944	22.12.1944	3.1945	stricken 10.1976
Catamount	LSD17	Newport News	8.1944	27.1.1945	4.1945	stricken 10.1976
Colonial	LSD18	Newport News	8.1944	28.2.1945	5.1945	stricken 10.1976
Comstock	LSD19	Newport News	1.1945	28.4.1945	7.1945	stricken 6.1976
Donner	LSD20	Boston N Yd, Charlestown	12.1944	1.4.1945	7.1945	stricken 11.1976
Fort Mandan	LSD21	Boston N Yd, Charlestown	3.1944	2.6.1945	10.1945	to Greece 1.1971 (Nafkratousa)
Fort Marion	LSD22	Gulf SB, Chickasaw	1944	22.5.1945	1.1946	stricken 10.1974
Fort Snelling	LSD23	Gulf SB, Chickasaw	11.1944	8.1945	(1956)	completed mercantile
Point Defiance	LSD24	Gulf SB, Chickasaw	1944	28.5.1945	(10.1945)	completed mercantile
San Marcos	LSD25	Philadelphia N Yd	9.1944	10.1.1945	4.1945	to Spain 7.1971 (Galicia)
Tortuga	LSD26	Boston N Yd, Charlestown	10.1944	21.1.1945	6.1945	stricken 10.1976
Wheatstone	LSD27	Boston N Yd, Charlestown	4.1945	18.7.1945	2.1946	stricken 9.1971

Ashland 1943

Belle Grove 1943

4490 / 9375 t, 139.5 x 22.0 x 4.8 m, 2 Skinner Uniflcw QuiPE (LSD1-8) or 2 sets Skinner geared steam turbines (LSD13-27), 2 Babcock & Wilcox boilers, 7400 (LSD1-8) or 7000 (LSD13-21, 25-27) or 9000 (LSD22-24) hp, 15.4 or 15.6 (LSD22-24) kts, 1770 t oil, 7400 nm (15 kts), complement 254; 1 x 1 – 127/38 Mk 12, (2 x 4 + 2 x 2) – 40/56 Bofors, 16 x 1 – 20/70 Oerlikon; 3 LCT(5) or 3

LCT(6) or 2 LCT(3) or 2 LCT(4) or 14 LCM(3) or 1450 t of cargo or 41 LVT or 47 DUKW (up to 92 LVT or 108 DUKW if additional decks were installed), 332 troops; SF or SG or SL or SU radar.

One of the most unusual landing ships of the Second World War. They were designed according to the technical design developed by the British Admiralty. A flooded docking well was arranged in the aft part of the hull, which housed 2-3 LCT with tanks or up to 14 LCM with a landing party. During the passage, the well was drained, before landing, the ship took ballast water into special tanks, and the draught aft increased by several meters, the docking well was filled with water, and the landing craft left using own engines. In total, 27 ship-docks were ordered, 4 were transferred to the RN under Lend-Lease.

Shadwell 24.1.1945 was damaged by Japanese air torpedo near the Philippines. *Fort Snelling* was cancelled in 1945 and completed as the mercantile vessel *Carib Queen*. Later she was acquired by the Navy and used as MSTS cargo vessel *Taurus*.

Tortuga 1945

CATSKILL class vehicle landing ships

Catskill	LSV1	Willamette Iron & Steel, Portland	7.1941	19.5.1942	6.1944	sold 11.1973
Ozark	LSV2	Willamette Iron & Steel, Portland	12.1941	15.6.1942	9.1944	stricken 4.1974
Osage	LSV3	Ingalls, Pascagoula	6.1942	30.6.1943	12.1944	to the MarAd 9.1961
Saugus	LSV4	Ingalls, Pascagoula	7.1942	4.9.1943	2.1945	stricken 7.1961
Monitor	LSV5	Ingalls, Pascagoula	10.1941	29.1.1943	6.1944	stricken 9.1961
Montauk	LSV6	Ingalls, Pascagoula	4.1942	14.4.1943	10.1944	stricken 9.1961

Osage 1944

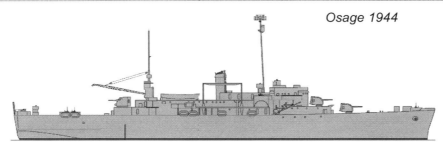

Ozark 1944

5875 (LSV1, 2) or 5625 (LSV3-6) / 9040 t, 138.8 (LSV1, 2) or 139.6 (LSV3-6) x 18.4 x 6.1 m, 2 sets General Electric geared steam turbines, 4 Combustion Engineering boilers, 11000 hp, 20.3 kts, complement 472-564; 4 x 1 (LSV1, 2) or (1 x 2 + 2 x 1) (LSV3-6) – 127/38 Mk 12, 4 x 2 – 40/56 Bofors (LSV3-6), 20 x 1 (LSV1, 2) or 6 x 2 (LSV3-6) – 20/70 Oerlikon, 14 LCV(P), 1 LCP(L) (LSV1, 2), 1 LCP(R) (LSV1, 2), 19 (LSV3, 4) or 21 (LSV5, 6) LVT, 44 (LSV1, 2) or 29 (LSV3, 4) or 31

(LSV5, 6) DUKW, 868 troops; SE or SF or SL or SO or SU radar.

The FY40 Program provided for the building of two minelayers of the *Terror* class and four netlayers of the close design. Immediately before laying down, these ships were proposed to be redesigned to fast landing transports, and the amount of works could be minimized due to the hull structure with an extensive covered deck aft, originally intended to accommodate mines or nets. Although the plan of conversion was not accepted, and the ships were laid down as mine- and netlayers, they were never commissioned in this configuration. With the entry of the USA into the Second World War, the building of landing ships was of paramount importance, and in 1943 shipbuilders returned to the conversion project, abandoned in 1941. The high speed compared to other landing ships and covered cargo deck predetermined

Montauk 1944

them a rather specific purpose: disembarkation of the first wave of "rangers" on DUKW and LVT vehicles. The latter were floated on a special ramp or by crane fitted aft. Besides the vehicles, every ship carried 14-19 LCVP on davits.

LST1 class tank landing ships

LST1	Dravo, Pittsburgh	7.1942	7.9.1942	12.1942	stricken 6.1946
LST2	Dravo, Pittsburgh	6.1942	19.9.1942	2.1943	to the UK 11.1944 (LST2)
LST3	Dravo, Pittsburgh	6.1942	19.9.1942	2.1943	to the UK 12.1944 (LST3)
LST4	Dravo, Pittsburgh	7.1942	9.10.1942	2.1943	to the UK 12.1944 (LST4)
LST5	Dravo, Pittsburgh	7.1942	3.10.1942	2.1943	to the UK 11.1944 (LST5)
LST6	Dravo, Wilmington	7.1942	21.10.1942	1.1943	sunk 18.11.1944
LST7	Dravo, Pittsburgh	7.1942	31.10.1942	3.1943	stricken 6.1946
LST8	Dravo, Pittsburgh	7.1942	29.10.1942	(3.1943)	to the UK 3.1943 (LST8)
LST9	Dravo, Pittsburgh	8.1942	14.11.1942	(3.1943)	to the UK 3.1943 (LST9)
LST10	Dravo, Pittsburgh	8.1942	25.11.1942	(2.1943)	commissioned as landing craft repair ship
LST11	Dravo, Pittsburgh	8.1942	18.11.1942	(3.1943)	to the UK 3.1943 (LST11)
LST12	Dravo, Pittsburgh	8.1942	7.12.1942	(3.1943)	to the UK 3.1943 (LST12)
LST13	Dravo, Pittsburgh	9.1942	1.1.1943	(4.1943)	to the UK 4.1943 (LST13)
LST14	Dravo, Pittsburgh	9.1942	9.12.1942	(3.1943)	commissioned as MTB depot ship
LST15	Dravo, Pittsburgh	9.1942	30.1.1943	(8.1943)	commissioned as battle damage repair ship
LST16	Dravo, Wilmington	9.1942	19.12.1942	3.1943	stricken 4.1946
LST17	Dravo, Pittsburgh	9.1942	8.1.1943	4.1943	target 11.1954
LST18	Dravo, Pittsburgh	10.1942	15.2.1943	4.1943	stricken 4.1946
LST19, 9.1945- LST(H)19	Dravo, Pittsburgh	10.1942	11.3.1943	5.1943	stricken 5.1946
LST20	Dravo, Pittsburgh	10.1942	15.2.1943	5.1943	stricken 6.1946

LST21	Dravo, Wilmington	9.1942	18.2.1943	4.1943	stricken 6.1946
LST22	Dravo, Pittsburgh	11.1942	29.3.1943	5.1943	stricken 4.1946
LST23, 9.1945- LST(H)23	Dravo, Pittsburgh	10.1942	13.3.1943	5.1943	stricken 7.1946
LST24	Dravo, Pittsburgh	11.1942	17.4.1943	6.1943	stricken 6.1946
LST25	Dravo, Wilmington	10.1942	9.3.1943	5.1943	stricken 10.1946
LST26	Dravo, Pittsburgh	11.1942	31.3.1943	6.1943	stricken 5.1946
LST27	Dravo, Pittsburgh	12.1942	27.4.1943	6.1943	stricken 11.1945
LST28	Dravo, Pittsburgh	12.1942	19.4.1943	6.1943	stricken 10.1946
LST29	Dravo, Pittsburgh	1.1943	17.5.1943	7.1943	stricken 5.1946
LST30	Dravo, Pittsburgh	1.1943	3.5.1943	7.1943	stricken 5.1946
LST31	Dravo, Pittsburgh	2.1943	5.6.1943	7.1943	stricken 8.1955
LST32	Dravo, Pittsburgh	2.1943	22.5.1943	7.1943	advance aviation base ship 9.1957
LST33	Dravo, Pittsburgh	2.1943	21.6.1943	8.1943	to Greece 8.1943 (Samos)
LST34	Dravo, Pittsburgh	3.1943	15.6.1943	7.1943	stricken 12.1947
LST35	Dravo, Pittsburgh	3.1943	30.6.1943	(8.1943)	to Greece 8.1943 (Chios)
LST36	Dravo, Pittsburgh	4.1943	10.7.1943	(8.1943)	to Greece 8.1943 (Limnos)
LST37	Dravo, Pittsburgh	4.1943	5.7.1943	(8.1943)	to Greece 8.1943 (Lesbos)
LST38, 9.1945- LST(H)38	Dravo, Pittsburgh	4.1943	27.7.1943	9.1943	stricken 5.1946
LST39	Dravo, Pittsburgh	4.1943	29.7.1943	9.1943	explosion 21.5.1944, repaired as auxiliary
LST40	Dravo, Pittsburgh	6.1943	7.8.1943	9.1943	to South Korea 2.1947
LST41, 9.1945- LST(H)41	Dravo, Pittsburgh	5.1943	17.8.1943	9.1943	stricken 6.1946
LST42, 9.1945- LST(H)42	Dravo, Pittsburgh	6.1943	17.8.1943	9.1943	stricken 9.1946
LST43	Dravo, Pittsburgh	6.1943	28.8.1943	10.1943	explosion 21.5.1944
LST44	Dravo, Pittsburgh	7.1943	11.9.1943	10.1943	target 23.7.1947
LST45	Dravo, Pittsburgh	6.1943	31.8.1943	10.1943	stricken 12.1948
LST46	Dravo, Pittsburgh	7.1943	16.9.1943	11.1943	stricken 6.1946
LST47	Dravo, Pittsburgh	7.1943	24.9.1943	11.1943	to the Philippines 9.1976 (Tarlac)
LST48	Dravo, Pittsburgh	8.1943	2.10.1943	11.1943	stricken 12.1947
LST49	Dravo, Pittsburgh	8.1943	9.10.1943	11.1943	stricken 7.1946
LST50	Dravo, Pittsburgh	8.1943	16.10.1943	11.1943	battle damage repair ship 11.1952
LST51	Dravo, Pittsburgh	8.1943	22.10.1943	12.1943	stricken 10.1947
LST52	Dravo, Pittsburgh	9.1943	20.10.1943	12.1943	stricken 4.1948
LST53	Dravo, Pittsburgh	9.1943	6.11.1943	12.1943	barrack ship 9.1954
LST54	Dravo, Pittsburgh	10.1943	13.11.1943	12.1943	stricken 11.1945
LST55	Dravo, Pittsburgh	10.1943	20.11.1943	1.1944	stricken 1.1946
LST56	Dravo, Pittsburgh	10.1943	27.11.1943	1.1944	stricken 7.1946
LST57	Dravo, Pittsburgh	10.1943	4.12.1943	1.1944	stricken 8.1955
LST58	Dravo, Pittsburgh	10.1943	11.12.1943	1.1944	stricken 11.1945
LST59	Dravo, Pittsburgh	11.1943	18.12.1943	1.1944	stricken 2.1946
LST60	Dravo, Pittsburgh	11.1943	24.12.1943	2.1944	stricken 11.1958
LST61	JeffBoat, Jeffersonville	6.1942	8.11.1942	2.1943	stricken 6.1946

LST62	JeffBoat, Jeffersonville	8.1942	23.11.1942	(3.1943)	to the UK 3.1943 (LST62)
LST63	JeffBoat, Jeffersonville	8.1942	19.12.1942	(3.1943)	to the UK 3.1943 (LST63)
LST64	JeffBoat, Jeffersonville	8.1942	8.1.1943	(3.1943)	to the UK 4.1943 (LST64)
LST65	JeffBoat, Jeffersonville	8.1942	7.12.1942	(3.1943)	to the UK 3.1943 (LST65)
LST66	JeffBoat, Jeffersonville	8.1942	16.1.1943	4.1943	stricken 5.1946
LST67	JeffBoat, Jeffersonville	9.1942	28.1.1943	4.1943	stricken 5.1946
LST68	JeffBoat, Jeffersonville	9.1942	8.3.1943	6.1943	stricken 6.1946
LST69	JeffBoat, Jeffersonville	9.1942	20.2.1943	5.1943	explosion 21.5.1944
LST70	JeffBoat, Jeffersonville	11.1942	8.2.1943	5.1943	stricken 5.1946
LST71	JeffBoat, Jeffersonville	11.1942	27.2.1943	6.1943	stricken 5.1946
LST72	JeffBoat, Jeffersonville	12.1942	17.3.1943	6.1943	stricken 6.1946
LST73	JeffBoat, Jeffersonville	12.1942	29.3.1943	6.1943	stricken 6.1947
LST74	JeffBoat, Jeffersonville	1.1943	31.3.1943	6.1943	stricken 1.1946
LST75	JeffBoat, Jeffersonville	1.1943	7.4.1943	6.1943	to the Philippines 12.1947 (Cotabato)
LST76	JeffBoat, Jeffersonville	1.1943	14.4.1943	6.1943	to the UK 12.1944 (LST76)
LST77	JeffBoat, Jeffersonville	2.1943	21.4.1943	7.1943	to the UK 12.1944 (LST77)
LST78	JeffBoat, Jeffersonville	2.1943	28.4.1943	7.1943	stricken 5.1946
LST79	JeffBoat, Jeffersonville	2.1943	8.5.1943	(7.1943)	to the UK 7.1943 (LST79)
LST80	JeffBoat, Jeffersonville	3.1943	18.5.1943	(7.1943)	to the UK 7.1943 (LST80)
LST81	JeffBoat, Jeffersonville	3.1943	28.5.1943	(7.1943)	to the UK 7.1943 (LSE1)
LST82	JeffBoat, Jeffersonville	3.1943	9.6.1943	(8.1943)	to the UK 8.1943 (LSE2)
LST83	JeffBoat, Jeffersonville	3.1943	14.6.1943	(8.1943)	commissioned as landing craft repair ship
LST84, 9.1945- LST(H)84	JeffBoat, Jeffersonville	4.1943	26.6.1943	8.1943	stricken 10.1947
LST117, 9.1945- LST(H)117	JeffBoat, Jeffersonville	4.1943	10.7.1943	8.1943	stricken 6.1973
LST118, 9.1945- LST(H)118	JeffBoat, Jeffersonville	4.1943	21.7.1943	9.1943	stricken 9.1947
LST119	JeffBoat, Jeffersonville	5.1943	28.7.1943	9.1943	stricken 6.1946
LST120	JeffBoat, Jeffersonville	5.1943	7.8.1943	9.1943	to South Korea 2.1947 (Munsan)
LST121, 9.1945- LST(H)121	JeffBoat, Jeffersonville	5.1943	16.8.1943	9.1943	stricken 5.1946
LST122	Missouri Valley Bridge, Evansville	6.1943	9.8.1943	9.1943	stricken 7.1946
LST123, 9.1945- LST(H)123	Missouri Valley Bridge, Evansville	6.1943	14.8.1943	9.1943	stricken 5.1946
LST124	Missouri Valley Bridge, Evansville	6.1943	18.8.1943	9.1943	stricken 8.1946
LST125	Missouri Valley Bridge, Evansville	6.1943	23.8.1943	9.1943	target 14.8.1946

LST126	Missouri Valley Bridge, Evansville	6.1943	28.8.1943	10.1943	stricken 6.1947
LST127	Missouri Valley Bridge, Evansville	6.1943	31.8.1943	10.1943	stricken 6.1947
LST128	Missouri Valley Bridge, Evansville	6.1943	3.9.1943	10.1943	stricken 4.1946
LST129	Missouri Valley Bridge, Evansville	7.1943	8.9.1943	10.1943	test ship 12.1944
LST130	Missouri Valley Bridge, Evansville	7.1943	13.9.1943	11.1943	stricken 12.1947
LST131	Missouri Valley Bridge, Evansville	7.1943	13.9.1943	11.1943	stricken 6.1947
LST132	Chicago Bridge, Seneca	6.1943	26.10.1943	(4.1944)	commissioned as battle damage repair ship
LST133	Chicago Bridge, Seneca	6.1943	2.11.1943	11.1943	sunk as target 11.5.1948
LST134	Chicago Bridge, Seneca	6.1943	9.11.1943	12.1943	stricken 10.1947
LST135	Chicago Bridge, Seneca	7.1943	16.11.1943	(4.1944)	commissioned as MTB depot ship
LST136	Chicago Bridge, Seneca	6.1943	10.12.1943	(3.1944)	commissioned as landing craft repair ship
LST137	American Bridge, Pittsburgh	10.1943	19.12.1943	1.1944	stricken 12.1945
LST138	American Bridge, Pittsburgh	10.1943	30.12.1943	2.1944	stricken 12.1945
LST139	American Bridge, Pittsburgh	11.1943	12.1.1944	2.1944	stricken 5.1946
LST140	American Bridge, Pittsburgh	11.1943	8.1.1944	2.1944	stricken 3.1946
LST141	American Bridge, Pittsburgh	11.1943	16.1.1944	2.1944	stricken 2.1946
LST157	Missouri Valley Bridge, Evansville	6.1942	31.10.1942	3.1943	to the UK 12.1944 (LST157)
LST158	Missouri Valley Bridge, Evansville	7.1942	16.11.1942	2.1943	sunk 11.7.1943
LST159	Missouri Valley Bridge, Evansville	7.1942	21.11.1942	2.1943	to the UK 3.1943 (LST159)
LST160	Missouri Valley Bridge, Evansville	7.1942	30.11.1942	2.1943	to the UK 3.1943 (LST160)
LST161	Missouri Valley Bridge, Evansville	7.1942	7.12.1942	2.1943	to the UK 3.1943 (LST161)
LST162	Missouri Valley Bridge, Evansville	7.1942	3.2.1943	(3.1943) / 2.1945	to the UK 3.1943-2.1945 (LST162), stricken 6.1946
LST163	Missouri Valley Bridge, Evansville	8.1942	4.2.1943	3.1943	to the UK 4.1943 (LST163)
LST164	Missouri Valley Bridge, Evansville	8.1942	5.2.1943	3.1943	to the UK 4.1943 (LST164)
LST165	Missouri Valley Bridge, Evansville	9.1942	2.2.1943	4.1943	to the UK 4.1943 (LST165)
LST166	Missouri Valley Bridge, Evansville	9.1942	1.2.1943	4.1943	stricken 6.1946
LST167	Missouri Valley Bridge, Evansville	9.1942	25.2.1943	4.1943	CTL 25.9.1943

LST168	Missouri Valley Bridge, Evansville	9.1942	25.2.1943	5.1943	stricken 4.1946
LST169	Missouri Valley Bridge, Evansville	10.1942	26.2.1943	5.1943	stricken 6.1946
LST170	Missouri Valley Bridge, Evansville	10.1942	27.2.1943	5.1943	stricken 7.1946
LST171	Missouri Valley Bridge, Evansville	10.1942	28.2.1943	6.1943	stricken 7.1946
LST172	Missouri Valley Bridge, Evansville	12.1942	12.5.1943	6.1943	stricken 6.1946
LST173	Missouri Valley Bridge, Evansville	12.1942	24.4.1943	6.1943	to the UK 12.1944 (LST173)
LST174	Missouri Valley Bridge, Evansville	1.1943	21.4.1943	6.1943	stricken 1.1946
LST175	Missouri Valley Bridge, Evansville	1.1943	18.4.1943	5.1943	stricken 5.1946
LST176	Missouri Valley Bridge, Evansville	1.1943	15.4.1943	5.1943	stricken 11.1973
LST177	Missouri Valley Bridge, Evansville	2.1943	16.5.1943	6.1943	stricken 4.1946
LST178	Missouri Valley Bridge, Evansville	2.1943	23.5.1943	6.1943	to the UK 12.1944 (LST178)
LST179	Missouri Valley Bridge, Evansville	2.1943	30.5.1943	7.1943	explosion 21.5.1944
LST180	Missouri Valley Bridge, Evansville	2.1943	3.6.1943	6.1943	to the UK 7.1943 (LST180)
LST181	Jeffboat, Jeffersonville	4.1943	3.7.1943	8.1943	stricken 4.1946
LST197	Chicago Bridge, Seneca	6.1942	13.12.1942	2.1943	stricken 6.1946
LST198	Chicago Bridge, Seneca	6.1942	17.1.1943	2.1943	to the UK 3.1943 (LST198)
LST199	Chicago Bridge, Seneca	6.1942	7.2.1943	3.1943	to the UK 3.1943 (LST199)
LST200	Chicago Bridge, Seneca	7.1942	20.2.1943	3.1943	to the UK 3.1943 (LST200)
LST201	Chicago Bridge, Seneca	7.1942	2.3.1943	4.1943	MTB depot ship 8.1944
LST202	Chicago Bridge, Seneca	7.1942	16.3.1943	4.1943	stricken 8.1946
LST203	Chicago Bridge, Seneca	7.1942	25.3.1943	4.1943	wrecked 1.10.1943
LST204	Chicago Bridge, Seneca	7.1942	3.4.1943	4.1943	stricken 6.1946
LST205, 9.1945-LST(H)205	Chicago Bridge, Seneca	8.1942	13.4.1943	5.1943	stricken 6.1946
LST206	Chicago Bridge, Seneca	8.1942	21.4.1943	6.1943	stricken 6.1946
LST207	Chicago Bridge, Seneca	9.1942	29.4.1943	6.1943	stricken 4.1946
LST208	Chicago Bridge, Seneca	9.1942	22.5.1943	6.1943	stricken 7.1946
LST209	Chicago Bridge, Seneca	9.1942	29.5.1943	6.1943	stricken 11.1958
LST210	Chicago Bridge, Seneca	9.1942	5.6.1943	7.1943	stricken 1.1946
LST211	Chicago Bridge, Seneca	9.1942	5.6.1943	7.1943	stricken 12.1945
LST212	Chicago Bridge, Seneca	12.1942	12.6.1943	7.1943	stricken 11.1945
LST213, 9.1945-LST(H)213	Chicago Bridge, Seneca	12.1942	16.6.1943	7.1943	stricken 3.1947
LST214	Chicago Bridge, Seneca	12.1942	22.6.1943	(7.1943) / 1.1944	to the UK 7.1943- 1.1944 (LST214), stricken 4.1946

LST215	Chicago Bridge, Seneca	1.1943	26.6.1943	(7.1943)	to the UK 7.1943 (LST215)
LST216	Chicago Bridge, Seneca	1.1943	4.7.1943	(8.1943)	to the UK 8.1943 (LST216)
LST217	Chicago Bridge, Seneca	2.1943	13.7.1943	(8.1943)	to the UK 8.1943 (LST217)
LST218	Chicago Bridge, Seneca	2.1943	20.7.1943	8.1943	to South Korea 5.1955 (Bibong)
LST219	Chicago Bridge, Seneca	2.1943	27.7.1943	8.1943	stricken 12.1948
LST220	Chicago Bridge, Seneca	3.1943	3.8.1943	8.1943	stricken 5.1948
LST221	Chicago Bridge, Seneca	3.1943	7.8.1943	9.1943	stricken 7.1946
LST222, 9.1945-LST(H)222	Chicago Bridge, Seneca	3.1943	17.8.1943	9.1943	to the Philippines 7.1972 (Mindoro Occidental)
LST223, 9.1945-LST(H)223	Chicago Bridge, Seneca	3.1943	24.8.1943	9.1943	for disposal 3.1947
LST224	Chicago Bridge, Seneca	4.1943	31.8.1943	9.1943	stricken 4.1946
LST225	Chicago Bridge, Seneca	4.1943	4.9.1943	10.1943	stricken 8.1946
LST226	Chicago Bridge, Seneca	4.1943	14.9.1943	10.1943	stricken 6.1946
LST227	Chicago Bridge, Seneca	5.1943	21.9.1943	10.1943	to South Korea 3.1955 (Deokbong)
LST228	Chicago Bridge, Seneca	5.1943	25.9.1943	10.1943	wrecked 20.1.1944
LST229	Chicago Bridge, Seneca	5.1943	5.10.1943	11.1943	stricken 10.1947
LST230	Chicago Bridge, Seneca	5.1943	12.10.1943	11.1943	to the Philippines 9.1976 (Laguna)
LST231	Chicago Bridge, Seneca	6.1943	19.10.1943	(2.1944)	commissioned as landing craft repair ship
LST237	Missouri Valley Bridge, Evansville	2.1943	8.6.1943	(7.1943)	to the UK 7.1943 (LST237)
LST238	Missouri Valley Bridge, Evansville	3.1943	15.6.1943	(7.1943)	to the UK 7.1943 (LST238)
LST239	Missouri Valley Bridge, Evansville	3.1943	18.6.1943	(7.1943)	to the UK 7.1943 (LST239)
LST240	Missouri Valley Bridge, Evansville	3.1943	25.6.1943	7.1943	stricken 6.1947
LST241	Missouri Valley Bridge, Evansville	3.1943	29.6.1943	7.1943	stricken 6.1946
LST242, 9.1945-LST(H)242	Missouri Valley Bridge, Evansville	3.1943	3.7.1943	8.1943	stricken 10.1947
LST243, 9.1945-LST(H)243	Missouri Valley Bridge, Evansville	4.1943	9.7.1943	8.1943	stricken 7.1947
LST244	Missouri Valley Bridge, Evansville	5.1943	14.7.1943	8.1943	stricken 7.1946
LST245	Missouri Valley Bridge, Evansville	5.1943	17.7.1943	8.1943	stricken 5.1946
LST246	Missouri Valley Bridge, Evansville	5.1943	22.7.1943	8.1943	stricken 3.1948
LST247, 9.1945-LST(H)247	Missouri Valley Bridge, Evansville	5.1943	30.7.1943	8.1943	stricken 8.1946
LST261	American Bridge, Pittsburgh	9.1942	23.1.1943	5.1943	stricken 3.1946
LST262	American Bridge, Pittsburgh	9.1942	13.2.1943	6.1943	stricken 6.1946

LST263	American Bridge, Pittsburgh	9.1942	27.2.1943	6.1943	stricken 11.1958
LST264	American Bridge, Pittsburgh	9.1942	13.3.1943	7.1943	stricken 6.1946
LST265	American Bridge, Pittsburgh	10.1942	24.4.1943	7.1943	stricken 1.1946
LST266	American Bridge, Pittsburgh	11.1942	16.5.1943	8.1943	stricken 11.1958
LST267	American Bridge, Pittsburgh	11.1942	6.6.1943	8.1943	stricken 7.1946
LST268, 9.1945-LST(H)268	American Bridge, Pittsburgh	11.1942	18.6.1943	8.1943	stricken 10.1947
LST269	American Bridge, Pittsburgh	12.1942	4.7.1943	8.1943	stricken 12.1947
LST270	American Bridge, Pittsburgh	1.1943	18.7.1943	9.1943	sold 5.1950
LST271	American Bridge, Pittsburgh	1.1943	25.7.1943	9.1943	stricken 6.1946
LST272	American Bridge, Pittsburgh	2.1943	1.8.1943	9.1943	stricken 9.1946
LST273	American Bridge, Pittsburgh	2.1943	8.8.1943	9.1943	stricken 10.1946
LST274	American Bridge, Pittsburgh	3.1943	15.8.1943	9.1943	stricken 6.1947
LST275	American Bridge, Pittsburgh	4.1943	22.8.1943	10.1943	stricken 9.1946
LST276, 9.1945-LST(H)276	American Bridge, Pittsburgh	5.1943	29.8.1943	10.1943	to Singapore 6.1973
LST277	American Bridge, Pittsburgh	5.1943	5.9.1943	10.1943	to Chile 2.1973 (Comandante Toro)
LST278	American Bridge, Pittsburgh	6.1943	12.9.1943	10.1943	test ship 2.1945
LST279	American Bridge, Pittsburgh	7.1943	19.9.1943	10.1943	to Taiwan 6.1955 (Chung Chi)
LST280	American Bridge, Pittsburgh	7.1943	26.9.1943	11.1943	to the UK 10.1944 (LST280)
LST281	American Bridge, Pittsburgh	6.1943	30.9.1943	11.1943	stricken 5.1954
LST282	American Bridge, Pittsburgh	7.1943	3.10.1943	11.1943	sunk 15.8.1944
LST283	American Bridge, Pittsburgh	8.1943	10.10.1943	11.1943	stricken 3.1947
LST284	American Bridge, Pittsburgh	8.1943	17.10.1943	11.1943	stricken 6.1946
LST285	American Bridge, Pittsburgh	8.1943	24.10.1943	12.1943	stricken 8.1947
LST286	American Bridge, Pittsburgh	8.1943	27.10.1943	12.1943	stricken 5.1946
LST287	American Bridge, Pittsburgh	8.1943	31.10.1943	12.1943	to the Philippines 9.1976 (Samar Oriental)
LST288	American Bridge, Pittsburgh	9.1943	7.11.1943	12.1943	to South Korea 3.1956 (Gyebong)
LST289	American Bridge, Pittsburgh	9.1943	21.11.1943	12.1943	to the UK 11.1944 (LST289)

LST290	American Bridge, Pittsburgh	9.1943	5.11.1943	1.1944	stricken 11.1945
LST291	American Bridge, Pittsburgh	9.1943	14.11.1943	12.1943	stricken 5.1954
LST292	American Bridge, Pittsburgh	9.1943	28.11.1943	1.1944	stricken 4.1946
LST293	American Bridge, Pittsburgh	10.1943	12.12.1943	1.1944	stricken 12.1945
LST294	American Bridge, Pittsburgh	10.1943	15.12.1943	1.1944	stricken 1.1946
LST295	American Bridge, Pittsburgh	10.1943	24.12.1943	2.1944	stricken 4.1946
LST301	Boston N Yd, Charlestown	6.1942	15.9.1942	(11.1942)	to the UK 11.1942 (LST301)
LST302	Boston N Yd, Charlestown	6.1942	15.9.1942	(11.1942)	to the UK 11.1942 (LST302)
LST303	Boston N Yd, Charlestown	7.1942	21.9.1942	(11.1942)	to the UK 11.1942 (LST303)
LST304	Boston N Yd, Charlestown	7.1942	21.9.1942	(11.1942)	to the UK 11.1942 (LST304)
LST305	Boston N Yd, Charlestown	7.1942	10.10.1942	(12.1942)	to the UK 12.1942 (LST305)
LST306	Boston N Yd, Charlestown	7.1942	10.10.1942	12.1942	stricken 2.1959
LST307	Boston N Yd, Charlestown	9.1942	9.11.1942	12.1942	stricken 7.1946
LST308	Boston N Yd, Charlestown	9.1942	9.11.1942	1.1943	for disposal 12.1947
LST309	Boston N Yd, Charlestown	9.1942	23.11.1942	1.1943	stricken 6.1947
LST310	Boston N Yd, Charlestown	9.1942	23.11.1942	1.1943	stricken 3.1946
LST311	New York N Yd, Brooklyn	9.1942	30.12.1942	1.1943	to the UK 11.1944 (LST311)
LST312	New York N Yd, Brooklyn	9.1942	30.12.1942	1.1943	stricken 8.1946
LST313	New York N Yd, Brooklyn	9.1942	30.12.1942	1.1943	sunk 10.7.1943
LST314	New York N Yd, Brooklyn	9.1942	30.12.1942	1.1943	sunk 9.6.1944
LST315	New York N Yd, Brooklyn	10.1942	28.1.1943	2.1943	to the UK 11.1944 (LST315)
LST316	New York N Yd, Brooklyn	10.1942	28.1.1943	2.1943	stricken 3.1946
LST317	New York N Yd, Brooklyn	10.1942	28.1.1943	2.1943	stricken 3.1946
LST318	New York N Yd, Brooklyn	10.1942	28.1.1943	2.1943	sunk 9.8.1943
LST319	Philadelphia N Yd	8.1942	5.11.1942	(12.1942)	to the UK 12.1942 (LST319)
LST320	Philadelphia N Yd	8.1942	5.11.1942	(12.1942)	to the UK 12.1942 (LST320)
LST321	Philadelphia N Yd	8.1942	5.11.1942	(12.1942)	to the UK 12.1942 (LST321)
LST322	Philadelphia N Yd	8.1942	5.11.1942	(1.1943)	to the UK 1.1943 (LST322)
LST323	Philadelphia N Yd	8.1942	5.11.1942	(1.1943)	to the UK 1.1943 (LST323)
LST324	Philadelphia N Yd	8.1942	5.11.1942	(1.1943)	to the UK 1.1943 (LST324)
LST325	Philadelphia N Yd	8.1942	27.10.1942	2.1943	to Greece 5.1964 (Syros)
LST326	Philadelphia N Yd	11.1942	11.2.1943	2.1943	to the UK 12.1944 (LST326)

LST327	Philadelphia N Yd	11.1942	11.2.1943	3.1943	stricken 12.1945
LST328	Philadelphia N Yd	11.1942	11.2.1943	(5.1943)	commissioned as battle damage repair ship
LST329	Philadelphia N Yd	11.1942	11.2.1943	(5.1943)	commissioned as battle damage repair ship
LST330	Philadelphia N Yd	11.1942	11.2.1943	(6.1943)	commissioned as MTB depot ship
LST331	Philadelphia N Yd	11.1942	11.2.1943	3.1943	to the UK 11.1944 (LST331)
LST332	Philadelphia N Yd	10.1942	24.12.1942	2.1943	stricken 3.1946
LST333	Norfolk N Yd, Portsmouth	7.1942	15.10.1942	11.1942	sunk 22.6.1943
LST334	Norfolk N Yd, Portsmouth	7.1942	15.10.1942	11.1942	stricken 6.1946
LST335	Norfolk N Yd, Portsmouth	7.1942	15.10.1942	12.1942	stricken 1.1946
LST336	Norfolk N Yd, Portsmouth	7.1942	15.10.1942	12.1942	to the UK 11.1944 (LST336)
LST337	Norfolk N Yd, Portsmouth	7.1942	8.11.1942	12.1942	to the UK 12.1944 (LST337)
LST338	Norfolk N Yd, Portsmouth	7.1942	8.11.1942	12.1942	stricken 6.1947
LST339	Norfolk N Yd, Portsmouth	7.1942	8.11.1942	12.1942	stricken 6.1947
LST340	Norfolk N Yd, Portsmouth	7.1942	8.11.1942	12.1942	test ship 10.1944
LST341	Norfolk N Yd, Portsmouth	8.1942	8.11.1942	12.1942	stricken 4.1946
LST342	Norfolk N Yd, Portsmouth	8.1942	8.11.1942	12.1942	sunk 18.7.1943
LST343	Norfolk N Yd, Portsmouth	10.1942	15.12.1942	1.1943	to South Korea 2.1947 (Danyang)
LST344	Norfolk N Yd, Portsmouth	10.1942	15.12.1942	1.1943	stricken 9.1974
LST345	Norfolk N Yd, Portsmouth	10.1942	15.12.1942	1.1943	stricken 1.1946
LST346	Norfolk N Yd, Portsmouth	10.1942	15.12.1942	1.1943	to the UK 11.1944 (LST346)
LST347	Norfolk N Yd, Portsmouth	11.1942	7.2.1943	2.1943	to the UK 12.1944 (LST347)
LST348	Norfolk N Yd, Portsmouth	11.1942	7.2.1943	2.1943	sunk 20.2.1944
LST349	Norfolk N Yd, Portsmouth	11.1942	7.2.1943	2.1943	wrecked 26.2.1944
LST350	Norfolk N Yd, Portsmouth	11.1942	7.2.1943	2.1943	stricken 3.1946
LST351	Norfolk N Yd, Portsmouth	11.1942	7.2.1943	2.1943	to the UK 12.1944 (LST351)
LST352	Norfolk N Yd, Portsmouth	11.1942	7.2.1943	2.1943	to the UK 12.1944 (LST352)
LST353	Charleston N Yd	7.1942	12.10.1942	11.1942	explosion 21.5.1944
LST354	Charleston N Yd	7.1942	13.10.1942	11.1942	stricken 6.1946
LST355	Charleston N Yd	9.1942	16.11.1942	12.1942	stricken 10.1947
LST356	Charleston N Yd	9.1942	16.11.1942	12.1942	stricken 9.1960
LST357	Charleston N Yd	10.1942	14.12.1942	2.1943	stricken 7.1946
LST358	Charleston N Yd	10.1942	15.12.1942	2.1943	to the UK 12.1944 (LST358)
LST359	Charleston N Yd	11.1942	11.1.1943	2.1943	sunk 20.12.1944
LST360	Charleston N Yd	11.1942	11.1.1943	2.1943	to the UK 11.1944 (LST360)
LST361	Bethlehem, Quincy	8.1942	10.10.1942	(11.1942)	to the UK 11.1942 (LST361)
LST362	Bethlehem, Quincy	8.1942	10.10.1942	(11.1942)	to the UK 11.1942 (LST362)
LST363	Bethlehem, Quincy	9.1942	26.10.1942	(11.1942)	to the UK 11.1942 (LST363)

LST364	Bethlehem, Quincy	9.1942	26.10.1942	(12.1942)	to the UK 12.1942 (LST364)
LST365	Bethlehem, Quincy	10.1942	11.11.1942	(11.1942)	to the UK 11.1942 (LST365)
LST366	Bethlehem, Quincy	10.1942	11.11.1942	(12.1942)	to the UK 12.1942 (LST366)
LST367	Bethlehem, Quincy	10.1942	24.11.1942	(12.1942)	to the UK 12.1942 (LST367)
LST368	Bethlehem, Quincy	10.1942	24.11.1942	(1.1943)	to the UK 1.1943 (LST368)
LST369	Bethlehem, Quincy	10.1942	24.11.1942	1.1943	to the UK 11.1944 (LST369)
LST370	Bethlehem, Quincy	10.1942	12.12.1942	1.1943	stricken 4.1946
LST371	Bethlehem, Quincy	10.1942	12.12.1942	1.1943	to the UK 11.1944 (LST371)
LST372	Bethlehem, Quincy	11.1942	19.1.1943	1.1943	stricken 8.1946
LST373	Bethlehem, Quincy	11.1942	19.1.1943	1.1943	to the UK 12.1944 (LST373)
LST374	Bethlehem, Quincy	11.1942	19.1.1943	1.1943	stricken 3.1946
LST375	Bethlehem, Quincy	11.1942	28.1.1943	2.1943	stricken 6.1947
LST376	Bethlehem, Quincy	11.1942	1.2.1943	2.1943	sunk 9 6.1944
LST377	Bethlehem, Quincy	11.1942	1.2.1943	2.1943	stricken 7.1946
LST378	Bethlehem, Quincy	12.1942	6.2.1943	2.1943	stricken 3.1947
LST379	Bethlehem, Quincy	12.1942	6.2.1943	2.1943	stricken 3.1946
LST380	Bethlehem, Quincy	12.1942	10.2.1943	2.1943	to the UK 11.1944 (LST380)
LST381	Bethlehem, Quincy	12.1942	10.2.1943	2.1943	to the UK 12.1944 (LST381)
LST382	Bethlehem, Quincy	12.1942	3.2.1943	2.1943	to the UK 11.1944 (LST382)
LST383	Newport News	6.1942	28.9.1942	10.1942	to the UK 11.1944 (LST383)
LST384	Newport News	6.1942	28.9.1942	11.1942	stricken 6.1946
LST385	Newport News	6.1942	28.9.1942	11.1942	to the UK 11.1944 (LST385)
LST386	Newport News	6.1942	28.9.1942	11.1942	to the UK 12.1944 (LST386)
LST387	Newport News	6.1942	28.9.1942	11.1942	stricken 7.1946
LST388	Newport News	6.1942	28.9.1942	11.1942	stricken 2.1947
LST389	Newport News	6.1942	15.10.1942	11.1942	stricken 6.1959
LST390	Newport News	6.1942	15.10.1942	11.1942	stricken 9.1947
LST391	Newport News	7.1942	28.10.1942	12.1942	to Greece 5.1960 (Rodos)
LST392	Newport News	7.1942	28.10.1942	12.1942	stricken 6.1946
LST393	Newport News	7.1942	11.11.1942	12.1942	stricken 3.1947
LST394	Newport News	7.1942	11.11.1942	12.1942	to the UK 12.1944 (LST394)
LST395	Newport News	9.1942	23.11.1942	12.1942	stricken 5.1946
LST396	Newport News	9.1942	23.11.1942	12.1942	explosion 18.8.1943
LST397	Newport News	9.1942	23.11.1942	12.1942	stricken 6.1946
LST398	Newport News	9.1942	23.11.1942	1.1943	stricken 8.1947
LST399	Newport News	9.1942	23.11.1942	1.1943	stricken 11.1973

LST400	Newport News	9.1942	23.11.1942	1.1943	to Taiwan 9.1958 (Chung Suo)
LST401	Bethlehem-Fairfield, Baltimore	8.1942	16.10.1942	(11.1942)	to the UK 11.1942 (LST401)
LST402	Bethlehem-Fairfield, Baltimore	8.1942	9.10.1942	(12.1942)	to the UK 12.1942 (LST402)
LST403	Bethlehem-Fairfield, Baltimore	8.1942	24.10.1942	(12.1942)	to the UK 12.1942 (LST403)
LST404	Bethlehem-Fairfield, Baltimore	8.1942	28.10.1942	(12.1942)	to the UK 12.1942 (LST404)
LST405	Bethlehem-Fairfield, Baltimore	8.1942	31.10.1942	(12.1942)	to the UK 12.1942 (LST405)
LST406	Bethlehem-Fairfield, Baltimore	9.1942	28.10.1942	(12.1942)	to the UK 12.1942 (LST406)
LST407	Bethlehem-Fairfield, Baltimore	9.1942	5.11.1942	(12.1942)	to the UK 12.1942 (LST407)
LST408	Bethlehem-Fairfield, Baltimore	9.1942	31.10.1942	(12.1942)	to the UK 12.1942 (LST408)
LST409	Bethlehem-Fairfield, Baltimore	9.1942	15.11.1942	(1.1943)	to the UK 1.1943 (LST409)
LST410	Bethlehem-Fairfield, Baltimore	9.1942	15.11.1942	(1.1943)	to the UK 1.1943 (LST410)
LST411	Bethlehem-Fairfield, Baltimore	9.1942	9.11.1942	(12.1942)	to the UK 12.1942 (LST411)
LST412	Bethlehem-Fairfield, Baltimore	9.1942	16.11.1942	(1.1943)	to the UK 1.1943 (LST412)
LST413	Bethlehem-Fairfield, Baltimore	10.1942	10.11.1942	(1.1943)	to the UK 1.1943 (LST413)
LST414	Bethlehem-Fairfield, Baltimore	10.1942	21.11.1942	(1.1943)	to the UK 1.1943 (LST414)
LST415	Bethlehem-Fairfield, Baltimore	10.1942	21.11.1942	(1.1943)	to the UK 1.1943 (LST415)
LST416	Bethlehem-Fairfield, Baltimore	10.1942	30.11.1942	(2.1943)	to the UK 2.1943 (LST416)
LST417	Bethlehem-Fairfield, Baltimore	10.1942	24.11.1942	(1.1943)	to the UK 1.1943 (LST417)
LST418	Bethlehem-Fairfield, Baltimore	11.1942	30.11.1942	(1.1943)	to the UK 1.1943 (LST418)
LST419	Bethlehem-Fairfield, Baltimore	11.1942	30.11.1942	(2.1943)	to the UK 2.1943 (LST419)
LST420	Bethlehem-Fairfield, Baltimore	11.1942	5.12.1942	(2.1943)	to the UK 2.1943 (LST420)
LST421	Bethlehem-Fairfield, Baltimore	11.1942	5.12.1942	(1.1943)	to the UK 1.1943 (LST421)
LST422	Bethlehem-Fairfield, Baltimore	11.1942	10.12.1942	(2.1943)	to the UK 2.1943 (LST422)
LST423	Bethlehem-Fairfield, Baltimore	12.1942	14.1.1943	(2.1943)	to the UK 2.1943 (LST423)
LST424	Bethlehem-Fairfield, Baltimore	11.1942	12.12.1942	(2.1943)	to the UK 2.1943 (LST424)
LST425	Bethlehem-Fairfield, Baltimore	11.1942	12.12.1942	(2.1943)	to the UK 2.1943 (LST425)
LST426	Bethlehem-Fairfield, Baltimore	11.1942	11.12.1942	(2.1943)	to the UK 2.1943 (LST426)

LST427	Bethlehem-Fairfield, Baltimore	11.1942	19.12.1942	(2.1943)	to the UK 2.1943 (LST427)
LST428	Bethlehem-Fairfield, Baltimore	11.1942	22.12.1942	(2.1943)	to the UK 2.1943 (LST428)
LST429	Bethlehem-Fairfield, Baltimore	11.1942	11.1.1943	(2.1943)	to the UK 2.1943 (LST429)
LST430	Bethlehem-Fairfield, Baltimore	11.1942	22.12.1942	(2.1943)	to the UK 2.1943 (LST430)
LST446	Kaiser, Vancouver	6.1942	18.9.1942	11.1942	stricken 10.1946
LST447	Kaiser, Vancouver	7.1942	22.9.1942	12.1942	sunk 6 4.1945
LST448	Kaiser, Vancouver	7.1942	26.9.1942	12.1942	sunk 5 10.1943
LST449	Kaiser, Vancouver	7.1942	30.9.1942	12.1942	stricken 3.1946
LST450, 9.1945-LST(H)450	Kaiser, Vancouver	7.1942	4.10.1942	1.1943	stricken 4.1946
LST451	Kaiser, Vancouver	7.1942	6.10.1942	1.1943	stricken 9.1946
LST452	Kaiser, Vancouver	7.1942	10.10.1942	1.1943	stricken 7.1946
LST453	Kaiser, Vancouver	7.1942	10.10.1942	1.1943	landing craft repair ship 8.1944
LST454	Kaiser, Vancouver	7.1942	14.10.1942	1.1943	stricken 5.1946
LST455	Kaiser, Vancouver	8.1942	17.10.1942	1.1943	landing craft repair ship 8.1944
LST456	Kaiser, Vancouver	8.1942	20.10.1942	2.1943	stricken 6.1973
LST457	Kaiser, Vancouver	8.1942	23.10.1942	2.1943	stricken 9.1947
LST458	Kaiser, Vancouver	9.1942	26.10.1942	2.1943	stricken 7.1946
LST459	Kaiser, Vancouver	9.1942	29.10.1942	2.1943	stricken 6.1946
LST460	Kaiser, Vancouver	9.1942	31.10.1942	2.1943	sunk 21.12.1944
LST461	Kaiser, Vancouver	9.1942	3.11.1942	2.1943	stricken 9.1947
LST462	Kaiser, Vancouver	10.1942	6.11.1942	2.1943	stricken 5.1946
LST463	Kaiser, Vancouver	10.1942	9.11.1942	2.1943	stricken 6.1946
LST464, 9.1945-LST(H)464	Kaiser, Vancouver	10.1942	12.11.1942	2.1943	stricken 6.1946
LST465	Kaiser, Vancouver	12.1942	9.1.1943	2.1943	stricken 4.1946
LST466	Kaiser, Vancouver	10.1942	18.11.1942	3.1943	stricken 4.1946
LST467	Kaiser, Vancouver	10.1942	21.11.1942	3.1943	stricken 6.1946
LST468	Kaiser, Vancouver	10.1942	24.11.1942	3.1943	stricken 6.1946
LST469	Kaiser, Vancouver	10.1942	27.11.1942	3.1943	stricken 5.1946
LST470	Kaiser, Vancouver	10.1942	30.11.1942	3.1943	stricken 6.1946
LST471	Kaiser, Vancouver	10.1942	3.12.1942	3.1943	stricken 4.1946
LST472	Kaiser, Vancouver	10.1942	7.12.1942	3.1943	sunk 21.12.1944
LST473	Kaiser, Vancouver	11.1942	9.12.1942	3.1943	stricken 4.1946
LST474	Kaiser, Vancouver	11.1942	12.12.1942	3.1943	stricken 4.1946
LST475	Kaiser, Vancouver	11.1942	16.12.1942	3.1943	stricken 6.1946
LST476	Kaiser, Richmond	8.1942	10.10.1942	4.1943	stricken 10.1947
LST477, 9.1945-LST(H)477	Kaiser, Richmond	8.1942	29.10.1943	2.1943	stricken 8.1947
LST478	Kaiser, Richmond	8.1942	7.11.1942	3.1943	stricken 8.1947
LST479	Kaiser, Richmond	8.1942	4.10.1942	4.1943	stricken 3.1946
LST480	Kaiser, Richmond	8.1942	29.10.1942	5.1943	explosion 21.5.1944
LST481	Kaiser, Richmond	9.1942	2.12.1942	5.1943	stricken 4.1946
LST482, 9.1945-LST(H)482	Kaiser, Richmond	9.1942	17.12.1942	3.1943	stricken 8.1955
LST483	Kaiser, Richmond	9.1942	30.12.1942	5.1943	stricken 8.1955

LST484	Kaiser, Richmond	9.1942	2.1.1943	4.1943	stricken 8.1946
LST485	Kaiser, Richmond	12.1942	9.1.1943	5.1943	stricken 8.1946
LST486, 9.1945-LST(H)486	Kaiser, Richmond	12.1942	16.1.1943	5.1943	target 23.7.1947
LST487	Kaiser, Richmond	1.1943	23.1.1943	4.1943	stricken 5.1946
LST488, 9.1945-LST(H)488	Kaiser, Richmond	1.1943	5.3.1943	5.1943	to the Philippines 7.1972 (Surigao del Norte)
LST489	Kaiser, Richmond	1.1943	2.4.1943	(7.1943)	commissioned as landing craft repair ship
LST490	Kaiser, Richmond	1.1943	3.4.1943	(8.1943)	commissioned as landing craft repair ship
LST491	Missouri Valley Bridge, Evansville	7.1943	23.9.1943	12.1943	stricken 6.1975
LST492	Missouri Valley Bridge, Evansville	8.1943	30.9.1943	12.1943	stricken 6.1947
LST493	Missouri Valley Bridge, Evansville	8.1943	4.10.1943	12.1943	wrecked 12.4.1945
LST494	Missouri Valley Bridge, Evansville	8.1943	11.10.1943	12.1943	stricken 8.1946
LST495	Missouri Valley Bridge, Evansville	8.1943	16.10.1943	12.1943	stricken 6.1946
LST496	Missouri Valley Bridge, Evansville	8.1943	22.10.1943	12.1943	sunk 11.6.1944
LST497	Missouri Valley Bridge, Evansville	8.1943	27.10.1943	12.1943	stricken 1.1946
LST498	Missouri Valley Bridge, Evansville	8.1943	1.11.1943	1.1944	stricken 11.1945
LST499	Missouri Valley Bridge, Evansville	9.1943	5.11.1943	1.1944	sunk 8.6.1944
LST500	Missouri Valley Bridge, Evansville	9.1943	10.11.1943	1.1944	stricken 8.1947
LST501	JeffBoat, Jeffersonville	6.1943	22.9.1943	11.1943	stricken 9.1947
LST502	JeffBoat, Jeffersonville	6.1943	25.9.1943	12.1943	stricken 12.1947
LST503	JeffBoat, Jeffersonville	7.1943	8.10.1943	12.1943	to Taiwan 4.1955 (Chung Kuang)
LST504	JeffBoat, Jeffersonville	7.1943	19.10.1943	12.1943	stricken 8.1955
LST505	JeffBoat, Jeffersonville	8.1943	27.10.1943	12.1943	stricken 9.1947
LST506	JeffBoat, Jeffersonville	8.1943	14.11.1943	1.1944	stricken 8.1947
LST507	JeffBoat, Jeffersonville	9.1943	16.11.1943	1.1944	sunk 28.4.1944
LST508	JeffBoat, Jeffersonville	9.1943	10.11.1943	1.1944	stricken 1.1947
LST509	JeffBoat, Jeffersonville	10.1943	23.11.1943	1.1944	to South Vietnam 4.1970 (Qui Nhơn)
LST510	JeffBoat, Jeffersonville	9.1943	30.11.1943	1.1944	stricken 11.1958
LST511	Chicago Bridge, Seneca	7.1943	30.11.1943	1.1944	stricken 1.1946
LST512	Chicago Bridge, Seneca	7.1943	10.12.1943	1.1944	stricken 2.1957
LST513	Chicago Bridge, Seneca	8.1943	17.12.1943	(5.1944)	commissioned as landing craft repair ship
LST514	Chicago Bridge, Seneca	8.1943	24.12.1943	(5.1944)	commissioned as battle damage repair ship
LST515	Chicago Bridge, Seneca	9.1943	31.12.1943	1.1944	to the Philippines 11.1969 (Bataan)
LST516	Chicago Bridge, Seneca	9.1943	7.1.1944	1.1944	stricken 10.1958
LST517	Chicago Bridge, Seneca	9.1943	15.1.1944	2.1944	stricken 1.1946

LST518	Chicago Bridge, Seneca	9.1943	20.1.1944	(6.1944)	commissioned as battle damage repair ship
LST519	Chicago Bridge, Seneca	9.1943	25.1.1944	2.1944	stricken 11.1962
LST520	Chicago Bridge, Seneca	9.1943	31.1.1944	2.1944	to Taiwan 10.1958 (Chung Shu)
LST521	Chicago Bridge, Seneca	10.1943	13.12.1943	3.1944	stricken 11.1959
LST522	Chicago Bridge, Seneca	10.1943	11.2.1944	3.1944	stricken 1.1948
LST523	JeffBoat, Jeffersonville	10.1943	6.12.1943	2.1944	sunk 19.6.1944
LST524	JeffBoat, Jeffersonville	10.1943	13.12.1943	2.1944	stricken 10.1947
LST525	JeffBoat, Jeffersonville	10.1943	20.12.1943	2.1944	stricken 9.1974
LST526	JeffBoat, Jeffersonville	10.1943	27.12.1943	2.1944	stricken 1.1946
LST527	JeffBoat, Jeffersonville	10.1943	3.1.1944	2.1944	stricken 10.1958
LST528	JeffBoat, Jeffersonville	11.1943	11.1.1944	2.1944	stricken 11.1960
LST529	JeffBoat, Jeffersonville	11.1943	17.1.1944	3.1944	to South Vietnam 12.1963 (Thị Nại)
LST530	JeffBoat, Jeffersonville	11.1943	25.1.1944	3.1944	stricken 6.1973
LST531	Missouri Valley Bridge, Evansville	9.1943	24.11.1943	1.1944	sunk 23.4.1944
LST532	Missouri Valley Bridge, Evansville	9.1943	28.11.1943	1.1944	to Singapore 6.1973
LST533	Missouri Valley Bridge, Evansville	9.1943	1.12.1943	1.1944	stricken 9.1974
LST534	Missouri Valley Bridge, Evansville	10.1943	8.12.1943	1.1944	stricken 1.1946
LST535	Missouri Valley Bridge, Evansville	10.1943	21.12.1943	2.1944	to Taiwan 10.1958 (Chung Wan)
LST536	Missouri Valley Bridge, Evansville	10.1943	27.12.1943	2.1944	to South Korea 2.1947
LST537	Missouri Valley Bridge, Evansville	10.1943	31.12.1943	2.1944	to China 5.1946 (Chungting)
LST538	Missouri Valley Bridge, Evansville	10.1943	5.1.1944	2.1944	to the UK 12.1944 (LST538)
LST539	Missouri Valley Bridge, Evansville	11.1943	10.1.1944	2.1944	stricken 7.1946
LST540	Missouri Valley Bridge, Evansville	11.1943	14.1.1944	2.1944	wrecked 20.8.1947
LST541	Missouri Valley Bridge, Evansville	11.1943	25.1.1944	2.1944	stricken 11.1945
LST542	Missouri Valley Bridge, Evansville	11.1943	28.1.1944	2.1944	stricken 11.1959
LST543	Missouri Valley Bridge, Evansville	12.1943	1.2.1944	3.1944	stricken 7.1947
LST544	Missouri Valley Bridge, Evansville	12.1943	4.2.1944	3.1944	stricken 9.1946
LST545	Missouri Valley Bridge, Evansville	12.1943	12.2.1944	3.1944	target 12.5.1948
LST546	Missouri Valley Bridge, Evansville	12.1943	16.2.1944	3.1944	to the Philippines 7.1972 (Surigao del Sur)
LST547	Missouri Valley Bridge, Evansville	12.1943	19.2.1944	3.1944	stricken 10.1947
LST548	Missouri Valley Bridge, Evansville	12.1943	22.2.1944	4.1944	stricken 1.1960

LST549	Missouri Valley Bridge, Evansville	1.1944	25.2.1944	4.1944	stricken 12.1947
LST550	Missouri Valley Bridge, Evansville	1.1944	9.3.1944	4.1944	stricken 11.1973
LST551	Missouri Valley Bridge, Evansville	1.1944	11.3.1944	4.1944	stricken 6.1970
LST552	Missouri Valley Bridge, Evansville	1.1944	14.3.1944	4.1944	stricken 5.1946
LST553	Missouri Valley Bridge, Evansville	1.1944	16.3.1944	4.1944	to the US Army 4.1947
LST554	Missouri Valley Bridge, Evansville	1.1944	18.3.1944	4.1944	stricken 9.1946
LST555	Missouri Valley Bridge, Evansville	2.1944	22.3.1944	4.1944	stricken 1.1946
LST556	Missouri Valley Bridge, Evansville	2.1944	7.4.1944	5.1944	stricken 4.1946
LST557	Missouri Valley Bridge, Evansville	2.1944	11.4.1944	5.1944	to China 5.1946 (Chunghsing)
LST558	Missouri Valley Bridge, Evansville	2.1944	14.4.1944	5.1944	stricken 9.1947
LST559	Missouri Valley Bridge, Evansville	2.1944	18.4.1944	5.1944	stricken 6.1946
LST560	Missouri Valley Bridge, Evansville	2.1944	21.4.1944	5.1944	stricken 6.1946
LST561	Missouri Valley Bridge, Evansville	2.1944	25.4.1944	5.1944	stricken 6.1958
LST562	Missouri Valley Bridge, Evansville	2.1944	28.4.1944	5.1944	stricken 7.1946
LST563	Missouri Valley Bridge, Evansville	3.1944	1.5.1944	5.1944	wrecked 21.12.1944
LST564	Missouri Valley Bridge, Evansville	3.1944	4.5.1944	5.1944	stricken 5.1946
LST565	Missouri Valley Bridge, Evansville	3.1944	8.5.1944	5.1944	stricken 7.1946
LST566	Missouri Valley Bridge, Evansville	3.1944	11.5.1944	5.1944	stricken 11.1973
LST567	Missouri Valley Bridge, Evansville	3.1944	15.5.1944	6.1944	stricken 10.1947
LST568	Missouri Valley Bridge, Evansville	3.1944	18.5.1944	6.1944	scuttled 7.3.1946
LST569	Missouri Valley Bridge, Evansville	3.1944	20.5.1944	6.1944	stricken 10.1946
LST570	Missouri Valley Bridge, Evansville	4.1944	22.5.1944	6.1944	stricken 6.1946
LST571	Missouri Valley Bridge, Evansville	4.1944	25.5.1944	6.1944	stricken 4.1946
LST572	Missouri Valley Bridge, Evansville	4.1944	29.5.1944	6.1944	stricken 6.1973
LST573	Missouri Valley Bridge, Evansville	4.1944	31.5.1944	6.1944	stricken 10.1947
LST574	Missouri Valley Bridge, Evansville	4.1944	5.6.1944	6.1944	stricken 7.1946
LST575, 1.1945-LST(M)575	Missouri Valley Bridge, Evansville	5.1944	9.6.1944	6.1944	barrack ship 3.1945

LST576	Missouri Valley Bridge, Evansville	5.1944	12.6.1944	7.1944	stricken 6.1946
LST577	Missouri Valley Bridge, Evansville	5.1944	16.6.1944	7.1944	sunk 11.2.1945
LST578	Missouri Valley Bridge, Evansville	5.1944	19.6.1944	7.1944	to Taiwan 1958 (Chung Pang)
LST579	Missouri Valley Bridge, Evansville	5.1944	22.6.1944	7.1944	to Singapore 1976 (Intrepid)
LST580	Missouri Valley Bridge, Evansville	5.1944	26.6.1944	7.1944	stricken 10.1947
LST581	Missouri Valley Bridge, Evansville	5.1944	29.6.1944	7.1944	stricken 6.1972
LST582	Missouri Valley Bridge, Evansville	5.1944	1.7.1944	7.1944	stricken 10.1947
LST583	Missouri Valley Bridge, Evansville	5.1944	5.7.1944	8.1944	stricken 9.1974
LST584	Missouri Valley Bridge, Evansville	5.1944	8.7.1944	8.1944	stricken 7.1946
LST585	Missouri Valley Bridge, Evansville	5.1944	12.7.1944	8.1944	stricken 8.1946
LST586	Missouri Valley Bridge, Evansville	6.1944	15.7.1944	8.1944	stricken 9.1947
LST587	Missouri Valley Bridge, Evansville	6.1944	19.7.1944	8.1944	stricken 6.1972
LST588	Missouri Valley Bridge, Evansville	6.1944	22.7.1944	8.1944	stricken 7.1946
LST589	Missouri Valley Bridge, Evansville	6.1944	26.7.1944	8.1944	to China 4.1947 (Chung 106)
LST590	Missouri Valley Bridge, Evansville	6.1944	29.7.1944	8.1944	stricken 6.1973
LST591	Missouri Valley Bridge, Evansville	6.1944	2.7.1944	8.1944	stricken 9.1947
LST592	Missouri Valley Bridge, Evansville	6.1944	5.8.1944	9.1944	stricken 7.1946
LST593	Missouri Valley Bridge, Evansville	6.1944	9.8.1944	9.1944	stricken 5.1946
LST594	Missouri Valley Bridge, Evansville	7.1944	12.8.1944	9.1944	stricken 3.1947
LST595	Missouri Valley Bridge, Evansville	7.1944	16.8.1944	9.1944	stricken 3.1947
LST596	Missouri Valley Bridge, Evansville	7.1944	21.8.1944	9.1944	stricken 9.1946
LST597	Missouri Valley Bridge, Evansville	7.1944	28.8.1944	9.1944	stricken 9.1947
LST598	Missouri Valley Bridge, Evansville	7.1944	29.8.1944	9.1944	stricken 7.1946
LST599	Missouri Valley Bridge, Evansville	7.1944	2.9.1944	9.1944	stricken 12.1947
LST600	Chicago Bridge, Seneca	10.1943	28.2.1944	3.1944	stricken 6.1969
LST601	Chicago Bridge, Seneca	10.1943	4.3.1944	3.1944	stricken ~1972
LST602	Chicago Bridge, Seneca	10.1943	9.3.1944	3.1944	to Mexico 5.1972 (Manzanillo)
LST603	Chicago Bridge, Seneca	11.1943	14.3.1944	4.1944	to South Vietnam 4.1969 (Vũng Tàu)

LST604	Chicago Bridge, Seneca	10.1943	20.3.1944	4.1944	MTB depot ship 8.1944
LST605	Chicago Bridge, Seneca	9.1943	29.3.1944	4.1944	stricken 7.1946
LST606	Chicago Bridge, Seneca	11.1943	3.4.1944	4.1944	stricken 6.1946
LST607	Chicago Bridge, Seneca	12.1943	7.4.1944	4.1944	to the Philippines 9.1976 (Leyte del Sur)
LST608	Chicago Bridge, Seneca	12.1943	11.4.1944	4.1944	stricken 2.1947
LST609	Chicago Bridge, Seneca	12.1943	15.4.1944	5.1944	stricken 1.1946
LST610	Chicago Bridge, Seneca	12.1943	19.4.1944	5.1944	stricken 12.1947
LST611	Chicago Bridge, Seneca	12.1943	26.4.1944	5.1944	National Reserve 10.1956
LST612	Chicago Bridge, Seneca	12.1943	29.4.1944	5.1944	stricken 7.1946
LST613	Chicago Bridge, Seneca	1.1944	2.5.1944	5.1944	stricken 6.1975
LST614	Chicago Bridge, Seneca	1.1944	6.5.1944	5.1944	stricken 10.1946
LST615	Chicago Bridge, Seneca	2.1944	9.5.1944	5.1944	stricken 4.1946
LST616	Chicago Bridge, Seneca	2.1944	12.5.1944	5.1944	to Indonesia 5.1961 (Teluk Bajur)
LST617	Chicago Bridge, Seneca	2.1944	15.5.1944	6.1944	stricken 7.1946
LST618	Chicago Bridge, Seneca	2.1944	19.5.1944	6.1944	to US Army 10.1946
LST619	Chicago Bridge, Seneca	3.1944	22.5.1944	6.1944	stricken 10.1947
LST620	Chicago Bridge, Seneca	3.1944	30.5.1944	6.1944	stricken 6.1946
LST621	Chicago Bridge, Seneca	3.1944	2.6.1944	6.1944	stricken 7.1946
LST622	Chicago Bridge, Seneca	3.1944	8.6.1944	6.1944	stricken 4.1946
LST623	Chicago Bridge, Seneca	3.1944	12.6.1944	6.1944	to Singapore 1971 (Perseverance)
LST624	Chicago Bridge, Seneca	3.1944	16.6.1944	7.1944	stricken 2.1947
LST625	Chicago Bridge, Seneca	3.1944	20.6.1944	7.1944	stricken 5.1954
LST626	Chicago Bridge, Seneca	3.1944	27.6.1944	7.1944	stricken 6.1972
LST627	Chicago Bridge, Seneca	4.1944	1.7.1944	7.1944	to the Netherlands 6.1946
LST628	Chicago Bridge, Seneca	4.1944	4.7.1944	7.1944	stricken 7.1946
LST629	Chicago Bridge, Seneca	4.1944	8.7.1944	7.1944	to Singapore 1976 (Excellence)
LST630	Chicago Bridge, Seneca	4.1944	13.7.1944	8.1944	stricken 6.1973
LST631	Chicago Bridge, Seneca	4.1944	18.7.1944	8.1944	stricken 7.1946
LST632	Chicago Bridge, Seneca	4.1944	21.7.1944	8.1944	stricken 1.1947
LST633	Chicago Bridge, Seneca	5.1944	27.7.1944	8.1944	stricken 9.1947
LST634	Chicago Bridge, Seneca	5.1944	1.8.1944	8.1944	stricken 7.1946
LST635	Chicago Bridge, Seneca	5.1944	7.8.1944	8.1944	for disposal 7.1946
LST636	Chicago Bridge, Seneca	5.1944	11.8.1944	8.1944	stricken 12.1947
LST637	Chicago Bridge, Seneca	5.1944	18.8.1944	9.1944	stricken 6.1946
LST638	Chicago Bridge, Seneca	5.1944	23.8.1944	9.1944	stricken 3.1948
LST639	Chicago Bridge, Seneca	5.1944	28.8.1944	9.1944	stricken 9.1947
LST640	Chicago Bridge, Seneca	5.1944	31.8.1944	9.1944	to China 7.1946
LST641	Chicago Bridge, Seneca	6.1944	4.9.1944	9.1944	stricken 7.1946
LST642	Chicago Bridge, Seneca	6.1944	8.9.1944	9.1944	wrecked 10.2.1948
LST643	Chicago Bridge, Seneca	6.1944	12.9.1944	10.1944	stricken 6.1973
LST644	Chicago Bridge, Seneca	6.1944	15.9.1944	(9.1944)	commissioned as landing craft repair ship
LST645	Chicago Bridge, Seneca	6.1944	20.9.1944	(2.1945)	commissioned as landing craft repair ship
LST646	Chicago Bridge, Seneca	6.1944	25.9.1944	10.1944	stricken 4.1946
LST647	Chicago Bridge, Seneca	7.1944	28.9.1944	10.1944	stricken 12.1947

LST648	Chicago Bridge, Seneca	7.1944	3.10.1944	10.1944	stricken 2.1947
LST649	Chicago Bridge, Seneca	7.1944	6.10.1944	10.1944	to Singapore 1976 (Resolution)
LST650	Chicago Bridge, Seneca	7.1944	10.10.1944	(2.1945)	commissioned as landing craft repair ship
LST651	Chicago Bridge, Seneca	7.1944	16.10.1944	11.1944	stricken 12.1947
LST652, 9.1945-LST(H)652	Chicago Bridge, Seneca	7.1944	19.10.1944	11.1944	stricken 5.1961
LST653	American Bridge, Pittsburgh	11.1943	23.1.1944	4.1944	stricken 3.1947
LST654	American Bridge, Pittsburgh	12.1943	30.1.1944	3.1944	stricken 7.1946
LST655	American Bridge, Pittsburgh	12.1943	6.2.1944	3.1944	stricken 7.1946
LST656	American Bridge, Pittsburgh	12.1943	18.2.1944	4.1944	stricken 7.1946
LST657	American Bridge, Pittsburgh	12.1943	25.2.1944	4.1944	stricken 5.1961
LST658	American Bridge, Pittsburgh	12.1943	13.3.1944	4.1944	for disposal 6.1946
LST659	American Bridge, Pittsburgh	12.1943	20.3.1944	4.1944	stricken 2.1947
LST660	American Bridge, Pittsburgh	1.1944	24.3.1944	4.1944	stricken 6.1946
LST661	American Bridge, Pittsburgh	1.1944	30.3.1944	4.1944	stricken 7.1948
LST662	American Bridge, Pittsburgh	1.1944	5.4.1944	5.1944	stricken 1.1946
LST663	American Bridge, Pittsburgh	1.1944	8.4.1944	5.1944	stricken 7.1946
LST664	American Bridge, Pittsburgh	1.1944	13.4.1944	5.1944	stricken 6.1973
LST665	American Bridge, Pittsburgh	2.1944	18.4.1944	5.1944	stricken 7.1946
LST666	American Bridge, Pittsburgh	2.1944	24.4.1944	5.1944	stricken 7.1946
LST667	American Bridge, Pittsburgh	2.1944	27.4.1944	5.1944	stricken 7.1946
LST668	American Bridge, Pittsburgh	3.1944	30.4.1944	5.1944	stricken 7.1946
LST669	American Bridge, Pittsburgh	3.1944	3.5.1944	5.1944	stricken 9.1946
LST670	American Bridge, Pittsburgh	3.1944	6.5.1944	5.1944	stricken 6.1946
LST671	American Bridge, Pittsburgh	3.1944	11.5.1944	6.1944	stricken 8.1946
LST672	American Bridge, Pittsburgh	4.1944	14.5.1944	6.1944	stricken 7.1946
LST673	American Bridge, Pittsburgh	4.1944	22.5.1944	6.1944	stricken 8.1946
LST674	American Bridge, Pittsburgh	4.1944	26.5.1944	6.1944	stricken 6.1946
LST675	American Bridge, Pittsburgh	4.1944	2.6.1944	6.1944	damaged 4.4.1945, never repaired

LST676, 1.1945-LST(M)676	American Bridge, Pittsburgh	4.1944	6.6.1944	6.1944	barrack ship 3.1945
LST677, 1.1945-LST(M)677	American Bridge, Pittsburgh	4.1944	15.6.1944	7.1944	barrack ship 3.1945
LST678	American Bridge, Pittsburgh	4.1944	16.6.1944	6.1944	barrack ship 3.1945
LST679	American Bridge, Pittsburgh	5.1944	20.6.1944	7.1944	stricken 7.1946
LST680	American Bridge, Pittsburgh	5.1944	26.6.1944	7.1944	stricken 8.1946
LST681	American Bridge, Pittsburgh	5.1944	1.7.1944	7.1944	stricken 10.1946
LST682	JeffBoat, Jeffersonville	12.1943	31.1.1944	3.1944	stricken 9.1946
LST683	JeffBoat, Jeffersonville	11.1943	7.2.1944	3.1944	stricken 7.1946
LST684	JeffBoat, Jeffersonville	12.1943	12.2.1944	4.1944	stricken 3.1946
LST685	JeffBoat, Jeffersonville	12.1943	18.2.1944	4.1944	stricken 11.1958
LST686	JeffBoat, Jeffersonville	1.1944	24.2.1944	4.1944	stricken 8.1946
LST687	JeffBoat, Jeffersonville	12.1943	28.2.1944	4.1944	stricken 7.1946
LST688	JeffBoat, Jeffersonville	1.1944	5.3.1944	4.1944	stricken 9.1946
LST689	JeffBoat, Jeffersonville	1.1944	9.3.1944	5.1944	stricken 10.1959
LST690	JeffBoat, Jeffersonville	1.1944	14.3.1944	5.1944	stricken 8.1946
LST691	JeffBoat, Jeffersonville	1.1944	23.3.1944	5.1944	stricken 6.1946
LST692	JeffBoat, Jeffersonville	2.1944	31.3.1944	5.1944	stricken 6.1975
LST693	JeffBoat, Jeffersonville	2.1944	7.4.1944	5.1944	stricken 7.1946
LST694	JeffBoat, Jeffersonville	2.1944	16.4.1944	5.1944	stricken 2.1958
LST695	JeffBoat, Jeffersonville	2.1944	24.4.1944	5.1944	stricken 11.1945
LST696	JeffBoat, Jeffersonville	2.1944	27.4.1944	5.1944	stricken 8.1946
LST697	JeffBoat, Jeffersonville	3.1944	1.5.1944	5.1944	stricken 8.1946
LST698	JeffBoat, Jeffersonville	3.1944	5.5.1944	6.1944	stricken 12.1945
LST699	JeffBoat, Jeffersonville	3.1944	9.5.1944	6.1944	stricken 7.1946
LST700	JeffBoat, Jeffersonville	3.1944	13.5.1944	6.1944	stricken 8.1946
LST701	JeffBoat, Jeffersonville	4.1944	18.5.1944	6.1944	stricken 8.1946
LST702	JeffBoat, Jeffersonville	4.1944	22.5.1944	6.1944	stricken 8.1946
LST703	JeffBoat, Jeffersonville	4.1944	28.5.1944	6.1944	stricken 7.1946
LST704	JeffBoat, Jeffersonville	4.1944	3.6.1944	6.1944	stricken 9.1946
LST705	JeffBoat, Jeffersonville	4.1944	7.6.1944	7.1944	stricken 9.1946
LST706	JeffBoat, Jeffersonville	5.1944	12.6.1944	7.1944	stricken 7.1946
LST707	JeffBoat, Jeffersonville	5.1944	16.6.1944	7.1944	stricken 7.1946
LST708	JeffBoat, Jeffersonville	5.1944	20.6.1944	7.1944	stricken 7.1946
LST709	JeffBoat, Jeffersonville	5.1944	24.6.1944	7.1944	stricken 8.1946
LST710	JeffBoat, Jeffersonville	5.1944	28.6.1944	7.1944	barrack ship 8.1945
LST711	JeffBoat, Jeffersonville	5.1944	3.7.1944	7.1944	to the US Army 8.1946
LST712	JeffBoat, Jeffersonville	5.1944	7.7.1944	8.1944	stricken 8.1946
LST713	JeffBoat, Jeffersonville	6.1944	11.7.1944	8.1944	stricken 7.1946
LST714	JeffBoat, Jeffersonville	6.1944	15.7.1944	8.1944	stricken 6.1946
LST715	JeffBoat, Jeffersonville	6.1944	20.7.1944	8.1944	stricken 11.1973
LST716	JeffBoat, Jeffersonville	6.1944	25.7.1944	8.1944	to China 2.1948 (Chung Chien)
LST717	JeffBoat, Jeffersonville	6.1944	29.7.1944	8.1944	to China 2.1948
LST718	JeffBoat, Jeffersonville	6.1944	3.8.1944	8.1944	sold 6.1948
LST719	JeffBoat, Jeffersonville	6.1944	8.8.1944	8.1944	stricken 3.1947
LST720	JeffBoat, Jeffersonville	7.1944	12.8.1944	9.1944	stricken 7.1946

LST721	JeffBoat, Jeffersonville	7.1944	7.8.1944	9.1944	stricken 8.1946
LST722	JeffBoat, Jeffersonville	7.1944	21.8.1944	9.1944	stricken 9.1974
LST723	JeffBoat, Jeffersonville	7.1944	25.8.1944	9.1944	stricken 6.1947
LST724	JeffBoat, Jeffersonville	7.1944	29.8.1944	9.1944	stricken 7.1946
LST725	JeffBoat, Jeffersonville	7.1944	2.9.1944	9.1944	stricken 7.1946
LST726	JeffBoat, Jeffersonville	7.1944	6.9.1944	9.1944	stricken 7.1946
LST727	JeffBoat, Jeffersonville	8.1944	10.9.1944	10.1944	stricken 8.1946
LST728	JeffBoat, Jeffersonville	8.1944	14.9.1944	10.1944	stricken 7.1946
LST729	JeffBoat, Jeffersonville	8.1944	18.9.1944	10.1944	stricken 8.1946
LST730	Dravo, Pittsburgh	12.1943	29.1.1944	3.1944	stricken 7.1946
LST731, 9.1945-LST(H)731	Dravo, Pittsburgh	12.1943	12.2.1944	4.1944	stricken 11.1958
LST732	Dravo, Pittsburgh	1.1944	19.2.1944	4.1944	to China 7.1946 (Chung Shun)
LST733	Dravo, Pittsburgh	1.1944	26.2.1944	4.1944	stricken 7.1946
LST734	Dravo, Pittsburgh	1.1944	4.3.1944	4.1944	stricken 6.1946
LST735	Dravo, Pittsburgh	1.1944	11.3.1944	4.1944	to Taiwan 5.1957 (Chung Hai)
LST736	Dravo, Pittsburgh	2.1944	18.3.1944	5.1944	stricken 7.1946
LST737	Dravo, Pittsburgh	2.1944	25.3.1944	5.1944	to the US Army 11.1946
LST738	Dravo, Pittsburgh	2.1944	1.4.1944	5.1944	sunk 15.12.1944
LST739	Dravo, Pittsburgh	2.1944	8.4.1944	5.1944	stricken 7.1946
LST740	Dravo, Pittsburgh	2.1944	8.4.1944	5.1944	stricken 4.1946
LST741	Dravo, Pittsburgh	3.1944	15.4.1944	5.1944	stricken 9.1946
LST742	Dravo, Pittsburgh	3.1944	22.4.1944	5.1944	stricken 2.1961
LST743	Dravo, Pittsburgh	2.1944	19.4.1944	5.1944	stricken 6.1946
LST744	Dravo, Pittsburgh	3.1944	29.4.1944	5.1944	stricken 8.1946
LST745	Dravo, Pittsburgh	3.1944	29.4.1944	5.1944	stricken 8.1946
LST746	Dravo, Pittsburgh	3.1944	6.5.1944	6.1944	stricken 7.1946
LST747	Dravo, Pittsburgh	4.1944	20.5.1944	6.1944	stricken 7.1946
LST748	Dravo, Pittsburgh	4.1944	13.5.1944	6.1944	for disposal 5.1948
LST749	Dravo, Pittsburgh	4.1944	20.5.1944	6.1944	sunk 21.12.1944
LST750	Dravo, Pittsburgh	4.1944	30.5.1944	6.1944	sunk 28.12.1944
LST751	Dravo, Pittsburgh	4.1944	27.5.1944	6.1944	stricken 10.1946
LST752	Dravo, Pittsburgh	4.1944	3.6.1944	7.1944	stricken 7.1946
LST753	Dravo, Pittsburgh	4.1944	10.6.1944	7.1944	stricken 7.1946
LST754	American Bridge, Pittsburgh	5.1944	6.7.1944	7.1944	stricken 7.1946
LST755	American Bridge, Pittsburgh	5.1944	11.7.1944	8.1944	to China 5.1946 (Chung Hai)
LST756	American Bridge, Pittsburgh	5.1944	15.7.1944	8.1944	stricken 4.1948
LST757	American Bridge, Pittsburgh	6.1944	21.7.1944	8.1944	stricken 7.1946
LST758	American Bridge, Pittsburgh	6.1944	25.7.1944	8.1944	stricken 11.1976
LST759	American Bridge, Pittsburgh	6.1944	29.7.1944	8.1944	stricken 10.1958
LST760	American Bridge, Pittsburgh	6.1944	3.8.1944	8.1944	stricken 7.1946
LST761	American Bridge, Pittsburgh	6.1944	7.8.1944	9.1944	target 1959

LST762	American Bridge, Pittsburgh	6.1944	11.8.1944	9.1944	stricken 4.1975
LST763	American Bridge, Pittsburgh	6.1944	16.8.1944	9.1944	stricken 8.1946
LST764	American Bridge, Pittsburgh	7.1944	21.8.1944	9.1944	stricken 7.1946
LST765	American Bridge, Pittsburgh	7.1944	26.8.1944	9.1944	stricken 7.1946
LST766	American Bridge, Pittsburgh	7.1944	30.8.1944	9.1944	stricken 6.1946
LST767	American Bridge, Pittsburgh	7.1944	4.9.1944	9.1944	stricken 3.1946
LST768	American Bridge, Pittsburgh	7.1944	8.9.1944	10.1944	stricken 6.1946
LST769	American Bridge, Pittsburgh	7.1944	12.9.1944	10.1944	stricken 7.1946
LST770	American Bridge, Pittsburgh	8.1944	17.9.1944	10.1944	stricken 7.1946
LST771	American Bridge, Pittsburgh	8.1944	21.9.1944	10.1944	stricken 6.1946
LST772	Chicago Bridge, Seneca	8.1944	24.10.1944	11.1944	sunk as target 19.3.1958
LST773	Chicago Bridge, Seneca	8.1944	27.10.1944	(10.1944)	commissioned as MTB depot ship
LST774	Chicago Bridge, Seneca	8.1944	31.10.1944	11.1944	stricken 8.1946
LST775	Dravo, Pittsburgh	4.1944	10.6.1944	7.1944	National Reserve 1948
LST776	Dravo, Pittsburgh	5.1944	17.6.1944	7.1944	stricken 5.1946
LST777	Dravo, Pittsburgh	5.1944	24.6.1944	7.1944	stricken 8.1946
LST778	Dravo, Pittsburgh	5.1944	24.6.1944	7.1944	stricken 6.1946
LST779	Dravo, Pittsburgh	5.1944	1.7.1944	8.1944	stricken 7.1946
LST780	Dravo, Pittsburgh	5.1944	10.7.1944	8.1944	stricken 7.1946
LST781	Dravo, Pittsburgh	6.1944	15.7.1944	8.1944	stricken 8.1946
LST782	Dravo, Pittsburgh	6.1944	22.7.1944	8.1944	stricken 6.1946
LST783	Dravo, Pittsburgh	6.1944	11.7.1944	8.1944	stricken 6.1950
LST784	Dravo, Pittsburgh	6.1944	29.7.1944	9.1944	BU 1959
LST785	Dravo, Pittsburgh	6.1944	5.8.1944	9.1944	stricken 6.1946
LST786	Dravo, Pittsburgh	5.1944	22.7.1944	8.1944	patrol craft depot ship 1970
LST787	Dravo, Pittsburgh	7.1944	12.8.1944	9.1944	stricken 7.1946
LST788	Dravo, Pittsburgh	7.1944	19.8.1944	9.1944	stricken 6.1946
LST789	Dravo, Pittsburgh	6.1944	5.8.1944	9.1944	stricken 7.1946
LST790, 9.1945- LST(H)790	Dravo, Pittsburgh	6.1944	19.8.1944	9.1944	stricken 7.1946
LST791	Dravo, Pittsburgh	7.1944	26.8.1944	9.1944	stricken 7.1946
LST792	Dravo, Pittsburgh	6.1944	2.9.1944	10.1944	stricken 7.1946
LST793	Dravo, Pittsburgh	7.1944	2.9.1944	10.1944	stricken 7.1946
LST794	Dravo, Pittsburgh	7.1944	16.9.1944	10.1944	target 22.5.1958
LST795	Dravo, Pittsburgh	7.1944	9.9.1944	10.1944	stricken 7.1946
LST796	Dravo, Pittsburgh	8.1944	16.9.1944	10.1944	stricken 6.1946
LST797	JeffBoat, Jeffersonville	8.1944	22.9.1944	10.1944	stricken 7.1946
LST798	JeffBoat, Jeffersonville	8.1944	26.9.1944	10.1944	stricken 8.1946
LST799	JeffBoat, Jeffersonville	8.1944	3.10.1944	10.1944	stricken 11.1960
LST800	JeffBoat, Jeffersonville	8.1944	10.10.1944	11.1944	stricken 7.1946
LST801	JeffBoat, Jeffersonville	9.1944	14.10.1944	11.1944	stricken 8.1946

LST802	JeffBoat, Jeffersonville	9.1944	19.10.1944	11.1944	to Japan 7.1960 (Hayatomo)
LST803	JeffBoat, Jeffersonville	9.1944	23.10.1944	11.1944	stricken 4.1958
LST804	JeffBoat, Jeffersonville	9.1944	27.10.1944	11.1944	to China 7.1946 (Chung 101)
LST805	JeffBoat, Jeffersonville	9.1944	31.10.1944	11.1944	stricken 7.1946
LST806	Missouri Valley Bridge, Evansville	7.1944	7.9.1944	9.1944	stricken 7.1946
LST807	Missouri Valley Bridge, Evansville	7.1944	11.9.1944	10.1944	stricken 7.1946
LST808	Missouri Valley Bridge, Evansville	8.1944	15.9.1944	10.1944	CTL 20.5.1945
LST809	Missouri Valley Bridge, Evansville	8.1944	19.9.194	10.1944	stricken 8.1946
LST810	Missouri Valley Bridge, Evansville	8.1944	21.9.1944	10.1944	stricken 8.1946
LST811	Missouri Valley Bridge, Evansville	8.1944	23.9.1944	10.1944	stricken 7.1946
LST812	Missouri Valley Bridge, Evansville	8.1944	27.9.1944	10.1944	stricken 1946
LST813	Missouri Valley Bridge, Evansville	8.1944	30.9.1944	10.1944	stricken 7.1946
LST814	Missouri Valley Bridge, Evansville	8.1944	4.10.1944	10.1944	stricken 5.1946
LST815	Missouri Valley Bridge, Evansville	8.1944	7.10.1944	10.1944	to France 5.1948 (Odet)
LST816	Missouri Valley Bridge, Evansville	9.1944	11.10.1944	11.1944	stricken 7.1946
LST817	Missouri Valley Bridge, Evansville	9.1944	14.10.1944	11.1944	stricken 2.1947
LST818	Missouri Valley Bridge, Evansville	9.1944	18.10.1944	11.1944	stricken 8.1946
LST819	Missouri Valley Bridge, Evansville	9.1944	21.10.1944	11.1944	stricken 4.1975
LST820	Missouri Valley Bridge, Evansville	9.1944	25.10.1944	11.1944	stricken 2.1946
LST821	Missouri Valley Bridge, Evansville	9.1944	27.10.1944	11.1944	patrol craft depot ship 1970
LST822	Missouri Valley Bridge, Evansville	9.1944	1.11.1944	11.1944	to the Philippines 9.1976 (Aurora)
LST823	Missouri Valley Bridge, Evansville	9.1944	4.11.1944	11.1944	stricken 1.1946
LST824	Missouri Valley Bridge, Evansville	9.1944	8.11.1944	11.1944	stricken 4.1975
LST825	Missouri Valley Bridge, Evansville	10.1944	11.11.1944	12.1944	to the Philippines 11.1969 (Cagayan)
LST826	Missouri Valley Bridge, Evansville	10.1944	14.11.1944	12.1944	wrecked 9.10.1945
LST827	Missouri Valley Bridge, Evansville	10.1944	16.11.1944	12.1944	stricken 3.1958
LST828	Missouri Valley Bridge, Evansville	10.1944	22.11.1944	12.1944	stricken 5.1947
LST829	American Bridge, Pittsburgh	8.1944	26.9.1944	10.1944	for disposal 3.1948

LST830	American Bridge, Pittsburgh	8.1944	30.9.1944	10.1944	stricken 7.1946
LST831	American Bridge, Pittsburgh	8.1944	6.10.1944	11.1944	for disposal 12.1947
LST832	American Bridge, Pittsburgh	8.1944	11.10.1944	11.1944	stricken 7.1946
LST833	American Bridge, Pittsburgh	8.1944	16.10.1944	11.1944	stricken 6.1947
LST834	American Bridge, Pittsburgh	9.1944	20.10.1944	11.1944	stricken 10.1946
LST835	American Bridge, Pittsburgh	9.1944	25.10.1944	11.1944	stricken 10.1959
LST836	American Bridge, Pittsburgh	9.1944	29.10.1944	11.1944	to Singapore 7.1971 (Endurance)
LST837	American Bridge, Pittsburgh	9.1944	3.11.1944	11.1944	stricken 8.1946
LST838	American Bridge, Pittsburgh	9.1944	8.11.1944	12.1944	patrol craft depot ship 1970
LST839	American Bridge, Pittsburgh	9.1944	12.11.1944	12.1944	to Indonesia 7.1970 (Teluk Bone)
LST840	American Bridge, Pittsburgh	9.1944	15.11.1944	12.1944	to Taiwan 7.1958 (Chung Fu)
LST841	American Bridge, Pittsburgh	10.1944	20.11.1944	12.1944	stricken 6.1947
LST842	American Bridge, Pittsburgh	10.1944	24.11.1944	12.1944	to the Philippines 1.1948 (Pampanga)
LST843	American Bridge, Pittsburgh	10.1944	29.11.1944	12.1944	to the Philippines 12.1947 (Bulacan)
LST844	American Bridge, Pittsburgh	10.1944	3.12.1944	12.1944	stricken 9.1947
LST845	American Bridge, Pittsburgh	10.1944	7.12.1944	1.1945	stricken 2.1961
LST846	American Bridge, Pittsburgh	10.1944	12.12.1944	1.1945	stricken 9.1970
LST847	American Bridge, Pittsburgh	11.1944	17.12.1944	1.1945	stricken 7.1946
LST848	American Bridge, Pittsburgh	11.1944	21.12.1944	1.1945	to South Vietnam 4.1970 (Nha Trang)
LST849	American Bridge, Pittsburgh	11.1944	30.12.1944	1.1945	to South Korea 1.1959 (Wibong)
LST850	Chicago Bridge, Seneca	8.1944	3.11.1944	11.1944	stricken 11.1958
LST851	Chicago Bridge, Seneca	8.1944	8.11.1944	11.1944	stricken 5.1946
LST852	Chicago Bridge, Seneca	8.1944	13.11.194	(4.1945)	commissioned as landing craft repair ship
LST853	Chicago Bridge, Seneca	8.1944	17.11.1944	12.1944	to South Korea 12.1958 (Suyeong)
LST854	Chicago Bridge, Seneca	8.1944	20.11.1944	12.1944	to Barbados 7.1975 (Northpoint)
LST855	Chicago Bridge, Seneca	9.1944	27.11.1944	12.1944	target 19.3.1958
LST856	Chicago Bridge, Seneca	9.1944	1.12.1944	12.1944	stricken 7.1946
LST857	Chicago Bridge, Seneca	9.1944	6.12.1944	12.1944	test ship 5.1958
LST858	Chicago Bridge, Seneca	10.1944	11.11.1944	(12.1944)	commissioned as landing craft repair ship

LST859	Chicago Bridge, Seneca	9.1944	15.12.1944	1.1945	to Taiwan 8.1958 (Chung Cheng)
LST860	Chicago Bridge, Seneca	9.1944	19.12.1944	1.1945	stricken 7.1946
LST861	Jeffboat, Jeffersonville	9.1944	4.11.1944	11.1944	stricken 4.1947
LST862	Jeffboat, Jeffersonville	9.1944	9.11.1944	12.1944	for disposal 10.1947
LST863	Jeffboat, Jeffersonville	10.1944	14.11.1944	12.1944	stricken 7.1946
LST864	Jeffboat, Jeffersonville	10.1944	18.11.1944	12.1944	stricken 5.1947
LST865	Jeffboat, Jeffersonville	10.1944	22.11.1944	12.1944	to the Philippines 12.1947 (Albay)
LST866	Jeffboat, Jeffersonville	10.1944	27.11.1944	12.1944	stricken 7.1946
LST867	Jeffboat, Jeffersonville	10.1944	1.12.1944	12.1944	stricken 7.1946
LST868	Jeffboat, Jeffersonville	10.1944	6.12.1944	12.1944	stricken 6.1947
LST869	Jeffboat, Jeffersonville	10.1944	11.12.1944	1.1945	stricken 8.1946
LST870	Jeffboat, Jeffersonville	11.1944	15.12.1944	1.1945	stricken 8.1946
LST871, 9.1945- LST(H)871	Jeffboat, Jeffersonville	11.1944	20.12.1944	1.1945	stricken 11.1946
LST872	Jeffboat, Jeffersonville	11.1944	28.12.1944	1.1945	stricken 8.1946
LST873	Jeffboat, Jeffersonville	11.1944	3.1.1945	1.1945	stricken 9.1946
LST874	Missouri Valley Bridge, Evansville	10.1944	25.11.1944	12.1944	stricken 7.1946
LST875	Missouri Valley Bridge, Evansville	10.1944	29.11.1944	12.1944	stricken 7.1946
LST876	Missouri Valley Bridge, Evansville	10.1944	2.12.1944	12.1944	stricken 7.1946
LST877	Missouri Valley Bridge, Evansville	10.1944	6.12.1944	1.1945	stricken 7.1946
LST878	Missouri Valley Bridge, Evansville	10.1944	10.12.1944	1.1945	stricken 7.1946
LST879	Missouri Valley Bridge, Evansville	11.1944	13.12.1944	1.1945	stricken 9.1946
LST880	Missouri Valley Bridge, Evansville	11.1944	16.12.1944	1.1945	stricken 11.1958
LST881	Missouri Valley Bridge, Evansville	11.1944	20.12.1944	1.1945	stricken 3.1947
LST882	Missouri Valley Bridge, Evansville	11.1944	23.12.1944	1.1945	stricken 8.1946
LST883	Missouri Valley Bridge, Evansville	11.1944	30.12.1944	1.1945	stricken 1.1960
LST884	Dravo, Pittsburgh	7.1944	30.9.1944	10.1944	damaged 1.4.1945, never repaired
LST885	Dravo, Pittsburgh	8.1944	23.9.1944	10.1944	stricken 7.1946
LST886	Dravo, Pittsburgh	8.1944	30.9.1944	11.1944	stricken 6.1946
LST887	Dravo, Pittsburgh	8.1944	7.10.1944	11.1944	to Indonesia 11.1960 (Tandjung Nusanive)
LST888	Dravo, Pittsburgh	8.1944	14.10.1944	11.1944	stricken 9.1960
LST889	Dravo, Pittsburgh	9.1944	14.10.1944	11.1944	stricken 7.1946
LST890	Dravo, Pittsburgh	9.1944	21.10.1944	11.1944	stricken 7.1946
LST891	Dravo, Pittsburgh	8.1944	28.10.1944	11.1944	stricken 7.1946
LST892	Dravo, Pittsburgh	9.1944	28.10.1944	11.1944	stricken 8.1946
LST893	Dravo, Pittsburgh	9.1944	4.11.1944	12.1944	stricken 6.1946
LST894	Dravo, Pittsburgh	9.1944	11.11.1944	12.1944	stricken 7.1946
LST895	Dravo, Pittsburgh	10.1944	11.11.1944	12.1944	stricken 3.1948
LST896	Dravo, Pittsburgh	10.1944	18.11.1944	12.1944	wrecked 9.10.1945

LST897	Dravo, Pittsburgh	9.1944	25.11.1944	12.1944	stricken 8.1946
LST898	Dravo, Pittsburgh	10.1944	25.11.1944	12.1944	to Thailand 8.1962 (Chang)
LST899	Dravo, Pittsburgh	10.1944	2.12.1944	1.1945	stricken 8.1946
LST900	Dravo, Pittsburgh	10.1944	9.12.1944	1.1945	to South Korea 12.1958 (Bukhan)
LST901	Dravo, Pittsburgh	10.1944	9.12.1944	1.1945	stricken 4.1975
LST902	Dravo, Pittsburgh	11.1944	16.12.1944	1.1945	stricken 8.1970
LST903	Dravo, Pittsburgh	10.1944	23.12.1944	1.1945	stricken 11.1958
LST904	Dravo, Pittsburgh	11.1944	23.12.1944	1.1945	stricken 11.1958
LST905	Dravo, Pittsburgh	11.1944	30.12.1944	1.1945	to the Philippines 11.1969 (Ilocos Norte)
LST906	Bethlehem, Hingham	1.1944	11.3.1944	4.1944	wrecked 18.10.1944
LST907	Bethlehem, Hingham	1.1944	18.3.1944	4.1944	to Venezuela 11.1946 (Capana)
LST908	Bethlehem, Hingham	2.1944	28.3.1944	5.1944	stricken 8.1946
LST909	Bethlehem, Hingham	2.1944	3.4.1944	5.1944	stricken 7.1946
LST910	Bethlehem, Hingham	2.1944	8.4.1944	5.1944	stricken 7.1946
LST911	Bethlehem, Hingham	2.1944	12.4.1944	5.1944	stricken 7.1946
LST912	Bethlehem, Hingham	3.1944	22.4.1944	5.1944	wrecked 30.12.1966
LST913	Bethlehem, Hingham	3.1944	26.4.1944	5.1944	stricken 3.1947
LST914	Bethlehem, Hingham	2.1944	18.4.1944	5.1944	sold 6.1960
LST915	Bethlehem, Hingham	3.1944	3.5.1944	5.1944	stricken 7.1946
LST916	Bethlehem, Hingham	3.1944	29.4.1944	5.1944	to the US Army 6.1946
LST917	Bethlehem, Hingham	3.1944	6.5.1944	5.1944	stricken 7.1946
LST918	Bethlehem, Hingham	4.1944	7.5.1944	5.1944	stricken 7.1946
LST919	Bethlehem, Hingham	4.1944	17.5.1944	5.1944	stricken 9.1946
LST920	Bethlehem, Hingham	4.1944	29.5.1944	6.1944	stricken 3.1947
LST921	Bethlehem, Hingham	5.1944	2.6.1944	6.1944	sunk 14.8.1944
LST922	Bethlehem, Hingham	4.1944	7.6.1944	6.1944	stricken 8.1946
LST923	Bethlehem, Hingham	5.1944	11.6.1944	7.1944	stricken 8.1946
LST924	Bethlehem, Hingham	5.1944	17.6.1944	7.1944	stricken 7.1946
LST925	Bethlehem, Hingham	5.1944	30.6.1944	7.1944	stricken 12.1945
LST926	Bethlehem, Hingham	5.1944	24.6.1944	7.1944	stricken 7.1946
LST927	Bethlehem, Hingham	5.1944	28.6.1944	7.1944	stricken 10.1946
LST928	Bethlehem, Hingham	6.1944	5.7.1944	7.1944	barrack ship 7.1955
LST929, 9.1945-LST(H)929	Bethlehem, Hingham	6.1944	8.7.1944	8.1944	to China 5.1946
LST930, 9.1945-LST(H)930	Bethlehem, Hingham	6.1944	12.7.1944	8.1944	stricken 7.1946
LST931, 9.1945-LST(H)931	Bethlehem, Hingham	6.1944	19.7.1944	8.1944	stricken 7.1946
LST932	Bethlehem, Hingham	6.1944	22.7.1944	8.1944	stricken 7.1946
LST933	Bethlehem, Hingham	6.1944	26.7.1944	8.1944	stricken 8.1946
LST934	Bethlehem, Hingham	6.1944	29.7.1944	8.1944	for disposal 5.1946
LST935	Bethlehem, Hingham	7.1944	5.8.1944	8.1944	stricken 8.1946
LST936	Bethlehem, Hingham	7.1944	9.8.1944	9.1944	stricken 6.1946
LST937	Bethlehem, Hingham	7.1944	12.8.1944	9.1944	to China 5.1946 (Chung 102)
LST938	Bethlehem, Hingham	7.1944	15.8.1944	9.1944	stricken 6.1962
LST939	Bethlehem, Hingham	7.1944	23.8.1944	9.1944	stricken 7.1946
LST940	Bethlehem, Hingham	7.1944	26.8.1944	9.1944	stricken 8.1946

LST941	Bethlehem, Hingham	7.1944	30.8.1944	9.1944	stricken 7.1946
LST942	Bethlehem, Hingham	8.1944	6.9.1944	9.1944	stricken 7.1946
LST943	Bethlehem, Hingham	8.1944	9.9.1944	9.1944	stricken 9.1946
LST944	Bethlehem, Hingham	8.1944	13.9.1944	10.1944	stricken 1.1946
LST945	Bethlehem, Hingham	8.1944	16.9.1944	10.1944	for disposal 5.1946
LST946	Bethlehem, Hingham	8.1944	20.9.1944	10.1944	stricken 7.1946
LST947	Bethlehem, Hingham	8.1944	23.9.1944	10.1944	stricken 10.1946
LST948	Bethlehem, Hingham	8.1944	28.9.1944	(3.1945)	commissioned as landing craft repair ship
LST949, 9.1945-LST(H)949	Bethlehem, Hingham	8.1944	30.9.1944	10.1944	stricken 9.1946
LST950, 9.1945-LST(H)950	Bethlehem, Hingham	9.1944	4.10.1944	10.1944	stricken 6.1947
LST951, 9.1945-LST(H)951	Bethlehem, Hingham	9.1944	7.10.1944	10.1944	stricken 9.1946
LST952, 9.1945-LST(H)952	Bethlehem, Hingham	9.1944	11.10.1944	11.1944	stricken 1.1947
LST953	Bethlehem, Hingham	9.1944	15.10.1944	11.1944	stricken 11.1958
LST954	Bethlehem, Hingham	9.1944	18.10.1944	(4.1945)	commissioned as landing craft repair ship
LST955	Bethlehem, Hingham	9.1944	22.10.1944	(4.1945)	commissioned as landing craft repair ship
LST956	Bethlehem, Hingham	1.1944	21.8.1944	(3.1945)	commissioned as battle damage repair ship
LST957	Bethlehem, Hingham	9.1944	30.10.1944	11.1944	stricken 1.1948
LST958	Bethlehem, Hingham	10.1944	31.10.1944	11.1944	stricken 3.1946
LST959	Bethlehem, Hingham	10.1944	4.11.1944	11.1944	stricken 7.1946
LST960	Bethlehem, Hingham	10.1944	8.11.1944	12.1944	stricken 8.1946
LST961	Bethlehem, Hingham	10.1944	11.11.1944	12.1944	stricken 8.1946
LST962	Bethlehem, Hingham	10.1944	17.11.1944	(5.1945)	commissioned as landing craft repair ship
LST963	Bethlehem, Hingham	10.1944	18.11.1944	(5.1945)	commissioned as landing craft repair ship
LST964	Bethlehem, Hingham	10.1944	22.11.1944	12.1944	stricken 8.1946
LST965	Bethlehem, Hingham	10.1944	25.11.1944	12.1944	stricken 7.1946
LST966	Bethlehem, Hingham	11.1944	6.12.1944	(6.1945)	commissioned as MTB depot ship
LST967	Bethlehem, Hingham	11.1944	2.12.1944	(4.1945)	commissioned as battle damage repair ship
LST968	Bethlehem, Hingham	11.1944	9.12.1944	1.1945	stricken 8.1946
LST969	Bethlehem, Hingham	11.1944	13.12.1944	1.1945	stricken 8.1946
LST970	Bethlehem, Hingham	11.1944	16.12.1944	1.1945	stricken 8.1946
LST971	Bethlehem, Hingham	11.1944	20.12.1944	(5.1945)	commissioned as landing craft repair ship
LST972	Bethlehem, Hingham	11.1944	22.12.1944	1.1945	stricken 8.1946
LST973	Bethlehem, Hingham	11.1944	27.12.1944	1.1945	to France 11.1951 (Golo)
LST974	Bethlehem, Hingham	11.1944	31.12.1944	1.1945	for disposal 5.1946
LST975	Bethlehem, Hingham	12.1944	6.1.1945	2.1945	to South Vietnam 4.1962 (Cam Ranh)
LST976	Bethlehem, Hingham	12.1944	10.1.1945	(2.1945)	commissioned as battle damage repair ship

LST977	Bethlehem, Hingham	12.1944	15.1.1945	(2.1945)	commissioned as MTB depot ship
LST978	Bethlehem, Hingham	12.1944	20.1.1945	2.1945	stricken 7.1946
LST979	Bethlehem, Hingham	12.1944	23.1.1945	2.1945	stricken 8.1946
LST980	Boston N Yd, Charlestown	12.1943	27.1.1944	2.1944	stricken 4.1975
LST981	Boston N Yd, Charlestown	12.1943	27.1.1944	3.1944	stricken 8.1946
LST982	Boston N Yd, Charlestown	12.1943	10.2.1944	3.1944	stricken 7.1946
LST983	Boston N Yd, Charlestown	12.1943	10.2.1944	3.1944	stricken 9.1974
LST984	Boston N Yd, Charlestown	1.1944	25.2.1944	4.1944	stricken 7.1946
LST985	Boston N Yd, Charlestown	1.1944	25.2.1944	4.1944	stricken 7.1946
LST986	Boston N Yd, Charlestown	1.1944	5.3.1944	4.1944	stricken 8.1946
LST987	Boston N Yd, Charlestown	2.1944	5.3.1944	4.1944	stricken 6.1960
LST988	Boston N Yd, Charlestown	2.1944	12.3.1944	4.1944	stricken 9.1957
LST989	Boston N Yd, Charlestown	2.1944	12.3.1944	4.1944	stricken 11.1946
LST990	Boston N Yd, Charlestown	2.1944	27.3.1944	5.1944	stricken 9.1946
LST991	Boston N Yd, Charlestown	2.1944	27.3.1944	5.1944	to War Dept. 1946
LST992	Boston N Yd, Charlestown	3.1944	7.4.1944	5.1944	stricken 9.1946
LST993	Boston N Yd, Charlestown	3.1944	7.4.1944	5.1944	to China 2.1948 (Chunghsun)
LST994	Boston N Yd, Charlestown	3.1944	17.4.1944	5.1944	stricken 8.1946
LST995	Boston N Yd, Charlestown	3.1944	2.5.1944	5.1944	stricken 9.1946
LST996	Boston N Yd, Charlestown	3.1944	2.5.1944	5.1944	stricken 5.1946
LST997	Boston N Yd, Charlestown	3.1944	12.5.1944	5.1944	stricken 4.1947
LST998	Boston N Yd, Charlestown	4.1944	14.5.1944	5.1944	stricken 7.1946
LST999	Boston N Yd, Charlestown	4.1944	14.5.1944	5.1944	stricken 9.1946
LST1000	Boston N Yd, Charlestown	4.1944	26.5.1944	6.1944	stricken 8.1946
LST1001	Boston N Yd, Charlestown	4.1944	24.5.1944	6.1944	stricken 6.1946
LST1002	Boston N Yd, Charlestown	4.1944	3.5.1944	6.1944	for disposal 5.1946
LST1003	Boston N Yd, Charlestown	4.1944	3.5.1944	(11.1944)	commissioned as landing craft repair ship
LST1004	Bethlehem, Quincy	1.1944	3.3.1944	3.1944	stricken 2.1947
LST1005	Bethlehem, Quincy	2.1944	11.3.1944	4.1944	collision 30.12.1945
LST1006	Bethlehem, Quincy	2.1944	11.3.1944	4.1944	stricken 8.1948
LST1007	Bethlehem, Quincy	2.1944	20.3.1944	4.1944	stricken 4.1946
LST1008	Bethlehem, Quincy	2.1944	23.3.1944	4.1944	to China 5.1946 (Chung 122)
LST1009	Bethlehem, Quincy	2.1944	23.3.1944	4.1944	to the US Army 7.1946
LST1010	Bethlehem, Quincy	2.1944	29.3.1944	4.1944	to South Korea 3.1955 (Unbong)
LST1011	Bethlehem, Quincy	2.1944	29.3.1944	4.1944	stricken 7.1946
LST1012	Bethlehem, Quincy	3.1944	8.4.1944	4.1944	stricken 7.1946
LST1013	Bethlehem, Quincy	3.1944	16.4.1944	5.1944	UNRRA service 10.1946
LST1014	Bethlehem, Quincy	3.1944	16.4.1944	5.1944	stricken 4.1946
LST1015	Bethlehem, Quincy	3.1944	20.4.1944	5.1944	for disposal 5.1946
LST1016	Bethlehem, Quincy	3.1944	25.4.1944	5.1944	stricken 7.1946
LST1017	Bethlehem, Quincy	3.1944	25.4.1944	5.1944	to China 12.1946 (Chungchi)
LST1018	Bethlehem, Quincy	3.1944	6.5.1944	5.1944	stricken 6.1947
LST1019	Bethlehem, Quincy	3.1944	6.5.1944	5.1944	stricken 9.1946
LST1020	Bethlehem, Quincy	4.1944	10.5.1944	5.1944	stricken 6.1948
LST1021	Bethlehem, Quincy	4.1944	16.5.1944	5.1944	to the UK 12.1944 (LST1021)

LST1022	Bethlehem, Quincy	4.1944	16.5.1944	5.1944	stricken 1.1948
LST1023	Bethlehem, Quincy	4.1944	17.5.1944	5.1944	stricken 8.1946
LST1024	Bethlehem, Quincy	4.1944	22.5.1944	5.1944	stricken 7.1946
LST1025	Bethlehem, Quincy	4.1944	22.5.1944	5.1944	stricken 8.1946
LST1026	Bethlehem, Quincy	5.1944	2.6.1944	6.1944	stricken 8.1946
LST1027	Bethlehem, Quincy	5.1944	2.6.1944	6.1944	stricken 4.1947
LST1028	Boston N Yd, Charlestown	5.1944	18.6.1944	7.1944	stricken 12.1945
LST1029	Boston N Yd, Charlestown	5.1944	18.6.1944	7.1944	sold 10.1946
LST1030	Boston N Yd, Charlestown	5.1944	25.6.1944	7.1944	to China 2.1948 (Chungchuan)
LST1031	Boston N Yd, Charlestown	5.1944	25.6.1944	7.1944	stricken 1.1946
LST1032	Boston N Yd, Charlestown	6.1944	9.7.1944	8.1944	stricken 8.1970
LST1033, 9.1945-LST(H)1033	Boston N Yd, Charlestown	6.1944	9.7.1944	8.1944	stricken 8.1946
LST1034	Boston N Yd, Charlestown	6.1944	26.7.1944	9.1944	sold 10.1946
LST1035	Boston N Yd, Charlestown	6.1944	26.7.1944	9.1944	stricken 7.1946
LST1036	Boston N Yd, Charlestown	7.1944	24.8.1944	(1.1945)	commissioned as landing craft repair ship
LST1037	Boston N Yd, Charlestown	7.1944	24.8.1944	(2.1945)	commissioned as landing craft repair ship
LST1038	Dravo, Pittsburgh	10.1944	6.1.1945	2.1945	stricken 11.1958
LST1039	Dravo, Pittsburgh	11.1944	6.1.1945	2.1945	stricken 7.1946
LST1040	Dravo, Pittsburgh	12.1944	13.1.1945	2.1945	sold 10.1946
LST1041	Dravo, Pittsburgh	11.1944	20.1.1945	2.1945	stricken 6.1960
LST1042	Dravo, Pittsburgh	12.1944	20.1.1945	2.1945	stricken 6.1946
LST1043	Dravo, Pittsburgh	12.1944	27.1.1945	2.1945	stricken 8.1946
LST1044	Dravo, Pittsburgh	11.1944	3.2.1945	3.1945	stricken 7.1946
LST1045	Dravo, Pittsburgh	12.1944	3.2.1945	3.1945	stricken 8.1946
LST1046	Dravo, Pittsburgh	12.1944	10.2.1945	3.1945	stricken 7.1946
LST1047	Dravo, Pittsburgh	12.1944	17.2.1945	3.1945	to the US Army 6.1946
LST1048	Dravo, Pittsburgh	1.1945	17.2.1945	3.1945	stricken 8.1959
LST1049	Dravo, Pittsburgh	1.1945	24.2.1945	3.1945	stricken 2.1948
LST1050	Dravo, Pittsburgh	12.1944	3.3.1945	4.1945	to China 1.1947 (Chunglien)
LST1051	Dravo, Pittsburgh	1.1945	3.3.1945	4.1945	stricken 6.1946
LST1052	Dravo, Pittsburgh	1.1945	6.3.1945	4.1945	stricken 8.1946
LST1053	Dravo, Pittsburgh	1.1945	6.3.1945	4.1945	stricken 7.1946
LST1054	Dravo, Pittsburgh	2.1945	17.3.1945	4.1945	stricken 7.1946
LST1055	Dravo, Pittsburgh	2.1945	24.3.1945	4.1945	stricken 2.1947
LST1056	Dravo, Pittsburgh	1.1945	24.3.1945	5.1945	sold 1.1947
LST1057	Dravo, Pittsburgh	2.1945	31.3.1945	5.1945	stricken 9.1946
LST1058	Dravo, Pittsburgh	2.1945	7.4.1945	5.1945	stricken 9.1946
LST1059	Dravo, Pittsburgh	3.1945	14.4.1945	5.1945	sold 1.1947
LST1060	Bethlehem, Hingham	12.1944	29.1.1945	2.1945	stricken 4.1947
LST1061	Bethlehem, Hingham	12.1944	3.2.1945	3.1945	stricken 7.1946
LST1062	Bethlehem, Hingham	12.1944	6.2.1945	3.1945	stricken 7.1946
LST1063	Bethlehem, Hingham	1.1945	11.2.1945	3.1945	for disposal 6.1948
LST1064	Bethlehem, Hingham	1.1945	14.2.1945	3.1945	stricken 10.1959
LST1065	Bethlehem, Hingham	1.1945	17.2.1945	3.1945	stricken 6.1947
LST1066	Bethlehem, Hingham	1.1945	21.2.1945	3.1945	stricken 6.1973
LST1067	Bethlehem, Hingham	1.1945	27.2.1945	3.1945	stricken 6.1973
LST1068	Bethlehem, Hingham	1.1945	3.3.1945	3.1945	stricken 9.1957

LST1069	Bethlehem, Hingham	2.1945	7.3.1945	3.1945	stricken 6.1975
LST1070	Bethlehem, Hingham	2.1945	9.3.1945	4.1945	auxiliary 1.1947
LST1071	Bethlehem, Hingham	2.1945	14.3.1945	4.1945	stricken 11.1959
LST1072	Bethlehem, Hingham	2.1945	20.3.1945	4.1945	stricken 6.1975
LST1073	Bethlehem, Hingham	2.1945	22.3.1945	4.1945	to Brazil 5.1971 (Garcia d'Avila)
LST1074	Bethlehem, Hingham	2.1945	27.3.1945	4.1945	stricken 11.1958
LST1075	Bethlehem, Hingham	3.1945	3.4.1945	4.1945	to China 12.1946 (Chungcheng I)
LST1076	Bethlehem, Hingham	3.1945	14.4.1945	5.1945	to Greece 3.1971 (Kriti)
LST1077	Bethlehem, Hingham	3.1945	18.4.1945	5.1945	stricken 4.1978
LST1078	Bethlehem, Hingham	3.1945	25.4.1945	5.1945	auxiliary 1.1949
LST1079	Bethlehem, Hingham	3.1945	27.4.1945	5.1945	stricken 11.1959
LST1080	Bethlehem, Hingham	4.1945	2.5.1945	5.1945	to South Korea 10.1958 (Hwasan)
LST1081	American Bridge, Pittsburgh	11.1944	5.1.1945	1.1945	stricken 11.1958
LST1082	American Bridge, Pittsburgh	11.1944	26.1.1945	2.1945	stricken 4.1975
LST1083	American Bridge, Pittsburgh	11.1944	14.1.1945	2.1945	stricken 6.1972
LST1084	American Bridge, Pittsburgh	11.1944	19.1.1945	2.1945	stricken 9.1974
LST1085	American Bridge, Pittsburgh	12.1944	13.1.1945	2.1945	auxiliary 1.1949
LST1086	American Bridge, Pittsburgh	12.1944	28.1.1945	2.1945	to Greece 1960 (Ikaria)
LST1087	American Bridge, Pittsburgh	12.1944	3.2.1945	3.1945	stricken 9.1947
LST1088	American Bridge, Pittsburgh	12.1944	11.2.1945	3.1945	stricken 11.1973
LST1089	American Bridge, Pittsburgh	12.1944	17.2.1945	3.1945	to West Germany 10.1960 (Bochum)
LST1090	American Bridge, Pittsburgh	12.1944	24.2.1945	4.1945	stricken 11.1960
LST1091	American Bridge, Pittsburgh	1.1945	3.3.1945	4.1945	to Taiwan 10.1958 (Chung Chih)
LST1092	American Bridge, Pittsburgh	1.1945	3.3.1945	(5.1945)	commissioned as aircraft engines repair ship
LST1093	American Bridge, Pittsburgh	1.1945	11.4.1945	(6.1945)	commissioned as aircraft repair ship
LST1094	American Bridge, Pittsburgh	1.1945	21.4.1945	(6.1945)	commissioned as aircraft engines repair ship
LST1095	American Bridge, Pittsburgh	1.1945	25.3.1945	(6.1945)	commissioned as aircraft repair ship
LST1096	Jeffboat, Jeffersonville	11.1944	10.1.1945	2.1945	stricken 4.1975
LST1097	Jeffboat, Jeffersonville	11.1944	16.1.1945	2.1945	auxiliary 1.1949
LST1098	Jeffboat, Jeffersonville	12.1944	27.1.1945	(6.1945)	commissioned as salvage craft depot ship
LST1099	Jeffboat, Jeffersonville	12.1944	8.2.1945	(6.1945)	commissioned as salvage craft depot ship

LST1100	Jeffboat, Jeffersonville	12.1944	20.2.1945	(7.1945)	commissioned as salvage craft depot ship
LST1101	Missouri Valley Bridge, Evansville	11.1944	3.1.1945	1.1945	to West Germany 11.1960 (Bottrop)
LST1102	Missouri Valley Bridge, Evansville	11.1944	10.1.1945	1.1945	auxiliary 1.1949
LST1103	Missouri Valley Bridge, Evansville	11.1944	13.1.1945	1.1945	stricken 6.1947
LST1104	Missouri Valley Bridge, Evansville	12.1944	17.1.1945	2.1945	stricken 5.1947
LST1105	Missouri Valley Bridge, Evansville	12.1944	20.1.1945	2.1945	stricken 6.1946
LST1106	Missouri Valley Bridge, Evansville	12.1944	24.1.1945	2.1945	stricken 10.1946
LST1107	Missouri Valley Bridge, Evansville	12.1944	29.1.1945	2.1945	stricken 7.1946
LST1108	Missouri Valley Bridge, Evansville	12.1944	1.2.1945	2.1945	stricken 9.1946
LST1109	Missouri Valley Bridge, Evansville	12.1944	6.2.1945	2.1945	stricken 6.1946
LST1110	Missouri Valley Bridge, Evansville	12.1944	9.2.1945	3.1945	to Taiwan 8.1958 (Chung Chiang)
LST1111	Missouri Valley Bridge, Evansville	1.1945	9.4.1945	(7.1945)	commissioned as barrack ship
LST1112	Missouri Valley Bridge, Evansville	1.1945	12.4.1945	(6.1945)	commissioned as barrack ship
LST1113	Missouri Valley Bridge, Evansville	1.1945	17.4.1945	(6.1945)	commissioned as barrack ship
LST1114	Missouri Valley Bridge, Evansville	1.1945	20.4.1945	(6.1945)	commissioned as barrack ship
LST1115	Chicago Bridge, Seneca	9.1944	22.12.1944	(6.1945)	commissioned as landing craft repair ship
LST1116	Chicago Bridge, Seneca	10.1944	28.12.1944	(5.1945)	commissioned as landing craft repair ship
LST1117	Chicago Bridge, Seneca	10.1944	2.1.1945	(6.1945)	commissioned as landing craft repair ship
LST1118	Chicago Bridge, Seneca	10.1944	5.1.1945	(6.1945)	commissioned as landing craft repair ship
LST1119	Chicago Bridge, Seneca	10.1944	11.1.1945	(6.1945)	commissioned as battle damage repair ship
LST1120	Chicago Bridge, Seneca	10.1944	16.1.1945	2.1945	stricken 2.1948
LST1121	Chicago Bridge, Seneca	10.1944	19.1.1945	(7.1945)	commissioned as battle damage repair ship
LST1122	Chicago Bridge, Seneca	10.1944	24.1.1945	2.1945	stricken 5.1972
LST1123	Chicago Bridge, Seneca	11.1944	29.1.1945	2.1945	stricken 5.1975
LST1124	Chicago Bridge, Seneca	11.1944	1.2.1945	(6.1945)	commissioned as landing craft repair ship
LST1125	Chicago Bridge, Seneca	11.1944	6.2.1945	(8.1945)	commissioned as MTB depot ship
LST1126	Chicago Bridge, Seneca	11.1944	9.2.1945	2.1945	stricken 7.1970
LST1127	Chicago Bridge, Seneca	11.1944	14.2.1945	(7.1945)	commissioned as battle damage repair ship

LST1128	Chicago Bridge, Seneca	11.1944	19.2.1945	3.1945	to Indonesia 11.1958 (Teluk Langsa)
LST1129	Chicago Bridge, Seneca	11.1944	22.2.1945	3.1945	stricken 11.1958
LST1130	Chicago Bridge, Seneca	12.1944	27.2.1945	3.1945	wrecked 23.3.1948
LST1131	Chicago Bridge, Seneca	12.1944	2.3.1945	(7.1945)	commissioned as landing craft repair ship
LST1132	Chicago Bridge, Seneca	12.1944	7.3.1945	(7.1945)	commissioned as landing craft repair ship
LST1133	Chicago Bridge, Seneca	12.1944	10.3.1945	(9.1945)	commissioned as MTB depot ship
LST1134	Chicago Bridge, Seneca	12.1944	16.3.1945	4.1945	to Thailand 5.1966 (Phangan)
LST1135	Chicago Bridge, Seneca	12.1944	21.3.1945	4.1945	stricken 8.1948
LST1136	Chicago Bridge, Seneca	12.1944	26.3.1945	(7.1945)	commissioned as landing craft repair ship
LST1137	Chicago Bridge, Seneca	1.1945	30.3.1945	(8.1945)	commissioned as landing craft repair ship
LST1138	Chicago Bridge, Seneca	1.1945	5.4.1945	4.1945	stricken 2.1961
LST1139	Chicago Bridge, Seneca	1.1945	9.4.1945	4.1945	stricken 8.1946
LST1140	Chicago Bridge, Seneca	1.1945	13.4.1945	5.1945	stricken 8.1949
LST1141	Chicago Bridge, Seneca	1.1945	18.4.1945	5.1945	to Thailand 3.1970 (Lanta)
LST1142	Chicago Bridge, Seneca	1.1945	23.4.1945	5.1945	stricken 11.1958
LST1143	Chicago Bridge, Seneca	1.1945	27.4.1945	(10.1945)	commissioned as landing craft repair ship
LST1144	Chicago Bridge, Seneca	2.1945	2.5.1945	5.1945	stricken 6.1960
LST1145	Chicago Bridge, Seneca	2.1945	7.5.1945	(9.1945)	commissioned as landing craft repair ship
LST1146	Chicago Bridge, Seneca	2.1945	11.5.1945	5.1945	stricken 11.1976
LST1147	Chicago Bridge, Seneca	2.1945	21.5.1945	(10.1945)	commissioned as landing craft repair ship
LST1148	Chicago Bridge, Seneca	2.1945	23.5.1945	6.1945	stricken 9.1974
LST1149	Chicago Bridge, Seneca	2.1945	25.5.1945	(12.1945)	commissioned as landing craft repair ship
LST1150	Chicago Bridge, Seneca	3.1945	30.5.1945	6.1945	stricken 9.1974
LST1151	Chicago Bridge, Seneca	3.1945	4.6.1945	(11.1945)	commissioned as landing craft repair ship
LST1152	Chicago Bridge, Seneca	3.1945	8.6.1945	6.1945	to Taiwan 10.1958 (Chung Ming)

1625-1780 / 3640-4080 t, 100.0 x 15.2 x 4.3 m, 2 General Motors diesels, 1800 hp, 12 kts, 590 t diesel oil, 24000 nm (9 kts), complement 91-125; 1 x 1 – 76/50 Mk 10/18/20 (LST1-541, earlier), 4 x 1 (LST1-541, earlier) or (1 x 2 + 5 x 1) (LST1-541, later) or (2 x 2 + 4 x 1) (LST542-1152) – 40/56 Bofors, 6 (LST1-541, earlier) or 12 (other) x 1 – 20/70 Oerlikon; 4 (sometimes 2 or 6) LCVP, 20 25t tanks or 500t cargo, 163 troops; SE or SF or SL or SO or SU radar (not on all).

Tank landing ships were originally intended to transport tanks across the Atlantic. They were designed according to the technical requirements of the British Admiralty, according to which they were supposed to transport 20 medium tanks across the Atlantic with their subsequent

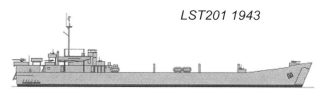

LST201 1943

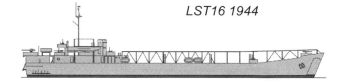

LST16 1944

LST914

LST742

was limited to 2366 t (with 500-t cargo weight) with 1.2 / 3.0-m draught fwd/aft.

A total of 1152 ships of LST (Mκ 2) class were ordered. LST85-116, 182-196 (Jefferson Boat), LST142-156, 296-300 (American Bridge), LST232-236 (Chicago Bridge), LST248-260 (Missouri Valley Bridge), LST431-445 (Bethlehem-Fairfield) were cancelled in September 1942.

1943 - 1944, some ships (inc. *LST16*, *18* etc): flight deck was fitted, "air group" consisted of 2-6 observation planes (L-4).

LST333 was torpedoed by German submarine *U593* off Dellis, Algeria 22.6.1943. *LST158* was bombed by German aircraft 1.7.1943 off Licata (Sicily). *LST313* was sunk by German aircraft 10.7.1943 off Gela (Sicily). *LST342* was torpedoed by Japanese submarine *RO106* off the Solomon Islands 18.7.1943. *LST318* was sunk by German aircraft 9.8.1943 at Coronia, Sicily. *LST396* sank after accidental fire and explosion off the Solomon Islands 18.8.1943. *LST167* was severely damaged by Japanese aircraft at Vella Lavella 25.9.1943 and stricken as CTL. *LST203* ran aground off Noumea (Ellice Islands) 1.10.1943. *LST448* was bombed by Japanese aircraft 1.10.1943 off Vella Lavella and sunk 5.10.1943 off the Solomon Islands in tow. *LST228* ran aground at the Azores 19.1.1944 and became a total loss. *LST348* was torpedoed by German submarine *U410* 20.2.1944 off Anzio. *LST349* ran aground off Ponza, Italy, 26.2.1944. *LST507* was sunk by German MTB 28.4.1944 in the English Channel, *LST531* was torpedoed by German MTB 28.4.1944 in Lyme Bay (England). *LST43*, *LST69*, *LST179*, *LST353* and *LST480* were destroyed by an ammunition explosion in Pearl Harbor 21.5.1944. *LST499* was mined off the coast of Normandy 8.6.1944. *LST314* and *LST376* were torpedoed by German MTBs 9.6.1944 off the coast of Normandy and in the English Channel, respectively. *LST496* was mined off the coast of Normandy 11.6.1944. *LST523* was mined off the coast of Normandy 19.6.1944. *LST282* was sunk by German guided glide bomb off the coast of Southern France 15.8.1944. *LST6* was mined *en route* from Rouen to Portland (UK) 18.11.1944. *LST359* was torpedoed by German submarine *U870* in the East Atlantic 20.12.1944. *LST472* was sunk by Japanese aircraft off Mindoro 21.12.1944. *LST460* was sunk by Japanese aircraft 21.12.1944 off Mindoro. *LST447* was sunk 6.4.1945 by kamikaze off Okinawa. *LST493* ran aground at Plymouth (UK) 12.4.1945 *LST534* was badly damaged by kamikaze at Okinawa 22.6.1945 and never completely repaired.

LST39 was lost in an accidental explosion of the ammunition in Pearl Harbor 21.5.1944, stricken, later salvaged and used for spare parts. *LST327* was badly damaged 27.8.1944 by a mine in the English Channel. *LST387* was badly damaged 22.6.1943 by a torpedo from German submarine *U593* 22.6.1943

disembarkation through the bow door. When designing, the British experience in building such ships was used. To distinguish the US-built ships, they received the designation Mk 2, while the British-built *Boxer* class was designated LST Mk 1.

Compared to the British prototype, the Mk 2 was 6 knots slower, but the use of the diesel machinery instead of turbines allowed to exceed the required cruising range many times over, receiving 24000 nm at 9 knots. The tanks were carried in the hold (on the so-called "tank" deck) and on the upper deck. Cargo and tanks were transferred from the upper deck to the "tank" deck by a lift which, starting with *LST513* (except *LST531*), was replaced by a simple ramp. *LST542* and later ships had a slightly lighter construction, strengthened AA armament and powerful distilling plant.

When fully loaded, the ships had a displacement of more than 4000 t and fwd/aft draught of 2.3 / 4 m, respectively, therefore during beaching the displacement

LST975

between Algiers and Bizerte, but later repaired. *LST921* was torpedoed by German submarine *U764* off Bristol 14.8.1944. *LST906* grounded at Leghorn (Italy) 18.10.1944. *LST738* was sunk by Japanese aircraft off Mindoro 15.12.1944. *LST563* ran aground on Clipperton Island in the Eastern Pacific 21.12.1944. *LST749* was sunk by Japanese aircraft off the Philippines 21.12.1944. *LST750* was sunk by Japanese aircraft off Leyte 28.12.1944. *LST577* was torpedoed by Japanese submarine *RO50* off the Philippines 11.2.1945. *LST884* was badly damaged by kamikaze 1.4.1945 at Okinawa, never repaired, the hulk sank 6.5.1946. *LST675* was badly damaged by Japanese aircraft at Okinawa 4.4.1945 and never repaired. *LST808* was hit by kamikaze 20.5.1945 off Ieshima and later totally destroyed.

LST1153 class tank landing ships

| LST1153 | Boston N Yd, Charlestown | 19.7.1945 | 24.4.1947 | 3.9.1947 | stricken 5.1973 |
| LST1154 | Boston N Yd, Charlestown | 4.8.1945 | 19.7.1946 | 24.5.1949 | aviation base ship 2.1962 |

LST1153 1947

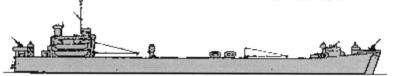

2250 / 6000 t, 116.4 x 16.5 x 4.4 m, 2 sets Westinghouse / General Electric geared steam turbines, 2 Babcock & Wilcox boilers, 6000 hp, 14 kts, 10000 nm (10 kts), complement 181; 2 x 1 – 127/38 Mk 12, 2 x 2 – 40/56 Bofors, 2 x 1 – 20/70 Oerlikon; 20 tanks or 500 t cargo, 175 troops; SU radar.
Failed attempt to increase the speed of the LST, using the steam turbine machinery. Building of LST1155 was cancelled in January 1946.

LSM1 class medium landing ships

LSM1	Brown SB, Houston	2.1944	23.3.1944	5.1944	stricken 1946
LSM2	Brown SB, Houston	2.1944	23.3.1944	5.1944	stricken 1946
LSM3	Brown SB, Houston	3.1944	9.4.1944	5.1944	stricken 1946
LSM4	Brown SB, Houston	3.1944	9.4.1944	5.1944	stricken 1947
LSM5	Brown SB, Houston	3.1944	9.4.1944	5.1944	wrecked 6.7.1948
LSM6	Brown SB, Houston	3.1944	9.4.1944	5.1944	stricken 1946
LSM7	Brown SB, Houston	3.1944	24.4.1944	5.1944	stricken 1946
LSM8	Brown SB, Houston	3.1944	24.4.1944	5.1944	stricken 1946
LSM9	Brown SB, Houston	3.1944	24.4.1944	5.1944	stricken 1946
LSM10	Brown SB, Houston	3.1944	24.4.1944	5.1944	stricken 1946
LSM11	Brown SB, Houston	3.1944	30.4.1944	5.1944	stricken 1947
LSM12	Brown SB, Houston	3.1944	30.4.1944	5.1944	sunk 4.4.1945
LSM13	Brown SB, Houston	3.1944	30.4.1944	6.1944	to China 5.1946 (Yongming)
LSM14	Brown SB, Houston	3.1944	30.4.1944	6.1944	sold 1.1948
LSM15	Brown SB, Houston	4.1944	7.5.1944	6.1944	foundered 9.10.1945
LSM16	Brown SB, Houston	4.1944	7.5.1944	6.1944	stricken 1946
LSM17	Brown SB, Houston	4.1944	7.5.1944	6.1944	to France 4.1954 (LSM17)
LSM18	Brown SB, Houston	4.1944	7.5.1944	6.1944	stricken 1946
LSM19	Brown SB, Houston	4.1944	14.5.1944	6.1944	to South Korea 7.1956 (Girin)
LSM20	Brown SB, Houston	4.1944	14.5.1944	6.1944	sunk 5.12.1944
LSM21	Brown SB, Houston	4.1944	14.5.1944	6.1944	stricken 1946
LSM22	Brown SB, Houston	4.1944	14.5.1944	6.1944	stricken 1946
LSM23	Brown SB, Houston	4.1944	21.5.1944	6.1944	stricken 1946
LSM24	Brown SB, Houston	4.1944	21.5.1944	6.1944	stricken 1946
LSM25	Brown SB, Houston	4.1944	21.5.1944	6.1944	stricken 1946

LSM26	Brown SB, Houston	4.1944	21.5.1944	6.1944	scuttled 24.3.1947
LSM27	Brown SB, Houston	5.1944	28.5.1944	6.1944	stricken 1946
LSM28	Brown SB, Houston	5.1944	28.5.1944	7.1944	stricken 1946
LSM29	Brown SB, Houston	5.1944	28.5.1944	7.1944	stricken 1946
LSM30	Brown SB, Houston	5.1944	28.5.1944	7.1944	to South Korea 4.1956 (Geomun)
LSM31	Brown SB, Houston	5.1944	6.6.1944	7.1944	stricken 1946
LSM32	Brown SB, Houston	5.1944	6.6.1944	7.1944	stricken 1946
LSM33	Brown SB, Houston	5.1944	6.6.1944	7.1944	stricken 1946
LSM34	Brown SB, Houston	5.1944	6.6.1944	7.1944	stricken 1946
LSM35	Brown SB, Houston	5.1944	14.6.1944	7.1944	stricken 1946
LSM36	Brown SB, Houston	5.1944	14.6.1944	7.1944	stricken 1946
LSM37	Brown SB, Houston	5.1944	14.6.1944	7.1944	stricken 1957
LSM38	Brown SB, Houston	5.1944	14.6.1944	7.1944	stricken 1948
LSM39	Brown SB, Houston	5.1944	22.6.1944	7.1944	stricken 1946
LSM40	Brown SB, Houston	5.1944	22.6.1944	7.1944	stricken 1946
LSM41	Brown SB, Houston	5.1944	22.6.1944	8.1944	stricken 1947
LSM42	Brown SB, Houston	5.1944	22.6.1944	8.1944	to China 6.1946 (Hua 208)
LSM43	Brown SB, Houston	6.1944	30.6.1944	7.1944	to China 6.1946
LSM44	Brown SB, Houston	6.1944	30.6.1944	7.1944	stricken 1946
LSM45	Brown SB, Houston	6.1944	30.6.1944	7.1944	to Greece 11.1958 (Ipopliarchos Grigoropoulos)
LSM46	Brown SB, Houston	6.1944	30.6.1944	8.1944	stricken 1946
LSM47	Brown SB, Houston	6.1944	30.6.1944	8.1944	stricken 11.1946
LSM48	Brown SB, Houston	6.1944	7.7.1944	8.1944	stricken 1946
LSM49	Brown SB, Houston	6.1944	7.7.1944	8.1944	stricken 1946
LSM50	Brown SB, Houston	6.1944	7.7.1944	8.1944	stricken 1946
LSM51	Brown SB, Houston	6.1944	24.7.1944	8.1944	stricken 1946
LSM52	Brown SB, Houston	6.1944	14.7.1944	8.1944	stricken 1946
LSM53	Brown SB, Houston	6.1944	14.7.1944	8.1944	stricken 1946
LSM54	Brown SB, Houston	6.1944	14.7.1944	8.1944	to South Korea 5.1956 (Pungdo)
LSM55	Brown SB, Houston	6.1944	21.7.1944	8.1944	UNRRA service 5.1946
LSM56	Brown SB, Houston	6.1944	21.7.1944	8.1944	stricken 1946
LSM57	Brown SB, Houston	6.1944	21.7.1944	8.1944	to South Korea 5.1958 (Wolmi)
LSM58	Brown SB, Houston	6.1944	21.7.1944	8.1944	to France 4.1954 (LSM58)
LSM59	Brown SB, Houston	7.1944	29.7.1944	8.1944	sunk 21.6.1945
LSM60	Brown SB, Houston	7.1944	29.7.1944	8.1944	nuclear tests 7.1946
LSM61	Brown SB, Houston	7.1944	29.7.1944	9.1944	stricken 1946
LSM62	Brown SB, Houston	7.1944	29.7.1944	8.1944	to China 5.1946
LSM63	Brown SB, Houston	7.1944	5.8.1944	8.1944	stricken 1946
LSM64	Brown SB, Houston	7.1944	5.8.1944	9.1944	stricken 1946
LSM65	Brown SB, Houston	7.1944	5.8.1944	9.1944	stricken 1946
LSM66	Brown SB, Houston	7.1944	5.8.1944	9.1944	stricken 1946
LSM67	Brown SB, Houston	7.1944	14.8.1944	9.1944	stricken 1946
LSM68	Brown SB, Houston	7.1944	14.8.1944	9.1944	stricken 1946
LSM69	Brown SB, Houston	7.1944	14.8.1944	9.1944	to China 2.1948
LSM70	Brown SB, Houston	7.1944	14.8.1944	9.1944	stricken 1946
LSM71	Brown SB, Houston	7.1944	22.8.1944	9.1944	stricken 1946
LSM72	Brown SB, Houston	7.1944	22.8.1944	9.1944	stricken 6.1946
LSM73	Brown SB, Houston	7.1944	22.8.1944	9.1944	stricken 1946
LSM74	Brown SB, Houston	7.1944	22.8.1944	9.1944	stricken 1946

LSM75	Brown SB, Houston	8.1944	30.8.1944	9.1944	stricken 1946
LSM76	Brown SB, Houston	8.1944	30.8.1944	9.1944	to China 6.1946 (Meijian)
LSM77	Brown SB, Houston	8.1944	30.8.1944	9.1944	stricken 1946
LSM78	Brown SB, Houston	8.1944	7.9.1944	9.1944	stricken 1946
LSM79	Brown SB, Houston	8.1944	7.9.1944	9.1944	stricken 1946
LSM80	Brown SB, Houston	8.1944	7.9.1944	10.1944	to China 2.1948
LSM81	Brown SB, Houston	8.1944	7.9.1944	10.1944	stricken 1946
LSM82	Brown SB, Houston	8.1944	7.9.1944	10.1944	stricken 1946
LSM83	Brown SB, Houston	8.1944	15.9.1944	10.1944	stricken 1946
LSM84	Brown SB, Houston	8.1944	15.9.1944	10.1944	to South Korea 7.1956 (Neongna)
LSM85	Brown SB, Houston	8.1944	15.9.1944	10.1944	to France 5.1954 (LSM85)
LSM86	Brown SB, Houston	8.1944	15.9.1944	10.1944	to Argentina 2.1948 (BDM2)
LSM87	Brown SB, Houston	8.1944	23.9.1944	10.1944	stricken 1946
LSM88	Brown SB, Houston	8.1944	23.9.1944	10.1944	to China 2.1948
LSM89	Brown SB, Houston	8.1944	23.9.1944	10.1944	stricken 1946
LSM90	Brown SB, Houston	8.1944	23.9.1944	10.1944	stricken 1946
LSM91	Brown SB, Houston	9.1944	30.9.1944	10.1944	stricken 1946
LSM92	Brown SB, Houston	9.1944	30.9.1944	10.1944	stricken 1946
LSM93	Brown SB, Houston	9.1944	30.9.1944	10.1944	stricken 1946
LSM94	Brown SB, Houston	9.1944	30.9.1944	10.1944	stricken 1946
LSM95	Brown SB, Houston	9./1944	7.10.1944	10.1944	stricken 1946
LSM96	Brown SB, Houston	9.1944	7.10.1944	10.1944	to South Korea 4.1956 (Bian)
LSM97	Brown SB, Houston	9.1944	7.10.1944	10.1944	stricken 1946
LSM98	Brown SB, Houston	9.1944	7.10.1944	11.1944	stricken 1946
LSM99	Brown SB, Houston	9.1944	14.10.1944	11.1944	stricken 1957
LSM100	Brown SB, Houston	9.1944	14.10.1944	11.1944	stricken 1946
LSM101	Brown SB, Houston	9.1944	14.10.1944	11.1944	stricken 1957
LSM102	Brown SB, Houston	9.1944	14.10.1944	11.1944	to Greece 11.1958 (Ipopliarchos Tournas)
LSM103	Brown SB, Houston	9.1944	21.10.1944	11.1944	stricken 1946
LSM104	Brown SB, Houston	9.1944	21.10.1944	11.1944	stricken 1958
LSM105	Brown SB, Houston	9.1944	21.10.1944	11.1944	stricken 1957
LSM106	Brown SB, Houston	9.1944	21.10.1944	11.1944	stricken 1958
LSM107	Brown SB, Houston	10.1944	28.10.1944	11.1944	stricken 1958
LSM108	Brown SB, Houston	10.1944	28.10.1944	11.1944	stricken 1958
LSM109	Brown SB, Houston	10.1944	28.10.1944	11.1944	sold 11.1956
LSM110	Brown SB, Houston	10.1944	28.10.1944	11.1944	to France 1.1954 (LSM110)
LSM111	Brown SB, Houston	10.1944	4.11.1944	11.1944	stricken 1946
LSM112	Brown SB, Houston	10.1944	4.11.1944	11.1944	to China 5.1946 (Hua 201)
LSM113	Brown SB, Houston	10.1944	4.11.1944	11.1944	to Chile 3.1947 (Guardiamarina Contreras)
LSM114	Brown SB, Houston	10.1944	4.11.1944	12.1944	stricken 7.1946
LSM115	Brown SB, Houston	10.1944	11.11.1944	12.1944	stricken 1946
LSM116	Brown SB, Houston	10.1944	11.11.1944	12.1944	stricken 1958
LSM117	Brown SB, Houston	10.1944	11.11.1944	12.1944	stricken 1946
LSM118	Brown SB, Houston	10.1944	11.11.1944	12.1944	stricken 1958
LSM119	Brown SB, Houston	10.1944	18.11.1944	12.1944	stricken 1957
LSM120	Brown SB, Houston	10.1944	18.11.1944	12.1944	stricken 1957
LSM121	Brown SB, Houston	10.1944	18.11.1944	12.1944	stricken 1958
LSM122	Brown SB, Houston	10.1944	18.11.1944	12.1944	stricken 1946
LSM123	Brown SB, Houston	11.1944	25.11.1944	12.1944	stricken 1946

LSM124	Brown SB, Houston	11.1944	25.11.1944	12.1944	to China 6.1946
LSM125	Brown SB, Houston	11.1944	25.11.1944	12.1944	to France 1.1954 (LSM125)
LSM126	Charleston N Yd	1.1944	15.3.1944	4.1944	stricken 1946
LSM127	Charleston N Yd	1.1944	15.3.1944	4.1944	stricken 1946
LSM128	Charleston N Yd	2.1944	1.4.1944	5.1944	stricken 1946
LSM129	Charleston N Yd	2.1944	1.4.1944	5.1944	stricken 1946
LSM130	Charleston N Yd	3.1944	12.4.1944	5.1944	stricken 1946
LSM131	Charleston N Yd	3.1944	12.4.1944	5.1944	stricken 1946
LSM132	Charleston N Yd	3.1944	13.4.1944	5.1944	stricken 1947
LSM133	Charleston N Yd	3.1944	13.4.1944	5.1944	stricken 1946
LSM134	Charleston N Yd	3.1944	23.4.1944	5.1944	stricken 7.1946
LSM135	Charleston N Yd	3.1944	23.4.1944	5.1944	sunk 25.5.1945
LSM136	Charleston N Yd	3.1944	19.4.1944	5.1944	stricken 1946
LSM137	Charleston N Yd	3.1944	18.4.1944	5.1944	wrecked 9.10.1945
LSM138	Charleston N Yd	3.1944	1.5.1944	6.1944	stricken 1946
LSM139	Charleston N Yd	4.1944	1.5.1944	6.1944	stricken 1946
LSM140	Charleston N Yd	4.1944	18.5.1944	6.1944	stricken 1946
LSM141	Charleston N Yd	4.1944	15.5.1944	6.1944	stricken 1946
LSM142	Charleston N Yd	4.1944	15.5.1944	6.1944	stricken 1946
LSM143	Charleston N Yd	4.1944	10.5.1944	6.1944	stricken 1946
LSM144	Charleston N Yd	4.1944	10.5.1944	6.1944	stricken 1946
LSM145	Charleston N Yd	4.1944	14.5.1944	6.1944	stricken 1946
LSM146	Charleston N Yd	4.1944	14.5.1944	6.1944	to China 2.1948
LSM147	Charleston N Yd	4.1944	14.5.1944	6.1944	to China 2.1948
LSM148	Charleston N Yd	5.1944	27.5.1944	7.1944	stricken 1946
LSM149	Charleston N Yd	5.1944	27.5.1944	7.1944	sunk 5.12.1944
LSM150	Charleston N Yd	5.1944	2.6.1944	7.1944	stricken 1946
LSM151	Charleston N Yd	5.1944	2.6.1944	7.1944	stricken 1946
LSM152	Charleston N Yd	5.1944	3.6.1944	7.1944	stricken 1946
LSM153	Charleston N Yd	5.1944	3.6.1944	7.1944	to China 6.1946 (Hua 209)
LSM154	Charleston N Yd	5.1944	22.6.1944	7.1944	to China 2.1948
LSM155	Charleston N Yd	5.1944	19.6.1944	7.1944	to China 5.1946 (Meicheng)
LSM156	Charleston N Yd	5.1944	22.6.1944	8.1944	stricken 1946
LSM157	Charleston N Yd	5.1944	19.6.1944	8.1944	to China 6.1946 (Meilo)
LSM158	Charleston N Yd	5.1944	16.6.1944	7.1944	stricken 1946
LSM159	Charleston N Yd	5.1944	16.6.1944	7.1944	to China 2.1948
LSM160	Charleston N Yd	6.1944	27.6.1944	8.1944	stricken 1946
LSM161	Charleston N Yd	6.1944	27.6.1944	8.1944	stricken 6.1965
LSM162	Charleston N Yd	6.1944	26.6.1944	8.1944	stricken 1946
LSM163	Charleston N Yd	6.1944	26.6.1944	8.1944	stricken 1946
LSM164	Charleston N Yd	6.1944	11.7.1944	8.1944	stricken 1946
LSM165	Charleston N Yd	6.1944	11.7.1944	8.1944	stricken 1947
LSM166	Charleston N Yd	6.1944	24.7.1944	8.1944	stricken 1946
LSM167	Charleston N Yd	6.1944	24.7.1944	8.1944	stricken 1958
LSM168	Charleston N Yd	6.1944	25.7.1944	9.1944	stricken 1957
LSM169	Charleston N Yd	6.1944	20.7.1944	9.1944	damaged 15.2.1945, never repaired
LSM170	Charleston N Yd	6.1944	20.7.1944	9.1944	stricken 1946
LSM171	Charleston N Yd	6.1944	20.7.1944	9.1944	scuttled 1948
LSM172	Charleston N Yd	6.1944	20.7.1944	9.1944	stricken 1947
LSM173	Charleston N Yd	6.1944	21.7.1944	9.1944	stricken 1946
LSM174	Charleston N Yd	6.1944	21.7.1944	9.1944	stricken 1946

LSM175	Charleston N Yd	7.1944	3.8.1944	9.1944	to Vietnam 8.1961 (Hương Giang)
LSM176	Charleston N Yd	7.1944	12.8.1944	9.1944	stricken 1946
LSM177	Charleston N Yd	7.1944	12.8.1944	9.1944	stricken 1946
LSM178	Charleston N Yd	7.1944	16.8.1944	10.1944	stricken 1946
LSM179	Charleston N Yd	7.1944	16.8.1944	10.1944	stricken 1946
LSM180	Charleston N Yd	8.1944	26.8.1944	10.1944	stricken 1946
LSM181	Charleston N Yd	8.1944	26.8.1944	10.1944	stricken 1946
LSM182	Charleston N Yd	7.1944	28.8.1944	10.1944	stricken 1946
LSM183	Charleston N Yd	7.1944	28.8.1944	10.1944	stricken 1946
LSM184	Charleston N Yd	8.1944	7.9.1944	10.1944	stricken 1946
LSM185	Charleston N Yd	8.1944	7.9.1944	10.1944	stricken 1946
LSM186	Charleston N Yd	7.1944	5.9.1944	10.1944	stricken 1946
LSM187	Charleston N Yd	7.1944	5.9.1944	10.1944	stricken 1946
LSM200	Charleston N Yd	9.1944	17.10.1944	12.1944	stricken 1957
LSM201	Dravo, Wilmington	12.1943	26.2.1944	4.1944	stricken 1946
LSM202	Dravo, Wilmington	1.1944	15.3.1944	4.1944	stricken 1946
LSM203	Dravo, Wilmington	1.1944	10.4.1944	5.1944	stricken 1946
LSM204	Dravo, Wilmington	1.1944	29.3.1944	5.1944	stricken 1958
LSM205	Dravo, Wilmington	2.1944	14.4.1944	5.1944	stricken 1946
LSM206	Dravo, Wilmington	2.1944	22.4.1944	5.1944	stricken 1946
LSM207	Dravo, Wilmington	3.1944	29.4.1944	5.1944	stricken 1946
LSM208	Dravo, Wilmington	3.1944	10.5.1944	6.1944	to China 5.1946
LSM209	Dravo, Wilmington	3.1944	18.5.1944	6.1944	stricken 1946
LSM210	Dravo, Wilmington	3.1944	23.5.1944	6.1944	stricken 1946
LSM211	Dravo, Wilmington	3.1944	29.5.1944	6.1944	stricken 1946
LSM212	Dravo, Wilmington	4.1944	3.6.1944	7.1944	stricken 1958
LSM213	Dravo, Wilmington	4.1944	8.6.1944	7.1944	stricken 1946
LSM214	Dravo, Wilmington	4.1944	13.6.1944	7.1944	stricken 1946
LSM215	Dravo, Wilmington	5.1944	23.6.1944	7.1944	stricken 1946
LSM216	Dravo, Wilmington	5.1944	28.6.1944	7.1944	to Dominican Republic 11.1946 (San Rafael)
LSM217	Dravo, Wilmington	5.1944	5.7.1944	8.1944	stricken 1946
LSM218	Dravo, Wilmington	5.1944	11.7.1944	8.1944	to China 6.1946
LSM219	Dravo, Wilmington	5.1944	17.7.1944	8.1944	stricken 1947
LSM220	Dravo, Wilmington	6.1944	15.7.1944	8.1944	stricken 1946
LSM221	Dravo, Wilmington	6.1944	29.7.1944	8.1944	stricken 1946
LSM222	Dravo, Wilmington	7.1944	5.8.1944	8.1944	stricken 1946
LSM223	Dravo, Wilmington	6.1944	15.8.1944	9.1944	stricken 1946
LSM224	Dravo, Wilmington	6.1944	22.8.1944	9.1944	stricken 1946
LSM225	Dravo, Wilmington	7.1944	29.8.1944	9.1944	to China 6.1946
LSM226	Dravo, Wilmington	7.1944	4.9.1944	9.1944	to France 4.1954 (LSM226)
LSM227	Dravo, Wilmington	7.1944	9.9.1944	10.1944	to Greece 11.1958 (Ipolpiarchos Daniolos)
LSM228	Dravo, Wilmington	7.1944	30.7.1944	10.1944	stricken 1946
LSM229	Dravo, Wilmington	8.1944	25.9.1944	10.1944	stricken 1958
LSM230	Dravo, Wilmington	8.1944	30.9.1944	10.1944	stricken 1946
LSM231	Dravo, Wilmington	8.1944	9.10.1944	10.1944	stricken 1958
LSM232	Dravo, Wilmington	8.1944	14.10.1944	11.1944	stricken 1958
LSM233	Western Pipe & Steel, San Francisco	2.1944	4.7.1944	8.1944	stricken 1946

LSM234	Western Pipe & Steel, San Francisco	3.1944	4.7.1944	8.1944	stricken 1946
LSM235	Western Pipe & Steel, San Francisco	3.1944	4.7.1944	8.1944	stricken 1946
LSM236	Western Pipe & Steel, San Francisco	3.1944	4.7.1944	9.1944	stricken 1958
LSM237	Western Pipe & Steel, San Francisco	3.1944	30.7.1944	9.1944	stricken 1946
LSM238	Western Pipe & Steel, San Francisco	4.1944	30.7.1944	9.1944	stricken 1947
LSM239	Western Pipe & Steel, San Francisco	4.1944	31.7.1944	9.1944	stricken 1947
LSM240	Western Pipe & Steel, San Francisco	4.1944	31.7.1944	9.1944	stricken 1946
LSM241	Western Pipe & Steel, San Francisco	5.1944	20.8.1944	10.1944	stricken 1946
LSM242	Western Pipe & Steel, San Francisco	5.1944	20.8.1944	10.1944	stricken 1946
LSM243	Western Pipe & Steel, San Francisco	5.1944	3.9.1944	10.1944	stricken 1946
LSM244	Western Pipe & Steel, San Francisco	6.1944	3.9.1944	10.1944	stricken 1946
LSM245	Western Pipe & Steel, San Francisco	7.1944	17.9.1944	11.1944	stricken 1946
LSM246	Western Pipe & Steel, San Francisco	8.1944	17.9.1944	11.1944	stricken 1946
LSM247	Western Pipe & Steel, San Francisco	8.1944	1.10.1944	11.1944	stricken 1946
LSM248	Western Pipe & Steel, San Francisco	8.1944	1.10.1944	11.1944	to China 5.1946 (Hua 202)
LSM249	Western Pipe & Steel, San Francisco	8.1944	15.10.1944	11.1944	to China 6.1946
LSM250	Western Pipe & Steel, San Francisco	8.1944	15.10.1944	12.1944	stricken 1957
LSM251	Western Pipe & Steel, San Francisco	8.1944	15.10.1944	12.1944	stricken 1947
LSM252	Western Pipe & Steel, San Francisco	9.1944	29.10.1944	12.1944	stricken 1946
LSM253	Federal, Newark	2.1944	17.4.1944	5.1944	stricken 1947
LSM254	Federal, Newark	2.1944	17.4.1944	5.1944	stricken 1946
LSM255	Federal, Newark	2.1944	22.4.1944	5.1944	stricken 1946
LSM256	Federal, Newark	2.1944	22.4.1944	5.1944	to China 9.1946
LSM257	Federal, Newark	3.1944	12.5.1944	5.1944	stricken 1946
LSM258	Federal, Newark	3.1944	12.5.1944	6.1944	stricken 1946
LSM259	Federal, Newark	4.1944	26.5.1944	6.1944	stricken 1946
LSM260	Federal, Newark	4.1944	26.5.1944	6.1944	stricken 1946
LSM261	Federal, Newark	4.1944	3.6.1944	6.1944	stricken 1946
LSM262	Federal, Newark	4.1944	3.6.1944	6.1944	stricken 1958
LSM263	Federal, Newark	5.1944	17.6.1944	7.1944	stricken 1946
LSM264	Federal, Newark	5.1944	26.6.1944	7.1944	stricken 1946
LSM265	Federal, Newark	5.1944	30.6.1944	7.1944	stricken 3.1946
LSM266	Federal, Newark	5.1944	3.7.1944	7.1944	stricken 1946
LSM267	Federal, Newark	5.1944	12.7.1944	8.1944	to Argentina 2.1948 (BDM1)

LSM268	Federal, Newark	5.1944	17.7.1944	8.1944	to South Korea 2.1955 (Yeodo)
LSM269	Federal, Newark	6.1944	17.7.1944	8.1944	stricken 1958
LSM270	Federal, Newark	6.1944	25.7.1944	8.1944	stricken 1958
LSM271	Federal, Newark	6.1944	29.7.1944	9.1944	scuttled 8.2.1947
LSM272	Federal, Newark	6.1944	9.8.1944	9.1944	stricken 1946
LSM273	Federal, Newark	7.1944	26.8.1944	9.1944	stricken 1947
LSM274	Federal, Newark	7.1944	4.9.1944	9.1944	stricken 1958
LSM275	Federal, Newark	8.1944	11.9.1944	10.1944	cable repair ship 7.1952
LSM276	Federal, Newark	8.1944	20.9.1944	10.1944	stricken 1958
LSM277	Federal, Newark	7.1944	27.9.1944	10.1944	stricken 1946
LSM278	Federal, Newark	7.1944	6.10.1944	10.1944	stricken 1946
LSM279	Federal, Newark	8.1944	14.10.1944	10.1944	stricken 1946
LSM280	Federal, Newark	9.1944	21.10.1944	11.1944	to China 2.1948
LSM281	Federal, Newark	9.1944	27.10.1944	11.1944	scuttled 6.3.1947
LSM282	Federal, Newark	9.1944	6.11.1944	11.1944	to China 6.1946 (Hua 207)
LSM283	Federal, Newark	10.1944	15.11.1944	11.1944	stricken 1946
LSM284	Federal, Newark	10.1944	22.11.1944	12.1944	stricken 1946
LSM285	Federal, Newark	10.1944	30.11.1944	12.1944	to China 6.1946 (Meiyi)
LSM286	Federal, Newark	10.1944	7.12.1944	12.1944	stricken 1946
LSM287	Federal, Newark	11.1944	14.12.1944	12.1944	stricken 1946
LSM288	Federal, Newark	11.1944	22.12.1944	1.1945	stricken 1958
LSM289	Federal, Newark	11.1944	29.12.1944	1.1945	stricken 1958
LSM290	Federal, Newark	11.1944	8.1.1945	1.1945	stricken 1946
LSM291	Federal, Newark	12.1944	15.1.1945	1.1945	stricken 1957
LSM292	Federal, Newark	12.1944	22.1.1945	2.1945	to China 2.1948
LSM293	Federal, Newark	12.1944	2.2.1945	2.1945	stricken 1946
LSM294	Federal, Newark	12.1944	10.2.1945	2.1945	stricken 1946
LSM295	Charleston N Yd	9.1944	17.10.1944	12.1944	to Chile 3.1947 (Aspirante Isaza)
LSM296	Charleston N Yd	10.1944	30.10.1944	12.1944	stricken 1958
LSM297	Charleston N Yd	10.1944	30.10.1944	12.1944	stricken 1958
LSM298	Charleston N Yd	10.1944	13.11.1944	12.1944	stricken 1958
LSM299	Charleston N Yd	10.1944	13.11.1944	12.1944	stricken 1958
LSM300	Charleston N Yd	10.1944	19.11.1944	1.1945	stricken 1958
LSM301	Charleston N Yd	10.1944	19.11.1944	1.1945	to Greece 12.1953 (Aktion)
LSM302	Charleston N Yd	10.1944	14.11.1944	1.1945	stricken 1946
LSM303	Charleston N Yd	10.1944	14.11.1944	1.1945	to Greece 12.1953 (Amvrakia)
LSM304	Charleston N Yd	10.1944	27.11.1944	1.1945	stricken 1958
LSM305	Charleston N Yd	10.1944	27.11.1944	1.1945	stricken 1958
LSM306	Charleston N Yd	10.1944	27.11.1944	1.1945	stricken 1958
LSM307	Charleston N Yd	10.1944	14.11.1944	1.1945	stricken 1946
LSM308	Charleston N Yd	11.1944	9.12.1944	1.1945	to China 5.1946
LSM309	Charleston N Yd	11.1944	9.12.1944	1.1945	stricken 1958
LSM310	Pullman Standard Car, Chicago	2.1944	29.4.1944	5.1944	stricken 1946
LSM311	Pullman Standard Car, Chicago	2.1944	2.5.1944	5.1944	stricken 1946
LSM312	Pullman Standard Car, Chicago	3.1944	17.5.1944	6.1944	stricken 1946
LSM313	Pullman Standard Car, Chicago	3.1944	24.5.1944	6.1944	stricken 1958
LSM314	Pullman Standard Car, Chicago	3.1944	6.1944	7.1944	stricken 1946
LSM315	Pullman Standard Car, Chicago	3.1944	6.1944	7.1944	stricken 1958
LSM316	Pullman Standard Car, Chicago	4.1944	18.6.1944	7.1944	to France 1.1954 (LSM316)
LSM317	Pullman Standard Car, Chicago	4.1944	24.6.1944	7.1944	stricken 1947
LSM318	Pullman Standard Car, Chicago	4.1944	6.1944	8.1944	sunk 7.12.1944

LSM319	Pullman Standard Car, Chicago	4.1944	16.7.1944	8.1944	to Australia 7.1959 (Harry Chauvel)
LSM320	Pullman Standard Car, Chicago	5.1944	20.6.1944	8.1944	stricken 1958
LSM321	Pullman Standard Car, Chicago	5.1944	27.7.1944	8.1944	stricken 1946
LSM322	Pullman Standard Car, Chicago	5.1944	3.8.1944	9.1944	stricken 1946
LSM323	Pullman Standard Car, Chicago	5.1944	11.8.1944	9.1944	stricken 1946
LSM324	Pullman Standard Car, Chicago	5.1944	18.8.1944	9.1944	stricken 1958
LSM325	Pullman Standard Car, Chicago	5.1944	25.8.1944	9.1944	stricken 1946
LSM326	Pullman Standard Car, Chicago	5.1944	1.9.1944	10.1944	stricken 1946
LSM327	Pullman Standard Car, Chicago	6.1944	15.9.1944	10.1944	stricken 1946
LSM328	Pullman Standard Car, Chicago	6.1944	22.9.1944	10.1944	stricken 1946
LSM329	Pullman Standard Car, Chicago	6.1944	28.9.1944	10.1944	stricken 1958
LSM330	Pullman Standard Car, Chicago	6.1944	6.10.1944	11.1944	stricken 1958
LSM331	Pullman Standard Car, Chicago	6.1944	13.10.1944	11.1944	stricken 1958
LSM332	Pullman Standard Car, Chicago	7.1944	20.10.1944	11.1944	stricken 1958
LSM333	Pullman Standard Car, Chicago	6.1944	13.10.1944	11.1944	to Thailand 10.1946 (Kut)
LSM334	Pullman Standard Car, Chicago	7.1944	3.11.1944	12.1944	stricken 1946
LSM335	Pullman Standard Car, Chicago	7.1944	10.11.1944	12.1944	stricken 1958
LSM336	Pullman Standard Car, Chicago	8.1944	17.11.1944	12.1944	to China 6.1946 (Hua 205)
LSM337	Pullman Standard Car, Chicago	8.1944	30.11.1944	12.1944	to China 2.1948
LSM338	Pullman Standard Car, Chicago	8.1944	5.12.1944	1.1945	to Thailand 10.1946 (Phai)
LSM339	Pullman Standard Car, Chicago	8.1944	8.12.1944	1.1945	to China 12.1946
LSM340	Pullman Standard Car, Chicago	8.1944	22.12.1944	1.1945	stricken 1947
LSM341	Pullman Standard Car, Chicago	9.1944	29.12.1944	2.1945	stricken 1958
LSM342	Pullman Standard Car, Chicago	9.1944	12.1.1945	2.1945	stricken 1947
LSM343	Pullman Standard Car, Chicago	9.1944	19.1.1945	2.1945	stricken 1958
LSM344	Pullman Standard Car, Chicago	10.1944	26.1.1945	2.1945	stricken 1947
LSM345	Pullman Standard Car, Chicago	10.1944	2.2.1945	3.1945	stricken 1947
LSM346	Pullman Standard Car, Chicago	10.1944	9.2.1945	3.1945	stricken 1947
LSM347	Pullman Standard Car, Chicago	10.1944	16.2.1945	3.1945	stricken 1947
LSM348	Pullman Standard Car, Chicago	11.1944	23.2.1945	3.1945	stricken 1947
LSM349	Pullman Standard Car, Chicago	11.1944	2.3.1945	3.1945	to China 8.1946
LSM350	Pullman Standard Car, Chicago	11.1944	9.3.1945	4.1945	stricken 1947
LSM351	Pullman Standard Car, Chicago	11.1944	20.3.1945	4.1945	stricken 1947
LSM352	Pullman Standard Car, Chicago	12.1944	23.3.1945	4.1945	stricken 1946
LSM353	Pullman Standard Car, Chicago	12.1944	31.3.1945	4.1945	stricken 1947
LSM354	Brown SB, Houston	11.1944	25.11.1944	12.1944	to Indonesia 3.1959
LSM355	Brown SB, Houston	11.1944	2.12.1944	12.1944	to France 1.1954 (LSM355)
LSM356	Brown SB, Houston	11.1944	2.12.1944	12.1944	stricken 1947
LSM357	Brown SB, Houston	11.1944	2.12.1944	12.1944	stricken 1958
LSM358	Brown SB, Houston	11.1944	2.12.1944	1.1945	stricken 1958
LSM359	Brown SB, Houston	11.1944	9.12.1944	1.1945	stricken 1957
LSM360	Brown SB, Houston	11.1944	9.12.1944	1.1945	stricken 1957
LSM361	Brown SB, Houston	11.1944	9.12.1944	1.1945	wrecked 9.10.1945
LSM362	Brown SB, Houston	11.1944	9.12.1944	1.1945	stricken 1958
LSM363	Brown SB, Houston	11.1944	16.12.1944	1.1945	stricken 1958
LSM364	Brown SB, Houston	11.1944	16.12.1944	1.1945	stricken 1958
LSM365	Brown SB, Houston	11.1944	16.12.1944	1.1945	stricken 1958
LSM366	Brown SB, Houston	11.1944	16.12.1944	1.1945	stricken 1957
LSM367	Brown SB, Houston	12.1944	23.12.1944	1.1945	stricken 1958
LSM368	Brown SB, Houston	12.1944	23.12.1944	1.1945	stricken 1947
LSM369	Brown SB, Houston	12.1944	23.12.1944	1.1945	stricken 1957

LSM370	Brown SB, Houston	12.1944	23.12.1944	1.1945	to Venezuela 7.1959
LSM371	Brown SB, Houston	12.1944	30.12.1944	1.1945	stricken 1957
LSM372	Brown SB, Houston	12.1944	30.12.1944	1.1945	stricken 1958
LSM373	Brown SB, Houston	12.1944	30.12.1944	1.1945	stricken 1.1960
LSM374	Brown SB, Houston	12.1944	30.12.1944	1.1945	to China 5.1946
LSM375	Brown SB, Houston	12.1944	6.1.1945	1.1945	stricken 1947
LSM376	Brown SB, Houston	12.1944	6.1.1945	1.1945	to China 7.1946
LSM377	Brown SB, Houston	12.1944	6.1.1945	2.1945	stricken 1948
LSM378	Brown SB, Houston	12.1944	6.1.1945	2.1945	stricken 1950
LSM379	Brown SB, Houston	12.1944	13.1.1945	2.1945	stricken 1947
LSM380	Brown SB, Houston	12.1944	13.1.1945	2.1945	stricken 1948
LSM381	Brown SB, Houston	12.1944	13.1.1945	2.1945	stricken 1948
LSM382	Brown SB, Houston	12.1944	13.1.1945	2.1945	stricken 1947
LSM383	Brown SB, Houston	12.1944	20.1.1945	2.1945	stricken 1.1947
LSM384	Brown SB, Houston	12.1944	20.1.1945	2.1945	stricken 1946
LSM385	Brown SB, Houston	12.1944	20.1.1945	2.1945	stricken 1947
LSM386	Brown SB, Houston	12.1944	20.1.1945	2.1945	stricken 1946
LSM387	Brown SB, Houston	1.1945	27.1.1945	2.1945	to China 2.1947
LSM388	Brown SB, Houston	1.1945	27.1.1945	2.1945	stricken 1947
LSM389	Charleston N Yd	11.1944	12.12.1944	1.1945	stricken 1958
LSM390	Charleston N Yd	11.1944	12.12.1944	1.1945	to Denmark 5.1954 (Beskytteren)
LSM391	Charleston N Yd	11.1944	17.12.1944	2.1945	to China 5.1946
LSM392	Charleston N Yd	11.1944	17.12.1944	2.1945	to Denmark 6.1954 (Vindhunden)
LSM393	Charleston N Yd	12.1944	29.12.1944	3.1945	to China 5.1946
LSM394	Charleston N Yd	12.1944	29.12.1944	3.1945	stricken 1958
LSM395	Charleston N Yd	12.1944	2.1.1945	3.1945	stricken 1958
LSM396	Charleston N Yd	12.1944	2.1.1945	3.1945	to Peru 4.1959 (Lomas)
LSM397	Charleston N Yd	12.1944	6.1.1945	7.1945	stricken 1958
LSM398	Charleston N Yd	12.1944	6.1.1945	8.1945	research ship 6.1957
LSM399	Charleston N Yd	12.1944	16.1.1945	8.1945	to Greece 11.1958 (Ipopliarchos Roussen)
LSM400	Charleston N Yd	12.1944	18.1.1945	8.1945	to Chile 3.1947 (Aspirante Goycolea)
LSM413	Charleston N Yd	2.1945	3.3.1945	8.1945	stricken 1958
LSM414	Dravo, Wilmington	8.1944	20.10.1944	11.1944	stricken 1947
LSM415	Dravo, Wilmington	9.1944	27.10.1944	11.1944	stricken 1958
LSM416	Dravo, Wilmington	9.1944	2.11.1944	11.1944	stricken 1958
LSM417	Dravo, Wilmington	9.1944	8.11.1944	11.1944	to Chile 3.1947 (Aspirante Morel)
LSM418	Dravo, Wilmington	9.1944	14.11.1944	12.1944	stricken 1958
LSM419	Dravo, Wilmington	10.1944	18.11.1944	12.1944	to South Korea 2.1955 (Dokdo)
LSM420	Dravo, Wilmington	10.1944	25.11.1944	12.1944	stricken 1947
LSM421	Dravo, Wilmington	10.1944	30.11.1944	12.1944	stricken 1958
LSM422	Dravo, Wilmington	10.1944	7.12.1944	12.1944	to France 2.1954 (LSM422)
LSM423	Dravo, Wilmington	10.1944	12.12.1944	1.1945	to China 2.1948 (Meicheng)
LSM424	Dravo, Wilmington	10.1944	12.12.1944	1.1945	stricken 1958
LSM425	Dravo, Wilmington	11.1944	23.12.1944	1.1945	stricken 6.1946
LSM426	Dravo, Wilmington	11.1944	30.12.1944	1.1945	stricken 1947
LSM427	Dravo, Wilmington	11.1944	6.1.1945	2.1945	to China 2.1948
LSM428	Dravo, Wilmington	11.1944	12.1.1945	3.1945	stricken 1948

LSM429	Dravo, Wilmington	12.1944	18.1.1945	2.1945	stricken ~1958
LSM430	Dravo, Wilmington	12.1944	27.1.1945	2.1945	to China 6.1946 (Hua 204)
LSM431	Dravo, Wilmington	12.1944	2.2.1945	2.1945	to China 9.1946 (Meipeng)
LSM432	Dravo, Wilmington	12.1944	5.2.1945	2.1945	wrecked 11.1.1947
LSM433	Dravo, Wilmington	12.1944	12.2.1945	3.1945	to China 1.1947 (Meiho)
LSM434	Dravo, Wilmington	1.1945	17.2.1945	3.1945	stricken 1948
LSM435	Dravo, Wilmington	1.1945	23.2.1945	3.1945	stricken 1947
LSM436	Dravo, Wilmington	1.1945	28.2.1945	3.1945	stricken 1948
LSM437	Dravo, Wilmington	1.1945	10.3.1945	3.1945	stricken 1947
LSM438	Dravo, Wilmington	1.1945	14.3.1945	4.1945	stricken 1947
LSM439	Dravo, Wilmington	2.1945	19.3.1945	4.1945	to China 2.1948
LSM440	Dravo, Wilmington	2.1945	24.3.1945	4.1945	stricken 1947
LSM441	Dravo, Wilmington	2.1945	30.3.1945	4.1945	stricken 1958
LSM442	Dravo, Wilmington	2.1945	6.4.1945	4.1945	to China 3.1947 (Meihung)
LSM443	Dravo, Wilmington	2.1945	11.4.1945	5.1945	stricken 1948
LSM444	Dravo, Wilmington	3.1945	17.4.1945	5.1945	civil service 11.1957
LSM445	Dravo, Wilmington	3.1945	24.4.1945	5.1945	drone control ship 6.1957
LSM446	Dravo, Wilmington	3.1945	28.4.1945	5.1945	drone control ship 6.1957
LSM447	Western Pipe & Steel, San Francisco	9.1944	13.11.1944	12.1944	stricken 1947
LSM448	Western Pipe & Steel, San Francisco	9.1944	13.11.1944	1.1945	stricken 1958
LSM449	Western Pipe & Steel, San Francisco	10.1944	3.12.1944	1.1945	stricken 6.1947
LSM450	Western Pipe & Steel, San Francisco	10.1944	3.12.1944	1.1945	stricken 1947
LSM451	Western Pipe & Steel, San Francisco	10.1944	10.12.1944	1.1945	stricken 1947
LSM452	Western Pipe & Steel, San Francisco	10.1944	10.12.1944	2.1945	stricken 1947
LSM453	Western Pipe & Steel, San Francisco	10.1944	22.12.1944	2.1945	to China 6.1946
LSM454	Western Pipe & Steel, San Francisco	10.1944	22.12.1944	2.1945	stricken 1947
LSM455	Western Pipe & Steel, San Francisco	11.1944	27.12.1944	2.1945	stricken 1959
LSM456	Western Pipe & Steel, San Francisco	11.1944	28.12.1944	2.1945	to China 2.1947 (Meihua)
LSM457	Western Pipe & Steel, San Francisco	12.1944	17.3.1945	3.1945	to China 7.1946 (Meisong)
LSM458	Western Pipe & Steel, San Francisco	12.1944	28.1.1945	3.1945	stricken 1948
LSM459	Brown SB, Houston	1.1945	27.1.1945	2.1945	wrecked 2.11.1946
LSM460	Brown SB, Houston	1.1945	27.1.1945	2.1945	stricken 1948
LSM461	Brown SB, Houston	1.1945	3.2.1945	3.1945	to China 8.1946 (Meiping)
LSM462	Brown SB, Houston	1.1945	3.2.1945	3.1945	to South Korea 2.1955 (Gadeok)
LSM463	Brown SB, Houston	1.1945	3.2.1945	3.1945	to the Philippines 3.1961 (Isabela)
LSM464	Brown SB, Houston	1.1945	3.2.1945	3.1945	stricken 1947
LSM465	Brown SB, Houston	1.1945	10.2.1945	3.1945	stricken 1947
LSM466	Brown SB, Houston	1.1945	10.2.1945	3.1945	stricken 1947
LSM467	Brown SB, Houston	1.1945	10.2.1945	3.1945	stricken 9.1946

LSM468	Brown SB, Houston	1.1945	10.2.1945	3.1945	stricken 1946
LSM469	Brown SB, Houston	1.1945	17.2.1945	3.1945	stricken 1958
LSM470	Brown SB, Houston	1.1945	17.2.1945	3.1945	to China 7.1946 (Meiwei)
LSM471	Brown SB, Houston	1.1945	17.2.1945	3.1945	to France 5.1954 (LSM471)
LSM472	Brown SB, Houston	1.1945	17.2.1945	3.1945	to Taiwan 2.1959 (Mei Wei)
LSM473	Brown SB, Houston	2.1945	24.2.1945	3.1945	stricken 1958
LSM474	Brown SB, Houston	2.1945	24.2.1945	3.1945	to Taiwan 2.1959 (Mei Han)
LSM475	Brown SB, Houston	2.1945	3.3.1945	3.1945	to China 7.1946 (Meihan)
LSM476	Brown SB, Houston	2.1945	3.3.1945	3.1945	stricken 1958
LSM477	Brown SB, Houston	2.1945	3.3.1945	4.1945	to Australia 7.1959 (Brudenell White)
LSM478	Brown SB, Houston	2.1945	3.3.1945	4.1945	to France 4.1954 (LSM478)
LSM479	Brown SB, Houston	2.1945	24.2.1945	4.1945	to France 4.1954 (LSM479)
LSM480	Brown SB, Houston	2.1945	24.2.1945	4.1945	stricken 1958
LSM481	Brown SB, Houston	2.1945	10.3.1945	4.1945	to Turkey 9.1952 (Marmaris)
LSM482	Brown SB, Houston	2.1945	10.3.1945	4.1945	to China 5.1946 (Meigong)
LSM483	Brown SB, Houston	2.1945	10.3.1945	4.1945	to Dominican Republic 3.1958 (Sirio)
LSM484	Brown SB, Houston	2.1945	10.3.1945	4.1945	to Turkey 10.1952 (Mordoğan)
LSM485	Brown SB, Houston	2.1945	17.3.1945	4.1945	stricken 1947
LSM486	Brown SB, Houston	2.1945	17.3.1945	4.1945	stricken 1947
LSM487	Brown SB, Houston	2.1945	17.3.1945	4.1945	stricken 1947
LSM488	Brown SB, Houston	2.1945	17.3.1945	4.1945	stricken 1958
LSM489	Brown SB, Houston	2.1945	3.1945	4.1945	to China 5.1946
LSM490	Brown SB, Houston	3.1945	24.3.1945	4.1945	to Turkey 10.1952 (Meriç)
LSM491	Brown SB, Houston	3.1945	24.3.1945	4.1945	to West Germany 9.1958 (Eidechse)
LSM492	Brown SB, Houston	3.1945	24.3.1945	5.1945	to Norway 10.1952 (Vale)
LSM493	Brown SB, Houston	3.1945	30.3.1945	5.1945	to Norway 10.1952 (Vidar)
LSM494	Brown SB, Houston	3.1945	31.3.1945	5.1945	stricken 1958
LSM495	Brown SB, Houston	3.1945	31.3.1945	5.1945	stricken 1958
LSM496	Brown SB, Houston	3.1945	31.3.1945	5.1945	stricken 1958
LSM497	Brown SB, Houston	3.1945	7.4.1945	5.1945	stricken 1958
LSM498	Brown SB, Houston	3.1945	7.4.1945	5.1945	stricken 1958
LSM499	Brown SB, Houston	3.1945	7.4.1945	5.1945	stricken 1958
LSM500	Brown SB, Houston	3.1945	7.4.1945	5.1945	MTB depot ship 5.1953
LSM537	Brown SB, Houston	5.1945	1945	11.1945	to West Germany 9.1958 (Krokodil)
LSM538	Brown SB, Houston	5.1945	1945	11.1945	to Dominican Republic 3.1958 (Antares)
LSM539	Brown SB, Houston	5.1945	1945	12.1945	to Ecuador 1.1958 (Jambelí)
LSM540	Brown SB, Houston	5.1945	8.1945	12.1945	stricken 1.1960
LSM541	Brown SB, Houston	5.1945	1945	12.1945	to Greece 6.1958 (Ipopliarchos Krystallidis)
LSM542	Brown SB, Houston	5.1945	1945	12.1945	to Venezuela 7.1959
LSM543	Brown SB, Houston	5.1945	1945	12.1945	to Venezuela 7.1959 (Los Roques)
LSM544	Brown SB, Houston	1945	1945	1.1946	stricken 1959
LSM545	Brown SB, Houston	1945	1945	1.1946	stricken 1959
LSM546	Brown SB, Houston	1945	1945	1.1946	to South Korea 2.1955 (Daecho)
LSM547	Brown SB, Houston	1945	1945	1.1946	stricken 1958

LSM548	Brown SB, Houston	1945	1945	2.1946	to Venezuela 2.1959 (Los Monjes)
LSM549	Brown SB, Houston	1945	7.12.1945	(3.1946)	commissioned as salvage vessel
LSM550	Brown SB, Houston	8.1945	7.12.1945	(3.1946)	commissioned as salvage vessel
LSM551	Brown SB, Houston	8.1945	7.12.1945	(3.1946)	commissioned as salvage vessel
LSM552	Brown SB, Houston	8.1945	7.12.1945	(4.1946)	commissioned as salvage vessel
LSM553	Charleston N Yd	2.1945	3.3.1945	9.1945	to West Germany 9.1958 (Salamander)
LSM554	Charleston N Yd	3.1945	22.3.1945	9.1945	to Peru 4.1959 (Atico)
LSM555	Charleston N Yd	3.1945	22.3.1945	9.1945	to Ecuador 11.1958 (Tarqui)
LSM556	Charleston N Yd	3.1945	10.4.1945	10.1945	stricken 1958
LSM557	Charleston N Yd	3.1945	10.4.1945	10.1945	to Greece 10.1958 (Ipolpliarchos Merlin)
LSM558	Charleston N Yd	4.1945	28.4.1945	11.1945	to West Germany 9.1958 (Viper)

LSM4 1944

LSM437

520 / 1095 t, 62.0 x 10.5 x 2.1 m, 2 diesels, 2880 hp, 12.5-13.2 kts, 4900 nm (12 kts), complement 60; 1 x 2 – 40/56 Bofors, 4 x 1 – 20/70 Oerlikon; 5 medium or 3 heavy tanks or 6 LVT or 9 DUKW, 48-65 troops; SE or SF or SL or SO or SU radar.

Medium tank landing ships, designed in 1943 to fill the gap between tank landing ships (LST) and large tank landing craft (LCT). Unlike the latter, they were able to make long routes on the high seas. This was the basis for changing the originally planned classification from LCT(7) to LSM. A distinctive feature of the LSM was the asymmetric outline profile: the superstructure was not placed on a centerline, being shifted to the starboard side, keeping the cargo deck open.

In total, 558 ships were ordered under the FY44 and FY45 Programs, 498 were completed according to the original design. The remaining 60 were completed as fire support ships of the LSM(R) class.

LSM20 was sunk by kamikaze 5.12.1944 in Surigao Strait. *LSM149* 5.12.1944 beached at Sansapore, New Guinea and declared a total loss. *LSM318* 7.12.1944 was hit by kamikaze near Ormoc. *LSM12* was sunk by a Japanese explosive boat at Okinawa 4.4.1945. *LSM135* was sunk by kamikaze off Okinawa 25.5.1945. *LSM59* was sunk by kamikaze off Okinawa 21.6.1945. *LSM169* was damaged by mine off Mariveles Harbor 15.2.1945 and was never repaired.

LSM(R) class medium amphibious fire support ships

LSM(R)188	Charleston N Yd	8.1944	12.9.1944	11.1944	damaged 29.3.1945, repaired as auxiliary
LSM(R)189	Charleston N Yd	8.1944	12.9.1944	11.1944	stricken 1946
LSM(R)190	Charleston N Yd	8.1944	21.9.1944	11.1944	sunk 4.5.1945
LSM(R)191	Charleston N Yd	8.1944	21.9.1944	11.1944	stricken 1946
LSM(R)192	Charleston N Yd	9.1944	4.10.1944	11.1944	stricken 1946
LSM(R)193	Charleston N Yd	9.1944	4.10.1944	11.1944	stricken 1946
LSM(R)194	Charleston N Yd	8.1944	7.10.1944	11.1944	sunk 4.5.1945
LSM(R)195	Charleston N Yd	8.1944	7.10.1944	11.1944	sunk 3.5.1945
LSM(R)196	Charleston N Yd	9.1944	12.10.1944	12.1944	stricken 1946
LSM(R)197	Charleston N Yd	9.1944	12.10.1944	12.1944	stricken 1946

LSM(R)198	Charleston N Yd	9.1944	14.10.1944	12.1944	stricken 1946
LSM(R)199	Charleston N Yd	9.1944	14.10.1944	12.1944	stricken 1946
LSM(R)401	Charleston N Yd	1.1945	22.1.1945	4.1945	stricken 5.1973
LSM(R)402	Charleston N Yd	1.1945	22.1.1945	4.1945	stricken 10.1958
LSM(R)403	Charleston N Yd	1.1945	26.1.1945	4.1945	stricken 1955
LSM(R)404	Charleston N Yd	1.1945	25.1.1945	4.1945	stricken 1970
LSM(R)405	Charleston N Yd	1.1945	6.2.1945	5.1945	stricken 5.1973
LSM(R)406	Charleston N Yd	1.1945	6.2.1945	5.1945	stricken 1960
LSM(R)407	Charleston N Yd	1.1945	12.2.1945	5.1945	stricken 1958
LSM(R)408	Charleston N Yd	1.1945	12.2.1945	5.1945	stricken 1958
LSM(R)409	Charleston N Yd	1.1945	18.2.1945	5.1945	stricken 1970
LSM(R)410	Charleston N Yd	1.1945	18.2.1945	5.1945	stricken 1960
LSM(R)411	Mare Island N Yd, Vallejo	2.1945	25.2.1945	5.1945	stricken 1960
LSM(R)412	Mare Island N Yd, Vallejo	2.1945	25.2.1945	5.1945	stricken 1973
LSM(R)501	Brown SB, Houston	3.1945	21.4.1945	5.1945	auxiliary 10.1955
LSM(R)502	Brown SB, Houston	3.1945	21.4.1945	6.1945	stricken 1958
LSM(R)503	Brown SB, Houston	3.1945	21.4.1945	6.1945	stricken 1958
LSM(R)504	Brown SB, Houston	3.1945	21.4.1945	6.1945	stricken 10.1960
LSM(R)505	Brown SB, Houston	3.1945	28.4.1945	6.1945	stricken 10.1958
LSM(R)506	Brown SB, Houston	3.1945	28.4.1945	5.1945	stricken 10.1958
LSM(R)507	Brown SB, Houston	3.1945	28.4.1945	6.1945	stricken 10.1958
LSM(R)508	Brown SB, Houston	3.1945	28.4.1945	6.1945	drone aircraft control ship 5.1960
LSM(R)509	Brown SB, Houston	4.1945	5.5.1945	6.1945	stricken 10.1958
LSM(R)510	Brown SB, Houston	4.1945	5.5.1945	7.1945	stricken 2.1960
LSM(R)511	Brown SB, Houston	4.1945	5.5.1945	7.1945	stricken 2.1960
LSM(R)512	Brown SB, Houston	4.1945	5.5.1945	7.1945	stricken 5.1973
LSM(R)513	Brown SB, Houston	4.1945	19.5.1945	7.1945	stricken 5.1973
LSM(R)514	Brown SB, Houston	4.1945	19.5.1945	7.1945	stricken 2.1960
LSM(R)515	Brown SB, Houston	4.1945	19.5.1945	7.1945	stricken 5.1973
LSM(R)516	Brown SB, Houston	4.1945	19.5.1945	7.1945	stricken 10.1958
LSM(R)517	Brown SB, Houston	4.1945	2.6.1945	7.1945	stricken 2.1960
LSM(R)518	Brown SB, Houston	4.1945	2.6.1945	7.1945	stricken 10.1958
LSM(R)519	Brown SB, Houston	4.1945	2.6.1945	7.1945	stricken 10.1958
LSM(R)520	Brown SB, Houston	4.1945	2.6.1945	7.1945	stricken 2.1960
LSM(R)521	Brown SB, Houston	5.1945	4.6.1945	8.1945	stricken 10.1958
LSM(R)522	Brown SB, Houston	5.1945	9.6.1945	8.1945	stricken 5.1973
LSM(R)523	Brown SB, Houston	5.1945	9.6.1945	8.1945	stricken 2.1960
LSM(R)524	Brown SB, Houston	5.1945	9.6.1945	8.1945	stricken 10.1958
LSM(R)525	Brown SB, Houston	5.1945	16.6.1945	8.1945	stricken 4.1970
LSM(R)526	Brown SB, Houston	5.1945	16.6.1945	8.1945	stricken 10.1958
LSM(R)527	Brown SB, Houston	5.1945	16.6.1945	8.1945	to South Korea 9.1960 (Siheung)
LSM(R)528	Brown SB, Houston	5.1945	16.6.1945	9.1945	stricken 10.1958
LSM(R)529	Brown SB, Houston	6.1945	7.7.1945	9.1945	stricken 10.1958
LSM(R)530	Brown SB, Houston	6.1945	7.7.1945	9.1945	stricken 10.1958
LSM(R)531	Brown SB, Houston	6.1945	7.7.1945	9.1945	stricken 5.1973
LSM(R)532	Brown SB, Houston	6.1945	7.7.1945	10.1945	to West Germany 9.1958 (Otter)
LSM(R)533	Brown SB, Houston	6.1945	14.7.1945	10.1945	stricken 10.1958
LSM(R)534	Brown SB, Houston	6.1945	14.7.1945	10.1945	to West Germany 9.1958 (Natter)
LSM(R)535	Brown SB, Houston	6.1945	14.7.1945	11.1945	stricken 1958
LSM(R)536	Brown SB, Houston	6.1945	14.7.1945	11.1945	stricken 5.1970

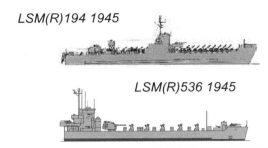

LSM(R)194 1945

LSM(R)536 1945

LSM(R)536 post-war

783 (LSM(R)188-195) or 826 (LSM(R)196-199) or 994 (LSM(R)401-412, 501-536) / 1175 t, 62.0 x 10.5 x 1.7 (LSM(R)188-195) or 1.8 (LSM(R)196-199) or 2.1

(LSM(R)401-412, 501-536) m, 2 diesels, 2880 hp, 13 kts, 4900 nm (LSM(R)188-199) or 3000 nm (LSM(R)401-412, 501-536) (12 kts), complement 81 (LSM(R)188-199) or 143 (LSM(R)401-412, 501-536); 1 x 1 – 127/38 Mk 12, 1 (LSM(R)188-199) or 2 (LSM(R)401-412, 501-536) x 2 – 40/56 Bofors, 3 x 1 (LSM(R)188-199) or 4 x 2 (LSM(R)401-412, 501-536) – 20/70 Oerlikon, 4 x 1 – 107/10 chemical mortars, (75 x 4 Mk 36 + 30 x 6 Mk 30) (LSM(R)188-195) or (85 x 1 Mk 51) (LSM(R)196-199) or (5 x 2 automatic) (LSM(R)401-412, 501-536) – 127 RL; SG or SU radar.

Fire support ships in the medium landing ship hulls. The first 12 ships differed from the prototype only in a large number of rocket launchers and a 127-mm gun aft. On subsequent ships, the superstructure was moved from starboard to aft; the open landing deck was eliminated, and the upper deck was made continuous, placing on it 127-mm rocket launchers and a 127-mm gun fwd of the superstructure.

LSM(R)188 was damaged off Okinawa by a kamikaze 29.3.1945 and was never repaired as a combat ship. *LSM(R)190*, *LSM(R)194* and *LSM(R)195* were sunk by kamikaze off Okinawa 4.5.1945, 4.5.1945 and 3.5.1945, respectively.

APD class fast amphibious troop transports

Yokes	APD69	Consolidated, Orange	8.1943	27.11.1943	12.1944	stricken 4.1964
Pavlic	APD70	Consolidated, Orange	9.1943	18.12.1943	12.1944	stricken 4.1967
Odum	APD71	Consolidated, Orange	10.1943	19.1.1944	1.1945	to Chile 11.1966 (Serrano)
Jack C. Robinson	APD72	Consolidated, Orange	11.1943	8.1.1944	2.1945	to Chile 12.1966 (Orella)
Bassett	APD73	Consolidated, Orange	11.1943	15.1.1944	2.1945	stricken 5.1967
John P. Gray	APD74	Consolidated, Orange	12.1943	18.3.1944	3.1945	stricken 3.1967
Crosley	APD87	Philadelphia N Yd	10.1943	12.2.1944	10.1944	stricken 6.1960
Cread	APD88	Philadelphia N Yd	10.1943	12.2.1944	7.1944	stricken 6.1960
Ruchamkin	APD89	Philadelphia N Yd	2.1944	15.6.1944	9.1944	to Columbia 11.1969 (Córdoba)
Kirwin	APD90	Philadelphia N Yd	2.1944	16.6.1944	11.1944	stricken 9.1974
Kinzer	APD91	Charleston N Yd	9.1943	19.12.1943	11.1944	to Taiwan 4.1965 (Yu Shan)
Register	APD92	Charleston N Yd	10.1943	20.1.1944	1.1945	to Taiwan 9.1966 (Tai Shan)
Brock	APD93	Charleston N Yd	10.1943	20.1.1944	2.1945	stricken 6.1960
John Q. Roberts	APD94	Charleston N Yd	11.1943	11.2.1944	3.1945	stricken 6.1960
William M. Hobby	APD95	Charleston N Yd	11.1943	11.2.1944	4.1945	to South Korea 5.1967 (Jeju)
Ray K. Edwards	APD96	Charleston N Yd	12.1943	19.2.1944	6.1945	stricken 6.1960
Arthur L. Bristol	APD97	Charleston N Yd	12.1943	19.2.1944	6.1945	stricken 6.1964

Truxton	APD98	Charleston N Yd	12.1943	9.3.1944	7.1945	to Taiwan 11.1965 (Chang Shan)
Upham	APD99	Charleston N Yd	12.194	9.3.1944	7.1945	stricken 6.1960
Ringness	APD100	Bethlehem, Hingham	12.1943	5.2.1944	10.1944	stricken 9.1974
Knudson	APD101	Bethlehem, Hingham	12.1943	5.2.1944	11.1944	stricken 7.1972
Rednour	APD102	Bethlehem, Hingham	12.1943	12.2.1944	12.1944	stricken 3.1967
Tollberg	APD103	Bethlehem, Hingham	12.1943	12.2.1944	1.1945	stricken 11.1964
William J. Pattison	APD104	Bethlehem, Hingham	1.1944	15.2.1944	2.1945	stricken 6.1960
Myers	APD105	Bethlehem, Hingham	1.1944	15.2.1944	3.1945	stricken 6.1960
Walter B. Cobb	APD106	Bethlehem, Hingham	1.1944	23.2.1944	4.1945	stricken 1.1966
Earle B. Hall	APD107	Bethlehem, Hingham	1.1944	1.3.1944	5.1945	stricken 2.1965
Harry L. Corl	APD108	Bethlehem, Hingham	1.1944	1.3.1944	6.1945	to South Korea 1.1966 (Asan)
Belet	APD109	Bethlehem, Hingham	1.1944	3.3.1944	6.1945	to Mexico 12.1963 (California)
Julius A. Raven	APD110	Bethlehem, Hingham	1.1944	3.3.1944	6.1945	to South Korea 1.1966 (Ungpo)
Walsh	APD111	Bethlehem, Hingham	2.1944	28.4.1945	7.1945	stricken 5.1966
Hunter Marshall	APD112	Bethlehem, Hingham	3.1944	5.5.1945	7.1945	stricken 6.1960
Earhart	APD113	Bethlehem, Hingham	3.1944	12.5.1945	7.1945	to Mexico 12.1963 (Papaloapan)
Walter S. Gorka	APD114	Bethlehem, Hingham	4.1944	26.5.1945	8.1945	stricken 6.1960
Rogers Blood	APD115	Bethlehem, Hingham	4.1944	2.6.1945	8.1945	stricken 6.1960
Francovich	APD116	Bethlehem, Hingham	4.1944	5.6.1945	9.1945	stricken 4.1964
Joseph M. Auman	APD117	Consolidated, Orange	11.1943	5.2.1944	4.1945	to Mexico 12.1963 (Tehuantepec)
Don O. Woods	APD118	Consolidated, Orange	12.1943	19.2.1944	5.1945	to Mexico 12.1963 (Usumacinta)
Beverly W. Reid	APD119	Consolidated, Orange	1.1944	4.3.1944	6.1945	stricken 9.1974
Kline	APD120	Bethlehem, Quincy	5.1944	27.6.1944	10.1944	to Taiwan 1.1966 (Ao Shan)
Raymond W. Herndon	APD121	Bethlehem, Quincy	6.1944	15.7.1944	11.1944	stricken 9.1966
Scribner	APD122	Bethlehem, Quincy	6.1944	1.8.1944	11.1944	stricken 8.1966
Diachenko *(ex-Alex Diachenko)*	APD123	Bethlehem, Quincy	7.1944	15.8.1944	12.1944	stricken 9.1974
Horace A. Bass	APD124	Bethlehem, Quincy	8.1944	12.9.1944	12.1944	stricken 9.1974
Wantuck	APD125	Bethlehem, Quincy	8.1944	25.9.1944	12.1944	stricken 3.1958
Gosselin	APD126	Defoe, Bay City	2.1944	4.5.1944	12.1944	stricken 4.1964
Begor	APD127	Defoe, Bay City	3.1944	25.5.1944	3.1945	stricken 5.1975
Cavallaro	APD128	Defoe, Bay City	3.1944	15.6.1944	3.1945	to South Korea 10.1959 (Gyeongnam)
Donald W. Wolf	APD129	Defoe, Bay City	4.1944	22.7.1944	4.1945	stricken 3.1965
Cook	APD130	Defoe, Bay City	5.1944	26.8.1944	4.1945	stricken 11.1969
Walter X. Young	APD131	Defoe, Bay City	5.1944	30.9.1944	5.1945	stricken 5.1962
Balduck	APD132	Defoe, Bay City	6.1944	27.10.1944	5.1945	stricken 7.1975
Burdo	APD133	Defoe, Bay City	7.1944	25.11.1944	6.1945	stricken 4.1966
Kleinsmith	APD134	Defoe, Bay City	8.1944	27.1.1945	6.1945	to Taiwan 5.1960 (Tien Shan)
Weiss	APD135	Defoe, Bay City	10.1944	15.2.1945	7.1945	stricken 9.1974
Carpellotti	APD136	Defoe, Bay City	10.1944	10.3.1945	7.1945	stricken 1959

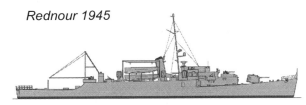

Rednour 1945

Joseph M. Auman 1945

Brock 1945

1725 / 2114 t, 93.3 x 11.3 x 3.8 m, 2 General Electric steam turbo-generators, 2 boilers, 2 electric motors, 12000 hp, 23.6 kts, 347 t oil, 5500 nm (15 kts), complement 203; 1 x 1 – 127/38 Mk 12, 3 x 2 or 4 x 2 (APD55) or (1 x 4 + 3 x 2) (APD63, 86) – 40/56 Bofors, 6 x 1 – 20/70 Oerlikon, 2 DCR; 4 LCVP, 162 troops, deck cargo (except APD55, 63, 86); SA, SF or SL or SU radars, QGA sonar (mostly).

In 1944 when the number of escorts in the Atlantic became sufficient, many of destroyer escorts of the *Buckley* and *Rudderow* classes were converted to fast transports for service in the Pacific. They received a superstructure expanded to the sides, all ASW equipment (except two DC racks), part of the artillery and torpedoes were removed. After conversion, such a transport could carry up to 162 rangers and 4 LCVP for their landing.

In addition to the above, many old destroyers and destroyer escorts were converted to fast transports, as follows: APD1 of the *Caldwell* class; APD2-9, 14-17, 19-22 and 25 of the *Wickes* class; APD10-13, 18, 23, 24, 29, and 31-36 of the *Clemson* class; APD37-40, 42-57, 59-63, 65, 66, 75-81, 84-86 of the "TE" (*Buckley*) class, and APD139 of the "TEV" (*Rudderow*) class.

Conversion of DE635 (planned APD41), DE636 (APD58), DE214 (APD64), DE665 (APD67), DE666 (APD68), DE790 (APD82), DE791 (APD83) of the "TE" class and DE684 (APD137), DE685 (APD138) of the "TEV" class was cancelled.

DOYEN class amphibious transports

Doyen	APA1	Consolidated, Wilmington	1941	9.7.1942	5.1943	for disposal 6.1946
Feland	APA11	Consolidated, Wilmington	1941	10.11.1942	6.1943	for disposal 1946

Doyen 1945

4351 / 6720 t, 126.3 x 17.1 x 5.6 m, 2 sets Westinghouse geared steam turbines, 2 Babcock & Wilcox boilers, 8000 hp, 19 kts, 1772 t oil, 9500 nm (15 kts), complement 472; 4 x 1 – 76/50 Mk 20, 2 x 2 – 40/56 Bofors, 10 x 1 – 20/70 Oerlikon; 14 LCVP, 1 LCPL, 1 LCPR, 400 t of cargo, 845 troops; radar.

Assault transports (APA and AKA) served to deliver troops and cargo directly to a beaching place. The main difference between APA / AKA and AK / AP was the large number of LCVP, LCM and LCP (L) craft carried on board; with their help, people and cargo were delivered to the shore.

Initially, such ships were not outlined as separated sub-type and were registered as AP and AK. In February 1943, assault transports received APA and AKA indexes.

Two *Doyen* class ships, designed on the eve of the war for amphibious operations in the Caribbean, became the first USN assault transports. The vast majority of the remaining APA and AKA were converted from merchant cargo and cargo-passenger vessels or constructed in the hulls of standard cargo vessels, built in large numbers during the war years. Purpose-designed assault transports of the *Gilliam* (APA) and *Artemis* (AKA) classes were the exception.

In addition to the large landing transport ships of APA and AKA classes, small landing parties and sabotage groups were landed by fast landing transports (APD), converted from obsolete destroyers of the *Wickes* and *Clemson* classes, and destroyer escorts of *Buckley* and *Rudderow* classes.

Doyen and *Feland* were purpose-built P1-S2-L2 class.

HARRIS class amphibious transports

Harris (ex-President Grant, ex-Pine Tree State)	AP8, 2.1943-APA2	Bethlehem, Sparrows Point	1920	1921	(11.1921) / 8.1940	stricken 1946
Zeilin (ex-President Jackson, ex-Silver State)	AP9, 11.1942-APA3	Newport News	1920	1921	(5.1921) / 1.1942	stricken 6.1946
Leonard Wood (ex-Western World, ex-Nutmeg State)	AP25, 2.1943-APA12	Bethlehem, Sparrows Point	1921	1921	(5.1922) / 6.1941	stricken 1946
Hunter Liggett (ex-Pan American, ex-Palmetto State)	AP27, 2.1943-APA14	Bethlehem, Sparrows Point	1921	1921	(2.1922) / 6.1941	to the MarCom 9.1946

Hunter Liggett 1944

12400-14174 / 21300-21900 t, 163.1 x 22.0 x 9.3 m, 2 sets Bethlehem geared steam turbines, 8 Yarrow boilers, 12000 hp, 17.5 kts, 4449 t oil, 13700 nm (15 kts), complement 693; 4 x 1 – 76/50 Mk 10/17, 4 x 1 – 12.7 MG; 22 LCVP, 2 – 4 LCM(3), 3991 t of cargo, 1650 – 1900 troops.

Former passenger liners of the *Hog Islander* class. By 1945, all ships were armed with 4 x 1 - 76/50 Mk10/18/20, 2 x 2 - 40/56 Bofors, 10 x 1 - 20/70 Oerlikon, radar.

Zeilin was damaged by a kamikaze 12.1.1945 at Luzon.

McCAWLEY class amphibious transports

McCawley (ex-Santa Barbara)	AP10, 2.1943-APA4	Furness, Haverton Hill, UK	1928	(1928) / 9.1940	sunk 30.6.1943
Barnett (ex-Santa Clara)	AP11, 2.1943-APA5	Furness, Haverton Hill, UK	1928	(1928) / 9.1940	stricken 5.1946

McCawley

9304-9432 / 14080 t, 148.3 x 19.4 x 7.9 m, 2 Busch-Sulzer diesels, 8000 hp, 14.5 kts, 4449 t diesel oil, 9000 nm (12 kts), complement 304; 4 x 1 – 76/50 Mk 10/17, 4 x 1 – 12.7 MG; 22 LCVP, 2 – 4 LCM(3), 3991 t of cargo, 1650 – 1900 troops.

Former passenger liners of Grace Liners Co. By 1945, *Barnett* carried 4 x 1 - 76/50 Mk 10/18, 2 x 2 - 40/56 Bofors, 18 x 1 - 20/70 Oerlikon; 2 LCM(3), 23 LCVP, 1 LCPL, 1 LCPR, 1700 t of cargo, 1382 troops, radar.

McCawley 30.6.1943 was badly damaged by Japanese aircraft at Rendova and later sunk by US MTB.

HEYWOOD class amphibious transports

Heywood (ex-City of Baltimore, ex-Steadfast)	AP12, 2.1943-APA6	Bethlehem, San Francisco	1919	1919	(5.1919) / 1941	for disposal 7.1946
Fuller (ex-City of Newport News, ex-Archer)	AP14, 2.1943-APA7	Bethlehem, San Francisco	1919	1919	(2.1919) / 4.1941	to the MarCom 7.1946
William P. Biddle (ex-City of San Francisco, ex-City of Hamburg, ex-Eclipse)	AP15, 2.1943-APA8	Bethlehem, San Francisco		1919	(2.1919) / 2.1941	stricken 6.1946

Neville (ex-City of Norfolk, ex-Independence)	AP16, 2.1943-APA9	Bethlehem, San Francisco	1918	(11.1918) / 5.1941	stricken 8.1946

Heywood 1945

8789 / 14450 t, 154.5 x 17.1 x 7.8 m, 1 De Laval geared steam turbine, 4 Babcock & Wilcox boilers, 9500 hp, 16.8 kts, 1523 t oil, 9000 nm (12 kts), complement 550; 4 x 1 – 76/50 Mk 10/17, 4 x 1 – 12.7 MG; 22 LCVP, 2 – 4 LCM(3), cargo, 1278 troops.
Former passenger liners of Baltimore Mail Line.
By 1945, all carried 4 x 1 – 76/50 Mk 10/17, 2 x 2 – 40/56 Bofors, 16 x 1 – 20/70 Oerlikon, 4 LCM(6), 21 LCVP, 1 LCPL, 1 LCPR, 2900 t of cargo, 1275 troops, radar.

HARRY LEE class amphibious transports

Harry Lee (ex-Exochorda)	AP17, 2.1943-APA10	New York SB, Camden	11.1929	18.10.1930	(1.1931) / 12.1940	to Turkey 4.1948
Joseph Hewes (ex-Excalibur)	AP50	New York SB, Camden	11.1929	5.8.1930	(12.1930) / 5.1942	sunk 11.11.1942
John Penn (ex-Excambion)	AP51, 2.1943-APA23	New York SB, Camden	10.1930	28.5.1931	(8.1931) / 4.1942	sunk 13.8.1943
Edward Rutledge (ex-Exeter)	AP52	New York SB, Camden	8.1930	4.4.1931	(6.1931) / 4.1942	sunk 7.12.1942

John Penn 1943

9989 / 14520 t, 144.9 x 18.8 x 7.7 m, 1 set Parsons geared steam turbines, 4 Babcock & Wilcox boilers, 7200 hp, 16 kts, 1462 t oil, 12500 nm (12 kts), complement 453; 4 x 1 – 76/50 Mk 10/17, 4 x 1 – 12.7 MG; 22 LCVP, 2 – 4 LCM(3), cargo, troops.

Former cargo-passenger vessels of American Export Lines.
By 1945, survived ships carried 4 x 1 - 76/50 Mk 10/17, 2 x 2 - 40/56 Bofors, 16 x 1 - 20/70 Oerlikon; 2 LCM(3), 13 LCVP, 1 LCPL, 1 LCPR, 1200 t of cargo, 1118 troops; radar.
Joseph Hewes (planned APA22) was sunk by German submarine *U173* 11.11.1942 off the Moroccan coast, *Edward Rutledge* (planned APA24) was torpedoed by German submarine *U130* 12.11.1942 in the same area. *John Penn* was sunk by Japanese torpedo bombers off Lunga Point (Guadalcanal) 13.8.1943.

JOSEPH T. DICKMAN class amphibious transports

Joseph T. Dickman (ex-President Roosevelt, ex-President Pierce, ex-Peninsula State)	AP26, 2.1943-APA13	New York SB, Camden	7.1920	6.7.1921	(2.1922) / 6.1941	to the MarCom 1.1947
Henry T. Allen (ex-President Jefferson, ex-Wenatchee)	AP30, 2.1943-APA15	New York SB, Camden	6.1918	24.5.1919	(5.1921) / 4.1942	to the MarCom 2.1946
J. Franklin Bell (ex-President McKinley, ex-Keystone State)	AP34, 2.1943-APA16	New York SB, Camden	5.1919	15.5.1920	(5.1921) / 4.1942	to the MarCom 2.1947
American Legion (ex-Badger State)	AP35, 2.1943-APA17	New York SB, Camden	1.1919	11.10.1919	(7.1921) / 8.1941	stricken 3.1946

12400-14174 / 21300-21900 t, 163.1 x 22.1 x 9.2 m, 2 sets Curtis geared steam turbines, 8 Yarrow boilers, 10000 hp, 16.7 kts, 4449 t oil, 13700 nm (15 kts), complement 693; 4 x 1 – 76/50 Mk 10/17, 4 x 1 – 12.7 MG; 33 LCVP, 2 – 4 LCM(3), 3991 t of cargo, 1650 – 1900 troops.

Former passenger liners of the *Hog Islander* class.
By 1945, all ships were armed with 4 x 1 - 76/50 Mk10/18/20, 2 x 2 - 40/56 Bofors, 10 x 1 - 20/70 Oerlikon, radar.

Joseph T. Dickman 1943

PRESIDENT JACKSON class amphibious transports

President Jackson	AP37, 2.1943-APA18	Newport News	10.1939	7.6.1940	(10.1940) / 1.1942	stricken 10.1958
President Adams	AP38, 2.1943-APA19	Newport News	6.1940	31.6.1941	11.1941	stricken 10.1958
President Hayes	AP39, 2.1943-APA20	Newport News	12.1939	4.10.1940	(2.1941) / 12.1941	stricken 10.1958
Thomas Stone (ex-*President Van Buren*)	AP59, 2.1943-APA29	Newport News	8.1940	1.5.1941	(9.1941) / 5.1942	damaged 26.11.1942, never repaired
Thomas Jefferson (ex-*President Garfield*)	AP60, 2.1943-APA30	Newport News	2.1940	20.11.1940	(3.1941) / 8.1942	stricken 10.1958

10210-10305 / 16175 t, 149.7 x 21.2 x 8.1 m, 1 set Newport News geared steam turbines, 2 Babcock & Wilcox boilers, 8500 hp, 17 kts, 1340 t oil, 10700 nm (15 kts), complement 512; 4 x 1 – 76/50 Mk 10/17, 8 x 1 – 20/70 Oerlikon or 4 x 1 – 12.7 MG; 32 LCVP, 3 LCM(3), 3500 t of cargo, 1382 troops; radar (on some).
These transports were built in standard C3-A type hulls.
By 1945, survived ships carried 4 x 1 - 76/50 Mk 10/17, (2 x 2 + 2 x 1) - 40/56 Bofors, 12 x 1 - 20/70 Oerlikon; 4 LCM(6), 23 LCVP, 2 LCPL, 1 LCPR, 3500 t of cargo, 1379 troops; radar
Thomas Stone 7.11.1942 was damaged by a torpedo in

President Hayes

the Mediterranean, 25-26.11.1942 damaged again by an aircraft at the coast of Algeria and ran aground.

CRESCENT CITY class amphibious transports

Crescent City (ex-*Del Orleans*)	AP40, 2.1943-APA21	Bethlehem, Sparrows Point	1939	17.2.1940	(8.1940) / 10.1941	to the MarCom 9.1946
Charles Carroll (ex-*Del Uruguay*)	AP58, 2.1943-APA28	Bethlehem, Sparrows Point	3.1942	1942	8.1942	stricken 10.1958
Monrovia (ex-*Del Argentina*)	AP64, 2.1943-APA31	Bethlehem, Sparrows Point	3.1942	19.9.1942	12.1942	stricken 11.1968
Calvert (ex-*Del Orleans*)	AP65, 2.1943-APA32	Bethlehem, Sparrows Point	1942	19.9.1942	10.1942	stricken 8.1966

8409 / 14247 t, 151.8 x 17.2 x 8.1 m, 1 set General Electric geared steam turbines, 2 Babcock & Wilcox boilers, 7800 hp, 17 kts, 1751 t oil, 15500 nm (15 kts), complement 534; 1 x 1 – 127/38 Mk 12, 4 x 1 – 76/50 Mk 20, 8 x 1 – 20/70 Oerlikon; 22 LCVP, 2 – 4 LCM(3), 2300 t of cargo, 1160 troops; radar.
Standard C3 Delta type hulls.

Charles Carroll 1943

By 1945, all ships carried 1 x 1 - 127/38 Mk 12, 4 x 1 - 76/50 Mk 20, (1 x 2 + 1 x 1) - 40/56 Bofors, 11 x 2 - 20/70 Oerlikcn; 4 LCM(6), 20 LCVP, 3 LCPL, 2 LCPR, 2700 t of cargo, 1237 troops; radar.

ARTHUR MIDDLETON class amphibious transports

Arthur Middleton (ex-African Comet)	AP55, 2.1943- APA25	Ingalls, Pascagoula / Bethlehem, San Francisco	7.1940	28.6.1941	9.1942	stricken 10.1958
Samuel Chase (ex-African Meteor)	AP56, 2.1943- APA26	Ingalls, Pascagoula	8.1940	25.8.1941	6.1942	stricken 10.1958
George Clymer (ex-African Planet)	AP57, 2.1943- APA27	Ingalls, Pascagoula	10.1940	27.9.1941	6.1942	stricken 1967

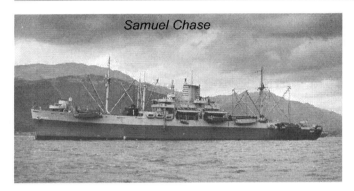
Samuel Chase

10812-11760 / 18000 t, 149.1 x 21.3 x 8.3 m, 1 set General Electric geared steam turbines, 2 Foster Wheeler boilers, 8500 hp, 16.5 kts, 1392 t oil, 11000 nm (15 kts), complement 578; 1 x 1 - 127/38 Mk 12, 4 x 1 – 76/50 Mk 20, 8 x 1 – 20/70 Oerlikon, 4 x 1 – 12.7 MG; 22 LCVP, 2 – 4 LCM(3), cargo, 1304 troops; radar.
Standard C3-P type hulls.
By 1945, ships carried 1 x 1 - 127/38 Mk 12, 4 x 1 - 76/50 Mk 20, 2 x 2 - 40/56 Bofors, 10 x 1 - 20/70 Oerlikon; 4 LCM(6), 18 LCVP, 3 LCPL, 2 LCPR, 2700 t of cargo, 1240 troops; radar.

BAYFIELD class amphibious transports

Bayfield (ex-Sea Bass)	APA33	Western Pipe & Steel, San Francisco	11.1942	15.2.1943	6.1943	stricken 10.1968
Bolivar (ex-Sea Angel)	APA34	Western Pipe & Steel, San Francisco	5.1942	7.9.1942	3.1943	stricken 7.1946
Callaway (ex-Sea Mink)	APA35	Western Pipe & Steel, San Francisco	6.1942	10.10.1942	4.1943	stricken 9.1946
Cambria (ex-Sea Swallow)	APA36	Western Pipe & Steel, San Francisco	7.1942	10.11.1942	5.1943	stricken 9.1971
Cavalier	APA37	Western Pipe & Steel, San Francisco	12.1942	15.3.1943	7.1943	stricken 10.1968
Chilton (ex-Sea Needle)	APA38	Western Pipe & Steel, San Francisco	9.1942	29.12.1942	5.1943	stricken 7.1972
Clay (ex-Sea Carp)	APA39	Western Pipe & Steel, San Francisco	10.1942	23.1.1943	6.1943	stricken 9.1946
Custer (ex-Sea Eagle)	APA40	Ingalls, Pascagoula	1942	6.11.1942	7.1943	stricken 6.1946
Du Page (ex-Sea Hound)	APA41	Ingalls, Pascagoula	1942	19.12.1942	2.1943	stricken 6.1946
Elmore (ex-Sea Panther)	APA42	Ingalls, Pascagoula	1942	29.1.1943	3.1943	stricken 5.1946
Fayette (ex-Sea Hawk)	APA43	Ingalls, Pascagoula	1942	25.2.1943	4.1943	stricken 5.1946
Fremont (ex-Sea Corsair)	APA44	Ingalls, Pascagoula	1942	31.3.1943	5.1943	stricken 6.1973
Henrico (ex-Sea Darter)	APA45	Ingalls, Pascagoula	1942	31.3.1943	6.1943	stricken 6.1973
Knox	APA46	Ingalls, Pascagoula	2.1943	17.7.1943	9.1943	stricken 5.1946

Lamar	APA47	Ingalls, Pascagoula	3.1943	28.8.1943	11.1943	stricken 4.1946
Leon (ex-*Sea Dolphin*)	APA48	Ingalls, Pascagoula	2.1943	19.6.1943	9.1943	stricken 1946
Alpine (ex-*Sea Arrow*)	APA92	Western Pipe & Steel, San Francisco	4.1943	10.7.1943	9.1943	stricken 5.1946
Barnstable (ex-*Sea Snapper*)	APA93	Western Pipe & Steel, San Francisco	5.1943	5.8.1943	10.1943	stricken 4.1946
Burleigh	APA95	Ingalls, Pascagoula	7.1943	3.12.1943	4.1944	stricken 7.1946
Cecil (ex-*Sea Angler*)	APA96	Western Pipe & Steel, San Francisco	6.1943	27.9.1943	2.1944	to the MarCom 5.1946
Dade (ex-*Lorain*)	APA99	Ingalls, Pascagoula	11.1943	14.1.1944	4.1944	to the MarCom 2.1946
Mendocino	APA100	Ingalls, Pascagoula	9.1943	11.2.1944	5.1944	stricken 3.1946
Montour	APA101	Ingalls, Pascagoula	10.1943	10.3.1944	6.1944	stricken 5.1946
Riverside	APA102	Ingalls, Pascagoula	11.1943	13.4.1944	6.1944	stricken 5.1946
Westmoreland	APA104	Ingalls, Pascagoula	12.1943	28.4.1944	7.1944	stricken 6.1946
Hansford (ex-*Gladwin*, ex-*Sea Adder*)	APA106	Western Pipe & Steel, San Francisco	12.1943	25.4.1944	10.1944	to the MarCom 6.1946
Goodhue (ex-*Sea Wren*)	APA107	Western Pipe & Steel, San Francisco	1.1944	31.5.1944	11.1944	stricken 1946
Goshen (ex-*Sea Hare*)	APA108	Western Pipe & Steel, San Francisco	1.1944	29.6.1944	12.1944	to the MarCom 5.1946
Grafton (ex-*Sea Sparrow*)	APA109	Western Pipe & Steel, San Francisco	3.1944	10.8.1944	12.1944	to the MarCom 5.1946

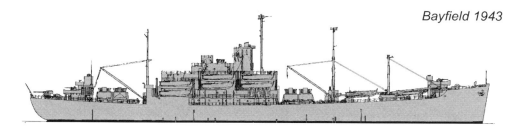

Bayfield 1943

8100 / 16100 t, 150.0 x 21.2 x 8.1 m, 1 set General Electric geared steam turbines, 2 Combustion Engineering or Foster Wheeler boilers, 8500 hp, 18 kts, 1282 t oil, 10450 nm (12 kts), complement 575; 2 x 1 – 127/38 Mk 12, (2 – 4) x 2 – 40/56 Bofors, 18 x 1 – 20/70 Oerlikon; 24 – 26 LCVP, 2 LCM(3), 5500 t of cargo, 1500 troops; radar.

Bayfield class transports were built in standard C3-S-A2 type hulls.

By 1945, all ships carried 2 x 1 - 127/38 Mk 12, (2 - 4) x 2 - 40/56 Bofors, 18 x 1 - 20/70 Oerlikon; 4 LCM(6), 18 – 21 LCVP, 2 – 3 LCPL, 1 – 2 LCPR, radar.

Alpine 17.11.1944 was damaged in Leyte Gulf by a kamikaze. *Callaway* and *Dupage* were damaged by kamikazes 7 and 10.1.1945, respectively, off the Philippines. *Cavalier* 30.1.1945 was damaged by a torpedo from Japanese submarine *RO46*. *Bolivar* 3.3.1945

Barnstable 1944

was damaged at Iwo Jima by Japanese coastal guns. *Alpine* and *Elmore* 1.4.1945 and *Chilton*, *Goodhue* and *Henrico* 2.4.1945 were damaged by Japanese aircraft and kamikazes off Okinawa.

ORMSBY class amphibious transports

Ormsby (ex-Twillight)	APA49	Moore, Oakland	7.1942	20.10.1942	3.1943	stricken 4.1946
Pierce (ex-Northern Lights)	APA50	Moore, Oakland	7.1942	10.10.1942	6.1943	stricken 4.1946
Sheridan (ex-Messenger)	APA51	Moore, Oakland	8.1942	11.11.1942	7.1943	stricken 4.1946

Pierce

7300 / 13910 t, 140.0 x 19.2 x 7.3 m, 1 set General Electric geared steam turbines, 2 Foster-Wheeler boilers, 6000 hp, 16.5 kts, 1380 t oil, 12000 nm (15.5 kts), complement 524; 2 x 1 – 127/38 Mk 12, 4 x 2 – 40/56 Bofors, 12 x 2 – 20/70 Oerlikon; 26 LCVP, 2 LCM(3), 2700 t of cargo, 1548 troops; radar.
Built in standard C2-S-B1 type hulls.
By 1945, all ships can carry 2 LCM(6), 1 LCM(3), 19 LCVP, 1 LCPL, 1 LCPR, 2700 t of cargo, 1615 troops.

SUMTER class amphibious transports

Sumter (ex-Iberville)	APA52	Gulf SB, Chickasaw	4.1942	4.10.1942	9.1943	stricken 4.1946
Warren (ex-Jean Lafitte)	APA53	Gulf SB, Chickasaw	4.1942	7.9.1942	8.1943	stricken 4.1946
Wayne (ex-Afoundria)	APA54	Gulf SB, Chickasaw	4.1942	6.12.1942	8.1943	stricken 4.1946
Baxter (ex-Antinous)	APA94	Gulf SB, Chickasaw	3.1943	19.9.1943	5.1944	stricken 4.1946

Wayne

8355 / 12775 t, 142.9 x 19.2 x 7.1 m, 1 set General Electric geared steam turbines, 2 Babcock & Wilcox boilers, 6000 hp, 16.5 kts, 1235 t oil, 13500 nm (12 kts), complement 449; 2 x 1 – 127/38 Mk 12, 4 x 2 – 40/56 Bofors, 10 x 2 – 20/70 Oerlikon; 26 LCVP, 2 LCM(2), 1300 t of cargo, 1650 troops; radar.
Standard C2-S-E1 hulls.
By 1945, APA52-54 could carry 2 LCM(6), 3 LCM(3), 15 LCVP, 1 LCPL, 1 LCPR, 1300 t of cargo, 1442 troops. By 1945, APA94 could carry 3 LCM(3), 19 LCVP, 1 LCPL, 1 LCPR, 1400 t of cargo, 1730 troops.

WINDSOR class amphibious transports

Windsor (ex-Excelsior)	APA55	Bethlehem, Sparrows Point	7.1942	28.12.1942	6.1943	stricken 4.1946
Leedstown (ex-Wood, ex-Exchequer)	APA56	Bethlehem, Sparrows Point	8.1942	13.2.1943	7.1943	stricken 7.1946
Adair (ex-Exchester)	APA91	Bethlehem, Sparrows Point	1943	29.2.1944	7.1944	stricken 5.1946
Dauphin	APA97	Bethlehem, Sparrows Point	1944	10.6.1944	9.1944	to the MarCom 4.1946
Dutchess	APA98	Bethlehem, Sparrows Point	1944	26.8.1944	11.1944	for disposal 4.1946
Queens	APA103	Bethlehem, Sparrows Point	3.1944	12.9.1944	12.1944	stricken 6.1946
Shelby	APA105	Bethlehem, Sparrows Point	6.1944	25.10.1944	1.1945	stricken 6.1946

Windsor 1943

8276 / 13500 t, 144.3 x 20.3 x 7.6 m, 1 set Bethlehem geared steam turbines, 2 Babcock & Wilcox boilers, 8000 hp, 18.5 kts, 1627 t oil, 16000 nm (15 kts), complement 466-555; 2 x 1 – 127/38 Mk 12, 2 x 2 – 40/56 Bofors, 18 x 1 – 20/70 Oerlikon; 24 LCVP, 2 LCM(3), 1 LCPL, 1

LCPR, 3895 t of cargo, 1468 troops; radar.
Standard C3-S-A3 type hulls.

By 1945, all ships could carry 4 LCM(6), 16 LCVP, 1 LCPL, 1 LCPR, 1600 t of cargo, 1514 troops.

GILLIAM class amphibious transports

Gilliam	APA57	Consolidated, Wilmington	1943	28.3.1944	7.1944	nuclear tests 7.1946
Appling	APA58	Consolidated, Wilmington	1943	9.4.1944	8.1944	stricken 4.1947
Audrain	APA59	Consolidated, Wilmington	12.1943	21.4.1944	8.1944	stricken 8.1947
Banner	APA60	Consolidated, Wilmington	1.1944	3.5.1944	9.1944	nuclear tests 7.1946
Barrow	APA61	Consolidated, Wilmington	1.1944	11.5.1944	9.1944	nuclear tests 7.1946
Berrien	APA62	Consolidated, Wilmington	2.1944	20.5.1944	10.1944	stricken 8.1947
Bladen	APA63	Consolidated, Wilmington	3.1944	31.5.1944	10.1944	stricken 10.1953
Bracken	APA64	Consolidated, Wilmington	3.1944	10.6.1944	10.1944	scuttled 10.3.1948
Briscoe	APA65	Consolidated, Wilmington	3.1944	19.6.1944	10.1944	sunk as target 6.5.1948
Brule	APA66	Consolidated, Wilmington	4.1944	30.6.1944	10.1944	sunk as target 11.5.1948
Burleson	APA67	Consolidated, Wilmington	4.1944	11.7.1944	11.1944	stricken 9.1968
Butte	APA68	Consolidated, Wilmington	5.1944	20.7.1944	11.1944	nuclear tests 7.1946
Carlisle	APA69	Consolidated, San Pedro	1944	30.7.1944	11.1944	nuclear tests 7.1946
Carteret	APA70	Consolidated, Wilmington	1944	15.8.1944	11.1944	sunk as target 19.4.1948
Catron	APA71	Consolidated, Wilmington	1944	28.8.1944	11.1944	sunk as target 6.5.1948
Clarendon	APA72	Consolidated, Wilmington	1944	12.9.1944	12.1944	to the MarCom 9.1946
Cleburne	APA73	Consolidated, Wilmington	1944	27.9.1944	12.1944	to the MarCom 7.1947
Colusa	APA74	Consolidated, San Pedro	1944	7.10.1944	12.1944	stricken 3.1947
Cortland	APA75	Consolidated, Wilmington	1944	18.10.1944	12.1944	to the MarCom 3.1948
Crenshaw	APA76	Consolidated, Wilmington	1944	27.10.1944	1.1945	to the MarCom 6.1946
Crittenden	APA77	Consolidated, Wilmington	1944	6.11.1944	1.1945	scuttled 5.10.1947
Cullman	APA78	Consolidated, Wilmington	1944	17.11.1944	2.1945	stricken 7.1946
Dawson	APA79	Consolidated, Wilmington	1944	27.11.1944	2.1945	sunk as target 19.4.1948
Elkhart	APA80	Consolidated, Wilmington	1944	5.12.1944	2.1945	to the MarCom 6.1946
Fallon	APA81	Consolidated, Wilmington	1944	14.12.1944	2.1945	scuttled 11.3.1948
Fergus	APA82	Consolidated, Wilmington	1944	24.12.1944	2.1945	to the MarCom 9.1947
Fillmore	APA83	Consolidated, Wilmington	1944	4.1.1945	3.1945	to the MarCom 4.1948
Garrard	APA84	Consolidated, Wilmington	10.1944	13.1.1945	3.1945	stricken 5.1946
Gasconade	APA85	Consolidated, Wilmington	11.1944	23.1.1945	3.1945	sunk as target 21.7.1948
Geneva	APA86	Consolidated, Wilmington	1944	31.1.1945	3.1945	stricken 2.1947
Niagara	APA87	Consolidated, Wilmington	11.1944	10.2.1945	3.1945	sold 2.1950
Presidio	APA88	Consolidated, Wilmington	12.1944	17.2.1945	4.1945	stricken 8.1947

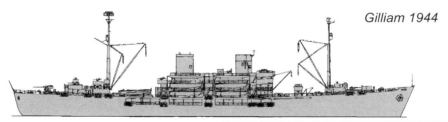

Gilliam 1944

4247 / 6800-7080 t, 129.9 x 17.7 x 4.7 m, 2 Westinghouse turbine-generators, 2 electric motors, 2 Babcock & Wilcox boilers, 6000 hp, 18 kts, 1475 t oil, 5250 nm (15 kts), complement 283; 1 x 1 – 127/38 Mk 12, 4 x 2 – 40/56 Bofors, 10 x 1 – 20/70 Oerlikon; 13 LCVP, 1 LCPL, 1 LCPR, 600 t of cargo, 986 troops; radar.
Purpose-designed S4-SE2-BD1 type hulls, shallow-draught, with twin-shaft machinery.

Audrain 1945

FREDERICK FUNSTON class amphibious transports

Frederick Funston	APA89	Seattle-Tacoma, Tacoma	1941	27.9.1941	(11.1942) / 4.1943	to the Army 4.1946
James O`Hara	APA90	Seattle-Tacoma, Tacoma	6.1941	30.12.1941	(12.1942) / 4.1943	to the Army 4.1946
Griggs	APA110	Ingalls, Pascagoula	1943	1944	12.1944	stricken 6.1946
Grundy	APA111	Ingalls, Pascagoula	1943	16.1.1944	1.1945	to the War Shipping Adm. 5.1946
Guilford	APA112	Ingalls, Pascagoula	1944	14.7.1944	5.1945	to the MarCom 5.1946
Sitka	APA113	Ingalls, Pascagoula	2.1944	23.6.1944	3.1945	stricken 6.1946
Hamblen	APA114	Ingalls, Pascagoula	1944	30.6.1944	6.1945	to the MarCom 5.1946
Hampton	APA115	Ingalls, Pascagoula	1944	25.8.1944	2.1945	to the MarCom 5.1946
Hanover	APA116	Ingalls, Pascagoula	1944	18.8.1944	3.1945	to the MarCom 5.1946

James O'Hara 1943

10967 / 14700 t, 150.1 x 21.2 x 7.6 m, 1 set Bethlehem geared steam turbines, 2 Foster Wheeler boilers, 8500 hp, 16.5 kts, 1649 t oil, 13000 nm (15 kts), complement 466-555; 1 x 1 – 127/38 Mk 12, 2 x 1 – 76/50 Mk 20, 2 x 2 – 40/56 Bofors, 16 x 1 – 20/70 Oerlikon; 24 LCVP, 2 LCM(3), 1 LCPL, 1 LCPR, 3895 t of cargo, 1468 troops. Standard C3-S1-A3 type hulls.
By 1945, all ships can carry 4 LCM(6), 16 LCVP, 1 LCPL, 1 LCPR, 1500t of cargo, 1593 troops.

HASKELL class amphibious transports

Haskell	APA117	California SB, Wilmington	5.1944	17.7.1944	8.1944	stricken 6.1946
Hendry	APA118	California SB, Wilmington	5.1944	6.8.1944	10.1944	stricken 3.1946
Highlands	APA119	California SB, Wilmington	6.1944	21.8.1944	10.1944	to the MarCom 2.1946
Hinsdale	APA120	California SB, Wilmington	6.1944	28.8.1944	10.1944	stricken 4.1946
Hocking	APA121	California SB, Wilmington	6.1944	25.7.1944	8.1944	to the MarCom 5.1946
Kenton	APA122	California SB, Wilmington	6.1944	1.9.1944	11.1944	stricken 4.1946
Kittson	APA123	California SB, Wilmington	6.1944	29.8.1944	12.1944	to the MarCom 3.1946
La Grange	APA124	California SB, Wilmington	6.1944	27.7.1944	9.1944	to the MarCom 10.1945
Lanier	APA125	California SB, Wilmington	6.1944	4.9.1944	11.1944	to the MarCom 3.1946
St. Mary`s	APA126	California SB, Wilmington	6.1944	1.8.1944	9.1944	stricken 2.1946
Allendale	APA127	California SB, Wilmington	7.1944	1.9.1944	11.1944	stricken 3.1946

Arenac	APA128	California SB, Wilmington	7.1944	14.9.1944	12.1944	stricken 10.1958
Marvin H. McIntyre (ex-Arlington)	APA129	California SB, Wilmington	5.1944	21.9.1944	11.1944	stricken 6.1946
Attala	APA130	California SB, Wilmington	7.1944	27.9.1944	11.1944	stricken 3.1946
Bandera	APA131	California SB, Wilmington	7.1944	6.10.1944	11.1944	stricken 5.1946
Barnwell	APA132	California SB, Wilmington	7.1944	30.9.1944	1.1945	stricken 10.1958
Beckham	APA133	California SB, Wilmington	7.1944	14.10.1944	12.1944	stricken 5.1946
Bland	APA134	California SB, Wilmington	8.1944	26.10.1944	12.1944	stricken 5.1946
Bosque	APA135	California SB, Wilmington	8.1944	28.10.1944	12.1944	stricken 3.1946
Botetourt	APA136	California SB, Long Beach	8.1944	19.10.1944	1.1945	stricken 7.1961
Bowie	APA137	California SB, Wilmington	8.1944	31.10.1944	12.1944	stricken 3.1946
Braxton	APA138	California SB, Wilmington	8.1944	3.11.1944	12.1944	stricken 7.1946
Broadwater	APA139	California SB, Wilmington	9.1944	5.11.1944	12.1944	stricken 3.1946
Brookings	APA140	California SB, Wilmington	9.1944	20.11.1944	12.1944	stricken 10.1958
Buckingham	APA141	California SB, Wilmington	9.1944	13.11.1944	1.1945	stricken 3.1946
Clearfield	APA142	California SB, Wilmington	9.1944	21.11.1944	12.1944	to the MarCom 3.1946
Clermont	APA143	California SB, Wilmington	9.1944	25.11.1944	1.1945	to the MarCom 3.1946
Clinton	APA144	California SB, Wilmington	9.1944	29.11.1944	1.1945	stricken 10.1958
Colbert	APA145	California SB, Wilmington	9.1944	1.12.1944	2.1945	to the MarCom 3.1946
Collingsworth	APA146	California SB, Wilmington	10.1944	2.12.1944	2.1945	stricken 3.1946
Cottle	APA147	Kaiser, Vancouver	10.1944	26.11.1944	12.1944	stricken 3.1946
Crockett	APA148	Kaiser, Vancouver	10.1944	28.11.1944	1.1945	stricken 10.1958
Audubon	APA149	Kaiser, Vancouver	10.1944	3.12.1944	12.1944	stricken 3.1946
Bergen	APA150	Kaiser, Vancouver	10.1944	5.12.1944	1.1945	stricken 5.1946
La Porte	APA151	Oregon SB, Portland	5.1944	30.6.1944	8.1944	to the War Shipping Adm. 3.1946
Latimer	APA152	Oregon SB, Portland	5.1944	4.7.1944	8.1944	to the MarAdm 2.1960
Laurens	APA153	Oregon SB, Portland	5.1944	11.7.1944	9.1944	to the MarCom 4.1946
Lowndes	APA154	Oregon SB, Portland	5.1944	18.7.1944	9.1944	stricken 5.1946
Lycoming	APA155	Oregon SB, Portland	5.1944	25.7.1944	9.1944	to the MarCom 3.1946
Mellette	APA156	Oregon SB, Portland	6.1944	4.8.1944	9.1944	stricken 7.1960

Napa	APA157	Oregon SB, Portland	6.1944	12.8.1944	10.1944	stricken 6.1946
Newberry	APA158	Oregon SB, Portland	6.1944	24.8.1944	10.1944	to the MarCom 3.1946
Darke	APA159	Oregon SB, Portland	6.1944	29.8.1944	10.1944	to the MarCom 4.1946
Deuel	APA160	Oregon SB, Portland	6.1944	9.9.1944	10.1944	stricken 1956
Dickens	APA161	Oregon SB, Portland	6.1944	8.9.1944	10.1944	to the MarCom 5.1946
Drew	APA162	Oregon SB, Portland	6.1944	14.9.1944	10.1944	to the MarCom 5.1946
Eastland	APA163	Oregon SB, Portland	7.1944	19.9.1944	10.1944	to the MarCom 4.1946
Edgecombe	APA164	Oregon SB, Portland	7.1944	24.9.1944	10.1944	to the MarCom 10.1958
Effingham	APA165	Oregon SB, Portland	7.1944	29.9.1944	11.1944	to the MarCom 5.1946
Fond du Lac	APA166	Oregon SB, Portland	7.1944	5.10.1944	11.1944	to the MarCom 4.1946
Freestone	APA167	Oregon SB, Portland	8.1944	9.10.1944	11.1944	to the War Shipping Adm. 4.1946
Gage	APA168	Oregon SB, Portland	8.1944	14.10.1944	11.1944	stricken 10.1958
Gallatin	APA169	Oregon SB, Portland	8.1944	17.10.1944	11.1944	stricken 5.1946
Gosper	APA170	Oregon SB, Portland	8.1944	20.10.1944	11.1944	stricken 5.1946
Granville	APA171	Oregon SB, Portland	9.1944	23.10.1944	11.1944	stricken 5.1946
Grimes	APA172	Oregon SB, Portland	9.1944	27.10.1944	11.1944	stricken 10.1947
Hyde	APA173	Oregon SB, Portland	9.1944	30.10.1944	11.1944	stricken 6.1946
Jerauld	APA174	Oregon SB, Portland	9.1944	3.11.1944	11.1944	to the MarCom 5.1946
Karnes	APA175	Oregon SB, Portland	9.1944	7.11.1944	12.1944	stricken 5.1946
Kershaw	APA176	Oregon SB, Portland	9.1944	12.11.1944	11.1944	stricken 10.1958
Kingsbury	APA177	Oregon SB, Portland	10.1944	16.11.1944	12.1944	stricken 5.1946
Lander	APA178	Oregon SB, Portland	9.1944	19.11.1944	12.1944	to the MarCom 4.1946
Lauderdale	APA179	Oregon SB, Portland	10.1944	23.11.1944	12.1944	to the MarCom 5.1946
Lavaca	APA180	Oregon SB, Portland	10.1944	27.11.1944	12.1944	stricken 10.1958
Oconto	APA187	Kaiser, Vancouver	4.1944	20.6.1944	9.1944	to the MarCom 5.1946
Olmsted	APA188	Kaiser, Vancouver	4.1944	4.7.1944	9.1944	stricken 7.1960
Oxford	APA189	Kaiser, Vancouver	4.1944	12.7.1944	9.1944	stricken 5.1946
Pickens	APA190	Kaiser, Vancouver	4.1944	21.7.1944	9.1944	to the MarCom 5.1946
Pondera	APA191	Kaiser, Vancouver	4.1944	27.7.1944	9.1944	stricken 6.1946
Rutland	APA192	Kaiser, Vancouver	5.1944	10.8.1944	9.1944	stricken 10.1958
Sanborn	APA193	Kaiser, Vancouver	5.1944	19.8.1944	10.1944	stricken 7.1960
Sandoval	APA194	Kaiser, Vancouver	5.1944	2.9.1944	10.1944	to the MarAdm 8.1970
Lenawee	APA195	Kaiser, Vancouver	5.1944	11.9.1944	10.1944	to the MarAdm 4.1968
Logan	APA196	Kaiser, Vancouver	5.1944	19.9.1944	10.1944	stricken 7.1960
Lubbock	APA197	Kaiser, Vancouver	6.1944	25.9.1944	10.1944	stricken 10.1958
McCracken	APA198	Kaiser, Vancouver	6.1944	29.9.1944	10.1944	stricken 10.1958
Magoffin	APA199	Kaiser, Vancouver	6.1944	4.10.1944	10.1944	stricken 2.1980

Marathon	APA200	Kaiser, Vancouver	7.1944	7.10.1944	10.1944	to the MarCom 5.1946
Menard	APA201	Kaiser, Vancouver	7.1944	11.10.1944	10.1944	stricken 9.1961
Menifee	APA202	Kaiser, Vancouver	7.1944	15.10.1944	11.1944	stricken 10.1955
Meriwether	APA203	Kaiser, Vancouver	7.1944	18.10.1944	11.1944	stricken 10.1958
Sarasota	APA204	Permanent Metals, Richmond	4.1944	14.6.1944	8.1944	stricken 7.1966
Sherburne	APA205	Permanent Metals, Richmond	5.1944	10.7.1944	9.1944	stricken 9.1958
Sibley	APA206	Permanent Metals, Richmond	5.1944	19.7.1944	10.1944	stricken 9.1958
Miffin	APA207	Permanent Metals, Richmond	5.1944	7.8.1944	10.1944	stricken 10.1958
Talladega	APA208	Permanent Metals, Richmond	6.1944	17.8.1944	10.1944	to the MarAdm 10.1946
Tazewell	APA209	Permanent Metals, Richmond	6.1944	22.8.1944	10.1944	stricken 10.1958
Telfair	APA210	Permanent Metals, Richmond	5.1944	30.8.1944	10.1944	stricken 11.1968
Missoula	APA211	Permanent Metals, Richmond	6.1944	6.9.1944	10.1944	stricken 10.1958
Montrose	APA212	Permanent Metals, Richmond	6.1944	13.9.1944	11.1944	stricken 11.1969
Mountrail	APA213	Permanent Metals, Richmond	6.1944	20.9.1944	11.1944	to the MarAdm 8.1970
Natrona	APA214	Permanent Metals, Richmond	6.1944	27.9.1944	11.1944	stricken 10.1958
Navarro	APA215	Permanent Metals, Richmond	6.1944	3.10.1944	11.1944	to the MarAdm 8.1970
Neshoba	APA216	Permanent Metals, Richmond	7.1944	7.10.1944	11.1944	stricken 10.1958
New Kent	APA217	Permanent Metals, Richmond	7.1944	12.10.1944	11.1944	stricken 10.1958
Noble	APA218	Permanent Metals, Richmond	7.1944	18.10.1944	11.1944	to Spain 12.1964 (Aragón)
Okaloosa	APA219	Permanent Metals, Richmond	8.1944	22.10.1944	11.1944	stricken 10.1958
Okanogan	APA220	Permanent Metals, Richmond	8.1944	26.10.1944	11.1944	stricken 6.1973
Oneida	APA221	Permanent Metals, Richmond	9.1944	31.10.1944	12.1944	stricken 10.1958
Pickaway	APA222	Permanent Metals, Richmond	9.1944	5.11.1944	12.1944	stricken 1.1970
Pitt	APA223	Permanent Metals, Richmond	9.1944	10.11.1944	12.1944	stricken 4.1947
Randall	APA224	Permanent Metals, Richmond	9.1944	15.11.1944	12.1944	stricken 7.1960
Bingham	APA225	Permanent Metals, Richmond	9.1944	20.11.1944	12.1944	stricken 7.1946
Rawlins	APA226	Kaiser, Vancouver	8.1944	21.10.1944	11.1944	stricken 10.1958
Renville	APA227	Kaiser, Vancouver	8.1944	25.10.1944	11.1944	stricken 9.1976
Rockbridge	APA228	Kaiser, Vancouver	9.1944	28.10.1944	11.1944	stricken 12.1968
Rockingham	APA229	Kaiser, Vancouver	9.1944	1.11.1944	11.1944	stricken 10.1958

Rockwell	APA230	Kaiser, Vancouver	9.1944	5.11.1944	11.1944	stricken 12.1958
Saint Croix	APA231	Kaiser, Vancouver	9.1944	9.11.1944	12.1944	stricken 4.1947
San Saba	APA232	Kaiser, Vancouver	9.1944	12.11.1944	12.1944	stricken 10.1958
Sevier	APA233	Kaiser, Vancouver	10.1944	16.11.1944	12.1944	stricken 6.1947
Bollinger	APA234	Kaiser, Vancouver	10.1944	19.11.1944	12.1944	stricken 5.1947
Bottineau	APA235	Kaiser, Vancouver	10.1944	22.11.1944	12.1944	stricken 7.1961
Bronx	APA236	Oregon SB, Portland	5.1945	14.7.1945	8.1945	stricken 10.1958
Bexar	APA237	Oregon SB, Portland	6.1945	25.7.1945	10.1945	stricken 9.1976
Dane	APA238	Oregon SB, Portland	6.1945	9.8.1945	10.1945	to the MarCom 8.1958
Glynn	APA239	Oregon SB, Portland	6.1945	9.8.1945	10.1945	stricken 7.1960
Harnett	APA240	Oregon SB, Portland	7.1945	-	-	cancelled 8.1945
Hempstead	APA241	Oregon SB, Portland	7.1945	-	-	cancelled 8.1945
Iredell	APA242	Oregon SB, Portland	8.1945	-	-	cancelled 8.1945

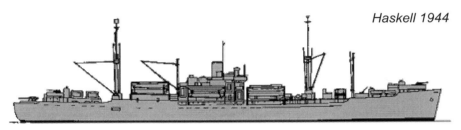

Haskell 1944

Glynn post-war

6873 / 14800-14880 t, 138.7 x 18.9 x 7.3 m, 1 set Westinghouse geared steam turbines, 2 Babcock & Wilcox boilers, 8500 hp, 16.5 kts, 1177 t oil, 7200 nm (15 kts), complement 536; 1 x 1 – 127/38 Mk 12, (1 x 4 + 4 x 2) – 40/56 Bofors, 10 x 1 – 20/70 Oerlikon; 21-22 LCVP, 2 LCM(3), 1 – 2 LCPL, 1 LCPR, 2900 t of cargo, 1561 troops; radar.

Standard VC-2-S-AP5 type hull (*Victory* class). Unnamed APA181-186 were cancelled in 1944, APA243 *Luzerne*, APA244 *Madeira*, APA245 *Maricopa*, APA246 *McLennan*, APA247 *Mecklenburg* in August 1945 (all Oregon SB, Portland).

By 1945, ships could carry 2 LCM(6), 22 LCVP, 1 LCPL, 1 LCPR, 1800 t of cargo and 1596 troops.

During the landing on Okinawa, as a result of kamikaze attacks. following ships received damages of varying severity: *Hinsdale* (31.3.1945 and 1.4.1945), *Telfair* (2.4.1945), *Sandoval* (28.5.1945) and *Lagrange* (13.8.1945).

ARCTURUS class amphibious cargo ships

Arcturus *(ex-Mormachawk)*	AK18, 2.1943-AKA1	Sun SB, Chester	7.1938	18.5.1939	(7.1939) / 10.1940	stricken 6.1946
Alchiba *(ex-Mormacdove)*	AK23, 2.1943-AKA6	Sun SB, Chester	8.1938	6.7.1939	(9.1939) / 8.1941	stricken 2.1946
Alcyone *(ex-Mormacgull)*	AK24, 11.1942-AKA7	Sun SB, Chester	1.1939	28.8.1939	(10.1939) / 6.1941	stricken 8.1946
Algorab *(ex-Mormacwren)*	AK25, 2.1943-AKA8	Sun SB, Chester	8.1938	15.6.1939	(8.1939) / 6.1941	stricken 12.1945
Betelgeuse *(ex-Mormaclark)*	AK28, 2.1943-AKA11	Sun SB, Chester	3.1939	18.7.1939	(11.1939) / 6.1941	stricken 3.1946

7293 / 13910 t, 140.0 x 19.2 x 8.0 m, 1 Sun Nordberg (AK18) or Sun Doxford diesel, 6000 hp, 16.5 kts, 1790 t diesel oil, complement 267-397; 1 x 1 – 127/38 Mk 12, 4 x 1 – 76/50 Mk 20, 4 x 1 – 12.7 MG; 15 – 16 LCVP, 8 LCM(3), 4410 t of cargo, 112 troops.

Arcturus class ships were ex-cargo vessels built for Moore-McCormack Lines, purchased by the Navy on the stocks. Standard C2 type hull.

By 1945, all ships carried 1 x 1 - 127/38 Mk 12, 2 x 2 - 40/56 Bofors, 16 x 1 - 20/70 Oerlikon; 6 LCM(6), 2

Alcyone 1942

LCM(3), 9 LCVP, 2 LCPL, 4410 t of cargo, 112 troops; radar.

PROCYON class amphibious cargo ships

Procyon (ex-Sweepstakes)	AK19, 2.1943-AKA2	Tampa SB	1.1940	14.11.1940	8.1941	stricken 4.1946
Bellatrix (ex-Raven)	AK20, 2.1943-AKA3	Tampa SB	1940	15.8.1941	2.1942	to Peru 7.1963 (Independencia)
Electra (ex-Meteor)	AK21, 2.1943-AKA4	Tampa SB	1940	18.11.1940	3.1942	BU 1973
Libra (ex-Jean Lykes)	AK53, 2.1943-AKA12	Federal, Kearny	1941	12.11.1941	5.1942	stricken 1.1977
Titania (ex-Harry Culbreath)	AK55, 2.1943-AKA13	Federal, Kearny	10.1941	28.2.1942	5.1942	stricken 7.1961
Oberon (ex-Delalba)	AK56, 2.1943-AKA14	Federal, Kearny	2.1942	28.3.1942	6.1942	stricken 7.1960

7476-8045 / 13910 t, 140.0-143.0 x 19.2 x 7.8 m, 1 Nordberg diesel (AK19-21) or 1 set General Electric geared steam turbines, 2 Foster-Wheeler boilers1d (AK53, 55, 56), 6000 hp, 16.5 kts, 1790 t diesel oil (AK19-21) or 2130 t oil (AK53, 55, 56), 22600 nm (AK19-21) or 18180 nm (AK53, 55, 56) (12 kts), complement 412; 1 x 1 – 127/38 Mk 12, 4 x 1 – 76/50 Mk 20, 4 x 1 – 12.7 MG; 15 – 16 LCVP, 8 LCM(3), cargo ,troops.
Standard C2-F type hulls.

By 1945, AKA2-4 carried 1 x 1 - 127/38 Mk 12, 4 x 1 - 76/50 Mk 20, 18 x 1 - 20/70 Oerlikon; 6 LCM(6), 2 LCM(3), 10 LCVP, 1 LCPL, 4515 t of cargo, 54 troops; radar. By 1945, AKA12-14 carried 1 x 1 - 127/38 Mk 12, 4

Procyon 1945

x 2 - 40/56 Bofors, 18 x 1 - 20/70 Oerlikon; 6 LCM(6), 3 LCM(3), 10 LCVP, 1 LCPL, 4605 t of cargo, 190 troops; radar.

FOMALHAUT amphibious cargo ship

Fomalhaut (ex-Cape Lookout)	AK22, 2.1943-AKA5	Pennsylvania S Yd, Beaumont	1940	25.1.1941	3.1942	underway ammunition replenishment ship 11.1944

7480 / 14225 t, 140.0 x 19.2 x 6.1 m, 1 Nordberg diesel, 4800 hp, 16 kts, 1235 t diesel oil, complement 267; 1 x 1 – 127/51 Mk 9/15, 4 x 1 – 76/50 Mk 20, 4 x 1 – 12.7 MG; 15 – 16 LCVP, 8 LCM(3), cargo , troops.
Standard C1-A type hull.

By late 1944, AKA5 presumably carried 1 x 1 - 127/51 Mk 15, 4 x 1 - 76/50 Mk 20, 2 x 1 - 40/56 Bofors, 12 x 1 - 20/70 Oerlikon; 2 LCM(3), 8 LCVP, 2 LCPL, 4500 t of cargo, 174 troops; radar.

Fomalhaut 1944

ALHENA amphibious cargo ship

Alhena (ex-Robin Kettering)	AK26, 11.1942-AKA9	Bethlehem, Sparrows Point	6.1940	18.1.1941	6.1941	stricken 8.1946

Alhena 1942

7101 / 11154 t, 146.2 x 20.1 x 6.3 m, 1 set Bethlehem

geared steam turbines, 2 Babcock & Wilcox boilers, 6300 hp, 16.6 kts, 2360 t oil, 11000 nm (12 kts), complement 446; 1 x 1 – 127/38 Mk 12, 4 x 1 – 76/50 Mk 10/18; 15 – 16 LCVP, 8 LCM(3), cargo, troops.
Standard C2-S type hull.
By 1945, AKA9 presumably carried 1 x 1 – 127/38 Mk 12, 4 x 2 – 40/56 Bofors, 18 x 1 – 20/70 Oerlikon; 6 LCM(6), 2 LCM(3), 10 LCVP, 1 :CPL, 4885 t of cargo, 162 troops; radar.

ALMAACK amphibious cargo ship

Almaack (ex-Executor)	AK27, 1.1943-AKA10	Bethlehem, Quincy	3.1940	21.9.1940	(10.1940) / 6.1941	stricken 8.1946

Almaack 1942

8600 / 14460 t, 144.2 x 20.3 x 8.7 m, 1 set geared steam turbines, 2 Babcock & Wilcox boilers, 8000 hp, 18.6 kts, 1659 t oil, 19345 nm (12 kts), complement 426; 1 x 1 – 127/38 Mk 12, 4 x 1 – 76/50 Mk 20; 15 – 16 LCVP, 8 LCM(3), cargo, troops.
Standard C3-E type hull.
By 1945, AKA10 presumably carried 1 x 1 – 127/38 Mk 12, 4 x 1 – 76/50 Mk 20/21, 18 x 1 – 20/70 Oerlikon; 6 LCM(6), 2 LCM(3), 8 LCVP, 1 LCPL, 5175 t of cargo, 167 troops; radar.

ANDROMEDA class amphibious cargo ships

Andromeda	AKA15	Federal, Kearny	9.1942	22.12.1942	3.1943	stricken 7.1960
Aquarius	AKA16	Federal, Kearny	4.1943	23.7.1943	8.1943	stricken 11.1946
Centaurus	AKA17	Federal, Kearny	1943	3.9.1943	10.1943	stricken 9.1946
Cepheus	AKA18	Federal, Kearny	1943	23.10.1943	12.1943	stricken 9.1946
Thuban	AKA19	Federal, Kearny	2.1943	26.4.1943	6.1943	stricken 1.1977
Virgo	AKA20	Federal, Kearny	3.1943	4.6.1943	7.1943	stricken 7.1961
Achernar	AKA53	Federal, Kearny	9.1943	3.12.1943	1.1944	to Spain 2.1965 (Castilla)
Algol (ex-James Baines)	AKA54	Moore, Oakland	12.1942	17.2.1943	11.1943	stricken 1.1977
Alshain	AKA55	Federal, Kearny	10.1943	26.1.1944	3.1944	stricken 7.1960
Arneb (ex-Mischief)	AKA56	Moore, Oakland	1943	6.7.1943	11.1943	stricken 8.1971
Capricornus (ex-Spitfire)	AKA57	Moore, Oakland	1943	14.8.1943	11.1943	stricken 1.1977
Chara	AKA58	Federal, Kearny	1943	15.3.1944	6.1944	ammunition transport 6.1966
Diphda	AKA59	Federal, Kearny	1944	11.5.1944	7.1944	stricken ~1960
Leo	AKA60	Federal, Kearny	3.1944	29.7.1944	8.1944	stricken 7.1960
Muliphen	AKA61	Federal, Kearny	5.1944	26.8.1944	10.1944	stricken 1.1977
Sheliak	AKA62	Federal, Kearny	6.1944	17.10.1944	12.1944	stricken 5.1946
Theenim	AKA63	Federal, Kearny	7.1944	31.10.1944	12.1944	stricken 5.1946

Uvalde (ex-Wild Pigeon)	AKA88	Moore, Oakland	3.1944	20.5.1944	8.1944	stricken 12.1968
Warrick (ex-Black Prince)	AKA89	Moore, Oakland	4.1944	29.5.1944	8.1944	stricken 7.1961
Whiteside (ex-Wings of the Morning)	AKA90	Moore, Oakland	4.1944	12.6.1944	9.1944	stricken ~1968
Whitley	AKA91	Moore, Oakland	5.1944	22.6.1944	9.1944	stricken 7.1960
Wyandot	AKA92	Moore, Oakland	5.1944	28.6.1944	9.1944	cargo ship 1.1969
Yancey	AKA93	Moore, Oakland	5.1944	8.7.1944	10.1944	stricken 1.1977
Winston	AKA94	Federal, Kearny	7.1944	30.11.1944	1.1945	stricken 9.1976
Marquette	AKA95	Federal, Kearny	1945	29.4.1945	6.1945	stricken 1.1960
Mathews	AKA96	Federal, Kearny	9.1944	22.12.1944	3.1945	stricken 11.1968
Merrick	AKA97	Federal, Kearny	10.1944	28.1.1945	3.1945	stricken 9.1976
Montague	AKA98	Federal, Kearny	1944	12.2.1945	4.1945	stricken 2.1960
Rolette	AKA99	Federal, Kearny	12.1944	11.3.1945	4.1945	stricken 7.1960
Oglethorpe	AKA100	Federal, Kearny	12.1944	15.4.1945	6.1945	stricken 11.1968
San Joaquin	AKA109	Federal, Kearny	8.1945	-	-	cancelled 8.1945

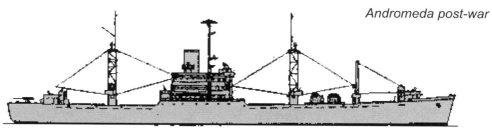

Andromeda post-war

8635 / 13910 t, 139.9 x 19.2 x 7.9 m, 1 set General Electric or De Laval (AKA16, 17) geared steam turbines, 2 Combustion Engineering (AKA15-17, 19, 20) or Foster Wheeler boilers, 6000 hp, 16.5 kts, 1553 t oil, 16040 nm (12 kts), complement 404; 1 x 1 – 127/38 Mk 12, 4 x 2 – 40/56 Bofors, (16 – 18) x 1 – 20/70 Oerlikon; 6 LCM(6), 2 LCM(3), 13 LCVP, 1 LCPL, 4900 t of cargo, 74-78 troops.

Standard C2-S-B1 type hulls. AKA110 *Sedgwick* and AKA111 *Whitfield* (both Federal, Kearny) were cancelled in August 1945.

Leo 27.2.1945 was damaged off Iwo Jima by gunfire from Japanese coastal batteries. *Wyandot* 28.3.1945 was damaged off Okinawa by Japanese aircraft. *Achernar* 2.4.1945 was damaged at Okinawa by kamikaze.

Virgo 1944

ARTEMIS class amphibious cargo ships

Artemis	AKA21	Walsh-Kaiser, Providence	11.1943	20.5.1944	8.1944	stricken 2.1947
Athene	AKA22	Walsh-Kaiser, Providence	1.1944	18.6.1944	9.1944	stricken 8.1947
Aurelia	AKA23	Walsh-Kaiser, Providence	2.1944	4.7.1944	10.1944	stricken 6.1946
Birgit	AKA24	Walsh-Kaiser, Providence	2.1944	18.7.1944	10.1944	stricken 5.1946
Circe	AKA25	Walsh-Kaiser, Providence	1944	4.8.1944	11.1944	stricken 5.1946
Corvus	AKA26	Walsh-Kaiser, Providence	1944	24.9.1944	11.1944	stricken 1946
Devosa	AKA27	Walsh-Kaiser, Providence	1944	12.10.1944	11.1944	stricken 1946
Hydrus	AKA28	Walsh-Kaiser, Providence	1944	28.10.1944	12.1944	stricken 6.1956
Lacerta	AKA29	Walsh-Kaiser, Providence	7.1944	10.11.1944	12.1944	stricken 1946
Lumen	AKA30	Walsh-Kaiser, Providence	7.1944	20.11.1944	12.1944	stricken 1946
Medea	AKA31	Walsh-Kaiser, Providence	8.1944	30.11.1944	1.1945	stricken 10.1946
Mellena	AKA32	Walsh-Kaiser, Providence	9.1944	11.12.1944	1.1945	stricken 7.1946

Ostara	AKA33	Walsh-Kaiser, Providence	10.1944	21.12.1944	1.1945	stricken 4.1946
Pamina	AKA34	Walsh-Kaiser, Providence	1944	5.1.1945	2.1945	survey ship 5.1946
Polana	AKA35	Walsh-Kaiser, Providence	12.1944	17.1.1945	2.1945	stricken 5.1946
Renate	AKA36	Walsh-Kaiser, Providence	1944	31.1.1945	2.1945	survey ship 7.1946
Roxane	AKA37	Walsh-Kaiser, Providence	12.1944	14.2.1945	3.1945	stricken 7.1946
Sappho	AKA38	Walsh-Kaiser, Providence	12.1944	3.3.1945	3.1945	stricken 10.1946
Sarita	AKA39	Walsh-Kaiser, Providence	12.1944	23.2.1945	3.1945	stricken 2.1947
Scania	AKA40	Walsh-Kaiser, Providence	1.1945	17.3.1945	4.1945	stricken 9.1947
Selinur	AKA41	Walsh-Kaiser, Providence	1.1945	28.3.1945	4.1945	stricken 5.1946
Sidonia	AKA42	Walsh-Kaiser, Providence	2.1945	7.4.1945	4.1945	stricken 4.1946
Sirona	AKA43	Walsh-Kaiser, Providence	2.1945	17.4.1945	5.1945	stricken 7.1946
Sylvania	AKA44	Walsh-Kaiser, Providence	2.1945	25.4.1945	5.1945	stricken 2.1947
Tabora	AKA45	Walsh-Kaiser, Providence	3.1945	3.5.1945	5.1945	stricken 7.1946
Troilus	AKA46	Walsh-Kaiser, Providence	3.1945	11.5.1945	6.1945	stricken 7.1946
Turandot	AKA47	Walsh-Kaiser, Providence	3.1945	20.5.1945	6.1945	stricken 4.1947
Valeria	AKA48	Walsh-Kaiser, Providence	4.1945	29.5.1945	6.1945	stricken 4.1946
Vanadis	AKA49	Walsh-Kaiser, Providence	4.1945	8.6.1946	7.1945	stricken 6.1946
Veritas	AKA50	Walsh-Kaiser, Providence	4.1945	16.5.1945	7.1945	stricken 4.1946
Xenia	AKA51	Walsh-Kaiser, Providence	5.1945	27.6.1945	7.1945	stricken 9.1946
Zenobia	AKA52	Walsh-Kaiser, Providence	1945	6.7.1945	8.1945	stricken 11.1946

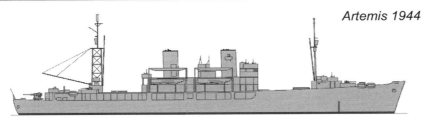

Artemis 1944

Zenobia

4087 / 6740 t, 129.9 x 17.7 x 4.7 m, 2 Westinghouse turbine-generators, 2 electric motors, 2 Babcock & Wilcox boilers, 6000 hp, 18 kts, 1400 t oil, 9500 nm (12 kts), complement 303; 1 x 1 – 127/38 Mk 12, 4 x 2 – 40/56 Bofors, 10 x 1 – 20/70 Oerlikon; 12 LCVP, 2 LCM(3), 1 LCPL, 2900 t of cargo, 252 troops; radar. Standard purpose-designed S4-SE2-BE1 type.

TOLLAND and RANKIN classes amphibious cargo ships

Tolland class

Tolland	AKA64	North Carolina SB, Wilmington	4.1944	26.6.1944	9.1944	stricken 7.1946
Shoshone	AKA65	North Carolina SB, Wilmington	5.1944	17.7.1944	9.1944	stricken 7.1946
Southampton	AKA66	North Carolina SB, Wilmington	5.1944	28.7.1944	9.1944	stricken 7.1946
Starr	AKA67	North Carolina SB, Wilmington	6.1944	18.8.1944	9.1944	stricken 6.1946
Stokes	AKA68	North Carolina SB, Wilmington	6.1944	31.8.1944	10.1944	stricken 7.1946
Suffolk	AKA69	North Carolina SB, Wilmington	7.1944	15.9.1944	10.1944	stricken 7.1946
Tate	AKA70	North Carolina SB, Wilmington	7.1944	26.9.1944	11.1944	stricken 7.1946
Todd	AKA71	North Carolina SB, Wilmington	8.1944	10.10.1944	11.1944	stricken 7.1946
Caswell	AKA72	North Carolina SB, Wilmington	1944	24.10.1944	12.1944	stricken 6.1946
New Hannover	AKA73	North Carolina SB, Wilmington	8.1944	31.10.1944	12.1944	stricken 8.1946
Lenoir	AKA74	North Carolina SB, Wilmington	9.1944	6.11.1944	12.1944	stricken 6.1946
Alamance	AKA75	North Carolina SB, Wilmington	9.1944	11.11.1944	12.1944	stricken 7.1946

Torrance	AKA76	North Carolina SB, Wilmington	1944	6.6.1944	6.1944	stricken 7.1946
Towner	AKA77	North Carolina SB, Wilmington	4.1944	18.6.1944	6.1944	stricken 6.1946
Trego	AKA78	North Carolina SB, Wilmington	4.1944	20.6.1944	7.1944	stricken 6.1946
Trousdale	AKA79	North Carolina SB, Wilmington	4.1944	3.7.1944	7.1944	stricken 5.1946
Tyrrell	AKA80	North Carolina SB, Wilmington	5.1944	30.7.1944	7.1944	stricken 5.1946
Valencia	AKA81	North Carolina SB, Wilmington	5.1944	22.7.1944	8.1944	stricken 5.1946
Venango	AKA82	North Carolina SB, Wilmington	6.1944	9.8.1944	8.1944	stricken 5.1946
Vinton	AKA83	North Carolina SB, Wilmington	6.1944	25.8.1944	9.1944	stricken 6.1946
Waukesha	AKA84	North Carolina SB, Wilmington	7.1944	6.9.1944	9.1944	stricken 7.1946
Wheatland	AKA85	North Carolina SB, Wilmington	7.1944	21.9.1944	10.1944	stricken 5.1946
Woodford	AKA86	North Carolina SB, Wilmington	7.1944	5.10.1944	10.1944	stricken 5.1946
Duplin	AKA87	North Carolina SB, Wilmington	1944	17.10.1944	10.1944	stricken 5.1946
Ottawa	AKA101	North Carolina SB, Wilmington	10.1944	29.11.1944	2.1945	stricken 3.1947
Prentiss	AKA102	North Carolina SB, Wilmington	10.1944	6.12.1944	2.1945	stricken 6.1946
Rankin class						
Rankin	AKA103	North Carolina SB, Wilmington	10.1944	22.12.1944	2.1945	stricken 1.1977
Seminole	AKA104	North Carolina SB, Wilmington	1944	28.12.1944	3.1945	stricken 9.1976
Skagit	AKA105	North Carolina SB, Wilmington	9.1944	18.11.1944	5.1945	stricken 7.1969
Union	AKA106	North Carolina SB, Wilmington	9.1944	23.11.1944	4.1945	stricken 1.1976
Vermilion	AKA107	North Carolina SB, Wilmington	10.1944	12.12.1944	6.1945	stricken 1.1977
Washburn	AKA108	North Carolina SB, Wilmington	10.1944	18.12.1944	5.1945	stricken 10.1976

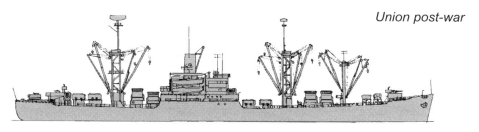

Union post-war

8635 / 13910 t, 139.9 x 19.2 x 7.9 m, 1 set General Electric geared steam turbines, 2 Combustion Engineering or Foster Wheeler boilers, 6000 hp, 16.5 kts, 1553 t oil, complement 404; 1 x 1 – 127/38 Mk 12, 4 x 2 – 40/56 Bofors, 16 x 1 – 20/70 Oerlikon; 6 LCM(6), 2 LCM(3), 13 LCVP, 1 :CPL, 5275 t of cargo, 62 troops; radar.
Standard C2-S-AJ3 type hulls
Tyrrell 2.4.1945 was damaged at Okinawa by a kamikaze. *Starr* 9.4.1945 was damaged at Okinawa by a Japanese suicide boat.

Tolland 1945

LCI(L) class landing craft infantry (large)

LCI(L)1	New York SB, Camden	7.1942	3.9.1942	10.1942	sunk 17.8.1943
LCI(L)2	New York SB, Camden	7.1942	5.9.1942	10.1942	stricken 1946
LCI(L)3	New York SB, Camden	7.1942	7.9.1942	10.1942	to the UK 10.1944 (LCI(L)3)
LCI(L)4	New York SB, Camden	7.1942	9.9.1942	10.1942	to the UK 10.1944 (LCI(L)4)
LCI(L)5	New York SB, Camden	7.1942	11.9.1942	10.1942	to the UK 10.1944 (LCI(L)5)
LCI(L)6	New York SB, Camden	7.1942	13.9.1942	(10.1942)	to the UK 10.1942 (LCI(L)6)
LCI(L)7	New York SB, Camden	8.1942	15.9.1942	(10.1942)	to the UK 10.1942 (LCI(L)7)
LCI(L)8	New York SB, Camden	8.1942	16.9.1942	10.1942	to the UK 10.1944 (LCI(L)8)
LCI(L)9	New York SB, Camden	8.1942	19.9.1942	10.1942	to the UK 10.1944 (LCI(L)9)
LCI(L)10	New York SB, Camden	8.1942	21.9.1942	10.1942	to the UK 10.1944 (LCI(L)10)

LCI(L)11	New York SB, Camden	8.1942	23.9.1942	10.1942	to the UK 11.1944 (LCI(L)11)
LCI(L)12	New York SB, Camden	8.1942	24.9.1942	10.1942	to the UK 10.1944 (LCI(L)12)
LCI(L)13	New York SB, Camden	9.1942	26.9.1942	10.1942	to the UK 10.1944 (LCI(L)13)
LCI(L)14	New York SB, Camden	9.1942	28.9.1942	11.1942	to the UK 10.1944 (LCI(L)14)
LCI(L)15	New York SB, Camden	9.1942	29.9.1942	11.1942	to the UK 10.1944 (LCI(L)15)
LCI(L)16	New York SB, Camden	9.1942	2.10.1942	11.1942	to the UK 10.1944 (LCI(L)16)
LCI(L)17, 7.1945- LCI(G)17	New York SB, Camden	1942	1942	11.1942	landing craft gun 7.1945, stricken 1946
LCI(L)18, 7.1945- LCI(G)18	New York SB, Camden	1942	1942	12.1942	landing craft gun 7.1945, stricken 1946
LCI(L)19, 7.1945- LCI(G)19	New York SB, Camden	1942	1942	12.1942	landing craft gun 7.1945, stricken 1946
LCI(L)20	New York SB, Camden	1942	1942	12.1942	sunk 22.1.1944
LCI(L)21, 7.1945- LCI(G)21	New York SB, Camden	1942	1942	12.1942	landing craft gun 7.1945, stricken 1946
LCI(L)22, 6.1944- LCI(G)22	New York SB, Camden	9.1942	18.10.1942	12.1942	landing craft gun 6.1944, stricken 1946
LCI(L)23, 6.1944- LCI(G)23	New York SB, Camden	1942	1942	12.1942	landing craft gun 6.1944, stricken 1946
LCI(L)24, 6.1944- LCI(G)24	New York SB, Camden	1942	1942	12.1942	landing craft gun 6.1944, stricken 1946
LCI(L)25	New York SB, Camden	1942	1942	12.1942	stricken 1946
LCI(L)26	New York SB, Camden	1942	1942	12.1942	stricken 1946
LCI(L)27	New York SB, Camden	1942	1942	12.1942	stricken 1946
LCI(L)28	New York SB, Camden	1942	1942	12.1942	stricken 1946
LCI(L)29	New York SB, Camden	1942	1942	12.1942	stricken 1946
LCI(L)30	New York SB, Camden	10.1942	5.11.1942	12.1942	stricken 1946
LCI(L)31, 6.1944- LCI(G)31, 7.1945- LCI(R)31	New York SB, Camden	1942	1942	12.1942	landing craft gun 6.1944, landing craft rocket 7.1945, stricken 1946
LCI(L)32	New York SB, Camden	1942	1942	12.1942	sunk 26.1.1944
LCI(L)33	New York SB, Camden	10.1942	2.11.1942	12.1942	to the UK 11.1944 (LCI(L)33)
LCI(L)34, 6.1944- LCI(G)34, 7.1945- LCI(R)34	New York SB, Camden	1942	1942	1.1943	landing craft gun 6.1944, landing craft rocket 7.1945, stricken 1946
LCI(L)35	New York SB, Camden	10.1942	4.11.1942	1.1943	to the UK 11.1944 (LCI(L)35)
LCI(L)36, 7.1945- LCI(G)36	New York SB, Camden	10.1942	5.11.1942	2.1943	landing craft gun 7.1945, stricken 1946
LCI(L)37	New York SB, Camden	1942	1942	2.1943	to the MarCom 6.1947
LCI(L)38	New York SB, Camden	1942	1942	2.1943	CTL 1946
LCI(L)39	New York SB, Camden	1942	1942	2.1943	stricken 1946
LCI(L)40	New York SB, Camden	1942	1942	12.1942	to Dominican Republic 1.1947 (Beller)
LCI(L)41, 7.1945- LCI(G)41, 9.1945- LCI(L)41	New York SB, Camden	1942	1942	12.1942	landing craft gun 7.1945, landing craft 9.1945, stricken 1946
LCI(L)42, 7.1945- LCI(G)42	New York SB, Camden	1942	1942	12.1942	landing craft gun 7.1945, stricken 1946
LCI(L)43, 7.1945- LCI(G)43	New York SB, Camden	1942	1942	12.1942	landing craft gun 7.1945, stricken 1946
LCI(L)44	New York SB, Camden	1942	1942	12.1942	stricken 1946

LCI(L)45, 7.1945- LCI(G)45, 9.1945- LCI(L)45	New York SB, Camden	1942	1942	12.1942	landing craft gun 7.1945, landing craft 9.1945, stricken 1946
LCI(L)46, 7.1945- LCI(G)46	New York SB, Camden	1942	1942	2.1943	landing craft gun 7.1945, stricken 1946
LCI(L)47	New York SB, Camden	11.1942	10.12.1942	2.1943	stricken 1946
LCI(L)48	New York SB, Camden	11.1942	10.12.1942	2.1943	to Dominican Republic 4.1947 (Palo Incado)
LCI(L)61, 6.1944- LCI(G)61	Consolidated, Orange	1942	1942	11.1942	landing craft gun 6.1944, stricken 1946
LCI(L)62	Consolidated, Orange	8.1942	27.9.1942	11.1942	stricken 1946
LCI(L)63	Consolidated, Orange	1942	1942	11.1942	stricken 1945
LCI(L)64, 6.1944- LCI(G)64	Consolidated, Orange	1942	1942	12.1942	landing craft gun 6.1944, stricken 1946
LCI(L)65, 6.1944- LCI(G)65	Consolidated, Orange	8.1942	4.10.1942	12.1942	landing craft gun 6.1944, stricken 1946
LCI(L)66, 6.1944- LCI(G)66	Consolidated, Orange	1942	1942	12.1942	landing craft gun 6.1944, stricken 1946
LCI(L)67, 6.1944- LCI(G)67	Consolidated, Orange	1942	1942	12.1942	landing craft gun 6.1944, stricken 1946
LCI(L)68, 6.1944- LCI(G)68	Consolidated, Orange	9.1942	11.10.1942	12.1942	landing craft gun 6.1944, stricken 1946
LCI(L)69, 6.1944- LCI(G)69	Consolidated, Orange	1942	1942	12.1942	landing craft gun 6.1944, stricken 1946
LCI(L)70, 6.1944- LCI(G)70	Consolidated, Orange	9.1942	25.10.1942	12.1942	landing craft gun 6.1944, stricken 1946
LCI(L)71, 7.1945- LCI(R)71	Consolidated, Orange	9.1942	25.10.1942	12.1942	landing craft rocket 7.1945, stricken 1946
LCI(L)72, 7.1945- LCI(R)72	Consolidated, Orange	1942	1942	12.1942	landing craft rocket 7.1945, stricken 1946
LCI(L)73, 6.1944- LCI(G)73, 7.1945- LCI(R)73	Consolidated, Orange	9.1942	8.11.1942	1.1943	landing craft gun 6.1944, landing craft rocket 7.1945, stricken 1946
LCI(L)74, 7.1945- LCI(R)74	Consolidated, Orange	1942	1942	1.1943	landing craft rocket 7.1945, stricken 1946
LCI(L)75	Consolidated, Orange	9.1942	8.11.1942	1.1943	to the UK 11.1944 (LCH75)
LCI(L)76	Consolidated, Orange	1942	1942	1.1943	sunk as target 1956
LCI(L)77, 6.1944- LCI(G)77	Consolidated, Orange	9.1942	1942	1.1943	landing craft gun 6.1944, stricken 1946
LCI(L)78, 6.1944- LCI(G)78	Consolidated, Orange	1942	1942	1.1943	landing craft gun 6.1944, stricken 1946
LCI(L)79, 6.1944- LCI(G)79	Consolidated, Orange	1942	6.12.1942	1.1943	landing craft gun 6.1944, stricken 1946
LCI(L)80, 6.1944- LCI(G)80	Consolidated, Orange	10.1942	6.12.1942	1.1943	landing craft gun 6.1944, stricken 1946
LCI(L)81, 6.1944- LCI(G)81	Consolidated, Orange	1942	1942	1.1943	landing craft gun 6.1944, stricken 1946
LCI(L)82, 6.1944- LCI(G)82	Consolidated, Orange	1942	1942	1.1943	landing craft gun 6.1944, sunk 4.4.1945
LCI(L)83	Consolidated, Orange	10.1942	13.12.1942	1.1943	stricken 1946
LCI(L)84	Consolidated, Orange	10.1942	13.12.1942	1.1943	stricken 1946
LCI(L)85	Consolidated, Orange	10.1942	1942	1.1943	sunk 6.6.1944
LCI(L)86	Consolidated, Orange	10.1942	20.12.1942	1.1943	stricken 1946

LCI(L)87	Consolidated, Orange	10.1942	20.12.1942	2.1943	stricken 1946
LCI(L)88	Consolidated, Orange	10.1942	20.12.1942	2.1943	stricken 1946
LCI(L)89	Consolidated, Orange	10.1942	30.12.1942	2.1943	stricken 1946
LCI(L)90	Consolidated, Orange	10.1942	12.1942	2.1943	stricken 1946
LCI(L)91	Consolidated, Orange	10.1942	12.1942	2.1943	sunk 6.6.1944
LCI(L)92	Consolidated, Orange	11.1942	3.1.1943	2.1943	sunk 6.6.1944
LCI(L)93	Consolidated, Orange	12.1942	1.1943	2.1943	sunk 6.6.1944
LCI(L)94	Consolidated, Orange	12.1942	17.1.1943	2.1943	stricken 1946
LCI(L)95	Consolidated, Orange	12.1942	17.1.1943	2.1943	stricken 1946
LCI(L)96	Consolidated, Orange	12.1942	17.1.1943	2.1943	stricken 1946
LCI(L)97	Bethlehem, Hingham	8.1942	24.9.1942	10.1942	to the UK 10.1942 (LCI(L)97)
LCI(L)98	Bethlehem, Hingham	8.1942	9.10.1942	(11.1942)	to the UK 11.1942 (LCI(L)98
LCI(L)99	Bethlehem, Hingham	8.1942	12.10.1942	11.1942	to the UK 11.1942 (LCI(L)99)
LCI(L)100	Bethlehem, Hingham	8.1942	15.10.1942	(11.1942)	to the UK 11.1942 (LCI(L)100)
LCI(L)101	Bethlehem, Hingham	8.1942	22.10.1942	(11.1942)	to the UK 11.1942 (LCH101)
LCI(L)102	Bethlehem, Hingham	8.1942	24.10.1942	(11.1942)	to the UK 11.1942 (LCI(L)102)
LCI(L)103	Bethlehem, Hingham	8.1942	31.10.1942	11.1942	to the UK 12.1942 (LCI(L)103)
LCI(L)104	Bethlehem, Hingham	8.1942	30.10.1942	(11.1942)	to the UK 11.1942 (LCI(L)104)
LCI(L)105	Bethlehem, Hingham	8.1942	7.11.1942	11.1942	to the UK 11.1942 (LCI(L)105)
LCI(L)106	Bethlehem, Hingham	8.1942	9.11.1942	12.1942	to the UK 12.1942 (LCI(L)106)
LCI(L)107	Bethlehem, Hingham	8.1942	14.11.1942	12.1942	to the UK 12.1942 (LCI(L)107)
LCI(L)108	Bethlehem, Hingham	8.1942	18.11.1942	(12.1942)	to the UK 12.1942 (LCI(L)108)
LCI(L)109	Bethlehem, Hingham	8.1942	20.11.1942	12.1942	to the UK 12.1942 (LCI(L)109)
LCI(L)110	Bethlehem, Hingham	8.1942	20.11.1942	12.1942	to the UK 12.1942 (LCI(L)110)
LCI(L)111	Bethlehem, Hingham	8.1942	27.11.1942	(12.1942)	to the UK 12.1942 (LCI(L)111)
LCI(L)112	Bethlehem, Hingham	8.1942	27.11.1942	12.1942	to the UK 12.1942 (LCI(L)112)
LCI(L)113	Bethlehem, Hingham	9.1942	30.11.1942	12.1942	to the UK 12.1942 (LCI(L)113)
LCI(L)114	Bethlehem, Hingham	9.1942	1.12.1942	(12.1942)	to the UK 12.1942 (LCI(L)114)
LCI(L)115	Bethlehem, Hingham	9.1942	5.12.1942	(12.1942)	to the UK 12.1942 (LCI(L)115)
LCI(L)116	Bethlehem, Hingham	9.1942	6.12.1942	(1.1943)	to the UK 1.1943 (LCI(L)116)
LCI(L)117	Bethlehem, Hingham	10.1942	7.12.1942	(1.1943)	to the UK 1.1943 (LCI(L)117)
LCI(L)118	Bethlehem, Hingham	10.1942	8.12.1942	(1.1943)	to the UK 1.1943 (LCI(L)118)
LCI(L)119	Bethlehem, Hingham	10.1942	10.12.1942	1.1943	to the UK 1.1943 (LCI(L)119)
LCI(L)120	Bethlehem, Hingham	10.1942	11.12.1942	(1.1943)	to the UK 1.1943 (LCI(L)120)
LCI(L)121	Bethlehem, Hingham	10.1942	14.12.1942	(1.1943)	to the UK 1.1943 (LCI(L)121)
LCI(L)122	Bethlehem, Hingham	10.1942	14.12.1942	(1.1943)	to the UK 1.1943 (LCI(L)122)
LCI(L)123	Bethlehem, Hingham	10.1942	19.12.1942	(1.1943)	to the UK 1.1943 (LCI(L)123)
LCI(L)124	Bethlehem, Hingham	10.1942	19.12.1942	(1.1943)	to the UK 1.1943 (LCI(L)124)
LCI(L)125	Bethlehem, Hingham	10.1942	26.12.1942	(1.1943)	to the UK 1.1943 (LCI(L)125)
LCI(L)126	Bethlehem, Hingham	10.1942	26.12.1942	(1.1943)	to the UK 1.1943 (LCI(L)126)
LCI(L)127	Bethlehem, Hingham	10.1942	29.12.1942	1.1943	to Canada 1.1943 (LCI(L)127)
LCI(L)128	Bethlehem, Hingham	10.1942	30.12.1942	1.1943	to the UK 1.1943 (LCI(L)128)
LCI(L)129	Bethlehem, Hingham	12.1942	31.12.1942	1.1943	to the UK 1.1943 (LCI(L)129)
LCI(L)130	Bethlehem, Hingham	12.1942	31.12.1942	1.1943	to the UK 1.1943 (LCI(L)130)
LCI(L)131	Bethlehem, Hingham	12.1942	7.1.1943	1.1943	to the UK 1.1943 (LCI(L)131)
LCI(L)132	Bethlehem, Hingham	12.1942	7.1.1943	(1.1943)	to the UK 1.1943 (LCI(L)132)
LCI(L)133	Bethlehem, Hingham	12.1942	11.1.1943	(2.1943)	to the UK 2.1943 (LCI(L)133)
LCI(L)134	Bethlehem, Hingham	12.1942	11.1.1943	(2.1943)	to the UK 2.1943 (LCI(L)134)
LCI(L)135	Bethlehem, Hingham	12.1942	13.1.1943	(2.1943)	to the UK 2.1943 (LCI(L)135)
LCI(L)136	Bethlehem, Hingham	12.1942	16.1.1943	(2.1943)	to the UK 2.1943 (LCI(L)136)
LCI(L)161	Federal, Newark	8.1942	10.10.1942	10.1942	to the UK 10.1942 (LCI(L)161)
LCI(L)162	Federal, Newark	8.1942	10.10.1942	10.1942	to the UK 10.1942 (LCI(L)162)

LCI(L)163	Federal, Newark	8.1942	12.10.1942	10.1942	to the UK 10.1942 (LCI(L)163)
LCI(L)164	Federal, Newark	8.1942	12.10.1942	11.1942	to the UK 11.1942 (LCI(L)164)
LCI(L)165	Federal, Newark	8.1942	17.10.1942	(11.1942)	to the UK 11.1942 (LCI(L)165)
LCI(L)166	Federal, Newark	8.1942	17.10.1942	(11.1942)	to the UK 11.1942 (LCI(L)166)
LCI(L)167	Federal, Newark	8.1942	22.10.1942	11.1942	to the UK 11.1942 (LCI(L)167)
LCI(L)168	Federal, Newark	8.1942	22.10.1942	11.1942	to the UK 11.1942 (LCI(L)168)
LCI(L)169	Federal, Newark	9.1942	2.11.1942	(11.1942)	to the UK 11.1942 (LCI(L)169)
LCI(L)170	Federal, Newark	9.1942	2.11.1942	11.1942	to the UK 11.1942 (LCI(L)170)
LCI(L)171	Federal, Newark	9.1942	11.11.1942	11.1942	to the UK 11.1942 (LCI(L)171)
LCI(L)172	Federal, Newark	9.1942	11.11.1942	(11.1942)	to the UK 11.1942 (LCI(L)172)
LCI(L)173	Federal, Newark	9.1942	11.11.1942	11.1942	to the UK 11.1942 (LCI(L)173)
LCI(L)174	Federal, Newark	9.1942	11.11.1942	11.1942	to the UK 11.1942 (LCI(L)174)
LCI(L)175	Federal, Newark	9.1942	19.11.1942	12.1942	to the UK 12.1942 (LCI(L)175)
LCI(L)176	Federal, Newark	9.1942	19.11.1942	12.1942	to the UK 12.1942 (LCI(L)176)
LCI(L)177	Federal, Newark	9.1942	27.11.1942	(12.1942)	to the UK 12.1942 (LCI(L)177)
LCI(L)178	Federal, Newark	9.1942	27.11.1942	(12.1942)	to the UK 12.1942 (LCI(L)178)
LCI(L)179	Federal, Newark	9.1942	7.12.1942	12.1942	to the UK 12.1942 (LCI(L)179)
LCI(L)180	Federal, Newark	9.1942	7.12.1942	12.1942	to the UK 12.1942 (LCI(L)180)
LCI(L)181	Federal, Newark	9.1942	14.12.1942	12.1942	to the UK 12.1942 (LCI(L)181)
LCI(L)182	Federal, Newark	9.1942	14.12.1942	12.1942	to the UK 12.1942 (LCI(L)182)
LCI(L)183	Federal, Newark	9.1942	21.12.1942	12.1942	to the UK 12.1942 (LCI(L)183)
LCI(L)184	Federal, Newark	9.1942	21.12.1942	12.1942	to the UK 12.1942 (LCI(L)184)
LCI(L)185	Federal, Newark	11.1942	4.1.1943	(1.1943)	to the UK 1.1943 (LCH185)
LCI(L)186	Federal, Newark	11.1942	4.1.1943	(1.1943)	to the UK 1.1943 (LCI(L)186)
LCI(L)187	Federal, Newark	11.1942	11.1.1943	(1.1943)	to the UK 1.1943 (LCI(L)187)
LCI(L)188	Federal, Newark	1942	1.1943	1.1943	stricken 1946
LCI(L)189	Federal, Newark	1942	1.1943	1.1943	stricken 1946
LCI(L)190	Federal, Newark	11.1942	18.1.1943	2.1943	stricken 1946
LCI(L)191, 6.1945- LCI(G)191, 9.1945- LCI(L)191	Federal, Newark	12.1942	25.1.1943	2.1943	landing craft gun 6.1945, landing craft 9.1945, stricken 1946
LCI(L)192, 7.1945- LCI(G)192	Federal, Newark	1942	1.1943	2.1943	landing craft gun 7.1945, stricken 1946
LCI(L)193	Federal, Newark	12.1942	30.1.1943	2.1943	to the UK 11.1944 (LCI(L)193)
LCI(L)194, 7.1945- LCI(G)194	Federal, Newark	1942	1943	2.1943	landing craft gun 7.1945, for disposal 8.1947
LCI(L)195, 7.1945- LCI(G)195	Federal, Newark	1942	1943	2.1943	landing craft gun 7.1945, stricken 1946
LCI(L)196, 7.1945- LCI(G)196	Federal, Newark	1942	1943	2.1943	landing craft gun 7.1945, stricken 1946
LCI(L)209	Geo Lawley, Neponset	8.1942	7.9.1942	10.1942	to the UK 10.1944 (LCI(L)209)
LCI(L)210	Geo Lawley, Neponset	8.1942	7.9.1942	10.1942	to the UK 10.1944 (LCI(L)210)
LCI(L)211	Geo Lawley, Neponset	9.1942	23.9.1942	10.1942	to the UK 10.1944 (LCI(L)211)
LCI(L)212	Geo Lawley, Neponset	9.1942	23.9.1942	10.1942	to the UK 10.1944 (LCI(L)212)
LCI(L)213	Geo Lawley, Neponset	9.1942	30.9.1942	10.1942	to the UK 10.1944 (LCI(L)213)
LCI(L)214	Geo Lawley, Neponset	9.1942	8.10.1942	10.1942	to the UK 10.1944 (LCI(L)214)
LCI(L)215	Geo Lawley, Neponset	9.1942	13.10.1942	11.1942	to the UK 10.1944 (LCI(L)215)
LCI(L)216	Geo Lawley, Neponset	9.1942	19.10.1942	11.1942	to the UK 11.1944 (LCI(L)216)
LCI(L)217	Geo Lawley, Neponset	9.1942	25.10.1942	11.1942	to the UK 11.1944 (LCI(L)217)
LCI(L)218	Geo Lawley, Neponset	10.1942	31.10.1942	11.1942	to the UK 10.1944 (LCI(L)218)
LCI(L)219	Geo Lawley, Neponset	1942	1942	11.1942	sunk 11.6.1944

LCI(L)220, 7.1945- LCI(G)220	Geo Lawley, Neponset	10.1942	12.11.1942	11.1942	landing craft gun 7.1945, to China 12.1946
LCI(L)221	Geo Lawley, Neponset	10.1942	14.11.1942	11.1942	stricken 1946
LCI(L)222	Geo Lawley, Neponset	1942	1942	12.1942	stricken 1946
LCI(L)223	Geo Lawley, Neponset	1942	1942	12.1942	stricken 1946
LCI(L)224, 7.1945- LCI(R)224	Geo Lawley, Neponset	1942	1942	12.1942	landing craft rocket 7.1945, stricken 1946
LCI(L)225, 7.1945- LCI(R)225	Geo Lawley, Neponset	1942	1942	12.1942	landing craft rocket 7.1945, stricken 1946
LCI(L)226, 7.1945- LCI(R)226	Geo Lawley, Neponset	1942	1942	12.1942	landing craft rocket 7.1945, stricken 1946
LCI(L)227	Geo Lawley, Neponset	1942	1942	12.1942	stricken 1946
LCI(L)228	Geo Lawley, Neponset	1942	1942	12.1942	stricken 1946
LCI(L)229	Geo Lawley, Neponset	11.1942	27.12.1942	1.1943	to the UK 11.1944 (LCI(L)229)
LCI(L)230, 7.1945- LCI(R)230	Geo Lawley, Neponset	11.1942	31.12.1942	1.1943	landing craft rocket 7.1945, stricken 1946
LCI(L)231	Geo Lawley, Neponset	11.1942	5.1.1943	1.1943	to the UK 11.1944 (LCI(L)231)
LCI(L)232	Geo Lawley, Neponset	1942	1.1943	1.1943	sunk 6.6.1944
LCI(L)233, 7.1945- LCI(G)233	Geo Lawley, Neponset	12.1942	13.1.1943	1.1943	landing craft gun 7.1945, stricken 1946
LCI(L)234, 7.1945- LCI(G)234	Geo Lawley, Neponset	12.1942	16.1.1943	1.1943	landing craft gun 7.1945, stricken 1946
LCI(L)235, 7.1945- LCI(G)235, 9.1945- LCI(L)235	Geo Lawley, Neponset	1.1943	21.1.1943	1.1943	landing craft gun 7.1945, landing craft 9.1945, stricken 1946
LCI(L)236, 7.1945- LCI(G)236, 9.1945- LCI(L)236	Geo Lawley, Neponset	1943	1.1943	1.1943	landing craft gun 7.1945, landing craft 9.1945, stricken 1946
LCI(L)237, 6.1944- LCI(R)237	Geo Lawley, Neponset	1.1943	30.1.1943	2.1943	landing craft rocket 6.1944, stricken 1946
LCI(L)238	New Jersey SB, Barber	1.1943	4.2.1943	2.1943	to the UK 11.1944 (LCI(L)238)
LCI(L)239	New Jersey SB, Barber	8.1942	12.9.1942	11.1942	to the UK 11.1942 (LCI(L)239)
LCI(L)240	New Jersey SB, Barber	8.1942	12.9.1942	11.1942	to the UK 11.1942 (LCI(L)240)
LCI(L)241	New Jersey SB, Barber	8.1942	12.9.1942	(11.1942)	to the UK 11.1942 (LCI(L)241)
LCI(L)242	New Jersey SB, Barber	8.1942	12.9.1942	(11.1942)	to the UK 11.1942 (LCI(L)242)
LCI(L)243	New Jersey SB, Barber	8.1942	12.9.1942	(11.1942)	to Canada 11.1942 (LCI(S)243)
LCI(L)244	New Jersey SB, Barber	8.1942	12.9.1942	(10.1942)	to India 10.1942 (LCI(L)244)
LCI(L)245	New Jersey SB, Barber	9.1942	10.1942	11.1942	to the UK 11.1942 (LCI(L)245)
LCI(L)246	New Jersey SB, Barber	9.1942	19.10.1942	11.1942	to the UK 12.1942 (LCI(L)246)
LCI(L)247	New Jersey SB, Barber	10.1942	20.11.1942	(12.1942)	to the UK 12.1942 (LCI(L)247)
LCI(L)248	New Jersey SB, Barber	10.1942	21.11.1942	12.1942	to the UK 12.1942 (LCI(L)248)
LCI(L)249	New Jersey SB, Barber	10.1942	15.12.1942	(12.1942)	to the UK 12.1942 (LCI(L)249)
LCI(L)250	New Jersey SB, Barber	10.1942	16.12.1942	(12.1942)	to the UK 12.1942 (LCI(L)250)
LCI(L)251	New Jersey SB, Barber	9.1942	18.10.1942	(12.1942)	to the UK 12.1942 (LCI(L)251)
LCI(L)252	New Jersey SB, Barber	9.1942	18.10.1942	(12.1942)	to the UK 11.1942 (LCI(L)252)
LCI(L)253	New Jersey SB, Barber	9.1942	18.10.1942	1.1943	to the UK 1.1943 (LCI(L)253)
LCI(L)254	New Jersey SB, Barber	9.1942	18.10.1942	1.1943	to the UK 1.1943 (LCI(L)254)
LCI(L)255	New Jersey SB, Barber	9.1942	18.10.1942	(1.1943)	to the UK 1.1943 (LCI(L)255)
LCI(L)256	New Jersey SB, Barber	9.1942	18.10.1942	(1.1943)	to the UK 1.1943 (LCI(L)256)
LCI(L)257	New Jersey SB, Barber	10.1942	30.12.1942	(2.1943)	to the UK 2.1943 (LCI(L)257)
LCI(L)258	New Jersey SB, Barber	10.1942	6.2.1943	(2.1943)	to the UK 2.1943 (LCI(L)258)
LCI(L)259	New Jersey SB, Barber	10.1942	19.2.1943	(3.1943)	to the UK 3.1943 (LCI(L)259)
LCI(L)260	New Jersey SB, Barber	10.1942	13.3.1943	(3.1943)	to Canada 12.1942 (LCI(L)260)

LCI(L)261	New Jersey SB, Barber	10.1942	19.3.1943	(3.1943)	to the UK 3.1943 (LCI(L)261)
LCI(L)262	New Jersey SB, Barber	10.1942	17.12.1942	(1.1943)	to the UK 1.1943 (LCI(L)262)
LCI(L)263	New Jersey SB, Barber	10.1942	18.12.1942	(1.1943)	to the UK 1.1943 (LCI(L)263)
LCI(L)264	New Jersey SB, Barber	11.1942	22.12.1942	1.1943	to Canada 1.1943 (LCI(L)264)
LCI(L)265	New Jersey SB, Barber	11.1942	23.12.1942	(1.1943)	to the UK 1.1943 (LCI(L)265)
LCI(L)266	New Jersey SB, Barber	11.1942	6.1.1943	(1.1943)	to the UK 1.1943 (LCI(L)266)
LCI(L)267	New Jersey SB, Barber	11.1942	16.1.1943	(2.1943)	to the UK 2.1943 (LCI(L)267)
LCI(L)268	New Jersey SB, Barber	11.1942	31.12.1942	1.1943	to the UK 1.1943 (LCI(L)268)
LCI(L)269	New Jersey SB, Barber	11.1942	7.1.1943	1.1943	to the UK 1.1943 (LCH269)
LCI(L)270	New Jersey SB, Barber	11.1942	12.1.1943	(1.1943)	to the UK 1.1943 (LCI(L)270)
LCI(L)271	New Jersey SB, Barber	11.1942	29.1.1943	(2.1943)	to the UK 2.1943 (LCI(L)271)
LCI(L)272	New Jersey SB, Barber	11.1942	10.2.1943	2.1943	to the UK 2.1943 (LCI(L)272)
LCI(L)273	New Jersey SB, Barber	11.1942	14.1.1943	2.1943	to the UK 2.1943 (LCI(L)273)
LCI(L)274	New Jersey SB, Barber	11.1942	22.1.1943	2.1943	to the UK 2.1943 (LCI(L)274)
LCI(L)275	New Jersey SB, Barber	12.1942	4.2.1943	2.1943	to the UK 2.1943 (LCH275)
LCI(L)276	New Jersey SB, Barber	12.1942	18.2.1943	(3.1943)	to the UK 3.1943 (LCI(L)276)
LCI(L)277	New Jersey SB, Barber	12.1942	26.2.1943	(3.1943)	to the UK 3.1943 (LCI(L)277)
LCI(L)278	New Jersey SB, Barber	1.1943	18.3.1943	(3.1943)	to the UK 3.1943 (LCI(L)278)
LCI(L)279	New Jersey SB, Barber	12.1942	30.1.1943	2.1943	to the UK 2.1943 (LCI(L)279)
LCI(L)280	New Jersey SB, Barber	12.1942	5.2.1942	2.1943	to the UK 2.1943 (LCI(L)280)
LCI(L)281	New Jersey SB, Barber	12.1942	12.2.1942	(3.1943)	to the UK 3.1943 (LCI(L)281)
LCI(L)282	New Jersey SB, Barber	1.1943	15.2.1943	(3.1943)	to the UK 3.1943 (LCI(L)282)
LCI(L)283	New Jersey SB, Barber	1.1943	17.2.1943	(3.1943)	to the UK 3.1943 (LCI(L)283)
LCI(L)284	New Jersey SB, Barber	1.1943	23.2.1943	(3.1943)	to the UK 3.1943 (LCI(L)284)
LCI(L)285	New Jersey SB, Barber	1.1943	24.2.1943	(3.1943) / 9.1944	to the UK 3.1943-9.1944 (LCI(L)285), stricken 1946
LCI(L)286	New Jersey SB, Barber	1.1943	17.2.1943	(3.1943)	to the UK 3.1943 (LCI(L)286)
LCI(L)287	New Jersey SB, Barber	1.1943	12.3.1943	(3.1943)	to the UK 3.1943 (LCI(L)287)
LCI(L)288	New Jersey SB, Barber	1.1943	27.2.1943	(3.1943)	to the UK 3.1943 (LCI(L)288)
LCI(L)289	New Jersey SB, Barber	1.1943	27.2.1943	(3.1943)	to the UK 3.1943 (LCI(L)289)
LCI(L)290	New Jersey SB, Barber	1.1943	11.2.1943	(3.1943)	to the UK 3.1943 (LCI(L)290)
LCI(L)291	New Jersey SB, Barber	2.1943	25.3.1943	(3.1943)	to the UK 3.1943 (LCI(L)291)
LCI(L)292	New Jersey SB, Barber	2.1943	22.3.1943	(3.1943)	to the UK 3.1943 (LCI(L)292)
LCI(L)293	New Jersey SB, Barber	2.1943	11.3.1943	(3.1943)	to the UK 3.1943 (LCI(L)293)
LCI(L)294	New Jersey SB, Barber	2.1943	25.3.1943	(3.1943)	to the UK 3.1943 (LCI(L)294)
LCI(L)295	New Jersey SB, Barber	2.1943	27.3.1943	(4.1943)	to the UK 4.1943 (LCI(L)295)
LCI(L)296	New Jersey SB, Barber	10.1942	21.11.1942	1.1943	to the UK 1.1943 (LCI(L)296)
LCI(L)297	New Jersey SB, Barber	10.1942	21.11.1942	1.1943	to the UK 1.1943 (LCI(L)297)
LCI(L)298	New Jersey SB, Barber	10.1942	21.11.1942	(1.1943)	to the UK 1.1943 (LCI(L)298)
LCI(L)299	New Jersey SB, Barber	10.1942	21.11.1942	(1.1943)	to the UK 1.1943 (LCI(L)299)
LCI(L)300	New Jersey SB, Barber	10.1942	21.11.1942	(1.1943)	to the UK 1.1943 (LCI(L)300)
LCI(L)301	New Jersey SB, Barber	10.1942	21.11.1942	(2.1943)	to the UK 2.1943 (LCI(L)301)
LCI(L)302	New Jersey SB, Barber	2.1943	31.3.1943	(4.1943)	to the UK 4.1943 (LCI(L)302)
LCI(L)303	New Jersey SB, Barber	2.1943	1.4.1943	(4.1943)	to the UK 4.1943 (LCI(L)303)
LCI(L)304	New Jersey SB, Barber	2.1943	25.2.1943	(3.1943)	to the UK 3.1943 (LCI(L)304)
LCI(L)305	New Jersey SB, Barber	2.1943	9.3.1943	(3.1943)	to the UK 3.1943 (LCI(L)305)
LCI(L)306	New Jersey SB, Barber	2.1943	26.3.1943	(4.1943)	to the UK 4.1943 (LCI(L)306)
LCI(L)307	New Jersey SB, Barber	2.1943	23.3.1943	(3.1943)	to the UK 3.1943 (LCI(L)307)
LCI(L)308	New Jersey SB, Barber	2.1943	25.3.1943	(4.1943)	to the UK 4.1943 (LCI(L)308)
LCI(L)309	New Jersey SB, Barber	2.1943	27.3.1943	(4.1943)	to the UK 4.1943 (LCI(L)309)
LCI(L)310	New Jersey SB, Barber	2.1943	31.3.1943	(4.1943)	to the UK 4.1943 (LCI(L)310)
LCI(L)311	New Jersey SB, Barber	3.1943	1.4.1943	(4.1943)	to the UK 4.1943 (LCI(L)311)

LCI(L)312	New Jersey SB, Barber	3.1943	30.3.1943	(4.1943)	to the UK 4.1943 (LCI(L)312)
LCI(L)313	New Jersey SB, Barber	11.1942	12.12.1942	(2.1943)	to the UK 2.1943 (LCI(L)313)
LCI(L)314	New Jersey SB, Barber	11.1942	12.12.1942	(2.1943)	to the UK 2.1943 (LCI(L)314)
LCI(L)315	New Jersey SB, Barber	11.1942	12.12.1942	(2.1943)	to the UK 2.1943 (LCI(L)315)
LCI(L)316	New Jersey SB, Barber	11.1942	12.12.1942	(2.1943)	to the UK 2.1943 (LCI(L)316)
LCI(L)317	New Jersey SB, Barber	11.1942	12.12.1942	(2.1943)	to the UK 2.1943 (LCH317)
LCI(L)318	New Jersey SB, Barber	11.1942	12.12.1942	(2.1943)	to the UK 2.1943 (LCI(L)318)
LCI(L)319	Brown SB, Houston	11.1942	12.1942	2.1943	stricken 1946
LCI(L)320	Brown SB, Houston	11.1942	21.12.1942	2.1943	stricken 1946
LCI(L)321	Brown SB, Houston	11.1942	21.1.1943	2.1943	stricken 1946
LCI(L)322	Brown SB, Houston	12.1942	3.2.1943	2.1943	stricken 1946
LCI(L)323	Brown SB, Houston	12.1942	22.1.1943	2.1943	stricken 1946
LCI(L)324	Brown SB, Houston	12.1942	1.1943	2.1943	stricken 1946
LCI(L)325	Brown SB, Houston	12.1942	29.1.1943	2.1943	stricken 1946
LCI(L)326	Brown SB, Houston	1942	1942	10.1942	stricken 1946
LCI(L)327	Brown SB, Houston	1942	1942	10.1942	destroyed as target 30.10.1947
LCI(L)328	Brown SB, Houston	7.1942	12.9.1942	10.1942	sold 11.1945
LCI(L)329	Brown SB, Houston	1942	1942	11.1942	scuttled 16.3.1948
LCI(L)330	Brown SB, Houston	7.1942	22.9.1942	11.1942	stricken 1946
LCI(L)331, 7.1945- LCI(R)331	Brown SB, Houston	1942	1942	11.1942	landing craft rocket 7.1945, stricken 1946
LCI(L)332	Brown SB, Houston	1942	1942	11.1942	stricken 1946
LCI(L)333	Brown SB, Houston	7.1942	26.9.1942	11.1942	stricken 1946
LCI(L)334	Brown SB, Houston	7.1942	3.10.1942	11.1942	stricken 1946
LCI(L)335	Brown SB, Houston	7.1942	9.10.1942	11.1942	stricken 1946
LCI(L)336	Brown SB, Houston	7.1942	13.10.1942	12.1942	stricken 1946
LCI(L)337, 7.1945- LCI(R)337	Brown SB, Houston	9.1942	21.10.1942	12.1942	landing craft rocket 7.1945, stricken 1.1946
LCI(L)338, 7.1945- LCI(R)338	Brown SB, Houston	9.1942	24.10.1942	11.1942	landing craft rocket 7.1945, stricken 1946
LCI(L)339	Brown SB, Houston	1942	1942	12.1942	sunk 4.9.1943
LCI(L)340, 7.1945- LCI(R)340	Brown SB, Houston	10.1942	31.10.1942	12.1942	landing craft rocket 7.1945, stricken 1946
LCI(L)341, 7.1945- LCI(R)341	Brown SB, Houston	10.1942	7.11.1942	12.1942	landing craft rocket 1.1944, stricken 1946
LCI(L)342, 7.1945- LCI(R)342	Brown SB, Houston	10.1942	7.11.1942	12.1942	landing craft rocket 7.1945, stricken 1946
LCI(L)343	Brown SB, Houston	10.1942	12.11.1942	1.1943	stricken 1946
LCI(L)344	Brown SB, Houston	10.1942	2.12.1942	1.1943	stricken 1946
LCI(L)345, 6.1944- LCI(G)345	Brown SB, Houston	1942	3.12.1942	1.1943	landing craft gun 6.1944, stricken 1946
LCI(L)346, 6.1944- LCI(G)346	Brown SB, Houston	10.1942	3.12.1942	1.1943	landing craft gun 6.1944, stricken 1946
LCI(L)347, 6.1944- LCI(G)347	Brown SB, Houston	10.1942	3.12.1942	1.1943	landing craft gun 6.1944, stricken 1946
LCI(L)348, 6.1944- LCI(G)348	Brown SB, Houston	11.1942	21.12.1942	1.1943	landing craft gun 6.1944, stricken 1946
LCI(L)349	Brown SB, Houston	11.1942	21.12.1942	1.1943	stricken 1946
LCI(L)350	Brown SB, Houston	11.1942	21.12.1942	2.1943	stricken 1946
LCI(L)351, 12.1944- LCI(G)351, 4.1945- LCI(M)351	Geo Lawley, Neponset	3.1943	8.4.1943	5.1943	landing craft gun 12.1944, landing craft mortar 4.1945, stricken 1946

LCI(L)352, 12.1944- LCI(G)352, 4.1945- LCI(M)352	Geo Lawley, Neponset	1943	1943	5.1943	landing craft gun 12.1944, landing craft mortar 4.1945, stricken 1946
LCI(L)353, 12.1944- LCI(G)353, 4.1945- LCI(M)353	Geo Lawley, Neponset	3.1943	30.4.1943	5.1943	landing craft gun 12.1944, landing craft mortar 4.1945, stricken 1946
LCI(L)354, 12.1944- LCI(G)354, 4.1945- LCI(M)354	Geo Lawley, Neponset	1943	1943	6.1943	landing craft gun 12.1944, landing craft mortar 4.1945, stricken 1946
LCI(L)355, 12.1944- LCI(G)355, 4.1945- LCI(M)355	Geo Lawley, Neponset	4.1943	20.5.1943	6.1943	landing craft gun 12.1944, landing craft mortar 4.1945, stricken 1946
LCI(L)356, 12.1944- LCI(G)356, 4.1945- LCI(M)356	Geo Lawley, Neponset	4.1943	27.5.1943	6.1943	landing craft gun 12.1944, landing craft mortar 4.1945, stricken 1946
LCI(L)357	Geo Lawley, Neponset	1943	1943	6.1943	stricken 1946
LCI(L)358	Geo Lawley, Neponset	1943	1943	6.1943	stricken 1946
LCI(L)359, 4.1945- LCI(M)359	Geo Lawley, Neponset	1943	1943	7.1943	landing craft mortar 4.1945, stricken 1946
LCI(L)360	Geo Lawley, Neponset	6.1943	29.6.1943	7.1943	stricken 1946
LCI(L)361	Geo Lawley, Neponset	6.1943	9.7.1943	7.1943	stricken 1946
LCI(L)362, 4.1945- LCI(M)362	Geo Lawley, Neponset	6.1943	16.7.1943	7.1943	landing craft mortar 4.1945, stricken 1946
LCI(L)363	Geo Lawley, Neponset	1943	1943	7.1943	stricken 1946
LCI(L)364	Geo Lawley, Neponset	1943	1943	6.1943	stricken 1946
LCI(L)365, 6.1944- LCI(G)365	Geo Lawley, Neponset	7.1943	3.8.1943	8.1943	landing craft gun 6.1944, damaged 10.1.1945, never repaired
LCI(L)366, 6.1944- LCI(G)366	Geo Lawley, Neponset	7.1943	9.8.1943	8.1943	landing craft gun 6.1944, stricken 1946
LCI(L)367, 12.1944- LC(FF)367	Geo Lawley, Neponset	1943	1943	8.1943	landing craft flotilla flagship 12.1944, stricken 1950
LCI(L)368, 12.1944- LC(FF)368	Geo Lawley, Neponset	8.1943	23.8.1943	8.1943	landing craft flotilla flagship 12.1944, stricken 1946
LCI(L)369, 12.1944- LC(FF)369	Geo Lawley, Neponset	1943	1943	8.1943	landing craft flotilla flagship 12.1944, stricken 1946
LCI(L)370, 12.1944- LC(FF)370	Geo Lawley, Neponset	8.1943	8.9.1943	9.1943	landing craft flotilla flagship 12.1944, to the MarCom 3.1948
LCI(L)371, 6.1944- LCI(G)371	Geo Lawley, Neponset	1943	1943	9.1943	landing craft gun 6.1944, stricken 1946
LCI(L)372, 6.1944- LCI(G)372	Geo Lawley, Neponset	1943	1943	9.1943	landing craft gun 6.1944, stricken 1946
LCI(L)373, 6.1944- LCI(G)373	Geo Lawley, Neponset	1943	1943	9.1943	landing craft gun 6.1944, stricken 1946
LCI(L)374	Geo Lawley, Neponset	9.1943	27.9.1943	(10.1943)	to the UK 10.1943 (LCI(L)374)
LCI(L)375	Geo Lawley, Neponset	9.1943	3.10.1943	(10.1943)	to the UK 10.1943 (LCI(L)375)
LCI(L)376	Geo Lawley, Neponset	9.1943	8.10.1943	(10.1943)	to the UK 10.1943 (LCI(L)376)
LCI(L)377	Geo Lawley, Neponset	9.1943	14.10.1943	(10.1943)	to the UK 10.1943 (LCI(L)377)
LCI(L)378	Geo Lawley, Neponset	9.1943	18.10.1943	(10.1943)	to the UK 10.1943 (LCI(L)378)
LCI(L)379	Geo Lawley, Neponset	10.1943	23.10.1943	(10.1943)	to the UK 10.1943 (LCI(L)379)
LCI(L)380	Geo Lawley, Neponset	10.1943	28.10.1943	(10.1943)	to the UK 10.1943 (LCI(L)380)
LCI(L)381	Geo Lawley, Neponset	10.1943	29.10.1943	(11.1943)	to the UK 11.1943 (LCI(L)381)
LCI(L)382	Geo Lawley, Neponset	10.1943	4.11.1943	(11.1943)	to the UK 11.1943 (LCI(L)382)

LCI(L)383	Geo Lawley, Neponset	10.1943	7.11.1943	(11.1943)	to the UK 11.1943 (LCI(L)383)
LCI(L)384	Geo Lawley, Neponset	10.1943	11.11.1943	(11.1943)	to the UK 11.1943 (LCI(L)384)
LCI(L)385	Geo Lawley, Neponset	10.1943	15.11.1943	(11.1943)	to the UK 11.1943 (LCI(L)385)
LCI(L)386	Geo Lawley, Neponset	11.1943	17.11.1943	(11.1943)	to the UK 11.1943 (LCI(L)386)
LCI(L)387	Geo Lawley, Neponset	11.1943	20.11.1943	(11.1943)	to the UK 11.1943 (LCI(L)387)
LCI(L)388	Geo Lawley, Neponset	11.1943	25.11.1943	(11.1943)	to the UK 11.1943 (LCI(L)388)
LCI(L)389	Geo Lawley, Neponset	11.1943	27.11.1943	11.1943	to the UK 11.1943 (LCI(L)389)
LCI(L)390	Geo Lawley, Neponset	11.1943	28.11.1943	11.1943	to the UK 12.1943 (LCI(L)390)
LCI(L)391	Geo Lawley, Neponset	11.1943	2.12.1943	12.1943	to the UK 12.1943 (LCI(L)391)
LCI(L)392	Geo Lawley, Neponset	1943	1943	12.1943	stricken 1946
LCI(L)393	Geo Lawley, Neponset	1943	1943	12.1943	stricken 1946
LCI(L)394	Geo Lawley, Neponset	1943	1943	12.1943	stricken 1946
LCI(L)395	Geo Lawley, Neponset	1943	1943	12.1943	stricken 1946
LCI(L)396, 6.1944- LCI(G)396	Geo Lawley, Neponset	1943	1943	12.1943	landing craft gun 6.1944, test ship 2.1945
LCI(L)397, 6.1944- LCI(G)397	Geo Lawley, Neponset	1943	1943	12.1943	landing craft gun 6.1944, stricken 1946
LCI(L)398, 7.1944- LCI(G)398	Geo Lawley, Neponset	12.1943	20.12.1943	12.1943	landing craft gun 7.1944, stricken 1946
LCI(L)399, 7.1945- LC(FF)399	Geo Lawley, Neponset	12.1943	23.12.1943	12.1943	landing craft flotilla flagship 7.1945, wrecked 16.12.1945
LCI(L)400, 3.1945- AMCU8	Geo Lawley, Neponset	12.1943	29.12.1943	12.1943	minehunter 1945, to the MarCom 1947
LCI(L)401, 7.1945- LCI(G)401	Geo Lawley, Neponset	1943	1.1944	1.1944	landing craft gun 7.1945, stricken 1946
LCI(L)402	Geo Lawley, Neponset	1943	1.1944	1.1944	stricken 1946
LCI(L)403, 7.1945- LCI(G)403	Geo Lawley, Neponset	12.1943	7.1.1944	1.1944	landing craft gun 7.1945, stricken 1946
LCI(L)404, 6.1945- LCI(G)404	Geo Lawley, Neponset	1.1944	9.1.1944	1.1944	landing craft gun 6.1945, to the Philippines 7.1948
LCI(L)405, 6.1944- LCI(G)405	Geo Lawley, Neponset	1.1944	12.1.1944	1.1944	landing craft gun 6.1944, stricken 1946
LCI(L)406, 6.1944- LCI(G)406	Geo Lawley, Neponset	1.1944	15.1.1944	1.1944	landing craft gun 6.1944, stricken 1946
LCI(L)407, 6.1944- LCI(G)407	Geo Lawley, Neponset	1.1944	16.1.1944	1.1944	landing craft gun 6.1944, stricken 1946
LCI(L)408, 7.1945- LCI(G)408	Geo Lawley, Neponset	1.1944	1.1944	1.1944	landing craft gun 7.1945, stricken 1946
LCI(L)409, 3.1945- AMCU9	Geo Lawley, Neponset	1.1944	20.1.1944	1.1944	minehunter 3.1945, to the MarCom 1947
LCI(L)410	Geo Lawley, Neponset	1.1944	22.1.1944	1.1944	stricken 1946
LCI(L)411	Geo Lawley, Neponset	1.1944	24.1.1944	1.1944	to the UK 11.1944 (LCI(L)411)
LCI(L)412, 7.1945- LCI(G)412	Geo Lawley, Neponset	1.1944	26.1.1944	1.1944	landing craft gun 7.1945, stricken 1946
LCI(L)413, 7.1945- LCI(G)413	Geo Lawley, Neponset	1944	1944	2.1944	landing craft gun 7.1945, stricken 1946
LCI(L)414, 7.1945- LCI(G)414	Geo Lawley, Neponset	1944	1944	2.1944	landing craft gun 7.1945, stricken 1946
LCI(L)415, 7.1945- LCI(G)415	Geo Lawley, Neponset	1944	1944	2.1944	landing craft gun 7.1945, stricken 1946
LCI(L)416	Geo Lawley, Neponset	1944	1944	2.1944	sunk 9.6.1944
LCI(L)417, 7.1945- LCI(G)417	Geo Lawley, Neponset	2.1944	9.2.1944	2.1944	landing craft gun 7.1945, to China 2.1948 (Liengli)

LCI(L)418, 7.1945- LCI(G)418	Geo Lawley, Neponset	1944	1944	2.1944	landing craft gun 7.1945, to China 2.1948 (Liengsheng)
LCI(L)419, 7.1945- LCI(G)419	Geo Lawley, Neponset	2.1944	14.2.1944	2.1944	landing craft gun 7.1945, for disposal 2.1946
LCI(L)420, 7.1945- LCI(G)420	Geo Lawley, Neponset	2.1944	16.2.1944	2.1944	landing craft gun 7.1945, to the Netherlands 1946
LCI(L)421, 7.1945- LCI(G)421	Geo Lawley, Neponset	1944	1944	2.1944	landing craft gun 7.1945, stricken 1946
LCI(L)422, 7.1945- LCI(G)422	Geo Lawley, Neponset	2.1944	2.1944	2.1944	landing craft gun 7.1945, for disposal 3.1946
LCI(L)423, 12.1944- LC(FF)423	New Jersey SB, Barber	1943	1943	6.1943	landing craft flotilla flagship 12.1944, stricken 1946
LCI(L)424, 12.1944- LC(FF)424	New Jersey SB, Barber	1943	1943	6.1943	landing craft flotilla flagship 12.1944, stricken 1946
LCI(L)425, 12.1944- LC(FF)425	New Jersey SB, Barber	1943	1943	6.1943	landing craft flotilla flagship 12.1944, to MarCom 11.1947
LCI(L)426, 12.1944- LC(FF)426	New Jersey SB, Barber	1943	1943	6.1943	landing craft flotilla flagship 12.1944, stricken 1946
LCI(L)427, 12.1944- LC(FF)427	New Jersey SB, Barber	1943	1943	7.1943	landing craft flotilla flagship 12.1944, stricken 1946
LCI(L)428, 7.1945- LCI(G)428	New Jersey SB, Barber	1943	1943	7.1943	landing craft gun 7.1945, stricken 1946
LCI(L)429	New Jersey SB, Barber	1943	1943	7.1943	stricken 1946
LCI(L)430	New Jersey SB, Barber	1943	1943	7.1943	stricken 1946
LCI(L)431, 4.1945- LCI(M)431	New Jersey SB, Barber	1943	1943	7.1943	landing craft mortar 4.1945, stricken 1946
LCI(L)432	New Jersey SB, Barber	1943	1943	7.1943	stricken 1946
LCI(L)433	New Jersey SB, Barber	1943	1943	7.1943	stricken 1946
LCI(L)434	New Jersey SB, Barber	1943	1943	7.1943	stricken 1946
LCI(L)435	New Jersey SB, Barber	4.1943	8.7.1943	7.1943	stricken 1946
LCI(L)436	New Jersey SB, Barber	1943	1943	7.1943	stricken 1946
LCI(L)437, 6.1944- LCI(G)437	New Jersey SB, Barber	1943	1943	7.1943	landing craft gun 6.1944, stricken 1946
LCI(L)438, 6.1944- LCI(G)438	New Jersey SB, Barber	1943	1943	8.1943	landing craft gun 6.1944, stricken 1946
LCI(L)439, 1.1944- LCI(G)439	New Jersey SB, Barber	4.1943	21.7.1943	8.1943	landing craft gun 1.1944, stricken 1946
LCI(L)440, 6.1944- LCI(G)440	New Jersey SB, Barber	1943	1943	8.1943	landing craft gun 6.1944, stricken 1946
LCI(L)441, 6.1944- LCI(G)441	New Jersey SB, Barber	4.1943	20.7.1943	8.1943	landing craft gun 6.1944, stricken 1946
LCI(L)442, 7.1944- LCI(G)442	New Jersey SB, Barber	5.1943	31.7.1943	8.1943	landing craft gun 7.1944, stricken 1946
LCI(L)443	New Jersey SB, Barber	5.1943	2.8.1943	8.1943	stricken 1946
LCI(L)444	New Jersey SB, Barber	1943	1943	8.1943	stricken 1946
LCI(L)445	New Jersey SB, Barber	1943	1943	8.1943	stricken 1946
LCI(L)446	New Jersey SB, Barber	1943	1943	8.1943	stricken 1946
LCI(L)447	New Jersey SB, Barber	1943	1943	8.1943	stricken 1946
LCI(L)448	New Jersey SB, Barber	1943	1943	8.1943	stricken 1946
LCI(L)449, 6.1944- LCI(G)449	New Jersey SB, Barber	6.1943	14.8.1943	8.1943	landing craft gun 6.1944, stricken 1946
LCI(L)450, 6.1944- LCI(G)450	New Jersey SB, Barber	1943	1943	8.1943	landing craft gun 6.1944, stricken 1946

LCI(L)451, 6.1944- LCI(G)451	New Jersey SB, Barber	6.1943	19.8.1943	8.1943	landing craft gun 6.1944, stricken 1946
LCI(L)452, 6.1944- LCI(G)452	New Jersey SB, Barber	1943	1943	8.1943	landing craft gun 6.1944, stricken 1946
LCI(L)453, 6.1944- LCI(G)453	New Jersey SB, Barber	1943	1943	8.1943	landing craft gun 6.1944, stricken 1946
LCI(L)454, 6.1944- LCI(G)454	New Jersey SB, Barber	7.1943	25.8.1943	9.1943	landing craft gun 6.1944, stricken 1946
LCI(L)455, 6.1944- LCI(G)455	New Jersey SB, Barber	7.1943	26.8.1943	9.1943	landing craft gun 6.1944, stricken 1946
LCI(L)456, 6.1944- LCI(G)456	New Jersey SB, Barber	7.1943	27.8.1943	9.1943	landing craft gun 6.1944, stricken 1946
LCI(L)457, 6.1944- LCI(G)457	New Jersey SB, Barber	7.1943	28.8.1943	9.1943	landing craft gun 6.1944, stricken 1946
LCI(L)458, 6.1944- LCI(G)458	New Jersey SB, Barber	7.1943	1.9.1943	9.1943	landing craft gun 6.1944, stricken 1946
LCI(L)459, 6.1944- LCI(G)459	New Jersey SB, Barber	1943	1943	9.1943	landing craft gun 6.1944, sunk 19.9.1944
LCI(L)460, 6.1944- LCI(G)460	New Jersey SB, Barber	1943	1943	9.1943	landing craft gun 6.1944, stricken 1946
LCI(L)461, 6.1944- LCI(G)461	New Jersey SB, Barber	1943	1943	9.1943	landing craft gun 6.1944, stricken 1946
LCI(L)462, 6.1944- LCI(G)462	New Jersey SB, Barber	1943	1943	9.1943	landing craft gun 6.1944, stricken 1946
LCI(L)463, 6.1944- LCI(G)463	New Jersey SB, Barber	1943	1943	9.1943	landing craft gun 6.1944, stricken 1946
LCI(L)464, 6.1944- LCI(G)464	New Jersey SB, Barber	1943	1943	9.1943	landing craft gun 6.1944, stricken 1946
LCI(L)465, 6.1944- LCI(G)465	New Jersey SB, Barber	1943	1943	9.1943	landing craft gun 6.1944, stricken 1946
LCI(L)466, 6.1944- LCI(L)466	New Jersey SB, Barber	1943	1943	9.1943	landing craft gun 6.1944, stricken 1946
LCI(L)467, 6.1944- LCI(G)467	New Jersey SB, Barber	8.1943	16.9.1943	9.1943	landing craft gun 6.1944, to the Netherlands 5.1946
LCI(L)468, 6.1944- LCI(G)468	New Jersey SB, Barber	8.1943	9.1943	9.1943	landing craft gun 6.1944, sunk 18.6.1944
LCI(L)469, 6.1944- LCI(G)469	New Jersey SB, Barber	8.1943	18.9.1943	9.1943	landing craft gun 6.1944, stricken 1946
LCI(L)470, 6.1944- LCI(G)470	New Jersey SB, Barber	1943	1943	9.1943	landing craft gun 6.1944, stricken 1946
LCI(L)471, 6.1944- LCI(G)471	New Jersey SB, Barber	8.1943	23.9.1943	9.1943	landing craft gun 6.1944, stricken 1946
LCI(L)472, 6.1944- LCI(G)472	New Jersey SB, Barber	8.1943	24.9.1943	10.1943	landing craft gun 6.1944, stricken 1946
LCI(L)473, 6.1944- LCI(G)473	New Jersey SB, Barber	1943	1943	10.1943	landing craft gun 6.1944, stricken 1946
LCI(L)474, 6.1944- LCI(G)474	New Jersey SB, Barber	1943	1943	10.1943	landing craft gun 6.1944, sunk 17.2.1945
LCI(L)475, 6.1944- LCI(G)475	New Jersey SB, Barber	1943	1943	10.1943	landing craft gun 6.1944, stricken 1946
LCI(L)476	New Jersey SB, Barber	8.1943	2.10.1943	10.1943	to France 1952 (Medecin Capitaine le Gall)
LCI(L)477	New Jersey SB, Barber	1943	1943	10.1943	stricken 1946
LCI(L)478	New Jersey SB, Barber	1943	1943	10.1943	to China 1946

LCI(L)479	New Jersey SB, Barber	1943	1943	10.1943	stricken 1946
LCI(L)480	New Jersey SB, Barber	1943	1943	10.1943	stricken 1946
LCI(L)481	New Jersey SB, Barber	1943	1943	10.1943	stricken 1946
LCI(L)482	New Jersey SB, Barber	1943	1943	10.1943	stricken 1946
LCI(L)483	New Jersey SB, Barber	1943	1943	10.1943	stricken 1946
LCI(L)484, 12.1944- LC(FF)484	New Jersey SB, Barber	1943	1943	10.1943	landing craft flotilla flagship 12.1944, stricken 1946
LCI(L)485, 12.1944- LC(FF)485	New Jersey SB, Barber	1943	1943	10.1943	landing craft flotilla flagship 12.1944, sunk as target 1956
LCI(L)486, 12.1944- LC(FF)486	New Jersey SB, Barber	1943	1943	10.1943	landing craft flotilla flagship 12.1944, stricken 1946
LCI(L)487	New Jersey SB, Barber	9.1943	10.1943	10.1943	to the UK 11.1944 (LCI(L)487)
LCI(L)488	New Jersey SB, Barber	9.1943	10.1943	10.1943	to the UK 11.1944 (LCI(L)488)
LCI(L)489	New Jersey SB, Barber	9.1943	22.10.1943	10.1943	to the UK 11.1944 (LCI(L)489)
LCI(L)490	New Jersey SB, Barber	9.1943	23.10.1943	11.1943	to the UK 11.1944 (LCI(L)490)
LCI(L)491	New Jersey SB, Barber	9.1943	27.10.1943	11.1943	to the UK 11.1944 (LCI(L)491)
LCI(L)492	New Jersey SB, Barber	9.1943	28.10.1943	11.1943	to the UK 11.1944 (LCI(L)492)
LCI(L)493	New Jersey SB, Barber	9.1943	30.10.1943	11.1943	to the UK 11.1944 (LCI(L)493)
LCI(L)494	New Jersey SB, Barber	9.1943	30.10.1943	11.1943	to the UK 11.1944 (LCI(L)494)
LCI(L)495	New Jersey SB, Barber	10.1943	3.11.1943	11.1943	to the UK 11.1944 (LCI(L)495)
LCI(L)496	New Jersey SB, Barber	10.1943	4.11.1943	11.1943	to the UK 11.1944 (LCI(L)496)
LCI(L)497	New Jersey SB, Barber	1943	1943	11.1943	CTL 6.6.1944
LCI(L)498	New Jersey SB, Barber	10.1943	6.11.1943	11.1943	to the UK 11.1944 (LCI(L)498)
LCI(L)499	New Jersey SB, Barber	10.1943	8.11.1943	11.1943	to the UK 11.1944 (LCI(L)499)
LCI(L)500	New Jersey SB, Barber	10.1943	10.11.1943	11.1943	to the UK 11.1944 (LCI(L)500)
LCI(L)501	New Jersey SB, Barber	10.1943	11.11.1943	11.1943	to the UK 11.1944 (LCI(L)501)
LCI(L)502	New Jersey SB, Barber	10.1943	13.11.1943	11.1943	to the UK 11.1944 (LCI(L)502)
LCI(L)503, 12.1944- LC(FF)503	New Jersey SB, Barber	1943	1943	11.1943	landing craft flotilla flagship 12.1944, for disposal 2.1948
LCI(L)504, 12.1944- LC(FF)504	New Jersey SB, Barber	10.1943	18.11.1943	11.1943	landing craft flotilla flagship 12.1944, stricken 1956
LCI(L)505	New Jersey SB, Barber	10.1943	19.11.1943	11.1943	to the UK 11.1944 (LCI(L)505)
LCI(L)506, 7.1945- LCI(G)506	New Jersey SB, Barber	1943	1943	11.1943	landing craft gun 7.1945, stricken 1946
LCI(L)507	New Jersey SB, Barber	10.1943	23.11.1943	11.1943	to the UK 12.1944 (LCI(L)507)
LCI(L)508	New Jersey SB, Barber	11.1943	24.11.1943	11.1943	to the UK 12.1944 (LCI(L)508)
LCI(L)509	New Jersey SB, Barber	11.1943	26.11.1943	12.1943	to the UK 12.1944 (LCI(L)509)
LCI(L)510	New Jersey SB, Barber	11.1943	17.11.1943	12.1943	to the UK 12.1944 (LCI(L)510)
LCI(L)511	New Jersey SB, Barber	11.1943	30.11.1943	12.1943	to the UK 12.1944 (LCI(L)511)
LCI(L)512	New Jersey SB, Barber	11.1943	1.12.1943	12.1943	to the UK 12.1944 (LCI(L)512)
LCI(L)513, 3.1945- AMCU10	New Jersey SB, Barber	11.1943	3.12.1943	12.1943	minehunter 3.1945, to the MarCom 1948
LCI(L)514, 7.1945- LCI(G)514	New Jersey SB, Barber	11.1943	12.1943	12.1943	landing craft gun 7.1945, to China 2.1948 (Liengp])
LCI(L)515, 3.1945- AMCU11	New Jersey SB, Barber	11.1943	4.12.1943	12.1943	minehunter 3.1945, stricken 1960
LCI(L)516, 7.1945- LCI(G)516	New Jersey SB, Barber	11.1943	12.1943	12.1943	landing craft gun 7.1945, stricken 1946
LCI(L)517, 7.1945- LCI(G)517	New Jersey SB, Barber	11.1943	12.1943	12.1943	landing craft gun 7.1945, to China 2.1948 (Chutien)
LCI(L)518	New Jersey SB, Barber	11.1943	12.1943	12.1943	to China 7.1946
LCI(L)519	New Jersey SB, Barber	11.1943	12.1943	12.1943	stricken 1946

LCI(L)520, 3.1944- LCI(H)520	New Jersey SB, Barber	11.1943	12.1943	12.1943	landing craft headquarters 3.1944, to Netherlands 1946
LCI(L)521	New Jersey SB, Barber	11.1943	12.1943	12.1943	to the USSR 7.1945 (DS-8)
LCI(L)522	New Jersey SB, Barber	11.1943	17.12.1943	12.1943	to the USSR 7.1945 (DS-2)
LCI(L)523	New Jersey SB, Barber	11.1943	12.1943	12.1943	to the USSR 7.1945 (DS-3)
LCI(L)524	New Jersey SB, Barber	11.1943	12.1943	12.1943	to the USSR 7.1945 (DS-4)
LCI(L)525	New Jersey SB, Barber	11.1943	12.1943	12.1943	to the USSR 7.1945 (DS-5)
LCI(L)526	New Jersey SB, Barber	11.1943	22.12.1943	12.1943	to the USSR 7.1945 (DS-46)
LCI(L)527	New Jersey SB, Barber	11.1943	12.1943	1.1944	to the USSR 7.1945 (DS-7)
LCI(L)528, 7.1945- LCI(G)528	New Jersey SB, Barber	11.1943	23.12.1943	1.1944	landing craft gun 7.1945, stricken 1946
LCI(L)529	New Jersey SB, Barber	11.1943	23.12.1943	1.1944	stricken 1946
LCI(L)530	New Jersey SB, Barber	12.1943	31.12.1943	1.1944	stricken 1946
LCI(L)531, 12.1944- LC(FF)531	New Jersey SB, Barber	12.1943	1.1944	1.1944	landing craft flotilla flagship 12.1944, for disposal 10.1947
LCI(L)532, 12.1944- LC(FF)532	New Jersey SB, Barber	12.1943	1.1944	1.1944	landing craft flotilla flagship 12.1944, to the MarCom 1.1948
LCI(L)533, 12.1944- LC(FF)533	New Jersey SB, Barber	12.1943	6.1.1944	1.1944	landing craft flotilla flagship 12.1944, stricken 1946
LCI(L)534	New Jersey SB, Barber	12.1943	1.1944	1.1944	stricken 1946
LCI(L)535, 12.1944- LC(FF)535	New Jersey SB, Barber	12.1943	1.1944	1.1944	landing craft flotilla flagship 12.1944, stricken 1946
LCI(L)536, 12.1944- LC(FF)536	New Jersey SB, Barber	12.1943	1.1944	1.1944	landing craft flotilla flagship 12.1944, stricken 1946
LCI(L)537	New Jersey SB, Barber	12.1943	1.1944	1.1944	to the UK 11.1944 (LCI(L)537)
LCI(L)538, 7.1945- LCI(G)538	New Jersey SB, Barber	12.1943	14.1.1944	1.1944	landing craft gun 7.1945, to Naval Academy 1946
LCI(L)539, 7.1945- LCI(G)539	New Jersey SB, Barber	12.1943	1.1944	1.1944	landing craft gun 7.1945, stricken 1946
LCI(L)540, 7.1945- LCI(G)540	New Jersey SB, Barber	12.1943	1.1944	1.1944	landing craft gun 7.1945, stricken 1946
LCI(L)541, 7.2945- LCI(G)541	New Jersey SB, Barber	12.1943	1.1944	1.1944	landing craft gun 7.1945, stricken 1946
LCI(L)542, 7.1945- LCI(G)542	New Jersey SB, Barber	12.1943	1.1944	1.1944	landing craft gun 7.1945, stricken 1946
LCI(L)543, 7.1945- LCI(G)543	New Jersey SB, Barber	12.1943	1.1944	1.1944	landing craft gun 7.1945, stricken 2.1955
LCI(L)544, 7.1945- LCI(G)544, 9.1945- LCI(L)544	New Jersey SB, Barber	12.1943	25.1.1944	1.1944	landing craft gun 7.1945, landing craft 9.1945, stricken 1956
LCI(L)545	New Jersey SB, Barber	12.1943	1.1944	2.1944	stricken 1946
LCI(L)546, 7.1945- LCI(G)546, 9.1945- LCI(L)546	New Jersey SB, Barber	1.1944	1.1944	2.1944	landing craft gun 7.1945, landing craft 9.1945, stricken 1946
LCI(L)547, 7.1945- LCI(G)547, 9.1945- LCI(L)547	New Jersey SB, Barber	1.1944	2.2.1944	2.1944	landing craft gun 7.1945, landing craft 9.1945, stricken 1946
LCI(L)548, 7.1945- LCI(G)548, 9.1945- LCI(L)548	New Jersey SB, Barber	1.1944	2.1944	2.1944	landing craft gun 7.1945, landing craft 9.1945, stricken 1946
LCI(L)549	New Jersey SB, Barber	1.1944	4.2.1944	2.1944	stricken 1946
LCI(L)550	New Jersey SB, Barber	1.1944	2.1944	2.1944	stricken 1946
LCI(L)551	New Jersey SB, Barber	1.1944	7.2.1944	2.1944	to the USSR 7.1945 (DS-48)

LCI(L)552	New Jersey SB, Barber	1.1944	8.2.1944	2.1944	stricken 1946
LCI(L)553	New Jersey SB, Barber	1.1944	2.1944	2.1944	sunk 6.6.1944
LCI(L)554	New Jersey SB, Barber	1.1944	2.1944	2.1944	to the USSR 7.1945 (DS-9)
LCI(L)555	New Jersey SB, Barber	1.1944	2.1944	2.1944	stricken 1946
LCI(L)556, 7.1945- LCI(G)556	New Jersey SB, Barber	1.1944	2.1944	2.1944	landing craft gun 7.1945, stricken 1946
LCI(L)557	New Jersey SB, Barber	1.1944	2.1944	2.1944	to the USSR 7.1945 (DS-10)
LCI(L)558, 6.1944- LCI(G)558	New Jersey SB, Barber	1.1944	2.1944	2.1944	landing craft gun 6.1944, to the Netherlands 1946
LCI(L)559, 6.1944- LCI(G)559	New Jersey SB, Barber	1.1944	2.1944	2.1944	landing craft gun 6.1944, to the Netherlands 6.1946
LCI(L)560, 6.1944- LCI(G)560	New Jersey SB, Barber	1.1944	2.1944	2.1944	landing craft gun 6.1944, stricken 1946
LCI(L)561, 6.1944- LCI(G)561	New Jersey SB, Barber	1.1944	2.1944	2.1944	landing craft gun 6.1944, stricken 1946
LCI(L)562	New Jersey SB, Barber	1.1944	24.2.1944	2.1944	stricken 1946
LCI(L)563, 7.1945- LCI(G)563	New Jersey SB, Barber	1.1944	25.2.1944	3.1944	landing craft gun 7.1945, stricken 1946
LCI(L)564, 6.1944- LCI(G)564	New Jersey SB, Barber	1.1944	2.1944	3.1944	landing craft gun 6.1944, to the MarCom 2.1948
LCI(L)565, 6.1944- LCI(G)565	New Jersey SB, Barber	1.1944	2.1944	3.1944	landing craft gun 6.1944, stricken 1946
LCI(L)566, 6.1944- LCI(G)566	New Jersey SB, Barber	2.1944	2.1944	3.1944	landing craft gun 6.1944, stricken 1946
LCI(L)567, 6.1944- LCI(G)567	New Jersey SB, Barber	2.1944	1.3.1944	3.1944	landing craft gun 6.1944, stricken 7.1946
LCI(L)568, 6.1944- LCI(G)568	New Jersey SB, Barber	2.1944	3.1944	3.1944	landing craft gun 6.1944, stricken 1946
LCI(L)569, 12.1944- LC(FF)569	New Jersey SB, Barber	2.1944	3.1944	3.1944	landing craft flotilla flagship 12.1944, stricken 1946
LCI(L)570, 7.1945- LCI(G)570, 9.1945- LCI(L)570	New Jersey SB, Barber	2.1944	3.1944	3.1944	landing craf gun 7.1945, landing craft 9.1945, to the MarCom 8.1947
LCI(L)571, 12.1944- LC(FF)571	New Jersey SB, Barber	2.1944	3.1944	3.1944	landing craft flotilla flagship 12.1944, stricken 1946
LCI(L)572, 12.1944- LC(FF)572	New Jersey SB, Barber	2.1944	3.1944	3.1944	landing craft flotilla flagship 12.1944, stricken 1946
LCI(L)573, 7.1945- LCI(G)573, 9.1945- LCI(L)573	New Jersey SB, Barber	2.1944	10.3.1944	3.1944	landing craft gun 7.1945, landing craft 9.1945, stricken 1946
LCI(L)574, 7.1945- LCI(G)574, 9.1945- LCI(L)574	New Jersey SB, Barber	2.1944	3.1944	3.1944	landing craft gun 7.1945, landing craft 9.1945, to the MarCom 11.1947
LCI(L)575, 12.1944- LC(FF)575	New Jersey SB, Barber	2.1944	3.1944	3.1944	landing craft flotilla flagship 12.1944, sunk as target 1956
LCI(L)576, 7.1945- LCI(G)576, 9.1945- LCI(L)576	New Jersey SB, Barber	2.1944	3.1944	3.1944	landing craft gun 7.1945, landing craft 9.1945, stricken 1946
LCI(L)577, 7.1945- LCI(G)577, 9.1945- LCI(L)577	New Jersey SB, Barber	2.1944	3.1944	3.1944	landing craft gun 7.1945, landing craft 9.1945, stricken 1946
LCI(L)578, 7.1945- LCI(G)578, 9.1945- LCI(L)578	New Jersey SB, Barber	2.1944	3.1944	3.1944	landing craft gun 7.1945, landing craft 9.1945, stricken 1946

LCI(L)579, 7.1945- LCI(G)579, 9.1945- LCI(L)579	New Jersey SB, Barber	2.1944	3.1944	3.1944	landing craft gun 7.1945, landing craft 9.1945, stricken 1946
LCI(L)580, 6.1944- LCI(G)580	New Jersey SB, Barber	2.1944	3.1944	3.1944	landing craft gun 6.1944, stricken 1946
LCI(L)581	New Jersey SB, Barber	2.1944	23.3.1944	3.1944	stricken 1946
LCI(L)582, 5.1945- LCI(M)582	New Jersey SB, Barber	2.1944	24.3.1944	4.1944	landing craft mortar 5.1945, stricken 1946
LCI(L)583	New Jersey SB, Barber	2.1944	28.3.1944	4.1944	stricken 1946
LCI(L)584	New Jersey SB, Barber	3.1944	3.1944	4.1944	to the USSR 6.1945 (DS-38)
LCI(L)585	New Jersey SB, Barber	3.1944	3.1944	4.1944	to the USSR 6.1945 (DS-45)
LCI(L)586	New Jersey SB, Barber	3.1944	31.3.1944	4.1944	to the USSR 6.1945 (DS-37)
LCI(L)587	New Jersey SB, Barber	3.1944	3.4.1944	4.1944	to the USSR 6.1945 (DS-33)
LCI(L)588, 3.1945- LCI(M)588	New Jersey SB, Barber	3.1944	4.1944	4.1944	landing craft mortar 3.1945, to the Netherlands 5.1946
LCI(L)589, 3.1945- AMCU7	New Jersey SB, Barber	3.1944	5.4.1944	4.1944	minehunter 3.1945, to the MarCom 1948
LCI(L)590	New Jersey SB, Barber	3.1944	4.1944	4.1944	to the USSR 6.1945 (DS-34)
LCI(L)591	New Jersey SB, Barber	3.1944	10.4.1944	4.1944	to the USSR 6.1945 (DS-35)
LCI(L)592	New Jersey SB, Barber	3.1944	11.4.1944	4.1944	to the USSR 6.1945 (DS-39)
LCI(L)593	New Jersey SB, Barber	3.1944	12.4.1944	4.1944	to the USSR 6.1945 (DS-31)
LCI(L)594, 5.1945- LCI(M)594	New Jersey SB, Barber	3.1944	17.4.1944	4.1944	landing craft mortar 5.1945, stricken 1946
LCI(L)595, 5.1945- LCI(M)595	New Jersey SB, Barber	3.1944	14.4.1944	4.1944	landing craft mortar 5.1945, stricken 1946
LCI(L)596, 5.1945- LCI(M)596	New Jersey SB, Barber	3.1944	4.1944	4.1944	landing craft mortar 5.1945, stricken 1951
LCI(L)597	New Jersey SB, Barber	3.1944	4.1944	4.1944	stricken 1946
LCI(L)598	New Jersey SB, Barber	3.1944	4.1944	4.1944	stricken 1946
LCI(L)599	New Jersey SB, Barber	3.1944	4.1944	4.1944	stricken 1946
LCI(L)600	New Jersey SB, Barber	3.1944	4.1944	4.1944	sunk 12.1.1945
LCI(L)601	New Jersey SB, Barber	3.1944	28.4.1944	5.1944	stricken 1946
LCI(L)602	New Jersey SB, Barber	3.1944	4.1944	5.1944	stricken 1946
LCI(L)603	New Jersey SB, Barber	4.1944	27.4.1944	5.1944	stricken 1946
LCI(L)604	New Jersey SB, Barber	4.1944	4.1944	5.1944	stricken 1946
LCI(L)605	New Jersey SB, Barber	4.1944	4.1944	5.1944	stricken 1946
LCI(L)606	New Jersey SB, Barber	4.1944	5.1944	5.1944	to Argentina 2.1948 (BDI4)
LCI(L)607	New Jersey SB, Barber	4.1944	5.1944	5.1944	stricken 1946
LCI(L)608	New Jersey SB, Barber	4.1944	5.1944	5.1944	stricken 1946
LCI(L)609	New Jersey SB, Barber	4.1944	5.1944	5.1944	stricken 1946
LCI(L)610	New Jersey SB, Barber	4.1944	5.1944	5.1944	stricken 1946
LCI(L)611	New Jersey SB, Barber	4.1944	5.1944	5.1944	stricken 1946
LCI(L)612	New Jersey SB, Barber	4.1944	5.1944	5.1944	stricken 1946
LCI(L)613	New Jersey SB, Barber	4.1944	5.1944	5.1944	stricken 1946
LCI(L)614	New Jersey SB, Barber	4.1944	5.1944	5.1944	stricken 1946
LCI(L)615	New Jersey SB, Barber	4.1944	5.1944	5.1944	to the MarCom 8.1949
LCI(L)616	New Jersey SB, Barber	4.1944	17.5.1944	5.1944	for disposal 6.1946
LCI(L)617	New Jersey SB, Barber	4.1944	5.1944	5.1944	for disposal 10.1947
LCI(L)618, 12.1944- LC(FF)618	New Jersey SB, Barber	4.1944	19.5.1944	5.1944	landing craft flotilla flagship 12.1944, stricken 1946
LCI(L)619	New Jersey SB, Barber	4.1944	5.1944	5.1944	stricken 1946
LCI(L)620	New Jersey SB, Barber	4.1944	24.5.1944	5.1944	sunk as target 10.8.1946

LCI(L)621	New Jersey SB, Barber	4.1944	25.5.1944	5.1944	stricken 1946
LCI(L)622	New Jersey SB, Barber	4.1944	5.1944	6.1944	stricken 1946
LCI(L)623	New Jersey SB, Barber	4.1944	5.1944	6.1944	stricken 1946
LCI(L)624	New Jersey SB, Barber	5.1944	5.1944	6.1944	stricken 1946
LCI(L)625	New Jersey SB, Barber	5.1944	5.1944	6.1944	stricken 1946
LCI(L)626	New Jersey SB, Barber	5.1944	5.1944	6.1944	stricken 1946
LCI(L)627, 12.1944- LC(FF)627	New Jersey SB, Barber	5.1944	2.6.1944	6.1944	landing craft flotilla flagship 12.1944, stricken 1956
LCI(L)628, 12.1944- LC(FF)628	New Jersey SB, Barber	5.1944	6.1944	6.1944	landing craft flotilla flagship 12.1944, stricken 1956
LCI(L)629	New Jersey SB, Barber	5.1944	6.6.1944	6.1944	stricken 1946
LCI(L)630, 12.1944- LCI(G)630, 4.1945- LCI(M)630	New Jersey SB, Barber	5.1944	6.1944	6.1944	landing craft gun 12.1944, landing craft mortar 4.1945, to China 2.1948 (Liengtseng)
LCI(L)631, 12.1944- LCI(G)631, 4.1945- LCI(M)631	New Jersey SB, Barber	5.1944	8.6.1944	6.1944	landing craft gun 12.1944, landing craft mortar 4.1945, to China 2.1948 (Lienghwa)
LCI(L)632, 12.1944- LCI(G)632, 4.1945- LCI(M)632	New Jersey SB, Barber	5.1944	9.6.1944	6.1944	landing craft gun 12.1944, landing craft mortar 4.1945, to China 1946 (Yungkan)
LCI(L)633, 12.1944- LCI(G)633, 4.1945- LCI(M)633	New Jersey SB, Barber	5.1944	6.1944	6.1944	landing craft gun 12.1944, landing craft mortar 4.1945, stricken 1951
LCI(L)634	New Jersey SB, Barber	5.1944	6.1944	6.1944	stricken 1946
LCI(L)635	New Jersey SB, Barber	5.1944	6.1944	6.1944	stricken 1946
LCI(L)636	New Jersey SB, Barber	5.1944	6.1944	6.1944	stricken 1946
LCI(L)637	New Jersey SB, Barber	5.1944	6.1944	6.1944	stricken 1946
LCI(L)638, 4.1945- LCI(M)638	New Jersey SB, Barber	5.1944	6.1944	6.1944	landing craft mortar 4.1945, stricken 1956
LCI(L)639	New Jersey SB, Barber	5.1944	6.1944	6.1944	stricken 1946
LCI(L)640	New Jersey SB, Barber	5.1944	6.1944	6.1944	stricken 8.1946
LCI(L)641	New Jersey SB, Barber	5.1944	6.1944	6.1944	stricken 1946
LCI(L)642, 3.1945- LCI(R)642	New Jersey SB, Barber	5.1944	6.1944	7.1944	landing craft rocket 3.1945, stricken 1946
LCI(L)643, 3.1945- LCI(R)643	New Jersey SB, Barber	5.1944	28.6.1944	7.1944	landing craft rocket 3.1945, stricken 1946
LCI(L)644, 3.1945- LCI(R)644	New Jersey SB, Barber	5.1944	29.6.1944	7.1944	landing craft rocket 3.1945, stricken 1946
LCI(L)645, 3.1945- LCI(R)645	New Jersey SB, Barber	6.1944	7.1944	7.1944	landing craft rocket 3.1945, stricken 1946
LCI(L)646, 3.1945- LCI(R)646	New Jersey SB, Barber	6.1944	7.1944	7.1944	landing craft rocket 3.1945, stricken 1946
LCI(L)647, 3.1945- LCI(R)647	New Jersey SB, Barber	6.1944	7.1944	7.1944	landing craft rocket 3.1945, stricken 1946
LCI(L)648, 3.1945- LCI(M)648	New Jersey SB, Barber	6.1944	7.1944	7.1944	landing craft mortar 3.1945, stricken 1946
LCI(L)649, 3.1945- LCI(R)649	New Jersey SB, Barber	6.1944	7.1944	7.1944	landing craft rocket 3.1945, stricken 1946
LCI(L)650, 3.1945- LCI(R)650	New Jersey SB, Barber	6.1944	7.1944	7.1944	landing craft rocket 3.1945, stricken 1946
LCI(L)651, 3.1945- LCI(R)651	New Jersey SB, Barber	6.1944	7.1944	7.1944	landing craft rocket 3.1945, stricken 1946
LCI(L)652	New Jersey SB, Barber	6.1944	13.7.1944	7.1944	stricken 9.1956

LCI(L)653	New Jersey SB, Barber	6.1944	14.7.1944	7.1944	stricken 1.1960
LCI(L)654	New Jersey SB, Barber	6.1944	18.7.1944	7.1944	sold 5.1960
LCI(L)655	New Jersey SB, Barber	6.1944	7.1944	7.1944	sunk as target 1956
LCI(L)656, 1.1945- LC(FF)656	New Jersey SB, Barber	6.1944	7.1944	7.1944	landing craft flotilla flagship 1.1945, sunk as target 1956
LCI(L)657, 1.1945- LC(FF)657	New Jersey SB, Barber	6.1944	7.1944	7.1944	landing craft flotilla flagship 1.1945, stricken 1946
LCI(L)658, 12.1944- LCI(G)658, 4.1945- LCI(M)658	Geo Lawley, Neponset	1944	2.1944	3.1944	landing craft gun 12.1944, landing craft mortar 4.1945, stricken 1946
LCI(L)659, 12.1944- LCI(G)659, 4.1945- LCI(M)659	Geo Lawley, Neponset	1944	2.1944	3.1944	landing craft gun 12.1944, landing craft mortar 4.1945, stricken 1946
LCI(L)660, 12.1944- LCI(G)660, 4.1945- LCI(M)660	Geo Lawley, Neponset	1944	3.1944	3.1944	landing craft gun 12.1944, landing craft mortar 4.1945, stricken 1946
LCI(L)661	Geo Lawley, Neponset	1944	3.1944	3.1944	stricken 1946
LCI(L)662	Geo Lawley, Neponset	1944	3.1944	3.1944	stricken 1946
LCI(L)663	Geo Lawley, Neponset	2.1944	6.3.1944	3.1944	stricken 1946
LCI(L)664	Geo Lawley, Neponset	3.1944	3.1944	3.1944	stricken 1951
LCI(L)665	Geo Lawley, Neponset	3.1944	14.3.1944	3.1944	to the USSR 6.1945 (DS-36)
LCI(L)666	Geo Lawley, Neponset	3.1944	16.3.1944	3.1944	to the USSR 7.1945 (DS-50)
LCI(L)667	Geo Lawley, Neponset	3.1944	3.1944	3.1944	to the USSR 6.1945 (DS-40)
LCI(L)668	Geo Lawley, Neponset	3.1944	22.3.1944	3.1944	to the USSR 6.1945 (DS-41)
LCI(L)669, 5.1945- LCI(M)669	Geo Lawley, Neponset	3.1944	22.3.1944	4.1944	landing craft mortar 5.1945, stricken 1946
LCI(L)670, 5.1945- LCI(M)670	Geo Lawley, Neponset	3.1944	28.3.1944	4.1944	landing craft mortar 5.1945, to Thailand 1946 (Prab)
LCI(L)671	Geo Lawley, Neponset	3.1944	30.3.1944	4.1944	to the USSR 7.1945 (DS-47)
LCI(L)672	Geo Lawley, Neponset	3.1944	3.4.1944	4.1944	to the USSR 7.1945 (DS-1)
LCI(L)673, 5.1945- LCI(M)673	Geo Lawley, Neponset	3.1944	6.4.1944	4.1944	landing craft mortar 5.1945, to Israel 3.1948
LCI(L)674, 5.1945- LCI(M)674	Geo Lawley, Neponset	3.1944	8.4.1944	4.1944	landing craft mortar 5.1945, stricken 1950
LCI(L)675	Geo Lawley, Neponset	4.1944	4.1944	4.1944	to the USSR 6.1945 (DS-42)
LCI(L)676	Geo Lawley, Neponset	4.1944	4.1944	4.1944	stricken 1946
LCI(L)677	Geo Lawley, Neponset	4.1944	4.1944	4.1944	scuttled 14.4.1947
LCI(L)678	Geo Lawley, Neponset	4.1944	4.1944	4.1944	destroyed 13.2.1946
LCI(L)679, 12.1944- LC(FF)679	Geo Lawley, Neponset	4.1944	4.1944	4.1944	landing craft flotilla flagship 12.1944, sunk as target 1956
LCI(L)680	Geo Lawley, Neponset	4.1944	4.1944	5.1944	stricken 1946
LCI(L)681	Geo Lawley, Neponset	4.1944	4.1944	5.1944	stricken 1946
LCI(L)682	Geo Lawley, Neponset	4.1944	5.1944	5.1944	stricken 1946
LCI(L)683	Geo Lawley, Neponset	4.1944	5.1944	5.1944	stricken 1946
LCI(L)684	Geo Lawley, Neponset	4.1944	5.1944	5.1944	sunk 12.11.1944
LCI(L)685	Geo Lawley, Neponset	5.1944	11.5.1944	5.1944	stricken 1946
LCI(L)686	Geo Lawley, Neponset	5.1944	5.1944	5.1944	stricken 1946
LCI(L)687	Geo Lawley, Neponset	5.1944	5.1944	5.1944	stricken 1946
LCI(L)688	Geo Lawley, Neponset	5.1944	20.5.1944	5.1944	to Argentina 2.1948 (BDI10)
LCI(L)689	Geo Lawley, Neponset	5.1944	5.1944	5.1944	to Argentina 2.1948 (BDI15)
LCI(L)690	Geo Lawley, Neponset	5.1944	25.5.1944	5.1944	stricken 1946
LCI(L)691	Geo Lawley, Neponset	5.1944	5.1944	6.1944	sunk as target 1956
LCI(L)692	Geo Lawley, Neponset	5.1944	6.1944	6.1944	stricken 1946

LCI(L)693	Geo Lawley, Neponset	5.1944	6.1944	6.1944	sunk as target 1956
LCI(L)694	Geo Lawley, Neponset	5.1944	6.6.1944	6.1944	sold 4.1960
LCI(L)695	Geo Lawley, Neponset	5.1944	6.1944	6.1944	stricken 1956
LCI(L)696	Geo Lawley, Neponset	5.1944	6.1944	6.1944	stricken 1956
LCI(L)697	Geo Lawley, Neponset	6.1944	6.1944	6.1944	stricken 1946
LCI(L)698	Geo Lawley, Neponset	6.1944	6.1944	6.1944	to France 1.1951 (L9029)
LCI(L)699	Geo Lawley, Neponset	6.1944	6.1944	6.1944	to France 1.1951 (L9034)
LCI(L)700	Geo Lawley, Neponset	6.1944	6.1944	6.1944	sunk as target 1956
LCI(L)701	Geo Lawley, Neponset	6.1944	24.6.1944	6.1944	sold 4.1960
LCI(L)702	Geo Lawley, Neponset	6.1944	7.1944	7.1944	to France 12.1953 (L9035)
LCI(L)703	Geo Lawley, Neponset	6.1944	8.7.1944	7.1944	sold 4.1960
LCI(L)704, 3.1945- LCI(R)704	Geo Lawley, Neponset	6.1944	7.1944	7.1944	landing craft rocket 3.1945, stricken 1946
LCI(L)705, 3.1945- LCI(R)705	Geo Lawley, Neponset	6.1944	7.1944	7.1944	landing craft rocket 3.1945, stricken 1946
LCI(L)706, 3.1945- LCI(R)706	Geo Lawley, Neponset	6.1944	7.1944	7.1944	landing craft rocket 3.1945, stricken 1946
LCI(L)707, 3.1945- LCI(R)707	Geo Lawley, Neponset	6.1944	7.1944	7.1944	landing craft rocket 3.1945, stricken 1946
LCI(L)708, 3.1945- LCI(R)708	Geo Lawley, Neponset	7.1944	7.1944	7.1944	landing craft rocket 3.1945, stricken 1946
LCI(L)709	Geo Lawley, Neponset	7.1944	20.7.1944	7.1944	stricken 1960
LCI(L)710	Geo Lawley, Neponset	7.1944	7.1944	7.1944	to France 1.1951 (L9036)
LCI(L)711	Geo Lawley, Neponset	7.1944	7.1944	8.1944	stricken 1946
LCI(L)712	Geo Lawley, Neponset	7.1944	8.1944	8.1944	stricken 1946
LCI(L)713	Geo Lawley, Neponset	8.1944	8.1944	9.1944	sold 2.1948
LCI(L)714	Geo Lawley, Neponset	8.1944	8.1944	9.1944	stricken 1946
LCI(L)715	Geo Lawley, Neponset	8.1944	8.1944	10.1944	to France 1.1951 (L9030)
LCI(L)716	Geo Lawley, Neponset	8.1944	8.1944	10.1944	stricken 1946
LCI(L)725, 6.1944- LCI(G)725	Commercial IW, Portland	11.1943	12.1943	12.1943	landing craft gun 6.1944, stricken 1946
LCI(L)726, 6.1944- LCI(G)726	Commercial IW, Portland	11.1943	17.12.1943	12.1943	landing craft gun 6.1944, stricken 1946
LCI(L)727, 6.1944- LCI(G)727	Commercial IW, Portland	11.1943	12.1943	1.1944	landing craft gun 6.1944, stricken 1946
LCI(L)728, 6.1944- LCI(G)728	Commercial IW, Portland	12.1943	12.1943	1.1944	landing craft gun 6.1944, stricken 1946
LCI(L)729, 6.1944- LCI(G)729	Commercial IW, Portland	12.1943	1.1944	1.1944	landing craft gun 6.1944, stricken 1946
LCI(L)730, 6.1944- LCI(G)730	Commercial IW, Portland	12.1943	1.1944	1.1944	landing craft gun 6.1944, stricken 1946
LCI(L)731	Commercial IW, Portland	12.1943	1.1944	1.1944	stricken 1946
LCI(L)732, 5.1945- LCI(R)732	Commercial IW, Portland	1.1944	1.1944	2.1944	landing craft rocket 5.1945, stricken 1946
LCI(L)733	Commercial IW, Portland	1.1944	1.1944	2.1944	stricken 1946
LCI(L)734	Commercial IW, Portland	1.1944	2.1944	2.1944	to Argentina 2.1948 (BDI8)
LCI(L)735	Commercial IW, Portland	1.1944	2.1944	2.1944	stricken 1946
LCI(L)736	Commercial IW, Portland	1.1944	2.1944	2.1944	stricken 1946
LCI(L)737	Commercial IW, Portland	1.1944	13.2.1944	2.1944	to Argentina 2.1948 (BDI11)
LCI(L)738	Commercial IW, Portland	1.1944	2.1944	3.1944	stricken 1946
LCI(L)739, 12.1944- LCI(G)739, 4.1945- LCI(M)739	Commercial IW, Portland	1.1944	27.2.1944	3.1944	landing craft gun 12.1944, landing craft mortar 4.1945, to Thailand 5.1947 (Sattakut)

LCI(L)740, 12.1944- LCI(G)740, 4.1945- LCI(M)740	Commercial IW, Portland 2.1944	3.1944	3.1944	landing craft gun 12.1944, landing craft mortar 4.1945, stricken 1946
LCI(L)741, 12.1944- LCI(G)741, 4.1945- LCI(M)741	Commercial IW, Portland 2.1944	3.1944	3.1944	landing craft gun 12.1944, landing craft mortar 4.1945, stricken 1946
LCI(L)742, 12.1944- LCI(G)742, 4.1945- LCI(M)742	Commercial IW, Portland 3.1944	6.4.1944	4.1944	landing craft gun 12.1944, landing craft mortar 4.1945, stricken 1946
LCI(L)743	Commercial IW, Portland 3.1944	3.1944	3.1944	stricken 1946
LCI(L)744, 6.1944- LCI(G)744, 9.1945- LCI(L)744	Commercial IW, Portland 3.1944	3.1944	3.1944	landing craft gun 6.1944, landing craft 9.1945, stricken 1946
LCI(L)745, 6.1944- LCI(G)745, 9.1945- LCI(L)745	Commercial IW, Portland 3.1944	3.1944	3.1944	landing craft gun 6.1944, landing craft 9.1945, stricken 1946
LCI(L)746, 6.1944- LCI(G)746, 9.1945- LCI(L)746	Commercial IW, Portland 3.1944	3.1944	4.1944	landing craft gun 6.1944, landing craft 9.1945, to Argentina 2.1948 (BDI5)
LCI(L)747, 6.1944- LCI(G)747, 9.1945- LCI(L)747	Commercial IW, Portland 3.1944	3.1944	4.1944	landing craft gun 6.1944, landing craft 9.1945, stricken 1946
LCI(L)748, 6.1947- LCI(G)748, 9.1945- LCI(L)748	Commercial IW, Portland 3.1944	3.1944	4.1944	landing craft gun 6.1944, landing craft 9.1945, to Argentina 2.1948 (BDI7)
LCI(L)749, 6.1944- LCI(G)749, 9.1945- LCI(L)749	Commercial IW, Portland 3.1944	4.1944	4.1944	landing craft gun 6.1944, landing craft 9.1945, stricken 1946
LCI(G)750, 6.1944- LCI(G)750, 9.1945- LCI(L)750	Commercial IW, Portland 3.1944	5.4.1944	4.1944	landing craft gun 6.1944, landing craft 9.1945, to Argentina 2.1948 (BDI4)
LCI(L)751, 6.1944- LCI(G)751	Commercial IW, Portland 3.1944	4.1944	4.1944	landing craft gun 6.1944, stricken 1946
LCI(L)752, 6.1944- LCI(G)752	Commercial IW, Portland 3.1944	9.4.1944	4.1944	landing craft gun 6.1944, stricken 1946
LCI(L)753, 6.1944- LCI(G)753, 9.1945- LCI(L)753	Commercial IW, Portland 3.1944	4.1944	4.1944	landing craft gun 6.1944, landing craft 9.1945, to Argentina 2.1948 (BDI12)
LCI(L)754, 12.1944- LCI(G)754, 4.1945- LCI(M)754	Commercial IW, Portland 3.1944	4.1944	5.1944	landing craft gun 12.1944, landing craft mortar 4.1945, stricken 1946
LCI(L)755, 3.1945- LCI(G)755, 4.1945- LCI(M)755	Commercial IW, Portland 4.1944	4.1944	5.1944	landing craft gun 3.1945, landing craft mortar 4.1945, stricken 1946
LCI(L)756, 12.1944- LCI(G)756, 4.1945- LCI(M)756	Commercial IW, Portland 4.1944	5.1944	5.1944	landing craft gun 12.1944, landing craft mortar 4.1945, stricken 1946
LCI(L)757, 12.1944- LCI(G)757, 4.1945- LCI(M)757	Commercial IW, Portland 4.1944	7.5.1944	5.1944	landing craft gun 12.1944, landing craft mortar 4.1945, stricken 1946
LCI(L)758	Commercial IW, Portland 4.1944	5.1944	5.1944	stricken 1946
LCI(L)759	Commercial IW, Portland 4.1944	5.1944	5.1944	stricken 1946

LCI(L)760, 12.1944- LCI(G)760, 4.1945- LCI(M)760	Commercial IW, Portland	4.1944	14.5.1944	5.1944	landing craft gun 12.1944, landing craft mortar 4.1945, stricken 1946
LCI(L)761	Commercial IW, Portland	4.1944	5.1944	5.1944	stricken 1946
LCI(L)762, 3.1945- LCI(R)762	Commercial IW, Portland	5.1944	5.1944	6.1944	landing ship rocket 3.1945, stricken 1946
LCI(L)763, 3.1945- LCI(R)763	Commercial IW, Portland	5.1944	28.5.1944	6.1944	landing craft rocket 3.1945, stricken 1.1946
LCI(L)764, 3.1945- LCI(R)764	Commercial IW, Portland	5.1944	28.5.1944	6.1944	landing craft rocket 3.1945, stricken 1946
LCI(L)765, 3.1945- LCI(R)765	Commercial IW, Portland	5.1944	6.1944	6.1944	landing craft rocket 3.1945, stricken 1946
LCI(L)766, 3.1945- LCI(R)766	Commercial IW, Portland	5.1944	6.1944	6.1944	landing craft rocket 3.1945, stricken 1946
LCI(L)767, 3.1945- LCI(R)767	Commercial IW, Portland	5.1944	6.1944	6.1944	landing craft rocket 3.1945, stricken 1946
LCI(L)768, 2.1949- LSIL768	Commercial IW, Portland	5.1944	6.1944	6.1944	to France 12.1953 (L9037)
LCI(L)769, 3.1945- LCI(R)769	Commercial IW, Portland	6.1944	6.1944	7.1944	landing craft rocket 3.1945, stricken 1946
LCI(L)770, 3.1945- LCI(R)770	Commercial IW, Portland	6.1944	6.1944	7.1944	landing craft rocket 3.1945, stricken 1946
LCI(L)771, 3.1945- LCI(R)771	Commercial IW, Portland	6.1944	27.6.1944	7.1944	landing craft rocket 3.1945, for disposal 11.1947
LCI(L)772, 3.1945- LCI(R)772	Commercial IW, Portland	6.1944	7.1944	7.1944	landing craft rocket 3.1945, stricken 1946
LCI(L)773	Commercial IW, Portland	6.1944	7.1944	7.1944	to the Army 2.1947
LCI(L)774	Commercial IW, Portland	6.1944	7.1944	7.1944	sunk as target 1956
LCI(L)775, 1.1945- LC(FF)775	Commercial IW, Portland	6.1944	7.1944	7.1944	landing craft flotilla flagship 1.1945, sunk as target 1956
LCI(L)776	Commercial IW, Portland	6.1944	7.1944	8.1944	sold 5.1960
LCI(L)777	Commercial IW, Portland	6.1944	17.7.1944	8.1944	stricken 9.1956
LCI(L)778	Commercial IW, Portland	6.1944	7.1944	8.1944	sunk as target 1956
LCI(L)779	Commercial IW, Portland	7.1944	8.1944	8.1944	stricken 1946
LCI(L)780	Commercial IW, Portland	7.1944	8.1944	8.1944	stricken 1946
LCI(L)782, 1.1945- LC(FF)782	New Jersey SB, Barber	6.1944	7.1944	8.1944	landing craft flotilla flagship 1.1945, sunk as target 1956
LCI(L)783, 1.1945- LC(FF)783	New Jersey SB, Barber	6.1944	7.1944	7.1944	landing craft flotilla flagship 1.1945, stricken 1951
LCI(L)784	New Jersey SB, Barber	6.1944	7.1944	8.1944	stricken 1946
LCI(L)785, 3.1945- LCI(R)785	New Jersey SB, Barber	6.1944	29.7.1944	8.1944	landing craft rocket 3.1945, stricken 1946
LCI(L)786, 1.1945- LC(FF)786	New Jersey SB, Barber	7.1944	7.1944	8.1944	landing craft flotilla flagship 1.1945, sold 12.1950
LCI(L)787	New Jersey SB, Barber	7.1944	8.1944	8.1944	to the MarCom 3.1948
LCI(L)788, 1.1945- LC(FF)788	New Jersey SB, Barber	7.1944	8.1944	8.1944	landing craft flotilla flagship 1.1945, stricken 1957
LCI(L)789, 1.1945- LC(FF)789	New Jersey SB, Barber	7.1944	8.1944	8.1944	landing craft flotilla flagship 1.1945, stricken 1957
LCI(L)790, 1.1945- LC(FF)790	New Jersey SB, Barber	7.1944	8.1944	8.1944	landing craft flotilla flagship 1.1945, stricken 1957
LCI(L)791, 1.1945- LC(FF)791	New Jersey SB, Barber	7.1944	8.1944	8.1944	landing craft flotilla flagship 1.1945, stricken 1957

LCI(L)792, 1.1945- LC(FF)792	New Jersey SB, Barber	7.1944	8.1944	8.1944	landing craft flotilla flagship 1.1945, stricken 1957
LCI(L)793, 1.1945- LC(FF)793	New Jersey SB, Barber	7.1944	8.1944	8.1944	landing craft flotilla flagship 1.1945, stricken 1957
LCI(L)794	New Jersey SB, Barber	7.1944	11.8.1944	8.1944	stricken 1946
LCI(L)795	New Jersey SB, Barber	7.1944	15.8.1944	8.1944	stricken 1946
LCI(L)796	New Jersey SB, Barber	7.1944	8.1944	8.1944	for disposal 5.1947
LCI(L)797	New Jersey SB, Barber	7.1944	8.1944	8.1944	stricken 1946
LCI(L)798	New Jersey SB, Barber	7.1944	8.1944	8.1944	stricken 1946
LCI(L)799	New Jersey SB, Barber	7.1944	21.8.1944	8.1944	stricken 1957
LCI(L)800	New Jersey SB, Barber	7.1944	8.1944	8.1944	stricken 1946
LCI(L)801, 12.1944- LCI(G)801, 4.1945- LCI(M)801	New Jersey SB, Barber	7.1944	23.8.1944	8.1944	landing craft gun 12.1944, landing craft mortar 4.1945, stricken 1946
LCI(L)802, 12.1944- LCI(G)802, 4.1945- LCI(M)802	New Jersey SB, Barber	7.1944	8.1944	8.1944	landing craft gun 12.1944, landing craft mortar 4.1945, stricken 1946
LCI(L)803, 12.1944- LCI(G)803, 4.1945- LCI(M)803	New Jersey SB, Barber	7.1944	8.1944	9.1944	landing craft gun 12.1944, landing craft mortar 4.1945, stricken 1946
LCI(L)804, 12.1944- LCI(G)804, 4.1945- LCI(M)804	New Jersey SB, Barber	7.1944	29.8.1944	9.1944	landing craft gun 12.1944, landing craft mortar 4.1945, stricken 1946
LCI(L)805, 12.1944- LCI(G)805, 4.1945- LCI(M)805	New Jersey SB, Barber	7.1944	8.1944	9.1944	landing craft gun 12.1944, landing craft mortar 4.1945, stricken 1946
LCI(L)806, 12.1944- LCI(G)806, 4.1945- LCI(M)806	New Jersey SB, Barber	8.1944	9.1944	9.1944	landing craft gun 12.1944, landing craft mortar 4.1945, stricken 1946
LCI(L)807, 12.1944- LCI(G)807, 4.1945- LCI(M)807	New Jersey SB, Barber	8.1944	9.1944	9.1944	landing craft gun 12.1944, landing craft mortar 4.1945, to the MarCom 3.1947
LCI(L)808, 12.1944- LCI(G)808, 4.1945- LCI(M)808	New Jersey SB, Barber	8.1944	9.1944	9.1944	landing craft gun 12.1944, landing craft mortar 4.1945, stricken 1946
LCI(L)809, 12.1944- LCI(G)809, 4.1945- LCI(M)809	New Jersey SB, Barber	8.1944	9.1944	9.1944	landing craft gun 12.1944, landing craft mortar 4.1945, stricken 1946
LCI(L)810, 12.1944- LCI(G)810, 4.1945- LCI(M)810	New Jersey SB, Barber	8.1944	9.1944	9.1944	landing craft gun 12.1944, landing craft mortar 4.1945, to the MarCom 3.1947
LCI(L)811	New Jersey SB, Barber	8.1944	9.1944	9.1944	stricken 1946
LCI(L)812	New Jersey SB, Barber	8.1944	9.1944	9.1944	stricken 1946
LCI(L)813	New Jersey SB, Barber	8.1944	9.1944	9.1944	stricken 1946
LCI(L)814	New Jersey SB, Barber	8.1944	13.9.1944	9.1944	stricken 1946
LCI(L)815	New Jersey SB, Barber	8.1944	15.9.1944	9.1944	stricken 1946
LCI(L)816	New Jersey SB, Barber	8.1944	9.1944	9.1944	stricken 1946
LCI(L)817	New Jersey SB, Barber	8.1944	9.1944	9.1944	stricken 1946
LCI(L)818	New Jersey SB, Barber	8.1944	9.1944	9.1944	to France 1.1951 (L9031)
LCI(L)819	New Jersey SB, Barber	8.1944	9.1944	9.1944	stricken 1946
LCI(L)820	New Jersey SB, Barber	8.1944	9.1944	9.1944	stricken 1946
LCI(L)821	New Jersey SB, Barber	8.1944	9.1944	9.1944	stricken 1946
LCI(L)866	New Jersey SB, Barber	8.1944	9.1944	10.1944	stricken 1946

LCI(L)867	New Jersey SB, Barber	8.1944	9.1944	10.1944	stricken 1956
LCI(L)868	New Jersey SB, Barber	8.1944	9.1944	10.1944	stricken 2.1951
LCI(L)869	New Jersey SB, Barber	8.1944	29.9.1944	10.1944	stricken 1.1960
LCI(L)870	New Jersey SB, Barber	9.1944	2.10.1944	10.1944	stricken 1960
LCI(L)871	New Jersey SB, Barber	9.1944	3.10.1944	10.1944	to France 1.1951 (L9033)
LCI(L)872	New Jersey SB, Barber	9.1944	11.10.1944	10.1944	to France 1.1951 (L9038)
LCI(L)873	New Jersey SB, Barber	9.1944	10.1944	10.1944	sunk as target 1956
LCI(L)874	New Jersey SB, Barber	9.1944	6.10.1944	10.1944	sold 6.1960
LCI(L)875	New Jersey SB, Barber	9.1944	9.10.1944	10.1944	to France 12.1953 (L9039)
LCI(L)876	New Jersey SB, Barber	9.1944	10.1944	10.1944	for disposal 3.1947
LCI(L)877	New Jersey SB, Barber	9.1944	10.1944	10.1944	to Chile 2.1947 (Grumete Díaz)
LCI(L)878	New Jersey SB, Barber	9.1944	10.1944	10.1944	to Chile 2.1947 (Cabo Bustos)
LCI(L)879	New Jersey SB, Barber	9.1944	13.10.1944	10.1944	stricken 1946
LCI(L)880	New Jersey SB, Barber	9.1944	10.1944	10.1944	stricken 1946
LCI(L)881	New Jersey SB, Barber	9.1944	10.1944	10.1944	stricken 1946
LCI(L)882	New Jersey SB, Barber	9.1944	18.10.1944	10.1944	stricken 7.1956
LCI(L)883	New Jersey SB, Barber	9.1944	19.10.1944	10.1944	sunk as target 1960
LCI(L)884	New Jersey SB, Barber	9.1944	20.10.1944	10.1944	stricken 1.1960
LCI(L)943	Consolidated, Orange	1.1944	10.2.1944	3.1944	to the USSR 6.1945 (DS-43)
LCI(L)944	Consolidated, Orange	1.1944	10.2.1944	4.1944	stricken 1.1961
LCI(L)945	Consolidated, Orange	1.1944	2.1944	3.1944	to the USSR 7.1945 (DS-6)
LCI(L)946	Consolidated, Orange	1.1944	16.2.1944	3.1944	to the USSR 7.1945 (DS-49)
LCI(L)947	Consolidated, Orange	1.1944	16.2.1944	4.1944	stricken 1951
LCI(L)948, 7.1945- LCI(G)948	Consolidated, Orange	1.1944	2.1944	3.1944	landing craft gun 7.1945, to the Netherlands 5.1946
LCI(L)949	Consolidated, Orange	1.1944	2.1944	3.1944	to the USSR 6.1945 (DS-44)
LCI(L)950	Consolidated, Orange	1.1944	2.1944	3.1944	to the USSR 6.1945 (DS-32)
LCI(L)951, 5.1945- LCI(M)951	Consolidated, Orange	1.1944	3.3.1944	3.1944	landing craft mortar 5.1945, stricken 1946
LCI(L)952, 5.1945- LCI(M)952	Consolidated, Orange	2.1944	7.3.1944	4.1944	landing craft mortar 5.1945, stricken 1950
LCI(L)953, 6.1944- LCI(G)953, 9.1945- LCI(L)953	Consolidated, Orange	2.1944	3.1944	4.1944	landing craft gun 6.1944, landing craft 9.1945, stricken 1946
LCI(L)954, 6.1944- LCI(G)954, 9.1945- LCI(L)954	Consolidated, Orange	2.1944	3.1944	4.1944	landing craft gun 6.1944, landing craft 9.1945, stricken 1957
LCI(L)955, 6.1944- LCI(G)955, 9.1945- LCI(L)955	Consolidated, Orange	2.1944	3.1944	4.1944	landing craft gun 6.1944, landing craft 9.1945, stricken 1946
LCI(L)956, 6.1944- LCI(G)956, 9.1945- LCI(L)956	Consolidated, Orange	2.1944	3.1944	4.1944	landing craft gun 6.1944, landing craft 9.1945, stricken 1946
LCI(L)957, 6.1944- LCI(G)957, 9.1945- LCI(L)957	Consolidated, Orange	2.1944	3.1944	4.1944	landing craft gun 6.1944, landing craft 9.1945, stricken 1946
LCI(L)958, 6.1944- LCI(G)958, 9.1945- LCI(L)958	Consolidated, Orange	2.1944	3.1944	4.1944	landing craft gun 6.1944, landing craft 9.1945, stricken 1946
LCI(L)959, 6.1944- LCI(G)959, 9.1945- LCI(L)959	Consolidated, Orange	2.1944	3.1944	4.1944	landing craft gun 6.1944, landing craft 9.1945, stricken 1946
LCI(L)960	Consolidated, Orange	2.1944	3.1944	4.1944	stricken 1946

LCI(L)961, 6.1944- LCI(G)961, 9.1945- LCI(L)961	Consolidated, Orange	2.1944	4.1944	4.1944	landing craft gun 6.1944, landing craft 9.1945, stricken 1946
LCI(L)962, 6.1944- LCI(G)962, 9.1945- LCI(L)962	Consolidated, Orange	2.1944	4.1944	4.1944	landing craft gun 6.1944, landing craft 9.1945, stricken 1950
LCI(L)963	Consolidated, Orange	2.1944	20.3.1944	5.1944	stricken 1.1960
LCI(L)964, 6.1944- LCI(G)964, 9.1945- LCI(L)964	Consolidated, Orange	3.1944	3.1944	4.1944	landing craft gun 6.1944, landing craft 9.1945, stricken 1946
LCI(L)965	Consolidated, Orange	3.1944	3.1944	4.1944	stricken 1946
LCI(L)966	Consolidated, Orange	3.1944	23.3.1944	4.1944	sunk as target 1960
LCI(L)967	Consolidated, Orange	3.1944	3.1944	4.1944	stricken 1946
LCI(L)968	Consolidated, Orange	3.1944	3.1944	4.1944	stricken 1946
LCI(L)969	Consolidated, Orange	2.1944	27.3.1944	4.1944	stricken 3.1957
LCI(L)970	Consolidated, Orange	3.1944	3.1944	4.1944	stricken 1951
LCI(L)971	Consolidated, Orange	3.1944	4.1944	4.1944	stricken 1951
LCI(L)972	Consolidated, Orange	3.1944	4.1944	4.1944	stricken 1946
LCI(L)973	Consolidated, Orange	3.1944	5.4.1944	5.1944	stricken 1.1960
LCI(L)974	Consolidated, Orange	3.1944	3.1944	4.1944	sunk 10.1.1945
LCI(L)975, 3.1945- LCI(G)975, 4.1945- LCI(M)975	Consolidated, Orange	3.1944	4.1944	4.1944	landing craft gun 3.1945, landing craft mortar 4.1945, stricken 1946
LCI(L)976	Consolidated, Orange	3.1944	10.4.1944	5.1944	stricken 1.1960
LCI(L)977	Consolidated, Orange	3.1944	4.1944	5.1944	scuttled 1946
LCI(L)978	Consolidated, Orange	3.1944	4.1944	5.1944	stricken 1.1952
LCI(L)979	Consolidated, Orange	3.1944	4.1944	5.1944	stricken 1946
LCI(L)980	Consolidated, Orange	3.1944	4.1944	5.1944	stricken 1946
LCI(L)981	Consolidated, Orange	3.1944	14.4.1944	5.1944	stricken 1946
LCI(L)982	Consolidated, Orange	3.1944	18.4.1944	5.1944	stricken 10.1958
LCI(L)983	Consolidated, Orange	3.1944	18.4.1944	5.1944	stricken 1946
LCI(L)984	Consolidated, Orange	3.1944	4.1944	5.1944	stricken 1946
LCI(L)985	Consolidated, Orange	3.1944	22.4.1944	5.1944	stricken 1956
LCI(L)986	Consolidated, Orange	3.1944	4.1944	5.1944	stricken 1946
LCI(L)987	Consolidated, Orange	3.1944	22.4.1944	5.1944	stricken 1946
LCI(L)988, 12.1944- LC(FF)988	Consolidated, Orange	3.1944	4.1944	5.1944	landing craft flotilla flagship 12.1944, damaged 1946, never repaired
LCI(L)989	Consolidated, Orange	3.1944	4.1944	5.1944	sunk as target 1956
LCI(L)990	Consolidated, Orange	3.1944	4.1944	5.1944	stricken 1946
LCI(L)991	Consolidated, Orange	4.1944	4.1944	5.1944	stricken 1946
LCI(L)992	Consolidated, Orange	4.1944	4.1944	5.1944	stricken 1946
LCI(L)993	Consolidated, Orange	4.1944	4.1944	5.1944	stricken 1946
LCI(L)994, 12.1944- LC(FF)994	Consolidated, Orange	4.1944	4.1944	5.1944	landing craft flotilla flagship 12.1944, sunk as target 1956
LCI(L)995, 12.1944- LC(FF)995	Consolidated, Orange	4.1944	4.1944	5.1944	landing craft flotilla flagship 12.1944, stricken 1956
LCI(L)996	Consolidated, Orange	4.1944	5.1944	5.1944	sunk as target 1956
LCI(L)997	Consolidated, Orange	4.1944	5.1944	5.1944	stricken 1946
LCI(L)998, 12.1944- LC(FF)998	Consolidated, Orange	4.1944	5.1944	5.1944	landing craft flotilla flagship 12.1944, sunk as target 1956
LCI(L)999	Consolidated, Orange	4.1944	5.1944	5.1944	stricken 1946
LCI(L)1000	Consolidated, Orange	4.1944	5.1944	6.1944	stricken 1956

LCI(L)1001	Consolidated, Orange	4.1944	13.5.1944	6.1944	stricken 8.1956
LCI(L)1002	Consolidated, Orange	4.1944	5.1944	6.1944	to the MarCom 3.1948
LCI(L)1003	Consolidated, Orange	4.1944	5.1944	6.1944	stricken 1946
LCI(L)1004	Consolidated, Orange	4.1944	5.1944	6.1944	stricken 1946
LCI(L)1005	Consolidated, Orange	4.1944	5.1944	6.1944	stricken 1946
LCI(L)1006	Consolidated, Orange	4.1944	5.1944	6.1944	stricken 1946
LCI(L)1007	Consolidated, Orange	4.1944	5.1944	6.1944	stricken 1946
LCI(L)1008	Consolidated, Orange	4.1944	27.5.1944	6.1944	stricken 1.1960
LCI(L)1009	Consolidated, Orange	4.1944	5.1944	6.1944	stricken 1946
LCI(L)1010, 12.1944- LCI(G)1010, 4.1945- LCI(M)1010	Consolidated, Orange	5.1944	5.1944	6.1944	landing craft gun 12.1944, landing craft mortar 4.1945, stricken 1946
LCI(L)1011, 12.1944- LCI(G)1011, 4.1945- LCI(M)1011	Consolidated, Orange	5.1944	5.1944	6.1944	landing craft gun 12.1944, landing craft mortar 4.1945, stricken 1946
LCI(L)1012, 12.1944- LCI(G)1012, 4.1945- LCI(M)1012	Consolidated, Orange	5.1944	5.1944	6.1944	landing craft gun 12.1944, landing craft mortar 4.1945, stricken 1946
LCI(L)1013	Albina, Portland	1944	1944	3.1944	stricken 1946
LCI(L)1014, 6.1944- LCI(G)1014, 9.1945- LCI(L)1014	Albina, Portland	1944	1944	3.1944	landing craft gun 6.1944, landing craft 9.1945, stricken 1946
LCI(L)1015, 6.1944- LCI(G)1015, 9.1945- LCI(L)1015	Albina, Portland	1944	1944	3.1944	landing craft gun 6.1944, landing craft 9.1945, stricken 1946
LCI(L)1016, 6.1944- LCI(G)1016, 9.1945- LCI(L)1016	Albina, Portland	1944	1944	4.1944	landing craft gun 6.1944, landing craft 9.1945, stricken 1946
LCI(L)1017, 6.1944- LCI(G)1017, 9.1945- LCI(L)1017	Albina, Portland	1944	1944	4.1944	landing craft gun 6.1944, landing craft 9.1945, stricken 1957
LCI(L)1018, 6.1944- LCI(G)1018, 9.1945- LCI(L)1018	Albina, Portland	1944	1944	4.1944	landing craft gun 6.1944, landing craft 9.1945, to Argentina 1948 (BDI13)
LCI(L)1019	Albina, Portland	1944	1944	4.1944	stricken 1946
LCI(L)1020	Albina, Portland	2.1944	5.4.1944	5.1944	stricken 1946
LCI(L)1021	Albina, Portland	1944	1944	5.1944	stricken 1951
LCI(L)1022	Albina, Portland	3.1944	17.4.1944	5.1944	stricken 1.1960
LCI(L)1023, 12.1944- LCI(G)1023, 4.1945- LCI(M)1023	Albina, Portland	3.1944	24.4.1944	5.1944	landing craft gun 12.1944, landing craft mortar 4.1945, stricken 1946
LCI(L)1024, 3.1945- LCI(R)1024	Albina, Portland	3.1944	29.4.1944	6.1944	landing craft rocket 3.1945, stricken 1946
LCI(L)1025	Albina, Portland	1944	1944	6.1944	to Chile 3.1947 (Eduardo Llanos)
LCI(L)1026, 3.1945- LCI(R)1026	Albina, Portland	1944	1944	6.1944	landing craft rocket 3.1945, stricken 1946
LCI(L)1027	Albina, Portland	4.1944	18.5.1944	6.1944	to Chile 3.1947 (Soldado Canave)
LCI(L)1028, 3.1945- LCI(R)1028	Albina, Portland	1944	1944	7.1944	landing craft rocket 3.1945, stricken 1946
LCI(L)1029, 3.1945- LCI(R)1029	Albina, Portland	1944	1944	7.1944	landing craft rocket 3.1945, stricken 1946

LCI(L)1030, 3.1945- LCI(R)1030	Albina, Portland	1944	1944	7.1944	landing craft rocket 3.1945, stricken 1946
LCI(L)1031, 1.1945- LC(FF)1031	Albina, Portland	1944	1944	7.1944	landing craft flotilla flagship 1.1945, stricken 1946
LCI(L)1032	Albina, Portland	1944	21.6.1944	8.1944	to the USAF 2.1951
LCI(L)1033	Albina, Portland	5.1944	27.6.1944	8.1944	stricken 1946
LCI(L)1052	Defoe, Bay City	2.1944	9.3.1944	3.1944	stricken 1.1960
LCI(L)1053	Defoe, Bay City	1944	1944	3.1944	stricken 1956
LCI(L)1054	Defoe, Bay City	1944	1944	3.1944	stricken 1949
LCI(L)1055, 3.1945- LCI(G)1055, 4.1945- LCI(M)1055	Defoe, Bay City	3.1944	25.3.1944	4.1944	landing craft gun 3.1945, landing craft mortar 4.1945, stricken 1946
LCI(L)1056, 12.1944- LCI(G)1056, 4.1945- LCI(M)1056	Defoe, Bay City	1944	1944	4.1944	landing craft gun 12.1944, landing craft mortar 4.1945, to S. Korea 1949 (Cheongjin)
LCI(L)1057, 12.1944- LCI(G)1057, 4.1945- LCI(M)1057	Defoe, Bay City	1944	1944	4.1944	landing craft gun 12.1944, landing craft mortar 4.1945, stricken 1946
LCI(L)1058, 12.1944- LCI(G)1058, 4.1945- LCI(M)1058	Defoe, Bay City	1944	1944	4.1944	landing craft gun 12.1944, landing craft mortar 4.1945, to the Philippines 7.1948
LCI(L)1059, 12.1944- LCI(G)1059, 4.1945- LCI(M)1059	Defoe, Bay City	1944	1944	4.1944	landing craft gun 12.1944, landing craft mortar 4.1945, to the Philippines 7.1948
LCI(L)1060, 12.1944- LCI(G)1060, 9.1945- LCI(L)1060	Defoe, Bay City	1944	1944	4.1944	landing craft gun 12.1944, landing craft 9.1945, to Argentina 2.1948 (BDI14)
LCI(L)1061	Defoe, Bay City	1944	1944	5.1944	stricken 1946
LCI(L)1062	Defoe, Bay City	1944	1944	5.1944	to MarCom 3.1948
LCI(L)1063	Defoe, Bay City	1944	1944	5.1944	stricken 1946
LCI(L)1064	Defoe, Bay City	1944	1944	5.1944	stricken 8.1946
LCI(L)1065	Defoe, Bay City	1944	1944	5.1944	sunk 24.10.1944
LCI(L)1066	Defoe, Bay City	1944	1944	5.1944	stricken 1946
LCI(L)1067	Defoe, Bay City	1944	1944	5.1944	to Argentina 2.1948 (BDI2)
LCI(L)1068, 3.1945- LCI(R)1068	Defoe, Bay City	5.1944	24.5.1944	5.1944	landing craft rocket 3.1945, stricken 1946
LCI(L)1069, 3.1945- LCI(R)1069	Defoe, Bay City	1944	1944	6.1944	landing craft rocket 3.1945, stricken 1946
LCI(L)1070, 3.1945- LCI(R)1070	Defoe, Bay City	5.1944	5.6.1944	6.1944	landing craft rocket 3.1945, stricken 1946
LCI(L)1071	Defoe, Bay City	1944	1944	6.1944	stricken 1957
LCI(L)1072	Defoe, Bay City	1944	1944	6.1944	to Chile 3.1947 (Grumete Tellez)
LCI(L)1073	Defoe, Bay City	1944	1944	6.1944	to Chile 3.1947 (Grumete Bolados)
LCI(L)1074	Defoe, Bay City	1944	1944	6.1944	stricken 1946
LCI(L)1075	Defoe, Bay City	1944	1944	7.1944	stricken 1946
LCI(L)1076	Defoe, Bay City	1944	1944	7.1944	stricken 1946
LCI(L)1077, 3.1945- LCI(R)1077	Defoe, Bay City	1944	1944	7.1944	landing craft rocket 3.1945, stricken 1946
LCI(L)1078, 3.1945- LCI(R)1078	Defoe, Bay City	7.1944	15.7.1944	7.1944	landing craft rocket 3.1945, stricken 1946
LCI(L)1079	Defoe, Bay City	1944	1944	7.1944	stricken 1946

LCI(L)1080, 1.1945- LC(FF)1080	Defoe, Bay City	1944	1944	8.1944	landing craft flotilla flagship 1.1945, sunk as target 1956
LCI(L)1081, 1.1945- LC(FF)1081	Defoe, Bay City	1944	1944	8.1944	landing craft flotilla flagship 1.1945, sunk as target 1956
LCI(L)1082, 1.1945- LC(FF)1082	Defoe, Bay City	7.1944	29.7.1944	8.1944	landing craft flotilla flagship 1.1945, sunk as target 1956
LCI(L)1083, 1.1945- LC(FF)1083	Defoe, Bay City	1944	1944	8.1944	landing craft flotilla flagship 1.1945, sunk as target 1956
LCI(L)1084	Defoe, Bay City	1944	1944	8.1944	stricken 1951
LCI(L)1085	Defoe, Bay City	1944	1944	8.1944	stricken 1947
LCI(L)1086	Defoe, Bay City	1944	1944	8.1944	stricken 1951
LCI(L)1087	Defoe, Bay City	8.1944	26.8.1944	8.1944	stricken 1946
LCI(L)1088, 12.1944- LCI(G)1088, 4.1945- LCI(M)1088	Defoe, Bay City	1944	1944	9.1944	landing craft gun 12.1944, landing craft mortar 4.1945, stricken 1946
LCI(L)1089, 12.1944- LCI(G)1089, 4.1945- LCI(M)1089	Defoe, Bay City	1944	1944	9.1944	landing craft gun 12.1944, landing craft mortar 4.1945, stricken 1946
LCI(L)1090	Defoe, Bay City	1944	1944	9.1944	sold 12.1950
LCI(L)1091	Defoe, Bay City	8.1944	14.9.1944	9.1944	stricken 1951
LCI(L)1092	Defoe, Bay City	1944	1944	9.1944	to France 1.1951 (L9032)
LCI(L)1093	Defoe, Bay City	9.1944	23.9.1944	9.1944	stricken 1.1960
LCI(L)1094	Defoe, Bay City	1944	1944	10.1944	stricken 1946
LCI(L)1095	Defoe, Bay City	1944	1944	10.1944	auxiliary 2.1948
LCI(L)1096	Defoe, Bay City	1944	1944	10.1944	stricken 1946
LCI(L)1097	Defoe, Bay City	1944	1944	10.1944	stricken 1956
LCI(L)1098	Defoe, Bay City	10.1944	17.10.1944	10.1944	stricken 1.1960

194 / 387 (LCI(L)1-349) or 209 / 385 (LCI(L)350-1098) t, 48.5 (LCI(L)1-349) or 48.9 (LCI(L)350-1098) x 7.2 x 1.5 (LCI(L)1-349) or 1.6 (LCI(L)350-1098) m, 8 General Motors diesels (2 shafts), 1880 hp, 15.5 kts, 120 (LCI(L)1-349) or 110 (LCI(L)350-1098) t diesel oil, 8700 (LCI(L)1-349) or 8000 (LCI(L)350-1098) nm (12 kts), complement 24 (LCI(L)1-349) or 29 (LCI(L)350-1098); 4 (LCI(L)1-349) or 5 (LCI(L)350-1098) x 1 – 20/70 Oerlikon, 180 (LCI(L)1-349) or 209 (LCI(L)350-1098) troops or 75 t of cargo, SO or SCR-517A radar.

LCI(L) was originally designed as a landing craft for sabotage operations. The appointment predetermined high speed requirements (at least 14 knots, and preferably about 20). Besides, the dimensions did not allow these craft to be carried aboard larger ships, so more attention was paid to seaworthiness. To meet these requirements, these ships received a more streamlined hull than the nearby flat-bottomed earlier landing craft. The landing was carried out along light gangway boards in the bow. LCI(L)137 – 160 (Bethlehem, Hingham) were cancelled in October 1942, LCI(L)49 – 60 (New York SB), LCI(L)197 – 208 (Federal, Newark) in November 1942, LCI(L)781, 845 – 865 and 929 - 942 (Commercial Iron Wks, Portland), LCI(L)838 – 844 and 902-910 (Geo Lawley), LCI(L)911 – 928 (New Jersey SB), LCI(L)1034 – 1051 (Albina) in June 1944, LCI(L)717 – 724, 822 -

LCI(L)351 1944

LCI(L)98

LCI(L)191 1943

LCI(G)725 and 726 1944

837 (Geo Lawley), LCI(L)885 – 901, 1110 - 1139 (New Jersey SB) and LCI(L)1099 – 1109 (Defoe) in August 1944.

They were built in two series, the main external difference between which was the shape and size of the wheelhouse: on *LCI(L)1 - 349* it was made rectangular, and on subsequent ships it had an oval shape and was notably taller. Many ships of the 2nd series, instead of the shaky gangway boards that did not justify themselves, were fitted with traditional bow doors and a descending ramp (*LCI(L)641 - 657, 691 - 716, 762 - 780, 782 - 821, 866 - 884, 1024 - 1098*).

Many LCI(L) were converted to assault command craft (landing craft flotilla flagships) (LC(FF)), fire support craft (LCI(G) with guns and LCI(R) with rockets), and smoke screen craft (LCI(M) (mortar)).

1944-1945, some LCI(L) were converted to LC(FF): draught was 1.8 m, 5 x 1 - 20/70 Oerlikon, HQ personnel,

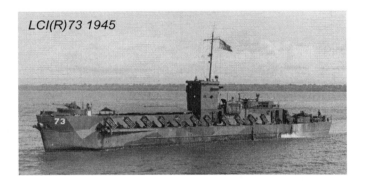

LCI(R)73 1945

complement 24. 1944-1945, some LCI(L) were converted to LCI(G): draught 1.8 m, 2 x 1 - 40/56 Bofors, 3 x 1 - 20/70 Oerlikon, 6 x 1 - 12.7 MG, 10 x 1 - 127 Mk 7 RL (version 1) or 3 x 1 - 40/56 Bofors, 2 x 1 - 20/70 Oerlikon, 5 x 1 - 12.7 MG, 8 x 1 - 127 Mk 7 RL (version 2) or 3 x 1 - 40/56 Bofors, 4 x 1 - 20/70 Oerlikon, 10 x 1 - 127 Mk 7 RL (version 3) or 1 x 1 - 76/50 Mk 20, 1 x 1 - 40/56 Bofors, 4 x 1 - 20/70 Oerlikon, 10 x 1 - 12.7/90 MG (version 4) or 1 x 1 - 40/56 Bofors, 3 x 1 - 20/70 Oerlikon, 24 x 1 - 127 Mk 7 RL (version 5), complement 70. 1944-1945, some LCI(L) were converted to LCI(R): draught 1.8 m, 1 x 1 - 40/56 Bofors, 6 x 1 - 127 RL, complement 34.

1945, some LCI(G) and LCI(L) were converted to LCI(M): draught 1.8 m, 1 x 1 - 40/56 Bofors, 3 x 1 - 107/9.5 chemical mortars, complement 53. 1945, *LCI(L)589, 400, 409, 513, 515; 1953, LSIL652 - 654, 694, 701, 703, 709, 776, 777, 869, 870, 874, 882 - 884, 944, 963, 966, 969, 973, 976, 982, 1001, 1008, 1022, 1052, 1053, 1093, 1098* were converted to minehunters (underwater locators) AMC(U). FM sonar and diving equipment were fitted. 1945, some LCI(G) and LCI(M) were converted to standard LCI(L) configuration

LCI(L)1 and *LCI(L)20* were sunk by Italian and German aircraft, *LCI(L)219* by German aircraft, *LCI(L)32* was stricken by German or Italian mine, *LCI(L)85, LCI(L)91, LCI(L)232, LCI(L)416* and *LCI(L)497* were sunk by German mines, *LCI(L)92, LCI(L)93* and *LCI(L)553* were sunk by German coastal guns. *LCI(L)339* was sunk by Japanese aircraft, *LCI(L)600* was sunk by a human torpedo from Japanese submarine *I36*. *LCI(L)684* and *LCI(L)1065* were sunk by Japanese Army. *LCI(G)82* and *LCI(G)365* were sunk by Japanese explosive boats, *LCI(G)456* was a victim of Japanese surface ships, *LCI(G)459* was sunk by a Japanese mine, *LCI(G)468* was badly damaged by Japanese aircraft and scuttled by the own crew, *LCI(G)474* and *LCI(G)974* were sunk by Japanese. *LCI(M)974* was sunk by Japanese explosive boat.

LCT(5) type landing craft tank

LCT1	Manitowoc SB	5.1942	10.6.1942	6.1942	
LCT2	Manitowoc SB	1942	1942	7.1942	to the UK 1942 (LCT2002)
LCT3	Manitowoc SB	6.1942	29.7.1942	8.1942	to France 1949
LCT4	Manitowoc SB	1942	1942	8.1942	to the UK 1942 (LCT2004)
LCT5	Manitowoc SB	1942	1942	(8.1942)	to the UK 1942 (LCT2005)
LCT6	Manitowoc SB	1942	1942	(8.1942)	to the UK 1942 (LCT2006)
LCT7	Manitowoc SB	7.1942	22.8.1942	9.1942	
LCT8	Manitowoc SB	1942	1942	9.1942	to the UK 1942 (LCT2008)
LCT9	Manitowoc SB	1942	1942	(9.1942)	to the UK 1942 (LCT2009)
LCT10	Manitowoc SB	1942	1942	(9.1942)	to the UK 1942 (LCT2010)
LCT11	Manitowoc SB	1942	1942	9.1942	to the UK 1942 (LCT2011)
LCT12	Manitowoc SB	1942	1942	9.1942	to the UK 1942 (LCT2012)
LCT13	Manitowoc SB	1942	1942	(9.1942)	to the UK 1942 (LCT2013)

LCT14	Manitowoc SB	1942	1942	(9.1942)	to the UK 1942 (LCT2014)
LCT15	Manitowoc SB	8.1942	27.8.1942	9.1942	
LCT16	Manitowoc SB	8.1942	31.8.1942	9.1942	
LCT17	Manitowoc SB	8.1942	3.9.1942	9.1942	
LCT18	Manitowoc SB	8.1942	5.9.1942	9.1942	
LCT19	Manitowoc SB	1942	1942	9.1942	sunk 14.7.1943
LCT20	Manitowoc SB	8.1942	9.9.1942	9.1942	
LCT21	Manitowoc SB	1942	1942	10.1942	sunk 1.1.1943
LCT22	Manitowoc SB	8.1942	15.9.1942	10.1942	sunk 6.6.1944
LCT23	Manitowoc SB	8.1942	9.1942	10.1942	sunk 3.5.1943
LCT24	Manitowoc SB	8.1942	20.9.1942	10.1942	
LCT25	Manitowoc SB	8.1942	9.1942	10.1942	stricken 3.1945
LCT26	Manitowoc SB	8.1942	9.1942	10.1942	foundered 25.2.1944
LCT27	Manitowoc SB	8.1942	9.1942	10.1942	wrecked 6.6.1944
LCT28	Manitowoc SB	9.1942	10.1942	10.1942	sunk 30.5.1943
LCT29	Manitowoc SB	9.1942	15.10.1942	10.1942	
LCT30	Manitowoc SB	9.1942	10.1942	10.1942	sunk 6.6.1944
LCT31	Manitowoc SB	9.1942	17.10.1942	10.1942	
LCT32	Manitowoc SB	9.1942	19.10.1942	10.1942	
LCT33	Manitowoc SB	9.1942	2.10.1942	10.1942	
LCT34	Manitowoc SB	9.1942	10.1942	11.1942	
LCT35	Manitowoc SB	9.1942	10.1942	11.1942	sunk 15.2.1944
LCT36	Manitowoc SB	9.1942	10.1942	11.1942	wrecked 26.2.1944
LCT37	Kansas City Steel	1942	1942	8.1942	to the UK 1942 (LCT2037)
LCT38	Kansas City Steel	1942	1942	(8.1942)	to the UK 1942 (LCT2038)
LCT39	Kansas City Steel	1942	1942	8.1942	to the UK 1942 (LCT2039)
LCT40	Kansas City Steel	1942	1942	8.1942	to the UK 1942 (LCT2040)
LCT41	Kansas City Steel	1942	1942	8.1942	to the UK 1942 (LCT2040)
LCT42	Kansas City Steel	1942	1942	(8.1942)	to the UK 1942 (LCT2042)
LCT43	Kansas City Steel	1942	1942	8.1942	to the UK 1942 (LCT2043)
LCT44	Kansas City Steel	1942	1942	(8.1942)	to the UK 1942 (LCT2044)
LCT45	Kansas City Steel	1942	1942	(8.1942)	to the UK 1942 (LCT2045)
LCT46	Kansas City Steel	1942	1942	9.1942	to the UK 1942 (LCT2046)
LCT47	Kansas City Steel	1942	1942	(9.1942)	to the UK 1942 (LCT2047)
LCT48	Kansas City Steel	1942	1942	(9.1942)	to the UK 1942 (LCT2048)
LCT49	Kansas City Steel	1942	1942	9.1942	to the UK 1942 (LCT2049)
LCT50	Kansas City Steel	1942	1942	9.1942	to the UK 1942 (LCT2050)
LCT51	Kansas City Steel	1942	1942	(9.1942)	to the UK 1942 (LCT2051)
LCT52	Kansas City Steel	1942	1942	(9.1942)	to the UK 1942 (LCT2052)
LCT53	Kansas City Steel	1942	1942	(9.1942)	to the UK 1942 (LCT2053)
LCT54	Kansas City Steel	1942	1942	(9.1942)	to the UK 1942 (LCT2054)
LCT55	Kansas City Steel	1942	1942	9.1942	to the UK 1942 (LCT2055)
LCT56	Kansas City Steel	1942	1942	9.1942	to the UK 1942 (LCT2056)
LCT57	Kansas City Steel	1942	1942	9.1942	to the UK 1942 (LCT2057)
LCT58	Kansas City Steel	9.1942	17.10.1942	10.1942	
LCT59	Kansas City Steel	9.1942	29.9.1942	9.1942	
LCT60	Kansas City Steel	9.1942	20.10.1942	10.1942	
LCT61	Kansas City Steel	9.1942	8.10.1942	10.1942	
LCT62	Kansas City Steel	10.1942	10.1942	10.1942	
LCT63	Kansas City Steel	10.1942	1.11.1942	11.1942	
LCT64	Kansas City Steel	10.1942	11.1942	11.1942	
LCT65	Kansas City Steel	10.1942	10.11.1942	11.1942	

LCT66	Kansas City Steel	10.1942	13.11.1942	11.1942	sunk 12.4.1945
LCT67	Kansas City Steel	10.1942	16.11.1942	11.1942	
LCT68	Kansas City Steel	10.1942	10.10.1942	11.1942	
LCT69	Kansas City Steel	10.1942	13.10.1942	10.1942	
LCT70	Kansas City Steel	10.1942	15.10.1942	11.1942	
LCT71	Kansas City Steel	10.1942	10.1942	11.1942	wrecked 11.9.1943
LCT72	Kansas City Steel	10.1942	24.10.1942	11.1942	
LCT73	Jones & Laughlin Steel, Pittsburgh	1942	1942	10.1942	to the UK 1942-1944 (LCT2073), to the UK 1944 (LCT2073)
LCT74	Jones & Laughlin Steel, Pittsburgh	1942	1942	10.1942	to the UK 1942-1944 (LCT2074), to the UK 1944 (LCT(A)2074)
LCT75	Jones & Laughlin Steel, Pittsburgh	1942	1942	10.1942	to the UK 1942 (LCT2075)
LCT76	Jones & Laughlin Steel, Pittsburgh	1942	1942	10.1942	to the UK 1942 (LCT2076)
LCT77	Jones & Laughlin Steel, Pittsburgh	1942	1942	10.1942	to the UK 1942 (LCT2077)
LCT78	Jones & Laughlin Steel, Pittsburgh	1942	1942	10.1942	to the UK 1942 (LCT2078)
LCT79	Jones & Laughlin Steel, Pittsburgh	1942	1942	10.1942	to the UK 1942 (LCT2079)
LCT80	Jones & Laughlin Steel, Pittsburgh	9.1942	27.10.1942	11.1942	stricken 7.1947
LCT81	Jones & Laughlin Steel, Pittsburgh	9.1942	31.10.1942	11.1942	
LCT82	Jones & Laughlin Steel, Pittsburgh	10.1942	13.11.1942	11.1942	
LCT83	Jones & Laughlin Steel, Pittsburgh	10.1942	11.1942	11.1942	
LCT84	Jones & Laughlin Steel, Pittsburgh	10.1942	6.11.1942	11.1942	
LCT85	Jones & Laughlin Steel, Pittsburgh	10.1942	27.11.1942	11.1942	
LCT86	Jones & Laughlin Steel, Pittsburgh	10.1942	2.12.1942	12.1942	
LCT87	Jones & Laughlin Steel, Pittsburgh	10.1942	4.12.1942	12.1942	
LCT88	Jones & Laughlin Steel, Pittsburgh	10.1942	9.12.1942	12.1942	
LCT119	Quincy Bargebuilders	1942	1942	8.1942	to the UK 1942 (LCT2119)
LCT120	Quincy Bargebuilders	1942	1942	8.1942	to the UK 1942 (LCT2120)
LCT121	Quincy Bargebuilders	1942	1942	(8.1942)	to the UK 1942 (LCT2121)
LCT122	Quincy Bargebuilders	1942	1942	8.1942	to the UK 1942 (LCT2122)
LCT123	Quincy Bargebuilders	1942	1942	8.1942	to the UK 1942 (LCT2123)
LCT124	Quincy Bargebuilders	1942	1942	(8.1942)	to the UK 1942 (LCT2124)
LCT125	Quincy Bargebuilders	7.1942	14.8.1942	9.1942	
LCT126	Quincy Bargebuilders	7.1942	16.8.1942	9.1942	
LCT127	Quincy Bargebuilders	7.1942	18.8.1942	9.1942	
LCT128	Quincy Bargebuilders	7.1942	19.8.1942	9.1942	
LCT129	Quincy Bargebuilders	7.1942	20.8.1942	9.1942	
LCT130	Quincy Bargebuilders	1942	1942	9.1942	to the UK 1942 (LCT2130)
LCT131	Quincy Bargebuilders	1942	1942	9.1942	to the UK 1942 (LCT2131)
LCT132	Quincy Bargebuilders	7.1942	23.8.1942	9.1942	
LCT133	Quincy Bargebuilders	8.1942	30.8.1942	9.1942	
LCT134	Quincy Bargebuilders	8.1942	4.9.1942	9.1942	
LCT135	Quincy Bargebuilders	8.1942	9.1942	9.1942	to the UK 1942 (LCT2135)
LCT136	Quincy Bargebuilders	8.1942	9.9.1942	10.1942	
LCT137	Quincy Bargebuilders	8.1942	24.8.1942	9.1942	
LCT138	Quincy Bargebuilders	1942	1942	9.1942	to the UK 1942 (LCT2138)
LCT139	Quincy Bargebuilders	8.1942	28.8.1942	9.1942	
LCT140	Quincy Bargebuilders	8.1942	31.8.1942	9.1942	
LCT141	Quincy Bargebuilders	8.1942	2.9.1942	10.1942	
LCT142	Quincy Bargebuilders	8.1942	10.9.1942	10.1942	
LCT143	Quincy Bargebuilders	8.1942	12.9.1942	11.1942	

LCT144	Quincy Bargebuilders	9.1942	17.10.1942	11.1942	
LCT145	Quincy Bargebuilders	8.1942	15.9.1942	9.1942	
LCT146	Quincy Bargebuilders	8.1942	17.9.1942	9.1942	
LCT147	Quincy Bargebuilders	8.1942	9.9.1942	10.1942	wrecked 6.1944
LCT148	Quincy Bargebuilders	8.1942	26.9.1942	10.1942	stricken 12.1944
LCT149	Quincy Bargebuilders	8.1942	28.9.1942	10.1942	
LCT150	Quincy Bargebuilders	1942	1942	10.1942	to the UK 1942 (LCT2150)
LCT151	Quincy Bargebuilders	9.1942	30.9.1942	10.1942	
LCT152	Quincy Bargebuilders	9.1942	18.9.1942	9.1942	
LCT153	Quincy Bargebuilders	9.1942	20.9.1942	10.1942	
LCT154	Quincy Bargebuilders	9.1942	9.1942	10.1942	sunk 31.8.1943
LCT155	Quincy Bargebuilders	9.1942	23.9.1942	10.1942	
LCT156	Quincy Bargebuilders	9.1942	9.10.1942	10.1942	
LCT157	Quincy Bargebuilders	9.1942	26.9.1942	9.1942	
LCT158	Quincy Bargebuilders	9.1942	12.10.1942	10.1942	
LCT159	Quincy Bargebuilders	9.1942	15.10.1942	10.1942	
LCT160	Quincy Bargebuilders	9.1942	1.10.1942	10.1942	
LCT161	Quincy Bargebuilders	9.1942	27.10.1942	10.1942	
LCT162	Quincy Bargebuilders	9.1942	21.10.1942	11.1942	
LCT163	Quincy Bargebuilders	9.1942	21.10.1942	11.1942	
LCT164	Quincy Bargebuilders	9.1942	24.10.1942	11.1942	
LCT165	Quincy Bargebuilders	9.1942	29.10.1942	11.1942	
LCT166	Quincy Bargebuilders	9.1942	30.10.1942	11.1942	
LCT167	Quincy Bargebuilders	9.1942	31.10.1942	11.1942	
LCT168	Quincy Bargebuilders	10.1942	3.11.1942	11.1942	
LCT169	Quincy Bargebuilders	10.1942	3.11.1942	11.1942	
LCT170	Quincy Bargebuilders	10.1942	4.11.1942	11.1942	
LCT171	Quincy Bargebuilders	10.1942	10.11.1942	11.1942	
LCT172	Quincy Bargebuilders	10.1942	7.11.1942	11.1942	
LCT173	Quincy Bargebuilders	10.1942	21.11.1942	11.1942	
LCT174	Quincy Bargebuilders	10.1942	18.11.1942	11.1942	
LCT175	Quincy Bargebuilders	10.1942	30.10.1942	10.1942	foundered 21.2.1945
LCT176	Quincy Bargebuilders	10.1942	12.12.1942	12.1942	
LCT177	Quincy Bargebuilders	10.1942	8.11.1942	11.1942	
LCT178	Quincy Bargebuilders	10.1942	8.11.1942	11.1942	
LCT179	Quincy Bargebuilders	10.1942	8.11.1942	11.1942	
LCT180	Quincy Bargebuilders	10.1942	12.10.1942	10.1942	
LCT181	Quincy Bargebuilders	9.1942	4.11.1942	11.1942	
LCT182	Quincy Bargebuilders	9.1942	4.11.1942	11.1942	foundered 7.8.1944
LCT183	Quincy Bargebuilders	9.1942	8.10.1942	10.1942	
LCT184	Quincy Bargebuilders	9.1942	20.10.1942	10.1942	
LCT185	Bison SB, North Tonawanda	8.1942	8.1942	8.1942	foundered 24.1.1944
LCT186	Bison SB, North Tonawanda	8.1942	8.1942	8.1942	to the UK 1942 (LCT2186)
LCT187	Bison SB, North Tonawanda	1942	1942	(8.1942)	to the UK 1942 (LCT2187)
LCT188	Bison SB, North Tonawanda	1942	1942	8.1942	to the UK 1942 (LCT2188)
LCT189	Bison SB, North Tonawanda	1942	1942	(8.1942)	to the UK 1942 (LCT2189)
LCT190	Bison SB, North Tonawanda	1942	1942	(8.1942)	to the UK 1942 (LCT2190)
LCT191	Bison SB, North Tonawanda	1942	1942	(8.1942)	to the UK 1942 (LCT2191)
LCT192	Bison SB, North Tonawanda	1942	1942	(8.1942)	to the UK 1942 (LCT2192)
LCT193	Bison SB, North Tonawanda	1942	1942	8.1942	to the UK 1942-1944 (LCT2193), to the UK 1944 (LCT2193)

LCT194	Bison SB, North Tonawanda	1942	1942	(8.1942)	to the UK 1942 (LCT2194)
LCT195	Bison SB, North Tonawanda	8.1942	17.9.1942	9.1942	
LCT196	Bison SB, North Tonawanda	8.1942	9.1942	10.1942	foundered 27.9.1943
LCT197	Bison SB, North Tonawanda	1942	1942	9.1942	sunk 6.6.1944
LCT198	Bison SB, North Tonawanda	9.1942	22.9.1942	9.1942	
LCT199	Bison SB, North Tonawanda	9.1942	24.9.1942	9.1942	
LCT200	Bison SB, North Tonawanda	9.1942	9.1942	9.1942	sunk 6.1944
LCT201	Bison SB, North Tonawanda			10.1942	
LCT202	Bison SB, North Tonawanda			10.1942	
LCT203	Bison SB, North Tonawanda			10.1942	
LCT204	Bison SB, North Tonawanda			10.1942	
LCT205	Bison SB, North Tonawanda			10.1942	
LCT206	Bison SB, North Tonawanda			10.1942	
LCT207	Bison SB, North Tonawanda			10.1942	
LCT208	Bison SB, North Tonawanda			10.1942	sunk 20.6.1943
LCT209	Bison SB, North Tonawanda			10.1942	sunk 10.6.1944
LCT210	Bison SB, North Tonawanda			10.1942	
LCT211	Bison SB, North Tonawanda			10.1942	
LCT212	Bison SB, North Tonawanda			10.1942	
LCT213	Bison SB, North Tonawanda			10.1942	
LCT214	Bison SB, North Tonawanda			11.1942	
LCT215	Bison SB, North Tonawanda			11.1942	sunk 9.1943
LCT216	Bison SB, North Tonawanda			11.1942	
LCT217	Bison SB, North Tonawanda			11.1942	
LCT218	Bison SB, North Tonawanda			11.1942	
LCT219	Bison SB, North Tonawanda			11.1942	
LCT220	Bison SB, North Tonawanda			11.1942	sunk 13.2.1944
LCT221	Bison SB, North Tonawanda			11.1942	
LCT222	Bison SB, North Tonawanda			11.1942	
LCT223	Bison SB, North Tonawanda			11.1942	
LCT224	Bison SB, North Tonawanda			11.1942	
LCT225	Bison SB, North Tonawanda	10.1942	11.1942	11.1942	to the UK 1942 (LCT2225)
LCT226	Bison SB, North Tonawanda	1942	1942	12.1942	to the UK 1942 (LCT2226)
LCT227	Bison SB, North Tonawanda	1942	1942	12.1942	to the UK 1942 (LCT2227)
LCT228	Bison SB, North Tonawanda	1942	1942	12.1942	to the UK 1942 (LCT2228)
LCT229	Bison SB, North Tonawanda	1942	1942	12.1942	to the UK 1942 (LCT2229)
LCT230	Bison SB, North Tonawanda	10.1942	11.1942	12.1942	to the UK 1942 (LCT2230)
LCT231	Bison SB, North Tonawanda	1942	1942	(12.1942)	to the UK 1942 (LCT2231)
LCT232	Bison SB, North Tonawanda	1942	1942	12.1942	to the UK 1942 (LCT2232)
LCT233	Bison SB, North Tonawanda	1942	1942	12.1942	to the UK 1942 (LCT2233)
LCT234	Bison SB, North Tonawanda	1942	1942	(12.1942)	to the UK 1942 (LCT2234)
LCT235	Bison SB, North Tonawanda	1942	1942	12.1942	to the UK 1942 (LCT2235)
LCT236	Bison SB, North Tonawanda	1942	1942	12.1942	to the UK 1942 (LCT2236)
LCT237	Pidgeon Thomas Iron, Memphis			9.1942	
LCT238	Pidgeon Thomas Iron, Memphis	1942	1942	10.1942	to the UK 1942 (LCT2238)
LCT239	Pidgeon Thomas Iron, Memphis	1942	1942	(10.1942)	to the UK 1942 (LCT2239)
LCT240	Pidgeon Thomas Iron, Memphis	1942	1942	10.1942	to the UK 1942 (LCT2240)
LCT241	Pidgeon Thomas Iron, Memphis			10.1942	sunk 15.9.1943
LCT242	Pidgeon Thomas Iron, Memphis			10.1942	sunk 2.12.1943
LCT243	Pidgeon Thomas Iron, Memphis	8.1942	9.1942	10.1942	to the UK 1942 (LCT2243)
LCT244	Pidgeon Thomas Iron, Memphis			10.1942	sunk 8.6.1944
LCT245	Pidgeon Thomas Iron, Memphis			11.1942	

LCT246	Pidgeon Thomas Iron, Memphis	9.1942	9.1942	11.1942	to the UK 1942 (LCT2246)
LCT247	Pidgeon Thomas Iron, Memphis			11.1942	
LCT248	Pidgeon Thomas Iron, Memphis			11.1942	
LCT249	Pidgeon Thomas Iron, Memphis			10.1942	
LCT250	Pidgeon Thomas Iron, Memphis			11.1942	
LCT251	Pidgeon Thomas Iron, Memphis			11.1942	
LCT252	Pidgeon Thomas Iron, Memphis			11.1942	
LCT253	Pidgeon Thomas Iron, Memphis			11.1942	sunk 21.1.1945
LCT254	Pidgeon Thomas Iron, Memphis			11.1942	
LCT255	Pidgeon Thomas Iron, Memphis			11.1942	
LCT256	Pidgeon Thomas Iron, Memphis			11.1942	
LCT257	Pidgeon Thomas Iron, Memphis			11.1942	
LCT258	Pidgeon Thomas Iron, Memphis			11.1942	
LCT259	Pidgeon Thomas Iron, Memphis			11.1942	
LCT260	Pidgeon Thomas Iron, Memphis			12.1942	
LCT261	Pidgeon Thomas Iron, Memphis	10.1942	11.1942	12.1942	to the UK 1942 (LCT2261)
LCT262	Pidgeon Thomas Iron, Memphis	10.1942	11.1942	12.1942	to the UK 1942 (LCT2262)
LCT263	Pidgeon Thomas Iron, Memphis	10.1942	11.1942	(12.1942)	to the UK 1942 (LCT2263)
LCT264	Pidgeon Thomas Iron, Memphis	10.1942	11.1942	12.1942	to the UK 1942 (LCT2264)
LCT265	Pidgeon Thomas Iron, Memphis	10.1942	11.1942	12.1942	to the UK 1942 (LCT2265)
LCT266	Pidgeon Thomas Iron, Memphis	10.1942	11.1942	12.1942	to the UK 1942 (LCT2266)
LCT267	Pidgeon Thomas Iron, Memphis	1942	1942	(12.1942)	to the UK 1942 (LCT2267)
LCT268	Missouri Valley Bridge, Evansville			9.1942	
LCT269	Missouri Valley Bridge, Evansville	1942	1942	9.1942	to the UK 1942 (LCT2269)
LCT270	Missouri Valley Bridge, Evansville	8.1942	9.1942	9.1942	to the UK 1942 (LCT2270)
LCT271	Missouri Valley Bridge, Evansville			9.1942	
LCT272	Missouri Valley Bridge, Evansville	9.1942	9.1942	9.1942	to the UK 1942 (LCT2272)
LCT273	Missouri Valley Bridge, Evansville	1942	1942	10.1942	to the UK 1942 (LCT2273)
LCT274	Missouri Valley Bridge, Evansville			10.1942	
LCT275	Missouri Valley Bridge, Evansville	9.1942	10.1942	10.1942	to the UK 1942 (LCT2275)
LCT276	Missouri Valley Bridge, Evansville			11.1942	
LCT277	Missouri Valley Bridge, Evansville			11.1942	
LCT278	Missouri Valley Bridge, Evansville			10.1942	
LCT279	Missouri Valley Bridge, Evansville			11.1942	
LCT280	Missouri Valley Bridge, Evansville			11.1942	
LCT281	Missouri Valley Bridge, Evansville	1942	1942	(12.1942)	to the UK 1942 (LCT2281)
LCT282	Missouri Valley Bridge, Evansville	1942	1942	12.1942	to the UK 1942 (LCT2282)
LCT283	Missouri Valley Bridge, Evansville	1942	1942	(12.1942)	to the UK 1942 (LCT2283)
LCT284	Missouri Valley Bridge, Evansville	1942	1942	(12.1942)	to the UK 1942 (LCT2284)
LCT285	Missouri Valley Bridge, Evansville	1942	1942	(12.1942)	to the UK 1942 (LCT2285)
LCT286	Missouri Valley Bridge, Evansville	1942	1942	12.1942	to the UK 1942 (LCT2286)
LCT287	Missouri Valley Bridge, Evansville	1942	1942	12.1942	to the UK 1942 (LCT2287)
LCT288	Darby Products, Kansas City			9.1942	
LCT289	Darby Products, Kansas City	8.1942	9.1942	9.1942	to the UK 1942 (LCT2289)
LCT290	Darby Products, Kansas City			9.1942	
LCT291	Darby Products, Kansas City	8.1942	9.1942	9.1942	to the UK 1942 (LCT2291)
LCT292	Darby Products, Kansas City	8.1942	9.1942	9.1942	to the UK 1942 (LCT2292)
LCT293	Darby Products, Kansas City			9.1942	sunk 11.10.1943
LCT294	Darby Products, Kansas City			9.1942	sunk 6.6.1944
LCT295	Darby Products, Kansas City	8.1942	9.1942	9.1942	to the UK 1942 (LCT2295)
LCT296	Darby Products, Kansas City	9.1942	9.1942	9.1942	to the UK 1942 (LCT2296)
LCT297	Darby Products, Kansas City	9.1942	9.1942	9.1942	to the UK 1942 (LCT2297)

LCT298	Darby Products, Kansas City			10.1942	
LCT299	Darby Products, Kansas City			10.1942	
LCT300	Darby Products, Kansas City			10.1942	
LCT301	Darby Products, Kansas City	1942	1942	10.1942	to the UK 1942 (LCT2301)
LCT302	Darby Products, Kansas City	1942	1942	10.1942	to the UK 1942 (LCT2302)
LCT303	Darby Products, Kansas City	1942	1942	10.1942	to the UK 1942 (LCT2303)
LCT304	Darby Products, Kansas City	1942	1942	10.1942	to the UK 1942 (LCT2304)
LCT305	Darby Products, Kansas City			10.1942	sunk 6.6.1944
LCT306	Darby Products, Kansas City	1942	1942	10.1942	to the UK 1942 (LCT2306)
LCT307	Darby Products, Kansas City	1942	1942	10.1942	to the UK 1942 (LCT2307)
LCT308	Omaha Steel Works			11.1942	
LCT309	Omaha Steel Works	1942	1942	11.1942	to the UK 1942 (LCT2309)
LCT310	Omaha Steel Works	1942	1942	11.1942	to the UK 1942 (LCT2310)
LCT311	Omaha Steel Works			11.1942	sunk 9.8.1943
LCT312	Omaha Steel Works	1942	1942	(11.1942)	to the UK 1942 (LCT2312)
LCT313	Omaha Steel Works	9.1942	9.1942	11.1942	to the UK 1942 (LCT2313)
LCT314	Omaha Steel Works			12.1942	
LCT315	Omaha Steel Works			12.1942	sunk 23.3.1944
LCT316	Omaha Steel Works			10.1942	
LCT317	Omaha Steel Works			11.1942	
LCT318	Omaha Steel Works			11.1942	
LCT319	Omaha Steel Works			11.1942	sunk 27.8.1943
LCT320	Omaha Steel Works			9.1942	
LCT321	Omaha Steel Works			10.1942	
LCT322	Omaha Steel Works			10.1942	
LCT323	Omaha Steel Works			10.1942	
LCT324	Omaha Steel Works			10.1942	
LCT325	Omaha Steel Works			10.1942	
LCT326	Omaha Steel Works			10.1942	
LCT327	Omaha Steel Works			10.1942	
LCT328	Omaha Steel Works			11.1942	
LCT329	Omaha Steel Works			11.1942	
LCT330	Omaha Steel Works			10.1942	
LCT331	Omaha Steel Works	1942	1942	(11.1942)	to the UK 1942 (LCT2331)
LCT332	Decatur Iron & Steel			8.1942	sunk 6.6.1944
LCT333	Decatur Iron & Steel			8.1942	
LCT334	Decatur Iron & Steel	6.1942	8.1942	8.1942	to the UK 1942 (LCT2334)
LCT335	Decatur Iron & Steel	1942	1942	(8.1942)	to the UK 1942 (LCT2335)
LCT336	Decatur Iron & Steel	6.1942	8.1942	8.1942	to the UK 1942 (LCT2336)
LCT337	Decatur Iron & Steel	6.1942	8.1942	9.1942	to the UK 1942 (LCT2337)
LCT338	Decatur Iron & Steel	6.1942	8.1942	9.1942	to the UK 1942 (LCT2338)
LCT339	Decatur Iron & Steel	6.1942	8.1942	9.1942	to the UK 1942 (LCT2339)
LCT340	Decatur Iron & Steel			9.1942	sunk 9.2.1944
LCT341	Decatur Iron & Steel	1942	1942	(9.1942)	to the UK 1942 (LCT2341)
LCT342	Decatur Iron & Steel			10.1942	sunk 29.9.1943
LCT343	Decatur Iron & Steel	6.1942	8.1942	10.1942	to the UK 1942 (LCT2343)
LCT344	Decatur Iron & Steel	1942	1942	(10.1942)	to the UK 1942 (LCT2344)
LCT345	Decatur Iron & Steel	6.1942	8.1942	10.1942	to the UK 1942 (LCT2345)
LCT346	Decatur Iron & Steel			10.1942	
LCT347	Decatur Iron & Steel			11.1942	
LCT348	Decatur Iron & Steel			11.1942	
LCT349	Decatur Iron & Steel			11.1942	

LCT350	Decatur Iron & Steel			11.1942	
LCT351	Decatur Iron & Steel			10.1942	
LCT352	Decatur Iron & Steel			11.1942	sunk 2.4.1945
LCT353	Decatur Iron & Steel			11.1942	garbage lighter 9.1946
LCT354	Decatur Iron & Steel			11.1942	
LCT355	Decatur Iron & Steel			11.1942	
LCT356	Decatur Iron & Steel			11.1942	
LCT357	Decatur Iron & Steel			11.1942	
LCT358	Decatur Iron & Steel			11.1942	
LCT359	Decatur Iron & Steel			11.1942	
LCT360	Decatur Iron & Steel			12.1942	
LCT361	Decatur Iron & Steel	11.1942	12.1942	12.1942	to the UK 1942 (LCT2361)
LCT362	Decatur Iron & Steel			12.1942	sunk 6.6.1944
LCT363	Decatur Iron & Steel	1942	1942	12.1942	to the UK 1942 (LCT2363)
LCT364	Decatur Iron & Steel			12.1942	sunk 6.6.1944
LCT365	Mount Vernon Bridge			10.1942	
LCT366	Mount Vernon Bridge			10.1942	sunk 9.9.1943
LCT367	Mount Vernon Bridge			10.1942	
LCT368	Mount Vernon Bridge			10.1942	
LCT369	Mount Vernon Bridge			10.1942	
LCT370	Mount Vernon Bridge			10.1942	
LCT371	Mount Vernon Bridge			10.1942	
LCT372	Mount Vernon Bridge			10.1942	
LCT373	Mount Vernon Bridge			10.1942	
LCT374	Mount Vernon Bridge			10.1942	
LCT375	Mount Vernon Bridge			10.1942	
LCT376	Mount Vernon Bridge			10.1942	
LCT377	Mount Vernon Bridge			10.1942	
LCT378	Mount Vernon Bridge			11.1942	
LCT379	Mount Vernon Bridge			11.1942	
LCT380	Mount Vernon Bridge			11.1942	
LCT381	Mount Vernon Bridge			11.1942	
LCT382	Mount Vernon Bridge			11.1942	
LCT383	Mount Vernon Bridge			11.1942	
LCT384	Mount Vernon Bridge			11.1942	
LCT385	Mount Vernon Bridge			11.1942	
LCT386	Mount Vernon Bridge			11.1942	
LCT387	Mount Vernon Bridge			11.1942	
LCT388	Mount Vernon Bridge			11.1942	
LCT389	Mount Vernon Bridge			11.1942	
LCT390	Mount Vernon Bridge			12.1942	
LCT391	Mount Vernon Bridge			12.1942	
LCT392	Mount Vernon Bridge			12.1942	
LCT393	Mount Vernon Bridge			12.1942	
LCT394	Mount Vernon Bridge			12.1942	
LCT395	Mount Vernon Bridge			12.1942	
LCT396	Mount Vernon Bridge			12.1942	
LCT397	Mount Vernon Bridge			12.1942	
LCT398	Mount Vernon Bridge	1942	1942	(12.1942)	to the UK 1942 (LCT2398)
LCT399	Mount Vernon Bridge	12.1942	12.1942	12.1942	to the UK 1942 (LCT2399)
LCT400	Mount Vernon Bridge			1.1943	
LCT401	New York SB, Camden			8.1942	

LCT402	New York SB, Camden	1942	1942	8.1942	to the UK 1942 (LCT2402)
LCT403	New York SB, Camden			8.1942	
LCT404	New York SB, Camden			8.1942	
LCT405	New York SB, Camden			8.1942	
LCT406	New York SB, Camden			8.1942	
LCT407	New York SB, Camden			8.1942	
LCT408	New York SB, Camden			8.1942	
LCT409	New York SB, Camden			8.1942	
LCT410	New York SB, Camden			8.1942	
LCT411	New York SB, Camden			8.1942	
LCT412	New York SB, Camden			8.1942	scuttled 1946
LCT413	New York SB, Camden			8.1942	sunk 6.1944
LCT414	New York SB, Camden			8.1942	scuttled 1946
LCT415	New York SB, Camden			8.1942	
LCT416	New York SB, Camden			8.1942	
LCT417	New York SB, Camden			8.1942	
LCT418	New York SB, Camden			8.1942	
LCT419	New York SB, Camden			8.1942	
LCT420	New York SB, Camden	1942	1942	(9.1942)	to the UK 1942 (LCT2420)
LCT421	New York SB, Camden	1942	1942	9.1942	to the UK 1942 (LCT2421)
LCT422	New York SB, Camden	1942	1942	(9.1942)	to the UK 1942 (LCT2422)
LCT423	New York SB, Camden	1942	1942	9.1942	to the UK 1942 (LCT(R)2423)
LCT424	New York SB, Camden	1942	1942	9.1942	to the UK 1942 (LCT2424)
LCT425	New York SB, Camden	1942	1942	9.1942	to the UK 1942 (LCT2425)
LCT426	New York SB, Camden	1942	1942	9.1942	to the UK 1942 (LCT2426)
LCT427	New York SB, Camden	1942	1942	9.1942	to the UK 1942 (LCT2427)
LCT428	New York SB, Camden	1942	1942	9.1942	to the UK 1942 (LCT2428)
LCT429	New York SB, Camden	1942	1942	9.1942	to the UK 1942 (LCT2429)
LCT430	New York SB, Camden	1942	1942	9.1942	to the UK 1942 (LCT2430)
LCT431	New York SB, Camden			9.1942	
LCT432	New York SB, Camden	8.1942	8.1942	(9.1942)	to the UK 1942 (LCT2432)
LCT433	New York SB, Camden	8.1942	8.1942	(9.1942)	to the UK 1942 (LCT2433)
LCT434	New York SB, Camden			9.1942	
LCT435	New York SB, Camden	8.1942	8.1942	9.1942	to the UK 1942 (LCT2435)
LCT436	New York SB, Camden	8.1942	8.1942	9.1942	to the UK 1942 (LCT2436)
LCT437	New York SB, Camden	1942	1942	9.1942	to the UK 1942 (LCT2437)
LCT438	New York SB, Camden	9.1942	9.1942	9.1942	to the UK 1942 (LCT2438)
LCT439	New York SB, Camden	9.1942	9.1942	9.1942	to the UK 1942 (LCT2439)
LCT440	New York SB, Camden	9.1942	9.1942	9.1942	to the UK 1942 (LCT2440)
LCT441	New York SB, Camden	9.1942	9.1942	9.1942	to the UK 1942 (LCT2441)
LCT442	New York SB, Camden	9.1942	9.1942	9.1942	to the UK 1942 (LCT2442)
LCT443	New York SB, Camden			9.1942	
LCT444	New York SB, Camden	9.1942	9.1942	9.1942	to the UK 1942 (LCT2444)
LCT445	New York SB, Camden	9.1942	9.1942	9.1942	to the UK 1942 (LCT2445)
LCT446	New York SB, Camden			9.1942	
LCT447	New York SB, Camden			9.1942	
LCT448	New York SB, Camden			9.1942	
LCT449	New York SB, Camden			9.1942	
LCT(R)450	New York SB, Camden	9.1942	9.1942	9.1942	to the UK 1942 (LCT(R)2450)
LCT451	New York SB, Camden			9.1942	
LCT(R)452	New York SB, Camden	9.1942	18.9.1942	9.1942	
LCT453	New York SB, Camden	9.1942	9.1942	(10.1942)	to the UK 1942 (LCT2453)

LCT454	New York SB, Camden	1942	1942	10.1942	to the UK 1942 (LCT2454)
LCT455	New York SB, Camden	9.1942	9.1942	(10.1942)	to the UK 1942 (LCT2455)
LCT456	New York SB, Camden	9.1942		10.1942	
LCT457	New York SB, Camden			10.1942	
LCT458	New York SB, Camden			10.1942	sunk 7.6.1944
LCT459	New York SB, Camden			10.1942	sunk 19.9.1944
LCT460	New York SB, Camden			10.1942	
LCT461	New York SB, Camden	9.1942	9.1942	(10.1942)	to the UK 1942 (LCT2461)
LCT462	New York SB, Camden			10.1942	
LCT463	New York SB, Camden			10.1942	
LCT(R)464	New York SB, Camden	9.1942	29.9.1942	10.1942	
LCT465	New York SB, Camden			10.1942	
LCT466	New York SB, Camden			10.1942	
LCT467	New York SB, Camden			10.1942	
LCT468	New York SB, Camden			10.1942	
LCT469	New York SB, Camden			10.1942	
LCT470	New York SB, Camden			10.1942	
LCT471	New York SB, Camden			10.1942	
LCT472	New York SB, Camden			10.1942	
LCT(R)473	New York SB, Camden	10.1942	7.10.1942	10.1942	
LCT474	New York SB, Camden			10.1942	
LCT475	New York SB, Camden			10.1942	
LCT476	New York SB, Camden			10.1942	to France 1949
LCT477	New York SB, Camden	1942	1942	10.1942	to the UK 1942 (LCT2477)
LCT478	New York SB, Camden	10.1942	10.1942	(10.1942)	to the UK 1942 (LCT2478)
LCT479	New York SB, Camden	10.1942	10.1942	(10.1942)	to the UK 1942 (LCT2479)
LCT480	New York SB, Camden	10.1942	10.1942	(10.1942)	to the UK 1942 (LCT2480)
LCT481	New York SB, Camden	10.1942	10.1942	10.1942	
LCT482	New York SB, Camden			10.1942	
LCT483	New York SB, Camden	10.1942	10.1942	11.1942	to the UK 1942 (LCT2483)
LCT484	New York SB, Camden	1942	1942	11.1942	to the UK 1942 (LCT2484)
LCT485	New York SB, Camden	1942	1942	11.1942	to the UK 1942 (LCT2485)
LCT486	New York SB, Camden			11.1942	sunk 7.6.1944
LCT487	New York SB, Camden	10.1942	10.1942	11.1942	to the UK 1942 (LCT2487)
LCT488	New York SB, Camden	1942	1942	11.1942	to the UK 1942 (LCT2488)
LCT489	New York SB, Camden			11.1942	
LCT490	New York SB, Camden	10.1942	10.1942	11.1942	to the UK (LCT2490)
LCT491	New York SB, Camden	10.1942	10.1942	(11.1942)	to the UK 1942 (LCT2491)
LCT492	New York SB, Camden			11.1942	
LCT493	New York SB, Camden			11.1942	
LCT494	New York SB, Camden			11.1942	
LCT495	New York SB, Camden			11.1942	
LCT496	New York SB, Camden			11.1942	sunk 2.10.1943
LCT497	New York SB, Camden			11.1942	
LCT498	New York SB, Camden	1942	1942	11.1942	to the UK 1942 (LCT2498)
LCT499	New York SB, Camden	1942	1942	11.1942	to the UK 1942 (LCT2499)
LCT500	New York SB, Camden	1942	1942	11.1942	to the UK 1942 (LCT2500)

143 / 286 t, 34.8 x 10.0 x 1.27 m, 3 Grey Marine diesels, *LCT1 1943*
675 hp, 8 kts, 1200 nm (7 kts), complement 11; 2 x 1 –
20/70 Oerlikon or (1 x 1 – 20/70 Oerlikon, 2 x 1 – 12.7
MG); 4 medium or 3 heavy tanks or 150 t of cargo (LCT)

LCT401

or rocket launchers (LCT(R))

The design was completed at the end of 1941 according to the British terms of reference. Hull could be disassembled into 3-5 parts for transportation over long distances. Some craft were completed as fire support LCT(R) (landing craft, tank (rocket)).

LCT19 was sunk by German aircraft 14.7.1943. *LCT21* was sunk aboard the s/s *Arthur Middleton en route* from the USA to the Mediterranean by German submarine *U73* 1.1.1943. *LCT22* and *LCT27* grounded at Normandy 6.6.1944. *LCT23* was sunk by an underwater explosion 3.5.1943. *LCT26* lost due to weather conditions 25.2.1944. *LCT28* was sunk by a mine 30.5.1943. *LCT30* was mined 6.6.1944. *LCT35* was sunk by German aircraft 15.2.1944. *LCT36* stranded 26.2.1944.

LCT89 – 118 (Jones & Laughlin) were cancelled in 1942.

LCT(6) type landing craft tank

LCT501	Manitowoc SB			8.1943	to Peru 8.1947 (Zarumilla)
LCT502	Bison SB, North Tonawanda			8.1943	
LCT503	Bison SB, North Tonawanda			8.1943	
LCT504	Bison SB, North Tonawanda			8.1943	
LCT505	Bison SB, North Tonawanda			8.1943	
LCT506	Bison SB, North Tonawanda			8.1943	
LCT507	Bison SB, North Tonawanda			8.1943	
LCT508	Bison SB, North Tonawanda			9.1943	
LCT509	Bison SB, North Tonawanda	6.1943	4.7.1943	9.1943	harbor craft 3.1966
LCT510	Bison SB, North Tonawanda			9.1943	
LCT511	Bison SB, North Tonawanda			9.1943	
LCT512	Bison SB, North Tonawanda			9.1943	to China 1946
LCT513	Bison SB, North Tonawanda			9.1943	
LCT514	Bison SB, North Tonawanda			9.1943	
LCT515	Bison SB, North Tonawanda			9.1943	to China 1946
LCT516	Bison SB, North Tonawanda			9.1943	
LCT517	Bison SB, North Tonawanda			9.1943	
LCT518	Bison SB, North Tonawanda			9.1943	
LCT519	Bison SB, North Tonawanda			10.1943	
LCT520	Bison SB, North Tonawanda	7.1943	15.8.1943	10.1943	stricken 1951/56
LCT521	Bison SB, North Tonawanda			9.1943	
LCT522	Bison SB, North Tonawanda			10.1943	
LCT523	Bison SB, North Tonawanda			9.1943	
LCT524	Bison SB, North Tonawanda	7.1943	25.8.1943	9.1943	harbor craft 5.1958
LCT525	Bison SB, North Tonawanda			9.1943	
LCT526	Bison SB, North Tonawanda			9.1943	
LCT527	Bison SB, North Tonawanda			9.1943	
LCT528	Bison SB, North Tonawanda			9.1943	
LCT529	Bison SB, North Tonawanda	8.1943	2.9.1943	10.1943	harbor craft 5.1958
LCT530	Bison SB, North Tonawanda			10.1943	
LCT531	Bison SB, North Tonawanda			9.1943	to S. Korea 1960 (Mulkae 71)
LCT532	Bison SB, North Tonawanda			9.1943	
LCT533	Bison SB, North Tonawanda			9.1943	
LCT534	Bison SB, North Tonawanda			9.1943	
LCT535	Bison SB, North Tonawanda			9.1943	
LCT536	Bison SB, North Tonawanda			9.1943	
LCT537	Bison SB, North Tonawanda			10.1943	

LCT538	Bison SB, North Tonawanda		10.1943	
LCT539	Bison SB, North Tonawanda		10.1943	harbor craft 1960s
LCT540	Bison SB, North Tonawanda		10.1943	
LCT541	Bison SB, North Tonawanda		10.1943	
LCT542	Bison SB, North Tonawanda		10.1943	
LCT543	Bison SB, North Tonawanda		10.1943	
LCT544	Bison SB, North Tonawanda		10.1943	
LCT545	Bison SB, North Tonawanda		10.1943	
LCT546	Bison SB, North Tonawanda		10.1943	
LCT547	Bison SB, North Tonawanda		10.1943	
LCT548	Bison SB, North Tonawanda		10.1943	sunk 10.1944
LCT549	Bison SB, North Tonawanda		10.1943	
LCT550	Bison SB, North Tonawanda	9.1943 3.10.1943	10.1943	harbor craft 5.1958
LCT551	Bison SB, North Tonawanda		10.1943	
LCT552	Bison SB, North Tonawanda		10.1943	
LCT553	Bison SB, North Tonawanda		10.1943	
LCT554	Bison SB, North Tonawanda		10.1943	
LCT555	Bison SB, North Tonawanda		10.1943	sunk 6.6.1944
LCT556	Bison SB, North Tonawanda		11.1943	
LCT557	Bison SB, North Tonawanda		11.1943	
LCT558	Bison SB, North Tonawanda		11.1943	
LCT559	Bison SB, North Tonawanda		11.1943	to the USSR 1946 (DT-3)
LCT560	Bison SB, North Tonawanda		11.1943	
LCT561	Bison SB, North Tonawanda		11.1943	to the USSR 1945 (DS-12)
LCT562	Bison SB, North Tonawanda	10.1943 23.10.1943	11.1943	harbor craft 5.1958
LCT563	Bison SB, North Tonawanda		11.1943	to the USSR 1946 (DT-4)
LCT564	Bison SB, North Tonawanda		11.1943	
LCT565	Bison SB, North Tonawanda		11.1943	
LCT566	Bison SB, North Tonawanda		11.1943	
LCT567	Bison SB, North Tonawanda		11.1943	
LCT568	Bison SB, North Tonawanda		11.1943	
LCT569	Bison SB, North Tonawanda		11.1943	
LCT570	Bison SB, North Tonawanda		11.1943	
LCT571	Bison SB, North Tonawanda		11.1943	
LCT572	Bison SB, North Tonawanda		11.1943	sunk 6.1944
LCT573	Bison SB, North Tonawanda		11.1943	
LCT574	Pidgeon Thomas Iron, Memphis		8.1943	
LCT575	Pidgeon Thomas Iron, Memphis		8.1943	
LCT576	Pidgeon Thomas Iron, Memphis		8.1943	
LCT577	Pidgeon Thomas Iron, Memphis		9.1943	
LCT578	Pidgeon Thomas Iron, Memphis		9.1943	
LCT579	Pidgeon Thomas Iron, Memphis		9.1943	sunk 4.10.1944
LCT580	Pidgeon Thomas Iron, Memphis		9.1943	
LCT581	Pidgeon Thomas Iron, Memphis		9.1943	
LCT582	Pidgeon Thomas Iron, Memphis		9.1943	sunk 22.1.1944
LCT583	Pidgeon Thomas Iron, Memphis		9.1943	
LCT584	Pidgeon Thomas Iron, Memphis		9.1943	
LCT585	Pidgeon Thomas Iron, Memphis		9.1943	
LCT586	Pidgeon Thomas Iron, Memphis		10.1943	
LCT587	Pidgeon Thomas Iron, Memphis		10.1943	
LCT588	Pidgeon Thomas Iron, Memphis		10.1943	to Turkey 1967 (Ç201)
LCT589	Pidgeon Thomas Iron, Memphis		10.1943	

LCT590	Pidgeon Thomas Iron, Memphis			10.1943	
LCT591	Pidgeon Thomas Iron, Memphis			10.1943	
LCT592	Pidgeon Thomas Iron, Memphis	9.1943	20.10.1943	10.1943	harbor craft 5.1958
LCT593	Pidgeon Thomas Iron, Memphis			10.1943	sunk 6.6.1944
LCT594	Pidgeon Thomas Iron, Memphis			10.1943	to Greece 1946
LCT595	Pidgeon Thomas Iron, Memphis			11.1943	
LCT596	Pidgeon Thomas Iron, Memphis			11.1943	
LCT597	Pidgeon Thomas Iron, Memphis			11.1943	sunk 6.6.1944
LCT598	Pidgeon Thomas Iron, Memphis			11.1943	
LCT599	Pidgeon Thomas Iron, Memphis			11.1943	
LCT600	Pidgeon Thomas Iron, Memphis	10.1943	16.11.1943	11.1943	harbor craft 5.1958
LCT601	Pidgeon Thomas Iron, Memphis			11.1943	
LCT602	Pidgeon Thomas Iron, Memphis			11.1943	
LCT603	Pidgeon Thomas Iron, Memphis			12.1943	
LCT604	Pidgeon Thomas Iron, Memphis			12.1943	
LCT605	Pidgeon Thomas Iron, Memphis			12.1943	
LCT606	Pidgeon Thomas Iron, Memphis			12.1943	
LCT607	Pidgeon Thomas Iron, Memphis			12.1943	to Greece 1946
LCT608	Pidgeon Thomas Iron, Memphis			12.1943	to Turkey 1967 (Ç202)
LCT609	Pidgeon Thomas Iron, Memphis			12.1943	
LCT610	Pidgeon Thomas Iron, Memphis			2.1943	ferry 6.1951
LCT611	Pidgeon Thomas Iron, Memphis			12.1943	
LCT612	Pidgeon Thomas Iron, Memphis			1.1944	sunk 6.6.1944
LCT613	Pidgeon Thomas Iron, Memphis			1.1944	
LCT614	Pidgeon Thomas Iron, Memphis			1.1944	
LCT615	Pidgeon Thomas Iron, Memphis			1.1944	
LCT616	Pidgeon Thomas Iron, Memphis			1.1944	
LCT617	Pidgeon Thomas Iron, Memphis			1.1944	
LCT618	Pidgeon Thomas Iron, Memphis			1.1944	
LCT619	Pidgeon Thomas Iron, Memphis			1.1944	to Greece 1946
LCT620	Pidgeon Thomas Iron, Memphis			1.1944	to Greece 1946
LCT621	Pidgeon Thomas Iron, Memphis			1.1944	
LCT622	Bison SB, North Tonawanda			11.1943	to France 1952 (L9085)
LCT623	Bison SB, North Tonawanda			11.1943	
LCT624	Bison SB, North Tonawanda			11.1943	
LCT625	Bison SB, North Tonawanda			11.1943	to Greece 1946
LCT626	Bison SB, North Tonawanda			11.1943	
LCT627	Bison SB, North Tonawanda			12.1943	to the UK 1943 (LCT2627)
LCT628	Bison SB, North Tonawanda			12.1943	to the UK 1943 (LCT2628)
LCT629	Bison SB, North Tonawanda	11.1943	13.12.1943	1.1944	harbor craft 5.1958
LCT630	Bison SB, North Tonawanda			1.1944	
LCT631	Bison SB, North Tonawanda			1.1944	
LCT632	Bison SB, North Tonawanda			1.1944	
LCT633	Bison SB, North Tonawanda			1.1944	
LCT634	Bison SB, North Tonawanda			1.1944	
LCT635	Bison SB, North Tonawanda			1.1944	to France 1946 (LCT635)
LCT636	Bison SB, North Tonawanda			1.1944	
LCT637	Bison SB, North Tonawanda	12.1943	18.1.1944	1.1944	harbor craft 3.1966
LCT638	Bison SB, North Tonawanda	12.1943	20.1.1944	1.1944	stricken 1958
LCT639	Bison SB, North Tonawanda			1.1944	ferry 6.1951
LCT640	Bison SB, North Tonawanda			1.1944	to Israel 1959
LCT641	Bison SB, North Tonawanda			1.1944	

LCT642	Bison SB, North Tonawanda			1.1944	
LCT643	Bison SB, North Tonawanda			1.1944	
LCT644	Bison SB, North Tonawanda	1.1944	26.1.1944	1.1944	harbor craft 5.1958
LCT645	Bison SB, North Tonawanda			1.1944	
LCT646	Bison SB, North Tonawanda	1.1944	27.1.1944	1.1944	harbor craft 3.1966
LCT647	Bison SB, North Tonawanda			1.1944	
LCT648	Bison SB, North Tonawanda			1.1944	
LCT649	Bison SB, North Tonawanda			1.1944	to Denmark 1.1962 (Odin)
LCT650	Bison SB, North Tonawanda			2.1944	
LCT651	Bison SB, North Tonawanda			2.1944	
LCT652	Bison SB, North Tonawanda			2.1944	
LCT653	Bison SB, North Tonawanda			2.1944	
LCT654	Bison SB, North Tonawanda			2.1944	
LCT655	Bison SB, North Tonawanda			2.1944	
LCT656	Bison SB, North Tonawanda			2.1944	
LCT657	Bison SB, North Tonawanda			2.1944	
LCT658	Bison SB, North Tonawanda			2.1944	
LCT659	Bison SB, North Tonawanda			2.1944	
LCT660	Bison SB, North Tonawanda			2.1944	
LCT661	Bison SB, North Tonawanda			2.1944	
LCT662	Pidgeon Thomas Iron, Memphis			1.1944	
LCT663	Pidgeon Thomas Iron, Memphis			2.1944	
LCT664	Pidgeon Thomas Iron, Memphis			2.1944	harbor craft 1958
LCT665	Pidgeon Thomas Iron, Memphis			2.1944	
LCT666	Pidgeon Thomas Iron, Memphis	1.1944	5.2.1944	2.1944	to Turkey 1967 (Ç203)
LCT667	Pidgeon Thomas Iron, Memphis			2.1944	to Turkey 1967 (Ç204)
LCT668	Pidgeon Thomas Iron, Memphis			2.1944	harbor craft 1958
LCT669	Pidgeon Thomas Iron, Memphis			2.1944	
LCT670	Pidgeon Thomas Iron, Memphis			2.1944	
LCT671	Pidgeon Thomas Iron, Memphis			2.1944	
LCT672	Pidgeon Thomas Iron, Memphis			2.1944	
LCT673	Pidgeon Thomas Iron, Memphis			3.1944	to Israel 1959
LCT674	Pidgeon Thomas Iron, Memphis			3.1944	
LCT675	Pidgeon Thomas Iron, Memphis			3.1944	
LCT676	Pidgeon Thomas Iron, Memphis			3.1944	
LCT677	Pidgeon Thomas Iron, Memphis	2.1944	8.3.1944	3.1944	harbor craft 5.1958
LCT678	Pidgeon Thomas Iron, Memphis			3.1944	
LCT679	Pidgeon Thomas Iron, Memphis			3.1944	
LCT680	Pidgeon Thomas Iron, Memphis			3.1944	
LCT681	Pidgeon Thomas Iron, Memphis			3.1944	
LCT682	Pidgeon Thomas Iron, Memphis			3.1944	
LCT683	Pidgeon Thomas Iron, Memphis			3.1944	
LCT684	Pidgeon Thomas Iron, Memphis			4.1944	
LCT685	Pidgeon Thomas Iron, Memphis			4.1944	
LCT686	Pidgeon Thomas Iron, Memphis	3.1944	4.4.1944	4.1944	harbor craft 5.1958
LCT687	Pidgeon Thomas Iron, Memphis			4.1944	
LCT688	Pidgeon Thomas Iron, Memphis			4.1944	
LCT689	Pidgeon Thomas Iron, Memphis			4.1944	
LCT690	Pidgeon Thomas Iron, Memphis			4.1944	
LCT691	Pidgeon Thomas Iron, Memphis			4.1944	
LCT692	Pidgeon Thomas Iron, Memphis			4.1944	
LCT693	Pidgeon Thomas Iron, Memphis			4.1944	

LCT694	Pidgeon Thomas Iron, Memphis			5.1944	
LCT695	Pidgeon Thomas Iron, Memphis			5.1944	
LCT696	Pidgeon Thomas Iron, Memphis			5.1944	to France 1946 (L9090)
LCT697	Pidgeon Thomas Iron, Memphis			5.1944	
LCT698	Pidgeon Thomas Iron, Memphis			5.1944	
LCT699	Pidgeon Thomas Iron, Memphis			5.1944	
LCT700	Pidgeon Thomas Iron, Memphis			5.1944	to Taiwan 1958 (He Zhi)
LCT701	Pidgeon Thomas Iron, Memphis			5.1944	
LCT702	Pidgeon Thomas Iron, Memphis			5.1944	
LCT703	Quincy Bargebuilders			12.1943	sunk 6.6.1944
LCT704	Quincy Bargebuilders			12.1943	
LCT705	Quincy Bargebuilders			12.1943	scuttled 1946
LCT706	Quincy Bargebuilders			12.1943	
LCT707	Quincy Bargebuilders			1.1944	
LCT708	Quincy Bargebuilders			1.1944	
LCT709	Quincy Bargebuilders	11.1943	26.12.1943	1.1944	harbor craft 3.1966
LCT710	Quincy Bargebuilders			1.1944	
LCT711	Quincy Bargebuilders			1.1944	
LCT712	Quincy Bargebuilders			1.1944	
LCT713	Quincy Bargebuilders			1.1944	sunk 6.1944
LCT714	Quincy Bargebuilders			1.1944	sunk 6.1944
LCT715	Quincy Bargebuilders			2.1944	to Denmark 1961
LCT716	Quincy Bargebuilders	12.1943	14.1.1944	2.1944	harbor craft 3.1966
LCT717	Quincy Bargebuilders			2.1944	
LCT718	Quincy Bargebuilders			2.1944	
LCT719	Quincy Bargebuilders			2.1944	
LCT720	Quincy Bargebuilders			2.1944	to France 1952 (L9091)
LCT721	Quincy Bargebuilders			2.1944	
LCT722	Quincy Bargebuilders			2.1944	
LCT723	Quincy Bargebuilders			2.1944	
LCT724	Quincy Bargebuilders			2.1944	
LCT725	Quincy Bargebuilders			3.1944	
LCT726	Quincy Bargebuilders			3.1944	
LCT727	Quincy Bargebuilders			3.1944	
LCT728	Quincy Bargebuilders			3.1944	
LCT729	Quincy Bargebuilders			3.1944	
LCT730	Quincy Bargebuilders			3.1944	
LCT731	Quincy Bargebuilders			3.1944	
LCT732	Quincy Bargebuilders			3.1944	
LCT733	Quincy Bargebuilders			3.1944	
LCT734	Quincy Bargebuilders			3.1944	
LCT735	Quincy Bargebuilders			3.1944	
LCT736	Quincy Bargebuilders			3.1944	
LCT737	Quincy Bargebuilders			3.1944	
LCT738	Quincy Bargebuilders			3.1944	
LCT739	Quincy Bargebuilders			4.1944	
LCT740	Quincy Bargebuilders			4.1944	
LCT741	Quincy Bargebuilders			4.1944	
LCT742	Quincy Bargebuilders	2.1944	11.3.1944	4.1944	harbor craft 5.1958
LCT743	Quincy Bargebuilders	2.1944	14.3.1944	4.1944	harbor craft 3.1966
LCT744	Quincy Bargebuilders			4.1944	to the USSR 1946 (DT-5)
LCT745	Quincy Bargebuilders			4.1944	to the USSR 1946 (DT-6)

LCT746	Quincy Bargebuilders			4.1944	
LCT747	Quincy Bargebuilders			4.1944	
LCT748	Quincy Bargebuilders			4.1944	
LCT749	Quincy Bargebuilders			4.1944	
LCT750	Quincy Bargebuilders			4.1944	
LCT751	Quincy Bargebuilders			5.1944	
LCT752	Quincy Bargebuilders			5.1944	
LCT753	Quincy Bargebuilders			5.1944	to Thailand 1946 (Talibong)
LCT754	Quincy Bargebuilders			5.1944	
LCT755	Quincy Bargebuilders			5.1944	
LCT756	Quincy Bargebuilders			5.1944	
LCT757	Quincy Bargebuilders			5.1944	
LCT758	Quincy Bargebuilders			5.1944	
LCT759	Quincy Bargebuilders			5.1944	
LCT760	Quincy Bargebuilders			5.1944	
LCT761	Quincy Bargebuilders			5.1944	
LCT762	Quincy Bargebuilders			5.1944	
LCT763	Missouri Valley Bridge, Evansville	10.1943	1.12.1943	12.1943	to Greece 1961 (Kythnos)
LCT764	Missouri Valley Bridge, Evansville	11.1943	23.12.1943	12.1943	harbor craft 5.1958
LCT765	Missouri Valley Bridge, Evansville			1.1944	to Denmark 1961
LCT766	Missouri Valley Bridge, Evansville			1.1944	to Greece 1959
LCT767	Missouri Valley Bridge, Evansville			1.1944	
LCT768	Missouri Valley Bridge, Evansville			1.1944	
LCT769	Missouri Valley Bridge, Evansville			2.1944	
LCT770	Missouri Valley Bridge, Evansville			2.1944	
LCT771	Missouri Valley Bridge, Evansville			2.1944	
LCT772	Missouri Valley Bridge, Evansville			2.1944	
LCT773	Missouri Valley Bridge, Evansville			2.1944	
LCT774	Missouri Valley Bridge, Evansville			3.1944	
LCT775	Mount Vernon Bridge			12.1943	
LCT776	Mount Vernon Bridge	11.1943	30.12.1943	12.1943	harbor craft 3.1966
LCT777	Mount Vernon Bridge			1.1944	sunk 6.6.1944
LCT778	Mount Vernon Bridge	11.1943	7.1.1944	1.1944	
LCT779	Mount Vernon Bridge			2.1944	to W. Germany 1958 (LCU1)
LCT780	Mount Vernon Bridge			2.1944	harbor craft 1960s
LCT781	Mount Vernon Bridge			2.1944	
LCT782	Mount Vernon Bridge			2.1944	
LCT783	Mount Vernon Bridge	2.1944	21.2.1944	2.1944	
LCT784	Mount Vernon Bridge			2.1944	
LCT785	Mount Vernon Bridge			3.1944	
LCT786	Mount Vernon Bridge			3.1944	
LCT787	Mount Vernon Bridge			3.1944	
LCT788	Mount Vernon Bridge	3.1944	25.3.1944	3.1944	harbor craft 5.1958
LCT789	Mount Vernon Bridge			3.1944	
LCT790	Mount Vernon Bridge			4.1944	
LCT791	Mount Vernon Bridge			4.1944	
LCT792	Mount Vernon Bridge			4.1944	
LCT793	Mount Vernon Bridge			4.1944	
LCT794	Mount Vernon Bridge			5.1944	
LCT795	Mount Vernon Bridge			5.1944	
LCT796	Mount Vernon Bridge			5.1944	
LCT797	Mount Vernon Bridge			5.1944	

LCT798	Mount Vernon Bridge		6.1944	
LCT799	Mount Vernon Bridge		6.1944	to France 1946 (L9092)
LCT800	Mount Vernon Bridge		6.1944	to Thailand 1946 (Rawi)
LCT801	Mount Vernon Bridge		6.1944	
LCT802	Mount Vernon Bridge		7.1944	
LCT803	Mount Vernon Bridge		7.1944	
LCT804	Mount Vernon Bridge		7.1944	
LCT805	Mount Vernon Bridge		7.1944	
LCT806	Mount Vernon Bridge		7.1944	
LCT807	Mount Vernon Bridge		8.1944	
LCT808	Mount Vernon Bridge		8.1944	
LCT809	Kansas City Steel		12.1943	
LCT810	Kansas City Steel		1.1944	to Denmark 1961
LCT811	Kansas City Steel		1.1944	
LCT812	Kansas City Steel		1.1944	scuttled 1946
LCT813	Kansas City Steel		1.1944	
LCT814	Kansas City Steel		2.1944	
LCT815	Kansas City Steel		2.1944	
LCT816	Kansas City Steel		2.1944	scuttled 1946
LCT817	Kansas City Steel		2.1944	
LCT818	Kansas City Steel		2.1944	scuttled 1946
LCT819	Kansas City Steel		2.1944	
LCT820	Kansas City Steel		2.1944	
LCT821	Kansas City Steel		3.1944	
LCT822	Kansas City Steel		3.1944	
LCT823	Kansas City Steel		3.1944	sunk 27.9.1944
LCT824	Kansas City Steel		3.1944	
LCT825	Kansas City Steel		3.1944	
LCT826	Kansas City Steel		4.1944	
LCT827	Kansas City Steel	3.1944	30.3.1944	4.1944	to Greece 1959 (Skiathos)
LCT828	Kansas City Steel		4.1944	
LCT829	Kansas City Steel		4.1944	
LCT830	Kansas City Steel		4.1944	
LCT831	Kansas City Steel		4.1944	
LCT832	Kansas City Steel		5.1944	
LCT833	Kansas City Steel		5.1944	
LCT834	Kansas City Steel		5.1944	to France 1946 (L9086)
LCT835	Kansas City Steel		5.1944	
LCT836	Kansas City Steel		5.1944	
LCT837	Kansas City Steel		5.1944	
LCT838	Kansas City Steel		5.1944	
LCT839	Kansas City Steel		6.1944	
LCT840	Kansas City Steel	5.1944	3.6.1944	6.1944	harbor craft 5.1958
LCT841	Kansas City Steel		6.1944	
LCT842	Kansas City Steel		6.1944	to Greece 1959
LCT843, 3.1945-AMCU1	Kansas City Steel	5.1944	21.6.1944	6.1944	minehunter 3.1945
LCT844, 3.1945-AMCU2	Kansas City Steel	5.1944	28.6.1944	7.1944	minehunter 3.1945
LCT845	Kansas City Steel		7.1944	

LCT846	Kansas City Steel			7.1944	
LCT847	Kansas City Steel			7.1944	
LCT848	Kansas City Steel			8.1944	
LCT849	Kansas City Steel			8.1944	to China 1946 (He Zhong)
LCT850	Kansas City Steel			8.1944	
LCT851	Darby Products, Kansas City	10.1943	15.12.1943	12.1943	harbor craft 3.1966
LCT852	Darby Products, Kansas City	11.1943	24.12.1943	1.1944	to Greece 1959 (Skopelos)
LCT853	Darby Products, Kansas City			1.1944	
LCT854	Darby Products, Kansas City			1.1944	diving tender 1951
LCT855	Darby Products, Kansas City			1.1944	to Peru 8.1947 (Salto)
LCT856	Darby Products, Kansas City			1.1944	
LCT857	Darby Products, Kansas City			2.1944	
LCT858	Darby Products, Kansas City			2.1944	
LCT859	Darby Products, Kansas City			2.1944	
LCT860	Darby Products, Kansas City			2.1944	
LCT861	Darby Products, Kansas City	1.1944	15.2.1944	2.1944	to Thailand 1946 (Adang)
LCT862	Darby Products, Kansas City			2.1944	
LCT863	Darby Products, Kansas City			2.1944	
LCT864	Darby Products, Kansas City			3.1944	
LCT865	Darby Products, Kansas City			3.1944	
LCT866	Darby Products, Kansas City			3.1944	
LCT867	Darby Products, Kansas City			3.1944	
LCT868	Darby Products, Kansas City			3.1944	
LCT869	Darby Products, Kansas City	2.1944	21.3.1944	3.1944	harbor craft 5.1958
LCT870	Darby Products, Kansas City			4.1944	
LCT871	Darby Products, Kansas City			4.1944	
LCT872	Darby Products, Kansas City			4.1944	
LCT873	Darby Products, Kansas City			4.1944	
LCT874	Darby Products, Kansas City			4.1944	scuttled 1946
LCT875	Darby Products, Kansas City			4.1944	
LCT876	Darby Products, Kansas City			5.1944	
LCT877	Darby Products, Kansas City	3.1944	2.4.1944	5.1944	harbor craft 5.1958
LCT878	Darby Products, Kansas City			5.1944	
LCT879	Darby Products, Kansas City			5.1944	
LCT880	Darby Products, Kansas City			5.1944	
LCT881	Darby Products, Kansas City			5.1944	
LCT882	Darby Products, Kansas City			5.1944	
LCT883	Darby Products, Kansas City			6.1944	
LCT884	Darby Products, Kansas City			6.1944	
LCT885	Darby Products, Kansas City			6.1944	
LCT886	Darby Products, Kansas City			6.1944	
LCT887, 3.1945- AMCU3	Darby Products, Kansas City	5.1944	18.6.1944	6.1944	minehunter 3.1945
LCT888, 3.1945- AMCU4	Darby Products, Kansas City	5.1944	23.6.1944	6.1944	minehunter 3.1945
LCT889, 3.1945- AMCU5	Darby Products, Kansas City	5.1944	29.6.1944	7.1944	minehunter 3.1945

LCT890, 3.1945- AMCU6	Darby Products, Kansas City	6.1944	4.7.1944	7.1944	minehunter 3.1945
LCT891	Darby Products, Kansas City			7.1944	
LCT892	Darby Products, Kansas City			7.1944	to China 1946 (He Qun)
LCT893	Missouri Valley Bridge, Evansville			3.1944	
LCT894	Missouri Valley Bridge, Evansville			3.1944	
LCT895	Missouri Valley Bridge, Evansville			3.1944	
LCT896	Missouri Valley Bridge, Evansville			4.1944	
LCT897	Missouri Valley Bridge, Evansville			4.1944	
LCT898	Missouri Valley Bridge, Evansville			4.1944	
LCT899	Missouri Valley Bridge, Evansville			4.1944	
LCT900	Missouri Valley Bridge, Evansville			4.1944	
LCT901	Missouri Valley Bridge, Evansville			4.1944	
LCT902	Missouri Valley Bridge, Evansville			5.1944	
LCT903	Missouri Valley Bridge, Evansville			5.1944	
LCT904	Missouri Valley Bridge, Evansville	4.1944	13.5.1944	5.1944	to Thailand 1946 (Khorum)
LCT905	Missouri Valley Bridge, Evansville			5.1944	
LCT906	Missouri Valley Bridge, Evansville			5.1944	
LCT907	Missouri Valley Bridge, Evansville			6.1944	
LCT908	Missouri Valley Bridge, Evansville			6.1944	
LCT909	Missouri Valley Bridge, Evansville			6.1944	
LCT910	Missouri Valley Bridge, Evansville			6.1944	
LCT911	Missouri Valley Bridge, Evansville			6.1944	
LCT912	Missouri Valley Bridge, Evansville			7.1944	
LCT913	Missouri Valley Bridge, Evansville			7.1944	
LCT914	Mare Island N Yd, Vallejo			10.1943	
LCT915	Mare Island N Yd, Vallejo			10.1943	
LCT916	Mare Island N Yd, Vallejo			10.1943	
LCT917	Mare Island N Yd, Vallejo	8.1943	16.10.1943	10.1943	harbor craft 3.1966
LCT918	Mare Island N Yd, Vallejo			10.1943	
LCT919	Mare Island N Yd, Vallejo			10.1943	
LCT920	Mare Island N Yd, Vallejo			10.1943	
LCT921	Mare Island N Yd, Vallejo			10.1943	
LCT922	Mare Island N Yd, Vallejo			10.1943	
LCT923	Mare Island N Yd, Vallejo			10.1943	
LCT924	Mare Island N Yd, Vallejo			11.1943	
LCT925	Mare Island N Yd, Vallejo			11.1943	
LCT926	Mare Island N Yd, Vallejo			11.1943	
LCT927	Mare Island N Yd, Vallejo			11.1943	
LCT928	Mare Island N Yd, Vallejo			11.1943	
LCT929	Mare Island N Yd, Vallejo			11.1943	
LCT930	Mare Island N Yd, Vallejo			11.1943	
LCT931	Mare Island N Yd, Vallejo			11.1943	
LCT932	Mare Island N Yd, Vallejo			11.1943	
LCT933	Mare Island N Yd, Vallejo			11.1943	
LCT934	Mare Island N Yd, Vallejo			11.1943	
LCT935	Mare Island N Yd, Vallejo			11.1943	
LCT936	Mare Island N Yd, Vallejo			11.1943	
LCT937	Mare Island N Yd, Vallejo			11.1943	
LCT938	Mare Island N Yd, Vallejo			11.1943	
LCT939	Mare Island N Yd, Vallejo			12.1943	

LCT940	Mare Island N Yd, Vallejo			12.1943	
LCT941	Mare Island N Yd, Vallejo			12.1943	
LCT942	Mare Island N Yd, Vallejo			12.1943	
LCT943	Mare Island N Yd, Vallejo			12.1943	
LCT944	Mare Island N Yd, Vallejo			12.1943	
LCT945	Mare Island N Yd, Vallejo			12.1943	
LCT946	Mare Island N Yd, Vallejo			12.1943	
LCT947	Mare Island N Yd, Vallejo			12.1943	
LCT948	Mare Island N Yd, Vallejo			12.1943	
LCT949	Mare Island N Yd, Vallejo			12.1943	
LCT950	Mare Island N Yd, Vallejo			12.1943	
LCT951	Mare Island N Yd, Vallejo			12.1943	
LCT952	Mare Island N Yd, Vallejo			12.1943	
LCT953	Mare Island N Yd, Vallejo			12.1943	
LCT954	Mare Island N Yd, Vallejo			12.1943	
LCT955	Mare Island N Yd, Vallejo			12.1943	
LCT956	Mare Island N Yd, Vallejo			1.1944	
LCT957	Mare Island N Yd, Vallejo			1.1944	
LCT958	Mare Island N Yd, Vallejo			1.1944	
LCT959	Mare Island N Yd, Vallejo			1.1944	
LCT960	Mare Island N Yd, Vallejo	11.1943	11.1.1944	1.1944	harbor craft 5.1958
LCT961	Mare Island N Yd, Vallejo			1.1944	sunk 21.5.1944
LCT962	Mare Island N Yd, Vallejo			1.1944	
LCT963	Mare Island N Yd, Vallejo			1.1944	sunk 21.5.1944
LCT964	Mare Island N Yd, Vallejo			1.1944	
LCT965	Mare Island N Yd, Vallejo			1.1944	
LCT966	Mare Island N Yd, Vallejo			1.1944	
LCT967	Mare Island N Yd, Vallejo			1.1944	
LCT968	Mare Island N Yd, Vallejo			1.1944	
LCT969	Mare Island N Yd, Vallejo			1.1944	
LCT970	Mare Island N Yd, Vallejo			2.1944	
LCT971	Mare Island N Yd, Vallejo	11.1943	30.1.1944	2.1944	to Greece 1959 (Kimolos)
LCT972	Mare Island N Yd, Vallejo			2.1944	
LCT973	Mare Island N Yd, Vallejo	11.1943	2.2.1944	2.1944	harbor craft 3.1966
LCT974	Mare Island N Yd, Vallejo			2.1944	harbor craft 1958
LCT975	Mare Island N Yd, Vallejo			2.1944	
LCT976	Mare Island N Yd, Vallejo			2.1944	
LCT977	Mare Island N Yd, Vallejo			2.1944	
LCT978	Mare Island N Yd, Vallejo			2.1944	
LCT979	Mare Island N Yd, Vallejo	12.1943	11.2.1944	2.1944	harbor craft 5.1958
LCT980	Mare Island N Yd, Vallejo	12.1943	14.2.1944	2.1944	harbor craft 5.1958
LCT981	Mare Island N Yd, Vallejo			2.1944	
LCT982	Mare Island N Yd, Vallejo			2.1944	
LCT983	Mare Island N Yd, Vallejo			2.1944	sunk 21.5.1944
LCT984	Mare Island N Yd, Vallejo			2.1944	sunk 9.6.1944
LCT985	Mare Island N Yd, Vallejo			2.1944	
LCT986	Mare Island N Yd, Vallejo			2.1944	
LCT987	Mare Island N Yd, Vallejo			2.1944	
LCT988	Mare Island N Yd, Vallejo			2.1944	sunk 9.6.1944
LCT989	Mare Island N Yd, Vallejo	10.1943	24.2.1944	2.1944	harbor craft 3.1966
LCT990	Mare Island N Yd, Vallejo	11.1943	30.1.1944	2.1944	
LCT991	Mare Island N Yd, Vallejo			3.1944	

LCT992	Mare Island N Yd, Vallejo		3.1944	
LCT993	Mare Island N Yd, Vallejo		3.1944	
LCT994	Mare Island N Yd, Vallejo		3.1944	
LCT995	Mare Island N Yd, Vallejo		3.1944	sunk 21.4.1945
LCT996	Mare Island N Yd, Vallejo		3.1944	
LCT997	Mare Island N Yd, Vallejo		3.1944	
LCT998	Mare Island N Yd, Vallejo		3.1944	
LCT999	Mare Island N Yd, Vallejo		3.1944	
LCT1000	Mare Island N Yd, Vallejo		3.1944	
LCT1001	Mare Island N Yd, Vallejo		3.1944	
LCT1002	Bison SB, North Tonawanda		2.1944	
LCT1003	Bison SB, North Tonawanda		2.1944	
LCT1004	Bison SB, North Tonawanda		2.1944	
LCT1005	Bison SB, North Tonawanda		2.1944	
LCT1006	Bison SB, North Tonawanda		2.1944	
LCT1007	Bison SB, North Tonawanda		2.1944	
LCT1008	Bison SB, North Tonawanda		2.1944	
LCT1009	Bison SB, North Tonawanda	2.1944 25.2.1944	2.1944	
LCT1010	Bison SB, North Tonawanda		2.1944	
LCT1011	Bison SB, North Tonawanda		2.1944	
LCT1012	Bison SB, North Tonawanda		2.1944	
LCT1013	Bison SB, North Tonawanda		2.1944	scuttled 1946
LCT1014	Bison SB, North Tonawanda		3.1944	
LCT1015	Bison SB, North Tonawanda		3.1944	to the USSR 1946 (DT-7)
LCT1016	Bison SB, North Tonawanda		3.1944	
LCT1017	Bison SB, North Tonawanda		3.1944	
LCT1018	Bison SB, North Tonawanda		3.1944	
LCT1019	Bison SB, North Tonawanda		3.1944	
LCT1020	Bison SB, North Tonawanda		3.1944	
LCT1021	Bison SB, North Tonawanda		3.1944	
LCT1022	Bison SB, North Tonawanda		3.1944	
LCT1023	Bison SB, North Tonawanda		3.1944	
LCT1024	Bison SB, North Tonawanda		3.1944	
LCT1025	Bison SB, North Tonawanda		3.1944	
LCT1026	Bison SB, North Tonawanda		3.1944	
LCT1027	Bison SB, North Tonawanda		4.1944	
LCT1028	Bison SB, North Tonawanda		4.1944	
LCT1029	Bison SB, North Tonawanda		4.1944	sunk 2.3.1945
LCT1030	Bison SB, North Tonawanda		4.1944	
LCT1031	Bison SB, North Tonawanda		4.1944	
LCT1032	Bison SB, North Tonawanda		4.1944	
LCT1033	Bison SB, North Tonawanda		4.1944	
LCT1034	Bison SB, North Tonawanda		4.1944	
LCT1035	Bison SB, North Tonawanda		4.1944	
LCT1036	Bison SB, North Tonawanda		4.1944	
LCT1037	Bison SB, North Tonawanda		4.1944	
LCT1038	Bison SB, North Tonawanda		4.1944	
LCT1039	Bison SB, North Tonawanda		4.1944	
LCT1040	Bison SB, North Tonawanda		4.1944	harbor barge 1950s
LCT1041	Bison SB, North Tonawanda		4.1944	
LCT1042	Bison SB, North Tonawanda		4.1944	to Denmark 1961
LCT1043	Bison SB, North Tonawanda		4.1944	

LCT1044	Bison SB, North Tonawanda			4.1944	
LCT1045	Bison SB, North Tonawanda			4.1944	
LCT1046	Bison SB, North Tonawanda			4.1944	to the USSR 5.1945 (DS-14)
LCT1047	Bison SB, North Tonawanda			4.1944	to the USSR 4.1945 (DS-11)
LCT1048	Bison SB, North Tonawanda			4.1944	
LCT1049	Bison SB, North Tonawanda			4.1944	
LCT1050	Bison SB, North Tonawanda			4.1944	sunk 27.7.1945
LCT1051	Bison SB, North Tonawanda			4.1944	to Vietnam 1956
LCT1052	Bison SB, North Tonawanda			4.1944	
LCT1053	Bison SB, North Tonawanda			4.1944	to the Netherlands 1945
LCT1054	Bison SB, North Tonawanda			4.1944	to the Netherlands 1945
LCT1055	Bison SB, North Tonawanda			4.1944	to the Netherlands 1945
LCT1056	Bison SB, North Tonawanda	4.1944	22.4.1944	4.1944	harbor craft 5.1958
LCT1057	Mare Island N Yd, Vallejo			3.1944	
LCT1058	Mare Island N Yd, Vallejo			3.1944	
LCT1059	Mare Island N Yd, Vallejo			3.1944	
LCT1060	Mare Island N Yd, Vallejo			3.1944	
LCT1061	Mare Island N Yd, Vallejo			3.1944	
LCT1062	Mare Island N Yd, Vallejo			3.1944	
LCT1063	Mare Island N Yd, Vallejo			3.1944	
LCT1064	Mare Island N Yd, Vallejo			3.1944	
LCT1065	Mare Island N Yd, Vallejo			3.1944	
LCT1066	Mare Island N Yd, Vallejo			3.1944	
LCT1067	Mare Island N Yd, Vallejo			4.1944	
LCT1068	Mare Island N Yd, Vallejo			4.1944	
LCT1069	Mare Island N Yd, Vallejo			4.1944	
LCT1070	Mare Island N Yd, Vallejo			4.1944	
LCT1071	Mare Island N Yd, Vallejo			4.1944	
LCT1072	Mare Island N Yd, Vallejo			4.1944	
LCT1073	Mare Island N Yd, Vallejo			4.1944	
LCT1074	Mare Island N Yd, Vallejo			4.1944	
LCT1075	Mare Island N Yd, Vallejo			4.1944	sunk 10.12.1944
LCT1076	Mare Island N Yd, Vallejo			4.1944	
LCT1077	Mare Island N Yd, Vallejo			4.1944	
LCT1078	Mare Island N Yd, Vallejo			4.1944	scuttled 1946
LCT1079	Mare Island N Yd, Vallejo			4.1944	
LCT1080	Mare Island N Yd, Vallejo			4.1944	
LCT1081	Mare Island N Yd, Vallejo			4.1944	
LCT1082	Mare Island N Yd, Vallejo	3.1944	2.5.1944	5.1944	harbor craft 5.1958
LCT1083	Quincy Bargebuilders			5.1944	
LCT1084	Quincy Bargebuilders			5.1944	
LCT1085	Quincy Bargebuilders	4.1944	29.4.1944	6.1944	
LCT1086	Quincy Bargebuilders	4.1944	2.5.1944	6.1944	harbor craft 5.1958
LCT1087	Quincy Bargebuilders			6.1944	
LCT1088	Quincy Bargebuilders			6.1944	
LCT1089	Quincy Bargebuilders			6.1944	to Thailand 1946 (Phetra)
LCT1090	Quincy Bargebuilders			6.1944	sunk 26.3.1945
LCT1091	Quincy Bargebuilders			6.1944	
LCT1092	Quincy Bargebuilders			6.1944	
LCT1093	Quincy Bargebuilders			6.1944	
LCT1094	Quincy Bargebuilders			6.1944	
LCT1095	Quincy Bargebuilders			7.1944	

LCT1096	Quincy Bargebuilders			7.1944	
LCT1097	Quincy Bargebuilders			7.1944	
LCT1098	Quincy Bargebuilders			7.1944	
LCT1099	Quincy Bargebuilders			7.1944	
LCT1100	Quincy Bargebuilders			7.1944	
LCT1101	Quincy Bargebuilders			7.1944	
LCT1102	Pidgeon Thomas Iron, Memphis			5.1944	
LCT1103	Pidgeon Thomas Iron, Memphis			6.1944	
LCT1104	Pidgeon Thomas Iron, Memphis			6.1944	
LCT1105	Pidgeon Thomas Iron, Memphis			6.1944	
LCT1106	Pidgeon Thomas Iron, Memphis			6.1944	
LCT1107	Pidgeon Thomas Iron, Memphis			6.1944	
LCT1108	Pidgeon Thomas Iron, Memphis			6.1944	
LCT1109	Pidgeon Thomas Iron, Memphis			6.1944	
LCT1110	Pidgeon Thomas Iron, Memphis			6.1944	
LCT1111	Pidgeon Thomas Iron, Memphis			6.1944	
LCT1112	Pidgeon Thomas Iron, Memphis			6.1944	scuttled 1946
LCT1113	Pidgeon Thomas Iron, Memphis			7.1944	scuttled 1946
LCT1114	Pidgeon Thomas Iron, Memphis			7.1944	scuttled 1946
LCT1115	Pidgeon Thomas Iron, Memphis			7.1944	scuttled 1946
LCT1116	Pidgeon Thomas Iron, Memphis			7.1944	
LCT1117	Pidgeon Thomas Iron, Memphis			7.1944	to the Philippines 1948
LCT1118	Pidgeon Thomas Iron, Memphis			7.1944	
LCT1119	Pidgeon Thomas Iron, Memphis			7.1944	
LCT1120	Pidgeon Thomas Iron, Memphis			7.1944	
LCT1121	Pidgeon Thomas Iron, Memphis			7.1944	
LCT1122	Pidgeon Thomas Iron, Memphis			7.1944	
LCT1123	Pidgeon Thomas Iron, Memphis			7.1944	
LCT1124	Pidgeon Thomas Iron, Memphis	6.1944	26.7.1944	8.1944	harbor craft 5.1958
LCT1125	Pidgeon Thomas Iron, Memphis			8.1944	
LCT1126	Pidgeon Thomas Iron, Memphis	7.1944	1.8.1944	8.1944	harbor craft 3.1966
LCT1127	Pidgeon Thomas Iron, Memphis			8.1944	
LCT1128	Pidgeon Thomas Iron, Memphis			8.1944	
LCT1129	Pidgeon Thomas Iron, Memphis			8.1944	
LCT1130	Quincy Bargebuilders			7.1944	
LCT1131	Quincy Bargebuilders			7.1944	
LCT1132	Quincy Bargebuilders			7.1944	
LCT1133	Quincy Bargebuilders			7.1944	
LCT1134	Quincy Bargebuilders			7.1944	
LCT1135	Quincy Bargebuilders			8.1944	
LCT1136	Bison SB, North Tonawanda	4.1944	26.4.1944	4.1944	harbor craft 5.1958
LCT1137	Bison SB, North Tonawanda			4.1944	
LCT1138	Bison SB, North Tonawanda			4.1944	
LCT1139	Bison SB, North Tonawanda			5.1944	
LCT1140	Bison SB, North Tonawanda			5.1944	
LCT1141	Bison SB, North Tonawanda			5.1944	
LCT1142	Bison SB, North Tonawanda			5.1944	
LCT1143	Bison SB, North Tonawanda			5.1944	to China 1946 (He Cheng)
LCT1144	Bison SB, North Tonawanda			5.1944	
LCT1145	Bison SB, North Tonawanda			5.1944	to China 1946 (He Zhen)
LCT1146	Bison SB, North Tonawanda			5.1944	
LCT1147	Bison SB, North Tonawanda			5.1944	

LCT1148	Bison SB, North Tonawanda			5.1944	
LCT1149	Bison SB, North Tonawanda			5.1944	
LCT1150	Bison SB, North Tonawanda			5.1944	
LCT1151	Bison SB, North Tonawanda			5.1944	sunk 26.1.1945
LCT1152	Bison SB, North Tonawanda			5.1944	
LCT1153	Bison SB, North Tonawanda			5.1944	
LCT1154	Bison SB, North Tonawanda			5.1944	
LCT1155	Bison SB, North Tonawanda	5.1944	20.5.1944	5.1944	
LCT1156	Bison SB, North Tonawanda	5.1944	24.5.1944	5.1944	harbor craft 5.1958
LCT1157	Bison SB, North Tonawanda	5.1944	24.5.1944	5.1944	
LCT1158	Bison SB, North Tonawanda	5.1944	28.5.1944	5.1944	
LCT1159	Bison SB, North Tonawanda	5.1944	28.5.1944	5.1944	harbor craft 5.1958
LCT1160	Bison SB, North Tonawanda	5.1944	28.5.1944	6.1944	
LCT1161	Bison SB, North Tonawanda	5.1944	28.5.1944	6.1944	to Peru 8.1947 (Pirura)
LCT1162	Bison SB, North Tonawanda	5.1944	31.5.1944	6.1944	harbor craft 5.1958
LCT1163	Bison SB, North Tonawanda			6.1944	to the USSR 8.1945 (DT-1)
LCT1164	Bison SB, North Tonawanda			6.1944	
LCT1165	Bison SB, North Tonawanda	5.1944	3.6.1944	6.1944	harbor craft 3.1966
LCT1166	Bison SB, North Tonawanda			6.1944	
LCT1167	Bison SB, North Tonawanda			6.1944	
LCT1168	Bison SB, North Tonawanda			6.1944	
LCT1169	Bison SB, North Tonawanda			6.1944	
LCT1170	Bison SB, North Tonawanda			6.1944	
LCT1171	Bison SB, North Tonawanda			6.1944	to China 1946
LCT1172	Bison SB, North Tonawanda			6.1944	
LCT1173	Bison SB, North Tonawanda			6.1944	
LCT1174	Bison SB, North Tonawanda			6.1944	
LCT1175	Bison SB, North Tonawanda			6.1944	scuttled 1946
LCT1176	Bison SB, North Tonawanda			6.1944	to the USSR 8.1945 (DT-2)
LCT1177	Bison SB, North Tonawanda			6.1944	
LCT1178	Bison SB, North Tonawanda			6.1944	
LCT1179	Bison SB, North Tonawanda			6.1944	
LCT1180	Bison SB, North Tonawanda			6.1944	
LCT1181	Bison SB, North Tonawanda			7.1944	
LCT1182	Bison SB, North Tonawanda			7.1944	
LCT1183	Bison SB, North Tonawanda			7.1944	
LCT1184	Bison SB, North Tonawanda			7.1944	
LCT1185	Bison SB, North Tonawanda			7.1944	
LCT1186	Bison SB, North Tonawanda			7.1944	
LCT1187	Bison SB, North Tonawanda			7.1944	scuttled 1946
LCT1188	Bison SB, North Tonawanda			7.1944	
LCT1189	Bison SB, North Tonawanda			7.1944	
LCT1190	Bison SB, North Tonawanda			7.1944	
LCT1191	Bison SB, North Tonawanda			7.1944	sunk 10.1945
LCT1192	Bison SB, North Tonawanda			7.1944	
LCT1193	Bison SB, North Tonawanda			7.1944	
LCT1194	Bison SB, North Tonawanda			7.1944	
LCT1195	Bison SB, North Tonawanda	5.1944	24.5.1944	7.1944	harbor craft 5.1958
LCT1196	Bison SB, North Tonawanda			7.1944	
LCT1197	Bison SB, North Tonawanda			7.1944	
LCT1198	Bison SB, North Tonawanda			7.1944	
LCT1199	Bison SB, North Tonawanda			7.1944	

LCT1200	Bison SB, North Tonawanda			7.1944	
LCT1201	Bison SB, North Tonawanda			7.1944	
LCT1202	Bison SB, North Tonawanda			8.1944	
LCT1203	Bison SB, North Tonawanda	7.1944	29.7.1944	8.1944	harbor craft 3.1966
LCT1204	Bison SB, North Tonawanda			8.1944	
LCT1205	Bison SB, North Tonawanda			8.1944	
LCT1206	Bison SB, North Tonawanda			8.1944	
LCT1207	Bison SB, North Tonawanda			8.1944	
LCT1208	Bison SB, North Tonawanda			8.1944	
LCT1209	Bison SB, North Tonawanda			8.1944	
LCT1210	Bison SB, North Tonawanda			8.1944	
LCT1211	Bison SB, North Tonawanda			8.1944	
LCT1212	Bison SB, North Tonawanda			8.1944	to Taiwan 1959 (He Qi)
LCT1213	Bison SB, North Tonawanda			8.1944	to China 1946 (He Zhong)
LCT1214	Bison SB, North Tonawanda			8.1944	
LCT1215	Bison SB, North Tonawanda			8.1944	
LCT1216	Bison SB, North Tonawanda			8.1944	
LCT1217	Bison SB, North Tonawanda			8.1944	
LCT1218	Bison SB, North Tonawanda			8.1944	to Taiwan 1959 (He Hui)
LCT1219	Bison SB, North Tonawanda			8.1944	
LCT1220	Bison SB, North Tonawanda			8.1944	
LCT1221	Bison SB, North Tonawanda			8.1944	to Vietnam 1960 (HQ535)
LCT1222	Bison SB, North Tonawanda			8.1944	
LCT1223	Bison SB, North Tonawanda			9.1944	
LCT1224	Bison SB, North Tonawanda	8.1944	30.8.1944	9.1944	harbor craft 5.1958
LCT1225	Bison SB, North Tonawanda			9.1944	to Taiwan 1959 (He Chun)
LCT1226	Bison SB, North Tonawanda			9.1944	
LCT1227	Bison SB, North Tonawanda			9.1944	to Greece 1946
LCT1228	Bison SB, North Tonawanda			9.1944	
LCT1229	Bison SB, North Tonawanda	8.1944	6.9.1944	9.1944	to Greece 1959 (Kea)
LCT1230	Bison SB, North Tonawanda			9.1944	to Denmark 1961
LCT1231	Bison SB, North Tonawanda			9.1944	
LCT1232	Bison SB, North Tonawanda	8.1944	10.9.1944	9.1944	harbor craft 3.1966
LCT1233	Bison SB, North Tonawanda			9.1944	
LCT1234	Pidgeon Thomas Iron, Memphis			8.1944	
LCT1235	Pidgeon Thomas Iron, Memphis			8.1944	
LCT1236	Pidgeon Thomas Iron, Memphis	7.1944	18.8.1944	8.1944	harbor craft 5.1958
LCT1237	Pidgeon Thomas Iron, Memphis			8.1944	scuttled 1946
LCT1238	Pidgeon Thomas Iron, Memphis			9.1944	
LCT1239	Pidgeon Thomas Iron, Memphis			9.1944	
LCT1240	Pidgeon Thomas Iron, Memphis			9.1944	
LCT1241	Pidgeon Thomas Iron, Memphis			9.1944	
LCT1242	Pidgeon Thomas Iron, Memphis			9.1944	
LCT1243	Pidgeon Thomas Iron, Memphis			9.1944	
LCT1244	Pidgeon Thomas Iron, Memphis			9.1944	to Taiwan 1959 (He Yao)
LCT1245	Pidgeon Thomas Iron, Memphis			9.1944	
LCT1246	Quincy Bargebuiders			8.1944	
LCT1247	Quincy Bargebuiders			8.1944	
LCT1248	Quincy Bargebuiders			8.1944	
LCT1249	Quincy Bargebuiders			8.1944	
LCT1250	Quincy Bargebuiders	8.1944	8.1944	8.1944	harbor craft 5.1958
LCT1251	Quincy Bargebuiders			8.1944	

LCT1252	Quincy Bargebuiders			8.1944	
LCT1253	Quincy Bargebuiders			8.1944	
LCT1254	Quincy Bargebuiders			8.1944	
LCT1255	Quincy Bargebuiders			8.1944	
LCT1256	Quincy Bargebuiders			8.1944	
LCT1257	Quincy Bargebuiders			9.1944	
LCT1258	Quincy Bargebuiders			9.1944	
LCT1259	Quincy Bargebuiders			9.1944	
LCT1260	Quincy Bargebuiders			9.1944	to Thailand 1946 (Mataphon)
LCT1261	Quincy Bargebuiders			9.1944	
LCT1262	Quincy Bargebuiders			9.1944	
LCT1263	Quincy Bargebuiders			9.1944	
LCT1264	Quincy Bargebuiders			9.1944	
LCT1265	Quincy Bargebuiders			9.1944	
LCT1266	Quincy Bargebuiders			9.1944	
LCT1267	Quincy Bargebuiders			9.1944	
LCT1268	Quincy Bargebuiders			9.1944	
LCT1269	Quincy Bargebuiders			9.1944	
LCT1270	Quincy Bargebuiders			9.1944	
LCT1271	Kansas City Steel			8.1944	to Taiwan 1958 (He Yong)
LCT1272	Kansas City Steel			8.1944	
LCT1273	Kansas City Steel	7.1944	28.8.1944	8.1944	to Chile 5.1960 (Gr. Tellez)
LCT1274	Kansas City Steel			9.1944	
LCT1275	Kansas City Steel			9.1944	
LCT1276	Kansas City Steel			9.1944	
LCT1277	Kansas City Steel			9.1944	
LCT1278	Missouri Valley Bridge, Evansville			7.1944	to Taiwan 1959 (He Jian)
LCT1279	Missouri Valley Bridge, Evansville			7.1944	
LCT1280	Missouri Valley Bridge, Evansville			7.1944	
LCT1281	Missouri Valley Bridge, Evansville			8.1944	
LCT1282	Missouri Valley Bridge, Evansville			8.1944	
LCT1283	Missouri Valley Bridge, Evansville	6.1944	22.7.1944	8.1944	harbor craft 5.1958
LCT1284	Missouri Valley Bridge, Evansville			8.1944	
LCT1285	Missouri Valley Bridge, Evansville			8.1944	
LCT1286	Missouri Valley Bridge, Evansville	7.1944	10.8.1944	8.1944	harbor craft 5.1958
LCT1287	Missouri Valley Bridge, Evansville			8.1944	
LCT1288	Missouri Valley Bridge, Evansville			9.1944	
LCT1289	Mare Island N Yd, Vallejo			4.1944	
LCT1290	Mare Island N Yd, Vallejo			5.1944	
LCT1291	Mare Island N Yd, Vallejo			5.1944	
LCT1292	Mare Island N Yd, Vallejo			5.1944	
LCT1293	Mare Island N Yd, Vallejo			5.1944	to Greece 1946
LCT1294	Mare Island N Yd, Vallejo			5.1944	to Denmark 1961
LCT1295	Mare Island N Yd, Vallejo			5.1944	
LCT1296	Mare Island N Yd, Vallejo			5.1944	
LCT1297	Mare Island N Yd, Vallejo			5.1944	to Greece 1946
LCT1298	Mare Island N Yd, Vallejo			5.1944	
LCT1299	Mare Island N Yd, Vallejo			5.1944	
LCT1300	Mare Island N Yd, Vallejo			5.1944	to Greece 1946
LCT1301	Mare Island N Yd, Vallejo			5.1944	to France 1952 (LCT1301)
LCT1302	Mare Island N Yd, Vallejo			5.1944	to France 1952 (LCT1302)
LCT1303	Mare Island N Yd, Vallejo			6.1944	

LCT1304	Mare Island N Yd, Vallejo			5.1944	
LCT1305	Mare Island N Yd, Vallejo			6.1944	
LCT1306	Mare Island N Yd, Vallejo			6.1944	
LCT1307	Mare Island N Yd, Vallejo			6.1944	
LCT1308	Mare Island N Yd, Vallejo			6.1944	
LCT1309	Mare Island N Yd, Vallejo			6.1944	
LCT1310	Mare Island N Yd, Vallejo			6.1944	
LCT1311	Mare Island N Yd, Vallejo			6.1944	
LCT1312	Mare Island N Yd, Vallejo			6.1944	
LCT1313	Mare Island N Yd, Vallejo			6.1944	
LCT1314	Mare Island N Yd, Vallejo			6.1944	
LCT1315	Mare Island N Yd, Vallejo			6.1944	
LCT1316	Mare Island N Yd, Vallejo			6.1944	
LCT1317	Mare Island N Yd, Vallejo	4.1944	1944	6.1944	
LCT1318	Mare Island N Yd, Vallejo			7.1944	
LCT1319	Mare Island N Yd, Vallejo			6.1944	
LCT1320	Mare Island N Yd, Vallejo			7.1944	
LCT1321	Mare Island N Yd, Vallejo			7.1944	
LCT1322	Mare Island N Yd, Vallejo			7.1944	
LCT1323	Mare Island N Yd, Vallejo			7.1944	
LCT1324	Mare Island N Yd, Vallejo			7.1944	
LCT1325	Mare Island N Yd, Vallejo			7.1944	
LCT1326	Mare Island N Yd, Vallejo			7.1944	
LCT1327	Mare Island N Yd, Vallejo			7.1944	
LCT1328	Mare Island N Yd, Vallejo			7.1944	
LCT1329	Mare Island N Yd, Vallejo			7.1944	
LCT1330	Mare Island N Yd, Vallejo			7.1944	harbor craft 1950s
LCT1331	Mare Island N Yd, Vallejo			7.1944	
LCT1332	Mare Island N Yd, Vallejo			7.1944	
LCT1333	Mare Island N Yd, Vallejo			8.1944	
LCT1334	Mare Island N Yd, Vallejo			7.1944	
LCT1335	Mare Island N Yd, Vallejo			8.1944	
LCT1336	Mare Island N Yd, Vallejo			8.1944	
LCT1337	Mare Island N Yd, Vallejo			8.1944	
LCT1338	Mare Island N Yd, Vallejo			8.1944	
LCT1339	Mare Island N Yd, Vallejo			8.1944	
LCT1340	Mare Island N Yd, Vallejo			8.1944	
LCT1341	Mare Island N Yd, Vallejo			8.1944	
LCT1342	Mare Island N Yd, Vallejo			8.1944	
LCT1343	Mare Island N Yd, Vallejo			8.1944	
LCT1344	Mare Island N Yd, Vallejo			8.1944	
LCT1345	Mare Island N Yd, Vallejo			8.1944	
LCT1346	Mare Island N Yd, Vallejo			8.1944	
LCT1347	Mare Island N Yd, Vallejo			8.1944	
LCT1348	Mare Island N Yd, Vallejo			8.1944	
LCT1349	Mare Island N Yd, Vallejo			9.1944	
LCT1350	Mare Island N Yd, Vallejo			9.1944	
LCT1351	Mare Island N Yd, Vallejo			9.1944	
LCT1352	Mare Island N Yd, Vallejo			9.1944	
LCT1353	Mare Island N Yd, Vallejo			9.1944	
LCT1354	Mare Island N Yd, Vallejo			9.1944	
LCT1355	Mare Island N Yd, Vallejo			9.1944	

LCT1356	Mare Island N Yd, Vallejo			9.1944	
LCT1357	Mare Island N Yd, Vallejo			9.1944	
LCT1358	Mare Island N Yd, Vallejo			9.1944	sunk 4.5.1945
LCT1359	Mare Island N Yd, Vallejo			9.1944	
LCT1360	Mare Island N Yd, Vallejo			9.1944	
LCT1361	Mare Island N Yd, Vallejo			9.1944	
LCT1362	Mare Island N Yd, Vallejo	8.1944	26.9.1944	10.1944	stricken 4.1953
LCT1363	Mare Island N Yd, Vallejo	8.1944	29.9.1944	10.1944	harbor craft 5.1958
LCT1364	Mare Island N Yd, Vallejo			10.1944	
LCT1365	Mare Island N Yd, Vallejo			10.1944	
LCT1366	Mare Island N Yd, Vallejo			10.1944	
LCT1367	Mare Island N Yd, Vallejo			10.1944	to Taiwan 1959 (He Deng)
LCT1368	Mare Island N Yd, Vallejo			10.1944	
LCT1369	Mare Island N Yd, Vallejo			10.1944	
LCT1370	Mare Island N Yd, Vallejo			10.1944	
LCT1371	Mare Island N Yd, Vallejo			10.1944	
LCT1372	Mare Island N Yd, Vallejo			10.1944	
LCT1373	Mare Island N Yd, Vallejo			10.1944	harbor craft 1960s
LCT1374	Mare Island N Yd, Vallejo	9.1944	2.11.1944	11.1944	
LCT1375	Mare Island N Yd, Vallejo			11.1944	
LCT1376	Mare Island N Yd, Vallejo	9.1944	7.11.1944	11.1944	harbor craft 5.1958
LCT1377	Mare Island N Yd, Vallejo			11.1944	
LCT1378	Mare Island N Yd, Vallejo	9.1944	13.11.1944	11.1944	harbor craft 5.1958
LCT1379	Mare Island N Yd, Vallejo	9.1944	16.11.1944	11.1944	to Greece 1962 (Karpathos)
LCT1380	Mare Island N Yd, Vallejo			11.1944	
LCT1381	Mare Island N Yd, Vallejo			11.1944	
LCT1382	Mare Island N Yd, Vallejo	10.1944	25.11.1944	11.1944	to Greece 1962 (Kasos)
LCT1383	Mare Island N Yd, Vallejo			11.1944	to Denmark 1961
LCT1384	Mare Island N Yd, Vallejo	10.1944	1.12.1944	12.1944	harbor craft 5.1958
LCT1385	Mare Island N Yd, Vallejo	10.1944	5.12.1944	12.1944	harbor craft 3.1966
LCT1386	Mare Island N Yd, Vallejo	10.1944	8.12.1944	12.1944	harbor craft 5.1958
LCT1387	Mare Island N Yd, Vallejo			12.1944	
LCT1388	Mare Island N Yd, Vallejo	10.1944	14.12.1944	12.1944	harbor craft 3.1966
LCT1389	Mare Island N Yd, Vallejo			12.1944	
LCT1390	Mare Island N Yd, Vallejo			12.1944	
LCT1391	Mount Vernon Bridge			9.1944	
LCT1392	Mount Vernon Bridge			9.1944	
LCT1393	Mount Vernon Bridge			9.1944	
LCT1394	Mount Vernon Bridge			10.1944	
LCT1395	Mount Vernon Bridge			10.1944	
LCT1396	Mount Vernon Bridge			10.1944	to Chile 1960 (Gr. Bolados)
LCT1397	Mount Vernon Bridge			10.1944	to Taiwan 1959 (He Feng)
LCT1398	Mount Vernon Bridge	10.1944	30.10.1944	10.1944	harbor craft 5.1958
LCT1399	Mount Vernon Bridge			11.1944	
LCT1400	Mount Vernon Bridge			11.1944	
LCT1401	Mount Vernon Bridge			11.1944	
LCT1402	Mount Vernon Bridge			12.1944	
LCT1403	Pidgeon Thomas Iron, Memphis			9.1944	
LCT1404	Pidgeon Thomas Iron, Memphis			9.1944	
LCT1405	Pidgeon Thomas Iron, Memphis			10.1944	
LCT1406	Pidgeon Thomas Iron, Memphis			10.1944	
LCT1407	Pidgeon Thomas Iron, Memphis			10.1944	

LCT1408	Pidgeon Thomas Iron, Memphis			10.1944	
LCT1409	Pidgeon Thomas Iron, Memphis			10.1944	
LCT1410	Pidgeon Thomas Iron, Memphis			10.1944	
LCT1411	Pidgeon Thomas Iron, Memphis	9.1944	10.10.1944	10.1944	harbor craft 5.1958
LCT1412	Pidgeon Thomas Iron, Memphis			10.1944	
LCT1413	Pidgeon Thomas Iron, Memphis			10.1944	
LCT1414	Pidgeon Thomas Iron, Memphis			10.1944	
LCT1415	Pidgeon Thomas Iron, Memphis			11.1944	
LCT1416	Pidgeon Thomas Iron, Memphis			11.1944	
LCT1417	Pidgeon Thomas Iron, Memphis			11.1944	
LCT1418	Pidgeon Thomas Iron, Memphis			11.1944	
LCT1419	Pidgeon Thomas Iron, Memphis			11.1944	
LCT1420	Pidgeon Thomas Iron, Memphis			11.1944	
LCT1421	Pidgeon Thomas Iron, Memphis			11.1944	to Cambodia 1962 (T915)
LCT1422	Pidgeon Thomas Iron, Memphis			11.1944	to Denmark 1961
LCT1423	Pidgeon Thomas Iron, Memphis			11.1944	
LCT1424	Pidgeon Thomas Iron, Memphis			11.1944	
LCT1425	Pidgeon Thomas Iron, Memphis			12.1944	
LCT1426	Pidgeon Thomas Iron, Memphis			12.1944	
LCT1427	Pidgeon Thomas Iron, Memphis			12.1944	
LCT1428	Pidgeon Thomas Iron, Memphis			12.1944	
LCT1429	Pidgeon Thomas Iron, Memphis			12.1944	to Taiwan 1959 (He Chao)
LCT1430	Bison SB, North Tonawanda	9.1944	10.9.1944	9.1944	harbor craft 5.1958
LCT1431	Bison SB, North Tonawanda			9.1944	to Iran 1964 (Queshm)
LCT1432	Bison SB, North Tonawanda			9.1944	
LCT1433	Bison SB, North Tonawanda			9.1944	
LCT1434	Bison SB, North Tonawanda			9.1944	to the USSR 5.1945 (DS-17)
LCT1435	Bison SB, North Tonawanda			9.1944	to the USSR 5.1945 (DS-18)
LCT1436	Bison SB, North Tonawanda			9.1944	to the USSR 5.1945 (DS-19)
LCT1437	Bison SB, North Tonawanda			9.1944	to the USSR 5.1945 (DS-20)
LCT1438	Bison SB, North Tonawanda			9.1944	to the USSR 5.1945 (DS-13)
LCT1439	Bison SB, North Tonawanda			9.1944	
LCT1440	Bison SB, North Tonawanda			9.1944	
LCT1441	Bison SB, North Tonawanda			10.1944	
LCT1442	Bison SB, North Tonawanda			10.1944	to the USSR 5.1945 (DS-15)
LCT1443	Bison SB, North Tonawanda			10.1944	
LCT1444	Bison SB, North Tonawanda			10.1944	
LCT1445	Bison SB, North Tonawanda			10.1944	to the USSR 5.1945 (DS-16)
LCT1446	Bison SB, North Tonawanda	1944	1944	10.1944	harbor craft 5.1958
LCT1447	Bison SB, North Tonawanda			10.1944	
LCT1448	Bison SB, North Tonawanda			10.1944	
LCT1449	Bison SB, North Tonawanda			10.1944	
LCT1450	Bison SB, North Tonawanda			10.1944	
LCT1451	Bison SB, North Tonawanda	9.1944	10.9.1944	10.1944	oiler 4.1956
LCT1452	Bison SB, North Tonawanda			10.1944	to Taiwan 1959 (He Teng)
LCT1453	Bison SB, North Tonawanda			10.1944	
LCT1454	Bison SB, North Tonawanda			10.1944	
LCT1455	Bison SB, North Tonawanda			10.1944	
LCT1456	Bison SB, North Tonawanda			10.1944	
LCT1457	Bison SB, North Tonawanda			10.1944	
LCT1458	Bison SB, North Tonawanda			10.1944	to Chile 1960 (Grumete Díaz)
LCT1459	Bison SB, North Tonawanda	10.1944	22.10.1944	10.1944	salvage craft 1958

LCT1460	Bison SB, North Tonawanda			10.1944
LCT1461	Bison SB, North Tonawanda			10.1944
LCT1462	Bison SB, North Tonawanda	10.1944	28.10.1944	11.1944
LCT1463	Bison SB, North Tonawanda			11.1944
LCT1464	Bison SB, North Tonawanda			11.1944
LCT1465	Bison SB, North Tonawanda			11.1944

160 / 309-320 t, 36.3 x 10.0 x 1.2 m, 3 Grey Marine diesels, 675 hp, 8 kts, 700 nm (7 kts), complement 13; 2 x 1 – 20/70 Oerlikon; 4 medium or 3 heavy tanks or 150t of cargo.

Further development of LCT(5). The hull could be disassembled into 3-5 parts for transportation over long distances.

LCT501 1943

1945, *LCT843, 844, 887, 888, 889, 890* were converted to minehunters (underwater locators). FM sonar and diving equipment were fitted.

LCF(L)2 type AA support landing craft

LCF(L)2	Tees-Side Bridge, Middlesborough, UK	11.8.1941	(11.1941) / 1944	to the UK 1944 (LCF(L)2)

369 (std) t, 48.8 x 9.5 x 1.6 m, 3 Paxman diesels, 1380 hp, 11 kts, 40 t diesel oil, 2000 nm (10 kts); 8 x 1 – 40/39 pompom, 4 x 1 – 20/70 Oerlikon.

RN LCF(L) Mk 2-class AA support craft. Temporarily served under the USN flag during the Normandy landings.

LCF(3)-type AA support landing craft, LCT(R)3-type rocket support landing craft, LCG(L)3-type large support landing craft

LCF(L)3	Tees-Side Bridge, Middlesbrough, UK	17.12.1941	(1942) / 1944	to the UK 1944 **(LCF(L)3**
LCF(L)4	Tees-Side Bridge, Middlesbrough, UK	16.1.1942	(5.1942) / 1944	to the UK 1944 (LCF(L)4)
LCF(L)5	Tees-Side Bridge, Middlesbrough, UK	17.2.1942	(1942) / 1944	to the UK 1944 (LCF(L)5)
LCF(L)6	Stockton, Thornaby, UK	14.2.1942	(2.1942) / 1944	to the UK 1944 (LCF(L)6)
LCF(L)9	General SN Co, Deptford, UK	1942	(3.1943) / 1944	to the UK 1944 (LCF(L)9)
LCF(L)10	General SN Co, Deptford, UK	1942	(3.1943) / 1944	to the UK 1944 (LCF(L)10)
LCF(L)12	Tilbury Dredging, UK	21.12.1942	(1943) / 1944	to the UK 1944 (LCF(L)12)
LCF(L)14	Stockton, Thornaby, UK	31.8.1942	(9.1942) / 1944	to the UK 1944 (LCF(L)14)
LCF(L)11	Pollock, Faversham, UK	24.11.1942	(3.1943) / 1944	to the UK 1944 (LCF(L)11)
LCF(L)7	Russell, Barking, UK	28.9.1942	(1.1943) / 1944	to the UK 1944 (LCF(L)7)
LCF(L)8	Russell, Barking, UK	27.10.1942	(2.1943) / 1944	to the UK 1944 (LCF(L)8)
LCT(R)366	Findlay, Old Kirkpatrick, UK	1942	(6.1942) / 1944	to the UK 1944 (LCT(R)366)
LCT(R)368	Findlay, Old Kirkpatrick, UK	1942	(1942) / 1944	to the UK 1944 (LCT(R)368)
LCF(L)15	Arrol, Meadowside, UK	8.10.1942	(1942) / 1944	to the UK 1944 (LCF(L)15)
LCF(L)16	Arrol, Meadowside, UK	11.10.1942	(1942) / 1944	to the UK 1944 (LCF(L)16)
LCF(L)17	Redpath Brown, Meadowside, UK	1942	(1942) / 1944	to the UK 1944 (LCF(L)17)
LCF(L)18	Redpath Brown, Meadowside, UK	1942	(1942) / 1944	to the UK 1944 (LCF(L)18)
LCT(R)423	Arrol, Meadowside, UK	18.2.1943	(1943) / 1944	to the UK 1944 (LCT(R)423)
LCG(L)424	Arrol, Meadowside, UK	22.2.1943	(1943) / 1944	to the UK 1944 (LCG(L)424)
LCT(R)425	Arrol, Meadowside, UK	19.3.1943	(1943) / 1944	to the UK 1944 (LCT(R)425)
LCG(L)426	Arrol, Meadowside, UK	6.4.1943	(1943) / 1944	to the UK 1944 (LCG(L)426)
LCT(R)447	Redpath Brown, Meadowside, UK	1943	(1943) / 1944	to the UK 1944 (LCT(R)447)
LCT(R)448	Redpath Brown, Meadowside, UK	1943	(1943) / 1944	to the UK 1944 (LCT(R)448)
LCT(R)449	Redpath Brown, Meadowside, UK	1943	(1943) / 1944	to the UK 1944 (LCT(R)449)
LCT(R)450	Redpath Brown, Meadowside, UK	1943	(1943) / 1944	to the UK 1944 (LCT(R)450)
LCT(R)452	Redpath Brown, Meadowside, UK	1943	(1943) / 1944	to the UK 1944 (LCT(R)452)
LCT(R)464	Arrol, Meadowside, UK	27.12.1943	(1944) / 1944	to the UK 1944 (LCT(R)464)

LCT(R)473	Arrol, Meadowside, UK	26.1.1944	(1944) / 1944	to the UK 1944 (LCT(R)473)
LCT(R)481	Findlay, Old Kirkpatrick, UK	1944	(1944) / 1944	to the UK 1944 (LCT(R)481)
LCT(R)482	Findlay, Old Kirkpatrick, UK	1944	(1944) / 1944	to the UK 1944 (LCT(R)482)
LCT(R)483	Findlay, Old Kirkpatrick, UK	1944	(1944) / 1944	to the UK 1944 (LCT(R)483)

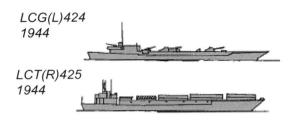

LCG(L)424
1944

LCT(R)425
1944

LCF(L): 440 / 515 t, 58.1 x 9.5 x 1.7 m, 2 Paxman diesels, 920 hp, 10 kts, 24 t diesel oil, 2700 nm (9 kts), complement 68 (*LCF(L)3-6*) or 76 (*LCF(L)7-18*); 8 (*LCF3-6*) or 4 (*LCF7-18*) x 1 – 40/39 pompom, 4 (*LCF3-6*) or 8 (*LCF7-18*) x 1 – 20/70 Oerlikon.
LCT(R): 560 t, 58.1 x 9.5 x 1.7 m, 2 Paxman diesels, 920 hp, 10.5 kts, 24 t diesel oil, 2700 nm (9 kts), complement 17-18; 2 x 1 – 20/70 Oerlikon, 1044 (or 936 in tropical variant) x 1 – 127 barrage RL.
LCG(L): 500 t, 58.1 x 9.5 x 1.7 m, 2 Paxman diesels, 920 hp, 10.5 kts, 24 t diesel oil, 2700 nm (10.5 kts), complement 45-48; 2 x 1 – 120/45 QF Mk IX, 2 x 1 – 40/39 pompom or 3 – 5 x 1 – 20/70 Oerlikon.
British fire support versions of the LCT Mk 3 landing craft, temporarily serving under the US flag during the landings in Normandy and Southern France.

LCG(L)4-type large support landing craft

| LCG(L)811 | Findlay, Old Kirkpatrick, UK | 1944 | (1944) / 1944 | to the UK 1944 |

570 t, 57.1 x 11.8 x 1.4 m, 2 Paxman diesels, 920 hp, 10 kts, 51 t diesel oil, 1100 nm (8 kts), complement 47-48; 2 x 1 – 120/45 BL Mk I, 7 x 1 – 20/70 Oerlikon.
RN LCG(L)4-class support craft temporarily transferred to the USN during Normandy landings.

LCS(L)3-type amphibious fire support craft

LCS(L)(3)1	Geo Lawley, Neponset	4.1944	15.5.1944	6.1944	BU 12.1950
LCS(L)(3)2	Geo Lawley, Neponset	5.1944	10.6.1944	7.1944	to France 8.1950 (Arbaléte)
LCS(L)(3)3	Geo Lawley, Neponset	6.1944	5.7.1944	7.1944	BU 12.1950
LCS(L)(3)4	Geo Lawley, Neponset	7.1944	15.7.1944	8.1944	to France 8.1950 (Arquebuse)
LCS(L)(3)5	Geo Lawley, Neponset	7.1944	27.7.1944	8.1944	BU 6.1947
LCS(L)(3)6	Geo Lawley, Neponset	7.1944	3.8.1944	8.1944	BU 2.1951
LCS(L)(3)7	Geo Lawley, Neponset	7.1944	9.8.1944	8.1944	sunk 16.2.1945
LCS(L)(3)8	Geo Lawley, Neponset	7.1944	11.8.1944	8.1944	BU 11.1946
LCS(L)(3)9	Geo Lawley, Neponset	7.1944	8.1944	9.1944	to France 8.1950 (Hallebarde)
LCS(L)(3)10	Geo Lawley, Neponset	8.1944	19.8.1944	9.1944	to France 8.1950 (Javeline)
LCS(L)(3)11	Geo Lawley, Neponset	8.1944	22.8.1944	9.1944	BU 1950
LCS(L)(3)12	Geo Lawley, Neponset	8.1944	24.8.1944	9.1944	to Japan 6.1953 (Sekichiku)
LCS(L)(3)13	Geo Lawley, Neponset	8.1944	26.8.1944	9.1944	to Japan 6.1953 (Oniyuri)
LCS(L)(3)14	Geo Lawley, Neponset	8.1944	28.8.1944	9.1944	to Japan 2.1953 (Sumire)
LCS(L)(3)15	Geo Lawley, Neponset	8.1944	3.9.1944	9.1944	sunk 22.4.1945
LCS(L)(3)16	Geo Lawley, Neponset	8.1944	4.9.1944	9.1944	stricken 12.1950
LCS(L)(3)17	Geo Lawley, Neponset	8.1944	4.9.1944	9.1944	BU 1.1951
LCS(L)(3)18	Geo Lawley, Neponset	8.1944	6.9.1944	9.1944	to Japan 6.1953 (Yamayuri)
LCS(L)(3)19	Geo Lawley, Neponset	9.1944	11.9.1944	10.1944	BU 12.1950
LCS(L)(3)20	Geo Lawley, Neponset	9.1944	13.9.1944	10.1944	to Japan 7.1953 (Himeyuri)
LCS(L)(3)21	Geo Lawley, Neponset	9.1944	20.9.1944	10.1944	BU 3.1951
LCS(L)(3)22	Geo Lawley, Neponset	9.1944	22.9.1944	10.1944	to Japan 3.1953 (Nogiku)
LCS(L)(3)23	Geo Lawley, Neponset	9.1944	29.9.1944	10.1944	BU 3.1951
LCS(L)(3)24	Geo Lawley, Neponset	9.1944	1.10.1944	10.1944	to Japan 5.1953 (Ezogiku)
LCS(L)(3)25	Geo Lawley, Neponset	9.1944	8.10.1944	10.1944	to Japan 6.1953 (Suzuran)
LCS(L)(3)26	Commercial IW, Portland	7.1944	13.8.1944	8.1944	sunk 16.2.1945

LCS(L)(3)27	Commercial IW, Portland	7.1944	13.8.1944	8.1944	to Japan 4.1953 (Azami)
LCS(L)(3)28	Commercial IW, Portland	7.1944	19.8.1944	9.1944	to France 8.1950 (Pertuisane)
LCS(L)(3)29	Commercial IW, Portland	7.1944	27.8.1944	9.1944	BU 1.1951
LCS(L)(3)30	Commercial IW, Portland	7.1944	27.8.1944	9.1944	BU 12.1950
LCS(L)(3)31	Commercial IW, Portland	8.1944	2.9.1944	9.1944	BU 1.1947
LCS(L)(3)32	Commercial IW, Portland	8.1944	10.9.1944	9.1944	stricken 11.1950
LCS(L)(3)33	Commercial IW, Portland	8.1944	10.9.1944	9.1944	sunk 19.2.1945
LCS(L)(3)34	Commercial IW, Portland	8.1944	16.9.1944	9.1944	to Italy 7.1951 (Alano)
LCS(L)(3)35	Commercial IW, Portland	8.1944	17.9.1944	10.1944	to France 3.1953 (Étendard)
LCS(L)(3)36	Commercial IW, Portland	8.1944	17.9.1944	10.1944	BU 2.1951
LCS(L)(3)37	Commercial IW, Portland	9.1944	23.9.1944	10.1944	damaged 1945, never repaired
LCS(L)(3)38	Commercial IW, Portland	9.1944	1.10.1944	10.1944	to Italy 7.1951 (Bracco)
LCS(L)(3)39	Commercial IW, Portland	9.1944	1.10.1944	10.1944	BU 10.1947
LCS(L)(3)40	Commercial IW, Portland	9.1944	7.10.1944	10.1944	BU 10.1947
LCS(L)(3)41	Commercial IW, Portland	9.1944	8.10.1944	10.1944	BU 10.1947
LCS(L)(3)42	Commercial IW, Portland	9.1944	8.10.1944	10.1944	BU 10.1947
LCS(L)(3)43	Commercial IW, Portland	9.1944	14.10.1944	10.1944	BU 10.1947
LCS(L)(3)44	Commercial IW, Portland	10.1944	22.10.1944	11.1944	BU 10.1947
LCS(L)(3)45	Commercial IW, Portland	10.1944	22.10.1944	11.1944	sold 10.1947
LCS(L)(3)46	Commercial IW, Portland	10.1944	27.10.1944	11.1944	BU 10.1947
LCS(L)(3)47	Commercial IW, Portland	10.1944	29.10.1944	11.1944	BU 10.1947
LCS(L)(3)48	Albina, Portland	5.1944	7.7.1944	8.1944	BU 10.1947
LCS(L)(3)49	Albina, Portland	6.1944	20.7.1944	8.1944	sunk 16.2.1945
LCS(L)(3)50	Albina, Portland	6.1944	29.7.1944	9.1944	BU 10.1947
LCS(L)(3)51	Albina, Portland	6.1944	5.8.1944	9.1944	BU 9.1947
LCS(L)(3)52	Albina, Portland	6.1944	14.8.1944	9.1944	to Japan 7.1953 (Sasayuri)
LCS(L)(3)53	Albina, Portland	6.1944	22.8.1944	9.1944	BU 1.1952
LCS(L)(3)54	Albina, Portland	7.1944	5.9.1944	10.1944	to S. Korea 10.1952 (Boseongman)
LCS(L)(3)55	Albina, Portland	7.1944	2.9.1944	10.1944	BU 12.1950
LCS(L)(3)56	Albina, Portland	8.1944	7.9.1944	10.1944	to Taiwan 2.1954 (Lian Ren)
LCS(L)(3)57	Albina, Portland	8.1944	14.9.1944	10.1944	to Japan 1.1953 (Kiku)
LCS(L)(3)58	Albina, Portland	8.1944	22.9.1944	11.1944	to Japan 7.1953 (Susuki)
LCS(L)(3)59	Albina, Portland	9.1944	2.10.1944	11.1944	BU 12.1950
LCS(L)(3)60	Albina, Portland	9.1944	7.10.1944	11.1944	to Japan 9.1953 (Keido)
LCS(L)(3)61	Albina, Portland	9.1944	14.10.1944	11.1944	BU 5.1951
LCS(L)(3)62	Albina, Portland	9.1944	23.10.1944	12.1944	to Italy 7.1951 (Mastino)
LCS(L)(3)63	Albina, Portland	10.1944	2.11.1944	12.1944	to Italy 7.1951 (Molosso)
LCS(L)(3)64	Albina, Portland	10.1944	7.11.1944	12.1944	to Italy 7.1951 (Segugio)
LCS(L)(3)65	Albina, Portland	10.1944	14.11.1944	12.1944	to France 6.1958 (Oriflamme)
LCS(L)(3)66	Albina, Portland	10.1944	23.11.1944	1.1945	sold 1.1948
LCS(L)(3)67	Albina, Portland	11.1944	2.12.1944	1.1945	to Japan 7.1953 (Karukaya)
LCS(L)(3)68	Albina, Portland	11.1944	7.12.1944	1.1945	to Japan 6.1953 (Hamayu)
LCS(L)(3)69	Albina, Portland	11.1944	14.12.1944	1.1945	BU 3.1951
LCS(L)(3)70	Albina, Portland	11.1944	22.12.1944	1.1945	BU 1.1951
LCS(L)(3)71	Albina, Portland	12.1944	5.1.1945	2.1945	BU 12.1950
LCS(L)(3)72	Albina, Portland	12.1944	8.1.1945	2.1945	to Japan 4.1953 (Shiragiku)
LCS(L)(3)73	Albina, Portland	12.1944	16.1.1945	2.1945	BU 1.1951
LCS(L)(3)74	Albina, Portland	12.1944	30.1.1945	2.1945	to Japan 9.1953 (Suisen)
LCS(L)(3)75	Albina, Portland	1.1945	9.2.1945	3.1945	to Japan 2.1953 (Fuji)
LCS(L)(3)76	Albina, Portland	1.1945	15.2.1945	3.1945	to Japan 4.1953 (Kaido)

LCS(L)(3)77	Albina, Portland	1.1945	26.2.1945	3.1945	to S. Korea 1.1952 (Yeongheungman)
LCS(L)(3)78	Albina, Portland	1.1945	28.2.1945	3.1945	to Japan 2.1953 (Bara)
LCS(L)(3)79	Commercial IW, Portland	10.1944	29.10.1944	11.1944	to Japan 4.1953 (Rindo)
LCS(L)(3)80	Commercial IW, Portland	10.1944	7.11.1944	11.1944	to France 8.1950 (Rapière)
LCS(L)(3)81	Commercial IW, Portland	10.1944	12.11.1944	11.1944	to Taiwan 2.1954 (Lian Zhi)
LCS(L)(3)82	Commercial IW, Portland	10.1944	12.11.1944	11.1944	to Japan 3.1953 (Yamagiku)
LCS(L)(3)83	Commercial IW, Portland	10.1944	17.11.1944	11.1944	to Japan 5.1953 (Hinagiku)
LCS(L)(3)84	Commercial IW, Portland	10.1944	19.11.1944	12.1944	to Japan 5.1953 (Sawagiku)
LCS(L)(3)85	Commercial IW, Portland	10.1944	30.11.1944	12.1944	to Japan 5.1953 (Tsuta)
LCS(L)(3)86	Commercial IW, Portland	11.1944	30.11.1944	12.1944	to S. Korea 1952 (Yeongilman)
LCS(L)(3)87	Commercial IW, Portland	11.1944	3.12.1944	12.1944	to Japan 3.1953 (Hamagiku)
LCS(L)(3)88	Commercial IW, Portland	11.1944	3.12.1944	12.1944	to Japan 4.1953 (Ajisai)
LCS(L)(3)89	Commercial IW, Portland	11.1944	7.12.1944	12.1944	to Japan 5.1953 (Hasu)
LCS(L)(3)90	Commercial IW, Portland	11.1944	17.12.1944	12.1944	to Japan 5.1953 (Shida)
LCS(L)(3)91	Commercial IW, Portland	11.1944	17.12.1944	1.1945	to S. Korea 1952 (Ganghwaman)
LCS(L)(3)92	Commercial IW, Portland	11.1944	22.12.1944	1.1945	BU 3.1951
LCS(L)(3)93	Commercial IW, Portland	12.1944	23.12.1944	1.1945	BU 3.1951
LCS(L)(3)94	Commercial IW, Portland	12.1944	23.12.1944	1.1945	to Japan 5.1953 (Suiren)
LCS(L)(3)95	Commercial IW, Portland	12.1944	3.1.1945	1.1945	to Taiwan 2.1954 (Lian Yong)
LCS(L)(3)96	Commercial IW, Portland	12.1944	6.1.1945	1.1945	to Japan 6.1953 (Shobu)
LCS(L)(3)97	Commercial IW, Portland	12.1944	6.1.1945	1.1945	BU 3.1951
LCS(L)(3)98	Commercial IW, Portland	12.1944	13.1.1945	2.1945	to Japan 3.1953 (Aoi)
LCS(L)(3)99	Commercial IW, Portland	12.1944	13.1.1945	2.1945	BU 12.1950
LCS(L)(3)100	Commercial IW, Portland	1.1945	27.1.1945	2.1945	to Japan 3.1953 (Akane)
LCS(L)(3)101	Commercial IW, Portland	1.1945	27.1.1945	2.1945	to Japan 4.1953 (Tsutsuji)
LCS(L)(3)102	Commercial IW, Portland	1.1945	3.2.1945	2.1945	to Japan 4.1953 (Himawari)
LCS(L)(3)103	Commercial IW, Portland	1.1945	3.2.1945	2.1945	to Japan 9.1953 (Yaguruma)
LCS(L)(3)104	Commercial IW, Portland	1.1945	17.2.1945	2.1945	to Japan 1.1953 (Ran)
LCS(L)(3)105	Commercial IW, Portland	1.1945	17.2.1945	3.1945	to France 12.1953 (Framée)
LCS(L)(3)106	Commercial IW, Portland	2.1945	24.2.1945	3.1945	to Japan 3.1953 (Isogiku)
LCS(L)(3)107	Commercial IW, Portland	2.1945	24.2.1945	3.1945	to Japan 1.1953 (Yuri)
LCS(L)(3)108	Commercial IW, Portland	2.1945	10.3.1945	3.1945	BU 3.1951
LCS(L)(3)109	Geo Lawley, Neponset	10.1944	10.10.1944	10.1944	to Japan 6.1953 (Kana)
LCS(L)(3)110	Geo Lawley, Neponset	10.1944	12.10.1944	10.1944	to Japan 3.1953 (Fuyo)
LCS(L)(3)111	Geo Lawley, Neponset	10.1944	17.10.1944	11.1944	to Japan 2.1953 (Keshi)
LCS(L)(3)112	Geo Lawley, Neponset	10.1944	19.10.1944	11.1944	BU 3.1951
LCS(L)(3)113	Geo Lawley, Neponset	10.1944	22.10.1944	11.1944	BU 3.1951
LCS(L)(3)114	Geo Lawley, Neponset	10.1944	26.10.1944	11.1944	to Japan 4.1953 (Hiiragi)
LCS(L)(3)115	Geo Lawley, Neponset	10.1944	28.10.1944	11.1944	to Japan 2.1953 (Ayame)
LCS(L)(3)116	Geo Lawley, Neponset	10.1944	30.10.1944	11.1944	to Japan 5.1953 (Yamabuki)
LCS(L)(3)117	Geo Lawley, Neponset	10.1944	4.11.1944	11.1944	BU 3.1951
LCS(L)(3)118	Geo Lawley, Neponset	10.1944	6.11.1944	11.1944	to Italy 7.1951 (Spinone)
LCS(L)(3)119	Geo Lawley, Neponset	10.1944	8.11.1944	11.1944	to Japan 7.1953 (Kikyo)
LCS(L)(3)120	Geo Lawley, Neponset	11.1944	14.11.1944	11.1944	to Japan 4.1953 (Iwagiku)
LCS(L)(3)121	Geo Lawley, Neponset	11.1944	16.11.1944	12.1944	BU 12.1950
LCS(L)(3)122	Geo Lawley, Neponset	11.1944	18.11.1944	12.1944	BU 2.1951
LCS(L)(3)123	Geo Lawley, Neponset	11.1944	24.11.1944	12.1944	BU 8.1947
LCS(L)(3)124	Geo Lawley, Neponset	11.1944	27.11.1944	12.1944	BU 12.1950
LCS(L)(3)125	Geo Lawley, Neponset	11.1944	1.12.1944	12.1944	BU 5.1951
LCS(L)(3)126	Geo Lawley, Neponset	11.1944	5.12.1944	12.1944	to Japan 5.1953 (Renge)
LCS(L)(3)127	Geo Lawley, Neponset	11.1944	6.12.1944	12.1944	wrecked 5.3.1945

LCS(L)(3)128	Geo Lawley, Neponset	12.1944	9.12.1944	12.1944	stricken 12.1950
LCS(L)(3)129	Geo Lawley, Neponset	12.1944	13.12.1944	12.1944	to Japan 6.1953 (Botan)
LCS(L)(3)130	Geo Lawley, Neponset	12.1944	13.12.1944	1.1945	to Japan 1.1953 (Hagi)

250 / 387 t, 48.2 x 7.2 x 1.7 m, 8 General Motors diesels (2 shafts), 2320 hp, 15.5 kts, 76 t diesel oil, 5500 nm (12 kts), complement 71. (1 x 1 - 76/50 Mk 20/21, 2 x 2 - 40/56 Bofors) (LCS(L)1 - 10, 26 - 30, 41 - 50, 58 - 60, 79, 80, 90, 91) or (2 x 2 + 1 x 1) - 40/56 Bofors (LCS(L)11 - 25, 31 - 40, 51 - 57, 61 - 66, 81 - 89, 109 – 124) or 3 x 2 – 40/56 Bofors (LCS(L)67 - 78, 92 - 108, 125 – 130), 4 x 1 - 20/70 Oerlikon, 4 x 1 – 12.7 MG, 10 x 1 - 127 Mk 7 RL, radar.

Fire support ships in the hulls of LCI(L) class large infantry landing craft, the further development of LCI(G). They had more powerful diesels and, as a result, were faster.

LCS(L)(3)7, LCS(L)(3)26 and *LCS(L)(3)49* were sunk by Japanese explosive boats off Mariveles Harbor (Philippines) 16.2.1945, *LCS(L)(3)15* was sunk by kamikaze off Okinawa 22.4.1945, *LCS(L)(3)33* was sunk by Japanese coastal artillery (or by kamikaze) off

LCS(L)55 1944

LCS(L)50

Okinawa 12.4.1945. *LCS(L)(3)127* ran aground off San Clemente Island (California) 5.3.1945.

Landing craft mechanized '38-ft prototype'

LCM13563 (1938)
20 (std) t, 11.6 x 4.1 x 1.1 m, 2 Ford petrol engines, 150

hp, 6 kts; 2 x 1 – 7.6 MG; 2 6.5-t or 1 9-t tank.
The first LCM prototype.

Landing craft mechanized '40-ft prototype'

LCM13564 (1939)
11 (std) t, 12.2 x 3.8 x 0.6 m, 8-10 kts.

The second LCM prototype.

Landing craft mechanized 'Norfolk prototype'

Norfolk N Yd: LCM13975 (1940)
19 / 32 t, 13.7 x 3.9 x 0.8 m, 1 diesel, 330 hp, 9 kts.

The third LCM prototype.

Landing craft mechanized, final prototypes

LCM13977, 13978
24 (std) t, 13.7 x 4.3 x 0.8 m, 2 petrol engines, 200 hp,

9.5 kts, 75 nm (7.5 kts); 2 x 1 – 12.7 MG, 12 t of cargo.
The final LCM prototypes, built in 1941.

LCM(2) type landing craft mechanized

American Car & Founfry: TKL1 – 8 (1941)
Higgins, New Orleans: LCM(2)1909 – 1913, 2084 – 2091, 2254 – 2283, 2910 – 2921, 3701 – 3724, 3791 – 3794, 4574 – 4628 (1942)

20 / 32 t, 14.6 x 4.0 x 0.9 m, 2 petrol engines or diesels, 350 hp, 8.5 kts; 12 t of cargo.
Landing Craft. Mechanized, Mark 2. 8 TKLs were built for the US Army in 1941, 139 LCMs for the Navy in 1942.

LCM(3) type landing craft mechanized

TKL9 – 28, 398 – 437, 455 – 474, 546, 547, 810 – 834, 839 – 852, 873 – 912, 944 – 1004 and 27 other, LCM(3)4629 – 4678, 4754 – 4814, 7350 – 7424, 7960 – 7999, 8197 – 8273, 8350 – 8459, 11956 – 12680, 14270

– 14369, 14402 – 14441, 14844 – 14918, 18186 – 18385, 18486 – 18560, 21061 – 21309, 24174, 24435 – 24461, 27992 – 30781, 35952 – 35991, 46330 – 49104, 51721 – 52329, 52350 – 52497, 52798 – 52849, 52988

– 53537, 68969 – 69888 (partly), 74389 – 77388 (partly) (1942-1945)
24 / 52 t, 15.3 x 4.3 x 1.4 m, 2 diesels, 330 hp, 8 kts (loaded), 140 nm (8 kts), complement 4; 2 x 1 – 12.7 MG; 1 tank or 60 troops or 27 t of cargo.
Landing craft, mechanized, Mark 3. 8631 units were built

by Higgins, W. A. Robinson, Drier Steel & Brewer DD, Walsh-Steers, Beth Wilmington, Boston N Yd, Norfolk N Yd, Charleston N Yd, American C & F and other builders; 1255 in 1942, 3765 in 1943, 3360 in 1944 and 71 in 1945.

LCM(6) type landing craft mechanized

LCM(6)52498 – 52797, 52850 – 52987, 53538 – 53677, 68969 – 69888 (partly), 74389 – 77388 (partly) (1943-1945)
25 / 56 t, 17.1 x 4.3 x 1.2 m, 2 diesels, 450 hp, 9 kts, 130 nm (9 kts), complement 5; 2 x 1 – 12.7 MG; 1 tank or 60 troops or 31 t of cargo.
Landing craft, mechanized, Mark 6. 2718 were built during the war: 52 in 1943, 1850 in 1944 and 828 in 1945. Building was re-commenced in 1950 and was finalized only in 1987.

LCC(1) and LCC(2) types landing craft control

LCC(1/2)25470-25529, 39044 – 39058 (partly) (1943-1944)
30 t, 17.1 x 4.1 (LCC(1) or 4.6 (LCC(2) x 1.2 m, 2 diesels, 450 hp, 13.5 kts, complement 14; 3 x 2 – 12.7 MG; SO

radar.
Landing craft, control. 99 were built in 1943-1944 by Albina Marine, Consolidated SB, and Charleston NYd.

LCV type landing craft vehicle

7 / 11 t, 11.1 x 3.3 x 0.9 m, 1 diesel or petrol engine, 225-250 hp, 9 kts, 100 nm (9 kts), complement 3; 2 x 1 – 7.6 MG; 36 troops or 4.5 t of cargo.

Landing craft, vehicle. 2366 were built by Chris-Craft Corp, Higgins and Owens Yacht: 110 in 1941, 1870 in 1942 and 306 in 1943.

LCP(L) type landing craft personnel (large)

5.9 / 8.2 t, 11.2 x 3.3 x 1.1 m, 1 diesel or petrol engine, 150 or 250 hp, 8 kts, 50 or 130 nm (8 kts), complement 3; 2 x 1 – 7.6 MG; 30-36 troops or 3-3.7 t of cargo.
Landing craft, personnel (large). 2193 were built during the war by Chris-Craft Corp, Higgins, Matthews, Owens

Yacht, Richardson Boat, Marinette Marine, Watercraft America, Bollinger and Peterson Builders: 564 in 1941, 307 in 1942, 282 in 1943, 547 in 1944 and 550 in 1945. These craft were built also in 1954-1994.

LCP(R) type landing craft personnel (ramp)

5.9 / 8.2 t, 10.9 x 3.3 x 1.1 m, 1 diesel or petrol engine, 150-250 hp, 11 kts, 50 or 130 nm (8 kts), complement 3; 2 x 1 – 7.6 MG; 30-36 troops or 3-3.7 t of cargo.
Landing craft, personnel (ramp). 2631 were built by

Chris-Craft Corp., Higgins, Matthews and Richardson Boat: 1563 in 1942, 24 in 1943, 705 in 1944 and 343 in 1945.

LCVP type landing craft vehicle personnel

9 / 13 t, 11.2 x 3.2 x 0.9m, 1 diesel or petrol engine, 225-250 hp, 8 kts, 850 nm (6 kts), complement 3-4; 2 x 1 – 12.7 MG; 36 troops or 1 light tank or 3.7 t of cargo.
Landing craft, vehicle personnel. 23358 were built before the war end by Chamberlin, Chris-Craft, Dodge Boat & Plane, Higgins, Matthews, Owens Yacht, Richardson

Boat, Shelburne SY, Lunn Laminates, Puget Sound N Yd and Marinette Marine: 215 in 1942, 8027 in 1943, 9290 in 1944 and 5865 in 1945. 750 LCV and LCVP were transferred to the United Kingdom in 1943-1944. Practically identical LCVP were built after war, in 1950-1969.

LCS(1) and LCS(2) types landing craft support

LCS(S)1: 9.8 t, 11.2 x 3.3 x 1.1 m, 1 petrol engine, 250 hp, 12 kts, 115 nm (12 kts), complement 6; 2 x 1 – 12.7 MG or 3 x 1 – 7.6 MG or (1 x 1 – 12.7 + 2 x 1 – 7.6) MG, 2 x 1 – 127 barrage RL.
LCS(S)2: 10.3 t, 11.2 x 3.3 x 1.1 m, 1 diesel, 225 hp, 11.5 kts, 135 nm (11.5 kts), complement 6; 1 x 1 – 12.7 MG, 2 x 1 – 7.6 MG, 2 x 12 – 114 barrage RL.

Landing craft, support. 559 were built: 151 Mk 1 in 1942, 145 Mk 2 in 1943 and 263 Mk 2 in 1944. 2 were transferred to the Soviet Union, 1 to the United Kingdom.

AUXILIARY VESSELS INTENDED FOR COMBAT SUPPORT

Destroyer tenders

Melville	AD2	New York SB, Camden	2.3.1915	12.1915	stricken 4.1947

7700 t, 127.3 x 16.6 x 6.1 m, 1 set geared steam turbines, 2 boilers, 4000 hp, 14.7 kts, complement 425;
2 x 1 – 127/51, 4 x 1 – 76/50, 2 x 2 – 40/56, 8 x 1 – 20/70

Dobbin	AD3	Philadelphia N Yd	5.5.1921	7.1924	sold 12.1946
Whitney	AD4	Boston N Yd	12.10.1923	9.1924	stricken 1.1947

8325 / 12450 t, 147.6 x 18.6 x 7.4 m, 1 set geared steam turbines, 4 boilers, 7000 hp, 16 kts, complement 414; 4
x 1 – 127/38, 4 x 2 – 40/56, 6 x 2 – 20/70.

Black Hawk	AD9	Cramp, Philadelphia	1913	5.1918	stricken 8.1946

5690 / 8900 t, 128.1 x 18.4 x 6.5 m, 1 VQE, 3 boilers, 3285 hp, 12.5 kts, complement 825; 4 x 1 – 76/50, 2 x
2 – 40/56, 16 x 1 – 20/70.

Bridgeport	AD10	Bremer Vulcan, Vegesack, Germany	14.8.1901	8.1917	stricken 10.1941

7175 t, 136.4 x 16.6 x 8.9 m, 2 VQE, 2 boilers, 12.5 kts, complement 552; 8 x 1 – 127/51.

Altair	AD11	Skinner & Eddy, Seattle	10.5.1919	12.1921	stricken 6.1946
Denebola	AD12	Skinner & Eddy, Seattle	1919	11.1921	stricken 5.1946

10400 t, 129.2 x 16.5 x 6.3 m, 1 set geared steam turbines, 2 boilers, 2500 hp, 10.5 kts, complement 608;
1 x 1 – 127/51, 3 x 2 – 40/56.

Rigel	AD13	Skinner & Eddy, Seattle	1918	2.1922	repair ship 4.1941, stricken 7.1946

6807 / 10000 t, 129.2 x 16.5 x 6.2 m, 1 set geared steam turbines, 2 boilers, 2500 hp, 11.5 kts, complement 482;
4 x 1 – 76/50, 4 x 2 – 40/56, 6 x 2 – 20/70.

Dixie	AD14	New York SB, Camden	27.5.1939	4.1940	stricken 6.1982
Prairie	AD15	New York SB, Camden	9.12.1939	8.1940	stricken 3.1993
Piedmont	AD17	Tampa SB		12.1942	1.1944	to Turkey 10.1982 (Derya)

Sierra	AD18	Tampa SB	23.2.1943	3.1944	stricken 10.1993
Yosemite	AD19	Tampa SB	16.5.1943	3.1944	stricken 1.1994

Dixie 1940

14037 / 18000 t, 161.8 x 22.4 x 7.8 m, 2 sets geared steam turbines, 4 boilers, 11000 hp, 19.6 kts, complement 1262; 4 x 1 – 127/38, 4 x 2 – 40/56, 23 x 1 – 20/70.

Cascade	AD16	Western Pipe & Steel, San Francisco	6.6.1942	3.1943	stricken 11.1974

11755 / 16600 t, 150.1 x 21.2 x 8.3 m, 1 set geared steam turbines, 2 boilers, 8500 hp, 18.4 kts, complement 857; 2 x 1 – 127/38, 3 x 2 – 40/56, (2 x 4 + 4 x 1) – 20/70.

Hamul	AD20	Federal, Kearny	6.4.1940	1.1943	stricken 1962
Markab	AD21	Ingalls, Pascagoula	21.12.1940	1.1942	stricken 9.1976

8560 / 14800 t, 150.2 x 21.3 x 7.5 m, 1 set geared steam turbines, 2 boilers, 8500 hp, 18.4 kts, complement 864; 1 x 1 – 127/38, 4 x 1 – 76/50, 2 x 2 - 40/56, 20 x 1 (AD20) or 8 x 2 (AD21) – 20/70.

Klondike	AD22	Todd-Pacific, San Pedro	12.8.1944	7.1945	stricken 9.1974
Arcadia	AD23	Todd-Pacific, San Pedro	19.11.1944	9.1945	stricken 7.1973
Everglades	AD24	Todd-Pacific, San Pedro	28.1.1945	5.1946	stricken 5.1989
Frontier	AD25	Todd-Pacific, San Pedro	25.3.1945	3.1946	stricken 12.1972
Shenandoah	AD26	Todd-Pacific, Tacoma	29.3.1945	8.1945	stricken 4.1980
Yellowstone	AD27	Todd-Pacific, Tacoma	12.4.1945	1.1946	stricken 9.1974
Grand Canyon	AD28	Todd-Pacific, Tacoma	27.4.1945	4.1946	stricken 9.1978
Isle Royale	AD29	Todd-Pacific, Tacoma	19.9.1945	7.1946	stricken 9.1976
Great Lakes	AD30	Todd-Pacific, Tacoma	-	-	cancelled 1.1946
Tidewater	AD31	Charleston N Yd	30.6.1945	2.1946	stricken 6.1978
Canopus	AD33	Mare Island N Yd, Vallejo	-	-	cancelled 8.1945
Arrowhead	AD35	Puget Sound N Yd	-	-	cancelled 8.1945
Bryce Canyon	AD36	Charleston N Yd	7.3.1946	9.1950	stricken 6.1981

Everglades post-war

11755 / 16635 t, 150.1 x 21.2 x 8.3 m, 1 set geared steam turbines, 2 boilers, 8500 hp, 18.4 kts, complement 826; 1 (AD22-25) or 2 (AD26-36) x 1 – 127/38, 2 (AD22-25) or 4 (AD26-36) x 2 – 40/56, 20 (AD22-25) or 22 (AD26-36) x 1 – 20/70.

New England	AD32	Tampa SB	-	-	cancelled 8.1945

14037 / 16750 t, 161.5 x 22.4 x 7.3 m, 2 sets geared steam turbines, 4 boilers, 12000 hp, 19.6 kts; 4 x 1 – 127/38, 4 x 2 – 40/56.

Alcor	AD34	Federal, Kearny	1928	11.1944	stricken 8.1946

12250 t, 135.7 x 18.3 x 7.8 m, 1 set geared steam turbines, 4 boilers, 7100 hp, 16.5 kts, complement 734; 1 x 1 – 127/51, 4 x 1 – 76/50.

Submarine tenders

Bushnell	AS2	Seattle Dry Dock	9.2.1915	11.1915	survey vessel 12.1937

4550 t, 106.9 x 13.9 x 5.6 m, 1 set geared steam turbines, 2 boilers, 2500 hp, 13.9 kts, complement 356; 1 x 1 – 127/38, 4 x 1 – 76/50.

Holland	AS3	Puget Sound N Yd, Bremerton	12.4.1926	6.1926	internal combustion engine repair ship 8.1945

8100 / 12614 t, 156.5 x 18.6 x 7.4 m, 1 set geared steam turbines, 2 boilers, 7000 hp, 16 kts, complement 798; 4 x 1 – 127/38, 4 x 2 – 40/56, 12 x 1 – 20/70.

Beaver	AS5	Newport News	27.11.1909	10.1918	internal combustion engine repair ship 6.1945

4737 / 6494 t, 115.9 x 14.4 x 6.2 m, 1 VTE, 6 boilers, 3650 hp, 16.5 kts, complement 480; 1 x 1 – 127/51, 4 x 1 – 76/50, 8 x 1 – 20/70.

Camden	AS6	Flensburger Schiffbau, Germany	1900	2.1919	auxiliary 9.1940

6075 t, 134.7 x 14.5 x 7.3 m, 1 VQE, 2 boilers, 12 kts, complement 345; 4 x 1 – 102/50, 2 x 1 – 76/50.

Canopus	AS9	New York SB, Camden	1919	1.1922	scuttled 10.4.1942

5975 / 7750 t, 114.0 x 15.8 x 7.4 m, 12 kts, complement 314; 2 x 1 – 127/38, 4 x 1 – 76/50.
Canopus was damaged by Japanese bomber at Mariveles (Luzon, Philippines) 29.12.1941 and scuttled 10.4.1942 to avoid capture by the Japanese.

Argonne	AS10	American International SB, Hog Island	24.2.1907	7.1924	auxiliary 7.1940

8400 / 11400 t, 136.6 x 17.8 x 5.7 m, 1 set geared steam turbines, 6 boilers, 6000 hp, 15.5 kts, complement 610; 4 x 1 – 127/51, 4 x 1 – 76/50.

Fulton	AS11	Mare Island N Yd, Vallejo	27.12.1940	9.1941	stricken 12.1991
Sperry	AS12	Mare Island N Yd, Vallejo	17.12.1941	5.1942	stricken 9.1982
Bushnell	AS15	Mare Island N Yd, Vallejo	14.9.1942	4.1943	stricken 11.1980
Howard W. Gilmore	AS16	Mare Island N Yd, Vallejo	16.9.1943	5.1944	stricken 12.1980
Nereus	AS17	Mare Island N Yd, Vallejo	12.2.1945	10.1945	stricken 10.1971
Orion	AS18	Moore DD, Oakland	14.10.1942	9.1943	stricken 9.1993
Proteus	AS19	Moore DD, Oakland	12.11.1942	1.1944	stricken 9.1992

15250 / 18000 t, 161.5 x 22.4 x 7.8 m, 3 diesel-generators, 2 electric motors, 11520 hp, 15.4 kts, complement 1300; 4 x 1 – 127/38, 4 x 2 – 40/56, 23 x 1 – 20/70.

Howard W. Gilmore post-war

Griffin	AS13	Sun SB, Chester	11.10.1939	7.1941	stricken 8.1972
Pelias	AS14	Sun SB, Chester	14.11.1939	9.1941	stricken 8.1972

8613 / 14500 t, 150.1 x 21.2 x 7.4 m, 1 diesel, 8500 hp, 16.5 kts, complement 1500; 4 x 1 – 76/50, (10 – 20) x 1 – 20/70.

| **Otus** | AS20 | Federal, Kearny | 2.11.1940 | 3.1941 | internal combustion engine repair ship 6.1945 |

12930 t, 127.4 x 18.3 x 6.3 m, 1 set geared steam turbines, 2 boilers, 4000 hp, 14.7 kts, complement 644;   1 x 1 – 127/38, 4 x 1 – 76/50, 12 x 1 – 20/70.

| **Antaeus** | AS21 | Newport News | 9.1.1932 | 5.1941 | auxiliary 9.1943 |

7800 / 8350 t, 122.9 x 18.6 x 6.2 m, 2 sets geared steam turbines, 4 boilers, 13000 hp, 20 kts, complement 440: 1   x 1 – 102/50, 2 x 1 – 76/50.

| **Euryale** | AS22 | Federal, Kearny | 15.4.1943 | 12.1943 | stricken 12.1971 |

7600 / 15400 t, 150.2 x 21.2 x 7.8 m, 1 set geared steam turbines, 2 boilers, 8500 hp, 16 kts, complement 1403: 1   x 1 – 127/38, 4 x 1 – 76/50, 2 x 2 – 40/56, 22 x 1 – 20/70.

Aegir	AS23	Ingalls, Pascagoula	15.9.1943	9.1944	stricken 6.1971
Anthedon	AS24	Ingalls, Pascagoula	15.10.1943	9.1944	stricken 1969
Apollo	AS25	Ingalls, Pascagoula	6.11.1943	9.1944	stricken 7.1963
Clytie	AS26	Ingalls, Pascagoula	26.11.1943	1.1945	BU 1971

Anthedon 1944

11760 / 16500 t, 150.1 x 21.2 x 8.2 m, 1 set geared steam turbines, 2 boilers, 8500 hp, 18.4 kts, complement 1460; 1 x 1 – 127/38, 2 x 2 – 40/56, 20 x 1 – 20/70.

PT boat tenders

| **Niagara** | AGP1 | Bath Iron Wks | 7.6.1929 | 1.1943 | sunk 22.5.1943 |

1922 t, 81.4 x 10.8 x 5.2 m, 2 diesels, 3000 hp, 16 kts, complement 139; 2 x 1 – 76/50.   *Niagara* was sunk 22.5.1943 by Japanese aircraft between Tulagi and New Guinea.

| **Hilo** | AGP2 | Bath Iron Wks | 18.7.1931 | 1.1943 | stricken 3.1946 |

2350 t, 85.1 x 11.7 x 5.2 m, 2 diesels, 6000 hp, 14.5 kts,   complement 105; 1 x 1 – 76/50.

| **Jamestown** | AGP3 | Pusey & Jones, Wilmington | 1928 | 1.1943 | stricken 3.1946 |

2250 t, 89.7 x 11.6 x 4.9 m, 2 diesels, 6000 hp, 15 kts,   complement 259; 2 x 1 – 76/50, 6 x 1 – 20/70.

Portunus	AGP4	Philadelphia N Yd	11.2.1943	6.1943	stricken 11.1946
Varuna	AGP5	Dravo, Wilmington	9.12.1942	8.1943	stricken 5.1946
Orestes	AGP10	Chicago Bridge, Seneca	16.11.1943	4.1944	stricken 4.1947
Silenus	AGP11	Chicago Bridge, Seneca	20.3.1944	8.1944	stricken 4.1946
Alecto	AGP14	Bethlehem-Hingham, Baltimore	15.1.1945	7.1945	stricken 6.1947
Callisto	AGP15	Bethlehem-Hingham, Baltimore	29.11.1944	6.1945	stricken 4.1947
Antigone	AGP16	Chicago Bridge, Seneca	27.10.1944	6.1945	stricken 6.1947
Brontes	AGP17	Chicago Bridge, Seneca	6.2.1945	8.1945	stricken 4.1946
Chiron	AGP18	Chicago Bridge, Seneca	10.3.1945	9.1945	stricken 3.1946
Pontus	AGP20	Chicago Bridge, Seneca	2.3.1943	8.1944	stricken 5.1946

1780 / 4100 t, 100.0 x 15.3 x 3.4 m, 2 diesels, 1800 hp, 11.5 kts, complement 289; 2 x 4 – 40/56, 8 x 2 – 20/70.

Alecto 1945

Oyster Bay	AGP6	Lake Washington, Houghton	23.5.1942	11.1943	stricken 4.1946
Mobjack	AGP7	Lake Washington, Houghton	2.8.1942	10.1943	stricken 8.1946
Wachapreague	AGP8	Lake Washington, Houghton	10.7.1943	5.1944	stricken 6.1946
Willoughby	AGP9	Lake Washington, Houghton	21.8.1943	6.1944	stricken 7.1946

1766 / 2800 t, 94.8 x 12.5 x 4.1 m, 4 diesels (2 shafts), 6400 hp, 18 kts, complement 215; 2 x 1 – 127/38, (1 x 4 + 2 x 2) – 40/56, 4 x 2 – 20/70.

Oyster Bay 1944

Acontius	AGP12	Pusey & Jones, Wilmington	12.10.1943	6.1944	stricken 4.1946
Cyrene	AGP13	Pusey & Jones, Wilmington	8.2.1944	9.1944	stricken 4.1947

5826 / 10590 t, 126.0 x 18.3 x 6.9 m, 1 set geared steam turbines, 2 boilers, 4000 hp, 14 kts, complement 289; 1 x 1 – 127/38, 4 x 2 – 40/56, 12 x 1 – 20/70.

Repair ships

Medusa	AR1	Puget Sound N Yd, Bremerton	16.4.1923	9.1924	sold 8.1950

10620 / 13000 t, 147.7 x 21.4 x 6.3 m, 1 set geared steam turbines, 2 boilers, 7000 hp, 16 kts, complement 840; 6 x 1 – 76/50, 2 x 2 – 40/56, 8 x 1 – 20/70.

Prometheus	AR3	Mare Island N Yd, Vallejo	5.12.1908	12.1914	stricken 7.1946

8940 t, 142.2 x 18.4 x 5.9 m, 2 VTE, 3 boilers, 7500 hp, 16 kts, complement 737; 2 x 1 – 127/51, 4 x 1 – 76/50, 2 x 2 – 40/56

Vestal	AR4	New York N Yd, Brooklyn	19.5.1908	9.1913	stricken 9.1946

9789 t, 142.1 x 18.4 x 7.9 m, 1 VTE, 3 boilers, 7500 hp, 16 kts, complement 783; 3 x 1 – 76/50, 2 x 2 – 40/56.

Vulcan	AR5	New York SB, Camden	14.12.1940	6.1941	stricken 7.1992
Ajax	AR6	Los Angeles SB, San Pedro	22.8.1942	10.1943	stricken 5.1989
Hector	AR7	Los Angeles SB, San Pedro	11.11.1942	2.1944	to Pakistan 4.1989 (Moawin)
Jason	AR8	Los Angeles SB, San Pedro	3.4.1943	(6.1944)	commissioned as heavy hull repair ship

8975 / 16200 t, 161.7 x 22.4 x 7.1 m, 2 sets geared steam turbines, 4 boilers, 11000 hp, 19.2 kts, complement 1058; 4 x 1 – 127/38, 4 x 2 – 40/56, 23 x 1 – 20/70.

Ajax post-war

Delta	AR9	Newport News	2.4.1941	7.1942	stricken 10.1977
Briareus	AR12	Newport News	14.2.1941	11.1943	stricken 1.1977

8975 / 14000 t, 149.6 x 21.2 x 7.2 m, 1 set geared steam turbines, 2 boilers, 8500 hp, 16.5 kts, complement 900;   1 x 1 – 127/38, 4 x 1 – 76/50, 2 x 2 – 40/56, 10 x 2 – 20/70.

Alcor	AR10	Federal, Kearny	1928	12.1941	destroyer tender 11.1944

12250 t, 135.7 x 18.3 x 7.8 m, 1 set geared steam turbines, 4 boilers, 7100 hp, 16.5 kts, complement 734;   1 x 1 – 127/51, 4 x 1 – 76/50.

Rigel	AR11	Skinner & Eddy, Seattle	1918	12.1941	stricken 7.1946

6807 / 10000 t, 129.2 x 16.5 x 6.3 m, 1 set geared steam turbines, 2500 hp, 11.5 kts, complement 482; 4 x 1 –   76/50, 4 x 2 – 40/56, 6 x 2 – 20/70.

Amphion	AR13	Tampa SB	15.5.1945	1.1946	stricken 3.1977
Cadmus	AR14	Tampa SB	5.8.1945	4.1946	stricken 1.1974
Deucalion	AR15	Tampa SB	-	-	cancelled 8.1945
Mars	AR16	Tampa SB	-	-	cancelled 8.1945

Amphion post-war

7826 / 16900 t, 150.1 x 21.2 x 8.4 m, 1 set geared steam turbines, 2 boilers, 8500 hp, 16.5 kts, complement 920; 2 x 1 – 127/38, 4 x 2 – 40/56, 22 x 1 – 20/70.

Assistance	AR17	Bethlehem-Fairfield, Baltimore	20.6.1944	(1.1945)	to the UK 1.1945 (Assistance)
Diligence	AR18	Bethlehem-Fairfield, Baltimore	31.7.1944	(1945)	to the UK 1945 (Diligence)
Xanthus	AR19	Bethlehem-Fairfield, Baltimore	31.7.1944	5.1945	stricken 9.1962
Laertes	AR20	Bethlehem-Fairfield, Baltimore	14.9.1944	3.1945	sold 7.1972
Dionysus	AR21	Bethlehem-Fairfield, Baltimore	10.10.1944	4.1945	to the MarAd 12.1960

5801 / 14350 t, 134.7 x 17.4 x 7.0 m, 1 set geared steam turbines, 2 boilers, 2500 hp, 12.5 kts, complement 525;   1 x 1 – 127/38, 3 x 1 – 76/50, 2 x 2 – 40/56, 12 x 1 – 20/70.

Repair ships, internal combustion engines

Oglala	ARG1	Cramp, Philadelphia	1907	5.1943	stricken 7.1946

3746 t, 117.8 x 15.9 x 4.9 m, 2 VTE, 8 boilers, 7000 hp, 17 kts, complement 425; 1 x 1 – 127/38, 4 x 1 – 76/50, 2   x 2 – 40/56, 8 x 1 – 20/70.

Luzon	ARG2	Bethlehem-Fairfield, Baltimore	14.5.1943	10.1943	stricken 9.1961
Mindanao	ARG3	Bethlehem-Fairfield, Baltimore	13.5.1943	11.1943	stricken 9.1961
Tutuila	ARG4	Bethlehem-Fairfield, Baltimore	12.9.1943	4.1944	stricken 2.1972
Oahu	ARG5	Bethlehem-Fairfield, Baltimore	9.9.1943	4.1944	stricken 7.1963
Cebu	ARG6	Bethlehem-Fairfield, Baltimore	18.10.1943	4.1944	stricken 9.1962
Culebra Island	ARG7	Bethlehem-Fairfield, Baltimore	23.11.1943	5.1944	stricken 9.1962
Leyte, 5.1945- **Maui**	ARG8	Bethlehem-Fairfield, Baltimore	18.2.1944	8.1944	stricken 9.1962
Mona Island	ARG9	Bethlehem-Fairfield, Baltimore	11.5.1944	10.1944	stricken 9.1962
Palawan	ARG10	Bethlehem-Fairfield, Baltimore	12.8.1944	5.1945	stricken 7.1963
Samar	ARG11	Bethlehem-Fairfield, Baltimore	19.10.1944	6.1945	stricken 9.1962

Basilan	ARG12	Bethlehem-Fairfield, Baltimore	21.3.1944	(10.1944)	commissioned as auxiliary
Burias	ARG13	Bethlehem-Fairfield, Baltimore	27.3.1944	(10.1944)	commissioned as auxiliary
Dumaran	ARG14	Bethlehem-Fairfield, Baltimore	22.5.1944	(12.1944)	commissioned as aircraft repair ship
Masbate	ARG15	Bethlehem-Fairfield, Baltimore	5.8.1944	(3.1945)	commissioned as aircraft repair ship
Kermit Roosevelt	ARG16	Bethlehem-Fairfield, Baltimore	5.10.1944	5.1945	stricken 1.1960
Hooper Island	ARG17	Bethlehem-Fairfield, Baltimore	18.10.1944	7.1945	stricken 7.1960

5801 / 14350 t, 134.7 x 17.4 x 7.0 m, 1 set geared steam turbines, 2 boilers, 2500 hp, 12.5 kts, complement 525; 1 x 1 – 127/38, 3 x 1 – 76/50, 2 x 2 – 40/56, 12 x 1 – 20/70.

Kermit Roosevelt post-war

Holland	ARG18	Puget Sound N Yd, Bremerton	12.4.1926	8.1945	stricken 6.1952

8100 / 12614 t, 156.5 x 18.6 x 7.4 m, 1 set geared steam turbines, 2 boilers, 7000 hp, 16 kts, complement 798; 4 x 1 – 127/38, 4 x 2 – 40/56, 12 x 1 – 20/70.

Beaver	ARG19	Newport News	27.11.1909	6.1945	stricken 8.1946

4737 / 6494 t, 115.9 x 14.4 x 6.2 m, 1 VTE, 6 boilers, 3650 hp, 16.5 kts, complement 480; 1 x 1 – 127/51, 4 x 1 – 76/50, 8 x 1 – 20/70.

Otus	ARG20	Federal, Kearny	2.11.1940	6.1945	stricken 9.1946

12930 t, 127.4 x 18.3 x 6.3 m, 1 set geared steam turbines, 2 boilers, 4000 hp, 14.7 kts, complement 644; 1 x 1 – 127/38, 4 x 1 – 76/50, 12 x 1 – 20/70

Aircraft repair ships

Chourre	ARV1	Bethlehem-Fairfield, Baltimore	22.5.1941	12.1944	stricken 1961
Webster	ARV2	Bethlehem-Fairfield, Baltimore	5.8.1944	3.1945	stricken 1962

5801 / 14350 t, 134.7 x 17.4 x 7.0 m, 1 set geared turbines, 2 boilers, 2500 hp, 12.5 kts, complement 525; 1 x 1 – 127/38, 3 x 1 – 76/50, 2 x 2 – 40/56, 12 x 1 – 20/70.

Aircraft repair ships (engine)

Aventius	ARV(E)3	American Bridge, Pittsburgh	24.3.1945	5.1945	to Chile 8.1963 (Aguila)
Chloris	ARV(E)4	American Bridge, Pittsburgh	21.4.1945	6.1945	stricken 6.1973
Fabius	ARV(E)5	American Bridge, Pittsburgh	11.4.1945	6.1945	stricken 1960s
Megara	ARV(E)6	American Bridge, Pittsburgh	25.4.1945	6.1945	stricken 6.1973

1780 / 4100 t, 100.0 x 15.3 x 3.4 m, 2 diesels, 1800 hp, 11.5 kts, complement 289; 2 x 4 – 40/56, 12 x 1 – 20/70.

Fabius

Repair ships, battle damage

Aristaeus	ARB1	Philadelphia N Yd	11.2.1943	5.1943	stricken post-war
Oceanus	ARB2	Philadelphia N Yd	11.2.1943	5.1943	stricken 7.1961
Phaon	ARB3	Dravo, Pittsburgh	30.4.1943	8.1943	stricken 7.1961
Zeus	ARB4	Chicago Bridge, Seneca	26.10.1943	4.1944	stricken 6.1973
Midas	ARB5	Chicago Bridge, Seneca	24.12.1943	5.1944	stricken 4.1976
Nestor	ARB6	Chicago Bridge, Seneca	20.1.1944	6.1944	stricken 1.1946
Sarpedon	ARB7	Bethlehem, Hingham	21.8.1944	3.1945	stricken 4.1976
Telamon	ARB8	Bethlehem, Hingham	10.1.1945	2.1945	stricken 6.1973
Ulysses	ARB9	Bethlehem, Hingham	2.12.1944	4.1945	stricken 1961
Demeter	ARB10	Chicago Bridge, Seneca	19.1.1945	7.1945	sold 1958
Diomedes	ARB11	Chicago Bridge, Seneca	11.1.1945	6.1945	to West Germany 6.1961 (Wotan)
Helios	ARB12	Chicago Bridge, Seneca	14.2.1945	7.1945	to Brazil 1.1962 (Belmonte)

Sarpedon 1945

1781 / 3960 t, 100.0 x 15.3 x 3.4 m, 2 diesels, 1800 hp, 11.6 kts, complement 286; 2 x 4 – 40/56, 8 x 1 – 20/70.

Heavy-hull repair ship

Jason	ARH1	Los Angeles SB, San Pedro	3.4.1943	6.1944	stricken 6.1995

8975 / 16200 t, 161.7 x 22.4 x 7.1 m, 2 sets geared steam turbines, 4 boilers, 11000 hp, 19.2 kts, complement 1058; 4 x 1 – 127/38, 4 x 2 – 40/56, 23 x 1 – 20/70.

Repair ships, landing craft

Achelous	ARL1	Dravo, Pittsburgh	25.11.1942	4.1943	stricken 6.1973
Amycus	ARL2	Kaiser, Richmond	2.4.1943	7.1943	stricken 6.1970
Agenor	ARL3	Kaiser, Richmond	3.4.1943	8.1943	to France 3.1951 (Vulcain)
Adonis	ARL4	JeffBoat, Jeffersonville	14.6.1943	8.1943	stricken 1.1960
	ARL5	JeffBoat, Jeffersonville	28.5.1943	(7.1943)	to the UK 7.1943 (LSE(L)1)
	ARL6	JeffBoat, Jeffersonville	9.6.1943	(7.1943)	to the UK 7.1943 (LSE(L)2)
Atlas	ARL7	Chicago Bridge, Seneca	19.10.1943	2.1944	stricken 6.1972
Egeria	ARL8	Chicago Bridge, Seneca	23.11.1943	3.1944	sold 6.1980
Endymion	ARL9	Chicago Bridge, Seneca	17.12.1943	5.1944	stricken 6.1972
Coronis	ARL10	Boston N Yd	8.6.1944	11.1944	sold ~1965
Creon	ARL11	Boston N Yd	24.8.1944	1.1945	stricken post-war
Poseidon	ARL12	Boston N Yd	24.8.1944	2.1945	stricken 7.1961
Menelaus	ARL13	Bethlehem, Hingham	20.12.1944	5.1945	stricken 6.1960
Minos	ARL14	Chicago Bridge, Seneca	15.9.1944	10.1944	stricken 1.1960
Minotaur	ARL15	Chicago Bridge, Seneca	29.9.1944	2.1945	to S. Korea 1955 (Duk So)
Myrmidon	ARL16	Bethlehem, Hingham	28.9.1944	3.1945	stricken 4.1960
Numitor	ARL17	Bethlehem, Hingham	18.10.1944	4.1945	stricken 4.1960
Pandemus	ARL18	Chicago Bridge, Seneca	10.10.1944	2.1945	stricken 10.1968
Patroclus	ARL19	Bethlehem, Hingham	22.10.1944	4.1945	stricken 8.1952
Pentheus	ARL20	Chicago Bridge, Seneca	22.12.1944	6.1945	stricken 1.1960

Proserpine	ARL21	Chicago Bridge, Seneca	28.12.1944	5.1945	stricken 9.1960
Romulus	ARL22	Bethlehem, Hingham	15.11.1944	5.1945	stricken 10.1960
Satyr	ARL23	Chicago Bridge, Seneca	13.11.1944	4.1945	stricken 6.1975
Sphinx	ARL24	Bethlehem, Hingham	18.11.1944	5.1945	stricken 4.1977
Stentor	ARL26	Chicago Bridge, Seneca	11.11.1944	4.1945	stricken 7.1960
Tantalus	ARL27	Chicago Bridge, Seneca	2.1.1945	6.1945	stricken 2.1947
Typhon	ARL28	Chicago Bridge, Seneca	5.1.1945	6.1945	stricken 7.1960
Amphitrite	ARL29	Chicago Bridge, Seneca	1.2.1945	6.1945	stricken 7.1961
Askari	ARL30	Chicago Bridge, Seneca	2.3.1945	7.1945	stricken 2.1979
Bellerophon	ARL31	Chicago Bridge, Seneca	7.3.1945	7.1945	stricken 10.1977
Bellona	ARL32	Chicago Bridge, Seneca	26.3.1945	7.1945	stricken 6.1946
Chimaera	ARL33	Chicago Bridge, Seneca	30.3.1945	8.1945	stricken 7.1961
Daedalus	ARL35	Chicago Bridge, Seneca	26.3.1945	10.1945	sold 10.1960
Gordius	ARL36	Chicago Bridge, Seneca	7.5.1945	9.1945	stricken 2.1961
Indra	ARL37	Chicago Bridge, Seneca	21.5.1945	10.1945	stricken 1984
Krishna	ARL38	Chicago Bridge, Seneca	25.5.1945	12.1945	stricken 10.1971
Quirinius	ARL39	Chicago Bridge, Seneca	4.6.1945	11.1945	to Venezuela 1962 (Guayana)
Remus	ARL40	Kaiser, Richmond	10.10.1942	8.1944	stricken 8.1946
Achilles	ARL41	Kaiser, Richmond	17.10.1942	8.1944	stricken 8.1946
Aeolus	ARL42	Boston N Yd	23.11.1942	(1.1943)	cancelled 9.1945
Cerberus	ARL43	New York N Yd, Brooklyn	28.1.1943	(2.1943)	cancelled 9.1945
Conus	ARL44	New York N Yd, Brooklyn	28.1.1943	(2.1943)	cancelled 9.1945
Feronia	ARL45	Philadelphia N Yd	24.12.1942	(2.1943)	cancelled 9.1945
Chandra	ARL46	Norfolk N Yd, Portsmouth	7.2.1943	(2.1943)	cancelled 9.1945
Minerva	ARL47	Bethlehem, Quincy	19.1.1943	(1.1943)	cancelled 9.1945

1781 / 3960 t, 100.0 x 15.3 x 3.4 m, 2 diesels, 1800 hp, 11.6 kts, complement 286; 2 x 4 – 40/56, 8 x 1 – 20/70.

Atlas post-war

Oilers

Kanawha	AO1	Mare Island N Yd, Vallejo	11.7.1914	6.1915	sunk 8.4.1943
Cuyama	AO3	Mare Island N Yd, Vallejo	17.6.1916	4.1917	stricken 1946

5723 / 14800 t, 145.1 x 17.2 x 8.1 m, 2 VTE, 4 boilers, 14 kts, complement 317; 2 x 1 – 127/38, 2 x 2 – 40/56, 2 x 2 – 20/70.

Kanawha was sunk by Japanese aircraft off Tulagi (Solomon Islands) 8.4.1943.

Maumee	AO2	Mare Island N Yd, Vallejo	17.4.1915	10.1916	auxiliary 7.1945

5723 / 14700 t, 145.1 x 17.1 x 8.1 m, 4 diesels (2 shafts), 5000 hp, 14.3 kts, complement 363; 2 x 1 – 127/38, 4 x 2 – 40/56, 2 x 2 – 20/70.

Brazos	AO4	Boston N Yd	1.5.1919	10.1919	stricken 2.1946
Neches	AO5	Boston N Yd	2.6.1920	10.1920	sunk 23.1.1942
Pecos	AO6	Boston N Yd	23.4.1921	8.1921	sunk 1.3.1942

5723 / 14700 t, 145.1 x 17.1 x 8.1 m, 2 VTE, 4 boilers, 5200 hp, complement 255; 2 x 1 – 127/38, 4 x 2 – 40/56, 4 x 2 – 20/70.

Neches was torpedoed by Japanese submarine *I172* 23.1.1942 between Hawaii and Alaska. *Pecos* was sunk by air group of Japanese carrier *Soryu* off Christmas Island 1.3.1942.

Patoka	AO9	Newport News	26.7.1919	10.1919	seaplane tender 10.1939-6.1940, auxiliary 8.1944
Sapelo	AO11	Newport News	24.12.1919	2.1920	stricken 11.1945
Ramapo	AO12	Newport News	11.9.1919	11.1919	stricken 1.1946
Trinity	AO13	Newport News	3.7.1920	9.1920	stricken 7.1946
Rapidan	AO18	Newport News	29.10.1919	1.1922	stricken 10.1946
Salinas	AO19	Newport News	16.3.1920	12.1921	stricken 2.1946
Sepulga	AO20	Newport News	21.4.1920	1.1922	stricken 3.1946
Tippecanoe	AO21	Newport News	5.6.1920	3.1922	stricken 4.1946

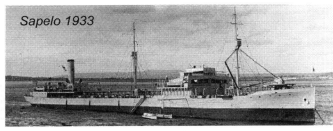

Sapelo 1933

5400 / 16800 t, 136.6 x 18.4 x 8.4 m, 1 VQE, 2 boilers, 2800 hp, 11.2 kts, complement 301; 2 x 1 – 127/38, 4 x 2 – 40/56, 4 x 2 – 20/70.

Robert L. Barnes	AO14	McDougall, Duluth	1918	10.1918	auxiliary 7.1938

1630 / 3850 t, 78.8 x 13.2 x 4.6 m, 1 VTE, 2 boilers, 8 5 kts, complement 54.

Kaweah	AO15	Cramp, Philadelphia	1919	12.1921	stricken 11.1945
Laramie	AO16	Cramp, Philadelphia	1920	12.1921	stricken 11.1945
Mattole	AO17	Cramp, Philadelphia	16.3.1920	12.1921	stricken 11.1945

4410 / 14950 t, 136.0 x 17.7 x 7.8 m, 1 VTE, 3 boilers, 2800 hp, 11.3 kts, complement 252; 2 x 1 – 127/38, 4 x 2 – 40/56, 4 x 2 – 20/70.

Cimarron	AO22	Sun SB, Chester	7.1.1939	3.1939	stricken 10.1968
Neosho	AO23	Federal, Kearny	29.4.1939	8.1939	sunk 7.5.1942
Platte	AO24	Bethlehem, Sparrows Point	8.7.1939	12.1939	stricken 1971
Sabine	AO25	Bethlehem, Sparrows Point	27.4.1940	12.1940	stricken 12.1976
Salamonie	AO26	Newport News	18.9.1940	4.1941	stricken 9.1969
Kaskaskia	AO27	Newport News	29.9.1939	10.1940	stricken 1.1959
Sangamon	AO28	Federal, Kearny	4.11.1939	10.1940	CVE 2.1942
Santee	AO29	Sun SB, Chester	4.3.1939	10.1940	CVE 1.1942
Chemung	AO30	Bethlehem, Sparrows Point	9.9.1939	7.1941	stricken 5.1971
Chenango	AO31	Sun SB, Chester	1.4.1939	6.1941	CVE 3.1942
Guadalupe	AO32	Newport News	26.1.1940	6.1941	stricken 5.1975
Suwanee	AO33	Federal, Kearny	4.3.1939	7.1941	CVE 2.1942
Ashtabula	AO51	Bethlehem, Sparrows Point	22.5.1943	8.1943	stricken 9.1991
Cacapon	AO52	Bethlehem, Sparrows Point	12.6.1943	9.1943	stricken 8.1973
Caliente	AO53	Bethlehem, Sparrows Point	25.8.1943	10.1943	stricken 12.1973
Chikaskia	AO54	Bethlehem, Sparrows Point	2.10.1943	11.1943	stricken 12.1976
Elokomin	AO55	Bethlehem, Sparrows Point	19.10.1943	11.1943	stricken 1970
Aucilla	AO56	Bethlehem, Sparrows Point	20.11.1943	12.1943	stricken 12.1976
Marias	AO57	Bethlehem, Sparrows Point	21.12.1943	2.1944	stricken 12.1992

Manatee	AO58	Bethlehem, Sparrows Point	18.2.1944	4.1944	stricken 8.1973
Mississinewa	AO59	Bethlehem, Sparrows Point	28.3.1944	5.1944	sunk 20.11.1944
Nantahala	AO60	Bethlehem, Sparrows Point	29.4.1944	6.1944	stricken 7.1973
Severn	AO61	Bethlehem, Sparrows Point	31.5.1944	7.1944	stricken 7.1974
Taluga	AO62	Bethlehem, Sparrows Point	10.7.1944	8.1944	stricken 2.1962
Chipola	AO63	Bethlehem, Sparrows Point	21.10.1944	11.1944	stricken 8.1973
Tolovana	AO64	Bethlehem, Sparrows Point	6.1.1945	2.1945	stricken 4.1975
Allagash	AO97	Bethlehem, Sparrows Point	14.4.1945	8.1945	stricken 6.1973
Caloosahatchee	AO98	Bethlehem, Sparrows Point	2.6.1945	10.1945	stricken 7.1994
Canisteo	AO99	Bethlehem, Sparrows Point	6.7.1945	12.1945	stricken 8.1992
Chukawan	AO100	Bethlehem, Sparrows Point	28.8.1945	1.1946	stricken 7.1972

7470 / 25440 t, 168.7 x 22.9 x 9.9 m, 2 sets geared steam turbines, 4 boilers, 13500 hp, 18.3 kts, complement 303; 1 (AO25, 27, 30, 32, 51-64) or 4 (AO22, 24, 26, 28-29) – 127/38, 3 x 1 – 76/50 (AO27, 32), 4 x 2 (AO22, 24-26, 28-30, 51-64) or 6 x 1 (AO27, 32) – 40/56, 4 x 2 – 20/70 (AO22, 24-26, 28-30, 51-64).
Neosho was damaged by Japanese carrier aircraft in the Coral Sea 7.4.1942 and later sunk by gunfire from destroyer *Henley*. *Mississinewa* was sunk by Japanese

Cimarron 1942

Kaiten-type human torpedoes 20.11.1944 at Ulithi, Caroline Islands.

Chicopee	AO34	Sun SB, Chester	6.9.1941	2.1942	stricken 2.1946
Housatonic	AO35	Sun SB, Chester	2.8.1941	2.1942	stricken 3.1946

5375 / 22325 t, 158.6 x 20.7 x 9.4 m, 1 set geared steam turbines, 2 boilers, 9000 hp, 18 kts, complement 279; 1 x 1 – 127/38, 4 x 1 – 76/50, 4 x 2 – 40/56, 4 x 2 – 20/70.

Kennebec	AO36	Bethlehem, Sparrows Point	19.4.1941	2.1942	stricken 1.1959
Merrimack	AO37	Bethlehem, Sparrows Point	1.7.1941	2.1942	stricken 2.1959
Winooski	AO38	Bethlehem, Sparrows Point	12.11.1941	1.1942	stricken 10.1946
Kankakee	AO39	Bethlehem, Sparrows Point	24.1.1942	5.1942	stricken 1.1973
Lackawanna	AO40	Bethlehem, Sparrows Point	16.5.1942	7.1942	stricken 6.1946
Neosho	AO48	Bethlehem, Sparrows Point	23.12.1941	9.1942	stricken 1.1946

6013 / 21580 t, 152.9 x 20.7 x 9.4 m, 1 set geared steam turbines, 2 boilers, 12000 hp, 16.7 kts, complement 254; 1 x 1 – 127/38, 4 x 1 – 76/50, 4 x 2 – 40/56, 4 x 2 – 20/70.

Kennebec post-war

Mattaponi	AO41	Sun SB, Chester	17.1.1942	5.1942	stricken 10.1970
Monongahela	AO42	Sun SB, Chester	30.5.1942	9.1942	stricken 2.1959
Tappahannock	AO43	Sun SB, Chester	18.4.1942	6.1942	stricken 7.1976
Patuxent	AO44	Sun SB, Chester	25.7.1942	10.1942	stricken 3.1946
Neches	AO47	Sun SB, Chester	11.10.1941	9.1942	stricken 10.1970

6809 / 22325 t, 158.6 x 20.7 x 9.4 m, 1 set geared steam turbines, 2 boilers, 12800 hp, 17.5 kts, complement 242;   1 x 1 – 127/38, 4 x 1 – 76/50, 4 x 2 – 40/56, 4 x 2 – 20/70.

| **Big Horn** | AO45 | Sun SB, Chester | 2.5.1936 | 4.1942 | auxiliary 2.1945 |

4150 / ~14000 t, 134.7 x 19.6 x 8.4 m, 1 set geared steam turbines, 2 boilers, 3080 hp, 12.5 kts, complement 150; 2 x 1 – 76/50, 2 x 1 – 40/56.

| **George G. Henry**, 4.1942-
Victoria | AO46 | Union Iron Wks, San Francisco | 9.4.1917 | 4.1942 | stricken 1.1946 |

4650 / 15150 t, 138.2 x 17.1 x 8.5 m, 1 VTE, 3 boilers, 3200 hp, 10 kts, complement 175; 1 x 1 – 127/38, 4 x   1 – 76/50, 2 x 2 – 40/56, 4 x 2 – 20/70.

Suamico	AO49	Sun SB, Chester	30.5.1942	8.1942	stricken 11.1974
Tallulah	AO50	Sun SB, Chester	25.6.1942	9.1942	stricken 3.1986
Pecos	AO65	Sun SB, Chester	17.8.1942	10.1942	stricken 10.1974
Cache	AO67	Sun SB, Chester	7.9.1942	11.1942	stricken 3.1986
Millicoma	AO73	Sun SB, Chester	21.1.1943	3.1943	stricken 3.1986
Saranac	AO74	Sun SB, Chester	21.12.1942	2.1943	barge 6.1946
Saugatuck	AO75	Sun SB, Chester	7.12.1942	2.1943	stricken 2.1995
Schuylkill	AO76	Sun SB, Chester	16.2.1943	4.1943	stricken 3.1986
Cossatot	AO77	Sun SB, Chester	28.2.1943	4.1943	stricken 9.1974
Chepachet	AO78	Sun SB, Chester	10.3.1943	4.1943	stricken 1.1980
Cowanesque	AO79	Sun SB, Chester	11.3.1943	5.1943	sold 7.1972

Tallulah post-war

5782 / 22380 t, 160.0 x 20.7 x 9.4 m, 1 set geared steam turbines, 2 boilers, 6000 hp, 15.1 kts, complement 230; 1 x 1 - 127/38, 4 x 1 - 76/50, 2 x 2 - 40/56, 4 x 2 - 20/70.

| **Atascosa** | AO66 | Sun SB, Chester | 7.9.1942 | 11.1942 | stricken 2.1946 |

5730 / 24660 t, 166.9 x 21.4 x 9.5 m, 1 set geared steam turbines, 2 boilers, 8200 hp, 15.5 kts, complement 282; 1 x 1 – 127/38, 4 x 1 – 76/50, 4 x 2 – 40/56, 4 x 2 – 20/70.

Chiwawa	AO68	Bethlehem, Sparrows Point	25.6.1942	12.1942	stricken 9.1946
Enoree	AO69	Bethlehem, Sparrows Point	29.8.1942	1.1943	stricken 2.1959
Escalante	AO70	Bethlehem, Sparrows Point	29.9.1942	1.1943	stricken 1.1946
Neshanic	AO71	Bethlehem, Sparrows Point	31.10.1942	2.1943	stricken 1.1946
Niobrara	AO72	Bethlehem, Sparrows Point	28.11.1942	3.1943	stricken 2.1959

Chiwawa 1945

5650 / 22030 t, 153.0 x 20.7 x 9.4 m, 1 set geared steam turbines, 2 boilers, 7000 hp, 15.3 kts, complement 213; 1 x 1 – 127/38, 4 x 1 – 76/50, 4 x 2 – 40/56, 4 x 2 – 20/70.

Escambia	AO80	Marinship, Sausalito	25.4.1943	10.1943	stricken 1957
Kennebago	AO81	Marinship, Sausalito	9.5.1943	12.1943	stricken 7.1946
Cahaba	AO82	Marinship, Sausalito	19.5.1943	1.1944	stricken 9.1959
Mascoma	AO83	Marinship, Sausalito	31.5.1943	2.1944	stricken 6.1959
Ocklawaha	AO84	Marinship, Sausalito	9.6.1943	3.1944	stricken 3.1971

Pamanset	AO85	Marinship, Sausalito	25.6.1943	4.1944	stricken 9.1957
Ponaganset	AO86	Marinship, Sausalito	10.7.1943	5.1944	stricken 4.1947
Sebec	AO87	Marinship, Sausalito	29.7.1943	3.1944	stricken 9.1957
Tomahawk	AO88	Marinship, Sausalito	10.8.1943	4.1944	stricken 1959
Pasig	AO91	Marinship, Sausalito	15.7.1944	(12.1944)	commissioned as distilling ship
Abatan	AO92	Marinship, Sausalito	6.8.1944	(1.1945)	commissioned as distilling ship
Soubarissen	AO93	Marinship, Sausalito	12.8.1944	1.1945	stricken 7.1961
Anacostia	AO94	Marinship, Sausalito	24.9.1944	2.1945	stricken 12.1957
Caney	AO95	Marinship, Sausalito	8.10.1944	3.1945	stricken 5.1959
Tamalpais	AO96	Marinship, Sausalito	29.10.1944	5.1945	stricken 12.1967
Cohocton	AO101	Marinship, Sausalito	28.6.1945	8.1945	stricken 1958
Concho	AO102	Marinship, Sausalito	25.7.1945	-	cancelled 8.1945
Conecuh	AO103	Marinship, Sausalito	10.8.1945	-	cancelled 8.1945
Contoocook	AO104	Marinship, Sausalito	-	-	cancelled 8.1945

5782 / 22380 t, 160.0 x 20.7 x 9.4 m, 1electric motor, 1 steam turbine-generator, 2 boilers, 10000 hp, 15.1 kts, complement 267; 1 x 1 – 127/38, 4 x 1 – 76/50, 4 x 2 – 40/56, 4 x 2 – 20/70.

Escambia 1943

Pasig	AO89	Newport News	24.11.1917	1.1943	stricken 10.1943

7165 / ~20000 t, 157.5 x 20.7 m, 1 VTE, 3 boilers, 3000 hp, 10.2 kts, 1 x 1 – 102/50.

Shikellamy	AO90	Bethlehem, Wilmington	26.3.1921	4.1943	gasoline tanker 7.1943

10800 t, 119.4 x 16.2 x 7.3 m, 1 VTE, 2400 hp, 9.5 kts, complement 62; 1 x 1 – 127/38, 2 x 2 – 40/56, 4 x 2 – 20/70.

Mispillion	AO105	Sun SB, Chester	10.8.1945	12.1945	stricken 2.1995
Navasota	AO106	Sun SB, Chester	30.8.1945	2.1946	stricken 1.1992
Passumpsic	AO107	Sun SB, Chester	31.10.1945	4.1946	stricken 12.1991
Pawcatuck	AO108	Sun SB, Chester	19.2.1946	5.1946	stricken 9.1991
Waccamaw	AO109	Sun SB, Chester	30.3.1946	6.1946	stricken 10.1991

7236 / 25400 t, 168.7 x 22.9 x 9.9 m, 1 set geared steam turbines, 4 boilers, 6750 hp, 18 kts, complement 304; 1 x 1 – 127/38, 4 x 1 – 76/50, 4 x 2 – 40/56, 4 x 2 – 20/70.

Mispillion post-war

Colliers

Neptune	AC8	Maryland Steel, Sparrows Point	21.1.1911	12.1914	stricken 5.1938

19375 t, 165.3 x 19.8 x 8.4 m, 1 steam turbine, 12.9 kts, complement 104; 4 x 1 – 102/50.

Proteus	AC9	Newport News	14.9.1912	7.1913	stricken 12.1940
Nereus	AC10	Newport News	26.4.1913	9.1913	stricken 12.1940

19000 t, 159.2 x 19.2 x 8.4 m, 1 VTE, 2 boilers, 15 kts, complement 158; 4 x 1 – 102/50.

Ammunition ships

Pyro	AE1	Puget Sound N Yd, Bremerton	16.12.1919	8.1920	stricken 7.1946
Nitro	AE2	Puget Sound N Yd, Bremerton	16.12.1919	4.1921	stricken 12.1945

11000 / 14110 t, 147.6 x 18.6 x 8.1 m, 1 set geared steam turbines, 2 boilers, 5300 hp, 16 kts, complement 319; 1 x   1 – 127/51, 4 x 1 – 76/50, 2 x 2 – 40/56.

Lassen	AE3	Tampa SB	10.1.1940	3.1941	stricken 7.1961
Kilauea, 3.1943- **Mount Baker**	AE4	Tampa SB	6.8.1940	5.1941	stricken 12.1969
Rainier	AE5	Tampa SB	1.3.1941	12.1941	stricken 8.1970
Shasta	AE6	Tampa SB	9.7.1941	1.1942	stricken 7.1969

6350 / 13855 t, 140.0 x 19.2 x 8.1 m, 1 diesel, 6000 hp, 15.3 kts, complement 280; 1 x 1 – 127/38, 4 x 1 – 76/50,   2 x 2 – 40/56, 8 x 2 – 20/70.

Mauna Loa	AE8	Tampa SB	14.4.1943	10.1943	stricken 10.1976
Mazama	AE9	Tampa SB	15.8.1943	3.1944	stricken 9.1970
Akutan	AE13	Tampa SB	17.9.1944	2.1945	stricken 7.1960

6350 / 14225 t, 140.0 x 19.2 x 8.1 m, 1 diesel, 6000 hp, 15.3 kts, complement 281; 1 x 1 – 127/38, 4 x 1 – 76/50,   2 x 2 – 40/56, 8 x 2 – 20/70.

Sangay	AE10	Pennsylvania SY, Beaumont	5.4.1942	3.1943	stricken 7.1960

6400 / 14050 t, 125.7 x 18.3 x 7.2 m, 1 diesel, 4150 hp, 14.8 kts, complement 308; 1 x 1 – 127/38, 3 x 1 – 76/50,   2 x 2 – 40/56, 12 x 1 – 20/70.

Mount Hood	AE11	North Carolina SB, Wilmington	30.11.1943	7.1944	explosion 10.11.1944
Wrangell	AE12	North Carolina SB, Wilmington	14.4.1944	10.1944	stricken 10.1976
Firedrake	AE14	North Carolina SB, Wilmington	12.5.1944	12.1944	stricken 1971
Vesuvius	AE15	North Carolina SB, Wilmington	26.5.1944	1.1945	stricken 8.1973
Mount Katmai	AE16	North Carolina SB, Wilmington	6.1.1945	7.1945	stricken 8.1973
Great Sitkin	AE17	North Carolina SB, Wilmington	20.1.1945	8.1945	stricken 7.1973
Paricutin	AE18	North Carolina SB, Wilmington	30.1.1945	7.1945	stricken 6.1973
Diamond Head	AE19	North Carolina SB, Wilmington	3.2.1945	8.1945	stricken 3.1973

Firedrake post-war

13910 t, 140.0 x 19.2 x 8.6 m, 1 set geared steam turbines, 2 boilers, 6000 hp, 16.4 kts, complement 267; 1 x 1 – 127/38, 4 x 1 – 76/50, 2 x 2 – 40/56, 8 x 1 – 20/70. *Mount Hood* 10.11.1944 sunk after internal explosion at Manus Island, Admiralty Islands.

Stores ships

Bridge	AF1	Boston N Yd	18.5.1916	6.1917	sold 12.1947

9500 t, 129.3 x 16.8 x 6.9 m, 2 VTE, 2 boilers, 5000 hp, 14 kts, complement 282; 1 x 1 – 127/38, 4 x 1 – 76/50, 1   x 2 – 40/56, 8 x 1 – 20/70.

Arctic	AF7	Moore DD, Oakland	1918	11.1921	stricken 5.1946
Boreas	AF8	Moore DD, Oakland	1919	12.1921	stricken 3.1946
Yukon	AF9	Moore DD, Oakland	1919	12.1921	stricken 4.1946

6100 / 12600 t, 127.1 x 16.2 x 8.1 m, 1 set geared steam turbines, 4 boilers, 2800 hp, 11 kts, complement 268; 1 x 1 – 127/51, 4 x 1 – 76/50, 8 x 1 – 20/70.

Aldebaran	AF10	Newport News	21.6.1939	1.1941	stricken 6.1973

13910 t, 140.1 x 19.2 x 7.9 m, 1 set geared steam turbines, 2 boilers, 6000 hp, 16.4 kts, complement 287; 1 x 1 – 127/38, 4 x 1 – 76/50, 10 x 1 – 20/70.

Polaris	AF11	Sun SB, Chester	22.4.1939	4.1941	stricken 10.1957

13910 t, 140.0 x 19.2 x 7.9 m, 1 diesel, 6000 hp, 16.4 kts, complement 253; 1 x 1 – 127/38, 4 x 1 – 76/50, 10 x 1 – 20/70.

Mizar	AF12	Bethlehem, Quincy	6.2.1932	6.1941	stricken 4.1946
Tarazed	AF13	Newport News	14.11.1931	6.1941	stricken 1.1946
Talamanca	AF15	Newport News	15.8.1931	1.1942	stricken 12.1945
Merak	AF21	Bethlehem, Quincy	23.4.1932	5.1942	stricken 1946
Ariel	AF22	Newport News	15.8.1931	5.1942	stricken 7.1946

11875 t, 136.3 x 18.4 x 7.9 m, 2 electric motors, 2 steam turbine-generators, 4 boilers, 11000 hp, 18.5 kts, complement 238; 1 x 1 – 127/38, 4 x 1 – 76/50, (8 – 12) x 1 – 20/70.

Tarazed 1942

Uranus	AF14	Maskinbygger Helsingør, Denmark	14.9.1935	10.1941	stricken 5.1946

3540 t, 90.4 x 12.0 x 5.3 m, 2 VTE, 2 boilers, 1140 hp, 11.5 kts, complement 93; 2 x 1 – 76/50, 6 x 1 – 20/70.

Pastores	AF16	Workman Clark, Belfast, UK	17.8.1913	2.1942	stricken 3.1946
Calamares	AF18	Workman Clark, Belfast, UK	2.9.1913	4.1943	stricken 5.1946

13750 t, 148.4 x 16.8 x 8.3 m, 2 VQE, 3 (AF16) or 4 (AF18) boilers, 6500 hp, 14 kts, complement 248; 1 x 1 – 127/51 (AF16), 1 x 1 – 127/38 (AF18), 4 x 1 – 76/50 (AF16), 8 x 1 – 20/70.

Antigua	AF17	Bethlehem, Quincy	1932	-	never commissioned

6893 t, 136.6 x 18.4 x 7.5 m, 1 electric motor, 16.5 kts, complement 114; 1 x 1 – 127/38, 4 x 1 – 76/50, 8 x 1 – 20/70.

Roamer	AF19	Maskinbygger Helsingør, Denmark	14.9.1935	8.1942	stricken 7.1946

4600 t, 97.1 x 13.0 x 5.5 m, 1 diesel, 1850 hp, 12 kts, complement 114; 2 x 1 – 76/50, 4 x 1 – 20/70.

Pontiac	AF20	Nakskov Skibsverft, Denmark	3.10.1936	5.1942	foundered 30.1.1945

5410 (std) t, 136.6 x 18.3 x 5.8 m, 1 diesel, 4300 hp, 15.5 kts, complement 166; 2 x 1 – 76/50, 2 x 2 – 20/70.

Pontiac foundered 30.1.1945 in the gale off Halifax, later salvaged but stricken as CTL.

| **Cygnus** | AF23 | Cammell Laird, Birkenhead, UK | 22.3.1924 | 8.1942 | stricken 1946 |

7170 t, 102.6 x 14.6 x 7.2 m, 1 VTE, 3 boilers, 2500 hp,   12 kts, complement 112; 2 x 1 – 76/50, 6 x 1 – 20/70.

| **Delphinus** | AF24 | Workman Clark, Belfast, UK | 5.5.1915 | 8.1942 | stricken 6.1946 |

5230 t, 100.3 x 13.5 x 7.0 m, 1 VTE, 3 boilers, 2500 hp,   6 x 1 – 20/70.
12 kts, complement 107; 1 x 1 – 102/50, 1 x 1 – 76/50,

| **Taurus** | AF25 | Workman Clark, Belfast, UK | 12.8.1921 | 10.1942 | stricken 1.1946 |

6600 t, 99.2 x 12.3 x 7.2 m, 1 steam turbine, 3 boilers,   1 – 76/50, 6 x 1 – 20/70.
2500 hp, 11.5 kts, complement 114; 1 x 1 – 102/50, 1 x

| **Octans** | AF26 | Workman Clark, Belfast, UK | 1917 | 6.1943 | stricken 3.1946 |

11600 t, 134.2 x 16.6 x 8.0 m, 2 VTE, 4 boilers, 6000 hp,   8 x 1 – 20/70.
13.5 kts, complement 227; 1 x 1 – 127/38, 4 x 1 – 76/50,

| *Pictor* | AF27 | Laird, Birkenhead, UK | 1910s | - | cancelled 5.1944 |

6000 t

| **Hyades** | AF28 | Gulf SB, Chickasaw | 12.6.1943 | 8.1944 | stricken 10.1976 |
| **Graffias** | AF29 | Gulf SB, Chickasaw | 12.12.1943 | 10.1944 | stricken 5.1974 |

15300 t, 142.9 x 19.2 x 8.5 m, 1 set geared steam   1 x 1 – 127/38, 4 x 1 – 76/50, 12 x 1 – 20/70.
turbines, 2 boilers, 6000 hp, 15.5 kts, complement 252;

Adria	AF30	Pennsylvania SY, Beaumont	16.4.1944	12.1944	stricken 7.1960
Arequipa	AF31	Pennsylvania SY, Beaumont	4.5.1944	1.1945	stricken 9.1961
Corduba	AF32	Pennsylvania SY, Beaumont	11.6.1944	1.1945	stricken ~1960
Karin	AF33	Pennsylvania SY, Beaumont	22.6.1944	2.1945	stricken 9.1961
Kerstin	AF34	Pennsylvania SY, Beaumont	16.7.1944	2.1945	stricken 6.1950
Latona	AF35	Pennsylvania SY, Beaumont	10.8.1944	2.1945	stricken ~1950
Lioba	AF36	Pennsylvania SY, Beaumont	27.8.1944	3.1945	stricken 7.1960
Malabar	AF37	Pennsylvania SY, Beaumont	17.9.1944	3.1945	stricken 7.1960
Merapi	AF38	Pennsylvania SY, Beaumont	4.10.1944	3.1945	stricken 7.1960
Palisana	AF39	Pennsylvania SY, Beaumont	21.10.1944	4.1945	stricken 6.1946
Athanasia	AF41	Pennsylvania SY, Beaumont	12.10.1944	4.1945	stricken 1.1946
Bondia	AF42	Pennsylvania SY, Beaumont	9.11.1944	4.1945	stricken 5.1973
Gordonia	AF43	Pennsylvania SY, Beaumont	30.11.1944	5.1945	stricken 1.1946
Laurentia	AF44	Pennsylvania SY, Beaumont	12.12.1944	6.1945	stricken 1970
Lucidor	AF45	Pennsylvania SY, Beaumont	25.1.1945	7.1945	stricken ~1946
Octavia	AF46	Pennsylvania SY, Beaumont	18.1.1945	6.1945	stricken 10.1946
Valentine	AF47	Pennsylvania SY, Beaumont	3.2.1945	7.1945	sold 1.1967

Merapi post-war

3139 / 7435 t, 103.2 x 15.3 x 6.4 m, 1 diesel, 1700 hp,
11.5 kts, complement 84; 1 x 1 – 76/50, 6 x 1 – 20/70.

Saturn	AF40	Bremer Vulcan, Vegesack, Germany	26.5.1939	4.1944	stricken 8.1946

5088 / 9760 t, 129.0 x 16.9 x 7.3 m, 1 electric motor, 1 steam turbine-generator, 2 boilers, 5600 hp, 17.5 kts, complement 205; 1 x 1 – 127/38, 2 x 1 – 76/50, 2 x 1 – 40/56, 4 x 1 – 20/70.

US COAST GUARD

JAMES GUTHRIE cutter

James Guthrie		1893	1895	to War Dept. 12.1937

149 t, 10 kts, complement 10.

This ancient vessel served as patrol until 1937.

APACHE cutter

Apache *(ex-Galveston)*	Reeder, Baltimore	1890	18.12.1890	8.1891	sold 12.1937

708 t, 57.9 x 8.8 x 2.2 m, 1 VTE, 2 single-end boilers, 1200 hp, 12 kts, complement 41; 3 x 1 – 76/50 Mk 2/3/5/6.
Iron-hulled revenue service cutter.

Apache

GRESHAM cutter

Gresham	WPG85	Globe I W, Cleveland	1.1896	12.9.1896	(5.1897) / 5.1943	sold 4.1944

936 / 1190 t, 62.6 x 9.8 x 3.4 m, 1 VTE, 4 single-end boilers, 2500 hp, 17 kts, complement 73; 4 x 1 – 76/50 Mk 2/3/5/6.
The last representative of 4-ship class of the USCG cutters, rigged for sail. Steel-hulled. Served on the Great Lakes. *Gresham* was sold in 1935 but recommissioned in May 1943.

Gresham

PAMLICO cutter

Pamlico	CG15, 11.1941- WPR57	Pusey & Jones, Wilmington	1906	8.3.1907	7.1907	sold 7.1947

455 t, 48.2 x 9.1 x 1.7 m, 2 VTE, 1 Babcock & Wilcox boiler, 600 hp, 9.8 kts, 2000 nm (8 kts), complement 33; 2 x 1 – 57/45 Driggs-Schroeder.
Shallow-draught USCG cutter, designed for inland waters. In 1942 she was reclassified as a river gunboat.

Pamlico 1927

TAHOMA class cutter

Yamacraw	CG21	New York SB, Camden	1907	24.10.1908	5.1909	sold 12.1937

1006 / 1082 t, 58.2 x 9.8 x 4.3 m, 1 VTE, 14.1 kts, complement 69; 2 x 1 – 76/50 Mk 2/3/5/6.   Steel-hulled.

MIAMI class cutter

Unalga	CG53, 11.1941- WPG53	Newport News	10.2.1912	5.1912	for disposal 10.1945

1181 t, 57.9 x 9.9 x 4.3 m, 1 VTE, 1300 hp, 13 kts; 2 x 1 – 102/50 Mk 9, 2 x 1 – 76/50 Mk 2/3/5/6, 2 DCR.   1943: - 2 x 1 – 76/50; + 2 x 1 – 20/70 Oerlikon, 2 DCT, radar.

OSSIPEE class cutters

Ossipee	CG26, 11.1941- WPG50	Newport News	1915	1.5.1915	7.1915	sold 9.1946
Tallapoosa	CG27, 11.1941- WPG52	Newport News	1915	1.5.1915	8.1915	sold 7.1946

Ossipee 1927

964 / 997 t, 50.5 x 9.8 x 3.6 m, 1 VTE, 2 Babcock & Wilcox boilers, 1000 hp, 12.7 kts, 3500 nm, complement 72; 2 x 1 – 76/50 Mk 10, 2 x 1 – 57/50 Driggs-Schroeder.
1941, both: - 2 x 1 - 57/50; + 1 x 1 - 76/23 Mk 4/9/13/14, 2 DCR.
1942 - 1943, both: - 1 x 1 - 76/23; + 2 x 1 - 20/70 Oerlikon, 2 x 4 Mousetrap ASWRL, 4 DCT, radar.

HAIDA class cutters

Haida	WPG45	Union Construction Wks, Oakland	9.1920	19.4.1921	10.1921	sold 1.1948
Modoc	WPG46	Union Construction Wks, Oakland	10.1921	1.10.1922	12.1922	for disposal 2.1947
Mojave	WPG47	Union Construction Wks, Oakland	1920	7.9.1921	12.1921	for disposal 7.1947
Tampa	WPG48	Union Construction Wks, Oakland	9.1920	19.4.1921	9.1921	for disposal 2.1947

Modoc

1506 / 1955 t, 73.2 x 11.9 x 5.0 m, 1 electric motor, 1 General Electric turbo-generator, 2 Babcock & Wilcox boilers, 2600 hp, 15 kts, 300 t oil, 5500 nm (9 kts), complement 122; 2 x 1 – 127/51 Mk 7/8, 1 x 1 – 76/50 Mk 10 (WPG46), 2 x 1 – 57/50 Driggs-Schroeder, 1 x 1 – 37/50 Driggs-Schroeder (WPG45, 47, 48)
The first cutters with a turbo-electric machinery. They served as prototypes for 10 'Lake' class cutters.
1941, *Modoc*: - 2 x 1 - 57/50; + 2 x 1 - 12.7 MG, 4 DCT, 2 DCR, QCJ-3 sonar.
1942, *Haida, Mojave, Tampa*: - 2 x 1 - 57/50, 1 x 1 - 37/50; + 1 x 1 - 76/50 Mk 20, 2 x 1 - 12.7 MG, 4 DCT, 2 DCR, QCJ-2/3 sonar.
1943, *Haida; Mojave, Tampa*: - 2 x 1 - 127/51, 2 x 1 - 12.7 MG; + 1 x 1 - 76/50 Mk 20, 4 x 1 - 20/70 Oerlikon, 2 x 4 Mousetrap ASWRL, SA, SL radars.
1945, *Modoc*: - 2 x 1 - 127/51, 1 x 1 - 76/50, 2 x 1 - 12.7 MG; + 2 x 1 - 76/50 Mk 20, SF-1, SC-3 radars.
1945, *Mojave*: - SA, SL radars, QCJ-3 sonar; + SF-1, SC-3 radars, QCL-2 sonar. 1945, *Tampa*: - SA, SL radars; + SF-1, SC-3 radars.

CORWIN class cutters

Forward		Defoe, Bay City	1925	1925	1925	buoy tender 9.1940
Nansemond		Defoe, Bay City	1926	1926	1926	buoy tender 9.1940
Patriot, 3.1938- *unnamed* 3.1938- YP69	Defoe, Bay City	1925	1926	6.1926	to the USN 3.1938, for disposal 11.1946
Perry		Defoe, Bay City	1926	1926	1926	USN auxiliary 12.1937
Petrel		Defoe, Bay City	1926	1926	1926	buoy tender 9.1940

210 (std) t, 30.4 x 7.0 x 1.4 m, 2 Grey diesels, 300 hp, 12 kts, complement 15; 1 x 1 – 76/23 Mk 9/13.

These cutters were intended to chase rum-runners during Prohibition but were too slow. 7 sister-ships served in the USN as patrol boats during the war.

ACTIVE class cutters

Active	WPC125, 2.1942- WSC125	New York SB, Camden	7.1926	30.11.1926	1.1927	sold 9.1963
Agassiz	WPC126, 2.1942- WSC126	New York SB, Camden	7.1926	30.11.1926	1.1927	sold 10.1969
Alert	WPC127, 2.1942- WSC127	New York SB, Camden	7.1926	30.11.1926	1.1927	sold 10.1969
Antietam, 6.1943- **Bedloe**	WPC128, 2.1942- WSC128	New York SB, Camden	7.1926	30.11.1926	1.1927	foundered 14.9.1944
Bonham	WPC129, 2.1942- WSC129	New York SB, Camden	7.1926	30.11.1926	1.1927	sold 12.1959
Boutwell	WPC130, 2.1942- WSC130	New York SB, Camden	8.1926	27.1.1927	2.1927	sold 5.1964
Cahoone	WPC131, 2.1942- WSC131	New York SB, Camden	8.1926	27.1.1927	2.1927	sold 12.1968
Cartigan	WPC132, 2.1942- WSC132	New York SB, Camden	8.1926	27.1.1927	3.1927	sold 4.1969
Colfax *(ex-Montgomery)*	WPC133, 2.1942- WSC133	New York SB, Camden	12.1926	22.3.1927	4.1927	sold 1.1956
Crawford	WPC134, 2.1942- WSC134	New York SB, Camden	8.1926	27.1.1927	2.1927	sold 8.1947
Diligence	WPC135, 2.1942- WSC135	New York SB, Camden	8.1926	27.1.1927	2.1927	sold 1.1963
Dix	WPC136, 2.1942- WSC136	New York SB, Camden	8.1926	27.1.1927	3.1927	sold 6.1948
Ewing	WPC137, 2.1942- WSC137	New York SB, Camden	12.1926	15.3.1927	3.1927	sold 1.1969
Faunce	WPC138, 2.1942- WSC138	New York SB, Camden	12.1926	15.3.1927	3.1927	sold 6.1948
Frederick Lee	WPC139, 2.1942- WSC139	New York SB, Camden	12.1926	15.3.1927	3.1927	sold 5.1966
General Greene	WPC140, 2.1942- WSC140	New York SB, Camden	12.1926	14.2.1927	3.1927	preserved 11.1968
Harriet Lane	WPC141, 2.1942- WSC141	New York SB, Camden	7.1926	30.11.1926	1.1927	sold 6.1948
Jackson	WPC142, 2.1942- WSC142	New York SB, Camden	12.1926	14.2.1927	3.1927	foundered 14.9.1944
Kimball	WPC143, 2.1942- WSC143	New York SB, Camden	2.1927	25.4.1927	5.1927	sold 2.1970

Legare	WPC144, 2.1942- WSC144	New York SB, Camden	12.1926	14.2.1927	3.1927	sold 11.1968
Marion	WPC145, 2.1942- WSC145	New York SB, Camden	12.1926	15.3.1927	4.1927	sold 3.1963
McLane	WPC146, 2.1942- WSC146	New York SB, Camden	12.1926	22.3.1927	4.1927	sold 11.1969
Morris	WPC147, 2.1942- WSC147	New York SB, Camden	12.1926	4.4.1927	4.1927	for disposal 8.1970
Nemaha	WPC148, 2.1942- WSC148	New York SB, Camden	12.1926	4.4.1927	4.1927	sold 6.1948
Pulaski	WPC149, 2.1942- WSC149	New York SB, Camden	12.1926	4.4.1927	4.1927	sold 7.1948
Reliance	WPC150, 2.1942- WSC150	New York SB, Camden	2.1927	18.4.1927	4.1927	sold 6.1948
Rush	WPC151, 2.1942- WSC151	New York SB, Camden	2.1927	18.4.1927	4.1927	sold 6.1948
Tiger	WPC152, 2.1942- WSC152	New York SB, Camden	2.1927	18.4.1927	4.1927	sold 6.1948
Travis	WPC153, 2.1942- WSC153	New York SB, Camden	2.1927	18.4.1927	4.1927	sold 11.1962
Vigilant	WPC154, 2.1942- WSC154	New York SB, Camden	2.1927	25.4.1927	5.1927	sold 1.1956
Woodbury	WPC155, 2.1942- WSC155	New York SB, Camden	2.1927	22.5.1927	6.1927	USN tug 7.1948
Yeaton	WPC156, 2.1942- WSC156	New York SB, Camden	2.1927	2.5.1927	5.1927	sold 7.1970

Frederick Lee 1944

220 / 289 t, 38.1 x 7.1 x 2.1 m, 2 diesels, 600 hp, 13.3 kts, 2500 nm (12 kts), complement 38; 1 x 1 – 76/23 Mk 4/7/11/13/14.
Cutters of this class were intended to intercept rum runners during Prohibition. They turned out to be of little use for this purpose due to their low speed.
1941, all: + 2 DCR.
1942 - 1943, all: + 2 x 1 - 20/70 Oerlikon, 2 x 4 Mousetrap ASWRL.
1943 - 1944, many: - 1 x 1 - 76/23; + 1 x 1 - 40/56 Bofors, SO radar
Antietam and *Jackson* were lost 14.9.1944 at Cape Hatteras in a storm.

NORTHLAND cutter-icebreaker

Northland	WPG49	Newport News	8.1926	5.2.1927	5.1927	to Israel 3.1946 (Eilath)

Northland 1943

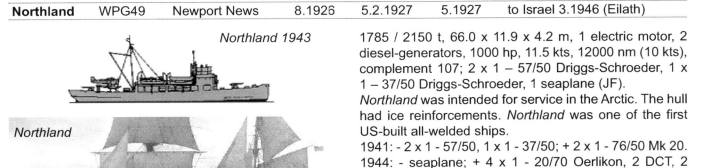

Northland

1785 / 2150 t, 66.0 x 11.9 x 4.2 m, 1 electric motor, 2 diesel-generators, 1000 hp, 11.5 kts, 12000 nm (10 kts), complement 107; 2 x 1 – 57/50 Driggs-Schroeder, 1 x 1 – 37/50 Driggs-Schroeder, 1 seaplane (JF).
Northland was intended for service in the Arctic. The hull had ice reinforcements. *Northland* was one of the first US-built all-welded ships.
1941: - 2 x 1 - 57/50, 1 x 1 - 37/50; + 2 x 1 - 76/50 Mk 20.
1944: - seaplane; + 4 x 1 - 20/70 Oerlikon, 2 DCT, 2 DCR, SC-1, SF radars, QCJ-3 sonar.

'LAKE' class cutters

Chelan	WPG45	Fore River, Quincy	11.1927	19.5.1928	9.1928	to the UK 5.1941 (Lulworth)
Pontchartrain	WPG46	Fore River, Quincy	11.1927	16.6.1928	10.1928	to the UK 4.1941 (Hartland)
Tahoe	WPG47	Fore River, Quincy	12.1927	12.6.1928	11.1928	to the UK 4.1941 (Fishguard)
Champlain	WPG48	Fore River, Quincy	5.1928	11.10.1928	1.1929	to the UK 5.1941 (Sennen)
Mendota	WPG49	Fore River, Quincy	6.1928	27.11.1928	3.1929	to the UK 4.1941 (Culver)
Itasca	WPG50	General Engineering, Alameda		16.11.1929	7.1930	to the UK 5.1941 (Gorleston)
Sebago	WPG51	General Engineering, Alameda		2.10.1930	9.1930	to the UK 5.1941 (Walney)
Saranac	WPG52	General Engineering, Alameda		12.4.1930	10.1930	to the UK 4.1941 (Banff)
Shoshone	WPG53	General Engineering, Alameda		11.9.1930	1.1931	to the UK 5.1941 (Landguard)
Cayuga	WPG54	Staten Island SB, Port Richmond		7.10.1931	3.1932	to the UK 5.1941 (Totland)

1662 / 2075 t, 76.2 x 12.8 x 3.9 m, 1 electric motor, 1 General Electric turbine-generator, 2 Babcock & Wilcox boilers, 3350 hp, 17 kts, 300 t oil, complement 97; 1 x 1 – 127/51 Mk 7/8, 1 x 1 – 76/50 Mk 10, 2 x 1 – 57/50 Driggs-Schroeder.

The cutters intended for service in the North Atlantic (ice situation observation, for which their hulls were reinforced). The machinery included a fairly common in the USA turbo-electric scheme. They were distinguished by good habitability for their size; however, they had a number of shortcomings, which did not allow them to be considered full-fledged combat ships: the hull had insufficient division into watertight compartments, the bulkheads did not reach the upper deck, which, moreover, was largerly wooden (not steel, sheathed with wood, but solid wooden, as on sailing frigates).

Sebago 1941

Tahoe pre-war

165-ft 'B' class cutters

Argo	WPC100	John Mathis, Camden		12.11.1932	1.1933	sold 11.1955
Ariadne	WPC101	Lake Union, Seattle		23.3.1934	10.1934	sold 9.1969
Atalanta	WPC102	Lake Union, Seattle		16.6.1934	9.1934	sold 12.1954
Aurora	WPC103	Bath Iron Wks	1.1931	28.11.1931	12.1931	sold 12.1968
Calypso	WPC104	Bath Iron Wks	1.1931	1.1.1932	1.1932	USN auxiliary 5.1941-1.1942, sold 11.1955
Cyane	WPC105	Lake Union, Seattle		30.8.1934	9.1934	sold 12.1954
Daphne	WPC106	Bath Iron Wks	1.1931	27.1.1932	2.1932	sold 12.1954
Dione	WPC107	Manitowoc SB		30.6.1934	10.1934	sold 2.1964
Galatea	WPC108	John Mathis, Camden		17.12.1932	2.1933	sold 7.1948
Hermes	WPC109	Bath Iron Wks	1.1931	23.2.1932	3.1932	sold 5.1958
Icarus	WPC110	Bath Iron Wks	1.1931	19.3.1932	4.1932	sold 7.1948
Nemesis	WPC111	Marietta, Point Pleasant		7.7.1934	10.1934	sold 2.1966
Nike	WPC112	Marietta, Point Pleasant		7.7.1934	10.1934	sold 5.1966

Pandora	WPC113	Manitowoc SB		30.6.1934	11.1934	sold 11.1959
Perseus	WPC114	Bath Iron Wks		11.4.1932	4.1932	sold 11.1959
Thetis	WPC115	Bath Iron Wks	1.1931	9.11.1931	12.1931	sold 7.1948
Triton	WPC116	Marietta, Point Pleasant		7.7.1934	11.1934	sold 1.1969

Galatea 1945

Argo post-war

334 / 370 t, 50.3 x 7.2 x 2.3 m, 2 Winton diesels, 1340 hp, 16 kts, 1600 nm (13 kts), complement 50; 1 x 1 – 76/23 Mk 4/7/11/13/14, 1 x 1 – 37/50 Driggs-Schroeder. The 165-ft 'B' class cutters were built during Prohibition and were intended primarily to intercept rum runners. A total of 18 ships were built; one (WPC187 *Electra*) was converted to the presidential yacht *Potomac* in 1935.

1941, all: - 1 x 1 - 37/50; + 1 DCT, 2 DCR

1943 - 1944, all: - 1 x 1 - 76/23; + 2 x 1 - 76/50 Mk 20, 2 x 1 - 20/70 Oerlikon, 2 x 4 Mousetrap Mk 20 ASWRL, 1 DCT, SO or SU radar.

165-ft 'A' class cutters

Algonquin	WPG75	Pusey & Jones, Wilmington	25.7.1934	10.1934	sold 7.1948
Comanche	WPG76	Pusey & Jones, Wilmington	16.9.1934	12.1934	sold 11.1948
Escanaba	WPG77	Defoe, Bay City	1.10.1932	11.1932	explosion 13.6.1943
Mohawk	WPG78	Pusey & Jones, Wilmington	1.10.1934	1.1935	sold 11.1948
Onondaga	WPG79	Defoe, Bay City	2.8.1934	9.1934	sold 12.1954
Tahoma	WPG80	Defoe, Bay City	5.9.1934	10.1934	sold 10.1955

Onondaga

1005 t, 50.3 x 11.0 x 3.7 m, 1 set Westinghouse or De Laval (WPG77, 79, 80) geared steam turbines, 2 Foster Wheeler or Babcock & Wilcox (WPG77, 79, 80) boilers, 1500 hp, 12.5 kts, 156 t oil, 3300 nm (10 kts), complement 61; 2 x 1 – 76/50 Mk 10.

Development of the *Tallapoosa* with a hull reinforced for ice navigation. 165-ft 'A' class.

1942 - 1943, *Algonquin, Comanche, Escanaba, Mohawk, Tahoma*: + (2 - 3) x 1 - 20/70 Oerlikon, 2 x 4 Mousetrap ASWRL, 4 DCT, 2 DCR, SO or SU radar.

1942 - 1943, *Onondaga*: + 3 x 1 - 20/70 Oerlikon, 4 DCT, 2 DCR, SO or SU radar.

Escanaba was sunk off the coast of Greenland 13.6.1943 as a result of internal explosion.

'TREASURY' class cutters

George M. Bibb, 7.1937- **Bibb**	WPG31, 2.1945-WAGC31	Charleston N Yd	8.1935	14.1.1937	3.1937	scuttled 28.11.1987
George W. Campbell, 7.1937- **Campbell**	WPG32, 3.1945-WAGC32	Philadelphia N Yd	5.1935	3.1.1936	6.1936	sunk as target 29.11.1984
William J. Duane, 7.1937- **Duane**	WPG33, 3.1944-WAGC6, 7.1945-WPG33	Philadelphia N Yd	5.1935	3.6.1936	8.1936	scuttled 27.11.1987
Alexander Hamilton, 7.1937- **Hamilton**	WPG34	New York N Yd, Brooklyn	9.1935	6.1.1937	3.1937	sunk 30.1.1942

Samuel D. Ingham, 7.1937- **Ingham**	WPG35, 10.1944-WAGC35	Philadelphia N Yd	5.1935	3.6.1936	9.1936	preserved 5.1988
John C. Spencer, 7.1937- **Spencer**	WPG36, 9.1944-WAGC36	New York N Yd, Brooklyn	9.1935	6.1.1937	3.1937	training hulk 1.1974
Roger B. Taney, 7.1937- **Taney**	WPG37, 1.1945-WAGC37	Philadelphia N Yd	5.1935	3.6.1936	10.1936	preserved 12.1986

2216 / 2660 t, 99.7 x 12.5 x 3.8 m, 2 sets Westinghouse geared steam turbines, 2 Babcock & Wilcox boilers, 5250 hp, 19 kts, 561 t oil, 9500 nm (11 kts), complement 123; 2 x 1 – 127/51 Mk 7/8/14/15, 2 x 1 – 57/50 Driggs-Schroeder, 1 x 1 – 37/50 Driggs-Schroeder, 1 seaplane (JF, J2F).

After the commissioning of the 'Lake' class cutters, the development of large cutters stopped for several years, caused by the direction of funding for the building of the large class of medium-sized cutters (so-called 165-ft class). Only in 1934 were the requirements for the next class of large cutters prepared, according to which the speed was increased to 20kts. A seaplane was also provided.

The original design was the same 'Lake', the hull of which was lengthened to 316 feet. She did not receive further development, since at the same time the Navy prepared a much more successful design of the *Erie* gunboat, created according to similar technical requirements. After making the necessary changes dictated by the specifics of the Coast Guard service, the "naval" design was transformed to the 'Treasury': the most successful Coast Guard cutter of the Second World War.

The origin of the design was predetermined by the significant differences between the new ships and the remaining cutters. The hull had longitudinal framing. Traditional single-shaft turbo-electrical machinery was replaced by twin-shaft geared steam turbines. Thus, the hull was reinforced for icebreaking.

It was originally planned to build ten ships of this class, but the last three were reordered on the cheaper *Owasco* design for financial reasons.

1941, *Bibb, Hamilton*: - 2 x 1 - 127/51, 2 x 1 - 57/50, 1 x 1 - 37/50, seaplane; + 3 x 1 - 76/50 Mk 20, 2 x 1 - 12.7 MG, 1 DCT, 2 DCR. 1941, *Campbell, Duane, Ingham, Spencer*: - 2 x 1 - 57/50, 1 x 1 - 37/50, seaplane; + 1 x 1 - 127/51 Mk 7/8/14/15, 3 x 1 - 76/50 Mk 20, 4 x 1 - 12.7 MG, 1 DCT, 2 DCR. 1941, *Taney*: - 2 x 1 - 57/50, 1 x 1 - 37/50, seaplane; + 4 x 1 - 76/50 Mk 20, 1 DCT, 2 DCR. 1943, *Bibb*: - 2 x 1 - 12.7 MG; + 1 x 1 - 127/51 Mk 7/8/14/15, 1 x 1 - 76/50 Mk 20, 2 x 1 - 20/70 Oerlikon, 1 x 24 Hedgehog AWSRL, 1 DCT. 1943, *Campbell*: - 1 x 1 - 127/51, 4 x 1 - 12.7 MG; + 1 x 1 - 76/50 Mk 20, 2 x 1 - 20/70 Oerlikon, 1 x 24 Hedgehog ASWRL, 1 DCT, Type 271, SC, SG, SC-3, SGa radars. 1943, *Duane, Ingham,*

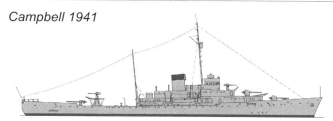

Campbell 1941

Campbell 1943

Spencer: - 1 x 1 - 127/51, 4 x 1 - 12.7 MG; + 1 x 1 - 76/50 Mk 20, 2 x 1 - 20/70 Oerlikon, 1 x 24 Hedgehog Mk 10 ASWRL, 5 DCT. 1943, *Taney*: - 2 x 1 - 127/51, 4 x 1 - 76/50; + 4 x 1 - 127/38 Mk 12, 6 x 1 - 20/70 Oerlikon, 1 x 24 Hedgehog ASWRL, 5 DCT, SK, SG-1, Mk 26 radars, QC sonar.

1944, *Duane, Ingham, Spencer*: - 2 x 1 - 127/51, 4 x 1 - 76/50, 1 x 24 Hedgehog ASWRL, 6 DCT, 2 DCR; + 2 x 1 - 127/38 Mk 12, 3 x 2 - 40/56 Bofors, 2 x 1 - 20/70 Oerlikon, SC-3/2/4, SGa, Mk 26 radars, QC sonar.

1945, *Bibb*: - 1 x 1 - 127/51, 4 x 1 - 76/50, 1 x 24 Hedgehog ASWRL, 2 DCT, 2 DCR; + 2 x 1 - 127/38 Mk 12, 3 x 2 - 40/56 Bofors, 2 x 1 - 20/70 Oerlikon, SK, SG-1, Mk 26 radars, QC sonar. 1945, *Campbell*: - 2 x 1 - 127/51, 4 x 1 - 76/50, 1 x 24 Hedgehog ASWRL, 2 DCT, 2 DCR; + 2 x 1 - 127/38 Mk 12, 3 x 2 - 40/56 Bofors, 4 x 1 - 20/70 Oerlikon, Mk 26 radar, QC sonar. 1945, *Taney*: - 2 x 1 - 127/38, 2 x 1 - 20/70, 1 x 24 Hedgehog ASWRL, 6 DCT, 2 DCR; + 6 x 2 - 40/56 Bofors.

Hamilton 29.1.1942 was torpedoed by German submarine *U132* and sunk next day by the ships of own convoy 17 nm of Reykjavik (Iceland).

'WIND' class cutters-icebreakers

Northwind	WAG278	Western Pipe & Steel, San Francisco	6.1942	28.12.1942	(2.1944)	to the USSR 2.1944 (Severnyy Vetyer)
Eastwind	WAG279	Western Pipe & Steel, San Francisco	6.1942	6.2.1943	6.1944	sold 1972
Southwind	WAG280	Western Pipe & Steel, San Francisco	7.1942	8.3.1943	7.1944	to the USSR 3.1945 (Kapitan Belousov)
Westwind	WAG281	Western Pipe & Steel, San Francisco	8.1942	31.3.1943	9.1944	to the USSR 2.1945 (Severnyy Polius)
Northwind	WAG282	Western Pipe & Steel, San Francisco	7.1944	25.2.1945	7.1945	sold 1.1989

Eastwind 1944

Eastwind post-war

3500 / 6515 t, 82.0 x 19.4 x 7.9 m, 3 electric motors (1 bow, 2 stern), 6 Fairbanks-Morse diesel-generators, 12000 hp, 16.8 kts, 1370 t diesel oil, 50000 nm (11 kts), complement 316; 2 x 2 – 127/38 Mk 12, 3 x 4 – 40/56 Bofors, 6 x 1 – 20/70 Oerlikon, 1 x 24 Hedgehog ASWRL, 6 DCT, 2 DCR, 1 seaplane (J2F); SF or SG or SL or SU, Mk 12/22 or Mk 25 radars.

Registered as large cutters, the '*Wind*' class ships were icebreakers with the armament similar to those of the *Owasco* class cutters. Unlike the latter, their building had a much higher priority, since the ships were supposed to be used for supply of US bases in Greenland, as well as to guide Arctic convoys.

The design provided for a bow screw to disperse ice, but it proved inappropriate and was removed.

1945, all: the fwd shaft was removed, the fore engine room was converted to a cargo hold.

'INDIAN TRIBES' class cutters

Owasco	WPG39	Western Pipe & Steel, San Francisco	11.1943	18.6.1944	5.1945	sold 10.1974
Winnebago	WPG40	Western Pipe & Steel, San Francisco	12.1943	2.7.1944	6.1945	sold 10.1974
Chautauqua	WPG41	Western Pipe & Steel, San Francisco	12.1943	14.5.1944	8.1945	sold 1976
Sebago (ex-*Wachusett*)	WPG42	Western Pipe & Steel, San Francisco	6/1943	28.5.1944	9.1945	for disposal 4.1972
Iroquois	WPG43	Western Pipe & Steel, San Francisco	1943	1944	2.1946	sold 6.1965
Wachusett (ex-*Huron*)	WPG44	Western Pipe & Steel, San Francisco	1943	1944	3.1946	sold 11.1974
Escanaba (ex-*Otsego*)	WPG64	Western Pipe & Steel, San Francisco	1943	1945	3.1946	sold 1974
Winona	WPG65	Western Pipe & Steel, San Francisco	1943	1945	4.1946	sold 1976
Klamath	WPG66	Western Pipe & Steel, San Francisco	1943	1945	6.1946	sold 11.1974
Minnetonka	WPG67	Western Pipe & Steel, San Francisco	1943	1945	7.1946	sold 1976
Androscoggin	WPG68	Western Pipe & Steel, San Francisco	1943	1945	9.1946	sold 10.1974

| Mendota | WPG69 | Coast Guard Yd, Baltimore | 1943 | 1944 | 6.1945 | sold 1974 |
| Pontchartrain (ex-Okeechobee) | WPG70 | Coast Guard Yd, Baltimore | 7.1943 | 29.2.1944 | 7.1945 | sold 1974 |

2216 / 2660 t, 77.7 x 13.1 x 4.9 m, 1 electric motor, 2 Westinghouse steam turbine-generators, 2 Foster Wheeler boilers, 4000 hp, 19 kts, 390 t oil, 12200 nm (12 kts), complement 276; 2 x 2 – 127/38 Mk 12, 2 x 4 – 40/56 Bofors, 4 x 1 – 20/70 Oerlikon, 1 x 24 Hedgehog ASWRL, 6 DCT, 2 DCR, SF or SG or SL or SU, Mk 12/22 or Mk 25 radars, QC sonar.

'Treasury' class cutters, with all their advantages, had one significant drawback: high, by Coast Guard standards, cost. For this reason, the building of the last three ships of this class was abandoned, and they were reordered according to the new, cheaper and more compact design. They returned to a single-shaft turbo-electric machinery, as in the 'Lake' class, leaving the armament and speed requirements unchanged compared to the 'Treasury'.

Three cutters were originally planned, but ten more were added in the summer of 1941 to replace the 'Lake' class ships transferred to the Royal Navy.

The low priority of the program during the war years led to the fact that the ships ordered in 1941 were launched only in 1944-1945. The only positive feature of this long-term building was the ability to take into account the experience of operations. The main guns

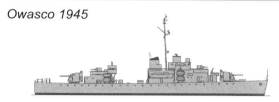

Owasco 1945

Owasco post-war

became dual-purpose, AA armament was strengthened. Seaplanes were abandoned.

Cutters converted from merchant vessels

More than 1000 t displacement

North Star	WPG59	1932 / 5.1941	2200	68.6 x 12.5 x 5.7	13	2 x 1 – 76/50, 6 – 20/70, 1 seaplane, 2 DCR	USN auxiliary 1.1944
Nourmahal	WPG122	1928 / 8.1940	2250	65.7 x 12.7 x 6.7	13.7	2 x 1 – 102/50, 2 DCR	USN 6-12.1943, stricken 5.1946
Cobb (ex-Governor Cobb)	WPG181	1906 / 7.1943	3500	91.5 x 16.8 x 5.8	14.7	2 x 1 – 127/38, 6 – 20/70, 2 Mousetrap ASWRL, 4 DCT, 2 DCR, 2 helicopters (from 1944)	sold 3.1947
Bodkin (ex-Burke, ex-Nokomis)	WPG182	1914 / (1942)	1000	74.1 x 9.7 x 3.9	16		conversion cancelled 7.1943
Mayflower (ex-Butte, ex-Mayflower)	WPG183	1896 / 10.1943	2690	83.2 x 11.0 x 6.0	12	1 x 1 – 127/61, 2 x 1 – 76/50, 6 – 20/70, 1 Hedgehog ASWRL, 4 DCT, 2 DCR	disposed 1.1947
Sea Cloud (ex-Hussar II)	WPG284	1931 / 4.1942	3077	96.0 x 15.0 x 5.8	12	2 x 1 – 76/50, 5 – 20/70, 1 Hedgehog ASWRL, 4 DCT	USN auxiliary 4.1943

Marita *(ex-Kaspar, ex-Seghill, ex-Kilmacrennan)*	WPY175	1918 / 11.1942	*1450*	55.8 x 9.2 x 5.2	7	2 x 1 – 76/50, 4 – 20/70	sold 5.1945

North Star 1941

Numbers written in *Italic* indicate displacement

500-1000 t displacement
WPYc3 **Amethyst** *(ex-Samona II)* (1931 / 3.1944, 525 t – stricken 3.1946)

100-500t displacement
Requisitioned: 23 (1942), 29 (1943), 1 (1944)
Lost: 1 (1942), 3 (1943)
Discarded: 18 (1943), 22 (1944), 1 (1945), 8 (post-war)

Cutters, former USN 110-ft submarine chasers

New York Yacht, Launch & Engine, Morris Heights: SC229 (8.1942- WPC335 Boone), SC231 (8.1942- WPC336 Blaze), SC238 (7.1943- WPC365 Bowstring) (1918)
Geo Lawley, Neponset: WPC372 Belleville (ex-SC258) (1917/1942)

Discarded: WPC365, 372 (1945), WPC335, 336 (1946)
75 / 85 t, 33.5 x 4.5 x 1.7 m, 3 Standard petrol engines, 660 hp, 18 kts, 1000 nm (12 kts), complement 27; 1 x 1 – 76/23 Mk 14, 2 x 1 – 7.6 MG, 1 DCT.
110-ft submarine chasers of the US Navy, transferred to the Coast Guard in 1919-1920. Wooden-hulled.

74-ft cutters

John Mathis, Camden: CG104, 107 – 109, 279, 282 – 285, 287 – 292 (1924-1925)
Defoe, Bay City: CG115 – 122, 124, 125, 127 - 129 (1924-1925)
Crowninshield, Fall River: CG130 – 132, 135 - 139 (1924-1925)
Dachel-Carter, Benton Harbor: CG140 – 141, 143, 145, 147, 148 (1924-1925)
T. H. Soule, Freeport: CG150, 151, 153 - 159 (1924-1925)
New York Launch & Engine: CG160 - 169 (1924-1925)
Rice Bros, East Boothbay: CG170 – 174, 178, 179 (1924-1925)
Southern Shipyard, Newport News: CG180, 183 – 187, 189 (1924-1925)
Portsmouth N Yd: CG190, 192 (1924-1925)
Chance, Annapolis: CG193, 195, 197, 200 - 202 (1924-1925)
Kingston Dry Dock: CG205, 206, 210 - 212 (1924-1925)

Vineyard SB, Milford: CG213 - 220 (1924-1925)
Colonna`s, Norfolk: CG223, 224, 226 – 229, 231, 232 (1924-1925)
Luders, Stamford: CG233 - 242 (1924-1925)
Gibbs Gas Engine, Jacksonville: CG244, 246, 249, 250, 293 – 300 (1924-1925)
A. W. DeYoung, Alameda: CG253 – 255, 257 - 260, 262 (1924-1925)
Lake Union, Seattle: CG264 – 266, 268, 270, 271, 277 (1924-1925)
Lost: W74327 (1944)
Discarded: W74300-74326, 7428-74351 (1946-1948)
37 t, 22.9 x 4.2 x 1.2 m, 1 petrol engine, 400 hp, 13.5 kts, 1 x 1 – 37/50 Driggs-Schroeder.
In 1942 52 survived boats were renumbered W74300-74351. Some units served under the USN flag during the war.
Early 1940s, almost all survived: - 1 x 1 – 37/50; + 1 x 1 – 20/70 Oerlikon, 2 DCR.

78-ft cutters

Southern SY, Newport News: CG400 – 405 (1942- W78300 – 78305) (1931)
Discarded: W78300-78305 (1946-1948)
43 t, 24.1 x 4.4 x 1.2 m, 2 petrol engines, 1200 hp, 21

kts; 1 x 1 – 37/50 Driggs-Schroeder
Early 1940s, almost all: - 1 x 1 – 37/50; + 1 x 1 – 20/70 Oerlikon, 2 DCR.

38-ft cutters

Gibbs Gas Engine, Jacksonville: CG2385 – 2399 (1931)
Corsair, Trenton: CG4300 – 4305 (1931-1932)
Freeport Point: CG4306 – 4320 (1936)
Stephens Bros, Stockton: CG4321 – 4326 (1937)

Discarded: W38301-38340 (1945-1946)
11.6 m.
In 1942 40 survived launches were renumbered W38301 – 38340.

72-ft cutters

Chance, Annapolis: CG439 (1942- W72005) (1933), CG440, 441 (1942- W72300, 72301)
Discarded: W72005, 72300, 72301 (1945-1947)
27 t, 21.9 x 4.6 x 1.1 m, 4 petrol engines (2 shafts), 1600

hp, 34 kts; 1 x 1 – 37/50 Driggs-Schroeder, 1 DCR.
Early 1940s, almost all: - 1 x 1 – 37/50; + 1 x 1 – 20/70 Oerlikon, 1 DCR.

80-ft cutters

Gibbs Gas Engine, Jacksonville: CG406 – 411 (1942- W80300 - 80305) (1937)
Harbor Boat, Terminal Is: CG412 – 414 (1942- W80306 – 80308) (1937)
Discarded: W80300-80308 (1945-1946)

52 t, 24.7 x 4.8 x 1.2 m, 4 petrol engines (2 shafts), 1600 hp, 25 kts; 1 x 1 – 37/50 Driggs-Schroeder, 2 x 1 – 7.6 MG, 1 DCR.
Early 1940s, almost all: - 1 x 1 – 37/50; + 1 x 1 – 20/70 Oerlikon, 1 DCR.

65-ft cutters

William Whiting, Long Beach: CG442, 443 (1942- W65300, 65301) (1937)
Discarded: W65300, 65301 (1947)
30 t, 19.8 x 4.3 x 1.1 m, 4 petrol engines (2 shafts), 1600

hp, 28 kts; 1 x 1 – 37/50 Driggs-Schroeder, 1 DCR.
Early 1940s, both: - 1 x 1 – 37/50; + 1 x 1 – 20/70 Oerlikon, 1 DCR.

83-ft cutters

Wheeler SB, Brooklyn: CG450 – 476 (1942- W83300 – 83326) (1941), CG477 – 499 (1942- W83327 – 83348), CG600 – 634 (1942- W83349 – 83383), W83384 – 83388 (1942), W83389 – 83513 (1943), W83514 – 83529 (1944)
Transferred: Cuba – W83316, 83317, 83350, 83351, 83384 – 83386, 83395 (1943), Mexico – W83446, 83510 and 1 other (1943), Peru – W83315, 83338, 83423, 83423, 83495, 83496 (1944), Columbia – W83349,

83433 (1944), United Kingdom – W83399, 83401, 83402, 83407 (1944).
Lost: W83421 (1943), W83415, 83421, 83471 (1944), W83301, 83306 (1945), W83478 (1954), W83524 (1961)
Discarded: all survived (1946-mid-1960s)
50 t, 25.3 x 4.9 x 1.4 m, 2 petrol engines, 1200 hp, 23.5 kts, complement 10; 1 x 1 – 20/70 Oerlikon, 2 x 4 Mousetrap ASWRL (many), 4 DCR, SO radar (many), sonar.

SHIP-BASED AIRCRAFT

Fighters

F4B

Boeing F4B (168, 1929-1937)

F4B-4: 9.14 x 6.12 x 2.84 m, 21.1 m², 1068 / 1638 kg, 1 Pratt & Whitney R-1340-16, 550 hp, 303 km/h, 600 (254) km, 8.7 m/s, 8200 m, 1 seat; 2 x 7.6-mm Browning MG, 120 kg bombs.
F4B-1 (fighter, 27 built 8.1929-1930, serv. 8.1929-late 1937, 525-hp Pratt & Whitney R-1340-17 engine), **F4B-2** (fighter, 46 built 1930-1931, serv. 1930-late 1937), **F4B-3** (fighter, 21 built 1931-1932, serv. 1931-late 1937, metal construction), **F4B-4** (fighter, 74 built 1932-1.1933, serv. 1932-late 1937, 550-hp R-1340-16 engine, lifeboat).

BFC-2

Curtiss F11C / BFC (28, 1933-1938)

F11C-2: 9.60 x 7.62 x 3.23 m, 23.3 m², 1378 / 1869 kg, 1 Wright R-1820-78, 750 hp, 309 km/h, 843 km, 11.7 m/s, 7400 m, 1 seat; 2 x 7.6-mm Browning MG, 431 kg bombs (1 227-kg and 4 51-kg).
F11C-2 / BFC-2 (fighter-dive bomber, 28 built 3.1933-12.1934, serv. 3.1933-1938)

F2F-1

Grumman F2F (54, 1935-1940)

F2F-1: 8.69 x 6.53 x 2.77 m, 21.4 m², 1221 / 1745 kg, 1 Pratt & Whitney R-1820-78, 650 hp, 383 km/h, 1585 (225) km, 10120 m, 1 seat; 2 x 7.6-mm MG, 113 kg bombs.
F2F-1 (fighter, 54 built 2-8.1935, serv. 2.1935-9.1940)

F3F-2

Grumman F3F (162, 1936-1941)

F3F-3: 9.75 x 7.06 x 2.84 m, 24.2 m², 1490 / 2175 kg, 1 Wright R-1820-22, 950 hp, 425 km/h, 1577 (241) km, 10120 m, 1 seat; 2 x 7.6-mm MG, 113 kg bombs.
F3F-1 (fighter, 54 built 4.1936-1.1937, serv. 4.1936-10.1941, 650-hp Pratt & Whitney R-1535-84 engine, 1 x 12.7-mm and 1 x 7.6-mm MG, 386 km/h), **F3F-2** (fighter, 81 built 1.1937-1938, serv. 1.137-10.1941, 950-hp Wright R-1820-22 engine, 2 x 7.6-mm MG, 434 km/h), **F3F-3** (Fighter, 27 built 1938-5.1939, serv. 1938-10.1941, streamlined).

Brewster F2A Buffalo (162, 1939-1942)

F2A-3: 10.67 x 8.03 x 3.68 m, 19.4 m², 2146 / 3247 kg, 1 Wright R-1820-40, 1200 hp, 571 km/h, 1553 (415) km, 10120 m, 1 seat; 4 x 12.7-mm MG, 90 kg bombs.
F2A-1 (fighter, 11 built 12.1939-1940, serv. 12.1939-4.1942, 950-hp Wright R-1820-34 engine, 1 x 12.7-mm and 1 x 7.6-mm MG (early 1940 – 3 x 12.7 and 1 x 7.6), **F2A-2** (fighter, 43 built 9.1940-1941, serv. 9.1940-4.1942, 1200-hp R-1820-40 engine, 4 x 12.7-mm MG, 90 kg bombs, length decreased by 0.13 m, all were modified under F2A-3 standard 5.1941), **F2A-3** (fighter, 108 built 1941-4.1942, serv. 1941-4.1942, lengthened by 0.25 m, fuel stowage increased, armor protection

F2A-2 Buffalo

strengthened).

Grumman F4F / General Motors FM Wildcat (7568, 1940-1945)

F4F-4: 11.58 x 8.83 x 3.58 m, 24.2 m², 2673 / 3616 kg, 1 Pratt & Whitney R-1830-86, 1200 hp, 512 km/h, 1239 (249) km, 10067 m, 1 seat; 6 x 12.7-mm MG.
F4F-3 (fighter, 285 built 12.1940-1942, serv. 12.1940-11.1945, 1200-hp Pratt & Whitney R-1830-76 engine (later R-1830-86), 4 x 12.7-mm MG), **F4F-3A** (fighter, 95 built 1942, serv. 1942-11.1945, 1200-hp R-1830-90 engine, fixed wing), **F4F-3P** (fighter / photo reconnaissance plane, some converted 1941-1942 from F4F-3, photo camera additionally, folding wing), **F4F-4** (fighter, 1169 built 1942-5.1943, serv. 1942-11.1945, F4F-3 with 1200-hp R-1830-86 engine, 6 x 12.7-mm MG), **F4F-4P** (fighter / photo reconnaissance plane, some converted from F4F-4 1942-1943, serv. 1942-11.1945, photo camera

F4F-4 Wildcat

additionally), **F4F-7** (reconnaissance plane, 21 built in 1942, serv. 1942-11.1945, unarmed, 5900-km flight range), **FM-1** (fighter, 1221 built 8.1942-late 1943, serv. 8.1942-11.1945, F4F-4 with only 4 x 12.7-mm MG), **FM-2** (fighter-bomber, 4777 built late 1943-5.1945, serv. late 1943-11.1945, 1350-hp Wright R-1820-56W engine, 4 x 12.7-mm MG, 6 x 127-mm rockets or 2 113-kg bombs).

Vought F4U / Goodyear FG / Brewster F3A Corsair (12272, 1942-1955)

FG-1: 12.49 x 10.16 x 4.50 m, 29.2 m², 3987 / 5443 kg, 1 Pratt & Whitney R-2800-8, 2000 hp, 684 km/h, 1618 km, 11247 m, 1 seat; 6 x 12.7-mm MG.
F4U-4: 12.50 x 10.26 x 4.50 m, 29.2 m², 4238 / 6592 kg, 1 Pratt & Whitney R-2800-18W, 2450 hp, 717 km/h, 2510 km (with external tanks), 19.7 m/s, 11580 m, 1 seat; 6 x 12.7-mm MG, 1452 kg bombs or 2 298-mm or 8 127-mm rockets
F4U-1 (fighter, 2155 built 10.1942-8.1943, serv. 10.1942-12.1955, 2000-hp Pratt & Whitney R-2800-8 engine, 6 x 12.7-mm MG), **FG-1** (fighter, 299 built 2-8.1943, serv. 2.1943-12.1955, as F4U-1), **F4U-1A** (fighter, 665 built 8.1943-4.1944, serv. 8.1943-12.1955, 2000-hp R-2800-8 or R-2800-8W (on later planes) engine), **FG-1A** (fighter, 2089 built 8.1943-4.1944, serv. 8.1943-12.1955, as F4U-1A), **F3A-1** (fighter, 735 built 4.1943-7.1944, serv. 4.1943-12.1955, as F4U-1A), **F4U-1C** (fighter, 200 built 9.-late1943, serv. 9.1943-12.1955, 4 x 20-mm guns), **F4U-1D** (fighter-bomber, 1484 built 4.1944-9.1945, serv. 4.1944-12.1955, 6 x 12.7-mm MG, 908 kg bombs or

F4U-4 Corsair

(later) 8 127-mm rockets), **FG-1D** (fighter-bomber, 1620 built 4.1944-9.1945, serv. 4.1944-12.1955, as F4U-1D), **F4U-1P** (fighter – reconnaissance plane, some converted from F4U-1A 1944, serv. 1944-12.1955, F4U-1A with photo camera), **FG-1E** (night fighter, some converted from FG-1A 1944, serv. 1944-12.1955, FG-1A with APS-4 radar), **F4U-2** (night fighter, 34 converted from F4U-1 1944, F4U-1 with APS-6 radar), **F4U-4** (fighter-bomber, 2050 built early 1945-8.1947, serv. early 1945-12.1955, F4U-1A with 2450-hp R-2800-18W (later R-2800-42W) engine, 6 x 12.7-mm MG, 1452 kg bombs or 2 298-mm rockets or 8 127-mm rockets), **F4U-4C** (fighter-bomber, 297 built early 1945-8.1947, serv. early 1945-12.1955, 4

x 20-mm guns, 1452 kg bombs or 2 298-mm rockets or 8 127-mm rockets)
Postwar modifications: fighter-bomber F4U-5 (223 built 1947-1951), night fighter-bomber F4U-5N (214

built 1947-1951), night fighter-bomber with arctic equipment F4U-5NL (101 built 1947-1951), long range reconnaissance plane F4U-5P (30 built 1947-1951) and attacker AU-1 (110 built in 1951).

F6F-5 Hellcat

Grumman F6F Hellcat (12271, 1943-1953)

F6F-5: 13.06 x 10.24 x 4.11 m, 31.0 m², 4152 / 6991 kg, 1 Pratt & Whitney R-2800-10W, 2200 hp, 611 km/h, 2100 km, 11400 m, 1 seat; (2 x 20-mm guns and 4 x 12.7-mm MG) or 6 x 12.7-mm MG, 6 127-mm rockets or 908 kg bombs (2 454-kg)

F6F-3 (fighter, 4403 built 1.1943-4.1944, serv. 1.1943-8.1953, 2000-hp Pratt & Whitney R-2800-10 engine (later 2200-hp R-2800-10W), 6 x 12.7-mm MG), **F6F-3E** (fighter, 18 converted from F6F-3 11.1943-1944, serv. 11.1943-8.1953, F6F-3 with APS-4 radar), **F6F-3N** (night fighter, 149 converted from F6F-3 11.1943-1944, serv. 11.1943-8.1953, F6F-3 with APS-6 radar), **F6F-5** (fighter, 6434 built 4.1944-11.1945, serv. 4.1944-8.1953, 2200-hp R-2800-10W engine, 6 x 12.7-mm MG or (2 x 20-mm guns and 4 x 12.7-mm MG), 6 x 127-mm rockets or 2 454-kg bombs, no radar), **F6F-5E** (fighter, 1434 built with F6F-5N 4.1944-11.1945, serv. 4.1944-8.1953, F6F-5 with APS-4 radar), **F6F-5N** (night fighter, 1434 built with F6F-5E 4.1944-11.1945, serv. 4.1944-8.1953, F6F-5 with APS-6 radar), **F6F-5P** (fighter-reconnaissance plane, some converted from F6F-5 1944-1945, serv. 1944-8.1953, F6F-5 with photo camera)

F7F-3N Tigercat

Grumman F7F Tigercat (531, 1944-1956)

F7F-3: 15.70 x 13.83 x 5.05 m, 42.3 m², 7380 / 11666 kg, 2 Pratt & Whitney R-2800-34W, 2 x 2100 hp, 700 km/h, 1623-1913 (357) km, 23 m/s, 12405 m, 1 seat; 4 x 20-mm guns and 4 x 12.7-mm MG, 2 454-kg bombs or 8 127-mm rockets or 2 298-mm rockets under wing and 907-kg bomb or 298-mm rocket or Mk 13 torpedo under the fuselage.
F7F-1 (fighter-bomber, 36 built 4.1944-1945, serv. 4.1944-1956, 2 2100-hp Pratt & Whitney R-2800-22W engines, 1 seat, 4 x 20-mm guns and 4 x 12.7-mm MG, 1 454-kg bomb or 1 298-mm rocket or 1 908-kg

Mk 13 torpedo), **F7F-2N** (night fighter-bomber, 66 built 10.1944-3.1945, serv. 10.1944-1948, 2 seats, 4 x 20-mm guns and 4 x 12.7-mm MG (during the day), 2 227-kg bombs or 8 127-mm rockets or 2 298-mm rockets under wing and 1 454-kg bomb or 1 298-mm rocket or 1 Mk 13 torpedo under hull, APS-6 radar), **F7F-3** (fighter-bomber, 250 built 3.1945-6.1946, serv. 3.1945-1956, 1 seat, 2 2100-hp R-2800-34W engines, 4 x 20-mm guns and 4 x 12.7-mm MG, 2 454-kg bombs or 8 127-mm rockets or 2 298-mm rockets under the wing and 1 907-kg bomb or 1 298-mm rocket or 1 Mk 13 torpedo under hull, no radar), **F7F-3N** (night fighter-bomber, 106 built 5.1945-6.1946, serv. 5.1945-1956, 2 seats, 4 x 20-mm guns, 2 454-kg bombs or 8 127-mm rockets or 2 298-mm rockets under wing and 1 907-kg bomb or 1 298-mm rocket or 1 Mk 13 torpedo under hull, SCR-720 radar), **F7F-3P** (fighter-bomber-reconnaissance plane, 61 built 3-8.1945, serv. 3.1945-1956, 1 seat, 4 x 20-mm guns and 4 x 12.7-mm MG, 2 454-kg bombs or 8 127-mm rockets or 2 298-mm rockets under the wing, photo camera)
Postwar modification: night fighter-bomber F7F-4N (12 built in 1946).

Goodyear F2G Super Corsair (18, 1945-1946)

F2G-2: 12.50 x 10.29 x 4.90 m, 29.2 m², 4649 / 6620 kg, 1 Pratt & Whitney R-4360-4, 3650 hp, 724 km/h, 2500 (694) km, 22.4 m/s, 12500 m, 1 seat; 6 x 12.7-mm MG.
F2G-2 (fighter, 18 built 1945-1946, serv. 1945-1946)

F2G-1 Super Corsair

Ryan FR Fireball (66, 1945-1947)

FR-1: 12.19 x 9.86 x 4.15 m, 25.6 m², 3590 / 4806 kg, 1 Wright R-1820-72W + 1 General Electric J31-GE-3, 1425 hp + 726 kgf, 686 km/h, 1685 (475) km, 13135 m, 1 seat; 4 x 12.7-mm MG, 454 kg bombs or 8 127-mm rockets
FR-1 (fighter, 66 built 3-11.1945, serv. 3.1945-6.1947)

FR-1 Fireball

Grumman F8F Bearcat (1266, 1945-1955)

F8F-1: 10.82 x 8.43 x 4.16 m, 22.7 m², 3322 / 5780 hp, 1 Pratt & Whitney R-2800-34W, 2750 hp, 682 km/h, 2280 (272) km, 28.5 m/s, 11520 m, 1 seat; 4 x 12.7-mm MG, 454-kg bomb under the fuselage, 2 454-kg bombs or 2 298-mm rockets or 2 twin 12.7-mm MG or 8 76-mm rockets or 8 127-mm rockets under the wing.
F8F-1 (fighter, 765 built 5.1945-1946, serv. 5.1945-1955)
Postwar modifications: fighters F8F-1B (100 built 1946-1948) and F8F-2 (293 built 1947-1949), night fighters F8F-1N (36 built 1946) and F8F-2N (12 built 1947-1949) and fighter-reconnaissance plane F8F-2P (60 built

F8F-2 Bearcat

1947-1949)

McDonnel FH Phantom (61, 1947-1950)

FH-1: 12.42 x 11.81 x 4.32 m, 25.6 m², 3030 / 5458 kg, 2 Westinghouse J30-WE-20, 2 x 725 kgf, 771 km/h, 1578 (399) km, 21.5 m/s, 12527 m, 1 seat; 4 x 12.7-mm MG. First take-off in January 1945. 61 FH-1 fighters were built in 1947-1948.

FH-1 Phantom

Dive bombers

Vought SBU (124, 1935-1941)

SBU-1: 10.14 x 8.46 m, 2600 kg, 1 Pratt & Whitney R-1535-80, 690 hp, 330 km/h, 880 (224) km, 7200 m, 2 seats; 2 x 7.6-mm Browning MG, 227 kg bombs
SBU-1 (dive bomber – reconnaissance plane, 84 built 11.1935-1936, serv. 11.1935-4.1941, 690-hp Pratt & Whitney R-1535-80 engine), **SBU-2** (dive bomber – reconnaissance plane, 40 built in 1936-8.1937, serv. 1936-4.1941, 750-hp R-1535-98 engine).

SBU-1

Curtiss SBC Helldiver (257, 1937-1941)

SBC-4: 10.36 x 8.57 x 3.17 m, 29.5 m², 2066 / 3211 kg, 1 Wright R-1830-34, 950 hp, 377 km/h, 950 (282) km, 7315 m, 2 seats; 2 x 7.6-mm MG, 454 kg bombs.
SBC-3 (dive bomber – reconnaissance plane, 83 built 7.1937-3.1939, serv. 7.1937-1941, 700-hp Pratt & Whitney R-1535-82 engine), **SBC-4** (dive bomber – reconnaissance plane, 174 built 3.1939-4.1941, serv. 3.1939-1941, 950-hp Wright R-1820-34 engine)

SBC-4 Helldiver

SB2U-3 Vindicator

Vought SB2U Vindicator (169, 1937-1943)

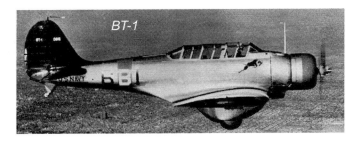

BT-1

SBD-5 Dauntless

Douglas SBD Dauntless (4923, 1940-1945)

SBD-6: 12.65 x 10.06 x 3.94 m, 30.2 m², 2964 / 4318 kg, 1 Wright R-1820-66, 1350 hp, 410 km/h, 1244 (298) km, 8.6 m/s, 7680 m, 2 seats; (2 x 12.7-mm + 2 x 7.6-mm) MG, 816 kg bombs (1 726-kg and 2 45-kg).

SBN-1

SB2C-5 Helldiver

Curtiss SB2C / Fairchild SBF / Canadian Car & Foundry SBW Helldiver (6214, 1942-1949)

SB2C-4: 15.16 x 11.18 x 4.01 m, 39.2 m², 4784 / 7537

SB2U-3: 12.80 x 10.36 x 3.12 m, 28.3 m², 2555 / 4272 kg, 1 Pratt & Whitney R-1535-02, 825 hp, 391 km/h, 1803 (244) km, 5.4 m/s, 7195 m, 2 seats; (2 – 5) x 12.7-mm MG, 454 kg bombs
SB2U-1 (dive bomber, 54 built 12.1937-8.1938, serv. 12.1937-11.1943, 825-hp Pratt & Whitney R-1535-96 engine, 2 x 7.6-mm MG, 454 kg bombs), **SB2U-2** (dive bomber, 58 built 8.1938-2.1939, serv. 8.1938-11.1943), **SB2U-3** (dive bomber, 57 built 2.1939-7.1941, serv. 2.1939-11.1943, 825-hp R-1535-02 engine, (2 – 5) x 12.7-mm MG, 454 kg bombs, increased flight range)

Northrop BT (54, 1938-1941)

BT-1: 14.54 x 9.87 m, 3425 kg, 1 Pratt & Whitney R-1535-94, 825 hp, 354 km/h, 1732 km, 7715 m, 2 seats; 2 x 7.6-mm MG, 454 kg bombs.
BT-1 (dive bomber, 54 built 4-10.1938, serv. 4.1938-early 1941).

SBD-1 (dive bomber, 57 built 6.1940-early 1941, serv. 6.1940-9.1945, 1000-hp Wright R-1820-32 engine, (2 x 12.7-mm + 1 x 7.6-mm) MG, 816 kg bombs, **SBD-2** (dive bomber, 87 built early 1941-spring 1942, serv. early 1941-9.1945, (1 x 12.7-mm + 1 x 7.6-mm) MG, 816 kg bombs, fuel stowage increased), **SBD-3** (dive bomber, 585 built spring 1942-10.1942, serv. spring 1942-9.1945, 1000-hp R-1820-52 engine, (2 x 12.7-mm + 2 x 7.6-mm) MG, 816 kg bombs, armor, **SBD-4** (dive bomber, 780 built 10.1942-mid-1943, serv. 10.1942-9.1945, many with radar), **SBD-5** (dive bomber, 2964 built mid-1943-3.1944, serv. mid-1943-9.1945, 1200-hp R-1820-60 engine), **SBD-6** (dive bomber, 450 built 3-8.1944, serv. 3.1944-9.1945, 1350-hp R-1820-66 engine)

Brewster SBN (30, 1940-1942)

SBN-1: 11.89 x 8.43 x 2.62 m, 24.1 m², 1851 / 3066 kg, 1 Wright R-1820-22, 950 hp, 409 km/h, 1633 km, 8625 m, 2 seats; (1 x 12.7-mm + 1 x 7.6-mm) MG, 227 kg bombs.
SBN-1 (dive bomber, 30 built 11.1940-3.1942, serv. 11.1940-late 1942)

kg, 1 Wright R-2600-20, 1900 hp, 457 km/h, 1876 (254) km, 8870 m, 2 seats; 2 x 20-mm guns, 2 x 7.6-mm MG, 725 kg bombs or 454-kg bomb and 4 127-mm rockets.
SB2C-1 (dive bomber, 200 built 12.1942-1943, serv. 12.1942-6.1949, 1700-hp Wright R-2600-8 engine, 4 x 12.7-mm and 2 x 7.6-mm MG, 725 kg bombs), **SB2C-1C** (dive bomber, 778 built 1943-1944, serv. 1943-6.1949, 2 x 20-mm guns and 2 7.6-mm MG, 725 kg bombs), **SBF-1** (dive bomber, 50 built 1943-1944, serv. 1943-6.1949, as SB2C-1C), **SBW-1** (dive bomber, 40 built 1943-1944, serv. 1943-6.1949, as SB2C-1C), **SB2C-3** (dive bomber, 1112 built early 1944-1944, serv. early

1944-6.1949, 1900-hp R-2600-20 engine), **SB2C-3E** (dive bomber, part of SB2C-3 built early 1944-1944, serv. early 1944-6.1949, SB2C-3 with APS-4 radar), **SBF-3** (dive bomber, 150 built early 1944-1944, serv. early 1944-6.1949, as SB2C-3), **SBW-3** (dive bomber, 413 built early 1944-1944, serv. early 1944-6.1949, as SB2C-3), **SB2C-4** (dive bomber, 2045 built mid-1944-1945, serv. mid-1944-6.1949, 2 x 20-mm guns and 2 x 7.6-mm MG, 725 kg bombs or 454 kg bomb and 4 127-mm rockets), **SB2C-4E** (dive bomber, part of SB2C-4 built mid-1944-1945, serv. mid-1944-6.1949, SB2C-4 with APS-4 radar), **SBF-4E** (dive bomber, 100 built mid-1944-1945, serv. mid-1944-6.1949, as SB2C-4E), **SBW-4E** (dive bomber, 270 built mid-1944-1945, serv. mid-1944-6.1949, as SB2C-4E), **SB2C-5** (dive bomber, 970 built 2-10.1945, serv. 2.1945-6.1949, as SB2C-4 with increased fuel stowage), **SBW-5** (dive bomber, 86 built 2-10.1945, serv. 2.1945-6.1949, as SB2C-5).

Brewster SB2A Buccaneer (60, 1943)

SB2A-3: 14.33 x 11.94 x 4.70 m, 35.2 m², 4501 / 6481 kg, 1 Wright R-2600-8, 1700 hp, 441 km/h, 2696 (259) km, 7590 m, 2 seats; 2 x 12.7-mm and 4 x 7.6-mm MG, 454 kg bombs
SB2A-3 (dive bomber, 60 built 1.1943-11.1943, serv. 1.1943-11.1943)

SB2A-4 Buccaneer

Torpedo bombers

Great Lakes TG (50, 1928-1931)

TG-1: 16.15 x 10.85 x 4.50 m, 60.9 m², 1783 / 3661 kg, 1 Pratt & Whitney R-1690-24, 525 hp, 183 km/h, 585 (172) km, 3085 m, 3 seats; 1 x 7.6-mm MG, 1 torpedo or 800 kg bombs
TG-1 (torpedo bomber-reconnaissance plane, 18 built 8.1928-1930, serv. 8.1928-3.1938, 525-hp Pratt & Whitney R-1690-24 engine), **TG-2** (torpedo bomber-reconnaissance plane, 32 built 1930-12.1931, serv. 1930-3.1938, 575-hp Wright R-1820-86 engine)

TG-2

Martin BM (32, 1932-1933)

BM-1: 12.50 x 8.80 m, 2785 kg, 1 Pratt & Whitney R-1690-44, 625 hp, 230 km/h, 850 km, 4600 m, 2 seats; 2 x 7.6-mm MG, 1 torpedo or 454 kg bombs
BM-1 (dive torpedo bomber, 16 built 10.1932-late 1932, serv. 10.1932-9.1938), **BM-2** (dive torpedo bomber, 16 built late 1932-1.1933, serv. late 1932-9.1938)

BM-1

Great Lakes BG (61, 1934-1941)

BG-1: 10.97 x 8.76 x 3.35 m, 35.7 m², 1770 / 2880 kg, 1 Pratt & Whitney R-1535-82, 750 hp, 303 km/h, 870 (278) km, 6125 m, 2 seats; 2 x 7.6-mm MG, 1 torpedo or 454 kg bombs.
BG-1 (dive torpedo bomber, 61 built 10.1934-11.1935, serv. 10.1934-6.1941)

BG-1

TBD-1 Devastator

TBF-1 Avenger

Grumman TBF / General Motors TBM Avenger (9835, 1942-1954)

TBM-3: 16.51 x 12.19 x 5.00 m, 45.5 m², 4853 / 8278 kg, 1 Wright R-2600-20, 1900 hp, 444 km/h, 1626 (236) km, 10.5 m/s, 9175 m, 3 seats; (3 x 12.7-mm + 1 x 7.6-mm) MG, 1 908-kg torpedo or 908 kg bombs or 8 127-mm rockets.
TBF-1 (torpedo bomber, 1525 built 3.1942-12.1943, serv. 3.1942-10.1954, 1700-hp Wright R-2600-8 engine, (1 x 12.7-mm + 2 x 7.6-mm) MG, 1 908-kg torpedo or 908 kg bombs or 8 127-mm rockets), **TBF-1C** (torpedo bomber, 764 built 7-12.1943, serv. 7.1943-10.1954, (3 x 12.7-mm + 1 x 7.6-mm) MG, 1 908-kg torpedo or 908 kg bombs or 8 127-mm rockets, ASB radar on some), **TBF-1CD** (torpedo bomber, some converted from TBF-1C 1943, serv. 1943-10.1954, ASD-1 radar), **TBF-1CP** (torpedo bomber – reconnaissance plane, some converted from TBF-1C 1945, serv. 1945-10.1954, TBF-1C with photo camera), **TBF-1D** (torpedo bomber, some converted from TBF-1 1943, serv. 1943-10.1954, TBF-1 with ASD-1 radar), **TBF-1E** (torpedo bomber, some converted from TBF-1 1944, serv. 1944-10.1954, TBF-1 with APS-4 radar), **TBF-1L** (torpedo bomber, some converted from TBF-1 1944, serv. 1944-10.1954, TBF-1 with a searchlight), **TBF-1P** (torpedo bomber –

BTD-1 Destroyer

Douglas TBD Devastator (130, 1937-1942)

TBD-1: 15.24 x 10.67 x 4.60 m, 39.2 m², 2539 / 4623 kg, 1 Pratt & Whitney R-1830-64, 900 hp, 331 km/h, 1152 (206) km, 3.7 m/s, 5945 m, 2 seats; 2 x 7.6 or (1 x 12.7-mm + 1 x 7.6-mm) MG, 1 908-kg torpedo or 545 kg bombs
TBD-1 (torpedo bomber, 130 built 5.1937-11.1939, serv. 5.1937-8.1942)

reconnaissance plane, some converted from TBF-1 1945, serv. 1945-10.1954, TBF-1 with photo camera), **TBM-1** (torpedo bomber, 550 built 11.1942-early 1944, serv. 11.1942-10.1954, as TBF-1), **TBM-1C** (torpedo bomber, 2332 built 7.1943-early 1944, serv. 7.1943-10.1954, as TBF-1C), **TBM-1D** (torpedo bomber, some converted from TBM-1 1943, serv. 1943-10.1954, as TBF-1D), **TBM-1E** (torpedo bomber, some converted from TBM-1 1944, serv. 1944-10.1954, as TBF-1E), **TBM-1L** (torpedo bomber, some converted from TBM-1 1944, serv. 1944-10.1954, as TBF-1L), **TBM-1P** (torpedo bomber – reconnaissance plane, some converted from TBM-1 1945, serv. 1945-10.1954, as TBF-1P), **TBM-3** (torpedo bomber, 2284 TBM-3 and TBM-3D built early 1944 – late 1944, serv. early 1944-10.1954, TBM-1C with 1900-hp R-2600-20 engine), **TBM-3D** (torpedo bomber, part of TBM-3 built early 1944-late 1944, serv. early 1944-10.1954, TBM-3 with APS-3 radar), **TBM-3E** (torpedo bomber, 2380 built late 1944-9.1945, serv. late 1944-10.1954, TBM-3 lightened by 1000 kg, 3 x 12.7-mm MG, 1 908-kg or 908 kg bombs or 8 127-mm rockets, APS-4 radar), **TBM-3H** (torpedo bomber, some converted from TBM-3 1944, serv. 1944-10.1954, TBM-3 with ASV radar), **TBM-3L** (torpedo bomber, some converted from TBM-3 1944, serv. 1944-10.1954, TBM-3 with a searchlight), **TBM-3P** (torpedo bomber – reconnaissance plane, some converted from TBM-3 1945, serv. 1945-10.1954, TBM-3 with photo camera), **TBM-3R** (some converted from TBM-3 1945, serv. 1945-10.1954, unarmed cargo plane, 7 passengers).
Post-war modifications, all were conversions of previously built planes: auxiliaries TBF-1J, TBM-1J and TBM-3J (1947), all-weather torpedo bomber TBM-3N (1946), ECM plane TBM-3Q (1946), ASW planes TBM-3S (1948) and TBM-3S2 (1950), auxiliary TBM-3U (1950) and submarine searchers TBM-3W (1948) and TBM-3W2 (1950).

Douglas BTD Destroyer (28, 1944-1945)

BTD-1: 13.72 x 11.76 x 5.05 m, 34.7 m², 5244 / 8618 kg, 1 Wright R-3350-14, 2300 hp, 554 km/h, 2382 (465) km, 7195 m, 1 seat; 2 x 20-mm guns, 1 torpedo or 1451 kg bombs
BTD-1 (torpedo bomber, 28 built 6.1944-10.1945, serv. 6.1944-10.1945)

Vought / Consolidated TBY Sea Wolf (180, 1944-1945)

TBY-2: 17.35 x 12.47 x 4.72 m, 8386 kg, 1 Pratt & Whitney R-2800-20, 2000 hp, 492 km/h, 2414 (346) km, 8290 m, 3 seats; 4 x 12.7-mm and 1 x 7.6-mm MG, 1 908-kg torpedo or 908 kg bombs or 8 127-mm rockets.
TBY-2 (torpedo bomber, 180 built 11.1944-9.1945, serv. 11.1944-3.1945)

TBY-2 Sea Wolf

Douglas AD Skyraider (ex-BT2D Dauntless II) (3081, 1946-1971)

AD-2: 15.47 x 11.84 x 4.75 m, 37.2 m², 8308 kg, 1 Wright R-3350-26W, 2800 hp, 607 km/h, 2567 km, 7350 m, 1 seat; 2 x 20-mm guns, 3629 kg of combat load on 15 points (1633 kg under the fuselage: 1 907-kg bomb or 1 torpedo, 2 x 1361 kg under the plane center: 2 907-kg bombs or 2 298-mm rockets or 2 CBU-28/A, CBU-37/A or M56 mine cassettes, 12 x 113.5 kg under the wing: 12 113.5-kg bombs or 12 127-mm HVAR rockets or 8 227-kg bombs or 6 XM-3 mine cassettes and 4 113.5-kg bombs), naval mines, rocket blocks, bomb cassettes, 7.6-mm sixtuple Minigun MG in containers, sixtuple 20-mm Vulcan guns were available, later up to 4767 kg of combat load
First BT2D took off in May 1945. Postwar modifications: attackers AD-1 (242 built 1946-1947), AD-2 (156 built 1947-1948), AD-3 (125 built 1948-1949), AD-4 (372 built 1949-1952), AD-4B (165 built + 28 converted from AD-4 1952-1953), AD-4L (63 converted from AD-4 1950-

AD-2 Skyraider

1952), AD-4NA (100 converted from AD-4N in 1950s), AD-5 (212 built 1951-1956), AD-6 (713 built 1953-1956), AD-7 (72 built 1956-1957), night attackers AD-3N (15 built 1948-1949), AD-4N (307 built 1950-1953), AD-4NL (37 converted from AD-4N in 1950s), AD-5N (218 built 1952-1956), ECM planes AD-1Q (35 built in 1947), AD-2Q (21 built 1947-1948), AD-3Q (23 built 1948-1949), AD-4Q (39 built 1949-1950), AD-5Q (54 converted from AD-5N in 1950s), AEW planes AD-3W (31 built 1948-1949), AD-4W (118 built 1950-1953 + 50 for FAA), AD-5W (217 built 1953-1956)

Martin AM Mauler (ex-BTM-1)(139, 1948-1953)

AM-1: 15.27 x 12.57 x 3.61 m, 46.1 m², 6855 / 11350 kg, 1 Pratt & Whitney R-4360-4W, 3000 hp, 557 km/h, 2452 (304) km, 9.4 m/s, 7812 m, 1 seat; 4 x 20-mm guns, up to 4086 kg of combat load on 14 wing points: 3 907-kg bombs and/or 3 227-kg bombs and/or 12 114-kg bombs and/or 2 298-mm Tiny Tim rockets and/or 12 127-mm HVAR rockets and/or 3 Mk13 torpedoes and/or 3 454-kg mines and/or 3 907-kg mines and/or 3 159-kg depth charges
First take off in 1944. In 1948-1949 121 AM-1 attackers

AM-1 Mauler

and 18 AM-1Q ECM planes were built.

Observation and reconnaissance planes

Curtiss O2C (30, 1934-1938)

O2C-1: 9.75 x 7.82 x 3.12 m, 28.6 m², 1140 / 1716 kg, 1 Pratt & Whitney R-1340-88, 450 hp, 237 km/h, 730 (215) km, 5300 m, 2 seats; 3 or 4 x 7.6-mm Browning MG, 227 kg bombs
O2C-1 (dive bomber, 30 built 1934, serv. 1934-7.1938)

O2C-1

O3U-6

Vought O3U and SU (309, 1930-1938)

SU-1: 10.97 x 8.37 x 3.45 m, 31,3 m², 1502 / 2161 kg. 1 Pratt & Whitney R-1690-42, 600 hp, 269 km/h, 1094 km, 5670 m, 2 seats; 3 x 7.6-mm Browning MG.
O3U-1 (observation plane, 87 built 1930-1931, mostly on floats, serv. 1930-1938, 425-hp Pratt & Whitney R-1340-C engine), **O3U-2 / SU-1** (observation/ reconnaissance plane, 29 built 1931-1932, serv. 1931-1938, 600-hp Pratt & Whitney R-1690-42 engine), **O3U-3** (observation plane, 76 built 1932-1933, mostly on floats, serv. 1932-1938, 550-hp R-1340/12 engine), **O3U-4 / SU-2** (observation/reconnaissance plane, 45 built 1933-1934, serv. 1933-1938, 600-hp R-1690-42 engine), **O3U-4 / SU-3** (observation/reconnaissance plane, 20 built 1934-1935, serv. 1934-1938), **O3U-6** (observation plane, 32 built 7.1935-1.1937, mostly on floats, serv. 1935-1938, 550-hp R-1340-12 or R-1340-18 engine, closed cabin), **SU-4** (reconnaissance plane, 20 built 7.1935-1.1937, serv. 7.1935-1938, 600-hp R-1690-42 engine)

Curtiss SOC / Navy SON Seagull (159, 1941-1944)

SOC-3A: 10.97 x 8.08 x 4.50 m, 31.8 m², 1718 / 2466 kg, 1 Pratt & Whitney R-1340-22, 600 hp, 266 km/h, 1086 (214) km, 4540 m, 2 seats; 2 x 7.6-mm MG, 295 kg bombs or 2 x 147-kg DCs.
SOC-2A (reconnaissance / observation plane, 40 converted from SOC-2 1941-1942, serv. 1941-1944), **SOC-3A** (reconnaissance / observation plane, 83 converted from SOC-3 1942, serv. 1942-1944), **SON-1** (reconnaissance / observation plane, 36 converted from SON-1 1942, serv. 1942-1944, wheel/float chassis)

SOC-3 Seagull

Piper NE Grasshopper (256, 1942-1945)

NE-1: 10.67 x 6.71 x 2.01 m, 16.6 m², 332 / 555 kg, 1 Continental O-170-3, 65 hp, 137 km/h, 306 km, 1.8 m/s, 2835 m, 2 seats.
NE-1 (observation plane, 230 built 11.1942-1945, serv. 11.1942-9.1945), **NE-2** (observation plane, 26 built 1945-9.1945, serv. 1945-9.1945)

Piper J-3

Stinson OY Voyager (458, 1944-1945)

OY-1: 10.36 x 7.34 x 2.41 m, 14.5 m², 703 / 916 kg, 1 Lycoming O-431-1, 185 hp, 209 km/h, 676 km, 4.0 m/s, 4815 m, 2 seats.
OY-1 (observation plane, 428 built 1.1944-8.1945, serv. 1.1944-9.1945), **OY-2** (observation plane, 30 built 1945-8.1945, serv. 1945-9.1945, as OY-1)

OY-1

Amphibians

Grumman JF / J2F Duck (627, 1935-1945)

J2F-6: 11.89 x 10.36 x 4.24 m, 38.0 m², 1996 / 3493 kg, 1 Wright R-1820-54, 900 hp, 306 km/h, 1207 (249) km, 7620 m, 2-3 seats; 1 x 7.6-mm Browning MG, 300 kg bombs or 2 x 147-kg DCs.
JF-1 (reconnaissance / rescue amphibian, 27 built 1935-1936, serv. 1935-~1942, 700-hp Pratt & Whitney R-1830 engine, unarmed), **JF-2** (reconnaissance / observation flying boat, 15 built 1936, serv. 1936-~1942, 750-hp Wright R-1820-20 engine), **J2F-1** (reconnaissance / rescue amphibian, 29 built 4.-late 1936, serv. 4.1936-1945, 750-hp Wright R-1820-20 engine), **J2F-2** (reconnaissance / rescue amphibian, 30 built 1936-1937, serv. 1936-1945, 750-hp R-1820-30 engine, 2 x 7.6 MG, 90 kg bombs), **J2F-3** (reconnaissance / rescue amphibian, 20 built 1937-1938, serv. 1937-1945, 750-hp

J2F-1 Duck

R-1820-36, unarmed), **J2F-4** (reconnaissance / rescue amphibian, 32 built 1938-1940, serv. 1938-1945, 750-hp R-1820-30 engine), **J2F-5** (reconnaissance / rescue amphibian, 144 built 1940-1945, serv. 1940-1945, 850-hp R-1820-50 engine, 1 x 7.6 MG, 300 kg bombs), **J2F-6** (reconnaissance / rescue amphibian, 330 built 1940-1945, 900-hp R-1820-54 engine).

Seaplanes and flying boats

Loening OL (94, 1926-1938)

OL-8: 13.72 x 10.59 x 3.89 m, 46.8 m², 1655 / 2451 kg, 1 Pratt & Whitney R-1340-4, 450 hp, 196 km/h, 1006 (170) km, 4360 m, 2 seats; 1 x 7.6-mm MG.
OL-6 (observation flying boat, 28 built 2.1926-1928, serv. 2.1926-3.1938, 3 seats, 440-hp Packard 1A-1500 engine), **OL-8** (observation flying boat, 20 built 1928-1930, serv. 1928-3.1938, 2 seats, 450-hp Pratt & Whitney R-1340-4 engine), **OL-8A** (observation amphibian, 20 built 1928-1930, serv. 1928-3.1938, OL-8 with carrier

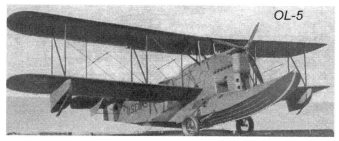

OL-5

arresting gear), **OL-9** (observation seaplane, 26 built 1930-7.1932, serv. 1930-3.1938, as OL-8).

Vought O3U (195, 1930-1942)

O3U-6: 10.97 x 8.37 x 3.45 m, 31.3 m², 1500 / 2161 kg, 1 Pratt & Whitney R-1340-12, 550 hp, 269 km/h, 1094 km, 5670 m, 2 seats; 3 x 7.6-mm MG.
O3U-1 (observation seaplane, partly wheeled, 87 built 7.1930-1932, serv. 7.1930-3.1942, 425-hp Pratt & Whitney R-1340-C engine), **O3U-3** (observation seaplane, partly wheeled, 76 built 1932-1934, serv. 1932-7.1942, 550-hp R-1340-12 engine), **O3U-6** (observation seaplane, partly wheeled, 32 built 1934-7.1935, serv.

O3U-1

1934-3.1942, 550-hp R-1340-12 or R-1340-18 engine)

Curtiss SOC / Navy SON Seagull (262, 1935-1946)

SOC-3: 10.97 x 8.08 x 4.50 m, 31.8 m², 1718 / 2466 kg, 1 Pratt & Whitney R-1340-22, 600 hp, 266 km/h, 1086 (214) km, 4540 m, 2 seats; 2 x 7.6-mm MG, 295 kg bombs or 2 147-kg DC.
SOC-1 (observation seaplane, 135 built 11.1935-1937, serv. 11.1935-11.1946, 600-hp Pratt & Whitney R-1340-18 engine), **SOC-3** (observation seaplane, 83 built 1937-8.1939, serv. 1937-11.1946, 600-hp Pratt &

SOC-4 Seagull

Whitney R-1340-22 engine, interchangeable wheels/ floats), **SON-1** (observation seaplane, 44 built 1937-

OS2U-2 Kingfisher

SO3C-1 Seamew

SC-1 Seahawk

8.1939, serv. 1937-11.1946, as SOC-3)

Vought OS2U / Navy OS2N Kingfisher (1518, 1940-1946)

OS2U-3: 10.96 x 10.27 x 4.60 m, 24.4 m², 1514 / 2260 kg, 1 Pratt & Whitney R-985-AN-2, 450 hp, 260 km/h, 1390 (191) km, 4.8 m/s, 5550 m, 2 seats; 2 x 7.6-mm MG, 295 kg bombs or 2 147-kg DC.
OS2U-1 (observation seaplane, 54 built 8.1940-1.1941, serv. 8.1940-5.1946, 450-hp Pratt & Whitney R-985-48 engine), **OS2U-2** (observation seaplane, 158 built 1-5.1941, serv. 1.1941-5.1946, 450-hp R-985-50 engine), **OS2U-3** (observation plane, 1006 built 5.1941-11.1942, serv. 5.1941-5.1946, 450-hp R-985-AN-2 engine), **OS2N-1** (observation plane, 300 built 5.1941-11.1942, serv. 5.1941-5.1946, 450-hp R-985-AN-2 or R-985-AN-8 engine)

Curtiss SO3C Seamew (545, 1942-1944)

SO3C-2: 11.56 x 10.60 x 4.32 m, 27.3 m², 2266 / 3175 kg, 1 Ranger V-770-8, 600 hp, 241 km/h, 1480 (188) km, 3.7 m/s, 5050 m, 2 seats; 2 x 7.6-mm MG, 90 kg bombs)
SO3C-1 (observation seaplane, 300 built 7.1942-1943, ser. 7.1942-3.1944, 520-hp Ranger V-770-6 engine, 2 x 7.6-mm MG, 90 kg bombs), **SO3C-2** (observation seaplane, 206 built 1943-late 1943, serv. 1943-3.1944, 600-hp Ranger V-770-8 engine), **SO3C-3** (observation seaplane, 39 built late 1943-1.1944, serv. late 1943-3.1944, lightened SO3C-2)

Curtiss SC Seahawk (576, 1944-1949)

SC-1: 12.50 x 11.09 x 5.49 m, 25.0 m², 2867 / 4082 kg, 1 Wright R-1820-62, 1350 hp, 500 km/h, 1000 (201) km, 12.7 m/s, 9000 m, 1 seat; 2 x 12.7-mm MG, 320 kg bombs
SC-1 (reconnaissance seaplane, 566 built 10.1944-9.1945, serv. 10.1944-10.1949, 1 seat, 1350-hp Wright R-1820-62 engine), **SC-2** (reconnaissance seaplane, 10 built 8-9.1945, serv. 8.1945-10.1949, 2 seats, 1426-hp R-1820-76 engine)

Helicopters

Sikorsky HNS Hoverfly (68, 1943-1947)

HNS-1: 11.60 x 14.65 x 3.78 m, 105.3 m², 913 / 1153 kg,
1 Warner R-550-3, 200 hp, 120 km/h, 209 km, 3.3 m/s.
2440 m, 2 seats.
HNS-1 (utility, 68 built 11.1943-12.1944, serv. 11.1943-
12.1947)

HNS-1 Hoverfly

Sikorsky HOS Hoverfly (105, 1944-1948)

HOS-1: 9.75 x 11.65 x 3.53 m, 74.7 m², 786 / 1352 kg, 1
Franklin O-405-9, 240 hp, 154 km/h, 481 (111) km, 4020
m, 1 seat; 1 passenger or 294 kg bombs (2 147-kg DC)
HOS-1 (utility, 105 built 10.1944-1.1946, serv. 10.1944-
1.1948)

HOS-1 Hoverfly

NAVAL WEAPONS

Guns

Machine guns

Caliber, mm	Bore Length, cal	No of bores	Type of mount	Guns used	Year	Ships used on	Maximal elevation angle, °	Shell mass, kg	Initial Velocity, m/s	Rate of fire of one bore, rounds per min	Fire range / AA ceiling, km
7.6	87.0	1	Lewis MG	0.30" Lewis MG	1917	many	80	0.010	823	400 - 500	1.8 / 1.2
7.6	80.0	1	Browning M1919A4	0.30" Browning M1919A4 MG	1918	many	80	0.010	853	400 - 500	1.8 / 1.2
7.6	80.0	1	Marlin MG	0.30" Marlin MG	1918	few	80	0.010	823	400 - 500	1.8 / 1.2
12.7	90.0	1	Mk 3	0.50" Browning M2 MG	1930	many	80	0.049	893	450 - 600	2.4 / 1.5
12.7	90.0	4	Mk 31	0.50" Browning M2 MG	1945	CV, CVE	80	0.049	860	550	2.0 / 1.3

| 12.7 | 72.0 | 2 | Dewandre turret | 0.50" Browning M2 MG | 1940 | PT | 80 | 0.049 | 866 | 750 - 850 | 2.0 / 1.3 |

Automatic guns

Caliber, mm	Bore Length, cal	No of bores	Type of mount	Guns used	Year	Ships used on	Maximal Elevation angle, °	Shell mass, kg	Initial Velocity, m/s	Rate of fire of one bore, rounds per min	Fire range / AA ceiling, km
20.0	70.0	1	Mk 1	20 mm/70 Oerlikon Mk 1	1940	few	87	0.123	844	250 - 320	4.4 / 3.0
20.0	70.0	1	Mk 2	20 mm/70 Oerlikon Mk 2, 3, 4	1941	many	87	0.123	844	450	4.4 / 3.0
20.0	70.0	1	Mk 4	20 mm/70 Oerlikon Mk 2, 3, 4	1942	many	87	0.123	844	450	4.4 / 3.0
20.0	70.0	1	Mk 5	20 mm/70 Oerlikon Mk 2, 3, 4	1942	many	87	0.123	844	450	4.4 / 3.0
20.0	70.0	1	Mk 6	20 mm/70 Oerlikon Mk 2, 3, 4	1942	many	90	0.123	844	450	4.4 / 3.0
20.0	70.0	1	Mk 10	20 mm/70 Oerlikon Mk 2, 3, 4	1943	many	90	0.123	844	450	4.4 / 3.0
20.0	70.0	1	Mk 12	20 mm/70 Oerlikon Mk 2, 3, 4	1943	many	90	0.123	844	450	4.4 / 3.0
20.0	70.0	1	Mk 14	20 mm/70 Oerlikon Mk 2, 3, 4	1943	many	90	0.123	844	450	4.4 / 3.0
20.0	70.0	4	Mk 15	20 mm/70 Oerlikon Mk 2, 3, 4	1943	CV, PT, BB	90	0.123	844	450	4.4 / 3.0
20.0	70.0	1	Mk 16	20 mm/70 Oerlikon Mk 2, 3, 4	1943	many	90	0.123	844	450	4.4 / 3.0
20.0	70.0	2	Mk 20	20 mm/70 Oerlikon Mk 2, 3, 4	1944	many	90	0.123	844	450	4.4 / 3.0
20.0	56.0	4	Mk 22	20 mm/56 T31	1944	few	90	0.123	844	450	4.4 / 3.0
20.0	70.0	2	Mk 24	20 mm/70 Oerlikon Mk 2, 3, 4	1944	many	90	0.123	844	450	4.4 / 3.0
20.0	56.0	2	Mk 25	20 mm/56 T31	1945	few	90	0.123	844	450	4.4 / 3.0
20.0	56.0	4	Mk 26	20 mm/56 T31	1946	few	90	0.123	844	450	4.4 / 3.0
27.9	74.6	4	Mk 2	1.1" Mk 1	1936	DD - BB	110	0.416	823	150	6.8 / 5.8
37.0	42.5	1	Mk 6?	1-pdr Maxim-Nordenfelt MG Mk 6	1897	many, later AA		0.480	610	75	3.2

Caliber, mm	Bore length, cal	No Of bores	Type of mount	Guns used	Year	Ships used on	Maximal elevation angle, °	Shell mass, kg	Initial Velocity, m/s	Rate of fire of one bore, rounds per min	Fire range / AA ceiling, km
37.0	30.0	1	Mk 7?	1-pdr Maxim-Nordenfelt MG Mk 7	1900	many, later AA		0.480	610	75	3.2
37.0	30.0	1	Mk 9?	1-pdr Maxim-Nordenfelt Mk 9		few		0.480	457	75	3.2
37.0	42.5	1	Mk 14?	1-pdr Baldwin Mk 14	1917	few		0.480	610	75	3.2
37.0	42.5	1	Mk 15?	1-pdr Baldwin Mk 15	1918	few		0.480	914	75	3.2
37.0	56.0	1	Mk 16	1-pdr Mk 16	1937?	few landing ships	90	0.567	914	120	7.0 / 5.7
37.0	61.0	1	Mk 14	1-pdr M4 fighter-gun	1944	PT		0.610	609	150	
37.0	71.0	1	Mk 1	1-pdr M9 fighter-gun	1944	PT		0.610	885	125	8.1
40.0	56.3	2	Mk 1	40 mm/56 Bofors Mk 1,2	1942	many	90	0.900	881	120	10.1 / 7.0
40.0	56.3	4	Mk 2	40 mm/56 Bofors Mk 1, 2	1943	DE - BB	90	0.900	881	120	10.1 / 7.0
40.0	56.3	1	Mk 3	40 mm/56 Bofors Mk 1, 2, M1	1944	many	90	0.900	881	120	10.1 / 7.0
40.0	56.3	4	Mk 4	40 mm/56 Bofors Mk 1, 2	1945	few	90	0.900	881	120	10.1 / 7.0

Light caliber guns

Caliber, mm	Bore length, cal	No Of bores	Type of mount	Guns used	Year	Ships used on	Maximal elevation angle, °	Shell mass, kg	Initial Velocity, m/s	Rate of fire of one bore, rounds per min	Fire range / AA ceiling, km
37.0	50.0	1	Mk 2?	1-pdr Driggs-Schroeder Mk 2		many		0.480	610	25	3.2
37.0	40.0	1	Mk 2?	1-pdr Driggs-Schroeder Mk 2 mod.1		many		0.480	610	25	3.2
37.0	40.0	1	Mk 3?	1-pdr Hotchkiss Mk 3		many		0.480	610	25	3.2
37.0	50.0	1	Mk 4?	1-pdr Driggs-Schroeder Mk 4		many		0.480	610	25	3.2
37.0	40.0	1	Mk 5?	1-pdr Hotchkiss Mk 5		many		0.480	610	25	3.2
37.0	40.0	1	Mk 8?	1-pdr Hotchkiss Mk 8		many		0.480	610	40	3.2
37.0	40.0	1	Mk 12?	1-pdr Driggs Mk 12		many		0.480	610	40	3.2
37.0	40.0	1	Mk 13?	1-pdr Hotchkiss Mk 13		few		0.480	610	40	3.2
37.0	53.0	1	M4	1-pdr M3 AT-gun	1943	PT	15	0.860	792		0.5
47.0	45.0	1	Mk 2?	3-pdr Driggs-Schroeder Mk 2		many	50	1.50	646	20 - 25	6.0

47.0	45.0	1	Mk 3?	3-pdr Driggs-Schroeder Mk 3		many	50	1.50	646	20 - 25	6.0
47.0	50.0	1	Mk 4?	3-pdr Hotchkiss Mk 4		many	50	1.50	671	40	6.2
47.0	50.0	1	Mk 5?	3-pdr Maxim-Nordenfelt Mk 5	1900	3 guns	50	1.50	671	40	6.2
47.0	45.0	1	Mk 7?	3-pdr Vickers Mk 7		10 guns	50	1.50	646	40	6.0
47.0	40.0	1	Mk 8?	3-pdr Hotchkiss-EOC Mk 8		few	50	1.50	618	20 - 25	5.9
47.0	50.0	1	Mk 9?	3-pdr Nordenfelt Mk 9		many	50	1.50	671	40	6.2
47.0	50.0	1	Mk 10?	3-pdr Hotchkiss Mk 10		many	50	1.50	671	40	6.2
47.0	50.0	1	Mk 11?	3-pdr US RF Gun and Power Mk 11		many	50	1.50	671	20 - 25	6.2
47.0	50.0	1	Mk 14?	3-pdr Driggs-Seabury Mk 14		few	50	1.50	671	40	6.2
57.0	45.0	1	Mk 6?	6-pdr Driggs-Schroeder Mk 6		many	60	2.74	683	20	7.3
57.0	45.0	1	Mk 7?	6-pdr Hotchkiss Mk 7		many	60	2.74	683	20	7.3
57.0	50.0	1	Mk 8?	6-pdr Driggs-Schroeder Mk 8		many	60	2.74	702	20	7.3
57.0	42.3	1	Mk 9	6-pdr Maxim-Nordenfelt Mk 9		many	70	2.74	683	35	8.0 / 3.1
57.0	42.3	1	Mk 10?	6-pdr Nordenfelt Mk 10		many	60	2.74	683	20	7.3
57.0	50.0	1	Mk 11?	6-pdr Driggs-Seabury Mk 11		many	60	2.74	702	20	7.3
57.0	32.0	1	Mk 12?	6-pdr Davis non-recoil Mk 12		few	38	2.74		20	
57.0	33.0	1	Mk 13?	6-pdr Davis non-recoil Mk 13		few	38	4.00		20	
60.0	12.0	1	M19	60mm M19 mortar	1941	many	85	1.36			1.8
76.2	50.1	1	Mk 2	3``/50 Mk 2, 3	1900	many	15	5.90	823	8 - 9	7.0
76.2	50.1	1	Mk 2	3``/50 Mk 5, 6, 8		many	15	5.90	823	15 - 20	7.0
76.2	50.1	1	Mk 4	3``/50 Mk 2, 3		many	15	5.90	823	8 - 9	7.0
76.2	50.1	1	Mk 4	3``/50 Mk 5, 6, 8		many	15	5.90	823	15 - 20	7.0
76.2	50.1	1	Mk 5	3``/50 Mk 2, 3		many	15	5.90	823	8 - 9	7.0
76.2	50.1	1	Mk 5	3``/50 Mk 5, 6, 8		many	15	5.90	823	15 - 20	7.0
76.2	50.1	1	Mk 7	3``/50 Mk 2, 3		many	15	5.90	823	8 - 9	7.0
76.2	50.1	1	Mk 7	3``/50 Mk 5, 6, 8		many	15	5.90	823	15 - 20	7.0
76.2	23.5	1	Mk 9	3``/23.5 Mk 4, 14	1900	many	75	5.90	503	8 - 9	8.1 / 5.5
76.2	23.0	1	Mk 9	3``/23 Mk 9, 13	1916	SS, YP	75	5.90	503	8 - 9	8.1 / 5.5
76.2	50.1	1	Mk 11	3``/50 Mk 5, 6, 8, 10, 17, 18	1916	many	85	5.90	823	15 - 20	13.4 / 9.3
76.2	23.5	1	Mk 13	3``/23.5 Mk 4, 14		many	75	5.90	503	8 - 9	9.2 / 5.5
76.2	23.0	1	Mk 13	3``/23 Mk 9, 13		SS, YP	75	5.90	503	8 - 9	9.2 / 5.5
76.2	23.5	1	Mk 14	3``/23.5 Mk 4, 14		many	75	5.90	503	8 - 9	9.2 / 5.5
76.2	23.0	1	Mk 14	3``/23 Mk 9, 13		SS, YP	75	5.90	503	8 - 9	9.2 / 5.5

Caliber, mm	Bore Length, cal	No of bores	Type of mount	Guns used	Year	Ships used on	Maximal elevation angle, °	Shell mass, kg	Initial velocity, m/s	Rate of fire of one bore, rounds per min	Fire range / AA ceiling, km
76.2	50.1	1	Mk 18	3``/50 Mk 18, 19	1919	SS	40	5.90	823	15 - 20	13.4
76.2	50.1	1	Mk 20	3``/50 Mk 20		many	85	5.90	823	15 - 20	13.4 / 9.3
76.2	50.1	1	Mk 21	3``/50 Mk 21		SS	85	5.90	823	15 - 20	13.4 / 9.3
76.2	50.1	1	Mk 22	3``/50 Mk 21, 22	1944	many	85	5.90	823	15 - 20	13.4 / 9.3
76.2	50.1	1	Mk 24	3``/50 Mk 21, 22		many	85	5.90	823	15 - 20	13.4 / 9.3
76.2	50.1	1	Mk 26	3``/50 Mk 22	1948	many	85	5.90	823	15 - 20	13.4 / 9.3
76.2	50.1	2	Mk 27	3``/50 Mk 22	1948	many	85	5.90	823	45 - 50	13.4 / 9.3
76.2	50.1	2	Mk 33	3``/50 Mk 22		many	85	5.90	823	45 - 50	13.4 / 9.3
76.2	50.1	1	Mk 34	3``/50 Mk 22		many	85	5.90	823	45 - 50	13.4 / 9.3
76.2	70.0	2	RF Mk 37	3``/70 Mk 26	1949	DDE, DL, CLC	90	6.80	1036	90 - 100	17.8 / 11.6
101.6	40.0	1	Mk 4	4``/40 Mk 1, 3, 4, 5, 6	1897	CL, PG	20	15.0	610	8 - 9	10.5
101.6	40.0	1	Mk 7	4``/40 Mk 1, 3, 4, 5, 6		CL, PG	20	15.0	610	8 - 9	10.5
101.6	40.0	1	Mk 9	4``/40 Mk 1, 3, 4, 5, 6		CL, PG	20	15.0	610	8 - 9	10.5
101.6	50.0	1	Mk 12	4``/50 Mk 9	1914	DD, SS, PG, PE	20	15.0	884	8 - 9	14.6
101.6	50.0	2	Mk 14	4``/50 Mk 9	1919	DD	20	15.0	884	8 - 9	14.6

Medium caliber guns

Caliber, mm	Bore Length, cal	No of bores	Type of mount	Guns used	Year	Ships used on	Maximal elevation angle, °	Shell mass, kg	Initial velocity, m/s	Rate of fire of one bore, rounds per min	Fire range / AA ceiling, km
106.7	9.5	1	Chemical mortar	4.2`` chemical mortar	1942	LFR	59	14.5			4.0
127.0	49.6	1	Mk 12	5``/50 Mk 5, 6		BB, CA	25	22.7	914	6 – 8	17.4
127.0	50.6	1	Mk 13	5``/51 Mk 7, 8, 15	1911	BB, CV, DD	15	22.7	960	8 - 9	14.6
127.0	50.6	1	Mk 15	5``/51 Mk 7, 8, 15		BB, CV, DD	20	22.7	960	8 - 9	15.5
127.0	25.0	1	Mk 17	5``/25 Mk 10, 11, 13	1926	BB, CA, CL	85	24.4	670	15 - 20	13.3 / 8.4
127.0	51.0	1	Mk 18	5``/51 Mk 9	1924	SS	25	22.7	960	8 - 9	17.2
127.0	25.0	1	Mk 19	5``/25 Mk 10, 11, 13		BB, CA, CL	85	24.4	670	15 - 20	13.3 / 8.4
127.0	38.0	1	Mk 21	5``/38 Mk 12	1934	DD, CV, CA	85	24.5	792	12 - 15	16.1 / 11.9

Caliber, mm	Bore Length, cal	No of bores	Type of mount	Guns used	Year	Ships used on	Maximal elevation angle, °	Shell mass, kg	Initial velocity, m/s	Rate of fire of one bore, rounds per min	Fire range / AA ceiling, km
127.0	38.0	2	Mk 22	5``/38 Mk 12		DD	35	24.5	792	15 - 22	15.6
127.0	25.0	1	Mk 23	5``/25 Mk 10, 11, 13		BB, CA, CL	85	24.4	670	15 - 20	13.3 / 8.4
127.0	38.0	1	Mk 24	5``/38 Mk 12		CV, CA, DD	85	24.5	792	12 - 15	16.1 / 11.9
127.0	38.0	1	Mk 25	5``/38 Mk 12		DD	85	24.5	792	15 - 22	16.1 / 11.9
127.0	25.0	1	Mk 27	5``/25 Mk 10, 11, 13		BB, CA, CL	85	24.4	670	15 - 20	13.3 / 8.4
127.0	38.0	2	Mk 28	5``/38 Mk 12		BB	85	24.5	792	15 - 22	16.1 / 11.9
127.0	38.0	2	Mk 29	5``/38 Mk 12		CL	85	24.5	792	15 - 22	16.1 / 11.9
127.0	38.0	1	Mk 30	5``/38 Mk 12		CA, DD, DE	85	24.5	792	15 - 22	16.1 / 11.9
127.0	38.0	1	Mk 30	5``/38 Mk 12		CVE	27	24.5	792	15 - 22	14.5
127.0	38.0	2	Mk 32	5``/38 Mk 12		CV, CB, CA, CL	85	24.5	792	15 - 22	16.1 / 11.9
127.0	38.0	2	Mk 38	5``/38 Mk 12		DD	85	24.5	792	15 - 22	16.1 / 11.9
127.0	54.0	1	Mk 39	5``/54 Mk 16	1945	CV	85	31.8	808	15 - 18	23.7 / 15.7
127.0	25.0	1	Mk 40	5``/25 Mk 17		SS	40	24.4	670	15 - 20	13.0

Heavy caliber guns

Caliber, mm	Bore Length, cal	No of bores	Type of mount	Guns used	Year	Ships used on	Maximal elevation angle, °	Shell mass, kg	Initial velocity, m/s	Rate of fire of one bore, rounds per min	Fire range / AA ceiling, km
152.4	52.6	1	Mk 13	6``/53 Mk 12, 14, 18	1923	CL	20	47.6	914	6 - 7	19.3
152.4	52.6	1	Mk 15	6``/53 Mk 12	1928	SS	25	47.6	914	6 - 7	21.3
152.4	52.6	2	Mk 16	6``/53 Mk 12, 14, 18	1923	CL	30	47.6	914	6 - 7	23.1
152.4	47.0	3	Mk 17?	6``/47 Mk 16	1938	CL	40 / 60	47.6 / 59.0	853 / 762	8 - 10 / 8 - 10	21.5 / 23.9
152.4	47.0	2	Mk 17 DP?	6``/47DP Mk 16	1948	CL	78	47.6 / 59.0	762 / 853	12 / 12	21.5 / 14.6 / 23.9
152.4	46.6	1	Mk 18?	6``/47 Mk 17	1936	PG	20	47.6	853	5 - 8	18.1
203.2	45.0	2	Mk 12	8``/45 Mk 6	1906	BB, CA	20	118	838	1 - 2	20.6
203.2	54.7	2	Mk 13?	8``/55 Mk 9, 11, 13, 14	1927	CV, CA	41	118	853	3 - 4	29.1
203.2	54.7	3	Mk 14?	8``/55 Mk 9, 11, 13, 14	1929	CA	41	118	853	3 - 4	29.1
203.2	54.7	3	Mk 15?	8``/55 Mk 9, 11, 12, 13, 14	1934	CA	41	118	853	3 - 4	29.1

203.2	54.7	3	Mk 16?	8``/55 Mk 12, 15	1939	CA	41	152	762	4	27.5
								118	823	4	27.3
203.2	55.0	3	Mk 17?	8``/55RF Mk 16	1948	CA	41	152	762	10	27.5
								118	823	10	27.3
304.8	49.1	2	Mk 9	12``/50 Mk 7	1912	BB	15	395	884	2 - 3	22.0
304.8	49.7	3	Mk 10?	12``/50 Mk 8	1944	BC	45	517	762	2.4 - 3	35.3
355.6	45.0	2	Mk 1?	14``/45 Mk 1, 2, 3, 5	1914	BB	15	635	792	1.25 - 1.75	21.0
355.6	45.0	3	Mk 2?	14``/45 Mk 1, 2, 3, 5	1916	BB	15	635	792	1.25 - 1.75	21.0
355.6	50.0	3	Mk 3?	14``/45 Mk 4, 6	1917	BB	15	635	853	1.75	22.0
355.6	50.0	3	Mk 4?	14``/45 Mk 4, 6	1920	BB	30	635	853	1.75	33.0
355.6	44.6	2	Mk 5?	14``/45 Mk 8, 9, 10, 12	1929	BB	30	680	792	1.25 - 1.75	31.4
355.6	44.6	3	Mk 6?	14``/45 Mk 8, 9, 10, 12	1929	BB	30	680	792	1.25 - 1.75	31.4
355.6	49.7	3	Mk 7?	14``/50 Mk 7, 11	1932	BB	30	680	823	1.75	33.7
406.4	44.7	2	Mk 1?	16``/45 Mk 1	1921	BB	30	957	792	1.5	31.4
406.4	49.7	2	Mk 2?	16``/50 Mk 2, 3	---	BB	46	1016	808	2	41.2
406.4	44.7	2	Mk 4?	16``/45 Mk 5, 8	1938	BB	30	1016	768	1.5	32.0
406.4	44.7	3	Mk 5?	16``/45 Mk 6	1941	BB	45	1225	701	2	33.7
406.4	49.7	3	Mk 6?	16``/50 Mk 7	1943	BB	50	1225	762	2	38.7

Surface-to-surface rockets

Surface-to-surface rockets

System	Year	Rocket	Rocket diameter, m	Warhead mass, kg	Shooting range, km	No of rails on launcher	No of rockets in a salvo
Mk 1	1942	4.5"	0.114	2.95	1.0	12	12
Mk 7	1943	4.5"	0.114	2.95	1.0	1	12 every 4 sec
Mk 8	1943	4.5"	0.114	2.95	1.0	12	12
Mk 24	1944	7.2" "Woofus"	0.183		0.26 or 0.42	120	120
Mk 30	1944	5" fin-stabilised	0.127			6	6
Mk 31	1944	5" fin-stabilised	0.127			4	4
Mk 32	1944	5" fin-stabilised	0.127			2	2
Mk 36	1944	5" fin-stabilised	0.127			4	4
Mk 50	1944	5" spin-stabilised	0.127		9.1	8	8
Mk 51	1944	5" spin-stabilised	0.127		4.6	1	12 every 4 sec
Mk 11	1945	4.5"	0.114	2.95	1.0	1	1

Torpedoes

Caliber, mm	Type	Year	Ships used on	Full mass, kg	Length, m	Explosive charge	Explosive mass, kg	Fire range, km	Speed, kts	Heading system	Max depth, m
450	18`` Mk 7	1912	K, O, R classes submarines	738	5.18	TNT	148	5.5	35	---	---
533	21`` Mk 8	1914	destroyers, PT boats	1383	6.51	TNT	211	14.6	26	---	---
533	21`` Mk 9	1915	battleships, S class submarines	914	5.00	TNT	95	6.4	27	---	---
533	21`` Mk 10	1918	S class submarines	1005	4.95	TNT	225	3.2	36	---	---
533	21`` Mk 11	1926	cruisers, destroyers	1593	6.88	TNT	227	5.5 9.2 13.7	46 34 27	---	---
533	21`` Mk 12	1930	cruisers, destroyers	1590	6.88	TNT	227	6.4 9.2 13.7	44 34 27	---	---
533	21`` Mk 14	1931	submarines	1488	6.25	torpex	292	4.1 8.2	46 31	---	---
533	21`` Mk 15	1935	cruisers, destroyers	1742	7.32	torpex	374	5.5 9.2 13.7	45 33.5 26.5	---	---
533	21`` Mk 23	1943	submarines	1488	6.25	torpex	292	4.1	46	---	---
569	22.4`` Mk 13	1944	PT boats	1005	4.09	torpex	262	5.8	33.5	---	---
533	21`` Mk 18	1944	submarines	1431	6.22	torpex	261	3.7	29	---	---
483	19`` Mk 27	1944	submarines	327	2.29	torpex	95	4.6	12	passive sonar	150
533	21`` Mk 16	1945	submarines	1814	6.25	torpex	428	12.5	46	---	---
533	21`` Mk 17	1945	destroyers	2087	7.32	torpex	399	16.5	46	---	---
569	22.4`` Mk 25	1945	PT boats	1046	4.09	torpex	329	2.3	40	---	---
533	21`` Mk 28	1945	submarines	1270	6.25	torpex	265	3.7	19.6	passive sonar	---
483	19`` Mk 32	1945	surface ships (ASW)	318	2.11	torpex	49	8.8	12	active sonar	120

Anti-submarine weapons

Depth charges

Type	Year	Mass, kg	Type and mass of explosive, kg	Sinking speed, m/s	Maximal depth setting, m	Type of piston
Mark 2	1917	191	TNT - 136	1.8	60	hydrostatic
Mark 3	1917	191	TNT - 136	1.8	90	hydrostatic
Mark 4	1918	338	TNT - 272	1.8	90	hydrostatic
Mark 6	~1939	191	TNT - 136	2.4 later 3.7	90 later 180	hydrostatic
Mark 7	~1939	338	TNT - 272	1.8 later 4	90 later 180	hydrostatic
Mark 8	1943	238	TNT - 122	3.5	150	magnetic
Mark 9	1943	154	torpex - 91	6.9	180 later 300	hydrostatic
Mark 14	1945	154	torpex - 91	7	300	acoustic
Mark 16	1946	197	torpex - 134	9.4	760	magnetic or acoustic

Depth charge racks

Type	Year	Number of DCs	Type of DCs
Mk 1 mod. 0	1918	8 or 13	Mk 2, 3
Mk 2	1919	5	Mk 2, 3
Mk 1 mod. 1	1934	5 / 3	Mk 6 / Mk 7
MK 3		8	Mk 6
Mk 4		4	Mk 6
Mk 5		7	Mk 6
Mk 6		5	Mk 6

Depth charge throwers

Type	Year	Fire range, km	Fire depth, m	Explosive type and mass, kg	DC mass, kg	Number and caliber of bores, mm
Mk 1 (Y-gun)	1917	0.027	90	TNT - 136	191	2 x 241
Mk 2	1918	0.027	90	TNT - 136	191	1 x 152
Mk 5 (Y-gun)	1918	0.027	90	TNT - 136	191	2 x 241
Mk 6 (K-gun)	1941	0.137	90 later 300	TNT – 136 later torpex - 91	191	1 x 241
Mk 7 (Y-gun)	1941	0.027	90	TNT - 136	191	2 x 241
Mk 10 Hedgehog	1942	0.26	180	torpex - 15.9	29.5	24 x 178
Mk 11 Hedgehog	1942	0.24	180	torpex - 15.9	29.5	24 x 178
Mk 20 Mousetrap	1942	0.26	180	torpex - 15.9	29.5	4 x 178
Mk 22 Mousetrap	1942	0.27	180	torpex - 15.9	29.5	8 x 178
Mk 15 Hedgehog	1948	0.24	180	torpex - 15.9	29.5	24 x 178
Mk 108 Weapon Alfa	1949	0.89	300		25	1 x (12 rpm)

Mines

Mines

Type	Year	Type of laying	Type of fuse	Carried on	Targets	Laying depth, m	Full mass, kg	Explosive mass, kg
Mk 1	1908	moored	contact	surface ships	surface ships			
Mk 2	1909	moored	contact	surface ships	surface ships			79
Mk 3	1910	moored	contact	surface ships	surface ships			54

Mk 4	1912	moored	contact	surface ships	surface ships			113
Mk 5	1914	moored	contact	surface ships	surface ships		771	227
drifting Mk 1	1915	drifting	contact + antenna	surface ships	surface ships			
Mk 6	1917	moored	antenna	surface ships	submarines	900	635	136
drifting Mk 2		drifting	magnetic + antenna	surface ships	surface ships			
drifting Mk 3	1923	drifting	antenna	surface ships	surface ships			
drifting Mk 4		drifting	acoustic + antenna	surface ships	surface ships			
drifting Mk 5	1924	drifting	acoustic + antenna	submarine Argonaut	surface ships			
drifting Mk 6	1925	drifting	antenna	surface ships (DCR)	drifting ships		318	164
Mk 10	1925	moored	contact	submarines (TT)	surface ships		798	136
Mk 10 mod. 1		moored	contact	submarines (TT)	surface ships		816 - 870	190
Mk 10 mod. 3		moored	magnetic	submarines (TT)	surface ships, submarines		816 - 870	190
Mk 10 mod. 7		moored	magnetic	PT boats	surface ships, submarines		816 - 870	190
Mk 10 mod. 11		moored	contact	submarine Argonaut	surface ships, submarines		816 - 870	227
Mk 11	1931	moored	antenna	submarine Argonaut	surface ships, submarines		850	227
Mk 12		ground	magnetic	submarines (TT)	surface ships, submarines		655 / 723	499 / 567
Mk 12 mod. 3		ground	magnetic	submarines (TT)	surface ships, submarines		630 / 680	481 / 544
Mk 16		moored	antenna	surface ships	submarines	900	925	272
Mk 16 mod. 2		moored	acoustic	surface ships	submarines	900	925	272
Mk 17		ground	magnetic	submarines (TT)	submarines		828	624
Mk 18		ground	magnetic	surface ships	surface ships, submarines		925	612
drifting Mk 7	1942	drifting	antenna	surface ships	surface ships			237
Mk 20		ground	by wires	surface ships	surface ships		197	136
Mk 27		mobile ground	magnetic	submarines (TT)	surface ships, submarines	could move up to 4.1 nm (10.5 kts)		398
Mk 37		ground	by wires	surface ships	surface ships		335	272

Radars

Radars

Type	Model	Year	Number of manu factured	Purpose	Carried on	Impulse power, kW	Wave length, m	Accu racy, m / °	Detection range, km surface	air
CXAM	CXAM	1940	6	air / surface search	CV, BB, CA, CL	15	1.5	270/3	up to 30	90 - 130
	CXAM-1	1941	14	air / surface search	CV, BB, CA, CL, AV	15	1.5	180/3	up to 30	90 - 130
SC	SC	1941	400	air / surface search	CV, BB, CA, CL, DD	100	1.5/1.36	180/3	up to 19	46 - 56
	SC-1	1942	ex-SC	air / surface search	CV, BB, CA, CL, DD	200	1.5/1.36	90/5	up to 37	92 - 112
	SC-2	1943	415	air / surface search	CV, BB, CA, CL, DD	20	1.5/1.36	90/3	up to 37	74 - 148
	SC-3	1943	200	air / surface search	CV, BB, CA, CL, DD	20	1.5/1.36	90/3	up to 37	74 - 148
	SC-4	1944	250	air / surface search	CV, BB, CA, CL, DD	20	1.5/1.36	90/3	up to 37	74 - 148
	SC-5	1945	100	air / surface search	CV, BB, CA, CL, DD	20	1.5/1.36	90/3	up to 37	74 - 148
SD	SD	1941	60	air search	SS	100	2.65	900/---	---	up to 37
	SDa	1942	ex-SD	air search	SS	100	2.65	900/---	---	up to 37
	SD-1	1942	20	air search	SS	100	2.65	900/---	---	up to 37
	SD-2	1942	60	air search	SS	100	2.65	900/---	---	up to 37
	SD-3	1942	125	air search	PT, later SS	100	2.65	900/---	---	up to 46
	SD-4	1943	104	air search	SS	130	2.65	900/---	---	circa 60
	SD-5	1944	85	air search	SS	130	2.65	900/---	---	circa 60
FA (Mk 1)	FA (Mk 1)	1941	10	surface search / main gun control (Mk34)	BB, CA, CL	40	0.4	180/20	up to 40	---

FC (Mk 3)	FC (Mk 3 Mod 0)	1941	139	main gun control	BB, CA, CL	15 - 20	0.4	36/10	11 - 27	up to 41
	Mk 3 Mod 1			main gun control	BB, CA, CL	15 - 20	0.4	36/10	11 - 27	up to 41
	Mk 3 Mod 2			main gun control	BB, CA, CL	15 - 20	0.4	36/10	11 - 27	up to 41
	Mk 3 Mod 3			main gun control	DD	15 - 20	0.4	36/10	11 - 27	up to 41
FD (Mk 4)	FD (Mk 4)	1941	667	DP gun control	CV, BB, CA, CL, DD (Mk33, Mk37)	15 - 20	0.4	36/10	11 - 27	up to 36
SA	SA	1942	400	air / surface search	CV, CA, CL, DD, FF	100	1.36	90/1	up to 22	56 - 74
	SA-1	1942	75	air / surface search	FF	100	1.65	90/2	up to 15	37 - 46
	SA-2	1943	865	air / surface search	CV, CA, CL, DD, FF	100	1.36	90/1	up to 22	56 - 74
	SA-3	1944	225	air / surface search	CV, CA, CL, DD, FF	100	1.36	90/1	up to 22	56 - 74
SE	SE	1942	few	surface search	DD and small ships	30	0.1	90/1	7 - 22	---
SF	SF	1942	600	surface search/gun control	FF, landing ships, ASW ships, SC	80	0.1	70/2	7 - 22	---
	SF-1	1943	1055	surface search/gun control	FF, landing ships, ASW ships, SC	80	0.1	70/2	7 - 22	---

SG	SG	1942	439	surface search	BB, CV, CA, CL, DD	25	0.1	180/2	up to 22	up to 14
	SGa	1943	ex-SG	surface search	BB, CV, CA, CL, DD	50	0.1	180/2	up to 41	up to 28
	SGb	1945	ex-SGa	surface search	BB, CV, CA, CL, DD	50	0.1	180/2	up to 41	up to 28
	SGc	1945	ex-SGa	surface search or air search	BB, CV, CA, CL, DD	50	0.1	180/2	up to 41	up to 28
	SGd	1945	ex-SGb	surface search or air search	BB, CV, CA, CL, DD	50	0.1	180/2	up to 41	up to 28
	SG-1	1943	516	surface search	BB, CV, CA, CL, DD	50	0.1	180/2	up to 41	up to 28
	SG-1b	1945	ex-SG-1	surface search	BB, CV, CA, CL, DD	50	0.1	180/2	up to 41	up to 28
	SG-1c	1945	ex-SG-1	surface search or air search	BB, CV, CA, CL, DD	50	0.1	180/2	up to 41	up to 28
	SG-1d	1945	ex-SG-1b	surface search or air search	BB, CV, CA, CL, DD	50	0.1	180/2	up to 41	up to 28
	SG-3	1945		surface search	BB, CV, CA, CL, DD	500	0.086	90/0.75	22 - 56	up to 41
	SG-4			surface search	BB, CV, CA, CL, DD	500	0.086	90/0.75	22 - 56	up to 41
	SG-5			air / surface search	BB, CV, CA, CL, DD	500	0.048	90/0.75	22 - 56	up to 41
	SG-6			air / surface search	DD, FF	125	0.048	90/0.75	22 - 56	up to 41
	SG-6b			air / surface search	DD, FF	125	0.048	90/0.75	22 - 56	up to 41
SJ	SJ	1942	160	surface search	SS	25	0.1	13/0.3	up to 12	---
	SJa	1943	ex-SJ	surface search	SS	50	0.1	13/0.3	up to 22	---
	SJ-1	1943	300	surface search	SS	50	0.1	13/0.3	up to 22	---
SCR-517	SCR-517A	1942	225	surface search	ASW ships, SC, PT	20 - 40	0.1	180/5		---
	SCR-517C	1943	225	surface search	ASW ships, SC, PT	20 - 40	0.1	180/5		---
SH	SH	1943	50	surface search, gun control	cargo vessels	30	0.1	22/0.25	up to 28	---

SK	SK	1943	250	air search	CV, BB, CA, CL	200	1.36	90/1	---	up to 185
	SK-2	1944	75	air search	CV, BB, CA, CL	200	1.36	90/1	---	up to 185
	SK-3	1945		air search	CV, BB, CA, CL	200	1.36	90/1	---	up to 185
SL	SL	1943	829	surface search	DE, FF	150	0.1	90/1	19 - 37	up to 28
	SLa	1944	ex-SL	surface search	DE, FF	150	0.1	90/1	19 - 37	up to 28
	SL-1	1944	480	surface search	DE, FF	150	0.1	90/1	19 - 37	up to 28
SM	SM	1943	23	fighter direction	CV	600 - 700	0.1	180/0.25	up to 46	up to 92
	SM-1	1943	26	fighter direction	CV	600 - 700	0.1	180/0.25	up to 46	up to 92
SN	SN	1943	775	surface search	portable	1	0.12		4 - 11	---
SO	SO	1943	525	surface search	SC, PT, landing ships	65	0.1	180/2	9 - 37	---
	SOa	1944	ex-SO	surface search	SC, PT, landing ships	65	0.1	180/2	9 - 37	---
	SO-1	1943	2047	surface search	SC, PT, landing ships	65	0.1	180/2	15 - 37	up to 28
	SO-2	1944	535	surface search	SC, PT, landing ships	65	0.1	180/4	9 - 37	up to 22
	SO-3	1944	350	surface search	SC, PT, landing ships	20	0.03	180/1	11 - 37	up to 19
	SO-4	1944	235	surface search	SC, PT, landing ships	40	0.03	180/1	13 - 41	up to 22
	SO-5	1945	2	surface search	SC, PT, landing ships	150	0.05	45/1	11 - 37	up to 19
	SO-6	1945	~100	surface search	SC, PT, landing ships	150	0.05	45/1	11 - 37	up to 19
	SO-8	1944	1700	surface search	SC, PT, landing ships	65	0.1	180/4	9 - 37	up to 22
	SO-9	1944	110	surface search	SC, PT, landing ships	65	0.1	180/4	9 - 37	up to 22
	SO-10	~1946	few	surface search	SC, PT, landing ships	285	0.05	55/1	13 - 41	up to 22
	SO-13	1944	587	surface search	SC, PT, landing ships	65	0.1	180/2	9 - 37	---

SQ	SQ	1943	700	surface search	portable	1	0.12		4,5 - 15	---
Mk 8	Mk 8 Mod 0	1943	205	main gun control	BB, CA, CL	15 - 20	0.1	13/	9 - 36	27
	Mk 8 Mod 1			main gun control	BB, CA, CL	20 - 30	0.1	13/	9 - 36	27
	Mk 8 Mod 2			main gun control	BB, CA, CL	20 - 30	0.1	13/	9 - 36	27
	Mk 8 Mod 3			main gun control	BB, CA, CL	20 - 30	0.1	13/	9 - 36	27
Mk 9	Mk 9	1943	30	AA gun control (Mk45)	CV, BB, CA, CL	20	0.1	13/0.3	up to 9	up to 9
Mk 10	Mk 10 Mod 2	1943	20	3`` AA gun control (Mk50)	BB, CA, CL	20 - 30	0.1	13/6	up to 18	up to 13
	Mk 10 Mod 3			3`` AA gun control (Mk50)	BB, CA, CL	20 - 30	0.1	13/6	up to 18	up to 13
	Mk 10 Mod 4			3`` AA gun control (Mk50)	BB, CA, CL	20 - 30	0.1	13/6	up to 18	up to 13
	Mk 10 Mod 5	1944	37	3`` AA gun control (Mk50)	BB, CA, CL	20 - 30	0.1	13/6	up to 18	up to 13
Mk 11	Mk 11 Mod 0	1943	few	AA gun control (rangefinder) (Mk49)	CV, BB, CA, CL, DD, DE	40 - 60	0.1	63/---	up to 11	up to 5
	Mk 11 Mod 1	1943	few	AA gun control (rangefinder) (Mk49)	CV, BB, CA, CL, DD, DE	40 - 60	0.1	63/---	up to 11	up to 5
Mk 12	Mk 12 Mod 0	1943	801	DP gun control (Mk33)	CV, BB, CA, CL, DD, DE	100 - 110	0.1	18/7	up to 36	up to 40
	Mk 12 Mod 1			DP gun control (Mk33)	CV, BB, CA, CL, DD, DE	100 - 110	0.1	18/7	up to 36	up to 40
	Mk 12 Mod 2			DP gun control (Mk33)	CV, BB, CA, CL, DD, DE	100 - 110	0.1	18/7	up to 36	up to 40
	Mk 12 Mod 3			DP gun control (Mk33)	CV, BB, CA, CL, DD, DE	100 - 110	0.1	18/7	up to 36	up to 40
Mk 13	Mk 13 Mod 0	1943		main gun control	BB, CA, CL	50	0.03	13/	9 - 36	27
	Mk 13 Mod 1			main gun control	BB, CA, CL	50	0.03	13/	9 - 36	27
	Mk 13 Mod 2			main gun control	BB, CA, CL	50	0.03	13/	9 - 36	27
Mk 18	Mk 18	1943	6	5`` AA gun control (Mk28)	BB	20 - 30	0.1	13/6	32	14 - 16
Mk 19	Mk 19	1943	200	AA gun control (Mk57)	BB, CV, CA, CL, DD	50	0.1	13/10	14	7

Mk 22	Mk 22 Mod 0	1943	995	height finder (Mk33)	CV, BB, CA, CL, DD, DE	25 - 35	0.1		up to 36	up to 40
	Mk 22 Mod 1		995	height finder (Mk33)	CV, BB, CA, CL, DD, DE	25 - 35	0.1		up to 36	up to 40
SP	SP 6-ft antenna	1944	300	fighter direction	CVЛ, CA, CL, DD	700 - 1000	0.1	180/0.5	20 - 46	46 - 92
	SP 8-ft antenna	1944		fighter direction	CV, BB	700 - 1000	0.1	180/0.5	28 - 65	65 - 130
SR	SR	1944	100	air search	CA, CL, DD	500	1.5/1.36	27/2	---	130 - 204
	SRa		ex-SR	air search	CA, CL, DD	500	1.5/1.36	27/2	---	130 - 204
	SRb		ex-SRa	air search	CA, CL, DD	500	1.5/1.36	27/2	---	130 - 204
	SR-1	1945	250	air search	CA, CL, DD	600	0.7	27/2	---	130 - 204
	SR-2	1945	18	air search	CV, CA, CL, DD, SS	300	0.5	90/1	---	130 - 204
	SR-3	1947	22	air search	CV, BB, CA, CL	500	0.25	90/2	---	148 - 185
	SR-6	1947	43	air search	CA, CL, DD, FF	500	0.25	90/2	---	74 - 92
ST	ST	1944	254	surface search	SS	30	0.03	13/20	6 - 15	---
	STa	1945	ex-ST	surface search	SS	30	0.03	13/20	6 - 15	---
	ST-1	1945	ex-ST	surface search	SS	30	0.03	13/20	6 - 15	---
SU	SU	1944	522	surface search/gun control	DE, FF	15	0.03	27/1	28 - 37	---
	SU-1	1944		surface search/gun control	DE, FF	15	0.03	27/1	28 - 37	---
	SU-2	1945	19	surface search/gun control	DE, FF, landing ships	15	0.03	27/1	28 - 37	---
	SU-3	1945		surface search/gun control	DE, FF, landing ships	15	0.03	27/1	28 - 37	---
	SU-4	1949		surface search/gun control	DE, FF, landing ships	15	0.03	27/1	28 - 37	---
Mk 26	Mk 26 Mod 3	1944	450	DP gun control (rangefinder)	DE, FF, auxiliary	40 - 60	0.1	130/---	up to 14	up to 9
	Mk 26 Mod 4	1944	328	DP gun control (rangefinder)	DE, FF, auxiliaries	40 - 60	0.1	130/---	up to 14	up to 9
Mk 27	Mk 27	1944	41	main gun control (Mk40, Mk55)	BB, CA, CL	50	0.1	27/6.5	up to 28	---
Mk 28	Mk 28 Mod 0	1944	~50	DP gun control (Mk33)	DD, DE	30	0.1	13/	---	13 - 18
	Mk 28 Mod 2		247	gun control 40-мм 3A (Mk63)	CV, BB, CA, CL, DD, DE	30	0.1	13/	---	13 - 18
	Mk 28 Mod 3		~50	DP gun control (Mk33)	DD, DE	30	0.1	13/	---	13 - 18

SS	SS	1945	300	surface search	SS	75 - 100	0.03	13/0.25	up to 22	---
	SS-1	1950	300	surface search	SS	75 - 100	0.03	13/0.25	up to 22	---
	SS-2	1952		surface search	SS	100	0.03	13/0.25	up to 22	---
	SS-2a		ex-SS-2	surface search	SS	100	0.03	13/0.25	up to 22	---
SV	SV	1945	80	air search	SS	500	0.086	13/1	---	20 - 41
	SVa	1945	ex-SV	air search	SS	500	0.086	13/1	---	20 - 41
	SV-1	1945	220	air search	SS	500	0.086	13/1	---	20 - 41
	SV-2	1948	few	height finder	SS	500	0.086	13/1	---	20 - 41
	SV-2A		ex-SV-2	height finder	SS	500	0.086	13/1	---	20 - 41
	SV-3	1950	17	air search	SS	500	0.086	13/1	---	20 - 41
	SV-4	1950	few	missile control	SS	500	0.086	13/1	---	20 - 41
	SV-4A		ex-SV-4	missile control	SS	500	0.086	13/1	---	20 - 41
	SV-5			missile control	SS	500	0.086	13/1	---	20 - 41
	SV-6			missile control (height finder)	SS	560	0.086	13/1	---	20 - 41
CXGQ	CXGQ	1945	35	surface search	SC, PT, landing ships	60	0.033	45/1	22 - 41	up to 28
SX	SX	1946	45	air search	CV, LCC	1000 500	0.086	180/1.2	---	up to 148
CXJG	CXJG	1947	14	surface search	SC, PT, landing ships	23	0.0125			

Made in the USA
Columbia, SC
05 May 2024

9499834c-5e33-40e3-947a-acf1263487b3R01